CRITICAL SURVEY
OF
SHORT FICTION
Fourth Edition

CRITICAL SURVEY
OF
SHORT FICTION

Fourth Edition

Volume 3
American Writers

Shirley Jackson - Richard Russo

Editor
Charles E. May
California State University, Long Beach

SALEM PRESS
Ipswich, Massachusetts   Hackensack, New Jersey

Copyright © 1981, 1987, 1993, 2001, 2012, Salem Press, A Division of EBSCO Publishing, Inc.

Some of the essays in this work, which have been updated, originally appeared in the following Salem Press publications, *Critical Survey of Short Fiction* (1981), *Critical Survey of Short Fiction, Supplement* (1987), *Critical Survey of Short Fiction, Revised Edition*, (1993; preceding volumes edited by Frank N. Magill), *Critical Survey of Short Fiction, Second Revised Edition* (2001; edited by Charles E. May).

The paper used in these volumes conforms to the American National Standard for Permanence of Paper for Printed Library Materials, X39.48-1992 (R1997).

LIBRARY OF CONGRESS CATALOGING-IN-PUBLICATION DATA

Critical survey of short fiction / editor, Charles E. May. -- 4th ed.
    p. cm.

Includes bibliographical references and index.
ISBN 978-1-58765-789-4 (set : alk. paper) -- ISBN 978-1-58765-790-0 (set, american : alk. paper) --
ISBN 978-1-58765-791-7 (vol. 1, american : alk. paper) -- ISBN 978-1-58765-792-4 (vol. 2, american : alk. paper) --
ISBN 978-1-58765-793-1 (vol. 3, american : alk. paper) -- ISBN 978-1-58765-794-8 (vol. 4, american : alk. paper) --
ISBN 978-1-58765-795-5 (set, british : alk. paper) -- ISBN 978-1-58765-796-2 (vol. 1, british : alk. paper) --
ISBN 978-1-58765-797-9 (vol. 2, british : alk. paper) -- ISBN 978-1-58765-798-6 (european : alk. paper) --
ISBN 978-1-58765-799-3 (world : alk. paper) -- ISBN 978-1-58765-800-6 (topical essays : alk. paper) --
ISBN 978-1-58765-803-7 (cumulative index : alk. paper)

1. Short story. 2. Short story--Bio-bibliography. I. May, Charles E. (Charles Edward), 1941-
PN3321.C7 2011
809.3'1--dc23

2011026000

First Printing

PRINTED IN THE UNITED STATES OF AMERICA

CONTENTS

CONTRIBUTORS

Randy L. Abbott
University of Evansville

Michael Adams
CUNY Graduate Center

Patrick Adcock
Henderson State University

Thomas P. Adler
Purdue University

A. Owen Aldridge
University of Illinois

Charmaine Allmon-Mosby
Western Kentucky University

Emily Alward
College of Southern Nevada

Andrew J. Angyal
Elon University

Jacob M. Appel
The Mount Sinai Medical School

Gerald S. Argetsinger
Rochester Institute of Technology

Karen L. Arnold
Columbia, Maryland

Marilyn Arnold
Brigham Young University

Leonard R. N. Ashley
Brooklyn College, City University of New York

Bryan Aubrey
Fairfield, Iowa

Stephen Aubrey
Brooklyn College

Edmund August
McKendree College

Jane L. Ball
Wilberforce University

David Barratt
Montreat College

Melissa E. Barth
Appalachian State University

Martha Bayless
University of Oregon

Alvin K. Benson
Utah Valley University

Stephen Benz
Barry University

Margaret Boe Birns
New York University

Nicholas Birns
Eugene Lang College, The New School

Elizabeth Blakesley
Washington State University Libraries

Richard Bleiler
University of Connecticut

Lynn Z. Bloom
University of Connecticut

Julia B. Boken
Indiana University, Southeast

Jo-Ellen Lipman Boon
Buena Park, California

William Boyle
University of Mississippi

Virginia Brackett
Park University

Harold Branam
Savannah State University

Gerhard Brand
California State University, Los Angeles

Alan Brown
Livingston University

Mary Hanford Bruce
Monmouth College

Carl Brucker
Arkansas Tech University

John C. Buchanan
Original Contributor

Stefan Buchenberger
Kanagawa University

Louis J. Budd
Original Contributor

Rebecca R. Butler
Dalton College

Susan Butterworth
Salem State College

Edmund J. Campion
University of Tennessee, Knoxville

Larry A. Carlson
Original Contributor

Amee Carmines
Hampton University

Thomas Gregory Carpenter
Lipscomb University

John Carr
Original Contributor

Warren J. Carson
University of South Carolina, Spartanburg

Mary LeDonne Cassidy
South Carolina State University

Thomas J. Cassidy
South Carolina State University

Hal Charles
Eastern Kentucky University

C. L. Chua
California State University, Fresno

David W. Cole
University of Wisconsin Colleges

Laurie Coleman
Original Contributor

Richard Hauer Costa
Texas A&M University

Ailsa Cox
Edge Hill University

Lisa-Anne Culp
Nuclear Regulatory Commission

Heidi K. Czerwiec
Univeristy of North Dakota

Dolores A. D'Angelo
American University

Anita Price Davis
Converse College

Frank Day
Clemson University

Danielle A. DeFoe
Sierra College

Bill Delaney
San Diego, California

Joan DelFattore
University of Delaware

Kathryn Zabelle Derounian
University of Arkansas-Little Rock

Joseph Dewey
University of Pittsburgh

Marcia B. Dinneen
Bridgewater State University

Thomas Du Bose
Louisiana State University-Shreveport

Stefan Dziemianowicz
Bloomfield, New Jersey

Wilton Eckley
Colorado School of Mines

K Edgington
Towson University

Robert P. Ellis
Northborough Historical Society

CONTRIBUTORS

Sonia Erlich
Lesley University

Thomas L. Erskine
Salisbury University

Christopher Estep
Original Contributor

Walter Evans
Augusta College

Jack Ewing
Boise, Idaho

Kevin Eyster
Madonna University

Nettie Farris
University of Louisville

Howard Faulkner
Original Contributor

James Feast
Baruch College

Thomas R. Feller
Nashville, Tennessee

John W. Fiero
University of Louisiana at Lafayette

Edward Fiorelli
St. John's University

Rebecca Hendrick Flannagan
Rrancis Marion University

James K. Folsom
Original Contributor

Ben Forkner
Original Contributor

Joseph Francavilla
Columbus State University

Timothy C. Frazer
Western Illinois University

Kathy Ruth Frazier
Original Contributor

Tom Frazier
Cumberland College

Rachel E. Frier
Rockville, Maryland

Terri Frongia
Santa Rosa Junior College

Miriam Fuchs
University of Hawaii-Manoa

Jean C. Fulton
Landmark College

Louis Gallo
Radford University

Ann Davison Garbett
Averett University

Marshall Bruce Gentry
Georgia College & State University

Jill B. Gidmark
University of Minnesota

M. Carmen Gomez-Galisteo
Esne-Universidad Camilo Jose Cela

Linda S. Gordon
Worcester State College

Julian Grajewski
Tuscon, Arizona

Charles A. Gramlich
Xavier University of Louisiana

James L. Green
Arizona State University

Glenda I. Griffin
Sam Houston State University

John L. Grigsby
Appalachian Research & Defense Fund of Kentucky, Inc.

William E. Grim
Ohio University

Elsie Galbreath Haley
Metropolitan State College of Denver

David Mike Hamilton
Original Contributor

Katherine Hanley
St. Bernard's School of Theology and Ministry

Michele Hardy
Prince George's Community College

Betsy Harfst
Kishwaukee College

Alan C. Haslam
Sierra College

CJ Hauser
Brooklyn College

Peter B. Heller
Manhattan College

Terry Heller
Coe College

Diane Andrews Henningfeld
Adrian College

DeWitt Henry
Emerson College

Cheryl Herr
Original Contributor

Allen Hibbard
Middle Tennessee State University

Cynthia Packard Hill
University of Massachusetts at Amherst

Jane Hill
Original Contributor

Nika Hoffman
Crossroads School for Arts & Sciences

William Hoffman
Fort Myers, Florida

Hal Holladay
Simon's Rock College of Bard

Kimberley M. Holloway
King College

Gregory D. Horn
Southwest Virginia Commmunity College

Sylvia Huete
Original Contributor

Edward Huffstetler
Bridgewater College

Theodore C. Humphrey
California State Polytechnic University, Pomona

Robert Jacobs
Central Washington University

Shakuntala Jayaswal
University of New Haven

Clarence O. Johnson
Joplin, Missouri

Eunice Pedersen Johnston
North Dakota State University

Theresa Kanoza
Lincoln Land Community College

William P. Keen
Washington & Jefferson College

Fiona Kelleghan
South Miami, Florida

Cassandra Kircher
Elon College

Paula Kopacz
Eastern Kentucky University

Uma Kukathas
Seattle, Washingtom

Rebecca Kuzins
Pasadena, California

Marvin Lachman
Santa Fe, New Mexico

Thomas D. Lane
Original Contributor

John Lang
Emory & Henry College

Carlota Larrea
Pennsylvania State University

Donald F. Larsson
Mankato State University

William Laskowski
Jamestown College

Norman Lavers
Arkansas State University

David Layton
University of California, Santa Barbar

Allen Learst
Oklahome State University

James Ward Lee
University of North Texas

Katy L. Leedy
Marquette University

Leon Lewis
Appalachian State University

Elizabeth Johnston Lipscomb
Randolph-Macon Women's College

Douglas Long
Pasadena, California

Michael Loudon
Eastern Illinois University

Robert M. Luscher
University of Nebraska at Kearney

Carol J. Luther
Pellissippi State Community College

R. C. Lutz
CII Group

Laurie Lykken
Century College

Andrew F. Macdonald
Loyola University

Joanne McCarthy
Tacoma Washington

Richard D. McGhee
Arkansas State University

S. Thomas Mack
University of South Carolina-Aiken

Victoria E. McLure
Texas Tech University

Robert J. McNutt
University of Tennessee at Chattanooga

Bryant Mangum
Original Contributor

Barry Mann
Alliance Theatre

Mary E. Markland
Argosy University

Patricia Marks
Valdosta State College

Wythe Marschall
Brooklyn College

Karen M. Cleveland Marwick
Hemel Hempstead, Hertfordshire, England

Charles E. May
California State University, Long Beach

Laurence W. Mazzeno
Alvernia College

Patrick Meanor
SUNY College at Oneonta

Martha Meek
Original Contributor

Ann A. Merrill
Emory University

Robert W. Millett
Original Contributor

Christian H. Moe
Southern Illinois University at Carbondale

Robert A. Morace
Daemen College

Christina Murphy
Original Contributor

Earl Paulus Murphy
Harris-Stowe State College

John M. Muste
Ohio State University

Donna B. Nalley
South University

Keith Neilson
California State University, Fullerton

William Nelles
*University of
Massachusetts-Dartmouth*

John Nizalowski
Mesa State College

Martha Nochimson
Mercy College

Emma Coburn Norris
Troy State University

Bruce Olsen
Austin Peay State University

Brian L. Olson
*Kalamazoo Valley Community
College*

James Norman O'Neill
Bryant College

Keri L. Overall
University of South Carolina

Janet Taylor Palmer
*Caldwell Community College &
Technical Institute*

Sally B. Palmer
*South Dakota School of Mines &
Technology*

Robert J. Paradowski
Rochester Institute of Technology

David B. Parsell
Furman University

Susie Paul
Auburn University, Montgomery

Leslie A. Pearl
San Diego, California

David Peck
Laguna Beach, California

William Peden
University of Missouri-Columbia

Chapel Louise Petty
Blackwell, Oklahoma

Susan L. Piepke
Bridgewater College

Constance Pierce
Original Contributor

Mary Ellen Pitts
Rhodes College

Victoria Price
Lamar University

Jere Real
Lynchburg, Virginia

Peter J. Reed
University of Minnesota

Rosemary M. Canfield Reisman
Sonoma, California

Martha E. Rhynes
*Oklahoma East Central
University*

James Curry Robison
Original Contributor

Mary Rohrberger
New Orleans, Louisiana

Douglas Rollins
Dawson College

Carl Rollyson
Baruch College, CUNY

Paul Rosefeldt
Delgado Community College

Ruth Rosenberg
Brooklyn, New York

Irene Struthers Rush
Boise, Idaho

David Sadkin
Hamburg, New York

David N. Samuelson
*California State University,
Long Beach*

Elizabeth D. Schafer
Loachapoka, Alabama

Barbara Kitt Seidman
Linfield College

D. Dean Shackelford
Concord College

M. K. Shaddix
Dublin University

Allen Shepherd
Original Contributor

Nancy E. Sherrod
Georgia Southern University

Thelma J. Shinn
Arizona State University

R. Baird Shuman
University of Illinois at Urbana-Champaign

Paul Siegrist
Fort Hays State University

Charles L. P. Silet
Iowa State University

Karin A. Silet
University of Wisconsin-Madison

Genevieve Slomski
New Britain, Connecticut

Roger Smith
Portland, Oregon

Ira Smolensky
Monmouth College

Katherine Snipes
Spokane, Washington

Sandra Whipple Spanier
Original Contributor

Brian Stableford
Reading, United Kingdom

John Stark
Original Contributor

Joshua Stein
Los Medanos College

Karen F. Stein
University of Rhode Island

Judith L. Steininger
Milwaukee School of Engineering

Ingo R. Stoehr
Kilgore College

Louise M. Stone
Bloomsburg University

William B. Stone
Chicago, Illinois

Theresa L. Stowell
Adrian College

Gerald H. Strauss
Bloomsburg University

Ryan D. Stryffeler
Western Nevada College

W. J. Stuckey
Purdue University

Catherine Swanson
Austin, Texas

Philip A. Tapley
Louisiana College

Terry Theodore
University of North Carolina at Wilmington

Maxine S. Theodoulou
The Union Institute

David J. Thieneman
Original Contributor

Lou Thompson
Texas Woman's University

Michael Trussler
University of Regina

Richard Tuerk
Texas A&M University-Commerce

Scott Vander Ploeg
Madisonville Community College

Dennis Vannatta
University of Arkansas at Little Rock

Jaquelyn W. Walsh
McNeese State University

Shawncey Webb
Taylor University

James Michael Welsh
Salisbury State University

James Whitlark
Texas Tech University

Barbara Wiedemann
Auburn University at Montgomery

Albert Wilhelm

Tennessee Technological University

Donna Glee Williams

North Carolina Center for the Advancement of Teaching

Patricia A. R. Williams

Original Contributor

Judith Barton Williamson

Sauk Valley Community College

Michael Witkoski

University of South Carolina

Jennifer L. Wyatt

Civic Memorial High School

Scott D. Yarbrough

Charleston Southern University

Mary F. Yudin

State College, Pennsylvania

Hasan Zia

Original Contributor

Gay Pitman Zieger

Santa Fe College

COMPLETE LIST OF CONTENTS

American Volume 1

American Volume 2

American Volume 3

American Volume 4

KEY TO PRONUNCIATION

To help users of the *Critical Survey of Short Fiction* pronounce unfamiliar names of profiled writers correctly, phonetic spellings using the character symbols listed below appear in parentheses immediately after the first mention of the writer's name in the narrative text. Stressed syllables are indicated in capital letters, and syllables are separated by hyphens.

VOWEL SOUNDS
Symbol: Spelled (Pronounced)

a:	answer (AN-suhr), laugh (laf), sample (SAM-puhl), that (that)
ah:	father (FAH-thur), hospital (HAHS-pih-tuhl)
aw:	awful (AW-fuhl), caught (kawt)
ay:	blaze (blayz), fade (fayd), waiter (WAYT-ur), weigh (way)
eh:	bed (behd), head (hehd), said (sehd)
ee:	believe (bee-LEEV), cedar (SEE-dur), leader (LEED-ur), liter (LEE-tur)
ew:	boot (bewt), lose (lewz)
i:	buy (bi), height (hit), lie (li), surprise (sur-PRIZ)
ih:	bitter (BIH-tur), pill (pihl)
o:	cotton (KO-tuhn), hot (hot)
oh:	below (bee-LOH), coat (koht), note (noht), wholesome (HOHL-suhm)
oo:	good (good), look (look)
ow:	couch (kowch), how (how)
oy:	boy (boy), coin (koyn)
uh:	about (uh-BOWT), butter (BUH-tuhr), enough (ee-NUHF), other (UH-thur)

CONSONANT SOUNDS
Symbol: Spelled (Pronounced)

ch:	beach (beech), chimp (chihmp)
g:	beg (behg), disguise (dihs-GIZ), get (geht)
j:	digit (DIH-juht), edge (ehj), jet (jeht)
k:	cat (kat), kitten (KIH-tuhn), hex (hehks)
s:	cellar (SEHL-ur), save (sayv), scent (sehnt)
sh:	champagne (sham-PAYN), issue (IH-shew), shop (shop)
ur:	birth (burth), disturb (dihs-TURB), earth (urth), letter (LEH-tur)
y:	useful (YEWS-fuhl), young (yuhng)
z:	business (BIHZ-nehs), zest (zehst)
zh:	vision (VIH-zhuhn)

CRITICAL SURVEY
OF
SHORT FICTION

Fourth Edition

J

Shirley Jackson

Born: San Francisco, California; December 14, 1916
Died: North Bennington, Vermont; August 8, 1965

Principal short fiction

The Lottery: Or, The Adventures of James Harris,
    1949 (also pb. as *The Lottery, and Other Stories*)
Come Along with Me: Part of a Novel, Sixteen
    Stories, and Three Lectures, 1968 (Stanley Edgar
    Hyman, editor)
Just an Ordinary Day, 1996 (Laurence Jackson
    Hyman and Sarah Hyman Stewart, editors)
Shirley Jackson Collected Short Stories, 2001
Novels and Stories, 2010

Other literary forms

Shirley Jackson's published books include novels, humorous fictionalized autobiographies, and children's books. Many of her stories, essays, and public speeches remain uncollected. Several works have been adapted to other media: "The Lottery" for television, *We Have Always Lived in the Castle* (1962) for stage, and *The Bird's Nest* (1954) and *The Haunting of Hill House* (1959) for the cinema.

Achievements

Shirley Jackson is probably best known for her short story "The Lottery," which was first published in the June 26, 1948, edition of *The New Yorker*. Like the majority of her works, both short stories and novels, "The Lottery" explores the darker side of the human psyche, often in a manner disturbing to the reader. In addition to using ordinary settings for extraordinary occurrences, Jackson often injects an element of the supernatural. This is seen, for example, in the story "The Visit" and in the novel *The Haunting of Hill House*. In addition, Jackson has published *Life Among the Savages* (1953), a highly humorous account of her home life. In 1961, Jackson received the Edgar Allan Poe Award for her story "Louisa, Please." She was awarded the Syracuse University Arents Pioneer Medal for Outstanding Achievement in 1965.

Biography

Shirley Hardie Jackson was born in California on December 14, 1916, and moved with her family to New York when she was sixteen. After an unsuccessful year at the University of Rochester, Jackson enrolled, at age twenty, in the University of Syracuse. This was to be the beginning of an independent life for the author, as she would finally be away from the dominating presence of her mother. At Syracuse, Jackson met Stanley Edgar Hyman, the man she would marry in 1940. Hyman achieved notoriety in his own right as a teacher, writer, and critic. The marriage between Jackson and Hyman was tumultuous in many ways but provided a stabilizing factor for Jackson. Her literary production increased markedly after the marriage and the birth of their four children. Jackson's own phobias, however, kept creeping into this successful, if odd, relationship. She was an agoraphobic and a depressive. Part of the latter affliction was exacerbated by her asthma and arthritis, as well as Hyman's extramarital affair in the early 1960's. In addition, Jackson had never really been a social person--she was much too individualistic to fit into any of the polite social molds. In 1963, Jackson began to turn around psychologically. Her husband made a new commitment to the marriage, and an enlightened psychiatrist began to help her work with the agoraphobia. Her writing continued to be an outlet for her. Although Jackson recovered emotionally, she never recovered physically. She was obese and a chain smoker. She died on August 8, 1965, at the age of forty-eight.

ANALYSIS

Shirley Jackson's stories seem to center on a single concern: Almost every story is about a protagonist's discovering or failing to discover or successfully ignoring an alternate way of perceiving a set of circumstances or the world. Jackson seems especially interested in how characters order their worlds and how they perceive themselves in the world. Often, a change in a character's perspective leads to anxiety, terror, neurosis, or even a loss of identity. While it is tempting to say that her main theme is the difference between appearance and reality, such a statement is misleading, for she seems to see reality as Herman Melville's Ishmael comes to see it, as a mirror of the perceiving soul. It is rarely clear that her characters discover or lose their grasp of reality; rather, they form ideas of reality that are more or less moral and more or less functional. For Jackson, reality is so complex and mysterious that one inevitably orders only part of it. A character may then discover parts that contradict a chosen order or that attract one away from the apparent order, but one can never affirm the absolute superiority of one ordering to another. In this respect, Jackson's fictional world resembles those of Stephen Crane and Ernest Hemingway. Perhaps the major differences between her fiction and theirs is that her protagonists are predominantly women; she explores some peculiarly feminine aspects of the problem of ideas of order.

Jackson's middle-class American women seem especially vulnerable to losing the security of a settled worldview. Their culture provides them with idealistic dream visions of what their lives should be, and they have a peculiar leisure for contemplation and conversation imposed upon them by their dependent roles. Men in her stories seem so busy providing that they rarely look at and think about the order of things. Her career women are more like these men. In "Elizabeth" and "The Villager," the protagonists succeed, albeit precariously, in preserving ideas of themselves and their worlds despite the contradictory facts that seem increasingly to intrude. In these two stories, one sees a sort of emotional cannibalism in the protagonists as they attempt to preserve belief in an order that reality seems no longer disposed to sustain. Several stories show a woman's loss of an ordering dream.

These divide into stories about women who experience the terror of loss of identity and those who may find a liberating and superior order in what would ordinarily be called infantile fantasy.

Among those who lose a dream are the protagonists of "The Little House" and "The Renegade." In "The Little House," a woman's first possession of her own small country house is ruined by the terrifying insinuations of her new neighbors; they leave her alone on her first night after relating to her their fears that the previous owner was murdered and that the murderer will return. In "The Renegade," a mother discovers an unsuspected cruelty in her neighbors and even in her children when her dog is accused of killing chickens. Although Jackson's humorous autobiographical stories are of a different order, the often anthologized "Charles" tells of a mother's discovery that the nemesis of the kindergarten whose antics her son reports each day is not the mythical Charles, but her own son, Laurie.

Shirley Jackson (AP Photo)

Perhaps the most successful escape into fantasy is Mrs. Montague's in "The Island." All her physical needs are provided by a wealthy but absent son and the constant attendance of Miss Oakes. Mrs. Montague lives in her dream of a tropical paradise, virtually untouched by her actual world. This escape is judged by the ironic frame of Miss Oakes's relative poverty and her inevitable envy, suffering, spite, and ugliness; she has no chance of such an escape herself. Some movements into fantasy are terrifying or at least ambiguous. In "The Beautiful Stranger," Margaret resolves a tension in her marriage by perceiving the man who returns from a business trip as a stranger, not her husband. By the end of the story, this fantasy has led to her losing herself, unable to find her home when she returns from a shopping trip. A similar but more ambiguous situation develops in "The Tooth," in which a woman escapes into a vision of an island to evade the pain of an aching tooth. Many of Jackson's protagonists conceive of an island paradise as an ideal order when their control of the immediate is threatened.

Some ideas of order remain impenetrable. In "Louisa, Please," a variation on Nathaniel Hawthorne's "Wakefield," a runaway daughter returns home after a long absence to discover that her family has built a life around her loss and will not be convinced of her return. In "Flower Garden" and "After You, My Dear Alphonse," protagonists find themselves unable to change or to abandon racist ideas because the ideas are too strong or because of community pressure.

"THE VISIT"

A closer look at three especially interesting stories reveals more about Jackson's themes and give some indication of her technical proficiency. In "The Visit," Margaret comes to visit a school friend, Carla Rhodes, for the summer. The beautiful Rhodes estate includes a dream house with numerous fantastic rooms. The house seems not quite real; nearly every room is covered with tapestries depicting the house in different hours and seasons, and there is a mysterious tower of which no one speaks. For Margaret, the house and the family are ideal, especially when Carla's brother, Paul, arrives with his friend, the Captain. This idyll lasts until the evening of Paul's departure, when Margaret discovers that Paul has been a hallucination or a ghost,

for the Captain is Carla's brother and no one else has seen Paul. This revelation clarifies several mysteries that have developed, especially that of Margaret's strange visit to the tower. Paul has told Margaret that an old aunt often secludes herself in the tower. When Margaret pays her a visit, she undergoes a not really frightening but certainly haunting experience with old Aunt Margaret. At the end of the story, the reader must conclude Aunt Margaret to be an apparition, that she is probably the Margaret who died for love and whose picture in mosaic appears on the floor of one room. Young Margaret has lost a phantom lover as old Margaret lost her Paul. Young Margaret realizes this at the same time that she is made aware of time's effect on the house: the age and weakness of the Rhodeses, the bitter darkness of their true son, and the physical decay of the buildings. Furthermore, she begins to doubt her own place and identity as she wonders if her visit to the house will ever end. The home of her dreaming now threatens to become an imprisoning nightmare.

In retrospect, the device by which Jackson encourages the reader to share Margaret's hallucination or haunting may seem contrived. This choice, however, seems effective because the more fully the reader shares Margaret's perceptions and the more subdued (without being absent) are the disturbing elements, the more fully will the reader share the shock of her awakening into nightmare. Also technically effective are the apparent connections with Poe's "The Fall of the House of Usher." Most important among these is the succession of mirror images: multiple pictures of the house, between the house and Mrs. Rhodes, among members of the family, between the two Margarets, and between the decline of the family and of the house. These connections seem deliberately chosen in part to emphasize the contrasts between Margaret and Poe's narrator. Because Margaret's response to the house is so positive, the shock of her discovery is greater by contrast. Furthermore, when she discovers this house to be like what one knows the House of Usher to be, one sees the analogy between her terror at imprisonment and that of Poe's narrator when he sees a universe unnaturally lit by a blood red moon, yet another image of the coffin lit from within. Margaret actually enters one of the dream worlds promised American girls. Under its spell, she overlooks its flaws and forgets about time, but when the Captain breaks the spell, pointing out signs of decay, Paul departs and Margaret becomes acutely aware of time as her nightmare begins.

"PILLAR OF SALT"

Time is often the destroyer of feminine ideals in Jackson's stories because they seem to depend on a suspension of time. In "Pillar of Salt," another Margaret loses her secure world. A trip to New York City with her husband forces a new perspective on her that produces her anxiety and, finally, paranoia. It remains unclear, however, whether her paranoia is illness or a healthy reaction to an inimical environment.

The couple's first week in the city is idyllic, and the fast pace is a pleasant change from New Hampshire. At a party at the end of the first week, however, Margaret begins to feel isolated, unnoticed among strangers who behave in strange ways. She learns there is a fire in the building but is unable to convince anyone else to leave. The fire turns out to be two buildings away, but she is the only one to heed the warning and flee the building. She comes to see this nightmarish experience as symbolic of her experience in New York and perhaps of her life as a whole. She begins to notice new details about the city: dirt, decay, speed, stifling crowds. She feels increasingly isolated and insignificant. Of this life she thinks, "She knew she was afraid to say it truly, afraid to face the knowledge that it was a voluntary neck-breaking speed, a deliberate whirling faster and faster to end in destruction." Even her friends' Long Island beach cottage shows the spreading blight; there they find a severed human leg on the sand. Margaret comes to believe that her former order was illusory. Upon returning to the city, she begins to hallucinate, to see the destruction of the city in fast motion. Windows crumble. Her bed shakes. Driven from her apartment, she finds herself unable to return, paralyzed in a fast-moving, anonymous crowd on the wrong side of a mechanical and murderous river of traffic.

Margaret comes to see herself in a modern Sodom, paralyzed not because she has disobeyed God, but because she has seen in prophetic vision the truth about the city: It is no home for human beings but rather is impersonally intent upon destruction. The allusion of the title and her critique of city life verify her perception; however, those who do not share her vision remain capable of functioning. As in "The Visit," the internal view of Margaret encourages a close identification between reader and character that makes judgment difficult until the reader can step back; but stepping back from "Pillar of Salt" plunges the reader deeper into mystery. In both stories, the protagonist moves from dream to nightmare, but in "Pillar of Salt," the reader is much less certain that the move is to a better or more accurate view of reality.

"THE LOTTERY"

Shirley Jackson's reputation rests primarily upon her most anthologized story, "The Lottery." Her lecture on this story (printed in *Come Along with Me*) suggests that her creation of a normal setting convinced many readers that the story was largely factual. In fact, the central problem of the story seems to be to reconcile the portrait of typical small-town life in which the characters seem just like the reader with the horrifying ritualistic killing these people carry out. Here, apparently incompatible ideas of order are thrust upon the reader for resolution, perhaps in order to complicate the reader's conceptions.

"The Lottery" develops by slowly raising the level of tension in the semipastoral setting until a series of carefully arranged revelations brings about a dramatic and shocking reversal. The villagers gather at midmorning on a late June day for an annual event, the lottery, around which a great deal of excitement centers. Jackson supplies details that arouse reader curiosity: Nearly all towns have a similar lottery; it is as old as the town; it has an elaborate ritual form that has decayed over time; every adult male *must* participate; some believe the orders of nature and of civilization depend on carrying it out correctly. The family of the man who draws the marked lot must draw again to determine the final winner. The tension built out of reader curiosity and the town's mood reverses toward the sinister when the "winner's" wife reveals that she does not want to win. Once this reversal is complete, the story moves rapidly to reveal the true nature of the lottery--to choose a victim for annual sacrifice by stoning. Jackson heightens the horror of this apparently unaccountable act with carefully chosen and placed details.

Several commentators have attempted to explain the story through reconstructing the meaning of the ritual and through carefully examining the symbols. Helen Nebeker sees the story as an allegory of "man trapped in a web spun from his own need to explain and control the incomprehensible universe around him, a need no longer answered by the web of old traditions." These attempts to move beyond the simple thriller seem justified by the details Jackson provides about the lottery. This ritual seems clearly to be a tradition of prehistoric origin, once believed essential for the welfare of the community. Even though its purpose has become obscure and its practice muddled, it continues to unify and sustain the community. Critics tend to underemphasize the apparent health and vitality of the community, perhaps feeling that this ritual essentially undercuts that impression. It is important to notice that one function of the lottery is to change the relationship between community and victim. The victim is chosen at random, killed without malice or significant protest, and lost without apparent grief. This story may be what Richard Eastman has called an open parable, a fable that applies at several levels or in several contexts. "The Lottery" creates an emotional effect of horror at the idea that perhaps in human civilization, the welfare of the many depends often on the suffering of the few: the victim race, the exploited nation, the scapegoat, the poor, the stereotyped sex, the drafted soldier. In these cases, instead of a ritual, other aspects of the social order separate oppressor and victim, yet the genuine order and happiness of the majority seems to depend on the destruction of others. In this respect, "The Lottery" resembles many stories of oppression, such as Franz Kafka's "The Bucket Rider" and some stories by Richard Wright; its purpose may be to jar readers into thinking about ways in which their lives victimize others.

Jackson places the reader of "The Lottery," which lacks a protagonist, in a position similar to that of the protagonists of "The Visit" and "Pillar of Salt." The story moves from a relatively secure agrarian worldview to an event which fantastically complicates that view. Here, as in most of her stories, Jackson emphasizes the complexity of reality. Nature and human nature seem unaccountable mixtures of the creative and destructive. Her best people are in search of ways to live in this reality without fear and cruelty.

OTHER MAJOR WORKS

LONG FICTION: *The Road Through the Wall*, 1948 (also pb. as *The Other Side of the Street*); *Hangsaman*, 1951; *The Bird's Nest*, 1954 (also pb. as *Lizzie*); *The Sundial*, 1958; *The Haunting of Hill House*, 1959; *We Have Always Lived in the Castle*, 1962.

PLAY: *The Bad Children*, pb. 1958.

NONFICTION: *Life Among the Savages*, 1953; *The Witchcraft of Salem Village*, 1956; *Raising Demons*, 1957.

CHILDREN'S LITERATURE: *Nine Magic Wishes*, 1963; *Famous Sally*, 1966.

BIBLIOGRAPHY

Bloom, Harold, ed. *Shirley Jackson*. Broomall, Pa.: Chelsea House, 2001. Compilation of previously published essays that analyze Jackson's short stories, including "The Lottery" and "Charles."

Cleveland, Carol. "Shirley Jackson." In *And Then There Were Nine . . . More Women of Mystery*, edited by Jane S. Bakerman. Bowling Green, Ohio.: Bowling Green State University Popular Press, 1985. The chapter on Jackson provides an overview of her major works and offers some useful critical insights.

Friedman, Lenemaja. *Shirley Jackson*. Boston: G. K. Hall, 1975. Friedman provides both a biographical and critical study of Jackson and offers information on her short stories and novels. Includes an extensive secondary bibliography.

Gelfant, Blanche H., ed. *The Columbia Companion to the Twentieth-Century American Short Story*. New York: Columbia University Press, 2000. Includes a chapter in which Jackson's short stories are analyzed.

Hall, Joan Wylie. *Shirley Jackson: A Study of the Short Fiction*. New York: Twayne, 1993. An introduction to Jackson's stories, with comments by Jackson herself, and a few short, previously published, critical articles by others. Discusses Jackson's interest in the occult, her fascination with dream situations, her focus on children, and her most famous story, "The Lottery."

Hattenhauer, Darryl. *Shirley Jackson's American Gothic*. New York: State University of New York, 2003. Makes a strong argument for Jackson's modernity. Analyzes her use of the supernatural as metaphor and illuminates the influences of Jackson's substance abuse, marital strife, and political leanings on her work. Devotes one chapter each to the short-story collections *The Lottery: Or, The Adventures of James Harris*, *Come Along with Me*, and *Just an Ordinary Day*.

Kittredge, Mary. "The Other Side of Magic: A Few Remarks About Shirley Jackson." In *Discovering Modern Horror Fiction*, edited by Darrell Schweitzer. Mercer Island, Wash.: Starmont House, 1985. A useful study of the use of magic and the supernatural in Jackson's works. The author draws interesting comparisons between Jackson's fiction and nonfiction works.

Murphy, Bernice M., ed. *Shirley Jackson: Essays on the Literary Legacy*. Jefferson, NC: McFarland, 2005. A collection of essays that sheds light on Jackson's better- and lesser-known works, primarily the novels. Some of the essays focus on more general topics, such as Jackson's New England gothic, domestic horror in her work, and a comparison of Jackson and writer Stephen King.

Oppenheimer, Judy. *Private Demons: The Life of Shirley Jackson*. New York: G. P. Putnam's Sons, 1988. This volume is the first extensive biography of Jackson; it is finely detailed and provides an excellent understanding of the author. Oppenheimer interviewed almost seventy persons for this book, including Jackson's family members, friends, and neighbors. Contains numerous photographs.

Parks, John G. "'The Possibility of Evil': A Key to Shirley Jackson's Fiction." *Studies in Short Fiction* 15, no. 3 (Summer, 1978): 320-323. Concentrates on Jackson's short stories, with Parks drawing useful comparisons with other authors, such as Flannery O'Connor and Nathaniel Hawthorne.

Rubinsein, Roberta. "House Mothers and Haunted Daughters: Shirley Jackson and Female Gothic." *Tulsa Studies in Women's Literature* 15 (Fall, 1996): 309-331. Explains how Jackson's fiction demonstrates her increasingly gothic representation of the bonds between mothers and daughters; discusses this theme in a number of Jackson's stories.

Schaub, Danielle. "Shirley Jackson's Use of Symbols in 'The Lottery.'" *Journal of the Short Story in English* 14 (Spring, 1990): 79-86. Discusses how Jackson distracts the reader's attention into thinking the story is a fable or fairy tale. Analyzes the symbolic use of setting, atmosphere, numbers, names, and objects in the story.

Stark, Jack. "Shirley Jackson's 'The Lottery.'" In *Censored Books*, edited by Nicholas Karolider, Lee Burgess, and John M. Kean. New York: Scarecrow Press, 1993. Discusses some of the reasons why the story was censored in schools and some of the values of teaching the story to teenagers. Argues that "The Lottery" encourages reflection on some of the issues teens need to understand in order to become good citizens.

Yarmove, Jay A. "Shirley Jackson's 'The Lottery.'" *The Explicator* 52 (Summer, 1994): 242-245. Discusses the importance of setting, historical time, and irony of character names in the allegorical meaning of the story. Compares the ending of the story to the ending of Thomas Hardy's novel *Tess of the D'Urbervilles*.

Terry Heller

HENRY JAMES

Born: New York, New York; April 15, 1843
Died: London, England; February 28, 1916

PRINCIPAL SHORT FICTION

A Passionate Pilgrim, 1875
Daisy Miller, 1878
An International Episode, 1878-1879 (serial), 1879 (book)
The Madonna of the Future, 1879
The Siege of London, 1883
Tales of Three Cities, 1884
The Author of Beltraffio, 1885
The Aspern Papers, 1888
The Lesson of the Master, 1892
The Private Life, Lord Beaupre, The Visits, 1893
The Real Thing, 1893
Terminations, 1895
Embarrassments, 1896
The Two Magics: The Turn of the Screw and Covering End, 1898
The Soft Side, 1900
The Better Sort, 1903
The Novels and Tales of Henry James, 1907-1909 (24 volumes)
The Finer Grain, 1910
A Landscape Painter, 1919
Travelling Companions, 1919
Master Eustace, 1920
Stories of Writers and Other Artists, 1944
Henry James: Selected Short Stories, 1950
Henry James: Eight Tales from the Major Phase, 1958
The Complete Tales of Henry James, 1962-1965 (12 volumes; Leon Edel, editor)
The Figure in the Carpet, and Other Stories, 1986
The Jolly Corner, and Other Tales, 1990
The Uncollected Henry James: Newly Discovered Stories, 2004

OTHER LITERARY FORMS

Henry James was a prolific writer who, from 1875 until his death, published a book or more every year. Other than short fiction, James wrote novels, dramas, biographies, autobiographies, reviews, travelogues, art and literary criticism, literary theory, and letters. James was a pioneer in the criticism and theory of fiction. Much of his criticism appears in Leon Edel and Mark Wilson's edition of *Henry James: Literary Criticism* (1984). James's creative method and the sources of many of his works are documented in *The Complete Notebooks of Henry James* (1987).

ACHIEVEMENTS

Henry James contributed to the development of the modernist novel, invented cryptic tales that border on the postmodern, and laid the groundwork for the contemporary theory of narrative. He completed more than twenty novels (two uncompleted novels were published posthumously). He also wrote 112 short stories, 7 travel books, 3 autobiographies, numerous plays, 2 critical biographies, and voluminous works of criticism. James brought the American novel to its fruition and gave it an international flavor. He transformed the novel of physical adventure to one of psychological intrigue. His character studies are probing and intense. His precise use of limited point of view invites the reader to become actively engaged in interpreting events and ferreting out meaning. His works also achieve a masterful blend of summarized action and dramatic scenes. In his short fiction, he created the forerunners of the modern antiheroes and invented metafictional stories about the nature of art and writing. Also, his critical works and many prefaces have given modern critics a vocabulary for discussing character and point of view. James edited a deluxe edition of his complete works, received honorary degrees from Harvard University and the University of Oxford, and was awarded the Order of Merit from King George V. His works have influenced Joseph Conrad, James Joyce, Virginia Woolf, and Graham Greene.

BIOGRAPHY

Henry James's career is usually divided into four periods: his formative years, his apprenticeship, his middle years, and his major phase. James was descended from Irish Protestants. His grandfather, a poor immigrant, lived out the American Dream and died one of the wealthiest men in the United States. James's father, Henry James, Sr., renounced the Calvinistic work ethic and indulged in the mysticism of Emanuel Swedenborg and the socialism of Charles Fourier.

Through most of his youth, James was shuttled back and forth between Europe and the United States, thus gaining an international perspective on art and life. He learned French and received a European education through a variety of tutors and schools. As a young man, he was exposed to the greatest museums and art galleries in the world. His eye for painting aided him in creating a painterly quality in his work. In 1858, his family moved to Newport, Rhode Island, which was to become the scene of some of his early works of fiction. In 1862, he went to Harvard University to study law but attended poet Robert Lowell's lectures and decided to pursue a literary career. In 1864, he published his first short story and continued to write stories and criticism for the rest of his life. In 1869, he spent a year abroad. With the death of his favorite cousin, Minnie, in 1870, he felt that his youth had come to an end.

James entered his apprentice years between 1865 and 1882. During these years, he published his first collection of short fiction, *A Passionate Pilgrim*, and his first significant novel, *Roderick Hudson* (1876). He achieved popular success with *Daisy Miller* and continued to write *The American* (1876-1877, serial; 1877, book), *Washington Square* (1880), and *The Portrait of a Lady* (1880-1881, serial; 1881, book). These works dealt with the international theme and explored the problems of American innocence exposed to the corrupting influence of European society.

In the 1880's, James began to take up some of the themes of the naturalists. With *The Bostonians* (1885-1886, serial; 1886, book) and *The Princess Casamassima* (1885-1886, serial; 1886, book), James began to

Henry James (Library of Congress)

treat the issues of social reformers. These novels, along with *The Tragic Muse* (1889-1890, serial; 1890, book), were not successful. Between 1890 and 1895, James attempted to establish his reputation as a dramatist, but he was unable to please theater audiences, and his play *Guy Domville* (pb. 1894, pr. 1895) was booed.

In 1897, James settled down in Lamb House in Sussex, and by 1900 he had entered his major phase and had written three richly textured novels: *The Wings of the Dove* (1902), *The Ambassadors* (1903), and *The Golden Bowl* (1904). He died in 1916 in London and was buried in the United States.

ANALYSIS

Henry James believed that an author must be granted his *donnée*, or central idea, and then be judged on the execution of his material. James's stories are about members of high society. The characters do not engage in dramatic actions but spend much of their time in cryptic conversations, which slowly reveal the intense psychological strain under which they are laboring. James's narrators are often

confused individuals trying to puzzle out and evaluate themselves and the people around them. Romance is frequently at the center of James's tales, but
his lovers have difficulty coming to terms with their
own feelings, and often love goes unrecognized and
unfulfilled. Marriage is often rejected by his characters, and when it does appear, it is often the scene of
heartaches and hidden resentments. Death and dying
are also a part of James's stories. Even though he focuses on the death of women and children, he avoids
both the macabre and the sentimental. His stories can
be divided into three categories: international romances, tales about writers and artists, and introspective narratives about wasted lives.

James has not been given the same recognition for
his short fiction that Nathaniel Hawthorne and Edgar
Allan Poe have received; yet James devoted much of
his literary life to the creation of short fiction and made
many attempts to master the form. Several times in his
life he expressed the desire to give up writing novels
and to devote himself solely to creating short fiction.
For half a century, James employed himself in the
writing of 112 pieces of short fiction, beginning with
"A Tragedy of Error" in 1864 and ending with "The
Round of Visits" in 1910. He began writing stories ten
years before he published his first novel, and over his
lifetime, his stories appeared in thirty-five different periodicals on both sides of the Atlantic.

James called his short fiction "tales," and he divided
his tales into types. The anecdote, which focuses on
one character and one incident, is a brief, compact, and
highly distilled story comparable to a sonnet. The
longer *nouvelle*, which often ran between twenty thousand and forty-five thousand words, allowed James
greater development in his short fiction, not for multi-
plying incidents but for probing the depths of a character's experience. James expanded his stories because
he wanted to explore the richness of human experience
that lies hidden behind the surface of everyday life.

James's major tales can be divided into three periods: His early stories focus on the international
theme; during his middle years, his stories center on
writers and artists; and his final stories focus on older
characters who have gone through life but never really
lived. James's international stories focus on taking

characters with set expectations and placing them in
foreign environments. *Daisy Miller* is one of James's
early novelettes and deals with a young American girl
who finds herself out of place in a European
environment.

DAISY MILLER

In *Daisy Miller*, young Frederick Winterbourne, an
American living in Europe, becomes fascinated with
the garrulous Daisy Miller, who is vacationing on the
Continent. The free-spirited Daisy amiably flirts with
Winterbourne. Although he is attracted to her, he is
aware that she and her negligent mother are the source
of gossip among European Americans, who are scan-
dalized by the forward ways of the unchaperoned
young American. After seeing Daisy in Vevey, he again
meets her in Rome, where she is frequently seen with
Giovanelli, who is thought to be an Italian adventurer.
Ostracized by her American compatriots, she continues
to be seen with Giovanelli and risks her life by spending
a moonlit night with him at the Colosseum, where she
contracts malaria and dies. The puzzled Winterbourne
attends her funeral and realizes that she is innocent.

In *Daisy Miller*, James explores the dilemma of an
innocent American woman who flouts the social codes
of European society. More than that, however, he explores the mind of Winterbourne, a Europeanized
American who tries to figure out whether Daisy is
naïve or reckless. Like other Jamesean heroes, Winterbourne cannot commit himself to a woman with whom
he is falling in love. Finding her attractive but shallow,
he is compelled to lecture her on mores, and when he
sees her at the Colosseum, he "cuts her dead." Unable
to break Winterbourne's stiffness, she sends him a message from her deathbed, noting that she was fond of
him. Convinced that he has been unjust to her, Winterbourne escapes into his studies and becomes entangled
with a foreign woman.

James's heroine, like Herman Melville's Billy
Budd, represents American innocence. Both have
found themselves in a world order that puts them at
risk, and both are sacrificed by those who should have
helped them. In addition to introducing the international theme, *Daisy Miller* introduces two Jamesean
types: the sacrificed woman and the egotist who rejects
her love. Though James later rejected his subtitle *A*

Study, the novelette *Daisy Miller* is a study of the complexity of human relationships. The enigmatic but vivacious Daisy is sacrificed at the Colosseum like the early Christians, while the reticent and regretful lover experiences a sense of loss as he retreats from the world of spontaneity and life.

THE ASPERN PAPERS

In "The Aspern Papers," James takes the international theme beyond the romance and weaves a darker and more complex tale. In order to obtain the letters of the American poet Jeffrey Aspern, an unnamed American editor takes up residence with Aspern's former mistress, Juliana Bordereau, and is willing to make love to her middle-aged niece, Miss Tita. He pays exorbitant rent for a room in their Venetian hideaway and spends lavishly to create a garden in their courtyard. Feeling that he is inspired by the mystic presence of Aspern and willing to take any measure to obtain the letters, he breaks into Juliana's drawer and is caught. He retreats, and the dying Juliana hides the papers in her mattress. After Juliana dies, Miss Tita offers to give him the papers if he will marry her. He rejects her proposal only to reconsider it too late, after Miss Tita has burned the papers.

The unnamed narrator goes by an alias. Later, he reveals his name to Miss Tita but not to the reader. He is one version of the unidentifiable American hero who either shuffles names, like James Fenimore Cooper's Leatherstocking, or assumes various identities, like Melville's heroes. He is a man without an identity, a parasite living on the reputation of a famous writer. He is also a typical American monomaniacal quester, fixed on an obsessive quest and willing to sacrifice all in pursuit of it. The narrator sees himself as part of a grandiose scheme; the garden that he plants becomes the symbol of a lost Eden. In Miss Tita, James again sets up a woman as a sacrificial victim. Like other Jamesean heroes (and heroes from American literature in general), the narrator rejects marriage. Also, in his quest for knowledge, he is willing to sacrifice the private lives of Juliana and Aspern.

"THE REAL THING"

In his next set of stories, which focus on artists and writers, James explores the relationship between life and art and the conflict between the artist's public and private life. In "The Real Thing," James tells the story of an unnamed artist who hires two highly polished aristocrats forced to earn their living as models. Major Monarch and his wife contrast with the artist's other models, Miss Churm, a feisty cockney, and Oronte, a low-life Italian. The artist discovers that his lower-class models can transform themselves into aristocrats, whereas the real aristocrats present either a static or a distorted picture of reality. He uses the Monarchs to create a set of illustrations upon which his future depends. An old friend tells him to get rid of the aristocrats because they are ruining his work and jeopardizing his career. The artist, however, respects and sympathizes with their plight but eventually has to dismiss them.

In "The Real Thing," James explores not only the relationship between art and life but also the human dilemma of an artist faced with the conflict of saving his career or upholding his responsibility to two people with whom he sympathizes. The story is built on a series of finely balanced contrasts. The Monarchs are pure aristocrats. The artist thinks that they have come to sit for a portrait, but they have come to be hired as models. The Monarchs are aristocrats, yet they cannot model aristocrats, whereas Miss Churm and Oronte are commoners who can easily transform themselves into gentry. Ironically, the Englishwoman models for Italian types, while the Italian model does Englishmen. The servant-class models start out waiting on the Monarchs, but later the Monarchs wait on the servants. Thus, class distinctions are reversed. The artist wants to paint artistic portraits for which the aristocratic Monarchs are suitable, yet he devotes himself to commercial illustrations, using a working woman who can impersonate an empress. The aristocrats display themselves like slaves at an auction, whereas the servants do their job without auditioning. The lower-class models are professionals; the aristocrats are amateurs. The artist friend is supposedly a good judge of models, but he is a second-rate painter. The greatest irony of all is that people who have no sense of self can become transformed into commercial art, while people holding on to their identity, their own clothes, and their own manners become too photographic, too typical, and too much the real thing. Although the artist must rid himself of the two aristocrats, his experience with them has moved him more deeply than his work with the professional models. The story is a gem of balance and contrast that transforms an aesthetic dilemma into an ethical one and explores the relationship of art to life, servant to master, self to role, portraiture to illustration, and commercial art to lived experience. "The Real Thing" is an often-anthologized story and a perfect illustration of James's craft in the anecdote or traditional short story.

"THE FIGURE IN THE CARPET"

The theme of the relationship between art and life is broadened in James's stories about writers. During his middle period, James created a series of stories in which a young would-be writer or critic surveys the life and work of a master writer. In "The Figure in the Carpet," a story about an eccentric writer who has gained significant critical attention, James probes the nature of criticism itself. An unidentified critic trying to gain a name for himself is called upon to review *The Middle*, the latest novel of the famous author Hugh Vereker, because the lead critic, George Corvick, has to meet his fiancé, Gwendolen Erme. The narrator writes a glowing review of Vereker's work, then attends a party in hope of seeing the great author. When a socialite presents Vereker with the narrator's review, he calls it "the usual twaddle." Vereker later apologizes to the critic but says that critics often misunderstand the obvious meaning, which stands out in his novels like a figure in a carpet. The critic probes Vereker for clues, but the author says that the clues run throughout his entire work. After searching for the secret meaning in Vereker's work, the critic gives up the quest as a hoax. His fellow critic Corvick, however, uses the quest for the narrative secret as an excuse to work more closely with his fiancé, Gwendolen. Frustrated in their efforts, Corvick leaves the country. While away, he writes Gwendolen that he has figured out the secret, and he and Gwendolen get married. When Corvick dies, Gwendolen will not reveal the secret to the narrator, who is even willing to marry her to obtain it. Gwendolen does marry a mediocre critic, Drayton Deane. After the deaths of Gwendolen, Vereker, and Vereker's wife, the narrator tries to obtain the secret from Deane, who knows nothing about it.

In "The Figure in the Carpet," James again turns to the monomanical unnamed narrator on a quest for secret knowledge hidden in a text. Like the narrator of "The Aspern Papers," the critic is willing to marry a woman to gain greater knowledge about an author's work. James said that the story was about misunderstood authors and the need for more analytical criticism. The story sets up typical Jamesean paradoxes. Is Vereker being honest or is "the figure" merely a hoax on critics? Does Corvick really know the secret or is he using his knowledge to win Gwendolen? What is the puzzling connection between interpreting a work and exploring the intimate relationships between men and women? Why do the many so-called possessors of the secret die? This story has been cited as a model for the critical act by many modern critics. Its metafictional qualities and its strange mixture of love and death with the act of interpretation give it a distinctly postmodern quality.

The stories written in James's later years take on a mystical tone. The artist is replaced by a sensitive individual who has alienated himself from the world. The characters are few and often focus on only two people. The characters remain obsessive, but now they are in pursuit of that part of themselves that haunts them. The Jamesean love story is played out into old age, with the woman as a patient bystander, a reflector of the man's battle with himself. The image of the hunt found in Cooper, Melville, and Ernest Hemingway is now symbolic of an internal quest for the terrors hidden within the self. The artists, who in earlier stories sought to gain a second chance or find a next time, now become egocentric gentlemen facing the life that they could have had. The venture into the wilderness becomes a metaphor for the descent into the unconscious.

"THE ALTAR OF THE DEAD"

In "The Altar of the Dead," George Stransom constantly memorializes the death of his bride, Mary Antrim, who died of a fever after their wedding day. Like a character from a Poe short story, he maintains an obsessive devotion to his dead love and is chained to the observance of the anniversary of his wife's death. While remembering his wife, he meets his friend Paul Creston and Paul's second wife. In a strange way, James returns to the international theme by making

Creston's new wife an American who has married for money. Stransom meditates on Creston's first wife and idealizes her in her death. Later the same day, Stransom learns of the death of his boyhood friend, Acton Hague, a man who betrayed Stransom in some undisclosed manner. Hague becomes the only dead friend whom Stransom rejects, as Stransom becomes more and more absorbed with the dead and creates an altar of candles to them. A mysterious woman becomes a fellow mourner at Stransom's shrine. It takes him months to learn her name and years to find out her address. He finally comes to her apartment after the death of her aunt, only to find that her room is a personal shrine to Acton Hague, who rejected the woman. Since Stransom cannot light a candle for Hague, the relationship ends. The loss of the woman casts a shadow over his daily devotions at his altar. Dismayed, he has a vision of his dead wife, Mary, smiling at him from heaven. Just then, the mysterious woman returns to him as he dies in her arms. The last candle on the altar is lit not only for Acton Hague but also for Stransom.

Stransom has left the world of the living and has become obsessed with the dead. He forms a distant relationship with a fellow mourner, but she is only a part of his isolated world. Her feelings are never considered. Instead of forming a meaningful relationship, he continues to withdraw from human love. Stransom, like other heroes in James's later tales, becomes an example of James's reticent lover, a man who has rejected life and embraced death. The death of Stransom in the woman's arms unites the love and death theme predominant in the later tales.

"The Beast in the Jungle"

"The Beast in the Jungle" is a powerful story about one man's quest for his illusive identity. John Marcher meets May Bartram when they are both in their thirties. Ten years earlier, Marcher revealed to her that he was singled out for a terrible fate. When Marcher recalls that he told her about his premonition, they form a relationship, and May begins to wait with him. Blindly, he rules out love as the strange fate that awaits him and forms a friendship with May, taking her to operas, giving her gifts, and spending hours talking about his fate. As the years pass, he becomes skeptical that the "beast" will ever come. He feels reluctant to take May

along with him on a "tiger hunt." Finally, May becomes ill. She knows his fate but will not tell him because she wants to make him a man like any other. He realizes that he might save her, but he is too preoccupied with his own destiny to become involved with her. She eventually tells him that his fate has already passed him by and that he never recognized it. When she dies, he contemplates that her death might be the terrible fate, but he rules out this premise. Marcher, an outsider at May's funeral, eventually goes abroad only to return to the grave of his friend to see another mourner stricken with grief. Suddenly, the beast leaps out at Marcher, as he realizes that he has failed to love and has been unable to feel deeply about anything. He has been an empty man who has watched his life from the outside but has failed to live it.

Marcher, like Stransom, is held prisoner to an obsession that removes him from the world of human relationships. He cannot give himself to another, so he must await his fate. James called the story a negative adventure. Indeed, Marcher's trek into the wilderness is his own confrontation with his unconscious fears. In his monomaniacal obsession, he sacrifices May, who becomes dedicated to waiting for him to discover his fate, while he prides himself on his disinterestedness. In "The Beast in the Jungle," as in other James stories, the woman becomes useful to the man as a siphon for his own obsessions. Marcher fails to recognize and accept love and wastes his life by projecting all his endeavors onto a nebulous future. He is so wrapped up in his own ego that he fails to believe that the death of a lifelong friend is a terrible fate. In the end, he is brought into the world of the dead. Like Stransom, he has lived outside the present and now has only a lost past on which to look back. Like Winterbourne at the funeral of Daisy Miller, he begins to realize what the woman has meant to him. The cemetery where he stands is compared to a garden, which can be seen as an Eden, where Marcher realizes his own ignorance and comes to a painful awareness of his loss of paradise. The cemetery is also called a wilderness, a wilderness that will take him beyond the settled life and into the terrible recesses of his own heart. Marcher is a version of the American future-oriented pioneer unattached to family and loved ones, an Emersonian hero caught in the void of his own solipsistic world. He also becomes one of the first modern antiheroes, inauthentic men who live outside themselves, men to whom nothing really happens.

"THE JOLLY CORNER"

Stransom becomes absorbed in the past, in the world of the dead, and he neglects to establish a relationship with the woman who mourns with him. Marcher becomes involved in a vacuous destiny, unable to see the love that surrounds him. In "The Jolly Corner," Spencer Brydon, another alienated man who rejects the present, pursues his obsession with a past that might have been. Having lived abroad, Brydon returns to New York after a thirty-three-year absence only to find that the world has changed around him. James again explores what happens to an individual who finds himself in an alien culture. When Brydon comes to settle some property that he owns in the United States, he begins to wonder about his talents as a businessman and contemplates the kind of man he might have been had he stayed in the United States. He eventually develops a morbid obsession with his alter ego, the other self that he might have been. One night, Brydon enters the empty house called the Jolly Corner in search of his doppelgänger. When he finally comes face to face with it, he faints at the monstrous sight. Upon recovery, he finds himself in the lap of Alice Staverton, who reassures him that she does not find his shadow self so horrible. In the end, he rejoices that he has gained knowledge about himself.

Spencer Brydon's return to the United States plays an ironic twist on James's international theme, as a Europeanized American returns to a United States from which he feels alienated and then conjures up an American self that horrifies him. Like Marcher, Brydon finds himself on a hunt stalking his secret self, his fate that might have been. Again, James uses the image of the hunt to symbolize an internal journey into the subconscious mind. As the doors of life's options open and close around Brydon in the haunted house of his lost youth, the monster leaps out at him as it did at Marcher. Both men, like Stransom, collapse upon the women they have neglected. Alice Staverton is the woman who waited and shared Brydon's destiny, the way that May Bartram did Marcher's. Alice not only knew his double but also accepted it. The use of the double figure was

popular in romantic and gothic literature, but in "The Jolly Corner," James gave a deeper psychological and philosophical undertone to the motif. In his last group of stories, James used the mystery adventure format to probe the inner psyche of his characters and to examine characters obsessed with living life outside the present.

James brought a greater psychological realism to the genre of short fiction, expanded its length in order to encompass an in-depth range of inner experiences, transformed the mystery story into metafictional narratives that have a distinctly postmodern quality, and reshaped the quest motif of American literature into existential probings about authenticating one's identity.

OTHER MAJOR WORKS

LONG FICTION: *Roderick Hudson*, 1876; *The American*, 1876-1877 (serial), 1877 (book); *The Europeans*, 1878; *Confidence*, 1879-1880 (serial), 1880 (book); *Washington Square*, 1880; *The Portrait of a Lady*, 1880-1881 (serial), 1881 (book); *The Bostonians*, 1885-1886 (serial), 1886 (book); *The Princess Casamassima*, 1885-1886 (serial), 1886 (book); *The Reverberator*, 1888; *The Tragic Muse*, 1889-1890 (serial), 1890 (book); *The Spoils of Poynton*, 1897; *What Maisie Knew*, 1897; *In the Cage*, 1898; *The Awkward Age*, 1898-1899 (serial), 1899 (book); *The Sacred Fount*, 1901; *The Wings of the Dove*, 1902; *The Ambassadors*, 1903; *The Golden Bowl*, 1904; *The Outcry*, 1911; *The Ivory Tower*, 1917; *The Sense of the Past*, 1917.

PLAYS: *Daisy Miller*, pb. 1883 (adaptation of his novel); *The American*, pr. 1891, pb. 1949 (adaptation of his novel); *Theatricals: Tenants and Disengaged*, pb. 1894; *The Reprobate*, pb. 1894, pr. 1919; *Guy Domville*, pb. 1894, privately, pr. 1895, pb. 1949; *Theatricals, Second Series: The Album and The Reprobate*, pb. 1895; *The High Bid*, pr. 1908, pb. 1949; *The Other House*, wr.1909, pb. 1949; *The Outcry*, wr.1909, pr. 1917, pb. 1949; *The Saloon*, pr. 1911, pb. 1949 (one-act); *The Complete Plays of Henry James*, pb. 1949 (Leon Edel, editor).

NONFICTION: *Transatlantic Sketches*, 1875; *French Poets and Novelists*, 1878; *Hawthorne*, 1879; *Portraits of Places*, 1883; *A Little Tour in France*, 1884; *The Art of Fiction*, 1884 (with Walter Besant; includes James's essay "The Art of Fiction"); *Partial Portraits*, 1888;

Essays in London, 1893; *William Wetmore Story and His Friends*, 1903; *English Hours*, 1905; *The American Scene*, 1907; *Views and Reviews*, 1908; *Italian Hours*, 1909; *A Small Boy and Others*, 1913 (memoir); *Notes of a Son and Brother*, 1914 (memoir); *Notes on Novelists*, 1914; *The Middle Years*, 1917; *The Art of the Novel: Critical Prefaces*, 1934 (R. P. Blackmur, editor); *The Notebooks of Henry James*, 1947 (F. O. Matthiessen and Kenneth B. Murdock, editors); *The Scenic Art*, 1948 (Allan Wade, editor); *Henry James Letters*, 1974-1984 (5 volumes; Leon Edel, editor); *Henry James: Literary Criticism*, 1984; *The Art of Criticism: Henry James on the Theory and Practice of Fiction*, 1986; *The Complete Notebooks of Henry James*, 1987; *Dear Munificent Friends: Henry James's Letters to Four Women*, 1999 (Susan E. Gunter, editor); *Henry James on Culture: Collected Essays on Politics and the American Social Scene*, 1999 (Pierre A. Walker, editor); *Dearly Beloved Friends: Henry James's Letters to Younger Men*, 2001 (Susan E. Gunter and Steven H. Jobe, editors); *The Complete Letters of Henry James, 1855-1872*, 2006 (Pierre A. Walker and Greg W. Zacharias, editors); *The Complete Letters of Henry James, 1872-1876*, 2008, 2009 (2 volumes; Pierre A. Walker and Greg W. Zacharias, editors).

Bibliography

Bell, Millicent. "'The Pupil' and the Unmentionable Subject." *Raritan* 16 (Winter, 1997): 50-63. Claims the story is about money, a subject that was once considered unmentionable by the genteel set. James focuses on the extinct code of manners and taste by which refined persons were not supposed to talk much about money.

Bloom, Harold, ed. *Henry James*. Broomall, Pa.: Chelsea House, 2001. Focuses on James's short fiction, reprinting critical analyses of several of his works, including "The Beast in the Jungle," "The Lesson of the Master," "The Jolly Corner," and *Daisy Miller*. Contains a biography of James, a list of characters in each story, a bibliography of James's works, and an index of themes and ideas.

Dewey, Joseph, and Brooke Horvath, eds. *"The Finer Thread, the Tighter Weave": Essays on the Short Fiction of Henry James*. West Lafayette, Ind.:

Purdue University Press, 2001. A collection of critical essays analyzing James's short fiction. Includes bibliography and index.

Gage, Richard P. *Order and Design: Henry James Titled Story Sequences*. New York: Peter Lang, 1988. Gage examines James's published short-story collections, such as *Terminations, Embarrassments*, and *The Soft Side*, in order to show how James collected his stories around a central theme. Focusing on the interrelatedness of James's works, Gage shows how James's stories can be divided into organized units based upon a holistic design.

Heldreth, Leonard. "The Ghost and the Self: The Supernatural Fiction of Henry James." In *The Celebration of the Fantastic*, edited by Donald E. Morse, Marshall B. Tymn, and Csilla Bertha. Westport, Conn.: Greenwood Press, 1992. Discusses two typical patterns in James's ghost stories: In one group, the supernatural force is a trace of the past compelling a character to make a change. In the second group, ghosts constitute an intrusion of the romantic relationship between two characters.

Hocks, Richard A. *Henry James: A Study of the Short Fiction*. Boston: Twayne, 1990. A good introduction to James's short fiction. Divides James's stories into three periods: the early social realism, the middle tales dealing with psychological and moral issues, and the later works of poetic expressionism. Detailed analyses of the major works are provided, along with selections of James's writings on short fiction and a collection of critical articles on selected works.

Horne, Philip. "Henry James and the Economy of the Short Story." In *Modernist Writers and the Marketplace*, edited by Ian Willison, Warwick Gould, and Warren Chernaik. London: Macmillan, 1996. Discusses some of the commercial and social constraints and opportunities that affected James's writing of short fiction in the last half of his career.

Kraft, James. *The Early Tales of Henry James*. Carbondale: Southern Illinois University Press, 1969. Kraft briefly covers James's theory of short fiction and gives considerable emphasis to James's little-known early stories. He focuses on James's development as a writer of short fiction, beginning with James's first story "A Tragedy of Error" (1864) and ending with "The International Episode" (1879). This book is not for the student interested in James's major works.

Lustig, T. J. *Henry James and the Ghostly*. Cambridge, England: Cambridge University Press, 1994. Discusses James's ghost stories and the significance of the "ghostly" for his work generally. Among the works discussed are "The Jolly Corner" and *The Turn of the Screw*. Lustig devotes a third of this study to *The Turn of the Screw*, which he argues is a story about reading.

Martin, W. R., and Warren U. Ober. *Henry James's Apprenticeship: The Tales, 1864-1882*. Toronto: P. D. Meany, 1994. An analysis of the stories James wrote in the first fifteen years of his career, suggesting how the vision he was creating in those stories prepared him to write his first masterpiece, *The Portrait of a Lady*. Discusses the sources of his basic theme of the victimized innocent.

Oates, Joyce Carol. "The Madness of Art: Henry James's 'The Middle Years.'" *New Literary History* 27 (Spring, 1996): 259-262. Discusses the story's buried theme of the strange marriage of artist and "greatest admirer."

Pearson, John H. *The Prefaces of Henry James: Framing the Modern Reader*. University Park: Pennsylvania State University Press, 1997. In Chapter 5 of this study, Pearson examines James's preface to volume 17 of his collected works, which contains such stories as "The Altar of the Dead," "The Beast in the Jungle," and "The Birthplace." Provides an intertextual reading of these stories as self-reflective tales in which author and reader are dialectically opposed.

Rawlings, Peter. "A Kodak Refraction of Henry James's 'The Real Thing.'" *Journal of American Studies* 32 (December, 1998): 447-462. Discusses "The Real Thing" and its treatment of the issues of representation and reproduction as an allegory in which the tyrannical forces of the real and the vulgar,

unless subjected to the processes of selection and idealization, can be all-vanquishing.

Scofield, Martin. "Henry James." In *The Cambridge Introduction to the American Short Story*. New York: Cambridge University Press, 2006. Analyzes a number of James's stories and novellas, placing his work in the broader context of, and discussing his contributions to, the development of the American short story.

Simon, Linda. *The Critical Reception of Henry James: Creating a Master*. Rochester: Camden House, 2007. A thorough study of the criticism of James's work, ranging from early magazine reviews to contemporary studies.

Vaid, Krishna Balden. *Technique in the Tales of Henry James*. Cambridge, Mass.: Harvard University Press, 1964. Covers all the major works, gives a comprehensive overview of James's writings on short fiction, and focuses on James's styles of narration and his careful balance of summary and scene. Contains an excellent chapter on James's later tales.

Wagenknecht, Edward. *The Tales of Henry James*. New York: Frederick Ungar, 1984. Contains brief analyses of fifty-five of James's major tales, as well as thumbnail sketches of other stories. Provides a good reference work for someone looking for short summaries and critical bibliographies (found in the footnotes) but lacks detailed criticism of individual works, as well as historical perspective.

Zacharias, Greg W., ed. *A Companion to Henry James*. Malden, Mass.: Wiley/Blackwell, 2008. Collection of essays analyzing James's work, including three that focus on his short fiction: "Bad Years in the Matrimonial Market: James's Shorter Fiction, 1865-1878," by Clair Hughes, "What Daisy Knew: Reading Against Type in *Daisy Miller: A Study*," by Sarah Wadsworth, and "Revisitings and Revisions in the New York Edition of *The Novels and Tales of Henry James*," by Philip Horne.

Paul Rosefeldt

SARAH ORNE JEWETT

Born: South Berwick, Maine; September 3, 1849
Died: South Berwick, Maine; June 24, 1909
Also known as: Alice Eliot, Sarah O. Sweet

PRINCIPAL SHORT FICTION

Deephaven, 1877 (linked sketches)
Old Friends and New, 1879
Country By-Ways, 1881
The Mate of the Daylight, and Friends Ashore, 1884
A White Heron, and Other Stories, 1886
The King of Folly Island and Other People, 1888
Strangers and Wayfarers, 1890
Tales of New England, 1890
A Native of Winby and Other Tales, 1893
The Life of Nancy, 1895
The Queen's Twin, and Other Stories, 1899
Stories and Tales, 1910
The Uncollected Short Stories of Sarah Orne Jewett,
    1971

OTHER LITERARY FORMS

Sarah Orne Jewett wrote four novels, and she published popular books for children, including *Play Days* (1878) and *Betty Leicester* (1890). Her main work of nonfiction was a history, *The Story of the Normans* (1887).

ACHIEVEMENTS

Sarah Orne Jewett is best known as a local colorist who captured with fidelity the life of coastal Maine in the late nineteenth century in sensitive and moving portraits, mainly of women's lives. Except for *The Country of the Pointed Firs* (1896), widely considered her masterpiece, Jewett's long fiction is thought less successful than her short stories. During her lifetime, she was considered one of the best short-story writers in America. Most of her stories appeared first in popular magazines such as *The Atlantic*, under the editorship of William Dean Howells, and *Harper's*. American literary historian F. O. Matthiessen said in his 1929 study of Jewett that she and Emily Dickinson were the two best women writers America had produced. Willa Cather offered Jewett similar praise and credited her with positively changing the direction of her literary career in a brief but rich acquaintance near the end of Jewett's life.

BIOGRAPHY

Sarah Orne Jewett spent most of her life in South Berwick on the coast of Maine, where she was born on September 3, 1849. Daughter of a country doctor, she aspired to medicine herself, but moved toward writing because of early ill health (which led her father to take her on his calls, for fresh air), the special literary education encouraged by her family, and her discovery as a teenager of her "little postage stamp of soil" in reading Harriet Beecher Stowe's *The Pearl of Orr's Island* (1862). Her father, especially, encouraged her to develop her keen powers of observation, and her grandfathers stimulated her interest in storytelling. After the death of her father in 1878, she began a lifelong friendship with Annie Fields that brought her into contact with leading writers in America and Europe, such as Henry James and George Eliot. The two friends traveled together in Europe, the Caribbean, and the United States, and after the death of Mr. Fields, they lived together for extended periods.

Jewett began writing and publishing at the age of nineteen. During her career she developed and maintained the purpose of helping her readers to understand and love the ordinary people of her native, and later she told stories about other misunderstood people, such as the Irish and southern whites. In her career, she produced more than twenty volumes of fiction for children and adults, history, prose sketches, and poetry. Her short stories show rapidly increasing subtlety and power. Her early books were well received, but beginning with *The Mate of the Daylight, and Friends Ashore* reviewers routinely praised her collections highly. It was not unusual for a reviewer to be a little puzzled by how much he or she liked Jewett's stories. A frequent response was that the stories seemed to lack plot and action and yet at the same time, they were absorbing and charming. Late twentieth century critics, notably feminist critics, have suggested that Jewett was developing a kind of storytelling in opposition to the popular melodramas with their fast-paced romance or adventure plots. Jewett's stories came more and more to focus on intimate relations of friendship, especially between older women, but eventually in one way or another between all kinds of people.

By the time Jewett wrote her masterpiece, the novella *The Country of the Pointed Firs*, she had fully developed a form of narration that pointed toward the James Joyce of *Dubliners* (1914). This novella, and a number of her best stories, such as "Miss Tempy's Watchers" and "The Queen's Twin," would set up a problem of tact, of how to overcome barriers to communion between two or more people, and then through a subtle process of preparation would make overcoming these barriers possible. The story would end with an epiphany that involved communion between at least two people. Though she wrote a variety of other kinds of stories in her career, this type of development was probably her major accomplishment, and it achieved its fullest realization in *The Country of the Pointed Firs*.

A tragic carriage accident on her birthday in 1902 left her in such pain that she gave up fiction writing and devoted herself to her friends. In the fall of 1908, she met Willa Cather, to whom she wrote several letters that inspired Cather to write about Nebraska. Cather recognized Jewett's help by dedicating to Jewett her first Nebraska novel, *O Pioneers!* (1913). Jewett died at her South Berwick home on June 24, 1909.

ANALYSIS

When a young reader wrote to Sarah Orne Jewett in 1899 to express admiration of her stories for girls, Jewett encouraged her to continue reading:

You will always have the happiness of finding friendships in books, and it grows pleasanter and pleasanter as one grows older. And then the people in books are apt to make us understand "real" people better, and to know why they do things, and so we learn sympathy and patience and enthusiasm for those we live with, and can try to help them in what they are doing, instead of being half suspicious and finding fault.

Here Jewett states one of the central aims of her fiction, to help people learn the arts of friendship. Chief among these arts is tact, which Jewett defines in *The Country of the Pointed Firs* as a perfect self-forgetfulness that allows one to enter reverently and sympathetically the sacred realms of the inner lives of others. In her stories, learning tact is often a major element, and those who are successful are often rewarded with epiphanies--moments of visionary union with individuals or with nature--or with communion--the feeling of oneness with another person that for Jewett is the ultimate joy of friendship.

Sarah Orne Jewett (Library of Congress)

"A WHITE HERON"

"A White Heron," which first appeared in *A White Heron and Other Stories*, is often considered Jewett's best story, perhaps because it goes so well with such American classics as Nathaniel Hawthorne's *The Scarlet Letter* (1850), Herman Melville's *Moby Dick* (1851), and William Faulkner's "The Bear" (1942). With these works, the story shares a central, complex symbol in the white heron and the major American theme of a character's complex relationship with the landscape and society. As a story about a young person choosing between society and nature as the proper spiritual guide for a particular time in her life, however, "A White Heron" is atypical for Jewett. One main feature that marks the story as Jewett's, however, is that the main character, Sylvia, learns a kind of tact during her adventure in the woods, a tact that grows out of an epiphany and that leads to the promise of continuing communion with nature that the story implies will help this somewhat weak and solitary child grow into a strong adult.

Sylvia, a young girl rescued by her grandmother, Mrs. Tilley, from the overstimulation and overcrowding of her city family meets a young ornithologist, who fascinates her and promises her ten dollars if she will tell him where he can find the white heron he has long sought for his collection. Childishly tempted by this magnificent sum and her desire to please the hunter, who knows so much of nature yet kills the birds, she determines to climb at dawn a landmark pine from which she might see the heron leave its nest. She succeeds in this quest, but finds she cannot tell her secret to the hunter. The story ends with the assertion that she could have loved the hunter as "a dog loves" and with a prayer to the woodlands and summer to compensate her loss with "gifts and graces."

Interesting problems in technique and tone occur when Sylvia climbs the pine. The narrative tone shifts in highly noticeable ways. As she begins her walk to the tree before dawn, the narrator expresses personal anxiety that "the great wave of human interest which flooded for the first time this dull little life should sweep away the satisfactions of an existence heart to heart with nature and the dumb life of the forest." This statement seems to accentuate an intimacy between reader and narrator; it states the position the narrative rhetoric has implied from the beginning and, in effect, asks if the reader shares this anxiety. From this point until Sylvia reaches the top of the tree, the narrator gradually merges with Sylvia's internal consciousness. During the climb, Jewett builds on this intimacy with Sylvia. Both narrator and reader are aware of sharing in detail Sylvia's subjective impressions of her climb and of her view, and this merging of the subjectivities of the story (character, narrator, and reader) extends beyond the persons to objects as the narrator unites with the tree and imagines its sympathy for the climber. The merging extends even further when Sylvia, the reader, and the narrator see with lyric clarity the sea, the sun, and two hawks that, taken together, make all three observers feel as if they could fly out over the world. Being atop the tallest landmark pine, "a great mainmast to the voyaging earth," one is, in a way, soaring in the cosmos as the hawks soar in the air. At this point of clarity and union, the narrative tone shifts again. The narrator speaks directly to Sylvia, commanding her to look at the point where the heron will rise. The vision of the heron rising from a dead hemlock, flying by the pine, and settling on a nearby bough is a kind of colloquy of narrator and character and, if the technique works as it seems to intend, of the reader, too. This shift in "place" involves a shift in time to the present tense that continues through Sylvia's absorption of the secret and her descent from the tree. It seems clear that the intent of these shifts is to transcend time and space, to unite narrator, reader, character, and the visible scene that is "all the world." This is virtually the same technical device that is the central organizing device of Walt Whitman's "Crossing Brooklyn Ferry," and the intent of that device seems similar as well. The reader is to feel a mystical, "transcendental" union with the cosmos that assures one of its life and one's participation in that life.

A purpose of this union is to make justifiable and understandable Sylvia's choice not to give the heron's life away because they have "watched the sea and the morning together." The narrator's final prayer makes sense when it is addressed to transcendental nature on behalf of the girl who has rejected superfluous commodity in favor of Spirit, the final gift of Ralph Waldo

Emerson's nature in his essay, "Nature." Though this story is atypical of Jewett insofar as it offers a fairly clearly transcendental view of nature and so presents a moment of communion with the nonhuman, it is characteristic of Jewett in that by subtly drawing reader and narrator into the epiphany, the story creates a moment of human communion.

"THE ONLY ROSE"

More typical of Jewett's best work is "The Only Rose," which was first published in *The Atlantic* in January, 1894, and was then collected in *The Life of Nancy*. This story is organized by three related epiphanies, each centering on the rose, and each involving a blooming.

In the first "miracle of the rose," Mrs. Bickford and Miss Pendexter are hypnotized into communion by contemplating the new bloom on Mrs. Bickford's poor bush. In this epiphany, Miss Pendexter enters into spiritual sympathy with Mrs. Bickford, realizing that her silence this time is unusual, resulting not from having nothing to say, but from "an overburdening sense of the inexpressible." They go on to share the most intimate conversation of their relationship. The blooming flower leads to a blooming in their friendship. It also leads, however, to Mrs. Bickford's dilemma: On which of her three dead husbands' graves should she place this single rose? Her need to answer this question points to a deeper need to escape from her comparatively isolated and ineffectual life by shifting from an ethic of obligation to an ethic of love. Her heart has been frozen since her first husband's death, and it is long past time now for it to thaw and bloom again. Miss Pendexter understands something of this and tactfully leaves Mrs. Bickford to work it out for herself.

The second miracle of the rose occurs almost at the end of the story, when John confesses his love for Lizzie to his Aunt Bickford as he drives her to the graveyard. The symbolic rose of young and passionate love moves him to speak, even though he is unsure of the propriety of speaking up to the wealthy aunt from whom he hopes to inherit. His story of young love and hope, however, takes Mrs. Bickford out of herself, and she forgets her troubles in sharing his joy. As a result, John blooms, blushing a "fine scarlet."

The final miracle is that while John is taking the flowers to the graves, Mrs. Bickford realizes which of her husbands should have the rose. At the same time that John is taking the rose for his Lizzie, Mrs. Bickford is giving it in her heart to Albert, the first husband whom she loved so passionately in her youth. Her realization of this event makes her blush "like a girl" and laugh in self-forgetfulness before the graveyard as she remembers that the first flower Albert gave her was just such a rose.

In the overall movement of the story, Mrs. Bickford is lifted out of herself and prepared for a richer and deeper communion with her friends and relatives. The single rose blossom seems mysteriously to impose an obligation upon her, but probably it really awakens the ancient spring of love within her that was perhaps covered over by grief at losing Albert so young and by the difficult life that followed his loss. When she finally struggles free of the weight of the intervening years, she recovers her hidden capacity for friendship and joy, for forgetting herself and joining in the happiness of others. She has epiphanies, rediscovers tact, and begins again to experience communion.

"MARTHA'S LADY"

"Martha's Lady" first appeared in *The Atlantic* in October, 1897, and was then collected in *The Queen's Twin, and Other Stories*. This story illustrates Jewett's mature control over her technique and material. She represents a kind of sainthood without falling into the syrupy sentimentality of popular melodrama.

Into a community beginning to show the effects of a Puritan formalism comes Helena Vernon, a young city woman who is un-self-consciously affectionate and beautiful and, therefore, a pleasure to please. She delights her maiden cousin, Harriet Pyne; charms the local minister, who gives her a copy of his *Sermons on the Seriousness of Life*; and transforms Martha, Harriet's new and awkward servant girl. In fact, Helena transforms to some extent everyone she meets in the village of Ashford, taking some of the starch out of their stiff and narrow way of life. After Helena leaves to marry, prosper, and suffer in Europe, Martha carries her memory constantly in her heart: "To lose out of sight the friend whom one has loved and lived to please is to lose joy out of life. But if love is true, there comes presently a higher joy of pleasing the ideal, that is to say, the perfect friend." This is the ideal of sainthood that the narrative voice asks the reader to admire. Thanks largely to Martha's living this ideal of always behaving so as to please Helena, she and Harriet live a happy life together for forty years. Helena returns to visit, worn, but with the same youthful spirit, and to reward with a kiss what she recognizes as Martha's perfect memory of the services Helena enjoyed as a girl. This recognition acknowledges Martha's faithfulness to her ideal and creates that moment of communion that is the ultimate reward for such faithfulness.

What prevents this story from dissolving into mush? Nearly all the special features of Jewett's technical facility are necessary. She avoids overelaboration. It is not difficult for an alert reader to notice the parallel to the Christ story type; a liberating figure enters a legalistic society to inspire love in a group of followers, which results in an apotheosis after her departure. The disciple remains true to the ideal until the liberator comes again to claim the disciple. Jewett could have forced this analogy on the reader, but she does not. Only a few details subtly suggest the analogy--character names, calling Martha a saint, and her relics--but these need not compel the reader in this direction, which, in fact, adds only a little to the story's power.

While avoiding overelaboration, Jewett also avoids internal views. On the whole, the story is made of narrative summary and brief dramatic scenes. Emotion is revealed through action and speech; this technical choice produces less intensity of feeling than, for example, the intimate internal view of Sylvia in "The White Heron." The result is a matter-of-factness of tone that keeps Martha's sainthood of a piece with the ordinary world of Ashford. This choice is supported by nearly every other technical choice of the story--the attention to detail of setting, the gentle but pointed humor directed against religious formalism, and the emergence of Martha from the background of the story. Jewett's intention seems to be on the one hand to prevent the reader from emoting in excess of the worth of the object, but on the other hand to feel strongly and warmly the true goodness of Martha's faithfulness to love. Another purpose of this narrative approach is to demonstrate tact. In "A White Heron," both Sylvia and

the reader enter the quest for the heron with mixed motives, but the nature of the journey--its difficulties, its joys, the absorption it requires--tends to purify motives and to prepare the spirit for epiphany. Sylvia's vision from atop the pine culminates in communion with the wild bird, a vision she has earned and that she may repeat if she realizes its value.

Jewett's light touch, her own tact in dealing with such delicate subjects, is one of her leading characteristics, and it flowers magnificently in the fiction of the last ten years of her writing career. While the stories discussed here illustrate Jewett's most powerful and moving storytelling, they do not illustrate so fully another of the main characteristics of her stories--humor. Humor is often present in her stories and can be found in more abundance than might be expected in "The Only Rose" and "Martha's Lady." She also wrote a number of funny stories that discriminating readers such as Cather would not hesitate to compare with the work of Mark Twain. "The Guests of Mrs. Timms," though more similar to the stories of Jane Austen than Twain, is a popular story of the humorous ironies that result when a socially ambitious widow calls on another widow of higher status without announcing her visit in advance. Among her best humorous stories are "Law Lane," "All My Sad Captains," "A Winter Courtship," and "The Quest of Mr. Teaby," but there are many others that are a delight to read.

OTHER MAJOR WORKS

LONG FICTION: *A Country Doctor*, 1884; *A Marsh Island*, 1885; *The Country of the Pointed Firs*, 1896; *The Tory Lover*, 1901.

POETRY: *Verses: Printed for Her Friends*, 1916.

NONFICTION: *Letters of Sarah Orne Jewett*, 1911 (Annie Fields, editor); *Sarah Orne Jewett Letters*, 1956 (Richard Cary, editor).

CHILDREN'S LITERATURE: *Play Days: A Book of Stories for Children*, 1878; *The Story of the Normans*, 1887; *Betty Leicester: A Story for Girls*, 1890.

BIBLIOGRAPHY

Auten, Janet Gebhart. "'Nothing Much Happens in This Story': Teaching Sarah Orne Jewett's 'A White Heron.'" In *Short Stories in the Classroom*, edited by Carole L. Hamilton and Peter Kratzke. Urbana, Ill.: National Council of Teachers of English, 1999. Recounts several experiences in teaching the story to high school students, making suggestions about the value of the story in exploring conflicts of interest and expanding the canon.

Blanchard, Paula. *Sarah Orne Jewett: Her World and Her Work*. Reading, Mass.: Addison-Wesley, 1994. Offers biographical information and critical interpretation of Jewett's works.

Breitwieser, Mitchell. "Losing Deephaven: Sarah Orne Jewett, Regionalism, and the Art of Loss." In *National Melancholy: Mourning and Opportunity in Classic American Literature*. Stanford, Calif.: Stanford University Press, 2007. Breitwieser's study of American writers' struggle to understand mourning devotes a chapter to *Deephaven*, in which he discusses the circumstances in Jewett's life that led her to write this collection of sketches and her treatment of grief, mourning, and depression in the stories.

Cary, Richard, ed. *Sarah Orne Jewett*. New York: Twayne, 1962. This critical study of Jewett includes a chronology, a biographical sketch, and descriptive analyses of most of her published works. Cary divides Jewett's works into thematic groups and shows how she is a product of her New England background. Supplemented by annotated bibliographies of Jewett's books and of secondary sources.

_____. *Appreciation of Sarah Orne Jewett: Twenty-Nine Interpretive Essays*. Waterville, Maine: Colby College Press, 1973. Collects a good cross section of criticism of Jewett's major writing from 1885 until 1972. Contains biographical sketches, extended reviews, examinations of her technique, interpretations of some individual works, and evaluations of her career.

Castor, Laura. "Making the Familiar Strange: Representing the House in Sarah Orne Jewett's 'The Landscape Chamber' and Linda Hogan's 'Friends and Fortunes.'" In *The Art of Brevity: Excursions in Short Fiction Theory and Analysis*, edited by Per Winther, Jakob Lothe, and Hans H. Skei. Columbia: University of South Carolina Press, 2004. A comparison of the two short stories.

Church, Joseph. "Romantic Flight in Jewett's 'White Heron.'" *Studies in American Fiction* 30, no. 1 (Spring, 2002): 21. Examines the autobiographical and psychological elements of "A White Heron." Discusses Jewett's use of symbolism and analyzes events and characters in the story.

Donovan, Josephine. *Sarah Orne Jewett*. New York: Frederick Ungar, 1980. This critical study includes a chronology and an examination of Jewett's literary career, charting the development of her major themes through her works. Donovan is especially interested in Jewett's feminist themes. Provides primary and secondary bibliographies.

Matthiessen, F. O. *Sarah Orne Jewett*. Boston: Houghton Mifflin, 1929. This short biographical study remains readily available in many libraries. Matthiessen surveys Jewett's life without going into great detail.

Nagel, Gwen L., ed. *Critical Essays on Sarah Orne Jewett*. Boston: G. K. Hall, 1984. This collection's sixteen contemporary reviews of Jewett's books, reprints of eight critical essays published from 1955 to 1983, and eight original essays provide biographical information and interpretations of her works. The introduction surveys the history of critical writing on Jewett.

Palmer, Stephanie C. "Travel Delays in the Commercial Countryside: Bret Harte and Sarah Orne Jewett." In *Together by Accident: American Local Color Literature and the Middle Class*. Lanham, Md.: Lexington Books, 2009. Examines the travel motif in selected works by the two authors, devoting considerable attention to Jewett's short story "The Life of Nancy."

Roman, Margaret. *Sarah Orne Jewett: Reconstructing Gender*. Tuscaloosa: University of Alabama Press, 1992. A survey of Jewett's life and art, focusing on her rejection of the limited role of woman in the nineteenth century. Argues that "A White Heron" raises doubts that men and women can join together and suggests hope for a symbolic androgyny instead. Argues that Jewett rejects male/female sexual categories in her fiction.

Scofield, Martin. "Rebecca Harding Davis, Sarah Orne Jewett, and Mary Wilkins Freeman." In *The Cambridge Companion to the American Short Story*. New York: Cambridge University Press, 2006. Defines Jewett's contribution to the development of the American short story and analyzes several of her stories.

Silverthorne, Elizabeth. *Sarah Orne Jewett: A Writer's Life*. Woodstock, N.Y.: Overlook Press, 1993. Silverthorne describes the increasing interest in Jewett's treatment of women, ecology, and regional life. Silverthorne had access to letters and manuscripts unavailable to previous biographers, and she takes full advantage of Jewett scholarship in this biography.

Slote, Ben. "Jewett at the Fair: Seeing Citizens in 'The Flight of Betsey Lane.'" *Studies in American Fiction* 36, no. 1 (Spring, 2008): 51-76. Describes how Jewett's travels to the world's fair in Chicago influenced her handling of American patriotism in this short story, which is about an old woman's trip to a fair. Notes how this story focuses on the residents of a poorhouse.

Terry Heller

ADAM JOHNSON

Born: South Dakota; July 12, 1967

PRINCIPAL SHORT FICTION

Emporium, 2002
"The Denti-Vision Satellite," 2004
"Hurricanes Anonymous," 2009

OTHER LITERARY FORMS

Though he is known primarily for his short fiction, Adam Johnson is also the author of the novel *Parasites Like Us*, published in 2003. *Parasites Like Us* traces the journey of anthropologist Hank Hannah as he researches the history of a destructive, plundering culture called the Clovis People. He gets embroiled in a dubious archaeological discovery when two of his prize students take their anthropology fellowship research too far. The apocalyptic tale is a satirical social commentary on human culture and the culture of academia. Additionally, it is a character-driven story about one man's life. *Parasites Like Us*, much like Johnson's short fiction, exhibits a keen interest in the evolution of society and technology and its ramifications for the human experience. It is fitting that the main characters of this book are all anthropologists.

ACHIEVEMENTS

Adam Johnson consistently has received awards, fellowships, and accolades since his appearance on the fiction scene. At Arizona State University he was a recipient of the Swarthout Writing Award. He also received a Kingsbury Fellowship from Florida State University. He was a Stegner Fellow at Stanford University for two years and received scholarships from both the Bread Loaf and Sewanee Writers' Conferences. Johnson was named Debut Writer of the Year by Amazon.com in 2002 after the release of his story collection *Emporium*, and in 2003 he was selected for the Barnes and Noble Discover Great Writers series. His novel *Parasites Like Us* received the California Book Award.

In 2009, Johnson received the Whiting Writers' Award, which is given to emerging American writers. He also was nominated for the New York Public Library's prestigious Young Lions Award. In 2010, he received a grant from the National Endowment for the Arts for creative writing and also won the Gina Berriault Award.

BIOGRAPHY

Adam Johnson was born in South Dakota in 1967 and was raised in Arizona. In interviews, he has stated that he signed up for writing classes because it would be an easy A, only to discover he had great passion and talent for writing. He received his B.A. from Arizona State University in 1992. He then pursued both an M.A. and an M.F.A., which he was awarded by McNeese State University in 1996. He received his Ph.D. from Florida State in 2001. Johnson became an associate professor at Stanford University, heading, with Tom Kealey, the Stanford Graphic Novel Project, in which a group of Stanford students study the graphic novel and then write and illustrate their own as a collective in only six weeks.

Johnson often travels to research the subjects of his stories. For his story "Hurricanes Anonymous," which is about a United Parcel Service (UPS) driver post-Hurricane Katrina, Johnson visited New Orleans's Ninth Ward after the storm to observe the city and interview inhabitants. He even accompanied several UPS drivers on local routes. He also has visited North Korea.

Johnson settled in California with his wife, Stephanie Harrell, who is also a writer; they have three children. Johnson's writing mentors include Robert Olen Butler, Tobias Wolff, Ron Carlson, and Sheila Ortiz-Taylor. Some of his favorite writers include Paul Theroux, E. Annie Proulx, Robert O'Connor, Robert Stone, Toni Morrison, and Herman Melville.

ANALYSIS

Adam Johnson's worlds are places full of danger and uncertainty, where a character might lose a loved one, be uprooted from his home, or have everything he believes to be true reversed at a moment's notice. The most meaningful relationships in his stories occur between unlikely pairs of people, who are brought into each other's lives by chance or circumstance. These fleeting but profound connections call to mind the concept of "karass," which was invented and loosely defined by Kurt Vonnegut in *Cat's Cradle* (1963) as strangers whose lives become linked, by sharing some moment or experience with lifelong significance, even though their interaction may be brief.

The dedication to Johnson's story collection *Emporium* makes a cohesive statement of purpose: "to the boxy loop of youth." The stories all involve young people, often coming of age, and Johnson uses exaggerated situations to evoke the grandness of feeling that accompanies many of the milestones of youth.

Johnson's work also is characterized by the extremity of the situations in which his characters find themselves. They accept danger and violence as part of their everyday realities. As a result, Johnson is able to evoke in his readers and his characters an intensity of emotion that corresponds to such violence. This extremity of emotion conveys the intensity of teenage feelings as much as it describes how people respond to violence and fear. Johnson uses thematic elements borrowed from science fiction, popular culture, comic books, and video games to bring to light the utter strangeness of so many aspects of growing up. It is through his use of the surreal that Johnson best reveals for the reader what is worth noting about the everyday.

"TEEN SNIPER"

"Teen Sniper" was published originally in *Harper's* and was later collected in *Emporium*. The story is set in a future when being a police sniper is normal occupation. Tim, the story's narrator, is the best and youngest sniper alive. Still, he feels alienated from his team, mostly older African American men. As a result, Tim's only friend is a bomb detection and disposal robot called ROMS, whom he tries to teach to act more "cool," so the robot will have more friends, something Tim desires himself.

As the story begins, Tim is having trouble with the emotional repercussions of his job as a sniper. He cannot distance himself from the humanity of his targets, and he begins working with a psychiatrist to replace the images of violence he sees with images of flowers. The official company line from the police department on Tim's emotional response to his assignments is that it is an unnecessary and possibly false sensation.

Tim meets and falls for one of his coworker's daughters, Seema, and in an attempt to woo her, he acts like the older snipers, writing off his old friend ROMS in the process. His actions, however, only frighten her to the extent she tells him to get lost. In a fit of despair Tim reconciles with ROMS, who gives him the preprogrammed hostage negotiation advice to be himself and share a meal to promote social interaction with Seema. When ROMS is "killed" in an explosion, the grieving Tim takes the robot's advice and successfully begins a friendship with Seema. This triumph of ROMS's advice leaves Tim and the reader believing that real emotional responses, even in an age of robots and sniping, are not as irrelevant as the police sniper department would have one believe.

This story is a classic bildungsroman turned on its head and made new. The setting and Tim's job aside, his budding interest in girls, confusion over how to become a man, and difficulty in dealing with the hard facts of life are all typical themes in a traditional coming-of-age story. In "Teen Sniper," however, Johnson makes the circumstances of Tim's life extreme: at age thirteen Tim murders people for a living; the masculine role models surrounding him are superfit mercenary snipers; the girl Tim likes can pin him in jujitsu. Johnson uses exaggerated situations to convey how large those coming-of-age emotions feel to a boy of thirteen. Through these heightened examples, he addresses the way in which the evolution of society has made growing up more difficult, and certainly more rapid, than it has been in the past.

"TRAUMA PLATE"

"Trauma Plate" was originally published in *The Virginia Quarterly Review* and later collected in *Emporium*. The story takes place in an imagined not-so-distant future. The three main characters are a husband, wife, and daughter, who own a mom-and-pop bulletproof vest store that is slowly being put out of business by the giant chain, Armor Emporium. The story is told in three third-person sections, following first the father, then the mother, and then the daughter. Each story skips ahead in time. As time progresses, Ruthie, the daughter, grows into a teenager in a world where her parents' marriage becomes more strained, the neighborhood becomes distinctly more violent, and though bulletproof-vest use increases the family store increasingly becomes devastated. By the last section it seems the majority of people are wearing bulletproof vests on a daily basis. Ruthie, who had for years been an excellent swimmer, becomes so uncomfortable taking her vest off that she swims a race at her school meet in record time, wins, and puts on her vest after making the decision to never take it off again.

While this is a story about a future where weapons are everywhere and people always feel the need to wear a bulletproof vest, it is mostly about love. At the end, Ruthie asks her boyfriend to shoot her in the vest, aiming for the metal square protecting her heart, the trauma plate. If he hits her here, she reasons, the odds that she will be shot in the heart a second time are so small statistically that she thinks she can stop wearing her vest. In the final scene, as Ruthie anticipates the shot, she feels great relief and love, knowing that her boyfriend will be the one to do this for her, that he will wound her just enough so that she will be free to live without her vest.

Johnson uses the symbol of the bulletproof vest, even a whole store of them, to show how much love and protection the parents want to offer their daughter. Of course, Johnson shows that even the parents are baffled by the changes they see in the world around them. Their inability to realize their dreams or sell their inventory as they grow older shows how futile these reserves of vests are to protect Ruthie, or themselves, from the dangers of the world. Johnson uses the hyperbolic gesture of giving one's child a bulletproof vest to make a relevant statement about the relationship between parents and children, and the gesture has meaning that reaches beyond the scope of the imagined future he has depicted here.

"CLIFF GODS OF ACAPULCO"

"Cliff Gods of Acapulco" was originally published in *Esquire* in April, 1999, and is collected in *Emporium*. An inventory of the story's components (Las Vegas high jinks, vicious caiman, severed toes, marijuana, indoor parachuting, sex inside a facility for indoor parachuting) sounds more like daredevil journalism than literary fiction, but the story is as innovative in its form as in its content. Johnson is interested in writing a story that is emotionally perceptive and action-packed. The story follows a nonlinear course as the first-person narrator embarks on what turns out to be a misadventure with a friend named Jimbo to visit his friend Marty, who was horribly injured in a car crash several years ago. The two visit Marty's odd home, where wolves prowl the fenced perimeter. The friend's father loses a toe when baiting a caiman and is rushed to the hospital. The next day Marty, Jimbo, and the narrator visit Tasha, Marty's girlfriend, and she lets them indoor parachute at the attraction where she works. Jimbo and Marty go off in search of marijuana while Tasha and the narrator parachute in tandem and have sex, during which the narrator experiences an epiphany. He thinks about all the different people in his life who have had danger and violence swoop down upon them without warning and who spend the rest of their lives seeking out danger, even the artificial variety.

While all of this is going on, it is explained that the narrator's father, who is working in Africa, is dying, unbeknown to the narrator. The story includes the narrator's thoughts of his mother, a stewardess who has lost a coworker in a violent accident, and of future conversations he imagines he will have with his stepfather, Ted, an unlikely father substitute, about the passing of the narrator's real father.

By intercutting the story of the trip with old memories and scenes that will take place in the future, Johnson accomplishes the feat of encapsulating the narrator's entire process of dealing with the death of his father, from the narrator's ignorant moments before it has happened to his profoundest grief, and even moving into the future, where he will come to terms with the loss. Moreover, the narrator manages to accomplish this emotional trajectory through a series of scenes that take place before his father has died. Johnson uses the characters in each scene to address indirectly the way one deals with loss and inexplicable violence through the trappings of consumerism: exotic pets, college football, amusement-park rides, and air travel, to name a few. In the last scene, after the narrator's indoor parachuting epiphany, he finds himself is in a future conversation with his stepfather Ted. The narrator seems willing to give human relationships a chance, despite the fact that there is never any certainty that one will not lose the person one loves and that that person might not be the one for whom one had hoped.

"HURRICANES ANONYMOUS"

While the characters in "Hurricanes Anonymous" seem to come from the same family of well-meaning screw-ups and tenderhearted hell-raisers as those in *Emporium*, the story marks a departure from Johnson's early work. In *Emporium*, the characters face futuristic, human-created dangers, such as technology, gun culture, artificial intelligence, and caged animals. In "Hurricanes Anonymous," however, the main character, Randall, instead faces perils that have existed for eons: a storm and fatherhood. In the story, set in the aftermath of Hurricane Katrina, Randall's son's mother, Marnie, has disappeared, leaving Randall to take care of his estranged son, Geronimo. The story is longer and more patient than much of Johnson's early work, and the main character is older than many of the previous antiheroes. A constant, however, between this piece and the stories of *Emporium*, is the way in which the terrible trappings of bureaucracy drive the characters into crises and the ever-present commentary on the futility of the characters' attempts to be in control of their lives.

OTHER MAJOR WORKS

LONG FICTION: *Parasites Like Us*, 2003.

BIBLIOGRAPHY

Kakutani, Michiko. "An Out-of-Kilter World, Just Down the Interstate." *The New York Times*, April 2, 2002. Perceptive review of *Emporium* takes note of Johnson's common themes.

Mendelsohn, Daniel. "Road to Nowhere." *New York* (May 13, 2002). Notes Johnson's ability to create characters with warmth but with a biting satiric edge.

Reyn, Irina. "Violence and Strip Malls: Stories Paint a World Unsettlingly Familiar." *San Francisco Chronicle*, April 14, 2002, p. RV-3. Review discusses Johnson's ability to meld science fiction with the "familiar present."

CJ Hauser

CHARLES JOHNSON

Born: Evanston, Illinois; April 23, 1948

PRINCIPAL SHORT FICTION

The Sorcerer's Apprentice, 1986

*Soulcatcher, and Other Stories: Twelve Powerful
Tales About Slavery,* 2001

Dr. King's Refrigerator, and Other Bedtime Stories,
2005

OTHER LITERARY FORMS

Charles Johnson worked as a cartoonist from 1965
to 1972 before turning to prose fiction. His first novel,
Faith and the Good Thing, was published in 1974, followed by *Oxherding Tale* (1982), *Middle Passage*
(1990), and *Dreamer* (1998). *Being and Race: Black
Writing Since 1970* (1988) includes essays on literary
theory and culture, while *I Call Myself an Artist* (1999)
has essays, interviews, reviews, and an autobiographical sketch. *Turning the Wheel: Essays on Buddhism
and Writing* (2003) contains essays on the importance
of Buddhist practice and principles in Johnson's life as
an African American intellectual and artist.

ACHIEVEMENTS

Middle Passage won the National Book Award for
Fiction in 1990. *Booker*, a Public Broadcasting Service
(PBS) teleplay, received a Writers Guild Award and the
Prix Jeunesse in 1985. *The Sorcerer's Apprentice* was a
finalist for the 1987 PEN/Faulkner Award. The story
"Kwoon" was reprinted in 1993's *Prize Stories: The O.
Henry Awards*. Johnson is a l998 MacArthur fellow,
and in 2002 he received an American Academy of Arts
and Letters Award for Literature.

BIOGRAPHY

Charles Richard Johnson was born in the Chicago
suburb of Evanston, Illinois, on April 23, 1948. A
voracious reader who resolved to complete one book
per week when he entered high school, Johnson aspired to be a visual artist and took a two-year correspondence course in cartooning while still in school.
He entered Southern Illinois University in 1966, majoring in journalism, and began a lifelong study of
martial arts in 1967. Johnson published his first book
of political drawings, *Black Humor*, in 1970, followed by *Half-Past Nation Time* in 1972, while producing a show called *Charlie's Pad* for PBS, which
was to run for ten years starting in 1969.

Johnson married Joan New in 1970 and began the
first of six novel-length manuscripts that he wrote
during the next two years, while working toward a
master's degree in philosophy at Southern Illinois. He
entered a doctoral program at the State University of
New York at Stony Brook in 1973, published the novel
Faith and the Good Thing in 1974, and in 1976 accepted a position in the English Department of the University of Washington.

Oxherding Tale, the novel that elevated Johnson to
national prominence as a writer, appeared in 1982 after
being rejected by twenty-five publishing houses. The
short stories that Johnson had been placing in magazines since 1977 were collected as *The Sorcerer's Apprentice* in 1986, and his theoretical overview of African American literature, *Being and Race: Black
Writing Since 1970*, was issued in 1988. Johnson's
novel *Middle Passage* won the National Book Award,
making Johnson the second black man (after Ralph Ellison) to be so honored. In spite of his success in several fields, Johnson has continued what he describes as
"the same life and labor--that of devoting myself to a
genuinely philosophical black American fiction."

ANALYSIS

From the beginning of his writing life, Charles
Johnson sought to combine a deep interest in the dominant aesthetic and philosophical concerns of the

Western intellectual tradition with the specific issues and historical consequences of three centuries of chattel slavery and economic discrimination. In response to the numerous stereotypes and misconceptions about African American life that have accumulated in American culture, Johnson observed, "Good fiction sharpens our perception; great fiction *changes* it." Assuming that pioneering African American writers such as Zora Neale Hurston have shattered the silence surrounding the African American experience, Johnson has attempted to open the field, further asserting, "We know, of course, more than oppression and discrimination." Describing his objective as "whole sight," Johnson has worked toward a "cross-cultural fertilization" in his fiction that draws on the full range of technical strategies, which he calls "our inheritance as writers."

One of the most influential people in Johnson's development was the writer and theorist John Gardner, who stressed the importance of what Johnson calls "imaginative storytelling reinforced by massive technique." In his first short-fiction collection, *The Sorcerer's Apprentice*, Johnson's technical facility is evident in stories that range from straight realism to fable, fantasy, folktale, allegory, and quasi-autobiographical confession, mingling modes within stories, while establishing an authentic, convincing narrative voice that reflects the psychological condition of his protagonists. The pattern of development in his stories is from what he calls "ignorance to knowledge, or from a lack of understanding to some greater understanding." This understanding is often an aspect of the character's quest for identity, a kind of progression in which Johnson resists a fixed notion of the self in favor of what he calls the "expansive." The stories in the collection touch on some of the most fundamental aspects of African American life to reveal what Rudolph Byrd calls "the richness of the black world."

"THE EDUCATION OF MINGO"

Each of the stories in *The Sorcerer's Apprentice* has a specific philosophic concept at the core of the narrative. "The Education of Mingo," which opens the collection, is informed by the argument that humans are ultimately not responsible for their actions if there is an omniscient deity in control of the universe. The story is

grounded in a down-to-earth situation involving a white man, Moses Green, who has trained an African slave, Mingo, to echo all of his desires, attitudes, preferences, and predilections. As Mingo begins to act beyond the specific instructions of his master, anticipating Green's subconscious and instinctual urges, the servant-master relationship is presented as a reciprocal form of entrapment, in which neither is truly free nor completely himself. The costs of this arrangement are Green's permanent connection to his slave and Mingo's restriction to his status as menial, no matter how skilled or accomplished he becomes. The story is both a commentary on three centuries of slavery and a vivid expression of the inner conflicts of an essentially good man, whose well-meaning attempt to educate someone he regards as completely ignorant must lead to a disastrous, violent conclusion because of his own massive ignorance of Mingo's mind. The interlocking destiny of Green and Mingo, the secret sharers of each other's lives, points the story toward an indeterminate future, in which the racial clash of American life remains to be resolved. As the writer Michael Ventura has observed,

Charles Johnson (WireImage)

the stories in *The Sorcerer's Apprentice* often "reveal the underside of the last or next," so that the brothers in the succeeding story, "Exchange Value," Cooter and Loftis, are also trapped in an interlocking relationship that wrecks their ability to think with moral clarity or any sense of self-preservation.

"CHINA"

Located at the center of the collection, "China" is the most energetically affirmative story in *The Sorcerer's Apprentice*, closer in mood to Johnson's celebrated novels, *Oxherding Tale* and *Middle Passage*, than to his short fiction. Rudolph Lee Jackson, the protagonist, is a middle-aged man whose entire life has been a catastrophe of caution and avoidance. His marriage is devoid of passion and communication, and he is physically feeble, psychically terrified, and steadily deteriorating from even this diminished condition. The story is not an open allegory, but Jackson is presented as an emblem of the frightened, semibourgeois, not-quite-middle-class African American man, nearly completely emasculated by a retreat from the daily assaults of a racist society and further discouraged by the constant critical sarcasm of his wife Evelyn, whose disappointment and fear are understandable in terms of Jackson's apparent acceptance of defeat.

Johnson has criticized novels in which "portraits of black men . . . are so limited and one-sided" that they seem immoral. The direction of "China" is an opening away from what Johnson calls "an extremely narrow range of human beings"--exemplified by Jackson, who has a "distant, pained expression that asked: *Is this all?*"--toward a kind of self-actualization and fulfillment, which Jackson achieves through a difficult, painful, but energizing course in the philosophy and practice of martial arts. In some of his most engaging, vivid writing, Johnson describes the revitalization and growth that lead to Jackson's symbolic rebirth as a man, as he becomes more and more involved in the life of the kwoon. Initially, Evelyn resists everything about Jackson's enthusiastic, disciplined transformation, but at the story's conclusion, she is, despite her reservations and fears, awakened to the possibility of a life without the artificial, self-imposed limits that African Americans have adopted as a kind of protection from the pain of a three-centuries-long legacy of racial oppression.

"ALĒTHIA"

"ALĒTHIA" is the most explicitly philosophical of Johnson's short stories. It is narrated by a book-ruled professor, whose ordered, intellectually contained life is fractured when a student pulls him into a forest of uncontrolled passion, the necessary complement to his mental fortress. The two sides of human existence are expressed in the contrast between the professor's measured discourse and the raw reality of the netherworld to which his guide takes him. The word "alēthia" is drawn from the philosopher Max Scheler's term concerning a process that "calls forth from concealedness," and it stands for the revelation of an inner essence that has been previously suppressed--the "ugly, lovely black life (so it was to me) I'd fled so long ago in my childhood." Johnson's presentation of the professor is a commentary on the retreat that a preoccupation with the purely mental may produce and a statement about the futility of repressing aspects of the true self.

SOULCATCHER

The stories in Johnson's second short fiction collection, *Soulcatcher, and Other Stories: Twelve Powerful Tales About Slavery*, were written at the request of the producer Orlando Bagwell as companion pieces to the 1998 PBS series *Africans in America: America's Journey Through Slavery*. Johnson's stories, composed over the course of a month, were first printed in a companion volume to the television program, accompanying Patricia Smith's account of the historical events from the Middle Passage to the beginning of the Civil War. In his introduction, Johnson says he hopes the tales "serve as a time machine for readers, transporting them back to an African American past" and also that he sought to make the stories "aesthetically vivid" by using a distinct narrative style for each one. He accomplishes this by assuming a unique, highly original authorial voice for each piece.

The stories are told from the points of view of various historical characters, and Johnson uses a rich range of narrative strategies to recount their experiences. Fittingly, authorial omniscience is the technique used in "Transmission," in which a young African boy captured on a slave ship realizes he must take on the role of griot to preserve and honor his people's history and experiences. "Confession" is told in first person by the runaway slave Tiberius, who acknowledges participation in the Stono Rebellion to his captors while describing his awakening to the madness and injustice of slavery. The intimacy of first person captures Martha Washington's terror as she records in her diary her fears that her slaves are plotting against her, when they discover that her husband's will guarantees their manumission after her death. "Poetry and Politics," told entirely in dialogue, reveals the complex relationship between the poet Phyllis Wheatley and her mistress and their views on the role of the artist. Wheatley explains to her sympathetic slaveholder her uneasiness at not doing more with her talent to fight for her people's liberation but expresses her reluctance to be a pamphleteer at the expense of her art.

The question of the role of the writer and artist in revealing, shaping, and preserving the past is at the heart of all the stories and is central to the very project of the volume. Johnson uses numerous innovative artistic forms to wrestle with questions about the American past, and his portraits of whites and African Americans responding to the immorality and inhumanity of slavery suggest that in the end art is not only more powerful and enduring but also more practically useful than polemic when it comes to changing human lives and minds.

DR. KING'S REFRIGERATOR, AND OTHER BEDTIME STORIES

Johnson's third short-story collection, *Dr. King's Refrigerator, and Other Bedtime Stories*, has not earned the same admiration from critics as his earlier volumes, and some reviewers have complained that the eight short pieces, five of which were commissioned for the Humanities Washington reading series, feel "experimental," unpolished, and lacking in depth. The subtitle of the collection signals that perhaps the tales should not be taken too seriously and might better be viewed as moral fables that employ a different form from conventional narratives. Many of the pieces feature themes familiar to readers of Johnson's longer works, weaving together Western philosophy, Buddhism, aesthetics, and race to ponder questions about the position of the self in the modern world. In the Kafkaesque "Sweet Dreams," which opens the collection, a faceless bureaucrat notifies the protagonist he is overdue in his

"dream tax," and the man is too defeated by the system to do anything but submit to his fate; his self has nowhere to retreat but his dreams. "Executive Decision," about a white, liberal executive who must choose between hiring a dynamic, spirited white woman and a serious, reserved African American man, is a meditation on affirmative action and the worth of the individual self. René Descartes's notion of the indubitable nature of the self is the subject of "The Queen and the Philosopher." In the story Queen Christina of Sweden not only questions Descartes's idea of the metaphysical isolation of the self but also forces him to engage with her hard-driven unyielding ego on freezing northern winter mornings, leading to the famous philosopher's eventual demise.

"DR. KING'S REFRIGERATOR"

The question of the self as isolated, and in particular as socially isolated, is explored tenderly in the collection's title story. The protagonist of the tale is Martin Luther King, Jr., before he achieved fame as a civil rights activist. After staying up late, struggling to find a subject for his Sunday sermon, the young King raids the refrigerator for a snack and sees the food his wife has prepared for her ladies' prayer group. When he beholds the bounty of food from around the world--pineapples from Hawaii, truffles from England, sauerkraut from Germany, and pasta from Italy--he has an epiphany about the interconnectedness of all things. He feels profound thanks for those who have come before him and for all things in creation. Johnson's fusion of Buddhist notions of life's connectedness and King's ideals of the contributions of all people to the bounty enjoyed by humankind is skillfully done. The various morals of the story--that the truth is right before people, that love and humanity connect all people, that artistic inspiration and spiritual revelation come from the most mundane places--are sharp and clear, but, as was the case with King's own sermons, the truths are no less forceful because they are overtly told.

"KWOON"

The most anthologized story in *Dr. King's Refrigerator* is "Kwoon," originally published in 1991 and winner of a 1993 O. Henry Award. The protagonist of the tale is David Lewis, a martial arts teacher who lives in his ramshackle studio, or *kwoon*, where he has dedicated himself to mentoring to the youth in his poor Chicago neighborhood. Lewis lives by principles of simplicity and humility and seeks to lead his students to better themselves and be of use to the world, as was done for him. Everything changes when a brash, angry new student, Ed Morgan, enters the class. A former merchant seaman who has perfected almost every form of hand-to-hand combat in the most undisciplined fashion, Morgan beats up his teacher, leaving him barely alive. After the incident, Lewis questions his principles, practice, and almost everything else he has believed in, but ultimately the humility that he learned in his discipline enables him to conquer his dejection and win the respect of Morgan. Like the other stories in the collection, "Kwoon" explores the question of the nature of the self and ego but adds a particular richness with its Buddhist ruminations on the uncertain and elusive nature of enlightenment and its depiction of the true meaning of forgiveness and honor.

OTHER MAJOR WORKS

LONG FICTION: *Faith and the Good Thing*, 1974; *Oxherding Tale*, 1982; *Middle Passage*, 1990; *Dreamer*, 1998.

NONFICTION: *Black Humor*, 1970 (cartoons and drawings); *Half-Past Nation Time*, 1972 (cartoons and drawings); *Being and Race: Black Writing Since 1970*, 1988; *Africans in America: America's Journey Through Slavery*, 1998 (with Patricia Smith); *I Call Myself an Artist: Writings by and About Charles Johnson*, 1999 (Rudolph P. Byrd, editor); *King: The Photobiography of Martin Luther King, Jr.*, 2000 (photographs by Bob Adelman); *Turning the Wheel: Essays on Buddhism and Writing*, 2003; *Passing the Three Gates: Interviews with Charles Johnson*, 2004 (Jim McWilliams, editor).

TELEPLAYS: *Charlie Smith and the Fritter Tree*, 1978; *Booker*, 1984; *The Green Belt*, 1996.

EDITED TEXT: *Black Men Speaking*, 1997 (with John McCluskey, Jr.).

BIBLIOGRAPHY

African American Review 30, no. 4 (Winter, 1996). A special issue of the journal devoted to Johnson's work. Most of the essays consider Johnson's novels, but there are some references to the short fiction. The strength of the issue is the variety of viewpoints it presents, ranging from political assessments to philosophical excursions. Uneven but often informative.

Beavers, Herman. "Bondage and Discipline: The Pedgogy of Discomfort in *The Sorcerer's Apprentice*." In *Charles Johnson: The Novelist as Philosopher*, edited by Mark C. Conner and William R. Nash. Jackson: University Press of Mississippi, 2007. Beavers's essay concentrates on the pedagogical practice outlined in *The Sorcerer's Apprentice*, which he describes as the story's characters ability to free themselves from the bondage of wanting to be more. Through their enactment of failed pedagogies, the characters evade the limitations of Western concepts of selfhood, achieving progress on the "Way" of enlightenment through misguidedness and incompleteness.

Byrd, Rudolph P., ed. *I Call Myself an Artist: Writings by and About Charles Johnson*. Bloomington: Indiana University Press, 1999. An intelligently chosen, eclectic collection of works by Charles Johnson, which includes an autobiographical essay and several essays explaining his aesthetic perspective and theories of literary composition. There are also two interviews with Johnson and an extensive section of critical discussions of Johnson's work, including an essay by the editor on *The Sorcerer's Apprentice*, which explains Johnson's employment of the philosophical perspectives of Alfred North Whitehead.

Gleason, William. "'Go There': The Critical Pragmatism of Charles Johnson." In *Charles Johnson: The Novelist as Philosopher*, edited by Mark C. Conner and William R. Nash. Jackson: University Press of Mississippi, 2007. Gleason amplifies the understanding of Johnson's philosophical imagination by identifying some of the ways in which his work resonates with a cosmopolitan, pluralist strain of American pragmatism. Gleason says the author's "critical pragmatism," or his complex relationship with reading, instruction, and democracy, is on emphatic display in the stories in *Soulcatcher*.

_____. "The Liberation of Perception: Charles Johnson's *Oxherding Tale*." *Black American Literature Forum* 25 (Winter, 1991): 705-728. One of the most perceptive critiques of the spiritual dimension of Johnson's writing, an important component often overlooked by other commentators.

Little, Jonathan. *Charles Johnson's Spiritual Imagination*. Columbia: University of Missouri Press, 1997. A critical study of Johnson's work, with a chapter on *The Sorcerer's Apprentice*, arguing that the short fiction, in contrast to novels such as *Oxherding Tale* and *Middle Passage*, offers a pessimistic view of human existence, dwelling on the "nightmarish and destructive side of his (Johnson's) integrative aesthetic and social vision." The individual stories are approached with insight and are effectively related to Johnson's other work. Little concludes with an assertion that "the short stories often resonate with more power, depth and ambiguity" than the longer books.

Nash, William R. *Charles Johnson's Fiction*. Chicago: University of Illinois Press, 2003. Nash discusses Johnson's fascination with the Black Arts Movement, his dismissal of separatist black politics and racialist thought, his adoption of Western and Eastern philosophies, and his belief that race is a blinding, limiting category that impedes the exploration of individual and collective identity. The concluding chapter of the book discusses the stories in *Soulcatcher*, which Nash says create a "confusing thematic picture" because of the author's changing stances on aesthetics and the role of the artistic in politics but invite readers to see and understand the problem of slavery for themselves.

Packer, ZZ. "'Dr. King's Refrigerator': Thinking Outside the Icebox." *The New York Times*, March 6, 2005. ZZ Packer's review praises Johnson's quirky writing style and views the light stories as narrative versions of Zen koans used to focus the mind during meditation. She also welcomes Johnson's use of philosophical themes, which she says in these stories are used not to impress or confound but to provoke and delight.

Ventura, Michael. "Voodoo and Subtler Powers." *The New York Times Book Review*, March 30, 1986, p. 7. Ventura's thoughtful essay contends that *The Sorcerer's Apprentice* might best be understood as a "good short novel," in that each story works as a commentary or extension of the next or previous one. His sense of central themes and ongoing concerns is illuminating.

Leon Lewis
Updated by Uma Kukathas

DENIS JOHNSON

Born: Munich, Germany; July 1, 1949

PRINCIPAL SHORT FICTION
Jesus' Son, 1992
"*Train Dreams,*" 2002

OTHER LITERARY FORMS

Denis Johnson has published several volumes of poetry, the best-known being *The Incognito Lounge and Other Poems* (1982), and a number of novels, including *Angels* (1983), *Already Dead: A California Gothic* (1997), *Tree of Smoke* (2007), and *Nobody Move* (2009). He has also written plays, a screenplay, book reviews, news copy, and essays ("School's Out," 1999).

ACHIEVEMENTS

Denis Johnson received a National Poetry Series Award for *The Incognito Lounge, and Other Poems*, a Whiting Writers Award from the Whiting Foundation in 1986 for "exceptionally promising emerging talent," a Guggenheim Fellowship in 1986, and a Lannan Fellowship in Fiction in 1993. His short-story collection *Jesus' Son* was adapted as a film released in 1999;

"Train Dreams," a lengthy story about the life and death of a hermit widower in the West, was awarded the Aga Khan Prize for Fiction from *The Paris Review* in 2002 and an O. Henry Prize as one of the best short stories of 2003. In 2007, *Tree of Smoke* received a National Book Award and was a finalist for a Pulitzer Prize.

BIOGRAPHY

Denis Johnson, the son of a United States diplomat, was born in Munich, West Germany, in 1949. He grew up in countries such as the Philippines and Japan, wherever his father was posted. These frequent moves inculcated in Johnson a sense that relationships and life were unsustainable. In the United States, he went to school in Washington, D.C., and while overseas he attended the American School. Later, Johnson attended the Iowa Writers' Workshop at the University of Iowa. He had one son with his first wife before their marriage ended in divorce; years later, he remarried.

Johnson, intermittently a teacher and a journalist, has always been a writer and often alludes to a troubled period when he was addicted to heroin and alcohol. In 1969, when he was only twenty, he published his first volume of poetry, which received immediate acclaim. In 1983, he published the first of his novels. He has also been a foreign news correspondent, covering such hot spots as the war in Somalia. Johnson is well traveled and has made homes in such disparate places as Washington, D.C., Iowa, Massachusetts, and Arizona. In 2006-2007, Johnson held the Mitte Chair in Creative Writing at Texas State University in San Marcos, Texas.

ANALYSIS

Denis Johnson writes about lost souls who have faint hopes of finding, if not God, at least some meaning in their lives. His themes and violent descriptions echo the works of Flannery O'Connor and Robert Stone, two of his major influences. Johnson portrays the marginal in American society: the addicts, alcoholics, homeless, beggars, and crooks, as well as those who simply cannot or will not adapt to mainstream culture, a culture that itself is crumbling and has helped create the characters it rejects. Johnson's characters seem able to survive on hope and human resilience, no matter how outcast or alienated they may be. Ultimately, Johnson's themes are metaphysical. The alienation of his characters implies the existence of someone or a something from which to be alienated.

Johnson's finely detailed works are often episodic and surreal but told in a colloquial, almost intimate manner. He balances a wry detachment from his characters with a tenderness for even the most criminal of them. Johnson's narrators are often addicts. Therefore, the narrator's voice is alternately dreamy and brutally factual, shifting from a detachment, which speaks casually of bullets and blood, to an unexpected, intimate recognition of the characters' common humanity. The sudden intrusion of compassion in otherwise cold narratives has the effect of producing both Christlike and pathological states within the same character.

By juxtaposing fact and fantasy, realism and surrealism, saintliness and destructive craziness, Johnson flirts with altering the short-story form itself, producing a variation that intrigues as well as appalls. As the reader watches losers spiral downward through the consciousness of a narrator, who is also "not all there," he or she feels empathy for them and recognizes the implicit suggestion that, through a shared humanity, the difference between Johnson's misfits and the rest of society is one of degree only and that in some respects everyone is "not all there."

"CAR CRASH WHILE HITCHHIKING"

The narrator, high on drugs, hitches a ride in an Oldsmobile and senses an imminent crash the minute he hears the "sweet voices of family inside it." After the wreck, the narrator, holding the family's baby, wanders toward the other car that was involved in the accident. Seeing that the broadsided car has been smashed, he assumes all inside are dead and walks past it. Flagging down a passing truck, he tells the truck driver to go for help. Because the truck driver cannot turn around on the narrow bridge, the narrator leaves the truck, sees another car nearing the scene, and approaches it. Then he perceives that the man in the smashed car is not dead but soon will be. At the hospital, he hears the wife shriek when she learns of her husband's death. The narrator remarks her scream made him "feel wonderful to be alive" and that he had "gone looking for that feeling everywhere," exhibiting the addict's relentless search for a rush.

Years later, in a hospital detoxification ward, the narrator experiences a flashback to the accident scene. The ambiguous last phrase, "you ridiculous people, you expect me to help you," expresses either contempt for those who might count on him or the self-loathing and guilt beneath an addict's thrill-seeking veneer.

"EMERGENCY"

The narrator, working as a hospital clerk, befriends Georgie, an emergency room orderly, who steals pills (which the narrator takes) and is always high. Terrence Weber comes in with a knife stuck in his one good eye. Explaining that his wife stabbed him, Weber claims the knife has affected his brain because his body will no longer do what his mind directs it to do. The emergency room physician calls for the best eye surgeon, brain surgeon, and anesthetist, then orders Georgie to prepare Weber for surgery, even though he knows Georgie is "not right."

As the specialists argue over how best to remove the knife, Georgie returns from preparing the patient with the knife in hand. Stunned, no one says anything. When the narrator asks how Weber is doing, Georgie replies, "Who?"

Later, Georgie and the narrator, still high, become lost. When Georgie hits a rabbit, he cries, "Rabbit stew," picks up the rabbit, and skins it with Weber's knife. When he finds tiny rabbit fetuses inside the corpse, he declares, "We killed the mother but saved the children," then hands them to the narrator, who warms them in his shirt. As darkness approaches, the two stumble upon what the narrator hallucinates is a military graveyard with large angels hovering overhead. In a rare lucid moment, Georgie recognizes the place as a drive-in cinema. When the screen goes blank, they argue over whether or not to go home. Georgie resists driving until he remembers that the rabbits need milk. The narrator tells him to forget about the rabbits, which have been crushed inside his shirt. The rabbits' deaths provoke Georgie's wrath, but the narrator acknowledges he is unclear about how or when the deaths occurred. His only clear memory is of the morning's mystical beauty.

Before Georgie and the narrator return to the hospital, they pick up a friend of the narrator, a serviceman named Hardee, who is absent without leave and headed for Canada. Georgie declares that he will take Hardee to Canada. When asked what he does for a living, Georgie replies, "I save lives." Ironically, despite Georgie's drug-crazed recklessness, he probably could get Hardee to Canada, just as he succeeded in removing Weber's knife. The reader does not learn anything more about Hardee because of the drugged narrator's fragmented narration, which, like their lives, is in a state of emergency.

When they return to work, the Lord's Prayer is playing over the intercom. Weber, miraculously unscathed, comes to say goodbye to Georgie, who does not recognize him. The infusion of the sacred into this story implies that the protagonists' successes may be providential.

"BEVERLY HOME"

Living in Phoenix, the narrator decides to look for a job because members of his Narcotics Anonymous group think he should. He finds work at the Beverly Home, an old-age home that also houses the disabled, some of whom are so deformed they make "God look like a senseless maniac." During his free time, the narrator rides the bus and strolls in the desert. One evening, he hears a woman singing in the shower. Entranced, he hides behind some greenery and peeps at her. The narrator reveals his cowardice and violence when he states that he would break in and rape the woman if he had a mask to wear. Peeping at the woman becomes an obsession for him, particularly after he discovers that the woman and her husband are Amish, an oddity in Phoenix. Hoping to see them make love (he never does), he watches their daily movements, including an extraordinary act of contrition: a foot washing by the repentant husband.

When not working or peeping, the narrator dates first a dwarf and then a woman whose childhood encephalitis has left her with spasms and who is thus "unwholesome and very erotic." The narrator thirsts for, but is afraid of, making connections of either a spiritual or an earthly nature. Beverly Home's hall seems a room for souls waiting to be reborn. He has sex with the dwarf while the television is on so he will not have to get to know her. The closest he gets to either God or a real relationship is peeping at the Amish couple. The parallels between the Beverly Home misfits and the narrator are obvious to the reader but not to the narrator, who gratefully concludes that he is improving, despite living among "weirdos."

"DIRTY WEDDING"

"Dirty Wedding" deals with the narrator's anguish over his girlfriend's abortion. As he and Michelle approach the abortion clinic, picketers sprinkle holy water on them and pray, and the narrator wishes he knew their prayer. Hating himself, he tells lies to make Michelle leave him, but she stays until, as the narrator says, "She really knew me."

Thrown out of the abortion clinic for making wisecracks, the narrator aimlessly rides the city's public transportation. As in "Beverly Home," when the narrator illustrates his alienation by peeping through the window at the married couple, the narrator of "Dirty Wedding" peers into the windows of buildings as the train he is riding rushes past.

After Michelle's abortion, he cannot look strangers in the eye. Fixating on one man, who seemingly has an appointment, the narrator follows him. When the man confronts him, the narrator thinks the man is Jesus Christ. Later, the narrator says that he would have felt the same way about anyone he followed, thus revealing his need for direction.

Back on the train, the narrator muses on what motel maids stuff into trash cans; thoughts about throwaways lead him to thinking about Michelle's fetus. He reveals his sense of loss as he wonders if the fetus could imagine a world outside the womb, if its darkness would get darker in death, and if it would know or care about being aborted.

Abruptly the narrator shifts the subject to Michelle. Michelle ran off with a man named John Smith, then died from a drug overdose. Afterward, Smith heard her ghost calling to him and also died. Illustrating his convenient sense of victimization, the narrator brands Michelle a traitor and a killer. Once she shot him five times, not to kill him but to "eat his heart," to wound him the way a mother can devastate a child. He concludes that arguments about the morality of abortion are beside the point. "It," the wrong, in this situation is

not the abortion. "It" is "What the mother and father did together," implying destructive personal relations and motives, as well as premarital sex. The narrator's union with Michelle is dirty not because they aborted their child but because of the way they treated each other.

OTHER MAJOR WORKS

LONG FICTION: *Angels*, 1983; *Fiskadoro*, 1985; *The Stars at Noon*, 1986; *Resuscitation of a Hanged Man*, 1991; *Already Dead: A California Gothic*, 1997; *The Name of the World*, 2000; *Tree of Smoke*, 2007; *Nobody Move*, 2009.

PLAYS: *Shoppers: Two Plays*, pb. 2002 (includes *Hellhound on My Trail* and *Shoppers Carried by Escalators into the Flames*); *Soul of a Whore*, pr. 2003.

SCREENPLAY: *Hit Me*, 1998.

POETRY: *The Man Among the Seals*, 1969; *Inner Weather*, 1976; *The Incognito Lounge, and Other Poems*, 1982; *The Veil*, 1987; *The Throne of the Third Heaven of the Nations Millennium General Assembly*, 1995.

NONFICTION: *Seek: Reports from the Edges of America and Beyond*, 2001.

BIBLIOGRAPHY

Donnelly, Daria. "Flannery O'Connor in Reverse--*Jesus' Son*." *Commonweal*, August 13, 1993. This review alleges that *Jesus' Son* owes much to Flannery O'Connor. Unlike similar allusions in the work of O'Connor, the spiritual allusions in *Jesus' Son* rest on incertitude, rather than on faith. The passive spiritual hopefulness of Johnson's fiction is reflected in the addicted narrator of *Jesus' Son*. Through the nonlinear, drunken narrative, reality is rendered both comically and tragically. Donnelly thinks that much of the power of *Jesus' Son* is in the complex rendering of the narrator, who exhibits both lust and indifference, as well a longing for love and God.

Farrin, J. Scott. "Eloquence and Plot in Denis Johnson's *Jesus' Son*: The Merging of Premodern and Modernist Narrative." In *The Postmodern Short Story: Forms and Issues*, edited by Farhat Iftekharrudin, et al., under the auspices of the Society for the Study of the Short Story. Westport, Conn.: Praeger, 2003. Analyzes the narrative style of the collection.

Gates, David. *Newsweek*, February 8, 1993, p.67. Reviews *Jesus' Son* positively, calling it "masterfully bleak." Gates particularly stresses the narrative form, praising Johnson's depiction of the narrator's drugged, hallucinatory mind as he tells his stories. The surreal tone is exhilarating, according to Gates, for it reflects the irrational lives of the addicts. In the same way, the stories' enigmatic forms are appropriate to the subject matter.

Kristulent, Steve. Review of *Already Dead*, by Denis Johnson. *Oyster Boy Review* 9 (May-August, 1998). This review deals not only with this particular novel but also with Johnson as a social critic. Kristulent compares Johnson to such European novelists as Milan Kundera and Robert Musil, who believe that every personal choice is also a political one. He also considers Johnson's work to be particularly American, comparing him to John Dos Passos in his emphasis on contemporary fringe groups.

McManus, James. Review of *Jesus' Son*, by Denis Johnson. *New York Times Book Review*, December 27, 1992, p.5. McManus argues that *Jesus' Son* is a masterpiece of moral deterioration. Its disjointed narrative illustrates both diseases and Christlike states of mind, as well as a condition in which salvation remains possible but improbable.

Miles, Jack. "An Artist of American Violence." *The Atlantic*, June, 1993, 121-127. Miles praises Johnson's skill in portraying the mind of the addict and criminal, but he thinks the characters' poetic language is linguistically unrealistic. Miles calls the characters' spiritual longings "pre-religious," a yearning for God, a result of having lost faith in people. Argues that Johnson's most innovative contribution is the narrator's intermittent, direct addresses to the reader; these intimate asides bring the reader closer not only to the narrator but also to the more shattering moments in the narrative.

Parrish, Timothy. "Denis Johnson's *Fiskadoro*: Postcolonial America." In *From the Civil War to the Apocalypse: Postmodern History and American Fiction*. Amherst: University of Massachusetts Press, 2008. Discusses the relationship of fiction and history in Johnson's novel. Parrish argues that Johnson and many other postmodern novelists "compel" readers to accept their narratives as true in the same way that historians expect readers to assume the truth of their accounts.

_____. "Denis Johnson's *Jesus' Son:* The Kingdom Come." *Critique* 43, no. 1 (2001): 17-29. Discusses the theme of transformation in Johnson's writing and speculates why the author writes the kind of stories he does.

Smith, Robert McClure. "Addiction and Recovery in Denis Johnson's *Jesus' Son*." *Critique* 42, no. 2 (2001): 180-191. Analyzes the spiritual concerns explored in Johnson's short-story collection.

Wiggins, Marianne. "Talk into My Bullet Hole." *The Nation* 256 (February 15, 1993): 121. Praises *Jesus' Son* for depicting characters with serious flaws and scars, such as addictions and craziness. Wiggins argues that what makes the book memorable is that Johnson at times endows the characters with an essential, shared humanity. She claims that reading the stories is like reading a subconscious ticker tape.

Woodrell, Daniel. Review of *Jesus' Son*, by Denis Johnson. *Washington Post Book World*, February 21, 1993, p.C1. Comments on the strengths and weaknesses of *Jesus' Son*. Woodrell praises the fragmentary style that reflects the narrator's mind-set and states that in the best stories the narrator's disjointed consciousness is portrayed so that his anguish conveys a kind of majesty. However, the stories fail to reveal much more of the character of the narrator than the reader is shown in the beginning, and the characters in *Jesus' Son* are not as large of heart as the characters in *Angels*.

Mary Hanford Bruce

BRET ANTHONY JOHNSTON

Born: Corpus Christi, Texas; December 23, 1971

PRINCIPAL SHORT FICTION

Corpus Christi, 2004
"*Republican,*" 2007
"*Calcutta,*" 2007
"*The End of Summer,*" 2008
"*Caiman,*" 2009
"*Boy,*" 2009
"*Soldier of Fortune,*" 2010

OTHER LITERARY FORMS

Bret Anthony Johnston has published nonfiction in periodicals ranging from *The New York Times Magazine* and *Men's Journal* to *McSweeney's, The Oxford American*, and *Shenandoah*. His journeyman pieces tend to build toward a fragmentary memoir, centered on his Corpus Christi upbringing, his engagement in southern pop culture (southern heavy metal music, although violent, reveals an "overlooked soulfulness"), his touring with a professional skateboarding team in his late teens, his ambivalence toward getting a college education, and his relationship with his working-class father. *McSweeney's* calls Johnston "one of skateboarding's most discerning and yet heartfelt observers." In terms of an aesthetic related to writing, much after the fashion of Ernest Hemingway's "grace under pressure," perhaps Johnston's most significant essay is "Danny Way and the Gift of Fear": "Think Picasso, Hemingway, Dvorak. Think Laird Hamilton, Chuck Yeager. And, yes, think Tyson. Consider the likelihood that these men don't possess qualities the rest of us lack, but instead have within them intense voids, empty and expansive chambers of possibility." Johnston also has edited *Naming the World, and Other Exercises for the Creative Writer* (2007), exercises for fiction writers collected from such notable writers and teachers as

Elizabeth Strout, Richard Bausch, Joyce Carol Oates, Katherine Min, and sixty-one others.

ACHIEVEMENTS

Corpus Christi (2004) was named a Best Book of the Year by *The Independent of London* and *The Irish Times*, and the collection has received the *Southern Review*'s Annual Short Fiction Award, the Glasgow Prize for Emerging Writers, the Texas Institute of Letters' Debut Fiction Award, the Christopher Isherwood Prize, and the James Michener Fellowship. It was shortlisted for Ireland's Frank O'Connor International Short Story Award, "the richest short story prize in the world." In 2006, the National Book Foundation honored Johnston with a new National Book Award for writers younger than age thirty-five.

Jonhston's stories have been reprinted in such anthologies as *New Stories from the South: The Year's Best* for the years 2003, 2004, 2005, 2008, and 2010, *Best American Short Stories*, and *Prize Stories: The O. Henry Awards*. "Republican" won the Cohen Award from *Ploughshares*. The Cohen Award honors the best poem and story published each year in the magazine. Johnston has been the recipient of a National Endowment for the Arts Literature Fellowship. In 2007, *Pages* magazine named Johnston one of "The Next Generation of Literary Lions." The honor went also to Zadie Smith, David Mitchell, Jonathan Safran Foer, and Andrew Sean Greer.

BIOGRAPHY

Bret Anthony Johnston was born in Corpus Christi, Texas, on December 23, 1971, into a working-class family. His father, Jay Johnston, was a supervisor at the Corpus Christi Army Depot, and his mother, Donna Stakes, was an office manager. Bret Anthony Johnston went to Corpus Christi public schools until he graduated from Richard King High School in 1990. He attended Del Mar Community College in Corpus Christi, then transferred to Texas A and M, Corpus Christi. At Del Mar and Texas A and M, Johnston, encouraged by a few professors, started to write seriously.

Johnston went on to attend Miami University (1996-1998) and the Iowa Writers' Workshop (2000-2002), where Frank Conroy and Ethan Canin mentored him. He held the post of assistant professor at California State University, San Bernardino, from 2003 to 2006. In 2006, he took the post of Briggs Copeland Lecturer at Harvard University and in 2007 became director of creative writing at Harvard. He settled in Arlington, Massachusetts, and has made frequent trips to Texas.

ANALYSIS

As he explores lives wounded by loss and the contradictions of love, Bret Anthony Johnston pushes his characters to the limits of what they can understand and can bear to hear and say. Along with his preoccupation with time and the capacities of memory and imagination to resist oblivion, his primary subject is the experience of life lived over the limit. He highlights the decisive and defining moments to which one is responsible, even when one is powerless over them. The moments of violence in his stories are like internal hurricanes, as if, in addition to punishment by outside forces, one is mysteriously at the mercy of oneself.

CORPUS CHRISTI

A critic praised *Corpus Christi* for its "ten hard-eyed, soulful, and life-affirming stories," which are emotionally powerful and technically adroit. However, Johnston is at his best, Mark Rozzo argues, in the triptych of stories-- "I See Something You Don't See," "The Widow," and "Buy for Me the Rain"--that depicts the "thorny relationship between Minnie Marshall, whose cancer has metastasized in her brain, and her son, Lee, who has abandoned his own life to drive her to the clinic, change her diapers, and, ultimately, convey her to the next world. It's a stunning and complex portrait of an indelible alliance." Elizabeth Egan labels Johnston "a slightly more upbeat [Raymond] Carver, [whose] genius lies in weaving a web of optimism around a series of difficult and occasionally depressing topics."

Perhaps the only apprentice-level story in the collection is "Outside the Toy Store," in which the pathos seems formulaic. It is about the accidental meeting of adulterous lovers in a shopping mall, five years after the breakup of their affair. The narrator has lost his wife and then his daughter from cancer; his dog is dead, killed in a hit and run. His grief, however, is what the other woman refuses to share. Tragedy is a stigma, repulsive to those with luckier lives.

The title story, "Corpus Christi," features a cast of different characters with broken hearts and lives "on the other side of things." The primary character is Charlie Banks, whose wife, Edie, was placed in the mental hospital when she broke down after a miscarriage. Charlie sits next to Dwana, who has ridden on a motorcycle with Omar to visit her brother, Donnie, who was committed for an act of psychopathic rage. Each character has a dramatized point of view, one alternating ironically with other and emphasizing their coincidental intersections.

As Charlie leaves the hospital, speeding in his Lexus, he is blindsided by Omar's motorcycle with Dwana on it. In surreal, visionary prose, Johnston describes the accident. Charlie finds Omar dead, but Dwana alive. From her dazed point of view, the reader gets a key to Johnston's theory of character: "to understand who they essentially were, you only had to know what they'd lost. This was explicitly clear. Everyone could be seen that way." Charlie then remembers Edie the morning before she was committed, suddenly smoking, agitated, and admitting to taking pills in an attempt at suicide. At this point, Johnston suddenly shifts the narrative perspective to "years later," so that Charlie is remembering the rest of the night's outcome "as nothing more than coincidence." An ambulance speeds Dwana away without her knowing that Omar is dead. Charlie returns to his empty house, drinks bourbon, and turns on all the lights, alone. His mother-in-law calls from her nursing home; she has not been told about the miscarried baby. Charlie pretends that the baby is alive and that Edie is sleeping. He holds the phone out and tells his mother-in-law to listen to the baby snoring, and this act of deception carries him to a place of bewilderment. Against this elegiac negativism, however, Johnston adds another twist.

The story ends in Edie's point of view in the hospital as she remembers their happiness and her solitary maternal ecstasy, when she, pregnant and naked, waded alone in the ocean on a late morning. She remembers her realization, before the miscarriage and her depression, that "[h]er life had become more than it had been. Here we are." Ending on this note both softens and heightens the pathos, as if outcomes have no stability in time. She will, of course, be released from the hospital and will attempt to return to Charlie, but "years later" she will leave him "because he remind[s] her of all she'd lost."

UNCOLLECTED STORIES

In "Republican," Johnston returns to the setting and material of *Corpus Christi: Stories*. An absent mother and a grieving father drive this story of sixteen-year-old Jay's coming of age. The father runs a pawn shop, and, despite the family's working-class status, he has acquired a Fleetwood Cadillac on default and Elvis Presley's guitar, possessions that will figure in the story like Anton Chekhov's famous gun on the mantel. By story's end, Jay has won the heart of the cook's stepdaughter, Melinda, whom he met in the Tex-Mex restaurant where they all worked; the cook is playing the Presley guitar; and Melinda is driving them wildly in the Cadillac. Even more astonishing than this confluence, however, is the car's convertible roof, which Jay's father had slashed in anger when Jay's mother left. Jay had neglected to repair the roof, but Jay's father has fixed it in secret. As the rain begins, Melinda raises the roof, and Jay recognizes his father's "coded, sheltering lessons of sorrow."

In "Soldier of Fortune," Johnston continues to mine the Gulf Coast milieu and male passages to adulthood. In this rich and perfectly orchestrated masterpiece, the reader discovers near the end that the narrator is a thirty-five-year-old writer, Josh, who has just heard about the death in combat of the older girl next door on whom he had had crush on when he was fourteen. The neighbor, Holly, had since married, had children, and had a distinguished military career. However, the reader is first drawn into the story through Josh's remembered teenage fantasies, first about war games with his best male friend, then about sex with Holly, about whom Josh's father warns him: "she was trouble

and if he caught me alone with her, he'd whip my ass." In fact, Holly, who has sex with older boys and with the school geology teacher, will initiate Josh to sex and to much else that awakens his writer's heart.

In a household accident, Holly's younger brother Sam suffers severe burns, and the entire family relocates to be nearby a distant burn unit, leaving Josh in charge of feeding the family's dog (with Josh's father's blessing, given the tragedy). In the family's absence, Josh uses the key to their house and is tempted by a voyeuristic intimacy. The nature of Sam's accident remains grist for lurid exaggeration by Josh's friends at school, who imagine that he must have shot himself playing with his father's Luger pistol. Someone says there is a bloodstain under the pool table. Josh knows better and fights the combat-minded buddy who asserts this, thereby defending the harder truth of real tragedy. Josh then succumbs to snooping in Holly's bedroom, fixated on a photograph of her and her brother as a memento. One night, Holly catches him. She has returned in secret and alone. She applauds his snooping, and as she offers to answer his questions, he suddenly guesses the deepest intimacy: that Sam is her child. As she invites Josh to have sex, he expects that "countless mysteries [would part] around me like currents," including the mystery of who the father might be (probably the geology teacher but possibly Josh's father), "but Holly offered none of this." Instead she weeps in his arms: "I just want him to be okay." Johnston weaves together the disparate motifs of guns, war, tragedy, gender, imagination, sex, and family love; he shows how stories are speculations about other lives and how they progress from fantasies to clairvoyant empathy and due regard. Nothing is forced.

Other uncollected stories begin as exercises and become authentic art. "Boy" is a witty variation on Jamaica Kincaid's well-known story "Girl," in which an Antiguan mother lectures her daughter about how to be a respectable island woman. Students of writing often attempt this variation, attempting to highlight the tyranny of the male gender. While most of these attempts are lax, Johnston's comes fully and complexingly alive.

"Calcutta" and "The End of Summer" were both written for *Esquire* magazine and are reminiscent of Hemingway's "Hills Like White Elephants." The theme of infidelity occurs in "In the Tall Grass" in *Corpus Christi: Stories* in the milieu of hardship, but in the later stories the mirror held up to the worldly seems more moralistic. Privileged and modish drifters reap the whirlwind of their vanities.

"Caiman" plays with elements of southern gothic and with Grace Paley's sense of "open destiny" in stories. A working-class father brings home a baby alligator, bought at roadside, as a pet for his seven-year-old, who "liked bedtime stories with fantastic monsters and twisty, unexpected endings" and who is an affectionate trickster, who loves to hide and "jump out screaming and laughing." The man's wife opposes monsters, trickery, and the alligator as an appropriate pet; she is also preoccupied by a news story about a girl her son's age who has disappeared and who possibly has been molested and murdered by her uncle. As the two discuss the inappropriateness of the alligator and the possibility of family depravity, the wife comes around to allowing the alligator but insists that the husband lie to his son about the girl and "make up a story for him, something with a happy outcome." Then they discover that their son has been hiding and eavesdropping and already knows about the alligator and the girl. They join in anticipation of loving play with him, where love is like violence ("I wanted to bite down, to crush your perfect bones and swallow your body whole") and the parents devolve into alligators, "bodies low to the ground like strange and ancient creatures." The author is having serious fun with his readers.

OTHER MAJOR WORKS

EDITED TEXT: *Naming the World, and Other Exercises for the Creative Writer*, 2007

BIBLIOGRAPHY

Egan, Elizabeth. "All Sorts of Stories Blow Through Patch of Texas." *San Francisco Chronicle*, June 20, 2004. In this review of *Corpus Christi: Stories*, the writer notes that Johnston has a "pitch-perfect ear for dialogue and a dead-on eye for conjuring an entire universe with one simple detail."

Henry, DeWitt. "Storms of Fate on the Gulf Coast." *Boston Sunday Globe*, June 27, 2004, p. D7. Review of *Corpus Christi: Stories* examines the plot twists perfected by Johnston.

Poissant, David James. "*Naming the World and Other Exercises for the Creative Writer*." *Ploughshares* 35, no. 1 (Spring, 2009). This review offers Johnston's theories on writing: perhaps it cannot be taught, but it can be learned.

DeWitt Henry

EDWARD P. JONES

Born: Washington, D.C.; October 5, 1950
Also known as: Edward Paul Jones

PRINCIPAL SHORT FICTION
Lost in the City, 1992
All Aunt Hagar's Children, 2006

OTHER LITERARY FORMS

Edward P. Jones wrote the novel *The Known World* (2003), which won the Pulitzer Prize for fiction, the National Book Critics Circle Award, and the International IMPAC Dublin Literary Award. The novel is different from his short fiction in that it is set in pre-Civil War times. The book tells the story of a freed slave who becomes a land owner in Virginia. He will own as many as thirty slaves to work his land.

ACHIEVEMENTS

Despite having only a small amount of published work, Jones has received major awards for his stories. His first book, *Lost in the City*, received the Hemingway Foundation/PEN Award and was nominated for the National Book Award. His first novel also was nominated for the National Book Award and won, among other prizes, a Pulitzer Prize. Following the publication of his second book of short stories, *All Aunt Hagar's Children*, Jones received a Lannan Foundation Award and a what is known as a "genius award" fellowship from the MacArthur Foundation. Three of his short stories were selected by the O. Henry Awards.

BIOGRAPHY

Edward Paul Jones was born October 5, 1950, in Washington, D.C., the setting for his stories and a place he has left only rarely. His books are dedicated to his mother, Jeanette S. M. Jones, who raised him as a single parent. In interviews, Jones describes the poverty of his childhood and how he barely knew his father. Despite moments of near homelessness, upon graduation for Cardozo High School, he received a college scholarship to Holy Cross. An M.F.A. degree from the University of Virginia followed. In 2009, Jones began teaching at George Washington University.

Jones's mother has been the major influence upon his writing. Though she could neither read nor write, her advice and her struggles to support Jones, his sister, and his brother left a strong mark on his imagination. Jones started writing after reading stories in his sister's copy of *Essence* magazine. He believed he could write a better story, so he did, and that story submission began the group of stories that would grow into *Lost in the City*. Despite the strong reviews and awards his work earned, Jones continued to work for an organization that produced a newsletter for people who prepared taxes. When he heard about an African American who owned slaves before the Civil War, Jones was struck by the possibilities of that story for a novel. For most of a decade, he collected books on the subject, as his imagination worked on the narrative. Finally, on vacation, he began writing. During the second week of that vacation, he received the notification that he had been laid off from his job. That shock pushed him to the completion of his first novel. Despite his success, he still feels the effect of poverty on his life. He does not have a driver's license or a car. A description of his apartment notes that he does not own a bed, since the floor was where he slept while he was growing up.

ANALYSIS

Jones says his goal is writing is to describe the lives of African Americans living in Washington, D.C. His two collections of short stories have shown glimpses at varied experiences of people outside of the political spotlight in the U.S. capital. Like William Faulkner and Louise Erdrich, Jones sets out to describe a particular place, its people, their challenges and dreams, and their place in private history.

LOST IN THE CITY

Jones's first collection, *Lost in the City*, can be labeled a short-story cycle. Most collections are a gathering of short stories of random themes and topics, in which there is no connection between the stories but the style and interests of the particular author. A short-story cycle tends to follow a particular person or group of people, but without the narrative arc found in a novel. A novel might be divided into smaller units, but those chapters may not be complete stories. In a short-story cycle, each story can stand alone, yet each is a part of a pattern that gives a sense of unity to the book as a whole.

Often, short-story cycles are organized around a setting. Examples include Russell Banks's *Trailerpark* (1981), which is made up of stories about different inhabitants of a trailer park, and Sherwood Anderson's *Winesburg, Ohio* (1919), which is a loose group of stories about the inhabitants of a small town who are all in some way lonely and isolated.

Lost in the City is often compared to the short-story cycle *Dubliners* (1914) by James Joyce, a masterpiece that Jones notes was on his mind as he wrote. For example, each story in *Lost in the City* describes the life of a different person, building to a big picture of the ways people live in that culture. Though the people in each story are unrelated and do not appear in multiple stories, still, by the end of the book, the reader gets a sense of how different attempts to deal with poverty, racism, and the problems they create--hopelessness, violence, the breakdown of the family---develop into a detailed picture of society. As Jones describes these characters and their lives, he uses a language similar to their own speech and thought patterns, though typically utilizing a third-person, distant, objective narrator. Similar to *Dubliners*, *Lost in the City* moves from stories about childhood and adolescence, through adulthood, and ends with characters in old age. However, throughout this cycle, the recognition of death is always apparent.

Lost in the City opens with the story "The Girl Who Raised Pigeons," which describes Betsy Ann Morgan's childhood fascination with pigeons and her father's attempt to shelter her from the bad aspects of life. After incessantly pestering her father, he finally builds her a cage and gets her a pair of pigeons, which she raises. However, the birds do not always remain in their cages. They sometimes fly off and disappear, and, worse, rats attack and kill them. Betsy Ann grows up and begins to escape the careful circle within which her single father wishes she would remain. She gets in trouble, for instance, when another girl convinces her they could get away with shoplifting from a local store. Though Betsy Ann recognizes that her pigeons will die, her father cannot accept that possibility, so he disassembles the cages and gets rid of the birds. The story ends with Betsy Ann wandering off, exploring the town on her own, not caring about how much her father worries.

As the collection's title suggests, being lost in the city is a major theme of the book. Stories are full of people who feel lost, unconnected to others. Sometimes they glimpse strangers they cannot quite connect with, as in the story "An Orange Line Train to Ballston," in which a single mother tries to get up the nerve to talk to a man who regularly rides the same train. The title

Edward P. Jones (AP Photo/Rogelio V. Solis)

story "Lost in the City" describes how lost a woman feels in her own life. Lydia Walsh is awakened at 3 a.m. with a phone call notifying her that her aged mother has died. As Lydia dresses to go to the hospital, she looks over all the trappings of her financial success, but she cannot recall the name of the man sound asleep in her bed. When Lydia gets in a cab, she does not ask the driver to take her directly to the hospital; she asks him to just drive, to get her "lost in the city," much as she feels lost in her own life.

Other stories describe other characters who have become lost in their lives. "The Night Rhonda Ferguson Was Killed" follows a high school girl, Cassandra, through another bad afternoon. She is angry because her parents died in a car accident, and she is lashing out at anyone who crosses her path. Without permission, she has taken the car belonging to her sister's husband, with whom she lives. As she drives around with some friends, they visit a pair of pregnant teens. Though she swears she will not end up like them, she is clearly looking for a boyfriend. The story ends with the news that her friend Rhonda Ferguson has been shot. Rhonda appeared to be on the path to success, unlike Cassandra, but Rhonda's death is one more blow for Cassandra.

Another story, "Young Lions," tells of how Caesar has started on a criminal path. As a teen, he was thrown out of his house by his father for committing a petty crime. After working with a mentor, who is trying to go straight, Caesar is beginning to make his own plans. He drags his girlfriend into a scheme to rob a developmentally disabled adult, Anna. At first his girlfriend helps fool Anna into giving her Anna's life savings, but then the girlfriend realizes how wrong this act will be for Caesar. He beats her, and she runs off with Anna's money, leaving Caesar alone in the rain.

Later stories in the collection show parents worried about their lost children. In the often anthologized story "A New Man," Woodrow Cunningham comes home from work to find his teenage daughter alone with two male friends. When Cunningham throws out the boys, his daughter runs off as well. She will never return. He and his wife search the city for their lost daughter. Oddly, Cunningham continues his search, even after it has become hopeless. He has become fascinated with these little glimpses of different lives, as

he goes door to door with a picture of his lost daughter. He even begins creating new stories about her, as a way looking for a different life.

The book ends with a portrait of Marie, an eighty-six-year-old woman, trying to make sense of a confusing world. She is called down to the Social Security office and gets tangled in the bureaucracy, with a letter signed by a worker Marie has been told has died. She continues to go to the office, when summoned, but never sees anyone. After her morning is wasted waiting, she is sent home. A college student introduces himself to her; he is interested in collecting oral histories. After spending hours telling him her life story, Marie realizes that she hates her life. The story and the book end with her putting away all the mementos of her life, in a place where she will not see them again.

This ending focuses on a central theme for the book-that of memories, all too often lost. Over and over, throughout the book, characters pull out old photos or other objects to help them recall faces they can no longer picture in memory. No matter the ties, or the worries and concerns, the characters in this collections seems to drift apart.

ALL AUNT HAGAR'S CHILDREN

Following the publication of his novel *The Known World*, Jones published in 2006 his second collection of short stories. At first appearance, this book may not show the unity of his first collection, but, subtly or obviously, his second collection, *All Aunt Hagar's Children*, connects with *Lost in the City*; for one, each book has fourteen stories. In some cases, the connections are subtle. The first story in *All Aunt Hagar's Children*, "In the Blink of God's Eye," describes how a young married couple moves to Washington, D.C., in 1901. The husband wants children, but their marriage comes apart over an infant, an abandoned child that his wife takes in and treats as her own. While it may not be apparent at first, there is a small and subtle connection between both initial stories in the collections. Fifty years later, this infant will be a minor character in "The Girl Who Raised Pigeons." The abandoned baby will give the main character her first set of pigeons.

Other stories work as sequels to previous stories. One of the strongest in the collection, noted by the editors of the O. Henry Award, is "Old Boys Old Girls." It revisits Caesar, a young criminal, introduced in the first collection. In this story, his crimes, in particular murder, put him in jail. In cool detail, the story describes Caesar's years in jail, time that leaves him both physically and mentally scarred. As horrible things happen to him, his brother and sister attempt to connect with him. He rejects their early attempts to talk to him, but years later, when he is released, his brother tracks him down. They invite him to Sunday dinner. All seems to go well, though Caesar finds it almost impossible to let down his guard around the adults. His niece is able to talk to him, though, and she is the only person with whom he feels a bit safe. As they part, he grabs the little girl's shoe, as if to shake good-bye. He gets a glimpse of the frightened and disgusted look on his sister's face, as she worries what he might do. His realization that he will never be trusted costs him his last shred of humanity. He returns to the horrible apartment building where he lives and realizes that the troubled woman there, the only person he talks to, has died. He washes her body, cleans her whole apartment, and notifies the authorities. Caesar feels completely lost and heads off without a plan in the world. With each decision, he flips a coin, letting its random fall determine his course of action. The story ends suspended in air with a flip of that coin.

A major theme for this collection is a contrast between people such as Caesar, who have lost their moral compass, and those who still have a clear sense of right and wrong. The book explores what happens to people who believe that there are no rules and how they will destroy others around them.

OTHER MAJOR WORKS

LONG FICTION: *The Known World*, 2003.

BIBLIOGRAPHY

Graham, Maryemma. "An Interview with Edward P. Jones." *African American Review* 42 (Fall, 2008): 421. A lengthy interview that discusses all of Jones's works.

Jones, Edward P. "In the Name of the Mother." *Essence.* 36, no. 8 (December, 2005): 140. Jones's story of his relationship with his mother.

Mason, Wyatt. "Ballad for Americans: The Stories of Edward P. Jones." *Harper's* (September, 2006): 87. A overview of Jones's short stories and their place in American literature.

Tucker, Neely. "The Known World of Edward P. Jones." *The Washington Post*, November 15, 2009. An article describing Jones's life in Washington, D.C., and its relationship to his work.

Yardley, Jonathan. "Shining City, Tarnished Dreams." *The Washington Post*, August 27, 2006. A review of *All Aunt Hagar's Children*.

Brian L. Olson

THOM JONES

Born: Aurora, Illinois; January 26, 1945

PRINCIPAL SHORT FICTION

The Pugilist at Rest, 1993
Cold Snap, 1995
Sonny Liston Was a Friend of Mine, 1999

OTHER LITERARY FORMS

Thom Jones is best known for his short stories, although a novella-length story, "You Cheated, You Lied," appears in *Sonny Liston Was a Friend of Mine.* Jones has, however, worked on various screenplays.

ACHIEVEMENTS

Thom Jones appeared on the literary scene in the early 1990's with a flurry of awards. His first story, "The Pugilist at Rest," was chosen for *Best American Short Stories* in 1992 and won first prize in the 1993 *O. Henry Awards.* His first book, also titled *The Pugilist at Rest,* was shortlisted for the 1993 National Book Award. The story "I Want to Live" was chosen for *Best American Short Stories* in 1993. "Cold Snap" was chosen for *Best American Short Stories* in 1994, and "Way Down Deep in the Jungle" appeared in *Best American Short Stories* in 1995. Jones was a Guggenheim Fellow in 1994 and 1995.

BIOGRAPHY

Thom Jones was born in Aurora, Illinois, in 1945, the first of three children. His father was a professional fighter, who became an engineer in the aerospace industry. After his father left when Jones was a child, his mother remarried. Jones spent most of his childhood with his grandmother, who ran a grocery store. His interest in boxing came from his father, who often took Jones, beginning when he was seven, to the gym for boxing lessons.

Jones entered the Marine Corps in 1963, preparing to go to Vietnam. However, after receiving a head injury in a boxing match, he became epileptic and was not deployed overseas. On discharge from the service,

he went to school at the University of Hawaii and then earned a degree in English from the University of Washington. He was accepted into the Iowa Writers' Workshop at the University of Iowa, from which he received an M.F.A. in 1973. He bounced back and forth between work in Aurora as a janitor and work in Chicago and Seattle as an advertising copywriter. He got married and worked as a janitor for twelve years at North Thurston High School in Lacey, Washington, a suburb of Olympia, where his wife was librarian. In 1986, he began rehabilitation treatment for alcoholism, after which he became diabetic.

Jones said that one morning in 1992, after he got home from the graveyard shift, he watched the *Today* show on television. He was drinking ale when he saw a former classmate from Iowa, Tracy Kidder, being interviewed. Jones said that he was as low as he could get and decided at that moment to start writing again. In his biographical comments in the 1993 *O. Henry Award Prize Stories,* Jones said he wrote the story "The Pugilist at Rest" in a sort of "controlled ecstatic frenzy." He recounted that one day, just as he was getting ready to go to work, his agent called to tell him that *The New Yorker* had accepted "The Pugilist at Rest." About two minutes later, he said, she called to say that *Esquire* had accepted another story. Just as he started out the door to go to work, she called a third time to tell him that *Harper's* was going to publish the story "I Want to Live."

Between 1992 and 1999, Jones published three collections of stories, went on book tours, did readings, taught part time, and conducted seminars and writers' workshops. He taught at the Iowa Writers' Workshop as a guest instructor between 1994 and 1996. However, since the publication of his third collection, he has done some screenplay writing. He settled in Olympia, Washington.

ANALYSIS

Some critics have suggested that Thom Jones is a realist who introduces readers to a segment of society not often seen--captives of veterans' hospitals, wanderers around the fringes of prize-fighting gyms, whacked-out refugees of disillusionment, existential absurdists in a drug-induced world of their own. However, Jones's stories are less realistic than hallucinatory, more figural than sociological, more metaphoric than mimetic. When readers enter a Jones story, they put normality aside and live momentarily in a world that most of them recognize from those rare moments of hallucination when they are feverish or highly medicated. Characteristic of Jones's style is the runaway voice of characters spaced out, speeded up, and thus somehow in touch with a strange magic that transcends the everyday world and throws readers into a nether world between fantasy and reality.

"The Pugilist at Rest"

The title story of Jones's enthusiastically received first collection of stories is typical of the style and narrative method that early readers found irresistible. The voice of the narrator, who describes training and fighting as a Marine and a boxer, sounded so raw and convincing that many early reviewers declared, incorrectly, that Jones had served in Vietnam. The story begins with a young recruit, called Hey Baby, being razzed for a letter he wrote to a girlfriend. When Hey Baby begins harassing the narrator's buddy Jorgeson, a guy who admires Jack Kerouac and wants to practice Zen Buddhism, the narrator hits him in the temple with the butt of his M-14, fracturing his skull.

After boot camp, when the narrator runs into Jorgeson again at Camp Pendleton in Southern California, Jorgeson has become a gung-ho Marine. The only Vietnam War scene in the story describes a battle in which the narrator's gun jams and he watches helplessly as many of his comrades are killed, including his buddy Jorgeson, all of which Jones recounts in gruesome detail. The story then shifts to the narrator's discussion of the concept of bravery, referencing the gladiator Theogenes, a powerful boxer who is depicted in a famous Roman statue named "The Pugilist at Rest." The narrator says he has discovered a reservoir of malice and sadism in his soul that poured out in Vietnam, where he served three tours, seeking payback for the death of Jorgeson and his other comrades. After returning home from Vietnam, he takes up boxing and gets hit so hard and so repeatedly by another boxer that he develops epileptic seizures, which cause a kind of aura that he describes as being satori. The story ends with his realization that good and evil are only illusions and his growing

that his vision of Supreme Reality is nothing more than the demons visited on madmen. Jones provided a bit of welcome ragged, rough-edged relief to the clean lines of M.F.A. storytelling at the end of the 1980's, but it is probably his linking a rambling macho voice with the seeming erudition suggested by his quotations from Arthur Schopenhauer that made early critics so enthusiastic about this story.

"Quicksand"

Jones has suggested that his stories often begin with an overheard line around which he develops a distinctive voice. Then, "like a method actor," he says, he falls into character and writes "instinctively without a plan or an idea as to what will happen." Jones creates a persona for his possessed writing style in the character Ad Magic, featured in the story "The White Horse" in *The Pugilist at Rest* and "Quicksand" in *Cold Snap*. Whereas Ad Magic winds up in India after a seizure of epileptic amnesia in the earlier story, in the new piece, he is a direct-mail wizard in Africa, writing fund appeal letters for the Global Aid Society hunger effort. Ad Magic, who takes his name from his ability to lapse into a

Thom Jones (Time & Life Pictures/Getty Images)

trancelike state and tap into a writing frenzy, is, like other Jones characters, suffering from a variety of pains, ills, and drugs. In this story, his thumb, which has been broken, throbs with pain, and he has malaria, complete with chills, hypnagogic dreams, and "visceral evacuation."

Typical of Jones's physically tormented characters, Ad Magic is caught in the quicksand of Africa's heart of darkness, "sinking deeper and deeper," filled with existential angst and a sense of absurdity, feeling like a marionette in a Punch and Judy show and realizing that life is nothing but a big cartoon. As Ad Magic says at one point, "Life's a dream." He is filled with anger at the lies, duplicity, and deceit at the heart of life; however, he gleefully engages in deceit himself by sending small baggies of crushed-up Milk Bones with his appeal letter, telling recipients that it is the only food that poor Africans have to eat. "Quicksand," whose title comes from a 1960's song by Martha and the Vandellas, ends much as the earlier Ad Magic story does: with Jones's fevered persona caught up in one of his frenzied writing seizures and, as usual, going too far.

"Cold Snap"

In the title story to Jones's second collection, the central character, Richard, is sent back from Africa after contracting malaria, having a "manic episode," and losing his medical license for drug abuse. Like Ad Magic, with his broken thumb, Richard, the character in this story, has a throbbing thumb, which he cut while trying to assemble a battery tester and for which he must go to doctor where he gets the inevitable pain pills. Richard's younger sister, Susan, a schizophrenic, who in one of her many suicide attempts puts a bullet through her temple and gives herself a perfect lobotomy, is the most important figure in this story, for she provides him with his best hope for finding some relief from his own episodes of depression.

Richard, who says he is in one of his Fyodor Dostoevski moods, cures himself temporarily by putting a gun to his head, spinning the cylinder, and pulling the trigger. The relief he experiences he attributes to what he calls the Van Gogh effect, for Vincent Van Gogh said he felt like a million dollars when he cut off his ear. However, Richard's more promising and possibly more lasting "island of stability" occurs when Susan tells him about her dream of the two of them driving a 1967 Dodge around heaven, where he will not have to ask any more existential questions. The story ends as they sit in the front seat of his car and eat the lunch he brought-- "the best little lunch of a lifetime"--while outside it rains and inside the radio plays the Shirelles singing "This Is Dedicated to the One I Love."

"Forty, Still at Home"

The problem with Jones's stories in his third collection is that his characters are selfish, self-indulgent, and often just plain mean. The most obnoxious is Matthew, an out-of-work man who, as the title indicates, is "Forty, Still at Home," and whose idea of a "commendable feat" is to sleep for twenty-two out of twenty-four hours. When he finds his cancer-racked mother's dead body in bed, he searches her safe and is as delighted to find a prescription for morphine as he is to find her money. To avoid probate, he zips her in a sleeping bag, puts her in the freezer, takes some morphine, and hops back in bed, feeling "absolutely, positively, right-on-the-money cap-*ee*-tal." Although this is supposed to be funny, it just comes off as quintessential adolescent meanness.

"Tarantula"

In "Tarantula," thirty-eight pages are devoted to making life hell for John Harold Hammermeister, an ambitious, admittedly not very likable young academic, who takes the job as assistant principal at W. E. B. Du Bois High School in urban Detroit. Hammermeister, who has big plans of climbing the ladder to the position of state superintendent, keeps a tarantula on his desk to intimidate students and faculty, but he meets his comeuppance in a janitor, who reads Joseph Conrad and who stabs the tarantula with a number one Dixon pencil. Then, with the help of another janitor, he puts duct tape over Hammermeister's eyes and mouth and beats his legs, knees, and elbows with a baseball bat. All great satiric fun, with ex-janitor Jones self-indulgently enjoying himself.

"Sonny Liston Was a Friend of Mine"

One of the better stories in the collection is the title story, which deals with an adolescent male who tries to find some heroic or romantic meaning in the world. Although Sonny Liston is not really a friend of Kid Dynamite, the young boxer in the title story, he does meet him once (as Jones said he did when he was a young man), and Liston signs a picture for him, "To the Kid, from your friend, Sonny Liston." The story is an engaging combination of young boy stuff (throwing snowballs at school, being awkward with a girlfriend, trying to cope with a stepfather) and adult stuff (fighting in the Golden Gloves, trying to establish a career, coping with a dangerous nemesis). Although the Kid wins his big fight by a split decision, he loses in the long run because a cut over his eye puts him out of the tournament. The story ends with the inevitable realization that "the real world, which had seemed so very far away all these years, was upon him."

BIBLIOGRAPHY

Bloom, James D. "Cultural Capital and Contrarian Investing: Robert Stone, Thom Jones, and Others." *Contemporary Literature* 36 (1995): 490-507. Discusses how characters in Jones's stories "Break on Through" and "Rocket Man" from *The Pugilist at Rest* blindly idolize Jim Morrison and the rock group the Doors.

Kelleher, Ray. "The New Machoism: An Interview with Thom Jones." *Poets and Writers Magazine* 23 (May/June, 1995): 28-37. Kelleher provides a biographical sketch and describes Jones's writing and medication regimen. Jones talks about his epileptic auras, comparing them to the experience of a Zen satori, and how he writes stories complete in one sitting. When he creates a character, it is like method acting, for he becomes that character.

McCarron, Kevin. "'The Crack-House Flicker': The Sacred and the Absurd in the Short Stories of Dennis Cooper, Dennis Johnson, and Thom Jones." *Yearbook of English Studies* 31 (2001): 50-61. Discusses the relationship between religion and narcotics in the stories in *The Pugilist at Rest* and *Cold Snap.* Argues that experiences with the sacred and the absurd in Jones's stories are related to use of various drugs and that Jones's characters yearn for experiences that reject the corporeality of the body and its eventual and final death.

McGuane, Thomas. "Unhappy Warriors." *The New York Times Book Review*, June 13, 1993, p. 7. An important long review of *The Pugilist at Rest*, in which author McGuane discusses Jones's "absolute authority" in presenting his soldier characters in the Vietnam War stories as "warriors," who often face a grotesque and ignominious death. Claims that Jones's boxing characters are like soldiers imagining themselves engaged in a Nietzschean will to power.

Solotaroff, Ted. "S*emper Fi*, Nietzsche." *The Nation*, September 6, 1993. This is a significant review of *The Pugilist at Rest*, in which Solotaroff argues that with his macho elitism Jones comes close to being a fictionist of the radical right. Provides an analysis of the title story and brief comments on "Wipeout" and "Rocket Man."

Charles E. May

K

DAVID MICHAEL KAPLAN

Born: New York, New York; April 9, 1946

PRINCIPAL SHORT FICTION
Comfort, 1987
Skating in the Dark, 1991

OTHER LITERARY FORMS

In addition to his short-story collections, David Michael Kaplan has written *Revision: A Creative Approach to Writing and Rewriting Fiction* (1997), which shows writers how to be their own editors, offers writing strategies, and points out common errors.

ACHIEVEMENTS

David Michael Kaplan's stories have been anthologized in publications such as *American Short Fiction*, *The Best American Short Stories*, *Prize Stories: The O. Henry Awards, Sudden Fiction International*, and *The Sound of Writing*. In 1999, he won the Nelson Algren Short Story Award, and he has also received grants and awards from the National Endowment for the Arts, the Corporation of Yaddo, the Illinois Arts Council, the Pennsylvania Council on the Arts, and the CINE New York International Film and Television Festival.

BIOGRAPHY

David Michael Kaplan was born in New York City on April 9, 1946, to Sidney and Minnie Marie Henson Kaplan. He married twice, the second time to Joyce Winer in 1988. He earned his bachelor's degree at Yale University (1967) and his master's of fine arts at the University of Iowa (1987). Before teaching at the latter institution from 1985 through 1987 and thereafter at Loyola University in Chicago, Kaplan was the creative director of Shadowstone Films in Durham, North Carolina, from 1971 through 1976 and the production director of National Television News in Los Angeles from 1976 through 1984.

ANALYSIS

The stories in David Michael Kaplan's first collection, *Comfort*, have two primary themes: difficult, often sad, parent-child relationships and the magical or mystical. The former theme focuses on children physically and/or emotionally estranged from a parent through abandonment, divorce, misunderstanding, or death, followed by a search for reconciliation. Stylistically, Kaplan tries to practice what he teaches in his writing workshops. As his course descriptions read, "Revision is where the story gets made: we all know this hoary maxim from writers' workshops and creative writing books." Kaplan emphasizes the need to engage the reader's interest right from the start, to create the imaginative "reality" of the fictional world, and to establish the authority of the narrative voice so that the reader may willingly suspend disbelief. Kaplan does not always offer a resolution to the strange connections and the unbridgeable distances between the characters he creates. For instance, in "Summer People," which was revised for his second collection, an estranged and divorced son, who has spent his adult life trying to get away from his father's excessively judgmental attitude, is reunited with his widower parent. Long-standing conflicts and resentments flare up, and the son has a confrontation with the father after they close up their old summer house for the last time. Still, there is no reconciliation.

"Love, Your Only Mother," in the first collection, is the most typical variation on Kaplan's primary theme. It is about a mother who left her daughter with the girl's father thirty years earlier and whose only contact with her daughter, who is now married with a daughter of her own, has been the occasional bizarre and untraceable postcard from various locations in the West. The postcards--sixty-three in all--have never revealed where the mother is, only where she was sometime before. Thus, the postcards are more terrifying than comforting.

In another story, "In the Realm of the Heron," a father takes his eleven-year-old daughter on a lakeside vacation in the wake of his wife's sudden, accidental death. The young widower has not been able to cope with his daughter's unexpressed rage and refusal to accept her loss. One day, the father insists on taking his daughter to an old deserted house that he discovered while rowing in a nearby lake. Instead of the idyllic retreat that he envisioned, the girl finds a dead heron nailed to a wall. In this instance, the experience provides the daughter with the opportunity to deal with her bereavement.

In "Elisabetta, Carlotta, Catherine," a young woman, abandoned by her mother long ago, searches for a girl in a photograph, which also depicts her prematurely deceased father. She thus presumes the girl in the picture to be his illegitimate daughter. In searching for a posthumous reconciliation with her dead parent, the daughter goes to Barbados and watches a strange ritual, a voodoo ceremony involving the raising of a demon, who is supposed to be able to reveal one's heart's desire in exchange for something the petitioner treasures. Elisabetta offers the demon the photograph of her father and the child, for whom she has been searching on the island. The photograph is consumed in the demon's flames, but Elisabetta does not get her wish. This story, then, like "Doe Season," touches base with both major themes.

Indeed, Kaplan uses the surreal or the supernatural as a plot device and as a way to enrich the understanding of his stories. This becomes apparent in his treatment of dreamlike fantasies, levitation, voodoo, witchery, transformation, ghostly visitations, and the like, as in "A Mexican Tale" or "Elias Schneebaum," two horror tales in which the supernatural provides the plot itself.

"COMFORT"

The title story of domestic realism in Kaplan's first collection is about two young women, Laurie and Michaela, former Skidmore College classmates now sharing an apartment in Saratoga, New York, while

holding down nondescript jobs. On this warm spring evening, the girls are expecting a visit from the current boyfriend of Laurie's mother, Ted Bremmer. Laurie has a generally low opinion of her parent's consorts, including Ted Bremmer, who is currently on assignment in Saratoga. Laurie had met him on a previous occasion and disapproved of his behavior then. Michaela suggests that Laurie test his faithfulness by trying to seduce him. When Laurie objects, Michaela jokingly volunteers.

Potent drinks followed by Ted's wine and Michaela's attraction for the middle-aged man do the rest. The more Michaela makes a play for Ted, the more incensed Laurie feels. When it becomes evident to Laurie that Ted, in fact, has spent a good part of the night in Michaela's room and thus has failed the "test," she calls him at his motel but hangs up after uttering an expletive.

The tension of the story flows from whether Laurie will now become even more estranged from her mother, given the evidence that the woman's current boyfriend is no better than her previous "jerks." In addition, there is a question of whether Laurie and Michaela will continue to be friends or Laurie's strong sense of betrayal by her roommate will end their earlier close ties. Accordingly, there is little comfort to be found in this or several other stories in the collection.

"DOE SEASON"

Widely considered to be the showpiece of Kaplan's first collection, *Comfort*, this fantasy story is about a precocious nine-year-old girl, Andy, who is initiated into the adult world of sexuality and death on the occasion of a deer hunt. On a cold winter morning in the Pennsylvania woods, she witnesses the gutting of a doe, which she reluctantly accepted an invitation to kill the previous day. It is the only one bagged by an otherwise all-male party of three--her father, his friend Charlie, and the latter's eleven-year-old son Mac.

That night Andy experiences a surreal, dreamlike vision of herself stepping out of the tent just as the doe's ghost enters the hunters' camp. The animal helplessly allows the girl to approach closely enough to touch it and palpate the inside of its gaping wound. As Andy cups the doe's beating heart, its warmth nearly sears her hand. She is struck by the horror and beauty of it all. The next morning, when the hunting party finds the dead doe and her father begins to eviscerate it, Andy runs away.

Here, as in several other stories, Kaplan deals with the complicated ties between parents and children. In this case, the conflict revolves around how Andy relates to her mother, who makes only a brief appearance in the story, as well as how Andy resists her father's teasing of her hoydenish qualities. In fact, the story ends with her not responding to her boyish nickname Andy but insisting on the use of her full name, Andrea. The deer hunt has hastened the girl's passage from tomboyhood to premature womanhood.

Skating in the Dark

This is a collection of twelve interrelated stories presented as a novel. It traces the coming-of-age, marriage, and divorce of Frank Kresky over a forty-year period, from 1951 to 1990. During that time he tries to find out who he is. Frank first appears at age seven, growing up in a small western Pennsylvania town and dreading piano lessons from a nun ("Piano Lessons"). By age fifteen he likes to break into houses, including the one he shares with his parents ("Break-In"). Age twenty-five finds him in Crete ("Governotou") agonizing over what he should be and whether he should marry Jena. It is the summer of 1969, and he has supposedly been deferred from the Vietnam War draft because of his job as an "educator" writing standardized achievement tests. Seven years later, now married, Frank takes Jena back to Crete to visit his old haunts and do what had been enjoyable the first time around, but the fun has gone out of it ("Tombs"), and the couple is evidently drifting apart.

In the title story, "Skating in the Dark," set in January, 1972, when Frank is twenty-eight years old, he and his wife of three years, now living and working in Southern California, travel back east for a family visit and break into his parents' summer home, where they learn they are doomed to say things they do not mean and that deceptions and lies are bound to mark their future conjugal life.

The remaining stories deal with the aftereffects of Frank's divorce, as well as the ill health, decline, and death of his parents. The final tale, "In the Night," set in August, 1990, when Frank is forty-six, shows him

trying to help a girlfriend, Allie, out of a major crisis in her life, affording him some kind of redemptive quality.

Thus, this collection is about a sterile, childless marriage and about parent-child relationships. At the close, Frank still seems to be trying to find himself. He is still afraid of life and of growing up; for him, looking back--skating in the dark--is at best a sad, elegiac experience. Reading *Skating in the Dark*, then, is a little like thumbing through a photograph album from which most of the happy pictures are missing, a series of episodes recording the sadder and more troublesome moments of a man's life. The stories of the unengaging hero's coming-of-age as he fumbles through his rough-and-tumble life, searching for a persona he can accept, do not lead to anything pleasurable. Accordingly, as in Kaplan's first collection, *Comfort*, the atmosphere is morose.

Other major works

NONFICTION: *Revision: A Creative Approach to Writing and Rewriting Fiction*, 1997.

Bibliography

Cameron, Peter. "Melancholy in the 50's." Review of *Skating in the Dark*, by David Michael Kaplan. *The New York Times*, September 8, 1991, sec. VII, p. 41. A short-story writer's book review of Kaplan's second collection finds that the protagonist's prolonged sensitivity to hurt seems more like unchecked moping.

Hall, Sharon K., ed. "David Michael Kaplan." *Contemporary Literary Criticism: Yearbook 1987* 50 (1988): 55-58. A profile and various review synopses of Kaplan's first short-story collection, *Comfort*.

"*Skating in the Dark*." Review of *Skating in the Dark*, by David Michael Kaplan. *Kirkus Reviews* 59 (August 1, 1991): 956. A critical reading of Kaplan's second collection finds it a little too calculating and, with two or three exceptions, lacking in real power.

"*Skating in the Dark*." Review of *Skating in the Dark*, by David Michael Kaplan. *Publishers Weekly* 238 (August 2, 1991): 62. A laudatory review of the collection sees it as neatly sidestepping "muzzy nostalgia traps" in the protagonist's movement toward a more redeemable life.

Wood, Susan. "Children Without Parents." Review of *Comfort*, by David Michael Kaplan. *The New York Times*, June 4, 1987, sec. VII, p. 41. A review of Kaplan's first collection finds its stories "affecting"

because of their common focus on the extraordinary moments of recognition in ordinary lives.

Peter B. Heller

GARRISON KEILLOR

Born: Anoka, Minnesota; August 7, 1942

PRINCIPAL SHORT FICTION

G. K. the DJ, 1977
Happy to Be Here: Stories and Comic Pieces, 1982
Lake Wobegon Days, 1985
Leaving Home: A Collection of Lake Wobegon Stories, 1987
We Are Still Married: Stories and Letters, 1989
The Book of Guys, 1993
Truckstop, and Other Lake Wobegon Stories, 1995
Wobegon Boy, 1998
Life Among the Lutherans, 2009

OTHER LITERARY FORMS

Garrison Keillor (GAR-ih-suhn KEE-lur) began his literary career in 1960 as a radio comedian, appearing on Minnesota Public Radio. From 1974 to 1987, he hosted a live weekly radio show based in St. Paul, Minnesota, entitled *A Prairie Home Companion*, a variety format that included original monologues that he called "News from Lake Wobegon." Offered as a premium to Minnesota Public Radio contributors, Keillor's *The Selected Verse of Margaret Haskins Durber* (1979) includes fourteen poems about Minnesota that he had read or sung on the air. The short fiction that he subsequently published is largely rooted in the twenty-minute monologues that he composed for his radio shows and that revolve around the places and characters of the mythical Lake Wobegon, Minnesota, in Mist (missed) County. Some of his monologues have been released on audiocassette tapes, videocassettes, and compact-disc recordings. Beginning in 1989, Keillor hosted from New York City the weekly radio broadcast

American Radio Company of the Air, a variety format, which likewise included original monologues, some of which have been anthologized in print or on tape. In 1999, Keillor published the novel *Me: By Jimmy (Big Boy) Valente, Governor of Minnesota, as Told to Garrison Keillor*.

ACHIEVEMENTS

Garrison Keillor, along with Spalding Gray and Eric Bogosian, achieved fame as one of the most accomplished monologuists in the last half of the twentieth century. Keillor's written production initially grew out of both his live and his recorded performances and succeeded largely because his reputation as a performer preceded the publications. He is a homespun humorist with a droll, low-key, tongue-in-cheek style. His rambling tales emanated from poking fun at the fictional characters of his mythical Lake Wobegon, Minnesota, "the little town that time forgot and that decades cannot improve."

Besides having created and hosted nationally acclaimed radio shows and published best-selling books, Keillor has continued to be a regular contributor to *The New Yorker*. He received a Grammy Award for his recording of *Lake Wobegon Days* and two Awards for Cable Excellence for the Disney Channel productions of *A Prairie Home Companion*. He has also received a George Foster Peabody Broadcasting Award and an Edward R. Murrow Award. He has appeared with the Chicago, Minnesota, Milwaukee, San Francisco, Pittsburgh, and National symphony orchestras, and in a performance entitled *Lake Wobegon Tonight*, at the Apollo Theatre in London. He has received a Gold Medal Award for spoken English from the American Academy of Arts and Letters in 1990, and he was inducted into the Museum of Broadcast Communications and the Radio Hall of Fame in 1994.

BIOGRAPHY

His roots in small-town Minnesota provided Gary Edward Keillor with the particular brand of midwestern humor that brought him fame and on which he continued to capitalize even after relocating to New York City. He was the third of six children in the family of John P. Keillor, a railway mail clerk and carpenter, and Grace Denham. When Garrison Keillor was in the eighth grade, he adopted the pen name "Garrison" in place of his given names because, he said, he believed that it sounded "more formidable." He grew up just north of Minneapolis, Minnesota, south of the small town of Anoka, what has since become Brooklyn Park. After his 1960 graduation from Anoka High School, Keillor enrolled in the University of Minnesota, wrote a regular column, published stories in the student magazine *The Ivory Tower*, which he later edited, and was student announcer for KUOM, the university radio station. He received a B.A. in English and journalism in 1966, went to New York in an unsuccessful attempt to land a job as a writer, returned to work on a master's degree in English, and then took a job with KSJR-FM in Collegeville, the first station in the Minnesota Public Radio network.

Keillor spent fourteen years on and off, from 1968 to 1982, as a disc jockey in St. Paul, Minnesota. His earliest program, *The Prairie Home Morning Show*, eventually included anecdotes about a mythical midwestern place that he called Lake Wobegon, situated in the similarly mythical Mist County. One of the hallmarks of the program was inclusion of advertisements from bogus sponsors: Powdermilk Biscuits, Jack's Auto Repair, Bertha's Kitty Boutique, and Ralph's Pretty Good Grocery, among others. Besides broadcasting, Keillor was busy writing. He sold his first story, "Local Family Keeps Son Happy," to *The New Yorker* in 1970, then moved with his wife and small son to a farm near Freeport, Minnesota. He was divorced in 1976.

Modeled after the Grand Ole Opry in Nashville, Tennessee, Keillor's *A Prairie Home Companion* aired on July 6, 1974. The monologues, advertisements, and musical entertainment were highlights of the program. Eleven years later, one of the show's monologues concerned a twenty-fifth high school class reunion in

Garrison Keillor (Getty Images)

which the narrator, Keillor, rekindles an acquaintance with a foreign exchange student that blossoms into a romance. The monologue was biographical in the sense that, at his own class reunion at Anoka High School, Keillor established a real-life relationship with Ulla Skaerved, a Danish exchange student twenty-five years earlier, and they were married on December 29, 1985, in Denmark.

A Prairie Home Companion continued in weekly radio broadcasts for thirteen years, culminating in a farewell performance on June 13, 1987. During these years, Keillor anthologized his monologues in recordings and in books. Perhaps a disenchantment with his celebrity status and an irritation with newspaper reporters in St. Paul, who printed what Keillor believed to be private information about himself, resulted in Keillor and his new wife relocating to Denmark for a short while, then settling in New York City. There, he continued to write for *The New Yorker* and host a weekly radio broadcast entitled *American Radio Company of the Air*.

In the mid-1990's, Keillor resumed live broadcasts of *A Prairie Home Companion*, but for his return to radio he began touring the United States and no longer limited himself to performing his shows in Minnesota. He still continued to tell witty stories about the residents of the fictional town of Wobegon, Minnesota. In 1999, Keillor wrote a fictional autobiography of a resident of Wobegon and a witty satire of Governor Jesse Ventura of Minnesota. The similarities between the fictional governor named Jimmy Valente and Jesse Ventura are so striking that Keillor felt the need to state that readers should not assume that his book, a satire of the state of American politics in the late twentieth century, has anything to do with Jesse Ventura.

ANALYSIS

Garrison Keillor's upbringing in a small town in central Minnesota is the single greatest influence on his work. Many of the experiences and characters that appear in his short fiction are rooted in memories of events that happened to him there or of people whom he knew. In fact, the name for his radio show, *A Prairie Home Companion*, is taken from a cemetery in Moorhead, Minnesota, called Prairie Home Lutheran Cemetery.

The theme of religion--specifically Christianity--is the most frequently explored concept in Keillor's work. He has, in fact, described *A Prairie Home Companion* as "a gospel show." Growing up, Keillor and his family were members of the Plymouth Brethren, a Protestant sect of Anglican dissenters that closely resembles the "fundamentalists" and the "Sanctified Brethren" in his published works. His upbringing was a conservative one, in which drinking, smoking, dancing, attending films, and watching television were frowned upon; consequently Keillor writes with a conservative, instructional, and highly moral tone. A piece in one of his early books is entitled "Your Wedding and You: A Few Thoughts on Making It More Personally Rewarding, Shared by Reverend Bob Osman." Here, Keillor offers, tongue in cheek, prudent advice and practical suggestions on how to tailor a wedding ceremony to fit the personalities of the bride and groom. A couple he calls Sam and Judy, for example, "chose to emphasize their mutual commitment to air and water

quality, exchanging vows while chained to each other and to the plant gate of a major industrial polluter."

LAKE WOBEGON STORIES

Throughout Lake Wobegon stories, Keillor writes about ordinary events that evoke a natural piety, *memento mori*, along with an awareness of the transience of all things. His philosophy is consistent with the Christian doctrine that life is basically good. Some of the pieces, for example, offer metaphors for the Christian promise of eternal life. A quotation from "State Fair," a piece that appears in *Leaving Home*, perhaps best illustrates this point of view. In it, the narrator remembers riding the Ferris wheel as a child:

> We go up and I think of people I knew who are dead and I smell fall in the air, manure, corn dogs, and we drop down into blazing light and blaring music. Every summer I'm a little bigger, but riding the ferris wheel, I feel the same as ever, I feel eternal. . . . The wheel carries us up high, high, high, and stops, and we sit swaying, creaking, in the dark, on the verge of death. . . . Then the wheel brings me down to the ground. We get off and other people get on. Thank you, dear God, for this good life and forgive us if we do not live it enough.

In other pieces, however, rebellion against his repressive upbringing surfaces in sarcasm, not all of it gentle or good-humored. The most notable example of this is an extended complaint, the "longest footnote in American fiction," entitled "Ninety-Five Theses Ninety-Five," which appears in *Lake Wobegon Days*. One of Keillor's important themes here is righteous anger at how the Midwest has shaped him. Keillor uses the character Johnny Tollefson, a fictional angry son, who returns to Lake Wobegon with a new wife from Boston, intent on nailing a set of written complaints about the repressive effects of putative parents and neighbors to the door of the Lutheran church, but "something in his upbringing made him afraid to pound holes in a good piece of wood." So, instead, the treatise becomes "lost" on the overloaded desk of the town's newspaper editor and ultimately appears as a footnote that spans twenty-three pages.

In this complaint, Keillor rails against religious strictures, fear of sexuality, fastidiousness, and his resultant ineptness at sustaining interpersonal relationships. A milder complaint is thesis seven, which states,

> You have taught me to fear strangers and their illicit designs, robbing me of easy companionship, making me a very suspicious friend. Even among those I know well, I continue to worry: what do they *really* mean by liking me?

These complaints become increasingly bitter; thesis fourteen, for example, states:

> You taught me to trust my own incompetence and even now won't let me mash potatoes without your direct supervision. "Don't run the mixer so fast that you get them all over," you say, as if in my home, the walls are covered with big white lumps. I can't mow a lawn or hang tinsel on a Christmas tree or paint a flat surface in your presence without you watching, worried, pointing out the unevenness.

Thesis twenty-one shows Keillor's anger at having been brought up to feel guilty. "Suffering was its own reward, to be preferred to pleasure. As Lutherans, we viewed pleasure with suspicion. Birth control was never an issue with us. Nor was renunciation of pleasures of the flesh. We never enjoyed them in the first place."

This is an imposing example of Keillor's sarcasm, but it is just as important to bear in mind his knack for comedy, which is, ultimately, more prevalent in his work. With deliberate pacing and mild surprise, many of his stories are gentle, nostalgic, and quiet. Finally, he celebrates, rather than satirizes, the Sanctified Brethren. He believes that, despite ridiculous situations and smallness or meanness in certain people, "life is a comedy" because "God is the author, and God writes an awful lot of comedy." Although he laughs at how foolish humankind can be, it is a good-natured laughter that has his characters' best interests at heart.

When one of Keillor's characters, Clarence Bunsen, discovers that what he thought was a heart attack in the shower one day really was not, he is so grateful that he drops a check into the collection plate at church the following Sunday. Moments later he realizes that he had mistakenly made the check out for three hundred dollars instead of thirty, thus cleaning out his bank account.

Lake Wobegon's visitation by twenty-four Lutheran ministers ends in a disaster that is really humorous. Pastor Ingqvist had arranged an outing for the clergy on a pontoon boat owned by Wally of the Sidetrack Tap, but the combined weight of the earnest ministers, each holding a can of beer, was too much for the *Agnes D.* She took on more water than Wally could bail out, forcibly introducing eight of the clergy to the Baptist heresy of full immersion. Soon, all the ministers were standing chin deep in water, faces uplifted, unable to call out for help "because their voices were too deep and mellow" and "trying to understand this experience and its deeper meaning."

Family gatherings at which his great uncle and aunt told long tales were also influential on Keillor. Keillor often calls himself a "shy person," and, in fact, humorously advocates "shy rights" in some of his tales. His quietly reserved and remote personality is immediately evident in listening to his radio broadcasts. Not surprisingly, one of Keillor's main themes is an idealization of home and family relationships, and another is the evanescence of home. Many of his tales, as well as the title of one of his books, concern his relationship with home.

HAPPY TO BE HERE

Happy to Be Here collected witty and urbane pieces that Keillor initially wrote for periodical publication. Though the book includes no Lake Wobegon material, it pokes fun at small-town life in its sly humor and bucolic optimism. Keillor uses an ordinary Minnesota farm as his setting for the ideal "home": "Found paradise. Here it is, and it is just what I knew was here all along. . . . I'm happy to be here." Here also Keillor parodies the styles of writing in magazines such as *Life* and *Rolling Stone*, the swagger of political figures and the unchecked optimism, grand designs, and little moral dilemmas of his midwestern characters. Two of the pieces, "WLT" and "The Slim Graves Show," draw on his radio experience, and many offer rules to live by or recount lessons that he has learned from life.

LAKE WOBEGON DAYS

Prompted by the popularity of the monologues in *A Prairie Home Companion* broadcasts, Keillor offered in *Lake Wobegon Days* an extended history and geography of the mythical town of Lake Wobegon. Although giving abundant detail of a specific place, Keillor insists on the universality of his myth because he believes that places like it exist everywhere. The book has a pattern of development that is both chronological and seasonal. It chronicles the founding of the town by early settlers and the establishment of its traditions. Emphasizing the cycle of seasons, it also recounts the personal story of a little boy growing up among the Sanctified Brethren, envious of Catholics and Lutherans, who becomes a restless adolescent.

Leaving Home: A Collection of Lake Wobegon Stories is the title of Keillor's second book of Lake Wobegon stories, published after Keillor ended his association with Minnesota Public Radio and moved to Denmark and then, soon afterward, to New York City. If *Lake Wobegon Days* defined the stable and slightly sentimentalized mid-American town, *Leaving Home* portrays it in flux and recombination, emphasizing the transience of all things. Every story recounts some kind of leave-taking or homecoming: a waitress quitting her job at the Chatterbox Café, a boy joining the Army, Father Emil retiring from Our Lady of Perpetual Responsibility Catholic Church, family members returning to Lake Wobegon for Christmas. During the time of the book's writing, Keillor married a second time and left Minnesota, so the book is significant biographically as well as artistically. Keillor laments in the book's introduction that his home territory, Minneapolis and St. Paul, has changed and not for the better. The Met Stadium, he notes, has been replaced by "a polyester ball field with a roof over it, a ghostly greenish plastic baseball mall, and all those lovely summer nights were lost." The book ends with Keillor taking leave of his characters: "This is my last view of [the residents of Lake Wobegon] for a while. If you see them before I do, say hello from me and give them my love."

WE ARE STILL MARRIED

We Are Still Married: Stories and Letters is a challenging set of essays about life on the edge. The stories are cryptic, cynical, suave, and aggressive. In several,

Keillor expresses explicit anger at the media. "My Life in Prison" is a vicious parody about what journalists have done to him. The title story is the piece that closes the book, which describes the near destruction of an ordinary marriage once the media move in to examine it. There is violence in the book as well as sadness and some midcareer anxiety. The restrooms in New York City's subways are described as a hell unmatched by even the most primitive rural Minnesota gas stations, "full of garbage, filth, killer bees, Nazis, crack heads, [and] flies who carry AIDS." Annie Szemanski is a tobacco-spitting, brass-kneed feminist baseball player in "What Did We Do Wrong?" who insults and abuses her ardent fans. Even the five sketches devoted to Lake Wobegon characters are more complicated and sophisticated than his earlier stories were, depicting raw emotion and a bit of meanness.

WOBEGON BOY

In 1997, Keillor's fictional autobiography of a male resident of Wobegon was published. Readers sense that this narrator represents the persona created by Keillor for the monologues he gave in performances of *A Prairie Home Companion*. Each chapter is a touching story told by the narrator. Perhaps the most moving is the one Keillor entitled "The Wake." Keillor evokes the universal use of humor as a defense mechanism by family members attending a wake and the difficulty that people have in talking about the lives of recently deceased family members. In this story, the narrator's father has just died, and the narrator has returned to Wobegon for the funeral. As they are approaching the cemetery, the narrator tells his friend Diana that his dad is not in the coffin but in Buenos Aires. This remark represents a clear effort to deny reality, but many people who are grieving seek to deny reality. Keillor also describes a curious group of strange characters, including a retired senator who now lives in a trailer park in Florida and several cousins who tell tall tales. This story illustrates nicely how people use humor to get through painful experiences, such as a wake or a burial.

LIFE AMONG THE LUTHERANS

Life Among the Lutherans is a collection of twenty-five stories and three songs, dating from 1983 through 2009. Edited by Holly Harden, they are adaptations of the Lake Wobegon monologues delivered by Keillor during his weekly radio show. The overall tone is that of the homespun, good-humored tale, leisurely told by a good-natured narrator, who pokes gentle fun at his neighbors and himself. However, the evolution in Keillor's writing occurring over three decades is especially apparent. The earliest Keillor fiction is largely apolitical and free of the rancor so often associated with political advocacy. In "Minister's Retreat," though, the narrator refers to the long chain of sorry characters from the Republican South who attempted to overthrow a presidency (the Bill Clinton impeachment is not named but is clearly indicated). In "Memorial Day," the narrator--who, granted, is not Keillor but a persona invented by him--speaks bitterly of the arrogant and deceitful old men who send young men to die in purposeless wars. The narrator of "Potato Salad" declares he is a Democrat and explains why. In "Ninety-Five Theses," a writer who has fled Lake Wobegon returns to submit an anonymous manifesto, mimicking Martin Luther's famous protest. The author's charges against his parents, his fellow townspeople, and his fellow Lutherans--of having instilled in him prejudices, feelings of guilt, an unhealthy fear of sex, and a grim theology--are amusing at one level, but the suggestion is strong that the small-town values with which he grew up have marred him for life.

Several of Keillor's beloved monologues, some previously published elsewhere, are included. "Pontoon Boat" tells the tale of the ill-starred outing in the *Agnes D.*, which sinks (in five feet of water) during a pleasure cruise for twenty-four Lutheran ministers, visiting Lake Wobegon on the five-day Meeting the Pastoral Needs of Rural America tour. "Gospel Birds" tells the story of the appearance of Ernie and Irma Lundeen and their Performing Gospel Birds during the Wednesday-night service at the Lake Wobegon Lutheran Church. Some of the birds do tricks, the parrots recite verses of scripture, Ernie testifies to his wayward past life as a circus performer, and Irma dresses as various animals entering the ark. In the finale, a dove circles the sanctuary three times, then lands on the ark, whereupon a cloud of birds is released and proceeds to take up the collection. In "Raking Leaves," Eunice Ingqvist brings her two nephews to Lake Wobegon for a proper Lutheran baptism. Eunice's sister, Nancy, has been

attending a church in Minneapolis that does not require a belief in God. Nancy's twice-divorced boyfriend is the church janitor. He belongs to Alcoholics Anonymous and the Sons of Emotionally Distant Fathers Support Group. He wears long hair and a Grateful Dead T-shirt. Eunice feels that Nancy's boys clearly are in need of the protective Lutheran imprint. The reader may note a slightly different tone from one piece to the next, as they were performed and/or written in fifteen separate years over a total span of twenty-seven years. Some things, however, remain constant in Keillor's Lake Wobegon fiction: his unerring sense of the absurd, his (usually) light comedic touch, and his deft depiction of midwestern language and behavior.

More than one critic of Keillor's work has compared his particular brand of humor and storytelling with that of Mark Twain. Both authors are distinctly American, offering homespun profundities and cracker-barrel philosophies that are regional in inception and origin. Both writers tell tall tales with digressive anecdotes. Both mock pretense, portray comic suffering, and reveal the near-universal indignities of youth. As platform performers, both share the belief that a good tale should be heard as well as read, and both pose as overeager, inept but perceptive witnesses to life experiences. The rich imagination evident in the writings of both authors can be enjoyed by scholars of humor as well as by people who simply want to laugh.

OTHER MAJOR WORKS

LONG FICTION: *WLT: A Radio Romance*, 1991; *Me: By Jimmy (Big Boy) Valente, Governor of Minnesota, as Told to Garrison Keillor*, 1999; *Lake Wobegon Summer 1956*, 2001; *Love Me*, 2003; *Pontoon: A Novel of Lake Wobegon*, 2007; *Liberty: A Lake Wobegon Novel*, 2008; *A Christmas Blizzard*, 2009; *Pilgrims: A Novel of Lake Wobegon*, 2009.

SCREENPLAY: *A Prairie Home Companion*, 2006.

POETRY: *Seventy-Seven Love Sonnets*, 2009.

NONFICTION: *In Search of Lake Wobegon*, 2001 (photographs by Richard Olsenius); *Homegrown Democrat: A Few Plain Thoughts from the Heart of America*, 2004.

CHILDREN'S LITERATURE: *Cat, You Better Come Home*, 1995; *The Old Man Who Loved Cheese*, 1996; *The*

Sandy Bottom Orchestra, 1996 (with Jenny Lind Nilsson); *Daddy's Girl*, 2005.

EDITED TEXTS: *The Best American Short Stories 1998*, 1998 (with Katrina Kenison); *Good Poems*, 2002; *Good Poems for Hard Times*, 2005.

BIBLIOGRAPHY

Fedo, Michael. *The Man from Lake Wobegon*. New York: St. Martin's Press, 1987. Fedo's biography of Keillor, from early childhood until his departure from Minnesota, is unauthorized. Keillor refused to be interviewed by Fedo and encouraged his staff and the performers on his show to do likewise. Still, Fedo reveals close particulars of Keillor's personal life, his interests and influences, and the phenomenon of his popularity. Particularly useful is Fedo's four-page bibliography, which includes published interviews and articles about Keillor.

Lee, Judith Yaross. *Garrison Keillor: A Voice of America*. Jackson: University Press of Mississippi, 1991. Analysis of Keillor's stories in *Lake Wobegon Days*, *Leaving Home*, and other uncollected short fictions. Examines Keillor's methods of composition and such literary ancestors of his creation of Lake Wobegon as William Faulkner's Yoknapatawpha, James Joyce's Dublin, and Sherwood Anderson's Winesburg.

Narveson, Robert D. "Catholic-Lutheran Interaction in Keillor's *Lake Wobegon Days* and Hassler's *Grand Opening*." In *Exploring the Midwestern Literary Imagination*, edited by Marcia Noe. Troy, N.Y.: Whitston, 1993. Compares descriptions of Catholic and Lutheran interaction in small towns in Keillor's fiction with anthropological studies. Suggests that such social interactions in fiction may be conditioned more by the demands exerted by fiction's thematic significance and related symbolic patterns than by their correspondence to external reality.

"Periscope." *Newsweek* 150, no. 26 (December 24, 2007): 9-10, 14, 16-18. A short news item dealing with Keillor's activities toward the end of the decade. Illustrated with a portrait of the subject.

"Post People." *The Saturday Evening Post* 279, no. 1 (January/February, 2007): 16. Concerns Keillor's business ventures. Over time, his *Prairie Home Companion*, with the books, the audio presentations, a cable television broadcast, and a motion picture--all in addition to the original radio program--has become big business. Illustrated with a portrait of the subject.

Scholl, Peter A. *Garrison Keillor*. New York: Twayne, 1993. Examines Keillor's humorous and pastoral fiction and the place of Minnesota in literature. Includes a bibliography and an index.

_____. "Garrison Keillor." In *Dictionary of Literary Biography, 1987 Year-Book*, edited by J. M. Brook. Detroit: Gale Research, 1988. A good introduction to Keillor's life and works, giving insights into Keillor's personality, motivation, and career. Recounts the early influences of his literary heroes and of the Grand Ole Opry. Discusses Keillor's childhood, education, and individual published works in some detail and chronicles Keillor's involvement in radio broadcasting.

_____. "Garrison Keillor and the News from Lake Wobegon." *Studies in American Humor* 4 (Winter, 1985-1986): 217-228. Comparing Keillor to Will Rogers and Twain, Scholl stresses the regional, homespun character of Keillor's work. He also draws a distinction between two Keillors, "that of wandering storyteller in exile from Lake Wobegon and that of the urbane wit and writer for *The New Yorker*." Scholl discusses the unique brand of storytelling that Keillor uses in his monologues, a combination of spontaneity and studied elegance that is evident in the oral narratives as well as on the printed page. He stresses Keillor's focus on the "continuity and resilience of human life" and on the belief that "God is good."

Skow, John. "Let's Hear It for Lake Wobegon!" *Reader's Digest* 128 (February, 1986): 67-71. The inviting and immediate tone of this article makes it very engaging. It details a public performance of a segment of *A Prairie Home Companion* and, in doing so, relates explicitly the tone and mood that infuses all Keillor's work. Some biographical information gives insight into Keillor's career as a performer.

Traub, James. "The Short and Tall Tales of Garrison Keillor." *Esquire* 97 (May, 1982): 108-117. This article, in part an interview, contains an early yet detailed look at Keillor's performance techniques. Formative influences from childhood, college, and adulthood are recounted. Much attention is paid to

Keillor's method and technique of written composition as well as the evolution of *A Prairie Home Companion*.

Jill B. Gidmark; Edmund J. Campion
Updated by Patrick Adcock

JAMAICA KINCAID

Born: Saint John's, Antigua; May 25, 1949
Also Known As: Elaine Cynthia Potter Richardson

PRINCIPAL SHORT FICTION
At the Bottom of the River, 1983

OTHER LITERARY FORMS

In addition to her short stories, Jamaica Kincaid has written four novels, *Annie John* (1985), *Lucy* (1990), *The Autobiography of My Mother* (1996), and *Mr. Potter* (2002); a book-length essay concerning her native island Antigua entitled *A Small Place* (1988); a children's book, *Annie, Gwen, Lilly, Pam, and Tulip* (1986), with illustrations by Eric Fischl, and several nonfiction works, including *My Brother* (1997), *My Garden (Book)* (1999), and *Among Flowers: A Walk in the Himalaya.* In 1998, she edited *My Favorite Plant: Writers and Gardeners on the Plants They Love*; in 2005, she edited *The Best American Travel Writing 2005.*

ACHIEVEMENTS

Jamaica Kincaid's short-story collection *At the Bottom of the River* received the Morton Dauwen Zabel Award from the American Academy of Arts and Letters in 1983. Her novel *Annie John* was one of three finalists for the international Ritz Paris Hemingway Award in 1985. Her short story "Xuela" was included in *The Best American Short Stories 1995*; "In Roseau" was included in *The Best American Short Stories 1996.*

Kincaid is the recipient of the Anifeld-Wolf Book Award and The Lila-Wallace-*Reader's Digest* Fund Award. She was also nominated for the 1997 National Book Award for *My Brother* and received the 2000 Prix Femina Étranger for this work. Kincaid was elected in 2004 to the American Academy of Arts and Letters, and five years later she was elected to the American Academy of Arts and Sciences.

BIOGRAPHY

Born in 1949, Jamaica Kincaid, then Elaine Cynthia Potter Richardson, lived with her homemaker mother and carpenter father on Antigua, a small West Indian island measuring nine by twelve miles. The family was impoverished: Their house had no running water or electricity. The young girl's chores included drawing water from a community faucet and registering with the public works so that the "night soil men" would dispose of the family's waste. Even so, her childhood was idyllic. She was surrounded by the extraordinary beauty of the island, was accepted by her community, and was loved and protected by her mother. When Kincaid was nine, however, her mother gave birth to the first of three more children--all boys. At that point, the closeness that Kincaid had enjoyed was at first disturbed and then destroyed. She credits the lies that she began to tell her mother as the catalyst for her fiction writing: "I wasn't really lying. I was protecting my privacy or protecting a feeling I had about something. But lying is the beginning of fiction. It was the beginning of my writing life." Also at this time, she began to comprehend the insidious impact of colonialism. (Antigua was a British colony until 1967, and only in 1981 did it receive full independence.) The Antiguans' docile acceptance of their inferior status enraged her. Thus the serenity she had known as a child was displaced by loneliness and anger.

In 1966, Kincaid, seeking to disassociate herself from her mother, left Antigua; she did not return for nineteen years, and then only after she was a naturalized citizen of the United States and an established writer. Arriving in Scarsdale, New York, the seventeen-year-old Kincaid worked as a live-in babysitter. She did not open her mother's letters, and when, after a few months, she took an au pair position in New York City, she did not send her mother her new address. For the next three years, she cared for the four young girls of Michael Arlen, a writer for *The New Yorker* and a future colleague when she herself would become a staff writer for the magazine. Her childhood and early New York experiences are fictionalized in *At the Bottom of the River*, *Annie John*, and *Lucy*.

During her first few years in New York, she wanted to continue her education at a university but found her Antiguan schooling to be inferior; instead, she first studied for a high school diploma, took a few photography courses at a community college, and then attended Franconia College in New Hampshire on a scholarship, leaving after a year because, although only in her twenties, she felt too old. After jobs as a secretary and receptionist, she wrote for a teen magazine. In 1973, she changed her name to Jamaica Kincaid, perhaps suggesting that she had achieved her own identity. Associating with New York writers and artists, she met George Trow (*Lucy* is dedicated to him), who wrote "Talk of the Town" for *The New Yorker*. She collaborated on a few columns, and eventually one of her pieces was accepted by editor William Shawn, who was known for encouraging fledgling writers. In 1978, the magazine published her first short story, "Girl." Soon after, she married Allen Shawn, the editor's son.

In 1983, her first collection, *At the Bottom of the River*, was published to generally favorable reviews, as was her subsequent work, which has earned for her a devoted following. She continued to write short stories, usually published in *The New Yorker*, and give lectures and readings. She and Allen Shawn, a composer and professor at Bennington College, along with their two children--Annie, named after her mother, and

Jamaica Kincaid (AP Photo/Francois Mori)

Harold--settled in Bennington, Vermont, before the couple divorced. Until June, 2009, Kincaid taught at Harvard University, holding a joint appointment in the departments of English and of African and African American studies. In July, 2009, she joined the faculty of Claremont McKenna College, where she was a professor of literature.

ANALYSIS

Jamaica Kincaid is noted for her lyrical use of language. Her short stories and novels have a hypnotic, poetic quality that results from her utilization of rhythm and repetition. Her images, drawn from her West Indian childhood, recall Antigua, with its tropical climate, Caribbean food, local customs, and folklore laced with superstitions. Many of her stories move easily from realism to surrealistic fantasy, as would a Caribbean folktale. She is also praised for her exploration of the strong but ambiguous bond between mother and daughter and her portrayal of the transformation of a girl into a woman. Thus her work touches upon the loss of innocence that comes when one moves out of the Eden that is childhood. These are the features that are found not only in her short fiction but also in her novels, the chapters of which *The New Yorker* originally published as short stories, and in *Annie, Gwen, Lilly, Pam, and Tulip*, a children's book that was part of a project designed by the Whitney Museum of American Art, the original publisher, which sought to bring together contemporary authors and artists for a series of limited editions aimed primarily at collectors.

Kincaid's concern with racism, colonialism, classicism, and sexism is rooted in her history: "I never give up thinking about the way I came into the world, how my ancestors came from Africa to the West Indies as slaves. I just could never forget it. Or forgive it." She does not hesitate to tackle these issues in her writing. In her nonfictional *A Small Place*, she directs the force of her language toward an examination of her native island of Antigua, presenting the beauty as well as the racism and corruption rooted in its colonial past. In her fiction, these same issues are not slighted; for example, *Annie John* and *Lucy* address various forms of oppression and exploitation.

Kincaid's short stories, strongly autobiographical, are often set in the West Indies or incorporate images from the islands and include many events from her youth and young adulthood. In general, her stories chronicle the coming-of-age of a young girl. Because the mother-daughter relationship is central to the process, Kincaid often examines the powerful bond between them, a bond that the child must eventually weaken, if not break, in order to create her own identity. Kincaid has been accurately called "the poet of girlhood and place."

"GIRL"

The first of the ten stories in *At the Bottom of the River* is the often praised and quoted "Girl." Barely two pages in length, the story outlines the future life of a young girl growing up on a small Caribbean island. The voice heard belongs to the girl's mother as she instructs her daughter in the duties that a woman is expected to fulfill in a culture with limited opportunities for girls. Twice the girl interrupts to offer a feeble protest, but her mother persists.

The girl is taught how to wash, iron, and mend clothes; how to cook fritters and pepper pot; how to grow okra; and how to set the table--in short, everything that will enable her to care for a future husband. She is told how to smile, how to love a man, and how to get rid of an unborn baby should it be necessary. Most important, however, her mother warns her about losing her reputation because then the girl (and this is unsaid) loses her value as a potential wife. Almost as a refrain, the mother cautions, "On Sundays try to walk like a lady and not like the slut you are so bent on becoming" or "This is how to behave in the presence of men who don't know you very well, and this way they won't recognize immediately the slut I have warned you against becoming." On the island, the girl's most important asset is her virginity.

The language is a prime example of Kincaid's ability to work a hypnotic spell. The story consists of a series of variations on particular instruction: "This is how to sew on a button; this is how to make a buttonhole for the button you have just sewed on; this is how to hem a dress when you see the hem coming down and so to prevent yourself from looking like the slut I know you are so bent on becoming." The rhythm and repetition create a lyric poetic quality that is present to some degree in all Kincaid's fiction. Her prose demands to be read out loud.

"Girl" suggests the child's future life on the island, but several stories in the collection re-create the atmosphere of her present existence. The story "In the Night" recounts her daily experiences. Thus, details such as crickets or flowers that would be important to her are recorded, often in the form of lists or catalogs: "The hibiscus flowers, the flamboyant flowers, the bachelor's buttons, the irises, the marigolds, the whiteheadbush flowers, lilies, the flowers on the daggerbush," continuing for a full paragraph. Here cataloging, a familiar feature of Kincaid's prose, represents a child's attempt to impose an order on her surroundings. The young narrator does not question her world but only reports what she observes. Thus witchcraft exists side by side with more mundane activities: "Someone is making a basket, someone is making a girl a dress or a boy a shirt . . . someone is sprinkling a colorless powder outside a closed door so that someone else's child will be stillborn." This melding of the common-place with the supernatural occurs frequently in Kincaid's fiction. The narrator's troubles, such as wetting the bed, are those of a child and are easily resolved by her mother. Her plans for the future, marrying a woman who will tell her stories, also are typical of a child. This is an idyllic world before the fall from innocence, a world in which everything is ordered, listed, and cataloged. Nothing is threatening, since the all-powerful mother protects and shields.

"HOLIDAYS"

In several other stories, including "Wingless" and "Holidays," the girl is again shown to be occupied by the usually pleasant sensations of living: walking barefoot, scratching her scalp, or stretching, but sometimes, as illustrated in "Holidays," experiencing pain: "spraining a finger while trying to catch a cricket ball; straining a finger while trying to catch a softball; stepping on dry brambles while walking on the newly cut hayfields." The trauma, however, is clearly limited to physical sensations. When the child thinks of the future, the images are those of wishful thinking, similar to daydreams. This tranquil state of youth, however, is only temporary, as "Wingless" implies. The narrator, wingless, is still in the "pupa stage."

"THE LETTER FROM HOME"

In "The Letter from Home," the narrator's growing awareness makes it impossible for her to maintain the comforting simplicity of her child's world. Questions about life and death intrude: "Is the Heaven to be above? Is the Hell below?" These inquiries, however, are set aside in favor of the present physical reality--a cat scratching a chair or a car breaking down. Even love and conception are reduced to the simplest terms: "There was a bed, it held sleep; there was movement, it was quick, there was a being." She is not ready to confront the idea of death, so when death beckons, she "turned and rowed away."

"WHAT I HAVE BEEN DOING LATELY"

Just as the philosophical questions about life and death disrupt the bliss of childhood, so does the journey toward selfhood, which Kincaid symbolically represents as a journey over rough or impassable terrain or water. In "What I Have Been Doing Lately," the obstacle is water: "I walked for I don't know how long

before I came to a big body of water. I wanted to get across it but I couldn't swim. I wanted to get across it but it would take me years to build a boat. . . . I didn't know how long to build a bridge." Because the journey is difficult, as any passage to adulthood would be, the narrator is hesitant, afraid of finding the world not beautiful, afraid of missing her parents, so she goes back to bed: She is not ready yet. Soon, however, she will not have the option of retreating and waiting.

"MY MOTHER"

The journey toward selfhood necessitates a separation from the mother, as is suggested in the story "My Mother." The protection that was vital during childhood becomes stifling in adolescence: "Placing her arms around me, she drew my head closer and closer to her bosom, until finally I suffocated." Furthermore, the girl's feelings are ambiguous. Realizing that she has hurt her mother, she cries, but then she uses those tears to create a pond, "thick and black and poisonous," to form a barrier over which they "watched each other carefully." The all-protecting mother of the earlier stories transforms herself into a mythic monster and thus threatens the emerging selfhood of the daughter. The daughter, however, also grows "invincible" like her mother, and she, too, metamorphoses into a similar beast. Strong as the daughter has become, however, she can never vanquish her mother: "I had grown big, but my mother was bigger, and that would always be so." Only after the daughter completes her own journey toward selfhood is her mother no longer a threat: "As we walked along, our steps became one, and as we talked, our voices became one voice, and we were in complete union in every way. What peace came over me then, for I could not see where she left off and I began, or where I left off and she began."

"AT THE BOTTOM OF THE RIVER"

The concluding and title story is also the longest in the collection, at about twenty pages. "At the Bottom of the River" suggests answers to the questions raised in the other stories. Again, Kincaid employs the symbol of a journey through forbidding terrain to suggest traveling through life. What is the purpose of the journey, for what does one ultimately face but death? One man, overwhelmed, does nothing. Another discovers meaning in his family, his work, and the beauty of a sunrise, but still he struggles and "feels the futility." How can one live with the paralyzing knowledge that "dead lay everything that had lived and dead also lay everything that would live. All had had or would have its season. And what should it matter that its season lasted five billion years or five minutes?" One possible response is suggested in the life of "a small creature" that lives in the moment, aware only of the sensation of grass underfoot or of the sting of a honeybee.

The narrator, who at first knew only the love of her mother, suffers from its necessary withdrawal. Adrift, she embarks on a symbolic journey in which she submerges herself in a river-fed sea. Discovering a solution at the bottom of the river, she emerges with a commitment to the present. Death, because it is natural, cannot be destroyed, but the joys derived from the commonplace--books, chairs, fruit--can provide meaning, and she "grow[s] solid and complete."

"XUELA"

Kincaid's story "Xuela" became the first chapter of her novel *The Autobiography of My Mother*. Like many of her other stories, it is set against a rich description of the botany and geography of tropical Dominica, and it continues Kincaid's meditation on the theme of mothers and daughters. Xuela, the daughter who shares her mother's name, also shares with many Kincaid women an anger at the mother who has rejected her and a fury at the world which little understands--and little cares--about her needs.

In the story's first sentence, the reader learns that Xuela's mother died in giving her birth, and the rest of the story is the record of the first seven years of Xuela's life. Her father places the infant in the care of Eunice, his laundry woman, and visits her every two weeks when he delivers the dirty clothes; he cares for the clothes as little as he cares for his baby daughter either physically or emotionally, oblivious as he is to his laundrywoman's lack of affection for her foster child.

The child, however, knows very well that her foster mother has no use for her, and she grows ever more bitter and withdrawn. When she breaks Eunice's treasured china plate, she cannot bring herself to utter the words "I'm sorry." Like the turtles she captures and carelessly kills, Xuela has withdrawn into a shell which threatens to destroy her with enforced isolation.

At that point her father sends Xuela to school. The few other students are all boys; like their teacher they are "of the African people" and unable to respond to the powerful element of Carib Indian in Xuela's ancestry. The teacher wears her own African heritage like a penance and is quick to label Xuela's intelligence as a sign of her innate evil. When the child is found writing letters to her father, he removes her from the school and takes her to live with him and his new wife, another woman who has no love for the child. Like her insensitive teacher, her father's power as a jailer seems to suggest the destructive powers of colonialism, another Kincaid theme.

Through all these trials, the child is sustained by a vision of her mother, who appears to her in sleep. In the dream, she sees her true mother descending a ladder to her, but always the dream fades before she can see more than her mother's heels and the hem of her robe. Frustrating as it is, the dream also comes to represent the presence of the only person outside herself that Xuela can identify with unreserved love.

The story's themes of the mother who, from the child's point of view, has willfully withdrawn her love joins with the theme of the child's wakening to the use of sexuality to replace her lost mother's love, linking this story to the rest of Kincaid's work.

Kincaid's stories are praised for their strong images, poetic language, and challenging themes, and they are criticized for their lack of plot and sometimes obscure symbolism. Any reader, however, who, without reservations, enters Kincaid's fictive world will be well rewarded.

OTHER MAJOR WORKS

LONG FICTION: *Annie John*, 1985; *Lucy*, 1990; *The Autobiography of My Mother*, 1996; *Mr. Potter*, 2002.

NONFICTION: *A Small Place*, 1988; *My Brother*, 1997; *My Garden (Book)*, 1999; *Talk Stories*, 2001; *Among Flowers: A Walk in the Himalaya*, 2005.

CHILDREN'S LITERATURE: *Annie, Gwen, Lilly, Pam, and Tulip*, 1986 (with illustrations by Eric Fischl).

EDITED TEXTS: *The Best American Essays 1995*, 1995; *My Favorite Plant: Writers and Gardeners on the Plants They Love*, 1998; *The Best American Travel Writing 2005*, 2005.

BIBLIOGRAPHY

Bloom, Harold, ed. *Jamaica Kincaid*. Philadelphia: Chelsea House, 1998. A collection of individually authored essays on Kincaid, this critical study also includes bibliographical references and an index.

Bouson, J. Brooks. *Jamaica Kincaid: Writing Memory, Writing Back to the Mother*. Albany: State University of New York Press, 2005. An examination of Kincaid's life, including her relationship with her mother, her homeland of Antigua, and her conflicting relations with her father and brother.

Braziel, Jana Evans. "Alterrains of 'Blackness' in *At the Bottom of the River*." In *Caribbean Genesis: Jamaica Kincaid and the Writing of New Worlds*. Albany: State University of New York Press, 2009. Braziel examines all Kincaid's works to describe how she transforms genres, particularly the genres of autobiography, biography, and history, in order to depict "genealogy, genesis, and genocide" in the Caribbean. Devotes one chapter to a discussion of *At the Bottom of the River*.

De Abruna, Laura Nielsen. "Jamaica Kincaid's Writing and the Maternal-Colonial Matrix." In *Caribbean Women Writers*, edited by Mary Condé and Thorunn Lonsdale. New York: St. Martin's Press, 1999. Discusses Kincaid's presentation of women's experience, her use of postmodern narrative strategies, and her focus on the absence of the once-affirming mother or mother country that causes dislocation and alienation.

Edwards, Justin D. "Early Stories: *At the Bottom of the River*." In *Understanding Jamaica Kincaid*. Columbia: University of South Carolina Press, 2007. An introductory overview to Kincaid's work, including a chapter about her short-story collection. Edwards describes how Kincaid's works express her interests in familial relations, Caribbean culture, and the aftermath of colonialism and exploitation.

Ellsberg, Peggy. "Rage Laced with Lyricism." Review of *A Small Place*. *Commonweal* 115 (November 4, 1988): 602-604. In her review of *A Small Place* with references to *At the Bottom of the River* and *Annie John*, Ellsberg justifies the anger that is present in *A Small Place*, anger that is occasioned by exploitation.

Emery, Mary Lou. "Refiguring the Postcolonial Imagination: Tropes of Visuality in Writing by Rhys, Kincaid, and Cliff." *Tulsa Studies in Women's Literature* 16 (Fall, 1997): 259-280. Emery uses one of Jean Rhys's novels to illustrate a dialectical relationship between the European means of visualization and image-making in postcolonial literatures as something not just of the eye. Argues that the use of the rhetorical trope of ekphrasis (an artistic hybrid) reflects the cultural hybrid nature of postcolonial literature.

Garis, Leslie. "Through West Indian Eyes." *The New York Times Magazine* 140 (October, 7, 1990): 42. Based on an interview with Kincaid, this six-page article is the best source of information about Kincaid's life. Contains details about her childhood in Antigua, her relationship with her mother, her early interest in books, her early years in New York, and her marriage to Allen Shawn. Includes illustrations.

Gelfant, Blanche H., ed. *The Columbia Companion to the Twentieth-Century American Short Story*. New York: Columbia University Press, 2000. Includes a chapter in which Kincaid's short stories are analyzed.

Kincaid, Jamaica. "A Lot of Memory: An Interview with Jamaica Kincaid." Interview by Moira Ferguson. *The Kenyon Review*, n.s. 16 (Winter, 1994): 163-188. Kincaid discusses the inspiration for her writing and the reasons she wrote her first book in an experimental style; describes the influence of the English tradition on fiction in the Caribbean; and comments on the nature of colonial conquest as a theme she explores through the metaphor of gardening.

Lee, Hermoine. "Jamaica Kincaid." In *A Reader's Companion to the Short Story in English*, edited by Erin Fallon, et al., under the auspices of the Society for the Study of the Short Story. Westport, Conn.: Greenwood Press, 2001. Aimed at the general reader, this essay provides a brief biography of Kincaid followed by an analysis of her short fiction.

Milton, Edith. "Making a Virtue of Diversity." Review of *At the Bottom of the River*, by Jamaica Kincaid. *The New York Times Book Review*, January 15, 1984, 22. Milton presents the major criticism of

Kincaid's fiction--that the stories are obscure, plotless, and too visionary. Milton also discusses the strong Caribbean folktale influence evident in Kincaid's stories.

Onwordi, Iki. "Wising Up." Review of *At the Bottom of the River* and *Annie John*, by Jamaica Kincaid. *The Times Literary Supplement* (November 29, 1985): 1374. A brief review in which Onwordi discusses the works' similarities, especially in language and themes.

Simmons, Diane. *Jamaica Kincaid*. New York: Twayne, 1994. An introductory overview to Kincaid's life and works, including a chapter devoted to an analysis of *At the Bottom of the River*.

Snodgrass, Mary Ellen. *Jamaica Kincaid: A Literary Companion*. Jefferson, N.C.: McFarland, 2008. Aimed at students, teachers, and general readers, this book contains eighty-four alphabetical entries providing information about the themes, plots, characters, humor, and symbols in Kincaid's writings. Also includes a chronology of her life and a character name chart.

Barbara Wiedemann
Updated by Ann Davison Garbett

STEPHEN KING

Born: Portland, Maine; September 21, 1947
Also known as: Richard Bachman, Eleanor Druse, John Swithen

PRINCIPAL SHORT FICTION
Night Shift, 1978
Different Seasons, 1982
Skeleton Crew, 1985
Dark Visions, 1988 (with Dan Simmons and George R. R. Martin)
Four Past Midnight, 1990
Nightmares and Dreamscapes, 1993
Hearts in Atlantis, 1999
Everything's Eventual: Fourteen Dark Tales, 2002
Just After Sunset, 2008
Blockade Billy, 2010
Full Dark, No Stars, 2010

OTHER LITERARY FORMS
Stephen King is one of the most prolific and best-selling authors in the United States. He is best known for writing horror novels, though he has expanded into other genres, including mystery, crime, science fiction, fantasy, and literary fiction. Many of his novels have been made into films, and he has written several

screenplays, including original works specifically for the screen, such as *Cat's Eye* (1984) and *Sleepwalkers* (1992). His teleplay *Storm of the Century* (1999) was also published in novel form. A few of his poems have been included in his short-story collections, and he has written two notable works of nonfiction: *Danse Macabre* (1981), a detailed analysis of the horror genre in literature, film, and television, and *On Writing: A Memoir of the Craft* (2000), a combination memoir and "how to" book on writing fiction. In 2003, he began contributing a regular column, "The Pop of King," to the magazine *Entertainment Weekly*, and he collaborated on the first story arc for the comic book *American Vampire* (2010).

ACHIEVEMENTS
Stephen King became, in a relatively short time, one of the most popular writers in the United States. Nearly every book he has published has reached the best-seller lists, whether in hardback or paperback, and has often remained there for months. He is respected in the field of horror fiction, and several of his books have received World Fantasy Award nominations. He has received the World Fantasy Award for his short story "Do the Dead Sing?" (1981), a British Fantasy Award for *Cujo* (1981), and a Hugo Award for his nonfiction work

Danse Macabre. He has won special recognition for his contributions to horror fiction by both the British Fantasy Awards and the World Fantasy Awards. Despite the popularity of his novels, he has received greater critical recognition for his short fiction. In 1986, *Skeleton Crew* won the Locus Award for best collection. Two of the most acclaimed film adaptations of his work, *Stand by Me* (1986) and *The Shawshank Redemption* (1994), were adaptations of shorter works. The short story "The Man in the Black Suit" won the O. Henry Award for Best American Short Story in 1996. He received the Medal for Distinguished Contribution to American Letters in 2003 from the National Book Foundation, and he was invited to edit the annual collection of *Best American Short Stories* in 2007. That same year, he received the Grand Master Award from the Mystery Writers of America.

BIOGRAPHY

Stephen Edwin King was born in 1947 in Maine, where he lived the majority of his life. His parents had adopted his elder brother, David, several years before King was born, since his mother was told that she would be unable to have children. King's father abandoned the family when King was two years old. After his parents' separation, King's mother moved the family to Indiana, then Connecticut, and finally, in 1958, back to Maine to be near her aging parents. King's mother was a strict Methodist with fundamentalist leanings, and David and King attended church and Bible school several times a week.

King began to show an interest in writing at age seven or eight, partly to amuse himself during frequent periods of illness. His mother often read to her sons, including some of Classic Comics' adaptations of famous novels; King was impressed by H. G. Wells's *The Time Machine* (1895) and *The War of the Worlds* (1898). King was always an avid reader and loved adventure stories and science fiction; thus, even his juvenile work was influenced by fantasy and horror. At the age of twelve, he sent stories to the magazines *Fantastic* and *Fantasy and Science Fiction*; soon afterward, he discovered the stories of H. P. Lovecraft and began reading a range of horror fiction, including the works of Lovecraft, Edgar Allan Poe, several gothic

novelists, and Richard Matheson, whose horror novels, set in modern times, greatly influenced King.

King entered high school in 1962, and in 1965 his story "I Was a Teenage Grave Robber" appeared in *Comics Review*, a fan magazine. He wrote all through high school and printed several of his stories on his brother's offset printing press. In 1966, he entered the University of Maine at Orono and made his first professional sale, of "The Glass Floor," to *Startling Mystery Stories.* He also began work on two manuscripts that were eventually published under the pseudonym Richard Bachman in the 1970's. At the university, he received encouragement from several of his professors and was influenced by such naturalist writers as Thomas Hardy and Theodore Dreiser. He wrote a column, "King's Garbage Truck," for the university newspaper and was active in campus politics. In his senior year, while he was working at the college library, he met fellow student Tabitha Spruce, whom he married in 1971. King graduated from the University of Maine in 1970 with a degree in English and a teaching certificate; unable to find work as a teacher, however,

Stephen King (AP Photo/Mark Lennihan, file)

he took a job in an industrial laundry, an experience on which he drew for several of his stories. In 1971, he was hired to teach high school English at Maine's Hampden Academy, where he spent two years.

In 1973, King sold his first novel, _Carrie: A Novel of a Girl with Frightening Power_ (1974), to Doubleday. New American Library's purchase of the paperback rights allowed King to quit teaching and write full time. In 1976, the film version of _Carrie_ gave King's popularity a boost, but he was already selling quite well and producing virtually a novel per year. In 1979, King wrote his first screenplay, _Creepshow_ (1982), and in 1986 Metro-Goldwyn-Mayer/United Artists released _Maximum Overdrive_, which King had both scripted and directed. The reading world was shocked in June of 1999 when King was struck by a vehicle while he was taking a stroll near his summer home in Lewiston, Maine. He sustained multiple fractures to his right leg and hip, broken ribs, and a collapsed lung. Although grateful to be alive, King regretted most not being able to write during his long recuperation. However, he soon began writing again, gaining greater critical recognition by completing his seven-book fantasy series, _The Dark Tower_, and by becoming an outspoken advocate for the importance of the short story.

ANALYSIS

Stephen King credits writers Matheson and Robert Bloch, in addition to Lovecraft and Poe, with showing him that the horror story could be brought out "of the foggy moors and the castles and into those 7-Eleven stores and suburbia." He said, "The [horror] genre exists on three basic levels, separate but independent, and each one a little bit cruder than the one before. There's terror on top, the finest emotion any writer can induce; then horror; and, on the very lowest level of all, the gag instinct of revulsion." King's stories easily fit the various levels of horror that he describes. Not particularly worried about style, he aims for the impact of plot. Not all King's stories can be labeled solely horror; many have elements of science fiction, and many of his best stories contain a strong sense of psychological tension. Most of the stories, however, even those that cannot neatly be pegged as belonging to a particular genre, attempt to create a sense of uneasiness. King explains

their popularity by how they serve as emotional releases for his readers:

> When you've got a lot of free-floating anxieties, the horror story or movie helps to conceptualize them, shrink them down to size, make them concrete so they're manipulable. . . . [There's] probably some minor catharsis involved."

Increasingly, he has used the short story form as an opportunity to experiment, both with his subject matter and with style.

"JERUSALEM'S LOT"

The kind of horror with which King is most often associated, that of things that go bump in the night, is well represented in his short-story collections. Two of the stories, "Jerusalem's Lot" and "One for the Road," are connected by setting and plot elements to King's novel _'Salem's Lot_ (1975). In "Jerusalem's Lot," set in 1850 and told in a series of letters and journal entries, Charles Boone, hoping to regain his strength after a serious illness, moves into his ancestral home along with his friend Calvin McCann. They hear noises in the walls and attribute them to rats, but they soon learn that the townspeople of Preacher's Corners believe otherwise. Between the stories they glean from a woman in town and a journal that McCann finds in the house, Boone and McCann discover that Boone's mad great-uncle, Philip Boone, had joined with a malign preacher to unleash the evils found in a satanic bible called _The Mysteries of the Worm_. Boone tries to eradicate the evil by burning the book, but when he starts to set the pages on fire, his friend McCann is killed by an enormous worm. Boone commits suicide, and the story ends with a note written in 1971 by a distant Boone relative who disbelieves the evidence of the letters of Charles Boone but mentions hearing rats behind the walls of the ancestral home.

"Jerusalem's Lot" has all the trappings of horror in the gothic tradition: a house shunned by the townspeople, inexplicable noises behind the walls, an abandoned town, religion that has been twisted to serve evil, and a monster in the cellar. The tale, written originally for a college class in gothic fiction, is perhaps the only King story from his early career that takes place not in modern suburbia but in the past, in a setting somewhat akin to the lonely moors and castles of the gothic writers.

"ONE FOR THE ROAD"

"One for the Road," though also set in Jerusalem's Lot, is a modern vampire story. The car Gerard Lumley and his family are in has gone off the road in a bad snowstorm near Jerusalem's Lot. Lumley leaves his wife and child to find help. When he returns, both his wife and daughter have become vampires. King commented that "I've always believed that if you think the very worst, then, no matter how bad things get . . . they'll never get as bad as *that*. If you write a novel where the bogeyman gets somebody else's children, maybe they'll never get your own children." Fear for loved ones is a common theme in King's stories. Because Lumley is afraid for his wife and daughter, he risks his own life to get help for them. While he is gone, the worst happens to his wife and daughter: They have become something alien, something that no longer loves him.

"THE MONKEY"

In "The Monkey," King creates a high level of tension from the protagonists's fear for his family, especially for his younger son. When Hal was young, he discovered a toy monkey with a worn-out mechanism for clanging the cymbals strapped to the monkey's paws. When someone near Hal was about to die, the monkey clashed the cymbals. Hal attempts several times to get rid of the monkey, finally throwing it down his aunt's well. Years later, when Hal and his family are clearing the attic of his aunt's house after her death, Hal's elder son finds the monkey. In a desperate attempt to be rid of the maniacal toy, Hal rows out to the middle of the lake and drops the monkey into the water, nearly drowning as his boat breaks up, while his younger son watches. "The Monkey" is an effective story that evokes terror, the highest on King's list of horror-story levels. Like all King's stories, it is intensely visual. His settings and characters are familiar and easy to empathize with, and King forcefully uses the monkey as a symbol of evil that survives despite all efforts to keep away from it.

"TRUCKS" AND "THE MANGLER"

Numerous King stories deal with the destruction wrought by mechanical devices. "The Monkey" is perhaps the most effective, as the monkey is never *seen* to do anything other than strike its cymbals when it should not be able to do so. The connection between the clash of cymbals and death is made in the mind of Hal, and though it seems to be supported by the evidence, the connection could be pure coincidence. In "The Mangler" and "Trucks," however, the machines are clear agents of wholesale destruction. "The Mangler" is set in an industrial laundry: A mangler is a machine that irons and folds material fed into it. This mangler develops a taste for blood and sucks several workers into its internal mechanism: "A devil had taken over the inanimate steel and cogs and gears of the mangler and had turned it into something with its own life." After two men unsuccessfully attempt to exorcise the machine, the mangler tears itself loose from its moorings and moves toward the town.

"Trucks" concerns vehicles that turn against their owners, running them down when they try to escape. The trucks encircle a diner, crashing into it after their human hostages refuse to acknowledge a Morse code signal beeped out on a horn to refuel the vehicles. Both "Trucks" and "The Mangler" envisage machines that were built to serve human beings, turning to demand sacrifice and service themselves. King has commented that he finds machines frightening because he does not understand how they work. Both stories, while they play on one's fear of death and mutilation, are also darkly amusing.

"THE WOMAN IN THE ROOM"

In many of his stories, however, King treats death in a far more realistic manner, and in some ways these stories are more disturbing than stories such as "The Mangler." While "The Mangler" graphically describes violent death--fitting into King's third level in the horror genre, the "gag instinct of revulsion"--the plot is clearly unrealistic. It is one of those stories that takes the fear of death and makes it manipulable and even laughable. Industrial accidents do happen but not because machines turn malevolent. A story such as "The Woman in the Room," however, is more introspective and is based on King's own feelings when his mother was dying of cancer. It is highly realistic in both plot and emotion. In it, a son visits his mother in the hospital, where she has just had a "cortotomy," an operation to destroy the pain center in her brain so that she will not be in agony from the cancer in her stomach. The operation has also destroyed 60 percent of her motor control. Seeing her weak, unable to move freely, and with no hopes of recovery, the protagonist, Johnny, considers giving her some Darvon pills that he found in her medicine cabinet at home to end her suffering and her life. During his visit, his mother says, "I wish I was out of this. I'd do anything to be out of this." Finally, he brings the pills to the hospital, shows his mother the box, and shakes six pills into his hand. She looks at them and tacitly agrees to end her life by swallowing all six. Her last request is for Johnny to see if her legs are together: She wants to die with some dignity. She also tells Johnny that he has always been a good son.

"The Woman in the Room" reflects on a very personal, touching level the incredible difficulty of watching a loved one experience a painful death. King's style is as plain and as colloquial as ever; he does not try to elevate it to suit the subject. The story is told in the present tense, and the very artlessness and transparency of King's style give the story an air of honesty. It is by no means a horror story, yet it evokes what King calls "the finest emotion any writer can induce"--terror: fear that one's parents will get cancer; fear that one will be faced with the same painful dilemma as Johnny; or, ultimately, fear that one will end up lying in agony in a hospital bed, as Johnny's mother did.

"THE BODY"

Another psychologically honest story is "The Body," which became the 1986 film *Stand by Me*. In it, four twelve-year-old boys walk along a railway track in search of the corpse of a boy who has been hit by a train. The intense friendship among the boys, their silly jokes, and twelve-year-old bravado strike the reader as real and true to life. Because they are young, the idea of finding the body excites them, making this trip an adventure. It is not until they actually see the boy's body that they finally confront the reality of death:

> The kid was dead. The kid wasn't sick, the kid wasn't sleeping. The kid wasn't going to get up in the morning anymore . . . or catch poison ivy or wear

out the eraser on the end of his Ticonderoga No. 2 during a hard math test. The kid was dead.

Their quest and their discovery of the body are a rite of passage to which each of the boys reacts slightly differently; soon after they return to town, to their usual lives and to school, they drift apart, growing up in different directions, affected in different ways by what they experienced on that brief trip. King's plain, unornamented style again renders a believable and realistic story.

"THE BALLAD OF THE FLEXIBLE BULLET"

"The Ballad of the Flexible Bullet" is quite different from most of King's other short stories. It is not horror, but neither is it completely realistic. The story concerns a paranoid writer who believes that a "Fornit" inhabits his typewriter to help him write. His editor, humoring him, goes along with the idea and says that he has a Fornit, too. Soon, the editor, who has begun to drink heavily, begins finding messages on his typewriter from his Fornit when he wakes up from his periodic blackouts. The last message warns him that the writer's Fornit is about to be killed. When the writer hears this warning, he buys a gun to protect his Fornit but ends up killing himself after he watches his Fornit die. The flexible bullet of the title is madness; it kills just as surely as a lead bullet does, but in an unpredictable way. The story walks a neat tightrope between dismissing the Fornits as products of a deranged mind and admitting their existence: The writer's wife wonders if madness is catching when she thinks she hears the dying screams of the Fornit from inside the typewriter.

"The Ballad of the Flexible Bullet" ends in violent death. The writer attempted to kill his wife and the housekeeper and her son before shooting himself. No matter which type of story King is writing, he usually seems to return to terror, horror, or the gag reflex. King has commented that "the horror story makes us children. That's the primary function of the horror story--to knock away all this stuff . . . to take us over taboo lines, to places we aren't supposed to be." King does not limit this function of his stories to those of the horror genre; whether his characters are confronting death by mutilation from a mad mangler or death by cancer, King takes his readers over taboo lines, making them confront by proxy such subjects as madness, fear, and death.

"THE MAN IN THE BLACK SUIT"

With the publication of "The Man in the Black Suit" in the October 31, 1993, issue of *The New Yorker*, King created what might be considered one of his most "literary" stories. This story received popular and critical acclaim, both camps voicing appreciation for King's storytelling ability and his perceptiveness in delving into the deep recesses of humanity. More important, "The Man in the Black Suit" creates a psychological depth that many of King's other stories lack.

"The Man in the Black Suit" is the story of a nine-year-old boy coming face to face with the devil. The story is recounted as the boy, grown old to the age of eighty, faces quickly approaching death in his nursing-home bed. The further one moves into the narrative, the more apparent the complexity of the situation becomes, and how it fits into the King canon is appreciated.

In the classical American tradition, King allows his protagonist, Gary, to make a decision that will have lasting consequences for his sanity and spirituality. When Gary goes off on an afternoon fishing expedition, he must promise his parents that he will go no farther than where "Castle Stream forks." However, like Nathaniel Hawthorne's Young Goodman Brown (whose story King cites as an influence), Gary decides to go farther, and his decision governs the remainder of his life. As he moves deeper into the wilderness, Gary becomes more apprehensive, indicating to the reader that something evil lives in the wild. After catching two fish, Gary decides to take a nap. Awakened from his nap by a bee on his nose, Gary comes into contact with "the man in the black suit," very out of place in the wilderness. Gary knows immediately that the man is the devil and is afraid of him. The demon threatens Gary, but the boy is able to escape, eventually meeting his father who had come to join him fishing. The father intimates that Gary may have merely dreamed his encounter with the devil, but the boy knows the truth.

Although he does write a psychologically complex work, King retains many devices that tie this story to earlier ones. The boy remembers this particular event many years after it occurred, a plot device used in *It* (1986), *The Green Mile* (1996), and "The Body." His protagonist is a teacher and writer of sorts, the type of character prominent in numerous other works. King allows wickedness to emerge from a setting that houses stored-up evil, as happened in *It, 'Salem's Lot*, and *Pet Sematary* (1983). However, the most prevalent King element is the old man's realization that "what you write down sometimes leaves you forever," echoing King's argument that by writing about the things that terrify one the most, one is able to elude them.

EVERYTHING'S EVENTUAL: FOURTEEN DARK TALES

In his introductory essay, King attempts to establish himself as a serious writer of short stories in this collection. He laments the shrinking market for short fiction, and he describes the challenge of continuing to write stories as a duty. *Everything's Eventual* is almost like King's version of the Beatles' *White Album*. It contains a wide range of stories, varying in length, subject matter, tone, and style. These stories chart his interests and influences, and the variety helps to explain part of King's appeal and his persistent mixing of high and low culture. He includes "The Man in the Black Suit," noting afterward the influence of Hawthorne's "Young Goodman Brown." He also invokes Franz Kafka, Albert Camus, and Jean-Paul Sartre as inspirations for two of the stories. Another story springs from his interest in bathroom graffiti, and "Autopsy Room Four" owes much to an episode of *Alfred Hitchcock Presents*.

The collection shows a growing complexity in King's work. "All That You Love Will Be Carried Away" focuses on a man who checks into a hotel room with the intention of committing suicide. Like Willy Loman in Arthur Miller's *Death of a Salesman* (1949), nothing this man has accomplished amounts to much in his mind. However, his one hobby, collecting graffiti samples in a journal, seems closest to his heart. He feels intuitively that there is some substance there, but nothing in American culture seems to validate the worth of such a project. In many ways, the story could be seen as an allegory for King's own career as a writer of popular fiction.

Likewise, in "L. T.'s Theory of Pets," King presents a deceptively simple story about the nature of storytelling, pets, marriage, and loss. Much of the story's tone is light, as suggested by the double pun of the name "L. T. DeWitt." The first two-thirds of the story consists of L. T. telling a rollicking story about the breakup of his marriage and the couple's pets. The tone and style owe more to Mark Twain's Southwestern humor and oral tradition than to the horror stories of Poe. The final third of the story shifts to the real-life complexities of marriage. While King tosses in some references to a murdering Axe Man, this story, like "All That You Love Will Be Carried Away," suggests a greater degree of reflection and introspection than much of King's early work.

The rest of the collection demonstrates King's increasing interest in different genres. In "The Death of Jack Hamilton," King abandons the supernatural by presenting a fictional imagining of one of the late events in the life of the Great Depression-era gangster John Dillinger. King also includes a long story, "The Little Sisters of Eluria," as a supplement to his epic *Dark Tower* fantasy novels.

Just After Sunset

King wrote *Just After Sunset*, a collection of fourteen stories, soon after having served as the editor for *Best American Short Stories*, and the work suggests King's continued growth as a respected writer of short fiction. While his previous collection, *Everything's Eventual*, still contains a number of traditional horror pieces, *Just After Sunset* moves further from the familiar trappings of conventional horror. Two of the stories, "Willa" and "Ayana," explore concepts of the afterlife, and two others, "Harvey's Dream" and "Graduation Afternoon," are experimental transcriptions from dreams.

"The Things They Left Behind" focuses specifically on the aftereffects of the terrorist attacks on September 11, 2001, and, as such, is one of the most self-consciously serious stories in the collection. In addition to the subject matter, King peppers the story with literary allusions. The first two pages carry references to Jorge Luis Borges, Gabriel Garcia Márquez, Tom Robbins, Vladimir Nabokov, and Henry David Thoreau. King's references to Borges and Garcia Márquez seem most pertinent since the story shares much with the tradition of Magical Realism. The narrator should have died in the World Trade Center attack, but he inexplicably took the day off. Nearly a year later, a number of unusual

objects belonging to his former coworkers mysteriously turn up in his apartment. The story never explains the appearance of the objects or the nature of their power; King's focus, instead, rests completely on the narrator and his attempts to reconcile feelings of guilt, grief, memory, and confusion.

Full Dark, No Stars

As the title suggests, *Full Dark, No Stars* is as dark as anything in the King canon. The three novellas and one short story provide an examination of the motivations and repercussions of crime. No one in the stories is fully innocent, and each of the scenarios raises serious moral and ethical dilemmas. The first novella, *1922*, takes King far from the familiar terrain of Maine and modern suburbia. It is set in a pre-Depression-era Nebraska farm and is presented as the confession of a man who admits in the opening paragraph to having murdered his wife. The story is densely textured with echoes of other literary works, including William Shakespeare's *Macbeth* (1606) Poe's "The Tell-Tale Heart," and Lovecraft's "The Rats in the Walls." The style of the narration is less breezy than much of King's work, and the suggestions of supernatural elements are clearly products of the narrator's imagination. The second novella, *Big Driver*, is a rape and revenge story, brutal and morally complicated. As with *1922*, King provides hints of the supernatural, including an intelligent, talking global positioning system device, but King clearly labels these elements as the protagonist's fanciful means of talking to herself and her devolving psychological state. Again, the horror from the story comes from the realism of the crime and the darkness of the revenge. King appears less interested in the sensational aspects of these two stories and more focused on the moral ambiguities.

The lone short story, "Fair Extension," comes closer in style to some of King's early work than the other works from this collection. King presents a contemporary story, much like a fable, in which the protagonist makes a deal with the devil. However, King shows little interest in spending time with the demonic elements, only hinting at the salesman's true identity. His real focus is cultural. The story explores the lengths to which seemingly average people will go to achieve the American Dream. He laces the story with broader references to external events, from the serious, such as the destruction of the World Trade Center, to the frivolous, such as Kiefer Sutherland's arrest for drunk driving. The devil's bargain can be seen as symbolic of the deal many make for success in a capitalist system. The story is more political in nature than most of King's work, and it also provides the overall theme for the four stories in this collection. Each examines how far average individuals under duress are willing to violate their sense of ethics and morality.

OTHER MAJOR WORKS

LONG FICTION: *Carrie*, 1974; *'Salem's Lot*, 1975; *The Shining*, 1977; *The Stand*, 1978, unabridged edition 1990; *The Dead Zone*, 1979; *Firestarter*, 1980; *Cujo*, 1981; *Christine*, 1983; *Cycle of the Werewolf*, 1983 (illustrated by Berni Wrightson); *Pet Sematary*, 1983; *The Talisman*, 1984 (with Peter Straub); *The Eyes of the Dragon*, 1984, 1987; *The Bachman Books: Four Early Novels by Stephen King*, 1985 (includes *Rage*, *The Long Walk*, *Roadwork*, and *The Running Man*); *It*, 1986; *Misery*, 1987; *The Tommyknockers*, 1987; *The Dark Half*, 1989; *Needful Things*, 1991; *Gerald's Game*, 1992; *Dolores Claiborne*, 1993; *Insomnia*, 1994; *Rose Madder*, 1995; *Desperation*, 1996; *The Green Mile*, 1996 (six-part serialized novel); *Bag of Bones*, 1998; *Storm of the Century*, 1999 (adaptation of his teleplay); *The Girl Who Loved Tom Gordon*, 1999; *Black House*, 2001 (with Peter Straub); *Dreamcatcher*, 2001; *From a Buick Eight*, 2002; *The Journals of Eleanor Druse: My Investigation of the Kingdom Hospital Incident*, 2004 (as Eleanor Druse); *The Colorado Kid*, 2005; *Cell*, 2006; *Lisey's Story*, 2006; *Duma Key*, 2008; *Under the Dome*, 2009.

LONG FICTION (AS RICHARD BACHMAN): *Rage*, 1977; *The Long Walk*, 1979; *Roadwork*, 1981; *The Running Man*, 1982; *Thinner*, 1984; *The Regulators*, 1996; *Blaze*, 2007.

LONG FICTION (DARK TOWER SERIES): *The Gunslinger*, 1982, revised 2003 (illustrated by Michael Whelan); *The Drawing of the Three*, 1987 (illustrated by Phil Hale); *The Waste Lands*, 1991 (illustrated by Ned Dameron); *Wizard and Glass*, 1997 (illustrated by Dave McKean); *Wolves of the Calla*, 2003 (illustrated by Bernie Wrightson); *Song of Susannah*, 2004 (illustrated by Darrel Anderson); *The Dark Tower*, 2004 (illustrated by Michael Whelan).

NONFICTION: *Danse Macabre*, 1981; *Black Magic and Music: A Novelist's Perspective on Bangor*, 1983; *Bare Bones: Conversations on Terror with Stephen King*, 1988 (Tim Underwood and Chuck Miller, editors); *On Writing: A Memoir of the Craft*, 2000; *Faithful: Two Diehard Red Sox Fans Chronicle the Historic 2004 Season*, 2004 (with Stewart O'Nan).

SCREENPLAYS: *Creepshow*, 1982 (with George Romero; adaptation of his book); *Cat's Eye*, 1984; *Silver Bullet*, 1985 (adaptation of *Cycle of the Werewolf*); *Maximum Overdrive*, 1986 (adaptation of his short story "Trucks"); *Pet Sematary*, 1989; *Sleepwalkers*, 1992.

TELEPLAYS: *The Stand*, 1994 (based on his novel); *Storm of the Century*, 1999; *Rose Red*, 2002.

CHILDREN'S LITERATURE: *The Girl Who Loved Tom Gordon: A Pop-up Book*, 2004 (text adaptation by Peter Abrahams, illustrated by Alan Dingman).

EDITED TEXT: *The Best American Short Stories 2007*, 2007.

MISCELLANEOUS: *Creepshow*, 1982 (adaptation of the D. C. Comics); *Nightmares in the Sky*, 1988.

BIBLIOGRAPHY

Beahm, George W. *The Stephen King Story*. Kansas City, Mo.: Andrews and McMeel, 1992. A good biography of King. Includes bibliographical references and an index.

King, Stephen. *Bare Bones: Conversations on Terror with Stephen King*. Edited by Tim Underwood and Chuck Miller. New York: McGraw-Hill, 1988. Though many of the interviews collected in this volume become somewhat repetitive, they provide a good sense of what, in King's own words, he is trying to do in his fiction and why he does it. The interviews were held between 1979 and 1987; the opening transcript of a talk King gave at the Billerica Public Library is most useful.

_____. *Danse Macabre*. New York: Everest House, 1981. King researched and wrote this critical work on horror fiction and film at the instigation of his editor. He focuses on works since the 1940's and discusses novels, B-films, and horror comics to support his thesis that monsters such as Godzilla are a way of making tangible the fear of such things as nuclear war.

_____. *On Writing: A Memoir of the Craft*, Tenth Anniversary Edition. New York: Scribner, 2010. First published in 2000, this book is a combination memoir and instruction guide for the craft of writing fiction. In the first third of the book, King relates his life story, focusing on his development as a writer. The middle section of the book provides his practical insights into what makes good writing. The final section includes some exercises for would-be writers. This book was remarkably successful and is one of the best of its kind.

Miller Power, Brenda, Jeffrey D. Wilhelm, and Kelly Chandler, eds. *Reading Stephen King: Issues of Censorship, Student Choice, and Popular Literature*. Urbana, Ill.: National Council of Teachers of English, 1997. Examines issues at the heart of horror fiction. Includes bibliographical references and an index.

Rogak, Lisa. *Haunted Heart: The Life and Times of Stephen King*. New York: Thomas Dunne Books, 2009. While this basic professional biography was not particularly well received, it bears the distinction of being one of the few full-length biographies of King.

Rolls, Albert P. *Stephen King: A Biography*. Westport, Conn.: Greenwood Press, 2009. This relatively short biography focuses solely on King's professional life and is part of the Greenwood Biography series, designed in particular for high school libraries.

Spignesi, Stephen J. *The Complete Stephen King Encyclopedia: The Definitive Guide to the Works of America's Master of Horror*. Chicago: Contemporary Books, 1991. First published with the title *The Shape Under the Sheet*, this is an important guide for all students of King. Includes bibliographical references and indexes.

Underwood, Tim, and Chuck Miller, eds. *Fear Itself: The Horror Fiction of Stephen King, 1976-1982*. San Francisco: Underwood-Miller, 1982. This is another collection of articles on King's work. The articles vary in quality, with Ben Indick's "King and the Literary Tradition of Horror" providing a good introduction to the history of the horror genre. Douglas Winter's essay, "The Night Journeys of Stephen King," discusses several of the short stories. Includes a bibliography.

Winter, Douglas E. *The Art of Darkness: The Life and Fiction of the Master of the Macabre, Stephen King*. Rev. ed. New York: New American Library, 1989. Winter provides a perceptive critical overview of King's work, with long articles on each novel up to *The Talisman* and a chapter on the short stories in *Night Shift* and *Skeleton Crew*. Winter also includes summaries of King's short stories, a short biography of King, and extensive bibliographies both of King's work and of books and articles written about him.

Winter, Stanley, Christopher Golden, and Hank Wagner. *The Complete Stephen King Universe: A Guide to the Worlds of Stephen King*. New York: St. Martin's Griffin, 2006. This ambitious work serves as a handbook for King's entire canon, offering summaries and analyses of all of his major works. It is particularly unique in that the authors have organized the book into sections based on King's various "universes," such as the world of the Dark Tower novels, Jerusalem's Lot, and Derry, Maine.

Karen M. Cleveland Marwick; Tom Frazier
Updated by Thomas Gregory Carpenter

BARBARA KINGSOLVER

Born: Annapolis, Maryland; April 8, 1955

PRINCIPAL SHORT FICTION

Homeland, and Other Stories, 1989

OTHER LITERARY FORMS

Barbara Kingsolver is known primarily for her longer fiction, which includes *The Bean Trees* (1988), *Animal Dreams* (1990), *Pigs in Heaven* (1993), *The Poisonwood Bible* (1998), *Prodigal Summer* (2000), and *The Lacuna* (2009). She has written a collection of poetry, *Another America/Otra America* (1992); the collection's form invites awareness of diverse perspectives, with Kingsolver's poetry and its Spanish translations printed on facing pages

Kingsolver also writes travel articles, book reviews, and essays, and she is the author of several nonfiction books, including *Last Stand: America's Virgin Lands* (2002), featuring photographs by Annie Griffiths Belt, and *Small Wonder* (2002). *Holding the Line: Women in the Great Arizona Mine Strike of 1983* (1989) compellingly presents the plight of miners in southern Arizona's copper mining "company towns." A selection of her essays in *High Tide in Tucson: Essays from Now or Never* (1995) offers thoughts on parenting, home ownership, cultural habits, travel, and writing. Her observations on the natural order of things, from child rearing to exploring a volcanic crater in Hawaii, range from self-deprecatingly humorous to awe-inspired; all celebrate one's connection to and citizenship in the world. In 2007, she published another nonfiction book, *Animal, Vegetable, Miracle: A Year of Food Life*, cowritten with Steven L. Hopp and Camille Kingsolver, in which she recounted the year she and her family ate only locally grown food, much of which they grew and canned themselves.

ACHIEVEMENTS

Barbara Kingsolver has won many writing awards. In 1986 the Arizona Press Club gave her its feature-writing award. She received American Library Association awards for *The Bean Trees* in 1989 and for *Homeland, and Other Stories* in 1990. The Edward Abbey Ecofiction award (1990) for *Animal Dreams* and the prestigious PEN/West Fiction Award (1991) added to her reputation. In 1993 and 1994, respectively, she received the Los Angeles Book Award and the Mountain and Plains Booksellers Association Award for *Pigs in Heaven*. Her first three novels were *New York Times* Notable Books and she also received an Enoch Pratt Library Youth-to-Youth Book Award for *The Bean Trees*. In 1995, an honorary doctorate was conferred on her by DePauw University. *Animal, Vegetable, Miracle* won numerous prizes, including the James Beard Award.

Kingsolver was named one the most important writers of the twentieth century by *Writer's Digest* In 2000, she received the National Humanities Medal, America's highest honor for service through the arts. True to her activist principles, in 1998 she founded the Bellwether Prize, given in support of literature promoting social change.

BIOGRAPHY

Barbara Kingsolver was born in Annapolis, Maryland, on April 8, 1955. Her childhood was spent mostly in eastern Kentucky's rural Nicholas County. She began writing before she entered high school. In 1977 she earned her undergraduate degree magna cum laude in biology from DePauw University in Indiana. Work toward her master's of science degree at the University of Arizona at Tucson included a creative writing class. Between her stints as a student, she lived for a time in Greece and France. After completing her master's degree, she worked as a science writer for the University of Arizona and began to write feature articles, which have appeared in national publications such as *Smithsonian*, *Harper's*, and *The New York Times*. In 1985 she married Joseph Hoffman and wrote *The Bean Trees* in insomniac interludes during her pregnancy with her daughter Camille. She later settled in Tucson, Arizona, with husband Steven Hopp, Camille, and her second daughter, Lily. Kingsolver has been a political activist all her adult life.

ANALYSIS

Barbara Kingsolver's short stories are notable for their clear-eyed, sometimes ironic, and always empathic look at the daily lives of ordinary people. Her narrators are mostly female or compassionate omniscient voices telling stories of homecomings, intergenerational misunderstandings, and mundane events, such as scheduling errands or getting to know one's neighbors. She pays close attention to the tensions that control events like Thanksgiving dinners and accurately captures the dynamics of husband and wife and of mother and daughter. In her stories, characters struggle to understand who they are in the context of family history and their present circumstances. The epiphanies of Kingsolver's women are small but searingly personal. They range from deciding not to have a child to a sudden understanding of a mother's point of view. In a *News Hour* online interview with David Gergen, editor-at-large for *U.S. News and World Report*, Kingsolver explained her fascination with the quotidian episodes in families' and couples' lives:

> We need new stories. We need stories that can help us construct, reconstruct the value of . . . solidarity, of not . . . the lone solo flier, but the family, the community, the value of working together.

Kingsolver's short fiction is not minimalist. She belongs to generations of storytellers who create settings rich in sensual and situational detail. Her characters are clearly situated and her stories have a satisfying beginning, middle, and end, as do the stories of nineteenth century writers such as Sarah Orne Jewett and Mary E. Wilkins Freeman. She is also distinctly contemporary because her characters reach an episode's end when they achieve some insight or understanding of their condition. They do not, however, find sentimental or easy answers.

Each story concludes with characters more able to cope with the literal and emotional landscapes of their lives.

Like poet and essayist Adrienne Rich, Kingsolver embraces the political. She believes art should reflect the world she sees daily, so she writes, for example, about the plight of mine workers in the American Southwest and the displacement of American Indians. College professors, aging hippies, and small-town eccentrics all wrestle with bigotry and stereotyping as they move through their lives. Kingsolver's characters avoid the cynicism of many contemporary fictional voices, seeking instead a synthesis that will see them through or the moral vision that will allow them to rise above prejudices they cannot control. She combines the narrative structure of nineteenth century realists with the frank look at life espoused by John Steinbeck, one of her inspirations. Kingsolver's characters offer an alternative to ironic, angry characters. They struggle with the inequities of American life without losing their ability to maintain human connection. Kingsolver creates characters who confront life without relinquishing hope. Her vision is distinctive and welcome.

Barbara Kingsolver (AP Photo/File)

HOMELAND, AND OTHER STORIES

Kingsolver's collection of short fiction is divided between stories in which the difficulties of small-town life are controlled by the fears and sensibilities of people wed to the status quo and those in which the clash between alternative lifestyles and the ordinary routines of existence is prominent. With one exception, the narrators are women or feature omniscient narrators, whose voices elucidate women's lives and points of view. The stories frequently have a postmodern view of time, jumping nonchronologically from one episode or memory to the next, the changes marked by spaces in the text, as well as by narrated events. Kingsolver interestingly blurs the line between character and narrator by interspersing narrative passages with snippets of dialogue. Often the narrator's contributions could just as easily be spoken by the main character; this shared quality underlines the universal relevance of private stories.

Kingsolver's stories, built around family routines, usually emphasize a thoughtful female character grappling with a problem. These issues range from spending quality time with a child ("Quality Time"), facing the need to break off a love affair ("Stone Dreams"), coping with suffering the failure of a long-standing relationship ("Blueprints"), and fighting economic and social injustice ("Why I Am a Danger to the Public") to deciding whether or not to have a child ("Covered Bridges"). Another theme is how one comes to terms with one's past. "Survival Zone" and "Extinctions" have dual tensions: The eternal city/country dilemma surfaces differently in each story, and each considers the opportunities for a life in the larger world as opposed to a well-known existence. "Rose Johnny" tackles the divisive and mean-spirited effects of racial prejudice in a small southern town. A young girl, curious and kindhearted, tells the story, which highlights the socially sanctioned cruelty of adults. Kingsolver's characters realize the beginnings of personal solutions or they relate histories that reveal insights won after the scrutiny of their pasts. Either way, readers know life always goes on in its complicated and demanding way. Survival is mandatory; understanding possible.

"HOMELAND"

The title story of Kingsolver's collection *Homeland, and Other Stories* retrospectively tells the tale of an aging Cherokee grandmother's last days. Gloria St. Clair, Great Mam's granddaughter, a grown woman with her own grown children, narrates a family history that begins with the Cherokee Trail of Tears. Great Mam's band had eluded relocation by hiding and was finally allowed to settle where they chose. Still, they called the refugee years "The Time When We Were Not." Gloria's reference initiates the reader into history as a personal experience. A reminiscence of the family's trip back to Great Mam's birthplace, the Hiwassee Valley in Tennessee, follows. Gloria's father, a coal miner just back to work after a season of wildcat strikes, decides this trip is necessary for his mother, who is in her waning days; he plans it despite his wife's skepticism.

Great Mam and Gloria's special relationship evolves along with the story. During lazy afternoons or quiet evenings in the dark, Great Mam tells Gloria stories of the animals "as if they were relatives [her] parents had neglected to tell [her] about." The trip, with the three children bumping along in the back of a pickup truck, as well as the fact that they sleep three to a bed, reveals the family's economic situation. Gloria's mother represents a third dynamic, the social status quo; she is thankful God spared her children a "Cherokee nose." Mrs. Murray rises above the common-law, racially mixed marriage of her husband's parents. Gloria balances between her mother and her love for the soft-spoken woman, who tells her how the world began and calls her Waterbug. She fatalistically laments her lack of attention to stories she now knows were rare treasures. The trip fails because the home of a once-proud people now houses a troop of sideshow Indians in Cherokee Park. Great Mam does not get out of the truck but remarks to Gloria, "I've never been here before." Great Mam's death is unremarkable, personal, and poignant for Gloria and a troublesome irritation for her mother--the three of them a perfect metaphor for the pain of America's position on "the Indian question."

"ISLANDS ON THE MOON"

Annemarie and her mother Magda are intimate antagonists because Annemarie thinks her mother "doesn't seem mid-forties, she seems like Grandma

Moses in moonstone earrings." Annemarie has been alienated from her mother, an aging hippie with wild hair, since her father's death, and her aggravation only increases when Magda turns up pregnant at the same time that she does. As it turns out, Annemarie is not presently married and is contemplating remarrying her first husband. Her own son, Kevin, is moving steadily beyond her reach. Magda breaks her practice of keeping her distance because she wants Annemarie to accompany her when she has amniocentesis, a test to which she would not have agreed had her doctor not threatened to drop her as a patient if she refused. On the way to the clinic, the two have an automobile accident and are rushed to the hospital. The shock of the accident and their time side by side in the hospital free a torrent of resentments from Annemarie. Her persistence prompts Magda to say, "I never knew what you expected from me, Annemarie. I never could be the mother you wanted." When Annemarie makes the ultimate accusation that Magda does not miss her husband, Magda recounts her husband's obsessive attempts to try to think of all the things she would need to remember to do after he was gone. Stunned, Annemarie understands her error. "How could I not ever have known that, that it wrecked your life, too?" she asks her mother. At the story's end, Annemarie reaches over to touch her unborn sister, establishing a tenuous bond which now has a chance to flourish.

OTHER MAJOR WORKS

LONG FICTION: *The Bean Trees*, 1988; *Animal Dreams*, 1990; *Pigs in Heaven*, 1993; *The Poisonwood Bible*, 1998; *Prodigal Summer*, 2000; *The Lacuna*, 2009.

POETRY: *Another America/Otra America*, 1992.

NONFICTION: *Holding the Line: Women in the Great Arizona Mine Strike of 1983*, 1989; *High Tide in Tucson: Essays from Now or Never*, 1995; *Last Stand: America's Virgin Lands*, 2002 (photographs by Annie Griffiths Belt); *Small Wonder*, 2002; *Animal, Vegetable, Miracle: A Year of Food Life*, 2007 (with Steven L. Hopp and Camille Kingsolver).

EDITED TEXT: *The Best American Short Stories, 2001*, 2001.

BIBLIOGRAPHY

Austenfeld, Thomas, ed. *Critical Insights: Barbara Kingsolver*. Pasadena, Calif: Salem Press, 2010. Collection of original and reprinted essays providing critical readings of Kingsolver's work, including discussions of the sociopolitical realities in her writings, Kinsgsolver and the critics, and a general overview of her fiction. Also includes a biography, a chronology of major events in her life, a complete list of her works, and a bibliography listing resources for further research.

Fleischner, Jennifer, ed. *A Reader's Guide to the Fiction of Barbara Kingsolver: "The Bean Trees," "Homeland, and Other Stories," "Animal Dreams," "Pigs in Heaven."* New York: Harper Perennial, 1994. A good resource for the student new to Kingsolver's work.

Gaard, Greta. "Living Connections with Animals and Nature." In *Eco-Feminism: Women, Animals, Nature*, edited by Greta Gaard. Philadelphia: Temple University Press, 1993. Discusses the implications of a personal/political commitment to the natural world.

Houston, Lynn Marie, and Jennifer Warren. *Reading Barbara Kingsolver*. Santa Barbara, Calif.: Greenwood Press/ABC-CLIO, 2009. This introductory overview to Kingsolver's life and work devotes one chapter to a discussion of *Homeland, and Other Stories*.

Kingsolver, Barbara. Interview by Lisa See. *Publishers Weekly* 237 (August 31, 1990): 46. Kingsolver discusses her early literary influences and her research and writing methods.

Marshall, John. "Fast Ride on 'Pigs.'" Review of *Pigs in Heaven*, by Barbara Kingsolver. *Seattle Post-Gazette*, July 26, 1993, p. 1. This review gives an overview of Kingsolver's writing.

Snodgrass, Mary Ellen. *Barbara Kingsolver: A Literary Companion*. Jefferson, N.C.: McFarland, 2004. An introductory overview of Kingsolver's life and works. Contains 122 encyclopedic entries providing information about characters, dates, historical figures and events, allusions, literary motifs, and themes in her writings. Also includes an annotated chronology of her life, a comprehensive bibliography, and an index.

Wagner-Martin, Linda. *Barbara Kingsolver*. Philadelphia: Chelsea House, 2004. An overview of King

solver's life and works designed for students, teachers, and general readers.

Karen L. Arnold

MAXINE HONG KINGSTON

Born: Stockton, California; October 27, 1940
Also known as: Maxine Hong

PRINCIPAL SHORT FICTION

The Woman Warrior: Memoirs of a Girlhood Among Ghosts, 1976
China Men, 1980

OTHER LITERARY FORMS

Maxine Hong Kingston has written the novel *Tripmaster Monkey: His Fake Book*, 1989; her essays include the collection *Hawai'i One Summer* (1987). She acted as an adviser on a 1994 stage adaptation of her collections *The Woman Warrior* and *China Men*.

ACHIEVEMENTS

Maxine Hong Kingston's accolades include the National Book Critics Circle award for best nonfiction work for *The Woman Warrior* in 1976, the *Mademoiselle* magazine award in 1977, the Ainsfield-Wolf Race Relations Award in 1978, *Time* magazine's listing of *The Woman Warrior* in its top ten nonfiction works of the decade in 1979, a National Education Association writing fellowship in 1980, inclusion of *China Men* in the American Library Notable Books List, National Endowment for the Arts Writers Awards in 1980 and 1982, a John Simon Guggenheim Memorial Foundation Fellowship in 1981, a Stockton Arts Commission Award in 1981, the American Book Award for nonfiction for *China Men* in 1981, a Hawaii Award for Literature in 1982, a Hawaii Writers Award in 1983, a PEN/West Fiction Award for *Tripmaster Monkey* in 1989, a California Governor's Art Award in 1989, a Major Book Collection Award in 1990, an American Academy

of Arts and Letters award in 1990, and a Brandeis University National Women's Committee award.

BIOGRAPHY

Born the daughter of Chinese immigrants Tom and Ying Lang Hong in Stockton, California, Maxine Hong Kingston grew up torn between her parents' traditional East Asian culture and the culture of America. While her parents worked to support their family by operating a laundry, Kingston suffered, according to the autobiographical information in her books, much conflict over simultaneous identity as an American and a Chinese person. She addressed her struggles through writing, an activity begun at age nine. She benefited from immersion in Chinese traditional tales as she projected herself into roles of strong female figures from Chinese mythology.

Kingston earned a bachelor of arts degree from the University of California at Berkeley, then married actor Earll Kingston in 1962. Following the birth of their son, Joseph, Kingston taught high school English and later taught at the Honolulu Business College. While teaching at the Mid-Pacific Institute in Honolulu from 1970 to 1977, she wrote for publications and engaged in a long but ultimately successful search for a literary agent to represent *The Woman Warrior*. This book was published by Alfred A. Knopf in 1976 and won several awards. Kingston relocated to the mainland, where she became the McAndless Distinguished Professor in the Humanities at Eastern Michigan University, and in 1990 she became the Chancellor's Distinguished Professor at the University of California at Berkeley. In 1987, a limited edition (150 copies) of an eleven-essay collection, *Hawai'i One Summer*, was published by a San Francisco press. She was elected to the American Academy of Arts and Sciences in 1992.

Kingston then spent approximately eighteen months helping the Berkeley Repertory Theatre stage an adaptation of *The Woman Warrior* and *China Men*. Coproduced by the Huntington Theatre Company in Boston and the Center Theatre Group in Los Angeles, the drama, by playwright Deborah Rogin, opened to mixed reviews.

ANALYSIS

Maxine Hong Kingston's first two books defied conventional categorization. While the grantors of several critical awards labeled them nonfiction, their format is that of traditional short fiction, with each chapter able to stand alone as its own story. Kingston's use of Chinese mythology to chronicle her life and those of her ancestors not only entertains but also provides a gritty, often disturbing, education in Chinese culture, particularly in its regressive attitudes toward women. One *Washington Post* critic labeled Kingston's stories "intense" and "fierce," noting that they form "a strange, sometimes savagely terrifying and, in the literal sense, wonderful" reading. Feminist critics find themes such as the marginalization of women and their routine sacrifice to social ideals of great interest. Also intriguing is the theme of mother/daughter relationships. While Kingston's mother seems at moments ruthless and even cruel, at other times she stands as a paragon of emotional strength, a figure well worth Kingston's imitation. The fact that Kingston dedicates *The Woman Warrior* to her parents reveals her overall positive feelings toward their influence and her Chinese background.

Kingston notes Chinese literary classics as influences on her writing, along with works by Mark Twain, Gertrude Stein, Virginia Woolf, and William Carlos Williams. While Stein's works affect Kingston's use of dialogue, Kingston looks to Woolf for expertise in handling large expanses of time. She does not rely on the traditional use of chronology for continuity but rather on the strong individual voices of her mythological characters juxtaposed with her own modern, or postmodern, voice as narrator and sometimes as protagonist. She also cites as important her viewing of Chinese opera as a child, in which the application of a mixture

Maxine Hong Kingston (AP Photo/Eric Risberg)

of the fantastic and the realistic greatly impressed her.

"NO NAME WOMAN"

"No Name Woman" originally appeared as a chapter of *The Woman Warrior* in 1976. It has since been anthologized, most notably by feminist critics Sandra M. Gilbert and Susan Gubar in *The Norton Anthology of Literature by Women: The Tradition in English* (1985). Kingston uses legend to complement and inform fact as she relates select childhood experiences, one of which involves her hearing the story of an aunt who first shames her Chinese family by becoming pregnant by a man who is not her husband, then commits suicide. Horrifying details recall the ransacking by neighbors of the family home as "punishment" for her aunt's immoral act:

> At first they threw mud and rocks. . . . Then they threw eggs and began slaughtering our stock. We could hear the animals scream their deaths.

With a terrifying lack of emotion, the narrator's mother adds,

Your aunt gave birth in the pigsty that night. The next morning when I went for the water, I found her and the baby plugging up the well.

Ostensibly, the story proves a cautionary tale; having begun menstruation, Kingston stands warned of the shame that may result from her body's reproductive capability. However, she focuses instead on the injustice faced by females within traditional Chinese society. More important, Kingston recognizes multiple benefits to her mother's story. When her mother cautions her not to tell her father that she knows this tale, that act of confidence mitigates the seeming lack of respect for Kingston on the part of her mother. The story supports the theme of cultural conflict made apparent in the narrator's thought that her aunt's true punishment was not death, "but the family's deliberately forgetting her." It also allows Kingston's emphasis on the importance of writing: "My aunt haunts me--her ghost drawn to me because now, after fifty years of neglect, I alone devote pages of paper to her."

"WHITE TIGERS"

The narrator begins this chapter by summarizing the Chinese myth of Fa Mu Lan, a sword fighter and heroine of China. She contemplates the possible roles that Chinese women may assume and the power of the woman warrior, quickly adding the thought that helps perpetuate Kingston's emphasis on the power of words: "At last I saw that I too had been in the presence of great power, my mother talking-story." Then the narrator's voice becomes that of a girl who tells of her quest to become a sword fighter, beginning with a journey up a mountain and into the sky, where she receives training from two guide figures familiar to the traditional quest. Various symbols important to Chinese mythology find their way into the tale: the white heron for valor, the dragon for challenge, and the walnut tree, an Asian symbol of life.

As she meets the call to adventure that marks the beginning of most quest stories, the girl journeys through a barren land, representing the loss of fertility stolen from her country by marauders. Various trickster figures appear in the form of animals, all important to the future sword fighter's heroic development. Kingston imbues the story with multiple mystical elements:

When I could point at the sky and make a sword appear, a silver bolt in the sunlight, and control its slashing with my own mind, the old people said I was ready to leave.

However, she herself has stated that readers should not focus on Chinese stereotypes in her writing. She places the story early in her collection to "show that the childish myth is past. . . . The White Tigers is not a Chinese myth but one transformed by America." This story continues Kingston's contemplation of the female role, her own in particular, within her traditional and her modern culture.

CHINA MEN

Kingston's *China Men* may be viewed as a work complementary to *The Woman Warrior*. It echoes the first book's approach to grounding narrative in history and has been categorized variously as nonfiction and as historical fiction. Those supporting the second view defend the label "historical fiction" by arguing that Kingston's portrayal of China exceeds mere history. Instead, she grounds her "truths" in the individual experiences of her characters, all members of her own family, rather than in facts found in historical accounts. Of the six chapters and twelve stories/anecdotes, only one varies from this approach. "The Laws" offers a summary of laws that discriminated against Chinese immigrants beginning in 1868. For example, a 1924 immigration law excluded all Chinese females from entry into the United States. Furthermore, marriage to a Chinese female by an American male, or vice versa, would cause the American to lose his or her citizenship.

Kingston employs this story to clarify the aspirations that first drew the Chinese to America, a country imbued with mystical characteristics and labeled the "Gold Mountain" by those who idealized its appeal. She illuminates the ordeals suffered by Chinese immigrants, including the physical quest that brought them to America, through nonlinear narratives of their experiences in World Wars I and II and in the Vietnam War. "On Discovery," the title of her first chapter, refers to her own discovery of her heritage, as well as to the discovery made by a Chinese mythical male scholar, Tang Ao, of the "Land of Women." In a role reversal illuminating gender expectations, Tang Ao undergoes the painful process of having his feet bound as he becomes a slave to the females who rule the land. Critics note that by locating her mythical land in America, Kingston comments both on American culture's "demasculinization" of the Chinese immigrant and on China's demoralizing and often inhumane treatment of women. In the story "The Adventures of Lo Bun Sun," she adopts Daniel Defoe's familiar tale of *The Life and Strange Surprizing Adventures of Robinson Crusoe, of York, Mariner, Written by Himself* (1719) to expose Crusoe, and by extension other English speakers, as trickster imperialists, whose motivations remain based on greed leading to a desire for power.

The collection acts as an homage not only to Kingston's family members, made clear in the chapters "The Father from China" and "The American Father," but also to all male Chinese immigrants and their second- and third-generation offspring. The twelve tales celebrate their native culture, their adopted culture, and their physical, spiritual, and intellectual contributions to both. Throughout her collection, Kingston entertains and informs, while also criticizing racist behavior and systems that co-opt social relationships to form hierarchies in which one group assumes the right to control another based on an arbitrary and capricious cultural order.

OTHER MAJOR WORKS

LONG FICTION: *Tripmaster Monkey: His Fake Book*, 1989.

NONFICTION: *Hawai'i One Summer*, 1987; *Conversations with Maxine Hong Kingston*, 1998 (Paul Skenazy and Tera Martin, editors); *To Be the Poet*, 2002.

MISCELLANEOUS: *The Fifth Book of Peace*, 2003 (fiction and nonfiction).

BIBLIOGRAPHY

Cheung, King-Kok. *Articulate Silences: Hisaye Yamamoto, Maxine Hong Kingston, Joy Kogawa*. Ithaca, N.Y.: Cornell University Press, 1993. A discussion of the three authors' use of what Cheung terms "double-voiced discourse" as they demonstrate the arbitrary nature of "truth" and "history" through appropriation and subversion of their culture's dominant discourse.

Flota, Brian. *A Survey of Multicultural San Francisco Bay Literature, 1955-1979: Ishmael Reed, Maxine Hong Kingston, Frank Chin, and the Beat Generation*. Lewiston, N.Y.: Edwin Mellen Press, 2009. Describes how several Bay Area writers created works of multicultural literature long before the "multicultural boom" of the late 1980's and early 1990's. Includes an analysis of *The Woman Warrior*.

Gao, Yan. *The Art of Parody: Maxine Hong Kingston's Use of Chinese Sources*. New York: Peter Lang, 1996. Discusses all Kingston's works, emphasizing her skill in avoiding mythological stereotypes as she adapts Chinese stories to shape her vision of American culture.

Grice, Helena. *Maxine Hong Kingston*. Manchester, England: Manchester University Press, 2006. This introductory overview of Kingston's works devotes one chapter each to *The Woman Warrior* and *China Men*.

Huntley, E. D. *Maxine Hong Kingston: A Critical Companion*. Westport, Conn.: Greenwood Press, 2001. Provides an overview of Kingston's life, works, and her place within the Asian American literary tradition. Devotes one chapter each to *The Woman Warrior* and *China Men*.

Kingston, Maxine Hong. *Conversations with Maxine Hong Kingston*, edited by Paul Skenazy and Tera Martin. Jackson: University Press of Mississippi, 1998. Collection of interviews of Kingston conducted by various interviewers.

Sabine, Maureen. *Maxine Hong Kingston's Broken Book of Life: An Intertextual Study of "The Woman Warrior" and "China Men."* Honolulu: University of Hawaii Press, 2004. Focuses on the thematic and other connections between the two collections, suggesting that the women and men in the Hong family may be "struggling for dialogue with each other" although they appear to be textually apart.

Simmons, Diane. *Maxine Hong Kingston*. New York: Twayne, 1999. Introductory overview containing complete biography of Kingston, discussion of her works, a chronology of hr life, conversations with Kingston, and a bibliography.

Skandera-Trombley, Laura, ed. *Critical Essays on Maxine Hong Kingston.* New York: G. K. Hall, 1998. An interesting and informative collection made all the more valuable by the inclusion of an interview with, and a statement by, Kingston that elucidates her view of the critical reception of her works.

Smith, Jeanne Rosier. *Writing Tricksters: Mythic Gambols in American Ethnic Literature.* Berkeley: University of California Press, 1997. Discusses Kingston's three major works as focused on Chinese trickster myths and figures, particularly the monkey, stressing the trickster nature of Kingston's narrative itself, which remains subversive and paradoxical.

Wang, Jennie. "Maxine Hong Kingston." In *A Reader's Companion to the Short Story in English*, edited by Erin Fallon, et al., under the auspices of the Society for the Study of the Short Story. Westport, Conn.: Greenwood Press, 2001. Aimed at the general reader, this essay provides a brief biography of Kingston followed by an analysis of her short fiction.

Wong, Sau-Ling Cynthia, ed. *Maxine Hong Kingston's "The Woman Warrior": A Casebook.* New York: Oxford University Press, 2002. A collection of essays about the collection that includes discussion of Kingston's reception in China.

Virginia Brackett

JOHN KNOWLES

Born: Fairmont, West Virginia; September 16, 1926
Died: Near Fort Lauderdale, Florida; November 29, 2001

PRINCIPAL SHORT FICTION
Phineas: Six Stories, 1968

OTHER LITERARY FORMS

In addition to his short fiction, John Knowles (nohlz) published several novels, including *A Separate Peace* (1959), *Indian Summer* (1966), *Spreading Fires* (1974), *A Stolen Past* (1983), and *The Private Life of Axie Reed* (1986), and the nonfiction book *Double Vision: American Thoughts Abroad* (1964). He also wrote articles for *The Saturday Evening Post, Story, New World Writing, Reader's Digest,* and *Holiday* and a memoir, *Backcasts: Memories and Recollections of Seventy Years as a Sportsman* (1993).

ACHIEVEMENTS

John Knowles established his literary reputation in the 1960's when *A Separate Peace*, his first published novel, won the William Faulkner Foundation Award for a first novel, the Rosenthal Award of the National Institute of Arts and Letters, and an Independent Schools Education Board award. *A Separate Peace* explores the process of growing up, and it became a favorite with younger people in the 1960's, along with William Golding's *Lord of the Flies* (1954) and J. D. Salinger's *The Catcher in the Rye* (1951). In the novel, Knowles reveals the typical precise craftsmanship and handling of characteristic themes that run throughout all of his later work.

BIOGRAPHY

John Knowles, the third of four children of James Myron and Mary Beatrice Shaw Knowles, was born in the coal mining town of Fairmont, West Virginia, in 1926. After attending public schools in Fairmont through the ninth grade, Knowles left home at fifteen to attend Phillips Exeter Academy in New Hampshire. He entered the prestigious preparatory school in the fall of 1942 as a "lower middler," or sophomore. He found Phillips Exeter very challenging. In 1943, he attended a special summer wartime session there and joined a group called the Suicide Society, the members of which jumped from a tall tree on the campus into a river below. Because of a bad fall from this tree, Knowles was on crutches for a while with a foot injury. After graduating from Exeter in 1945, he enlisted in the U.S. Army Air Forces' Aviation Cadet Program, qualifying as a pilot.

Subsequently, Knowles attended Yale University, where he majored in English and was on the editorial board of the *Yale Daily*. While at Yale he also submitted stories to the *Yale Record*, the university's humor magazine, was invited to join Yale's Wiffenpoofs, and was a member of the varsity swimming team. For his senior essay at Yale he wrote a novel. Knowles graduated from Yale in 1949 and went to work as a reporter and drama critic for the Hartford *Courant*. In 1952, he became a freelance writer and lived for the next several years in Europe. There he wrote a novel called "Descent to Proselito," which was accepted for publication but withdrawn by Knowles on the advice of writer Thornton Wilder, and published his first story, "A Turn in the Sun," in *Story* magazine.

When he returned to the United States in 1955, Knowles settled in New York City. A year later he published the story "Phineas" in *Cosmopolitan* magazine; "Phineas" was the germ of his critically acclaimed, award-winning, and extremely popular novel *A Separate Peace*. Knowles moved to Philadelphia, where he worked as an associate editor of *Holiday* magazine and started writing *A Separate Peace*.

When it was clear that *A Separate Peace* was a very successful novel, Knowles resigned his position at *Holiday* to travel abroad again. During this two-year trip he gathered material for a travel book and published another novel. Now an established writer, Knowles returned from Europe to live in New York City. Throughout the 1960's he traveled, served as writer-in-residence at the University of North Carolina and at Princeton University, and completed another novel and a book of short fiction entitled *Phineas: Six Stories*. After his father died in 1970, Knowles moved to Southampton on Long Island, where he wrote five novels and was part of a coterie of writers that included Truman Capote and Irwin Shaw. In 1988, Knowles moved to Fort Lauderdale, Florida. He died near Fort Lauderdale on November 29, 2001.

ANALYSIS

John Knowles wrote about environments he himself had experienced, and his descriptive technique is one of his most appealing qualities. He frequently uses place descriptions to indicate the environmental shaping of his protagonists' personalities, and he ties these descriptions to the themes in his work. Knowles was interested in the self-knowledge derived from his protagonists' continual attempts to integrate the two elements of the American character, savagery and cautious Protestantism, into a reasonable whole. His later novels continue to explore the strategies his protagonists invent to reconcile this dualism.

PHINEAS

Phineas consists of six stories, "A Turn with the Sun," "Summer Street," "The Peeping Tom," "Martin the Fisherman," "Phineas," and "The Reading of the Will," which are not linked thematically but which possess a universality that leaves the reader with an insight into the condition of humankind. Structurally, all the stories are orthodox and follow the traditional plot structure, but their final effect is aimed at more than one level, with a symbolic timelessness coming from the context of each story. The plot is only half of each story; the other half is the matrix of the earth from which the author, the story, and the phenomenon of life emerge.

"A TURN WITH THE SUN"

The first story in the volume, "A Turn with the Sun," is set in New Hampshire, and although the immediate locale is Devon, a sophisticated prep school, nature plays a larger role in the story. The plot is simple and concerns the attempts of Lawrence Stewart to break the barrier of the "foggy social bottomland where unacceptable first year boys dwell" and to win a close friend. Lawrence, the protagonist, has entered Devon in the fall in the fourth form and instantly finds out that he possesses nothing distinct to make him accepted by his "sophisticated" peers. Like Knowles himself, he is from an unknown and small West Virginia town, he does not have outstanding athletic ability, his clothes are wrong, his vocabulary is common, and he engages in conversation about the wrong things. He is assigned to live in a small house with "six other nebulous flotsam," and as early as his fourth day at school, Lawrence shows signs of becoming a person to be considered. Lawrence is standing on the bridge and does not have anything in mind when he dives from it. He is similar to other Devon students when he initially plunges from the bridge, an unknown newcomer, but his dive is so remarkable that when he breaks the surface of the water he becomes to his peers a boy to be regarded. His achievement is capped by an invitation to dinner from Ging Powers, a senior from his own town, who previous to his dive has religiously avoided him.

The dinner that evening is Lawrence's waterloo. In his own mind he is sure that this is the beginning of a new career at Devon. As he walks into the dining room, he sees his host and his friends huddled at a corner table. Ging then introduces him to Vinnie Ump, the vice-chairman of the senior council, and Charles Morrell, the sportsman laureate of Devon, an outstanding football, baseball, and hockey player. During the course of the conversation, Lawrence realizes that Ging is a social climber and immediately feels superior to him. He also understands by looking at Morrell that the important aspect of the athlete is not his ability but his unique personality, the "unconscious authority" that his diverse skills give him. Then his own visions of being the next Captain Marvel get the better of him, and he lies, "I have some cousins, two cousins, you know--they're in clubs at Harvard. . . . " Suddenly aware that the others are interested, Lawrence goes on with his diatribe on the clubs of Harvard, capping it eventually with a restatement of his dive from the bridge. When Morrell asserts that "I saw you do it," Lawrence is overwhelmed because the most important athlete in school saw him in his moment of triumph. He envisions the distinct possibility of becoming Morrell's protégé and jumps at the chance by talking continuously about his house and family and anything he can think of to make himself sound important.

His downfall occurs when he asks which of the men at chapel the first day of school was the dean; when the other boys describe him, Lawrence responds in his loudest voice, "Like my beagle, that's the way he looks, like the beagle I've got at home, my beagle looks just like that right after he's had a bath." The consternation of the three seniors calls Lawrence's attention to the elderly couple making their way toward the door; his questions ("Was that the dean? . . . Did he hear me?") go unanswered momentarily, and Lawrence responds symbolically by slipping under the table. Only then does Lawrence realize the ridiculousness of his position, "under a table in the Anthony Wayne Dining Room of the Devon Inn, making a fool of himself." Immediately Ging, Morrell, and Vinnie make excuses and begin to leave. Morrell asks Lawrence, "Are you British?" and "Is that why you talk so queer?" Numbed, Lawrence can only smother his sobs and keep his anguish to himself.

After this evening, all Lawrence's attempts to be "regarded" backfire, until suddenly with the change of seasons he is redeemed to an extent. He plays intramural football and makes the junior varsity swimming team; that winter his housemates start accepting him and calling him "Varsity." However, there are still sensitive incidents, and he has confrontations with several of his housemates regarding his undistinguished background.

When Lawrence returns to Devon after the spring break, the bleakness of winter has given way to the peripheral beauty of spring. Then unexpectedly he begins to slip in his studies. For two successive French classes he is unprepared, but the undercutting from his peers does not bother him. Soon after this he achieves a "minor triumph" when he scores his first goal for his intramural team, but the event is actually of little magnitude and does nothing to further his quest to be "regarded." The day of this "minor triumph" turns out to be the final day of his life. After a shower Lawrence goes to the trophy room and fantasizes that 1954 will be the year that he will win the Fullerton Cup, the trophy awarded to the outstanding athlete of each year. Then he suddenly realizes the "finiteness of the cup" and that with the passage of time the cup and the inscriptions on it will all fade from human memory. The room suddenly feels like a crypt, and he steps outside to the freshness and aroma of spring. That night Lawrence, a good swimmer, accidentally drowns in the river that flows between the playing fields. Bruce and Bead, who have gone swimming with him, try to save him, but fail. At a conference two days later Bruce remembers distinctly that Lawrence "had looked different, standing up there on the bridge." The dean asks if Lawrence had looked happy. "Something like that. He wasn't scared, I know that," Bruce answers, unable to fathom the enigma.

Structurally "A Turn with the Sun" is reminiscent of the work of Katherine Mansfield, James Joyce, and Sherwood Anderson and sharply distinct from the contemporary mode of stories with a surreal surface structure. The story begins in medias res with Lawrence scoring a winning goal in a spring lacrosse game. Then the story recounts how he made a remarkable dive the previous September on his fourth day at Devon. There is no formal introduction or exposition. The positioning of words in the first sentence, however, together with the punctuation and the soft vowel sounds grouped together, suggests the softness of dusk and is in direct contrast to Lawrence's experience. Moreover, the serene setting sets the area of thematic concern. The atmosphere created in the first sentence is maintained throughout the story. Everything that Lawrence does or experiences is set against a backdrop of changing seasons, of a beautiful nature indifferent to the upheavals around it. The important images and recurring motifs-- the steamy heat, the bridge and the stream, the quest for athletic glory--come together at the end of the story to symbolize how Lawrence never "found" himself during his short stay at Devon. Thus "A Turn with the Sun" achieves microcosmic proportions not through the story line but by repetitive patterns. Parallel scenes (the two dives), motifs, and events juxtaposed with each other create metaphors and achieve symbolic levels; thus Lawrence's accidental death assumes universal meaning.

"PHINEAS"

The narrative technique of flashback that Knowles deploys in "A Turn with the Sun" is also used in the title story of the collection. The flashback in "Phineas" is framed by a prologue and an epilogue in the present tense designed to link the narrative to the present moment. The setting is Devon, the same as that used in the earlier story, and the cast of characters includes the narrator and his roommate, Phineas or "Finny." Thematically the focus in this story is more on the process of initiation of the young narrator than on the quest to be "regarded." When the narrator arrives at Devon during the summer session, he is thrown off by the outgoing attitude of his roommate, Phineas. At the very moment of arrival, Finny lectures him on all subjects, "beginning with God and moving undeviatingly through to

sex." The narrator chooses not to reveal his own confidences, however, because he takes an immediate dislike to Phineas.

Phineas is an excellent athlete. He excels in soccer, hockey, and lacrosse and has the queer notion that an athlete is "naturally good at everything at once." When the narrator asks him why he chose these teams, he replies nonchalantly that they give him the freedom to develop and display his individual talent-- "to create without any imposed plan." This lack of discipline makes Finny a weak student, and the narrator begins to suspect that Finny is interfering with his studies because "He hated the fact that I could beat him at this... . He might be the best natural athlete in school, the most popular boy, but I was winning where it counted." The narrator suddenly feels that he is equal to Finny and that Finny has human frailties after all.

One evening in summer, five students, including Finny and the narrator, go to the river with the intention of jumping into it from a tree which leans out slightly over the river's edge. Finny jumps into the river impetuously, expecting the others to follow. Everybody refuses except the narrator, who "hated" the idea but jumps anyway because he does not want to "lose" to Phineas. A similar tree episode is the central incident in Knowles's novel *A Separate Peace*. Soon after this event, Phineas draws up a charter for the Super Suicide Society of the Summer Session, inscribing his name and the narrator's as charter members and enrolling Chet, Bobby, and Leper as trainees. The society meets almost every evening and all members are required to attend and jump.

On a Thursday evening, the day before a French examination, Phineas goes to the narrator's room and asks him to attend a meeting of their select society because Leper has finally agreed to jump. The narrator is visibly irritated and says sarcastically, "Okay, we go. We watch little lily-liver Leper not jump from a tree, and I ruin my grade." Finny is taken aback at this and says simply, "I didn't know you needed to study. . . . I thought it just came to you." The narrator realizes for the first time that Phineas has assumed that the narrator's intellectual capacity comes as easily as his own natural ability at sports. Truth dawns on the narrator and he realizes that Phineas has never been jealous of him or considered him a rival--he has simply considered himself a far "superior" person. This realization causes the narrator, as they both climb the tree by the river, to shake the limb, and Phineas falls into the river with a "sickening natural thud." One of his legs is shattered in the fall and he is maimed for life.

Later, when the narrator goes to see Phineas at the infirmary, his guilt almost makes him reveal the truth. When he asks Phineas if he remembers how he fell, Phineas answers "I just fell, that's all." The narrator finally has a total conception of Phineas's character and realizes that he has not been jealous of Phineas's popularity, background, or skill at sport--he has envied Finny's total and complete honesty.

"Phineas" has a universal quality stemming from its classic initiation theme. The narrator is initiated into the ways of men within three months of his first meeting with Phineas. Phineas himself is not only the touchstone but also a symbol of an ideal state of being. His lack of human frailties sets him apart from the snobbish class struggle and the Machiavellian quest for athletic fame which Knowles satirizes in "Phineas" and "A Turn with the Sun." This quest is responsible for the undertone of pessimism in both stories, for it makes victims not only of the involved but also of the innocent. Thus Lawrence is drowned and Phineas is maimed for life, a victim of his roommate's moment of jealousy in a self-seeking, hostile world.

This negative view of human striving contrasts sharply with the serenity of nature in Knowles's stories. Unlike Thomas Hardy's nature, which reflects the aimlessness of human life, Knowles's nature is beautiful, peaceful, and distant. "Phineas" opens with a nostalgic description of an old Massachusetts town with its "ancient impregnable elm" and proceeds to Devon, where the pace of summer is sketched in a beautiful metaphor: "Summer moved on in its measureless peace." The story ends with the approach of dusk, which seems to have a special meaning for Knowles; similarly, "A Turn with the Sun" opens with a soothing detailed description of the sun going down, and "Martin the Fisherman" ends with the "warm crimson glow" of the sun setting over the ocean. This peaceful beauty is in stark contrast to the social and moral conflict in the stories and symbolizes the other half of life--the latent allure beneath the external conflagration of life.

Epiphany is an element common to all of Knowles's stories. The sudden realization, the dawning of the truth, is quite marked in "Phineas" but is more subtle in "Martin the Fisherman," a short vignette in which the patron of a Basque fishing boat finally sees the problem of his crew from their perspective after he gets an accidental dunking in the sea. In "The Reading of the Will," Christopher Curtin realizes that his father did not leave him anything because he, Christopher, did not need any help. Everything was left to Christopher's mother, except a mysterious manila envelope. This was left to Ernie, Christopher's older brother. When Christopher brings the envelope to Ernie's hospital room in Cairo, he has to sit outside while Ernie opens it.

OTHER MAJOR WORKS

LONG FICTION: *A Separate Peace*, 1959; *Morning in Antibes*, 1962; *Indian Summer*, 1966; *The Paragon*, 1971; *Spreading Fires*, 1974; *A Vein of Riches*, 1978; *Peace Breaks Out*, 1981; *A Stolen Past*, 1983; *The Private Life of Axie Reed*, 1986.

NONFICTION: *Double Vision: American Thoughts Abroad*, 1964; *Backcasts: Memories and Recollections of Seventy Years as a Sportsman*, 1993.

BIBLIOGRAPHY

Bloom, Harold, ed. *John Knowles's "A Separate Peace."* New York: Bloom's Literary Criticism, 2009. Collection of essays analyzing the novel, including discussions of its narrative methods, use of counterpoint and double vision, and use of symbolic names. Although the essays focus on a *Separate Peace*, they can pertain to the short stories in *Phineas*, which feature similar characters, plots, themes, and narrative styles as the novel.

Bryant, Hallman Bell. *A Separate Peace: The War Within.* Boston: Twayne, 1990. One of Twayne's masterwork studies, this is a helpful guide for the student of the novel. Includes bibliographical references and an index.

Degnan, James. "Sex Ex Machina and Other Problems." *The Kenyon Review* 31 (Spring, 1969): 272-277. By analyzing "Phineas," the source of material for *A Separate Peace*, Degnan shows how Knowles succeeds when he adheres to treating the torments of the sensitive intelligent male adolescent. In other novels, however, he fails because he leaves this theme.

Holborn, David G. "A Rationale for Reading John Knowles' *A Separate Peace*." In *Censored Books: Critical Viewpoints*, edited by Nicholas J. Karolides, Lee Burress, and John M. Kean. Metuchen, N.J.: Scarecrow Press, 1993. An essay championing the novel and its importance in the literary canon.

McEwen, Fred. "John Knowles: Overview." In *Twentieth-Century Young Adult Writers*, edited by Laura Standley Berger. London: St. James Press, 1994. A standard introduction to the author and his works.

Weber, Ronald. "Narrative Method in *A Separate Peace*." *Studies in Short Fiction* 3 (Fall, 1965): 63-72. To show how Knowles's narrative method relates to his themes, Weber explores comparisons with J. D. Salinger's *The Catcher in the Rye*. He shows how, because he is such a precise craftsman, Knowles provides the clearer statement about life.

Zia Hasan
Updated by Louise M. Stone and
James Norman O'Neill

L

JHUMPA LAHIRI

Born: London, England; July 11, 1967

Interpreter of Maladies, 1999
Unaccustomed Earth, 2008

OTHER LITERARY FORMS

In addition to her short-fiction collection, Jhumpa Lahiri (JUHM-pah lah-heer-ee) has written a nonfiction work, *Accursed Palace: The Italian Palazzo on the Jacobean Stage,1603-1625*, which was published in 1997. Her first novel, *The Namesake*, was published in 2003.

ACHIEVEMENTS

Despite her modest output, Jhumpa Lahiri has received an impressive number of awards and honors. Recipient of the Henfield Award and the Fiction Prize (from *Transatlantic Review* and *Louisville Review* respectively), she has been hailed in *The New Yorker*'s "Future of American Fiction" issue as one of the country's best young writers, has had one story, "Interpreter of Maladies," selected for both *The Best American Short Stories 1999* and *Prize Stories: The O. Henry Awards*, and was appointed the 1999 Margaret Bridgman Fellow in Fiction at the Bread Loaf Writers' Conference. Lahiri won the Pulitzer Prize for Fiction in 2000, a Guggenheim Fellowship in 2002, and for *Unaccustomed Earth* the International Frank O'Connor Award in 2008. She was named vice president of the PEN American Center in 2005, and in 2010 she was named a member of the Committee on the Arts and Humanities.

BIOGRAPHY

Although her parents were from Calcutta, Jhumpa Lahiri was born in London on July 11, 1967, and raised in Rhode Island, where she began writing while still in grade school. After completing her undergraduate education at Barnard College in New York City (B.A., 1989), she worked as a research assistant at a nonprofit organization before enrolling in Boston University's writing program (M.A., 1993); "Interpreter of Maladies" first appeared in the program's literary magazine, *Agni*. In the course of earning a doctorate in Renaissance studies (Boston University, 1997), Lahiri realized that she had considerably more interest in imaginative writing than in scholarship. A two-year fellowship at the Fine Arts Work Center in Provincetown (1997-1999) gave her time to write as well as to secure an agent, a coveted acceptance from *The New Yorker*, and a book contract from Houghton Mifflin. Her apprenticeship complete and the making of her international reputation under way, Lahiri settled in New York City. In 2001, Lahiri married Alberto Vourvoulias-Bush, a journalist. She and her husband moved to Brooklyn, New York, with their two children.

ANALYSIS

The publication of Salman Rushdie's Booker McConnell Prize-winning novel *Midnight's Children* (1980) generated enormous western interest in and appetite for contemporary Indian writing, albeit chiefly fiction written in English by writers living outside India. In Britain, the new generation of Indian writers is large and varied. In the United States, where the Indian population is proportionately smaller and less visible, the kinds of Indian writing favored by publishers and readers are in general limited to the exotic and the poignant. Much to her credit, Lahiri has avoided exploiting the former while investing the latter with an emotional depth made all the more effective by a restrained, Chekhovian style that is worlds away from both the Rabelaisian extravagance of Rushdie and the mere cleverness of his many imitators.

Lahiri's roots, in fact, predate Rushdie's, extending back to another transplanted Bengali writer, Bharati Mukherjee, whose early stories also concern the complexities of the Indian immigrant experience. In dealing with the lives of the Americanized offspring of that earlier immigrant generation, Lahiri is interested less in the clash of cultures than in the commonplace disasters that slowly erode the fragile foundations of her characters' everyday lives. It is for this new generation of young, well-educated Indian Americans that Lahiri's stories provide a shock of recognition not unlike Hanif Kureishi's films and fictions did in Britain and Philip Roth's early fiction did in the 1950's for young American Jews, the sense that "someone understands us!" The cultural displacement that Lahiri's characters experience so acutely has wider implications, however, insofar as it serves as an "index of a more existential sense of dislocation."

Jhumpa Lahiri (AP Photo/Gino Domenico)

"INTERPRETER OF MALADIES"

The title story of Lahiri's debut collection offers an excellent introduction to her highly accomplished but unassuming art. At first glance "Interpreter of Maladies" looks like a case of yet another Indian writer exploiting a distant homeland to satisfy the American appetite for the foreign and faraway. The story does not exploit, however; it explores. Its Indian setting acts as a necessary backdrop for a complex portrayal of that sense of disappointment and displacement central to Lahiri's vision. A young, thoroughly Americanized Indian couple, Mr. and Mrs. Das, both born in the United States, pay a visit to the Sun Temple in Konarak, under the watchful eye of their guide and driver, Mr. Kapasi, from whose perspective, but not in whose voice, the story is told. Thus, it is the couple, not the country, that appears strange to Mr. Kapasi, who takes note of, and quiet exception to, a family that acts as if "they were all siblings." Although appalled by their effusive, even excessive informality, Mr. Kapasi also finds himself attracted, especially as they take pains to include him in their little circle and even more when Mrs. Das pays him an unexpected compliment, saying how important his regular, weekday job is, interpreting patients' maladies for a doctor.

Lahiri quickly sketches Mr. Kapasi's life as a series of disappointments. Having once dreamed of becoming a scholar of languages, he has had to settle for much less: first, as a teacher of English at a local grammar school, and then, in order to pay his dead son's medical bills, as an interpreter of maladies and weekend tour guide. Not surprisingly, Mrs. Das's compliment goes to his head. Her promise to send him a copy of the group photo that her husband has just taken leads this otherwise hopeless husband of an embittered wife to fantasize a chaste but satisfying epistolary relationship with the attractive, twenty-eight-year-old Mrs. Das. It is an imaginary airmail affair of the heart that appears at once touching and ridiculous, especially played against the backdrop of the temple's erotic friezes. However, when Mrs. Das, whose own marriage is none too happy, tells Mr. Kapasi of her secret symptoms--the child fathered by another man, the "terrible urges to throw things away"--he proves inadequate, even "insulted that Mrs. Das should ask him to interpret her common, trivial little secret." Failing to understand the depth of her despair, he responds in a way that serves as the ironic measure of his own failures of nerve and compassion: "Is it really pain you feel, Mrs. Das, or is it guilt?" Even the scrap of dignity he salvages from rescuing her son from hungry monkeys is quickly stripped away when he alone sees the paper on which he had written his address (and pinned his hopes) fall from Mrs. Das's bag and blow away in the wind.

"A TEMPORARY MATTER"

"A Temporary Matter" is an even more painful rendering of what Lahiri has described as "the dilemma, the difficulty, and often the impossibility of communicating emotional pain to others, as well as expressing it to ourselves." The title refers to a disruption in electrical service while workmen repair a damaged line."It's good of them to warn us," says the wife, Shoba. There had been no warning months before when her child was stillborn, and she and her husband had been left to drift apart even while living together, she into her job as a proofreader (correcting other people's mistakes), he, "still a student at thirty-five," into a still-unfinished dissertation on agrarian revolts in India. Darkness forces them together, dining together by candlelight and passing the time telling stories that become "an exchange of confessions--the little ways they'd hurt or disappointed each other, and themselves." The experience is painfully intimate, fraught with risk as well as possibility, but when the line is repaired, it is the reader's turn to be caught off guard, unprepared first for Shoba's declaring that she is leaving Shukumar, then for the way he avenges himself, telling his rebellious wife what she had neither known nor wanted to know: their child's sex. It was a secret he had kept even after holding their dead son "because he still loved her then, and it was the one thing in her life that she had wanted to be a surprise." The story ends with the two together yet alone, each weeping "for the things they now knew."

"WHEN MR. PIRZADA CAME TO DINNER"

Lahiri found writing "When Mr. Pirzada Came to Dinner" difficult because it draws on two aspects of her own experience. One is the way her parents' lives in America were largely defined by their Indianness, which caused them to look back, and occasionally travel back, to India, in part to compensate for the "malnourished version of family" they experienced as immigrants. (This is a subject more fully rendered in "Mrs. Sen's.") The other is the way that, as the daughter of Indian immigrants, Lahiri came to feel that she could never really be at home either in the India her parents yearned for or in America. "When Mr. Pirzada Came to Dinner" is not so much about its title character, then, as it is about its Lahiri-like narrator, a woman in her early thirties looking back to 1971, when she was ten and Mr. Pirzada, a visiting researcher from Dacca, was a frequent guest in her home. It is a time when East Pakistan becomes Bangladesh and ten-year-old Lilia comes to feel her Indianness in much more complex terms than before. She learns, for example, that despite language and appearance, the "impeccably suited" and formal-sounding Mr. Pirzada is not Indian and that the war in East Pakistan that her parents and their guest follow so intently on television has no place at her school, where she and her classmates study the American Revolution. Seemingly, all ends well: India comes to the Bangladeshis' aid; Mr. Pirzada is reunited with his family in a homeland at once familiar and new; and Lilia grows up, learning along the way from books about a war halfway around the world that had once mystified her. Nonetheless, the story ends elegiacally, with Lilia's feeling the "absence" that haunts all of Lahiri's characters.

"THE THIRD AND FINAL CONTINENT"

"The Third and Final Continent" is another story Lahiri found difficult to write, not because it is autobiographical (though it does draw on her parents' experiences) but because of the challenge of narrating the story in a man's voice. Although it is her restrained style, Indian characters, and immigrant themes that have attracted most attention, it is Lahiri's virtuoso handling of narrative voices and points of view that is arguably the most impressive feature of her writing: the Faulkner-inspired "we" of "The Treatment of Bibi Haldar," the young white boy in "Mrs. Sen's," the young (again white) woman from Michigan in "Sexy" who feels so displaced in a Boston in which her well-off Indian lover feels so at home. Perhaps the great challenge Lahiri faced in writing this story was to avoid sounding sentimental, which is just what "The Third and Final Continent" did seem when it first appeared in *The New Yorker*. As the last of the nine stories in *Interpreter of Maladies*, however, "The Third and Final Continent" leaves a different impression. Here, the artful simplicity of the narrator's seemingly uneventful odyssey from Calcutta to London in 1964 and then to Boston on the very day in 1969 when men first set foot on the moon, seems quietly triumphant rather than sentimental. The story's and the narrator's modesty and humility compel the reader's attention, focusing not on the narrator's travails but instead on the summer he rented a room in the home of an elderly and cantankerous lady, whom he treated with typically Indian formality and sincere, if understated, affection. His subsequent life, humbly and briefly narrated at story's end, is ordinary enough--marriage, job, home, children--yet it leads the reader to wonder whether in marveling at achievements, such as the moon landing, the reader may have missed entirely the kinds of commonplace triumphs that "The Third and Final Continent" celebrates--triumphs so conspicuously absent in Lahiri's other stories.

Unaccustomed Earth

Although the stories in *Unaccustomed Earth* focus on immigrants who "must strike their roots into unaccustomed earth," Lahiri develops her theme more deeply than that, using geography not as a social message but as a metaphor for crossing borders. The title story is paradigmatic. Ruma, a mother at age thirty-eight, has left her job in a New York law firm to follow her husband to Seattle to raise their child. Her father, at age seventy, has retired after his wife's death and now spends his time taking European tours. The story takes place during the father's visit while Ruma's husband is out of town. For sixty pages, nothing much seems to happen as Ruma tries to come to terms with her father's newfound freedom, and he comes to know and love his young grandson. Then in the last few pages, because Lahiri knows how to manage the rhythm of the short story almost as masterfully as her mentors William Trevor and Alice Munro, the story tightens as a secret is revealed and the daughter realizes her father is also a man with an identity of his own.

"Hell-Heaven" also focuses on a parent-child relationship, this time a wife who has her own secret and a daughter who seeks a surrogate mother until she finally understands her own mother's private loss. When a man takes his wife to the wedding of a young woman he once knew in "A Choice of Accommodations," the past threatens their relationship until Lahiri tightens the ending with an encounter that reminds them that the only past that matters is their own. In "Only Goodness," a woman tries to cope with guilt for introducing her brother to alcohol when he was in high school, a habit that he has never been able to break. As the brother spirals out of control and the young woman becomes a successful professional, the story turns unexpectedly when she trusts him and must pay for her mistake.

Part 2 of *Unaccustomed Earth* is made up of three loosely linked stories. "Once in a Lifetime" is told by sixteen-year-old Hema, who is attracted to Kaushik, nineteen, when he comes to the United States from India with his parents to live with her family because, as the reader discovers at the end, his mother is dying. In "Year's End," Kaushik tells of his father's remarriage and his attempts to come to terms with his new young mother and her two daughters. In the final story, "Going Ashore," Hema is thirty-seven and in Rome alone, where she meets Kaushik again, and they have a brief, intense love affair, which, as is always the case with great loves, cannot be fulfilled. Because of their realistic detail and their casual narrative flow, these stories are called "novelistic" erroneously by critics. However, make no mistake, when the temporal narrative flow tightens into a vortex at the end, and the seemingly irrelevant details transfigure into significance, a reader finds himself or herself in the hands of a master of the short story.

Other major works

long fiction: *The Namesake*, 2003.

nonfiction: *Accursed Palace: The Italian Palazzo on the Jacobean Stage, 1603-1625*, 1997.

Bibliography

Bellafante, Ginia. "Windows into Life." *Time* 154 (August 2, 1999): 91. Bellafante maintains that Lahiri and Gish Jen--who wrote *Who's Irish: Stories* (1999)--are two of the best young writers who have published collections of short stories. Lahiri's strength is her "gift for illuminating the full meaning of brief relationships" of various kinds.

Crain, Caleb. "Subcontinental Drift." *The New York Times Book Review*, July 11, 1999, p. 11-12. In Lahiri's seductive, "elegantly constructed" stories, "the pang of disappointment turns into a sudden hunger to know more" on the part of both characters and readers.

Curtis, Sarah. "Strangers and Neighbours." *The Times Literary Supplement*, October 22, 1999, 25. In these stories of "isolation and displacement," Lahiri goes well beyond typical Indian-immigrant fiction, utilizing her "ability to delineate in telling detail the mores of both [Indian and American] societies" in order to "illuminate human nature" in general.

Kakutani, Michiko. "Liking America, but Longing for India." *The New York Times*, August 6, 1999, p. E48. Praising Lahiri's "wonderfully distinctive new voice" and "eloquent and assured style," Kakutani contends that the "cultural displacement" that connects Lahiri's stories serves as "a kind of index of a more existential sense of dislocation."

Keesey, Anna. "Four New Collections Show the Elastic Quality of Short Fiction." *Chicago Tribune*, August 8, 1999, p. 4. Lahiri's fiction "deals tenderly with the difficulties of the expatriate." Although not averse to including "vivid, aromatic details" of Indian life, she is most effective when retrained and austere.

Mhatre, Lee. "Review of *Unaccustomed Earth*, by Jhumpa Lahiri." *Confrontation* 102 (Winter, 2008/ Spring, 2009): 202-205. Long positive review praising Lahiri's expertise in depicting the lives of Begali professionals and their adaptations and resistance to western culture.

O'Grady, Megan. Review of *The Interpreter of Maladies*, by Jhumpa Lahiri. *The Village Voice* 104 (April 19, 1999): 59-60. According to O'Grady, *The Interpreter of Maladies* "speaks to anyone who has ever felt like a foreigner--at home or abroad." Although marriage may be her "richest domain," the "awe she invokes in her characters as they cross barriers of nations and generations" is present in all nine stories.

Todd, Tamsin. "At the Corner Delhi." *The Washington Post*, October 7, 1999, p. C8. After Arundhati Roy (*The God of Small Things*), Lahiri has been anointed "the next subcontinental sensation"; fortunately her fiction proves her a worthy candidate, for she is original, "accomplished, insightful, and deeply American."

Robert A. Morace
Updated by Charles E. May

RING LARDNER

Born: Niles, Michigan; March 6, 1885
Died: East Hampton, New York; September 25, 1933

PRINCIPAL SHORT FICTION

Bib Ballads, 1915
Gullible's Travels, Etc., 1917
Treat 'em Rough, 1918
Own Your Own Home, 1919
The Real Dope, 1919
How to Write Short Stories, 1924
The Love Nest, and Other Stories, 1926
Round Up: The Stories of Ring Lardner, 1929
Lose with a Smile, 1933
*Ring Around the Bases: The Complete Baseball
    Stories of Ring Lardner,* 1992 (Matthew J.
    Bruccoli, editor)
*The Annotated Baseball Stories of Ring W. Lardner,
    1914-1919,* 1995 (George W. Hilton, editor)

OTHER LITERARY FORMS

Ring Lardner is known chiefly as a short-story writer, but in his own time was better known as a sportswriter, columnist, and humorist. He also wrote two novel-length works, *You Know Me Al* (1915, serial; 1916, book) and *The Big Town* (1921), and he tried his hand at writing musical comedies, with *June Moon* (pr. 1929), written in collaboration with George S. Kaufman, being his only successful one. Most of Lardner's nonfictional prose remains uncollected, although a few works have appeared in book form, including an early piece about the return of the Chicago White Sox from a worldwide tour; a book about successful business and professional men, *Regular Fellows I Have Met* (1919); three humorous essays, "The Young Immigrunts" (1920), "Symptoms of Being Thirty-Five" (1921), and "Say It with Oil" (1923); and a burlesque autobiography, *The Story of a Wonder Man* (1927).

ACHIEVEMENTS

Ring Lardner added significantly to a tradition dating back at least as far as Mark Twain's *The Adventures of Huckleberry Finn* (1884). Using first-person monologue--usually humorous, always steeped in colloquialisms, occasionally in the form of correspondence--Lardner allowed his characters to reveal themselves, warts and all. As such, the superficiality and insincerity of his narrators is starkly contrasted with the often harsh truths they unintentionally reveal. This allowed Lardner to illustrate some of the less edifying aspects of American society and human nature in general. He also captured the spoken language and slang of ordinary people, rendering it as an art form unto itself. Thus, in addition to their entertainment value, Lardner's stories provide a telling picture of American manners and morals during the first third or so of the twentieth century. Finally, Lardner was a pioneer in the fruitful marriage between the game of baseball and American letters, laying the foundation for later works by prominent authors such as Mark Harris (*Bang the Drum Slowly,* 1956), W. P. Kinsella (*Shoeless Joe,* 1982, filmed as *Field of Dreams,* 1989), Bernard Malamud (*The Natural,* 1952), and Philip Roth (*The Great American Novel,* 1973).

BIOGRAPHY

Ringgold Wilmer Lardner was born into a wealthy, genteel family and educated at home by his mother and a tutor before he attended the public high school. After a brief stay at the Armour Institute in Chicago, where his father sent him to study mechanical engineering, he held a series of jobs with newspapers, chiefly as a sportswriter, which led him into writing fiction about ball players and athletes. He married Ellis Abbott in 1911; they had four sons. He died of a heart attack in 1933.

ANALYSIS

The question that inevitably arises in any discussion of Ring Lardner's stories is: What is Lardner's attitude toward his characters and by extension toward the culture out of which they come? Is Lardner, in other words, a misanthrope who hated not only his own characters but also himself, or is he, rather, a disappointed idealist who found in the world of his immediate experience constant instances of cruelty, vulgarity, and insensitivity? Those who point to Lardner's sheltered upbringing and the apparently happy family life both of his early years and of his later married life favor the latter view, while those who wish to find in his fiction some affirmation of the goodness of human beings prefer the former. Obviously, no final answer to the question is possible.

"CHAMPION"

If one reads an early story, such as "Champion," one sees a heavy-handed author stacking the cards against his brutal hero, Midge Kelly. Midge beats his crippled brother to steal his half dollar and, when their mother objects, beats her too. Thereafter Midge's life is a succession of victories and brutalities: He becomes a prizefighter who wins fight after fight and, at the same time, does in those who have befriended him. Although his crippled brother is sick and unable to get out of bed and longs to have a letter from his famous brother, Midge refuses to write. When his wife and son are ill and destitute, he tears up a letter from his wife begging for help. He fires the manager who has helped make him a champion fighter and heaps money on a woman who is obviously using him, although he later casts her off, too, and then takes for himself the wife of his new manager. Through the obvious card-stacking one sees Lardner's intention. He hates brutality and he hates the way brutality is not only ignored but also rewarded in society. Midge Kelly is not a believable character; he is a symbol on which Lardner heaps all of the abuse he can muster. If it were not for the brutality, "Champion" would be a maudlin tearjerker.

The truth seems to be that, underneath the pose of the realist, observer, and reporter of American crudities, Lardner was a sensitive, even a sentimental man. The monologue form exactly suited his need to keep the sentimentality out of sight while letting his crude,

Ring Lardner (Library of Congress)

vulgar, insensitive types condemn themselves out of their own mouths, but it was also a way of allowing the victims of the bullies to engage the reader's sympathies without having to make them stereotyped victims: cripples who are beaten, mothers knocked down by their sons, abandoned wives and babies. Lardner's best stories present the reader with a story in which the real author has all but disappeared while his narrator tells his ironically revealing, self-condemning tale.

"HAIRCUT"

One of the best of Lardner's stories, "Haircut," is told by a barber who is giving a haircut to an unnamed stranger in a small midwestern town. The hero of the barber's tale is Jim Kendall, a practical joker, whom the barber describes as "all right at heart" but whom the reader quickly sees as a man who enjoys inflicting pain on other human beings under the guise of being funny. To pay his wife back for getting his paycheck (he gives her no money to run the household), Kendall tells her to meet him with their children outside the tent of a visiting circus. Instead of joining her there with the tickets as he promised, he hides out in a saloon to savor the joke he is playing on his family. Meanwhile, a new doctor in the town, "Doc" Stair, appears on the scene, and feeling sorry for the mother with the crying children, buys the tickets for them. When Kendall hears how Doc Stair spoiled his fun, he gets furious and vows revenge. He tricks a young woman, Julie Gregg, who is "sweet on" Doc Stair, into coming into the doctor's office late at night. No one is there but Kendall and his friends hiding in the dark. When Julie calls out the doctor's first name, "Oh, Ralph," Kendall and his crowd leap out and mimic her. When she retreats, they chase her home. Another frequent victim of Kendall's jokes, a "cuckoo" named Paul, who is fond of Julie and the doctor and who hears the doctor say that a man like Kendall ought not to be allowed to live, invites himself to go duck hunting with Kendall. Kendall gives Paul his gun to hold, the gun goes off, and Kendall is killed. Doc Stair, the coroner, rules the shooting accidental. Although in this story the chief villain is given his comeuppance, a subtler cruelty is revealed by the barber who says of Kendall that in letting a man like Paul hold his gun, he probably got what he deserved.

"GOLDEN HONEYMOON"

Another of Lardner's best stories, "Golden Honeymoon," is a gentler satire; indeed, critics have disagreed about whether this is the portrait of a happy marriage or a vicious attack on marriage in general. Doubtless the truth lies somewhere in between, for the old man who tells the story of his and his wife's trip to Florida on their golden honeymoon is a boring windbag. He is impressed with himself and his son, who is "high up in rotary"; with the commonplace, vulgar details of their trips to cafeterias, church socials, card games, and films; and with their encounter with his wife's old beau. The main action of the story concerns the conflict that arises between the couple over the reappearance fifty years later of the suitor, who is married to a woman the narrator describes as a rotten cardplayer. Although he is not as brutal or despicable as other Lardner narrators, he has many of the same faults: insensitivity, vanity, pettiness, and even a little cruelty. When he wins a game of checkers, he gloats; when he loses at horseshoes, he pouts. When his wife hurts her back on the croquet court, he laughs at her, and when he is beaten at horseshoes, he quarrels with

his wife and she quits speaking to him. The story ends "happily"--that is, the two make up and get "kind of spoony"--but the essential portrait remains that of a boring, vain, pompous old man.

"SOME LIKE THEM COLD"

"Some Like Them Cold" is a story told through the exchange of letters between a young woman named Mabelle Gillespie, who allows herself to be picked up by a young man in the La Salle Street station in Chicago. Chas. F. Lewis (as he signs his letters) is on his way to New York to break into the songwriting business. He is a typical Lardner monologuist--vain, crude, and cruel--and Mabelle is the familiar Lardner victim--sensitive, trusting, and foolish. Her letters to Lewis play up her virtues as a "home body"; his become increasingly short, emphasizing how well he is getting on in the Big Town and offering accounts of women who chase him. After he announces his marriage to a woman whom he had earlier described as cold and indifferent to home life, he advises Mabelle not to speak to "strange men who you don't know nothing about as they may get you wrong and think you are trying to make them." "Some Like Them Cold" was later converted by Lardner into the successful musical comedy *June Moon*.

"EX PARTE"

A story technically subtler is "Ex Parte," told in the first person by a man attempting to justify his part in the breakup of his marriage. As he tells it, he and his wife were happy on their honeymoons but as soon as they moved into the house he had bought as a surprise for her (he had promised they would choose a house together), their marriage began to go bad. The trouble is that the house and furniture (picked out by a decorator) are too shiny and new-looking to suit his wife; she hates the house and admires the converted barn and early American furniture of her school friend. Even the nicks and burns on her friend's dining room table seem beautiful to her. The narrator, after consuming a large quantity of "early American Rye," goes home and mutilates their table with a blow torch. His wife leaves him, and he is now trying to get his friends to take his side in the quarrel.

What is unusual about this story is that, instead of the typical opposition of bully and victim, there is rather a battle between two people equally insensitive and shallow: the husband who likes bright, shiny new things and the wife who likes antiques. For both, marriage is simply a matter of having the right things.

To call Ring Lardner either a misanthrope or a humorist, or even a realist who observed American manners, is to miss the point. Lardner was a moralist, like his friend F. Scott Fitzgerald, and, although at times he could be merely funny or sentimental or tiresome, his best stories are homilies, camouflaged by humor, on meanness, cruelty, and vanity. Lardner had a remarkable ear for a certain kind of native American speech, and he used that talent for giving his stories the ring of truth and passing on to succeeding generations a small but enduring collection of excellent short stories.

OTHER MAJOR WORKS

LONG FICTION: *You Know Me Al*, 1915 (serial), 1916 (book); *The Big Town*, 1921.

PLAY: *June Moon*, pr. 1929 (with George S. Kaufman).

NONFICTION: *My Four Weeks in France*, 1918; *Regular Fellows I Have Met*, 1919; "The Young Immigrunts," 1920; "Symptoms of Being Thirty-Five," 1921; "Say It with Oil," 1923; *What of It?*, 1925; *The Story of a Wonder Man*, 1927; *Letters from Ring*, 1979 (Clifford M. Caruthers, editor; revised as *Letters of Ring Lardner*, 1995).

BIBLIOGRAPHY

Blythe, Hal, and Charlie Sweet. "Lardner's 'Haircut.'" *The Explicator* 55 (Summer, 1997): 219-221. Poses the question of why Whitey would tell his tale of homicide to a stranger; argues that Whitey feels guilty because he has been involved and thus, like the Ancient Mariner, he stops strangers to tell his tale.

Bruccoli, Matthew J., and Richard Layman. *Ring Lardner: A Descriptive Bibliography*. Pittsburgh: University of Pittsburgh Press, 1976. This highly accessible and useful summary of Lardner's work provides a good starting point for getting a sense of Lardner's overall achievements, range, and productivity.

Cowlishaw, Brian T. "The Reader's Role in Ring Lardner's Rhetoric." *Studies in Short Fiction* 31 (Spring, 1994): 207-216. Argues that readers of Lardner's stories perceive a set of corrective lessons conveyed satirically by an implied author. Readers who accept the role of implied reader and thus align themselves with the implied author as perceptive and intelligent people accept these lessons and thus fulfill the basic purpose of satire, which is social correction.

Duffy, Dennis. "Owl Eyes and Incinerators: Ring Lardner's Role in *The Great Gatsby* Revisited." *ANQ* 22, no. 4 (Fall, 2009): 42-46. Discusses the friendship of Lardner and F. Scott Fitzgerald and examines Lardner's influence on Fitzgerald's novel *The Great Gatsby*. Discusses Lardner's short story "Reunion" and explains how its depiction of an incinerating plant was similar to Fitzgerald's description of "the valley of ashes" in *The Great Gatsby*.

Elder, Donald. *Ring Lardner*. Garden City, N.Y.: Doubleday, 1956. This early biography is helpful because it includes much firsthand testimony from those who knew Lardner throughout his career, including the very early days when his affection for baseball and overall philosophy of life were formed.

Friedrich, Otto. *Ring Lardner*. Minneapolis: University of Minnesota Press, 1965. An admirably concise work that discusses Lardner's command of different dialects. Puts the darker side of Lardner's psyche into the context of myths and misconceptions popular at the time he wrote. Friedrich, an expert on the historical period both in the United States and Europe, provides a lucid and insightful introduction to Lardner's main themes and techniques.

Geismar, Maxwell. *Ring Lardner and the Portrait of Folly*. New York: Thomas Y. Crowell, 1972. Probably the most ambitious work of literary criticism devoted entirely to Lardner. Geismar draws a full-blown critique of American materialism out of Lardner's work, arguing that Lardner's sarcasm and satire masked a deeply felt idealism.

Gelfant, Blanche H., ed. *The Columbia Companion to the Twentieth-Century American Short Story*. New York: Columbia University Press, 2000. Includes a chapter in which Lardner's short stories are analyzed.

Lardner, James. "Ring Lardner at 100--Facing a Legacy." *The New York Times Book Review*, March 31, 1985, 3. James Lardner reflects on the life and work of his grandfather, Ring Lardner, and describes the Ring Lardner Centennial Conference held at Albion College in Michigan. James discusses Ring Lardner's satire, although he contends that his grandfather gives his characters more depth than one usually associates with satire.

Lardner, Ring. *Letters of Ring Lardner*. Edited by Clifford M. Caruthers. Washington, D.C.: Orchises, 1995. Lardner's correspondence reveals biographical details of his life.

Lardner, Ring, Jr. *The Lardners: My Family Remembered*. New York: Harper & Row, 1976. Lardner's third son, a successful screenwriter, provides a charming portrait of the Lardner family. As portrayed here, Ring Lardner, Sr., was humble and completely unpretentious about his work. He was also a good family man and had an interesting circle of friends, including F. Scott Fitzgerald.

Peterson, Scott D. "Do You Know Me Now? Cultural Reflection and Resistance in Ring Lardner's *You Know Me, Al*." *Nine: A Journal of Baseball History and Culture* 18, no. 2 (Spring, 2010): 38-48. A critique of Lardner's novel, examining his use of vernacular humor and the novel's place in early twentieth century baseball fiction. Much of what is said about this novel can also pertain to Lardner's short fiction and sports journalism.

Robinson, Douglas. *Ring Lardner and the Other*. New York: Oxford University Press, 1992. Examines Lardner's themes in his fiction. Includes bibliographical references and an index.

Yardley, Jonathan. *Ring*. New York: Random House, 1977. This well-written, thorough biography is especially good at drawing the strong connection between Lardner as journalist and Lardner as short-story writer. According to Yardley, the journalistic desire for unadorned facts leads logically to Lardner's unflinching examination of human nature and American society through the medium of fiction.

W. J. Stuckey
Updated by Ira Smolensky

DAVID LEAVITT

Born: Pittsburgh, Pennsylvania; June 23, 1961

PRINCIPAL SHORT FICTION
Family Dancing, 1984
A Place I've Never Been, 1990
Arkansas: Three Novellas, 1997
The Marble Quilt: Stories, 2001
Collected Stories, 2003

OTHER LITERARY FORMS

In addition to his short-story collections, David Leavitt (LEH-viht) writes novels: *The Lost Language of Cranes* was published in 1986, *Equal Affections* in 1989, *While England Sleeps* in 1993 and revised in 1995, *The Page Turner* in 1998, *Martin Bauman: Or, A Sure Thing* in 2000, *The Body of Jonah Boyd* in 2004, and *The Indian Clerk* in 2007. He has written nonfiction, including *Florence, A Delicate Case* in 2002 and *The Man Who Knew Too Much: Alan Turing and the Invention of the Computer* in 2005. With Mark Mitchell, he wrote *Italian Pleasures* (1996) and *In Maremma: Life and a House in Southern Tuscany* (2001) and edited *The Penguin Book of Gay Short Stories* (1994) and *Pages Passed from Hand to Hand: The Hidden Tradition of Homosexual Literature in English from 1748 to 1914* (1997).

ACHIEVEMENTS

While still a student at Yale University, David Leavitt won the Willets Prize for Fiction in 1982 for his story "Territory," and a subsequent story, "Counting Months," won the 1984 O. Henry Award. His first published collection of short fiction, *Family Dancing*, was nominated for best fiction from the National Book Critics Circle in 1984, and in 1985 it was a finalist for the PEN/Faulkner Award for Fiction. *While England Sleeps* was a finalist for the *Los Angeles Times* Fiction Prize, and *The Indian Clerk* was a finalist for the PEN/Faulkner Award and shortlisted for the IMPAC/Dublin Award. Leavitt received a National Endowment for the Arts grant in 1985 and a John Simon Guggenheim Foundation Fellowship in 1989; that same year, he was also foreign writer-in-residence at the Institute of Catalan Letters in Barcelona, Spain.

BIOGRAPHY

David Leavitt was born June 23, 1961, in Pittsburgh, Pennsylvania. His father, Harold Jack, was a professor, and his mother, Gloria, was a housewife who battled cancer for many years. This struggle is reflected in many of Leavitt's stories and particularly in one novel, *Equal Affections*, which deals with cancer and its impact on family life.

The young Leavitt grew up in Palo Alto, California, and some elements of his adolescence are found in a 1985 *Esquire* magazine article, "The New Lost Generation," in which Leavitt discusses and compares the late 1960's and early 1970's generation of youth to his own of the late 1970's and early 1980's. Leavitt attended Yale University, where he published, at age twenty-one and while still a student, his first short story in *The New Yorker*. He received his B.A. from Yale University in 1983 and worked for a time as a reader and editorial assistant at Viking Penguin in New York, where he was, he said in interviews, a reader of the "slush" manuscripts, those that came in over the transom and not shepherded by literary agents.

Leavitt's first collection of short fiction was published by Alfred A. Knopf and received considerable literary acclaim in 1984. That volume, *Family Dancing*, did, however, generate some negative criticism for its limited choice of themes. Nevertheless, Leavitt was soon considered to be among a promising group of young American writers first appearing in the 1980's. In addition to two stories in *The New Yorker*, he published short fiction in *Harper's*. His first novel, *The Lost Language of Cranes*, appeared in 1986 and generated controversy over its straightforward depiction of a homosexual youth's lifestyle compared to the closeted sexuality of the boy's father, who kept his homosexual yearnings in secret. Leavitt's second novel, *Equal Affections*, appeared in 1989 and centers on a family in which a dominant mother figure fights a long battle with cancer. One child in the family is homosexual and living with his lover in the East, while a daughter is a lesbian folksinger caught up in the world of concerts, travel, and performing. A second collection of short fiction, which picks up many themes from the first collection and also some of its characters in later stages of their lives (much as the southern writer Ellen Gilchrist has done with her fictional characters in several short-story collections), was published in 1990 under the title *A Place I've Never Been*. Three other collections followed, including *Arkansas*, *The Marble Quilt*, and *Collected Stories*, which contains selections from all previous volumes except *Arkansas*. In 1993, Leavitt and his life partner, the author Mark Mitchell, moved to Italy, first to Florence and then to a farm house in southern Tuscany. In 2000, Leavitt divided his residency between Italy and Gainesville, Florida, where he began to teach creative writing at the University of Florida and edit the journal *Subtropics*. Leavitt's transatlantic pattern of residence has informed, over time, his fiction since he often resorts to what nineteenth century American novelist Henry James referred to as "the international theme," casting light on the confrontation between American and European value systems.

ANALYSIS

David Leavitt is one of a number of openly homosexual writers whose work began to appear in the 1970's and 1980's but who, in spite of their declared sexual orientation, attracted a far wider audience than that normally restricted to gay writers. While Leavitt (and other writers) may deal in their fiction with the topic of homosexuality and the difficulties posed by heterosexual society for those who are gay or are so perceived, that theme is not the entire focus of his fiction, and his handling of the homosexual experience is not of some isolated, hidden world (as gay and lesbian writing tended to be in the decades of the 1940's and 1950's). Instead, the homosexual experience in Leavitt's work is directly related to the family experience of which parents, brothers, sisters, and relatives are an integral part. Homosexuals are present, every day and all around, rather as early gay activists liked to say: "We are everywhere." To that generalization, Leavitt's characters add the assertion, "and we are just like you, for the most part." To this theme of homosexual identity can be added two other concerns to which it can be linked. One is the recurring fragility of human life and the threat to it by terminal illness, such as cancer, acquired immunodeficiency syndrome (AIDS), or even a sudden fatal allergy. Another discernible theme is the fragility of the contemporary American family, particularly because of the fragmenting effect of divorce.

Leavitt's systematic return to certain topics, especially the complexities of familial relationships and the effects of sexual orientation on the formation of individual identity, in his short fiction offers readers a vivid portrayal of contemporary American social mores, rendered all the more acute by the author's ability to select situations and details that become metaphors for his stories' issues. In a discussion of other contemporary fiction writers whom he admires, Leavitt has suggested that these authors are concerned with the shattering of the familial, or parental, edifice. Many today write of a world "where very little can be taken for granted or counted on, where potentially dangerous change looms around every corner, and where marriages and families, rather than providing havens, are themselves the fulcrum of the most sweeping upheavals." His comment about the works of a number of other contemporary writers could, quite easily, be applied to his own work.

"DEDICATED"

Several stories in Leavitt's collections deal with the complications resulting from the confrontations of heterosexual and homosexual lives. This difficult intersection is seen particularly in a group of stories involving the characters of Celia, Nathan, and Andrew, from their

David Leavitt (Getty Images)

initial encounters as college students to their later lives; as their sexual relationships change, new ones develop, and the later loves affect their friendships.

In "Dedicated," the final story in the *Family Dancing* collection, the trio of Nathan (dark and Jewish, from a wealthy family), Andrew (blond and the definitive WASP, white Anglo-Saxon Protestant), and Celia (attracted to and friends with both Nathan and Andrew) is introduced at the residence of Nathan's parents, while they spend a leisurely weekend away from their Manhattan jobs. In a story seen primarily from Celia's point of view, the contentious sexual relationship between Nathan and Andrew is explored in the present-time setting of the story and also in flashbacks to college, to scenes in New York, and to scenes from a European trip, when Nathan and Andrew became lovers in Florence. The story centers on Celia's somewhat frustrated attempts to comprehend her attraction to homosexual men, which she sees not as an accident but as what she terms "a career."

Celia is a confidant to both Andrew, who professes not to love Nathan, and Nathan, who likes talking endlessly and analytically with her. While Nathan and Andrew constantly attempt to define for her their conflicting affair, Celia tries to determine why she is attracted only to men who, ultimately, can be attracted only to one another. Additionally, there are discussions among the trio in which issues, such as whether one should be a gay activist or whether to discuss one's homosexuality with one's parents, are argued. The complexities of Nathan's and Andrew's lives are further explored in scenes in which both Nathan and Andrew tell Celia of their first night of love together, and she becomes aware of the discrepancy of their points of view while experiencing her own ongoing sense of isolation from the men and their lives. She finally realizes that her happiness with each results in part from their unhappiness with each other. She also notices how much of her awareness comes from her repeated partings with the two young men.

"A PLACE I'VE NEVER BEEN"

In Leavitt's second collection, *A Place I've Never Been*, he again deals with the trio in several stories. In the book's title story, Nathan returns from a lengthy trip to Europe to find his apartment in shambles and immediately calls on Celia, who continues to be for him a dependable prop in his life. Nathan's former lover, Martin, has tested positive for human immunodeficiency virus (HIV), and Nathan vows to give up sex entirely. In Nathan's absence, Celia has discovered her own sense of being and has come to understand her own beauty and appeal. She also knows that as long as she is the only solace in Nathan's life, she cannot have a life of her own, and Nathan now is paralyzed by his fear of getting AIDS--or, worse, giving AIDS to someone he loves.

"WHEN YOU GROW TO ADULTERY"

In "When You Grow to Adultery," Andrew resurfaces, having long been separated from Nathan and Celia, the friends of his college years. Andrew momentarily is suspended between his relationship with his established lover, Allen, and his new attraction to an architect named Jack Seldon. Andrew thus is torn between his love for Allen (who needs Andrew) and his need for Jack, a need that is underscored by the story's final scene, where, as Andrew and Allen make love at the house of Allen's parents, Andrew traces Jack's name on Allen's back.

"I SEE LONDON, I SEE FRANCE"

In the story "I See London, I See France," Celia goes to Europe with Seth, a man she has met through a telephone dating service, and she discovers on their first date that they share a love of Italy. At the heart of Celia's life is an essential unhappiness about what her life is and has been and the impossibility of ever making it anything truly different. That realization comes to her vividly as she and Seth visit a "beautiful" couple, Alex and Sylvie Foster, and their two daughters, Adriana and Francesca, at the Fosters' Italian farmhouse, Il Mestolo. Yet, after an idyllic afternoon at the Italian house, Celia Hoberman, who grew up with her mother, Rose, and her grandmother, Lena, in an apartment in Queens, also comes to know that she, too, can change her life and live in Italy, but she will never break the umbilical cord that life uses to attach everyone to his or her undeniable past.

"TERRITORY" AND "AYOR"

Other problems associated with sexual orientation appear in stories such as "Ayor," "Houses," and "My Marriage to Vengeance" in *A Place I've Never Been* and in the story "Territory" in *Family Dancing*. In "Territory," a young man, Neil, whose mother supports liberal causes, brings his male lover, Wayne, home to visit. The confrontation with his lover brings about a subtle epiphany of suppressed feelings of guilt and responsibility between mother and son. The same kind of shared responsibility of one friend for another's life is seen, too, in "Ayor," in which an unnamed narrator (Nathan, possibly?) tells of his sexual longing for a college friend, Craig Rosen, who later becomes the narrator's guide to the seedy underside of New York's homosexual life. After a trip to France--where the narrator has an affair with a young Frenchman named Laurent--the he again meets Craig, who tells him that he has been raped by a man in Spain, a revelation that conjures up for the narrator a complex of feelings questioning the extent to which human beings are, indeed, somewhat responsible for all the lives upon which they impinge.

"MY MARRIAGE TO VENGEANCE"

In "My Marriage to Vengeance," Ellen Britchkey is invited to the wedding of her former lesbian lover, Diane Helaine Winters. In this story, Leavitt fully explores both the ironies and the humor inherent in this situation: Ellen's being a lesbian is just how things are, while with Diana, it is merely the exploration of one of several options in life, which leads the narrator (Ellen) to comment, "Rich people are like that, I have noticed. They think a love affair is like a shared real estate venture they can just buy out of when they get tired of it." In actuality, Ellen comes to see, after witnessing Diane cry in desperation about her own wedding, that Diane simply has made a life of compromise for herself, but Ellen also knows that for many like Diane, dishonest compromise in life is easier than difficult honesty.

"HOUSES"

A similar theme is explored in "Houses," in which Paul, a real estate broker married to Susan, suddenly and impetuously enters into a sexual relationship with a local dog groomer, Ted, who cares for the couple's dog. Paul and Ted meet on their first "date" at a local restaurant frequented by gay customers, the Dunes, and begin a three-month affair. Eventually, however, Paul decides to return to his wife, only to find that she views their marriage as something false and questions whether he ever truly loved her and if he really was not thinking of men as he made love to her. Paul's business occupation with houses is also a personal one, since he professes to "love" houses. After his second departure from his wife, he lives hit-or-miss in a succession of empty houses, a poignant symbol of his sexual life. As he states his condition at one point, it is possible in one's heart to love two different people in differing ways, but it is not possible to do so in life.

"THE LOST COTTAGE"

As Leavitt examines subtly the many ways in which homosexuality alters perceptions of family relationships and values, so, too, does he look regularly at how divorce can suddenly create a major shift in family values and alliances. In "The Lost Cottage," a story in *Family Dancing*, Leavitt presents the Dempson family, in which the parents, Lydia and Alex, six months earlier, had announced to their children that they were divorcing. Yet, in spite of the changed nature of the parents' relationship to each other, the family--at the mother Lydia's insistence--still assembles, as they have for twenty-six years, at their summer cottage on Cape Cod.

The Dempsons' three children are Mark, a gay man who lives in Manhattan doing odd jobs; Ellen, an unmarried lawyer; and Douglas, who, with his girlfriend of five years, conducts oceanographic research in Hawaii. All gather at the family cottage, "Under the Weather," where Lydia attempts to continue the same family rituals they long have observed each summer. Yet, the summer's reunion soon disintegrates as Lydia is unable to bear her husband's new relationship, an anxiety that is heightened to crisis proportions for the family when Alex's new girlfriend, Marian Hollister, shows up in the New England village to be near him as he spends time with his family and former wife. Amid the growing tensions set off by Marian's presence, Lydia reveals the blunt fact of her own--and her family's--problem: She still loves her husband, Alex, and always has, and, even if he has left her, he cannot escape the simple fact of that love.

The situation among the family, however, is one that cannot be resolved by any family member; the complexities set in motion by the parents' divorce are such that they are as insurmountable as Mark's trying to comprehend his brother's heterosexual indulgence of his girlfriend's demands. It is a confusion also mirrored in Mark's sister, who cannot understand Mark's ability to go to bed with someone he has just met. The shifts that occur in human relationships--such as homosexual and heterosexual desire--may simply be, ultimately, inexplicable and irreconcilable despite the good intentions of all involved. The tragedy is, as Ellen tells her family at one point, not that they do not care but that they do.

Sexual complications and divorce's ramifications are two principal themes in Leavitt's short fiction. The impact of terminal illness forms a third major topic. In the stories "Counting Months" and "Radiation" (in *Family Dancing*), the manifestations of family problems surrounding the last days of cancer patients and their medical treatment are explored. In "Gravity" (in Leavitt's second collection), a mother's reaction to her son's fatal AIDS is seen. This invocation of fatal illness (especially that of cancer) is one to which the author frequently returns, and it is again treated in his novel *Equal Affections*, where the mother, Louise Cooper, has been involved in a twenty-year struggle with cancer.

"SPOUSE NIGHT"

Another story, "Spouse Night," also presents a group of characters whose lives have been suddenly altered by the loss of a mate. The title refers to a post-death support meeting, in which people attempt to come to grips with their individual losses. Arthur has lost his wife, Claire, to a sudden and quickly fatal skin disease, while his new companion, Mrs. Eve Theodorous, recently has lost her husband, Spiro. The survivors have begun a tentative sexual affair and even have acquired a new "child," a puppy that Mrs. Theodorous envies for its ability to forget its family connections and for being spared the sense of loss that humans must accept. Arthur's hesitancy in committing himself to his new relationship with Mrs. Theodorous is emphasized in his passionate scene of grief, when he attempts to scatter his wife's ashes from a boat in the harbor. This scene suggests in vivid detail (which Leavitt is so good at selecting) the anguish encountered in transitional moments in life from one form of commitment to another.

ARKANSAS

Leavitt chose to give his third collection of short fiction the idiosyncratic title *Arkansas: Three Novellas*. The only connection with that state is explained in a quotation he attributes to Victorian writer Oscar Wilde: "I should like to flee like a wounded hart into Arkansas." Ostracized and financially ruined by imprisonment for "gross indecency" (sodomy), Wilde wanted to hide in some remote wilderness. Leavitt's own embarrassment was far less serious but apparently had a comparable effect.

When Leavitt published the novel *While England Sleeps*, he created a furor gleefully reported on both sides of the Atlantic. Stephen Spender, once a prominent English poet, accused Leavitt of plagiarism and sued for libel, charging the young American with borrowing too freely from his autobiography *World Within World* (1948), which includes an account of an intimate relationship with a young man who served as a

volunteer in the Spanish Civil War of the 1930's. Leavitt felt disgraced when his publishers pulled his novel out of bookstores. Instead of flying like a wounded hart to Arkansas, however, he fled Manhattan for the remote wilderness of Los Angeles, California.

"THE TERM PAPER ARTIST"

Leavitt briefly describes his humiliation in "The Term Paper Artist," then gives a hilarious account of being propositioned by a student at a major Southern California university. Eric offers sex in exchange for a ghostwritten term paper comparing and contrasting E. M. Forster's *A Room with a View* (1908) and Henry James's *Daisy Miller* (1878). Leavitt, paralyzed by writer's block, seizes this win-win opportunity. He would enjoy the sexual adventure with a raunchy but virginal young male and the challenge of writing about two homosexual authors with whom he is thoroughly familiar. Rereading their famous novels reminds him of the love for literature that inspired him to make it the focus of his career.

Word gets around that a prominent professional writer can be talked into exchanging high-quality papers for sex. He finds himself in a wonderland instead of a wasteland. Though shocked by the callous attitude of his rowdy young "clients" toward both homosexuality and turning in ghostwritten papers, he finds their coarse amorality arousing and adopts their sardonic attitude as a way of coping with the Spender debacle. Instead of corrupting these rowdy young men, they are corrupting him. Then he meets Ben, a confused, sensitive virgin. Their relationship transforms Ben's life when he realizes he has always been a latent homosexual and comes out of the closet with relief and gratitude.

"SATURN STREET" AND "THE WOODEN ANNIVERSARY"

"Saturn Street" recounts a tragic love affair with an actor the narrator encounters when he volunteers to deliver meals to housebound AIDS victims. Here again Leavitt demonstrates a talent for capturing the sunstruck anomie of sprawling Los Angeles. "The Wooden Anniversary," about dissolute homosexual expatriates in Italy, seems included to pad this slender volume. All three novellas show Leavitt's growing maturity and self-confidence in a confusing but infinitely varied and amusing world, his severance of emotional dependence on family, his abandonment of guilt and self-flagellation, his willingness to face the challenges of homosexuality, and, especially, his power to recover from any setback through the healing magic of creative writing.

THE MARBLE QUILT

In *The Marble Quilt*, Leavitt's fourth collection of short works, he revisits familiar themes, but this time, perhaps because of his own relocation to Italy in 1993, his settings are most often in Europe. Even so, the protagonists are American, such as the family making the grand tour in "Crossing St. Gotthard" or the expatriate ex-lovers in the title story. Both tales explore the nature of individual identity, complicated by familial relationships and sexual orientation.

In "Crossing St. Gotthard," an American woman, her two sons, and her nephew, installed in their first-class railway compartment, face, in their separate ways, the train's approach to the nine-mile-long St. Gotthard Tunnel, the Swiss link between northern and southern Europe. Irene Pratt, whose husband and favorite son had died recently in a freak accident, equates the utter blackness of the tunnel to the darkness of the grave; her nephew, Harold, a frail, bookish young man whose spot on the tour is underwritten by his wealthy aunt, sees the tunnel as the entrance to Italy, whose art and culture and permissive stance toward sexual matters may finally give him the courage to act on his heretofore hidden desires. The tunnel, like the tropes in so many of Leavitt's stories, represents a passageway of momentous consequence, an opportunity to confront one's fears and perhaps forge a new, more confident identity.

The title story in the collection makes explicit reference to a mosaic floor, such as those found in the churches of Rome, whose tesserae are pieced together in intricate patterns like a quilt. On the surface, the tale, a murder mystery of sorts, features a protagonist, a young American translator living in Germany, who voluntarily submits to an interview by the Roman police, who are investigating the brutal murder of his ex-lover, an English teacher in Rome found tied to his kitchen table, bludgeoned to death. In the story, marble takes on many meanings. During his residency in

Rome, the murdered man, Thomas Carlomusto, had become a collector of marble, perhaps because its apparent permanency stood in sharp contrast to the dissolution of his relationship with his former partner, the translator Vincent Burke. The two men had first been drawn together in San Francisco during the height of the AIDS crisis, and their bond, Thomas hoped, would serve to keep them invulnerable to the disease. However, largely because of Vincent's promiscuity, their relationship was not as solid as it may have seemed to others and to Thomas himself. Ultimately the reader never learns the identity of the murderer; it may have been an anonymous stranger that Thomas picked up on the street. Vincent shares some of the guilt, for he blames himself for the change in his ex-partner after they broke up; Thomas had become both "sullen and brazen" after his move to Rome, perhaps in acknowledgment that he no longer trusted life. He tells Vincent during one of the Vincent's infrequent visits to the city that "no one ever really owns marble. It'll outlive us all."

OTHER MAJOR WORKS

LONG FICTION: *The Lost Language of Cranes*, 1986; *Equal Affections*, 1989; *While England Sleeps*, 1993, revised 1995; *The Page Turner*, 1998; *Martin Bauman: Or, A Sure Thing*, 2000; *The Body of Jonah Boyd*, 2004; *The Indian Clerk*, 2007.

NONFICTION: *Italian Pleasures*, 1996 (with Mark Mitchell); *In Maremma: Life and a House in Southern Tuscany*, 2001 (with Mitchell); *Florence: A Delicate Case*, 2002; *The Man Who Knew Too Much: Alan Turing and the Invention of the Computer*, 2005.

EDITED TEXTS: *The Penguin Book of Gay Short Stories*, 1994 (with Mark Mitchell); *Pages Passed from Hand to Hand: The Hidden Tradition of Homosexual Literature in England from 1748 to 1914*, 1997 (with Mitchell); *Selected Stories*, 2001 (of E. M. Forster; with Mitchell).

BIBLIOGRAPHY

Bleeth, Kenneth, and Julie Rivkin. "The 'Imitation David': Plagiarism, Collaboration, and the Making of a Gay Literary Tradition in David Leavitt's 'The Term Paper Artist.'" *PMLA* 116 (October, 2001):

1349-1363. The article analyzes Leavitt's "The Term Paper Artist" in light of the author's contention that copying is an accepted, long-standing means of cultural transmission in gay literary genealogy.

Bohlen, Celestine. "Writer on the Rebound: This Time, He Takes Liberties with His Own Life." *The New York Times*, February 25, 1997, p. C11. Notes that while Leavitt's book *While England Sleeps* was pulled from the presses after the English poet Spender filed a plagiarism suit because of sexual suggestions concerning his autobiography, Leavitt's story "The Term Paper Artist" features a character called David Leavitt who has gone home to his father's house to brood over a vengeful English poet's accusation of plagiarism.

Kekki, Lasse. *From Gay to Queer: Gay Male Identity in Selected Fiction by David Leavitt and in Tony Kushner's Play "Angels in America I-II."* Bern, Switzerland: Peter Lang, 2003. The author devotes four out of seven sections of the book to Leavitt's fiction, including the three novellas in *Arkansas*; each work is analyzed through the critical lens of contemporary queer theory.

Klarer, Mario. "David Leavitt's 'Territory': René Girard's Homoerotic 'Trigonometry' and Julia Kristeva's 'Semiotic Chora.'" *Studies in Short Fiction* 28 (Winter, 1991): 63-76. Argues that the mother-son-lover triangle in the story "Territory" calls for two different theoretical frames for analysis: Girard's "erotic triangle" in his 1965 book *Deceit, Desire, and the Novel* and Kristeva's theory of a "semiotic territory" in her 1984 book *Revolution in Poetic Language*.

Leavitt, David. "Interview with David Leavitt." Interview by Sam Staggs. *Publishers Weekly* 237 (August 24, 1990): 47-49. In this interview, Leavitt refers to his collection of stories *A Place I've Never Been* as the first book of "the middle years" of his career; Staggs claims the stories in Leavitt's collection reveal the maturity that his earlier work hinted at, with several excellent stories exploiting the theme of Americans in Europe.

Lo, Mun-Hou. "David Leavitt and the Etiological Maternal Body." *Modern Fiction Studies* 41 (Fall/Winter, 1995): 439-465. Discusses the figure of the mother in some stories from Leavitt's debut collection *Family Dancing*; comments on Leavitt's obsessive interest in the specter of the strong mother, even as this interest can take the form only of looking everywhere except directly at the relationship between maternity and homosexuality.

Rivkin, Julie. "Writing the Gay '80's with Henry James: David Leavitt's *A Place I've Never Been* and Alan Hollinghurst's *The Line of Beauty*." *Henry James Review* 26 (Fall, 2005): 282-292. The author claims that James, in his biography, subject matter, and style, heavily influenced Leavitt's story collection *A Place I've Never Been* and Hollinghurst's novel *The Line of Beauty*.

White, Edmund. "Out of the Closet, onto the Bookshelf." *The New York Times Magazine*, June 16, 1991, pp. 22-24. White writes about the 1980's generation of openly homosexual writers and how the AIDS epidemic has both decimated their ranks and at the same time created a maturity of creative writing as writers react to the disease and its threat.

Jere Real; Bill Delaney
Updated by S. Thomas Mack

Andrea Lee

Born: Philadelphia, Pennsylvania; January 1, 1953

Other literary forms

Each of Andrea Lee's books can read like a novel, as the individual essays and stories tend to connect through themes, characters, or tone. The collection *Sarah Phillips,* for instance, is often regarded as such, as each story revolves around the title character. In *Lost Hearts in Italy* (2006), Lee's first novel, she gives readers the story in its entirety, rather than in separate installments, as the stories of *Sarah Phillips* first made their way to print. The novel proves consistent with the overarching themes of Lee's work: place, relationships, identity, and sexuality.

Achievements

Andrea Lee's collection of essays *Russian Journal* was nominated for the National Book Award, and Lee was a finalist. In 1984, she won the Jean Stein Award from the American Academy and Institute of Arts and Letters. In 2002, she won an O. Henry Award for her story "Anthropology," published in *The Oxford American.* Lee's razor-sharp intellect permeates her work; she commonly makes reference to high literature or esoteric historical knowledge and inserts Italian and Latin phrases in her work. Nevertheless, the pages remain light and spirited and turn like those of an easy read. Lee manages to inject playfulness and looseness into sensitive and challenging cultural dynamics. Her voice reflects the new generation, a voice that feels the residue of history and bears its burden but transcends it,

too. Lee's personal circumstances afford her insight into a unique but certainly not singular experience. Thus, she provides yet another version of the African American story, in which light-colored skin, relative wealth, and elite education carve a different path for a young African American woman. The distinctiveness of the narratives of Lee's characters brings awareness both to the individuality and to the universality of every human story.

Biography

Born in 1953, Andrea Lee spent the early part of her life in a middle-class suburb of Philadelphia. Her mother was an elementary school teacher, and her father was a Baptist minister. Her parents had one other child, Lee's brother. Both of her parents were active in the Civil Rights movement, an influence that makes its way into "In the Pulpit" in *Interesting Women* and into other stories. Lee was writing avidly by the age of four.

As a teenager, Lee turned to writing and literature both for recreation and for reflection. She worked feverishly on literary assignments at her girls' high school. Lee was one of the first African Americans to attend the school; most of the student population was wealthy and white. Reading and writing stories served as a place to illuminate and contemplate the world around her.

At eighteen, Lee moved to Cambridge, Massachusetts, to attend Harvard University, where she earned her bachelor's and master's degrees. At twenty-five, Lee traveled to Russia with her husband, Tom, a fellow graduate student at Harvard (whom she later divorced). She tried her hand at journalism and was highly prolific during her year abroad. Several of the essays she wrote during that period appeared in her collection *Russian Journal.* Just three years later, Lee published several of her short stories in *Sarah Phillips.*

When her children were young, Lee's writing efforts manifested mostly in essays and articles, which she saw published in a number of high-profile journals and magazines. She worked on staff for *The New Yorker* for several years and has continued to contribute essays on occasion. Additionally, Lee has contributed to *The New York Times Book Review*, *The New York Times Magazine*, *The Oxford American*, *O, The Oprah Magazine*, and *Vogue*.

Among her literary loves, Lee names Rudyard Kipling, Isak Dinesen, Ivan Turgenev, Henry Louis Gates, Jr., Philip Roth, Toni Morrison, V. S. Naipaul, and Alberto Moravia. The roster reflects the range of voices and worlds that Lee absorbs and then channels through her writing. She is a globetrotter, through literature and travel.

This worldliness surfaces throughout her stories. In fact, various aspects of Lee's life appear in her writing. Many of her protagonists are well-educated, attractive, divorced, remarried, African American, or racially mixed women. Several of these women are writers, world travelers, mothers, and children of civil rights activists. It is as if Lee writes her persona into varied settings and situations. The author's familiarity with her characters lends itself to depth and insight; she builds worlds of fully realized, complex characters. The author's work includes essays for various publications and her full-length novel *Lost Hearts in Italy*, which builds upon themes explored in earlier books.

Lee returns to the United States regularly but resides in Turin, Italy, with her husband, who is native to Italy. Her zeal for world travel has not diminished, and she has continued to explore nearly every continent with her family. She has two children, Alexandra and Charles.

ANALYSIS

Some critics have posited that Andrea Lee's work is limited by her personal narrative and that she has not been able to shed the lens of privilege and elite scholarship. Certainly, the consistency with which she draws characters of a certain class and educational background leaves little room to delve into less familiar worlds. In her novel *Lost Hearts in Italy*, each chapter ends with the voice of a marginal character--a servant,

a fortune teller, a fruit vendor. Lee manages these "others" with an awkward and at times presumptuous sense of respect and diplomacy. They are never fully realized characters; they are the other voices, the other factors, that serve to illuminate something about those that are more central to the story. Nonetheless, one person's limitation is another's concentration. Lee paints, again and again, the world she knows, which allows the reader to go more deeply there, to a place that largely is unpainted and unrecognized as part of the African American female experience.

Pain and suffering, for instance, look different in Lee's world. The author applies an awareness of cultural phenomena that may include or exclude certain people; Lee keenly observes prejudices, perceptions, and reactions. These issues do not oppress, however; they interest, they sadden, they resonate, they frustrate, and at times they create apathy and further detachment. Beneath this approach lies a feeling of empowerment, if sometimes through distance, on the part of the writer.

Though limited in ways and troubling to some, Lee's perspective on long-standing cultural issues feels fresh. The author gains enough distance to speak with candor on subjects long submerged. Sexuality, infidelity, socioeconomic disparity, the disconnect between men and women, the power and market value of appearance and physicality--Lee tackles all of these face front, with an objectivity that puts them in their place but a sensitivity that holds the reader's concern and interest.

Lee's writing exemplifies and emboldens the voice of the individual, yet many of her insights touch upon truths that are part of the universal human experience.

RUSSIAN JOURNAL

Through her first and most decorated work, *Russian Journal*, readers witness Lee's flawless prose and stunning ability to create a sensory experience on paper. Her descriptions are rich, nearly edible; even as she meanders through darkness or bleakness, her style possesses so much vitality that the page retains a certain lightness of being. She achieves this lightness, in part, by constantly situating herself as an outsider. She establishes an intimacy with her subjects, enough to allow for close observation and reflection. She captures the complicated relationship between Russia and the

United States without compromising the spontaneity and creativity with which she renders a scene. Whether she is depicting a mealtime conversation, a popular song playing, or the changing of the guard before Vladimir Lenin's tomb, broad cultural issues are present and undeniable, but the scenes retain a certain simplicity of meaning. The scenes may bear cultural significance, but they also can be, simply, something she perceived, something that occurred, part of her day abroad. There is a level of detachment in what she portrays that lends itself to striking clarity.

This chronicle of her time in Russia sets in motion her expatriate lifestyle. She speaks to an awareness of her appearance in comparison to those in her surroundings, and she considers how others see her. Her look is difficult to pinpoint, which causes discomfort, intrigue, attraction, pity, or distrust, depending on the viewer. Lee's self-consciousness about her appearance, particularly surrounding the color of her skin, emerges in subsequent stories and characters.

SARAH PHILLIPS

Stringing together a collection of stories, each published initially in *The New Yorker*, Lee formed a connected, quasi-chronological piece centered on the title character. The character's life and plight so closely resemble the author's own that the book can read like a memoir. The book grapples with tensions in the varied experiences of African Americans, across class and generations. Like Lee, Sarah Phillips came from middle-class, suburban, African American parents--a teacher and a preacher--who were steeped in Civil Rights activism and grounded in the Philadelphia black community. Unlike her parents (or Lee's parents, incidentally), Sarah grew up attending mostly white, privileged schools, where she was estranged from many of her African American peers. The collection explores that estrangement, all the questions raised by it, and consequently the places, situations, and relationships to which Sarah is led as a result. There is a level of unconsciousness and reactivity operating in Sarah, while the writing itself is deeply self-aware.

The collection is framed by a construction of home and homelessness, a sense of place and identity. The collection opens with "In France," in which Sarah describes escapades with her peers in France. The book closes with "A Funeral at New African," in which her father's illness causes Sarah to return home, where she feels more strange than familiar. She leaves again, after his untimely death, indicating that the quest for place continues for her.

INTERESTING WOMEN

In this aptly titled short-story collection, the renaissance author quickly, fluidly, and confidently moves through countries, characters, languages, and literary styles. She tours the reader around the United States, Italy, France, and beyond--nearly every continent is represented. Her characters are writers, mothers, socialites, students, models--many categories of women make appearances. Given the global span of the content and the author's erudite prose style, it is only logical that within the first few pages of the collection, Lee's characters are already spouting full Italian sentences. References to Mephistopheles or Jonathan Swift or a Roman epic are as commonplace and easily applied to a scene as an article or a pronoun.

Lee not only dabbles in varied subject matter but also adopts different prose forms. "The Golden Chariot," which first appeared in *Zoetrope*, is a short play: A cross-country, family road trip is related through a series of monologues by each member of the family. "The Visit" is an extended address and sequence of thoughts, woman to woman. There is no traditional dialogue, yet communication is exchanged. The visit lasts only twenty-four hours, yet years are covered. Lee successfully bridges gaps of five or six years in a sentence or two without losing her reader, which creates a multilayered, multidimensional story. She is, unquestionably, a master of construction with words.

The women of Lee's stories are explorers, moving through journeys of self-realization. "The Birthday Present," a story that has raised eyebrows and questions, kicks off the collection and features Ariel, an American woman living in Italy with her Italian husband and children. Motivated by a friend's challenge, Ariel hires two young prostitutes as birthday presents for her middle-aged husband. The arrangement becomes an occasion for Ariel to explore her identity as a wife in a relationship that has matured toward the banality of marriage.

Sexual exploration is a crucial component in Lee's women. "The Prior's Room" features Anna, a young woman in the prime of naïve beauty. So volatile is the expectation of this phase of womanhood that her "grandparents shied away from giving her a post-graduation summer in Paris and, instead, sent her to polish her French in tamer surroundings." This attempt to control Anna's green sexuality sets the scene for her solo border-crossing adventure, to see just how far attraction will take her. "Winter Barley" portrays a more mature, yet equally profound exploration for Elizabeth, as she finds companionship with an older man. Their affair is passionate, yet they have the wisdom of years, and Elizabeth watches herself attach and detach from a relationship that has its limits.

Lee covers vast ground--physically and conceptually--in short stories. At times, she could afford to pause and settle more deeply into her subject and to allow her reader time to develop investment. Nonetheless, her stories are salvaged by moments of heartfelt centeredness and connection to the characters. Lee loves her characters and the relationships they form.

OTHER MAJOR WORKS

LONG FICTION: *Lost Hearts in Italy*, 2006.

BIBLIOGRAPHY

Danoff, Douglas. "The Preacher's Daughter: Andrea Lee, the Nice Minister's Kid Who Writes Spicy Fiction, Releases a Can't-Miss Summer Read." *Essence* 37, no. 2 (June, 2006): 93. Danoff reviews Lee's novel *Lost Hearts in Italy*.

Hogue, W. Lawrence. "The Limits of Modernity: Andrea Lee's *Sarah Phillips*." *MELUS* 19, no. 4 (1994): 75. Critic Hogue observes the insightful, problematic, and sometimes limiting nature of the perspective rendered in *Sarah Phillips*.

Lee, Andrea. "Altered State." *The New Yorker* 84, no. 19 (June 30, 2008): 36. Personal essay in which Lee contemplates childhood, home, past, and present.

_____. "Books That Made a Difference to Andrea Lee: Russia! Africa! Suburban New Jersey in the 1950's!" *O, The Oprah Magazine* 7, no. 9 (September, 2006): 270. Lee cites her literary influences.

_____. "From Italy: Guilt, Politics, and Eros in a Jar." *The New Yorker* (March 6, 1995): 36. Lee observes cultural tendencies, personal and political, in the United States and Italy through a close look at a particular food.

_____. "A River Flows Through Us: Her Worldly Twelve-Year-Old Wasn't the Sort to Read *Tom Sawyer*. Or Was He?" *O, The Oprah Magazine* 8, no. 9 (September, 2007): 258. Provides biographical information about the author, her son, and their exploration of a literary classic.

Smith, Valerie. Foreword to *Sarah Phillips*. Boston: Northeastern, 1984. Smith discusses the value of this undervalued, often misunderstood text as it contributes to a literary conversation on race, class, culture, and alienation.

Sonia Erlich

JOAN LEEGANT

Born: New York, New York; May 1, 1950

PRINCIPAL SHORT FICTION
An Hour in Paradise, 2003

OTHER LITERARY FORMS
Wherever You Go (2010) is the first long-fiction work of Joan Leegant.

ACHIEVEMENTS
Joan Leegant's *An Hour in Paradise: Stories* was a finalist for the National Jewish Book Award and won the L. L. Winship /PEN New England Award in 2004. It also was named the Edward Lewis Wallant Award winner for Jewish fiction by the Maurice Greenberg Center for Judaic Studies in 2002.

BIOGRAPHY
A native New Yorker who has divided most of her life between the greater Boston area and Israel, Joan Leegant began writing fiction just before she turned forty. The ten stories included in *An Hour in Paradise*, her first book, were written over a four-year period and first appeared in literary magazines such as *Prairie Schooner, Nimrod, New England Review*, and *American Literary Review*. While in her late twenties, Leegant spent three years in Jerusalem, and the impetus for her collection of stories is drawn largely from that experience. With an undergraduate degree from Harvard University, Leegant pursued a law degree from Boston University and worked as an attorney for more than ten years. Married with two sons, Leegant found herself slowly beginning to spend more time writing. After nearly seven years of writing essays, songs, poems, and various nonfiction, Leegant sought an M.F.A. at Vermont College. This education, over two years, gave her the discipline and experience to

begin writing fiction.

During the final revisions of her collection of short stories, Leegant was in Tel Aviv with her husband. Torn between being in Israel, where many of her stories are based, and seeking isolation in New England's writer's colonies, the author sought a blending of inspiration and sustained attention.

Leegant taught writing at Harvard University for eight years, and she returned to Israel to teach at Tel Aviv's Bar-Ilan University from 2007 to 2010. Leegant also was a guest lecturer of the U.S. State Department in Israel, where she focused on American literature, writing, and teacher training. When not in Israel, Leegant makes her home outside Boston, where she routinely takes a fifteen-minute walk or a ten-minute drive to her rented office, where she prefers to work through the hours of midnight to 5 a.m.

ANALYSIS
A Yiddish proverb states, "Even an hour in paradise is worthwhile." In this collection of ten elegant stories, Leegant presents characters who are searching. The author's original title for the work was "Seekers in the Holy Land," which is the title of one of the stories in the book. It is a more apt book title, more exact in description, but the given title, "An Hour in Paradise," captures the spirit of the collection and the ephemeral quality that several of the stories possess. There's a mystical atmosphere that shrouds the scenes in a number of the stories, an encounter with the divine, the unknowable and unexplainable guiding hand.

Not all the stories possess this quality, but the memorable ones have it. "The Tenth," "How to Comfort the Sick and Dying," and "The Lament of the Rabbi's Daughters" exhibit this quality of the invisible force, which produces "The Tenth" man for the minyan but does not stop there. It offers Siamese twins, showing the quirky influence of a mischievous force that does more than quietly work behind the scenes; instead it shouts to attract attention.

In "How to Comfort the Sick and Dying," Reuven Schweller, a recovering alcoholic and drug abuser, in an effort at rehabilitation, finds himself charged with visiting a man dying of acquired immunodeficiency syndrome (AIDS). The situation requires him to reach within himself, to overcome his selfish interests. The dying man's only request during each visit is that he be told a story. The stories Reuven tells are infected with the virus of his own sordid past. To her credit, Leegant avoids sentimentality and heavy-handedness, reaching not for an attractive moral but for a plainer message about survival and persistence.

Leegant has included a few stories that seem outside the theme. One of these is "Accounting," a play on words. This deals with an ungrateful child, a young man who has been a curse to his parents. His mother enables him, and his father waits in vain for his son to become a decent man. In this story, Leegant replaces the divine with the human. There is no magic, no gentle winds blowing fair weather. It is a stark world, a bleak existence. It is a reality that only a loving parent can understand. There are no small miracles or simple joys, only large sacrifices and complicated relationships.

"THE TENTH"

In a Boston shul, a rabbi frets about finding the required tenth man for the morning minyan, a prayer service. He turns to Nathan Lefkowitz, an elderly man with a solid track record for finding the tenth man. Lefkowitz leaves the shul, as on so many other occasions in the past when he has had to recruit on the streets. On this particular morning Lefkowitz is in luck. Rather than having to ask, he is approached. It is not by exactly one man and not by exactly two men. Siamese twins stop to ask if he is Nathan Lefkowitz, the person searching for the tenth man for morning minyan. Lefkowitz admits to being one and the same, and the twins accompany him back to the shul, where a grateful rabbi is waiting to lead the prayer.

The rabbi, however surprised at seeing Siamese twins at minyan, does not delay or pause to ask questions. Instead, the morning prayer proceeds as usual, and when it is over, the Siamese twins are the first ones out the door. The rabbi has time to consider what just

happened. Did he really have ten men for morning prayer, or did he have eleven? Should Siamese twins count as one, as two, or not at all? Being a conscientious rabbi, he canvasses the neighborhood, looking for the Siamese twins, hoping to offer them the comfort and hospitality of the shul, to reach out to these new-found adherents of the faith.

The twins are nowhere to be found. No one has seen them. If one did see them, even once, the rabbi reasons, could one forget them? The rabbi returns to the apartment building where Lefkowitz met the twins. They do not live in the apartment building. They had not visited. They had not been seen by anyone living there. Did they really exist? Could it be they existed for only that time, that place, and that purpose?

In the mysterious appearance and disappearance of the Siamese twins, Leegant presents an opening of a door through which the mystical walks into the realm of the ordinary religious observance. This first story in the collection sets the table for a series of similar influences from forces both divine and human.

"HOW TO COMFORT THE SICK AND DYING"

Reuven Schweller was once Robert Smith, a drug addict, a man who knowingly and willingly sold poisons to teenagers and was himself almost beyond help. In fact, his last stop, his last chance, is a new life. He has new clothes, a new look, a new name, and the same old demons living in his bowels, waiting to erupt in fresh torment. The Rebbe sends Reuven into the world, specifically to visit the sick. Reuven is given an assignment, to visit every day a man named Ash, an AIDS patient dying in a neighborhood hospital.

This is an understated story, though one of human frailty, crushing guilt, and feelings of unworthiness. Reuven is lost, trying to bring comfort to a dying man. There is only so much he can do, provide a friendly face, a sympathetic ear, a helping hand. These are small considerations, but Reuven is not even equal to these minimal challenges. He is asked by Ash to tell a story.

Reuven's stories, however, like an abused child's drawings, tell a different tale, one steeped in the ugliness of the storyteller's life. Reuven sees this exercise, this attempt to comfort a dying man, as yet another lost cause in his life. He backslides.

Night finds him with a liquor bottle in hand, perched on the ground beneath a bridge where other men are embracing their own demons. Reuven glories in his inadequacy, righteously recounting his miserable life. A passing derelict reaches out his hand to Reuven, as if to pat his head, but stops short and walks away. Reuven begins to feel different, to pull himself together. He hurries to the hospital to visit Ash, to offer comfort to a dying man.

In this story, Leegant pulls back from the brink of an easy answer, favoring a shade of gray over black and white. Reuven could have found his faith, could have been a success, a positive example. Instead, Reuven is fallible, a man who comes to terms with his damaged self, one who finally chooses to persist in comforting the sick and dying rather than joining them.

"Accounting"

Solomon and Ruth Hirsch have one child, a grown son, Eliot. Eliot is a liar, a thief, a cheat, and an adulterer. He is divorced from wife Pam, and they have two children. Solomon, Ruth, and Pam all know the truth about Eliot, though to the world outside the family he seems charming, respectful, and successful. He is, in fact, none of these things.

Eliot is a user, and his parents are a seemingly bottomless pool of forgiveness. Ruth makes excuses for Eliot, denies the obvious truth, and searches desperately for alternative explanations for her son's behavior. Solomon, the stoic father, loves his wife and son and bears the burden of providing the illusion of normalcy. To keep peace in the family, Solomon gives up his business, relinquishing control to his son. The accounting firm's employees have never been happier. Eliot is a thoughtful boss, a dynamic leader, an inspirational figure who lives and breathes charisma. Of course, this is all a facade.

The reckoning comes from the Internal Revenue Service, when a second or third notice finally finds its way into Solomon's hands. Tens of thousands of dollars in back taxes were never paid. Rather than confront Eliot, banish him from the business and the family, Solomon chooses to become a martyr to his son's bad judgment. Solomon takes the weight of the tax burden on his shoulders, and he slowly walks up the stairs to begin digging out from under the financial ruin.

Leegant presents the flip side of parenting, the endless responsibility, the constant ingratitude, the sad and painful reality that enabling mothers and fathers confront as they seek to save face and preserve the myth of the perfect family. There is no divine spark in this scenario, no invisible guiding hand to right the ship. Solomon takes on the role of accountant, balancing the family's books between Eliot's misdeeds and the state of denial that has become the family's reality.

"The Diviners of Desire: A Modern Fable"

Yakov and Ruti Shtarr, husband and wife, live in Jerusalem. Ruti, also known as Madame Shtarr, has an impressive reputation as a matchmaker. Yakov, more grounded, is an amateur sociologist. Yakov's personal research is studying American youth who come to Jerusalem. Why do so many of them come, and what are they looking for in Jerusalem? What would possess young Americans, spoiled by wealth and opportunities, to come to Jerusalem in search of anything?

Shoshana Borenstein, twenty-two years old with flowing red hair, is a young American searching for something in Jerusalem while teaching at a local girls' school. Leibel Frehn, a neighborhood butcher in Jerusalem, loves selling his best cuts of meat, making recommendations to his customers. Frehn's real passion, however, is getting to know his customers, speculating on their lives based on their orders at the butcher's counter. The butcher, a people person, is well connected in the neighborhood and is good friends with Yakov and Ruti. This is how Yakov comes to know about Shoshana, another young American to interview for his private research.

It is not long before Shoshana becomes a client of Ruti. Ruti, who prides herself on her abilities as a matchmaker, is hesitant to take on Shoshana's case. Ruti is thinking about retiring. Shoshana, though a lovely girl, is a little shy and an American. Finding the right one for Shoshana might be more work than Ruti wants.

Meanwhile, Frehn keeps a watchful eye on Shoshana's butcher shop purchases. Lately, she has ordered enough meat for a specific recipe she wants to try that serves two. Frehn thinks this is a good sign. However, the days pass, and Shoshana does not return to the shop. Frehn begins to worry about her absence. It could mean a number of things: She made the recipe for two people and it did not pan out; she never made the recipe at all; she left the neighborhood or returned to America. After a little snooping, Frehn learns that Shoshana is still living in the neighborhood, and he deduces that she has not made the recipe or otherwise she would have returned to the butcher shop for another order.

Steven Epstein, another young American, new to the neighborhood, finds his way to Frehn's shop. A conversation ensues, and Frehn learns that Steven is a scholar, a Ph.D. candidate. The subject of his doctorate, which he is in Israel to research, is why young Americans come to Israel. Of course, Frehn introduces him to his friend Yakov.

Meanwhile, Ruti despairs over her red-haired American client. Ruti is ready to give up and admit defeat. She writes a letter to this effect and sends it along with Yakov to deliver, since he is taking Steven to meet Shoshana because she would be an excellent interview for his research. Meanwhile, Frehn takes it upon himself to make a stew for Shoshana. He delivers the fragrant stew with its enticing aroma that fills the apartment just as Yakov and Steven knock on her door. Steven sees Shoshana, smells the wonderful stew, and says, "Why have we not met before?" Ruti's letter stays in Yakov's pocket, undelivered.

In this story humans provide the semblance of divine chance. Leegant uses Yakov and Frehn to arrange the right conditions for young romance. The point of the story, perhaps, is that sometimes things can not be left to chance, that humans must intercede with life to manipulate the circumstances for a desirable outcome.

Like a clever trick, what seems amazing can be easily understood if one knows the secrets behind the magic.

OTHER MAJOR WORKS

LONG FICTION: *Wherever You Go*, 2010.

BIBLIOGRAPHY

Bayard, Louis. "Was That Elijah? Stories by a Writer Who Know How to Avoid the Perils of Connecting Faith and Fiction." *The New York Times Book Review*, October 5, 2003, p. 18. A review of *An Hour in Paradise*, this article focuses on how Leegant avoids the trap of falling too far toward faith in her fiction. Stories discussed include "The Tenth," "Lucky in Love," and "The Lament of the Rabbi's Daughters."

Fichtner, Margaria. "Finding a Tenth for Minyan: Outing Big Family Secrets in *An Hour in Paradise*." *The Miami Herald*, August 14, 2003. This review of *An Hour in Paradise* gives an overview of the story plots and especially highlights "The Tenth," "Henny's Wedding," and "How to Comfort the Sick and Dying."

Miron, Susan. "A Short Story Collection Suffused with Jewish Lore and Driven by Unforgettable Characters." *The Jewish Daily Forward*, September 12, 2003. This review of *An Hour in Paradise* discusses the "wondrous, sometimes miraculous, experiences" detailed in Leegant's short-story collection.

Randy L. Abbott

URSULA K. LE GUIN

Born: Berkeley, California; October 21, 1929
Also known as: Ursula Kroeber

PRINCIPAL SHORT FICTION

The Word for World Is Forest, 1972
The Wind's Twelve Quarters, 1975
Orsinian Tales, 1976
The Water Is Wide, 1976
Gwilan's Harp, 1981
The Compass Rose, 1982
The Visionary: The Life Story of Flicker of the Serpentine, with Wonders Hidden, 1984
Buffalo Gals and Other Animal Presences, 1987
Fish Soup, 1992
A Fisherman of the Inland Sea: Science Fiction Stories, 1994
Solitude, 1994 (novella)
Unlocking the Air, and Other Stories, 1996
Tales from Earthsea, 2001
The Birthday of the World, and Other Stories, 2002
Changing Planes, 2003

OTHER LITERARY FORMS

Ursula K. Le Guin (UR-sew-lah kay leh-GWIHN) is best known for her novels, especially the Earthsea books, which include *A Wizard of Earthsea* (1968), *The Tombs of Atuan* (1971), *The Farthest Shore* (1972), and *Tehanu: The Last Book of Earthsea* (1990). Other well-known novels include *The Left Hand of Darkness* (1969), *The Lathe of Heaven* (1971), *The Dispossessed: An Ambiguous Utopia* (1974), *Always Coming Home* (1985), and the four linked novellas *Four Ways to Forgiveness* (1995). She also published poetry, including *Wild Angels* (1975), *Hard Words and Other Poems* (1981), and *Going Out with Peacocks and Other Poems* (1994). *The Language of the Night: Essays on Fantasy and Science Fiction* (1979) and

Dancing at the Edge of the World: Thoughts on Words, Women, and Places (1988) are important collections of her critical writing. Le Guin edited *The Norton Book of Science Fiction: North American Science Fiction, 1960-1990* (1993) and *Steering the Craft: Exercises and Discussions on Story Writing for the Lone Navigator or the Mutinous Crew* (1998) and translated *Tao Te Ching: A Book About the Way and the Power of the Way* (1997).

ACHIEVEMENTS

Ursula K. Le Guin is recognized as a leading American writer of science fiction and fantasy. Her short stories, especially "The Ones Who Walk Away from Omelas," winner of a 1974 Hugo Award, often appear in college literature anthologies. Le Guin has received many awards and honors for her work. *The Left Hand of Darkness* and *The Dispossessed* received both the Nebula and Hugo Awards. Volumes of the Earthsea books earned awards for adolescent literature, including the *Boston Globe*/Horn Book Award for *A Wizard of Earthsea*, a Newbery Honor Book Citation for *The Tombs of Atuan*, and the National Book Award for Children's Literature for *The Farthest Shore*. Her other awards include a Hugo Award for *The Word for World Is Forest*, a Nebula and Jupiter Award in 1975 for "The Day Before the Revolution," and Jupiter Awards for *The Dispossessed* and "The Diary of the Rose." She was given a Gandalf Award in 1979, an American Book Award nomination and the Janet Heidinger Kafka Prize for Fiction for *Always Home* in 1986, and Nebula Awards for *Tehanu* in 1991 and for *Solitude* in 1995.

BIOGRAPHY

Ursula Kroeber was born on October 21, 1929, in Berkeley, California, the daughter of anthropologist Alfred L. Kroeber and author Theodora Kroeber. She received her B.A. from Radcliffe College in 1951 and her M.A. from Columbia University in 1952. While on a Fulbright Fellowship in Paris in 1953, she married Charles A. Le Guin. They had three children: daughters Elisabeth and Caroline and a son, Theodore. She taught French at Mercer University and the University of Idaho before settling in Portland, Oregon, in 1959. In 1962, she began publishing fantasy and science fiction. In addition to writing, she has been active in the Democratic Party, in writing workshops, and in tai chi chuan, a Chinese form of exercise.

ANALYSIS

As literary scholars and critics give more attention to fantasy and science fiction, Ursula K. Le Guin attracts a large share of their interest, because she creates possible worlds that cast an informative light on perennial human problems, she explores gender issues that make her fiction popular among feminist readers, and she is precise and powerful in her use of language.

Ursula K. Le Guin (Bettmann/CORBIS)

When Le Guin writes about her craft and her works, she often refers to Jungian psychology and Daoist philosophy as major components of her worldview. In her 1975 essay "The Child and the Shadow," Le Guin uses Jungian psychology to support her contention that fantasy is "the language of the night," an important means by which the collective unconscious speaks to the growing individual. In Le Guin's understanding of Jungian thought, consciousness, the part of the self that can be expressed in everyday language, emerges from the unconscious as a child matures. The individual's unconscious is shared in its essentials with all other humans and so is called the collective unconscious.

To become an adult, an individual must find ways of realizing the greatest potential of the unconscious. For Le Guin, these are summed up in the recognition by the individual that on unconscious levels, he or she is identical with all other humans. This recognition releases the irrational forces of social binding, such as compassion, love, creativity, and the sense of belonging to the human community. A major problem in achieving this recognition is learning to deal with "the shadow." Choosing to be one person involves choosing not to be other persons whom one could be. Both the positive and the negative choices must be maintained to sustain an identity; the negative choices become one's shadow. The process of achieving adulthood is blocked by the shadow, an unconscious antiself with which one must deal in order to take possession of the rest of the unconscious.

For Le Guin, a child becomes an adult when he or she is able to cease projecting evil impulses onto others and to recognize that these impulses are part of the self. This process, she believes, is symbolically represented in the many fairy tales and fantasies in which an animal helps the protagonist to discover and attain his true identity. Such stories speak to the unconscious, telling the child by means of myth and symbol how to achieve wholeness of self.

Le Guin's writings tend to equate Daoism, a Chinese philosophy expressed about two thousand years ago in the *Dao De Jing*, with Jungian psychology. This goal of wholeness, as expressed in the Circle of Life or in the yin and yang symbol of Daoist philosophy, is a recurrent theme in her fiction. The Circle of Life is a diagram of the dynamic relationship between being and nonbeing in the universe. Le Guin celebrates the balancing of such oppositions.

This metaphysic leads to an ethic of passive activity. All acts in the world of being imply their opposites, the assertion of being activating the potential for nonbeing of the end one seeks. Acts of coercion aimed at controlling human behavior are especially prone to produce equal and opposite reactions. Therefore, Le Guin's successful characters do not try to influence people's actions by direct persuasion or by force but rather by being models of the desired activity.

Le Guin's science fiction differs from her fantasy and psychomyths in that the distinguishing feature of the story's world is technology rather than magic. Her best science-fiction stories accept the unique technology as a given and center on fully realized characters coming to terms with the problems or implications of that technology. "The Eye Altering" recounts the struggle of colonists trying to adjust to a new planet that does not quite mesh with their metabolism, especially the difficulties they encounter when they discover that they are bearing children who, in fact, are better suited to this new planet than to Earth. In "The Diary of the Rose," the psychoscope, a therapeutic tool, allows a form of mind reading. An apprentice analyst confronts the problem of how to treat a patient who seems perfectly sane but who is accused of political deviation. Several of Le Guin's best science-fiction stories became the seeds of later novels or developed in relation to her novels. "Winter's King" led to *The Left Hand of Darkness*. Written after *The Dispossessed*, "The Day Before the Revolution" is about the death of Odo, the woman who founded Odonianism, the anarchist philosophy of the Anarres society in *The Dispossessed*. In "The New Atlantis," Le Guin combines psychomyth and science fiction. While a future America sinks into the sea under the weight of political tyranny and ecological sin, a mythical new world awakens and rises from the sea. In each of these stories, the fates of fully realized characters are more central than the science-fiction settings and technology.

Though Le Guin's stories nearly always contain multiple layers of meaning that repay rereading, they are usually also engaging and entertaining on first reading. She interests the reader in her characters or she sets up her problems in images and symbols that stimulate the imagination and lead to speculation. Many of her stories are also witty. Sometimes the wit is broad, as in "The Author of the Acacia Seeds," which tells of efforts to translate the writings of ants. Sometimes, her wit is more subtle, as in "Sur," an account of the "real" first expedition to the South Pole, made by a group of women who kept their feat a secret to avoid embarrassing Roald Amundsen.

This brief account cannot deal with many of Le Guin's themes. She has shown significant interest in feminism and other political and social themes. Her family background in anthropology contributed to her interest in imagining cultures and contact between alien cultures. Over the span of her career, she has tended to move from more traditional forms of fantasy and science fiction toward imagining alternative cultures and their interactions.

"DARKNESS BOX"

Several of these aspects of Le Guin's worldview appear in "Darkness Box," one of her early publications. "Darkness Box" is a fairy tale/allegory that takes place in a world of cycles. In this world, time does not pass. There is no source of light, though it is always midmorning. Certain events repeat themselves exactly and perpetually. A young prince rides with his army to the seashore to repel an invasion by his rebel brother. The brother always comes from the sea; he is always defeated and killed. At the same time that he leaves, the prince returns to the palace of his father, who had exiled the brother. The prince always rides out again with his army to meet the restored and returning invaders. Into this cycle intrudes what appears to be a unique set of events that are sequential rather than cyclical. The son of a witch finds a box on the shore and gives it to the prince. The king recognizes it as a box he cast into the sea and warns the prince not to open it. The prince's longing for music that ends, for wholeness, leads him to knock the box open and restrains him from closing it. Darkness spills out, the darkness of shadows and their opposite, the sun. He begins to experience conflict, death, and the passing of time. Having achieved a shadow, he has entered into time and being.

Read as a Jungian myth of maturation, the tale represents the collective unconscious as a place of unrealized potentials for identity. The prince is a potential ego, his exiled brother a potential shadow, their endless battle a portent of the struggle consciousness must undergo to create a mature personality. Opening the box that lets out darkness becomes a symbolic representation of the birth of the ego, the entrance into time, and self-creation with real consequences for the self, such as the creation of a shadow and the acceptance of mortality.

Read as a Daoist allegory, the tale represents nonbeing, the dark half of the Circle of Life, as a place of unrealized potential for being. Nonbeing is timeless and changeless yet full of possibilities. In this reading, opening the box realizes some of the potentials for being. A real world begins, a world of cause and effect in time, a world bounded by nonbeing as reflected in the introduction of true death. Though not all of Le Guin's stories so directly communicate the Jungian and Daoist aspects of her worldview, many become richer and deeper when viewed in this context.

Le Guin defines fantasy as the manipulation of myths and symbols to communicate with the unconscious. Some of her fantasies she called psychomyths: "more or less surrealistic tales, which share with fantasy the quality of taking place outside any history, outside of time, in that region of the living mind which . . . seems to be without spatial or temporal limits at all."

"The Ones Who Walk Away from Omelas"

"The Ones Who Walk Away from Omelas" is probably Le Guin's best-known psychomyth. This story combines fiction and essay in an unusual way. The narrator describes the beautiful and happy city of Omelas beginning its summer festival. Gradually, she reveals that this is an imagined city. The narrator cautions the reader against doubting that a utopian city filled with joy might also be a place of dynamic and meaningful life. The reader is encouraged to follow his or her own fancy in imagining a truly happy city. She suggests attitudes toward technology, sexual pleasure, and drug use that would foster happiness, then returns to a description of the festival.

Guessing that the reader will be skeptical even after helping to imagine this wonderful city, she then reveals two more facts. First, the happiness of Omelas depends upon one small child being locked forever in a dark room, deprived of all comfort and affection. Any effort to provide care and justice for that child would destroy the happiness of Omelas. Second, there are people who cannot bear to accept their happiness under this condition. These are the ones who walk away. The narrator cannot tell where they are going, perhaps because a place where there really is "justice for all" is so hard to imagine.

Structured as a mutually imagined myth, this story seems designed to provoke examination of the tendencies of human imagination. Why must people find a dark side of beauty in order to believe in it? Why is happiness unimaginable without suffering? How do people manage to find ways of accepting life under these terms? Why are some people unable to accept that living inevitably entails gaining from the suffering of others? What would justice for all entail? Would it really be antithetical to happiness? While this story is somewhat different in form from her more typical fantasies, it seems to share with them the central aim of fantasy Le Guin described in "The Child and the Shadow": to reduce the reader's inclination "to give up in despair or to deny what he sees, when he must face the evil that is done in the world, and the injustices and grief and suffering that we must all bear, and the final shadow at the end of all."

A Fisherman of the Inland Sea

The importance of imagination in achieving balance continues in *A Fisherman of the Inland Sea*. The volume begins with an eleven-page introduction in which Le Guin dichotomizes readers into "us"--science fiction readers--and people who cannot or will not program their videocassette recorders (VCRs), which is how she characterizes those who spurn the genre. She also explains thematic aspects of the eight stories in the collection, the last three of which are space exploration fantasies that involve imagined cultures and technologies she has previously developed, namely the Hanish world and the ansible. She adds to these a time-space device called a "churten" drive, which allows instantaneous transmission of matter across any points in space.

"The First Contact with the Gorgonids" is a straight-forward "justice served" narrative that explains how the much-abused housewife, Annie Laurie Debree, became the hero of Grong Crossing, at the expense of her difficult husband, Jerry. The second story, "Newton's Sleep," explores the psychological impact of an earth-wide holocaust on the surviving escapees. "Ascent of the North Face" is predicated on the language pun of the title and rolls out in journal-entry style. "The Rock That Changed Things" depicts the evolutionary dynamic of an oppressed race as it attains autonomy, reminiscent of *The Word for World Is Forest*. The fifth story, "The Kerastion," describes a coherent set of cultural behaviors that involve the production of a musical instrument from human flesh. Taken together, these five stories show Le Guin to be varied in approach and treatment and interested in different subjects.

The trilogy of space stories begins with "The Shobies' Story." The Hanish-Gethenian-Human crew of ten take a test flight using a new "churten" drive. Their noninterval "transilence" to a distant location becomes problematic as they seek to interpret their separate realities. They are able to reintegrate into a unified story of their travel only out of a willingness to achieve group harmony. The next test, described in "Dancing to Ganam," involves a smaller crew of Cetians and Hanish that includes Dalzul, a charismatic leader. Their arrival in another world, where they are treated as gods, ends in Dalzul's sacrifice, apparently as a willed conclusion from the collective group. The collection's title story, "Another Story: Or, A Fisherman of the Inland Sea," continues the "churten" theme. The narrator, Hideo, begins with the fable of a fisherman who catches the attention of the sea king's daughter, agrees to stay with her for a night, then finds that more than one hundred years have passed in the short time of his absence. Hideo leaves home and a nascent love interest, Isidri, in order to study temporal physics. Eventually, he becomes disjunct in time, when experimenting with the churten drive, and arrives back at home fifteen years earlier, just after he had decided to leave. Instead, he chooses to stay and follow a different path. Hideo then accepts the love of Isidri but wonders what has happened in the temporal paradox of his future.

CHANGING PLANES

Changing Planes is a collection of light, comic, and satirical stories unified by a pun on "planes": airplanes and levels or realms of existence. The opening sketch presents Sita Dulip stranded in an airport by delays and cancellations. Ill fed, uncomfortable, frustrated, and bored, "she discovers that, by a mere kind of twist and a slipping bend, easier to do than to describe, she can go anywhere--be anywhere--because she is *already between planes*." Sita could be a hotel maid or a heart surgeon; she is everywoman, indeed every person.

One of the most intriguing stories in the collection, "The Social Dreaming of the Frin," describes a plane on which the natives synchronize their rapid-eye-movement (REM) sleep and share dreams. Because Frinthians, including the sentient animals, can send and receive all kinds of dreams, including wish fulfillments, stress dreams, erotic dreams, nightmares and even visions of the future, their dreams are collective and chaotic. The mechanism of dream sharing is not understood but the effect of dream sharing--far greater than the individually perceived collective unconscious --is to create an extraordinarily close communal bond. Like much of Le Guin's fiction, "The Social Dreaming of the Frin" depends not on the patterned, conflict-driven plot common in popular fiction and not on well- developed characters, but instead on thoughtful exploration of an idea and an analytical, almost anthropological depiction of a society or a culture.

"Great Joy," a satirical story, tells of a plane recently colonized by Texas entrepreneurs, who persuade or coerce the natives of a newly discovered plane into staffing a collection of crudely commercial islands. Chief among them is Christmas Island, where the commercial Christmas season lasts through every hour of every day of the year. Frost and snow decorate the roofs and windows of the buildings in a tropical setting, and Santa again and again climbs down a chimney while Rudolph's nose blinks and in another setting the Star of Bethlehem shines over the manger. Other Great Joy ™ Islands include Fourth of July Island, Easter Island, Hollo-Een! Island, and New Year's Island, with its perpetual party and with the Times Square ball descending every twelve--or every six--hours. (Perhaps understandably the entrepreneurs did not develop a Labor Day Island, although they did consider Isla Cinco de Mayo, Kwanza! Afric-Island, and even, although briefly, Têt Everlasting.

In "Great Joy," as in "Sita Dulip's Method," Le Guin satirizes the tastelessness and immorality of corporate America and, indeed, of the corporate mentality generally. In "The Ire of the Veksi" and "Woeful Tales from Mahigul," she takes on the unfortunate human predilection for violence. The latter of these two stories presents a peaceful plane with a bloody history, ranging from the atrocities of a megalomaniac tyrant to a generations-long war over land bordering a peaceful trout stream, which ends up totally destroying not only the trout but also the very land that was the object of contention. One is reminded of the U. S. Army public relations officer in Vietnam who explained quite earnestly that it was necessary to destroy a village in order to save it.

Other stories in *Changing Planes* employ a comic technique reminiscent of W. S. Gilbert's topsy-turvy fantasies. "The Island of the Immortals," for instance, like the classical myth of Tithonus, shows immortality not to be the blessing that many people imagine but rather a terrible misfortune. "The Royals of Hegn" presents a plane in which almost every family is of royal blood and quite often connected to more than one royal family. Only one family, the Gats, are commoners, and hence the details of their lives--especially the scandalous details--draw widespread and intense interest, much as the lives of the royal family in Great Britain do on a plane full of commoners. While not devoid of serious intent, *Changing Planes* is a lighthearted collection, as its punning title suggests.

THE BIRTHDAY OF THE WORLD

In *The Birthday of the World*, Le Guin addresses familiar themes: the clash of cultures, apocalyptic militarism, cultural evolution on generation ships in space, and, repeatedly, love and the relationship between the sexes. The title story of the collection involves a culture in which a dynasty of married sister and brother reign jointly as God Herself and God Himself. The harmony of this culture is interrupted first by civil war and then by the advent of astronauts aboard a disabled spaceship, and things fall apart. However, the story ends on a note of hope.

The last story in the collection, "Paradises Lost," long enough to be a novella, also treats religious conflict--this time not the end but rather the birth and growth of a religion. The story follows the cultural evolution of generations of people in a self-sustaining community bound, necessarily at less than the speed of light, on a large spaceship from Earth to an Earth-like planet far off in interstellar space. Many travelers who never knew Earth and may die before reaching the ship's destination understandably come to value the journey above life on any planet and make of this conviction a new religion; other travelers remain true to the original mission. Le Guin's exploration of the conflict between the two value systems is gripping and insightful.

Among the love stories in this collection, "Mountain Ways" is of interest because it combines Le Guin's concern with gender roles and alternative sexuality. The characters in this story live in a culture in which marriage is a complex institution involving two men and two women. The protagonist of the story is constrained by circumstance to initiate a marriage in which one of the male roles is filled by a woman masquerading as a man. Le Guin, in her chatty introduction, calls the story a comedy of manners--true enough--but a comedy that threatens for a moment to become something far more grim. The stories of *The Birthday of the World* are without exception sensitive and provocative.

OTHER MAJOR WORKS

LONG FICTION: *Planet of Exile*, 1966; *Rocannon's World*, 1966; *City of Illusions*, 1967; *A Wizard of Earthsea*, 1968; *The Left Hand of Darkness*, 1969; *The Lathe of Heaven*, 1971; *The Tombs of Atuan*, 1971; *The Farthest Shore*, 1972; *The Dispossessed: An Ambiguous Utopia*, 1974; *Very Far Away from Anywhere Else*, 1976; *Leese Webster*, 1979; *Malafrena*, 1979; *The Beginning Place*, 1980; *The Eye of the Heron*, 1983; *Always Coming Home*, 1985; *Tehanu: The Last Book of Earthsea*, 1990; *Searoad: Chronicles of Klatsand*, 1991; *Four Ways to Forgiveness*, 1995 (four linked novellas); *The Telling*, 2000; *The Other Wind*, 2001; *Lavinia*, 2008.

POETRY: *Wild Angels*, 1975; *Hard Words, and Other Poems*, 1981; *In the Red Zone*, 1983; *Wild Oats and Fireweed: New Poems*, 1988; *Blue Moon over Thurman Street*, 1993; *Going Out with Peacocks, and Other Poems*, 1994; *Sixty Odd: New Poems*, 1999; *Incredible Good Fortune: New Poems*, 2006.

NONFICTION: *From Elfland to Poughkeepsie*, 1973; *The Language of the Night: Essays on Fantasy and Science Fiction*, 1979 (Susan Wood, editor); *Dancing at the Edge of the World: Thoughts on Words, Women, and Places*, 1988; *Napa: The Roots and Springs of the Valley*, 1989; *Steering the Craft: Exercises and Discussions on Story Writing for the Lone Navigator or the Mutinous Crew*, 1998; *The Wave in the Mind: Talks and Essays on the Writer, the Reader, and the Imagination*, 2004; *Cheek by Jowl*, 2009.

TRANSLATIONS: *The Twins, the Dream/Las Gemelas, el sueño*, 1996 (with Diana Bellessi); *Tao Te Ching: A Book About the Way and the Power of the Way*, 1997 (of Laozi); *Kalpa Imperial: The Greatest Empire That Never Was*, 2003 (by Angéla Gorodischer); *Selected Poems of Gabriela Mistral*, 2003.

CHILDREN'S LITERATURE: *The Adventure of Cobbler's Rune*, 1982; *The Visionary*, 1984; *A Visit from Dr. Katz*, 1988; *Catwings*, 1988; *Solomon Leviathan's 931st Trip Around the World*, 1988; *Catwings Return*, 1989; *Fire and Stone*, 1989; *A Ride on the Red Mare's Back*, 1992; *Wonderful Alexander and the Catwings*, 1994; *Tales of the Catwings*, 1997; *Tom Mouse and Ms. Howe*, 1998; *Tom Mouse*, 1998; *Jane on Her Own: A Catwings Tale*, 1999; *More Tales of the Catwings*, 2000; *Gifts*, 2004; *Voices*, 2006; *Powers*, 2007.

EDITED TEXTS: *Norton Book of Science Fiction: North American Science Fiction, 1960-1990*, 1993; *Selected Stories of H. G. Wells*, 2005.

BIBLIOGRAPHY

Atwood, Margaret. "The Queen of Quinkedom." *The New York Review of Books* 49, no. 14 (2002): 23. This review of *The Birthday of the World* is the appreciation of one highly accomplished author for the work of another. Atwood asserts the validity of science fiction in general and the artistry of Le Guin in particular. Atwood appreciates *The Birthday of the World* story by story.

Bittner, James W. *Approaches to the Fiction of Ursula K. Le Guin*. Ann Arbor, Mich.: UMI Research Press, 1984. This author discusses both Le Guin's short stories and novels, making connections among her works to show how certain themes are apparent in all of them.

Bucknall, Barbara J. *Ursula K. Le Guin*. New York: Frederick Ungar, 1981. The main emphasis in this book is a discussion of Le Guin's novels, mainly in chronological order. It does include one chapter devoted to her short fiction.

Collins, Jerre. "Leaving Omelas: Questions of Faith and Understanding." *Studies in Short Fiction* 27 (Fall, 1990): 525-535. Argues that "The Ones Who Walk Away from Omelas" can be read either as a religious allegory of the "suffering servant" or as an allegory of western capitalism; however, rejection of the capitalist exploitation story undermines the redemption story. Thus, Le Guin indirectly supports the scapegoat theodicy she tries to undermine.

Cummins, Elizabeth. *Understanding Ursula K. Le Guin*. Columbia: University of South Carolina Press, 1990. An analysis of Le Guin's work emphasizing the different worlds she has created (Earthsea, the Hanish World, Orsinia, and the West Coast) and how they provide the structure for all of her fiction.

De Bolt, Joe, ed. *Ursula K. Le Guin: Voyager to Inner Lands and to Outer Space*. Port Washington, N.Y.: Kennikat Press, 1979. This volume is a collection of critical essays that discusses Le Guin's work from a variety of perspectives, including those of anthropology, sociology, science, and Daoist philosophy.

Kaler, Anne K. "'Carving in Water': Journey/Journals and the Images of Women's Writings in Ursula Le Guin's 'Sur.'" *Literature, Interpretation, Theory* 7 (1997): 51-62. Claims that Le Guin's story "Sur" provides a cleverly coded map for women striving to be professional writers; to illustrate the paths that women writers must take into the tundras ruled by male writers, she uses the devices of disorder, dislocation, and reversal in the journey/journal.

Reid, Suzanne Elizabeth. *Presenting Ursula K. Le Guin*. New York: Twayne, 1997. This critical biography helps young readers to understand how Le

Guin's childhood, family, and life have helped to shape her work.

Spivack, Charlotte. *Ursula K. Le Guin.* Boston: Twayne, 1984. Begins with a brief chronology of important personal and professional milestones in Le Guin's life up to 1981 and then examines her background and her literary contributions. Includes annotated references, primary and secondary bibliographies, and an index.

Sturgis, Susanna J. "Alternative Universes." *The Women's Review of Books*, XXI (November, 2003): 15. Sturgis concludes that Le Guin's stories provide her readers not only with pictures of an imagined existence but also with a deeper understanding of themselves and their own world.

Walsh, William. "I Am a Woman Writer; I Am a western Writer: An Interview with Ursula Le Guin." *The Kenyon Review*, n.s. 17 (Summer/Fall, 1995): 192-205. Le Guin discusses such topics as the genre of science fiction, her readership, the feminist movement, women writers, and the Nobel Prize.

White, Donna R. *Dancing with Dragons: Ursula K. Le Guin and the Critics.* Columbia, S.C.: Camden House, 1999. Part of the Studies in English and American Literature, Linguistics, and Culture series, this volume examines Le Guin's works and critical reaction to them.

Terry Heller; Eunice Pedersen Johnston and
Scott Vander Ploeg
Updated by David W. Cole

J. ROBERT LENNON

Born: Easton, Pennsylvania; January 1, 1970

PRINCIPAL SHORT FICTION

Pieces for the Left Hand: One Hundred Anecdotes, 2005

OTHER LITERARY FORMS

Although J. Robert Lennon has written a great deal of short fiction in addition to *Pieces for the Left Hand*, he is probably best known for his novels. In addition to writing traditional forms of the novel and short story, Lennon maintains an active Internet blog and has published many essays, humor pieces, photographs, and reviews online and in other publications. Lennon self-published an e-book containing some of these and made still others available free on his Web site.

ACHIEVEMENTS

J. Robert Lennon's mainstream acclaim began in 1998 with a Barnes and Noble Discover Great New Writers Award for *The Light of Falling Stars* (1997). Soon after, his short story "The Fool's Proxy" was selected for publication in *Prize Stories, 2000: The O.*

Henry Awards; later, another short-story series, "Eight Pieces for the Left Hand," was reprinted in *Best American Short Stories, 2005*, before later inclusion in the collection *Pieces for the Left Hand*. Lennon has published dozens of uncollected short stories in such journals as *Fiction, Granta, Epoch,* and *McSweeney's* and in such magazines as *Playboy, Harper's,* and *The New Yorker*.

BIOGRAPHY

John Robert Lennon was born in 1970 in Easton, Pennsylvania, and raised in Phillipsburg, New Jersey. Lennon's interest in literature began early; as a young adult, he was absorbed in science fiction and horror novels, beginning a lifelong interest in genre fiction. In 1992, Lennon earned a B.A. in English from the University of Pennsylvania in Philadelphia. Following his undergraduate degree, Lennon moved to Missoula, Montana, and attended the University of Montana, completing an M.F.A. in creative writing in 1995. Lennon and his wife, author Rhiann Ellis, moved from Missoula to Ithaca, New York, in 1997. Lennon became an associate professor at Cornell University, where he has taught creative writing to both undergraduate and graduate students. In addition to writing and teaching, Lennon is an instrumentalist and composer; he has recorded solo albums under the name Inverse Room: *Simulacrum* (2002); *Pieces for the Left Hand* (2005), a companion piece for the short-story collection of the same name; and *American Recluse* (2007). He has recorded an album as part of the Bemus Point called *Infra Dig* (2005). In addition, Lennon has held several photography exhibitions. He and his wife settled in Ithaca, New York, with their two sons.

ANALYSIS

In terms of subject matter, J. Robert Lennon's work is extremely varied; he handles with equal proficiency literary-leaning fiction, such as "The Fool's Proxy," the uncollected "Three Cats and Five Women," and "Cloud," and comic, genre-inspired pieces, such as "Zombie Dan" and "Cul-de-Sac." The shorter near-anecdotes of *Pieces for the Left Hand* are probably his best-known short fiction. All of Lennon's fiction shares an interest, as one of his characters puts it in "Zombie Dan," of "how very much peculiarity the world [seems] capable of absorbing." The premises of Lennon's stories often involve chance, coincidence, and seemingly random events. Many times Lennon's characters are in the grip of loss, loneliness, or fear when these random events strike; the events initially seem insignificant, but they significantly affect Lennon's characters and their interpersonal relationships. These peculiar and uncanny situations may take place in small towns or in rural settings, where the drama is may be largely hidden from observers, outsiders, family, loved ones, and the principal characters themselves. In addition to exploring the unseen drama of everyday life, Lennon's work often exposes the flimsiness of self-identity; his characters aspire to be or perceive themselves in a certain way, but end up realizing that their persona is mere artifice or wishful thinking. Humor suffuses much of Lennon's short fiction as well, though it usually has a sharp edge; often, the unconventional situations in which his characters are entrenched are laughable on the surface, but for the characters are the result of, or are attempts to navigate, deep psychic pain, or to find closure for unresolved conflicts in their past. Lennon's work overall is an exploration of the human condition, told humorously, compassionately, and believably.

Though at times the situations his characters find themselves in are outlandish, Lennon suffuses them with charity and humanity, and his stories often end not with a blatant catharsis or epiphany but with a subtle, believable nudge toward them. That nudge toward understanding often enough includes a realization, or a resignation, that the past cannot ever be fully put to rest.

"THE FOOL'S PROXY"

Originally published in *Harper's* and designated an O. Henry Prize Story in 2000, "A Fool's Proxy" is set in the years following World War II and centers on Grant Person, a young man who leaves his family's ranch, setting out for New York City to see the Atlantic Ocean. Grant's experience leaving his isolated home reveals his ignorance and naïveté toward the outside world. As Grant leaves his hometown by train, his thinly conceived "proxy" identity begins to be revealed as well: Grant is posing as a war veteran, an identity that he unconvincingly presents to people he meets. As he embarks on the first leg of his journey toward Chicago, his family's legacy of death and tragedy is explored: His infant brother Wesley fell into a coma and died at home; his six-year-old brother Robert died from an accidental shotgun wound; his brother Thornton, the real war veteran, died at sea; his brother Edwin committed suicide. Grant decides eventually to head to Atlantic City after overhearing some talk of its carefree, carnivalesque atmosphere. He arrives there nearly penniless and, after a few days, convinces the owner of a sideshow to let him care for sideshow owner's pet parrot in return for a paltry wage. It becomes clear soon enough that Grant's Atlantic City existence is untenable; it seems poised to end soon after the story's conclusion, during which Grant is on the beach, watching soldiers returning from overseas come ashore and pretend to assault the vacationers there as if landing in Normandy. Grant's pain, loss, and loneliness hit him with real physical force, and he realizes that although he would rather die than go back home, going back home is inevitable.

"The Fool's Proxy" is an excellent example of Lennon's literary fiction; the main character, Grant, tries to escape his past--the tragedy of losing his brothers and the isolation of life in a small town--and discovers that his history will follow him wherever he goes. Grant not only tries to escape his origins but also tries to escape himself, another theme common to Lennon's work. Grant's attempt at self-reinvention as a veteran and an unmoored man seeking his luck and fortune is ultimately shown to be futile. Grant's short time in Atlantic City, though he is surrounded by people, is disconnected and uncomfortable. Even as he stumbles zombielike through his time there, it is clear that there will be no comfort or fulfillment. As in many of Lennon's stories, seemingly random, even slightly comic, events and situations propel Grant's final realization, including Grant's experience begging a job from a carnie to spend his nights with a parrot in a flophouse room. These comic elements make Grant's situation all the more poignant; even in romanticized, postwar Atlantic City, there will be no true happiness or reinvention for him.

PIECES FOR THE LEFT HAND

Pieces for the Left Hand, originally published in the United Kingdom in 2005 and reprinted for American audiences in 2009, is subtitled, "One Hundred Anecdotes," and indeed, few of the stories are longer than two pages. The stories, told in first person by an unnamed wanderer and observer, chronicle the events in a small, upstate New York town reminiscent of Ithaca. The collection is broken up into seven sections, each loosely delineating the subject matter of the stories therein. The style of the collection is that of short, anecdotal essays; the subject matter is fictional; and the prose is plain, clear, and expository. Like all of Lennon's work, however, the anecdotes in *Pieces for the Left Hand* focus on his characters' inner-workings--their reactions to loss or loneliness, their fears or paranoia, their conception of self--and the random, often comic or uncanny events that reveal the characters' hidden selves to themselves or to the people close to them. The stories in *Pieces for the Left Hand* also traffic in a good deal of irony and inflict on some characters what could be thought of as karmic comeuppance--physical, mental, or emotional.

Several critics have noted that *Pieces for the Left Hand*, although composed of very short stories, has a cumulative, novelistic effect. If this is the case, the main character of *Pieces for the Left Hand* as a whole is the fictional town itself, comprised of its inhabitants and their stories; in this way, typical of Lennon's sensibility, what would appear at face value to be a normal, wholesome, straightforward, all-American town proves that it has a secret, unknown life that it cannot escape and that refuses to be entirely contained, like a family history or like the subconscious. Just as his characters cannot escape their origins, the town in which the hundred anecdotes take place cannot escape its secrets, no matter how many subdivisions, malls, or manicured lawns spring up on top of it.

"THE PIPELINE"

The narrator's town university decides to handle its high summer cooling costs through a system that works by diverting water from a nearby lake through a system of pipes that eventually ends up in the walls of the college's classrooms and cools the air. Soon after construction begins, a group of students discovers the giant, unattached pipes: The school end has not yet been connected to a pump, and the lake end not yet to the lake. The students stumble upon this wonderful amusement park-style ride, and they don helmets and swimsuits and ride down the pipe on wheeled pallets and land in the lake below. Later that summer, the students disappear from their summer classes, and their bodies are eventually found in a pump station at the bottom of the lake; the lake side of the construction had been finished before the college side, unbeknownst to them. Construction is halted indefinitely. "The Pipeline" showcases the sinister, tragic side of life in Lennon's fictional town: In the pursuit of innocent fun, students die what can be assumed awful deaths. Although it is unclear if the pipes remain as half-constructed monuments, for the inhabitants of the town who remember the incident, the lake will always hold a reminder of the tragedy and of the lost possibility of the youths. Even when life returns to normal, as it inevitably does--as a ripple stitches itself back together on the glassy surface of a lake--knowledge and memory inescapably lie beneath.

"SHORTCUT"

The narrator describes falling asleep while driving on a country highway and waking suddenly to find himself on an interstate. After finding a motel and getting his bearings, he meets a woman at the hotel coffee shop over breakfast who will become his wife. Later, while looking at a map, he discovers the country road and the interstate were parallel and sixty miles apart, and he has no memory of crossing the intervening space or even how to do so. The narrator does not tell his wife for years, and when he does, she casually dismisses his version of the story and insists he must have found a shortcut. "Shortcut" has at its center Lennon's trope of the unexplainable or the uncanny completely altering the course of a character's life, at least in hindsight; whatever happened, the narrator was not aware of the pivotal actions that led him to his wife and the happiness of his later years. In stories such as "Shortcut," Lennon reveals that often lives are dictated more by chance than by intention or best-laid plans; in this story, at least, such seeming predestination seems to have been in the narrator's favor.

"Deaf Child Area"

The narrator and his wife, a young couple expecting their first child, rent a house where a family with a deaf daughter used to live and had erected a yellow cautionary sign near the road which read "deaf child area." After living there for some time, the sign begins to make the narrator and his wife irrationally uneasy and sleepless, as if the sign could wreak some unknown harm on their unborn child. The wife asks the husband to remove it. He does so, at first merely removing the sign portion, then later going so far as to dig out the post and haul it to a nearby lake. This remedies the couples' unease, and they both sleep well until their child is born healthy and sound. This story subtly points to the irrational, subconscious fear that parents can feel for their children; the couple likely, and the reader certainly, fears the malevolent irony of Lennon's town being directed toward their child. In this world, though there is no reason for their child to be born deaf, it is a real possibility it could be, simply because of the presence of the sign. Though it is not outwardly explored in the story, it is reasonable to assume that some of the couple's fear and unease is social in nature; they are likely disturbed by superstition and the unspoken stigma that "abnormal" people may carry. They worry that the outside world will look at that house and its inhabitants differently, as separate from the "normal" world, even if not with malice.

"Brevity"

As the final story in the collection, "Brevity" relates the story of a novelist in the narrator's town, who writes a thousand-page novel and, upon submitting it to a publisher, is advised to cut it in half. Once she begins cutting, however, she finds it difficult to stop, and ultimately distills her novel to a haiku: "Tiny Upstate town / Undergoes many changes / Nonetheless endures." No magazine will publish the haiku, but the eccentric author prints it on note cards, which she gives away to passersby. "Brevity" is a fitting finale to the collection as a literal exploration of a writer's mission to reduce a story to its barest essentials; it could be argued that Lennon does the same in *Pieces for the Left Hand* as a whole. He condenses the experience of a town and the lives of its inhabitants to their barest, strangest, most mysterious, and haunting components.

Other major works

LONG FICTION: *The Light of Falling Stars*, 1997; *The Funnies*, 1999; *Mailman*, 2003; *Happyland*, 2006 (serialized); *Castle*, 2009.

MISCELLANEOUS: *Video Game Hints, Tricks, and Cheats*, 2010 (e-book includes essays, exercises, riffs, gags, and other incidental writings).

Bibliography

Abell, Stephen. "Small-Town Screwballs and Surprises." *Spectator* (April 2, 2005): 50. Though somewhat unfavorable, this review, which criticizes Lennon's attempt to reduce and distill his subject matter to its barest essentials, reveals interesting thematic trends in the collection.

Bradfield, Scott. "Upstate." *The New York Times Book Review* (May 22, 2009): 17. This review essay provides an overview and discusses prevalent themes in *Pieces for the Left Hand*.

Lingan, John. "J. Robert Lennon: *Pieces for the Left Hand*." *The Review of Contemporary Fiction* 30, no. 1 (Spring, 2010): 261. This review provides an analytical overview of *Pieces for the Left Hand*, likening it to a mix of Sherwood Anderson's *Winesburg, Ohio*(1919) and Yasunari Kawabata's *Tenohira no shōsetsu* (1969; palm-of-the-hand stories).

Alan C. Haslam

JONATHAN LETHEM

Born: Brooklyn, New York; February 19, 1964

PRINCIPAL SHORT FICTION

"*Hugh Merrow,*" 1993
The Wall of the Sky, the Wall of the Eye, 1996
"*Mood Bender,*" 1998
"*Access Fantasy,*" 1998
"*K for Fake,*" 1999
Kafka Americana, 1999 (with Carter Scholz)
"*Martyr and Pesty,*" 2001
This Shape We're In, 2001
Men and Cartoons, 2004
How We Got Insipid, 2006
"*The King of Sentences,*" 2007

OTHER LITERARY FORMS

Jonathan Lethem (LEE-thuhm) has written prolifically and in many forms. One of his essays caused unusual controversy: "The Ecstasy of Influence: A Plagiarism," which appeared in *Harper's* in February, 2007, and which responds to American literary critic Harold Bloom's *The Anxiety of Influence* (1973). Lethem argues that authors should not worry about the "anxiety of influence"--the perceived need to write entirely new, original texts without borrowing from earlier writers, as though an homage or an appreciation means stealing intellectual property: If a wallet is stolen, it remains unavailable to its owner, but downloaded music is still available to the artist and the audience. Lethem tosses off the yoke of anxiety and celebrates "recasting," "situationism, pop art, and appropriationism." In Lethem's view, "appropriation, mimicry, quotation, allusion, and sublimated collaboration consist of a kind of *sine qua non* of the creative act, cutting across all forms and genres in the realm of cultural production." Lethem has written many introductions and forewords, the commissioning of which shows his value in the literary community, and he has edited anthologies that reveal his expansive interest in popular culture.

ACHIEVEMENTS

Jonathan Lethem earned critical acclaim with his first novel, *Gun, with Occasional Music* (1994), which won the 1995 Crawford and Locus Reader Awards for Best First Novel and was nominated for the Nebula Award. Several stories were also nominated for the Nebula. His collection *The Wall of the Sky, the Wall of the Eye* earned the 1997 World Fantasy Award. Lethem's novel *Motherless Brooklyn* (1999) won a National Book Critics Circle Award and achieved mainstream success. In 2003, he published *The Fortress of Solitude*, which became a *New York Times* best seller. In 2005, he received a MacArthur Fellowship, sometimes called a "genius grant." *Newsweek* magazine, in 1997, proclaimed Lethem among the "one hundred people to watch in the next century." Some of his works have been optioned for film adaptation, and many have been translated into a variety of foreign languages.

BIOGRAPHY

Jonathan Allen Lethem was born on February 19, 1964, in Brooklyn, New York, into an artistic family. His father, Richard Brown Lethem, is a painter, and his mother, Judith Lethem, who died when Jonathan Lethem was in his teens, was a political activist. His younger brother Blake is an artist, and his younger sister Mara is a photographer and writer.

Lethem attended the High School of Music and Art, a magnet public alternative high school in New York City boasting many notable alumni. In his youth and teens, Lethem was a voracious reader and enjoyed science fiction; at the age of fifteen he encountered and devoured the works of American science-fiction writer Philip K. Dick. Although Lethem's original intention was to specialize in the visual arts when he attended

Bennington College in Vermont in 1982, he grew more interested in writing and hitchhiked from Denver, Colorado, to Berkeley, California. For many years he worked in bookstores while honing his writing skills.

In 1987, Lethem married writer and artist Shelley Jackson; the marriage ended in divorce, as did a later marriage to Canadian film executive Julia Rosenberg. In 1996, Lethem moved to Brooklyn with his third wife, filmmaker Amy Barrett. He also has spent time in Berwick, Maine.

ANALYSIS

Jonathan Lethem's works are characterized by allusiveness in narrative tone and in theme; his sense of humor can be both broad and dry. His wit is multifaceted: His characters revel in puns, twisted clichés, and the intentional malapropism. His writing rarely uses intentional superficiality, as in the gossipy virtual-reality space of "Forever, Said the Duck." Lethem's early novels, which deftly pay homage to the noir detective genre (*Gun, with Occasional Music*), the post-apocalypse road novel (*Amnesia Moon*, 1995), the Don

Jonathan Lethem (AP Photo/Pat Wellenbach)

DeLillo homage campus comedy (*As She Climbed Across the Table*, 1997), the western (*Girl in Landscape*, 1998), the neurotic amateur detective (*Motherless Brooklyn*, 1999), and others, serve to demonstrate his skills as an adept pasticheur, though his later novels, and especially his short fiction, demonstrate his unique narrative voice.

Lethem's gift for homage appears in his short fiction, too. For example, "K for Fake," an intriguing Kafkaesque story about intellectual property, relies upon the reader's recognition of previous texts: German author Franz Kafka's body of work, the Orson Welles-directed film *F for Fake* (1975), and the real-life lawsuit brought by American artist Margaret Keane against her husband Walter, an event that drew media coverage in 1986.

Among Lethem's major themes are change, communication, maturation, evolution, and the ways that any or all of these can lead to interpersonal problems, especially between the sexes. His stories are salted and peppered with allusions to popular culture.

Some of these issues are dramatized by characters who fear interacting with strangers or who react to strangers bizarrely. For example, in "Sleepy People," a town is, inexplicably, under martial law and army agents try to corral people who are in unwakeable sleep, while others attempt to care for them.

Another story of miscommunication, "The King of Sentences," portrays two youthful managers of a bookstore who worship an author they have dubbed the King of Sentences. They determine to meet him, and after sending postcards and other forms of communication, they visit his town and wait by his post office box for him. The author is ungrateful for this attention (though the text implies that he is an unsuccessful writer) and orders them to meet him in a neutral motel room. The delighted pair follow him and, after baring their souls, he demands that they remove their clothing. They hasten to obey, and even when he rends their clothes so that they cannot safely return outside, they cling together in rapture after the author leaves. In a story about unmitigated and nuanced but unconsciously nuisance-filled fandom, Lethem tells an amusing and erudite tale.

Lethem's fiction often uses a plot structure based on a quest or a mystery, or both. In an early story, "Access Fantasy," a young man realizes that a realtor's advertising video (of an apartment for sale) contains the shadows of a murder, a man strangling a woman, occurring just off-screen; he makes great efforts to find the advertised apartment but winds up putting another young woman in grave danger. In Lethem's tales, there rarely are assured happy endings.

Lethem's minor characters are sometimes comical, but his major characters are fully rounded people who face the challenges of getting through youthful awkwardness and embarrassment, to advance to enlightenment and understanding, to discover maturity, and to learn positive and definitive communication, whether among a handful of friends at a small party or at a large party on the brink of becoming an orgy. The reader might sense that Lethem intentionally is holding back much of the real feelings and therefore seeks, like a detective, clues that will make, for example, enjoying being an avatar, a virtual meaning in a virtual space.

"LIGHT AND THE SUFFERER"

"Light and the Sufferer" is a cautionary tale, in which two brothers need to find a way to explain their actions to each other. They cannot quite accomplish that form of communication in their journey across New York in one hectic day, nor can they figure out the actions or motives of the gadabout extraterrestrials among them. The humans can always offer an excuse for making mistakes; the aliens, Sufferers (a human-given name), offer none. Paul is the older brother of Don, nicknamed "Light," who is a crack addict on the verge of flying to California from New York to start a drug-free, clean life.

Paul loves his brother well but unwisely, because Light keeps postponing the flight and acquires a gun and a booty of cocaine stolen from his dealer. Light refuses to show maturity by sticking to his original plans. He makes a series of bad decisions whose dangers escalate, and while Paul follows ineffectually and with misguided hope, they both become increasingly embroiled in a quest for a better life, although it can end only with Light's death. The tragedy is heralded by the appearance of a Sufferer, one of a pantherlike race of aliens who silently follow troubled humans, and

though Light makes light of its pursuit, Paul endeavors to intervene in his brother's plight.

The story is about failed though loving communication and persuasion. Light is proud of his "hip" acquaintance with the clandestine transactions with dealers. He appreciates his brother Paul, but Light decides to live and die by drugs rather than escape to California.

Young adults enjoy this story because it offers them scenes of living dangerously, demonstrations that their friends and family care about them, and proof that the decisions they make are their own. This tragedy of a failed intervention demonstrates how the older brother tries to save the younger but must hopelessly watch his brother's doom.

THIS SHAPE WE'RE IN

This Shape We're In is the story of an unlikely quest, narrated by a husband and father, Mr. Farbur (his name suggests the acronym FUBAR), who relates that his profession is "garbage hider," who, as that professional position punningly hints at, is an unrepentant alcoholic, and who admits "that there were *things I didn't wish to remember*" (Lethem's italics). Farbur's nominal quest, urged by his wife, is to seek his grown son who has become a beggar in a place called the Eye.

Farbur's real quest, however, is to remember his responsibilities, which he has, for years, drunk to forget, in another stance against maturation. Lethem's narrator is a witty, punning, riffing clown. (When a proselytizer tells Farbur, "In these great times, sir, it is a shame and a sorrow to see a man of your stature and accomplishment leading a band of two on so paltry a mission as that which brought you to our door." Farbur replies, "True, it's barely more than a paltry-raid.")

The title seems, at first glance, to refer to a spiritual or relational situation; the story soon proves that it refers to a physical construct, which is called by its inhabitants the Shape. The areas of the shape are named the stomach, the rump, the eyes, the nose, and so forth. The residents of the Shape do not agree on its actuality: Some believe it is an intergenerational starship whose builders' descendants have forgotten that they are traveling; others believe it is a shelter from an exterior "worldwide catastrophe." Farbur's observations, through one alleged Eye, offer an homage to the film *The Planet of the Apes* (1968): "a vast figurative sculpture, a titan in rotting green copper, jutted at an impossible angle from its place half-swallowed in the sand. The figure was a totem of a woman in a robe and a spiked headdress. She bore a torch to heaven. . . . Seabirds wheeled and clouds tumbled ever so slightly in the sky, but this panorama was a tape loop or I was a monkey's commanding officer," a joke almost as good as Farbur describing himself as looking like Marlon Brandon in *Mutiny on the Apocalypse Now*, a clever conflation of the titles of the 1962 film *Mutiny on the Bounty* and the 1979 film *Apocalypse Now*.

When Farbur finally finds his son, Farbur is given another alleged, entirely black Eye to look through, and Lethem mixes humor with popular culture while showing Farbur to be as immature as his son: "It might have been God's or Big Brother's unblinking eye. It might have been a vidscreen turned off."

One mystery, which the reader must follow clues to solve, surrounds the rise of a "militia craze that's sweeping the Young People of the Shape Today (which) knows no bounds." Farbur's interlocutor replies, "Martial memory," a joke on "partial memory," to which Farbur responds with anger and guilt. As he follows Balkan, his son's friend, the two encounter many military units of youths: "Everywhere troops of one definition or another were massing, being drummed into this or that obscure warlike fervor, whether under the guise of religious or scientific or merely paranoiac revelations provided by up-to-the-minute reports and rumors from the various competing eyes." Farbur and Balkan (whose name suggests the balkanization of this community) also learn of red phones in various places about the Shape, which allegedly lead to Central Command, wherever that might be and whoever might be there.

When Farbur remembers the truth from which he has been hiding, he understands that he *represents* Central Command and that his mission is to gather all the warriors and command them to wage war against the tourists in the fairground field in which the Shape is parked. As bathos goes, this takes the cake--why would anyone build a Trojan horse to infiltrate a park or playground?--but, comically, Farbur finally lurches toward his perceived friends. Again, the acronym FUBAR seems appropriate.

"VIVIAN RELF"

This is the story of two young people who "meet cute" several times, but the young man, Doran, misses his opportunity to befriend Vivian in the serious way in which he would like. They meet at a party, in their twenties, and believe they recognize each other. Doran fires off many questions to Vivian: Where did she attend school? Had she been to summer camp? Do they have friends in common? As the conversation continues, the two gradually realize they were mistaken in that déjà vu feeling. Doran cares profoundly about her, but he and Vivian slip away from each other.

When they meet two years later, at another party, they recognize each other again, and then later, they see each other at a baggage carousel in an airport. Lethem's use of the limited third-person narration allows the reader to view lovable Vivian through Doran's eyes but also limits a full knowledge of Vivian. Doran is happy to see her again, but during their conversation he goes through several emotional states: He is obsessed with her and giddy; after they part, he feels a profound desire to see her again.

Later, he writes a poem for and about her, though he is unsure that he will see her again. This romantic period of his life elaborates his nostalgia and the vision in which he describes Vivian. Therefore, he is startled when, years later, he learns that she has married a colleague in the arts world.

Invited to a dinner by entrepreneur Vander Polymus, Doran is entranced by the many important people in attendance, but Vivian is casual, saying that they have met only once before. Her husband, an arrogant blowhard, demands to know if they had been lovers; Vivian replies calmly in the negative. Doran feels increasingly worse as Vivian reveals that she did not like Doran's friends and has forgotten their other encounters. Doran feels embarrassed and frustrated; he thinks that he "might have known Vivian Relf better than anyone he actually knew," but he is like the character John Marcher in the story *The Beast in the Jungle*, a 1903 novella by American writer Henry James. Like Marcher, Doran learns his real feelings too late. Vivian appears blithely indifferent to him, while Doran's "soul creaked in irrelevant despair." It is a story about lostness and loss.

OTHER MAJOR WORKS

LONG FICTION: *Gun, with Occasional Music*, 1994; *Amnesia Moon*, 1995; *As She Climbed Across the Table*, 1997; *Girl in Landscape*, 1998; *Motherless Brooklyn*, 1999; *The Fortress of Solitude*, 2003; *You Don't Love Me Yet*, 2007; *Chronic City*, 2009.

NONFICTION: *The Disappointment Artist, and Other Essays*, 2005.

EDITED TEXT: *The Vintage Book of Amnesia: An Anthology of Writing on the Subject of Memory Loss*, 2000; *Da Capo Best Music Writing: The Year's Finest Writing on Rock, Pop, Jazz, Country, and More*, 2002 (with Paul Bresnick); *Four Novels of the 1960's*, 2007 (of Philip K. Dick); *Five Novels of the 1960's and 1970's*, 2008 (of Philip K. Dick); *Valis, and Later Novels*, 2009 (of Philip K. Dick).

BIBLIOGRAPHY

Gaffney, Elizabeth. "Jonathan Lethem: Breaking the Barriers Between Genres." *Publishers Weekly* 244, no. 13 (March 30, 1998). This biographical interview focuses on Lethem's first four novels.

Kelleghan, Fiona. "Private Hells and Radical Doubts: An Interview with Jonathan Lethem." *Science Fiction Studies* 25, no. 2 (July 1998): 225-240. Lethem discusses at length his writing style, habits, and philosophies and gives insights into many of his short stories.

Kellogg, Carolyn. "Tales to Tell on Either Coast." *Los Angeles Times*, February 13, 2011, p. E1. Profile of Lethem that recounts his decision to move to the West Coast and how he copes with the differences between New York and Claremont, California, where he has settled with his family.

Peacock, James. "Jonathan Lethem's Genre Evolutions." *Journal of American Studies* 43, no. 3 (December, 2009): 425-440. Describes the theme of evolution in Lethem's first two novels.

Rossi, Umberto. "From Dick to Lethem: The Dickian Legacy, Postmodernism, and Avant-Pop in Jonathan Lethem's *Amnesia Moon*." *Science Fiction Studies* 29, no. 1 (March, 2002): 15-33. Compares Lethem with seminal author Dick.

Schiff, James. "A Conversation with Jonathan Lethem." *The Missouri Review* 29, no. 1 (2006:) 116-134. This interview covers Lethem's parents and favorite writers as influences, the autobiographical impulse, his writing style, and the novels *Motherless Brooklyn* and *The Fortress of Solitude*.

Sharpe, Matthew. "Educating the Imagination: Jonathan Lethem." *Teachers and Writers* 33, no. 5 (May/June, 2002): 23-27. An interview with Lethem that begins with a story about his background as a writer and discusses some of his thoughts on writing and the writing process.

Fiona Kelleghan

JOHN L'HEUREUX

Born: South Hadley, Massachusetts;
   October 26, 1934

PRINCIPAL SHORT FICTION
   Family Affairs, 1974
   Desires, 1981
   Comedians, 1990

OTHER LITERARY FORMS

John L'Heureux (lah-ROO) began his literary career by publishing four volumes of poetry, written while he was a Jesuit. His autobiographical memoir, *Picnic in Babylon: A Jesuit Priest's Journal, 1963-67* (1967), chronicles and analyzes the years of theological study leading to his ordination as a priest. Since leaving the Jesuits in 1971, he has written several novels. The first two, *Tight White Collar* (1972) and *The Clang Birds* (1972), grew out of his experiences in religious life, whereas his later novels, especially *An Honorable Profession* (1991) and *The Handmaid of Desire* (1996), spring from his career in teaching.

ACHIEVEMENTS

Editors of *The Best American Short Stories* and *Prize Stories: The O. Henry Awards* have selected several of John L'Heureux's stories for inclusion in their annuals. He received creative writing fellowships from the National Endowment for the Arts in 1981 and 1986. At Stanford University he won the Dean's Award for Excellence in Teaching in 1983 and again in 1998.

BIOGRAPHY

John Clarke L'Heureux was born in South Hadley, Massachusetts, on October 26, 1934, the second son of Wilfred Joseph L'Heureux, a civil engineer, and his wife Mildred (Clarke) L'Heureux. While attending local schools, he began to write, mainly poetry. Upon graduating from high school, he spent a summer at the National Academy of Theatre Arts before entering Holy Cross College. In 1954, at the end of his sophomore year, he decided "on the grounds of coldest reason" to enter the Society of Jesus because it was "the best and most generous thing" he could do with his life. He began his ascetical training at Shadowbrook, the Jesuit novitiate, in Lenox, Massachusetts. When it burned down, he was sent to Wernersville, Pennsylvania, where he took his perpetual vows of poverty, chastity, and obedience in July, 1956.

In the course of his Jesuit training L'Heureux earned a licentiate in philosophy from Weston College in Massachusetts in 1959 and a licentiate in theology from Woodstock College in Maryland in 1967. He was ordained "a priest forever" on June 11, 1966. By this time his collections of poetry had begun to be published, starting with *Quick as Dandelions* in 1964. After the completion of his theological studies he began work for a doctorate in English at Harvard University, but seeing himself as primarily a creative writer, he left with his master's degree in 1968. While working as an editor for *The Atlantic Monthly*, he decided to leave the Society of Jesus, essentially because of difficulties with his vow of obedience (he wanted to be "his own man"). After being laicized in 1971, he married Joan Polston, a writer, on June 26. In the early 1970's, while he was a visiting professor at Tufts College and Harvard University, he alchemized his Jesuit experiences into two novels and into several short stories that were published in such magazines as *The Atlantic Monthly* and *The New Yorker*.

In 1973, L'Heureux began what would become a long and fruitful academic career at Stanford University. He expeditiously passed through the ranks of assistant professor (1973-1979) and associate professor (1979-1981) to full professor (beginning in 1981), while also serving as the director of the Creative Writing Program (1976-1994). He later became a professor emeritus at Stanford. L'Heureux has also led workshops for the Wallace Stegner Fellows, a program to nourish promising talent, through which he has influenced such writers as Ron Hansen, David Henry Hwang, Kathryn Harrison, Tobias Wolff, and many others. He continued to write novels, including *The Shrine at Altamira* (1992), *The Handmaid of Desire* (1996), *Having Everything*, (1999), and *The Miracle* (2002). Characteristically, he has taken care of life after L'Heureux by composing his own obituary and completing a "posthumous" novel, "Lies."

ANALYSIS

In an analysis of John L'Heureux's short fiction John Gardner compared him to Anton Chekhov, the stodgy old doctor who enjoyed clinically dissecting his characters' desperate desires and destructive loves. On initially encountering L'Heureux's characters, with their mind-forged manacles and emotional cages, imprisoned in a muddled world of hopeless disillusion, a reader might agree with Gardner's assessment, but a deeper reading reveals that above this surface of disorder and despair dwells a transcendent God who may or may not be enjoying the human comedy. For L'Heureux, the cord between the meaningless absurdity of life and the meaningfulness of religious faith is weak and easily frayed, but God is still able to write straight with crooked lines. L'Heureux seems to enjoy making his characters' lives as tortuous as possible, the better to bring out the irony of God, one of his favorite themes. Humans seem to make messes of their lives, and yet his characters, even though they may have lost the sense that anything transcends their troubled existences, somehow muddle through to an encounter with something (someone?) larger and more meaningful than themselves.

L'Heureux's stories, with their caustic insights and wicked wit, have been compared to the works of Iris Murdoch and Muriel Spark, two writers he admires. Despite the bleakness of life detailed in many of his stories, L'Heureux has said that he still believes in God, and he believes even more deeply in the amazing grace that can save the wretches about whom he writes. As a Jesuit priest, he was duty-bound to save the world, to do everything "for the greater glory of God" (Saint

Ignatius of Loyola's motto for the Society of Jesus, which he founded), but as a man of the world L'Heureux has said that he writes for his own salvation, not the world's. He sees his stories as "a pack of lies intended to entertain and illumine and dismay." Nevertheless, he does try to probe the mystery underlying or overarching the few truths he knows for certain, such as, that people carry within themselves the means of their own destruction--or salvation. In his stories he tries to create something good that will help people "appreciate the wonders of another person, or of being alive."

In several of his best-known and most successful stories L'Heureux portrays priests and former priests, whose crises often arise from the conflicts between their sacred and secular lives. His fictional creations often discover an ineradicable egocentricity that lies at the core of even their most spiritual activities. For some critics, L'Heureux's stories about the religious life are a lament for the world he lost when he left the Jesuits. For others, particularly those who have remained in the religious life, his depictions of priests and nuns who are more avid about sex than salvation, more eager for alcoholic spirits than the Holy Spirit, are demeaning and untrue to the lives they have experienced in their service of God. While the priests and nuns of L'Heureux's stories share little common ground with their fictional predecessors in the novels of Georges Bernanos andGraham Greene, or with the film incarnations played by Bing Crosby and Julie Andrews, their lives are not as totally lacking in redeeming spiritual value as some of his detractors contend. In his own defense L'Heureux emphasizes that his duty as a writer is to create people as they really are--on the way to redemption but not there yet.

"FOX AND SWAN"

Judging from interviews and several of his short stories, L'Heureux's break with the Jesuit Order after sixteen years of service occasioned much soul-searching, and it is understandable that he dealt with the feelings generated by this wrenching event, albeit in a transformed way, in some of his stories. Indeed, several of the stories in his first collection, *Family Affairs*, have the religious life as their subject, and for some critics his stories about priests and nuns are more convincing than those with secular protagonists. Martha

Foley selected "Fox and Swan" to appear in *The Best American Short Stories 1972*. The story focuses on Francis Xavier Madden, a Jesuit working for his doctorate at Harvard University, who is agonizing over his vocation (he is called "fox" by a girl who finds his beard "groovy"). He develops an intimate relationship with Caryl Henderson, a fellow doctoral student who is a devout Catholic. While waiting to be dispensed from his vows, Francis feels guilty about their sexual activities, whereas she sees their lovemaking as "the most beautiful thing in the world." Using humor and irony, L'Heureux deals with their carnalities compassionately, particularly in contrasting how a theologian and a red-blooded human being view sexual desires. Another conflict in the story is the decision facing Francis about whether to pursue his doctorate or a career as a creative writer. He is fascinated by an image of swans whose legs are frozen in ice, making them easy prey for voracious foxes, and he writes a story about it. This story resolves one of his problems, because he decides to become a writer, but how many swans will this fox devour to survive?

"THE PRIEST'S WIFE"

This story, subtitled "Thirteen Ways of Looking at a Blackbird," has been anthologized several times and appears in 1980's *Prize Stories: The O. Henry Awards*. It also was an important part of *Desires*, L'Heureux's second collection of short fiction, whose stories continue his attempt to reconcile the best ideas and feelings he absorbed as a Jesuit and his new insights into the modern world, in which he chose to live and work. L'Heureux treats this story of the marriage of a former nun and a former priest with a tone of methodical detachment. He not only constructs the story in thirteen brief scenes but also uses lists within some of these scenes. For example, after the priest meets the woman who will become his wife, he is "of three minds what he ought to do": be a poet and write perfect love songs to God, be a professional writer for publication, or be an incorruptible creator of good things.

The marriage of the former priest and the former nun seems doomed from the start (it was "like having a buzzard sitting . . . square on your tombstone"). Unhappy in his job as a high school teacher and despondent over his avocation as a poet, he heaps abuse onto

his wife, who responds, "Why didn't you stay a priest and drink yourself to death?" After eleven endless months the couple separates, and she pursues a career as a writer while he works in an advertizing agency. They eventually resume their relationship, and on their anniversary his wife writes that "the river carrying them out of control at least carried them together."

"DEPARTURES"

An appearance in *The New Yorker* has traditionally indicated a high level of success for a short-story writer. "Departures," a widely anthologized story, which appeared in *The New Yorker* in 1980, occupies a special place in L'Heureux's oeuvre because he views its central character as closer to who he really is than any of his other creations. The story centers on a young seminarian who decides to become a priest because it will allow him to live an ordered life securely isolated from the chaos of the secular world. After several years of Jesuit training, he travels home to visit his parents. During his trip, he feels ill at ease in public. Instead of seeing people through the eyes of Christian charity, as fellow children of God, he is repelled by the vulgarities of the hoi polloi. They put him into such a sour mood that he refuses to let his mother embrace him when his train arrives; the pain in her eyes will haunt him for the rest of his life.

Though his parents live to see their son ordained, his priesthood is neither fulfilling nor joyful. He is bored with his life and drinks too much. Even in his priestly functions, the symbols of transcendence fail to work their magic in sanctifying his soul. After his father quickly dies of a heart attack and his mother dies slowly of Parkinson's disease, his spiritual aridity becomes pandemic, infecting all aspects of his life. The story ends at an Easter vigil service, during which the priest puts out the holy fire. When critics in religious publications complained that L'Heureux was too hard on the priests he so acidly depicts, he responded that he was not easy on himself as a Jesuit, but "if kindness means treating people a lot better than they deserve," then he feels that he has been "extraordinarily kind" to his characters, who happen to be priests.

"THE COMEDIAN"

In a famous poem, Robert Frost asked God to forgive his little jokes, and he in turn would forgive the great big joke of God's creating humanity. In L'Heureux's third collection of short fiction, *Comedians*, he often presents human life as just such a cosmic prank. In a pivotal story of this collection, "The Comedian," which William Abrahams chose for *Prize Stories: The O. Henry Awards* in 1986, L'Heureux's protagonist is not a priest but a stand-up comic named Corinne, who wants only two things from life: a lot of laughs and a successful career. When a doctor discovers her unexpected pregnancy, he suggests abortion, but she is not sure. She had been a Catholic "until the end of her first marriage," and she needs some time to think about her decision, which is made more complicated when she hears her fetus singing. Her husband thinks that this is a joke for her act, but L'Heureux seems to be using Corinne's singing fetus as a vehicle for her spiritual redemption.

Corinne continues to perform, but her boss tells her that her routine provokes laughter from the head, not the heart. It is true that she is having difficulty finding things to joke about, as she hates jokes that put down women, ridicule husbands, or make fun of people's looks, and she certainly cannot make a good joke about abortion (can anyone?).

When amniocentesis reveals that her fetus is deformed, Corinne decides to abort it, whereupon it promptly stops singing. On the abortion table, just before the doctor is to inject the fatal salt solution, she stops him, saying that she wants the baby, who begins to sing again. Even though her baby is born dumb (an ironic God getting the last laugh), she accepts her baby, who has become her way to transcend the profane chaos of her life.

OTHER MAJOR WORKS

LONG FICTION: *The Clang Birds*, 1972; *Tight White Collar*, 1972; *Jessica Fayer*, 1976; *A Woman Run Mad*, 1988; *An Honorable Profession*, 1991; *The Shrine at Altamira*, 1992; *The Handmaid of Desire*, 1996; *Having Everything*, 1999; *The Miracle*, 2002.

POETRY: *Quick as Dandelions*, 1964; *Rubrics for a Revolution*, 1967; *One Eye and a Measuring Rod*, 1968; *No Place for Hiding*, 1971.

NONFICTION: *Picnic in Babylon: A Jesuit Priest's Journal, 1963-67*, 1967.

BIBLIOGRAPHY

Colby, Vineta, ed. *World Authors, 1985-1990*. New York: H. W. Wilson, 1995. The article on L'Heureux begins with a helpful interview with the writer, who reflects on his life and writings, and includes a short biography and a long analysis of his poetry, short fiction, and novels. Also included are a list of his principal publications and a selection of articles about him.

Farrell, Michael J. "L'Heureux's People Perplexed by Ironic God." *National Catholic Reporter* 27 (May 11, 1990): 21, 30. Using the publication of *Comedians* as a pretext to explore the author's fiction about priests, Farrell analyzes L'Heureux's Catholic background and its effect on his short stories and novels. The article is enlivened by material gathered in an interview with L'Heureux.

Johnson, Greg. "Jokers Are Wild." *The Georgia Review* 44 (Winter, 1990): 713-722. In this essay review Johnson discusses five American writers who have linked humor with hostility in their critiques of modern life. He sees Flannery O'Connor and Iris Murdoch as influencing L'Heureux's fictional methods, which he incisively uses to probe the spiritual realities behind his characters' moral dilemmas.

Long, J. V. "John L'Heureux." In *American Short-Story Writers Since World War II*, edited by Patrick Meanor and Joseph McNicholas. Detroit: Gale Group, 2001. The entry on L'Heureux contains a brief biography followed by an analysis of his short fiction.

Stefano, Frances. "*Comedians* by John L'Heureux." *Theology Today* 47 (Fall, 1990): 319-324. Stefano analyzes the stories in L'Heureux's last collection from a theological perspective. She sees them as being ultimately about the light of God's grace becoming visible in a dark world of apparent randomness and waste. Though she finds L'Heureux's stories contrived and not as convincing as those of Flannery O'Connor, she is nonetheless enthralled by his overdrawn characters, whose actions are

"comically, sometimes terrifyingly, true to the strangeness of life."

Robert J. Paradowski

Yiyun Li

Born: Beijing, China; November 4, 1972

Principal short fiction

A Thousand Years of Good Prayers, 2005
Gold Boy, Emerald Girl, 2010

Other literary forms

The first novel of Yiyun Li (yee-yuhn lee), *The Vagrants*, was published in 2009 to critical acclaim. Set in a small provincial town in China, it provides a horrifyingly naturalistic slice of life during the politically tumultuous 1970's. Li also published in diverse periodicals several brief and revealing memoir pieces about growing up in China and migrating to the United States. In addition, she wrote the screenplay for Wayne Wang's prize-winning film adaptation of her story "A Thousand Years of Good Prayers"; she also assisted in the adaptation of her "The Princess of Nebraska" for Wang.

Achievements

Yiyun Li's literary accomplishment and promise were recognized by a MacArthur Foundation "genius grant" in 2010, and critics have praised her ability to capture the agony and the humanity of the Chinese people as they make the transition from communism to capitalism. Li's short fiction has been the recipient of the Pushcart Prize (2004), *The Paris Review*'s Plimpton Prize for new writers (2004), the Frank O'Connor International Short Story Award (2005), the Hemingway Foundation/PEN Award (2006), the Whiting Writers' Award (2006), and the *Guardian* First Book Award (2006). Her stories have been included repeatedly in *Best American Short Stories* and *O. Henry Prize Stories*. In 2007, *Granta* named Li one of the best American writers under thirty-five; in 2010, *The New Yorker* listed her among the top twenty fiction writers under forty years old.

Biography

Yiyun Li was born November 4, 1972, in Beijing, China. Her father, a son of peasants, was a nuclear physicist developing China's arsenal, while her mother was an elementary school teacher of bourgeois parentage. Li witnessed the transformations of post-Maoist China, living with her parents, sister, and maternal grandfather in an enclave for government intellectuals only a short bicycle ride from Tiananmen Square (site of the 1989 massacre). Li's family enclave was off-limits to the Red Guard during the Cultural Revolution (1966-1976), though Li's day-care class attended a denunciation ceremony preceding a public execution. As children, Li and her elder sister shared a cramped bedroom with their colorful maternal grandfather (born 1897), scion of a fabric merchant family; he spoke English, became a Shanghai publishing executive, fought in the Chinese Civil War/War of Liberation on the Kuomintang (Nationalist) side, and remained a perilously inveterate critic of Chairman Mao. Li was considered a child prodigy in mathematics and dreamed of becoming the Madame Curie of China; her parents discouraged her from writing, even in her diary, for that might be later construed as subversive activity. At age eighteen, Li spent a year of political reeducation and privation in the People's Liberation Army, then she attended Peking University in Beijing and earned a B.S. in cell biology in 1996.

That year, Li arrived in the United States to study at the University of Iowa, obtaining an M.S. in immunology in 2000. However, upon taking a community writing course to improve her English, Li discovered a hitherto unsuspected talent for creative writing; she was admitted to the University of Iowa Writers' Workshop and completed an M.F.A. in 2005. While attending the Writers' Workshop, Li published short stories in *The New Yorker* and *The Paris Review*.

Despite garnering several literary awards and obtaining recommendations from the likes of Salman Rushdie and *The New Yorker* editor David Remnick, Li's initial application for U.S. permanent residency was denied by the Immigration Service in 2006 on the grounds that she showed insufficient ability in the arts; eventually, however, Li was granted residency in 2008. She taught at Mills College, in California, from 2005 to 2008, establishing her residence in Oakland; in 2008, she began teaching at the University of California, Davis. Li also has been a contributing editor to the Brooklyn-based literary magazine *A Public Space*. Li, married to a computer engineer, has two sons. In September 2010, the MacArthur Foundation awarded Li a "genius grant" of $500,000.

Analysis

Yiyun Li's highly acclaimed fiction is appreciated internationally for the light it sheds on the lives of ordinary people in mainland China during the extraordinary 1960's to the twenty-first century. It is a light of unflinching realism suffused with profound human insight and understanding. Although the preponderance of Li's literary production concerns the human and political landscape of China, her literary imagination also is engaged with the transnational experience of Chinese immigrants to the United States. Generally, her narrative method is grounded in the great tradition of realism, in the style of Guy de Maupassant, Anton Chekhov, and Leo Tolstoy; on occasion, however, she employs a near surrealistic premise (as she does in "Immortality") to create an allegory in the mode of Franz Kafka's "In the Penal Colony" or Lu Xun's "Diary of a Madman." As a native Chinese educated to the university level in China before attempting to write in English, Li shows remarkable facility in her second language and has been compared favorably with the towering émigré fiction writers Joseph Conrad and Vladimir Nabokov. Li's resoundingly successful crafting of fiction stems from her ability to make real to English-speaking readers her fictional individuals of an unfamiliar society and culture, and to draw her readers into sharing her characters' anxieties and aspirations, delights and terrors, aches and elations.

An endlessly revisited theme of Chinese fiction is that of family: The fountainhead of this infinitely variable theme is the eighteenth century epic of family, Can Xueqin's *Hongloumeng* (1792; also known as *Hunglou meng*; English translation, *Dream of the Red Chamber*, 1958; also translated as *A Dream of Red Mansions*, 1978-1980, and The Story of the Stone), a novel comparable to Leo Tolstoy's *Anna Karenina* (1875-1877; English translation, 1886) or Émile Zola's nineteenth century Rougon-Macquart series. Many, if not all, of Li's stories are variations upon one or more of the myriad aspects of this theme: marriage (or celibacy), love (in its abundance and in its absence), parentage (including surrogacy), siblings (rivals and comrades), sexuality (straight and gay); indeed, the theme is elaborated in infinite and exquisite variety and detail through the people of Li's tales. Of course, these individuals do not exist in social vacuums, for family is the mediating nexus between individual and society, and hence the link to the societal and political contexts of Li's narratives.

"A Thousand Years of Good Prayers"

The interplay among the individual, the family, and society is apparent immediately in the title story of Li's debut volume. "A Thousand Years of Good Prayers" is a delicate but expansive exploration of the gulf of noncommunication between a retired Chinese scientist father and his newly divorced librarian daughter domiciled in the United States. The father habitually deals with top-secret research but his career was ruined by false office gossip about his having an affair. Hence, his embittering life experience in a secretive and accusatory society, symptomatic of Big Brother communism, has conditioned him to cultivate reticence. He longs to help his daughter sort out her life after divorce, but she, too, has acquired his reticence and cannot explain to him her marital break-up and her Romanian lover. Frustrated and lonely, the father makes a chance acquaintance with an elderly Iranian woman. Neither of them can speak much English, but they begin to meet regularly in a neighborhood park and form a heartwarming friendship through gestures, looks, and speaking in their own mutually incomprehensible tongues, liberated from the inhibition and societal danger of being understood by each other.

Indeed, each of the stories in this volume is a gem-like variation on the interplay among the individual, the family, and society. For instance, in "Persimmons," a brooding narrative communally told through a chorus of drought-stricken peasants, a father exacts a terrible vengeance upon callous judicial officials, one of whom killed his son. In "Immortality," Li employs a Kafkaesque near-surrealist premise of voluntary castration (grounded in Chinese history) to critique the cult of Chairman Mao, elaborating the illogic of the family benefits of castration and creating an unique eunuch who thrives on being a duplicate. In several other stories, their titles alone (for example, "Love in the Marketplace" and "Son") already indicate their relevance to the family theme.

"THE PRINCESS OF NEBRASKA"

Included in Li's first book, "The Princess of Nebraska" concerns a woman's decision about whether to start a family. It touches disturbingly on abortion and homosexuality, nativity and nationality. The woman is a Russian-named Chinese, Sasha, newly arrived in Nebraska for graduate school. She discovers, just before leaving Beijing, that she is pregnant from a tryst with Yang, a homosexual *Nan Dan* (a male actor playing female roles). The sexual triangle is completed by Boshen, Yang's former gay lover (now an émigré in Chicago), who is helping Sasha decide about an abortion.

The middle-aged Boshen has failed at doctoring, at gay activism, and at his attempt to return Yang to the Peking Opera after it expelled him for homosexual proclivities. The societal hypocrisy is patent: reward a man for female impersonation but punish him for homosexuality, venerate the Goddess of Mercy (Kuanyin) and ignore her transsexuality in having once been a male god. Yang is forced to prostitute himself until Boshen invites him to move in. Then Yang, apparently charmed by the fairy-tale possibilities of Julia Roberts's *Pretty Woman* (1990), extends his sexuality and impregnates Sasha.

When the narrative begins, Chicago is lighting up for Thanksgiving and Christmas, holidays of immigration and childbirth. The lighting of the trees becomes a moment of illumination for Sasha. She recalls how her Chinese mother became reconciled to living in Inner Mongolia because she gave birth to her children there: Birth, which determines nationality, happens to child and mother. As the story ends, Sasha realizes that finding the right time and place for birthing may be as unlikely as a Chinese girl from Outer Mongolia becoming a princess in Nebraska. However, making the best of her painful present could imbue any time and place with possibility and hope, especially during the season that celebrates America's first immigrants and Christianity's miraculous birth.

GOLD BOY, EMERALD GIRL

This second volume of Li's short fiction, comprising eight stories and a novella, continues to explore the themes of family. The dominant mood, however, is bleak, and Li's focus shifts from a linkage of self to society toward greater emphasis on the individual human psyche. The book's title story, for instance,

Yiyun Li (AP Photo/Vincent Yu)

describes the genesis of an unusual ménage à trois. The protagonist, Siyu, is a thirty-eight-year-old librarian, who, since her student days, has nursed an unspoken crush on another woman, seventy-one-year-old Professor Dai. Tenacity and devotion mark Siyu's character: When she was a student, she spent half an hour daily for two years seated in front of Professor Dai's office memorizing Charles Dickens's *Great Expectations* (1860-1861). Professor Dai has a forty-four-year-old gay son, Hanfeng, who has lived twenty years in the United States but is disillusioned with San Francisco and decides to repatriate to Beijing (his friends understandably are incredulous). Though mother and son are affectionate, he has not come out to his mother, but one gathers she knows. Professor Dai fixes up Siyu and Hanfeng on a date, and it is soon understood that they will marry and that all three will live together in separate bedrooms, each person complementing the others like gold and emerald in jewelry, never melded into an alloy, but each discretely enhancing the other.

KINDNESS

Li's *Kindness*, a novella included in *Golden Boy, Emerald Girl*, meditates on this highly desirable quality in human feeling, thought, and action. Kindness is kin to the compassion mandated by Buddha and Confucius and cousin to St. Paul's Christian charity. Kindness is thing of great fragility, easily shattered or distorted, and therefore all the more precious.

Kindness is also an artfully condensed bildungsroman about the pathos-filled formation of a psyche that selects isolation, an unlikely and ironic protagonist for a narrative with this title. The reader's curiosity is piqued. The narrator-protagonist is Moyan, a lonely forty-one-year-old spinster whose antisociability is rooted in her family, "the loneliest family in the world"--though, ironically, her family is formed in kindness. Her nondescript father, age fifty, marries her beautiful mother, age twenty, out of kindness, for she has been condemned as a nymphomaniac by their neighbors after falling in love with a married man. To reciprocate her husband's kindness, she kindly promises to give him twenty years of her life, one that she would rather end. In kindness and hoping to strengthen their marriage, they adopt Moyan, an orphan. However, Moyan's mother loses herself in romance novels, hardly noticing her. Moyan's father

strives to parent her, but he is a night-shift janitor who must sleep during daytime (when he sleeps in the bedroom, his wife goes out on endless errands, and when he is at work, she sleeps). Twenty years after they married, the wife punctually commits suicide.

It is not only her family that conditions Moyan's loneliness. A kind neighbor, Professor Shan, befriends her and tutors her in English from age twelve through college. Professor Shan is herself a recipient of kindness, for she had been an adopted orphan. She and Moyan start by reading Dickens (the novelist par excellence of orphans), proceed to Thomas Hardy (whom Moyan loves), then to D. H. Lawrence (whom Moyan considers mad, like her mother). As a teenager, Moyan forms an attachment to an older unhappily married man and is grievously saddened when he departs their neighborhood. Professor Shan comments: "The moment you admit someone into your heart you make yourself a fool. . . . When you desire nothing, nothing will defeat you"--the first sentiment being in the mean spirit of Dickens's Miss Havisham and the second almost worthy of Buddha. Thus is Moyan initiated into the economy of the closed heart.

Moyan's refusal to respond to amity is detailed vividly in the narrative of her year in military service when camaraderie in the face of hardship can be so strong. Even in the bitter cold of winter, however, when the women are permitted to bunk together for warmth, Moyan refuses. When her officer, Lieutenant Wei, becomes concerned about Moyan and asks how she can be helped to be happy, Moyan rejects her overture.

The novella closes on a quintessential image of aloneness, as Moyan walks past a shop window through which she sees a television showing one of her former fellow soldiers, Nan, an internationally famous singer. Moyan cannot hear Nan, but she remembers the day when Nan sang "The Last Rose of Summer" at a suddenly hushed firing range. It is a telling image of the gulf separating human beings, a gulf that may not be bridged in actuality but only in the imagination. Moyan's imagination recalls Thomas Moore's lyrics set to remembered music asserting the kindness of death. Indeed, Li's closing scene in this masterly novella is almost as exquisite and heartbreaking as that in James Joyce's "The Dead" (1914).

OTHER MAJOR WORKS
  LONG FICTION: *The Vagrants*, 2009.

BIBLIOGRAPHY

Faber, Michel. "Rotting Fruits of Revolution." *Guardian*, January 7, 2006, p. 16. *A Thousand Years of Good Prayers* employs traditional realism to portray perceptively a China roiled by "post-Marxist confusion."

Li, Yiyun. "Afterword." In *The Real Story of Ah-Q, and Other Tales of China* by Lu Xun. London: Penguin, 2009. A personal assessment of Lu Xun, the most influential Chinese fiction writer of the 1900's, by whom Li is anxious not to seem too influenced.

_____. "Why We Write." *Poets and Writers* 37 (January/February, 2009): 68-69. Li declares that she writes from curiosity and that her greatest influence is the Irish writer William Trevor, though she also admires Graham Greene, Iris Murdoch, Bernard Malamud, and others.

Mirsky, Jonathan. "Brutalized in China." *New York Review of Books*, March 11, 2009, p. 38. A China expert discusses and praises individual stories from *A Thousand Years of Good Prayers*.

Prose, Francine. "Straw into Gold." *The New York Times Book Review*, September 19, 2010, p. 10. Focuses on *Gold Boy, Emerald Girl* and compares Li's work to that of other Chinese artists and writers.

Tóibín, Colm. "A Thousand Prayers." *New York Review of Books*, November 30, 2006, p. 50. A wide-ranging assessment of *A Thousand Years of Good Prayers*, noting the stories' societal criticism and human dimension; also situates Li as an émigré writer of English.

                                        C. L. Chua and Christopher Estep

JACK LONDON

Born: San Francisco, California; January 12, 1876
Died: Glen Ellen, California; November 22, 1916

PRINCIPAL SHORT FICTION
  The Son of the Wolf, 1900
  The God of His Fathers, and Other Stories, 1901
  Children of the Frost, 1902
  The Faith of Men, and Other Stories, 1904
  Tales of the Fish Patrol, 1905
  Love of Life, and Other Stories, 1906
  Moon-Face, and Other Stories, 1906
  Lost Face, 1910
  South Sea Tales, 1911
  When God Laughs, and Other Stories, 1911
  A Son of the Sun, 1912
  Smoke Bellew, 1912
  The House of Pride, and Other Tales of Hawaii, 1912
  The Night-Born, 1913
  The Strength of the Strong, 1914
  The Turtles of Tasman, 1916
  The Human Drift, 1917
  The Red One, 1918
  On the Makaloa Mat, 1919
  Dutch Courage, and Other Stories, 1922
  Curious Fragments: Jack London's Tales of Fantasy Fiction, 1975 (Dale L. Walker, editor)

OTHER LITERARY FORMS

Jack London's more than fifty published books include plays, children's fiction, novels, sociological studies, essays, and short stories. Although generally known as a writer of short fiction, London is also remembered for two novels, *The Call of the Wild* (1903) and *The Sea-Wolf* (1904), both of which have been made into motion pictures several times. London is also credited with pioneering work in the development of tramp fiction (*The Road*, 1907) and science fiction (*The Star Rover*, 1915).

ACHIEVEMENTS

Jack London's numerous stories and his many novels capture with a bold and sometimes brutal reality the confrontation between humans and nature, which by some writers may easily have been portrayed romantically. Instead, London was at the forefront of the move toward naturalistic fiction and realism. He was influenced by social Darwinism, and his stories often reflect the idea that human beings, to survive, must adapt to nature yet are themselves creatures of nature, subject to forces they do not really understand. London was also interested in Marxism, and his work often employs a working-class hero.

London's realistic stories were very popular in the United States when they were first published and continue to be so. He has also achieved wide popularity abroad, with his work being translated into more than fifty languages. His stories in the naturalistic mode continue to influence writers.

BIOGRAPHY

Largely self-educated, John Griffith London was the product of California ranches and the working-class neighborhoods of Oakland. London's rise to fame came as a result of the Klondike gold rush. Unsuccessful in his attempt to break into the magazine market, he joined the flood of men rushing to make instant riches in the Yukon. Although he found little gold, he returned after the winter of 1897 with a wealth of memories and notes of the Northland, the gold rush, and the hardships of the trail. London married Elizabeth May Maddern in 1900, and the couple settled in Oakland, soon adding two daughters to the family. The marriage, however, was not successful, and London divorced his wife in 1905 and married Charmian Kittredge the same year. With Charmian, he sailed across the Pacific aboard a small yacht, intending to continue around the world on a seven-year voyage. The trip ended in Australia, however, when ill health forced London to abandon the voyage after only two years. London's last years were spent in the construction of a scientifically run ranch complex in Glen Ellen, Sonoma County, California. It was there that he died at age forty, on November 22, 1916. His death still has not been satisfactorily explained.

ANALYSIS

Jack London's fame as a writer came about largely through his ability to interpret realistically humans' struggle in a hostile environment. Early in his career, London realized that he had no talent for invention and that in his writing he would have to be an interpreter of the things that are rather than a creator of the things that might be. Accordingly, he turned to the Canadian Northland, the locale where he had gained experience, for his settings and characters. Later on he would move his setting to the primitive South Seas, after his travels had also made him familiar with that region. By turning to the harsh, frontier environment for his setting and themes, London soon came to be a strong voice heard over the genteel tradition of nineteenth century parlor-fiction writers. His stories became like the men and women about whom he wrote--bold, violent, sometimes primitive. London was able to give his stories greater depth by using his extraordinary powers of narrative and language, and by infusing them with a remarkable sense of irony.

"TO BUILD A FIRE"

"To Build a Fire" has often been called London's masterpiece. It is a story which contrasts the intelligence of human beings with the intuition of animals and suggests that humans alone cannot successfully face the harsh realities of nature. The story begins at dawn as a man and his dog walk along a trail which eventually could lead them, thirty-two miles away, to a companion's cabin and safety. The air is colder than the man has ever experienced before, and although the man does not know about the cold, the dog does. While the animal instinctively realizes that it is time to curl up in the snow and wait for warmer weather, the man lacks the imagination which would give him a grasp of the laws of nature. Such perception would have enabled him to see the absurdity of attempting to combat the unknown, especially since an old-timer had warned him about the dangers of the cold to inexperienced men. With his warm mittens, thick clothes, and heavy coat, the man feels prepared for the cold and protected while the dog longs for the warmth of a fire. As the man walks along the trail, he looks carefully for hidden traps of nature, springs under the snow beneath which pools of water lie, since to step into one of these pools would mean calamity. Once he forces the dog to act as a trail-breaker for him, and, when the dog breaks through and ice immediately forms on its extremities, the man helps the dog remove the ice.

At midday the man stops, builds a fire, and eats his lunch. The dog, without knowing why, feels relieved; he is safe. The man, however, does not stay beside the fire; he continues on the trail and forces the dog onward too. Finally, inevitably, the man's feet become wet. Although he builds a fire to dry out, snow puts out the fire, and before he can build another fire, the cold envelops him, and he freezes to death. The dog senses the man's death and continues on the trail toward the cabin, wherein lies food and the warmth of a fire.

The irony of the story is that the man, even with the benefit of all the tools with which civilization has provided him, fails in his attempt to conquer nature and instead falls victim to it, while the dog, equipped only with the instinct which nature has provided, survives. The story, representing London's most mature expression of pessimism, stresses the inability of human beings to shape their environment and conquer the unknown. Unlike the dog, they cannot draw from instinct since civilization has deprived them of it. They are therefore unfit and totally unequipped to face the unknown and conquer the cosmic power.

"LAW OF LIFE"

"Law of Life" exhibits another recurring theme in London's work--the inability of humans to assert positive values. It tells the story of the last moments of life for an old Native American. As the tale begins, the old man, son of the chief of the tribe, sits by a small fire with a bundle of wood nearby. The tribesmen are busy breaking camp in preparation for departure since they must go to new hunting grounds in order to survive. The old man, too old to benefit the tribe further, represents only a burden to the rest of his society and must therefore stay behind. As the man sits beside the fire, he remembers the days of his youth and an incident when he tracked an old moose. The animal had become separated from the rest of the herd and was being trailed by wolves. Twice the young Native American had come across the scene of a struggle between the moose and the wolves, and twice the moose had survived. Finally, the Native American witnessed the kill, the old moose

Jack London (Library of Congress)

dying so that the wolves might live. The moose-wolf analogy to the old Native American's situation is obvious, and as the story closes, the old Native American feels the muzzle of a wolf upon his cheek. At first he picks up a burning ember in preparation for battle, but then resigns himself to the inevitability of fate and extinguishes it.

London uses several vehicles to express his pessimism. Like the protagonist in "To Build a Fire," the old Native American is a man of limited vision. Encircled by an ever-constricting set of circumstances, he waits by a dying fire for his own death. Finally, as the moose-wolf analogy has foretold, the inevitability of nature dominates. As the story ends, the fire goes out, the wolves are no longer kept at bay, and the reader is left repulsed by the knowledge of the Native American's horrible death. London also employs a number of symbols in this story. The fire gives light which symbolizes life, as does the white snow which falls gently at the beginning of the story. As the fire ebbs, the man remembers the grey wolves, and at the end of the moose-wolf analogy, London writes of the dark point in the midst of the stamped snow, foretelling the end of the fire, and thus of life.

Although London's earlier stories embody a pessimism which reflects humans' helplessness in challenging the unknown, his later ones mark a dramatic changeover. Following an intensive study of Carl Jung and Sigmund Freud, London began writing stories in the last years of his life which reflected his discovery of some unique human quality that enabled humans to challenge successfully the cosmos and withstand the crushing forces of nature. One of London's last stories, also with a Northland setting, reflects this change of philosophy and contrasts markedly with the earlier "To Build a Fire" and "Law of Life."

"LIKE ARGUS OF ANCIENT TIMES"

"Like Argus of Ancient Times" begins as a largely autobiographical account of London's trek to Dawson City with a man known as "Old Man" or "John" Tarwater. Unlike the unnamed protagonist of "To Build a Fire," Tarwater is totally unequipped to face the rigors and challenges of the north. He is old and weak; furthermore, he arrives on the trail without money, camping gear, food, and proper clothing. Somehow he manages to join a group of miners, serve as their cook, and earn his passage to Dawson City. Although the winter snows force the group to make camp until spring, Tarwater (who is also called "Old Hero" and "Father Christmas") is driven by gold fever. He strikes out on his own, gets lost in a snowstorm, and falls to the ground, drifting off into a dreamlike world between consciousness and unconsciousness. Unlike London's earlier characters, Tarwater survives this confrontation with nature, awakens from his dream, turns toward the "rebirthing east," and discovers a treasure of gold in the ground. Couched in Jungian terms, the story is directly analogous to the Jungian concepts of the wandering hero who, undertaking a dangerous night journey in search of treasure difficult to attain, faces death, reaches the highest pinnacle of life, and emerges in the East, reborn. "Like Argus of Ancient Times" marks London's return to the many stories he wrote in which the hero feels the call of adventure, encounters difficulties and confronts nature, battles with death, and finally achieves dignity.

Often called the successor to Edgar Allan Poe, an imitator of Rudyard Kipling, or a leader of writers emerging from the nineteenth century, London wrote stories which mark the conflict between the primitive and the modern, between optimism and pessimism. He created fiction which combined actuality and ideals, realism and romance, and rational versus subjective responses to life. More than a new Poe, an imitator of Kipling, or a new genre writer, however, London is a legitimate folk hero whose greatness stems from his primordial vision and ability to center on the fundamental human struggles for salvation and fears of damnation.

OTHER MAJOR WORKS

LONG FICTION: *A Daughter of the Snows*, 1902; *The Call of the Wild*, 1903; *The Sea-Wolf*, 1904; *The Game*, 1905; *Before Adam*, 1906; *White Fang*, 1906; *The Iron Heel*, 1907; *Martin Eden*, 1908; *Burning Daylight*, 1910; *Adventure*, 1911; *The Abysmal Brute*, 1913; *The Valley of the Moon*, 1913; *The Mutiny of the Elsinore*, 1914; *The Scarlet Plague*, 1915; *The Star Rover*, 1915; *The Little Lady of the Big House*, 1916; *Jerry of the Islands*, 1917; *Michael, Brother of Jerry*, 1917; *Hearts of Three*, 1920; *The Assassination Bureau, Ltd.*, 1963 (completed by Robert L. Fish).

PLAYS: *Scorn of Women*, pb. 1906; *Theft*, pb. 1910; *The Acorn-Planter*, pb. 1916; *The Plays of Jack London*, pb. 2001.

NONFICTION: *The Kempton-Wace Letters*, 1903 (with Anna Strunsky); *The People of the Abyss*, 1903; *The War of the Classes*, 1905; *The Road*, 1907; *Revolution, and Other Essays*, 1910; *The Cruise of the Snark*, 1911; *John Barleycorn*, 1913; *Letters from Jack London*, 1965 (King Hendricks and Irving Shepard, editors); *No Mentor but Myself: Jack London on Writers and Writing*, 1979, revised and expanded 1999 (Dale L. Walker and Jeanne Campbell Reesman, editors); *The Letters of Jack London*, 1988 (three volumes; Earle Labor, Robert C. Leitz III, and I. Milo Shepard, editors).

CHILDREN'S LITERATURE: *The Cruise of the Dazzler*, 1902.

MISCELLANEOUS: *The Radical Jack London: Writings on War and Revolution*, 2008 (Jonah Raskin, editor).

BIBLIOGRAPHY

Auerbach, Jonathan. *Male Call: Becoming Jack London*. Durham, N.C.: Duke University Press, 1996. Auerbach reverses the trend of earlier London studies, emphasizing how London used his writing to reinvent himself. Above all, Auerbach argues, London wanted to become a successful author, and in that respect he shaped his life to suit his art. Includes detailed notes but no bibliography.

Berkove, Lawrence I., ed. *Critical Insights: Jack London*. Pasadena, Calif.: Salem Press, 2012. Collection of original and reprinted essays providing critical readings of London's work. Also includes a biography, a chronology of major events in London's life, a complete list of his works, and a bibliography listing resources for further research.

Bloom, Harold, ed. *Jack London*. Broomal, Pa.: Chelsea House, 2001. Offers plot summaries, lists of characters, and critical essays about the short stories "For the Love of a Man," "The She-Wolf," "The Apostate," and "To Build a Fire."

Furer, Andrew J. "Jack London's New Women: A Little Lady with a Big Stick." *Studies in American Fiction* 22 (Autumn, 1994): 185-214. Discusses London's representation of "new womanhood" that emphasizes physical power and capability and an economic and intellectual independence, but is nonetheless feminine and heterosexual.

Gelfant, Blanche H., ed. *The Columbia Companion to the Twentieth-Century American Short Story*. New York: Columbia University Press, 2000. Includes a chapter in which London's short stories are analyzed.

Hedrick, Joan D. *Solitary Comrade: Jack London and His Work*. Chapel Hill: University of North Carolina Press, 1982. Hedrick interweaves a discussion of London's stories and novels with details of his life in an attempt to see behind his self-created myth. She does some close reading of the stories and includes a useful bibliography and an index.

Hodson, Sara S., and Jeanne Campbell Reesman, eds. *Jack London: One Hundred Years a Writer*. San Marino, Calif.: Huntington Library Press, 2002. Collection of essays on London's life and works, including two focusing on his short fiction: "Fathers and Sons in Jack London's 'The House of Pride,'" by Gary Riedl and Thomas R. Tietze, and "Jack London's 'Second Thoughts': The Short Fiction of His Late Period," by Lawrence I. Berkove.

Kershaw, Alex. *Jack London: A Life*. New York: St. Martin's Press, 1997. Concentrates on the "powerful drama" of London's life. Includes notes, illustrations, bibliography, and several helpful maps.

Labor, Earle, and Jeanne Campbell Reesman. *Jack London*. Rev. ed. New York: Twayne, 1994. This clear introduction to London's life and work, first published in 1974, takes into account the twenty years of scholarship after the volume first appeared. This volume also takes issue with the widespread belief that the quality of London's work declined in the last decade of his life. Includes chronology, notes, and an annotated bibliography.

London, Jack. *The Letters of Jack London*. Edited by Earle Labor, Robert C. Leitz III, and I. Milo Shepard. 3 vols. Stanford, Calif.: Stanford University Press, 1988. Includes the most significant letters of the thousands London wrote during his lifetime. The editors have thoroughly annotated each letter, explaining references and identifying people. The correspondence includes love letters, letters to editors and publishers, and letters to fellow writers on London's ideas and methods, as well as correspondence to friends and family.

McClintock, James I. *White Logic: Jack London's Short Stories*. Grand Rapids, Mich.: Wolf House Books, 1975. Provides a detailed analysis of the short stories in a clear and useful way.

Reesman, Jeanne Campbell. "Frank Norris and Jack London." In *A Companion to the American Short Story*, edited by Alfred Bendixen and James Nagel. Malden, Mass.: Wiley-Blackwell, 2010. Discusses both writers as adherents to the naturalist school of literature, describing the characteristics of this literary style. Includes analyses of several of London's short stories.

_____. *Jack London's Racial Lives: A Critical Biography*. Athens: University of Georgia Press, 2009. Focuses on the issue of race in London's life and writings. Argues that while he promoted white supremacy in his novels and nonfiction, he satirized

racism and meaningfully portrayed racial charac-
ters--most often as protagonists--in his short fiction.
Reesman explains the reasons for this disparity, examining his childhood upbringing, socialist philosophy, and his experiences in the South Seas and
Hawaii.

_____. "'Never Travel Alone': Naturalism, Jack
London, and the White Silence." *American Literary
Realism* 29 (Winter, 1997): 33-49. Argues that even
in London's most naturalistic stories, readers find
the search for spirit, the desire for community, and
the need to address the Other. Provides a detailed
analysis of "To Build a Fire" to illustrate these
concepts.

Scofield, Martin. "O. Henry and Jack London." In *The
Cambridge Introduction to the American Short
Story*. New York: Cambridge University Press,
2006. Discusses the contributions of the two writers
to the development of the American short story and
analyzes some of London's short fiction.

Sinclair, Andrew. *Jack: A Biography of Jack London*.
London: Weidenfeld & Nicolson, 1978. A well-re-
searched, extensively documented biography that
focuses on London's life rather than his work. Includes a bibliography and many photographs.

David Mike Hamilton
Updated by Karen M. Cleveland Marwick

AUGUSTUS BALDWIN LONGSTREET

Born: Augusta, Georgia; September 22, 1790
Died: Oxford, Mississippi; July 9, 1870

PRINCIPAL SHORT FICTION

*Georgia Scenes, Characters, Incidents, Etc. in the
First Half Century of the Republic,* 1835

OTHER LITERARY FORMS

Although Augustus Baldwin Longstreet's unquestioned masterpiece is *Georgia Scenes, Characters, Incidents, Etc. in the First Half Century of the Republic*, he
also published a variety of books, pamphlets, letters,
and other materials, most of which deal with politics,
religion, or the South, and often with the intersection of
the three. Perhaps the most significant is *Letters on the
Epistle of Paul to Philemon: Or, The Connection of Apostolic Christianity with Slavery* (1845), a closely rea-
soned defense of slavery on biblical grounds. *A Voice
from the South, Comprising Letters from Georgia to
Massachusetts* (1847) vehemently sets forth antebellum
southern political positions. Late in life he published a
long-contemplated didactic novel on the folly of in-
dulging youth, *Master William Mitten: Or, A Youth of
Brilliant Talents Who Was Ruined by Bad Luck* (1864).

ACHIEVEMENTS

Augustus Baldwin Longstreet is best known for his
collection of humorous tales, *Georgia Scenes*. His use
of the tall-tale form, vernacular speech, and the setting
of the Georgia frontier (then considered part of the
"Southwest") marks him as foremost among the
Southwest humorists. In a form known for its combination of oral folklore with more traditional forms,
such as the sketch, Longstreet's contributions are
marked for their polished, literary quality. Like the
border region that composes his settings, Longstreet's
stories reveal a literary territory that combines genteel
prose with raucous renderings of local scenes and
characters. He often uses an Addisonian-type gentleman narrator who describes the less civilized, more
outrageous behavior of the "locals." Later writers,
such as Mark Twain and William Faulkner, make similar use of the contrast between exaggerated storytelling and vivid, even cynical, realism. Longstreet's
renderings of unique Georgia characters, who speak in
uncensored and often hilarious voices, place him
firmly within the tradition of southern literature.

BIOGRAPHY

Augustus Baldwin Longstreet was born in Augusta,
Georgia, on September 22, 1790. He was graduated

from Yale University and from the Litchfield Law School, then widely considered the finest in America, and returned to Augusta in 1814. He became a successful lawyer and subsequently a judge. He left the bench, became a farmer, and, a little later, a newspaper editor. It was during this period that he published, first periodically and then in book form, his *Georgia Scenes*. In 1838, Longstreet became a professing Christian and a most active Methodist minister; the next year he was appointed the first president of Emory College, a Methodist institution. In the following years he served as president of Centenary College in Louisiana, the University of Mississippi, and the University of South Carolina. Longstreet died on July 9, 1870, and was buried in Oxford, Mississippi.

ANALYSIS

Augustus Baldwin Longstreet's *Georgia Scenes* covers such a remarkably wide variety of behavior that he largely succeeds in his ambition to be a social historian. He vividly pictures men involved in such noble occupations as "The Horse-Swap," "The Fight," "The Militia Company Drill," and "The Foxhunt." He portrays women as charming their beaux with an impromptu concert in "The Song," engaging in polite battles of status and manipulation in "The Ball," or simply gossiping into the wee hours in "A Sage Conversation." Longstreet structures some "scenes," less typical but often more interesting, around elaborate practical jokes: "The Character of a Native Georgian" follows Ned Brace through an involved series of capers that bewilder dozens of people; in "The Debating Society," two young men confound their peers by putting up for discussion a completely incomprehensible question; and in "The Wax-Works," a group of touring rowdies try to swindle enough for their tavern bill by masquerading as wax figures at an exhibition.

"GEORGIA THEATRICS"

Longstreet combines many of these elements in the book's brief opening sketch, "Georgia Theatrics." The narrator begins in uncharacteristically precise fashion: "If my memory fail me not, the 10th of June, 1809, found me, at about eleven o'clock in the forenoon, ascending a long and gentle slope in what was called 'The Dark Corner' of Lincoln [County]." In a kind of

Augustus Baldwin Longstreet (Library of Congress)

thematic prelude to the volume as a whole, he explains that the corner was "Dark" from a "moral darkness" which, he avers, by "wonderful transitions," has been dispelled in the past quarter century. The narrator takes care, however, to distinguish the area's former "*moral* condition" from its "*natural* condition." The latter, in terms of physical contours, trees, streams, birds, and flowers, he characterizes as idyllic. Early in the sketch, as the narrator mounts a slope, the aura of Edenic grace shatters with a concatenation of "loud, profane, and boisterous voices," the source hidden in the undergrowth. Violent oaths give way to sounds of muffled blows and terrific thrashings; the narrator watches the largely obscured back of one man rise briefly, then plunge heavily, "and at the same instant I heard a cry in the accent of keenest torture, 'Enough! My eye's out!'" The victor rises bragging until he sees the narrator, then looks "excessively embarrassed." The narrator orders the swaggering bully to help him aid the horribly maimed victim, but the young victor defiantly replies that there has been no one else involved: "I was jist seein' how I could 'a' *fout*." He then bounds over to a plough that he had left in a fence corner several yards off. The narrator surveys the battlefield; in the soft dirt, he sees two thumbprints, about as far apart as a man's eyes:

> . . . would you believe it, gentle reader? his report was true. All that I had heard and seen was nothing more nor less than a Lincoln rehearsal, in which the youth who had just left me had played all the parts of all the characters in a court-house fight.

The brief sketch effectively introduces several of the book's dominant motifs: violence, crude humor, cultural conflict, close attention to physical detail, and a style that abruptly alternates between the narrator's polite affection and the powerful dialect of the lower classes.

"THE GANDER-PULLING"

Many of these elements reach a sort of climax in "The Gander-Pulling," a sketch which none of the others can top for sheer crudity and high spirits. Longstreet sets the scene in 1798, just beyond the outskirts of Augusta proper and not far from three very close satellite "towns." He opens reprinting an "advurtysement" for the gander-pulling, a notice every bit as enthusiastically unconventional in its phrasing as in its spelling. After elaborately describing the general area and petty rivalries of the neighboring towns, he details the immediate scene of action. The locals have outlined a circular path about forty yards in diameter around which the entrants will ride their horses. At one point on each side of the path, about ten feet apart, stands a post; between the posts a rope is slung loosely enough that a gander attached can vibrate in an arc of four or five feet. The gander-pull impresario, Ned Prator, first passes a hat into which each contestant tosses twenty-five cents, the sum to be the victor's prize. He next proceeds to bind the gander's feet and then to coat the bird's neck liberally with goose grease--inspiring in the narrator an ironic paean to the gander's former mate. Finally Prator attaches the gander to the rope directly over the path, stations men at the posts to whip any horse inclined to dawdle, arranges in a rough line the contestants mounted on their increasingly spooked horses, and sets them off.

The riders make three raucous but uneventful rounds until one man, riding a horse aptly named Miss Sally Spitfire, finally makes a solid grab, jerks the gander's neck close to his startled horse's head, while at the same instant each of the two lashers lays on with all his might. The crazed horse gives one look at the gander, feels both lashes, and bolts through the crowd carrying along a circus worth of bawling dogs, alarmed and belled cattle, and three tobacco-rollers, hauling over all in her path until she arrives at not just one airborne gander but a whole flock immediately at her feet. She stops suddenly enough to convert her rider into an unguided projectile. Gridiron, a second and rather more coolly rational horse, ignores his rider's whoops, kicks, and lashings, while he pauses to examine and consider Miss Sally Spitfire's experience, and then heaves a deep sigh:

> It was plain that his mind was now made up; but, to satisfy the world that he would do nothing rashly, he took another view, and then wheeled and went for Harrisburg as if he had set in for a year's running. Nobody whooped at Gridiron, for all saw that his running was purely the result of philosophic deduction.

One of two of the remaining contestants seems most certain to win on each succeeding round, especially after one breaks the neck, but finally a third jerks away the head to win the prize. He brags and struts outrageously, but, as he and his audience are all aware since he triumphed through luck rather than skill, his vaunting puts the whole crowd in a high good humor--except for one little man who lost his bet of six quarts of huckleberries: "*He* could not be reconciled until he fretted himself into a pretty little *piny*-woods fight, in which he got whipped, and then he went home perfectly satisfied."

Much of the piece's charm derives from the relaxed focus which easily shifts from the advertisement to the area's history to the field of competition to the organizer to the gander to the competitors to the horses to the victor and on to the end, no one element taking precedence over another. Longstreet focuses where and how he pleases to gain maximum local effect from each element of his sketch--which is precisely the sum of its parts. What the sketch does not have is a controlling fictional perspective that can compel the piece to do more than merely sum up its parts, more than exploit a fascinating, bizarre, and self-sufficient surface. Longstreet vividly represents the gander-pulling but merely represents it rather than significantly developing a meaningful experience arising out of that activity; consequently, he produces here one of his typical sketches rather than a story.

"THE SHOOTING-MATCH"

In the final section of *Georgia Scenes*, "The Shooting-Match," Longstreet does produce a genuine short story, although--compared to earlier pieces in the book--in some ways a rather bland one. About a year ago, the narrator tells the reader, traveling on business in northeastern Georgia, he encountered a small man carrying a massive old rifle and bound for a shooting match. The native, Billy Curlew, learns that this well-dressed stranger (the narrator) is the same person who, years ago as a child barely large enough to hold a shotgun, had earned a lasting reputation in a shooting match--and incidentally a fine silk handkerchief for Billy's father, who had bet on the boy. The narrator admits that the shot years before had been pure luck, but Billy talks him into coming along to see the fun.

When they arrive, Billy, unreservedly a partisan of the man who won his father's bet so long ago, startles the narrator by arranging for him to have a shot in the match, but none of the locals fear much from the strange dude. The narrator then vividly details the rules, target, prizes, contestants, and finally the shifting fortunes of all in the match. Hoping to delay his humiliation as long as possible, the narrator insists on shooting last. The dreaded time arrives, his arms cannot hold the ponderous rifle without trembling, and he paradoxically begins bragging (quite unconvincingly) to relieve somehow his own acute embarrassment. Finally, on impulse he halfheartedly fires and amazes absolutely everyone--except Billy--by making the second best shot of the day, missing first prize (won by Billy) by only fractions of an inch. Except for a handful of agnostics, the narrator converts the whole crowd, who promise to vote for him no matter which office he is seeking. When he objects that he is seeking no office, they insist he let them know when he does, for they

would all back him to the death. "If you ever come out for anything," Billy vows, "jist let the boys of Upper Hogthief know it, and they'll go for you to the hilt, against creation, tit or no tit, that's the *tatur*."

The story capitalizes on some nice ironies: Generous backwoods Billy seems fated to share in the narrator's humiliation but has judged better than anyone else. The narrator's nervous bragging during his ludicrous preliminaries ironically helps him to carry the day once he fires his shot. The narrator deserves a rich load of backwoods contempt for his lack of manliness but winds up with a whole region ready to back him to a man. Here Longstreet uses a fine rhetorical sensitivity to prepare, develop, and capitalize on his climactic surprise. Unlike a typical Georgia "scene," this story has no extraneous characters, no long descriptions or discussions of purely local interest, and no digressions to include bizarre comic incidents. Longstreet focuses not, as usual, on broadly representing typical scenes, characters, or actions, but more narrowly on re-creating the narrator's experience, an experience which encompasses his sympathy for the sympathetic Billy Curlew. Here Longstreet has created a genuine story by concentrating, uncharacteristically, on form at the expense of content. Later frontier humorists and local-color writers learned techniques which allowed them the best of both dimensions, but they could hardly have written as well as or as intelligently without the pioneering example of *Georgia Scenes*.

OTHER MAJOR WORKS

LONG FICTION: *Master William Mitten: Or, A Youth of Brilliant Talents Who Was Ruined by Bad Luck*, 1864.

NONFICTION: *Letters on the Epistle of Paul to Philemon: Or, The Connection of Apostolic Christianity with Slavery*, 1845; *A Voice from the South, Comprising Letters from Georgia to Massachusetts*, 1847; *Letters from President Longstreet to the Know-Nothing Preachers of the Methodist Church South*, 1855.

BIBLIOGRAPHY

Blair, Walter. *Native American Humor, 1800-1900*. New York: American Book, 1931. This classic in American humor studies provides a general discussion of nineteenth century humorists, an extensive bibliography (which is outdated but useful in its listing of "Individual Writers of Native American Humor"), and more than one hundred selections from a wide range of authors. The chapter on "Humor of the Old Southwest" discusses Longstreet among his contemporaries.

Brown, Carolyn S. *The Tall Tale in American Folklore and Literature.* Knoxville: University of Tennessee Press, 1987. Brown traces the origins of the popular tale in both folklore and literature. Chapter 3, "Flush Times: Varieties of Written Tales," has an extended analysis of Longstreet's *Georgia Scenes*. Brown does not oversimplify in her discussion of Longstreet's sketches but rather explores the complexity of his work within the tall-tale tradition.

Fitzgerald, Oscar Penn. *Judge Longstreet: A Life Sketch.* Nashville, Tenn.: Methodist Episcopal Church, 1891. Bishop Fitzgerald's biography covers Longstreet's life and work in eloquent terms--and at times does little to dispel some of the reigning legends surrounding Longstreet. Exaggerations aside, this biography distinguishes itself by the inclusion of many letters to and from Longstreet, allowing a more personal glimpse into the life of a complex and talented man.

Justus, James H. *Fetching the Old Southwest: Humorous Writing from Longstreet to Twain.* Columbia: University of Missouri Press, 2004. A study of Longstreet and the other humorists of the antebellum Southwest, focusing on the works written from 1834 to 1867 that led to the early writings of the area's most famous wit, Mark Twain. Contains analyses of the sketches in *Georgia Scenes* and numerous other references to Longstreet that are listed in the index.

King, Kimball. *Augustus Baldwin Longstreet.* Boston: Twayne, 1984. King's study provides an excellent general discussion of Longstreet's life and work. Much of the book discusses *Georgia Scenes* and gives a wealth of background material on both the writing and subject matter of this work. The annotated list of secondary sources is a useful component of this book.

Nimeiri, Ahmed. "Play in Augustus Baldwin Longstreet's *Georgia Scenes*." *Southern Literary Journal* 33, no. 2 (Spring, 2001): 44. Argues that the "distinguishing feature" of *Georgia Scenes* is "its depiction of play--in its two senses of contesting and role-playing--as the hallmark of antebellum southern life."

Rachels, David. "The Old Southwest: Mike Fink, Augustus Baldwin Longstreet, Johnson Jones Hooper, and George Washington Harris." In *A Companion to American Fiction, 1780-1865*, edited by Shirley Samuels. Malden, Mass.: Blackwell, 2004. Places Longstreet and *Georgia Scenes* in the context of Southwest antebellum legends and literature.

_____. "Oliver Hillhouse Prince, Augustus Baldwin Longstreet, and the Birth of American Literary Realism." *The Mississippi Quarterly* 51 (Fall, 1998): 603-619. Shows that Longstreet published "The Militia Company Drill," a work by Prince, as his own. Claims that because Prince did not receive recognition for the work, his role in the founding of American literary realism has been ignored.

Romine, Scott. "Negotiating Community in Augustus Baldwin Longstreet's *Georgia Scenes*." *Style* 30 (Spring, 1996): 1-27. Argues that rather than simply asserting and justifying class privilege, Longstreet undertakes a complex negotiation of class roles. Lyman Hall, the primary narrator, initially demonstrates a socionarrative style--that is, a social style reflected in narrative stylistics--that keeps the lower class at a social and moral distance; by the end of the text he is able to negotiate with the lower class a mutual perception of class roles.

Wade, John Donald. *Augustus Baldwin Longstreet: A Study of the Development of Culture in the South.* New York: Macmillan, 1924. This engaging biography of Longstreet, the result of Wade's extensive research, recounts the life of a literary man whose interests and activities ranged far beyond that of writing humorous sketches. Wade refers not only to *Georgia Scenes* but also to Longstreet's career as a lawyer and judge, his religious and political interests, and his terms as president of several leading universities in the South.

Wegmann, Jessica. "'Playing in the Dark' with Longstreet's *Georgia Scenes*: Critical Reception and
Reader Response to Treatments of Race and
Gender." *Southern Literary Journal* 30 (Fall, 1997):
13-26. Claims that *Georgia Scenes* advocates theories of a paternalistic, God-ordained slavery. In
many of its stories, an African American or a white

woman attempts to exert authority and, using humor
as a vehicle to trivialize, Longstreet subdues these
characters, bringing them back under white patriarchal rule.

Walter Evans
Updated by Ann A. Merrill

BARRY LOPEZ

Born: Port Chester, New York; January 6, 1945

PRINCIPAL SHORT FICTION

Desert Notes: Reflections in the Eye of a Raven,
    1976
Giving Birth to Thunder, Sleeping with His
    Daughter: Coyote Builds North America, 1978
River Notes: The Dance of Herons, 1979
Winter Count, 1981
Field Notes: The Grace Note of the Canyon Wren,
    1994
Lessons from a Wolverine, 1997
Light Action in the Caribbean, 2000
Resistance, 2004

OTHER LITERARY FORMS

Barry Lopez is as expansive as he is prolific. Though
he is primarily a writer of short fiction, he also has
written nonfiction (1978's *Of Wolves and Men* and
1986's *Arctic Dreams*) and several essay collections.
He has met with great success in his journalism career,
for which he has received a Pulitzer Prize. He often
collaborates with other artists, sculptors, illustrators,
and playwrights on his projects.

ACHIEVEMENTS

Barry Lopez has received almost every writing
honor over the course of his career. He received the National Book Award for *Arctic Dreams*; he received John
Burroughs and Christopher Medals for his book *Of
Wolves and Men*, which also was a National Book

Award finalist. He is a recipient of the Award in Literature from the American Academy of Arts and Letters
and received the Pulitzer Prize for feature writing in
2002 for "A Scary Abundance of Water." He received
two Pushcart Prizes, one each in fiction and nonfiction.
He also received the John Hay Medal, the Lannan Literary award, and the PEN Syndicated Fiction Award.
He won an Oregon Book Award two times and the Pacific Northwest Booksellers Award three times. He also
received fellowships from the Guggenheim, Lannan,
and McDowell Foundations, in addition to accepting
five National Science Foundation Antarctica Fellowships. In 2004, he was elected a Fellow of the Explorers
Club.

BIOGRAPHY

Barry Holstun Lopez is a writer, an explorer, and an
investigator of cultures. He was born in Port Chester,
New York, but grew up in Reseda, California, and New
York City, where he attended a Jesuit preparatory
school. In 1967, he moved to Oregon, where he settled
on the banks of the McKenzie River.

Lopez's artistic skills are diverse, and he worked as
a landscape photographer for many years. His first stories were published in 1966 and he became a full-time
writer in 1970. Perhaps because of his manifold interests, Lopez counts himself among the ranks of a community of artists with whom he sometimes collaborates
and from whom he often draws inspiration. He has collaborated with composer John Luther Adams, and
Lopez has spoken at galleries where the work of
sculptor Michael Singer and photographer Robert
Adams was on exhibition. Lopez also has written about

other artists, such as Lillian Pitt, Rick Bartow, Richard Rowland, and Alan Magee, whose monoprints are featured in Lopez's short-fiction collection *Resistance*.

Fine print limited editions of Lopez's book *Apologia* (1998), with artist Robin Eschner, are in the permanent collections of the Whitney Museum, the National Gallery, the J. Paul Getty Museum, the New York Public Library, Stanford University, and Yale University.

Lopez is not only a student of the world but also a teacher at various institutions. He served as the Welch Professor of American Studies at the University of Notre Dame, taught fiction at the Bread Loaf Writers' Conference, and became Visiting Distinguished Scholar at Texas Tech University. His achievements as a teacher are many. Among them are his collaboration with renowned biologist E. O. Wilson in creating an undergraduate major that includes the study of both sciences and humanities at Texas Tech University and his collaboration with Texas Tech's dean of libraries, William E. Tydeman, to initiate the Formby Lectures in Social Justice.

Barry Lopez (Getty Images)

ANALYSIS

Barry Lopez is as concerned with an animal or a landscape as he is with a human. Indeed, many of the stories in his collections focus on patiently described scenes from various terrains. Lopez has an eye for the smallest of details, and so do some of his characters, who tend to be observant people, constantly striving to lead more ethical, truthful, and peaceful lives. Readers of Lopez's work likely find themselves slowing down and taking time to appreciate his words with the same sort of patience and grace he uses to describe the worlds in his stories.

WINTER COUNT

This story collection takes its name from the American Indian form of history-keeping practiced by many different tribes. In a winter count, one writes a one- or two-sentence event that has happened in the past year, the time from last winter to this. The event symbolizes the year. These events may be personal or global, but it is important to note that these records are kept by individuals, not tribes, and that many different and differing winter counts exist for any given year. Some examples of winter counts that Lopez gives are "1847: Daughter of Turtle Head, her clothes caught on fire and she was burned up"; "1847: Three men who were women came": "1859: Ravens froze, fell over."

The collection is named for the winter count not only because that is the subject matter of its title story but also because Lopez uses the form of the winter count as an aesthetic and structural guide for the book. The stories of *Winter Count* are not concerned with moving from point A to point B or with pinning down universal observations. Instead, the stories are personal and anecdotal, like expanded winter count observations. Indeed, while most readers expect in their short fiction character development, structured action that comes to a climax, and resolution, Lopez instead prioritizes emotional honesty, patience, language, beauty, and truth. By constructing a collection around the aesthetic of the winter count, instead of the accepted norms of fiction writing, Lopez creates a unique yet ancient reading experience.

"WINTER COUNT 1973: GEESE, THEY FLEW OVER IN A STORM"

It is from the title story that the reader learns the definition of the winter count. In this story a man goes to give a lecture about the practice of winter count keeping, but he is not quite sure what is expected of him by the audience. He does not believe that there is anything definitive to say; there are only observations to be made. He gives the speech, the contents of which the reader learns of through the excerpts of historical winter counts the lecturer has collected. The lecturer fears that people will try to twist these winter counts into telling them something definitive. There is no definitive version of history, the lecturer stresses, only a myriad of personal experiences. Lopez writes: "He wished he were back in Nebraska with his students to warn them: it is too dangerous for everyone to have the same story. The same things do not happen to everyone."

It is fitting that each of the stories in this collection represents moments that are extremely important to a personal history and yet seemingly irrelevant to the greater scope of the world. Lopez does not seek to write a story or anecdote that is universal. Rather, he makes stories that are deeply personal or specific to the characters in them, while taking pains to write them in such a way that the humanity of the characters and the stories might speak to a universal audience.

"THE WOMAN WHO HAD SHELLS"

Among the stories of this collection, "The Woman Who Had Shells" seems emblematic of the idea of a winter count. In it, the narrator describes how early one morning, on Sanibel Island in Florida, he once watched a woman gather shells on the beach. He was moved by the delicate way she bent down and touched each shell, at one point cupping two shells to her cheeks. He compares her to an albatross, a seabird. To the narrator the woman is perfectly at home in this environment. He does not speak to her, and she leaves the beach. The memory of the occasion stays with the narrator; a year later, he sees the woman in a New York City restaurant. He approaches the woman and tells her of the time he saw her on the beach, looking at the shells. They begin to speak and soon have talked at length about topics from nature and art to politics. The woman and the

narrator go back to her apartment, where they continue to talk, until the narrator gets up to leave. At this point the woman leads the narrator to her bedroom and shows him her shell collection. He holds each, and then they say goodbye.

The structure of this story is much like that of many American Indian stories, where the primary concern is not to create a plot structure full of highs and lows of action but rather to capture a moment of significance that has meaning in and of itself and does not need to be tied to some greater plotline.

This moment between the narrator and the woman represents a meeting of kindred spirits by chance. It is not clear whether they will ever see each other again; it is not their relationship but this moment that is significant. This moment, one can imagine, might be the one the narrator would pick to write down if he were keeping a winter count of his life.

Elsewhere in the collection, Lopez writes: "The point, he told his students, was not this. There was no point. It was a slab of meat. It was a rhythm to dance to. It was a cloak that cut the wind when it blew hard enough to crack your soul." This is perhaps the most apt description of Lopez's stories from this collection. They are whole objects that do not instruct or inform the reader but rather are meant to be experienced and pondered .

RESISTANCE

Resistance comprises a series of linked stories involved with the American political and cultural climate of the early aughts. In between the stories are monoprints by the artist Magee, with whom Lopez collaborated for the book. The monoprints depict odd black-and-white renderings of faces that seem neither male nor female. The intensity and curiosity of the expressions on these faces interact with the troubled tales of the narrators in this book.

In an interview he gave in *January Magazine* in 2001, Lopez spoke a little about why he writes:

Every one of us has experienced to some degree--and some to a terrible degree--cruelty visited upon us in an unjust way. So I expect people to know all of that and what I want to do as a writer is write credibly about the other thing. That is: Is it possible to have a worthy life? Is it possible, for most of us who are not saints, to live in a place where we feel ethically comfortable with what we're doing and feel capable of love and capable of receiving love? Can we actually attain those things or are we just part of the disaster downline from the industrial revolution and the Age of Empire? And I think it is and that's what I write about.

Perhaps nowhere is this truer than in *Resistance*. The structure of this collection takes the form of a series of open letters. They read almost as treatises, and each one ends with the name of the narrator, his or her profession, and the name of a place outside the United States that the narrator is leaving on the occasion of the story. These stories are the accounts of people displeased with the way they are expected to live their lives and resist, in some way, the cultural and political norms. The stories detail their struggles. It is perhaps implied that each of the people in the collection has received a letter from the American government and decided he or she must go off the radar and into in hiding, immediately pursuant to the writing of this letter. This is further explained in the first story of the collection, "Apocalypse."

"APOCALYPSE"

In this story, an American expatriate living in Paris receives a letter from the U.S. government's "Inland Security" agency. He lives with his wife, and they are part of an international community of artists, writers, and philosophers, who, though they no longer live in proximity, communicate by letter and e-mail about their art, their thoughts, and their politics. Each of them, it turns out, also has received this letter. Lopez writes, "each of us was told of widespread irritation with our work and the government's desire to speak with us . . . our stratagems, the letter continued were those typical of 'terrorist cells.' They called for scrutiny, we had to desist."

Owen Daniels, the narrator, decides to leave Paris for somewhere Inland Security cannot find him. The reader gets the feeling that this story is a letter he posts in return to the Department of Inland Security before he leaves. It is an act of dissent, one of many enacted by the various characters in this book. All take issue with

various political, moral, or social realities they cannot abide. Their letters explain their struggles with these realities and some of them make peace.

"Apocalypse," as the first story of *Resistance*, serves as an introduction or lens, through which the subsequent stories might be read. Its final line reads almost as a mission statement for the book. Lopez writes: "these pages are our response to your intrusion, your order to be silent, your insistence that we have something to talk over."

Indeed Lopez's pages are exactly this. They are a response to the deeply complicated political climate of the United States and the world at the time of the book's publication in 2004. Inland Security, of course, seems a thinly veiled Department of Homeland Security, and throughout the book Lopez strives to give voice to the feelings and thoughts of many Americans, artists, and citizens, who desired to communicate their views at that time. The book is, in and of itself, one writer's act of *Resistance*. In this collection Lopez does what writers have done for generations: speak up and speak out.

OTHER MAJOR WORKS

LONG FICTION: *Crow and Weasel*, 1990 (novella).

NONFICTION: *Of Wolves and Men*, 1978; *Arctic Dreams: Imagination and Desire in a Northern Landscape*, 1986; *Crossing Open Ground*, 1988; *About This Life: Journeys on the Threshold of Memory*, 1998; *Apologia*, 1998; *The Rediscovery of North America*, 1990.

BIBLIOGRAPHY

Cosgrove, Ben. "Barry Lopez, Poet and Polemicist." *LA Weekly*, Thursday, July 29, 2004. This review of *Resistance* shows how Lopez aptly captures the "aftershocks of a changed world."

Lopez, Barry. "A Scary Abundance of Water: Growing up with the San Fernando Valley." *LA Weekly*, Wednesday, January 9, 2002. Long article in two parts in which Lopez describes his childhood filtered through the land in which he lived, Southern California's San Fernando Valley.

Martin, Christian."On Resistance: An Interview with Barry Lopez." *The Georgia Review* 60, no. 1 (Spring, 2006): 13-30. An interview with Lopez that discusses his literary influences and his thematic interests.

Shapiro, Michael. "The Big Rhythm: A Conversation with Barry Lopez on the McKenzie River." *Michigan Quarterly Review* 44, no. 4 (Fall, 2005):

583-610. In this wide-ranging interview, Lopez talks about the influence of landscape on his life and his work.

Wheeler, Sara. "Going Places." *The New York Times*, June 21, 1998. Review of Lopez's essays, which enumerates on themes that are reflected in his short fiction.

CJ Hauser

BETH LORDAN

Born: Pekin, Illinois; December 1, 1948

PRINCIPAL SHORT FICTION
And Both Shall Row, 1998
But Come Ye Back: A Novel in Stories, 2004

OTHER LITERARY FORMS

Beth Lordan is the author of the novel *August Heat* (1989), which has been highly praised for its Magical Realist evocation of American small-town life.

ACHIEVEMENTS

Beth Lordan received a National Endowment for the Humanities Fellowship in 1993, and her short fiction has won prizes from the New York State Council on the Arts and the Illinois Arts Council. *And Both Shall Row* was named one of *The New York Times'* notable books for 1998.

BIOGRAPHY

Ellenora Beth Lordan was born in Pekin, Illinois, on December 1, 1948. She has said that when she went to the University of Missouri just after graduation from a small and poor high school, she failed everything but western civilization. She took a job as a secretary in the entomology department at Cornell University, editing, copywriting, and typing professors' manuscripts. Taking advantage of the employee degree program there, she began work toward a B.A. in creative writing, which she finished in 1983, after nine years.

After graduation, she entered the M.F.A. program at Syracuse University, but pregnant and tired of the seventy-mile commute she decided to enter the graduate creative writing program at Cornell, closer to home, where she received her M.F.A. in 1987. Her first short story, "Running Out," appeared in *The Atlantic* in 1986. Her first novel, *August Heat*, was published in 1989. In 1991, she began teaching creative writing at Southern Illinois University at Carbondale, where she was named director of the creative writing program in 1992.

ANALYSIS

Beth Lordan's first collection of short stories focuses on a small number of people who live in the midwestern town of Clayborne. Often in her stories, Lordan's characters get a rare opportunity to glimpse, behind the routines and everyday demands of life, the special and the beautiful. In "Running Out," a carpenter who is out of work and down on his luck experiences a single day in which everything goes right. In "The Snake," a woman strikes back symbolically at her husband's betrayal by attacking heroically a snake that has invaded her house. In "The Cow Story," two lonely people almost, but not quite, break out of their loneliness and make a gesture toward each other. In "The Widow," an elderly woman discovers magic in the midst of the ordinary.

Lordan makes use of a familiar short-story tradition pioneered by Ivan Turgenev, Anton Chekhov, James Joyce, and Sherwood Anderson--the exploration of the complex secret lives of small-town people--thereby creating a world that, even though it seems ordinary and real, becomes extraordinary and magical. Like all great writers, Lordan crafts a world that, common and familiar, is at the same time strange and wonderful.

"THE WIDOW"

"The Widow" is a hauntingly magical story about the ultimate mystery of the other. The story begins cryptically with the sentence "The morning Warren Boyd dropped dead in his kitchen, he was the only living person on the farm." The sentence echoes poignantly in readers' minds when they discover that the other person in the house at the time is the spirit of Boyd's wife Ann, who has been hovering about him since her death three years earlier.

In addition to the supernatural suggestion that the wife, who, after having devoted her attentions to her husband for forty-two years, now as a spirit devotes herself to studying him, there is the matter of Warren's periodic transformations. The first time this occurred was after they had been married about a year, and she saw him out the upstairs window, walking as if under water, slowly and gracefully. In the folds of his clothes and on the hair of his head and in the stubble on his cheeks she saw "tiny air bubbles, gleaming like glass pearls." When Ann witnesses the mystery again, Warren, glowing in the darkness, does a series of somersaults across the lawn. The third event takes place after the death of their daughter, when Ann sees a soft brilliance rising from him, like mist off a barn roof; as he turns around and around in a circle, a bright color trails about him like veils in the rain.

Ann watches her husband for the rest of their lives together, and although he transforms again and again, it is never enough to completely offset the ordinary routine of their everyday experience. When she knows she is dying, she makes three wishes, the first of which is to remain with him until his death, hoping to see by then the meaning of his splendor. When Warren dies, the story ends with her making her second wish--for tears. It is understood that the third wish is that she will join him. No matter how long one may have known someone, Lordan's story suggests, at the very core of that person is an elusive magical mystery that too often one is unable to see.

"THE COW STORY"

The cow in this whimsical story chooses the afternoon of the only tornado in the history of the small village of Clayborne to escape her pasture and wander through the town. Lordan uses the cow running through the mysterious silence just before the tornado to introduce a magical setting for a restrained romantic encounter between Byron Doatze, the cow's owner, and Maude Nash, a fifty-three-year-old librarian.

When Maude invites Byron into her house out of the driving rain, their conversation is inconsequential but mildly flirtatious as they wait out the storm. Both know that something is happening, that they have moved from friendly joking to another level of possible intimacy, but neither has the nerve to make that intimacy actual. When the clock strikes midnight, both know that it is a moment when a decision must be made. They sit with their hands on the table looking at each other, knowing it would be hard to get from where they are into bed together: "They saw that this, after all, was coffee and cookies and a warm dry house in a rainstorm, in spite of the tornado and the cow."

Byron takes his cow home, smiling and saying to himself, "You damned jerk," while at the same time Maude smiles and says to herself, "You damn fool." The story ends with the reassertion of the everyday routine world, when the cow sighs and goes back to sleep. "The Cow Story" is a delicately done piece in which ordinary natural and domestic events--a storm, an escaped cow, and a casual conversation between two lonely people--take on an otherworldly beauty and mystery; it is a classic example of how story transforms the actual into the purely imaginary.

"AND BOTH SHALL ROW"

The long title story of Lordan's collection focuses on Margaret and May, sisters who, in their seventies, live together on the farm where they were born and raised. After May has a stroke and is unable to communicate, Margaret cares for her. This is about all that happens in the story in terms of plot, but the lyrical revelation of the relationship of the two, rather than simple events, is what moves the story along compellingly. The ultimate end of the novella is the fulfillment of the implications of the title, which is from the last lines of a song May was humming before her stroke: "Give me a boat that can carry two, and both shall row, my love and I."

The story is made up largely of May's memories and Margaret's talk, both of which focus primarily on the lifelong relationship of the two sisters. An important symbolic past event May remembers is a time when they were children and wore identical dresses, looking like ecstatic twin conspirators when they clipped their mother's roses for a game they never played. Another significant memory involves the two going to a dance during adolescence and Margaret purposely breaking the strap of her shoe to provide an excuse for leaving the dance early because of May. However, the most important event that both May and Margaret recall is Margaret's husband's divorcing her to marry May, something that Margaret accepted with seeming equanimity but which, fifty years later, still rankles her.

The most important story that Margaret recalls and tells is about her grown son Nick trying to shoot his wife and then turning the gun on himself. May recalls that the state trooper came to her house first with news of the death, thinking she was the mother. The blurring of identities and simultaneous separation of the two sisters is the central motif throughout the story, for even as Margaret accuses May of not comforting her after Nick's death, May recalls a vision of Margaret on that night when her eyes said that there was nothing she could do.

The lyrical confluence of the memories of Margaret and May culminates in Margaret's daughter's insisting that May be placed in a home for the elderly. In the last section of the story, May feels events come together like the end of a mystery story, as she realizes that the way Margaret is going to escape her daughter's plan is to kill May and then herself; May tries to shout to Margaret, "I don't belong to you, you can't decide that for me." However, as the story comes to an end, the two women become so blended into one entity that it is difficult to separate them; even their memories are inextricably entwined.

In the final scene, May shows Margaret the pills she has been saving, and Margaret adds to them what is left in the bottle. In a reenactment of tea parties she used to have for her dolls, Margaret divides the pills into six

each and goes to get a glass of water before telling one last story about a little doll she had that used to fit in her pocket--a doll called May Flower, which she identified with her sister.

Because of its dependence on memory and the gradual convergence of two characters into one entity, "And Both Shall Row" is not an easy story to read unless readers allow themselves to be engulfed and engaged in the closed-in subjective world of the two sisters. It is a highly lyrical story of reverie as reality, in which language casts a seductive spell that draws the reader more and more into a world that mixes memory and desire in an irresistible way.

BUT COME YE BACK

Lordan had just returned from a spring semester in Ireland when she wrote "The Man with the Lapdog," the first story in this "novel-in-stories" about an American man and his Irish-born wife retiring to her homeland, where the sea is near and the butter has a taste to it, but where he hates driving on the wrong side of the road and does not care for the Guinness. Although each story in *But Come Ye Back* is a perfectly formed independent fiction, the parts create an even greater whole. The reason is the reader's gradual discovery of, and growing concern for, the central characters. As the reader absorbs each story, the reader experiences shifting allegiances. At one point, Lyle seems like a gruff curmudgeon and his wife long-suffering; at another, Mary seems to be shrewishly sharp tongued and Lyle quietly self-sacrificing.

Like most couples who have lived together for many years, Lyle and Mary chafe against each other, finding it difficult to say how they really feel and occasionally fantasizing about being with someone else. For Lyle, it occurs when he meets an American couple on holiday and discovers that the husband is dying of cancer; he imagines meeting the wife again later. As opposed to the famous Anton Chekhov story ("The Lady with the Dog") of illicit love, from which Lordan's story, "The Man with the Lapdog," gets its name, Lyle quietly values his own relationship. For Mary, it is, of course, an Irish man about whom she momentarily pretends a different story from her marriage to the American who sometimes seems an ungrateful stranger in a strange land.

At the center of the book, after being introduced to the mysterious complexities of the relationship of this aging couple, the reader stumbles upon the story "Digging," ostensibly a chapter of exposition that provides historical background to their lives. However, inspired in part by Seamus Heaney's wonderful poem of the same name, "Digging," which appeared in *Best American Short Stories: 2002*, is more than just the story of how Lyle met Mary; it is a delightful fable in the voice of the traditional Irish fireside storyteller. *But Come Ye Back* concludes with a novella in which Mary gets her wish to be buried among her own people and in which Lyle, now in his seventies, comes gruffly together with his two grown sons and must decide whether to return to America or to stay where Mary seems most alive to him.

In an interview, Lordan justified her use of the popular linked stories format by saying that the individual stories seemed to be asking for one another, and that she wanted to duplicate the individuality and collectiveness of married couples, as well as of America and Ireland, in the book. She said she tried to create the experience the novel affords of going into another world and staying there a while, while using the dense language of the short story.

OTHER MAJOR WORK

LONG FICTION: *August Heat*, 1989.

BIBLIOGRAPHY

Cameron, Julia. "Weaving a Picture of a Small Town." *Los Angeles Times Book Review*, September 10, 1989, p. 13. Says that *August Heat* uses a form of literary pointillism to create a picture of a sour, dyspeptic town. Calls Lordan a fine writer who is perhaps sometimes too fine, too writerly; says her story could use some plot to thicken it.

Dougherty, Robin. "Between the Lines with Beth Lordan." *The Boston Globe*, January 25, 2004, p. H8. An interview story in which Lordan talks about the importance of the setting, her use of the novelistic linked story format, and her focus on older people in *But Come Ye Back*.

Glover, Charlotte L. "*And Both Shall Row*." Review of *And Both Shall Row*, by Beth Lordan. *Library Journal*, 123 (July, 1998): 39. A review that argues that storytelling does not get any better than this collection. Compares Lordan's characters to those of Garrison Keillor; says each story illuminates a different aspect of a community, providing a rich collage of experiences and emotions.

Hand, Elizabeth. "The Village Fairy Tale." Review of *August Heat*, by Beth Lordan. *The Washington Post*, August 22, 1989, p. E3. A review of Lordan's novel *August Heat* that says the book creates a vision of postwar small-town America so fully realized yet so strange to a modern sensibility that it seems like an American Brigadoon. Says Lordan's prose style recalls that of Eudora Welty and Carson McCullers.

Houston, Robert. "Luminous Husbands and Geriatric Cows." *The New York Times*, August 30, 1998, p. 19. Calls Lordan's *And Both Shall Row* a strong collection and praises Lordan's voice as "utterly assured and utterly distinctive." Says Lordan focuses on the kinds of experiences that go beyond words and the kinds of understandings that cannot be named but only described.

Kirkus Reviews. Review of *And Both Shall Row*, by Beth Lordan. 66 (June 15, 1998): 834. Claims that the title novella is the best of its kind since Tillie Olsen's *Tell Me a Riddle* (1961). Says the collection explores the buried visionary dimensions of rustic midwesterners. Compares the collection to Sherwood Anderson's *Winesburg, Ohio* (1919).

Publishers Weekly. Review of *And Both Shall Row*, by Beth Lordan. 245 (June 22, 1998): 83. Says that Lordan can weave a "dense tapestry out of the most mundane detail." Says her precise prose and subtle wisdom heighten an ominous tone in the stories. Claims that small, understated epiphanies bring the characters comfort in struggles over disappointment.

Wanner, Irene. "Collection Tells Tales of Emotion." Review of *And Both Shall Row*, by Beth Lordan. *The Seattle Times*, October 11, 1998, p. M10. This review suggests that whereas "The Snake" has the clearest conflict and the strongest ending, the title story creates the most memorable and fascinating character study.

Written and updated by Charles E. May

BRET LOTT

Born: Los Angeles, California; October 8, 1958

PRINCIPAL SHORT FICTION

A Dream of Old Leaves, 1989
How to Get Home: A Novella and Stories, 1996
The Difference Between Women and Men, 2005

OTHER LITERARY FORMS

Bret Lott is as well known as a novelist as he is as a writer of short fiction. When his novel *Jewel* (1991) was chosen as an Oprah Winfrey book club selection, his reputation rose, although he had published two novels before that. Since *Jewel* he has published novels, memoirs, and a volume of writing instruction. He also has edited two collections of short stories with religious themes.

ACHIEVEMENTS

Bret Lott's short fiction has won a variety of prizes, including the Pushcart Prize in 2000, the Chancellor's Medal from the University of Massachusetts in 2000, and the National Media Award from the National Down Syndrome Congress in 2000. He was named a Fulbright Senior American Scholar at Bar Ilan University in Tel Aviv, Israel, for 2006-2007. His novel *Jewel* was selected for the Oprah book club in 1999. He was appointed editor of the prestigious *Southern Review* in 2004 and has served as nonfiction editor of the journal *Crazyhorse.* He has been a member of the National Council on the Arts.

BIOGRAPHY

Bret Lott was born in Los Angeles, California, in 1958, and Southern California has provided settings for much of his fiction. His father was an executive in a corporation; his mother was a banker. However, his family had roots in the South. One set of grandparents was from near Hattiesburg, Mississippi. Because much of his adult life has been spent in Charleston, South Carolina, and in Baton Rouge, Louisiana, the South has informed his writing.

As a young adult, Lott worked at some of the jobs that often show up in his fiction, especially those in soft-drink sales. He also worked as a reporter for the *Daily Commercial News* in Los Angeles in 1980 and 1981.

Lott received a B.A. from California State University in 1981 and an M.F.A. from the University of Massachusetts, Amherst, in 1984. During that time he studied under writers James Baldwin and Jay Neugeboren. From 1984 to 1986, Lott taught English composition at Ohio State University. In 1986, he joined the English faculty of the College of Charleston in Charleston, South Carolina, leaving that position in 2004 to move to editorship of the *Southern Review* in Baton Rouge, Louisiana. He returned to the College of Charleston in 2007. He married Melanie Kai Swank in 1980; they have two sons.

ANALYSIS

Bret Lott's short fiction has focused on human relationships, especially in families and between parents and children and husbands and wives. Lott has said that he wants his work to stand in opposition to the bleak cynicism of much contemporary fiction. As an evangelical Christian, he finds such hopelessness contradictory to his understanding of the world, and he hopes that his work will counterbalance that worldview. He has cited the Catholic writer Flannery O'Connor as one of his literary heroes. Like O'Connor, Lott refrains from making explicitly religious statements in his work, and, like her, he often chooses to portray his characters at moments of great crisis in their lives, when they may be open to understanding both of themselves and of those around them.

The world of Lott's fiction is resolutely ordinary, especially regarding employment. It is a world in which many men work at low-paying jobs (the number of R. C. Cola route men in his stories is notable), a world in which people lose jobs because of the whims of their employers or the exigencies of the marketplace, a world in which people find themselves having to move to new cities to keep jobs they do not like. In general, Lott's characters live in modest homes and apartments; they drive ordinary Chevrolets and Fords; they are named ordinary names--David and Jill rather than Alexandra and Estaban.

Lott's characters face those crises that inform ordinary life. They get into fist fights at work; they squabble with their spouses; they get into illicit love affairs; they face bankruptcy; they deal with the death of loved ones (and not-so-loved ones), or they hear about the death of people outside their immediate world and recognize death's implication for themselves. The men spend months in unemployment, looking for work while their wives support the family. People get sick; they worry about their unborn children; they worry about their living children, who seem vulnerable in a frightening world. They endure painful family rifts in which parents refuse to attend a son's wedding or quit speaking to each other for years.

Lott is a meticulous observer of the tiny details that indicate an emotional response, and the action of many of his stories hinges on small gestures that suggest much more than they say. In "Things That Could Come," a couple stops for burgers on their way home from the hospital, the husband still raw in his new understanding of the possible dangers to his as-yet-unborn child. In "Christmas Presents," a father watches closely to see his son's reaction to the boy's new baby sister when she arrives home from the hospital.

A few of Lott's stories draw on the conventions of Magical Realism. In "Family," the quarreling parents discover that their children have disappeared. When at last the children surface, they have both shrunk and aged to become miniature adults, who--rather like their parents--are indifferent to any but themselves. In "The Difference Between Men and Women," an angry woman signals to her husband that their marriage is over by moving all their bedroom furniture, including a

Bret Lott (Getty Images)

heavy armoire containing his clothes, which she carries out of the bedroom.

The settings for Lott's stories are often the anonymous places of middle America; they contain housing developments and shopping malls, Bi-Lo groceries and small convenience stores. In some cases, Lott uses specific locations to underscore a story's themes. Thus, in the novella *After Leston*, the Los Angeles-area Watts riots create a motif for the stresses involved in a family's move to California. In several cases, a dual setting of East Coast and West Coast dramatizes family ties stretched thin.

"IN CALIFORNIA"

This story, from Lott's 1989 collection *A Dream of Old Leaves*, contains the seeds of his novel *Ancient Highway* (2008). In it, the narrator, Gordy, has been discharged from the Navy and has returned to his grandparents' home in Los Angeles. He feels far closer to his grandparents than to his parents, having stayed with the grandparents when he was a teenager after he ran away from home. Like many of Lott's young men, he is trying hard to figure out what to do with the rest of his life. He searches the newspaper want ads for a job and spends time with his grandfather, a former actor who makes caftans to sell at flea markets. Gordy also helps his grandmother, a former singer who has become a feisty old woman who is almost blind. Although his grandparents are not pressuring him, Gordy feels a deep need to find himself. On the day the story opens, he has two small triumphs. First, he accompanies his grandmother, a hard-core smoker, on a few blocks' walk to the liquor store, where she buys her cigarettes. He imagines that he is helping her, but events demonstrate that she is perfectly capable of managing the walk, even of crossing a busy boulevard. She tells him that this excursion is her last shred of independence. At the end of the story, Gordy is learning to operate a sewing machine and to make caftans with his grandfather. A few days earlier, his mother had phoned to make sure he had arrived, but she simply left a message without talking with him. She sends him a small card, which he stuffs in his pocket without reading, suggesting the great gulf between Gordy and his parents.

AFTER LESTON

The novella *After Leston*, from *How to Get Home*, is another example of Lott's use of short fiction as a seed for a long work; in this case the novel is *Jewel*. Jewel is the narrator of this story, which is set in a Los Angeles suburb on the second anniversary of her husband Leston's death. She misses Leston deeply, but Jewel's life is bound up in that of her last child, Brenda Kay, in her early twenties, who has Down syndrome. Jewel had brought the family to California to take advantage of the state's excellent educational facilities for learning-disabled children. Brenda Kay thrived, riding a bus to a school where she is taught not only academics but also arts and crafts. She particularly loves hooking rugs and has made several, including one as a gift for her father, almost as if she is not aware that he has died.

As Jewel prepares to commemorate Leston's death, she thinks of the upheaval the move to California caused her family. Leston had to close a business he loved and had a difficult time finding work in their new home. Ultimately he took a janitorial job, working with a black man whom he came to regard as a friend, until, on the eve of the Watts riots, his partner suddenly

cooled. After the riots, Leston drove his family through the ruins of the ghetto, in a sort of defiance. A few weeks later he died. Two years later, Jewel takes Brenda Kay to the tide pools for a picnic, honoring Leston's memory in a place he loved. To her surprise, she realizes that Brenda Kay also recognizes the significance of the place.

"EVERYTHING WILL COME BACK"

This story, from *The Difference Between Men and Women*, is a good example of Lott's use of family themes. In the story, the narrator in Massachusetts receives a phone call from his brother, Tim, in California. They are both married with children and, after the death of their parents, stay close through weekly phone calls, even though their lives have taken different directions. In this call, Tim relates how his neighbor's wife has died. Tim and the neighbor had once had a friendly rivalry in taking care of their lawns, mowing them at the same time every week. Tim, uncertain of how to reach out to his grieving neighbor, meticulously mows the neighbor's yard and prunes his lavish collection of azaleas and fruit trees. After the call, the narrator looks with love at his wife and family and then drives through the snowy countryside thinking of his parents and their love for each other, thoughts informed by the story of his brother's grieving neighbor.

"ROSE"

This story, very different from Lott's usual work, also comes from *The Difference Between Men and Women*. Its dedication reads "For Mr. Faulkner, with all respect," for this is a retelling of one of William Faulkner's best-known stories, "A Rose for Emily." Lott's version features Emily's indirect telling of her own version of the events of her life. Many of the details will be familiar to those who know Faulkner's story. Emily recalls her father driving off her suitors; she thinks of her role in the death of Homer Barron, her lover, and how she imposed her own will on the town to which she feels so superior. The difference in Lott's version is the gradual revelation that Emily bore a child as the result of her single union with Homer, a child who died, a child whom she named Rose and whose body she kept just as she had kept Homer's body. Unlike Homer, Rose is kept as documentation of the love Emily once received, not from Homer or the infant, but from the mother who died giving her birth.

OTHER MAJOR WORKS

LONG FICTION: *The Man Who Owned Vermont*, 1987; *A Stranger's House*, 1988; *Jewel*, 1991; *Reed's Beach*, 1993; *The Hunt Club*, 1998; *A Song I Knew by Heart*, 2004; *Ancient Highway*, 2008.

NONFICTION: *Fathers, Sons, and Brothers: The Men in My Family*, 1997 (essays); *Before We Get Started: A Practical Memoir of the Writer's Life*, 2005.

EDITED TEXTS: *The Best Christian Short Stories*, 2006; *Eyes to See, Volume Two*, 2008.

BIBLIOGRAPHY

Albin, C. D. "*The Best Christian Short Stories.*" *Christianity and Literature* 56, no. 4 (Summer, 2007): 716. In reviewing the stories of the collection, Albin gives considerable attention to Lott's religious perspective in selecting the stories, emphasizing his lack of "preachiness."

Bauer, Susan Wise. "Original Misunderstanding." *Books and Culture* 11, no. 5 (September/October, 2005): 31. In this generally negative review of *The Difference Between Men and Women*, the reviewer finds particular fault with Lott's style and plots, both of which she finds unnecessarily confusing,

Fugard, Lisa. "Home Movies." *The New York Times Book Review*, August 17, 2008, p. 13L. In this detailed review of *Ancient Highways*, the reviewer gives attention to Lott's interest in family relationships, his style, and the structure of the work. She finds the structure flawed.

Weinberg, Steve. "One Writer's Journey to Success." *The Writer* 118, no. 7 (July 2005): 48. This article reviews *Before We Get Started*, giving attention to the growth of Lott's career and his encouragement to writers who face rejection slips.

Ann Davison Garbett

H. P. LOVECRAFT

Born: Providence, Rhode Island; August 20, 1890
Died: Providence, Rhode Island; March 15, 1937

PRINCIPAL SHORT FICTION

The Dunwich Horror and Others, 1963
Dagon, and Other Macabre Tales, 1965
The Horror in the Museum, and Other Revisions, 1970

OTHER LITERARY FORMS

Except for his personal correspondence, H. P. Lovecraft's total output was quite modest, even considering his relatively short life. Like that of his illustrious predecessor, Edgar Allan Poe, almost all of Lovecraft's narratives are in the shorter forms, with at most three works qualifying as novelettes. Other than fiction, his writings consist of some poetry, a few essays on literature and science, and a voluminous amount of personal correspondence, much of which has been published. In addition to his own work, Lovecraft revised, rewrote, and "ghosted" a large number of works for other authors, including one short story for Harry Houdini. Although a number of his stories have served as the basis for films, the products have seldom resembled the originals. Indicative of this is the ironical fact that probably the most successful adaptation of Lovecraftian material was released under the title "Edgar Allan Poe's *Haunted Palace.*"

ACHIEVEMENTS

H. P. Lovecraft brought an intimate knowledge of the short story to his horror-story creations. Beginning as a ghostwriter and pulp-fiction hack, Lovecraft produced a body of tales that is still viewed as important by those who write fantasies on the dark side: Robert Bloch and Stephen King, to name only two who cite Lovecraft as an important influence on their own work. Of equal importance is Lovecraft's study of horror literature, *Supernatural Horror in Literature* (1945), in which he outlines the structure of the tale of terror. This work is still cited as an important study in the narrative structure of the horror story.

Biography

Except for a few trips with friends in the last years of his life and residence in New York City during part of his brief marriage to Sonia Greene, Howard Phillips Lovecraft spent almost all of his life in Providence, Rhode Island, living with aunts in genteel poverty on the diminishing family capital. Most of the money he made as a writer came from collaborative efforts and ghostwriting. As a pulp-fiction author he wrote too little to make much money and was too reticent to sell much of what he did produce. By far, the bulk of his writing was done for nonpaying amateur publications and in personal correspondence. Lovecraft died at age forty-six of intestinal cancer.

Analysis

The critical acceptance of H. P. Lovecraft as an important American writer, and as the finest exponent of dark fantasy since Poe, has not come quickly or easily. Much of this neglect was due to a blanket rejection of the "pulp writer," reinforced by the fact that Lovecraft published nothing in book form during his own lifetime. The primary outlet for his stories was *Weird Tales*, a pulp magazine whose circulation barely reached twenty thousand a month although its influence on horror fiction has been enormous. Moreover, Lovecraft's entire oeuvre was modest in size and, for reasons both personal and commercial, a considerable portion of it never saw print during his lifetime.

There are, perhaps, even more obvious reasons for this general critical dismissal: In many ways Lovecraft was a poor writer. The prose is often vague, ornate, and studded with overblown adjectives such as "eldrich," "uncanny," "hellish," and "weird." At a time when even the pulps featured the hard, lean prose of a Dashiell Hammett or James M. Cain, Lovecraft's purple verbosity sounded like a relic from the mid-nineteenth century. His characterization tends to be flat and undifferentiated. His plots sometimes collapse in the middle or disintegrate altogether, and his strain for sensational effect occasionally becomes painful. Lovecraft's characteristically italicized last-

line climaxes-- "*and the Monster was Real!!!*"--sometimes evoke more laughter than dread.

How, then, can the reader take this author seriously, let alone grant him status as an important writer? The answer lies in the two unique contributions Lovecraft made to the supernatural horror genre in particular and to modern literature in general: His original approach to dark fantasy revitalized the genre and has influenced every important new writer in the field, and the vision that animates his fictions transcended the limits of the popular genre to offer a provocative and significant view of modern human beings' predicament.

"The Outsider"

Because it has been so frequently anthologized, Lovecraft's best-known work is probably the somewhat uncharacteristic short story "The Outsider." An unnamed narrator laments his unhappy, bizarre youth. Having grown up bereft of human contact in a dismal, decaying castle, filled with damp "crumbling corriders" that smell like "piled-up corpses of dead generations," he resolves to escape by ascending a partly ruined black tower whose top "reaches above the trees into the unknown outer sky." After a difficult, perilous climb the narrator reaches a trapdoor, which he pushes open. To his amazement, he finds that he is not, as expected, on some "lofty eminence," but is, instead, "on *the solid ground*." Wandering about, he then comes upon a castle where a party is in full progress. As he enters, the guests run screaming. He assumes that there is a horrible presence lurking near him and becomes frightened. Sighting the beast, he overcomes his fears and approaches it, finally touching the thing's "*rotting outstretched paw*." Terrified, he flees back to the trapdoor but finds it blocked. Thus, he is forced to linger on the fringes of the world of the living, alienated from all contact with its inhabitants. In the last sentence of the story, the speaker reveals what he touched that so frightened him: *a cold and unyielding surface of polished glass.*"

The effect of this story on the reader is chilling--even if the story, when analyzed, is a bit absurd. Lovecraft succeeds in gaining the reader's sympathetic identification with the narrator so the revelation of its monstrous being is a shock, and the experience itself is almost archetypal. One ingenious critic has offered five separate and different interpretations of the tale: autobiographical, psychological (Jungian), metaphysical, philosophical, and political. Although none of these readings is completely satisfying, they all have some merit and illustrate the important point: "The Outsider" evokes emotional responses that are not fully explained by critical exegesis.

At the same time, the story turns essentially on a clever deception: The reader is tricked into identifying with a creature who turns out to be a corpse or zombie or ghoul or something of that sort, a fact that is not revealed until the punch line. The sensitive reader is likely to be moved and irritated by a story that seems both profound and trivial. This mixed reaction is characteristic of many of Lovecraft's stories, and any attempt to assess his importance must somehow take it into consideration.

Despite its popularity, "The Outsider" does not suggest the full range of the author's powers. At best it is a story with more resonance than substance, a very clever exercise in imitating Poe. To truly appreciate Lovecraft one must examine his central vision--the somewhat misnamed "Cthulhu Mythos." (The term was coined by August Derleth, but Cthulhu is not really the major figure in the hierarchy. Contemporary Lovecraftians prefer to call it the "Lovecraft Mythos.")

The Mythos did not spring full blown from Lovecraft's head but emerged in bits and pieces. In "Nyarlathotep," a fragment, Lovecraft presented the first important figure in his pantheon. "The Nameless City" introduced the "mad Arab, Abdul Alhazrad," author of the *Necronomicon*, a fictive text of magical spells and arcane knowledge which became the bible of the Mythos. The book itself was brought into "The Hound" and "The Festival," the latter story being the first set in the "Arkham, Massachusetts" region, site of most Mythos tales. It was not until 1926, however, that Lovecraft really consolidated his ideas and presented them in a single story, "The Call of Cthulhu."

The artistic assumption behind the Mythos is that by the 1920's the usual menaces of horror fiction--such as Satan, demons, werewolves, and vampires--had become overworked and obsolete. A new set of menaces, he felt, one more in keeping with contemporary views of humans and their place in the universe, was needed to breathe life into the genre.

The metaphysical assumption behind the Mythos is stated in the famous first paragraph of "The Call of Cthulhu":

> The most merciful thing in the world, I think, is the inability of the human mind to correlate all its contents. We live on a placid island of ignorance in the midst of black seas of infinity, and it was not meant that we should voyage far. The sciences, each straining in its own direction, have hitherto harmed us little; but some day the piecing together of dissociated knowledge will open up such terrifying vistas of reality, and of our frightful position therein, that we shall either go mad from the revelation or flee from the deadly light into the peace and safety of a new dark age.

In the Cthulhu Mythos, that "terrifying reality" consists of an order of beings, vast, powerful, and immortal, who hover at the edges of humans' consciousness, poised to enter their world and sweep them away like so much useless debris. These creatures--the "Great Old Ones" or "Ancient Ones," with exotic forbidding names and titles, such as "Cthulhu," "the messenger Nyarlathotep," "the blind, idiot god Azathoth," "the key to the gate Yog-Sothoth"--had dominated the earth long before human beings but lost the power eons ago for reasons that vary from story to story (in early tales, they tended to be supernatural creatures from another dimension; in later ones, they were usually powerful extraterrestrials).

The Old Ones remain on the periphery of human beings' reach in outer space or lie dormant in vast submerged cities, and they strive to reenter the human domain or to awaken from their enforced sleep. Since this reentry is barred to them without human assistance, the Old Ones have established contact with various degenerate groups, families, or individuals, who attempt to utilize the occult knowledge found in forbidden books such as the *Necronomicon* to summon their "masters."

Thus, the typical Mythos story pits the degenerate servants of the Old Ones against the harried but valiant human defenders (most often professors from Miskatonic University). In a few stories the Old Ones can be banished by various magical defenses, but, for the most part, once they are reanimated, they are invulnerable; only accident, luck, or whim saves humanity. Perhaps the most frightening thing about the Old Ones, however, is that, despite their horrendous appearances and destructive capacities, they are not truly evil or consciously malevolent. They simply regard humankind with total indifference and would destroy it for mere convenience without concern or rancor, as a human would step on a pesky insect.

"THE CALL OF CTHULHU"

The narrator of "The Call of Cthulhu" states that "he has had a glimpse" of that awful reality, which "like all dread glimpses of truth, flashed out from an accidental piecing together of separated things--in this case an old newspaper item and the notes of a dead professor." Lovecraft wisely maintains this fragmentary approach in narrating his tale. Instead of a simple chronology, the reader has isolated events and revelations which slowly form into a pattern. This indirect, quasi-journalistic approach also enables Lovecraft to mix real historical events, places, characters, and references with the fictional ones and to insert newspaper clippings and interviews into the text along with straight narrative; the effect is to give the story a strong feeling of authenticity that not only underscores the horrors described but also implies that horrors even more profound lurk just beyond the limits of perception.

"The Call of Cthulhu" is presented in three self-contained sections, which are brought together in the narrator's final conclusions. In the first section, "The Horror in Clay," he describes a set of notes left to him by his granduncle, George Gammell Angell, a Brown University professor emeritus of Semitic languages, who has recently died mysteriously after being jostled by a "nautical looking negro."

Angell's package contains a number of interesting items: a strange bas-relief covered with odd hieroglyphics, including a symbol suggesting "an octopus, a dragon, and a human caricature"; a document headed "Cthulhu Cult"; a number of notes on queer dreams, as well as references to secret cults; and occult, mythological, and anthropological texts. As the narrator examines these fragments, a frightening picture gradually coalesces, from dreams and hints, to accounts of the sinister machinations of the Cthulhu cults and the lore

surrounding the creature, to a final confrontation with the thing itself. This semidocumentary approach works brilliantly. The dreams of a young sculptor, as relayed to Angell and reinforced by a series of weird events around the world, give the reader a feeling of pervasive cosmic evil on the brink of erupting.

That evil is made more concrete in the second part, "The Tale of Inspector Legrasse," which chronicles the apprehension of a mysterious, bestial swamp cult in the midst of human sacrificial rituals. From the cultists and an old mestizo named Castro, the officers hear the story of the Great Old Ones, the first articulation of the Mythos in Lovecraft's stories.

In the third part, "The Madness from the Sea," the reader meets the dreaded Cthulhu itself in the grotesque experiences of Gustaf Johansen, a Norwegian sailor. Although Johansen has apparently been killed by the cultists, the narrator obtains his journal which describes the encounter. After meeting and subduing a boatload of bizarre, savage sailors, Johansen and his comrades discover a mysterious island and inadvertently release Cthulhu from his slumber. All but Johansen and one other are killed; chased by Cthulhu they flee and survive by ramming the monster head-on. The actual meeting with the beast is the least satisfying moment in the story. It is unlikely that any other writer, and certainly one not given to Lovecraft's extravagant use of language, could depict a creature as awful as the one suggested in the story prior to the actual meeting. Even the reader's disappointment in the monster, however, does not seriously undermine the power of Lovecraft's conception; the meeting with the creature is brief and sketchy, leaving the momentum of the story largely undamaged. Neither Lovecraft nor his successors ever made the mistake of bringing Cthulhu back to the surface again.

With "The Call of Cthulhu" Lovecraft established his Mythos, but the story is uncharacteristically expansive and fragmentary. It lacks one element that was typical of most of his best fiction--a solidly realized setting. The hierarchy of supernatural beings was only one side of Lovecraft's coin; the other was the very real, believable New England world into which they usually intruded-- "Arkham, Massachusetts," and environs. As the elements of his cosmic design grew and became more subtle and intricate, so, too, the world of Arkham became more concrete and familiar. Like William Faulkner's Yoknapatawpha County, the real area it was modeled after (Salem and vicinity) can easily be identified, but the fictional region takes on a separate identity of its own.

"THE DUNWICH HORROR"

Nowhere is the importance of this milieu better illustrated than in "The Dunwich Horror," as underscored by the fact that Lovecraft devotes the first five pages to convincing the reader that the township of Dunwich, located in northern Arkham County, is a particularly desolate, foreboding, and degenerate area. Only after thoroughly establishing this realistic environment and eerie atmosphere does he introduce the diabolical and perverse Whateley family, the subjects of the narrative.

Once an important, aristocratic family, the Whateley clan has split into two factions, one that clings to normality and some sense of respectability, and the other that has thoroughly degenerated into bestiality, viciousness, and black magic. The story proper begins with the birth of Wilbur Whateley to Lavinia, "a somewhat deformed albino woman of about 35"; the father is unknown. Lavinia's aged, half-mad, "wizard" father publicly rejoices and tells the villagers that "*some day yew folks'll hear a child o' Lavinny's a-callin' its father's name on the top o' Sentinel Hill!*" The child grows rapidly and strangely. At a year and a half he is as big as a four-year-old; at ten he is fully grown; at thirteen he assumes the role of an adult--and a height of more than seven feet. Other odd events occur around the Whateley household: Extra rooms are built for no apparent reason; whippoorwills crowd about the house and sing constantly; cattle mysteriously disappear--as does Lavinia; and finally the old man dies, mumbling incoherently about "Yog-Sothoth" and "the old ones as wants to come back."

Shortly thereafter Wilbur attempts to secure the Miskatonic University Library copy of the *Necronomicon.* He fails but excites the curiosity of the librarian, Henry Armitage. Some time later Wilbur is killed by a guard dog while attempting to steal the forbidden text during the night. When young Whateley's clothing is ripped off, he is revealed to be a monster whose torso is

covered with black fur, tentacles, unformed eyes, feelers, and the legs of a lizard; instead of blood a greenish-yellow ichor flows out. As people watch, the dead creature dissolves into a putrid mess.

With Wilbur dead, something in the house breaks loose and begins to terrorize the countryside. Armitage recruits two colleagues, and they study the dangerous, arcane books in hopes of finding a defense against the invisible creature, who leaves only huge footprints at the scenes of its carnage. At last they encounter the thing, make it momentarily visible with a powder spray, and deliver the magical chants. As it dissolves, it cries for help to "FATHER. YOG-SOTHOTH!" thus fulfilling old Whateley's prediction, but not in the manner he had desired. As usual, Lovecraft gives readers the final explanation of things in the last line: "You needn't ask how Wilbur called it out of the air. He didn't call it out. *It was his twin brother, but it looked more like the father than he did.*"

"The Dunwich Horror" is probably the most direct and visceral of Lovecraft's major horror stories. If it lacks some of the subtlety and complexity of other masterworks, such as "The Colour Out of Space," *At the Mountains of Madness* (1964), and "The Shadow Out of Time," it is a potent, memorable narrative that perhaps conveys the essence of the Mythos more clearly than any other single story.

OTHER MYTHOS TALES

Lovecraft continued to flesh out his Mythos for the rest of his life, producing a number of impressive stories, notably "Pickman's Model," "The Whisperer in Darkness," "The Shadow over Innsmouth," *At the Mountains of Madness,* "The Dreams in the Witch-House," and "The Shadow Out of Time." At the same time it should be remembered that at least half of Lovecraft's fictional output had little or nothing to do with the Cthulhu group. Even if there had been no Mythos, Lovecraft's place as America's foremost master of the macabre after Poe would have been assured by non-Cthulhuian works, such as "The Outsider," "The Rats in the Walls," "Cool Air" (after Poe's "The Facts in the Case of M. Valdemar"), the eerie science-fiction story "The Colour Out of Space," the Salem witchcraft novelette *The Case of Charles Dexter Ward* (1943), and his most enigmatic nightmare/heroic fantasy, *The Dream-*

Critical Survey of Short Fiction

Quest of Unknown Kadath (1943).

The thing that sets the Mythos narratives apart from Lovecraft's other fiction, however, is their collective power and the fact that the Mythos has continued to grow and prosper many years after its originator's death. Fortunately, however, the power of the original concept, at least in Lovecraft's own stories, comes through safely; in the end, it is this cosmic vision that gives Lovecraft his primary stature among modern horror writers. Lovercraft was a materialist in belief and attitude who viewed all supernatural ideas, whether conventionally religious or occult, as make-believe. The previously quoted opening paragraph from "The Call of Cthulhu" is a succinct summary of its author's own thinking. Thus, his Old Ones, with their indifferent cruelty and overwhelming powers, were, to Lovecraft, metaphors for a cruelly indifferent universe that provides a fragile, temporary refuge for the most ephemeral and insignificant of creatures--humans.

In essence, Lovercraft's cosmic view resembles that of many modern writers, including artists as different as Thomas Hardy and Robinson Jeffers. Like them, Lovecraft's art was an attempt to find a set of metaphors and images with which to express that worldview. The power of the Cthulhu Mythos lies in the fact that, despite the clumsiness, turgidity, and triteness of much of the writing, it presents a powerful metaphorical construct of the modern world and the extremely precarious place of human beings in it.

OTHER MAJOR WORKS

LONG FICTION: *The Case of Charles Dexter Ward*, 1943; *The Dream-Quest of Unknown Kadath*, 1943; *At the Mountains of Madness, and Other Novels*, 1964.

POETRY: *Collected Poems*, 1963; *A Winter Wish*, 1977.

NONFICTION: *Supernatural Horror in Literature*, 1945; *Selected Letters*, 1965-1976 (August Derleth and Donald Wandrei, editors); *Lovecraft at Last*, 1975 (with Willis Conover); *Lord of a Visible World: An Autobiography in Letters*, 2000 (S. T. Joshi and David E. Schultz, editors); *Mysteries of Time and Spirit: The Letters of H. P. Lovecraft and Donald Wandrei*, 2002 (S. T. Joshi and David E. Schultz, editors); *Collected Essays*, 2004-2007 (five volumes; S. T. Joshi, editor);

Letters from New York, 2005 (S. T. Joshi and David E. Schultz, editors).

MISCELLANEOUS: *The Outsider and Others*, 1939; *Beyond the Wall of Sleep*, 1943; *Marginalia*, 1944; *The Something About Cats*, 1949; *The Shuttered Room, and Other Pieces*, 1959; *The Dark Brotherhood, and Other Pieces*, 1966; *To Quebec and the Stars*, 1976; *Tales*, 2005 (includes short stories and novels; Peter Straub, editor).

BIBLIOGRAPHY

Airaksinen, Timo. *The Philosophy of H. P. Lovecraft: The Route to Horror*. New York: Peter Lang, 1999. Focuses on the themes of Lovecraft's stories, which are defined as "nihilism, cosmicism, the language of the unsayable, and the tension between science and magic." Discusses his writing style.

Burleson, Donald R. *H. P. Lovecraft: A Critical Study*. Westport, Conn.: Greenwood Press, 1983. A helpful consideration of Lovecraft's fiction, nonfiction, and poetry. Provides a good overview of his work and places him among other writers in the horror fiction genre.

_____. "Lovecraft's 'The Colour Out of Space.'" *The Explicator* 52 (Fall, 1993): 48-50. Focuses on the craft and intricacy of this short story.

Carter, Lin. *Lovecraft: A Look Behind the "Cthulhu Mythos."* New York: Ballantine, 1972. An extended examination of Lovecraft's mythic horror pantheon. Useful for following the development of his fictive world of demons and altered "realities."

Clements, Nicholaus. "Lovecraft's 'The Haunter of the Dark.'" *The Explicator* 57 (Winter, 1999): 98-100. Argues that the lightning in the story is not ordinary light but upward lightning, a dark light not ordinarily found in the known universe that comes from other dimensions of space.

Evans, Timothy H. "A Last Defense Against the Dark: Folklore, Horror, and the Uses of Tradition in the Works of H. P. Lovecraft." *Journal of Folklore Research* 42, no.1 (January-April, 2005): 99-135. Argues that Lovecraft's works "embodied much of the ideology that surrounded the interest in folklore and tradition in the United States in the 1920's and 1930's," such as the rejection of commercialism, mass culture, and immigration, and an interest in preserving American architecture and history.

Halpern, Paul, and Michael C. LaBossiere. "Mind Out of Time: Identity, Perception, and the Fourth Dimension in H. P. Lovecraft's 'The Shadow Out of Time' and 'The Dreams in the Witch House.'" *Extrapolation* 50, no. 3 (Fall, 2009): 512-533. Examines how Lovecraft uses contemporary science and philosophy, time travel, and the fourth dimension in the two stories. Maintains that these stories depict the supernatural "as a manifestation of science and the natural."

Joshi, S. T. *The Evolution of the Weird Tale.* New York: Hippocampus Press, 2004. Traces the development of American and British supernatural fiction during the nineteenth and twentieth centuries. Assesses Lovecraft's place in the cannon of horror fiction.

_____, ed. *H. P. Lovecraft: Four Decades of Criticism.* Athens: Ohio University Press, 1980. Contains essays by Barton Levi St. Armand, J. Vernon Shea, and Dirk W. Mosig, as well as a survey of Lovecraft criticism by Joshi.

_____. *H. P. Lovecraft: A Life.* West Warwick, R.I.: Necronomicon Press, 1996. A definitive biography by the foremost Lovecraft scholar. Joshi discusses the circumstances in which Lovecraft's stories originated and offers concise summaries, historical context, and critical remarks about these writings. Although generally sympathetic to Lovecraft, Joshi does describe his racism and ill treatment of his wife.

_____. *Primal Sources: Essays on H. P. Lovecraft.* New York: Hippocampus Press, 2003. Collection of Joshi's previously published essays on Lovecraft, including discussions of Lovecraft's philosophy, use of autobiography and pseudonyms in his works, his

depiction of the dream world and real world, and a political interpretation of his portrayal of alien civilizations. Some of the other essays analyze individual stories.

Lévy, Maurice. *Lovecraft: A Study in the Fantastic.* Translated by S. T. Joshi. Detroit: Wayne State University Press, 1988. A useful consideration of Lovecraft's fictional works as examples of the fantastic in literature. Helpful to those interested in genre study and critical theory.

Nelson, Victoria. "H. P. Lovecraft and the Great Heresies." *Raritan* 15 (Winter, 1996): 92-121. Compares the imaginative universe of Lovecraft to that of Daniel Paul Schreber. Claims that Lovecraft, obsessed by themes whose full dimensions he was unable or unwilling to grasp consciously, used his intense sensitivity to his own unconscious to give modern readers a unique body of work and a new variation on some very old religious and philosophical traditions of western culture.

Oakes, David. *Science and Destabilization in the Modern American Gothic: Lovecraft, Matheson, and King.* Westport, Conn.: Greenwood Press, 2000. A study of the role of science in the works of of Lovecraft, Richard Matheson, and Stephen King.

Schultz, David E., and S. T. Joshi. *An Epicure in the Terrible: A Centennial Anthology of Essays in Honor of H. P. Lovecraft.* London: Associated University Presses, 1991. Includes essays on Lovecraft's themes, the uses of isolation in his works of fiction, his cosmic vision, his unique mythology, his modernism, his use of the pulp-magazine tradition, and his relationship to Jorge Luis Borges.

Keith Neilson
Updated by Melissa E. Barth

M

CLARENCE MAJOR

Born: Atlanta, Georgia; December 31, 1936

PRINCIPAL SHORT FICTION

Fun and Games, 1990

OTHER LITERARY FORMS

Clarence Major has written more than twenty-five books in several genres, including the novels *All-Night Visitors* (1969), *NO* (1973), *My Amputations*, (1986), *Such Was the Season* (1987), *Painted Turtle: Woman with Guitar* (1988), and *One Flesh* (2003). He has published numerous collections of his poetry, including *Parking Lots: A Poem* (1992), *Configurations: New and Selected Poems, 1958-1998* (1999), *Waiting for Sweet Betty* (2002), and *Myself Painting* (2009). In addition, Major edited *The New Black Poetry* (1969), *Calling the Wind: Twentieth-Century African-American Short Stories* (1993), and other anthologies, and he has written several critical studies, including *The Dark and Feeling: Black American Writers and Their Work* (1974), *Dictionary of Afro-American Slang* (1970, reprinted in 1994 as *Juba to Jive: A Dictionary of African-American Slang*), and *Necessary Distance: Essays and Criticism* (2001). Achievements

Among his awards and grants, Clarence Major has received two Pushcart Prizes, one for poetry in 1976 and another for fiction in 1989. He was the recipient of a Fulbright-Hays Exchange Award in 1981-1983. His novel *My Amputations* won the western States Book Award, *Such Was the Season* was a Literary Guild Selection, *Painted Turtle: Woman with Guitar* was a *New York Times* notable book, *Fun and Games* was a finalist for the *Los Angeles Times* Book Critics Award, *Calling the Wind: Twentieth-Century African-American Short Stories* was a Book-of-the-Month Club selection, and

Configurations: New and Selected Poems was a finalist for the National Book Award

BIOGRAPHY

Clarence Major was born in Atlanta, Georgia, grew up on the South Side of Chicago, and served in the U.S. Air Force from 1955 to 1957. He studied at the Chicago Art Institute, graduated from the State University of New York at Albany, and earned a Ph.D. from the Union of Experimenting Colleges and Universities. Major taught at a number of universities, both in the United States and abroad, and since 1989 he has been teaching at the University of California at Davis. In addition to publishing his fiction and poetry, Major has exhibited and published paintings and photographs. He has also been an editor and columnist and has lectured widely. He has been married twice and has lived in various parts of the United States and for extended periods in France and Italy.

ANALYSIS

Clarence Major's short fiction has attracted much less critical attention than his novels, and yet, as Doug Bolling has noted, "his short fiction is valuable in its own right and deserves wide reading and critical discussion." Among other strengths, Major is capable of a range of fictional styles, from the conventional to the experimental. Nearly all of his fiction is marked by lyricism and a fascination with language, but even his most realistic short stories (like "My Mother and Mitch" and "Ten Pecan Pies") tend to challenge readers. His antimimetic, experimental fiction, as Bolling argues,

> helps us to see that fiction created within an aesthetic of fluidity and denial of "closure" and verbal freedom can generate an excitement and awareness of great value; that the rigidities of plot, characteriza-

tion, and illusioned depth can be softened and, finally, dropped in favor of new and valid rhythms.

Jerome Klinkowitz has written that the central achievement of Major's career

> has been to show just how concretely we live within the imagination--how our lives are shaped by language and how by a simple act of self-awareness we can seize control of the world and reshape it to our liking and benefit.

FUN AND GAMES

Clarence Major's short-story collection *Fun and Games* was nominated for the *Los Angeles Times* Book Critics Award in 1990. While the volume represents Major's short fiction through the 1980's, it is a good barometer of his continuing fictional interests and forms. The sixteen stories in the volume are divided into five parts: Section 1 contains three stories (including the realistic "My Mother and Mitch" and "Ten Pecan Pies"), section 2 also has three shorter and more surreal stories, section 3 contains six stories, section 4 has three, and section 5 comprises "Mobile Axis: A Triptych," three interconnected short fictions. While Major is capable of one form of social realism (as in "Letters"), he more regularly leans toward a staccato, fragmentary prose fiction in which the links are missing among characters and incidents (as in "The Horror" and the title story).

"The Exchange," for example is a fairly realistic, even comic story about a faculty exchange gone horribly wrong. When the narrator and his wife arrive on the opposite coast to begin the year-long exchange, they find a dilapidated house. Worse, when they return to their own home at the end of the year, their exchangees have turned the house into a replica of their own-- down to the moldy contents of the refrigerator. Likewise, the collection's title story is a first-person narration about a man's three or four girlfriends, who keep leaving him and returning. The story is comic and at the same an oblique commentary on transience and commitment in contemporary society. More common in *Fun and Games*, however, is "Mother Visiting," a short, three-page story that violates most of the conventions of fictional verisimilitude. While the story touches upon a number of contemporary

issues (notably sex and violence), its postmodernist style emphasizes the play of language over sense. Likewise, in the short story "Virginia," the dazzling use of language and image have replaced the demands of plot.

"MY MOTHER AND MITCH"

This story won the Pushcart Prize for fiction in 1989 and leads off the *Fun and Games* collection. In some ways it does not resemble Major's other short fiction, being a leaner and less experimental coming-of-age story. "My Mother and Mitch" centers on the date that Tommy Anderson's mother had with Mitch Kibbs when Tommy was a teenager in Chicago in 1951. Mitch had dialed a wrong number and then kept calling to talk with Tommy's mother, even after he discovered that she was black. The climax of the story comes when Mitch asks her to meet him in a restaurant, and Tommy watches the white man and his mother talking at the counter of a predominantly black eatery. The story is barely about interracial dating, for the couple never meet again after that night. What is more important is what the young Mitch discovers about his single mother: "I learned for the first time that she did not always know what she was doing. It struck me that she was as helpless as I sometimes felt." That knowledge makes the adolescent Tommy feel closer to his mother because, "there she was, just finding her way, step by step, like me. It was something wonderful anyway." The story may remind readers of Sherwood Anderson's "Death in the Woods," for Tommy is retelling the tale many years later and still trying to get it right and discover its meaning through the retelling. In its lean recreation of its spare events, the story may also remind readers of Raymond Carver and other minimalist short-story writers of the late twentieth century, who forsake long exposition and elaborate descriptions for the psychological revelations of a single voice.

"TEN PECAN PIES"

"Ten Pecan Pies" uses still another fictional style, here a third-person, more traditional narration. The story was first published in *Seattle Review*, is reprinted in the first section of *Fun and Games*, and may remind readers of William Faulkner or Truman Capote in its rural southern setting and voices. "Ten Pecan Pies" concerns one Christmas in the Flower household, when the patriarch Grady Flower has kept two bags of pecans to himself and will not let his wife Thursday make her annual Christmas pies. The other preparations for Christmas--finding and decorating a tree, for example--go on, but Grady hoards the pecans in his room until Christmas Eve, when Thursday finally shames her husband and then, when he gives in, "suddenly kisse[s] the side of his face. The first time in years." The story has other tensions--the drunken son Slick John killing the rabbits in front of his niece, Gal, for example--but the overwhelming feeling of the story is lyrical and nostalgic. Thursday douses the fire in the stove, and the story concludes, "Yet the warmth stayed."

"SCAT"

"Scat" was the only story of his own that Clarence Major selected for *Calling the Wind*, the collection of twentieth century African American fiction he edited in 1993, so readers can assume he thinks the story is important, but it is also representative of a certain comic-surreal style Major mastered. The story covers a nightmare cab ride the narrator and his white girlfriend take into New York City with a cabdriver who subjects them to a monologue about the dangers of Manhattan, where the couple want to go, and the relative safety of Brooklyn, where the cabdriver lives. In his frustration at the cabdriver's tales of the "superstitious practices" and "voodoo rites" in Manhattan, the narrator counters with his own stories of body snatching in Brooklyn. Readers conclude the story still not knowing who is crazier: the cabdriver, who talks knowingly of the "evil art of capnomancy," or the narrator, who speaks of "the Plot, I mean the Sacrifice" and seems equally deranged. Perhaps, if one pursues the definition of the tale's title, the story is the fictional equivalent of jazz singing with nonsense syllables, each voice trying to outdo the other.

"AN AREA IN THE CEREBRAL HEMISPHERE"

This story has been collected in Gloria Naylor's *Children of the Night: The Best Short Stories by Black Writers, 1967 to the Present* (1995) and is the best example of Major's postmodernist style, fragmentary and barely coherent but with a powerful edge to it. The story centers on a young African American woman, a visit by a friend, and the young woman's thoughts about her father and her own life. These events are parceled out in a style that dispels meaning: "The friend lit a cigarette and sat on the sounds of her own voice. Motion. And made a blowing sound," Major writes early in this story, and, a little later on, "And mother's couch was eaten by what might easily have been taxicabs with hooks on them. Anything can happen. (In any case, swift traffic was known to move through her living room.)" This metaphor of motion runs through the story, but it hardly ties together the various fragmented incidents and scraps of dialogue. What readers are left with is Major's brilliant and poetic use of language. Naylor titled the section containing this story "Breaking New Ground," which Major does with his experimental and poetic fictions.

OTHER MAJOR WORKS

LONG FICTION: *All-Night Visitors*, 1969; *NO*, 1973; *Reflex and Bone Structure*, 1975; *Emergency Exit*, 1979; *My Amputations*, 1986; *Such Was the Season*, 1987; *Painted Turtle: Woman with Guitar*, 1988; *Dirty Bird Blues*, 1996; *One Flesh*, 2003.

POETRY: *The Fires That Burn in Heaven*, 1954; *Love Poems of a Black Man*, 1965; *Human Juices*, 1966; *Swallow the Lake*, 1970; *Private Line*, 1971; *Symptoms and Madness*, 1971; *The Cotton Club*, 1972; *The Syncopated Cakewalk*, 1974; *Inside Diameter: The France Poems*, 1985; *Surfaces and Masks: A Poem*, 1988; *Some Observations of a Stranger at Zuni in the Latter Part of the Century*, 1989; *Parking Lots: A Poem*, 1992; *Configurations: New and Selected Poems, 1958-1998*, 1998; *Waiting for Sweet Betty*, 2002; *Myself Painting*, 2009.

NONFICTION: *Dictionary of Afro-American Slang*, 1970 (also known as *Juba to Jive: A Dictionary of African-American Slang*, 1994); *The Dark and Feeling: Black American Writers and Their Work*, 1974; *Necessary Distance: Essays and Criticism*, 2001; *Come by Here: My Mother's Life*, 2002; *Conversations with Clarence Major*, 2002 (Nancy Bunge, editor).

EDITED TEXTS: *Writers Workshop Anthology*, 1967; *Man Is Like a Child*, 1968; *The New Black Poetry*, 1969; *Calling the Wind: Twentieth-Century African-American Short Stories*, 1993; *The Garden Thrives: Twentieth-Century African-American Poetry*, 1996.

BIBLIOGRAPHY

Bell, Bernard W. *Clarence Major and His Art: Portraits of an African American Postmodernist*. Chapel Hill: University of North Carolina Press, 2001. Critical essays on Major's work are interspersed with essays, poems, and paintings by Major himself.

_____, ed. "Introduction: Clarence Major's Double Consciousness as a Black Postmodernist Artist." *African American Review* 28 (Spring, 1994): 5-10. Bell introduces this special issue of the journal, which includes eight "Writings by Clarence Major," a section of his artwork, as well as critical analyses of his poetry and fiction.

Bolling, Doug. "A Reading of Clarence Major's Short Fiction." *Black American Literature Forum* 13 (1979): 51-56. This early study of Major's short stories recognizes that the artist "works with 'process,' with open forms, with the inconclusive, and with the interplay of formal and informal tensions." One of the best analyses of Major's short fiction, the essay includes discussions of "Ten Pecan Pies," "Fun and Games," and "An Area in the Cerebral Hemisphere."

Fleming, Robert. "Thirty-Five Years as a Literary Maverick: Clarence Major Is Revered and Respected for His Literary Achievements--He's Just Not as Widely Known as He Should Be." *Black Issues Book Review* 6, no. 2 (March/April, 2004): 54-57. A review of two of Major's novels, *One Flesh* and *Such Was the Season*, that provides an overview of his life and literary career, details his achievements, and argues that he deserves greater recognition than he has received. Includes a selected bibliography of Major's work.

Klinkowitz, Jerome. "Clarence Major's Innovative Fiction." *African American Review* 28 (Spring 1994): 57-63. While dealing primarily with Major's novels, Klinkowitz recognizes the "anti-realistic (and even anti-mimetic)" strain to much of Major's fiction.

_____. *The Life of Fiction*. Urbana: University of Illinois Press, 1977. Chapter 8 of Klinkowitz's early study of a dozen postmodernist American writers focuses on Major and recognizes both the lyricism and the anticonventional strains of Major's fiction.

Major, Clarence. *Conversations with Clarence Major*, edited by Nancy Bunge. Jackson: University Press of Mississippi, 2002. Collection of interviews conducted with Major from 1969 through 2001, in which he discusses the diverse nature of his writings, particular works, the dynamic nature of language, his teaching of writing, and his views of nature, among many other subjects.

O'Brien, John. "Clarence Major." In *Interviews with Black Writers*. New York: Liveright, 1973. This fourteen-page interview with Major sheds light on the writer's life and work.

Weixlmann, Joe. "Clarence Major: A Checklist of Criticism." *Obsidian* 4, no. 2 (1978): 101-113. This checklist brings together some of the most important works of literary criticism written about Major's fiction.

David Peck

Bernard Malamud

Born: Brooklyn, New York; April 26, 1914
Died: New York, New York; March 18, 1986
Also known as: Peter Lumm

Principal short fiction
The Magic Barrel, 1958
Idiots First, 1963
Pictures of Fidelman: An Exhibition, 1969
Rembrandt's Hat, 1973
The Stories of Bernard Malamud, 1983
The People, and Uncollected Stories, 1989
The Complete Stories, 1997 (Robert Giroux, editor)

Other literary forms

Bernard Malamud (MAL-uh-muhd) devoted his writing career to fiction. In addition to his highly praised short stories, he wrote eight well-received novels: *The Natural* (1952), *The Assistant* (1957), *A New Life* (1961), *The Fixer* (1966), *The Tenants* (1971), *Dubin's Lives* (1979), *God's Grace* (1982), and *The People* (1989). He is also the author of many literary essays and reviews.

Achievements

Bernard Malamud is one of the best American writers of the last half of the twentieth century. In his eight novels and numerous short stories, he transcends the Jewish experience so ably chronicled by the so-called Jewish literary renaissance writers, such as Saul Bellow and Philip Roth, by using Jewish life as a metaphor for universal experience. Critic Robert Alter has proclaimed that Malamud's short stories, such as "The First Seven Years," "The Magic Barrel," "The Last Mohican," "Idiots First," and "Angel Levine," will be read "as long as anyone continues to care about American fiction written in the 20th century."

Both a traditionalist and an experimenter in his fiction, Malamud won rave reviews, literary plaudits, and many awards. *The Magic Barrel* brought a National Book Award in 1959. In 1967, *The Fixer* won for him a second National Book Award as well as a Pulitzer Prize. In addition, he was president of the International Association of Poets, Playwrights, Editors, Essayists, and Novelists (PEN Club) from 1979 to 1981.

Biography

Born on April 26, 1914, Bernard Malamud was the eldest of two sons of Max and Bertha Malamud. His parents, who had emigrated from Russia, ran a grocery store. Both Yiddish and English were spoken in the Malamud household, where much emphasis was placed on the cultural aspects of Judaism.

This milieu as well as his father's tales of life in czarist Russia provided much fodder for Malamud's fiction. He was also influenced by many trips to the Yiddish theater on Manhattan's Second Avenue, and by novels, such as his favorite Horatio Alger stories and a multivolume *Book of Knowledge* that his father gave him when he was nine.

Throughout his boyhood in the back room of the family store, where he wrote stories, and his high school days at Erasmus Hall in Brooklyn, where he was an editor of the literary magazine, Malamud was devoted to storytelling. In 1936, he was graduated from City College of New York. He had written a few stories in college and continued to write during a series of odd jobs. While working on an M.A. at Columbia University, he taught at Erasmus Hall Evening High School and wrote. In 1945, he married a Gentile, Ann de Chiara.

During the 1940's, Malamud's stories appeared in some noncommercial magazines. Then, in 1949, he sold the appropriately titled "The Cost of Living" to *Harper's Bazaar.* That same year, he moved with his family to Corvallis, Oregon, where he worked at

Oregon State University. Finally adjusting from the urban to the rural lifestyle, Malamud developed a new perspective and a weekly routine that allowed him much quality time for writing: He taught three days a week and wrote four. Without a Ph.D., he was forced to teach composition, not literature, so his favorite course was a compromise--a night workshop in short-story writing for townspeople. His stories began to appear in such noted magazines as *Partisan Review, Commentary*, and *Harper's Bazaar*.

The Natural, his first novel, appeared in 1952 to mixed reviews. Some critics were put off by what they saw as an obscure symbolism, while others applauded the masterful use of fable and its art of ancient story-telling in a modern voice. In 1956, the *Partisan Review* made Malamud a fellow in fiction and recommended him for a Rockefeller grant, which made it possible for Malamud to spend a year in Europe. In 1957, his next novel, *The Assistant*, was published, winning for him many awards and establishing him as a major Jewish American writer. The short-story collection *The Magic Barrel* came out in 1958, followed by his third novel, *A New Life*. In 1961, he moved to Bennington College, where he taught for more than twenty years. *Idiots First* was followed by *The Fixer*, which was researched during a trip to Russia.

From 1969 until his death in 1986, Malamud continued to publish both novels and short stories. His works include *Pictures of Fidelman: An Exhibition*, a collection of stories about one character; *The Tenants*, a novel; *Rembrandt's Hat*, another short-story collection; *Dubin's Lives*, a novel; *God's Grace*, a novel; and *The Stories of Bernard Malamud*, the last short-story collection published during his lifetime.

ANALYSIS

All Bernard Malamud's fiction seems based on a single affirmation: Despite its disappointments, horror, pain, and suffering, life is truly worth living. His work may be best understood in the context of mid-twentieth century American literature. When Malamud arrived upon the literary scene, he disagreed with the period's twin pillars of negativism and nihilism, and his work is a reaction to this prevailing trend. "The purpose of the writer," contends Malamud, "is to keep civilization

Bernard Malamud (David Lees/CORBIS)

from destroying itself." Therefore, his characters, no matter how bad their lot, push toward a better life, a new life. "My premise," notes the author, "is that we will not destroy each other. My premise is that we will live on. We will seek a better life. We may not become better, but at least we will seek betterment."

In this respect, for Malamud the most important element of fiction is form, a belief that appropriately reinforces his thematic beliefs. Literary form as "ultimate necessity" is the basis of literature. The writer's duty, he argues "is to create the architecture, the form." This element of structure, so prevalent in both his short and long fiction, runs counter to the practice of many of his contemporaries, who preferred the inherent formlessness of the so-called New Novel. The essence of this form, says Malamud, is "story, story, story. Writers who can't invent stories often pursue other strategies, even substituting style for narrative. I feel that story is the basic element of fiction."

This belief, however, raises the question of what for Malamud constitutes a good story. Here Malamud is likewise a traditionalist, returning to such nineteenth century influences as Fyodor Dostoevski, Leo Tolstoy, and Gustave Flaubert. Malamud's stories grow out of character. More often than not, the typical protagonist is the schlemiel (usually Jewish, though sometimes Italian). According to the author himself, "A Malamud character is someone who fears his fate, is caught up in it, yet manages to outrun it. He's the subject and object of laughter and pity." When Malamud began publishing his stories, the emphasis was often on case studies rather than elaborate personality development, a trend that irritated Malamud:

> The sell-out of personality is just tremendous. Our most important natural resource is Man. The times cry out for men of imagination and hope. Instead, our fiction is loaded with sickness, homosexuality, fragmented man, "other-directed" man. It should be filled with love and beauty and hope. We are underselling Man. And American fiction is at its weakest when we go in for journalistic case studies instead of rich personality development.

A typical Malamud story, then, is an initiation story, the classic American pattern. Malamud admits that his American literary roots lie in the works of Stephen Crane, Ernest Hemingway, and Sherwood Anderson. The story usually begins with a youth--or an older man with arrested personality development--who has led an unfulfilled life because of undeveloped emotions, failed relationships, and questionable morality. This protagonist then encounters a father figure--similar to the Hemingway tutor-tyro technique--who guides him through his odyssey by prodding him to ask the right questions, teaching him the meaning of suffering and spirituality, and ultimately coaxing him to accept the responsibility for his own life.

Because Malamud is Jewish, his protagonists are, more often than not, Jewish as well. Given Malamud's background--his father was a Jewish immigrant and passed on his knowledge of the Yiddish tradition of storytelling--this is to be expected. Malamud himself admits, "I write about Jews because I know them. But more important, I write about them because Jews are absolutely the very *stuff* of drama." By itself, this assertion is misleading, for unlike his fellow members of the Jewish literary renaissance, Malamud is not preoccupied with the uniqueness of the Jewish experience. The

Jew for Malamud is a metaphor for all human beings. "Jewishness is important to me," Malamud asserts, "but I don't consider myself only a Jewish writer. I have interests beyond that, and I feel I am writing for all men." Malamud's method, then, is synecdochic--by detailing the plight of his Jews, he reveals humankind's common humanity.

Throughout his career Malamud alternated writing novels with short stories. Of the two forms, he confesses to "having been longer in love with short fiction." One aspect of the short story that Malamud especially enjoys is "the fast payoff. Whatever happens happens quickly." A related matter is compression. Short fiction, Malamud argues, "packs a self in a few pages predicating a lifetime. . . . In a few pages a good story portrays the complexity of a life while producing the surprise and effect of knowledge--not a bad payoff."

Ironically, this fastness and compression are part of the ultimate illusion of Malamud's art. For him the writing of a short story is a long task that demands constant revision. "I would write a book, or a short story," Malamud admits, "at least three times--once to understand it, the second time to improve the prose, and a third to compel it to say what it still must say."

"THE FIRST SEVEN YEARS"

"The First Seven Years," which first appeared in the *Partisan Review* in 1950 and later in *The Magic Barrel*, is a straightforward tale set in the favorite Malamudian milieu, the New York Jewish ghetto. Feld, the shoemaker, decides to play matchmaker for his nineteen-year-old daughter, Miriam, whom he desires to attend college. Feld's choice is Max, a college boy, but the shoemaker is disappointed to learn that Max is a materialist (he wants to be an accountant), and for this reason his daughter rejects the chosen suitor. Simultaneously, Sobel, Feld's assistant, quits his job, and Feld has a heart attack.

The story turns on a typical Malamud irony. What Feld has failed to realize is that he, like Max, is a materialist and that his dreams of his daughter's having "a better life" are wrapped up in money, her marrying well. Malamud here also reverses the typical older-man-equals-tutor, younger-man-equals-tyro pattern. Apparently, Feld is teaching Sobel the shoemaker's trade, but in truth, Sobel is the instructor: He admits that he has worked cheaply and lived poorly for the past five years only to be around the woman whom he truly loves, Miriam. As Malamud might have punned, the assistant teaches the master the difference between soles and souls. Finally, Sobel agrees to remain an assistant for two more years before asking Miriam to marry him.

Malamud's symbolism is both simple and mythic. Feld suffers literally from a damaged heart and metaphorically from an organ that is too materialistic. The rebirth pattern is inherent in the story's time frame, which moves from winter toward spring. The seven-year cycle of fertility--Sobel's wait--suggests that he is in tune with larger forces in the universe. Interestingly, the story is also an early version of the tale on which Malamud would elaborate in *The Assistant*.

"THE MAGIC BARREL"

"The Magic Barrel" uses another familiar Malamud pattern, the fantasy. Here, he blends elements of the traditional fairy tale with Jewish folklore. The story in fact begins like a fairy tale, with the line "Not long ago there lived. . . . " In the story, Leo Finkle, a rabbinical student searching for a wife, is the prince; Salzman, the marriage broker with the "magic" barrel and his sudden appearances, is the supernatural agent; and Stella, Salzman's prostitute daughter, is the princess of the tale. The plot is likewise reminiscent of a fairy tale as the prince finally meets the princess and through the intervention of the supernatural agent has a chance at a happy ending.

Malamud's fairy tale borrows elements from Jewish folklore. The characters are certainly stereotypical: the marriage broker, the schlemiel, and the poor daughter. The setting is the usual lower-class milieu. With Leo helping Salzman at the end (each man plays both tutor and tyro), the plot has the familiar reversal, and the story is based on the age-old subject of parent as matchmaker. Even the theme is familiar: Love is a redemptive force earned through suffering and self-knowledge. Malamud also infuses his story with humor. Aside from the stock characters and stock situations, he uses puns (for example "Lily wilted"), hyperbole, and comic juxtaposition (prospective brides are described in the jargon of used-car salesmen). Finally, the story contains social criticism directed at the Jews. Leo

Finkle, the would-be rabbi, has learned the Jewish law but not his own feelings. He takes refuge in his self-pity (a frequent Malamud criticism), he wants a wife not for love but for social prestige, and he uses his religion to hide from life.

"ANGEL LEVINE"

"Angel Levine" is part fable, part fantasy, and an example of the typical Malamud theme, the brotherhood of all people. Manischevitz, a Malamudian Job-victim, seeks relief from his suffering and aid for his sick wife, Fanny. In the Malamudian world, help comes from human rather than divine sources; here, the aide is a Jewish African American angel, Angel Levine. In his narrow religious pride and prejudice, Manischevitz can only wonder why God has failed to send him help in the form of a white person. The tailor's subsequent refusal of aid, an act saturated with egotistical pride, fails to lead to relief.

Eventually, Manischevitz, in pursuit of aid, roams into Harlem, where, finding Angel Levine in Bella's bar, he overhears the essential Malamudian lesson about the divine spark in all persons: "It de speerit," said the old man. "On de face of de water moved de speerit. An' dat was good. It say so in de Book. From de speerit ariz de man. . . . " God put the spirit in all things.

Socially color-blind at last, Manischevitz can now believe that the same spirit dwells within every human, uniting them all. In a scene reminiscent of Felicity's vision at the end of Flaubert's "Un Cœur simple," Manischevitz is rewarded by the sight of a dark figure flying with dark wings. The final meaning of his experience he conveys to Fanny when he admits, "Believe me, there are Jews everywhere." Here, he is Malamud's rationalizer, mouthing the familiar theme of brotherhood.

"THE LAST MOHICAN"

"The Last Mohican" introduces the recurring Everyman character Arthur Fidelman (the stories about him were collected in *Pictures of Fidelman: An Exhibition*) and reveals Malamud's growth and artistry in enlarging the scope of his essentially Jewish materials. Although the setting is not New York City but Rome, the protagonist is familiar. Fidelman, "a self-confessed failure as a painter," is also a failure as a human being, a self-deluded egotist who knows little about his self. His teacher is the familiar aged Jew--this time called

Shimon Susskind in typical Malamudian gentle irony, "a Jewish refugee from Israel."

The essential lesson is again brotherhood. As Susskind persists in asking for help on his own terms, Fidelman inquires, "Am I responsible for you, Susskind?" The elderly Jew replies, "Who else . . . you are responsible. Because you are a man. Because you are a Jew, aren't you?" Like Dante descending into the depths of Hell, Fidelman must enter the personal hell of his own ego to learn the powerful lesson. Fearing that Susskind has stolen his manuscript-laden briefcase, Fidelman discovers the refugee in the Jewish ghetto of Rome, "a pitch black freezing cave." Susskind admits to burning the Giotto manuscript inside the case because "the spirit was missing."

This "rebirth of the spirit" story reads less like a Jewish parable than do many of Malamud's stories. Malamud has set the tale in Rome, and he has obviously undergirded it with mythic dimensions by using *Inferno* motifs (using, for example, "Virgilio" Susskind and a street named Dante). Some critics even contend this is the best of the stories in *The Magic Barrel*. Perhaps this story is more believable than others, for rather than merely learning an abstract lesson, Fidelman actually begins to care about Susskind, even forgiving him.

"Idiots First"

"Idiots First," the title story of his second collection, reveals Malamud's willingness to experiment. The story is a strange combination of fantasy and fable. Although set at night in his familiar territory, this New York is more of a dreamscape, a nightmare, than a realistic environment. No character motivation is provided, key information is omitted, and one Jewish character, Ginzburg, matter-of-factly introduced à la the fairy godmother in "Cinderella," follows an elderly Jew named Mendel, has the ability to freeze people, and seems to represent God/death. Malamud has either invented a new dramatic form or reverted to an old, nineteenth century American mode known as the romance.

Mendel, convinced that he will die that night, desperately seeks thirty-five dollars in order to send his retarded son to Uncle Leo in California. What is not made clear is that Mendel seems to have made a pact with Ginzburg--he will go willingly to his death if he is given time to take care of his son. Mendel is helped not by the rich (a pawnbroker or the supposedly philanthropic Mr. Fishbein), but by the poor, a dying rabbi who gives him a coat, and by death (or Ginzburg) himself, who gives him extra time.

Whereas earlier Malamud stories usually had contrivances, such as obvious symbols or preachy *raisonneurs*, "Idiots First" offers no such aid. On one level, the story seems almost metaphysical, a questioning of God/death for being so detached ("What will happen happens. This isn't my responsibility.") and wrathful (Ginzburg sees wrath mirrored in Mendel's eyes) that He no longer understands what it means to be human. In any case, this open-endedness and general ambiguity represent a new development.

"Black Is My Favorite Color"

"Black Is My Favorite Color," first appearing in *The Reporter* in 1963, is representative of another of Malamud's frequent concerns, the relationship among the races. Like "Angel Levine" before it and the novel *The Tenants* after it, this story explores the fragile love-hate bonds between Jews and African Americans.

Nat Lime, a white Jew who operates a liquor store in Harlem, professes to be color-blind ("there's only one human color and that's the color of blood"). Throughout his life, Lime has befriended "colored" people, but they all seem to resent his attempts. Buster Wilson, his would-be childhood buddy; Ornita Harris, the black woman to whom he proposes marriage; and Charity Sweetness, his current maid-- all reject his overtures of friendship and more.

This story is difficult to understand. Both Lime's words and his actions indicate that he is free of prejudice. He operates a business in black Harlem, and he hires black workers. In return, he is rejected by the three black people he truly likes and helps; twice, he is beaten and robbed by blacks, once obviously for dating a black woman. However, through it all, Lime retains his good sense as well as his good humor, and he pursues his cleaning lady everywhere ("Charity Sweetness--you hear me?--come out of that goddamn toilet!"). Malamud appears to be indicating that prejudice and divisiveness can reside in black people as well as white.

"THE GERMAN REFUGEE"

"The German Refugee," one of the few first-person stories in the Malamud canon, also illustrates the theme of brotherhood. The narrator, Martin Goldberg, relates his attempts to teach English to a German refugee, Oskar Gassner, who is scheduled to give a lecture in English about Walt Whitman's relationship to certain German poets.

Two distinct stories emerge: Oskar's anguish over his failure to comprehend English and the irony of Goldberg's failure to understand why. Thus, once again, each man is both tutor and tyro. While Martin teaches Oskar English, the German army begins its summer push of 1939. What the narrator fails to grasp is his pupil's deep involvement in his former country's fate and that of his non-Jewish wife, whom he left there.

To emphasize the irony, Malamud uses references to Whitman. Oskar ends up teaching his teacher the important lesson when he declares about the poet that "it wasn't the love of death they [German poets] had got from Whitman . . . but it was most of all his feeling for Brudermensch, his humanity." When Oskar successfully delivers his speech, the narrator feels only a sense of pride at what he taught the refugee, not the bonds of *Brudermensch* that have developed between them. When Oskar commits suicide, the narrator never sees that he is partially responsible.

"THE JEWBIRD"

"The Jewbird" is a modern, urban version of "The Raven." Just as the raven flew through the open window of Edgar Allan Poe's narrator and stayed to haunt his conscience, so Schwartz, this black jewbird, which looks "like a dissipated crow," flaps through the window of Harry Cohen's top-floor apartment and lingers to bedevil him. "Bird or devil," demands Poe's narrator; "How do I know you're a bird and not some kind of a goddman devil?" asks Cohen.

Malamud's beast fable, however, is concerned with more than nebulous guilt over a lost love. On the one hand, the tale is lighthearted with a considerable amount of hyperbole, sarcasm, and comic banter; on the other hand, "The Jewbird" focuses on a heavier theme, prejudice. When Schwartz first enters the Cohen apartment, the bird announces that it is running from "anti-Semeets." At the conclusion of the story, young Maurie Cohen goes in search of the bird, which had been driven from the apartment by his father. Finding the damaged jewbird by the river, the boy asks his mother who so hurt Schwartz, and his mother replies, "Anti-Semeets." In other words, Harry Cohen is anti-Semitic.

Malamud's story, however, is still more than a parable of anti-Semitism. Harry Cohen is a cruel man and an inherently selfish father who has little to do with his son. When Schwartz begins to help Maurie with his reading, math, violin lessons, and even games, the narrator notes that the bird "took on full responsibility for Maurie's performance in school." Harry Cohen is so self-absorbed that he has been unable to function successfully as a parent.

"REMBRANDT'S HAT"

Nathaniel Hawthorne once admitted that a few of his tales suffered from an inveterate love of allegory. The same diagnosis might apply to some of Malamud's stories. "Rembrandt's Hat," the title story from the collection that was published in 1973, is typical of the essentially two-person psychological dramas that Malamud does so well. Often in such stories, two people who apparently work closely together never grasp what is truly going on in each other. As a result, painful misunderstandings occur, with a major one and its subsequent suffering leading to self-knowledge as well as a greater understanding between the two. Feld and Sobel, Finkle and Salzman, Manischevitz and Levine, Goldberg and Gassner, Fidelman and Susskind--the names change, but the pattern remains.

In "Rembrandt's Hat," Rubin, a sculptor, and Arkin, an art historian, are colleagues at a New York art school, and they run into each other occasionally and utter polite, meaningless words. One day, Arkin makes a chance remark to Rubin that the latter's white headwear resembles a hat that Rembrandt wears in one of his self-portraits. From this point on, Rubin grows silent and starts shunning his colleague. Then, each wearing a different hat, the two art teachers go to great lengths to avoid each other. Ultimately, Arkin apologizes, Rubin weeps, and the two men resume their tenuous friendship.

The story turns on another prominent Malamud motif; like Henry James before him, Malamud uses art as a touchstone of character. For example, Fidelman's success as a human being is mirrored in his self-appraisal as an artist. Arkin, like some other Malamud characters, uses art to hide from life; it occurs to him that "he found it easier to judge paintings than to judge people." Rubin's self-portrait is sculpted in a single welded piece, a dwarf tree in the midst of an iron jungle. Thus, when Arkin makes the innocent comment, Rubin's inferiority complex interprets it as a comparison of the sculptor to the old master, Rembrandt, with the sculptor much less prominent. Finally, all the hats, from Arkin's white Stetson to Rubin's railroad engineer's cap, become self-Rorschach tests of the story's participants.

"Notes from a Lady at a Dinner Party"

"Notes from a Lady at a Dinner Party," appearing in *Rembrandt's Hat*, is a typical Malamud tale about the relationship between the sexes. In the Malamudian world, men and women desperately seek out each other, reach the verge of true commitment, but find it difficult to communicate, often to commit. Thus, Sobel silently pursues Miriam for seven years without revealing his true feelings, and Fidelman in "Naked Nude" finds it necessary to forge paintings in a whorehouse.

At a dinner party, Max Adler finds himself attracted to Karla Harris, the young wife of his former professor who is more than twice her age. Adler and Harris develop an alluring intimacy by secretly passing notes back and forth. An artist mired in the traditional role of wife-mother, Karla flirts with Adler, who, though previously daring only in his architecture, kisses her. After planning a late-night rendezvous at a nearby motel, they both get cold feet, part, and return to their separate lives of quiet desperation.

Both Karla and Adler are different versions of Malamud's self-limiting human beings. For the most part, Adler can only express his desires in architecture, while Karla's inner self comes out only in the relative safety of watercolors and romantic notes. In Malamud's twentieth century America, then, would-be lovers still cling to the courtly love tradition. Art is a medium not solely to express one's feelings but a place

to hide and sublimate. Love rarely blossoms. Adler is divorced. Karla is content to write enticing notes to strange men and keep getting pregnant by her aging husband. Other Malamud men never marry. Oskar Gassner and his wife live in two different countries and are separated by war. Mendel's wife has died. Feld claims his wife does not understand man-woman relationships. Fidelman ultimately becomes bisexual.

"God's Wrath"

"God's Wrath" is another story about parent-child relationships. As in his work focusing on the sexes and the races, Malamud indicates that there is very little communication between parents and children. Glasser, a retired sexton, is a Lear-like figure with three daughters (by two wives) who have all been disappointments. His hope for one child having a better life are pinned on his youngest daughter, Luci, who quits college, leaves her job, and moves out of his apartment. After a long search, Glasser finally locates Luci, learning that she has become a prostitute. "God's Wrath" offers little explanation for the reason things are the way they are, except that God occasionally winks an eye. The story's conclusion is once again open-ended. Unable to dissuade his daughter from a life of prostitution, Glasser stations himself at her haunts and calls down God's wrath on her. Interestingly, at this point, Malamud switches from the past to the present tense, which indicates a sort of never-ending tension between parent and child, a perpetual inability to communicate, and the ultimate ignorance about how a parent affects a child. In the midst of a pessimistic, naturalistic universe, Malamud suggests that certain conflicts are eternal.

Malamud is an acclaimed twentieth century master of the short story. Often writing realistic fantasy, he is able to imbue his initiating Jews with a mythic dimension, while simultaneously depicting social and spiritual squalor in a realistic manner. His tales contain a great depth of feeling that is occasionally marred by obvious moralizing and transparent mythology. He evinces a deep concern for his fellow human beings. His major flaw has been called the narrowness of his subject matter, the plight of the lower-class Jew, but this problem is only a misunderstanding when one realizes that the Jew is a symbol for people everywhere.

OTHER MAJOR WORKS

LONG FICTION: *The Natural*, 1952; *The Assistant*, 1957; *A New Life*, 1961; *The Fixer*, 1966; *The Tenants*, 1971; *Dubin's Lives*, 1979; *God's Grace*, 1982; *The People*, 1989.

NONFICTION: *Talking Horse: Bernard Malamud on Life and Work*, 1996 (Alan Cheuse and Nicholas Delbanco, editors).

BIBLIOGRAPHY

Abramson, Edward A. *Bernard Malamud Revisited.* New York: Twayne, 1993. Abramson's chapter on the short stories is a brief, general introduction, divided into such categories as fantasies, Italian stories, father-son stories, and sociopolitical stories. Echoes a familiar judgment that in his stories Malamud is a moralist in the tradition of Nathaniel Hawthorne and Henry James, but that he writes with the rhythms of Yiddish and the contours of the folktale.

Avery, Evelyn, ed. *The Magic Worlds of Bernard Malamud.* Albany: State University of New York Press, 2001. A wide-ranging collection of essays on Malamud and his writings, including personal memoirs by members of his family and friends. Three of the essays focus on his short fiction: "On 'The Magic Barrel,'" by Nicholas Delbanco, "America and the History of the Jews in Bernard Malamud's 'The Last Mohican,'" by Karen L. Polster, and "Not True Although Truth--the Holocaust's Legacy in Three Malamud Stories: 'The German Refugee,' 'Man in the Drawer,' and 'The Lady of the Lake,'" by Eileen H. Watts.

Bloom, Harold, ed. *Bernard Malamud.* New York: Chelsea House, 2000. Collection of essays that assess the entire spectrum of Malamud's writings, including a lengthy essay devoted to the short stories. Contains a chronology of his life and a bibliography.

Davis, Philip. *Bernard Malamud: A Writer's Life.* New York: Oxford University Press, 2007. A full-length biography of Malamud that provides analyses of his works and connects these writings to events in his life.

Field, Leslie A., and Joyce W. Field, eds. *Bernard Malamud and the Critics.* New York: New York University Press, 1970. A collection of critical essays that are separated into sections on the Jewish tradition; myth, ritual, and folklore; varied approaches; and specific novels and stories. Although the material is somewhat dated, this book is a valuable guide for scholars seeking to review early Malamud criticism. Contains a select bibliography and an index.

Gelfant, Blanche H., ed. *The Columbia Companion to the Twentieth-Century American Short Story.* New York: Columbia University Press, 2000. Includes a chapter in which Malamud's short stories are analyzed.

Giroux, Robert. "On Bernard Malamud." *Partisan Review* 64 (Summer, 1997): 409-413. A brief general discussion of the life and work of Malamud, commenting on his major novels and short-story collections, his reception of the Pulitzer Prize, and the National Book Award.

Malamud, Bernard. Introduction to *The Stories of Bernard Malamud.* New York: Farrar, Straus & Giroux, 1983. This untitled introduction offers invaluable insight into the mind and theories of Malamud. After a short literary autobiography, Malamud details his belief in form, his assessment of creative writing classes, and the reasons he loves the short story.

_____. "Reflections of a Writer: Long Work, Short Life." *The New York Times Book Review*, March, 1988, 5-16. Reprints a lecture presented at Bennington College in which Malamud offers numerous anecdotes and details about his life as a writer. He elaborates upon his influences, his various professions, his friends, and some of his theories.

Ochshorn, Kathleen. *The Heart's Essential Landscape: Bernard Malamud's Hero.* New York: Peter Lang, 1990. Chapters on each of Malamud's novels and his short-story collections. Seeks to continue a trend in Malamud criticism that views his heroes as tending toward the mensch (a person of honor and integrity) and away from the schlemiel (an inept, clumsy person). Includes a bibliography but no notes.

Richman, Sidney. *Bernard Malamud*. Boston: Twayne, 1966. Richman systematically appraises each of Malamud's works through *A New Life*. Richman also provides a chapter on Malamud's Jewishness, a select bibliography, and some personal correspondence with the writer. A must for students getting started on Malamud.

Sío-Castiñeira, Begoña. "Bernard Malamud." In *A Reader's Companion to the Short Story in English*, edited by Erin Fallon, et al., under the auspices of the Society for the Study of the Short Story. Westport, Conn.: Greenwood Press, 2001. Aimed at the general reader, this essay provides a brief biography of Malamud followed by an analysis of his short fiction.

_____. *The Short Stories of Bernard Malamud: In Search of Jewish Post-Immigrant Identity*. New York: Peter Lang, 1998. A good study of the short fiction and its major themes.

Sloan, Gary. "Malamud's Unmagic Barrel." *Studies in Short Fiction* 32 (Winter, 1995): 51-57. Argues that everything that Pinye Salzman does in "The Magic Barrel" can be accounted for in naturalistic terms. Maintains that the story is more dramatic and ingenious as a naturalistic story than as a supernatural fable.

Smith, Janna Malamud. *My Father Is a Book: A Memoir of Bernard Malmud*. Boston: Houghton Mifflin, 2006. An intimate and extensive biography of Malmud written by his daughter that recounts his personal life and writing career.

Watts, Eileen H. "Jewish Self-Hatred in Malamud's 'The Jewbird.'" *MELUS* 21 (Summer, 1996): 157-163. Argues that the interaction of assimilated Jew and the jewbird in the story reveals the political, social, and psychological fallout of the assimilated Jew as good tenant, the unassimilated Jew as bad, and the Gentile as landlord.

Hal Charles

PAULE MARSHALL

Born: Brooklyn, New York; April 9, 1929
Also known as: Valenza Pauline Burke

PRINCIPAL SHORT FICTION

Soul Clap Hands and Sing, 1961
Reena, and Other Stories, 1983 (also known as *Merle: A Novella and Other Stories*, 1985)

OTHER LITERARY FORMS

Paule (pohl) Marshall is best known for her 1959 novel *Brown Girl, Brownstones*, which tells the story of Barbadian immigrants striving to surmount poverty and racism in their new home, as seen through the eyes of the young heroine, Selina Boyce, daughter of a hardworking, ambitious mother and an easygoing, romantic father. Ten years later, her novel *The Chosen Place, the Timeless People* (1969) was published, followed by *Praisesong for the Widow* (1983), *Daughters* (1991),

and *The Fisher-King*, (2000). Marshall has also written a number of essays on African American woman writers and her own experience as an artist and has published an autobiography, *Triangular Road: A Memoir* (2009).

ACHIEVEMENTS

Paule Marshall was awarded a John Simon Guggenheim Memorial Foundation Fellowship in 1961, the Rosenthal Award from the National Institute of Arts and Letters in 1962 for *Soul Clap Hands and Sing*, a Ford Foundation grant for 1964-1965, a National Endowment for the Arts grant for 1967-1968, and the Before Columbus Foundation American Book Award in 1984 for *Praisesong for the Widow*. She also received the Langston Hughes Medallion Award (1986), the New York State Governor's Award for Literature (1987), the John Dos Passos Award for Literature (1989), and the John D. and Catherine T. MacArthur Fellowship (1992).

Marshall was designated as a Literary Lion by the New York Public Library in 1994, and she was inducted into the Celebrity Path at the Brooklyn Botanic Garden in 2001.

BIOGRAPHY

Paule Marshall was born Valenza Pauline Burke in Brooklyn in 1929, the daughter of Samuel and Ada Burke, émigrés from Barbados who arrived in the United States shortly after World War I. She thus grew up in a culture with its roots in the Caribbean, which she visited for the first time when she was nine years old, an experience that had a strong influence on her future writing. She wrote poetry as a child and listened to the talk of women, both preparing her for her career as a powerful and poetic writer. In the opening of *Reena, and Other Stories*, she describes the influence of her mother, woman relatives, and other female friends on her experience in an essay called "From the Poets in the Kitchen":

> They taught me my first lesson in the narrative art. They trained my ear. They set a standard of excellence. This is why the best of my work must be attributed to them; it stands as testimony to the rich legacy of language and culture they so freely passed on to me in the workshop of the kitchen.

Marshall attended Brooklyn College, receiving a B.A. cum laude in 1953; she was also a member of Phi Beta Kappa. She wrote her first novel, *Brown Girl, Brownstones*, while a graduate student at Hunter College. She married Kenneth E. Marshall in 1950; they had a child, Evan, but the marriage ended in 1963. In the meantime, Marshall worked as a librarian for the New York Public Libraries and as a staff writer for *Our World* magazine in New York; she also published her first collection of short stories for Atheneum, *Soul Clap Hands and Sing*. With the help of grants from the Ford Foundation and the National Endowment for the Arts, she completed her second novel, *The Chosen Place, the Timeless People*, which, like her earlier work, was critically well received but commercially only marginally successful.

On July 30, 1970, Marshall married Nourry Menard, and that autumn she took the position of lecturer on creative writing at Yale University. She also lectured on black literature at several colleges and universities, including the University of Oxford, Columbia University, Michigan State University, Lake Forest College, and Cornell University. In 1983, Marshall's third novel, *Praisesong for the Widow*, won the Before Columbus Foundation American Book Award. The Feminist Press published *Reena, and Other Stories*, which includes the novella *Merle*, excerpted from *The Chosen Place, the Timeless People*, and the short stories "Brooklyn" and "Barbados," which originally appeared in *Soul Clap Hands and Sing*. Other stories in *Reena, and Other Stories* appeared in various periodicals. This collection was reprinted in 1985 by Virago Press under the title *Merle: A Novella, and Other Stories*. In 1991, Marshall published the novel *Daughters*, which was also greeted with great critical acclaim.

ANALYSIS

Paule Marshall's first novel, *Brown Girl, Brownstones*, ushered in a whole new approach to the African American female protagonist; only Gwendolyn Brooks's *Maud Martha* (1953) and the earlier *Their Eyes Were Watching God* (1937) by Zora Neale Hurston had focused on an African American woman's search for identity within a black community and her own conscious, interior life. Marshall's work has been concerned from the beginning with a number of major themes: the experience of growing up African American in the United States; the clash of cultures between westerners and African Americans, West Indians and inhabitants of the American mainland; and the relationships between men and women.

SOUL CLAP HANDS AND SING

Marshall's first collection of shorter works, *Soul Clap Hands and Sing*, contains four longer short stories, almost novellas. They are given the titles of the settings: "Barbados," "Brooklyn," "British Guiana," and "Brazil." In each, the main character is an older man, and the stories explore how that man has failed to live his life fully, for whatever reasons. This failure is indicated by the title of the collection, taken from the William Butler Yeats poem "Sailing to Byzantium," which includes the lines "An aged man is but a paltry thing/ A tattered coat upon a stick, unless/ Soul clap its hands and sing." In each case, the failure of the man to allow his soul to "clap hands" has led to the emptiness or aridity of his life. Thus, he is forced to realize his failure to live truly through the intervention of a woman who, in some way, exposes his inadequacies.

"BARBADOS"

In "Barbados," Mr. Watford, who has returned to his native island after having worked single-mindedly throughout his adult life in the United States just so he can return for this purpose, lives like a white colonizer. He has built a house, bought plantation land, and planted coconut trees, which he tends faithfully, despite years of accumulated fatigue. He has never completely finished his house, however, and he lives in total isolation, proud of the fact that he needs no one and no one needs him. It takes a young native woman, foisted on him as a servant, to reveal the paucity of his life, the emptiness of his days. He recognizes that he has not been able to bear the responsibility for the meaninglessness of his life, but when he goes to confront the young woman with the hope of some renewal, he is capable only of attacking her verbally, to which she responds, "you ain't people, Mr. Watford, you ain't people." It is this knowledge that destroys him: He has not been able to be a part of the people who bore him, and has not found sustenance living the same way as those who oppressed him.

"BROOKLYN"

In "Brooklyn," an aging Jewish professor, who has been banned from teaching by the Red-baiters of the McCarthy era, attempts to coerce a young black woman who is taking his class to spend some time at his summer home. She refuses but in the end returns to his class for the final examination and takes him up on his invitation, only to express her outrage, as well as the freedom that she now feels. She has also felt like an outcast from her own people, while unable to trust whites. Now she has the courage to live not as her parents have taught her but as she chooses. Professor Max Berman, in contrast, is forced to recognize that it is his failure to believe in or stand up for anything that has resulted in his loneliness and misery. Interestingly, in "Barbados" the female

protagonist is not given a name, while here she is named only in dialogue as Miss Williams.

"BRITISH GUIANA"

"British Guiana" explores the present life of Gerald Motley, a man who is indeed a motley collection of races; he could have been taken for white, because of the British army officer who was one of his ancestors, or black, for the slave woman that officer had been intimate with, or East Indian, from some Hindu who also had a part in his creation. He has achieved a certain amount of success as the head of a radio station, but he knows that he has failed to live his life fully. Although as a young man he had shown a great ability and had rejected his middle-class background to organize a strike, he had been bought off by a job in radio, which forces him to copy the whites who have colonized his country. When he attempts to penetrate the jungle, to prove his worth to himself, he is prevented by another motley person, Sybil, an African Chinese woman with whom he is involved. He is forever conscious of his betrayal of himself and also of Sybil's part in this scheme, which results in a life of cynicism and taking the easy way. At the end of the story, when Sybil, whom he might have married, returns to visit, his last act is to bargain with her for a protégé who despises him but deserves a chance. In the conclusion, he realizes that he is going to die a failure by his own doing.

"BRAZIL"

The final story in the book, "Brazil," reminds the reader of Carson McCullers's *The Ballad of the Sad Café* (1951) because it is the story of what appears to be a strange love affair between a white woman of epic proportions and a black dwarf. In this story, the dwarf is a performer who goes by the name of O Grande Caliban and has teamed up with a blond of Germanic appearance to perform a comic and athletic act. He has decided that it is time to retire, but his mistress does not wish to do so. One of the interesting things about the story is the breaking of the traditional white reader's expectations; it is the undersized black man who is trying to end a relationship with the Aryan-looking female. He has become so famous as Caliban, however, that no one, not even his wife, knows him as he had been. He has been living a lie so long that he cannot convince people of the truth anymore, and so he ends by destroying everything.

REENA, AND OTHER STORIES

Reena, and Other Stories is a collection of previously printed works gathered together for the first time in 1983 by Feminist Press. It begins with Marshall's autobiographical essay, "From the Poets in the Kitchen," which had originally been published in *The New York Times Book Review's* series called "The Making of a Writer." This essay celebrates the women in Marshall's life who helped form her thought and shape her voice. The collection includes two of the stories discussed earlier, "Brooklyn" and "Barbados," previously published in *Soul Clap Hands and Sing.* Also included is a novella, *Merle*, which has been excerpted from her 1969 novel *The Chosen Place, the Timeless People* but was extensively reshaped and rewritten. Marshall wrote autobiographical headnotes to each story, which help to place them in the context of her experience and development as a writer.

"THE VALLEY BETWEEN"

The first story in the collection, "The Valley Between," was, as Marshall explained, "my very first published story, written when I could barely crawl, never mind stand up and walk as a writer." In it, the characters are white, a deliberate decision as Marshall herself was at the time married to Kenneth E. Marshall, a marriage she describes as "an early, unwise first marriage," and she wished to disguise the autobiographical elements in it. It is the story of a marriage falling apart because the wife (and mother of a small child) continues to grow, while the husband wishes her to remain the same, to be nothing more than a wife and mother. Published in August, 1954, it is a story well before its time in its depiction of the stifling expectations placed upon a woman of talent and energy.

"REENA"

The title story, "Reena," is unusual in that it was commissioned by *Harper's Magazine* for a special supplement on "The American Female," published in October, 1962. Intended by the editors to be an article on the African American woman, the story instead became a thinly disguised fiction concerning the women whom Marshall knew best: "those from an urban, working-class and lower middle-class, West Indian American background who, like [Marshall herself], had attended the free New York City colleges during the late forties and fifties."

A first-person narrator named Paulie recounts her meeting again after twenty years with a friend from her childhood, Reena, formally named Doreen. The friend-- a child who shapes her own life as best she can in a world that discriminates against women, African Americans, and particularly African Americans from the West Indies--had transformed herself into Reena, "with two ees!"

The meeting place is at the funeral of Aunt Vi, Reena's aunt, a woman who represents the strong, nurturing, enduring women "from the poets in the kitchen," and who will reappear in Marshall's fiction. Having been out of touch for so long, Reena and Paulie have much to discuss, and much of the story is Reena's recounting of what has been happening in her life: the struggle for meaningful work; her relationship with her family, particularly her mother; relationships with white men (usually unsuccessful) and with black men, who have to learn how to relate to and accept a strong, educated, ambitious black woman; childbearing; radical politics; and loneliness. In almost essayistic form, this story provides an intimate glimpse into the struggle, suffering, and successes of this group of African American women.

"TO DA-DUH, IN MEMORIAM"

"To Da-duh, in Memoriam" is based on a visit that Marshall made to her maternal grandmother in Barbados when she was nine. Da-duh is another of the ancestor figures who populate Marshall's fiction, like Aunt Vi in the previous story and Merle in the novella of that same name; as Marshall says, "Da-duh turns up everywhere."

MERLE

Another example of ancestor figures appears in the final selection in the collection, the novella *Merle*, from *Merle: A Novella, and Other Stories.* Merle is "Part saint, part revolutionary, part obeah woman," a woman who, wherever she goes, exhorts people to resist oppression, while on a personal level she is "still trying to come to terms with her life and history as a black woman, still seeking to reconcile all the conflicting elements to form a viable self."

Merle is the woman whom Marshall creates in various guises, calling into being a new character for twentieth century American literature. In her compelling portrayal of women in her works, she brings to life for her readers a vision of the direction in which the world should be going by showing readers the people whom the world desperately needs to listen to and perhaps emulate.

OTHER MAJOR WORKS

LONG FICTION: *Brown Girl, Brownstones*, 1959; *The Chosen Place, the Timeless People*, 1969; *Praisesong for the Widow*, 1983; *Daughters*, 1991; *The Fisher King*, 2000.

NONFICTION: *Triangular Road: A Memoir*, 2009; *Conversations with Paule Marshall*, 2010 (James C. Hall and Heather Hathaway, editors).

BIBLIOGRAPHY

Alexander, Simone A. James. *Mother Imagery in the Novels of Afro-Caribbean Women*. Columbia: University of Missouri Press, 2001. Compares Marshall's representation of mothers and the mother-daughter relationship with those of writers Jamaica Kincaid and Maryse Condé.

Brown, Lloyd W. "The Rhythms of Power in Paule Marshall's Fiction." *Novel: A Forum on Fiction* 7, no. 2 (Winter, 1974): 159-167. Focuses on Marshall's short story "To Da-Duh, in Memoriam," tracing her concern with the problems of African American women, tied to her commitment to feminism and racial equality. Brown argues that Marshall sees power as both a political goal of ethnic and feminist movements and a social and psychological phenomenon that affects racial and sexual roles, shapes cultural traditions, and molds the individual psyche.

Collier, Eugenia. "The Closing of the Circle: Movement from Division to Wholeness in Paule Marshall's Fiction." In *Black Women Writers, 1950-1980*, edited by Mari Evans. Garden City, N.Y.: Anchor Press/Doubleday, 1984. Collier finds in Marshall's writing a movement from the separated, segmented self to a discovery of wholeness and completion; this healing and wholeness is found within the context of the community. Contains good discussions of the short fiction. Collier's article is the first of two essays on Marshall in Evans's collection, which should be required reading for anyone interested in African American woman writers. Also contains a bibliography of criticism on Marshall and an index.

Coser, Stelamaris. *Bridging the Americas: The Literature of Paule Marshall, Toni Morrison, and Gayl Jones*. Philadelphia: Temple University Press, 1995. Compares and contrasts the fiction of the three authors, taking their cultural heritage into consideration.

Denniston, Dorothy Hamer. *The Fiction of Paule Marshall*. Knoxville: University of Tennessee Press, 1995. Examines Marshall's fiction as an imaginative reconstruction of African history and culture. Provides close readings of Marshall's work along with biographical information.

Gadsy, Meredith. "Refugees of a World on Fire: Kitchen Place and Refugee Space in the Poetics of Paule Marshall and Edwidge Danticat." In *Sucking Salt: Caribbean Women Writers, Migration, and Survival*. Columbia: University of Missouri Press, 2006. Analyzes works by Marshall and other Caribbean women writers to demonstrate how, through migration, their protagonists move into and through metropolitan spaces to create new realities for themselves, their families, and their communities.

Kapai, Leela. "Dominant Themes and Technique in Paule Marshall's Fiction." *College Language Association Journal* 16 (September, 1972): 49-59. Examines Marshall's use of folk tradition in her novels through *The Chosen Place, the Timeless People* and also in the short story "Reena." Kapai claims that Marshall places being a human being and the universal human experience before racial identity and states that Marshall is aware of her western heritage, even as she writes out of her personal experience as an African American. Contains some good, close readings.

Lock, Helen. "'Building Up from Fragments': The Oral Memory Process in Some Recent African-American Written Narratives." *College Literature* 22 (October, 1995): 109-120. Discusses Marshall and other writers as representative of a generation of African American literary artists whose sensibilities do not exclude orally constituted modes of thought. Argues that Marshall energizes the dialectic between oral and literate conceptions of memory by reasserting--through the medium of the written word--the value of an orally derived perception.

Macpherson, Heidi Slettedahl. "Perception of Place: Geopolitical and Cultural Positioning in Paule Marshall's Novels." In *Caribbean Women Writers*, edited by Mary Condé and Thorunn Lonsdale. New York: St. Martin's Press, 1999. Although the focus of this article is on Marshall's novels, it is a helpful discussion of her general use of fictionalized island backdrops; argues that while she acknowledges a geopolitical place, her representation of place moves beyond a specific locale.

Marshall, Paule. *Conversations with Paule Marshall.* Edited by James C. Hall and Heather Hathaway. Jackson: University Press of Mississippi, 2010. Collection of essays conducted from 1971 through 2009 in which Marshall discusses the sources of her writing, her involvement in the civil rights movement, and her understanding of the African diaspora and of the relationship between art and politics.

_____. "From 'Shaping the World of My Art.'" In *Shaping Memories: Reflections of African American Women Writers*, edited by Joanne Veal Gabbin. Jackson: University Press of Mississippi, 2009. An excerpt from one of Marshall's essays in which she describes how she creates her work.

McClusky, John, Jr. "And Called Every Generation Blessed: Theme, Setting, and Ritual in the Works of Paule Marshall." In *Black Women Writers, 1950-1980*, edited by Mari Evans. Garden City, N.Y.: Anchor Press/Doubleday, 1984. This essay, the second on Marshall in Evans's book, gives an overview of her achievement, evolution, and future directions in her writing.

Washington, Mary Helen. "Declaring (Ambiguous) Liberty: Paule Marshall's Middle-Class Women." In *Sister Circle: Black Women and Work*, edited by Sharon Harley and the Black Women and Work Collective. New Brunswick, N.J.: Rutgers University Press, 2002. Analyzes Marshall's depiction of black middle-class women in her novels and short fiction.

Waxman, Barbara Frey. "Dancing out of Form, Dancing into Self: Genre and Metaphor in Marshall, Shange, and Walker." *MELUS* 19 (Fall, 1994): 91-106. Discusses how texts by Marshall, Ntozake Shange, and Alice Walker articulate truths about the multiple selves of African American women by creating new mythopoetic genres and tropes that mediate between the word and the dance.

Mary LeDonne Cassidy
Updated by Theodore C. Humphrey

BOBBIE ANN MASON

Born: Mayfield, Kentucky; May 1, 1940

PRINCIPAL SHORT FICTION

Shiloh, and Other Stories, 1982
Love Life, 1989
*Midnight Magic: Selected Stories of Bobbie Ann
     Mason,* 1998
Zigzagging Down a Wild Trail, 2001
Nancy Culpepper, 2006

OTHER LITERARY FORMS

Bobbie Ann Mason has written novels, including
Spence + Lila (1988), *Feather Crowns* (1993), and *An
Atomic Romance* (2006); literary criticism; a memoir,
Clear Springs: A Memoir (1999); a biography, *Elvis
Presley* (2002); and popular-culture journalism. She
has also been the subject of numerous interviews and
tribute music videos.

ACHIEVEMENTS

Bobbie Ann Mason (MAY-suhn) has earned a place
in American literature with her short stories, which
have won two O. Henry Awards and two Pushcart
Prizes. She won the Ernest Hemingway Foundation
Award for first fiction in 1983 for her first collection of
short stories, *Shiloh, and Other Stories.* That collection
also earned Mason nomination for the National Book
Critics Circle Award (1982), the American Book Award
(1982), the PEN/Faulkner Award for Fiction, a National Endowment for the Arts Fellowship, and a Pennsylvania Arts Council grant (1983), a John Simon Guggenheim Memorial Foundation Fellowship, and an
American Academy of Arts and Letters Award (1984).
Mason received the Appalachian Medallion Award
(1991), and her novel *Feather Crowns* was co-winner
of the Southern Book Award for Fiction and a finalist
for the National Book Critics Circle Award (1994).

Clear Springs was a Pulitzer Prize finalist (1999). *Zigzagging down a Wild Trail* won the Southern Book
Critics Circle Award (2002), and Mason received the
Appalachian Heritage Writer's Award (2010). Mason's
writing for newspapers and magazines includes work
as a society columnist for the *Mayfield Messenger* in
Kentucky and as a writer of fan-magazine stories for
the Ideal Publishing Company in New York City. She
has also written "Talk of the Town" columns and feature articles for *The New Yorker.*

Mason's novels have reinforced her reputation. The
first of her novels, *In Country* (1985), was particularly
well received, and a film (also titled *In Country*) based
on the book was released by Warner Bros. in the fall of
1989. That year the Vietnam Veterans of America gave
Mason its first President's Citation, which honors a
nonveteran who promotes public understanding of the
war and its residual effects.

BIOGRAPHY

Bobbie Ann Mason was born in the Jackson Purchase area of rural Kentucky and grew up on her family's dairy farm. Her southern background appears to
have been a major force in shaping her fiction, as she
shared her father's love of the family's land. She attended a country school through the eighth grade and
then attended Mayfield High School. Her descriptions
of country schools in "State Champions" certainly ring
true, and her novel *Spence + Lila* (1988) fictionalizes a
part of her parents' experience. Another aspect of her
high school life echoes in her fiction: her love of rock
and roll.

Mason majored in English at the University of Kentucky in Lexington, where she wrote for the university
paper, *The Kernel.* While in college, she also wrote the
summer society column for the *Mayfield Messenger.*
After graduating with a B.A. in 1962, she spent fifteen
months in New York City, working for the Ideal Publishing Company, writing for fan magazines such as

Movie Life and *TV Star Parade*. In addition to her undergraduate degree, Mason earned an M.A. in literature from the State University of New York at Binghamton in 1966 and a Ph.D. in literature from the University of Connecticut in 1972. In her doctoral dissertation, she analyzed the garden symbolism in *Ada or Ardor: A Family Chronicle* (1969), by Vladimir Nabokov. Nabokov's artistry in presenting the details of his characters' lives apparently touched a chord in Mason, and she has described him as a major influence on her writing. While pursuing her Ph.D., she met Roger B. Rawlings at the University of Connecticut; they were married in 1969.

From 1972 to 1979, Mason was an assistant professor of English at Mansfield State College (which later became Mansfield University) in Pennsylvania, where she taught journalism as well as other English courses. She had been writing short stories during this period and had received encouraging responses from editors; they nevertheless rejected her stories for publication. In 1979, Mason stopped teaching to write fiction. She settled in rural Pennsylvania, sometimes giving readings and sometimes writing for *The New Yorker*. In 1990, she and her husband moved back to Kentucky, where she became writer-in-residence at the University of Kentucky. Her life, with its movement from rural to urban and back to rural living, mirrors a typical concern of her fiction: the tension between rural and urban life. Apparently her feelings match those of many of her protagonists.

ANALYSIS

Often compared with Ann Beattie, Raymond Carver, and Frederick Barthelme, Bobbie Ann Mason writes fiction that reads like life. Her characters struggle with jobs, family issues, and self-awareness and continually exude a lively sense of being. Those who people her stories often transcend circumstance without losing their rootedness in place. Often her characters struggle to live within a relationship but are frequently alone. Resonating with rock-and-roll music and family conflicts, her descriptions leave a reader sometimes feeling uncomfortably aware of a truth about families: Caring does not guarantee understanding or communication.

Mason's short stories are for the most part set in small towns in Kentucky and explore the lives of working-class people from small towns or farms. Kentucky, a North-South border state, is emblematic of Mason's concerns with borders, separations, and irrevocable decisions. Her stories typically explore a conflict between a character's past and future, a conflict that is often exemplified in a split between rural and urban leanings and a modern as opposed to a traditional life. Often the point of view in Mason's short fiction is limited omniscient. She is, however, adept with first-person narration as well. Readers are most often left with a sense of her characters' need to transcend their life scripts through action, frequently a quest. Her stories typically lack resolution, making them uncomfortably true to life.

SHILOH, AND OTHER STORIES

"Shiloh," the title story in Mason's first collection, is a story about love, loss, and history. A couple, Leroy and Norma Jean, have been married for sixteen years. They married when Norma Jean was pregnant with their son Randy, a child who died as an infant. Leroy is home recuperating from an accident in his truck. His leg is healing, but he is afraid to go back to driving a truck long distances. He takes on traditionally feminine activities in the story: He starts doing crafts, watches birds at the feeder, and remains the passenger in the car even after his leg has healed enough for him to drive.

The accident that forced Leroy to remain at home for months recuperating is the second crisis in the couple's marriage. The first crisis had been their baby's death. After the baby died, Leroy and Norma Jean remained married but emotionally isolated from each other:

> They never speak about their memories of Randy, which have almost faded, but now that Leroy is home all the time, they sometimes feel awkward around each other, and Leroy wonders if one of them should mention the child. He has the feeling that they are waking up out of a dream together.

Now that Leroy is at home, he "sees things about Norma Jean that he never realized before." Leroy's staying at home so much leads to several important changes for Norma Jean: She begins to lift weights, takes a writing course, and curses in front of her mother. In response to the repeated suggestion of Norma Jean's mother, the couple drives to the Shiloh battleground for a second honeymoon trip. At Shiloh, Norma Jean tells Leroy that she wants to leave him. The history of Shiloh is significant to the story of this marriage. Shiloh, an early battle in the Civil War, proved that the Civil War would be a long and bloody one. The story concludes with Leroy merging family history with battleground history and Norma Jean literally flexing her muscles. Their civil war will be Leroy fighting for union and Norma Jean seeking her independent self.

A contemporary history lesson on the fear of polio and communists, "Detroit Skyline, 1949" narrates in first person the summer spent by a nine-year-old girl, Peggy Jo, and her mother as they visit the mother's sister and her family in Detroit. The story reveals the conflict between rural and city life through the perceptions and desires of Peggy Jo. Seeing her aunt's neighborhood for the first time, Peggy Jo immediately knows that she wants to live "in a place like this, with neighbors." When she plays with the neighbor child, however, Peggy Jo is made to feel incompetent because she does not know how to roller-skate, so she instead spends her time watching television and examining newspaper articles and pictures in her aunt's scrapbook.

Peggy Jo feels isolated that summer. She observes the smoothness with which her mother and aunt converse, how natural their communication is. When she attends a birthday party for the neighbor child, Peggy Jo notes:

> I did not know what to say to the children. They all knew each other, and their screams and giggles had a natural continuity, something like the way my mother talked with her sister, and like the splendid houses of the neighborhood, all set so close together.

For Peggy Jo there is little "natural continuity" of speech or gesture within her aunt's household that summer. Her own comments are most often cut short, silenced, or discredited by the others. By the end of the summer, Peggy Jo realizes that her "own life [is] a curiosity, an item for a scrapbook."

Another of Mason's stories concerning rural isolation is "Offerings," in which the isolation is redemptive for Sandra, who stays in the couple's country home instead of traveling with her husband, Jerry, to Louisville, "reluctant to spend her weekends with him watching go-go dancers in smoky bars." She instead spends her time growing vegetables and tending her cats, ducks, and dogs. Her cobweb-strewn house is not her focus; the outdoors is. The offerings that Sandra makes are many: to her mother, tacit agreement to avoid discussing the separation from Jerry; to her grandmother, the fiction of Jerry's presence; and to the forces of nature around her, her tamed and dependent ducks. Sandra finds grace through the natural world, exemplified within the final image of the story: dewy spider webs that, in the morning, are trampolines enabling her to "spring from web to web, all the way up the hill to the woods." She cannot be honest with her grandmother and avoids truth in conversation with her mother, but she feels at peace and at home with her yard, the woods, and the wildlife there.

In "Residents and Transients," Mason's narrator also is married to a man who has gone away to work in Louisville. Mary, the narrator, is finding her place within a relationship as well as a location. Several images in this story reinforce the theme of stability as opposed to movement. The cats Mary cares for on the farm represent her dilemma of moving to Louisville. To Stephen, her lover, she explains that she has read about two basic types of cats, residents and transients. She cites difference of opinion by researchers over which type is truly superior: those who establish territories and stay there or those who show the greater curiosity by going from one place to another. Mary is drawn to the stability of her parents' old farmhouse, feeling the pull of the traditional value of place. The single image that succinctly and horrifically mirrors her dilemma is a rabbit, seen in the headlights as she is driving home. The rabbit at first appears to be running in place, but she realizes that its forelegs are still moving, despite the fact that its haunches have been run over. Throughout the story, Mary has been running in place, running from her relationship with her husband by taking a lover and running from her life with her husband by remaining in her parents' old home.

Mary's position at the end of the story is mirrored by the image of the odd-eyed cat, whose eyes shine red and green. The narrator has been waiting for some signal to move. Her husband's words do not convince; Mary thinks of them as words that are processed, computerized renderings. She needs more than words; she needs an integrated part of her world to spur her to act. Because her husband is no longer an integral part of her world, she listens and looks for other cues. The dying rabbit spurs her to action. The story ends with Mary "waiting for the light to change."

LOVE LIFE

Within Mason's second collection of short fiction, *Love Life*, the reader sees continued the skillful treatment of people's decisions and perceptions. "State Champions" is a reminiscence of twenty years past, so it offers a perspective different from that of other works. "State Champions" further explores Mason's theme of rural-versus-urban experience by recounting the success of the Cuba Cubs, Kentucky state champions in basketball in 1952. The narrator, Peggy (who appeared earlier in "Detroit Skyline, 1949" but is three years older when this story begins), had seen the team as glamorous, certainly larger than life. As an adult in upstate New York, Peggy is surprised to hear the team referred to as "just a handful of country boys who could barely afford basketball shoes." Although Peggy had shared in the excitement of the championship season, "State Champions" presents her perceptions of being different from the rest, even at that time. She rebelled against authority at school by talking back to the history teacher. She surprised her friend Willowdean with the assertion that she did not want to get pregnant and get married, a normal pattern for the girls at the high school. From her adult perspective, Peggy ascribes her own struggle for words with Glenn, the boy she cared about in 1952, to her status as a "country kid":

> I couldn't say anything, for we weren't raised to say things that were heartfelt and gracious. Country kids didn't learn manners. Manners were too embarrassing. Learning not to run in the house was about the extent of what we knew about how to act. We didn't learn to congratulate people; we didn't wish people

happy birthday. We didn't even address each other by name.

Ironically enough, what triggers Peggy's recollection of the state championship year is the comment by the New Yorker about the poor country boys' basketball team, certainly a comment not springing from a mannered upbringing.

In "Coyotes," Mason provides a third-person account from the perspective of a young man, Cobb, who embodies the ambivalence and sensitivity often seen in Mason's characters. He has asked Lynnette Johnson to marry him, and he continues to look for signs and indications that marriage is the right thing to do. Cobb sees a young clerk in a drugstore showing her wedding ring to a young couple. Their conversation is flat: no congratulations, no excitement. The matter-of-fact nature of the exchange haunts Cobb. He wants his marriage to be the subject of excitement, hugs, celebration. Marriage in general presents itself as a risk, leading him to look further for signs that his own marriage will work. He wonders if Lynnette will find more and more things about him that will offend her. For example, he fails to tell her about having hunted after she tells him that his sweatshirt, on which is written "Paducah, the Flat Squirrel Capital of the World," is in bad taste. He is reassured by their similarities--for example, the fact that they both pronounce "coyote" with an *e* sound at the end. Lynnette's past, with a mother who had attempted suicide, is something he recognizes to be significant to them, but he nevertheless speaks confidently with Lynnette about their future. Lynnette fears that her past will somehow intrude on their future, and so, in fact, does Cobb. Their relationship is, as is typical of Mason's fiction, freighted with all those tangled possibilities.

Past and future as conflicting forces also form a theme of "Private Lies," in which the male protagonist, Mickey, reestablishes his relationship with his former wife and decides to search for the child they gave up for adoption eighteen years earlier. Mickey's wife, Tina, has compartmentalized their lives with a regular television schedule and planned activities for their children. Tina has forbidden him to tell their children about his daughter. Mickey, however, cannot ignore the eighteenth birthday of his daughter. The story concludes with Mickey and his former wife, Donna, on the beach in Florida, the state in which they gave up their daughter for adoption. Donna insists that she does not want to find their daughter and that searching is a mistake. She nevertheless accompanies him to Florida, where Mickey seeks to stop telling lies (by silence) and where Donna still seeks to avoid the search, exemplified by her refusal to look inside shells for fear of what she may find in them. Mickey seeks the daughter who will be his bridge between past and future. He seeks to make a new present for himself, a present free of Tina's control.

Midnight Magic

All of the stories in *Midnight Magic* appeared in either *Shiloh, and Other Stories* or *Love Life*, but this collection provides a new arrangement and a new introduction by the author. The protagonist of the title story, Steve, is a young man whose personal power is no match for that of his showy "muscle" car. Like other Mason characters, he takes to the road in search of elusive secrets of life, but most of the time Steve merely drives in circles around his small hometown. When he finally heads for a specific destination (the Nashville airport to pick up his recently married friend), he is several hours late. His lateness for this appointment parallels his tardiness in maturing. After seeing a body lying beside the road, Steve tries to report it to a 911 emergency operator. Unfortunately, he cannot discover his specific geographic location just as he cannot define his place on the road of life. Steve's girlfriend, Karen, finds guidance in the spiritual teachings of Sardo, an ancient Native American now reincarnated in the body of a teenager. Steve also "wants something miraculous" but simply "can't believe in it." Thus, his persistent hope outstrips his fleeting faith.

Mason recalls that as a college student she associated late-night hours with a "mood of expectation" and "the sense that anything might happen." Thus, the title "Midnight Magic" suggests sympathy for a feckless but engaging misfit. In her introduction Mason describes Steve as a "guy who keeps imagining he'll get it together one day soon, who seeks transcendence and wants to believe in magic."

Another story with a confused male protagonist is "Big Bertha Stories." Written while Mason was working on *In Country*, this story also dramatizes the lingering effects of the war in Vietnam. Donald has come back from war physically, but he cannot make it all the way home emotionally. He operates a huge machine in a strip mine, and his destruction of the land recalls the horrors of war. Attempting to create some order in his life, Donald makes up stories about powerful superheroes. These stories begin with humor and high hopes but break off in chaos. Just as Donald cannot complete his journey home, he can never bring his fictions to a suitable conclusion. Having lost his youth in Vietnam, he becomes old prematurely and can no longer function as husband and father.

Still another story from *Midnight Magic* that tries to reconcile past with present is "Nancy Culpepper." Here the title character is apparently based on Mason herself, and she reappears in the story "Lying Doggo" and the novel *Spence + Lila*. The key symbols in "Nancy Culpepper" are photographs. Nancy recalls that the photographs from her wedding were fuzzy double exposures, just as the wedding itself was a superimposition of a strange new identity upon her southern rural past. Several years after the wedding she returns home to Kentucky to rescue old family pictures. She searches in particular for a likeness of her namesake, but this particular photograph is not found, just as her own sense of identity remains elusive.

Zigzagging Down a Wild Trail

Journeys are significant in *Zigzagging Down a Wild Trail*, which includes several stories from Mason's earlier collections. Protagonists travel geographical or psychological distances as they reevaluate past actions or cope with unanticipated life changes, often attempting to solve their problems by running away.

For Chrissie ("With Jazz"), a trip to her son's home leads her to several major reconsiderations. She realizes she has underestimated her son; also, she wonders about her responsibility in the breakup of her marriages and the death of her young daughter. Feeling generally unsuccessful, she attempts to escape her life by asking Jazz to take her to France, though he has already told her Kentuckians are out of place there. Similarly, Annie ("Rolling into Atlanta") reappraises her job and her ambitions after becoming involved with Wes, who gives her tickets to see the Rolling Stones.

Jackie ("Tobrah") travels to Tulsa to arrange the funeral of a father she has not seen for more than thirty-five years, only to discover that he has named her guardian of his five-year-old daughter, Tobrah. A custody challenge from Tobrah's aunt occurs at the same time Jackie learns she is not pregnant. Her reaction is to flee with Tobrah to a nearby Wildlife Center. Likewise, Liz ("Tunica") chooses to escape family problems by a bus trip to a casino. When the driver becomes lost, Liz equates the trip with a journey to Timbuktu or possibly even heaven.

For Bill ("Window Lights"), a first-person narrator, running away takes the form of emulating his grandmother, who dealt with family losses by retreating into a small section of her house and piecing quilts. In contrast, Mary ("Three-Wheeler") ends her self-imposed isolation on inherited family property as she speeds down the road on her uncle's three-wheeler, mentally reliving a motorcycle ride with the last man she truly loved.

For several Mason protagonists, returning to Kentucky leads to reconciliation. Attempting to explain the summer solstice to her father, Sandra ("The Funeral Side") realizes life's complexity and continuity as she learns truths about her mother's funeral and gains appreciation of both her father--who has maintained family's combination furniture store- funeral home-family dwelling--and the distant ancestor who began these businesses. Likewise, Wendy ("Night Flight") considers life in Florida an aberration from the normalcy of her traditional Kentucky life.

Searches are also significant. A television interview involving his job helps Boogie ("Thunder Snow") contact his wife, who is trapped in a snowstorm. Apprehensive about his forthcoming marriage, Charger ("Charger") believes if he drives to Texas to see why his father never returned, he can cope with any future.

NANCY CULPEPPER

Nowhere are Mason's Southern roots more evident than in *Nancy Culpepper*, which is dedicated to the memory of the writer's parents. Beginning with "Nancy Culpepper," which appeared first in *The New Yorker* in 1980 and later in *Shiloh, and Other Stories*,

Mason chronicles several generations of Culpeppers, emphasizing the importance of family--and extended family--in the development of personal identity.

Mason divides the stories chronologically, with the first three set between 1980 and 1982. The title story traces Nancy's attempts to establish her identity. Returning to Kentucky to help move her grandmother to a nursing home, Nancy explores family history, examining both the lifestyle of her Kentucky family and her life with her husband Jack and their son Robert in Pennsylvania. Apparently accepting Jack's theory that photographs are essential to preserve individuals' identities, Nancy searches for a photograph of her ancestor Nancy Culpepper (1833-1905), but when her mother and grandmother offer conflicting accounts, Nancy realizes that memories are transmitted through family lore.

The juxtaposition of family lore and photographic images is also at the center of "Blue Country," as Nancy receives word of her grandmother's fatal stroke while she and Jack are attending the wedding of longtime friends, where Jack plans to take photographs. The small talk at the wedding alternates with Nancy's telephone conversations with her mother, as Nancy agonizes about whether to return to Kentucky for the funeral. The color blue figures prominently: Nancy and Jack are staying at the Blue Lantern Inn, Nancy's grandmother is buried in a new blue dress with a corsage of blue flowers, and the story ends with the appearance of blue whales so spectacular that Jack, a professional photographer, forgets to snap the pictures he came to get.

A significant part of Nancy and Jack's family history is seen in "Lying Doggo," which ostensibly deals with the decline and death of Grover Cleveland, originally Jack's dog. Even after Jack is finally willing to euthanize Grover, Nancy and Robert find reasons for delay. The story ends with a party in Grover's honor--perhaps a kind of wake--as Grover may be dying or may be just "lying doggo."

Essential to the Culpeppers' history is Mason's novel *Spence + Lila*, set in 1982 as Lila's hospitalization for breast surgery brings together her husband Spence and their three adult children, Nancy, Catherine, and Lee. In this longest part of the collection,

Mason uses the memories and reflections of Lila and Spence to contrast their choice to remain close to home and parents with the independence of their children. The experiences of both generations mold their individual identities and collectively constitute a major element in their family lore.

Family history also figures prominently in "The Heirs" (set primarily in February, 2002) as Nancy's family home has been sold to a development consortium, and she is cleaning out the attic. Acutely aware of the changes since her parents' death, Nancy discovers a packet of letters dealing with attempts to cheat Nancy's great-aunts with dreams of a colonial grant to a distant ancestor.

"Proper Gypsies" (1994) and "The Prelude" (2005) deal with significant episodes in Nancy and Jack's marriage. In the former, a first-person narrative, Nancy discovers her vulnerability after a break-in at the London flat where she is staying after leaving Jack. In "The Prelude," Nancy awaits Jack's arrival in the Lake District, where they had honeymooned. As memories of the past combine with news of Jack's prostate cancer and the baby Robert and his girlfriend are expecting, Nancy and Jack realize that their minds function differently. However, Nancy concedes that life is essentially a series of pictures, and Jack shares her appreciation of the Romantic poets.

OTHER MAJOR WORKS

LONG FICTION: *In Country*, 1985; *Spence + Lila*, 1988; *Feather Crowns*, 1993; *An Atomic Romance*, 2005.

NONFICTION: *Nabokov's Garden: A Guide to "Ada,"* 1974; *The Girl Sleuth: A Feminist Guide to the Bobbsey Twins, Nancy Drew, and Their Sisters*, 1975, 1995; *Clear Springs: A Memoir*, 1999; *Elvis Presley*, 2002.

BIBLIOGRAPHY

Blythe, Hal, and Charlie Sweet. "The Ambiguous Grail Quest in 'Shiloh.'" *Studies in Short Fiction* 32 (Spring, 1995): 223-226. Examines the use of the Grail myth in "Shiloh"; claims the story is a contemporary version of Jessie Weston's "Waste Land." Argues that the myth lends universal significance to the minutiae-laden lives of a twentieth century western Kentucky couple in a troubled marriage.

Brinkmeyer, Robert H., Jr. "Never Stop Rocking: Bobbie Ann Mason and Rock-and-Roll." *Mississippi Quarterly: The Journal of Southern Culture* 42, no. 1 (1988-1989): 5-17. Footnoted with seven other articles and interviews, this essay explores Mason's use of rock music as a significant expression of contemporary culture.

Feinberg, Cara. "Poised for Possibility." *The Atlantic*, September, 2009. In an extended interview Mason discusses *Zigzagging Down a Wild Trail* and her writing of short stories generally.

Frey, Hillary. "Buying the Farm." Review of *Nancy Culpepper*, by Bobbie Ann Mason. *The New York Times Sunday Book Review*, August 13, 2006. The stories in this collection are analyzed in terms of the characters' life choices and the losses they feel when considering their pasts.

Giannone, Richard. "Bobbie Ann Mason and the Recovery of Mystery." *Studies in Short Fiction* 27 (Fall, 1990): 553-566. Claims that Mason's rural characters are caught between an incomprehensible otherworldly force and the loss of their this-worldly anguish; they are mystified by contemporary life while robbed of the mysteries of their lives. Discusses "Shiloh," "Retreat," and "Third Monday."

Morphew, G. O. "Downhome Feminists in *Shiloh, and Other Stories*." *The Southern Literary Journal* 21, no. 2 (1989): 41-49. In a considered treatment of Mason's down-home feminists, Morphew notes that the heroines want space within relationships, not equal pay for equal work. The essay notes differences between the actions of Mason's educated and uneducated heroines.

Pollack, Harriet. "From *Shiloh* to *In Country* to *Feather Crowns*: Bobbie Ann Mason, Women's History, and Southern Fiction." *The Southern Literary Journal* 28 (Spring, 1996): 95-116. Argues that Mason's fiction is representative of southern women authors who, without general recognition, have been transforming southern literature's characteristic attention to official history.

Price, Joanna. *Understanding Bobbie Ann Mason*. Columbia: University of South Carolina Press, 2000. These discussions of Mason's early fiction emphasize the interaction between the characters' rural roots and contemporary culture, with emphasis on the characters' sense of loss.

Rothstein, Mervyn. "Homegrown Fiction: Bobbie Ann Mason Blends Springsteen and Nabokov." *The New York Times Biographical Service* 19 (May, 1988): 563-565. This essay reports on Mason's love of rhythm and blues in high school and notes the semi-autobiographical details of *Spence + Lila.*

Ryan, Maureen. "Stopping Places: Bobbie Ann Mason's Short Stories." In *Women Writers of the Contemporary South*, edited by Peggy W. Prenshaw. Jackson: University Press of Mississippi, 1984. An overview of Mason's themes and character portraits, this sampling provides a brief treatment of many different works.

Thompson, Terry. "Mason's 'Shiloh.'" *The Explicator* 54 (Fall, 1995): 54-58. Claims that subdivisions play an important role in the story for gaining a full appreciation of the two main characters; argues that the subdivision is a metaphor for the marriage of the couple.

Wilhelm, Albert E. "Bobbie Ann Mason: Searching for Home." In *Southern Writers at Century's End*, edited by Jeffrey J. Folks and James A. Perkins. Lexington: University Press of Kentucky, 1997. Discusses the effect of American involvement in Vietnam in "Big Bertha Stories" and *In Country*. Argues that these two stories of soldiers' attempts to return home expand the theme of social dislocation to mythic proportions.

_____. *Bobbie Ann Mason: A Study of the Short Fiction*. New York: Twayne, 1998. This critical study of Mason's short fiction examines the influence of her femininity and her identity as a southerner on her writing. Includes such topics as the place that Kentucky plays in her work as well as a bibliography and index.

_____. "Private Rituals: Coping with Change in the Fiction of Bobbie Ann Mason." *Midwest Quarterly* 28, no. 2 (1987): 271-282. This article includes interview commentary from Mason as well as analysis of the rituals in several of the stories. Of the works he treats, Wilhelm examines "Shiloh" most closely.

Janet Taylor Palmer; Albert Wilhelm
Updated by Charmaine Allmon-Mosby

Mary McCarthy

Born: Seattle, Washington; June 21, 1912
Died: New York, New York; October 25, 1989

PRINCIPAL SHORT FICTION
The Company She Keeps, 1942
Cast a Cold Eye, 1950
The Hounds of Summer, and Other Stories, 1981

OTHER LITERARY FORMS

Mary McCarthy began writing as a drama critic for the *Partisan Review*. She wrote six novels; *The Group* (1963), the most widely read of these, was subsequently made into a film in Hollywood. She also wrote two autobiographies, as well as numerous articles and books on art and politics. Most groundbreaking among her nonfiction is the autobiography *Memories of a Catholic Girlhood* (1957), an idiosyncratic combination of fiction and nonfiction. In italicized bridges between each essay/story, McCarthy comments on the proportions of fact and fantasy in each selection. In her second autobiography, *How I Grew* (1987), she presents her life as an artist. Reviewers responded quite well to the second autobiography but typically noted the superiority of the first. McCarthy's literary criticism for *The New Republic* and *The Nation* earned her an important place in American literature.

ACHIEVEMENTS

Mary McCarthy's exceptional skill as a writer won her immediate recognition. An essay she wrote for the

College Entrance Examination Board (CEEB) was published anonymously in a CEEB journal of the early 1930's as an example of a high-scoring essay. Recognition for her excellence includes the 1949 *Horizon* literary prize for *The Oasis* (1949), an O. Henry short-story prize in 1957 for "Yellowstone Park," and in 1984 both the National Medal of Literature and the Edward MacDowell Medal for outstanding contributions to literature. McCarthy, a Guggenheim Fellow in both 1949 and 1959, was a member of the American Institute of Arts and Letters from 1960 until her death. Recognized for her astute observation of literary works, she was a judge for a number of fiction awards, including the Prix Formentor, the Booker Prize, and the National Book Award.

McCarthy's own writing style is classic: her sentences, architectural structures of balance and cadence; her rebellious point of view, a rainbow prism of satiric wit. The typical McCarthy story is realistic and satirical, revealing the self-deception of the supposedly intelligent and well educated. Her fiction is peopled with veiled portraits of those whom she knew well. Critical opinion tends to cast each of McCarthy's husbands, except James Raymond West, as the model for one or more of her male "antagonists": Harold Johnsrud for Harald Peterson in *The Group* and the husband in "Cruel and Barbarous Treatment"; Edmund Wilson for Miles Murphy in *A Charmed Life* (1955) and a legion of short-story husbands; and Bowden Broadwater for John Sinnot in *A Charmed Life* and a young American in "The Cicerone." Generally, McCarthy's characters are viewed ironically from a vantage point of cool detachment.

Biography

Mary Therese McCarthy's biography is unusually significant for understanding her fiction, since various clusters of biographical details seem to generate all her stories and characters. McCarthy's childhood began in Seattle with a doting, extravagant mother and a romantic, imaginative father. Her early life was an eden of picnics, parties, and stories that ended abruptly in 1918, when the flu killed both her parents within the same week. McCarthy was then remanded to the harsh and punitive custody of her Aunt Margaret and Uncle

Myers, but she survived in this new environment, which included beatings and deprivation, by excelling in school. These early triumphs led her to Vassar College, the crucible of her imaginative life and scene of her most popular work, *The Group*. All these details can be variously found in the lives of her fictional heroines, principally in that of Meg Sargent, the recurring figure in *The Company She Keeps*; indeed, Sargent was her great-grandmother's maiden name.

On her graduation from Vassar College, McCarthy married an actor, Harold Johnsrud, and at the same time she became drama critic for the *Partisan Review*; the marriage lasted three years, her career ten. By 1938, she had branched out into fiction and had a new marriage with writer and literary critic Edmund Wilson. After six cataclysmic years and one son, Reuel, McCarthy divorced Wilson and married Bowden Broadwater, from whom she was divorced in early 1961. Later in that year, McCarthy married James Raymond West, a State Department official, in Paris. She and West spent half of each year in their Paris home and half in Maine. During the last few years of her life,

Mary McCarthy (Washington Post/Getty Images)

McCarthy had several operations for hydrocephalus but continued to work on her memoirs, plan a study of gothic architecture, teach literature at Bard College, study German, and write literary criticism and commentary. She died in New York City on October 25, 1989, of cancer.

Analysis

Mary McCarthy's stories are, on the whole, about errors endemic to intellectuals, which lead them to indignity, despair, and sterility. McCarthy's typical intellectuals are political radicals or artists who fail to comprehend that their analytical acumen or talent does not raise them sufficiently from the common dilemma to empower them either to save the rest or to live more beautifully than do others. Meg Sargent, who, like Ernest Hemingway's Nick Adams, reappears continually in a series of short stories, is McCarthy's Every-intellectual, her voyage the purgatory of those with pretensions to education. "Cruel and Barbarous Treatment" is a good example of McCarthy's literary universe, and Meg's.

"Cruel and Barbarous Treatment"

In this story, Meg is going through a divorce, orchestrating the breakup of her marriage with the self-image of a diva in her greatest role. Meg considers herself to be a member of the intelligentsia, but McCarthy etches her as a grandiose fraud whose view of her situation is riddled with tired clichés. McCarthy comments on Meg economically by simply capitalizing strategically to turn Meg's thoughts into a series of buzz words. Meg is anxious to hear "What People Would Say" and "How Her Husband Would Take It." Finally, even the heroine realizes what she is doing. She will go ahead with her divorce, but she understands that The Young Man whom she thought she had waiting in the wings has been her factotum, not her passion. She will not be fool enough to fly into his arms. Unfortunately, her insight does not last, and on the train to Reno, she fabricates a new opera for her fellow passengers, deciding what to answer to queries concerning her destination. Neither will she be vulgar enough to blurt out "Reno" nor will she equivocate and reply "San Francisco." At first, she will say "'West,' with an air of vagueness and hesitation. Then, when pressed, she might go as far as to say 'Nevada.' But no farther."

"The Man in the Brooks Brothers Shirt"

The most pointed and, some might say, best treatment of McCarthy's theme is "The Man in the Brooks Brothers Shirt," her most widely anthologized story. In this story, Meg is traveling West to tell her aunt in Portland that she is to be married again. As a result of her trip, she realizes that she will never marry her new intended. The source of Meg's revelation is her encounter with Mr. Breen, a mid-level corporate executive in the steel business, whose wife Leonie and three children live comfortably in the Gate Hills section of Cleveland. Meg begins the trip flashing an advance copy of a very unimportant novel with which she intends to impress her suitor with her cultural superiority.

A political radical, Meg patronizes Breen's position in the corporate structure. Along with Meg's self-dramatized contempt for the man, however, McCarthy explores attitudes of which Meg is not aware. Meg is a poseur, and she envelops others in mythological poses. Despite her initial characterization of Breen as a "middle-aged baby, like a young pig, something in a seed catalogue . . . plainly Out of the Question," when Breen reveals that beneath his Brooks Brothers shirt beats a heart that wants to vote for Norman Thomas, Meg immediately romanticizes him as the last of the old breed of real American men. Stringing along behind her fantasy, she allows herself to get drunk in Breen's private compartment; the predictable revelry and sex follow in short order.

The next morning Meg is filled with shame, but Breen is wildly in love with her and wants to divorce Leonie and throw himself into an unconventional life with his Bohemian Girl. For Meg, sudden realization follows her drunken, sensual orgy; she begins to feel that she is not so much a free spirit, as she has always prided herself, but a sort of misfit. All the men in her life have suited her because they, like her, were in some way "handicapped" for American life. Although Breen seems to break the pattern, he does not. He is fifty, she thinks, over-the-hill. Would he, she wonders, have been in such hot pursuit if he were ten years younger?

What is clear, at least to the reader, is that each character is ambivalent about the characteristic of the other that holds the most attraction. Meg is contemptuous of Breen's conventionality, and Breen is critical of Meg's individualism. He tells her to shape up, because, if she does not, "In a few years you'll become one of those Bohemian horrors with oily hair and long earrings." The liberation that each affords the other does not mitigate these streaks of aversion. Meg and Breen do not run off together, but Meg also knows that she cannot marry her intended, and Breen manages to tryst with Meg several times before disappearing from her life. Meg has gained, through Breen, some humility about her elite self-image, but only temporarily; ultimately, she writes Breen off. Her last contact with him is a telegram she receives from him after the death of her father: "SINCEREST CONDOLENCES. YOU HAVE LOST THE BEST FRIEND YOU WILL EVER HAVE." Meg disposes of the missive, disgusted and embarrassed by Breen's middle-class sentimentality.

The portraits of Meg's individualism and Breen's conventionalism are ironic, but although both characters are supremely flawed, the story nevertheless treats Breen's limitations more charitably than Meg's. If Breen is corny, at least he fulfills the obligations of social convention to be nurturing, even if he is a bit obtuse. The nature of the intellect is to enlighten society, and Meg is too cliché-ridden to fulfill her obligations; all one sees are her limitations. In the end, her bohemian lifestyle is merely another form of convention. She shreds Breen's telegram at the end of the story because "It would have been dreadful if anyone had seen it." No bourgeoise could have better phrased the sentiment. McCarthy is a mistress of such deft, deflating touches. In the final ten words of the story she irretrievably nails Meg to the wall, just as she did at the end of "Cruel and Barbarous Treatment." She frequently uses a parting shot to devastate her protagonists.

McCarthy also grants her characters an occasional victory. When she does, the victory is hard-won and painfully small, but it can be lyrically affecting, as in "Ghostly Father, I Confess." In this story, Meg is now the wife of Frederick (perhaps based on Edmund Wilson) and is in analysis with Dr. James. Through numerous digressions, much is learned about other people in Meg's life, but the story takes place almost entirely during a session with her analyst. The beginning of the session is awash with stereotype; Meg stereotypes Dr. James, and he counters with the routine Freudian castration theory and dream interpretation. They move past this initial standoff, however, and begin to examine the effect of Meg's childhood on her terrible marriages. The details are all recognizable from McCarthy's own biography.

Meg explains how her marriage to Frederick shows that she is in a downward spiral initiated by the cruelty of her childhood guardians. James comes forward with a surprising inversion of Meg's rather obvious, although painfully arrived at, analysis, suggesting that "This marriage took more daring on your part than anything you have done since you left your father's house." He goes on to say that, with the marriage to Frederick, Meg has stopped denying the trauma of her childhood because she is now strong enough to face it and work through it. James quiets Meg's doubts by referring to her brains and beauty, which he tells her will overcome her problems. The session comes to a sudden close as James snaps shut his notebook, as though clicking the interview off. He is transformed, now uninvolved. Meg is upset by the abruptness but somewhat intoxicated by her discovery that James has given her five extra minutes and by his parting remark about her brains and beauty.

Once in the street, Meg is suddenly struck by the meaning of the dream for which James had given her an unsatisfying, conventional interpretation during the session. In her dream, she had seen herself loved by a Byronic figure who slowly metamorphosed into a Nazi war prisoner. She understands that the changing figure is her own mind revealing its true identity, not truly Byronic, after all, but a victim of rigidity and cruelty. As in the other stories, Meg has an insight into her fraudulent self-images, but this time the self-awareness seems to take hold. The story closes with the image of Meg in front of a window full of hot water bottles begging God to let her hold onto her uncomfortable revelation. McCarthy cryptically ends her narrative with the statement, "It was certainly a very small favor she was asking, but . . . she could not be too demanding, for, unfortunately, she did not believe in God."

McCarthy's sly portrait explores the enormity of trying to think at all. The mind tends to fall in love with its own creations and perpetrate frauds on itself. There is the fraud of the analyst who can turn his involvement on and off; the vanity of Meg's greed for five more minutes; the possible disingenuousness of James's remark about brains and beauty; the war between flesh and spirit, one of which desires the vulgar comfort of the hot water bottle, the other the irritant of enlightenment; and James's inordinate pleasure about his various interpretations, although readers do not know if they are true or false. Finally, there is the magnitude of the universe for which people desire the comfort of a caretaker, whom McCarthy would deny as a vulgarity equal to the hot water bottle. The mind is surely ninetenths dissembler, but Meg, by intuiting profoundly her own shabby role-playing has made an inroad on that great disabler of the intellect, its own narcissism. Such an inroad is the outer limit of McCarthy's concept of human achievement.

OTHER MAJOR WORKS

LONG FICTION: *The Oasis*, 1949; *The Groves of Academe*, 1952; *A Charmed Life*, 1955; *The Group*, 1963; *Birds of America*, 1971; *Cannibals and Missionaries*, 1979.

NONFICTION: *Sights and Spectacles, 1937-1956*, 1956; *Venice Observed*, 1956; *Memories of a Catholic Girlhood*, 1957; *The Stones of Florence*, 1959; *On the Contrary: Articles of Belief*, 1961; *Mary McCarthy's Theatre Chronicles, 1937-1962*, 1963; *Vietnam*, 1967; *Hanoi*, 1968; *The Writing on the Wall, and Other Literary Essays*, 1970; *Medina*, 1972; *The Mask of State*, 1974; *The Seventeenth Degree*, 1974; *Ideas and the Novel*, 1980; *Occasional Prose*, 1985; *How I Grew*, 1987; *Intellectual Memoirs: New York, 1936-1938*, 1992; *Between Friends: The Correspondence of Hannah Arendt and Mary McCarthy, 1949-1975*, 1995 (Carol Brightman, editor); *A Bolt from the Blue, and Other Essays*, 2002 (A. O. Scott, editor).

BIBLIOGRAPHY

Abrams, Sabrina Fuchs. *Mary McCarthy: Gender, Politics, and the Postwar Intellectual*. New York: P. Lang, 2004. Examines McCarthy's works of fiction and cultural criticism. Argues that McCarthy, a Catholic woman from the Northwest, stood at the periphery of New York City's predominantly Jewish male intellectual scene, and this "marginalized identity" shaped her satiric vision and her criticism of liberal pieties.

Brightman, Carol. *Writing Dangerously: Mary McCarthy and Her World*. New York: Clarkson Potter, 1992. Supplements but does not supersede Carol W. Gelderman's earlier biography. Like Gelderman, Brightman was able to interview her subject, and her book reflects not only inside knowledge but also (as its subtitle suggests) a strong grasp of the period in which McCarthy published. Includes a biographical glossary and notes.

Dickstein, Morris. "A Glint of Malice (Mary McCarthy)." In *A Mirror in the Roadway: Literature and the Real World*. Princeton, N.J.: Princeton University Press, 2005. A succinct overview and incisive analysis of McCarthy's works, in which Dickstein explains why the reputation of this once highly regarded writer eventually faded. His examination includes a discussion of some of her short stories

Epstein, Joseph. "Mary McCarthy in Retrospect." *Commentary* 95 (May, 1993): 41-47. Provides a summary of McCarthy's work, comments on her role in the intellectual life of America, and discusses the relationship of her life to her fiction.

Gelderman, Carol W. *Mary McCarthy: A Life*. New York: St. Martin's Press, 1988. Gelderman offers an objective biography of McCarthy. Although much of the narrative is familiar, the book is well written and amply documented. The photographs provide important perspective on McCarthy's childhood and a satisfying glimpse into her adult life. This biography makes good reading for a general audience, as well as for a student of McCarthy.

Gelfant, Blanche H., ed. *The Columbia Companion to the Twentieth-Century American Short Story*. New York: Columbia University Press, 2000. Includes a chapter in which McCarthy's short stories are analyzed.

Kiernan, Frances. *Seeing Mary Plain: A Life of Mary McCarthy*. New York: W. W. Norton, 2000. A comprehensive biography full of vivid details and anecdotes but marred by a lack of focus on certain essential aspects of McCarthy's life and work.

Kufrin, Joan. *Uncommon Women*. Piscataway, N.J.: New Century, 1981. In a book that examines women who have succeeded within several different fields, McCarthy is "The Novelist" for the chapter so named. The portrayal of the writer is friendly and informal, largely the transcription of an interview in McCarthy's home in Maine. McCarthy comments on her writing process of extensive revision. The two photographs capture a sense of fun and humor in McCarthy. A light and readable piece.

LIT: Literature Interpretation Theory 15, no. 1 (January-March, 2004). This entire issue is devoted to a reevaluation of McCarthy's fiction and literary criticism. While several of the articles focus on individual novels, their analyses can also pertain to the short fiction. Jaime Cleland's article, "Pink Pants and Pessaries: Mary McCarthy's Aesthetics of Embarrassment," discusses "Cruel and Barbarous Treatment," one of the stories in *The Company She Keeps*.

McCarthy, Mary. *Conversations with Mary McCarthy*. Edited by Carol W. Gelderman. Jackson: University Press of Mississippi, 1991. A series of interviews with the author, dating from 1962 to 1989.

McKenzie, Barbara. *Mary McCarthy*. New York: Twayne, 1966. McKenzie offers a one-page chronology of McCarthy's life, as well as an opening chapter providing biographical information. The fourth chapter, "The Key That Works the Person," discusses the short stories in *The Company She Keeps* and *Cast a Cold Eye*. The final chapter assesses McCarthy's overall contribution to literature. Includes notes, a bibliography, and an index.

Stock, Irvin. *Mary McCarthy*. Minneapolis: University of Minnesota Press, 1968. Stock's forty-seven-page essay includes overall critical comment on McCarthy's work, noting the moral concerns evident in her fiction. He summarizes and then provides analysis of *The Company She Keeps, Cast a Cold Eye*, and three of the novels. Stock's character studies are particularly incisive.

Stwertka, Eve, and Margo Viscusi, eds. *Twenty-Four Ways of Looking at Mary McCarthy: The Writer and Her Work*. Westport, Conn.: Greenwood Press, 1996. Reprints the twenty-four papers presented at a conference about McCarthy that was held at Bard College in 1993.

Wilford, Hugh. "An Oasis: The New York Intellectuals in the Late 1940's." *Journal of American Studies* 28 (August, 1994): 209-223. Wilford analyzes McCarthy's fictional portrayal of Europe-America Groups, a political organization created by New York intellectuals.

Martha Nochimson
Updated by Janet Taylor Palmer

JILL MCCORKLE

Born: Lumberton, North Carolina; July 7, 1958

PRINCIPAL SHORT FICTION
Crash Diet, 1992
Final Vinyl Days, and Other Stories, 1998
Creatures of Habit, 2001
Going Away Shoes, 2009

OTHER LITERARY FORMS

Jill McCorkle (muh-KOR-kuhl) began her writing career publishing novels. Her first book, *The Cheer Leader* (1984), incorporated similar themes, settings, and characters as those she first had explored in short stories she wrote in college. Elements in short stories she created influenced her other novels: *July Seventh, Tending to Virginia* (1987), *Ferris Beach* (1990), and *Carolina Moon* (1996). By the early twenty-first century, translations of her novels had been published in approximately fourteen languages. McCorkle has also written nonfiction, mostly book reviews, essays voicing her opinions and experiences, and literary criticism for periodicals and scholarly texts. She collaborated with Lee Smith on writing the musical *Good Ol' Girls* (2000). McCorkle read for audio recordings, including *The Best American Short Stories of the Century* (1999).

ACHIEVEMENTS

The New York Times placed five of Jill McCorkle's publications on its annual list of notable books. In 1993, the New England Booksellers Association presented McCorkle with its New England Book Award honoring all of her writing. Three years later, the literary periodical *Granta* recognized McCorkle as among the best young American novelists. In 1999, McCorkle's home state presented her with the North Carolina Award for Literature, and Longwood College

gave her its John Dos Passos Prize for Literature. Her short story "Intervention" was included in *The Norton Anthology of Short Fiction* (2006). Editors selected McCorkle's fiction for volumes of *The Best American Short Stories* in 2002, 2004, and 2009. Her work also was selected for *New Stories from the South* in 1988, 1991, 1993, 1996, 2004, and 2009 and chosen for *Best of the South: From the Second Decade of New Stories from the South* (2005). McCorkle's nonfiction appeared in the 2009 edition of *Best American Essays.*

BIOGRAPHY

Jill Collins McCorkle was born on July 7, 1958, in Lumberton, North Carolina, to John Wesley McCorkle, Jr., a U.S. Postal Service employee, and Melba Ann Collins, a pediatrician's secretary. Jill McCorkle listened to her grandmother's stories about their family and community, developing an affinity for storytelling. She graduated from Lumberton High School in 1976.

Attending the University of North Carolina, McCorkle took writing workshops from Max Steele, Lee Smith, and Louis D. Rubin, Jr. The campus literary periodical *Cellar Door* printed McCorkle's story "Mrs. Lela's Fig Tree" in 1979. Her story "Bare Facts" received the university's Jessie Rehder Prize. McCorkle earned a B.A. in 1980. Her professors suggested McCorkle attend graduate school at Hollins College, Smith's alma mater and where Rubin had helped establish the creative-writing program. Her fiction won Hollins's Andrew James Purdy Prize. In 1981, she completed an M.A., after writing her thesis, "From a Further Room."

On July 18, 1981, McCorkle married Stephen Alexander in her hometown. They moved to Florida, where McCorkle taught and worked as a librarian. McCorkle sent *The Cheer Leader* manuscript she had begun in college to Rubin for his insights, unaware he was establishing a press. She completed another manuscript, *July Seventh*, and also submitted it to Rubin, who decided to publish both books in 1984.

McCorkle returned to Chapel Hill in 1984 after her divorce at the request of Steele, so she could teach creative writing when a position was available. She worked as a secretary at the university's medical school and befriended medical student Dan Shapiro. By 1986, McCorkle had taught creative-writing classes at her alma mater and at Duke University in Durham. She married Shapiro in May, 1987, the same year her third book, *Tending to Virginia*, was published. They moved to Boston, Massachusetts, where McCorkle gave birth to a daughter, Claudia, and a son, Rob. She taught writing at Tufts University.

McCorkle's first short-story collection, *Crash Diet*, was published in 1992, and that fall she started teaching writing at Harvard University. Her story "Final Vinyl Days" was printed in *Elvis in Oz: New Stories and Poems from the Hollins Creative Writing Program* (1992). During the next decade, she taught in Bennington College's M.F.A. program and was a visiting writer at Brandeis University.

McCorkle and Smith appropriated elements of their stories to write the musical *Good Ol' Girls*. After Smith resigned from her North Carolina State University position in 2002, McCorkle moved to Hillsborough and began teaching writing in the school's M.F.A. program.

McCorkle's short stories appeared in periodicals, including *Ploughshares*, *Oxford American*, and *The Chattahoochee Review*. Editors selected McCorkle's stories for numerous anthologies, such as *The Cry of an Occasion: Fiction from the Fellowship of Southern Writers* (2001) and *Long Story Short: Flash Fiction by Sixty-Five of North Carolina's Finest Writers* (2009). She reviewed books for the *Hollins Critic* and several newspapers. McCorkle wrote the preface for the 2005 *New Stories from the South*.

Analysis

Jill McCorkle explores characters' motivations for their actions, especially their emotional responses to situations that confront them. Conflict is an important theme in her short fiction. McCorkle's characters often are betrayed by people they trust and are forced to make decisions that might permanently alter those relationships. Various challenges block characters from achieving desired goals and temptations, such as wanting to live elsewhere, securing different employment, or finding new romance. Her characters demonstrate that perseverance is essential.

Family, community, and memory shape McCorkle's short fiction. While many of her characters live in the South, McCorkle also appropriates northeastern settings, although southerners living there are among her archetypal casts, to show the universality of concerns, crises, and issues people contemplate. Her use of dialogue and depiction of interactions convey characteristics, stereotypes, and attitudes that set the tone of her stories. The theme of identity, relevant to both people and places in her stories, often proves appearances are deceptive. McCorkle juxtaposes humorous and macabre imagery to reveal absurdities. Defiance and confession intensify stories' comic and dramatic elements.

Crash Diet

Sudden loss confronts characters in many of the eleven stories in *Crash Diet*. Love bonds characters to spouses and family, while also provoking irreparable rifts. Themes of innocence, betrayal, misery, and resilience accompany narratives examining female characters adjusting to revelations and emotional injuries before transforming their lives so they can survive and affirm who they are and what they want without sacrificing their dignity, autonomy, and memories.

Ruthie and Jim receive the Goodnight Inn in Petrie, South Carolina, as a wedding present in "Gold Mine." Just graduated from high school, they live in a camper while renovating the motel and building their house. Ruthie decorates each room with a theme. The pair delights every night when travelers fill all their rooms. After I-95 diverts traffic from the highway passing their motel, the business falters. Jim criticizes Ruthie for renting a room to elderly Mrs. Adler, stating he does not want the empty motel to become a retirement home. He meets Barbara and abandons Ruthie, who continues tending their children and reminiscing about happy times at the Goodnight Inn. One night, she discovers Jim and Barbara in the motel's honeymoon suite. Facing truths about her past and present, which she has romanticized, Ruthie compromises to salvage a future.

Reminiscences comfort widow Anna Craven in "Departures." She mourns her husband Walter, who died unexpectedly on a business trip three years prior. Both nearing retirement age, the Cravens had planned activities to be together. Instead, Anna is alone, repeating Walter's last phone call in her mind and counting time increments since he has been gone. She endures her grown children's criticisms and unsolicited suggestions. Anna recalls the family's summer vacations at a beach, where she and Walter became entranced with another couple Anna and Walter called the Vanderbilts because of their elegance. She goes to airports, imagining stories for people who intrigue her and conclusions to dramas she witnesses. Anna remembers admiring the widowed Mrs. Vanderbilt's strength, wishing she had asked the woman how to counter loneliness. Anna resolves to live according to her desires, not others' dictates.

FINAL VINYL DAYS, AND OTHER STORIES

Transitions are essential for character development in the nine short fiction tales collected in *Final Vinyl Days, and Other Stories*. Depicting aspects of life cycles, the stories explore birth, childhood, adolescence, autonomy associated with careers and relationships, and death. Featuring moments and milestones in characters' lives, the stories share elements of grief and loss, even when protagonists are experiencing happiness or achieving desired goals.

Religious imagery provides structure in "Paradise." Georgia native Eve Lyn Wallace meets Adam, a Jewish New Yorker, at a Baptist wedding, at which she is bridesmaid for her friend who is marrying Adam's fraternity brother. Adam watches the ceremony in shock, unfamiliar with southern wedding traditions and pondering why his college friends who had pledged commitment to bachelorhood are marrying. After the ceremony, Adam and Eve share details about their lives but conceal facts, such as how Adam's parents' divorce impacted him. The wedding celebration, which includes throwing the groom in the pool, resembling a baptism, surrounds them. The lush setting forms their temporary Eden. They become a couple. Cultural differences, misunderstandings, and expectations threaten to split them apart, but they decide to marry, returning to the same wed-

ding site where they met. Their first child's birth foreshadows the consolidation of their futures.

Mortality motivates characters in "Last Request." Tina wonders what her mother means when she awakens briefly from a coma to insist Tina promise to remain married to her husband, even if she wants to leave him. Tina is bewildered by her mother's words because she is committed to Doug and questions whether her mother knows something she has not revealed to Tina. In a first-person narrative, Tina describes her childhood with her spoiled twin sister Twyla, who hedonistically enjoys life, while Tina dutifully obeys her mother's sometimes misguided orders. She compares the men they married, Tina's honest husband and Twyla's unethical lawyer spouse. Tina contemplates memories of her father and how her mother destroyed his clothing after he died, becoming aware of their infidelities. Recognizing truths in her mother's enigmatic command, Tina maintains her unconditional love for Doug, which validates her realization she should trust maternal advice.

CREATURES OF HABIT

Memories of childhood perceptions of places, people, and significant moments shape many of the twelve stories, each metaphorically titled for an animal, in *Creatures of Habit*. Settings often initially seem benign with nostalgic elements until dark tones emerge to reveal opportunities for evil to overtake innocence. Themes of routine and planning contrast with impulsiveness and spontaneity, which disrupt patterns and ordered lives and expectations. Death abruptly alters survivors' lives and their realizations regarding truths and deceptions people perpetuate for varied reasons. Secrets intensify misunderstandings and provoke conflicts.

Curiosity motivates the child narrator of "Billy Goats" and her playmates, as they roam their neighborhood in summer, 1970, observing people and sharing speculations. The children mimic goats crossing a bridge while evading a troll based on a children's story. Like those fictional goats, they recognize hazards in their surroundings. Their activities are framed by legal proceedings against Jeffrey MacDonald, a military captain accused of murdering his family violently in an adjacent town. The children wonder about a murder-suicide house in their town, where a violinist and her husband died, and a fence on which a boy was impaled twenty years previously. They are intrigued by eccentric Hank Carter, an honor student who became crazy. The narrator scrutinizes her community, aware that darkness can emerge anywhere and in anyone.

Pranks are central to "Snipe," in which a young girl, Caroline, strives to appease her older brother, Danny, a fourth grader, who controls her by telling lies to scare her. Taking advantage of Caroline's innocence, the contemptible boy plays practical jokes, such as blindfolding Caroline, then abandoning her. The children's family welcomes relatives who arrive for a Fourth of July gathering. The adults prepare Danny for a snipe hunt, a family rite of passage, in the dark woods surrounding their home and allow Caroline to accompany him. In the dark, unfamiliar noises frighten Danny, who confides a secret so extreme that Caroline ponders its veracity. When the truth about the family tradition is revealed, emboldened Caroline chooses to stick close to chastened Danny, out of love, not fear.

GOING AWAY SHOES

Lies, secrets, and memory provoke emotional chaos for characters in the eleven stories collected in *Going Away Shoes*. Female characters contemplate how past choices and events have shaped their present lives and potentially will impact their futures unless they make unexpected and often undesirable decisions. Protagonists often dwell on regrets and wish they could change their histories. As they face moral dilemmas, they experience epiphanies, which transform their perceptions of themselves, others, and their situations.

Darkness and fear establish sinister tones in "Magic Words." Paula Blake caters to her children's and husband's demands. As she drives to a motel for a tryst with a male colleague, linked characters and stories are introduced. Agnes Hayes, a retired schoolteacher, regrets nagging her deceased husband and hurting her son's feelings. An unnamed teenage boy terrorizes classmates and residents, including Agnes, whom he loathes for her insistence that he say "please," the magic word resonating as characters use it in this story. He intimidates and abuses a heartbroken girl, Lauren, who escapes his trap when Paula sees Laura barefoot

by the road and decides to help. As they drive around town, Paula ignores her buzzing phone, representing needy people in her life. Lauren ironically presents a real victim seeking her aid instead of the fictional woman Paula created as excuse to leave home.

The theme of salvation also is explored in "Intervention." Marilyn realizes her husband Sid is an alcoholic but resents the interference of and is unable to stop their adult children's plans to confront him regarding his drinking. They emphasize that Sid is a threat to Marilyn's safety because of a car accident in which they believe he was a drunken driver. Marilyn remembers when her children were toddlers and she had an affair. Ashamed of herself because the man's wife was pregnant, Marilyn drank heavily. Despite her betrayal, Sid forgave Marilyn and helped her recover, fixing their relationship and replanting grass in the scorched area where she had burned silk underwear she wore to meet her lover. Marilyn's love for her husband intensifies. After Sid rebuffs their children, pouring liquor down the drain, Marilyn vows to trust him with her life.

OTHER MAJOR WORKS

LONG FICTION: *The Cheer Leader*, 1984; *July Seventh*, 1984; *Tending to Virginia*, 1987; *Ferris Beach*, 1990; *Carolina Moon*, 1996.

PLAYS: *Good Ol' Girls*, pr. 2000 (with Lee Smith).

BIBLIOGRAPHY

Bennett, Barbara. *Understanding Jill McCorkle*. Columbia: University of South Carolina Press, 2000. Biographical information is supplemented by literary criticism of McCorkle's five novels, with analysis of *Crash Diet* and *Final Vinyl Days, and Other Stories* in two chapters. Bibliography.

Ellis, Sherry, ed. *Illuminating Fiction: A Collection of Author Interviews with Today's Best Writers of Fiction*. Los Angeles: Red Hen Press, 2009. Chapter featuring McCorkle provides her responses to questions addressing themes and literary elements in *Creatures of Habit* and prior collections

Elmore, Jenifer B. "Jill McCorkle." In *The History of Southern Women's Literature*, edited by Carolyn Perry and Mary Louise Weaks. Baton Rouge:

Louisiana State University Press, 2002. Comments regarding several stories in McCorkle's first and second short-fiction collections.

Gaines, Judith. "Yankee Interview." *Yankee*, 70, no. 6 (Summer, 2006): 122-124. McCorkle comments regarding her writing processes, readers' responses, and why her later works portray more darkness. Photograph of McCorkle.

Johnson, Greg. "Heart Troubles." *The Georgia Review* 46, no. 2 (Summer, 1992): 358-365. Review essay examining four short-story collections, including *Crash Diet*, compares McCorkle's style with that of other southern writers, identifying stories this critic considers her strongest and weakest, accompanied by explanations.

Kamps, Louisa. "Animal House." *The New York Times*, October 28, 2001, p. BR16. Reviewer dislikes many of the stories in *Creatures of Habit*, particularly the ones comparing men and women to apes and cats, while praising the tales using goat, snipe, and fish metaphors.

Town, Caren J. "'A Whole World of Possibilities Spinning Around Her': Female Adolescence in the Contemporary Southern Fiction of Josephine Humphreys, Jill McCorkle, and Tina Ansa." *Southern Quarterly* 42, no. 2 (Winter, 2004): 89-108. Discussion of themes and imagery in *Ferris Beach* is applicable to McCorkle's depiction of teenagers and young women in her short stories.

Wolitzer, Meg. "Hard Cases." *The New York Times*, July 19, 1998, p. BR23. Review of *Final Vinyl Days, and Other Stories* provides brief synopses of and lines from several stories; criticizes McCorkle's excessive use of popular culture references and praises her humor and insights.

Elizabeth D. Schafer

CARSON MCCULLERS

Born: Columbus, Georgia; February 19, 1917
Died: Nyack, New York; September 29, 1967

PRINCIPAL SHORT FICTION

The Ballad of the Sad Café: The Novels and Stories of Carson McCullers, 1951
The Ballad of the Sad Café and Collected Short Stories, 1952, 1955
The Shorter Novels and Stories of Carson Mc-Cullers, 1972

OTHER LITERARY FORMS

Carson McCullers's remarkable first novel, *The Heart Is a Lonely Hunter* (1940), established the themes that were to concern her in all her other writing: the spiritual isolation of individuals and their attempt to transcend loneliness through love. Thereafter, she wrote short stories, some poetry (mostly for children), four other novels, and two plays. The most popular of the novels, *The Member of the Wedding* (1946), she

adapted for the stage; the play was a great success on Broadway and was also made into an award-winning film. *The Heart Is a Lonely Hunter* and her somber Freudian novel, *Reflections in a Golden Eye* (1941), were also adapted for film. McCullers also wrote a number of significant essays, which are collected in *The Mortgaged Heart* (1971). The essays that are most important to understanding the method and content of her fiction, especially her use of the grotesque, are "The Russian Realists and Southern Literature" and "The Flowering Dream: Notes on Writing."

ACHIEVEMENTS

Carson McCullers was the winner of a number of literary awards during her lifetime, including membership in the National Institute of Arts and Letters, two John Simon Guggenheim Memorial Foundation Fellowships, and an Arts and Letters Grant. She also won the New York Drama Critics Circle Award, a Gold Medal, and the Donaldson Award (all for the play version of *The Member of the Wedding*). Her fiction and nonfiction works were published in a number of reputable magazines, including *The New Yorker, Harper's Bazaar, Esquire*, and *Mademoiselle*. For her story "A Tree. A Rock. A Cloud," she was nominated for an O. Henry Award.

A praiseworthy writer of short fiction, McCullers succeeds with objective narration, the theme of loneliness, and her lyric compression. While McCullers is perhaps not as great a writer of short stories as her peers Flannery O'Connor, Eudora Welty, and Katherine Anne Porter, she is nevertheless successful at affecting her readers' emotions. The brevity and compression of stories such as "The Jockey" and "The Sojourner" are remarkable based on any standards. Although her techniques are not as innovative as those of many other postmodern fiction writers, she influenced, among others, Truman Capote, Flannery O'Connor, and Anne Tyler, particularly with the expert use of the grotesque and the freakish and the portrayal of human alienation. Her knowledge of human psychology also makes her a great spokesperson for the complexity of human experience.

BIOGRAPHY

Carson McCullers, born Lula Carson Smith, was reared in a small southern town, a milieu that she used in much of her fiction. Exhibiting early talent in both writing and music, she intended to become a concert pianist but lost her tuition money for the Juilliard School of Music when she went to New York in 1935. This loss led her to get part-time jobs while studying writing at Columbia University. She earned early acclaim for her first novel, *The Heart Is a Lonely Hunter*, written when she was only twenty-two. Her friends included many prominent writers, including Tennessee Williams, W. H. Auden, Louis MacNeice, and Richard Wright. Her health was always delicate; she suffered early paralyzing strokes, breast cancer, and pneumonia. She stayed remarkably active in literature and drama, however, even when confined to bed and wheelchair. She died of a stroke at the age of fifty.

ANALYSIS

Carson McCullers's short stories (ruling out for the moment the novella *The Ballad of the Sad Café*) often explore the intense emotional content of seemingly undramatic situations. Plot is minimal, although there is often at least one unusual or grotesque element. "Wunderkind," for example, deals with the confused feelings of a gifted fifteen-year-old girl at a piano lesson. Her social development has been sacrificed to her musical talent; now her mastery of the keyboard is faltering and she is profoundly humiliated. The reader realizes that part of her difficulty is the awakening of sexual feelings for her teacher, Mister Bilderbach. Neither the teacher, who thinks of her as a child prodigy, nor the young girl herself understands her tension and clumsiness.

"THE JOCKEY"

"The Jockey" describes an even more ordinary situation--a brief encounter in a restaurant between a jockey and three other men identified as a trainer, a bookie, and a rich man whose horse the jockey has ridden. The dwarflike jockey, called Bitsy Barlow, is one of those grotesque figures who seem an embarrassing mistake in nature. The point of the story is the ironic contrast between the three "normal" men's callous pretense of sympathy for a rider's crippling accident on the track and the jockey's bitter grief for that rider, who is his closest friend. Although the jockey, because of his physical deformity, seems a caricature of humanity, the intensity of his sorrow makes the other men's callousness seem the more monstrous.

"MADAME ZILENSKY AND THE KING OF FINLAND"

"Madame Zilensky and the King of Finland" is, on the most obvious level, at least, a revelation of the emotional price of artistic excellence. Like "Wunderkind" and "The Jockey," the story concerns the subjective significance of seemingly minor events. Mr. Brook, head of a college music department, hires Madame Zilensky, a famous composer and teacher, for his faculty. He is tolerant of her several eccentricities, her tales of adventures in exotic places, and even her somewhat shocking assertion that her three sons are the offspring of three different lovers. When she claims to have seen the king of Finland, however, Mr. Brook realizes that she is a pathological liar, since Finland has no king. Mr. Brook is sensitive enough to intuit the motive for her prevarications: the terrible constriction of her actual experience. "Through her lies, she lived vicariously. The lies doubled the little of her existence that was left over from work and augmented the little rag end of her personal life."

Point of view is vital in this story. The pathetic emotional dependence of Madame Zilensky on fantasy is the explicit and obvious content, but the story's real focus is on the growing perception of Mr. Brook, who has himself led a somewhat dull, repetitive life in academia. It is his character which receives the more subtle delineation. He represents those countless ordinary people whose individuality has been subdued, but not utterly extinguished, by professional duties. When Mr. Brook, in his official capacity, feels he must reprimand Madame Zilensky for propagating lies about herself, he comes face to face with stark tragedy. The terrible emotional deprivation he is about to expose echoes in his own solitary soul. Compassion for her loneliness and his own makes him realize that truth is not the highest virtue.

This terrified retreat from reality into the most banal of polite conversation ironically combines tragedy and sardonic humor. To use the name of love in this context is surprising, at once accurate and absurd. A final symbolic image captures the grotesque irrationality embedded in the most familiar landscape. As Mr. Brook looks out of his office window later, he sees, perhaps for the hundredth time, a faculty member's old Airedale terrier waddling down the street. This time, however, something is strange: The dog is walking backward. He watches "with a kind of cold surprise" until the dog is out of sight, then returns to the pile of student papers on his desk.

This story is thematically typical of McCullers's fiction. Love, which has little or nothing to do with sexuality, is the only way to bridge the terrible isolation which separates individuals. Too many other factors in the situation, however--habit, social custom, human perversity, the demands of artistic creativity, or simply devotion to duty--conspire against the goal of giving love and comfort to one another. Each person is trapped, incommunicado, in the little cage he or she has chosen.

"A DOMESTIC DILEMMA"

The irrational persistence of love and its inadequacy to solve the everyday problems of existence are also apparent in "A Domestic Dilemma." Here, too, the

Carson McCullers (Library of Congress)

story is told from the point of view of a patient, kindly man whose attitude toward his alcoholic wife is a curious blend of compassion, love, and angry exasperation. He fears for the welfare of his two children. He comes home to the suburbs from his New York office to find his children unattended, playing with Christmas tree lights, a supper of cinnamon toast on the kitchen table, untouched except for one bite. The little boy complains, "It hurt. The toast was hot." His wife, Emily, had mistaken cayenne pepper for cinnamon.

The bewildered children do not understand the painful scene between mother and father, in which Emily vacillates drunkenly between belligerent defense of her behavior and tearful shame. Martin finally persuades her to go to bed and let him feed the children, bathe them, and put them to bed. He successfully reestablishes an atmosphere of tender solicitude, hoping the children will not remember their mother's puzzling behavior. How long will it be, he wonders, before they understand and despise her? There are moments when Martin hates his wife, imagining "a future of degradation and slow ruin" for himself and his children. When he finally lies down beside Emily and watches her sleeping, however, his anger gradually dissipates. "His hand sought the adjacent flesh and sorrow paralleled desire in the immense complexity of love."

One interpretation offered for "A Domestic Dilemma" points to the stresses of an urban lifestyle on a woman reared in an emotionally supportive small southern town. In suburbia, Emily is isolated from everyone she ever knew, while Martin commutes long distances into the inner city. Thus, it is social isolation that is destroying her. This interpretation has considerable validity, although the cause of her alcoholism is not really central to the story; isolation and loneliness occur in all kinds of social situations in McCullers's fiction, and small southern towns are as deadly as urban suburbs in that regard. Isolation is a metaphysical affliction more than a cultural one. Emily's social isolation is analogous to Bitsy Barlow's physical deformity or even Madame Zilensky's enslaving musical genius--one of the many accidents of nature or situation over which people have little control. Just as Mr. Brook's empathy for Madame Zilensky cannot alleviate her isolation, Martin's love for his wife will not necessarily save her from her unhappiness. In McCullers's fiction it is usually the act of love, not the comfort of being loved, that has power to transform the lover.

"A Tree. A Rock. A Cloud"

One of the most anthologized of McCullers's stories is "A Tree. A Rock. A Cloud," which was chosen for the 1942 *Prize Stories: The O. Henry Awards*, even though it may be inferior, in some ways, to "A Domestic Dilemma," "Wunderkind," and "Madame Zilensky and the King of Finland." It deals more philosophically and perhaps more ironically with the art of loving. The lover, in this case, is an old, boozy wanderer who waylays a newspaper delivery boy in a café. He is compulsively dedicated to explaining how he learned to love "all things both great and small." The quotation comes not from the story but from *The Rime of the Ancient Mariner* (1798), which is quite possibly its inspiration. The irony of Samuel Taylor Coleridge's Ancient Mariner waylaying an impatient wedding guest with his story of salvation through love is translated here into a somewhat different context.

Three persons, rather than two, are involved. Although the tale is addressed to the naïve newspaper delivery boy, it is overheard by Leo, the proprietor of the café, who is early characterized as bitter and stingy. When the wanderer accosts the boy and says distinctly, "I love you," the initial laughter of the men in the café and their immediate return to their own beer or breakfasts suggest both a widespread cynicism and an utter indifference concerning the welfare of the boy. Although Leo is also cynical and often vulgar, he listens to the conversation carefully. When the old man orders a beer for the boy, Leo brings coffee instead, reminding the other man, "He is a minor."

Although Leo soon understands that the old man's intention is not to proposition the boy, he continues to interject insulting remarks into the wanderer's sad tale of love for a wife who deserted him for another man. The old man struggles to explain the unifying effect of love on the fragmented psyche. Before his marriage, he says, "when I had enjoyed anything there was a peculiar sensation as though it was laying around loose in me. Nothing seemed to finish itself up or fit in with other things." His wife, however, transformed his experience of himself-- "this woman was something like an assembly line for my soul. I run these little pieces of myself through her and I come out complete." However, after years of frantic search for the lost wife, the man realizes with horror that he cannot even remember distinctly what she looked like. It was then that he began his "science" of love.

At this point, Leo explodes in exasperation:

Leo's mouth jerked with a pale, quick grin. "Well none of we boys are getting any younger," he said. Then with sudden anger he balled up a dishcloth he was holding and threw it down hard on the floor. "You draggle-tailed old Romeo!"

The wanderer solemnly explains that one must practice the art of loving by starting with small or inanimate things--a tree, a rock, a cloud--and graduate from one thing to another. He learned to love a goldfish next. Now he has so perfected the science of loving that he can love anything and everyone. By this time, Leo is screaming at him to shut up.

As an explanation of Platonic love, this, to be sure, may be feeble. The reactions of Leo and the boy do, however, provide depth to the story. The newsboy is puzzled and confused--presumably because he has yet to pass through adolescence, when the importance and complexity of love will become clearer to him. After the old man leaves, the boy appeals to Leo for answers. Was the man drunk? Was he a dope fiend? Was he crazy? To the first two questions Leo says, shortly, "No." To the last he is grimly silent. Probably Leo responds so emotionally to the old man's tale because it makes him too keenly aware of his own barren lovelessness. His role is somewhat analogous to that of Mr. Brook in this respect. He recognizes, perhaps, that the old man, unlike himself, has found a way to transcend his wretchedness. Can it be "crazy" to be at peace with oneself, in spite of outwardly miserable circumstances? If so, it is a craziness a sane man might covet. The boy, thinking of nothing else to say, comments that the man "sure has done a lot of traveling." As the story ends, McCullers emphasizes therefore that the story is about adolescent versus adult perceptions of love.

Autobiographical elements

McCullers's short fiction, like her most popular novel, *The Member of the Wedding*, has many autobiographical elements. Her own absorption in music and early aspirations to be a concert pianist are reflected in "Wunderkind" and "Madame Zilensky and the King of Finland." The particular mode of Madame Zilensky's escape from a narrowly focused existence is even more pertinent to McCullers's short, intense life. She escaped the limitations of her frail body through fantasy, transforming it into fiction and drama.

Even the situation in "A Domestic Dilemma" echoes her own life curiously altered. She lived both the Emily role, that is, the maimed personality who desperately needs love and companionship, and the Martin role, the hopeless lover of the psychologically crippled person. McCullers's husband, whom she divorced and later remarried, was an alcoholic whose drinking was aggravated by the fact that, although he fancied himself a writer, she was so much more successful than he. She has disguised the personal element in the situation by changing the presumed cause of the alcoholism (although she, too, knew the effect of migrating from a small southern town to New York) and by projecting her role more on the husband than the wife.

Both Martin and Mr. Brook exhibit qualities ordinarily ascribed to women--intuition, gentleness, patience, and unselfish love. McCullers's blurring of gender roles (Miss Amelia in *The Ballad of the Sad Café* is strikingly masculine) was probably not motivated by a feminist revolt against stereotyped sex roles; she was not a polemicist but a lyrical writer, projecting her own personality, feelings, dreams, and fears. If her men act like women, or vice versa, they behave this way because McCullers herself was decidedly androgynous. She loved both men and women and somehow contained them both. Some of her most ardent attractions were for women who repudiated her attentions (or at least did not remain in her vicinity), which may account for the wistful need for love in some of her fictional characters.

In spite of her personal sorrows and her emotional isolation and loneliness, McCullers was beloved by many friends and generous in her own affections. Even the odd triangular love affairs that appear in *The Member of the Wedding* and *Reflections in a Golden Eye* have some autobiographical parallels. Both Carson and her husband, according to McCullers's biographer, Virginia Spencer Carr, were intimately involved with Jack Diamond, a concert musician. It is not an accident that McCullers was one of the first American writers to deal openly (in *Reflections in a Golden Eye*) with repressed homosexuality. In the case of her husband, at least, his homosexual orientation was not always repressed; whether she was an active bisexual is more ambiguous.

McCullers' personal life and her fiction both seem marked by a curious combination of sophisticated intuition into human motives and an odd childlike quality that sometimes verges on immaturity. Most writers, for example, would not write of Mr. Brook that he could not speak until "this agitation in his insides quieted down," nor would many writers try to express the blurred Platonic idealism of "A Tree. A Rock. A Cloud." Although the situational irony of that story saves it from being naïvely expressed philosophy, one has a lingering impression that the writer is mocking a sentiment that she really wants to advocate.

The Ballad of the Sad Café

The Ballad of the Sad Café, sometimes grouped with novellas, sometimes with short stories, is the most successful of McCullers's ventures into the grotesque. The melancholy mood suggested by the title is appropriate; like many a folk ballad, it tells a mournful tale touched with sardonic humor. The story celebrates the love of a cross-eyed, mannish woman for a conceited, hunchbacked dwarf. It also involves a curious love triangle, for the climax is a grotesque battle between the protagonist, Miss Amelia, and her former husband for the affection of the dwarf.

True love, paradoxically, is both a cruel joke and the means of redemption, not only for the lover, Miss Amelia, but also for the whole ingrown, backwoods community, which otherwise dies of emotional starvation. The inhabitants of this stifling southern village, like a somber chorus in a Greek tragedy, observe and reflect the fortunes of Miss Amelia, their leading citizen. Cousin Lymon, the hunchback, appears out of nowhere at the door of Miss Amelia, who runs the town store and the best distillery for miles around. To everyone's amazement, instead of throwing him out, as she has done to others who claimed kinship, Miss Amelia takes in the wretched wanderer and even falls in love with him. Cousin Lymon becomes a pompous little king of the castle, although not, apparently, her bed partner. Love transforms the mean, hard, sexless Miss Amelia into a reasonable facsimile of a warmhearted woman. She opens a café in her store because Cousin Lymon likes company, and her place becomes the social center of the community. Miss Amelia blossoms; the community blooms with goodwill, until the arrival of another person who is to destroy this interlude of happiness and peace.

Miss Amelia had once married the town bad boy, who had unaccountably fallen in love with her. Her motivation had apparently been solely commercial, the hope of acquiring a strong helper in her business; when the bridegroom expected sexual favors, Miss Amelia had indignantly refused. After ten stormy days, she threw him out entirely, earning his undying hatred for causing him such frustration and humiliation; he turned to a life of crime and landed in the penitentiary. Now he is out of jail and returns with malevolent thoughts of

revenge. Poor Miss Amelia, now vulnerable in a new and surprising way, accepts his unwelcome presence in her café because Cousin Lymon is fascinated with him, and Miss Amelia and her former spouse become rivals for the affection of the dwarf.

This rivalry culminates in a ludicrous variation of the western showdown, solemnly witnessed by the whole community, when Miss Amelia and her former husband have a battle of fisticuffs in the café. Moreover, Miss Amelia, who has been quietly working out with a punching bag in preparation for the event, is winning. At the last moment, however, the traitorous Cousin Lymon leaps onto her back, and the two men together beat her senseless. Afterward, they vandalize her store and her still in the woods and flee. Miss Amelia thereafter closes her business and becomes a permanent recluse in a town now desolate and deserted.

Other major works

LONG FICTION: *The Heart Is a Lonely Hunter*, 1940; *Reflections in a Golden Eye*, 1941; *The Ballad of the Sad Café*, 1943, serial (1951, book); *The Member of the Wedding*, 1946; *Clock Without Hands*, 1961.

PLAYS: *The Member of the Wedding*, pr. 1950, pb. 1951 (adaptation of her novel); *The Square Root of Wonderful*, pr. 1957, pb. 1958.

NONFICTION: *Illumination and Night Glare: The Unfinished Autobiography of Carson McCullers*, 1999 (Carlos L. Dews, editor).

CHILDREN'S LITERATURE: *Sweet as a Pickle and Clean as a Pig*, 1964.

MISCELLANEOUS: *The Mortgaged Heart*, 1971 (short fiction, poetry, and essays; Margarita G. Smith, editor).

Bibliography

Bloom, Harold, ed. *Carson McCullers*. New ed. New York: Bloom's Literary Criticism, 2009. Collection of critical essays, including three focusing on McCullers's short fiction: "Expanding Southern Whiteness: Reconceptualizing Ethnic Differences in the Short Fiction of Carson McCullers," by Cynthia Wu, "Carson McCullers's Primal Scenes: *The Ballad of the Sad Café*," by Derek Fowler, and "The

Afterlife of Coverture: Contract and Gift in *The Ballad of the Sad Café*," by Naomi Morgenstern.

_____. *Carson McCullers' The Ballad of the Sad Café*. Philadelphia: Chelsea House, 2005. Collection of previously published essays about *The Ballad of the Sad Café*, including discussions of the work's narration; its construction of sex, gender, sexuality, the gothic, and the grotesque; comparisons to works by Eudora Welty and Katherine Anne Porter; and a comparison of *The Ballad of the Sad Café* with Mc-Cullers's novel *The Heart Is a Lonely Hunter*.

Carr, Virginia Spencer. *The Lonely Hunter: A Biography of Carson McCullers*. Garden City, N.J.: Anchor Press, 1975. Reprint. Athens: University of Georgia Press, 2003. This definitive biography offers an interesting read and provides significant biographical elements that are related to McCullers's works. The complexity, pain, and loneliness of Mc-Cullers's characters are matched by their creator's. Includes an extensive chronology of McCullers's life, a primary bibliography, and many endnotes; the 2003 edition features a new preface by Carr and a foreword by Tennessee Williams.

_____. *Understanding Carson McCullers*. Columbia: University of South Carolina Press, 1990. A thoughtful guide to McCullers's works; Chapter 4 is devoted to *The Ballad of the Sad Café*.

Clark, Beverly Lyon, and Melvin J. Friedman, eds. *Critical Essays on Carson McCullers*. New York: G. K. Hall, 1996. A collection of essays ranging from reviews of McCullers's major works to tributes by such writers as Tennessee Williams and Kay Boyle to critical analyses from a variety of perspectives. Most helpful to a study of the short story is Robert Philips's "Freaking Out: The Short Stories of Carson McCullers."

Cook, Richard M. *Carson McCullers*. New York: Frederick Ungar, 1975. A solid general introduction to McCullers's novels, short stories, and plays. Cook's analyses of the short stories and *The Ballad of the Sad Café* are especially good, and the book also includes chapters on each of the novels, Mc-Cullers's life, and her achievements. While admiring McCullers, Cook recognizes her limitations but nevertheless praises her success in portraying human suffering and isolation and in enabling readers to relate to the most grotesque of characters. Includes endnotes and primary and secondary bibliographies.

Gelfant, Blanche H., ed. *The Columbia Companion to the Twentieth-Century American Short Story*. New York: Columbia University Press, 2000. Includes a chapter in which McCullers's short stories are analyzed.

Gleeson-White, Sarah. *Strange Bodies: Gender and Identity in the Novels of Carson McCullers*. Tuscaloosa: University of Alabama Press, 2003. Approaches McCullers's short and long fiction from the perspectives of Mikhail Bakhtin's theory of the grotesque and of gender and psychoanalytical analyses.

James, Judith Giblin. *Wunderkind: The Reputation of Carson McCullers, 1940-1990*. Columbia, S.C.: Camden House, 1995. Examines McCullers's place in literature as a southern female author. Includes bibliography and index.

McDowell, Margaret B. *Carson McCullers*. Boston: Twayne, 1980. A good general introduction to Mc-Cullers's fiction, with a chapter on each of the novels, the short stories, and *The Ballad of the Sad Café*. Also included are a chronology, endnotes, and a select bibliography. Stressing McCullers's versatility, McDowell emphasizes the lyricism, the musicality, and the rich symbolism of McCullers's fiction, as well as McCullers's sympathy for lonely individuals.

Savigneau, Josyane. *Carson McCullers: A Life*. Translated by Joan E. Howard. Boston: Houghton Mifflin, 2001. The McCullers estate granted Savigneau access to McCullers's unpublished papers, which enables her to deepen the portrait presented by previous biographers.

Westling, Louise. *Sacred Groves and Ravaged Gardens: The Fiction of Eudora Welty, Carson McCullers, and Flannery O'Connor*. Athens: University of Georgia Press, 1985. Compares the works of three major southern writers of short fiction and novels. While Westling is not the first to use a feminist approach with McCullers, the book offers useful insight into the portrayal of the female characters and the issue of androgyny in McCullers's fiction. Westling's analysis of *The Ballad of the Sad Café* is particularly good. Supplemented by useful endnotes and a bibliography of secondary material.

Whitt, Jan, ed. *Reflections in a Critical Eye: Essays on Carson McCullers*. Lanham, MD: University Press of America, 2008. A collection of essays providing analyses of *The Ballad of the Sad Café* and McCullers's novels and offering biographical information about the author. Some key topics discussed are McCullers's links to feminism, gender identity, race relations, and southern culture.

Whitt, Margaret. "From Eros to Agape: Reconsidering the Chain Gang's Song in McCullers's *Ballad of the Sad Café*." *Studies in Short Fiction* 33 (Winter, 1996): 119-122. Argues that the chain gang was a rare visual example of integration in an otherwise segregated South. Notes the irony suggested through the song--that the men must be chained together to find harmony.

Katherine Snipes
Updated by D. Dean Shackelford

Thomas McGuane

Born: Wyandotte, Michigan; December 11, 1939

Principal short fiction
To Skin a Cat, 1986
Gallatin Canyon, 2006

Other literary forms

Thomas McGuane (muh-GWAYN) has written ten novels, including *Ninety-Two in the Shade* (1973), *Nothing but Blue Skies* (1992), and *The Cadence of Grass* (2002), along with two remarkable collections of short fiction. McGuane also has produced several nonfiction works, dealing with sport fishing, ranching, and horses, including *Some Horses* (1999) and *The Longest Silence: A Life in Fishing* (1999). He wrote several screenplays, including *The Missouri Breaks* (1975), which starred Marlon Brando and Jack Nicholson.

Achievements

Thomas McGuane is recognized nationally and internationally for his works that run the gamut from informative animal lore to deeply probing short fiction. His works have been translated into numerous languages, including Spanish and French. He received the Rosenthal Foundation award for *The Bushwhacked*

Piano (1971). McGuane was nominated for the National Book Award for *Ninety-Two in the Shade*. In 1988, he was given the Montana Governor's Literary Award. He received the Northwest Booksellers Association Award in 1992. The Wallace Stegner Award was given to McGuane in 2009 for his sustained contributions to the cultural identity of the West through literature.

Biography

Thomas Francis McGuane III was born on December 11, 1939, the son of Alice and Thomas Francis McGuane II. Thomas spent most of his childhood in Michigan, including much time at his family's summer home in northern Michigan. It was there that he acquired an affinity for sports that interact with nature, specifically fishing and hunting. His relationship with his father was strained, but his mother and her Irish family, rich in storytellers, was the source of McGuane's literary curiosity.

McGuane attended Cranbrook Kingswood School, a boarding school. Interspersed with his studies there, he worked on a ranch in Wyoming. His interests in ranching and sport fishing were soon to influence the themes in his writing. From 1955 to 1960, he spent time in Florida, principally in Key West. His fondness for the sea and the mountains was later manifested in McGuane's penchant for alternating between Key West and Livingston, Montana, from 1968 to 1974. Both areas appear prominently in his literature.

McGuane received a B.A. in English from Michigan State University in 1962. He followed this with an M.F.A. from Yale University in 1965, and then he went on to a Wallace Stegner Fellowship at Stanford University. While there, he worked on his first published novel, *The Sporting Club* (1969). When the screen rights to this work were sold, he bought a large cattle ranch in Paradise Valley, near Livingston, Montana. He has been offered several teaching positions in writing, but McGuane prefers life outside of academia.

McGuane married Portia Rebecca Crockett in 1962. After he completed his fellowship at Stanford, the pair moved to Livingston, where Thomas Francis McGuane IV was born in 1967. The couple divorced, and later Thomas McGuane married actor Margot Kidder. McGuane then entered a period of excessive overindulgence in the Hollywood scene. In a three-year span, his mother, father, and sister died. Again divorced, in 1977 McGuane married Laurie Buffett, the sister of a well-known musician from Key West, Jimmy Buffett. McGuane moved with his wife to a ranch in southwestern Montana, where they raise and train cutting horses.

Aɴᴀʟʏsɪs

Thomas McGuane has been characterized as writer of manly values in the manner of Ernest Hemingway. However, his writing is more comparable to that of Mark Twain (with his askew humor), Edward Abbey (with his not-too-subtle criticism of the modern West), and Ken Kesey (with his geographically specific settings). McGuane's short fiction is not full of romantic characters in their boots who win the West, with their long-skirted women in the background. It does not pander to youth and coming-of-age sentimentalism. These are tales of adults. They might be childish and immature, but they fight and take on the world directly and do not learn many lessons. McGuane's stories do not leave the reader with neat conclusions.

McGuane tells about men who experience a generalized anxiety disorder. They confront problems of marriage, infidelity, aging, financial problems, and trust. These themes easily give the author a platform from which subthemes, such as gender and class, can

be presented. Often, male characters in these works are at odds with one another over money. A typical structure presents an outsider, generally someone from the eastern part of the United States, who upsets the economic balance of a local man, who often works as a rancher or other occupation tied to what is portrayed as the traditional western way of life. The males take on bosses, bankers, lawyers, employees, and the world at large.

McGuane's men do things; they work the land and have jobs. They are busy, using tangible skills, such as horsemanship, fishing, or sailing. An adversarial relationship often develops between the working-class men and wealthy men who are imposing a new and dominant order over a traditional one. The local men work against nature, desperately holding an indifferent environment at bay, and into this setting comes disaster of one form or another. McGuane slowly builds a cumulative angst that inevitably ends with one side of the class struggle failing. Although the author consistently weaves a wry and oddly sarcastic humor throughout

Thomas McGuane (Getty Images)

his works, these are not cheerful tales. As McGuane has stated, it's not his job to keep the reader happy.

Throughout the works, women come and go. They are presented as intelligent, with active lives of their own. Unfortunately, they are drawn to the somewhat macho characters. Inevitably they learn of the flawed temperament of the men and try to reform them. When it becomes obvious that this will not happen, they are smart enough to get away. In McGuane's tales, the women are the only ones who learn anything.

The characters in these works are often ironic. They appear in unexpected settings, living intense, sometimes brutally funny lives. This includes reckless, charming, or despicable men whose lives appear completely believable through the generally third-person narrative of McGuane. His dialogs include absurd linguistics of his characters and their short, humorous, and biting comments. One refers to the outsider as the a---- from Connecticut. Another employs a colloquial term: sumbitch. Jail is called the crowbar hotel.

In each story, the protagonists realize that something has changed in their territory. Something or someone from another world has entered and the previous state of affairs has tilted and is threatened. They frantically attempt to carry on as before. They make poor choices and in the end pay the price.

McGuane leaves it to the reader to decide the right or wrong of the events in his fiction. The reader can grasp the author's conviction of the cathartic value of giving himself or herself to a physical task well done. Beyond that, the author lets the reader decide what, if anything, is to be learned from the experiences found in the stories. The American West that McGuane presents is already settled and occupied. It is a last frontier that outsiders enter with their erroneous preconceptions. In this final frontier, the Wild West often becomes the Weird West. The stranger who comes to start anew often ends up dead or defeated.

"Old Friends"

In "Old Friends," Erik Faucher leaves unmentioned troubles behind in Boston and heads out to Montana to join his longtime friend, John Biggs. Long ago they had attended boarding school and Yale University together. Biggs had left Boston years before and returned to his small-town Montana beginnings. McGuane often

presents friendships as adversarial, and this story is no exception. The time apart has left the two men with completely different viewpoints on life. Faucher has come to Montana to start over and desperately wants to be a cowboy. Biggs welcomes him with unopened arms.

Biggs has been commuting to North Carolina, where he is in the middle of a dispute between two small towns. He is the attorney negotiating with a company that will bring a flag-manufacturing factory to one of the towns, leaving the other to certain financial decline. This is one of the author's common themes in his short fiction: unfair and unexpected financial disruption, attached to an outside influences from the eastern United States.

Biggs takes Faucher to view the Montana countryside and into the nearby town. Each time Biggs shows his beloved environment to the newcomer, Faucher is bored by the whole thing. He is looking for the last frontier of cowboys, not the small ranching community that he finds. He is rude to the locals and keeps pressuring Biggs to show him the real West. The binds of their shared past begin to unravel. They reminisce about their unfulfilled lives, from divorces to errant offspring. Faucher brings home a woman whom he treats poorly. She eventually does what most women in McGuane's short fiction do: She leaves. Before leaving, she slaps Biggs and lets it be known that she blames him for the eastern's intrusion into her life.

In the end, Faucher is arrested for some unknown crime in Boston. He blames Biggs for not helping him more. The story ends with Biggs relating the whole thing to a stranger on an eastbound plane, wrapping the episode up by stating that he's glad it's over. The stranger replies by asking if Biggs really believes it is over. True to his literary style, the author spins a tale of a macho man who flees a complicated Eastern state, only to find that the perceived last frontier no longer awaits him.

"Vicious Circle"

"Vicious Circle" depicts another McGuane theme, that of the isolation and useless intimacy that life often presents in relationships between men and women. In this tale, the author leaves behind his usual focus on class wars and instead presents a man, John Briggs, who seeks the companionship of a woman, but he attempts to remain with her far after it becomes obvious that the relationship is destructive.

Briggs meets an attractive but alcoholic woman, Olivia. She quickly becomes inebriated in a bar where they have gone to become acquainted. Briggs takes her home and discovers her father has a strangely domineering power over her. As in other McGuane stories, the two male figures quickly develop adversarial roles. Uncomfortable about the odd family reality, Briggs nonetheless remains with the father while Olivia tries to return to normalcy upstairs. Briggs perceives this as a form of pleasant voyeurism. Eventually he is insulted enough to take his leave.

Briggs makes one poor decision after another. Through a series of odd events, he keeps reentering into Olivia's life. The last few chapters reveal the utter futility of this make-believe love affair. He foolishly accepts an invitation to Olivia's wedding. True to form, the author has the woman protagonist leave the hapless and useless man to his own unfulfilled life.

"Miracle Boy"

In "Miracle Boy," McGuane employs the first-person point of view. He seldom uses this style, but in this tale it successfully isolates the young protagonist, who narrates a story about family divisions, doubts, and the ambiguity that family history sometimes produces. He received the moniker "miracle boy" by convincing his dying grandmother to join the family in an important reunion when she had refused go downstairs. McGuane presents a complicated family of Irish dependency that is having trouble come to grips with the modern world around them. Generally McGuane uses the western United States to portray this juxtaposition. The author does maintain a nebulous connection with the Wild West; the unnamed boy often retreats to his room, where he reads *True West* magazine and watches films such as *Gunfight at the O.K. Corral* (1957). McGuane's tales often include the Eastern fantasy of the last frontier, and this story features insightful and humorous glimpses at life in the past. From the "I like Ike" decal (a reference to Dwight D. Eisenhower's presidential campaign) to Doc Holliday (a western character), slinking away on the television, the reader is taken on a drive down memory lane.

The boy's favorite uncle, Paul, comes in and out of the family portrait. As with other McGuane fiction, the men in this tale maintain senseless tensions with other males and females in and out of the family. Their pointless confrontations require the women to correct and re-create a family unity. The boy eventually is called on to perform another miracle: to bring his Uncle Paul to the family wake for the deceased grandmother. He fails. In the end, his mother concludes the story by orienting the boy sensibly between an orderly past and an unknown future.

"Aliens"

In this story, Homer Newland is retiring in Boston and dreams of returning to western America, where he grew up. That was long ago, and, at seventy-five years old, he can barely remember what it was like. He follows his dream and moves to Montana. He longs for female companionship and invites one of his girlfriends from his younger days in Boston to join him there. Madeleine accepts and come out West.

Once there, she finds Homer trying to convince her of the beauty of the location. However, she instead finds a man with a precarious relationship with his daughter and grandchild. The other men who appear, such as a rancher neighbor, are brusque and rude to her. In a slight twist of McGuane's usual view of an easterner who does not understand the West, this story features a westerner who returns home after a long absence and who sees everything through a filter of false happiness. As usual, the reader encounters a strong and intelligent woman who tries to understand and accept the male protagonist but, in the end, finds him and his paraplegic male friend unbearable fools. The work concludes with Madeleine escaping as quickly as she can.

Again, McGuane presents a modern American West that cannot be manipulated into being what it never was: a refuge for hapless dreamers. If one goes on a personal journey to find an imagined past, it is only a matter of time before disaster makes an appearance.

Other major works

LONG FICTION: *The Sporting Club*, 1969; *The Bushwhacked Piano*, 1971; *Ninety-Two in the Shade*, 1973; *Panama*, 1978; *Nobody's Angel*, 1982; *Something to*

Be Desired, 1984; *Keep the Change*, 1989; *Nothing but Blue Skies*, 1992; *The Cadence of Grass*, 2002; *Driving on the Rim*, 2010.

SCREENPLAYS: *Rancho Deluxe*, 1973; *Ninety-Two in the Shade*, 1975 (adaptation of this novel); *The Missouri Breaks*, 1975; *Tom Horn*, 1980 (with Bud Shrake).

NONFICTION: *An Outside Chance: Essays on Sport*, 1981; *Some Horses*, 1999; *The Longest Silence: A Life in Fishing*, 1999; *Some Horses*, 1999; *Conversations with Thomas McGuane*, 2007 (Beef Torrey, editor).

BIBLIOGRAPHY

Connors, Philip. *New West Reader: Essays on an Ever-Evolving Frontier*. New York: Nation Books, 2005. McGuane gives his viewpoints on how his works reflect the American West at the beginning of the twenty-first century. Includes bibliography.

Klinkowitz, Jerome. *The New American Novel of Manners: The Fiction of Richard Yates, Dan Wakefield, Thomas McGuane*. Athens: University of Georgia Press, 1986. Detailed examination of evolving American western fiction, with many relevant references to McGuane. Includes bibliography and index.

Torrey, Beef. *Conversations with Thomas McGuane*. Jackson: University Press of Mississippi, 2006. McGuane explains his unique viewpoint of the American West, his life, and his writings. Offers insightful on his work. Includes bibliography and index.

Westrum, Dexter. *Thomas McGuane*. Boston: Twayne, 1991. The definitive work on McGuane. Covers biographical and critical aspects of McGuane's publications to 1990. Contains extensive bibliography.

Paul Siegrist

REGINALD McKNIGHT

Born: Fürstenfeldbruck, West Germany (now in Germany); February 26, 1956

PRINCIPAL SHORT FICTION

Moustapha's Eclipse, 1988

The Kind of Light That Shines on Texas, 1992

White Boys, 1998

OTHER LITERARY FORMS

In addition to his short-story collections, Reginald McKnight has published the novels *I Get on the Bus* (1990) and *He Sleeps* (2001). He has also edited two collections of folk wisdom, *African American Wisdom* (1994) and *Wisdom of the African World* (1996).

ACHIEVEMENTS

Reginald McKnight is the recipient of a National Endowment for the Arts fellowship, an O. Henry Award, two Kenyon Review Awards for excellence, a PEN/Hemingway Special Citation, a Pushcart Prize, the Drue Heinz Literature Prize, the Watson Foundation Fellowship, the Whiting Writers' Award, and the Bernice M. Slote Award.

BIOGRAPHY

Reginald McKnight was born in Fürstenfeldbruck, Germany, to military parents in 1956. His father Frank was a U.S. Air Force noncommissioned officer, and his mother Pearl was a dietician. Because of his military background, McKnight has lived all over the world, moving a total of forty-three times. After a brief stint in the U.S. Marine Corps, McKnight earned an associate degree in anthropology (1978) from Pike Peak Community College and a B.A. in African literature (1981) from Colorado College. He received the Thomas J. Watson Fellowship to study folklore and literature in West Africa, enabling him to spend a year teaching and writing in Senegal. In 1987, he earned an M.A. in English with an emphasis in creative writing from the University of Denver. McKnight has taught at Arapahoe Community College, the University of Denver, the University of Maryland at College Park, Carnegie

Mellon University, the University of Michigan at Ann Arbor, and the University of Georgia at Athens. He married Michele Davis in 1985, and the couple had two daughters.

ANALYSIS

Reginald McKnight's work is a refreshing change from much of the black protest literature of the 1970's and 1980's. While white people are often presented as unpleasant, annoying, and mean-spirited, they are seldom presented as outrightly diabolical. McKnight deliberately refrains from political statement in his fiction, believing that art has the higher purpose of bringing a sense of joy to the reader, the type of joy that makes one think that "life is deep, limitless, and meaningful." However, he does not believe that art should be harmless. "It should get under your skin," he says. McKnight refuses to accept or to promote any singular concept of black identity; instead, he respects the diversity of black experience found in the United States and elsewhere.

Like many writers, McKnight draws heavily on personal experience to find subject matter for his stories. For example, several stories found in his collections are set in West Africa with an anthropologist as the narrator. Other stories include the painful experience of being one of a handful of black children in a school. His experience in the military is also woven into several stories. His stories, however, are no mere transcription of personal experience. He is equally successful in portraying the experiences of black working-class males.

Many of McKnight's stories are boldly experimental in point of view, tone, style, and concept. His stories set in West Africa are particularly notable for their non-western philosophical views and the incorporation of the fantastic. For example, in "The Homunculus: A Novel in One Chapter" (included in *The Kind of Light That Shines on Texas*), the protagonist is a young writer in a fairy-tale-like place who becomes so consumed with his writing that it becomes a flesh and blood likeness of himself. McKnight's work is characterized by his successful, convincing use of multiple voices.

"UNCLE MOUSTAPHA'S ECLIPSE"

"Uncle Moustapha's Eclipse," the title story of McKnight's first collection, *Moustapha's Eclipse*, is narrated in the broken English of a Senegalese interpreter working for an American anthropologist living in Africa. This story has the feel of a folktale; that is, it is clearly meant to teach a lesson. Uncle Moustapha is a successful peanut farmer, who lives in a small African village with his three wives and seven children. His only problem is that he constantly thinks of death; he would not have this problem if he had not adopted the white man's tradition of celebrating his birthday. On the eve of his sixtieth birthday (or at least what he has designated as his birthday), he goes to bed anticipating an eclipse of the sun, which has been predicted for the next day. On the following morning, a white scientist arrives to set up his viewing equipment on Uncle Moustapha's land. The scientist warns Moustapha not to view the eclipse directly with naked eyes. At first, Moustapha complies and views the eclipse properly through the scientific equipment. However, he quickly becomes overjoyed with the eclipse, believing that it was sent to him as a gift from Allah and his ancestors.

Moustapha runs to fetch his favorite wife, Fatima. They rush together to the baobab tree, which is believed to house the spirits of their ancestors. After a brief prayer, Moustapha experiences a rush of heightened sensory perceptions. He turns to stare at the eclipse with his eyes wide open, so that he can see "it all in supreme detail." As he returns home, the world seems more beautiful to him than ever before, except for a black shape that begins to flicker on and off in his left eye. The ending of the story is ambiguous. It is not clear whether he goes blind or it is death that is finally coming to Uncle Moustapha. However, he has no regrets because he has seen "what no other living soul has seen today." Clearly, he does not believe that going blind or even dying is too great a price to pay for such a magnificent experience.

"THE KIND OF LIGHT THAT SHINES ON TEXAS"

In this O. Henry Award-winning story, McKnight explores the ambivalence of friendship, not just between blacks and whites but also between blacks and blacks. Clinton Oates, the narrator, is one of three black children in his sixth-grade class in Waco, Texas. Oates, who is eager to prove himself inoffensive to whites, feels embarrassed by the presence of Marvin Pruitt, a black boy who fulfills most negative black stereotypes. Pruitt "smelled bad, was at least two grades behind, was hostile, dark skinned, homely, close-mouthed." Pruitt sleeps away most of the school day; the other black child is a large, passive girl who refuses to speak.

This class is full of older children, including a sixteen-year-old white bully, Kevin Oakley, who is just looking for a reason to fight with Oates. One day, their coach (who probably wants to see Oates get hurt) singles out the two boys for a game of "murder ball," using two hard-pumped volleyballs instead of the usual red rubber balls. Completely in fair play, Oates hits Oakley square in the face, causing a nosebleed and the boy's humiliation. Shortly afterward, in the locker room, Oakley threatens to attack Oates after school. Oates sees Marvin Pruitt, an innocent bystander, and asks, "How come you after me and not him?" Oates escapes from Oakley that afternoon by getting on the bus early, but he cannot escape the implications of what he had said in the locker room. Clearly, Oates meant that Pruitt deserved to be picked on or beaten up because he so neatly fit all the negative stereotypes of blacks. The next morning, Oakley predictably picks a fight with Oates. Surprisingly, Pruitt intervenes on Oates's behalf, with a disdainful "git out of my way, boy." This action shows that Pruitt is, without a doubt, morally superior to Oates, the nice young black who is only too eager to do his "tom-thing." The reader is left to believe that Pruitt knows exactly what Oates had meant in the locker room, but he still rises above this black-on-black racial insult. While never exactly friends, the black boys' relationship proves that blood is, indeed, thicker than water.

"Quitting Smoking"

This story, also collected in *The Kind of Light That Shines on Texas*, is narrated by a working-class black man, Scott Winters, who lives with his white lover Anna. Their relationship does not work, partly because Scott cannot stop smoking, partly because race becomes a barrier, and partly because Scott cannot bring himself to share his deepest secret with her. Scott began smoking in his late teens to hide the smell of reefer from his parents. He discovers that he likes the buzz

from cigarettes better than any other "high." When he meets Anna--a vegetarian, health nut, and feminist--he naturally and easily loses his desire to smoke and to eat meat. One night, Anna confides to him an incident of acquaintance rape. This confidence immediately reminds him of a time in his teens that he and three other males witnessed the abduction of a woman into a car. The woman struggled and screamed for help, but none of the young men intervened on her behalf. Nagged by this memory, Scott goes out and buys a pack of cigarettes.

What follows is a story of cigarette addiction that anyone who has ever smoked will find familiar. Scott continues to sneak out for smokes in the middle of the night. He begins to keep an arsenal of cover-up supplies in his truck--gum, toothpaste, mouthwash, deodorant, and air freshener. Cigarettes become his secret infidelity. When Anna confronts him with a cigarette she has found, Scott vows to quit but does not. Scott's deeper problem is that he cannot bring himself to confess to Anna what he had allowed to happen to the woman who had been abducted and perhaps raped or killed. One night, he makes elaborate preparations for this confession; he cleans the house, makes dinner, and buys wine and flowers. Scott tentatively approaches the subject by saying, "I wouldn't be surprised if you hated men." Anna, who has grown distant for other reasons, counters, "I'm surprised I don't hate black men. The guy who raped me was black." Scott, who feels this racial insult as an almost physical injury, immediately packs his bags and walks out the door. Both partners are guilty of erecting barriers that destroy the relationship, but only Anna chose to use race as a weapon.

"The White Boys"

This story opens with yet another move for a black military family. The Oates are, in many ways, a typical black middle-class family. Both parents are strict, even to the point of violence. Two particularly nasty beatings of the young protagonist Derrick are recounted in this narrative. His two siblings Dean and Alva are spared similar beatings, mostly because they are less conspicuous or odd than Derrick. Both parents greatly fear that one of their children will bring shame or trouble to their home. They know, only too well, that white people will conjure up the worst possible racial stereotypes at the slightest provocation. The day after they move in, Derrick provides this type of provocation by innocently scooping snow off of his neighbor's car. The neighbor, Sergeant Hooker, vehemently hates blacks, following his childhood experience of growing up in a predominantly black neighborhood in Baltimore. His mother, with whom he no longer communicates, even married a black man. Ironically, Hooker's best friend from childhood was also black. Furious over the Oates family moving next door, Hooker sets out to instill racial hatred equal to his own in his three sons. The youngest son Garrett is determined to hate Derrick, but a friendship begins to grow between the two boys. When Hooker discovers this friendship, he devises a diabolical scheme to scare Derrick away permanently. He plans to take Derrick and his three sons on a fishing trip, during which time the four whites will stage a mock lynching of Derrick. Garrett, unable to confront his father or to warn Derrick, comes up with his own scheme to save his friend. On the Friday before this fateful weekend, he calls Derrick a nigger, not just once but repeatedly. His act destroys their friendship (exactly what his father wanted) but saves Derrick from a far more horrific experience.

In an interview, McKnight has said that the stories in *White Boys* should produce this response: "It's too bad that blacks and whites don't get along very well today." This response is exactly what this story produces. There is every reason except race that the Hookers and Oateses should have been good friends and neighbors.

Other major works

LONG FICTION: *I Get on the Bus*, 1990; *He Sleeps*, 2001.

EDITED TEXTS: *African American Wisdom*, 1994; *Wisdom of the African World*, 1996.

Bibliography

Govan, Sandra Y. "A Stranger on the Bus: Reginald McKnight's *I Get on the Bus* as Complex Journey." In *Contemporary African American Fiction: New Critical Essays*, edited by Dana A.Williams. Columbus: Ohio State University Press, 2009. Provides an analysis of McKnight's first novel.

McKnight, Reginald. "A Conversation with Reginald McKnight." Interview by Xavier Nicholas. *Callaloo* 29, no. 2 (Spring, 2006): 304-321. McKnight emphasizes that although he was born in Germany when his military father was stationed there, he considers Colorado his home because it is where he experienced his major rites of passage. He also discusses his writing.

_____. "An Interview with Reginald McKnight." Interview by Renée Olander. *The Writer's Chronicle* 3 (February, 2000): 5-14. McKnight discusses his literary influences, his writing philosophies, the use of the word "nigger," and two of his works: *I Get on the Bus* and *White Boys*.

_____. "'Under the Umbrella of Black Civilization' A Conversation with Reginald McKnight." Interview by Bertram D. Ashe. *African American Review* 35, no. 3 (Fall, 2001): 427. An interview focusing on McKnight's short stories. He describes his talent to transform many different voices in his stories and explains the implication of the stories on his beliefs. Also provides an analysis of McKnight's racialist perspective.

_____. "We Are, in Fact, a Civilization." Interview by William Walsh. *Kenyon Review* 16, no. 2 (Spring, 1994): 27-42. McKnight addresses his background, writing style, and use of first- and third-person narrative.

Megan, Carolyn. "New Perceptions on Rhythm in Reginald McKnight's Fiction." *Kenyon Review* 16, no. 2 (Spring, 1994): 56-62. Megan examines the importance of sound and rhythm in McKnight's writing process. Her discussion includes the emotional responses evoked by this rhythm.

Nancy E. Sherrod

James Alan McPherson

Born: Savannah, Georgia; September 16, 1943

Principal short fiction
Hue and Cry, 1969
Elbow Room, 1977

Other literary forms

In addition to his short-fiction collections, James Alan McPherson (mehk-FEHR-suhn) has written the nonfiction works *Crabcakes* (1998) and *A Region Not Home: Reflections from Exile* (2000). He and Miller Williams edited *Railroad: Trains and Train People in American Culture* (1976), to which he contributed essays and a short story. He also collaborated with De-Witt Henry to edit *Fathering Daughters: Reflections by Men* (1998), a collection of essays on the father-daughter bond. In addition, McPherson has contributed several essays to *The Atlantic Monthly* and to *Reader's Digest.*

Achievements

The adroit characterizations and strong sense of place in James Alan McPherson's short fiction have attracted many readers and influenced a number of writers. His work has been anthologized and has appeared in *The Atlantic Monthly, Playboy, The New York Times Magazine, The Harvard Advocate, Reader's Digest, The Iowa Review, The Massachusetts Review,* and *Ploughshares.* John Updike included McPherson's story "The Gold Coast" in *The Best American Short Stories of the Century* (1999). McPherson's association with the Writer's Workshop at the University of Iowa and his teaching of courses in fiction writing have given him a forum from which he influences beginning writers across the United States. Though earlier critics noted similarities between McPherson and other African American writers, such

as James Baldwin and Ralph Ellison, his fiction later was examined in a much wider context, with critical attention focused on his unique use of language and his ability to create a mythical dimension to his stories.

"Gold Coast" won the prize for fiction awarded by *The Atlantic Monthly* in 1968. McPherson also won a literature award from the National Institute of Arts and Letters in 1970, and he was the recipient of a John Simon Guggenheim Memorial Foundation Fellowship in 1972. He became the first African American to win the Pulitzer Prize for Fiction when his short-story collection *Elbow Room* was awarded this honor in 1978; this collection was also nominated for the National Book Award. In 1981, his writing achievements earned him a MacArthur Fellowship.

Biography

James Alan McPherson earned degrees from Morris Brown College (B.A., 1965), Harvard Law School (LL.B., 1968), and the Iowa Writers' Workshop (M.F.A., 1971). He has taught at the University of Iowa, the University of California, Harvard University, Morgan State University, and the University of Virginia. He has held jobs ranging from stock clerk to newspaper reporter to contributing editor of *The Atlantic Monthly.* In the early 1980's, McPherson began teaching fiction writing in the Writers' Workshop at the University of Iowa in Iowa City. After publishing *Elbow Room,* McPherson primarily concentrated on writing on nonfiction essays that center on the need for African Americans to help define the cultural realities of contemporary American life. His first book in twenty years, *Crabcakes* (1998), focuses on his ultimate understanding of what makes people human.

Analysis

James Alan McPherson is one of the writers of fiction who form the second major phase of modern writing about the African American experience. Indebted, like all of his generation, to the groundbreaking and theme-setting work of Richard Wright, Ralph Ellison, and James Baldwin, McPherson shies away from doctrinaire argumentation about racial issues. Rather, he uses these issues to give his work a firmly American aura, which includes a preoccupation not only with what it means to be a black person in modern America but also with how the individual responds to a culture that often is plagued by subtle and not-so-subtle racial discriminations. Hence, there are times when blackness becomes for McPherson a metaphor for the alienation experienced by the individual in contemporary society.

This comprehensive concern with American culture informs all of McPherson's work, including those pieces that are included in the prose and poetry collection compiled by McPherson and Miller Williams, *Railroad: Trains and Train People in American Culture*. A celebration, a lament, and a plea, this volume deals with the passing of the great era of passenger railcar service in the United States. To McPherson, the liberating motion integral to the railroad is important, but so is the sense of place and time that builds for his characters much of their sense of self. McPherson's characters are often confined by the conventions of locale, yet McPherson is not a regional writer in the usual sense of the word; he can bring to life stories set in Tennessee, Virginia, Boston, Chicago, or London.

Because of the tension in his work between the individual and the community, McPherson's characters often feel alienated, lonely, and unable fully to reach or to maintain contact with acquaintances, friends, families, or lovers. However, such isolation may lead to a character's growth to near-tragic stature. The integrity of the individual is thus asserted even while a narrator may worry over the deep inability of any person to penetrate into the heart and mind of another. Such recognitions contribute to the sympathetic portrayal even of unpromising characters. It should be noted that the reader is not given solutions in McPherson's fiction, only access to degrees of awareness of the mysteries of race, sexuality, identity, and love. Reading McPherson, a reader may be reminded of Baldwin's presentation of agonizingly complex racial and sexual problems, of Saul Bellow's portrayal of characters battling absurdity and despair, and of the struggle of characters, both in

Baldwin and in Bellow, toward the ameliorating but no less mysterious experience of love.

"GOLD COAST"

McPherson's first volume of short fiction, *Hue and Cry*, is an often-grim affair, containing stories of loneliness, destitution, defeat, sexual alienation, and racial tension. A prime example of this early work is "Gold Coast." The narrator of this story is an "apprentice janitor" in a hotel near Harvard Square in Boston, a hotel that has seen better days and is now populated with aging singles or couples who are almost as disengaged from the mainstream of Boston life as is the superintendent of the building, James Sullivan. Listening to Sullivan and observing the people in the apartments, the narrator, Robert, seeks to gather information for the stories and books he hopes to write. For Robert, being a janitor is in some ways a whim; in addition to gleaning experiential details from rubbish bins, he is constructing his life along romantic lines. Hence, Robert notes that, almost nightly,

> I drifted off to sleep lulled by sweet anticipation of that time when my potential would suddenly be realized and there would be capsule biographies of my life on dust jackets of many books, all proclaiming: "He knew life on many levels. From shoeshine boy, free-lance waiter, 3rd cook, janitor, he rose to. . . . "

Naïve but witty, Robert humors Sullivan, putting up patiently with the Irishman's redundant reminiscing and opinionated ramblings on society and politics. Sullivan, however, comes to rely on Robert's company; he turns from the horrors of life in the filthy apartment he shares with his obscene, insane wife to interminable conversations with Robert.

Robert's sympathetic tolerance of Sullivan emanates from his sense of the pathetic isolation of Sullivan from human contact and from Robert's recognition for the first time of the terrors of aging. Robert is the archetypal youth coming to awareness of old age as a time of foreshortened expectations and straitened lifestyles, of possible despair and near dehumanization. The apprentice janitor can tolerate Sullivan and his new knowledge while his relationship with the rich, lovely Jean goes well, but Jean and he are soon torn apart by social forces. In fact, they play a game called

"Social Forces," in which they try to determine which of them will break first under social disapproval of their interracial relationship. When the game defeats them, Robert first is comforted by and then pulls back from his friendship with the dejected Sullivan, who is especially upset over the loss of his dog.

When Robert finally leaves his briefly held janitorial position, he does so with both relief and guilt over his abandonment of Sullivan. He knows, however, that he is "still young" and not yet doomed to the utter loneliness of the old man. McPherson suggests that the young, nevertheless, will inevitably come to such bleak isolation and that even the temporary freedom of youth is sometimes maintained at the expense of sympathy and kindness. There are dangers in being free, not the least of which are the burden of knowledge, the hardening of the self, and the aching realization of basic, but often unmet, human needs. This theme of loss is picked up in the volume's title story, "Hue and Cry," which includes this interchange between two characters:

> "Between my eyes I see three people and they are all unhappy. Why?"
>
> "Perhaps it is because they are alive. Perhaps it is because they once were. Perhaps it is because they have to be. I do not know."

These voices cannot make sense of the losses to which life dooms McPherson's characters, nor does Robert. He simply moves away from the hotel to enjoy, while he can, his youth and his sense of potential.

"A Solo Song: For Doc"

The theme of old age and its defeats is further developed in McPherson's well-received "A Solo Song: For Doc," a story which displays well the author's rhythmic and precise control of narration conceived of as speech. McPherson resolves to initiate readers of all races into a facet of their culture that is quickly passing out of sight. The narrator, an aging waiter on a railroad line, tells a young listener about the good old days in the service and about their embodiment, a waiter called Doc Craft. "So do you want to know this business, youngblood?" begins the teller of the tale, and he goes on, "So you want to be a Waiter's Waiter? The Commissary gives you a book with all the rules and tells

you to learn them. And you do, and think that is all there is to it." This "Waiter's Waiter" then proceeds to disillusion the "youngblood" by describing the difficult waiter's craft--the finesse, grace, care, and creativity required to make the job into an art and to make that art pay. The grace and dedication displayed by men of Doc Craft's generation are shown to be losing ground to the contemporary world of business in which men such as "Jerry Ewald, the Unexpected Inspector," lie in wait to trap heroes like Doc Craft and to remove them from the service that keeps them alive. The narrator specifies what kept Doc on the road: having power over his car and his customers, hustling tips, enjoying women without being married to them, getting drunk without having to worry about getting home. The shift from passenger to freight service on the railroad, however, spurs the company's attempt to fire Doc and also starts Doc's rise to heroic stature. Older ways of work and life yield to new technology. and, like the old-time railroad, Doc Craft is doomed; Ewald catches Doc on a technicality about iced tea service, and the waiter is fired.

Clearly, McPherson's thematic preoccupations and love of the railroad have coalesced in this story. He captures the complexity, richness, and hardships of the lives of African American traveling men, as well as the initiative and kinship developed by black workers. Movement, adventure, freedom, self-expression, craftsmanship, commitment, exuberance, and endurance--these qualities mark both Doc Craft and the railroad as valuable American entities. The passing of Doc carries McPherson's sense of the epic loss suffered by an America that has allowed the railroad, the metaphoric counterpart of imaginative integration of all kinds, to decay.

"Why I Like Country Music"

Even while remaining faithful to McPherson's characteristic themes, *Elbow Room*, his second volume, includes stories which reach a kind of comic perfection. One example is "Why I Like Country Music." The narrator, a southern-born black, addresses to his northern-born wife an explanation of his love of square-dance music. His wife will not believe or accept this preference, but the narrator quietly insists on it. In one sense, this insistence and the narration that justifies it may be viewed as evidence of the eternal and invincible isolation of the human heart from sympathetic understanding even by loved ones. The forces of memory and of individual development work to isolate human beings from one another. In addition, the narrator's insistence that the South Carolina traditions of his youth have given him preferences and ideas alien to those born in New York tends to strengthen this theme of the coherence but separateness of the self.

Such thematic reverberations, however, do not form the main concern of this story. Rather, the narrator recounts a comic case of childhood puppy love; he explains that he loves country music because it is permanently associated in his mind with a girl in his fourth-grade class whose name was Gweneth Larson. Born in Brooklyn and redolent of lemons, Gweneth is for the narrator an object of first love. The moments when he square danced with her in a school May Day celebration were etched in his mind as moments of surpassing joy and love. Far from exploring alienation, the story celebrates the endurance of such affection.

McPherson's comedy is never heavy-handed, but is always a matter of a light tone or a moment of incongruity. An example occurs when the narrator describes the calling of the Maypole teams to the playground for their performance:

> "Maypole teams *up*!" called Mr. Henry Lucas, our principal, from his platform by the swings. Beside him stood the white Superintendent of Schools (who said later of the square dance, it was reported to all the classes, "Lord, y'all square dance so *good* it makes me plumb *ashamed* us white folks ain't takin' better care of our art stuff").

"A Loaf of Bread"

A more somber story in *Elbow Room*, "A Loaf of Bread," addresses important issues associated with racism and assimilation by depicting the isolation of the African American middle class. As in many of his other stories, McPherson expresses hope for the evolution of a model of American identity toward which all Americans can proudly gravitate. In "A Loaf of Bread," he explores the difference between exploitation and participation of African Americans in American society.

Store owner Harold Green charges higher prices for goods in his store in an African American neighborhood than in the stores he owns in white neighborhoods. As an act of restitution for exploiting the black community, Green decides that the best solution is to open his store and give away his merchandise free of charge to members of the exploited black community. The ensuing frenzy leaves Green's store in complete disarray, totally depleted of merchandise.

Nelson Reed, the leader of the community protest against Green, returns to the store later in the day to pay Green one dollar for the loaf of bread that his wife had taken from the store that morning. Reed is evidently seeking the status of a participating consumer instead of an exploited one. Characteristic of McPherson's writing, characters in difficult situations struggle for some measure of success. However, Reed's attempt to receive equitable treatment as an American citizen is nullified by Green's response.

Similar to other fiction written by McPherson, the overall plot of "A Loaf of Bread" appears to argue for an American citizenship that eradicates racial boundaries and produces a coherent, color-blind American society. However, McPherson believes that racial exclusion continues to exist like an undeviated line from decades past and that acts of racial prejudice continue to demonstrate the pervasiveness of racial chauvinism. Furthermore, pointing fingers and using the "we/they" phrase in reference to other races only proliferates prejudice and isolation.

In "A Loaf of Bread," the hope for the black community to achieve unified American citizenship seems to be superseded by the lure of participating as a consumer in the marketplace. McPherson suggests that the African American middle class has abandoned the process of discarding some of the traditions of their fathers and embracing a sense of commonality with the white world. Consequently, the African American middle class becomes further isolated from the mainstream of American society. It is notable that in both his comic "Why I Like Country Music" and his somber "A Loaf of Bread," McPherson remains firmly focused on the human personality, which is for him the incentive for narration and the core of his art.

Oᴛʜᴇʀ ᴍᴀᴊᴏʀ ᴡᴏʀᴋs

NONFICTION: *Crabcakes*, 1998; *A Region Not Home: Reflections from Exile*, 2000.

EDITED TEXT: *Railroad: Trains and Train People in American Culture*, 1976 (with Miller Williams); *Fathering Daughters: Reflections by Men*, 1998 (with DeWitt Henry).

Bɪʙʟɪᴏɢʀᴀᴘʜʏ

Ashe, Bertram D. "The Best 'Possible Returns': Storytelling and Gender Relations in James Alan McPherson's 'The Story of a Scar.'" In *From Within the Frame: Storytelling in African-American Fiction*. New York: Routledge, 2002. Analyzes the theme and narrative technique of this short story, which concerns an encounter between a black man and a black woman who are sitting in a doctor's waiting room.

Beavers, Herman. "I Yam What You Is and You Is What I Yam: Rhetorical Invisibility in James Alan McPherson's 'The Story of a Dead Man.'" *Callaloo* 9 (1986): 565-577. Beavers discusses the linguistic and rhetorical characteristics of McPherson's dialogue and how his language shapes perceptions, specifically in "The Story of a Dead Man."

_____. *Wrestling Angels into Song: The Fictions of Ernest J. Gaines and James Alan McPherson*. Philadelphia: University of Pennsylvania Press, 1995. Compares and contrasts the works of the two writers, including a discussion of their triumvirate with Ralph Waldo Emerson and analyses of "A Solo Song: For Doc" and some of McPherson's other stories.

Cox, Joseph T. "James Alan McPherson." In *Contemporary Fiction Writers of the South*, edited by Joseph M. Flora and Robert Bain. Westport, Conn.: Greenwood Press, 1993. A brief introduction to McPherson's art, including a short biographical sketch, a summary and critique of the criticism of his work, and a discussion of his short-story themes of intolerance and general absence of grace and love in modern society.

DeWitt, Henry, et al. "About James Alan McPherson." *Ploughshares* 34, no. 2/3 (Fall, 2008): 187-201. A profile of McPherson, providing biographical information and a discussion of his writing.

Gelfant, Blanche H., ed. *The Columbia Companion to the Twentieth-Century American Short Story*. New York: Columbia University Press, 2000. Includes a chapter in which McPherson's short stories are analyzed.

Kurtzleben, James. "James Alan McPherson." In *A Reader's Companion to the Short Story in English*, edited by Erin Fallon, et al., under the auspices of the Society for the Study of the Short Story. Westport, Conn.: Greenwood Press, 2001. Aimed at the general reader, this essay provides a brief biography of McPherson followed by an analysis of his short fiction.

Laughlin, Rosemary M. "Attention, American Folklore: Doc Craft Comes Marching In." *Studies in American Fiction* 1 (1973): 221-227. Laughlin discusses McPherson's use of myth and folklore, as well as his ability to create new kinds of folklore in "A Solo Song: For Doc" based on his aesthetic use of language and his unique mythical style.

"McPherson, James Alan." *Current Biography* 57 (September, 1996): 34-38. A biographical sketch of McPherson, in which he states that he sees the United States as a land populated by diverse peoples who are connected by a larger heritage. He explains that his major theme in both fiction and nonfiction has been the common humanity that transcends race.

McPherson, James Alan. "Interview with James Alan McPherson." Interview by Bob Shacochis. *Iowa Journal of Literary Studies* 4 (1983): 6-33. Shacochis focuses on questions relating to McPherson's vision of his literary role and on specific works in his collections. Also contains some discussion of McPherson's obligations as a "black-American" author.

Reid, Calvin. "James Alan McPherson: A Theater of Memory." *Publishers Weekly* 244 (December 15, 1997): 36-37. A biographical profile of McPherson. Argues that McPherson presents a wonderfully accurate social tableau full of vivid characters and lively, true dialogue, which is delivered within narratives so universal and directly meaningful that the stories aspire to the mythic realm of folklore and legend.

Wallace, Jon. *The Politics of Style: Language as Theme in the Fiction of Berger, McGuane, and McPherson.* Durango, Colo.: Hollowbrook, 1992. A study of the importance of language in the fiction of three authors, including McPherson.

_____. "The Politics of Style in Three Stories by James Alan McPherson." *Modern Fiction Studies* 34 (Spring, 1988): 17-26. Wallace argues that in "The Story of a Dead Man," "The Story of a Scar," and "Just Enough for the City," characters use language to construct for themselves a defense against human involvement and human communities which often threaten to weaken their sense of self.

_____. "The Story Behind the Story in James Alan McPherson's *Elbow Room.*" *Studies in Short Fiction* 25 (Fall, 1988): 447-452. Wallace maintains that McPherson's stories are often attempts to create a new kind of mythology, or mythological space, in which to place the experiences of his characters in the larger context of American society. Because of this, Wallace argues that in McPherson's work the narrative form matters much more than either the particulars of the story or the characters.

Cheryl Herr
Updated by Edward Huffstetler
and Alvin K. Benson

DAVID MEANS

Born: Kalamazoo, Michigan; 1961

PRINCIPAL SHORT FICTION

A Quick Kiss of Redemption, and Other Stories, 1993
Assorted Fire Events, 2000
The Secret Goldfish, 2004
The Spot, 2010
"The Tree Line, Kansas, 1934," 2010

OTHER LITERARY FORMS

David Means has written two unpublished novels, one of which he has said he discarded.

ACHIEVEMENTS

David Means's second short-story collection, *Assorted Fire Events,* won the *Los Angeles Times* Book Prize for Fiction in 2000 and was shortlisted for the National Book Critics Circle Award for Fiction in 2001. His third collection, *The Secret Goldfish,* was shortlisted for the Frank O'Connor International Short Story Prize in 2006. He won a PEN/O. Henry Prize in 2006 for his story "Sault St. Marie."

BIOGRAPHY

David Means was born and grew up in Kalamazoo, Michigan. He received a B.A. in English from the College of Wooster, Ohio, and then moved to New York, where he received an M.F.A. in poetry from Columbia University. He settled in Nyack, New York, where he became a professor of English and creative writing at Vassar College.

ANALYSIS

Since his first collection, *A Quick Kiss of Redemption,* Means has progressively moved away from Chekhovian realism, taking more chances with experimental narrative structure. Pursuing tactics begun in *Assorted Fire Events* and made more evident in his third collection, *The Secret Goldfish,* Means takes increasing liberties in his fourth collection, *The Spot,* with narrative techniques that explore the nature and importance of storytelling.

"ASSORTED FIRE EVENTS"

The title piece of David Means's second book of short stories, which won the 2001 *Los Angeles Times* Book Award, is a poetic meditation on the universal human fascination with fire. The story describes and ponders the significance of several "fire events" in an attempt to explore what drives people to "play with fire" or "follow the fire truck" to a burning building.

The story has no single unified plot. Instead, as the title suggests, it recounts a series of events about fire, related to the others only insofar as they are of interest to the narrator.

In the first paragraph, the narrator recalls one winter, when he was thirteen and living in Michigan, when a man set fire to several cottages. This first event does not focus on the person who started the fire but on the boy's fascination with the effect of fire on a house. What he likes is the way the fire makes its way from the inside out, until there is no more inside, only outside. The skeletal remains after the fire ravages a house create a poetic image of something being stripped to the bone. For the second fire event, the narrator describes sitting in his study writing and listening to his children playing outside when a fire, caused by spontaneous combustion of varnish-soaked rags, breaks out in a nearby house. The narrator introduces the second event by saying that the sound of fire, like popcorn in hot oil just before the kernels explode, makes him laugh. The ironic juxtaposition of this sound against the sound of his children whooping and hollering with joy is what interests him.

The final and most extended event combines the horror and beauty of fire. When a young boy named Fenton tries to launch his homemade rocket ship with gasoline, the fire quickly gets out of control and engulfs him. The ironic juxtaposition of horrible destruction and comic effect is then suggested by a description of Fenton on fire, looking like an actor in a fire suit, a stunt person like a Charlie Chaplin tramp. This is "a holy event," says the narrator, for Fenton walked into the hot fire of hell and came out with a face hard to recognize as human. Ultimately, the narrator sees Fenton as Christ, for the boy has experienced an extreme mystery that he cannot explain and that the writer can only try to capture in assorted fire events. Style is everything in "Assorted Fire Events," for the story is an example of a writer's attempt to use language to explore the basic paradoxical mystery of fire as a powerful force that can burn away the extraneous and reduce one to pure essentials. Means's method for achieving this exploration is to reject linear narrative altogether and describe various fire events in such a way that, even as they are horrifying, they somehow are eerily beautiful.

THE SECRET GOLDFISH

Means--like Anton Chekhov, Flannery O'Connor, Raymond Carver, and Grace Paley--sees the world in a short-story way. This means that one should not read Means for a plot that rushes to an inevitable end or for easily recognizable characters, like the folks one meets every day. Instead one goes to Means for some scary and sacred sense that what happens is not as important as what it signifies and for the shock of recognition that those persons one thought are actually an enigma-- one knew one does not really know them at all. One goes to Means for mystery and the paradox understood by the great short-story writers from Edgar Allan Poe to Chekhov to Carver: If one removes everything extraneous from a scene, an object, a person, its meaning is revealed, stark and astonishing.

Means's short stories are seldom satisfied with linearity of plot and thus often become lists of connected mysteries. "Notable Dustman Appearances to Date" is a series of hallucinatory manifestations of famous faces in swirling dust kicked up by wind or smoke: Richard Nixon, Ernest Hemingway, Nikolai Gogol, Jesus. "Michigan Death Trips" is a catalog of catastrophic disruptions, as people abruptly disappear beneath the ice of a frozen lake, are struck suddenly on the highway, or are hit by a stray bullet from nowhere. "Elyria Man" lays bare mummified bodies found lying beneath the soil, as if patiently waiting to embody some basic human fear or need. In each of these stories, Means reveals the truth of our lives the way great art always has--by making the one see the world as it painfully is, not as one's comfortable habits hide it from one. In the short-story world of Means, a mundane tale of infidelity and divorce gets transformed by the metaphoric stillness of a neglected goldfish in a mucked-up tank, surviving in spite of the stagnation around it. As the story "Lightning Man" makes clear, the realm of reality that matters to Means is sacramental, ritualistic, miraculous--a world in which the old reassurances, such as that lightning never strikes twice in the same place, are shown to be nonsense. A man is struck seven times throughout his life by a powerful revelatory energy until he becomes a mythic creature, waiting for the inevitable eighth.

"THE BLADE"

Two stories in Means's fourth collection, *The Spot*--"The Blade" and "The Junction"--focus on tramps gathered around a campfire spinning yarns. In "The Blade," the central character, Ronnie, hesitates about telling his peers his "blade story," for he knows it will involve making explanations about how he spent a couple of years with an old tramp named Hambone, which would expose the old tramp to the ridicule of the men. Ronnie's blade story centers on his waking up one morning with Hambone holding a knife at Ronnie's throat, insisting that if Ronnie does not believe the good things the tramp has told Ronnie about the tramp's mother, he will kill Ronnie. However, Hambone has told Ronnie two stories: one characterizing Hambone's mother as a wonderful woman and another, two months earlier, in which Hambone said she did not have a decent bone in her body. Even though Ronnie tries to placate Hambone by agreeing that his mother was a great woman, the old man does not let up; Ronnie is forced to turn the knife and kill the tramp, making Ronnie's blade story one in which he wields the weapon.

"NEBRASKA"

Three stories in *The Spot* deal with another group of characters who live their lives on the road--thieves and scam artists. "Nebraska" focuses on a young woman involved in an armored-truck robbery in Nebraska, engineered by a man named Byron, with whom she lives. These are amateurs, members of the underground in the late 1960's, planning the robbery to finance bomb making to demolish the status quo, with Byron spouting a lot of rhetoric about striking out against the corrupt system. Although they make careful plans to execute the robbery, at the crucial moment, when Byron and his partner shoot two Brinks guards, the central female character, in charge of the getaway car, panics and drives away, leaving them literally holding the bag. The central tension in the story is the young woman's romantic identification with the Great Depression-era thieves Bonnie and Clyde--not the bank robbers, however, but Faye Dunaway and Warren Beatty, who starred in the 1967 film *Bonnie and Clyde*.

"THE GULCH"

In "The Gulch," three teenage boys crucify another boy on a homemade cross set up in a gulch to see if he will rise from the dead. The focus of the story is on various possible explanations for the murder, as news commentators and professors try to find reasons and precedents for the crime. A detective named Collard, who is investigating the case, thinks that when he retires, with a memory full of stories, the incident in the gulch will be the classic one he pulls out of his hat when the conversation gets boring. He knows, however, that his job is to find out who dreamed up the idea and made it true. Making an idea come true and making stories out of inexplicable acts constitute the themes of many of Means's stories in *The Spot*.

"THE KNOCKING"

"The Knocking," the shortest story in *The Spot*, is in many ways one of the most complex. The first-person male narrator complains of knocking noises emanating from the man who lives in an identical apartment above the narrator. The reader knows nothing about the narrator or the noisy neighbor--just a lot about the nature of the knocking--until three-quarters through the story, when the narrator says that the knocking often comes late in the day, when the man above knows that the narrator is in his deepest state of reverie, feeling a persistent sense of loss of his wife and kids. In the last two paragraphs, the narrator begins to identify with the knocker, remembering when narrator had gone around, fixing things at his house, trying to keep it in shape. "The Knocking" is about having nothing worthwhile to do and thus engaging in an activity that is irritating but that one cannot cease doing. The rhythm of the story echoes the repetitive, annoying, meaningless actions. Means creates a timeless universality that allows the reader to become deeply embedded in the story, caught up in a language event that is, paradoxically, both a personal obsession and an aesthetic creation.

"THE TREE LINE, KANSAS, 1934"

This story, which appeared in *The New Yorker* in 2010, shows how far Means has pushed his fiction toward narratives about the nature of narrative itself. Two Federal Bureau of Investigation (FBI) agents are on a stakeout in Kansas in 1934. The younger of the two, Barnes, insists that the criminal they are waiting for will not return; the older agent, Lee, says little but is fed up with Barnes's complaining. After five days of waiting, Barnes is taking a smoke in the trees when

Carson, the criminal, and his men drive up; Barnes walks out of the tree line and is cut down by, as the cliché goes, a hale of gunfire. On the surface, this is all that happens in the story.

However, this story quintessentially is about what all stories are about: Something appears to take place in time and space. The first paragraph emphasizes time by repeating: "Five days of trading field glasses. . . . Five days of surveillance. . . . Five days of listening to the young agent named Barnes. . . . Five days of listening to Barnes recount the pattern. . . . For five days Barnes talked. . . . Five days reduced to a single conversation. . . ." The last paragraph emphasizes not the passing of time but a "moment" when Lee "froze up" and Barnes steps forward out of the tree line, dulled by the "persistent tedium of a scene that had gone on for what seemed to his youthful mind an eternity" into "a single ferocious moment" of a "fury of gunfire." Moreover, space is emphasized in this story. The two men are hiding at the tree line, watching a farm; their pattern of behavior in space and time is to take turns going back into the trees to smoke and watching at the tree line. They try to feel assured that what has been imagined in the Chicago FBI office, using maps and line drawings, properly matches the Kansas reality they are watching. Thus, in time and space, the two men wait for something that is imminent. Barnes considers probability, trying to calculate the patterns of behavior as determined by Carson's previous movements. This is what all stories are about: time, space, expectation, perceiving patterns, and figuring probabilities--the transformation of the casual into the causal.

In the last paragraph, Barnes has been back in the tree line smoking, feeling a deeper relaxation. As he steps into the gunfire,

> his mind--young and foolish but beautiful nonetheless--remained partly back in the woods, taking in the solitude, pondering the way the future felt when a man was rooted to one place, waiting for an unlikely outcome, one that, rest assured, would never, ever arrive.

The pleasure the story provides lies not in the relationship between the two men but rather in the music it makes about waiting, about being caught in time and space, about trying to predict the future by making patterns out of the past.

BIBLIOGRAPHY

Crouch, Ian. "The Exchange: David Means." *The New Yorker*, July 20, 2010. Interview with Means discusses his fascination with landscape and violence in his short stories.

Row, Jess. "Turning Points." *The New York Times*, June 10, 2010. Review of *The Spot* acknowledges the unusual narrative flow in Means's stories that hinge on one event: "rather than moving in linear time, the narration pirouettes again and again around that one point."

Shengold, Nina. "Darkness on the Edge of Town." *Chronograph* (October 26, 2010). Shengold comments on the "high body count" in Means's stories but adds that Means can "jump-cut from harrowing cruelty to a image so gorgeous it makes you gasp." In this essay based on an interview, Means talks about his two "abortive" novels and comments on why the short story appeals to him more than the novel.

Charles E. May

MAILE MELOY

Born: Helena, Montana; January 1, 1972

PRINCIPAL SHORT FICTION
Half in Love, 2002
Both Ways Is the Only Way I Want It, 2009

OTHER LITERARY FORMS

Maile Meloy (MI-lee muh-LOY) has published two interconnected novels, *Liars and Saints* (2003) and *A Family Daughter* (2006). She wrote *Liars and Saints* as a stand-alone work, but she returned to the characters in the second novel, in which it becomes apparent that the daughter of the title has written *Liars and Saints* as a thinly disguised autobiographical work. In addition to her fiction, Meloy has published a number of book reviews for *The New York Times* and short nonfiction essays in *The New Yorker* and *Slate.* Her undergraduate honors thesis, "Landscape with Figures: The Georgic in Montana Literature," is included in *Writing Montana: Literature Under the Big Sky* (1996), and an undergraduate essay, "The Voice of the Looking-Glass," first appeared in the 1993 edition of *Modern American Prose: Fifteen Writers + Fifteen* and has since been widely anthologized.

ACHIEVEMENTS

Maile Meloy's short-story collection *Half in Love* received the Rosenthal Award from the American Academy of Arts and Letters, the PEN/Malamud Award for Excellence in Short Fiction, and the John C. Zacharis First Book Award. The story "Aqua Boulevard," included in *Half in Love,* was awarded the Aga Khan Prize by *The Paris Review. Both Ways Is the Only Way I Want It* was listed among the Ten Best Books of 2009 by *The New York Times Book Review. Liars and Saints* was shortlisted for Britain's Orange Prize for Fiction. Meloy has received a Guggenheim Fellowship

and in 2007 was listed as one of Best Young American Novelists by *Granta.* She was one of five finalists for the 2004 New York Public Library Young Lions of Fiction Award. "Landscape with Figures: The Georgic in Montana Literature" was awarded a Thomas T. Hoopes prize, one of Harvard's most prestigious undergraduate awards.

BIOGRAPHY

Maile Meloy grew up in Montana and later moved to California. Her parents, a teacher and a lawyer, divorced when she was young. Many of Meloy's stories are set in the West, and many of her plots feature troubled relationships. Her brother, Colin, is the lead singer for the band Decemberists and the author of a nonfiction work about the indie band the Replacements.

Meloy completed her bachelor's degree at Harvard, writing an honor's thesis on the western writer Wallace Stegner. She earned a master's degree in fine arts at the University of California, Irvine, a program whose graduates include Michael Chabon, Richard Ford, Alice Sebold, and Helena Viramontes. While at Irvine, she studied with Geoffrey Wolff--to whom *Both Ways Is the Only Way I Want It* is dedicated--and started many of the pieces that appear in *Half in Love.* Before beginning her studies in Irvine, she held a series of jobs, including a position as a script reader for Walt Disney Studios. Married, she settled in Los Angeles.

ANALYSIS

A member of Generation X and the offspring of the first wave of baby boomers, Meloy is often mentioned in the company of such writers as Jonathan Safran Foer, Gary Shteyngart, and Zadie Smith. Like many of her contemporaries, she places family relationships at the center of her work, but unlike the characteristic Generation X writer, she eschews postmodern irony and "hysterical realism," elaborate absurdist characterization and plotting. Instead, she favors a traditional, unadorned style that is deceptive in its simplicity. The conciseness of her writing is well suited for short fiction but drew some criticism from reviewers of her otherwise well-received first novel, *Liars and Saints*, which follows four generations of a family in 260 pages. Her second novel, *A Family Daughter*, has been more highly praised. Still ambitious in scope, it revisits the same family saga, this time centering the plot on a young woman who has written an autobiographical first novel, presumably *Liars and Saints*.

In both her long and short fiction, Meloy is known for creating characters who are flawed yet likable. Her narrative stance allows for understanding of a character's actions without passing judgment. In her short fiction, she works comfortably in first and third person, and in one story, "Ranch Girl," she uses second person. Her protagonists are both male and female; they vary in age from children to octogenarians. Some are financially comfortable; some are not. A good number are lawyers, but not high-powered ones. Most characters work hard and lead ordinary lives interrupted by infidelities, accidents, and death. What little violence there is in her stories occurs off stage, as do most life-changing events.

In her novels, plots take unexpected twists, and by "fictionalizing" the first novel with the second, Meloy complicates the storylines. In *Liars and Saints*, the character Abby Santerre discovers that her Uncle Jamie is not her grandmother's youngest son but the illegitimate child of Abby's aunt; Abby becomes involved in an incestuous relationship with Jamie (her first cousin), gives birth to his child, and dies young. In *A Family Daughter*, Abby is revealed to be the author of *Liars and Saints*. Alive and well, she is still involved with Jamie, but she is not the mother of his son, who has been adopted. Whether Jamie is her uncle or cousin remains unresolved. What matters is not the truth but how characters react to what appears to be the truth.

Plot and situation serve as a means to develop characterization, and this is especially evident in Meloy's short stories. Sometimes events are startling: In "Liliana," a man's grandmother appears on his doorstep two months after she has been reported drowned; a freak accident with a paint stirrer leaves a man seriously injured on his deck while his wife, inside, thinks

Maile Meloy (Getty Images)

he is upstairs asleep. More often, characters are blindsided by less-exotic occurrences, such as illness, infidelity, workplace hazards, bad weather, and road accidents. Whether innocent victims or responsible parties, Meloy's characters recognize accountability. In "Ranch Girl," when a police report states that the teenage driver killed in a car wreck had not been drinking, the victim's girlfriend accepts the statement as a well-intentioned gesture, but she rejects the sanitized version of events in favor of a scenario consistent with her boyfriend's behavior. In "Last of the White Slaves," a Saudi servant is punished severely for a theft he did not commit; however, he holds no resentment against his accuser or the legal system because he has stolen before without getting caught and, as a result, views his sentence as justified. Social injustices are facts of life rather than problems to be railed against. The young lawyers who populate many stories care for individual clients but are not crusaders.

Often, Meloy ends her stories on a note of uncertainty, leaving her characters torn between the comfort of the familiar and the promise of the unknown or, as the title of her second collection indicates, wanting it both ways. The significance lies not so much in the choice but in the individual's honest acknowledgment and acceptance of his or her ambivalence. Lack of closure, especially when combined with loss, can result in depressing literature, but many of Meloy's stories leave the reader with a sense of confidence that the characters will emerge intact.

HALF IN LOVE

"Tome," the opening story of the collection, traces the relationship between a young lawyer and her middle-aged client, Sawyer, a construction worker she has represented in a workman's compensation case. Unable to return to work and unsuccessful at adjusting to retirement, Sawyer has become increasingly angry and unreasonable. Although he has accepted a settlement that precludes his making additional claims, he is intent on filing suit against his former employers. Refusing to accept that he has no case, he takes hostage a guard at the building where his records are stored and demands that the lawyer come to the building to reexamine his file.

The hostage-taking comes as a surprise: Even though Sawyer has threatened violence in bursts of anger, his lawyer has been able to calm him quickly. Her confidence in her client transfers to the reader because she appears to be a reliable narrator. Furthermore, since the story is narrated in first person, past tense, the reader knows that the lawyer has survived to tell the tale. As a result, Sawyer remains a sympathetic character in spite of his volatility, and the relationship between the characters, rather than the events of the story, moves the narrative forward; the story ends with a small but significant insight.

"Garrison Junction" is considered by some reviewers the strongest piece in Meloy's first collection. Like many of her stories, it is set in Montana, where the climate and terrain demand adaptability. The story opens on a snowy winter evening, when Chase, a lawyer, and Gina, his girlfriend of ten years, have set off on a car trip, even though their route is hazardous. As Chase drives, Gina's nervousness about the treacherous road is intercut with her uneasiness about their relationship, which has been strained by a work-related separation, by Gina's suspicions that Chase has been

unfaithful, and, now, by an unplanned pregnancy. For Gina, the baby is "a happy accident," but Chase sees it as just "an accident."

Meloy has set the reader up to expect an auto accident to parallel the metaphoric one, and a crash does occur, but Chase and Gina are not involved. They learn the details secondhand while waiting at a roadside café in Garrison Junction for the wreckage to be cleared and the storm to pass. Another couple has been killed when their car, which they had stopped on the narrow road, was rammed from behind by a semi. Gina makes eye contact with the truck driver, who is among the stranded travelers at the café.

The café scene, which takes up two-thirds of the story, resembles Ernest Hemingway's "Hills Like White Elephants" in its slow pacing, its subject matter--a relationship strained by a pregnancy--and its limited point of view. Hemingway develops his narrative almost exclusively through dialogue, as if the narrator is a camera merely recording an overheard conversation between two people waiting for a train. Meloy uses a third person limited voice, restricting the point of view to Gina's perspective, her thoughts, her speculations. She envisions the victims just before the accident, wondering whether they were frightened and whether they were arguing. She imagines them too focused on the unknown ahead to pay attention to the dangers behind, an observation that could well apply to her current situation. She wonders what the truck driver is feeling and guesses at what Chase is thinking. Gina feels a connection with the driver, who represents both the possibility of escape into a different future and accountability for the actions and decisions that have brought her to the present moment. A later story in the collection, "Thirteen and a Half," revisits Chase, Gina, and their now-adolescent daughter, allowing readers to reflect on how the couple have negotiated their relationship.

In "Kite Whistler Aquamarine" Meloy weaves together two plot lines. The first-person narrator and her husband are both lawyers, but Cort, the husband, devotes much of his energy and a good bit of their joint income to raising horses. He has borrowed against their house to mate his best mare with a sire from distinguished bloodlines, but the mare has foaled early, in twenty-below weather, and the filly has frostbitten feet. The narrator, who is highly allergic to animals, is preoccupied with winning a custody case for a client about to be released from prison on appeal. Lauren, the client's daughter, has been living with foster parents whom the narrator finds self-righteous and smug; however, Lauren's mother, Ruth, convicted on drug charges, seems unable to provide a stable home environment. As Cort struggles to keep the filly alive, the narrator struggles to convince herself that Ruth, who plans to move into a tent in a field with a poacher, will be a fit mother.

Both Ways Is the Only Way I Want It

In "Travis, B," Meloy offers a version of the American cowboy that differs sharply from the stereotypical western hero. Chet Moran, part Cheyenne and partially crippled by a childhood case of polio, is a twenty-two-year-old ranch hand on a spread in eastern Montana, near the North Dakota border. One evening, his boredom takes him into town, where he wanders into an adult-education class and immediately falls for the teacher, Beth Travis. She had accepted the teaching position while still in law school but has been hired by a firm in Missoula, a nearly ten-hour drive across the state.

After class, Chet accompanies Beth to a nearby café. He is awkward in her presence, and she is too concerned about managing the long commute and her day job to notice his attentiveness. One evening, he rides his horse to the school and takes her on horseback to a café after class. However, he is too shy to express his feelings, and he does not realize that to Beth he is just a casual acquaintance. The story permits neither romance nor heroic endeavor. Although Chet behaves foolishly, abandoning the livestock to drive across Montana to find Beth after she quits teaching, he quickly realizes his mistake.

"Lovely Rita," set in Connecticut in the mid-1970's, centers on another young man who struggles with doing the right thing. Steven Kelly, who has lost both of his parents to cancer, works on the construction of a nuclear power plant with his friend Acey, a romantic who looks back on his high school days nostalgically--although he is still in his early twenties--and believes in luck. One night at a local bar, Acey meets a girl

Steven knew in grade school and falls immediately in love. At the plant, the other workers tease him mercilessly about "lovely Rita." A short time later, Acey is killed in an accident at work, and Rita asks Steven to arrange a raffle at the plant. The prize is herself. She claims she wants the money for a new start. When he realizes Rita cannot be dissuaded, he goes along with the plan, wrestling with mixed feelings, including his own desire to claim the winning ticket. Typical of Meloy's fiction, Rita turns out to have an understandable motive for her actions, and Stephen regains his moral balance without injuring anyone in the process.

OTHER MAJOR WORKS

LONG FICTION: *Liars and Saints*, 2003; *A Family Daughter*, 2006.

BIBLIOGRAPHY

Egan, Ken Jr. *Hope and Dread in Montana Literature*. Reno: University of Nevada Press, 2003. Egan's book, a critical-historical survey of Montana writers, gives an introduction to the history and regional literature that form a significant part of Meloy's cultural heritage.

Meloy, Maile. "Landscape with Figures: The Georgic in Montana Literature." In *Writing Montana: Literature Under the Big Sky*, edited by Rick Newby and Suzanne Hunger. Helena, Mont.: Falcon Press, 1996. Based on her undergraduate thesis, this essay provides insight into Meloy's writing in terms of the relationship between character and setting.

Miller, Laura. "An Author with Authority." *The New Yorker*, May 11, 2003. A look at Meloy and her work, with its at hard-bitten western flavor.

Sittenfeld, Curtis. "Irrational Behavior." *The New Yorker*, July 8, 2009. A review of *Both Ways Is the Only Way I Want It* praises Meloy's "clear, calm, and intelligent" prose that delivers "shocking" plot twists in a "low-key manner."

K. Edgington

HERMAN MELVILLE

Born: New York, New York; August 1, 1819
Died: New York, New York; September 28, 1891

PRINCIPAL SHORT FICTION

The Piazza Tales, 1856 (includes "Bartleby the
Scrivener," and "Benito Cereno")
The Apple-Tree Table, and Other Sketches, 1922
Great Short Works of Herman Melville, 1969
(Warner Berthoff, editor)

OTHER LITERARY FORMS

Herman Melville's published books include novels,
short stories, poetry, and sketches. He is best known for
his novels, particularly *Moby Dick: Or, The Whale*
(1851), *The Confidence Man: His Masquerade* (1857),
and *Billy Budd, Foretopman* (1924).

ACHIEVEMENTS

By the middle of the twentieth century, names
such as Moby Dick and Captain Ahab were well
known in the popular culture of the United States.
However, one must look to the 1920's and the revival
in Melville's work (notably *Moby Dick*) to see the beginning of what came to be his immense stature in
American literature. His most significant works received little popular or critical acclaim in his lifetime.
One reason for this may have been friction with nineteenth century American tastes. Problems also
stemmed from Melville's fascination with forces that
seemed (to him) to lie below the placid optimism of
his contemporary American culture. Readers were
disturbed by the author's tendency to view outward
appearances as pasteboard masks that concealed a
truer, darker reality. It should come as no surprise that
modern students sense an invitation to allegorize
Melville's works. Many believe that Melville, himself, perceived life in a symbolic way.

Many of the short pieces that Melville wrote for
various magazines represent conscious attempts,
through symbol and irony, to express disturbing layers
of meaning beneath a calm surface. In 1855-1856,
Melville finished a novel, *The Confidence Man*, rendering a bleak view of the possibility of faith in the
world as he knew it. Although Melville openly wrote
verse throughout his life, the manuscript that would become his novella, *Billy Budd, Foretopman*, was packed
away by his widow and not discovered until the 1920's.

Melville completed *Moby Dick* some forty years before Sigmund Freud began to penetrate the veneer of
conventional surfaces in his quest for the causes of
hysteria--the salient behavioral aberration of repressive
nineteenth century Europe. However, Melville (like his
contemporary Nathaniel Hawthorne) had already
begun to probe beyond the level of mundane appearances in his fiction. Even though some of Melville's
stories are lengthy by modern standards, the finest of
them exhibit exceptional merit in the short-story genre.
"Benito Cereno" and "Bartleby the Scrivener," for example, reveal a rich complexity and density that rival
those of modern masterpieces of the form.

BIOGRAPHY

Herman Melville withdrew from school at the age of
twelve after the death of his father. He worked in various
jobs--in a fur and cap store (with his brother), in a bank,
on a farm, and as a teacher in country schools. He made
two early sea voyages, one on a merchant ship to Liver-
pool in 1839, and one to the South Seas aboard the whaler
Acushnet, in 1841. After about eighteen months, Melville
and a friend deserted the whaler, and Melville spent a
month in the Taipi Valley on the island of Nuku Hiva.
Melville escaped the island aboard an Australian whaler
but was imprisoned when he and ten other crewmen refused service. Again, he escaped, spent some time on the
island of Mooréa, then several months in Hawaii. Eventually, he joined the U.S. Navy and returned home in 1844.

Out of these early sea adventures came Melville's two successful early novels, *Typee: A Peep at Polynesian Life* (1846) and *Omoo: A Narrative of Adventures in the South Seas* (1847). His experiences aboard the whaling ships led to a novel that was not to be successful in his lifetime, *Moby Dick*. The failure of *Moby Dick* and *Pierre: Or, The Ambiguities* (1852) left Melville financially and morally drained, but he would continue to produce fiction for a while, including the short stories that were guardedly constructed to seem unruffling to the sensibilities of the time but carried submerged patterns and disturbing undertones.

While still in the limelight of his early success, Melville married Elizabeth Shaw, daughter of a Massachusetts chief justice. They were to have four children; three died in young adulthood and the eldest son committed suicide in his eighteenth year (1867).

Melville was continually plagued by doubt, unrest, and marital problems. His later years were spent trying to adjust to his decline in status and seeking a comfortable living. In 1856, his father-in-law subsidized Melville's travels to the Mediterranean, the Holy Land, and England, where he visited Nathaniel Hawthorne. Unable to secure a naval commission during the Civil War, Melville sold his estate in Massachusetts and settled in New York. Finally, in 1866, he became an inspector in the New York Customs House until, some twenty years later, an inheritance enabled him to retire. He died September 28, 1891, at the age of seventy-two.

ANALYSIS

After the critical and commercial failure of *Moby Dick* and *Pierre*, Herman Melville, who was then supporting his wife and children, his mother, and his four sisters, was desperate for money. When he received an invitation from *Putnam's Monthly Magazine* to contribute short stories at the rate of five dollars a page, he accepted. He also sold short stories to *Harper's New Monthly Magazine*. Both magazines, however, had very strict editorial policies banning any material which might conceivably offend even the most sensitive reader on moral, social, ethical, political, or religious grounds. This was a shattering limitation to Melville, whose deepest personal and artistic convictions were bound up in the defiant heroes and themes of

highly unconventional metaphysical speculation of *Mardi and a Voyage Thither* (1849), *Moby Dick*, and *Pierre*. He genuinely questioned many of the ideas which, although they came to be freely debated, were sacrosanct in the nineteenth century. These included the existence of a personal God outside the human spirit, the importance of material goods, the existence of absolute good and absolute evil, and the right of established civil and religious authorities to impose sanctions against those who expressed ideas that differed from the ideas of the majority. Obviously, neither *Putnam's Monthly Magazine* nor *Harper's New Monthly Magazine* would publish stories which dealt openly with opinions that might be objectionable to many of their readers. This left Melville in an apparently unresolvable dilemma: ignore his own strongest beliefs, or allow those dependent on him to live in poverty.

Not only did Melville find a solution, but also he found one which, while not ideal from an artistic standpoint, gave him a great deal of rather diabolical satisfaction. Melville's short stories--all of which were written during this period and under these conditions--present bland and apparently harmless surfaces under which boil the same rebellion and the same questioning of established ideas that characterize his most controversial novels. Furthermore, these stories reflect, in allegorical terms, the same dilemma that produced them. Beneath apparently innocuous surface plots, Melville's short stories center on the image of an anguished human being who is cursed with the ability to see more than the world sees; faced with the hostility that results from his challenge to the established beliefs of a complacent majority, his protagonist either fights against, withdraws from, or surrenders to the world.

"BARTLEBY THE SCRIVENER"

One of the most effective devices that allowed Melville to achieve his artistic purpose was his use of reassuringly respectable elderly gentlemen as narrators. In the very act of allowing them to tell their own stories, Melville injected a subtle but savage mockery which both expressed and concealed his own attitudes. For example, the narrator of Melville's best-known short story, "Bartleby the Scrivener," which was collected in *The Piazza Tales*, is an elderly lawyer reminiscing about an incident that has occurred some time earlier.

Herman Melville (Library of Congress)

The lawyer's own blindness to the deeper meanings of life is suggested in the first paragraph of the story, when Melville describes Bartleby as "one of those beings of whom nothing is ascertainable." As the reader discovers, it is primarily the physical, external facts of Bartleby's life that are unknown; but to the materialistic lawyer, these are everything. He sees only surface reality, never inner truth, a point which is underlined in the narrator's next sentence: "What my own astonished eyes saw of Bartleby *that* is all I know of him."

The lawyer begins his story by describing the office on Wall Street which he occupied at the time of Bartleby's appearance. The significance of "Wall Street" becomes apparent immediately; the lawyer has surrounded himself with walls, and his windows command no other view. When the lawyer hires Bartleby as a scrivener, or copier of law documents, he assigns Bartleby a desk near a window which faces a wall only three feet away. On one side of Bartleby's desk is a ground glass door separating him from the other two copyists, and on the other side, the lawyer places a folding screen. Having imposed upon Bartleby his own claustrophobic setting, the lawyer gives him law documents to copy. For a while all goes well; Bartleby copies documents neatly and efficiently. On the third day, however, the lawyer asks Bartleby to examine his writing.

In ordering him to examine his writing, the lawyer means that Bartleby should read through the copy he has made while someone else reads aloud from the original. This is an extremely boring task, but an accepted part of every scrivener's work. Bartleby replies, "I would prefer not to." The lawyer reacts with characteristic indecision: He feels impelled to expel Bartleby from his office, but does nothing because he is unnerved by Bartleby's total lack of expression, by the absence of "anything ordinarily human about him."

Several days later, when Bartleby again refuses to examine his copy, the lawyer appeals to him in the name of two ideals which are of great importance to the lawyer himself: common usage and common sense. Bartleby is unmoved. Instead of asserting his own authority, the lawyer appeals not only to his other two scriveners but also to his office boy. All these uphold the lawyer's view. He then calls upon Bartleby in the name of "duty"; again, Bartleby fails to respond to the verbal cue.

The lawyer's inability to cope with Bartleby is anticipated in the story by his tolerance of the Dickensian eccentricities of his other two scriveners. The older one, Turkey, works well in the morning, but after a lunch which is implied to be mostly liquid, he becomes reckless, irascible, and messy. The younger copyist, Nippers, is dyspeptic. His irritability takes place in the morning, while the afternoons find him comparatively calm. Thus, the lawyer gets only one good day's work between them. Nevertheless, he always finds some rationalization for his lack of decisiveness.

The first rationalization he applies to his indecision regarding Bartleby is the difficulty of coping effectively with passive resistance. The lawyer feels that Bartleby's unaccountable displays of perversity must be the result of some involuntary aberration, and he reflects that tolerating Bartleby "will cost me little or nothing, while I lay up in my soul what will eventually prove a sweet morsel for my conscience." Even on the comparatively rare occasions when he is sufficiently irritated to confront Bartleby with a direct order to do something which Bartleby "would prefer not to," the lawyer always retires with dire resolutions, but no action.

One Sunday morning, as the lawyer walks toward Trinity Church "to hear a celebrated preacher," he decides to stop at his office. There he finds Bartleby in his shirt sleeves, together with evidence that he has been using the office as his home. The lawyer feels at first a sense of melancholy and pity at Bartleby's loneliness; but as the full realization of Bartleby's isolation dawns on the lawyer, his feelings turn to fear and repulsion. He reflects that Bartleby never reads, never converses, but only works and stands for long periods staring out at the dead walls. Bartleby's presence in the office at night and on Sunday, when the usually bustling Wall Street is silent and uninhabited, reminds the lawyer of Bartleby's essential difference from his own concept of humanity, which revolves around surface society. The lawyer rationalizes his unsympathetic response to these circumstances by reflecting that such depths of soul-sickness as Bartleby's repel the human heart because common sense rejects the idea of pity where there is no realistic hope of offering aid.

The lawyer makes an attempt, on Monday morning, to bring Bartleby inside the narrow circle of external reality, which is all the lawyer is capable of comprehending. He asks Bartleby for details of his life: place of birth, family, and the like. Bartleby refuses with his usual "I prefer not." The lawyer notices that he and his other copyists have begun to use that expression, and he fears that the influence of Bartleby will spread throughout the office. Bartleby further irritates the lawyer the next day by refusing to do even the one task he had, until then, been willing to do: copying law documents. When the lawyer asks the reason, Bartleby replies, "Do you not see the reason for yourself?" The lawyer does not see; and ironically, he attributes Bartleby's refusal to copy to trouble with his eyes. When Bartleby finally makes it clear, some days later, that his refusal is final, the lawyer decides to order him to leave. However, he feels a sense of pity for the scrivener because "he seemed alone, absolutely alone in the universe."

The lawyer gives Bartleby six days in which to get ready to leave; at the end of that time, Bartleby is still there. The lawyer gives him money, and, ordering Bartleby to be gone by the next day, leaves the office assuming that he will obey. The lawyer's self-congratulations on his masterly application of the doctrine of assumption end abruptly the next day when the lawyer discovers the scrivener still in the office. Then the lawyer rationalizes that it is his predestined fate to harbor Bartleby and that his charity will be amply repaid in the next world. The gibes of his friends and professional associates, however, undermine his resolve, and again he orders Bartleby to depart. When he does not, the lawyer finally takes decisive action. He packs up his own belongings and moves to a new office, leaving Bartleby alone in an empty room.

The lawyer soon finds, however, that he is not yet free of Bartleby. The landlord of the lawyer's former office, unable to move Bartleby from the building even after the new tenant has expelled him from the office itself, applies to the lawyer for help. The lawyer offers Bartleby several different jobs, and even suggests that he make his home with the lawyer for a time. Bartleby however, replies that he "would prefer not to make any change at all." The lawyer flees the building and stays incommunicado for several days. When he cautiously returns to his office, he finds that Bartleby has been removed to the Tombs, a prison in New York City. The lawyer visits the Tombs to offer comfort, but Bartleby will not speak to him. He adjures Bartleby to look at the blue sky and the green grass, but Bartleby replies, "I know where I am," and refuses to speak again. The lawyer leaves Bartleby in the prison yard, and on his way out arranges for him to be well fed but Bartleby refuses to eat. When the lawyer visits Bartleby again, several days later, he finds the scrivener curled up in a ball with his head against the prison wall, dead.

The narrator concludes the story by relating a rumor he has heard to the effect that Bartleby was once employed in a dead letter office. He reflects on the melancholy nature of such work, handling letters containing messages of charity and hope which arrived too late to relieve those to whom they had been sent. "On errands of life," reflects the lawyer, "these letters speed to death." The story ends with the line, "Ah Bartleby! Ah, humanity!"

Although the lawyer seems to be an honest and humane man, he is actually guilty of what Melville considers society's most prevailing sin: self-deception. He labels his pusillanimity prudence, his indecisiveness tolerance, his curiosity concern, as if by doing so he can create a reality which corresponds to his own illusions. He goes to a fashionable church not to worship the God in whom he professes to believe but "to hear a famous preacher." When he is upset by Bartleby's presence in his office on a Sunday, he does not turn to God for help. Rather, he stays away from church because his perturbation makes him unfit for the only function of churchgoing that he is aware of: the social function. He constantly thinks in terms of material entities, particularly money and food. The lawyer, however, is not an evil man. By the standards of the world, he is exceptionally charitable and forbearing. He feels for Bartleby's suffering, even if he never understands it; and if the help he offers his scrivener is not what Bartleby needs, still it is all the lawyer has to give. That is Melville's point: Even the best of those who think conventional thoughts, order their lives by conventional rules, and never question conventional commonplaces like "common sense" and "common usage," are incapable of understanding a man like Bartleby.

Bartleby is the only character in the story who makes a point of looking at the walls, who is actually aware of the limitations with which society, represented by the lawyer, has boxed him in. Bartleby's refusal to value meaningless tasks simply because they are important to a shallow and materialistic society reflects Melville's own rage at being ordered to produce literary pabulum by a society which will not even try to understand his ideas. Bartleby is placed in the same economic dilemma which produced the story in which he appears: produce what society values, regardless of individual needs and beliefs, or die. The solitary Bartleby died; and Melville, equally oppressed by being tied down to a family of dependent women and children, wrote "Bartleby the Scrivener."

"THE FIDDLER"

Not all the protagonists of Melville's short stories withdraw from the world. The narrator-protagonist of "The Fiddler," for example, responds to the world's contempt for his poetry by abandoning his art and

attempting to become a happy failure. The story opens as the young poet, Helmstone, storms out of doors after reading an unfavorable review of his recently published work. He meets a friend, Standard, who introduces him to Hautboy. The three attend a circus, where Helmstone rages at seeing the applause which the world has denied to his poetry being awarded to the antics of a clown. He marvels at the evident enjoyment of Hautboy, whom Helmstone identifies as a man of taste and judgment. Helmstone and Standard later visit Hautboy's home, where he entertains them by playing common tunes on a fiddle. Despite the simplicity of the tunes, Helmstone is struck by Hautboy's style; and Standard finally explains that Hautboy is actually a musical genius who has given up the fame he once had and retired to happy obscurity. The poet, resolved to imitate him, tears up his manuscripts, buys a fiddle, and goes to take lessons from Hautboy.

In "The Fiddler," Hautboy serves as a lesson in the worthlessness of fame because, having had it and rejected it, he is so outstandingly happy. This allows the poet to rationalize his own failure into a deliberate choice to turn his back on the world's opinion of his poetry. In this story, however, as in "Bartleby the Scrivener," the narrator's conformity to the standards of the world (in this case, by ceasing to produce poetry which the world does not appreciate) is an act of self-deception. Either Helmstone's poetry is meritorious but misunderstood by a world whose applause is reserved for clowns, in which case he has betrayed his art by abandoning it, or his poetry is genuinely inferior, in which case he has renounced nothing because he has had nothing, and his attitude of choice is a sham. This reflects another aspect of the situation that produced "The Fiddler." If the kind of literature Melville would have preferred to write was in fact the truth, then in ceasing to write it he was betraying himself; if it was not the truth, he was deceiving himself.

These two examples illustrate the complexity and depth which underlie the surface smoothness of Melville's short tales. His stories are allegorical in nature, expressing his ideas as parables rather than as expositions. Melville often makes his points by means of emblematic symbols, such as the walls in "Bartleby the Scrivener" and the clown in "The Fiddler." In his short stories, as in his novels, Melville emphasizes subjectivity, relativity, and ambiguity. Different characters see the same situation from different perspectives, and there is no omniscient force within the story which can resolve the resulting conflict. Reality is not static and absolute, but shifting and relative; ultimate truth, if it exists at all, is unattainable.

OTHER MAJOR WORKS

LONG FICTION: *Typee: A Peep at Polynesian Life*, 1846; *Omoo: A Narrative of Adventures in the South Seas*, 1847; *Mardi, and a Voyage Thither*, 1849; *Redburn: His First Voyage*, 1849; *White-Jacket: Or, The World in a Man-of-War*, 1850; *Moby Dick: Or, The Whale*, 1851; *Pierre: Or, The Ambiguities*, 1852; *Israel Potter: His Fifty Years of Exile*, 1855; *The Confidence Man: His Masquerade*, 1857; *Billy Budd, Foretopman*, 1924.

POETRY: *Battle-Pieces and Aspects of the War*, 1866; *Clarel: A Poem and Pilgrimage in the Holy Land*, 1876; *John Marr and Other Sailors*, 1888; *Timoleon*, 1891; *Collected Poems of Herman Melville*, 1947; *The Poems of Herman Melville*, 1976 (revised 2000; Douglas Robillard, editor).

NONFICTION: *Journal Up the Straits*, 1935; *Journal of a Visit to London and the Continent*, 1948; *The Letters of Herman Melville*, 1960 (Merrell R. Davis and William H. Gilman, editors); *Journals*, 1989 (text revised with historical note and annotations by Howard C. Horsford with Lynn Horth); *Correspondence*, 1993 (Lynn Horth, editor).

MISCELLANEOUS: *The Works of Herman Melville*, 1922-1924 (sixteen volumes); *The Writings*, 1968-1993 (fifteen volumes; Harrison Hayford, Hershel Parker, and G. Thomas Tanselle, editors); *Tales, Poems, and Other Writings*, 2001 (John Bryant, editor).

BIBLIOGRAPHY

Arsić, Branka. *Passive Constitutions: Or, Seven and One-Half Times Bartleby*. Stanford, Calif.: Stanford University Press, 2007. Examines the character of Bartleby while simultaneously addressing various themes in Melville's writing, including passivity, identity, the impersonal and neutral, sexuality, ethics, and drug addiction.

Bryant, John, ed. *A Companion to Melville Studies*. New York: Greenwood Press, 1986. A collection of scholarly articles, including a biography of Melville and discussions of some of his short stories and other works. Some of the essays provide insight into Melville's thoughts on religion and philosophy and assess his impact on modern culture.

Burkholder, Robert B., ed. *Critical Essays on Herman Melville's "Benito Cereno."* New York: G. K. Hall, 1992. Includes a few early reviews and sixteen previously published articles on Melville's novella, as well as three new articles written especially for this volume. Essays range from Newton Arvin's claim that the work is an artistic failure to more contemporary historicist critiques debating whether the work presents African Americans in a positive or a negative light.

Delbanco, Andrew. *Melville: His World and Work*. New York: Knopf, 2005. This insightful biography places Melville in his time and discusses the significance of his works, then and now.

Dillingham, William B. *Melville's Short Fiction 1853-1856*. Athens: University of Georgia Press, 1977. Dillingham provides footnoted, readable explications of the stories, with moderate allusion to possible sources and other works.

Fisher, Marvin. *Going Under: Melville's Short Fiction and the American 1850's*. Baton Rouge: Louisiana State University Press, 1977. Explores the short-fiction works in the context of Melville's cultural milieu of the 1850's. Discusses "The Fiddler," "The Lightning Rod Man," and "Bartleby the Scrivener," among other works.

Kelley, Wyn. *Herman Melville: An Introduction*. Malden, Mass.: Blackwell, 2008. An overview of Melville's life and works, including a chapter discussing his short fiction of the 1850's.

Kirby, David. *Herman Melville*. New York: Ungar, 1993. A short yet comprehensive guide to Melville's career, including chapters on his life, his early novels, *Moby Dick*, the later novels, and the tales and poems. Includes a chronology and a bibliography.

Leyda, Jay. *The Melville Log: A Documentary Life of Herman Melville, 1819-1891*. New York: Harcourt, Brace, 1951. This compilation of documents (letters, diary entries, and other materials) is carefully prepared chronologically with pages headed by year; it is published in two volumes and includes biographical sketches of Melville's associates.

McCall, Dan. *The Silence of Bartleby*. Ithaca, N.Y.: Cornell University Press, 1989. An extensive survey and analysis of literary criticism of "Bartleby the Scrivener."

Newman, Lea Bertani Vozar. *A Reader's Guide to the Short Stories of Herman Melville*. Boston: G. K. Hall, 1986. An overview of Melville's short fiction. Each chapter is divided into sections on a story's publication history, circumstances of composition, relationship to other works, profile of interpretive criticism, and bibliography.

Parker, Hershel. *Herman Melville: A Biography*. Vol. 1, 1819-1851, Vol. 2, 1851-1891. Baltimore: Johns Hopkins University Press, 1997-2002. This two-volume biography of Melville by the most distinguished authority on his life and art covers his life from birth in 1819, to the publication of *Moby Dick* in 1851, to his death in 1891. It is especially helpful on the early life of Melville and the controversies that arose from his early novel's being labeled obscene and blasphemous.

Robertson-Lorant, Laurie. *Herman Melville: A Biography*. New York: Clarkson Potter, 1996. Describes the personal, psychological, social, and intellectual aspects of Melville's life, as well as his travels and adventures in the South Seas and Europe.

Ryan, Steven T. "A Guide to Melville's 'Bartleby the Scrivener.'" In *A Companion to the American Short Story*, edited by Alfred Bendixen and James Nagel. Malden, Mass.: Wiley-Blackwell, 2010. A detailed analysis of the story, including discussion of the characters of Bartleby and the lawyer-narrator and the themes of communication and walls. Ryan notes that despite its title, the story is not a study of Bartleby but of the "justifiably unnamed" lawyer-narrator.

Scofield, Martin. "Herman Melville." In *The Cambridge Introduction to the American Short Story*. New York: Cambridge University Press, 2006. An overview and analysis of Melville's short fiction, including "Bartleby the Scrivener," "Paradise of Bachelors and Tartarus of Maids," and "The Bell-Tower."

Talley, Sharon. *Student Companion to Herman Melville*. Westport, Conn.: Greenwood Press, 2007. An introductory overview of Melville's life and works aimed at students and general readers. Includes chapters analyzing *The Piazza Tales* and other stories that Melville wrote for magazines.

Thompson, Graham. "The Rhetoric of the Office in Melville's 'Bartleby the Scrivener.'" In *Male Sexuality Under Surveillance: The Office in American Literature*. Iowa City: University of Iowa Press, 2003. Examines the boundaries of male friendship in Melville's story.

Updike, John. "The Appetite for Truth: On Melville's Shorter Fiction." *The Yale Review* 85 (October, 1997): 24-47. Discusses Melville's magazine short fiction of the mid-1850's, which Updike finds to be stiffer than Melville's earlier novels. Argues that as a novelist Melville was exalted by Shakespearean possibilities, but as a short-story writer he saw failure everywhere.

Joan DelFattore
Updated by Mary Rohrberger

LEONARD MICHAELS

Born: New York, New York; January 2, 1933
Died: Berkeley, California; May 10, 2003

PRINCIPAL SHORT FICTION

Going Places, 1969
I Would Have Saved Them If I Could, 1975
A Girl with a Monkey: New and Selected Stories,
    2000
The Collected Stories, 2007

OTHER LITERARY FORMS

Leonard Michaels is as well known for his 1981 novel *The Men's Club* as he is for his much admired short-story collections. He was also the author of the autobiographical *To Feel These Things: Essays* (1993) and the novel *Sylvia: A Fictional Memoir* (1992). *Shuffle* (1990) is a collection of essays and what Michaels called "autobiographical fiction." He collaborated with artist Frances Lerner on a coffee-table book entitled *A Cat* (1995), filled with almost one hundred observations about cats accompanied by Lerner's line drawings. After Michaels's death in 2003, *The Collected Stories* was published in 2007 and *The Essays of Leonard Michaels* appeared in 2009.

ACHIEVEMENTS

Leonard Michaels's first collection of stories, *Going Places,* was nominated for the National Book Award in 1969. He was a John Simon Guggenheim Memorial Foundation fellow in 1969 and a National Endowment for the Humanities fellow in 1970. He received a National Institute of Arts and Letters Award in Literature in 1971 and *The New York Times Book Review* Editor's Choice Award in 1975. His novel, *The Men's Club* was nominated for the American Book Award and the National Book Critics Circle Award in 1982.

BIOGRAPHY

Leonard Michaels was born in lower Manhattan on January 2, 1933, to Polish-Jewish immigrant parents; he grew up during the Depression in New York, where his father was a barber. He received his B.A. from New York University in 1953 and an M.A. in English literature from the University of Michigan in 1956. Michaels entered the Ph.D. program at the University of California at Berkeley, but later withdrew and moved back to Manhattan to devote his time to writing. During this time he married Sylvia Bloch, about whom he wrote a memoir, and made a living by teaching English classes at Paterson State College in Wayne, New Jersey.

After separating from his wife, who later committed suicide, Michaels went back to graduate school, this time at the University of Michigan, where he earned a Ph.D. in English and married Priscilla Older, with whom he had two sons. He published his first collection of short stories, *Going Places*, in 1969 while teaching English at the University of California at Davis; based on the reception for that book, he was hired to teach at the University of California, Berkeley. In 1977, Michaels divorced his second wife and married poet Brenda Lyn Hillman, with whom he had a daughter. In the late 1980's his third marriage also ended in divorce. Michaels wrote extensively about his marital difficulties in his fictional and autobiographical works. He died of cancer on May 20, 2003, at the age of seventy.

ANALYSIS

Leonard Michaels's stories are most often admired for his whimsical style. Reviewers admire Michael's fantastic plots and metaphorical style, which has been characterized as poetic realism. Combining fantasy and concrete realism, Michaels creates darkly terrifying worlds that keep readers laughing until they become appalled at what has made them laugh. As Michaels's recurring autobiographical persona, Phillip Leibowitz, encounters Conradian hearts of darkness and secret sharers in the jungle of New York City, he is always amazed at the mysterious multiplicity of the world around him.

"THE DEAL"

In this account of an encounter between a young woman and a group of fourteen- to fifteen-year-old boys over the woman's dropped glove, threat and tension shift back and forth between the boys and the young woman. The dangerous little dance between the woman and the gang (described by Michaels as a "monster of boys") begins harmlessly enough as she asks them if they have seen her dropped glove. The teasing game of "keep away" that the boys play shifts to a possible threat to the woman when she takes control by asking them what they want for the glove. Pushed to "make a deal," banter changes to barter as they demand ten dollars and she offers twenty-five cents.

The balance of power in the struggle shifts again when one of the boys demands a kiss for the return of the glove. Although she responds at first with nervousness, the woman switches to a businesslike tone as she agrees to the deal and goes with the boy to the doorway of her apartment. Female fear of male violence shifts to adolescent fear of female sexual power as the boy resists and is chided by the woman for being a chicken. The story shifts once more when after the kiss, the rest of the boys crowd into the doorway also demanding a kiss, pushing and shoving and knocking the woman down. The story ends with one of the leaders of the gang helping the woman open her door. When, once again reverting to a combination of childlike plea and male threat, he yells, "You give me something," she shuts the door in his face.

"MURDERERS"

Because of its combination of boyish Peeping-Tom comedy and horrifying, sexually stimulated violence, this has been Michaels's most anthologized story, appearing in contemporary American short-story anthologies edited both by Tobias Wolff and by Raymond Carver. The narrator of the story is Phillip Liebowitz, a young Jewish boy featured in a number of Michaels's stories, a preteen who, along with a small group of friends, climbs up to the roof of a building to watch a

bearded young rabbi and his sacramentally bald wife make love in their apartment across the way. As the boys become excited watching the couple, one begins to slide down the roof, his ring catching on a nail; while the ring finger remains, "the hand, the arm, the rest of him, were gone." At this point the rabbi sees them and calls out the window, "Murderers," shouting their names. The story ends abruptly with the boys being sent to a New Jersey camp overseen by World War II veterans.

A mere summary of the plot of the story does not convey its lyrical quality as the narrator, a grown man recollecting the event, places it within the context of coming-of-age and coming to terms with the terrible conjunctions that constitute human experience. He says that when the event occurred, he wanted "proximity to darkness, strangeness." Phillip considers the boys' voyeuristic observation of the rabbi and his wife the "beginning of philosophy." The rabbi he sees as "Mr. Life" as he dances to a rhumba on the phonograph, and the wife, with her many wigs, is for him "the world's lesson"; it little matters that one does not know what she "really" looks like, he says, for "what [i]s *reality*?" At the end of the story, Phillip lies in his bunkhouse listening to owls. Considering the mystery of the lessons he has learned about desire and death, mystery and danger, he listens to a sound he has never heard before, "the sound of darkness, blooming, opening inside you like a mouth."

"CITY BOY"

Second only to "Murderers" as an anthology favorite, "City Boy" also features Phillip Liebowitz, this time somewhat older and having sex with his girlfriend on the living room floor while the girl's parents sleep in the adjoining bedroom thirty feet away. Although the girl repeatedly says, "Phillip, this is crazy," he is so caught up in the encounter that he "burns" with the violence of it. Afterward, the two fall asleep, only to be awakened in the middle of the night by the girl's father who steps on Phillip's naked bottom in the dark.

The broad comedy of the encounter is emphasized by Phillip's reaction, springing "up like a frog out of the hand of a child"; he stands "spread-legged, bolt naked, great with eyes" face to face with the father, a sudden secret sharer, like two men "accidently met in hell." As the father threatens to kill him, Phillip runs out the door "naked as a wolf." The comedy increases as Phillip realizes that he needs poise, that without it the street was impossible; consequently he walks on his hands and pushes the elevator button with his toes, feeling he is in control of the situation. "I was a city boy," he thinks. "No innocent sh---kicker from Jersey. I was the A train, the Fifth Avenue bus. I could be a cop. My name was Phillip, my style New York City."

Thinking he can be cool, for a naked man is mysterious, Phillip goes out on the street, is turned away at the subway change booth, and runs into his girlfriend, who gives him his clothes and tells him that her father has had a heart attack and is in the hospital. As he accompanies her back to the apartment, Phillip feels as though he were in a trance, thinking, "This was life. Death!" When she gets a phone call that her father is going to be all right and that her mother is going to stay all night with him in the hospital, the story ends with her urging him to make love to her, as they "sank into the rug as if it were quicksand."

The fact that the story ends where it begins, with the primal sexual encounter, as if everything in between was inconsequential, suggests that this is another coming-of-age lesson for Phillip Leibowitz, who encounters in typically comic fashion basic elements of desire and danger. Being cast onto the city streets stark naked in the middle of the night is the ultimate comic image of vulnerability, punishment for transgressions, and the unaccommodated self.

OTHER MAJOR WORKS

LONG FICTION: *The Men's Club*, 1981; *Shuffle*, 1990; *Sylvia: A Fictional Memoir*, 1992.

PLAY: *City Boy*, pr. 1985.

SCREENPLAY: *The Men's Club*, 1986.

NONFICTION: *To Feel These Things: Essays*, 1993; *A Cat*, 1996; *Time Out of Mind: The Diaries of Leonard Michaels, 1961-1995*, 1999; *The Essays of Leonard Michaels*, 2009.

EDITED TEXTS: *The State of the Language*, 1980, 1990 (with Christopher Ricks); *West of the West: Imagining California*, 1989 (with Raquel Sheer and David Reid).

BIBLIOGRAPHY

DeCurtis, Anthony. "Self Under Siege: The Stories of Leonard Michaels." *Critique: Studies in Modern Fiction* 21 (1979): 101-111. Argues that in his first two collections of stories the most pressing problem Michaels's characters confront is maintaining their humanity in the face of the brutalization of modern life. Maintains his stories reveal the tenuous props that sustain continuity in the modern world. Discusses Michaels's imagery, his style, and his treatment of violence.

Ditsky, John. "A Men's Club: The Fiction of Leonard Michaels." *The Hollins Critic* 28 (December, 1991): 2-11. A survey of Michaels's work through *Shuffle*. Discusses autobiographical elements of his fiction, which Ditsky argues is energized by a tension between the academic intellectuality and indulgent sexuality embodied in his characters. Maintains that in Michaels's work sex becomes a language at odds with the purely verbal.

Donoghue, Denis. "Couples." *The New York Review of Books* 13 (July 10, 1969): 17-20. A review of *Going Places* in which Donoghue claims that the paradigm for Michaels's fiction is two people locked in violence, in which the people hardly matter except as conduits for the violence. Argues that the most powerful story in the collection, "The Deal," makes more stringent demands on the gothic genre than usual.

Lyons, Bonnie, and Bill Oliver. "An Interview with Leonard Michaels." *New England Review* 15 (Fall, 1993): 129-140. Michaels discusses his blurring of the lines between fiction and autobiography, his characters as embodiments of Jewish New York, and the influence of Isaac Babel on his fiction. He also comments on the frequent comparisons made between him and Philip Roth and the obligation writers have to speak the truth when writing about the Holocaust.

Michaels, Leonard. "My Yiddish." In *The Genius of Language: Fifteen Writers Reflect on Their Mother Tongues*, edited by Wendy Lesser. New York: Pantheon Books, 2004. Michaels meditates on Yiddish, his "mother tongue," describing the "Yiddish undercurrents" that are present in his English writings.

_____. *The Nachman Stories*. San Francisco: Arion Press, 2009. A posthumously published collection of Michaels's short stories featuring protagonist Raphael Nachman, a Los Angeles mathematician, some of which were included in previous collections. Also contains newly created critical and biographical essays by Robert Pinsky, Diana Ketchman, Morton Paley, and Robert Haas, as well as nine photographs of Michaels.

Segal, Lore. "Captivating Horrors." *The New Republic* 161 (July 19, 1969): 31-33. A review of *Going Places* that surveys several of the stories in the collection and concludes that the book poses the question of how it is possible to write about hideous things in a hilarious and beautiful way.

Simpson, Mona. "Proximity to Darkness." Review of *The Collected Stories*, by Leonard Michaels. *The New York Times Book Review*, June, 10, 2007, 14. Simpson, herself a short-story writer and novelists, reviews Michaels's short-fiction collection.

Woiwode, Larry. "Out of the Fifties." *Partisan Review* 44 (1977): 123-130. Fellow writer Woiwode praises *I Would Have Saved Them If I Could* as a mature, dense, complex work of fiction. Summarizing several of the stories in the collection, Woiwode notes Michaels's debt to Isaac Babel, Ernest Hemingway, Franz Kafka, and Samuel Beckett. Argues that Michaels's use of cultural figures, such as Sigmund Freud, Georg Wilhelm Friedrich Hegel, and Karl Marx, suggests that history pursues him.

Zweig, Paul. "Delicate Intentions." *Harper's Magazine* 251 (September, 1975): 68-69. Argues that in *I Would Have Saved Them If I Could*, Michaels uses a poet's twist to reduce civility to elements of sex, perverse daydreams, and inventive resentment. Calls the essaylike fragments in the book its thematic heart, placing it in the tradition of William Burroughs, Donald Barthelme, and Phillip Roth.

Charles E. May

SUE MILLER

Born: Chicago, Illinois; November 29, 1943

PRINCIPAL SHORT FICTION

"Given Names," 1981
"Leaving Home," 1982
"Tyler and Brina," 1985
"Calling," 1986
"The Lover of Women," 1986
Inventing the Abbotts, and Other Stories, 1987
"The Moms of Summer," 1991

OTHER LITERARY FORMS

Sue Miller's first novel *The Good Mother* was published in 1986 to effusive praise from many reviewers; it was on a number of best-seller lists for much of that year. Her second novel, *Family Pictures* (1990), also was a best seller; subsequent novels, *For Love* (1993) and *The Distinguished Guest* (1995), have generally been well received but not as enthusiastically as her first two. Miller has also written the novels *While I Was Gone* (1999), *The World Below* (2001), *Lost in the Forest* (2005), *The Senator's Wife* (2008), and *The Lake Shore Limited* (2010). In addition to her novels, she is the author of *The Story of My Father: A Memoir* (2003), in which she recounts her father's degeneration from Alzheimer's disease, and the editor of *Best American Short Stories 2002* (2003) and *Best New American Voices 2007* (2007).

ACHIEVEMENTS

Sue Miller's novel *Family Pictures* was nominated for the National Book Critics Circle Award in 1991. She received a Bunting Institute Fellowship from Radcliffe College, a McDowell Fellowship, and a John Simon Guggenheim Memorial Foundation Fellowship.

BIOGRAPHY

Sue Miller was born on the South Side of Chicago in 1943, into what she calls a family "ecclesiastical to its roots"; both grandfathers were preachers, and her father, also a minister, taught church history at the University of Chicago. She entered Radcliffe College at the age of sixteen and majored in history. By the time she was twenty, she had graduated and married a medical student. She taught high school English for a time, worked in a Head Start program, and was a cocktail waitress, a research assistant, and a model.

When her marriage failed, she supported her son as a preschool teacher and helped found the Harvard Day Care Center. She has said that one day she read a review of Robert Coover's first novel and was stunned because she remembered Coover as a boarder in her parent's basement apartment when he was a graduate student at the University of Chicago. "Suddenly," she says, "publishing a book was not such a remote thing."

In 1979, Miller attended the creative writing program at Boston University on a fellowship and began to publish stories in literary magazines; she also taught as an adjunct faculty member at Boston University, Tufts University, Emerson College, and the Massachusetts Institute of Technology. In 1983, she won a Bunting Fellowship at Radcliffe, during which time she finished half of *The Good Mother*. Her first novel was a best seller and in 1988 was made into a successful film staring Diane Keaton and Liam Neeson. Miller remarried, and she and her second husband, Douglas Bauer, settled in Boston. In 2008, she became a professor on English language at literature at Smith College.

ANALYSIS

Sex is the center of most of Sue Miller's short stories. In practically every story, men and women engage in quite explicitly described sex, but seldom is the act successful as a sign of intimacy and union. More often, whether Miller is describing sex from the point of view of a female or a male character, sex is an attempt at control or an act of desperate illusion. For example, the story "Slides" is structured around seven nude slides, which a woman's former husband photographed early in their marriage and have become irritating illusory images that get in the way of genuine intimacy. In

Miller's best-known story, "Inventing the Abbotts," a young man has sex with a wealthy young woman to try to climb the social ladder, while she has sex with him to rebel against her parents' control. In "Leaving Home," sex is a desperate attempt to hold on and hold things together.

One of the most fascinating aspects of Miller's short stories is her ability to assume the role of a male character and tell his story in the first person. Four of the eleven stories in *Inventing the Abbotts, and Other Stories*, including the title story, are told from the perspectives of male characters. This bit of gender ventriloquism has been all the more intriguing to readers because of the sexual drives of the men Miller creates as her personae. The effect on male readers is somewhat of a mild shock, as if one's gender secrets have been found out. As Jonathan Penner noted in a review of the collection, "When a female author employs a male viewpoint character to regard women, we are in a hall of mirrors, where sometimes we surprise or frighten ourselves."

"TYLER AND BRINA"

The central character in this story, Tyler, is a typical Miller male; the first two sentences delineate his central characteristic: "Tyler loved women. He was in love with women." Told in a straightforward, unadorned way, the story seems almost prototypical of a man who cannot resist women. What plot there is in the story centers on the disruption Tyler's obsession creates in his marriage to Brina. She wants a divorce and leaves him; he woos and pursues her; she gradually forgives him, accepting that he cannot help himself; he continues secretly to have sex with another woman; Brina moves back in with him; the other woman comes to the house; Brina sees her, and the story ends with Brina smashing the bottle of champagne she had bought to celebrate their reunion.

One side of Brina's face is dead, injured in a childhood accident. Miller uses this detail throughout the story as a metaphor to suggest that for her "some deep sorrow . . . lay under every fleeting joy." The metaphor allows Miller to evoke a striking conclusion to the story when Brina sees that Tyler will never change. She looks at him for a moment, the muscles shifting in the "live" side of her face, but when she turns, all he can see is the dead side, which shows a "vacant serenity as she looked down at the mess that lay around her feet." Brina will probably stay with Tyler, but she will have to turn her dead side to him and the world to make it possible.

"LEAVING HOME"

One of the shortest and most lyrical stories in *Inventing the Abbotts, and Other Stories*, "Leaving Home" is about a middle-aged woman, Leah, who has come to babysit for the young daughter of her son Greg and his wife Anita while they put on a twenty-fifth birthday party for Anita. Leah lives alone but has been seeing a man, enjoying her "long-awaited freedom, her claim to sexuality." The external conflict of the story is the friction in Greg and Anita's marriage, but the more significant emotional interest lies within Leah, who fears that Greg's marriage is going to fail and that he will lose not only his wife but also his daughter.

When Leah overhears Anita complaining to Greg about all the "mommy-daddy-baby" endless threesomeness of their life, she identifies with her daughter-in-law's lament that she does not exist as a woman

Sue Miller (Time & Life Pictures/Getty Images)

anymore, even as she resents the younger woman's self-centered disregard for her child and husband. The story ends with Leah overhearing Greg and Anita making love, but knowing that even though they still have sex it is not enough. Left with a sense of helplessness to guard her son against pain, she desires Joe, the man she has been seeing, for, like her son, she needs the "illusion of wholeness, of repair." The story poignantly portrays the difficulty of creating and sustaining intimacy when intimacy demands a sacrificial loss of self.

"INVENTING THE ABBOTTS"

Primarily because it was made into a 1997 Hollywood film, this is Miller's best-known short story. More like an abbreviated novel than a short story, the title story of Miller's collection focuses on the social-climbing desire of Jacey, a relatively poor young man, alternately, for the three Abbott sisters, who represent the wealthiest family in a small town. The narrator of the story is Jacey's younger brother Doug, who scorns the Abbotts and Jacey's social aspirations.

The story is a relatively conventional one, the basic conflicts arising from Jacey's sexual encounters with the Abbott sisters over the years and the Abbott family's socially snobbish reaction to those relationships. At a key point in the story, Jacey and Doug's mother, a working woman who raises her boys with good humor and common sense, tells Doug that if Jacey had not met the Abbotts, "he'd have had to invent them, one way or another." The story ends when, at Jacey and Doug's mother's funeral, the mother of the Abbott girls tells Jacey, "Well, I've no more daughters for you."

A recurring motif throughout the story is the theme of pretense or role-playing, something at which Doug is able to succeed more easily than Jacey. For example, early in the story, when Doug is first invited to one of the Abbotts' parties, he draws sideburns on his cheeks, like singer Elvis Presley, and Jacey refuses to go, saying that Doug will be the only one there "pretending to be someone else"; the mother simply tells Jacey to pretend he has never seen Doug before in his life. Near the end of the story, Doug, always on the fringes of Jacey's affairs, feels he is just "some bit actor in some part of their family drama." Later in the story when Doug goes off to Harvard University and becomes involved in theater groups, Doug feels he has chosen the right profession, saying, "I'm really much better at pretending than at being."

Throughout the story, the characters are involved in playing certain roles, yearning to be something they are not, and using others to achieve these goals. At first, while Jacey uses Eleanor Abbott to try to climb the social ladder, she uses him to rebel against her family. Later, when Doug falls in love with the oldest Abbott daughter, Alice, he feels she is using him for her own purposes. Finally, he has an affair with Phoebe, the youngest daughter, in an attempt to revenge himself for his ill treatment by the other sisters.

"Inventing the Abbotts" is derivative of a common F. Scott Fitzgerald theme--the attempt of a young man of modest means to leap across from one social class to another on the backs of wealthy young women. Jacey is not simply after money; for him the Abbott girls represent some sort of ideal; in fact, he tells his mother at one point, "Eleanor was just an *idea* I had." Originally entitled "The Lover of Women" when it appeared in *Mademoiselle*, the story is about a man who needs women, particularly young women unreachable because of their higher social class, in order to create an acceptable self-image.

OTHER MAJOR WORKS

LONG FICTION: *The Good Mother*, 1986; *Family Pictures*, 1990; *For Love*, 1993; *The Distinguished Guest*, 1995; *While I Was Gone*, 1999; *The World Below*, 2001; *Lost in the Forest*, 2005; *The Senator's Wife*, 2008; *The Lake Shore Limited*, 2010.

NONFICTION: *The Story of My Father: A Memoir*, 2003.

EDITED TEXTS: *Best American Short Stories 2002*, 2003; *Best New American Voices 2007*, 2007.

BIBLIOGRAPHY

Gussow, Mel. "Sue Miller Discovers a Trove of Domesticity." *The New York Times*, March 8, 1999, p. E1. This article, based on an interview and written on the occasion of the publication of Miller's novel *While I Was Gone*, provides a biographical sketch, discusses critical response to Miller's work, and comments on the novel's source in the life of Kath-

erine Ann Power, a 1960's activist involved in a robbery and the killing of a policeman in Boston.

Johnson, Sarah Anne. *Conversations with American Women Writers*. Hanover, N.H.:University Press of New England, 2004. In an interview entitled "Sue Miller: The Hot Dramas of the Domestic Scene," Miller describes her writing process, how she decides which point of view to use, her depiction of sex, her female characters, and other aspects of her work.

McNamara, Mary. "Authors--The People Behind the Books We Read." *Los Angeles Times*, April 14, 1999, p. E1. An interview-based article and discussion of Miller's *While I Was Gone*. Reacts against critics who characterize Miller's work as "domestic"; reviews her literary career; summarizes *While I Was Gone;* and provides a brief biographical sketch. Miller says she does not understand why she is perceived as a women's writer or a family writer, but she adds that at least women are still reading, asking: "Where are the people who were reading Philip Roth and Norman Mailer?"

Miller, Sue. Interview by Rosemary Herbert. *Publishers Weekly* 229 (May 2, 1986): 60-61. Miller discusses the evolution of her novel *The Good Mother* from a short story about a teenager's preoccupation with an aunt. She says she was dissatisfied with the simplistic answers of much postfeminist fiction and wished to trace the development of a woman who wanted to be someone other than who she became.

_____. "Virtual Reality: The Perils of Seeking a Novelist's Facts in Her Fiction." In *Writers on Writing: Collected Essays from The New York Times*. New York: Times Books, 2001. Miller's contribution to the series "Writers on Writing" focuses on the common reader question about how much of her fiction is autobiographical. Miller insists that writers can make a story out of anything and what is interesting about a story is not the thing that is in it, but what the writer makes of that thing; shaping is what writing is all about, she says, the struggle for meaning allowing the writer to "escape the tyranny of what really happened."

Penner, Jonathan. "Sense and Sensuality." *The Washington Post*, May 17, 1987, p. X9. In this review of *Inventing the Abbotts, and Other Stories*, Penner praises Miller for her ability to capture the male viewpoint, especially male sexual views of women. Singles out the stories "Tyler and Brina" and

"Leaving Home" for special praise, but argues that the title story, although the most ambitious, is too conversational and too engaged in summary and analysis.

Charles E. May

STEVEN MILLHAUSER

Born: New York, New York; August 3, 1943

PRINCIPAL SHORT FICTION

In the Penny Arcade, 1986
The Barnum Museum, 1990
Little Kingdoms: Three Novellas, 1993
The Knife Thrower, and Other Stories, 1998
Enchanted Night: A Novella, 1999
The King in the Tree: Three Novellas, 2003
Dangerous Laughter: Thirteen Stories, 2008

OTHER LITERARY FORMS

Edwin Mullhouse: The Life and Death of an American Writer, 1943-1954, by Jeffrey Cartwright, A Novel (1972) was Steven Millhauser's acclaimed debut novel. His next two novels, *Portrait of a Romantic* (1977) and *From the Realm of Morpheus* (1986), were less successful, to the point of relegating him to relative obscurity. *Martin Dressler: The Tale of an American Dreamer* (1996), however, restored his reputation; early collections of his short fiction were brought back into print, and new ones became easier to publish.

ACHIEVEMENTS

Martin Dressler won the Pulitzer Prize for fiction in 1997. Steven Millhauser received the Award in Literature from the American Academy of Arts and Letters in 1987 and earned a Lannan Fellowship. He also received a Prix Médicis Étranger in 1975, a World Fantasy Award in 1990, and a Lannan Literary Award for Fiction in 1994.

BIOGRAPHY

Steven Lewis Millhauser, like Edwin Mullhouse, the hero of his first novel, was born in early August of 1943, the son of a college English professor. As the events of that novel show, however, it is unwise to conflate the events of an author's life with those of his characters. When Millhauser unexpectedly won the Pulitzer Prize for his novel *Martin Dressler* in 1997, most news stories stressed Millhauser's deliberate avoidance of publicity, in a word, his shyness. Nevertheless, the salient features of his life can be noted.

Growing up in Connecticut, Millhauser wanted to be a writer from an early age. After receiving his undergraduate degree from Columbia University, he wrote fiction while living with his parents and working. He attended graduate school at Brown University, pursuing a Ph.D. in medieval and Renaissance studies, and he left after the success of his first novel. A series of academic appointments followed, including one at Skidmore College, where he shared a teaching position with his wife. He settled in Saratoga Springs with his wife and two children.

ANALYSIS

It seems clear enough at first where to place Steven Millhauser's short fiction. In its use of the fantastic and grotesque, it springs directly from the American tradition of Edgar Allan Poe and Nathaniel Hawthorne, with traces of Herman Melville. Millhauser's European forebears include E. T. A. Hoffmann and Franz Kafka; more recent international influences include Jorge Luis Borges and Vladimir Nabokov. That his work also coincides with that of other American postmodernists, such as Robert Coover and John Barth, is not surprising. His work, however, cannot be easily pigeonholed.

Like the writings of Borges and Nabokov, Millhauser's work is filled with doubles, slightly obtuse scholarly narrators, and at times a seemingly infinite series of regressions. The metafictional aspects of Borges's and Nabokov's work often leave readers feeling that they have missed out on some cosmic point or joke that only the authors and their acolytes share. In Millhauser's work, this layered effect gives his readers a sense of depth and a clear indication of the questions he is asking about the interrelationships among art, life, dreams, and reality. Similarly, the anguish that Kafka's characters undergo in his parables often seems too personal for readers to share; in Millhauser, such suffering arises not only out of the human condition but also out of the artistic dilemmas posed in so many of his stories. In short, Millhauser's fictional worlds, while often as mysterious as those of his predecessors, are both more accessible and more comprehensible--and admitting this removes none of their accompanying sense of wonder. His fantastic kingdoms, albeit rooted in reality, defamiliarize the mundane world of daylight and habit. Nevertheless, he is quite capable of writing the typically anthologized type of epiphanic, realistic short story, such as "A Protest Against the Sun" or "A Day in the Country."

Even though Millhauser has admitted that he often writes about "failures," they are often specifically American failures, who share a sense of vision with such quintessentially American figures as Thomas Edison and Walt Disney; his dreamers' machineries and domains are always doomed to failure, because they attempt to engulf and break down the borders between their experience and their dreams.

"August Eschenburg"

Some of Millhauser's most important stories are miniature portraits of the artist. This story is the first of these. Eschenburg is a designer and constructor of miniature automatons, and, like many of Millhauser's other artistic protagonists, explores with his lifelike creations the interstices between real life and the artificiality of the imagination; in Eschenburg's work, "realism itself [is] being pressed into the service of a higher law." Eschenburg's triumphs are overshadowed by

the successes of his artistic double (a characteristic Millhauser device), Hausenstein, whose figures are unabashedly sensual and satisfy the baser instincts of their audience. Thus it seems as if Hausenstein's appeal to the degraded tastes of the audience, the "Untermensch," as he calls them, has triumphed. Even as Eschenburg wanders out of the plot, the inner fire that led him to construct his analogues of life has not deserted him. "His ambition was to insert his dreams into the world, and if they were the wrong dreams, then he would dream them in solitude." He has failed, like so many of Millhauser's artistic protagonists, but he is not defeated.

"A Game of Clue"

One of the most striking aspects of Millhauser's short fiction is his ability to stretch the form by making a narrative out of unlikely subjects. In this case it is the juxtaposition of a normal, realistic narrative concerning four young people playing a popular board game with, in alternating paragraphs, descriptions of the actions of the well-known characters in that game, such as Colonel Mustard and Miss Scarlet. They and their surroundings are described with a scrupulousness bordering on the laborious. Even though the action "in" the game veers toward the licentious, as the Colonel attempts to seduce Miss Scarlet, the action is also paradoxically moving toward a sense of stasis. The mansion itself becomes a characteristic Millhauser edifice, with a series of rooms and secret passages branching off into labyrinthine infinity. The human characters playing the game are also trapped in a sense of stasis, as they silently wonder about their present problems and their futures: playing the game provides a balm, "a spot of time," as it were. A chance passerby looks on the game "and feels a yearning so deep that he wants to cry out in anguish, though in fact he continues steadily, even cheerfully, on his way."

"The Little Kingdom of Franklin J. Payne"

Franklin Payne is the first of Millhauser's early twentieth century American dreamers. His career loosely resembles that of pioneering American cartoonist Winsor McCay. Payne begins as an illustrator for that favorite site of Millhauser, the dime museum. Becoming an editorial cartoonist, Payne also draws comic strips, in which he explores the boundaries of reality and the imagination. When his characters become too unconstrained, deconstructing the panels that enclose them, they feel "a craving for the lines and shadows of the actual world." Payne soon meets his artistic double, Max Horn, whose own work is derivative and characterless. When Payne begins creating his own silent black-and-white cartoons, Horn, Disney-like, sets up his own assembly-line cartoon studio, which Payne rejects. His laborious technique of drawing each frame individually gives "the shimmer of a dream" to his work. Max ends up stealing Payne's wife, but he cannot steal Payne's soul. Payne's last work ends with his main character erasing himself; even though reality must be served, it is imperative

> to smash through the constriction of the actual, to unhinge the universe and let the impossible stream in, because otherwise--well, otherwise the world was nothing but an editorial cartoon.

"CATALOGUE OF THE EXHIBITION"

This portrait of the artist is presented in the form of a catalog commentary on the works the artist has created. Millhauser's triumph is to create a completely fictitious yet nonetheless highly believable major nineteenth century American painter. However, unlike Eschenburg's automatons or Payne's cartoons, Moorash's work is not grounded in realism; he is, according to Millhauser, a sort of American J. M. W. Turner--his paintings are romantically, fantastically abstract. Many of Millhauser's artists inhabit both the mundane day and the transfigured night, but Moorash is totally an inhabitant of the night. In his work "the world and the dreamer intermingle and dissolve." Moorash's menage echoes William Wordsworth's in England's Lake District: He lives with his sister, with whom he is uncomfortably close. The plot is out of Poe via Nabokov. Not only is Moorash doubled in the character of William Pinney, but also his sister is duplicated in Pinney's sister. As the catalog progresses, Moorash's work becomes more fantastic: "It is as if only by smashing what he once called 'the mimetic fetters' that Moorash could release into paint the human mystery." While others of Millhauser's artists walk into the sunset, the ending of this unabashedly romantic artist is suitably lurid and melodramatic.

THE KNIFE THROWER, AND OTHER STORIES

Millhauser's collection of stories shows him moving further away from the classic realistic mode of the short story. Some stories at first resemble that mode, such as "The Visit," in which the narrator visits an old friend, but the story soon takes a turn toward John Collier's *His Monkey Wife* (1930) as the friend turns out to be married to a large frog, who shows no sign of becoming a princess. Many of the stories are communally narrated, as a voice known only as "we" wonders what the young girls in the town are doing ("The Sisterhood of Night") or describes subterranean passageways ("Beneath the Cellars of Our Town").

The most significant stories in the collection characteristically concern artists, and in each case, Millhauser's vision has grown darker. In the title story, the knife thrower deliberately and artfully wounds his target, culminating in death. The theme is subtly linked to current American preoccupations with violence: "If such performances were encouraged, if they were even tolerated, what might we expect in the future?" "The New Automaton Theater" is a development of "August

Steven Millhauser (AP Photo/HO)

MILLHAUSER, STEVEN   *Critical Survey of Short Fiction*

Eschenburg," but the artist, Graum, deliberately enhances the artificiality of his creations and invites the audience to become one with them: "We yearn to mingle with these strange newcomers, to pass into their clockwork lives." Such a dissolution, the story hints, would be "terrifying." In "Paradise Park," Charles Sarabee, creator-designer of an early twentieth century amusement park, must resort to ever-increasing thrills to lure his audience. He becomes a modern Pied Piper, working toward "a magical or mystical park from which the unwary visitor would never return." In the dreams of Millhauser's artists begin not responsibilities but an escape from them, and his work increasingly identifies their siren-song lure and danger.

THE KING IN THE TREE: THREE NOVELLAS

"Listen. I'll tell you a story," innocently begins a recent widow, who is showing her home to a potential buyer. If this story is entitled "Revenge" and it is by Millhauser, the reader knows that it will be anything but innocent. As soon as the two enter the living room, the reader learns that the widow's husband had been having an affair; by the time the reader gets to the kitchen, he or she knows that the "other woman" is the potential buyer. The question that hovers over this extended monologue, which follows the silent buyer and the increasingly manic seller through each room of a house haunted by ghosts of betrayal, is where the revenge will take place. With poetic justice in the bedroom? In the attic among mementos of the widow's marriage? In the basement, where bodies are always buried? However, Millhauser--in the tradition of Poe, Hoffman, Borges, and Italo Calvino--has no simple act of violence in mind. In the end, it is the story itself that constitutes the only just revenge.

The most literary fiction in *The King in the Tree* is "An Adventure of Don Juan." Not an account of merely one more seduction, but rather a story about the great Lothario's growing boredom with easy conquests, the haunting decay of Venice, and his visit with an acquaintance, Augustus Hood, on his grand estate in the Arcadian beauty of the English countryside. There Don Juan meets a new challenge, the beautiful Georgiana, sister to Hood's wife, who is immune to the archetypal seducer's charms. Don Juan finds himself so drawn that he becomes, for the first time, sick with love. This is not, however, just a story of the woman Don Juan cannot have. There is also a secret behind the English-garden artifices of Hood, a man who lives in a world of contrivance and "skillful illusions." In the end, it is as though the Byronic hero happens upon the secret underworld of Percy Bysshe Shelley--an encounter that sends Don Juan back to the bridges and gondolas of Venice.

Millhauser's title story is a tour-de-force version of one of the great love stories of all time: the tale of Tristan, Queen Ysolt, and the tormented King of Cornwall. Told by Thomas, the king's faithful counselor, this is a classic fable of infidelity, jealousy, and court intrigue--complete with a beautiful queen, a handsome knight, an Iago-like chief steward, a demonic dwarf named Modor, and a claustrophobic world of lust, lies, alliances, betrayals, play-acting, whispers, mutilation, and murder. Because action in such a realm always turns back on itself, the reader may at times feel that the story goes on too long--as the king becomes suspicious, discovers all, seeks revenge, changes his mind, reconciles, only to suspect and seek revenge again. In the fictional world of Millhauser, there are always two parts to every action: the seemingly straightforward, visible one and the convoluted inward one, which is its true meaning. Millhauser is a brilliant romantic, for whom surface reality is merely an uninteresting illusion and ultimate reality is always artifice.

DANGEROUS LAUGHTER

While most short-story writers in the last three decades joined the realist rebellion against the fabulism of the 1970's, Millhauser stayed true to the fantastic tradition that extends from Poe and Kafka and thence to Borges, Barth, and Donald Barthelme--playfully and powerfully exploring the freedom of the imagination to reject the ordinary world of the merely real and explore the incredible world of purely aesthetic creation. Although the thirteen stories in *Dangerous Laughter* are divided into three categories--Vanishing Acts, Impossible Architectures, and Heretical Histories--they are united by the romantic quest for transcendence. Even the opening cartoon narrative, which uses fast-paced present tense to create the illusion that you are watching a Tom and Jerry animation, concludes with erasure of the physical and the reinstatement of illusion.

1190

The stories in the first group are intriguing in their transformation of the mundane into the miraculous. "The Disappearance of Elaine Coleman" is not a simple crime story. When the narrator and his former high school classmates look Coleman up in their yearbook, they cannot recall her, finally understanding that she did not suddenly disappear but rather gradually became more and more invisible. That the drive to transcend can begin in the most ordinary ways and lead to the most terrible results is explored in "Dangerous Laughter," a story of how, pushed to extremes, any activity can become both obsessive and powerfully significant. It begins with adolescents laughing at little until the laughing becomes an end in itself, part of the "kingdom of forbidden things."

The stories in the Impossible Architectures group, although similar to previous Millhauser stories about artificial and enclosed worlds, are less compelling. "The Dome" begins with transparent domes that cover houses, which then develop into larger domes to cover neighborhoods and then towns, until the entire country and then the world is transformed into a giant mall. Encountering a Millhauser story entitled "The Tower," the reader can guess that the issue is "How high?" Millhauser's trope explores the complications and implications of religious desire, but it is just too mechanical a metaphor. The Heretical Histories section presents stories about two "might-have-been" inventions that could have transformed the way people experience "reality." In "A Precursor of the Cinema," Harlan Crane, a late nineteenth century painter, creates a pigment that reproduces the object so faithfully that it actually moves on the canvas--a forerunner to current experiments with holographic images. In "The Wizard of West Orange," one of Edison's researchers creates a device called a haptograph, a wired suit which, when put on, simulates various sensations of touch and, significantly, creates new ones. However, the device's promise of revelation, transformation, and transcendence dooms it, for the ever-practical Edison knows it will never bring in profits. Millhauser's stories are not mere ingenuity; he is motivated by the same obsessions that drove William Blake--to see a world in a grain of sand and to affirm that the road of excess leads to the palace of wisdom.

OTHER MAJOR WORKS

LONG FICTION: *Edwin Mullhouse: The Life and Death of an American Writer, 1943-1954, by Jeffrey Cartwright, A Novel*, 1972; *Portrait of a Romantic*, 1977; *From the Realm of Morpheus*, 1986; *Martin Dressler: The Tale of an American Dreamer*, 1996.

BIBLIOGRAPHY

Alexander, Danielle, Pedro Ponce, and Alicita Rodríguez. *Review of Contemporary Fiction* 26 (Spring, 2006): 7-76. Long summary article covering Millhauser's fiction up through publication of *The King in the Tree*. This special issue on Millhauser also features an article on his novel *Martin Dressler* and his short story "Revenge," from *The King in a Tree*.

Byatt, A. S. "Reports from the Edge of Reality." *Washington Post Book World*, June 14, 1998, p. X1. A penetrating review of *The Knife Thrower, and Other Stories* by a fiction writer who explores much of the same territory as Millhauser does. Compares him to Hawthorne, Hoffmann, and Kafka.

Fowler, Douglas. "Steven Millhauser, Miniaturist." *Critique* 37 (Winter, 1996): 139-149. Places Millhauser firmly in the postmodernist tradition of Barthelme. Finds Millhauser "a fabulist disguised as a realist and a parodist."

Howe, Irving. "An Afterword." *Salmagundi* 92 (Fall, 1991): 110-114. An admittedly swift evaluation of "Catalogue of the Exhibition" by the eminent critic, who finds the story "a masterpiece." "The subject may be Romantic, the treatment is not." Contains an interesting note by Millhauser about his intentions.

Kinzie, May. "Succeeding Borges, Escaping Kafka: On the Fiction of Steven Millhauser." *Salmagundi* 92 (Fall, 1991): 115-144. Despite its title, this essay concentrates on Millhauser's second story collection, *The Barnum Museum*. Finds Borges's influence on Millhauser much stronger than Kafka's.

Millhauser, Steven. "Steven Millhauser: The Business of Dreaming." Interview by Jennifer Schuessler. *Publishers Weekly* (May 6, 1996): 56-57. One of the few interviews that Millhauser has given.

William Laskowski
Updated by Charles E. May

SUSAN MINOT

Born: Manchester, Massachusetts; December 7, 1956

PRINCIPAL SHORT FICTION
  Monkeys, 1986
  Lust, and Other Stories, 1989
  "Green Glass," 1991
  "House of Women," 1991
  "Japanese Lanterns," 1992

OTHER LITERARY FORMS

After the release of her first two collections of short fiction, Susan Minot (MIN-iht) published the novels *Folly* (1992), *Evening* (1998), and *Rapture* (2002). She collaborated with director Bernardo Bertolucci to write the screenplay for the film *Stealing Beauty* (1996); she and Michael Cunningham adapted her novel *Evening* for a film released in 2007. Minot has also written travel articles and an *Esquire* essay, "No Woman Is Convinced of Her Beauty." Her first volume of poetry, *Poems 4 A.M.*, appeared in 2002.

ACHIEVEMENTS

Susan Minot's short-story collection *Monkeys* was awarded the Prix Fémina Étranger and has been optioned for a film; her short fiction has also received an O. Henry Award and the Pushcart Prize, and her stories have been anthologized in *The Best American Short Stories.* In 1994, she was named *Victoria* magazine's first writer-in-residence.

BIOGRAPHY

Susan Minot was born in a north Boston suburb and grew up in a family of seven children that bears a strong resemblance to the one portrayed in *Monkeys.* She attended preparatory school at Concord Academy, where she worked on the school's literary magazine and spent summers with her family in North Haven, Maine. After beginning her college career at Boston University, Minot transferred to Brown University, where she studied creative writing and art, earning her B.A. in 1978. During her senior year, her mother was killed in a car accident; after graduation, she returned home to care for her father and youngest sister.

Minot earned an M.F.A. in 1983 from Columbia University, where she began writing the stories that would be collected in *Monkeys.* While attending Columbia she worked as an editorial assistant for *The New York Review of Books* (1981) and as an assistant editor for *Grand Street* (1982 to 1986), whose editor Ben Sonnenberg had published her first story, "Hiding." Before committing herself to writing full time, Minot worked as a carpenter, waitress, Greenpeace canvasser, and bookseller. After the critical success of *Monkeys,* she retreated to a small village in Tuscany for a brief sojourn, during which she wrote many of the pieces in *Lust, and Other Stories.* She married filmmaker Davis McHenry in 1988, and they made their home in New York, where she occasionally teaches writing workshops at Columbia.

ANALYSIS

In an eloquently understated style, Susan Minot explores the enigmas of familial and romantic love under stress. Her short-story cycle *Monkeys* focuses on the tensions within a large patrician family, whose mother provides a model of how to maintain love and joy in the midst of a troubled marriage. Even as the anxieties of adolescence, the growing need to express independence, and loss threaten family unity, new rituals and allegiances can work to mitigate and even transcend these forces. Her depictions of heterosexual relationships in *Lust, and Other Stories* are less optimistic, however, as her female protagonists exhibit problems in coping with the gulf between their stirrings of desire and its romantic fulfillment in ongoing relationships. Searching for commitment, they discover male attachment to be ephemeral and warily enter subsequent relationships emotionally wounded, seemingly fated to repeat self-destructive patterns.

Minot's family portrait in *Monkeys* has been likened to J. D. Salinger's Glass family, and her stories are clearly influenced by *The New Yorker* school of fiction. Her careful, polished, and somewhat understated style is marked by descriptive economy and a skillful use of detail, both of which provide oblique glimpses of her characters and develop ideas by implication. She notes that many of her stories begin in images and concurred with one interviewer's observation that her work contains numerous images of hiding and secrets.

With her 1998 novel *Evening*, Minot noted that she had diverged from the direction of her previous work, moving toward exploring material she had sought out "rather than a sorting through of material or concerns which life had presented me." The focus in her short fiction on the latter issues, however, has resulted in finely nuanced stories that exactingly anatomize the perplexities of uncertain relationships, whose contours are subtly shaped by influences of family and gender.

MONKEYS

Monkeys, although labeled a novel by some critics, is a collection of nine interrelated stories--seven of which were previously published in *The New Yorker* and *Grand Street*. Singly, each story conveys a significant incident that threatens the precarious unity of a large, privileged New England family; together the stories chronicle the ebb and flow of that coherence, which threatens to undergo dissolution when the mother, who has served as its nucleus, dies.

Rose Vincent, the mother whose nickname for her children provides the collection's title, provides love and continuity as she devises strategies to adapt to her husband Gus's alcoholism. Gus is most often flummoxed by, distracted by, or indifferent to his active brood, although he must ultimately take charge after Rose's death two-thirds of the way through the volume. The stories' most frequent point of view is that of Sophie, the second daughter, although other stories are related in the third person or through the eyes of other family members, all struggling to discover themselves, while at the same time maintain the ties that knit them together.

"Hiding," the volume's best story, artfully depicts the family's typical routine, with Gus characteristically aloof from its Sunday morning chaos before church. Later, on a skating excursion, the parents' differences are highlighted in their styles on the ice: Gus, a former Harvard University hockey player, powers determinedly in strong straight lines, while Rose, a former figure skater, glides stylishly in figure eights, which the impatient Gus fails to appreciate. Back home, Rose leads the children in an impromptu game of hiding from their father; his failure to seek them out, however, leaves Rose to hide her disappointment from the children in a sudden burst of domestic activity.

Subsequent stories foreshadow the breaches in the family that will widen as the children mature: In "Thanksgiving Day," a holiday dinner at the grandparents' home goes awry as Gus's father's memory fails and his temper flares. "Allowance" sketches a family vacation during which Gus's drinking, impatience with the children, and inability to leave work behind similarly spoil the family holiday. Little wonder that in "Wildflowers," the children perceive Rose's adoration of vacation neighbor Wilbur Kittredge, although the story's final scene depicts her more overwhelming exhilaration with motherhood.

In "Party Blues," Sophie's concluding memory of the aura of safety she relished as a child in the story "Madeline" contrasts with the confusion and chaos that adolescent love, alcohol, and drugs create during a party she and her siblings throw in their parents' absence--one which emulates the parties from which her parents have withdrawn as Gus's alcoholism has worsened. Danger of a return to this pattern in "The Navigator" provokes intervention by Gus's children, who may harbor some hope that his former abilities at a ship's helm will carry over into the family. Although some hope momentarily emerges that he will regain such capabilities, the story concludes with the dramatic shattering of a tranquil family picnic by the sound of his opening a can of beer.

While the "Accident" announced in the climactic story's title initially refers to son Sherman's drunk driving, the car accident that claimed Rose Vincent's life six months before is behind the family's current turmoil. With no mother to comfort him and a father who will not step forward to assume authority, Sherman's ache culminates in a wail that signals the danger of breakdown and despair. After the family muddles through the first Christmas after Rose's death in the penultimate story, "Wedlock," the volume concludes with the award-winning story "Thorofare," in which a provisional unity results after Gus takes the helm and leads the family on an improvised ceremony to dispose of Rose's ashes--a year and a half after her death. Illustrating individual style with a common purpose, each family member scatters a handful of ashes in a moving farewell. On shore, they regroup in an order that emulates their lineup in youth--a unity that is as evocative and promising as it is transitory, a loose coherence similar to the form of the collection as a whole.

LUST, AND OTHER STORIES

Minot's 1989 collection, *Lust, and Other Stories*, which contains twelve stories divided evenly into three sections, traces the curve of male-female relationships from early attraction through incipient breakups to the aftermath, when despair and desperation lead to the initiation of new relationships. Her female protagonists' instincts lead them in directions contrary to fulfillment, toward self-centered and distracted men threatened by commitment. The collection received somewhat mixed reviews, with *The New York Times Book Review* praising it as "superbly organized, poignant, and profound" and noting how the stories resonate and progressively accumulate meaning. *Time* magazine remarked that Minot's eye for "clinching detail" was less acute than in earlier short fiction and that the collection exhibited sameness in its focus on unmarried people in their thirties in "modish urban lofts and restaurants."

"Lust" opens the volume with an assembly of vignettes concerning sensuality and passionate encounters, where betrayal by the senses and by the male partners the narrator chooses seems inevitable. She melts easily into sensual abandon, although the results of her encounters gradually shift from erotic bliss and relief to the feeling that she is "sinking in muck," surrendering to sadness after desire is consummated and her partners disregard her. Passion thus gives way to ennui, and ultimately wary defensiveness: "You open your legs but can't, or don't dare anymore, to open your heart." Subsequent stories carry forward the same theme, as their protagonists drift

through relationships with abandon, often ending up like Ellen in "City Life," who "felt like something washed ashore after a shipwreck" after succumbing to a perfunctory seduction.

The slighter stories of the middle section project an autumnal ambience, as indifferent men seeking to maintain their emotional distance close down relationships before they become too involved. In "The Feather in the Toque," a bird that has unwittingly flown into the house becomes the metaphor for the girl who makes plans to extricate herself from such static relationships, with her only satisfaction being her plan to leave behind some small item as a warning to the next woman that others have preceded her.

"The Knot," which sketches the dissolution of a relationship through a series of conversational vignettes, is typical of the final group of stories. While the man is unable to provide the woman with the concentrated attention she desires and accuses her of craving unhappiness, even after they separate and establish equilibrium in new relationships, she discovers that her attraction to him still remains. "A Thrilling Life" perhaps best depicts Minot's female characters' tendency to seek men who will inevitably fall short of their hopes, even in the aftermath of a relationship that has failed for similar reasons. As the story's narrator confesses, her partner, Frank Manager,

> was not a candidate for the long run. He might just as well have been wearing a banner which said FRIVOLITY. . . . It was just what I was looking for.

Intrigued by his thrilling life, his tendency to be easily annoyed, and the rage that lurks beneath his charm, she sets herself up for jealousy and disappointment, even as she attempts to reason away her emotions and expect less.

Ultimately, Minot's female characters resign themselves to fatalistic acceptance that desire's vagaries will lead them astray, deluding themselves--as does the narrator of "The Man Who Would Not Go Away"--that they can settle for "one of those loose easy things." Thus, they drift through relationships, emotionally wounded and perpetually unfulfilled. As "dispatches from the sexual wars," *Time*'s reviewer remarks, Minot's stories show that "the news is not good for either side."

OTHER MAJOR WORKS

LONG FICTION: *Folly*, 1992; *Evening*, 1998; *Rapture*, 2002.

POETRY: *Poems 4 A.M.*, 2002.

SCREENPLAYS: *Stealing Beauty*, 1996; *Evening*, 2007 (based on her novel; with Michael Cunningham).

BIBLIOGRAPHY

Minot, Susan. "Interview with Susan Minot." Interview by Robley Wilson. *Short Story*, n.s. 2, no. 1 (1994): 112-118. Minot discusses her early experiences with writing, as well as the influence of early reading in Ernest Hemingway, F. Scott Fitzgerald, William Butler Yeats, William Faulkner, and J. D. Salinger. After experimenting briefly with metafiction, she discovered that it was not her "natural bent." She reviews her early career and experiences in Columbia's M.F.A. program, as well as the influence of New York City in stimulating her writing. Minot confirms the presence of numerous images of hiding in her work and comments on the relation they might have to her growing up in a large family.

_____. "Susan Minot: Understatement Is the Novelist's Preference, in Her Writing as Well as in Her Conversation." Interview by Marcelle Thiebaux. *Publishers Weekly* 16 (November, 1992): 42-43. Minot discusses her novel *Folly*, set in the patrician world she "always resisted" and her identification with her protagonist, who clings foolishly but bravely to slavish adoration of a man who spurned her. She comments on her "decorative" painting and her understated style. After remarking about her writing routine and future projects, Minot concludes, "There's more fictional material in unhappiness and disappointment and frustration than there is in happiness."

Nagel, James. "Susan Minot's *Monkeys* and the Cycle Paradigm." In *The Contemporary American Short-Story Cycle: The Ethnic Resonance of Genre*. Baton Rouge: Louisiana State University Press, 2001. Nagel seeks to define and examine the contemporary short-story cycle, analyzing eight works, including *Monkeys*, that were praised by critics but misidentified as novels. He argues that this genre, which features concentric instead of linear plot development, lends itself particularly well to themes of ethnic assimilation.

Picker, Lauren. "Talking with Susan Minot: A Private Affair." *Newsday* 15 (November, 1992): 34. Minot notes how her stories begin in images and reflects upon the genesis of her novel *Folly* in a vision of a woman on her deathbed. Though unwilling to discuss her private life in interviews, she recalls how success generated expectations that affected her relationship with her work. She concludes by contrasting the more focused and intense form of the short story with the novel, which depicts a larger world, in which one can live.

Pryor, Kelli. "The Story of Her Life: Writer Susan Minot Begins a New Chapter." *New York* 12 (June, 1989): 52-55. Pryor reviews Minot's career and praises *Monkeys* for its "coiled, understated language," "meticulous rendering of childhood," and "painful penchant for detail." She contrasts the "grand loss" of the mother depicted in *Monkeys* with *Lust*'s focus on "desire's smaller wounds." Minot notes how happiness is a "constant struggle" and "just does not last."

Smith, Dinitia. "The Minots: A Literary Clan Whose Stories Divide Them." *The New York Times*, May 27, 2004, p. 1. Recounts the literary efforts of Minot and her siblings. After Minot published *Monkeys*, some family members maintained that her portrait of an alcoholic father was an insult to her own father. Since then, her sister Eliza Minot and her brother George Minot have written their own fictional works based upon family experiences.

Robert M. Luscher

RICK MOODY

Born: New York, New York; October 18, 1961

PRINCIPAL SHORT FICTION

The Ring of Brightest Angels Around Heaven, 1995
Demonology, 2000
Right Livelihoods: Three Novellas, 2007

OTHER LITERARY FORMS

Before publishing his three collections of short fiction, Rick Moody had established a name as a novelist, publishing *Garden State* in 1991 and later *The Ice Storm,* the novel for which he remains best known, in 1994. *The Ice Storm* was later adapted for film and won best screenplay at the Cannes Film Festival in 1997. In addition to fiction writing, Moody also coedited *Joyful Noise: The New Testament Revisited* (1997), and in 2002 he published his most personal work, *The Black Veil: A Memoir with Digressions*, to critical acclaim.

ACHIEVEMENTS

Rick Moody's career began upon winning the Pushcart Press Editors Book Award for his novel *Garden State* in 1991; as a result, the novel was published the following year. Soon after that, critics took notice of Moody's short fiction. The title story of his first collection, *The Ring of Brightest Angels Around Heaven*, received the Aga Khan Award from *The Paris Review* in 1994, and in 1997 the title story from his second collection of fiction, *Demonology*, was awarded the O. Henry Prize. Moody went on to earn the American Academy of Arts and Letters' Addison Metcalf Award in 1998, and in 2000 Moody was awarded a Guggenheim Fellowship. His nonfiction also garnered success; his memoir, *The Black Veil*, earned the NAMI/Ken Book Award and the PEN Martha Albrand prize for memoir in 2002. His fourth novel, *The Diviners*, received the Mary Shelley Award in 2005.

BIOGRAPHY

Rick Moody was born Hiram Frederick Moody III in New York City in 1961 to parents Hiram F. Moody, Jr., and Margaret Maureen Davis. Soon after, his family relocated to the quiet, upper-class suburbs of Connecticut, where Rick Moody spent his boyhood. Throughout the years to come, Moody lived in various northeastern cities, an environment often reflected in the settings of his short stories and novels.

Moody was born into a family of book collectors and storytellers (his parents were both avid readers and his grandfather was a well-known publisher of the *New York Daily News*), and consequently his love for reading bloomed early. Moody admits to being a shy and quiet child. It was through the act of writing stories that he built his confidence; by the sixth grade

Rick Moody (AP Photo/Jeff Geissler)

he had begun the task of writing two novels, works he later abandoned.

While attending the prominent St. Paul's Academy in New Hampshire, Moody began his first serious attempts as a writer, penning the first of his stories and ultimately deciding to pursue writing as a career. He went on to attend Brown University, where he developed his craft under such teachers as John Hawkes, Robert Coover, and Angela Carter and where he began to experiment daringly with language and prose; these experiments evolved to become visible later in much of his short fiction. In 1983, Moody earned a degree in English from Brown and continued his studies at Columbia University, where he earned an M.F.A. in 1986.

After graduating, Moody began a career in publishing, working first as an editorial assistant for Simon and Schuster and later for Farrar, Straus and Giroux as an associate editor. In the midst of his accomplishments, however, Moody wrestled with personal demons and the lingering effects of his parents' painful divorce in 1970, and during these years he suffered depression and substance abuse. In 1987, he admitted himself briefly to a rehabilitation facility for treatment.

After years of struggling to become published, Moody found his career taking a positive turn. Upon leaving the world of publishing in 1991, Moody entered the field of teaching, finding an appointment at Bennington College in Vermont. His first novel, *Garden State*, was discovered and at last earned Moody a name as a novelist. Soon after, with the publication of *The Ice Storm*, Moody found himself firmly established in the literary community. Moody has continued to publish fiction and to work as an editor and a contributor to various projects and publications. He settled in Brooklyn, New York.

ANALYSIS

Rick Moody has established himself as one of the most talented writers of the late twentieth and early twenty-first centuries, among such authors as David Foster Wallace, Jonathan Franzen, and Michael Chabon, a generation of writers establishing the direction of contemporary American fiction. Although often hailed by critics as a modern-day John Cheever, Moody admits that he has been most influenced by the work of Saul Bellow, Thomas Pynchon, and notably Don DeLillo.

Moody's work often is difficult to categorize in one literary classification: His work ranges from traditional narratives to innovative linguistic experiments that challenge readers' expectations of structure and form. As demonstrated in his novel *The Ice Storm*, Moody has a reputation for exploring the lives of emotionally unhappy characters, who, dissatisfied and unfulfilled with their personal relationships, struggle to make some meaning out of their existence. Typically, his work offers no clear-cut answers to the problems characters suffer; there is often no catharsis. Similar characteristics also pervade his short stories, where characters struggle with the complexities of human emotion, with love and loss, with grief and depression, with addictions and disappointed lives.

What sets his collections of short fiction apart from his novels is Moody's inventive, at times perplexing experimentation with language, narrative structure, and voice. Moody defies the reader's expectations of narrative form and even his or her anticipations of the act of storytelling; the reader is always aware of the text, of its structure and limits. Moody's short stories are often more "experiments" than plot-driven narratives, and for this Moody has been both praised and criticized. Some critics claim that his employment of language works against plot and character development, resulting in a lack of emotional investment on the part of the reader.

For Moody, however, language and the ways in which language can be manipulated, formed, limited, and constrained are essential parts of the storytelling process. The language itself is the story, the means of revealing, expressing, sharing, and decoding human experience

Moody's first collection, *The Ring of Brightest Angels Around Heaven*, defies the standard conventions of storytelling. As some critics have argued, the stories are more involved with the exploration of ideas than with the unfolding of plot. At times the stories are darkly humorous, such as "Preliminary Notes," in which an emotionally detached narrator decides to record his wife's telephone calls, chronicling them neatly into a series of notes that slowly reveal the disintegration of his marriage. Other stories are more perplexing, such as the concluding story, "Primary Sources," in which Moody becomes a kind of text, as he prepares a personal annotated bibliography of various works that together create a portrait of Moody himself. He revisits this strategy in a later story, "Wilkie Fahnstock: The Boxed Set," from *Demonology*. This story is organized into two columns: One side details a man's life; the other side is a list of mixed tapes and playlists that create a character sketch of a man who is otherwise insignificant and unknown. The title story, a novella, is the centerpiece of the collection, and in it a voyeuristic narrator offers glimpses into the empty lives of various misfits, drug addicts, and sexual deviants as they struggle to cope with alienation, betrayal, and loss.

Moody's fractured and disjointed narratives are often vehicles for his characters who struggle with death and loss. This is a central theme to Moody's second collection of short fiction, *Demonology*, which is book-ended and punctuated by stories in which the characters must grapple with grief in all its strange manifestations. In the first and last stories, narrators suffer the death of a sister, and both offer their own elegies. Other stories in the collection (such as "Hawaiian Nights" and "The Double Zero") also share the theme of loss of a loved one.

Demonology continues with Moody's trademark experiments. Several of the stories are approached as assignments, on which Moody has imposed specific limits: In "Boys," virtually each sentence contains the words "boys" and "home." "Drawer" is composed of 650 words exactly, a limit that Moody took great pains to accomplish. "Ineluctable of the Vaginal," in which two graduate students discuss, with continually elevated rhetoric, postdeconstructionist theory, consists of a single paragraph comprising an ongoing comma splice.

Moody's *Right Livelihoods: Three Novellas* is darkly humorous and explores the anxiety-driven culture of a post-9/11 society, in which the protagonists find themselves convinced of varying conspiracies and terror plots. The final novella is said to be the most noteworthy of the collection, offering a postapocalyptic view of a Manhattan leveled by a suitcase bomb.

Moody admits that each novella was the result of an assignment, with *The Albertine Notes* being written upon the requests of Michael Chabon and Dave Eggers.

"THE GRID"

In this nonlinear story, an anonymous narrator stands beneath the window of a woman having a telephone conversation with the first boy she kissed. Our narrator discloses that he is about to embark upon the same venture and kiss the woman he is with for the first time. Moving between past and present, the narrative reveals glimpses into the lives of others who will soon share their first kisses, and other events that also will occur simultaneously: a man burgling an apartment, a couple watching below, relationships beginning and ending, revealing an intermingled web that somehow connects them all.

The story paints a pastiche of seemingly unrelated, disconnected moments, but their proximity makes readers see the connections. There is a tinge of bittersweetness to the story, as these individuals embark on something that seems filled with so much hope but that likely cannot last. Perhaps, however, that is Moody's point: Happiness can exist only in these brief, isolated, and disjointed moments.

"BOYS"

The story "Boys" comprises a single paragraph, in which the words "boy" and "house" appear in virtually every sentence. Throughout are various moments of the lives of twin boys, who remain unnamed, from the time they first enter the house swaddled in hospital blankets to the time they finally exit the house as adults following the funeral of their father. All of these disclosures are the details that make up the boys' lives, some of them humorous (tormenting their sister and burying her dolls in the backyard, the anxieties and awkwardness of their adolescence) and some of them painful (grieving the loss of their young sister and later their father).

Although the reader is aware of the formal limitations Moody imposes upon the text--the deliberate narrative structure--and although the description remains vague, the details of the characters' lives remain moving, universal, and distinctly human. Moody effectively conveys joy, anger, disappointment, grief, the sadness and longing that accompany adulthood, and the reverie for moments passed and loved ones gone. Again, Moody's experiment reveals something fundamental about the human condition. Though the particulars of people's lives are predictably heterogeneous, and when distilled to their fundamental elements often look like any other life, there are indelible moments of pathos in every one.

"DEMONOLOGY"

The title story of the collection bears certain similarities to the introductory story, "The Mansion on the Hill," in that the narrators ruminate on the death of their sister. Whereas the title story is clearly fiction, "Demonology" is a personal testimony of Moody's grief, inspired by the sudden death of his sister, Meredith.

Fragmented and nonlinear, this stream-of-consciousness narrative recounts various memories that make up the scope of the narrator's sister's life. The flashes intermingle with his interpretation of events, some of which he only imagines. The story reflects on two days in particular: Halloween and All Saints' Day, the final days of his sister's life. The narrator recalls images of costume-clad children, his sister in particular. Looking at the family photographs, some lying loose, on the shelves of his sister's home, the narrator is flooded with memories: how his sister once drank "demon rum," how he once carried her from a bar, how his sister had a gin and tonic before going out with the children for Halloween. Descriptions based on photographs move the narrator back and forth through time, conjuring fragmented images of his sister's life, until, suddenly, the memories culminate in tragedy: her collapse, her final deep breaths, her children in the hall, her boyfriend struggling to revive her.

In the final paragraph, Moody composes a list, a strategy he utilizes in an attempt to impose order on chaos, of things he should and should not do, writing that he "should have fictionalized [the story] more," made it less real. Nevertheless, in the end, what would it matter? The story offers no concrete lessons but is rather an elegy and an attempt to make sense of the profound grief that accompanies the loss of a loved one.

THE ALBERTINE NOTES

In the most successful of the three novellas, journalist Kevin Lee leads readers through a Manhattan-turned-wasteland after the detonation of a suitcase bomb. This is a darker New York, one with "post-apocalyptic, post-traumatic dimensions and obsessions." Nearly half the population is annihilated, and the city's remaining tenants consist of prostitutes and junkies addicted to the new drug Albertine, which puts users in a daze of fonder recollections, memories before the bomb. It is a world of drug cartels, industrial sex machines, and conspiracies, in which lost souls are connected only by their loneliness and longing to remember love. However, the price of remembering is also forgetting what is real. When rumors begin to circulate that people are inexplicably disappearing, namely "Addict Number One," Lee dives into the dark underbelly of this world in an attempt to trace the origin of Albertine and to investigate the rumors that this drug recalls memories not only of the past but also of the future. As he goes deeper into what seems to be a dream within a dream, or a memory within a memory, Lee ultimately will be led to question whether he is the origin, or "Addict Zero."

In this multilayered, unsettling narrative, the reader must continuously question what is and is not real. Moody's experimental narrative brings the reader into the story, asking the reader directly about memories of earlier events. The novella becomes a labyrinth of questions and layers of narrative, with the form of the text mirroring the Albertine-addled sensibility of the new world. In spite of the deliberately unsettling style, humorous moments permeate the narrative, specifically when the debate of origin enters academia, when deconstructionist and postcolonial theorists trace the Albertine sign system. Overall, *The Albertine Notes* is best understood as Moody's attempt to merge genre fiction with his own brand of postmodernism; whatever it means beyond that is for to the reader to decide.

OTHER MAJOR WORKS

LONG FICTION: *Garden State*, 1991; *The Ice Storm*, 1994; *Purple America*, 1997; *The Diviners*, 2005; *The Four Fingers of Death*, 2010.

NONFICTION: *The Black Veil: A Memoir with Digressions*, 2002.

EDITED TEXTS: *Joyful Noise: The New Testament Revisited*, 1997 (with Darcey Steinke).

BIBLIOGRAPHY

Dewey, Joseph. "Rick Moody." *Review of Contemporary Fiction*, 23, no. 2 (2003): 7-49. Provides extensive biographical information and excellent critical overview of Moody's fiction.

Moody, Rick. *The Black Veil: A Memoir with Digressions*. Boston: Little Brown, 2002. A memoir that details experiences of Moody's youth and his turbulent journey to becoming a writer.

Moore, John Frederick. "Moody Indigo." *Poets and Writers* 27, no. 2 (1999): 34-43. Provides helpful overview of Moody's life and career, prose style and themes.

Schillinger, Liesl. "Boomtown." *The New York Times Book Review*, June 3, 2007, p. 26. Provides in-depth review of *Right Livelihoods*.

Danielle A. DeFoe

LORRIE MOORE

Born: Glen Falls, New York; January 13, 1957
Also known as: Marie Lorena Moore

PRINCIPAL SHORT FICTION

Self-Help, 1985
Like Life, 1990
Birds of America, 1998
The Collected Stories of Lorrie Moore, 2008

OTHER LITERARY FORMS

Lorrie Moore is the author of the novels *Anagrams* (1986), *Who Will Run the Frog Hospital?* (1994), and *A Gate at the Stairs* (2009). She has also published a children's book, *The Forgotten Helper* (1987), and has edited the anthologies *I Know Some Things: Stories About Childhood by Contemporary Writers* (1992) and *The Best American Short Stories, 2004* (2004). *The Collected Stories of Lorrie Moore* was published in 2008 and featured selections from each of her three previously published collections, excerpts from *Anagrams*, and three previously uncollected stories that had appeared in *The New Yorker*.

ACHIEVEMENTS

Lorrie Moore's stories have been included in the annual *The Best American Short Stories* and *Prize Stories: The O. Henry Awards* series. In 1976, at the age of nineteen, she won *Seventeen* magazine's fiction contest. She also received a National Endowment for the Arts Fellowship (1989) and a Granville Hicks Memorial Fellowship (1983). In 1999, Moore was named the winner of the the *Irish Times* International Fiction Prize for *Birds of America*, and in 2004, she received the Rea Award for the Short Story. Moore was elected to the American Academy of Arts and Letters in 2006, and she is also a fellow of the Wisconsin Academy of Sciences, Arts and Letters. Her novel, *A Gate at the Stairs*, about a young midwestern woman's coming-of-age after the September 11, 2001, terrorist attacks, was a finalist for the 2010 PEN/Faulkner Award for Fiction and the Orange Prize for Fiction.

BIOGRAPHY

Lorrie Moore was born Marie Lorena Moore in Glen Falls, New York, in 1957. She is the second of four children born to professional, middle-class parents; her father was an insurance executive, and her mother was a nurse-turned-housewife. Although both of her parents had harbored literary ambitions in their youth, neither of them was particularly supportive of Moore's decision to become a writer, both believing that she should do something more practical.

Moore won a regents scholarship and attended St. Lawrence University in New York, which she followed with two years of paralegal work. In 1980, she enrolled in Cornell University's M.F.A. program; there she had the good fortune of studying under the novelist Alison Lurie, who proved to be very supportive of her writing. Upon Lurie's recommendation, Moore's work was accepted by literary agent Melanie Jackson, and in 1983, when she was twenty-six, Moore's first collection of short stories, *Self-Help*, was accepted for publication by Knopf.

Moore moved to Madison, Wisconsin, to accept an assistant professorship in the department of English at the University of Wisconsin. She had some difficulty adjusting to life in the Midwest, so for a while she continued to spend her summers in New York. Moore advanced to the position of full professor at the University of Wisconsin and settled in Madison with her husband, an attorney, and her son, Benjamin.

ANALYSIS

Lorrie Moore's work is often compared to that of such literary notables as Raymond Carver, Bobbie Ann Mason, Ann Beattie, and Flannery O'Connor. There are definitely overtones of O'Connor in the comic despair that pervades Moore's work. One can also perhaps find traces of Carver and Mason in her characters and subject matter. However, no one has written more convincingly and poignantly about the angst of the modern world than Moore. Her characters--an assortment of housewives, mothers, and career women (usually academic)--are typically isolated or disconnected from the larger world through no real character flaws of their own. These women can be bitingly sarcastic in their speech, but without fail they are eminently likable, sweet characters. In a world of upwardly mobile Americans, there are few panaceas for women who both think and feel. They cannot convince themselves to believe in God or the sanctity of marriage; relationships with the opposite sex offer little real comfort, and all efforts at self-help fail.

Given Moore's early success as a writer, it is not surprising to find some lack of maturity in her earliest work. Moore herself calls her first collection of stories, *Self-Help*, and her first novel, *Anagrams*, apprentice work. The stories in *Self-Help* bear the marks of a graduate workshop writing; all seem designed primarily to evoke laughter and thus have a stand-up comedic effect. These stories are saved, however, by the sad, underlying truths that slowly make their way to the surface and leave a lasting impression on the reader. Similarly, stories in her second collection, *Like Life*, are often too self-consciously clever. However, evidence of Moore's

mature writing is present in the stories "You're Ugly Too" and "Places to Look for Your Mind." Her novel *Who Will Run the Frog Hospital?* has some early pacing problems, but it proves to be a hauntingly sweet story of the friendship between two teenage girls, a friendship that nothing in adult life can quite match.

Finally, the stories in *Birds of America* are breathtakingly good. Moore's mordant sense of humor is still present, but she does not allow humor to eclipse plot and character development. Nearly every story is about characters in relationships--mothers and daughters, husbands and wives, or lovers--who cannot really connect or experience true intimacy. The last three stories of the collection are especially stunning: "Real Estate," in which a dying woman is saddled with her husband's choice of a house that needs massive renovation; "People Like That Are the Only People Here: Canonical Babbling in Peed Onk," in which a couple is faced with the cruel ironies of a baby with cancer; and "Terrific Mother," in which a childless woman accidentally kills a friend's baby and is left to struggle with this irreparable grief.

Lorrie Moore (AP Photo/Andy Manis)

"REAL ESTATE"

The story "Real Estate" from *Birds of America* is one of many stories by Moore that explores the futility of marriage. Ruth, who has already lost one lung to cancer, gets a premonition that she will die in the spring "after much boring flailing and flapping and the pained, purposeless work that constituted life." She also discovers yet another of her husband's love affairs and laughs for more than two pages. At Terence's (her husband) instigation, they begin to shop for a new house. Ruth finally consents to buy an old farmhouse with which her husband falls in love, but as with all his flings, he soon abandons the house. Ruth, a dying woman, is left to oversee the house's renovation. She also begins to battle the house's infestation with racoons, ants, bats, crows, squirrels, and finally a teenage punk.

Meanwhile, in a parallel plot, Noel, a lawn care person, is left by his girlfriend because, among other cultural deficiencies, he does not know a single song all the way through. Noel begins to drink a lot, gets fired, sleeps all day, and wanders the streets at night. He soon turns to burglary, but his motivation is not the acquisition of worldly goods. He holds a gun to his victims' heads, demanding that they sing a song all the way through. He ends up in Ruth's house, where Ruth shoots and kills him. The plot of "Real Estate" is as inevitable as the return of Ruth's lung cancer (she still smokes occasionally). Ruth's life demonstrates what can happen when basically kind, gentle women are pushed too far by the utterly selfish people around them.

"PEOPLE LIKE THAT ARE THE ONLY PEOPLE HERE"

"People Like That Are the Only People Here," from *Birds of America*, first appeared in *The New Yorker* in 1997. Although Moore keeps the details to herself, this story is probably her most autobiographical. Her son, Benjamin, suffered through a similar ordeal. In this story, the main characters do not receive names; they are known as the Mother, the Baby, and the Father. The Mother finds a blood clot in her baby's diaper and rushes him to a clinic at the children's hospital. She soon discovers that he has a cancerous lesion on his kidney and will require a nephrectomy, probably followed by chemotherapy. This story explores the various responses of parents whose children have catastrophic illnesses: self-blame, attempts to pray or bargain with God, thoughts of suicide or escape, and finally, just getting through the illness. As usual, Moore's humor is intact. God looks like a manager at Marshall Field's, who only offers the reassurance that not knowing the future is what makes us human. The narrator, a mother who writes, offers a number of succinct commentaries on what can only be Moore's own craft. For example, she says, "I do *the careful ironies of daydream*. I do *the marshy ideas upon which intimate life is built*." The Baby of this story survives the nephrectomy and does not have to go through chemotherapy, but other characters in the story are not as lucky. A child named Joey is expected to live only three more weeks after battling cancer for four and a half years. His father Frank has given up everything to save Joey--his career and his marriage--but now Joey is going to die anyway. One cannot help but wonder if Joey's mother did the right thing by leaving Frank and Joey, remarrying, and having a healthy child. Frank's sacrifice is one of the cruelest ironies in this story.

"TERRIFIC MOTHER"

In "Terrific Mother," also found in *Birds of America*, Adrienne, the thirty-five-year-old protagonist, accidentally kills a friend's baby when the picnic bench upon which she is sitting topples and the baby hits his head against a stone wall. Adrienne withdraws for a period of seven months until a friend and lover, Martin Porter, offers to marry her for purely practical reasons. He is going to a conference in northern Italy for a month, and if he and Adrienne are married, she can go with him. Ironically, this marriage of convenience turns out to be one of the best marriages in Moore's fiction. There is little to no romance between the couple, but Martin is infinitely kind and patient. At the conference in Italy, Adrienne finds academics mean-spirited and pretentious, so she escapes into the company of the other spouses and discovers an American masseuse named Ilke. Through massage, Adrienne begins to let go of some of her horrendous guilt. She even half falls in love with Ilke, but then realizes that Ilke is bored while she, Adrienne, is having a religious experience. When Adrienne discovers that Martin is also going to Ilke, she is as infuriated as she would be over a sexual infidelity. The story ends with Adrienne asking for Martin's forgiveness, and the reader is left to believe that here is a relationship that will work.

"You're Ugly Too"

"You're Ugly Too," found in *Like Life*, is one of Moore's most successful short stories. It has been published in *The New Yorker*, *Prize Stories: The O. Henry Awards*, and *The Best American Short Stories*. As in many of Moore's stories, the protagonist, Zoë Hendricks, finds it nearly impossible to connect with those around her. Zoë, an American history professor at a small liberal arts college in the Midwest, feels that she is dying, and she may, in fact, be dying because she has a tumor in her abdomen. Her students find her sarcastic, and she finds them inane. All of her efforts at romance or self-help have failed her. One refuge is her sister's place in New York, so Zoë heads for New York just after she discovers her tumor but before she hears the diagnosis. There she learns that her sister is getting married to her live-in boyfriend just at the point at which all the romance of their relationship has obviously died. At a Halloween party, her sister's boyfriend is already beginning to flirt shamelessly with other women. Zoë, dressed as a bonehead, is slated to meet Earl, a boorish man dressed up as a naked woman with rubber breasts and steel wool placed strategically over a body suit. Earl is, in many ways, a prototype of men who fail at intimacy. He interrupts Zoë's joke, changes the subject when she mentions her health (a serious concern), and then suggests ways to improve herself (wear the color blue). Finally, he whines that he prefers women with part-time jobs over professional women. Zoë nearly pushes him off the balcony, twenty floors up.

Other major works

LONG FICTION: *Anagrams*, 1986; *Who Will Run the Frog Hospital?*, 1994; *A Gate at the Stairs*, 2009.

CHILDREN'S LITERATURE: *The Forgotten Helper*, 1987.

EDITED TEXTS: *I Know Some Things: Stories About Childhood by Contemporary Writers*, 1992 (also known as *The Faber Book of Contemporary Stories About Childhood*, 1997); *The Best American Short Stories, 2004*, 2004.

Bibliography

Blades, John. "Lorrie Moore: Flipping Death the Bird." *Publishers Weekly* (August 24, 1997): 31-32. In this preview for the upcoming publication of *Birds of America*, Blade provides an overview of Moore's successes. Moore defends herself against assumptions that she has had it too easy as a writer, and she defends her use of humor, which some critics have found excessive. Moore considers both *Anagrams* and *Self-Help* apprentice books.

Gelfant, Blanche H., ed. *The Columbia Companion to the Twentieth-Century American Short Story*. New York: Columbia University Press, 2000. Includes a chapter in which Moore's short stories are analyzed.

Kelly, Alison. *Understanding Lorrie Moore*. Columbia: University of South Carolina Press, 2009. An introductory overview of Moore's life and works. Devotes one chapter apiece to analyses of the first three short-story collections.

Lee, Don. "About Lorrie Moore." *Ploughshares* (Fall, 1998): 224-229. An overview of Moore's life and work.

Moore, Lorrie. "The Booklist Interview: Lorrie Moore." Interview by Molly McQuade. *Booklist* (October 15, 1998): 402-403. Moore discusses the use of absurdity in her work, her pessimistic rather than cynical worldview, and the craft of writing stories.

_____. "More Moore." *New York*, August 31, 2009, p. 67. An interview, in which Moore explains how male and female writers describe women characters differently and admits that she always loved sad stories.

Weekes, Karen. Postmodernism in Women's Short Story Cycles: Lorrie Moore's *Anagrams*." In *The Postmodern Short Story: Forms and Issues*, edited by Farhat Iftekharrudin, et al., under the auspices of the Society for the Study of the Short Story. Westport, Conn.: Praeger, 2003. Explains why *Anagrams* should be defined as a short-story cycle instead of as a novel and analyzes this work.

Werner, Robin. "Lorrie Moore." In *A Reader's Companion to the Short Story in English*, edited by Erin Fallon, et al., under the auspices of the Society for the Study of the Short Story. Westport, Conn.: Greenwood Press, 2001. Aimed at the general reader, this essay provides a brief biography of Moore followed by an analysis of her short fiction.

Nancy E. Sherrod

WRIGHT MORRIS

Born: Central City, Nebraska; January 6, 1910
Died: Mill Valley, California; April 25, 1998

PRINCIPAL SHORT FICTION

Green Grass, Blue Sky, White House, 1970
Here Is Einbaum, 1973
The Cat's Meow, 1975
Real Losses, Imaginary Gains, 1976
Collected Stories, 1948-1986, 1986

OTHER LITERARY FORMS

In a career that began in 1942, Wright Morris published everything except plays and poems. Known primarily as a novelist, he was also a photographer and created books of photographs such as *The Inhabitants* (1946), with accompanying text, which presented his view of the artifacts of American lives. He even incorporated his photographs into a novel, *The Home Place* (1948). He was an essayist, offering his interpretations of literature and culture in general in works such as *The Territory Ahead* (1958, 1963). The first fifty years of Morris's life are examined in *A Cloak of Light: Writing My Life* (1985). He also published *Time Pieces: Photographs, Writing, and Memory* (1989), a nonfiction work.

ACHIEVEMENTS

Though often compared to midwestern writers such as Sherwood Anderson and Willa Cather, Wright Morris was hardly a mere regionalist. He wrote about all sections of the United States and many parts of Mexico and Europe. What most distinguishes his fiction is a distinctly original American writing style rooted in the vernacular and a consistently amused response to the efforts of his characters to cope with the daily reality of an increasingly complex world. Frequently categorized as unfairly unheralded, Morris was given many honors by the literary establishment. *The Field of Vision* (1956) received the National Book Award, and *Plains Song, for Female Voices* (1980) won the American Book Award. He was elected to the National Institute of Arts and Letters and the American Academy of Arts and Sciences in 1970 and was made an honorary fellow of the Modern Language Association in 1975 and a senior fellow of the National Endowment for the Humanities in 1976. He won the western Literature Association's Distinguished Achievement Award in 1979 and the Robert Kirsch Award of *The Los Angeles Times* in 1981. Morris's most notable achievement was the consistent quality of his writing. He was one of the few American authors to have written as well after he turned fifty as he did before that milestone.

BIOGRAPHY

Wright Marion Morris was born in Central City, Nebraska, on January 6, 1910. His mother, Ethel Grace (Osborn), died six days after his birth, and his father, William Henry Morris, reared his son (mostly alone) in rural Nebraska, Omaha, and Chicago. His father's efforts to find a new mother for Morris and to make a fortune in the egg business were rewarded with only limited success.

Between 1925 and 1930, Morris worked on a farm in Texas with his uncle. He later crossed the country in several run-down cars and lived in Chicago with his father, whose ill-fated enterprises encouraged Morris's early financial and emotional independence and propelled him into his long and productive writing career.

After briefly attending the City College of Chicago and Pacific Union College, Morris transferred to Pomona College and remained there from 1930 to 1933. In 1933, Morris traveled to Europe, where he remained for one year. He married Mary Ellen Finfrock in 1934. He supported himself by teaching drawing and swimming, while he learned the arts of fiction-writing and photography. After he had published several novels, Morris taught at several universities, including Princeton University, Sarah Lawrence College, and Swarthmore College. Divorced in 1961, Morris married Josephine Kantor that same year. He was a professor of English at San Francisco State University from 1962 until his retirement in 1975.

In 1992, Morris, then in his eighties, told an interviewer he had ceased writing. Only two more stories were published after the definitive *Collected Stories: 1948-1986*. One was "Uno Más" (One More), appearing in *The New Yorker* on February 6, 1989; the other was "What's New, Love?" about a waitress with a secret crush on a famous film star who frequents her coffee shop, published in *American Short Fiction*.

ANALYSIS

Wright Morris's novels, to a large extent, are about what it means to be American. They examine the unrelenting grasp of the American Dream and the often bizarre ways in which people attempt to live up to this ideal, which they only vaguely understand. His stories are more concerned with the everyday details of life, though these may also be bizarre. They are stories of character and mood more than plot or theme, written in a style which manages to be distinctive without calling attention to itself.

While the majority of his novels have Nebraska and California as their settings, Morris's short fiction roams all over the United States and Europe, presenting characters with extremely varied social, economic, educational, and ethnic backgrounds. Morris wrote stories sporadically for the first quarter century of his career, taking up the form in earnest only in 1969. Unusual among American writers for having refined his short-story skills after becoming firmly established as a novelist, he produced his best stories since turning seventy.

These stories look at the quiet side of the emotional turmoil people put themselves through each day. Such themes as the inability to communicate with or understand or feel for one another, loneliness, and the failure of relationships are presented without nostalgia for some simpler past, with little sentimentality or anger. Morris's objective stance toward the world of his characters creates a comic, compassionate, quirkily individualistic body of short fiction.

"THE RAM IN THE THICKET"

"The Ram in the Thicket," Morris's first published and best-known story, is an early version of what became the first two chapters of his novel *Man and Boy* (1951), but it stands on its own as a memorable portrait of one of Morris's frequent subjects in his early fiction: a weak husband in the grasp of a domineering wife. Roger Ormsby and his wife, known as Mother, are depicted preparing to go to the christening of the SS *Ormsby*, named for their only child, Virgil, missing in action during World War II.

The need to conceal emotions characterizes Ormsby and Mother, neither of whom allows the other to guess how they feel about their son's death. Although hearing that Virgil has been killed seems strangely "natural" to his father, Ormsby has "not been prepared to feel what he felt. Mother need never know it unless he slipped up and talked in his sleep." Mother, without saying so, blames Ormsby for the boy's death, since he gave Virgil an air rifle years earlier, thereby conditioning him for war. Since that time, she has considered them united against her, calling them *they* or *you* plural as if they were twin halves of a conspiracy: "Though the boy had been gone two years he still felt him *there*, right beside him, when Mother said *you*."

From the time of the air rifle, both father and son felt greater emotional distance from Mother, Virgil spending as much time as possible out-of-doors, Ormsby seeking solitude with his pipe in the basement. Once, Ormsby is surprised to find his son in his refuge, and the experience becomes the closest they ever share: "For two, maybe three minutes, there in the dark, they had been what Mother called them, they were *they*--and they were there in the basement because they were so much alike." When Ormsby receives the telegram he knows will tell him of Virgil's death, he takes it to the basement to read.

Mother is nationally prominent for her interest in bird-watching; she is constantly involved in that activity, the League of Women Voters, and other organizations and causes. She understands wildlife and politics better than she does those closest to her. She enjoys saying, in jest, that she prefers shoes to men but is actually truthful, since clothing is less complicated than people. Causes are her shelter as much as the basement is her husband's. Neither character is being held up to ridicule; the typical Morris character looks for excuses to hide his feelings, for ways of ignoring failures of communication.

The characters in "The Ram in the Thicket" could easily be comical caricatures, but Morris is not concerned with types. His creations come alive through their idiosyncrasies, such as the oriental rug Mother puts in the bathroom and the leftovers she refuses to throw away, carefully storing them in jars in the icebox, then forgetting about them, leaving Ormsby, when the contents have become moldy, to bury them behind the garage. Such details help create a sense of ordinary lives closely observed.

"The Safe Place"

"The Safe Place" is another Morris story incorporated into his longer fiction, appearing in a different form in *Ceremony in Lone Tree* (1960); it also has characters and situations resembling those in the short novel *War Games* (written in 1951-1952 but not published until 1972). A retired army colonel lives a dull Brooklyn existence with his wife until he is hit by a pie truck and almost killed. The cynical colonel spends his recovery in the hospital contemplating how life is full of senseless violence which ceaselessly swoops down upon the unsuspecting and innocent: "Life, to put it simply, was a battleground." He decides that the only way to avoid the world's dangers and foolishness is to stay in bed-- "the only safe place." In many ways, the colonel's view of the absurd world outside the hospital foreshadows that in Joseph Heller's death-obsessed *Catch-22* (1961).

The colonel becomes interested in another patient, Hyman Kopfman, who has had an arm and a leg amputated because of a blood ailment. When Kopfman identifies the problem in his body as America, the colonel senses a kinship between them: "What Hyman Kopfman knew was that the world was killing him." While the colonel is reserved, Kopfman enjoys talking about himself--apparently to himself-- "as if he were somebody else." The colonel listens in fascination to Kopfman's account of how his family left Vienna for Chicago when he was a boy, of how Kopfman, as he grew, began wearing his small father's clothes while his brother Paul wore their mother's old skirt and peasant blouse. The boys rarely left their apartment, making it into a self-contained world, a safe place. Below their apartment was another safe place: a walled garden where blind people came to walk.

The colonel decides that Kopfman's life has always been rather hopeless and that this hopelessness makes him lovable. That he is not aware of how hopeless he is touches the colonel even more. The colonel realizes that all Kopfman has ever wanted is to lead "the useless sort of life" that he himself has had. Kopfman's case inspires the colonel to get well despite having nothing to live for, while Kopfman, with his hunger for life, gets worse.

"The Safe Place" displays some of the common concerns of Morris's fiction. His characters always seem to be seeking safe places, like Ormsby's basement, which might not seem to be havens to others. Man survives in this absurd, violent world by tricking himself into believing that he has found a refuge, whether it be a place, a person, a job, a role in society, or a philosophy. "The Safe Place" is also one of several Morris stories contrasting American and European views of life; others include "The Character of the Lover," "Drrdla," "Fiona," "Here Is Einbaum," "In Another Country," "The Customs of the Country," and "Things That Matter." Whether Europeans in America or Americans in Europe, these characters always experience a feeling of dislocation.

Pets are central to Morris's delineation of character. Cats, dogs, and birds appear in the majority of his stories to help underscore certain facets of the humans around them, humans who belong to the pets more than the pets belong to the humans. Morris's use of animals ranges from the poignant, as in "Victrola," in which an elderly man's dog dies, to the comic, as when a man develops an affection for his neighbors' leghorn pullet in "Fellow Creatures."

Because his characters are independent and eccentric yet crave attention and love, it is appropriate that several Morris stories involve cats. The stray feline in "The Cat in the Picture" causes a marriage to break up. "Drrdla" explores how cats and women are alike, as a husband becomes attached to another stray, who rejects him for the man's unfaithful wife. "The Cat's Meow" is one of Morris's most effective humorous stories. A writer and his seventeen-pound cat are virtually inseparable, the cat lying on the man's desk during the four hours he writes each day:

> The cat faces him, his eyes blinking in the desk light, and the look he gives Morgan, and Morgan returns, is not something to be lightly dealt with, or even when soberly and thoughtfully dealt with, put into words.

Morris's animals and humans share this enigmatic quality.

"GLIMPSE INTO ANOTHER COUNTRY"

With its whimsical acceptance of the unusual, the unexpected, and the inexplicable, "Glimpse into Another Country" is most representative of Morris's later stories. On the plane from San Francisco to New York, Hazlitt, an elderly academic, is treated rudely by Mrs. Thayer, a fellow passenger, when he tries to make casual conversation with her and her husband. Soon after he arrives in Manhattan, Hazlitt goes to Bloomingdale's department store, seeing Mrs. Thayer on the way. In Bloomingdale's, he loses his driver's license and, in a sense, his identity, when the store is closed because of a bomb threat while a clerk is having his check approved.

The next day, he learns from a medical specialist that the health problem about which he has been worried is nonexistent. Considering himself "free of a nameless burden," Hazlitt returns to Bloomingdale's to retrieve his driver's license and impulsively buys an expensive strand of pearls to give to his wife. He cannot afford the gift, but "writing the numbers, spelling the sum out gave him a tingling sense of exhilaration."

Going to the Metropolitan Museum of Art, Hazlitt sees the ubiquitous Mrs. Thayer in the gift shop. In the museum's basement rest room, a group of boys, seemingly under the influence of drugs, force him to give

them the pearls. He returns to the gift shop for an Etruscan pin, the type of gift his wife will consider "sensible." From a bus outside, Mrs. Thayer waves to him, her now-friendly eyes giving him "all the assurances he needed."

Hazlitt, as opposed to the colonel in "The Safe Place," is not perturbed by these events, being slightly bemused by them. Unlike the stereotypical elderly person, Hazlitt also accepts the inevitability of change, as when he discovers that the museum's once-striking Fountain Court lunchroom has been renovated into blandness. More important are the usual Morris concerns, such as the protagonist's inability to communicate with either the relatively nonthreatening Thayers or the drugged youths. In the taxi from the airport, Hazlitt wants "to chat a bit with the driver, but the Plexiglas barrier between them seemed intimidating."

"Glimpse into Another Country" is primarily a comic view of contemporary life. Hazlitt, like many Morris characters, travels through life with an amused tolerance and detachment, refusing to take anything seriously since so many others are willing to assume that burden for him. The unusual and the everyday merge as he moves about as if in a dream. He sees a television picture of a milling crowd in India indifferently passing by dead or sleeping bodies: "The film gave Hazlitt a glimpse into a strange country where the quick and the dormant were accustomed to mingle. Perhaps . . . it was not the walkers but the sleepers who would range the farthest in their travels." For the Hazlitts of the world, so-called real life is carried on with even less logic than a dream.

"THE ORIGIN OF SADNESS"

With its characters stoically enduring the pains of emotional isolation on the plains, "The Origin of Sadness" is the Morris story most like his novels, particularly recalling *The Works of Love* (1952). Growing up in Osborn County, Kansas, shy, brooding, self-absorbed Schuler enjoys playing with an Indian companion because they do not have to talk much. He has as a pet a coyote pup, freed from a steel trap, that treats everyone else as an enemy. Schuler is expected to become a country doctor like his late father but is more interested in nature and becomes a paleontologist. Schuler's temperament is suited to an obsession with the remains of the distant past: "He did not find the immediate and shifting flux of time present real at all." As such, he is one of the few Morris characters with some understanding of his sense of displacement.

Schuler marries one of his students, Doreen Oakum, who is part Cherokee, because she shares "both his passion for bones and his talent for silence." Their life becomes "a matter of shared but secret communications." Typically for a Morris couple, there is little romance in their marriage. Doreen seems to feel more strongly about her parrot than her husband. However, what Schuler loves about her is "her detachment from the world that hummed and buzzed around her, her attachment to the invisible world within her."

Doreen's sudden death drives Schuler back to his birthplace as he experiences despair for the first time. As a snowstorm begins, Schuler, an Ice Age expert, makes his way to the arroyo where he had freed the coyote and discovers it to be full of tiny fossils, seemingly undisturbed since his last visit years before. He is concerned that he must bring destruction to the ageless setting by climbing the arroyo. His obsession with the past, his despair at the present, and the innocence of his youth converge as he falls, breaks his hip, and calmly lies awaiting an icy death. His final discovery is that the "deep freeze of all freezes was time itself." By understanding the past and its significance for the present, Schuler has sought to arrest time, and at the end, he recognizes the futility of his efforts.

During a public lecture, Schuler is once asked what he is really seeking; he replies, "What interests me is the origin of sadness." This search is similar to what motivates Morris as he takes ordinary people and situations and peels back the surface layers to uncover the human elements--or their absence--underneath. Morris's stories are unsentimental yet strangely moving, unusually amusing explorations into what it means to be human in the twentieth century.

"UNO MÁS"

Many of Morris's best short stories originally appeared in the nation's most prestigious literary magazine, *The New Yorker*. The title "Uno Más" might be taken to have the double meaning of a farewell to his readers. It concerns the problems of a California couple who have hired Maria, an illiterate Indian immigrant

from Oaxaca, Mexico, as an all-around cook, maid, and babysitter for their three small children. The story owes its broader implications to the fact that the United States is experiencing a deluge of immigration from south of the border, with the resulting impact on every aspect of American life, including language. The youngest family member becomes so strongly attached to Maria that his mother and father become alarmed: "Once Peanuts clutched the rope of Maria's braids, he would not let go." He only likes the food she prepares for him. He wants only Maria to bathe and dress him. He only wants to speak Spanish. His conventional middle-class parents fear they are losing their son. They were pleased that he was learning Spanish but fear he is in danger of becoming a non-English-speaking alien in his own country. The Drysdales themselves have become attached to Maria, who is so honest, devoted, industrious, and inexpensive. They do not have the heart to fire her but think they have found the solution when they recommend her to the wife of a successful avocado rancher who has three hellcat tomboys to raise and would like her daughters to grow up with Spanish as their second language. Mr. Drysdale railroads Maria on the pretext of taking her to a Mexican film. He drives for five hours to the Fresno ranch and dumps her on her new family. "Drysdale did not generally consider the Third World to be his personal problem, but the settling of Maria--into one place or another--gave him the disquiet of a winner's shame."

Peanuts is desolate. All the physical and psychological problems he exhibited before Maria's arrival reappear. The panicked parents capitulate. Drysdale drives all the way back to central California and returns exhausted after a nonstop round-trip. Maria, who has not tried to understand the changes these "gringos" have made in her life, calmly goes to the kitchen and washes the dishes stacked in the sink. Mrs. Drysdale, pregnant with the couple's fourth child, gives in to the inevitable. The whole family is obviously destined to succumb to the influence of a culture more ancient, and in some respects more humane, than their own.

Morris's short stories have a distinctive touch, a characteristic humanity and wisdom. They deal compassionately and humorously with seemingly incidental events in the lives of ordinary people which reflect in microcosm the growing complexity of the greater world.

OTHER MAJOR WORKS

LONG FICTION: *My Uncle Dudley*, 1942; *The Man Who Was There*, 1945; *The Home Place*, 1948; *The World in the Attic*, 1949; *Man and Boy*, 1951; *The Works of Love*, 1952; *The Deep Sleep*, 1953; *The Huge Season*, 1954; *The Field of Vision*, 1956; *Love Among the Cannibals*, 1957; *Ceremony in Lone Tree*, 1960; *What a Way to Go*, 1962; *Cause for Wonder*, 1963; *One Day*, 1965; *In Orbit*, 1967; *Fire Sermon*, 1971; *War Games*, 1972; *A Life*, 1973; *The Fork River Space Project*, 1977; *Plains Song, for Female Voices*, 1980.

NONFICTION: *The Inhabitants*, 1946; *The Territory Ahead*, 1958, 1963; *A Bill of Rites, a Bill of Wrongs, a Bill of Goods*, 1968; *God's Country and My People*, 1968; *Love Affair: A Venetian Journal*, 1972; *About Fiction: Reverent Reflections on the Nature of Fiction with Irreverent Observations on Writers, Readers, and Other Abuses*, 1975; *Wright Morris: Structures and Artifacts, Photographs, 1933-1954*, 1975; *Earthly Delights, Unearthly Adornments: American Writers as Image-Makers*, 1978; *Will's Boy*, 1981; *Photographs and Words*, 1982; *Picture America*, 1982; *Solo: An American Dreamer in Europe, 1933-1934*, 1983; *A Cloak of Light: Writing My Life*, 1985; *Time Pieces: Photographs, Writing, and Memory*, 1989.

MISCELLANEOUS: *Wright Morris: A Reader*, 1970.

BIBLIOGRAPHY

Bird, Roy K. *Wright Morris: Memory and Imagination*. New York: Peter Lang, 1985. An excellent appraisal of self-consciousness in Morris's fiction. Bird moves from a discussion of Morris's use of the past, namely the author's ambivalence toward it, to an analysis of his linguistic technique. The final chapter contains a detailed analysis of *The Fork River Space Project* and *Plains Song, for Female Voices*. Contains a bibliography.

Booth, Wayne C. "The Shaping of Prophecy: Craft and Idea in the Novels of Wright Morris." *American Scholar* 31 (1962): 608-626. An excellent reappraisal of Morris's work, focusing on *Love Among the Cannibals, The Territory Ahead*, and *Ceremony in Lone Tree*. Booth argues that Morris's fiction is structured around a distinction between the everyday time-bound world of "reality" and a more timeless world of platonic reality.

Crump, G. B. *The Novels of Wright Morris: A Critical Interpretation*. Lincoln: University of Nebraska Press, 1978. In an effort to demonstrate Morris's importance and clarify his contribution to modern fiction, Crump begins his study by addressing the major critical positions toward Morris's writing, thus isolating significant features of the author's work. Then he offers a new theoretical groundwork for criticizing the author's fiction: a major dualism between the real and the ideal.

Hamilton, James. "Wright Morris and the American Century." *Poets and Writers* 25 (November/December, 1997): 23-31. In this extended interview, Morris discusses his decision to stop writing, his feelings about America, and his family.

Hollander, John. "The Figure on the Page: Words and Images in Wright Morris's *The Home Place*." *Yale Journal of Criticism* 9 (Spring, 1996): 93-108. Discusses how Morris's *The Home Place* mixes text and photographs. Examines the work's original way of presenting word and image in a mode that appears to mix ekphrasis and illustration.

Howard, Leon. *Wright Morris*. Minneapolis: University of Minnesota Press, 1968. In this brief but insightful pamphlet surveying Morris's novels, Howard asserts that no other American novelist has approached Morris in the variety and shaping of the raw materials. According to Howard, Morris's unique medium is the high seriousness of brilliant comedy in which the absurd is laid bare with neither bitterness nor hope.

Knoll, Robert E., ed. *Conversations with Wright Morris: Critical Views and Responses*. Lincoln: University of Nebraska Press, 1977. This collection of lectures, interviews, critical essays, and photographs is one of the best sources of information about Morris and his work for the general reader. Much is illuminated in the discussions of Morris the novelist and Morris the photographer. Includes an extensive bibliography.

Madden, David. *Wright Morris*. New York: Twayne, 1964. This work assumes little or no prior knowledge of Morris's writing. Its main purpose is to examine each of Morris's novels (ending with *Cause for Wonder*) in quasi-chronological order so that the reader might see how the author's themes and methods develop from novel to novel. Madden also discusses characterization and the influence of setting (the Midwest) on Morris's work. Includes a bibliography of primary and secondary sources.

Morris, Wright. *A Cloak of Light: Writing My Life*. New York: Harper & Row, 1985. In this extremely informative and insightful autobiography, Morris sheds light not only on the formation of his character but also on his writing. Among other things, Morris discusses his faculty of image-making or what he calls time retrieval--a faculty that has served him well both as a photographer and as a writer.

Trachtenberg, Alan."Home Place." *Raritan* 26, no. 1 (Summer, 2006): 64-87. A critique of *The Home Place* and *The Inhabitants*, two books in which Morris combines words and pictures, creating the so-called photo-text. Discusses how Morris probes the meanings of home and place in these two books. Argues that the term "photographic" serves as an apt description of Morris's fiction, in which his "reflections on what is and has been seen" give these narratives their "distinctiveness."

_____. "Wright Morris's 'Photo-Texts.'" *Yale Journal of Criticism* 9 (Spring, 1996): 109-119. Discusses Morris's mixing of words and photographs in three works of fiction in which image and text stand beside each other in quite unexpected ways; shows how each work addresses similar questions about the role of images in the making of fiction.

Updike, John. "Wright Morris." *Due Considerations: Essays and Criticism*. New York: Alfred A. Knopf, 2007. Updike's essay on Morris recounts the two writers' relationship and provides an overview of Morris's life and literary career.

Michael Adams
Updated by Genevieve Slomski and Bill Delaney

WALTER MOSLEY

Born: Los Angeles, California; January 12, 1952

PRINCIPAL SHORT FICTION

Always Outnumbered, Always Outgunned: The Socrates Fortlow Stories, 1998
Futureland: Nine Stories of an Imminent World, 2001
Six Easy Pieces: Easy Rawlins Stories, 2003
The Tempest Tales: A Novel-in-Stories, 2008
The Right Mistake: The Further Philosophical Investigations of Socrates Fortlow, 2008

OTHER LITERARY FORMS

Walter Mosley (MOHZ-lee) is known primarily for his full-length crime-mystery fiction, especially the noir-flavored Easy Rawlins novels (ten between 1990 and 2007), the Fearless Jones novels (three since 2001), and the Leonid McGill novels (three since 2009). A prolific author who has released at least one major work nearly every year since 1990, Mosley also has published a children's book, a novella, and non-series novels that range across several genres, including fantasy, science fiction, and erotica. Nonfiction has become a part of Mosley's repertoire: Since 1999, he has published several politically and historically oriented works, a memoir, and a how-to book on novel writing. In 2010, his first play was produced, and Mosley has expressed an intention to further explore that writing form.

ACHIEVEMENTS

Walter Mosley first attracted attention for his fresh spin on the traditional private detective novel. His first novel, *Devil in a Blue Dress* (1990), introduced Ezekiel

"Easy" Rawlins. A synthesis of the attributes of Mosley's father, Easy is an African American, a World War II veteran, and a custodian at a Los Angeles-area African American high school. Often in league with boyhood friend Raymond "Mouse" Alexander, a small, charismatic, but violent man, Easy is called upon to act as a private detective in solving mysteries that involve African Americans. More than simple mysteries, the novels delve into social injustices and explore the relativistic nature of morality. *Devil in a Blue Dress* received nominations as best mystery for the Shamus Award (from the Private Eye Writers of America) and the Edgar Award (from the Mystery Writers of America). A later entry in the series, *Bad Boy Brawly Brown* (2002), was nominated for the Hammett Prize (from the International Association of Crime Writers). Mosley's novels have been translated into more than twenty languages for an enthusiastic worldwide audience.

BIOGRAPHY

Walter Ellis Mosley is the only child of Leroy Mosley, an African American World War II veteran originally from Louisiana who worked as head janitor at a public school, and Ella Slatkin, a clerk of Polish Jewish heritage. Born in the largely African American South Central Los Angeles area of Watts, Walter Mosley until the age of twelve attended Victory Baptist Elementary School. In 1965, just before the Watts riots--which resulted in extensive property damage, many deaths, injuries, and arrests--the Mosley family moved to a more stable middle-class neighborhood in west Los Angeles. Mosley became a member of the Afro-American Traveling Actors Association and traveled with the group to perform in Watts. He was affected profoundly by the violence he witnessed when he returned home after the performance was canceled.

Under the tutelage of his father, a natural storyteller with a philosophical bent, and of his mother, who encouraged her son to read a wide range of literature, the seed of writing was planted early in Mosley, though it would take time to bear fruit. After graduating from high school, Mosley traveled aimlessly around North America and wandered in Europe during the early 1970's. Returning to the United States, he attended

Goddard College, a liberal arts institution in Plainfield, Vermont. He dropped out and later enrolled at another Vermont school, Johnson State College, where he earned a B.A. in political science in 1977.

Mosley then became a computer programmer, in which capacity he worked for fifteen years for such companies as Dean Witter and Mobil Oil. He moved to New York City in the early 1980's. In New York, seeking a means to relieve the tedium of his occupation, Mosley enrolled in a writing course at Harlem's City College, where he was encouraged to draw from his own history and heritage for his work. He took the advice to heart, and in the mid-1980's he began publishing short fiction in such periodicals as *Black Renaissance Noir*, *The New Yorker*, *Los Angeles Times Magazine*, *Esquire*, *GQ*, and *Mary Higgins Clark Mystery Magazine*. Mosley met dancer-choreographer Joy Kellman and married her in 1987 (they divorced in 2001).

In 1990, the year before he earned a master's degree at City College of the City University of New York, Mosley's first mystery novel, *Devil in a Blue Dress*,

Walter Mosley (James Mitchell/ Ebony Collection via AP Images)

featuring amateur African American sleuth Easy Raw-lins, was released to instant critical acclaim. Because of the commercial success of the novel--which was filmed in 1995, with actor Denzel Washington as the major protagonist--and its many sequels, Mosley left computer programming and quit a doctoral course at City College to write full time. Since 1990, in addition to producing the popular Easy Rawlins series, he has begun two other crime series, has written several stand-alone novels in crime and other genres (including sci-ence fiction and erotica), a number of nonfiction works, five collections of short stories, and a play. He settled in New York, where he became artist-in-residence at New York University.

ANALYSIS

Many of Walter Mosley's major themes and stylistic characteristics have been present from his early pub-lished stories. His background as a member of two ethnic minorities (half Jewish, half African American), from an impoverished family, figures prominently in much of his work, which contains considerable auto-biographical material. His late father, both in occupa-tion and attitude, served as the inspiration for Mosley's best-known character, amateur private eye Easy Raw-lins. Mosley's upbringing in the depressed Los Angeles section of Watts provided the setting for the Rawlins series of novels, as well as for a multitude of short fic-tion. This work includes a story collection revolving around the exploits of Rawlins, *Six Easy Pieces*, and two collections that define the nature of Mosley's gut-level creation, the philosophical former convict strug-gling to do right, Socrates Fortlow: *Always Outnum-bered, Always Outgunned* and *The Right Mistake*.

One thread that runs throughout much of Mosley's long and short work is the commission, discovery, and resolution of crime. A fact of life, particularly in the desperate circumstances of the slums, where people with nothing to lose risk life and liberty to survive, crime for Mosley serves both as a catalyst that propels his characters into action and as a yardstick against which varying degrees of morality can be compared. Easy Rawlins, Socrates Fortlow, and Tempest Landry in *The Tempest Tales* are all flawed individuals who regularly break laws--stealing, breaking and entering,

threatening or perpetrating acts of violence--to prevent or avenge worse crimes.

A second major theme is the relationship among races, especially the continuing dominance of whites in American business, politics, economics, and law that undercuts full opportunity and justice for African Americans. As African Americans, Easy, Socrates, and Tempest in the course of their existence must con-stantly struggle against deep-seated prejudice from without and self-doubt about their true worth from within.

Stylistically, Mosley usually eschews literary pyro-technics. The author's particular strength is character-ization, revealed through telling description, action, and especially dialogue that demonstrates the author's keen ear. Speeches in the mouths of characters are laced with casual profanity, racial epithets, and gram-matical mistakes or mispronunciations--such as "ax" for "ask" or "chirren" for "children"--that indicate lack of or indifference to education. Mosley's characters, white, black, or otherwise, are well-rounded, specific individuals who come to life in the reader's mind.

Setting is also vital for Mosley. The streets of Watts in the Easy and Socrates stories (or New York in *The Tempest Tales*) add layers of meaning as they show the great gulf that exists between the haves and have-nots of the respective cities.

While plot is a significant consideration in Mosley's novels, it is of less importance in his short fiction. Many of his stories, which collectively form episodic novels with recurring characters, deal with small, subtle issues--relationships, the nature of friendship, the effects of poverty, longing and loneliness, the dif-ference between right and wrong--where the action oc-curs on a mental, rather than a physical, plane.

ALWAYS OUTNUMBERED, ALWAYS OUTGUNNED

This collection introduces Socrates Fortlow, who spent twenty-seven years locked up in an Indiana peni-tentiary for rape and homicide. Brutalized by his expe-riences in prison, Socrates upon his release drifts to Southern California to start a new and better life. Filled with inchoate rage that duels with a desire to overcome his violent nature, he takes up residence in a shack in the poorest area of Watts. He survives by redeeming soda cans and bottles and, over an eight-year period, forming a network of friends and acquaintances. With few expectations, but with huge reserves of hope and determination, Socrates asserts himself in the community, gaining respect for his quiet but authoritative ways.

In the first story, "The Crimson Shadow," Socrates becomes mentor to a wayward boy named Darryl. The relationship between man and boy grows and develops throughout the fourteen-story collection. Likewise, other colorful characters--disfigured World War II veteran Right Burke, welder Stony Wile, cowardly Markham Peal, hefty family man Howard Shakur, and no-nonsense restaurant owner Iula LaPort--appear periodically and serve as foils for the modern Socratic method of settling disputes. Separately and together, they interact with and are affected by Socrates's unique perspectives on life and his halting efforts to do the right thing through interrogation, reason, instinct, or persuasion.

Always Outnumbered, Always Outgunned presents a rich broth: a community of well-drawn individuals striving to rise above their circumstances, all orbiting around Socrates, a source of strength despite his faults. Prejudice is a constant presence in Socrates's new world as he seeks a job, interacts with police, survives illness and troubling dreams. Socrates endures to carry out, in his own small way, a vision of a better world, touching lives in the hope that tiny steps will inspire a great forward leap for humankind.

SIX EASY PIECES

There are seven stories in *Six Easy Pieces*, which shows private investigator Easy Rawlins at a particular point in his career. The first six stories were originally published one at a time in the 2002 Washington Square Press reprints of Easy Rawlins novels. Like the novels, the stories all contain reference to colors in their titles.

The stories in *Six Easy Pieces* unfold in the early 1960's, when Easy is employed as a custodian at Sojourner Truth High School. Easy lives comfortably in middle-class surroundings, with Bonnie, a beautiful Caribbean stewardess, and two adopted children: Feather, a young girl of mixed heritage, and Jesus, a Hispanic teen. Each story involves a particular problem Easy must solve: serial arson, murder, and misappropriation of funds. A deeper mystery runs throughout:

What has become of his lifelong friend Mouse? When last seen, Mouse apparently was fatally shot, but his body disappeared from the hospital where he allegedly died, and Easy feels obligated to find a definitive answer to the whereabouts of his friend's remains.

Six Easy Pieces supplements and reinforces the Easy Rawlins novels. Readers unfamiliar with the series can glimpse the protagonist at mid-career, while sampling the characterization, dialogue, plotting, and underlying moral dilemmas that made Mosley's groundbreaking novels popular.

THE TEMPEST TALES

Inspired by Langston Hughes's everyman character Jesse B. Semple, *The Tempest Tales* is a humorous fantasy concerning the tribulations of Tempest Landry, an ordinary African American who is the victim of mistaken identity. Wrongfully shot dead by police, Tempest is subjected to divine judgment, found wanting for his petty crimes, and ordered to hell. Tempest, however, argues against the sentence and is given a fresh chance to prove that he deserves heaven. He returns to Harlem, accompanied by an accounting angel in the appearance of an African American mortal. In a series of incidents, Tempest challenges the assumptions of "Angel" about right and wrong and falls in league with the devil (Basel Bob, or Beelzebub), who is disguised as a young man dressed in black. Meanwhile, Angel succumbs to human temptation--including falling in love and fathering a child--further confusing the issue of morality.

THE RIGHT MISTAKE

A little older, a little wiser, Socrates Fortlow is back, doing his part to change the world. This collection finds the ex-convict coming into possession of a house called the "Big Nickel," where he hosts regular weekly meetings with a motley group of neighborhood denizens--his adoptive ward Darryl, a gambler, a young lawyer, a Latino carpenter, an Asian martial arts instructor, a Jewish rag-picker, a pop singer, and others. Under the constant and clandestine scrutiny of suspicious police, the group attempts to develop creative solutions to perennial neighborhood problems: gang violence, prostitution, a variety of crimes, police profiling, and other issues. Though Socrates is still a primal force at the center of things, still very much an individual conscious of his violent nature, as a member of a community working toward common goals, he no longer has to work alone in fighting against society's ills and is stronger because of his reliance on friends.

OTHER MAJOR WORKS

LONG FICTION: *Devil in a Blue Dress*, 1990; *A Red Death*, 1991; *White Butterfly*, 1992; *Black Betty*, 1994; *RL's Dream*, 1995; *A Little Yellow Dog*, 1996; *Gone Fishin'*, 1996; *Blue Light*, 1998; *Walkin' the Dog*, 1999; *Fearless Jones*, 2001; *Bad Boy Brawly Brown*, 2002; *Fear Itself*, 2003; *Little Scarlet*, 2004; *The Man in My Basement*, 2004; *Cinnamon Kiss*, 2005; *Fear of the Dark*, 2006; *Fortunate Son*, 2006; *Killing Johnny Fry*, 2006; *The Wave*, 2006; *Blonde Faith*, 2007; *Diablerie*, 2008; *The Right Mistake; The Further Philosophical Investigations of Socrates Fortlow*, 2008; *The Tempest Tales*, 2008; *The Long Fall*, 2009; *Known to Evil*, 2010; *The Last Days of Ptolemy Grey*, 2010; *When the Thrill Is Gone*, 2011.

NONFICTION: *Workin' on the Chain Gang: Shaking Off the Dead Hand of History*, 2000; *What Next: A Memoir Toward World Peace*, 2003; *Life Out of Context: Which Includes a Proposal for the Non-violent Takeover of the House of Representatives*, 2006; *This Year You Write Your Novel*, 2007.

CHILDREN'S LITERATURE: *Forty-Seven*, 2005.

EDITED TEXTS: *Black Genius: African American Solutions to African American Problems*, 1999 (with others); *The Best American Short Stories, 2003*, 2003 (with Katrina Kenison).

BIBLIOGRAPHY

Bailey, Frankie Y. *African American Mystery Writers: A Historical and Thematic Study*. Jefferson, N.C.: McFarland, 2008. Written by a university professor of criminal justice, this book discusses the evolution of African American fiction from its beginnings to the present, particularly focusing on the historical, social, cultural, and judicial aspects as engendered in specific works by African American authors specializing in the crime-mystery genre.

Brady, Owen E., and Derek C. Maus, eds. *Finding a Way Home: A Critical Assessment of Walter Mosley's Fiction*. Jackson: University Press of Mississippi, 2008. This collection of essays focuses on the related concepts of home and belonging for African Americans, as expressed and developed across the breadth of Mosley's long and short fiction.

Penzler, Otto, ed. *Mystery, Crime, and Suspense Fiction by African-American Writers*. Oakland, Calif.: Pegasus, 2009. An anthology of the best mystery-crime genre fiction produced by African American writers since 1900--including a story by Mosley--with an insightful overview from mystery maven Penzler, which discusses elements common to the various entries of the collection.

Wilson, Charles E., Jr. *Walter Mosley: A Critical Companion*. Westport, Conn.: Greenwood, 2003. A study of Mosley's full range of writings, in terms of his heritage and upbringing, connecting such factors as influences and inspiration for his work.

Jack Ewing

N

Vladimir Nabokov

Born: St. Petersburg, Russia; April 23, 1899
Died: Montreux, Switzerland; July 2, 1977
Also known as: V. Sirin

OTHER LITERARY FORMS

During his fifty-year career as a writer, Vladimir Nabokov (VLAHD-eh-mehr NAB-uh-kawf) not only created short stories but also produced novels, poetry, drama, memoirs, translations, reviews, letters, critical essays, literary criticism, and the screenplay of his most famous novel, *Lolita* (1955). After his death, three volumes of lectures on literature that he had delivered to students at Wellesley, Stanford, and Cornell were scrupulously edited by Fredson Bowers and published as *Lectures on Literature* (1980), *Lectures on Russian Literature* (1981), and *Lectures on Don Quixote* (1983).

ACHIEVEMENTS

Vladimir Nabokov occupies a unique niche in the annals of literature by having become a major author in both Russian and English. He wrote nine novels, about forty stories, and considerable poetry in Russian before migrating to the United States in 1940. Thereafter, he not only wrote nine more novels and ten short stories in English but also translated into English the fiction that he had composed in his native language, sometimes with the collaboration of his son, Dmitri. Reversing his linguistic field, he translated his novel *Lolita* (1955) into Russian.

Nabokov's work has received considerable critical acclaim; a modern master, he has influenced such diverse literary figures as Anthony Burgess, John Barth, William H. Gass, Tom Stoppard, Philip Roth, John Updike, and Milan Kundera. Nabokov's fiction is never intentionally didactic or sociological; he detested moralistic, message-ridden writing. Instead, he delighted in playing self-consciously with the reader's credulity, regarding himself as a fantasist, a Prospero of artifice. He manipulates his characters as so many pieces on a chessboard, devising problems for absorbing, intricate games of which he and Jorge Luis Borges are the acknowledged modern masters. His precision of language, lexical command of multilingual allusions, and startling imagery have awed, delighted, and sometimes irritated critics and readers. Few writers have practiced art for the sake of art with such talent and discipline. Nabokov's advice to students suggests the best approach to his own fiction:

> In reading, one should notice and fondle details. . . . We must see things and hear things, we must visualize the rooms, the clothes, the manners of an author's people . . . above all, a great writer is always a great enchanter, and it is here that we come to the really exciting part when we try to grasp the individual magic of his genius and to study the style, the imagery, the pattern of his novels or poems.

BIOGRAPHY

Vladimir Vladimirovich Nabokov's life divides neatly into four phases, each lasting approximately twenty years. He was born on Shakespeare's birthday in 1899 to an aristocratic and wealthy family residing in St. Petersburg. His grandfather was state minister of justice for two czars; his father, Vladimir Dmitrievich, a prominent liberal politician, married a woman from an extremely wealthy family. Vladimir Vladimirovich, the first of two sons, was reared with much parental love and care, eloquently evoked in his lyrical memoir, *Conclusive Evidence: A Memoir* (1951), later expanded and retitled *Speak, Memory: An Autobiography Revisited* (1966).

In 1919, the October Revolution forced the Nabokovs to flee Russia. Vladimir, who had learned both French and English from governesses during his childhood, enrolled in the University of Cambridge, took a degree in foreign languages in 1923, and published two volumes of poetry the same year. Meanwhile, his father and the other family members settled in Berlin. There, Vladimir Dmitrievich was assassinated in 1922 by two right-wing extremist Russian expatriates who had intended their bullets for another victim. Vladimir took up residence in Berlin in 1923, and in 1925 he married a Jewish émigré, Véra Slonim, with whom he maintained a harmonious union. Between 1924 and 1929, he published twenty-two short stories in Russian-language exile newspapers and periodicals. Many of these stories were collected in *Vozvrashchenie Chorba* (the return of Chorb), whose contents were later translated into English and distributed among several collections of Nabokov's short stories.

To avoid confusion with his well-known father, the younger Nabokov assumed the pen name "V. Sirin," after a mythological, multicolored bird featured in ancient Russian literature; he used this name until leaving Europe in 1940. The Nabokovs stayed in Berlin until 1937, even though Vladimir never learned German and usually drew his German fictive personages unfavorably. In his writings during these years, he dramatized the autobiographical themes of political exile from Russia, nostalgia, grief, anguish, and other variations of vagrant rootlessness. His most important novels during the 1920's and 1930's are commonly judged to be *Zashchita Luzhina* (1929, serial; 1930, book; *The Defense*, 1964) and *Dar* (1937-1938, serial; 1952, book; *The Gift*, 1963).

Nabokov's third life-stage began in 1940, when, after a three-year stay in Paris, he was glad to escape the Nazi menace by emigrating to the United States. After a one-term lectureship at Stanford University, he distributed his time for the next seven years between teaching at Wellesley College and working as a research fellow in entomology at Harvard's Museum of Comparative Zoology, pursuing his passion for lepidoptera. During these years, he began to establish himself as an American writer of note and, in 1945, became a naturalized citizen. He published two novels, *The Real Life of Sebastian Knight* (1941) and *Bend Sinister* (1947); a brilliant but eccentric study of the Russian writer who had most deeply influenced him, *Nikolai Gogol* (1944); a number of stories and poems; and sections of his first autobiography. In 1948, Cornell University lured him away from Wellesley by offering him a tenured professorship. He became a celebrated ornament of the Ithaca, New York, campus for ten years,

Vladimir Nabokov (Library of Congress)

specializing in a course called Masters of European Fiction, alternately charming and provoking his students with witty lectures and difficult examinations.

Nabokov wrote *Lolita* during his summer vacations in the early 1950's, but the book was refused publication by several American firms and was first issued in 1955 by Olympia Press, a Parisian English-language publisher that usually featured pornography. By 1958, the work had become celebrated as well as notorious, and Putnam's issued it in New York. It became the year's sensational best seller, and Nabokov, taking an abrupt midyear leave from Cornell, thereupon moved to an elegant hotel on the banks of Switzerland's Lake Geneva for what were to prove nineteen more fecund years.

During this last arc of his career, Nabokov basked in the aura of worldwide recognition as an eminent writer yet continued to labor diligently: He revised his autobiography; resurrected his Russian long and short fiction in English translations; produced a four-volume translation of and commentary on Alexander Pushkin's novel in verse, *Yevgeny Onegin* (1833; Nabokov's English translation, *Eugene Onegin*, appeared in 1964); and wrote several new novels, including two--*Pale Fire* (1962) and *Ada or Ardor: A Family Chronicle* (1969)--worthy of consideration among the twentieth century's leading literary texts. Despite many losses and difficulties in his arduous life, Nabokov never yielded to self-pity, let alone despair. His career demonstrated not only artistic resourcefulness but also the personal virtues of resolution, resilience, and capacity for renewal.

Analysis

Vladimir Nabokov's early stories are set in the postczarist, post-World War I era, with Germany the usual location, and sensitive, exiled Russian men the usual protagonists. Many are nascent artists: wistful, sorrowful, solitary, sometimes despairingly disheartened. Many evoke a Proustian recollection of their Russian pasts as they try, and often as not fail, to understand an existence filled with irony, absurdity, and fortuity. These tales display Nabokov's abiding fascination with the interplay between reality and fantasy, between an outer world of tangs, scents, rain showers, sunsets, dawns,

butterflies, flowers, forests, and urban asphalt, and an inner landscape of recondite, impenetrable, mysterious feelings. He loved to mix the disheveled externals of precisely described furnishings, trappings, and drab minutiae with memories, myths, fantasy, parody, grandeur, hilarity, masks, nostalgia, and, above all, the magic of artistic illusion. He celebrates the unpredictable permutations of the individual imagination over the massive constraints of the twentieth century's sad history. He is the supreme stylist, dedicated to forging his vision in the most dazzling verbal smithy since James Joyce's.

"The Razor"

One of his first stories, "Britva" ("The Razor"), is a clever adaptation of motifs used in Nikolai Gogol's "Nos" ("The Nose") and Pushkin's "Vystrel" ("The Shot"). A White Russian émigré, Colonel Ivanov, now a barber in Berlin, recognizes a customer as the Red officer who had condemned him to death six years before. He toys with his victim, terrorizing him with caustic, cruel remarks, comparing his open razor to the sharp end of a sword, inverting the menace of their previous confrontation in Russia. In the end, however he shaves his former captor gently and carefully and releases him unharmed. By doing so, Ivanov also releases himself from his burning desire for vengeance. Nabokov uses the multivalent symbol of the razor compactly and densely: The acerbic Ivanov both sharpens and encases his razorlike temperament.

"The Doorbell"

In "Zvonok" ("The Doorbell"), Nabokov delineates a tragic encounter between past and present in a complex tale fusing realism and symbolism. A son, Galatov, has been separated from his mother for seven years, during which time he has fought in the post-1917 Russian civil war and wandered over Africa, Europe, and the Canary Islands. He learns that his mother's second husband has died and left her some real estate in Berlin. He searches for his mother there, meets her dentist, and through him obtains her address. Structurally, Galatov's visits to the dentist, a Dr. Weiner, anticipate his reunion with his mother: This Weiner is not Galatov's childhood dentist, yet he does happen to be his mother's. When Galatov finally meets his mother, he learns that she, too, is not the mother of his childhood: He meets, in the Berlin apartment, not the faded, dark-haired woman he left seven years earlier but an aged courtesan awaiting the arrival of a lover who is three years younger than her son. Galatov realizes that her fervent greeting of him had been intended for her paramour. When the doorbell announces the latter's arrival, Galatov learns, observing his mother's distraction and nervousness, that her new déclassé circumstances leave no room for him. He hurriedly departs, vaguely promising to see her again in a year or thereabouts. He knows now that not only has the mistress supplanted the mother but also his mother may never have cherished him as dearly as his previous need for her had deluded him into believing. The story's structural symmetry between memory and new reality is impressively achieved.

"A MATTER OF CHANCE"

"Sluchainost" ("A Matter of Chance") is one of Nabokov's most poignant tales. Its protagonist, Aleksey Luzhin--whose surname reappears five years later as that of the hero of *The Defense*--is a Russian exile who, like Galatov, has traveled to many places and worked many jobs. Currently, he is a waiter on a German train; having had no news of his wife, Elena, for five years, he is deeply depressed and has become addicted to cocaine. He plans his suicide for the night of August 1, the ninth anniversary of his wedding and the day of this story. On this particular trip, an old Russian princess, Maria Ukhtomski, is joined in her compartment by a young woman who arrived in Berlin from St. Petersburg the previous day, Elena Luzhina, who is seeking her lost husband. The story's rising action is full of suspense: Will the unsuspecting spouses find each other on the train? Luzhin sniffs cocaine in the toilet on the day he has resolved to make his last. The princess has known the Luzhin family and recalls its former aristocratic opulence. Ironically, when the now plebeian Luzhin announces the first seating for dinner, his cocaine-rotted mind can only dimly note the princess; he cannot connect her to his elegant past.

The links between the two plots never interlock. Elena, disturbed by a rudely aggressive fellow passenger, decides to forgo the dinner in the dining car where she would probably have met her husband. She loses her prized golden wedding ring in the vestibule of the train's wagon; it is discovered by another waiter as Luzhin leaves the wagon and jumps to his death before another train: "The locomotive came at him in one hungry bound." Missed chances abound--perhaps too many: Nabokov's uses of coincidence and his insistence of the malignity of haphazard events strain credulity.

"THE SCOUNDREL"

Perhaps Nabokov's most accomplished story of the 1920's is "Podlets" ("The Scoundrel," retitled by the author "An Affair of Honor" for its English publication). In his foreword to the English translation, Nabokov explains that "'An Affair of Honor' renders, in a drab expatriate setting, the degradation of a romantic theme whose decline had started with Chekhov's magnificent story 'The Duel' (1891)." Nabokov situates the duel within the traditional love triangle. The husband, an affluent banker named Anton Petrovich, returns home early from a business trip to find an arrogant acquaintance, Berg, nonchalantly getting dressed in his bedroom while his wife, Tanya, whom the reader never sees, is taking an interminable bath. Anton Petrovich challenges Berg to a duel. He pulls off his new glove and tries to throw it at Berg. Instead, it "slapped against the wall and dropped into the washstand pitcher." The ludicrous failure of Anton Petrovich's challenge sets the farcical, burlesque tone for the tale.

Anton Petrovich is a loving, tender, hardworking, amiable fellow whose major fault--abject cowardice--becomes his undoing. Anton Chekhov would have treated him gently and compassionately; Nabokov handles him disdainfully and absurdly, emphasizing his fondness for his shiny fountain pen, expensive shoes and socks, and monocle which "would gleam like a foolish eye on his belly." A duel is arranged but does not actually take place. Anton Petrovich, who has never fired a weapon, shakes with increasing fear at the prospect of confronting a former White Army officer who boasts of having killed hundreds. Before entering the woods where the combat is to occur, he and his caricatured seconds stop at a tavern for a round of beers. Anton Petrovich thereupon runs into the bar's backyard, slides and slips ridiculously down a slope, stumbles his way back to a train, and thence rides back to Berlin. He fantasizes that his craven flight will have been overshadowed by Berg's even earlier change of mind about dueling and that his wife will leave Berg and return to him, filled with love, delighted to satisfy him with an enormous ham sandwich.

Abruptly, Anton Petrovich awakens from his fiction. "Such things don't happen in real life," he reflects. He realizes that his reputation, his career, and his marriage are now ruined. He orders a ham sandwich and, animalistically, "grabbed the sandwich with both hands, immediately soiled his fingers and chin with the hanging margin of fat, and grunting greedily, began to munch." Nabokov has here begun to command the art of grotesquerie, precisely observed, relentlessly rendered, contemptuously concluded. Anton Petrovich would serve as a model for Albinus Kretschmar, cuckolded lover and failed artist in the novel *Kamera obskura* (1932; *Camera Obscura*, 1936; revised as *Laughter in the Dark*, 1938). Kretschmar in turn is a prototype for *Lolita*'s Humbert Humbert.

"THE ADMIRALTY SPIRE"

An amusing as well as saddening early exercise in playing mirror games, which were to become more and more convoluted in Nabokov's fiction, is his 1933 story "Admiralteyskaya Igla" ("The Admiralty Spire"). Its narrator addresses a trashy Soviet female writer who uses the pseudonymous male name Sergey Solntsev. He asserts that her cheap romantic novel, *The Admiralty Spire*, is a vulgar version of his first love affair, sixteen years earlier, with a young woman named Katya, whom the writer has renamed Olga. He accuses her of "pretentious fabrication" and of having "encroached with astonishing insolence on another person's past!" The letter proceeds to lecture the writer on the correct, nostalgic use of the sentimental past, but in the process of recall, the writer admits his distaste for Katya's "mendacity, her presumption, her vacuity" and deplores her "myopic soul" and the "triviality of [her] opinions." He did, however, once love her. The narrator ends with the speculation that the mediocre novelist he is addressing is probably Katya herself, "who, out of silly coquetry, has concocted a worthless book." He hopes against the odds that his presumption is erroneous. The atmosphere of overlapping dimensions of reality established here was to be splendidly employed in such later novels as *Pale Fire* and *Ada or Ardor*.

"CLOUD, CASTLE, LAKE"

In "Oblako, ozero, bashnya" ("Cloud, Castle, Lake"), the protagonist, a timid, intellectual bachelor, named Vasili Ivanovich, wins a pleasure trip at a charity ball for Russian expatriates in Berlin. He is the kind, meek, saintly soul familiar in Russian literature since Gogol's stories. He does not really want to take the journey but is intimidated by bureaucratic mazes into doing so. Obstacles thwart him persistently: Trying to settle down with a volume of Russian poetry, Vasili is instead bullied by a squadron of husky German fellow travelers, with monstrous knapsacks and hobnailed boots, into forced communal games that prove witless and humiliating. When the group pairs off, no one wants to romance him: He is designated "the loser and was forced to eat a cigarette butt." Unexpectedly, they come upon "a pure, blue lake," reflecting a large cloud and adjoining "an ancient, black castle." Overjoyed, Vasili wishes to surrender to the beautiful prospect and remain the rest of his life in the inn from which he can delight in this tableau. Unfortunately for Vasili, the group insists on dragging him back and beats him furiously during the return journey.

The tale is manifestly an allegory mourning the defeat of individuality and privacy in an ugly world determined to enforce total conformity. "Oh, but this is nothing less than an invitation to a beheading," protests Vasili as the group grimly denies him his room with a view. By no accident, Nabokov would soon write his novel, *Priglashenie na kazn'* (1935-1936, serial; 1938, book; *Invitation to a Beheading*, 1959), whose main character, Cincinnatus C., is condemned to death for not fitting into a totalitarian culture. Nabokov may have occasionally presented himself as an arrogant, coldhearted puppeteer lacking any world-mending concerns, but he does clearly condemn all cultures of regimentation and authoritarianism.

"SPRING IN FIALTA"

"Vesna v Fialte" ("Spring in Fialta") was to become the title work of a collection of Nabokov's short stories; some critics regard it as the masterpiece among his stories, although others prefer "Signs and Symbols." The narrator of "Spring in Fialta," Victor, is a Russian émigré businessman who, over the course of fifteen years, has had sporadic meetings with a charmingly casual, pretty, vital woman named Nina. These encounters are sometimes sexual but never last more than a few hours and occur outside their continuing lives and separate marriages. "Again and again," Victor notes, "she hurriedly appeared in the margin of my life, without influencing in the least its basic text." So, at least, he believes. He has his respectably bourgeois world "in which I sat for my portrait, with my wife, my young daughters, the Doberman pinscher." However, he finds himself also drawn to Nina's world of carefree sexuality mixed with "lies . . . futility . . . gibberish." This tension that Victor experiences is common in both life and literature, and Nabokov's characters are not immune. Although Nabokov appears to admire uxoriousness, as in the marriages of the Shades in *Pale Fire* or the Krugs in *Bend Sinister*, his protagonists are also mesmerized by *belles dames sans merci*--Margot (renamed Magda) in *Laughter in the Dark*, Lolita, Ada, and many more.

Nina is married to a gifted but repulsive Franco-Hungarian writer, Ferdinand; she also travels with the equally offensive but far less talented writer, Segur. Both men are artist figures: selfish, artificial, buoyant, heartless. Nina, while adaptable and "loyally sharing [Ferdinand's] tastes," is not really his muse: rather, she represents life's vulnerability, and her attempt to imitate Ferdinand's world proves fatal. When the car in which the three of them ride crashes into a truck, Ferdinand and Segur, "those invulnerable rogues, those salamanders of fate . . . had escaped with local and temporary injury . . . while Nina, in spite of her long-standing, faithful imitation of them, had turned out after all to be mortal." Life can only copy art, not replace it.

"SIGNS AND SYMBOLS"

In "Signs and Symbols," Nabokov wrote his most sorrowful story. An elderly, poor Russian émigré couple intend to pay a birthday visit to their son, institutionalized in a sanatorium, afflicted with "referential mania," in which "the patient imagines that everything happening around him is a veiled reference to his personality and existence." On their way to the sanatorium, the machinery of existence seems to malfunction: The subway loses its electric current between stations; the bus is late and crammed with noisy schoolchildren; they are pelted by pouring rain as they walk the last stretch of the way. Finally, instead of being able to see their son, they are informed that he has again attempted suicide and should not be disturbed. The couple return home with the present that they cannot give him, wordless with worry and defeat, the woman close to tears. On their way they see "a tiny, half-dead unfledged bird . . . helplessly twitching in a puddle."

After a somber supper, the husband goes to bed, and the wife reviews a family photo album filled with the faces of mostly suffering or dead relatives. One cousin is a "famous chess player"--Nabokov's oblique reference to Luzhin of *The Defense*, who commits suicide. In his previous suicide attempt, the son had wanted "to tear a hole in his world and escape." In the story's last section, the time is past midnight, the husband is sleepless and in pain, and the couple decide to bring their boy home from the institution; each parent will need to spend part of each night with him. Then the phone rings: a wrong number. When it rings a second time, the wife carefully explains to the same caller how she must have misdialed. After a while the phone rings for the third time; the story ends. The signs and symbols in all likelihood suggest that the last call is from the sanatorium, to announce that the son has succeeded in escaping this world.

Artistically, this story is virtually flawless: intricately patterned, densely textured, remarkably intense in tone and feeling. For once, Nabokov the literary jeweler has cut more deeply than his usual surfaces; for once, he has entered the frightening woods of tragic, unmitigated grief; for once, he has forsaken gamesmanship and mirror-play, punning and parody and other gambits of verbal artifice to face the grimmest horrors of a sometimes hopeless world.

OTHER MAJOR WORKS

LONG FICTION: *Mashenka*, 1926 (*Mary*, 1970); *Korol', dama, valet*, 1928 (*King, Queen, Knave*, 1968); *Zashchita Luzhina*, 1929 (serial), 1930 (book) (*The Defense*, 1964); *Soglyadatay*, 1930 (serial), 1938 (book) (*The Eye*, 1965); *Kamera obskura*, 1932 (*Camera Obscura*, 1936; revised as *Laughter in the Dark*, 1938); *Podvig*, 1932 (*Glory*, 1971); *Otchayanie*,

1934 (serial), 1936 (book) (*Despair*, 1937; revised 1966); *Priglashenie na kazn'*, 1935-1936 (serial), 1938 (book) (*Invitation to a Beheading*, 1959); *Dar*, 1937-1938 (serial), 1952 (book) (*The Gift*, 1963); *The Real Life of Sebastian Knight*, 1941; *Bend Sinister*, 1947; *Lolita*, 1955; *Pnin*, 1957; *Pale Fire*, 1962; *Ada or Ardor: A Family Chronicle*, 1969; *Transparent Things*, 1972; *Look at the Harlequins!*, 1974; *Novels, 1955-1962*, 1996; *Novels, 1969-1974*, 1996. *The Original of Laura (Dying Is Fun)*, 2009 (Dmitri Nabokov, editor).

PLAYS: *Dedushka*, pb. 1923; *Smert'*, pb. 1923; *Polius*, pb. 1924; *Tragediya gospodina Morna*, pb. 1924; *Chelovek iz SSSR*, pb. 1927; *Izobretenie Val'sa*, pb. 1938 (*The Waltz Invention*, 1966); *Sobytiye*, pr., pb. 1938.

SCREENPLAY: *Lolita*, 1962 (adaptation of his novel).

POETRY: *Stikhi*, 1916; *Dva puti*, 1918; *Gorny put*, 1923; *Grozd'*, 1923; *Stikhotvorenia, 1929-1951*, 1952; *Poems*, 1959; *Poems and Problems*, 1970.

NONFICTION: *Nikolai Gogol*, 1944; *Conclusive Evidence: A Memoir*, 1951; *Drugie berega*, 1954; *Speak, Memory: An Autobiography Revisited*, 1966 (revision of *Conclusive Evidence* and *Drugie berega*); *Strong Opinions*, 1973; *The Nabokov-Wilson Letters: Correspondence Between Vladimir Nabokov and Edmund Wilson, 1940-1971*, 1979 (Simon Karlinsky, editor); *Lectures on Literature*, 1980; *Lectures on Russian Literature*, 1981; *Lectures on Don Quixote*, 1983; *Vladimir Nabokov: Selected Letters, 1940-1977*, 1989.

TRANSLATIONS: *Anya v strane chudes*, 1923 (of Lewis Carroll's novel *Alice's Adventures in Wonderland*); *Three Russian Poets: Translations of Pushkin, Lermontov, and Tiutchev*, 1944 (with Dmitri Nabokov); *A Hero of Our Time*, 1958 (of Mikhail Lermontov's novel; with Dmitri Nabokov); *The Song of Igor's Campaign*, 1960 (of the twelfth century epic *Slovo o polki Igoreve*); *Eugene Onegin*, 1964 (of Alexander Pushkin's novel).

MISCELLANEOUS: *Novels and Memoirs, 1941-1951*, 1996.

BIBLIOGRAPHY

Alexandrov, Vladimir E. *Nabokov's Otherworld*. Princeton, N.J.: Princeton University Press, 1991. Alexandrov argues that "The central fact of both Nabokov's life and his art was something that could be described as an intuition about a transcendent realm of being." Showing how an awareness of this "otherworld" informs Nabokov's works, Alexandrov focuses on *Speak, Memory: An Autobiography Revisited* and on six of Nabokov's novels, but his study illumines Nabokov's short fiction as well, correcting the widely accepted view of Nabokov as an aloof gamesman preoccupied with verbal artifice for its own sake. Includes notes, a secondary bibliography, and an index.

Boyd, Brian. *Vladimir Nabokov: The Russian Years*. Princeton, N.J.: Princeton University Press, 1990.

_____. *Vladimir Nabokov: The American Years*. Princeton, N.J.: Princeton University Press, 1991. In the course of the two volumes of this critical biography, Boyd discusses virtually all Nabokov's stories. Boyd generally provides a brief summary of each story, relating it to Nabokov's development as an artist and noting recurring themes. Each volume includes illustrations, extensive notes, and an exceptionally thorough index.

Connolly, Julian W. *The Cambridge Companion to Nabokov*. New York: Cambridge University Press, 2005. Collection of essays analyzing various aspects of Nabokov's life and works, including "Nabokov's Short Fiction," by Priscilla Meyer. Some of the other essays discuss Nabokov's worldview, Nabokov and modernism, and his transition from writing in Russian to writing in English.

Field, Andrew. *Nabokov: His Life in Art*. Boston: Little, Brown, 1967. Field singles out several of Nabokov's stories for analysis. Of particular interest is his discussion of "The Potato Elf," which he describes as "a classic instance of a brilliantly executed short story whose compressed action is an essential function of its success." In Field's judgment, "The Potato Elf" is "Nabokov's greatest short story."

Foster, John Burt, Jr. "Nabokov's Art of Memory: Recollected Emotion in 'Spring in Fialta.'" In *The Russian Twentieth-Century Short Story: A Critical Companion*, edited by Lyudmila Parts. Brighton, Mass.: Academic Studies Press, 2010. Provides a critical reading of this story.

Gelfant, Blanche H., ed. *The Columbia Companion to the Twentieth-Century American Short Story*. New York: Columbia University Press, 2000. Includes a chapter in which Nabokov's short stories are analyzed.

Grayson, Jane, Arnold B. McMillin, and Priscilla Meyer, eds. *Reading Nabokov*. Vol. 2 in *Nabokov's World*. New York: Palgrave Macmillan, 2002. A collection of fifteen essays focusing on intertextuality in Nabokov's works and their literary reception. The index lists references to the short stories, and Dale E. Peterson analyzes some of Nabokov's short fiction in his essay "White (K)Nights: Dostoevskian Dreamers in Nabokov's Early Stories."

Kellman, Steven G., and Irving Malin, eds. *Torpid Smoke: The Stories of Vladimir Nabokov*. Atlanta, Ga.: Rodopi, 2000. Collection of essays examining Nabokov's short stories. Includes discussion of memory and dream in his short fiction, his approach to the supernatural in his early stories, and his Christmas stories, as well as analyses of some of the individual stories, including "Music," "Breaking the News," "The Assistant Producer," and "Mademoiselle O."

Morris, Paul Duncan. *Vladimir Nabokov: Poetry and the Lyric Voice*. Toronto: University of Toronto Press, 2010. A study focusing on Nabokov's English and Russian poetry, which Morris argues is a central part of Nabokov's identity as a writer. After analyzing his poetry, Morris examines the other genres in which Nabokov wrote, including a chapter devoted to "Nabokov and the Short Story: The Lyric Heights of a Small Alpine Form." Morris demonstrates how the short fiction, and all Nabokov's works, are shaped by his lyric sensibility.

Nicol, Charles. "'Ghastly Rich Glass': A Double Essay on 'Spring in Fialta.'" *Russian Literature Triquarterly*, no. 24 (1991): 173-184. One of two pieces devoted to Nabokov's short fiction in this special Nabokov issue, Nicol's article on "Spring in Fialta" has two concerns: "First, a consideration of the plot structure . . . and second, a further perspective on the vexed question of whether this story has any autobiographical relevance or personal reference to its author."

Nicol, Charles, and Gennady Barabtarlo. *A Small Alpine Form: Studies in Nabokov's Short Fiction*. New York: Garland, 1993. Contains sixteen essays on Nabokov's stories from a variety of critical points of view. The essays discuss themes, sources, parallels, and symbols in such stories as "Spring in Fialta," "Signs and Symbols," and several others.

Parker, Stephen Jan. *Understanding Vladimir Nabokov*. Columbia: University of South Carolina Press, 1987. An introductory guide to Nabokov for students and nonacademic readers. After a chapter on the self-reflexive aspects of Nabokov's narrative technique, the book focuses on individual analyses of five Russian novels and four American novels. The section on the short stories provides brief summary analyses of "Spring in Fialta," "Cloud, Castle, Lake," "Signs and Symbols," and "The Vane Sisters."

_____. "Vladimir Nabokov and the Short Story." *Russian Literature Triquarterly*, no. 24 (1991): 63-72. Parker worked with Nabokov and his wife Véra in the early 1970's to establish a precise chronology of Nabokov's short stories in Russian and to discuss possible titles for the English translations. Listed here are the results of their conversation and correspondence. Also included is a previously unpublished interview (conducted by mail) centering on the short story as a genre, with some characteristically provocative responses from Nabokov.

Shrayer, Maxim D. "Mapping Narrative Space in Nabokov's Short Fiction." *The Slavonic and East European Review* 75 (October, 1997): 624-641. Discusses the figurations of space in Nabokov's stories; emphasizes his rendering of three-dimensional space on an atomistic scale and the way in which a whole narrative serves as a travel guide to its own space. Compares Nabokov's method of rendering the narrative space with that of his Russian predecessors.

_____. *The World of Nabokov's Stories*. Austin: University of Texas Press, 1999. A detailed analysis of Nabokov's mastery of the short-story form and his worldview. Traces Nabokov's literary practice from the early 1920's to the 1930's, focusing on the Russian stories, such as "The Return of Chorb" and

"Cloud, Castle, Lake." Also discusses Nabokov's relationship to writers Anton Chekhov and Ivan Bunin.

Wyllie, Barbara. *Vladimir Nabokov*. London: Reaktion, 2010. Comprehensive overview of Nabokov's life and works. Examines Nabokov's preoccupations with time, memory, and mortality.

Gerhard Brand

ANTONYA NELSON

Born: Wichita, Kansas; January 6, 1961

PRINCIPAL SHORT FICTION

The Expendables, 1990
In the Land of Men, 1992
Family Terrorists: A Novella and Seven Stories, 1994
Female Trouble, 2002
Some Fun: Stories and a Novella, 2006
Nothing Right, 2009

OTHER LITERARY FORMS

Although Antonya Nelson is known mainly as a short-fiction writer, she has written a number of novels. Her first was in 1996, *Talking in Bed.* This was followed by *Nobody's Girl* (1998), *Living to Tell* (2000), and *Bound* (2010). The novels exhibit the same topics and plots as the short stories, handling them in much the same way. There is an obvious continuity between the two genres.

ACHIEVEMENTS

Antonya Nelson's short fiction has won her recognition as a careful craftsperson, writing in the realistic "slice-of-life" tradition. She lays bare the inadequacies and failures of lower middle-class American life, especially as lived west of the Mississippi and especially as it centers on family life. Her stories have been anthologized in *Prize Stories: The O. Henry Awards (*1992) and in *Best American Short Stories* (1993). *In the Land of Men, Talking in Bed*, and *Female Trouble* received attention in the *New York Times Book Review* Notable Books lists. In June, 1999, *The New York Times Magazine* selected her as one of the twenty best young fiction

writers in America. She won a Guggenheim Fellowship in 2000 and a Rea Short Story Award in 2003. Her short story "Listener" from her first volume won a Nelson Algren Award.

BIOGRAPHY

Antonya Nelson was one of five children born to Francis and Susan Nelson, in Wichita, Kansas. Her father was a professor and later professor emeritus in the English Department of Wichita State University; her mother was an instructor in the same department and a minor writer of fiction. After education in local schools, Nelson completed her undergraduate work at the University of Kansas, receiving her B.A. in 1983. The next year she married Robert L. Boswell, who at that time was a novelist and short-story writer. The marriage produced two children.

Nelson went on to complete her master of fine arts in creative writing in 1986 at the University of Arizona. Three years later she was appointed assistant professor at New Mexico State University, in the Department of English, as creative-writing specialist. By that time several of her short stories had appeared in magazines, but her first collection, *The Expendables*, did not appear until 1990, published by the University of Georgia Press.

Nelson's short stories began to appear more frequently, in such magazines as *Esquire, The New Yorker, Redbook*, and *Mademoiselle*. A further volume appeared in 1992, *In the Land of Men*, published by Morrow. It received favorable reviews. Her real breakthrough in terms of becoming known came with her third volume of short stories, which also included a novella. *Family Terrorists* was published in 1994 by Houghton Mifflin and became her first work to receive an overseas printing, in London in 1997 by the paperback imprint Picador.

Nelson began to receive invitations to become visiting writer or writer-in-residence. Residencies at Wichita State University in 1998 and Vermont Studio Center in 1999 were followed by a permanent post in the prestigious M.F.A. program at Warren Wilson College, Swannanoa, North Carolina. She lived partly in Las Cruces, New Mexico, and partly in Telluride, Colorado.

Nelson's first novel, *Talking in Bed*, appeared in 1996, to be followed by two more novels, *Nobody's Girl* and *Living to Tell*. She returned to short stories with *Female Trouble* in 2002 and *Some Fun* in 2006. The latter collection also included a significant novella, which gave its name to the overall collection. At this time she and her husband were jointly appointed to the Cullen Chair of Creative Writing at the University of Houston, for which they made a third home base for themselves in Texas. Their academic partnership has an interesting parallel to her parents'. A further collection of short stories, *Nothing Right*, appeared in 2009, to be shortly followed by the fourth novel, *Bound*, in 2010.

ANALYSIS

In some ways, Antonya Nelson's short stories mirror her life. They are often set in Kansas, Texas, New Mexico, or Colorado, places she has lived and knows well. She never strays east of the Mississippi in her settings, which are always contemporary. By and large her characters are from the middle class, some professional but mostly blue-collar, though she covers dropouts from those groups, too. Her style is, as might be expected from a creative-writing teacher, crisp, economic, and focused through specific viewpoints and perspectives. Its tone is neutral, even academic at times, and always controlled. She gains emotional shock through her open description of human sexuality rather than through allowing any strong emotions of anger or protest to spill out into the narrative.

In other ways, however, the stories differ remarkably from her own stable marriage and successful career as a writer and a teacher. Parents feature prominently, but nearly always as inadequate, almost to the

Antonya Nelson (Scott S. Warren/National Geographic Society/Corbis)

point where the reader feels social services should be involved. However, Nelson demands that they try to work out their own salvation, and outside intervention, apart from that of other family members or close family friends, is more or less ruled out. Generally, such attempts are only partially successful, leading the family members to live out warped or spoiled relationships. Variously, her parents can be typified as being abusive, alcoholic, divorced or divorcing, adulterous, and self-centered. They lack a moral framework for their lives and they lack spirituality. Nelson makes little attempt to portray them as attractive. If anything, the likable characters are children, struggling toward some sort of normal childhood, or their pets.

Moreover, her characters and stories exist without any sense of a wider society. She appears to believe, as did British prime minister Margaret Thatcher, that "there is no such thing as society." Even less is there any reference to a world outside. It is in small details that the stories place themselves in later twentieth century cultural history. It is in the feel of the fragmented family that the stories portray the aimless angst of Western civilization as it exists post-1960's, post-liberalism, post-Christianity. While Nelson's places are specific, they are cyphers: Those situated in the Midwest represent family life in some recognizable form; those in the West and Pacific are fragmented units searching for new relationships, a new life to build out of the shattered remains of a past.

Nelson's first volume of short stories, *The Expendables*, with its twelve stories, already lays out the pattern for future plots and characters. The title suggests some sort of underclass, disregarded by mainstream society. Unlike the underclass in the works of John Steinbeck, William Faulkner, and Eudora Welty, however, Nelson's underclass is portrayed without sympathy. They are inadequate, and there is no attempt to see them as otherwise, because their inadequacies usually are measured in terms of self-centeredness, of betrayal of trust and commitment, with few redeeming reasons or outcomes. "Cold Place," for example, is not just cold Wichita, but cold relationships in a marriage in crisis because of unfaithfulness. As in a number of stories, the perspective is that of a teenage daughter, for whom the inadequacies of the grown-ups are as bad as she thinks. Other stories deal with weddings and marriage, female friendship, and deaths in the family.

IN THE LAND OF MEN

Nelson's second volume contains fourteen stories. The title story concerns three brothers avenging their sister's rape, a biblical theme perhaps, but treated in a very modern way. There is no external code by which to proceed: The choice is left to the girl. Nelson ends the story before the girl decides what she wants her brothers to do with the rapist. The suggestion is that the brothers, too, are violating their sister by forcing on her such a choice. Other stories, it has been suggested, exemplify the emotional claustrophobia of familial relationships: harming rather than nurturing. Another story, "How Much We Could See," is set in Telluride, a typical Nelson move, setting her stories in places in which she lives.

In most stories, however, the town fails to take on specific features: It could be anywhere in the West. A holiday story turns bad when a teenager drowns. Two other stories feature members of the Link family, but

Nelson refuses to create a series of interlinking stories around this family or any other. She has stated she does not want to get into the business of creating maps, inventing histories, and specifying other information that interlinking stories demand. The name "Link" thus becomes deeply ironic: Her stories may repeat but they do not link. Such repeating plot motifs are the untimely deaths of mothers and the shooting or killing of pets.

FAMILY TERRORISTS

The title of this collection sums up well the family dynamics that Nelson typically portrays. There are no open battles in her families, which might invite outside societal intervention, but small acts of terrorism: betrayal, emotional blackmail, false expectations, petty unkindnesses. All of these are instantly recognizable in most families, and it is this recognition factor that provides the magnetic force to the stories. This is life as it is lived, without clear plot beginnings or ends; without overall perspectives, moral or spiritual; without clear goals or ambitions, but with a hedonistic force that is necessarily self-defeating. The families in this volume could be seen as typical, except that their failures are writ large. Nelson provides no solution, no handbook to find an exit to the warfare. The title story is a novella, a link perhaps to the three novels that followed this volume. It centers on the Link family, reassembling to witness the parents' remarriage. It culminates in exposure of secrets long held by the guilty father. Family life is seen as guilty activity.

"FEMALE TROUBLE"

"Female Trouble" is placed last of the thirteen stories that make up the volume by that name. The title given to the volume suggests stories that have a female protagonist, focusing on issues particular to women: motherhood and childlessness, daughters, sisters, managing a family, female friendship, marriage and divorce, pregnancy and abortion. Certainly, there are stories that do focus on these topics. However, such female issues as menopause and breast or cervical cancer, for example, are avoided.

In "Female Trouble," the protagonist is a man, and the story is told largely from his perspective. His "female trouble" comes in triplicate. McBride has a present mistress and a former one, who is in a psychiatric hospital near Tucson, not far from where he lives.

While visiting her, he meets another woman, who is suicidal. For some reason that is never really analyzed, McBride feels the need to begin an affair with her. In the end, he abandons her, and she then commits suicide. Meanwhile, his present and former mistresses become friends, a friendship from which McBride feels excluded. At the end of the story, he feels he is being pushed out of all female relationships, and he leaves, perhaps to start again.

None of the characters is presented as particularly attractive or with any redeeming qualities. Relationships are casual and promiscuous. The only people for whom the reader feels sorry are the suicidal woman's parents, who watch on the sidelines as McBride completes the destruction of their daughter. The environment is portrayed as bleak and trashy as the relationships. The gritty, sandy desert suggests the dried-out, desiccated nature of the quality of human love.

"Some Fun"

"Some Fun" is a novella that is the last fiction in the volume of that name. (It is preceded by six short stories, the most powerful of which is "Dick.") A recurring familial theme recurs: the strong woman married to a weaker man, feeling guilty about the decisions she has railroaded to satisfy her own desires.

The novella is nearly ninety pages long, as opposed to the fifteen or twenty pages of a typical Nelson short story. It is set in El Paso, Texas, and is told from the perspective of a fifteen-year-old girl, Claire. The story follows her transition from child to adult. Her maturity is forced on her by the behavior of her drunken childlike mother, whose inadequacies are a synthesis of those of typical Nelson mothers. Claire looks after her two small brothers and attempts to confront her mother with her alcoholism.

The father has left the family because his wife is just "too sad." In the sense that the story, like most Nelson stories, contains no humor at all and no cause for laughter, he is correct, though the woman he flees to seems to find even less fun in life. However, as a character, he is "sad," too, in his failure to support the family in a meaningful way. The two little boys live briefly with him and his girlfriend, but return to what emotional warmth there is with Claire and her mother. No one, of course, has much "fun."

The real emotional crises of the story center on Claire's aunt, who committed suicide, and the fear that Claire will do the same thing. Nelson typically refuses to bring in society around the death, which is at first believed to be murder. Instead, a single pathetic detective represents the forces of law and order. The other emotional events center on Claire's sexual encounters. These could have been far more damaging because of her mother's neglect as she tries to fulfill her own sexual needs. Claire emerges as a survivor, someone for whom a normal life is, at least, a possibility.

Nothing Right

This volume contains eleven stories, all about characters who can do "nothing right." Although Nelson claimed in one interview that she is as happy with male protagonists as female leads, the preponderance is toward female, especially strong women who trust in weak men. In "Some Fun," Nelson writes that her characters "demonstrate the inferiority of their lives . . . she [Claire] would have preferred not knowing." The reader feels that Nelson emphasizes this statement even more strongly in this collection: Does the reader really want to know? Nelson's intense focus on certain issues again is demonstrated by this volume, but her refusal to explore wider boundaries, to acknowledge other experiences, becomes a weakness rather than a strength.

The title story centers on motherhood, this time a surrogate motherhood resulting from a shiftless teenage pregnancy. However, the quality of motherhood seems instinctive rather than heroic. A pattern of failure remains generational, with only the faint hope something will happen to break it.

Other major works

Long fiction: *Talking in Bed*, 1996; *Nobody's Girl*, 1998; *Living to Tell*, 2000; *Bound*, 2010.

Bibliography

Kirsch, Adam. "*Nothing Right*: Short Stories by Antonya Nelson." *The New York Times*, February 6, 2009. A perceptive review of this volume of short stories, pointing up many of Nelson's recurring themes.

Levasseur, Jennifer, and Kevin Rabalais. "An Interview with Antonya Nelson." *Missouri Review* 13, no. 3 (Fall, 2000). The focus is on *Living to Tell*, but Nelson talks at some length on her other writings and her particular interests.

McInnis, Susan. "An Interview with Antonya Nelson." *Writer's Chronicle* 31 (September, 1998). Focuses especially on *Nobody's Girl*, but provides general comments about Nelson's fiction to that point.

David Barratt

GURNEY NORMAN

Born: Grundy, Virginia; July 22, 1937

PRINCIPAL SHORT FICTION

Kinfolks: The Wilgus Stories, 1977

OTHER LITERARY FORMS

Gurney Norman's first work of fiction was a novel entitled *Divine Right's Trip: A Folk-Tale* (1972), which was written for *The Last Whole Earth Catalog*. Between 1987 and 1991, he wrote the scripts for and narrated three hour-long documentaries on eastern Kentucky for Kentucky Educational Television. He has coedited several collections of essays and poetry, including *A Gathering at the Forks: Fifteen Years of the Hindman Settlement School* (1993), *Backtalk from Appalachia: Confronting Stereotypes* (1999), and *An American Vein: Critical Readings in Appalachian Literature* (2005).

ACHIEVEMENTS

Gurney Norman won a Wallace Stegner Fellowship at Stanford University in 1960. Morehead State University in Kentucky presented him with the Appalachian Treasure Award in 1996. Emory and Henry College honored his work at its annual Literary Festival in 1996. In 2009, Norman was named Kentucky's Poet Laureate for 2009-2010.

BIOGRAPHY

Born in Grundy, Virginia, on July 22, 1937, Gurney Norman grew up in a small coal-camp community near Hazard, Kentucky. He was enrolled in a Presbyterian boarding school in Letcher County,

Kentucky, at the age of nine, from which he graduated in 1955. He received a journalism degree from the University of Kentucky in 1959, and while there he studied literature and writing under two prominent Kentucky writers, Hollis Summers and Robert Hazel. Norman then received a Wallace Stegner Fellowship to California's Stanford University, studying under Frank O'Connor, Malcolm Cowley, and Wallace Stegner.

After spending two years in the Army, Norman moved back to Hazard, Kentucky, in 1963, and he became a reporter for a weekly newspaper, *The Hazard Herald*. In 1965, he moved back to Palo Alto, California, where he married and began writing reviews and organic gardening stories for *The Whole Earth Catalog*, a counter-culture publishing phenomenon begun in the late 1960's When the editor, Steward Brand, decided to compile a final issue of the catalog, Norman suggested including a novel in it, which he volunteered to write. *Divine Right's Trip* features a young hippie man from Kentucky making a road trip from California to Kentucky.

In 1977, Norman gathered together several of his short stories, which had appeared in small regional magazines and quarterlies, in a book entitled *Kinfolks: The Wilgus Stories*. In 1979, he joined the English Department at University of Kentucky to teach creative writing. He helped found the Southern Appalachian Writers Cooperative and in 1978 became a teacher at the Appalachian Writers Workshop at Hindman Settlement School in Kentucky. In 1990, he collaborated with filmmaker Andrew Garrison, who directed three film versions of stories from *Kinfolks*: "Fat Monroe," "Night Ride," and "Maxine." In 1996, Norman married Nyoka Hawkins, with whom he founded Old Cove Press. In 2009, the governor of Kentucky named Gurney Norman the state's poet laureate.

ANALYSIS

Gurney Norman's influence as a Kentucky writer far outweighs his body of work. He has written only one novel, *Divine Right's Trip*, best known for having been published in the margins of *The Last Whole Earth Catalog*, which sold more than two million copies in the fading years of the counter-culture movement of the late 1960's. His single stand-alone book is a small (a little more than one hundred pages) collection of ten short stories, published by a small press in Frankfort, Kentucky, in 1977. The stories were first published primarily in low-circulation regional magazines, such as *Kentucky Renaissance, Mountain Life and Work*, and *Appalachian South*. Norman is a tireless promoter of Kentucky writers and Appalachian culture. In the more than thirty years he has been teaching and administering the creative-writing program at the University of Kentucky in Lexington and serving on the staff at the annual Appalachian Writers Workshop in the mountain town of Hindman, Kentucky, he has encouraged the work of many young writers. As Kentucky Poet Laureate, he traveled across the state, speaking at schools and conferences about the culture of the mountains.

Norman has said that he realized several years ago that his kind of writing "just will not fit" the well-made novels that sell so widely and so well in America. He says he has hundreds of small narratives, personal and family stories, all about nine hundred words each, that he would like to transform from mere anecdote to fictional storytelling. Indeed, although his novel is patterned on the epic-journey structure, popular from Homer's *Odyssey* (c. 725 b.c.e.; English translation, 1614) to Jack Kerouac's *On the Road* (1957), Norman's real talent shows forth in Appalachian anecdotes and the stories of one young man's odyssey to adulthood in the mountains of eastern Kentucky in *Kinfolks: The Wilgus Stories*.

KINFOLKS: THE WILGUS STORIES

The central character in these linked stories is Wilgus Collier, whose parents appear only briefly in the first story; after their death, Wilgus spends his formative years living with his grandparents, his uncles, his aunts, and his cousins in the mountains of eastern Kentucky. In several of the stories, Wilgus is peacemaker in the battles between his grandmother and grandfather, his grandmother and her daughter Jenny, and his grandparents and their son Delmer. The three most important stories in the collection, the ones that were made into short films in 1990, are "Fat Monroe," "Night Ride," and "Maxine."

"FAT MONROE"

The opening story of *Kinfolks* is one of the best-loved stories in Norman's collection, not only because of its good-humored comedy and unforgettable main character, played to perfection by Ned Beatty in the film version of the story, but also because it introduces the family loyalty theme that unifies the collection. Wilgus Collier, the main character, appearing in all of the stories, is an eight-year-old mountain boy who hitches a ride home with a big fat man chomping on a cigar. The man spends the entire drive teasing the boy, sometimes making him laugh, sometimes irritating him. He refuses to call Wilgus by his real name, asks him how many wives he has, offers him a cigar, and says he thought the boy was thirty years old.

All this is only mildly annoying to Wilgus until the fat man starts saying bad things about Wilgus's father, claiming he has heard the father drinks whiskey, loses all his money on cards, is too worthless to work, and beats the boy and his mother. When Wilgus insists his daddy does not do such things and that he likes his daddy, Fat Monroe wants to know why, but the boy cannot explain. Fat Monroe starts laughing so hard that he begins to cough and tells the boy to hit him on the back before he dies. Wilgus beats the man on the back with his fists and starts crying. As they pull into Wilgus's yard, Fat Monroe gets out of the truck and shakes the father's hand, saying that he surely has raised a tough one. The two men laugh, and the father says that Wilgus is his defender. Wilgus watches the two friends walk away, arm in arm, before jumping out of the truck and running across the yard to his mother.

The story is a simple but effective account of a jolly fat man teasing a young boy so much that the boy gladly leaps at the opportunity to take out his frustration by beating on the man. Fat Monroe's behavior is typical of the harmless but aggravating way adults tease children in the mountains. The most important element of the story is the boy's attempt to defend the honor of his father, whom he loves, although it has never occurred to him to articulate why. When the truck rolls into the yard, the father is shirtless, clean, with a fresh shave and haircut. He looks so different Wilgus does not recognize him at first. His white skin makes him look not so much like the dusty laborer who spends most of his daylight life in the coal mines but rather like a vulnerable man. Having experienced the mystery of adult male camaraderie, Wilgus is happy to run to the comfort of his mother.

"NIGHT RIDE"

In this story, Wilgus, thirteen, is initiated into the world of young mountain men by his Uncle Delmer, who picks Wilgus up in Delmer's Ford and takes Wilgus on a wild ride, complete with fast driving, country music on the radio, bootleg beer, whiskey, and shooting at road signs with a pistol. Although Wilgus feels guilty about leaving his grandparents at home to do the work, he is too excited by the beer, the speed, and the shooting to brood about it. At one point, Delmer stops at a house, saying, "I've got to go in there and see a man about a horse." Wilgus knows Delmer is going in to see a woman but is happy to sit in the car, drinking beer and listening to the radio. However, a few minutes later, when Delmer storms out cursing, Wilgus knows things have not gone well.

Wilgus and his uncle continue on their wild ride around the narrow mountain roads of eastern Kentucky. When they take a break for Delmer, who is drunk, to urinate, he gives Wilgus the pistol to fire into the sky, declaring, "This is the wild side of life, ain't it, Wilgus?" They stop at a slagheap, which is burning in many different places, and walk onto it. Delmer tells Wilgus that Delmer and Wilgus's father had put some slate on this heap several years before, and it was still burning. Wilgus, also half drunk, is moved by the thought and tries to find words to account for his feelings, but Delmer begins shooting the pistol at the little fires. They talk about Delmer's brother, Wilgus's father, who is dead, and the woman that Delmer had gone to see earlier, and they listen to more country music on car radio. Delmer ruminates about how once the ocean used to fill this valley and the swamps grew ferns and flowers that turned into coal and slate that presently burns on the slagheap and may burn forever. In this classic instance of male bonding and marveling at mysteries, both Delmer and Wilgus are moved by the thought. When Delmer passes out, Wilgus thinks how much he loves old Delmer and the slate dump and the ride and their talk. However, he must drive the Ford and his Uncle Delmer back to the home place fifty miles away. This is a classic coming-of-age story, mountain style, in which fast cars, whiskey, and guns are part of the life that Wilgus knows but which will never be part of his life in the way they are part of the life of his Uncle Delmer.

"MAXINE"

This is the final Wilgus story in the book, the story of his experience with his cousin Maxine, just before he goes away to California. Maxine has been to Detroit to visit her daughter Cindy, and Wilgus picks Maxine up at the bus station in a small mountain town. He buys her a bottle of cheap wine, which she drinks as they drive home. Getting increasingly drunk, she complains about her daughter, who is pregnant, broke, and living with a worthless young man in a cheap hotel, looking like some kind of war orphan.

Wilgus already has graduated from the University of Kentucky and intends, with no precise plan or destination, to go to California for an adventure. When they arrive at Maxine's house, Maxine is intoxicated enough that she begins to confuse things she thinks with things she says. For example, when Wilgus says her house looks fine, that nobody has burned it down, she thinks, "I wouldn't care if they have," and then asks whether she said that. Because of her sorrow about her daughter Cindy and the effect of the wine, she leans onto Wilgus's arm and begins to cry, picturing her daughter as a baby and briefly dreaming that she is Cindy, come home with Wilgus. She berates herself, calling herself names, but Wilgus, always loyal to family, insists on how great she is.

At the end of the story, Wilgus undresses Maxine, lays her on the bed, and lies down beside her, Maxine thinking, "oh, lover." She tells Wilgus she loves him, and he says he loves her, too, before she falls asleep. In the last paragraph of the story, Maxine dreams that

Wilgus kisses her, strokes her face, touches her breasts. She dreams she hears his car start up and drive away, but that she is with him, that she is her daughter Cindy, riding away, heading west with Wilgus.

In this final Wilgus story, the young man who has been a peacemaker for his squabbling family, and who is the most intelligent, sensitive, mature person of the Collier clan, serves as comforter to a member of his family one final time, even as he leaves them to exist finally only in their dreams.

OTHER MAJOR WORKS

LONG FICTION: *Divine Right's Trip: A Folk-Tale*, 1972.

EDITED TEXTS: *A Gathering at the Forks: Fifteen Years of the Hindman Settlement School*, 1993 (with George Ella Lyon and Jim Wayne Miller); *Backtalk from Appalachia: Confronting Stereotypes*, 1999 (with Dwight Billings and Katherine Ledford); *An American Vein: Critical Readings in Appalachian Literature*, 2005 (with Sharon Hatfield and Danny Miller).

MISCELLANEOUS: *Time on the River, From This Valley, Wilderness Road*, Kentucky Educational Television, 1987-1991.

BIBLIOGRAPHY

Appalachian Heritage 33 (Summer, 2005). Forty pages of this issue are devoted to Norman, including an appreciation and recollection by his old college chum, Wendell Berry. The issue also contains a biographical sketch and tribute by *Appalachian Heritage* editor George Brosi.

Miller, Danny. "Kin and Kindness in Gurney Norman's *Kinfolks: The Wilgus Stories*." In *An American Vein: Critical Readings in Appalachian Literature*, edited by Danny Miller, Sharon Hatfield, and Gurney Norman. Athens: Ohio University Press, 2005. Miller discusses the theme of family relationships or mountain clannishness in the stories, from the family loyalty the young Wilgus shows in "Fat Monroe" in the first story to the support the adult Wilgus shows to his cousin Maxine in the final story.

Shannon, Beth Tashery, and J. W. Williamson. "Interview with Gurney Norman." In *Interviewing Appalachia: The Appalachian Journal Interviews, 1978-1992*, edited by Jerry Wayne Williams and Edwin T. Arnold. Knoxville: University of Tennessee Press, 1994. The Shannon interview took place in 1978; the Williamson interview was recorded in 1984. Norman talks about how he was influenced and aided by his teachers and colleagues Robert Hazel, Hollis Summers, Wendell Berry, Jim Baker Hall, Frank O'Connor, and others. Norman also talks about the difference between oral storytelling and writing, and his work in progress.

Charles E. May

FRANK NORRIS

Born: Chicago, Illinois; March 5, 1870
Died: San Francisco, California; October 25, 1902

PRINCIPAL SHORT FICTION

*A Deal in Wheat, and Other Stories of the New and
    Old West,* 1903
The Joyous Miracle, 1906
The Third Circle, 1909
Frank Norris of "The Wave," 1931 (Oscar Lewis,
    editor)

OTHER LITERARY FORMS

Frank Norris is best known for his novels *McTeague*
(1899), *The Octopus: A Spy of California* (1901), and
The Pit: A Story of Chicago (1903), along with book
reviews, interviews, football reports, editorials, features, translations, and short fiction. Earlier in his career he wrote several poems (including his first book,
Yvernelle: A Tale of Feudal France, 1892), a play (the
junior farce for 1892 at the University of California),
stories, and essays.

ACHIEVEMENTS

Frank Norris was the first full-blown practitioner of
Zolaesque naturalism in America. Like the nineteenth
century French writer Émile Zola, Norris often analyzed the effects of heredity, biological instincts, social
and cultural influences, and the physical environment
on individuals--a strategy that champions a less metaphysical and more scientific approach to looking at life.
Although these naturalistic novels are usually considered to be Norris's best writing, his reputation primarily grew during his lifetime because of his productivity and versatility (he wrote seven novels and
approximately three hundred essays, book reviews,
short stories, literary pieces, interviews, and poems).
When Norris made the economics of American

agriculture the subject of his unfinished trilogy--*The
Octopus* deals with the struggle between the wheat
growers and the railroad owners, *The Pit* depicts specu-
lators and the Chicago wheat exchange, and *The Wolf*
(never written) was to focus on the dispersal of wheat
in Europe--he contributed to the muckraking movement at the beginning of the twentieth century. The unfinished trilogy also helped establish the realistic tradition in twentieth century American fiction.

BIOGRAPHY

Although invariably associated with San Francisco
and naturalism, Benjamin Franklin Norris, Jr., was actually born in Chicago, the son of a wealthy wholesale
jeweler and a former actress (his parents were divorced
in 1894). The family moved to Oakland in 1884 and
across the bay to San Francisco the following year. Norris's education was desultory, all the more so because of
his unwillingness to follow in his father's footsteps as a
businessman. From 1887 to 1889 he was enrolled in the
Atelier Julien in Paris but had little success as an art student and never did begin the huge painting of the Battle
of Crecy he had planned. From 1890 to 1894 he pursued
the literary course at the University of California, but
because of a deficiency in mathematics he did not graduate. The next year was more fruitfully spent at Harvard
University where, as a student in Lewis E. Gates's
writing class, he began two novels, first *Vandover and
the Brute* and then *McTeague.*

In the winter of 1895 to 1896, Norris took a Richard
Harding Davis jaunt to South Africa and became involved in the abortive Uitlander Rebellion. He served
on the staff of *The Wave* from April, 1896, to February,
1898, much of the time as its subeditor. His serialized
novel *Moran of the Lady Letty* brought him to the attention of the editor and publisher S. S. McClure, for
whom he worked two years, including a brief stint as a
correspondent during the Spanish-American War. In
1900, Norris, with four novels already in print, became

a manuscript reader at Doubleday, Page and Company, his new publisher. That same year he married Jeannette Black of San Francisco and "discovered" and championed (unsuccessfully) Theodore Dreiser's novel *Sister Carrie* (1900). *The Octopus*, published the next year, was Norris's first financially successful book. Following the birth of a daughter in February, 1902, and the completion of *The Pit* in July, he began planning the sea cruise which would be part of his research for *The Wolf*, the projected third part of his "The Epic of the Wheat." While in San Francisco, however, Norris was stricken with appendicitis and died on October 25.

ANALYSIS

Except for Jeanette Gilder, in her review of the posthumous collection *The Third Circle*, no one has been so bold as to prefer Frank Norris's short fiction to his novels. In fact, a number of his critics seem to agree with Warren French, who, in a chapter of his *Frank Norris* (1962) entitled "Stubble," decries the fact that the stories have been "undeservedly rescued from the obscurity of the periodicals in which they first appeared." Most believe that Norris wrote the stories as potboilers or, in the case of the stories published in *The Wave*, as apprentice pieces (this despite the fact that drafts of *Vandover and the Brute* and *McTeague* had already been written) and that their value lies solely in whatever light they shed on his longer fiction. It is true that in his literary essays of 1901 and 1902 Norris did equate the short story with money and the novel with truth; moreover, in distinguishing between literature as construction and the more important literature as exploration, he did cite short-story writers Edgar Allan Poe, Frank R. Stockton, and Rudyard Kipling as examples of the former and novelists Gustave Flaubert, Thomas Hardy, and George Eliot as examples of the latter. Norris also contended (in May, 1902) that the continued increase in the publication of short fiction in American magazines, particularly the new low-priced magazines such as *McClure's*, would result in a decrease in the public's demand for short-story collections and ultimately would cause the short story to degenerate to the level of magazine ephemera.

During his years at *The Wave*, the period before his success as a novelist, Norris showed a much greater interest in the possibilities of short fiction. In May, 1897, he wrote that San Francisco was a true story city, where "things can happen"; although it was, he claimed, not yet settled enough for the purposes of the novelist, the city abounded with material for the writer of short stories. A few months earlier, in "The Decline of the Magazine Short Story," he had lamented the "absolutely stupid," "deadly dull" fiction published in the major American magazines. Echoing Hjalmar Boyesen's remarks concerning the "Iron Madonna," he charged that "It is the 'young girl' and the family center table that determine the standard of the American short story." Seeking to challenge this standard, Norris adopted various stylistic elements of those writers, such as Kipling, whom he distinguished from the writers of "safe" fiction. His failure to find a publisher for a collection of these stories does, to some extent, reflect upon their quality (and, as Norris suggests in his semiautobiographical novel *Blix* [1899], their being commercially out of fashion). Nevertheless, his persistence during late 1897 and 1898 in trying to secure the collection's publication reflects his more-than-passing interest in these writings.

"THE THIRD CIRCLE"

One of the best of his pieces for *The Wave* is "The Third Circle." Norris's use of a Chinatown setting in this story and of San Francisco and California locales for nearly all of the fiction of this period evidences the realist method of direct observation. He worked less in the tradition of the nostalgic local colorists than in the mode of Stephen Crane in investigating New York's demimonde and even more in the path established by Kipling and Richard Harding Davis in depicting settings that were both primitive and foreign to their readers. Basically, the story is a study in limited perception; in it Norris attempts to expose his readers to what he liked to call (in *The Octopus*) the "larger view."

The first half of the story concerns an engaged couple from the East and their "lark" in San Francisco's Chinatown. First they "discover" a quaint Chinese restaurant and then invite to their table a Chinese fortune-teller who turns out to be a Kanakan tattooist. Miss Harriet Ten Eyck thinks it would be "awfully queer and original" to have a tattoo, but her fiancé, young Hillegas, reminds her that their "lark" is one thing and the society in which they move quite another: "Let him do it on your finger, then. You never could wear an evening dress if it was on your arm." Once the tattoo is completed-- "a grotesque little insect, as much butterfly as anything else"--Hillegas goes off to find their waiter, leaving Harriet alone. Instead of the waiter, he finds a Chinese silk merchant to whom he at first speaks condescendingly. Much to his surprise, this "Chinaman" is articulate and cultured. "Here was a side of Chinese life he had not seen, nor even suspected." There is another side as well, as Hillegas discovers when he returns to find his fiancé gone: "He never saw her again. No white man ever did." This is that part of Chinatown Norris terms "the third circle," the part "no one ever hears of."

The second half of the story is set in the late 1890's, twenty years after Miss Ten Eyck's disappearance into white slavery. Here the narrator is no longer simply the teller of the tale, as in the first half, but a participant as well. Like the hapless eastern couple, he too makes a foray into Chinatown's third circle, but unlike them he has a guide, a "bum" and opium addict "who calls himself Manning." To a degree, the rest of the story follows a predictable course. The narrator tells Manning the story the reader has just read. Manning adds several details and mentions that there is a white slave, Sadie, who works in the opium joint he frequents who might know something further about Miss Ten Eyck. The debased Sadie, an alcoholic and opium addict, without the least desire to escape either her degradation or her addiction, is Harriet Ten Eyck, as the reader figures out long before Norris's rather unsurprising surprise ending: "She thrust out her left hand, and I saw a butterfly tattooed on her little finger."

Despite its unsatisfactory ending, the story does succeed as a study in perception, if not as a tale of suspense. As Norris (by way of *Hamlet*) points out in the opening sentence, "There are more things in San Francisco's Chinatown than are dreamed of in heaven and earth." Just as young Hillegas discovers aspects of life he had never before suspected and at first entirely misunderstands, so too does Norris's narrator; and readers--specifically the middle- and upper-middle-class

readers of *The Wave* for whom the story was written--discover aspects of their own immediate surroundings about which most San Franciscans had, like the easterner Hillegas, little or no knowledge. Although some readers will be offended by how readily Norris accepted the popular theory of the Chinese as a depraved and inferior race, he does describe the violence, slave trade, and opium traffic then to be found in Chinatown in convincing detail. More important, he makes clear that this depravity extends to the white population itself and that not even a proper middle-class woman such as Harriet Ten Eyck, or, Norris implies, the readers of *The Wave*, are entirely safe from its dangers.

"A REVERSION TO TYPE"

A similar vulnerability is also evident in Norris's more conventionally naturalistic stories. In "A Reversion to Type," for example, Paul Schuster, a forty-one-year-old floorwalker in a San Francisco department store, suddenly bolts from his "sober, steady, respectable life" and for a month lives as an outlaw in the California mining district where he murders the superintendent of the Little Bear mine. Schuster then returns to

Frank Norris (Library of Congress)

San Francisco and resumes his commonplace life. On his deathbed, he confesses his crimes but is not believed. A man of his character and steady habits, it is assumed, could not lapse into such criminal behavior. Norris's point is that Schuster's criminality is very much in character--in his hereditary character. As a prison official at San Quentin explains to the narrator (who has just told him Schuster's story), Schuster's grandfather was a "bad egg," a convicted highway robber.

"A Case for Lombroso" (which Norris at one time considered titling "A Story for Max Nordau") develops along the same lines. When two young people, Cresencia Hromada and the allegorically named Stayne, become sexually attracted to each other, her pride and morbid passion--both inherited characteristics--and his failure of will combine to turn their love into a perverse and ultimately destructive relationship.

NORRIS'S ROMANTICISM

Norris's interest in these and other rather unsavory subjects derives not from any personal morbidity but instead from his literary theory. Despite his admiration for the novels of William Dean Howells, Norris was impatient with realism's "teacup tragedies." Realism, he maintained, "confines itself to the type of normal life. . . . It notes only the surface of things." Romance, in contrast, explores "the unplumbed depths of the human heart, and the mystery of sex, and the problems of life, and the black unsearched penetralia of the soul of man." Whereas realism aimed for accuracy, romance went after truth. In such early writings as the stories "The Jongleur of Taillebois" and "Lauth" and the poem *Yvernelle: A Tale of Feudal France*, Norris did write superficially romantic works. Later, however, he developed his theory of naturalism, combining Romanticism's high drama and emphasis on variations from commonplace life with realism's contemporaneity and careful attention to detail.

NORRIS AND THE SHORT FORM

Norris's naturalistic style was more appropriate to his novels, in which the romantic and realistic elements could complement each other, than to his stories, in which his very definition of the genre worked to restrict his generally expansive imagination. Like many other critics of the late nineteenth century, Norris

propounded an evolutionary theory of literature. Magazines of the 1890's, he maintained, had only "limited space" for fiction; as a result, the short story was, of necessity, "reduced in some cases to the relation of a single incident by itself, concise, pungent, direct as a blow." (As an unfortunate corollary to this theory of extreme brevity, Norris held that the short-story writer must resort to various "tricks," such as surprise endings.) For the writer of short fiction the chief "difficulty lies not so much in the actual writing, in the condensing and suggesting, etc., as it does in the invention or selection . . . of the original idea, the motive." Taken to the limit, Norris's definition leads to the literary sketch, a form in which he worked often and with much success--for example, the thrice-weekly themes he submitted while a student in Lewis E. Gates's class at Harvard and the "Western City Types" series of 1896. In "Little Dramas of the Curbstone," Norris catenated three sketches into a single work, a technique he later used, with some modification, in one of his finest and best-known stories, "A Deal in Wheat."

"A DEAL IN WHEAT"

Written concurrently with *The Pit*, the second part of his epic trilogy, "A Deal in Wheat" is typical of Norris's work in three respects: its richly detailed portrayal of a phase of American life, its dramatic interest, and its emphasis on the "larger view." The first of the story's five parts (or sketches), "The Bear--Wheat at Sixty-Two," concerns the failure of one small Kansas farmer, Sam Lewiston. When, owing to the machinations of a "bearish" wheat trader in Chicago, the price of wheat plummets well below the cost of raising it, Lewiston is forced to sell his farm and, ironically, find employment in Chicago. In "The Bull--Wheat at a Dollar-Ten," the "bear," Truslow, having forced the price down too far, loses his hold on the market to a "bull," Horung, who for no particular reason and against the advice of his broker chooses not to gore "the Great Bear to actual financial death." That decision turns out to be costly--although not ruinous--for Horung.

In "The Pit," a lively account of actual trading in the wheat pit at Chicago's Board of Trade, an unknown bear begins to unload wheat on Horung. In "The Belt Line," a private detective named Cyrus Ryder (also a character in Norris's Three Crows stories of 1901-1902) explains that the wheat Horung has been forced to buy so as to keep the price artificially high does not in fact exist; Truslow has simply routed the same carloads around the city on the railroad belt line he owns, selling the same wheat over and over to make up the money he lost when Horung destroyed his corner some months earlier. The ploy merely amuses Horung, who, to cut his own losses, boosts the price to two dollars. In the fifth section, "The Bread Line," Sam Lewiston reappears. Now out of work and temporarily separated from his family, he is seen waiting outside a bakery at midnight, one of the growing number of unemployed forced to depend upon charity. That night there is no free bread, however, only a sign informing the men of the high price of wheat.

Like Hamlin Garland's "Under the Lion's Paw," a story it much resembles, "A Deal in Wheat" vividly dramatizes a social condition about which Norris clearly felt deep concern. Norris is especially successful in evoking sympathy for Sam Lewiston and the economic class he represents. Unfortunately, in the final three paragraphs, Norris abandons objective dramatization and becomes much more openly partisan. Lewiston, the reader learns in Norris's summing up, manages to secure a job and even to do modestly well in the city; in the newspapers, he reads about Truslow and Horung's deals in wheat and so attains a "larger view" which Norris chooses to make didactically overt rather than dramatically suggestive.

"PERVERTED TALES"

Among Norris's more than eighty-five works of short fiction, there are no truly great stories. His repeated preference for "life, not literature" virtually ensured a certain indifference to aesthetic craftsmanship, an indifference painfully apparent in his melodramatic passages and frequent overwriting. This is not to say that Norris had no understanding of the fine points of literary style, as his borrowings and his six "Perverted Tales," in particular his Stephen Crane parody "The Green Stone of Unrest," make clear. What chiefly characterizes his short fiction are his wide range of subjects and literary forms and his remarkable enthusiasm for writing itself. The works discussed in this entry are certainly his most significant, although there are others

which will repay a reader's careful attention: "His Sister" and "Dying Fires," dealing with writers very much like Norris; "A Memorandum of Sudden Death," written in the form of a recovered journal; "This Animal of a Buldy Jones," "Buldy Jones, *Chef de Claque*," and especially "The Associated Un-Charities" (mistitled "The Dis-Associated Charities" in *The Third Circle*) for their slapstick comedy. Finally, there are several nonfiction pieces, such as "Dago Conspirators" and "A Lag's Release," which are narratively so well constructed that they rise well above the level of the news report to the status of journalistic art.

OTHER MAJOR WORKS

LONG FICTION: *Moran of the Lady Letty*, 1898; *Blix*, 1899; *McTeague*, 1899; *A Man's Woman*, 1900; *The Octopus: A Spy of California*, 1901; *The Pit: A Story of Chicago*, 1903; *Vandover and the Brute*, 1914.

POETRY: *Yvernelle: A Tale of Feudal France*, 1892; *Two Poems and "Kim" Reviewed*, 1930.

NONFICTION: *The Responsibilities of the Novelist*, 1903; *The Surrender of Santiago*, 1917; *The Letters of Frank Norris*, 1956; *The Literary Criticism of Frank Norris*, 1964 (Donald Pizer, editor); *Collected Letters*, 1986.

MISCELLANEOUS: *The Complete Edition of Frank Norris*, 1928; *Novels and Essays*, 1986; *The Apprenticeship Writings of Frank Norris*, 1996 (two volumes; Joseph R. McElrath, Jr., and Douglas K. Burgess, editors).

BIBLIOGRAPHY

Boyd, Jennifer. *Frank Norris Spatial Form and Narrative Time*. New York: Peter Lang, 1993. Contains chapters on all Norris's novels, with discussions of his pictorialism, his relationship to Émile Zola and naturalism, and the structures of his longer fictional works. Includes notes and bibliography.

Dillingham, William. *Frank Norris: Instinct and Art*. Lincoln: University of Nebraska Press, 1969. Contains a biographical sketch and a survey of Norris's work. Dillingham argues that certain attitudes of the academicians, such as hard work and close observation, influenced Norris's conception of painting and writing. Stresses Norris's naturalism. Includes an annotated bibliography.

Graham, Don, ed. *Critical Essays on Frank Norris*. Boston: G. K. Hall, 1980. A collection of reviews and essays aimed at presenting Norris as a vital and still undefined writer. Among the contributors are Norris's contemporaries William Dean Howells, Willa Cather, and Hamlin Garland; literary critics include Donald Pizer and William Dillingham.

_____. *The Fiction of Frank Norris: The Aesthetic Context*. Columbia: University of Missouri Press, 1978. One of the few studies concerning itself with the aesthetics of Norris's work. Much attention is given to his four most literary novels--*Vandover and the Brute, McTeague, The Octopus*, and *The Pit*. Includes an excellent bibliography.

Lawlor, Mary. "Frank Norris and the Fiction of the Lost West." In *Recalling the Wild: Naturalism and the Closing of the American West*. New Brunswick, N.J.: Rutgers University Press, 2000. Examines the short and long fiction of Norris and works by other late nineteenth century writers to demonstrate the nation's changing ideas about the American West. Unlike earlier writers, who romantically depicted the West as an open frontier, Norris and other naturalist writers represented the region as a strictly material place that was geographically limited and limiting.

Lye, Colleen. "Meat Versus Rice: Frank Norris, Jack London, and the Critique of Monopoly Capitalism." In *America's Asia: Racial Form and American Literature, 1893-1945*. Princeton, N.J.: Princeton University Press, 2005. Examines some of Norris's short fiction that was published in periodicals in the 1890's, as well as works by Jack London, to demonstrate how these works reflected contemporary, and usually racist, views of the Chinese.

Marchand, Ernest. *Frank Norris: A Study*. Stanford, Calif.: Stanford University Press, 1942. The first full-length critical study of Norris, this overview situates his work against a social and intellectual, as well as a literary, background. Considers a wide variety of critical opinions about Norris's fiction. Includes an excellent bibliography.

Marut, David. "Sam Lewiston's Bad Timing: A Note on the Economic Context of 'A Deal in Wheat.'" *American Literary Realism* 27 (Fall, 1994): 74-80. Provides the economic and political context for Norris's story about how grain traders manipulate the market at the expense of the working class.

McElrath, Joseph R., Jr. "Beyond San Francisco: Frank Norris's Invention of Northern California." In *San Francisco in Fiction: Essays in a Regional Literature*, edited by David Fine and Paul Skenazy. Albuquerque: University of New Mexico Press, 1995. A discussion of the romantic transformation of the San Joaquin Valley in Norris's local-color sketches, as well as his treatment of San Francisco in some of his novels.

_____. *Frank Norris Revisited*. New York: Twayne, 1992. An updating and rewriting of a volume that first appeared in 1962 under the authorship of Warren French. This introductory study includes a chapter on the "novelist in the making," followed by subsequent chapters that discuss each of Norris's novels. Includes a chronology, notes, and an annotated bibliography.

McElrath, Joseph R., Jr. and Jesse S. Crisler *Frank Norris: A Life*. Urbana: University of Illinois Press, 2006. Meticulous and definitive biography, the result of its authors' thirty years of research. The authors provide new information and resolve some misconceptions about Norris.

Reesman, Jeanne Campbell. "Frank Norris and Jack London." In *A Companion to the American Short Story*, edited by Alfred Bendixen and James Nagel. Malden, Mass.: Wiley-Blackwell, 2010. Discusses both writers as adherents to the naturalist school of literature, describing the characteristics of this literary style. Includes analyses of several of Norris's short stories.

Walker, Franklin. *Frank Norris: A Biography*. New York: Russell & Russell, 1932. The first full-length biography of Norris, this study is uncritical of its subject. The book is also extraordinarily detailed and contains personal interviews with Norris's family and friends.

Robert A. Morace
Updated by Cassandra Kircher

BETH NUGENT

Born: New York, 1954

PRINCIPAL SHORT FICTION

City of Boys, 1992

OTHER LITERARY FORMS

Live Girls, the author's first novel, was published in 1996.

ACHIEVEMENTS

Beth Nugent has received grants from the National Endowment for the Arts, the Colorado Arts Council, and the Illinois Arts Council.

BIOGRAPHY

Caroline Bethune Nugent was born in upstate New York. She has one sibling, a brother. She did not begin writing until after college. She graduated with her bachelor's degree from Connecticut College in New London, Connecticut. Nugent moved to New York City after graduation and worked for American College Testing, where she edited tests for six months before quitting. Nugent also worked for *Redbook*, but she did not begin writing until she decided to pursue her master's in fine arts at the University of Iowa, which she achieved in 1982. Nugent moved to Evanston, Illinois, and taught writing at the School of the Art Institute of Chicago. Nugent's stories have appeared in *The New Yorker*, *North American Review*, *Mademoiselle*, *Black Warrior Review*, *The Best American Short Stories, 1985*, and the *Norton Anthology of Contemporary Short Fiction* (1988). Nugent became a professor at the University of Denver, where she has taught literature, fiction writing, and nonfiction writing.

ANALYSIS

Beth Nugent's writing is often described as bleak, yet *City of Boys: Stories* was well received and highly acclaimed. *Kirkus Reviews*, in April, 1992, called it an "uncompromising collection, powerful and unforgettable as well." Mark Bautz, writing for *The Washington Times*, described the stories as "edgy" and "haunting," but he warned "this book might be too intense for some readers."

Other critics focused on the emotionally barren characters that seem to lack any spark. Claire Messud, writing for *The Guardian* (London), described Nugent's vision as "so bleak and soulless as to be almost intolerable." Nugent's fiction is often compared to that of the American short-story master Raymond Carver. Messud argues that, like Carver, Nugent's "vision of America as a rootless, boring, and bored spiritual vacuum corresponds to the current literary myth of that country."

Carol Anshaw, writing in August, 1992, for *The Washington Post*, noted that "the inertia and stasis and passivity in these stories become less and less compelling. The point, having been made, then gets made again, and again." In 1993, a reviewer for *The Virginia Quarterly Review* observed, "City of malaise is more like it. Don't read too many of these stories at one sitting; the cumulative effect of so many haunted, disconnected characters is extremely depressing."

To dwell on the flatness of the characters, the lack of hope prevalent in the stories is to see only the outer grotesque beast without seeing the inner beauty. Nugent's stories are beautiful in their simplicity, in their spare but essential truths. Nugent's goal in these stories is to present characters in isolation, to show how characters continue to live despite the lack of support systems, friends, family, and a fabric of moral values. Nugent's characters are like desert plants, living in spite of conditions, adapting to survive. As one reviewer writing for *The Independent* noted, "There's not a single happy person in Beth Nugent's short stories." However, Nugent's stories are powerful and memorable because they strike a familiar chord with readers: Emptiness and desperation are as much expressions of the human condition as are fulfillment and contentment.

"ABATTOIR"

Teddy and his younger sister live in New York City in a flat above Madame Renalda's. Teddy works in produce at the local market, and his sister stays home all day and reads fashion magazines. Madame Renalda is a psychic, and her establishment is a front for prostitution. Teddy comes home from the market with fruits or vegetables; one night it is green beans, and the next night it is a pomegranate. Teddy and his sister eat dinner, often in front of the television while Teddy watches the New York Yankees. For baseball games Teddy misses, a VCR captures the day games and the late games on the West Coast.

Teddy and his sister have no father in the picture, and their mother lives across town with her second husband Stan and her cat Smokey. Their mother is dependent on drugs and further dependent on Stan to provide the drugs. Her life is a drugged-out haze, and telephone calls from her children are few and necessarily brief. In fact, some days she cannot even manage a phone conversation.

Teddy wants to get cable television. Think of all the extra games they could watch, he tells his sister. She does not care; she does not watch the games. She is under twenty-one, inexperienced, and living vicariously through the models she studies in the slick magazine ads. Teddy is overprotective and enabling, much like Stan is with the children's mother. The siblings live a limited and sheltered life. Teddy dreams of holding a position in middle management, reading business texts in his free time. He gets cable television, and all the sports channels are overwhelming, with baseball games on at all hours of the day or night.

Teddy's sister, as though released for a field trip, comes to visit him at the market. Teddy's supervisor in produce is Donny. Donny, a New York Mets fan, occasionally comes to the apartment to visit Teddy and his sister. Donny talks during the games, and Teddy, who sits on the floor directly in front of the television, has

trouble concentrating and enjoying the game when Donny talks so much. Anyway, Donny visits only to see Teddy's sister. Donny leers at her while they sit on the couch directly behind Teddy, who is absorbed in his baseball game.

When Donny begins to lose interest in Teddy's sister, Teddy is transferred from produce to meats. Teddy brings home hamburger, steak, and pork chops. Their small apartment begins to reek of fried flesh. Teddy learns he can make more money if he goes to work at the slaughterhouse, also known as an abattoir. He tries the new job, and he is appalled by the slaughtering, the blunt hammer used to knock out the animals, all the blood, and the dazed look on the faces of the animals as they somehow sense their fate. The story concludes with Teddy and his sister taking an impromptu trip to the Poconos in a rented car. They share a motel room with a single bed. Teddy's sister turns out the lights as they lie beside each other in the dark.

This story is typical of Nugent's collection. She captures the isolation, the loneliness, the desperation of these young people. Aside from the bleak, hopeless quality that pervades the story, there are also elements of love, responsibility, protection, and a hint of incest.

"ANOTHER COUNTRY"

Similar in theme to "Abattoir," this story features a young woman living in New York City. Catherine lives in a basement apartment with her middle-aged mother, once a beautiful woman, who exists only for a bottle of gin and the next man she meets. They live directly beneath Mr. Rosenberg, a wheelchair-bound chain smoker, who shamelessly eavesdrops on their conversations. As the two women move from room to room, they can hear the squeak of his wheelchair as he follows along one story above them.

Catherine has an older brother, Robbie, who is gay and has moved out of the apartment and lives elsewhere in the city. Catherine searches for Robbie as she walks the neighborhood, buying groceries and liquor for her mother. At home, her mother stares out the apartment's basement window at the feet of passing strangers. She goes out to meet men and brings them home to seventeen-year-old Catherine, introducing them as "uncles."

Catherine's father lives in New Jersey with his second wife, Roberta, and their three children. He remembers Catherine and Robbie on their birthdays. Catherine finds Robbie, and she tells him she wants to move to New Jersey and live with her father. Catherine has her father's address, and she undertakes the short trip to New Jersey, where she finds her father outside his house, working on his car.

After he recognizes Catherine, her father invites her into the house. Roberta brings her a Coke. Catherine's father is at a loss for words. Catherine has shown up uninvited, and her father stares at her, waiting for her to explain her presence at his house. Her father asks about Robbie and her mother; Catherine thanks him for the annual birthday card, and she leaves.

"Another Country" is New Jersey, so far removed from the basement apartment that it seems to be another land, a place remote, where familiar common customs no longer apply. Catherine turns her back on this fantasy of living with her father, a family man. She returns to her reality, a comfortable and predictable sameness, in which she has a part to play.

"COCKTAIL HOUR"

Originally published in *The New Yorker*, this story focuses on Sally and her friend Annie. Sally is new in town. An only child, Sally's parents move often. Though she has seen much of the country, Sally notes a dull sameness in every town they call home. Annie lives across the street from Sally, and Annie shares a bedroom with her brother Tommy. Sally and Annie meet when Sally is sent on a mission by her mother around the neighborhood to find a Pepsi to help alleviate the agony of her mother's hangover. Sally's parents love to party.

Sally's mother labors over the daily crossword puzzle, and the typical day goes by with dull routines until cocktail hour. At this appointed time, a gleam comes to the eyes of Sally's parents, who look forward to their daily imbibing. Meanwhile, Sally attends yet another new school, where she and Annie are becoming friends. Sally and Annie eat alone, but Annie barely eats at all. Sally notices that Annie has no other friends.

Annie, for entertainment, enjoys setting fires. Annie asks Sally if she, too, enjoys setting fires. Not really so inclined but wanting to fit in, Sally says yes. The two girls set small fires on the school's playground, watching four fires burn around the four poles that support the playground's swing set. To think, Annie tells Sally, we caused this, made these burned patches of ground.

Sally's parents love to host cocktail parties. New to the neighborhood, they use this excuse to host their new neighbors, including Annie's parents. The first to arrive at the party, Annie's parents are shy, awkward, unsophisticated, and uneducated in the social graces required for cocktail parties. They sit like two untouchables in an isolated leper colony situated in the middle of an otherwise teeming island paradise. The partiers navigate around them. Sally begins to freeze Annie out, breaking away from her to find other friends, more to her liking. Annie is clueless, needy, and desperate, hoping to make a connection without knowing how.

"LOCUSTS"

Susan's Aunt Louise, Uncle Woody, and cousin Francine are coming to stay for their customary annual visit. Susan is sixteen during this summer, the year of seventeen-year locusts. The noise from the insects permeates the air. Susan, called Susie by her relatives, has recovered from a bout of hepatitis. Susan is worried Francine, Susan's same age, will be bored by her lack of energy.

Francine longs for excitement and wants to meet boys. Susan will not be of much help to Francine. Aunt Louise is her father's sister. Though the annual visit is an intrusion that Susan's mother, Helen, obviously resents, Susan's father will never stand up to his domineering sister.

While Aunt Louise bullies Susan's parents, Uncle Woody tempts Susan with candy corn, treating her like she is a child. At night, when the house is quiet and everyone is supposed to be asleep, Susan can hear Uncle Woody creeping slowly along the hallway and stopping outside her room. One night, she wakes to find him lying beside her. The next morning Aunt Louise apologizes for Woody's behavior. Sometimes, she explains, Woody walks in his sleep and loses his way. He is afraid he must have given Susan an awful fright, Aunt Louise says regretfully.

Helen's birthday comes during the family visit, an event largely ignored by most of the family except for the gift of a trash compactor, which Uncle Woody swears Helen will absolutely love. Instead, Helen is saving her love for her friend Carol. Susan sees her mother and Carol kissing in the backyard when they think no one is looking. Helen is deeply unhappy with her life, as she looks back on her thirty-six years. "Whoever thought everything would be so awful?" she tells Susan. Susan tries to comfort her mother, reminding her that the family visit will soon be over and life will return to normal, not realizing that normal is her mother's problem.

OTHER MAJOR WORKS

LONG FICTION: *Live Girls*, 1996.

BIBLIOGRAPHY

Anshaw, Carol. "The Young and the Listless." *The Washington Post*, August 16, 1992, p. X4. Review of *City of Boys*, in which the reviewer observes women and young girl characters with no lives of their own.

Messud, Claire. "Books: The Young, the Bored and the Hopeless." *The Guardian* (London), August 20, 1992, p. 22. A critical review of *City of Boys*, and the reviewer notes that this collection is unlike many American short-story collections because of the author's intensity of vision. Scofield, Sandra. "Lovers Come and Go Like Summer Storms." *The New York Times Book Review*, June 14, 1992, p. 12. The reviewer claims Nugent has "a dark vision"; however, the author's message, that a family without a moral center cannot nurture its members, is well received.

Randy L. Abbott

O

JOYCE CAROL OATES

Born: Lockport, New York; June 16, 1938
Also known as: Rosamond Smith

PRINCIPAL SHORT FICTION

By the North Gate, 1963
Upon the Sweeping Flood, 1966
The Wheel of Love, 1970
Marriages and Infidelities, 1972
The Goddess and Other Women, 1974
The Hungry Ghosts: Seven Allusive Comedies, 1974
Where Are You Going, Where Have You Been?, 1974
The Poisoned Kiss, 1975
The Seduction, 1975
Crossing the Border, 1976
Night-Side, 1977
All the Good People I've Left Behind, 1978
The Lamb of Abyssalia, 1979
A Sentimental Education, 1980
Last Days, 1984
Raven's Wing, 1986
The Assignation, 1988
Heat, and Other Stories, 1991
Where Is Here?, 1992
Haunted: Tales of the Grotesque, 1994
Will You Always Love Me?, 1994
The Collector of Hearts, 1998
Faithless: Tales of Transgression, 2001
I Am No One You Know, 2004
The Female of the Species: Tales of Mystery and Suspense, 2005
High Lonesome: Stories, 1966-2006, 2006
The Museum of Dr. Moses: Tales of Mystery and Suspense, 2007
Wild Nights! Stories About the Last Days of Poe, Dickinson, Twain, James, and Hemingway, 2008
Dear Husband: Stories, 2009
Sourland, 2010
Give Me Your Heart: Tales of Mystery and Suspense, 2011

OTHER LITERARY FORMS

Joyce Carol Oates (ohts) is remarkable for the volume and breadth of her literary output. In addition to hundreds of short stories published in collections and various literary journals and popular magazines, Oates produced several volumes of poetry, plays, numerous novels, and edited texts. Furthermore, through interviews, essays, editorship of anthologies and journals, and positions at the University of Windsor and then Princeton University, she has engaged in an ongoing dialogue with the North American literary community.

ACHIEVEMENTS

Joyce Carol Oates received National Book Award nominations in 1968 and 1969; she won the award in 1970, for her novel *them* (1969). Other honors include O. Henry Awards in 1967, 1973, and 1983 for her short stories, John Simon Guggenheim Memorial Foundation and Rosenthal Fellowships, and election to the American Academy and Institute of Arts and Letters. She won the Heidemann Award for one-act plays and the Rea Award, both in 1990. Oates was nominated for a National Book Critics Circle Award and a Pulitzer Prize for *Black Water* (1992), and she was nominated for the Nobel Prize in Literature in 1993. She was a Pulitzer finalist again in 1995. In 1996, she won the Bram Stoker Award for Horror and the Fisk Fiction Prize for *Zombie* (1995).

BIOGRAPHY

Joyce Carol Oates was born on June 16, 1938, in Lockport, New York, a small city outside Buffalo. Her father was a tool and die designer, and her childhood was spent in a rural town where she attended a one-room schoolhouse. From earliest memory, she wanted to be a writer. As a child, she drew pictures to tell stories; later, she wrote the stories, sometimes producing handwritten books of up to two hundred pages, with carefully designed covers. Her youth was simple and happy, and she developed a closeness to her parents that flourished in her adult years.

In 1956, Oates graduated from Williamsville Central High School, where she had written for the school newspaper, and she entered Syracuse University under a New York State Regents Scholarship. During her freshman year, a tachycardiac seizure during a basketball game profoundly affected her view of life by bringing her face to face with her mortality. She continued writing, and in 1959 she was cowinner of the *Mademoiselle* college fiction award for "In the Old World." An excellent student, she was elected Phi Beta Kappa and graduated in 1960 at the top of her class.

She received a Knapp Fellowship to pursue graduate work at the University of Wisconsin, where she met Ph.D. candidate Raymond Joseph Smith. She and Smith were married on January 23, 1961. After receiving her M.A., Oates and Smith moved to Texas, where he taught in Beaumont, and she began doctoral work at William Marsh Rice University in Houston. With one of her stories appearing on the Honor Roll of Martha Foley's *Best American Short Stories*, however, Oates decided to devote herself to writing.

Her first collection of stories, *By the North Gate*, appeared in 1963, followed a year later by her first novel, *With Shuddering Fall* (1964). In 1967, *A Garden of Earthly Delights* appeared as the first novel in a thematic trilogy exploring the American obsession with money. The last of the trilogy, *them* (1969), earned Oates the 1970 National Book Award.

Oates taught at the University of Detroit from 1961 to 1967; then she and Smith moved to the University of Windsor in Ontario, Canada. A prolific author, Oates continued publishing stories in such periodicals as *The Literary Review* and *Cosmopolitan* and produced a steady flow of novels, stories, and poetry. Various other writings--essays, plays, reviews--add to the unusual breadth of her oeuvre.

In 1978, Oates became the Roger S. Berlind Distinguished Professor of Creative Writing at Princeton University in New Jersey. From their home, she and Smith edited *The Ontario Review* and ran a small publishing company. As her body of work grew, so did its formal and thematic diversity. *Bellefleur* (1980), *A Bloodsmoor Romance* (1982), and *Mysteries of Winterthurn* (1984) are experimental ventures into the genres of the family chronicle, the romance, and the gothic mystery, respectively. In the later 1980's, her work turned toward a modern naturalism.

Oates traveled and lectured widely, and in December, 1987, she was among a group of artists, writers, and intellectuals invited to greet Mikhail Gorbachev, then president of the Soviet Union, at the Soviet Embassy in Washington, D.C. During the 1990's, Oates produced a succession of works that were varied in format. From the novel *Foxfire: Confessions of a Girl Gang* (1993), about the members of an adolescent girl gang, to the gothic short stories in *Haunted: Tales of the Grotesque* and *The Collector of Hearts*, Oates continued to display her versatility and maintain her

Joyce Carol Oates (AP Photo/Jeff Zelevansky)

position as one of the world's eminent authors. In 1998, she moved into the children's market with *Come Meet Muffin*, an imaginative tale of a brave, adventuresome cat. Her novel *We Were the Mulvaneys*, published in 1996, was an Oprah Book Club Selection for 2001. Her husband died in 2008; she remarried in 2009. Her extensive expression as a writer, thinker, and teacher ensured Oates's role as a respected and vigorous participant in U.S. intellectual and literary life from the 1960's onward.

ANALYSIS

Joyce Carol Oates is a very American writer. Early in her career, she drew comparisons with such predecessors as Flannery O'Connor and William Faulkner. The chiefly rural and small-town milieu of her earlier work expanded over the years, as did her vision of passion and violence in the United States in the twentieth century.

It is difficult to separate Oates's short fiction from her novels, for she has consistently produced volumes in both genres throughout her career. Unlike many writers who produce both long and short fiction, Oates has never subordinated her stories to her novels: They represent in sum a no less considerable achievement, and Oates is by no means a novelist who sometimes writes stories, nor for that matter a storyteller who sometimes writes novels. Both forms figure centrally in her overall work. In many cases, her stories are crystallized versions of the types of characters and dramatic moments found in larger works; over the years, the themes and stylistic approaches in the two genres have maintained a parallel progression.

Oates concerns herself with the formulation of the American Dream and how it has changed and even soured through the decades of American prosperity and preeminence. Her characters are often prototypes of the nation, and their growth from naïveté to wisdom and pain reflect aspects of the national destiny that she sees in the evolving society around her. In her short stories, the naïveté is often the innocence of youth; many stories focus on adolescent girls becoming aware of the potential of their own sexuality and the dangers of the adult world. Like the United States, however, such characters retain an unbounded

youthful enthusiasm, an arrogant challenge to the future and the outside world.

An individual's relationship to the world around him or her is key to many of Oates's stories. Her fascination with images of the American Dream and the power of belief and self-creation implied therein translates to an awareness of her characters' self-perceptions, and, equally, their self-deceptions. Many of her characters have a built-in isolation: That is not to say that they are not involved with other people, but that their perceptions are necessarily limited, and that they are aware, though not always specifically, of those limits. Oates often establishes their subjectivity with remarkable clarity, allowing the reader to bring wider knowledge and perspective to the story to fill it out and complete the emotional impact. Isolation, detachment, and even alienation create the obstacles that her characters struggle to overcome. While Oates has been criticized for the darkness of her writing, as often as not her characters find redemption, hope, and even happiness. Neither the joy, however, nor the tragedy is ever complete, for human experience as Oates sees it is always a complex and mixed phenomenon.

Such complexity naturally emerges from human relationships, especially from those between the sexes. As a female writer, Oates had to deal with the "sexual question" merely in the act of sitting down at the typewriter, and her writing reveals a keen sensitivity to the interactions of men and women. While some of her works toward the end of the 1980's manifest a more explicitly feminist outlook, Oates has never been a feminist writer. Rather, her feminism--or humanism--is subsumed in her refusal to write the kind of stories and novels that women have traditionally written or to limit her male and female characters to typically male and female behaviors, attitudes, emotions, and actions. Oates does not make the sexes equivalent but celebrates the differences and examines feminine and masculine sexual and emotional life without preconceived assumptions. Thus, reading an Oates story is peering into a vision of the world where almost anything is possible between men and women. While they are eminently recognizable as the men and women of the contemporary United States, at the same time her characters are wholly independent and capable of full response to their inner lives.

Those inner lives often contain ugly possibilities. One of the major complaints that Oates faced, especially early in her career, regards the violence--often random, graphic, even obsessive--that characterizes much of her work. In a 1981 essay in *The New York Times Book Review* entitled "Why Is Your Writing So Violent?" Oates branded such criticism as blatantly sexist and asserted the female novelist's right to depict nature as she knows it. She clearly sees the United States as a nation where violence is a fact of life. In her novels, such violence takes the form of assassinations, mass murders, rapes, suicides, arsons, autopsies, and automobile accidents. In her short stories, the same events are treated with greater economy and precision but with no less commitment to the vivid portrayal of truth. She shies away from neither the physical details of pain and atrocity nor the psychological realities that accompany them. Even when the violence of her stories is a psychological violence performed by one character upon another, with no effusion of blood and guts, the effects are no less visceral. Oates's stories are deeply felt.

Violence, however, is never the ultimate point of an Oates story. Rather, the violence acts as either catalyst or climax to a dramatic progression: Through violent events, characters undergo inevitable transformations, and the suddenness of violence or the sharpness of pain, either felt or observed, jolts characters into a greater appreciation of life. Frequently, the violent event or action is very peripheral to the protagonist or prime action of the story. Rather, it is often anonymous, perpetrated by unseen hands for unknown reasons, presenting mysteries that will never be solved. Violence becomes an emphatic metaphor for the arbitrary hand of fate, destiny, chance, God--or whatever one wishes to call it. Oates generally portrays it without naming or quantifying it: For her, it is simply the way things are.

Beneath the passion, deep feeling, and violence of her stories is a meticulously intellectual mind, looking at the larger picture, in the wide array of approaches and devices that Oates employs over the range of hundreds of stories. She uses first-, second-, and third-person viewpoints, both male and female. Sometimes dialogue predominates; at other times, the prose is richly descriptive. Some of her stories turn on the use of imagery, tone, or rhythm, and plot is all but nonexistent; others are journalistically rich in event and sparse in stylistic embellishment. Some stories approach the length of novels, others are mere brushstrokes, several pages or even a single paragraph to express the crux of a character or dramatic situation. Some stories adhere to the traditional unity and structure of the short story, recounting a single event from beginning to end; others meander, circle in upon themselves, travel backward in time, or derive unity not from the narrative but from character or mood. In brief, Oates uses stories to explore the various tools available to her as a writer. As novelist John Barth noted, "Joyce Carol Oates writes all over the aesthetical map."

In addition, while each story has integrity as a complete work of fiction, Oates has devoted great attention to the composition of her collections, and each is unified structurally or thematically and forms an artistic whole as well as an anthology of smaller parts. For example, the stories in Oates's first collection, *By the North Gate*, are largely set in rural, small-town America and show individuals seeking to find order in their lives. *The Wheel of Love* consists of stories exploring varieties of love, and those in *The Goddess and Other Women* are all about women. The volume entitled *Marriages and Infidelities* contains reworkings of popular stories by such masters as Anton Chekhov, Henry James, Franz Kafka, and James Joyce; the stories deal with married people and marital issues and the literary approach itself suggests a "marriage" between Oates's tales and the originals on which they are modeled. The collection *The Hungry Ghosts* is unified by the stories' academic settings (places not unlike Oates's University of Windsor and Princeton) and the vein of satire that runs throughout. The stories in *The Poisoned Kiss* were, according to a prefatory note by Oates, written by a certain Ferdinand de Briao and deal with the exotic, rustic, and more authentically European material that such a gentleman--Oates's imaginary creation--would naturally devise. *Night-Side* and *The Seduction* contain stories that involve darker, psychologically ambiguous, sometimes surrealistic situations, and the stories in *Last Days* focus on individuals in upheaval and crisis, on the verge of emotional or physical breakdown. Many of the pieces in *Crossing the Border* are linked together by characters--Renée, Evan, Karl, Jake, Cynthia--who appear throughout, and many of those in *Raven's Wing* are set in small towns on the New Jersey coast.

"THE CENSUS TAKER"

A small rural town in mythical Eden County, based loosely on the region of western New York where Oates grew up, is the setting of "The Census Taker," one of the notable stories from *By the North Gate*. It is a simple story involving four relatively anonymous characters--a census taker, a boy, a girl, and a mother--and it is told in simple prose against a hazy, fairy-tale-like landscape. A census taker comes to a remote home to ask questions, but instead of finding the father who can give him the facts that he needs and send him on his way, he is faced with a pair of relentlessly inquisitive children who peel away the layers of his protective delusion in an effort to bring order to their young existence. Eventually, they wear away his confidence in the meaning of any answers, factual or existential, and he leaves without having taken the simplest measure of their household. At heart is the profound mystery of life, which, if not confronted with courage, will drive one to seek refuge in madness, blindness, or obsession.

"IN THE REGION OF ICE"

One of Oates's early triumphs in the short story, also dealing with obsession and madness, is a piece entitled "In the Region of Ice." First published in *The Atlantic Monthly* in 1965, and later in *The Wheel of Love*, it was an O. Henry Award winner. The protagonist of "In the Region of Ice" is Sister Irene, a lecturer on William Shakespeare at a small Catholic university. For all practical purposes, she lives "in the region of ice"--a region void of feeling and passion. Perfectly comfortable in front of a class, she is otherwise timid and essentially incapable of developing meaningful human contact.

Into her insulated existence comes Allen Weinstein, a brilliant but emotionally disturbed Jewish student. Obsessed with the reality of ideas, he comes to dominate one of Irene's classes, inspiring the hatred of his classmates but awakening intellectual and emotional life in the professor. The story, narrated through Irene's viewpoint, charts the emotional journey that she travels in response to Allen's erratic behavior. Their relationship, through her perception, becomes a dance of intellectual passion and spiritual magnetism.

Allen, however, stops coming to class and, after a prolonged absence, contacts Irene from a sanatorium with a plea that she intervene with his father. The Christian awakening and power that Irene feels as she approaches the Weinstein home disappear when she is faced with Allen's hateful, exasperated, unsympathetic father. Later, released from the sanatorium, Allen comes to Irene for emotional and financial support, but she painfully and inarticulately denies him, incapable of establishing a meaningful connection. While Allen is clearly on the edge of sanity, Irene's situation is more pathetic, for she is knowingly trapped within the trivial limits of her own selfhood. At the story's end, even the inevitable news of Allen's suicide provokes only a longing for feeling but no true emotional response.

"WHERE ARE YOU GOING, WHERE HAVE YOU BEEN?"

Another story that details the effects of a male intruder into the life of a female protagonist and the difficulty of connection between two very different people is "Where Are You Going, Where Have You Been?," one of Oates's most anthologized early stories. This tale of confused adolescence, based on a true story of a serial killer in Tucson, Arizona, is about Connie, a fifteen-year-old who abhors her parents, haunts suburban malls, and passes the hot summer nights with her equally precocious girlfriends. Through it all, however, she privately harbors innocent dreams of ideal love. One day, while home alone, she is approached by a strange man ominously named Arnold Friend, who is determined to seduce her and take her away. Rather than use force, Friend insinuates his way into Connie's mind and subdues her vulnerable and emerging sexuality. In the end, it is clear that he is leading her to some sort of death, spiritual or physical, and that his love is empty, but she is powerless against him.

Oates tells the story naturalistically but includes dreamy and surrealistic passages that suggest allegorical interpretation. The title implies both the uncertainty of adolescence and the changelessness of feminine behavior, or, possibly, the slow pace of social progress in improving women's lives. Subtly crafted and typically Oatesian, "Where Are You Going, Where Have You Been?" is in some ways a precursor to many later Oates stories. "How I Contemplated the World from the Detroit House of Correction and Began My Life Over Again" is a first-person account of a wayward adolescent girl in search of love and self-definition; the much later "Testimony" portrays a teenage girl who is so devoted to her older boyfriend that she serves as his accomplice in the abduction, rape, and murder of her perceived "rival"; and "April" is a simple sketch of two young adolescents rebelling against maternal authority. These four stories, and many others, portray moments in time when youth teeters on the brink of adulthood, when innocence is subtly transformed into sophistication, and when desire and love become stronger than life itself.

"THE SCREAM"

The struggles with desire, rebellion, and identity are subtler but no less intense in a story entitled "The Scream." It is a mood piece, in which little happens; the emotional impact is found in the images and the tension of stillness. The protagonist is a woman named Renée who, like many of the characters in the volume *Crossing the Border*, is an American living across the border in Canada. Floundering in a loving but lifeless marriage, she has been having an affair with a man for whom she feels passion but little trust.

The narrative of the story follows Renée as she wanders through an art museum, intentionally absent from an appointed rendezvous with her lover. An old man approaches her; she eavesdrops on talkative tourists; she peruses the art; she ruminates on her marriage, her affair, and her various uninteresting options. One photograph especially catches her attention: that of an Indian woman holding out a dead child, her face frozen in an anguished shriek. After gazing a long while at the photograph, losing herself in it, Renée swiftly leaves the museum and goes to meet her lover. The story ends as she stands outside their meeting place, no more determined to enter than when she started.

The power of the story lies in the photograph as an image. On one hand, the Indian woman's scream touches Renée's internal anguish, which is magnified by the relative paltriness of her particular discontent. On the other hand, the static quality of the photographic

image--the scream does not vanish when Renée looks away and back again--figures her own emotional paralysis. She can see and feel the inherent contradiction of her quandary--frozen in anguish--and through the experience at the museum can only barely begin to take action for self-liberation.

"IN THE AUTUMN OF THE YEAR"

An even more mature woman is at the center of "In the Autumn of the Year," which received an O. Henry Award in 1979, a year after its first publication in *The Bennington Review*, and which is included in the collection *A Sentimental Education*. Eleanor Gerhardt is a Pulitzer Prize-winning poet, an articulate spinster who has come to a small New England college to accept an award. Her host for the visit is Benjamin Holler, a man she knew when he was a boy in Boston when she was his father's mistress. She has never married, and her passion for Edwin Holler and the dramatic dissolution of their relationship form a memory that she sustains, though she did not seen him in the decades before his death. Upon meeting Benjamin, her consciousness shifts back and forth from the uneventful present to the tumultuous and deeply felt past. Oates uses balance to create powerful emotional dynamics. The juxtaposition of immediate experience and memory communicates the dislocation with which Eleanor perceives her existence in the "autumn" of her life.

The second half of the story comes suddenly and unexpectedly. In a seemingly casual conversation, Benjamin expresses accumulated anger and hatred at Eleanor and his father. Confronted with the sordidness of their affair and their responsibility for the emotional misery of his childhood, Eleanor finds her sentimental vision of the past shattered. Benjamin offers her the love letters and suicide threats that she sent to Edwin upon their separation, but she cannot face them and denies their authenticity. In the end, alone, she tosses the unopened letters in the fire, as if so doing will alleviate her guilt and folly. Benjamin's brutal honesty, however, has provided a missing piece to the puzzle of her life. Without the delusions by which her past drained her present of meaning, she is forced to face the past honestly and, recognizing its mixed qualities, to let go of it. Through this encounter, she can begin to take responsibility for her continued existence and her continued potential to think, feel, do, and live. As so often in Oates's stories, small encounters bring great transformations, and in pain there is redemption.

"RAVEN'S WING"

"Raven's Wing," a story in the volume of the same title, first appeared in *Esquire* and was included in *The Best American Short Stories 1985*. It is a subtle story that portrays a rather ordinary marriage and lacks the violence and passion of much of Oates's other work. Billy and Linda have been married for barely a year. Though Linda is five months pregnant, Billy treats her with indifference; Linda, in turn, baits, teases, and spites him. A horse-racing enthusiast, Billy becomes fascinated with a prize horse named Raven's Wing after it is crippled during a race. He finds a way to visit Raven's Wing in Pennsylvania, where it is recovering from major surgery, and, eye to eye with the animal, he feels a connection, an implicit mixture of awe, sympathy, and trust. The story ends soon thereafter in two brief scenes: Billy gives Linda a pair of delicate earrings and finds excitement in watching her put them on, and, weeks later, as he talks on the phone, Linda comes to him warmly, holding out a few strands of coarse black hair--a souvenir from Raven's Wing--and presses close against him.

In "Raven's Wing," rather than stating the characters' true feelings, of which they themselves are only hazily aware, Oates suggests them through the details of external reality. This is a story about perception--about how things appear differently through the blurring lens of familiarity and routine. Billy's fascination with the crippled horse betrays an unconscious awareness of his own crippled psyche, and the enormous, beautiful, and priceless creature's inevitable consignment to a stud farm is an ironic reminder of Linda's pregnancy and the very human power that a man and woman share to love, to support, and to create.

THE ASSIGNATION

The collection *The Assignation* is stylistically noteworthy, as Oates departs from standard forms and offers a variety of stories, character sketches, mood pieces, and other experiments in short fiction. Many of the pieces are deceptively short; lacking in plot information and often anonymous regarding character, they portray an emotional situation, interaction, or moment through the economic uses of detail and action. The first piece, "One Flesh," is no more than a paragraph suggesting the richly sensual relationship shared by an old couple. In "Pinch," a woman's fleeting emotions during a breast examination create a tense picture. In "Maximum Security," a woman's tour of a prison invokes a disturbing sense of isolation while invigorating her appreciation of nature and freedom. "Quarrel" and "Ace" are about how events of random violence affect, respectively, a homosexual couple's communication and a young street tough's sense of identity. In all these pieces, Oates provides the essentials of a fuller story and invites the reader's imagination to go beyond and within the story. The characters are no less unique, the prose no less picturesque, and the situations no less compelling; the economy with which Oates evokes these tales is testament to the depth of her craft.

WILL YOU ALWAYS LOVE ME?

Will You Always Love Me? is a collection of twenty-two narratives based upon childhood memories, suffering, and reason for hope. Oates cuts to the core of everyday life, revealing the truth about what people know but are not willing to admit. She portrays a profound commentary on the human condition by acting as a witness in describing the needs, cruelty, and violence displayed by humankind. Three of the stories, "You Petted Me, and I Followed You Home," "The Goose-Girl," and "Mark of Satan," won O. Henry Awards.

A lost dog is a central figure in "You Petted Me, and I Followed You Home," a story that first appeared in *TriQuarterly*. Dawn, who fears the erratic behavior and sudden violent acts of her husband, Vic, pets a little lost dog, which subsequently follows her and Vic home. Oates skillfully unveils how Dawn's feelings of fear for what lies ahead--of betrayal by loved ones and a terrible sense of lost feeling--parallel the feelings of the dog. By treating the dog with care and kindness, Dawn relays to Vic the need for similar consideration.

Oates examines some of the consequences that result from unbridled thoughts of passion in "The Goose-Girl," which first appeared in *Fiction*. Lydia, a respected suburban mother, helps her son Barry humiliate their new neighbor, Phoebe Stone. Phoebe, who reminds Lydia of the goose-girl in the fairy tales of the

Brothers Grimm, propositions Barry at a neighborhood party. Struggling with deep feelings of guilt, Barry eventually reveals the incident to his mother and pleads with her to call Phoebe. After allowing Barry time to worry, Lydia finally makes the call and wittingly embarrasses Phoebe over the proposed sexual encounter with her son.

In "Mark of Satan," which first appeared in *Antaeus*, Oates brings protagonist Flash to a renewed definition of self, even a renewal of spirit. During a visit from Thelma, a female missionary, Flash attempts to seduce her by drugging her lemonade. Thelma instinctively avoids the ploy and tells Flash that Satan is present in his home. Ironically, after Thelma leaves, she returns and prays for Flash. Finally, he realizes that someone cares about him, even though he does not deserve it.

Included in *The Best American Short Stories 1996*, "Ghost Girls" emerged from Oates's childhood image of a small country airport isolated between cornfields. Ingrid Boone, the child narrator, is intrigued by the mysterious lives led by her parents. Because she cannot fully comprehend or do anything about the strange adult world that surrounds her, Ingrid finds her life, influenced by the example of her attractive mother and her frequently absent father, spiraling downward into a tale of grotesque horrors. "Ghost Girls" is the seed of Oates's *Man Crazy* (1997), a novel of many stark images.

Perhaps the most concise articulation of the Oatesian aesthetic can be found in a story entitled "Love. Friendship," from *Crossing the Border*. In recollecting a friendship with a sensitive man who became obsessed with her marriage, the narrator Judith reflects:

> Our lives are narratives; they are experienced in the flesh, sometimes in flesh that comes alive only with pain, but they are recollected as poems, lyrics, condensed, illuminated by a few precise images.

Such descriptive narratives--lyrical, violent, experienced, recollected, full of precise images portraying real-life situations filled with deep heartfelt emotions--form the bulk of Oates's short fiction.

FAITHLESS: TALES OF TRANSGRESSION

The title story of *Faithless: Tales of Transgression*, originally published in *Kenyon Review*, earned a Pushcart Prize and appeared in *The Best American Mystery Stories* collection in 1998. "Faithless" tells the story of a woman's mysterious disappearance from the perspective of her adult granddaughter. The woman had left behind two very young daughters as well as a husband, and it is speculated that she ran off with another man, being dissatisfied with farm life, marriage to an older man, and her Lutheran faith. The story is filled with religious imagery: the grandmother's Bible, her gold cross, Reverend Dieckman and Mrs. Dieckman, who pray for the missing women's abandoned girls. Various rumors circulate about the missing woman's motivation for leaving home, none of them in her favor.

I AM NO ONE YOU KNOW

The title *I Am No One You Know* is an ironic one. Though many of Oates's characters appear on the surface to be bizarre and sensational, their similarities with common Americans provide readers with a point of entry into their stories. In "Three Girls," two young college students spot Marilyn Monroe in Strand Used Books in 1956 Manhattan. Monroe appears in disguise, wearing men's clothes and no makeup, her hair in a braid. In addition, like the two intellectual female poets watching her, Monroe is perusing books. She is, in fact, the third girl. The narrator becomes protective of Monroe, wishing no one to intrude upon her time as the third girl and even purchases her books for her, so she will not have to speak to the cashier. This non-iconic image of Monroe also appears in Oates's novel *Blonde*, published in 2001.

In "I'm Not Your Son, I Am No One You Know," the narrator visits his father in a nursing home. He is accompanied by his younger brother. Apparently not accustomed to visiting the home, the narrator is frightened by patients confusing him with their own sons. The narrator is warned by his brother that their father can no longer recognize himself in a mirror and will most likely not recognize the narrator, either. The climax of the visit involves a confrontation with another patient, an unlikable figure from the narrator's past.

"The Girl with the Blackened Eye" won an O. Henry Award and was selected for *The Best American Mystery Stories* for 2001. In this story, a high school student is abducted by a serial killer and survives, yet she resists telling her story to people new in her life, including her husband and daughters. She does, however, tell her readers. The story suggests that the people readers know perhaps have secret lives, perhaps are victims like the narrator of this story.

HIGH LONESOME: STORIES, 1966-2006

The large collection of short stories by Oates, *High Lonesome: Stories, 1966-2006*, serves as a valuable introduction to the short fiction of the famously prolific author. The collection includes eleven new stories in addition to twenty-five stories spanning her career and are grouped by decade of original publication. Stories from the past include "Where Are You Going, Where Have You Been?"; "How I Contemplated the World from the Detroit House of Correction, and Began My Life over Again"; "In the Region of Ice"; "Raven's Wing"; and "Mark of Satan." A new story, "Cousins," originally published in *Harper's*, was selected for *The Best American Short Stories* for 2005.

The collection's title story, "High Lonesome," takes place in a rural town, and, like many stories by Oates, is permeated with odors, in this case the odors of a farm. The narrator tells the story of his grandfather's arrest for solicitation for prostitution and suggests that, afterward, his life went downhill. He soon commits suicide. There is also the mystery of the brutal death of the narrator's cousin Drake, who arrested the grandfather. The story is connected by the image of the missing tip of the narrator's left forefinger, which reminds him of the past through its phantom pain. At the end of the story, the narrator acknowledges his loneliness and suggests that he would create a song to express that lonesome feeling if he knew how.

WILD NIGHTS! STORIES ABOUT THE LAST DAYS OF POE, DICKINSON, TWAIN, JAMES, AND HEMINGWAY

Oates fictionalizes the deaths of five iconic figures in American literature in *Wild Nights! Stories About the Last Days of Poe, Dickinson, Twain, James, and Hemingway*. The stories in this collection are arranged in chronological order. "Poe Posthumous; Or, The Light-House," presents Edgar Allan Poe as a lighthouse keeper and appears in the form of diary entries. Poe, whose only companion is a dog, chronicles his life as a naturalist at the lighthouse as well as his deteriorating mental state.

The collection's title refers to a poem by Emily Dickinson, which also appears in full as an epigraph. The Dickinson story, titled "EDickinsonRepliLuxe," involves a lonely childless couple who purchase a robotic replica of the poet in an attempt to alleviate their stilted existence. In preparation, the wife purchases the *Complete Poems of Emily Dickinson*, but has difficulty reading it; later, the wife is excited when she believes Dickinson to be writing poetry in her home. The husband and wife each have a different relationship with the Dickinson imitation: the wife considers her a companion, the husband considers her a possession.

"Grandpa Clemens and Angelfish, 1906," largely in epistolary form, is told in letters between Samuel Clemens, who is exhausted from playing the role of Mark Twain, and a young girl. Jealous, Clemens's spinster daughter Clara resents his relationships with girls, because he no longer shows affection for her. The happy innocent tone of the letters contrasts with the misery of the rest of the story, which reflects Clemens's daily life.

Henry James, who is, like Dickinson, one of Oates's favorite writers, is imagined as a volunteer in a London hospital during World War I in "The Master at St. Bartholomew's Hospital." Immediately, his sensitive nature is assaulted by the odors and sights and sounds of the ward of wounded and dying soldiers; however, he returns, day after day, to be of use: reading to soldiers (though not from his own works), writing letters, providing comfort. During his evenings at home, he writes in his diary and arranges an altar with objects collected as sacred relics from the hospital.

The emphasis of "Papa at Ketchum" is on mood rather than on plot. This story about Ernest Hemingway begins with Hemingway's suicide, then backtracks in time, meditating on Hemingway's experience in World War I, his father's suicide, Hemingway's guns, his alcoholism, and his inability to write. This final selection is the only story of the collection that does not include a diary entry, a letter, or a poem.

DEAR HUSBAND: STORIES

Dear Husband: Stories is a collection connected by the exploration of the dark side of American families. The title story, "Dear Husband," originally published in *The New Yorker* and selected for *The Best American Mystery Stories* for 2009, is told in the voice of Lauri

Lynn, a character based on Andrea Yates, a Texan who drowned her five children in the bathroom during a period of postpartum psychosis. The story is written in the form of a letter addressed to Lynn's husband, who was out of town on business at the time of the crime. The tone of the letter is calm and detached and suggests the motivation for the crime. Lynn seems to be suggest that her husband will be able to find a more perfect family after she has disposed of his current one.

"Landfill," also originally published in *The New Yorker* and similarly based on a true crime, was selected for *The Year's Best Fantasy and Horror* for 2007. The story, composed of a single long paragraph, tells the story of a missing college student, whose remains are found at the local landfill. Though the student had been missing for three weeks, his mother had refused to give up hope that he would be found alive. The young man apparently had been killed accidentally in a fraternity prank, but the story questions whether he might have been found alive had his disappearance been reported earlier.

Two of the collection's stories are told in epistolary form. "A Princeton Idyll," originally published in *Yale Review*, consists of a series of letters between a middle-aged woman and her grandparents' maid. The title of this story is identical to the title of a memoir that the grandfather of the initiator of the letters, Sophie, had worked on for a number of years before his death. Sophie writes to Muriel Kubelik in order to learn more about her family history and is unhappy with what she discovers. "Dear Joyce Carol," consists of a series of letters between a stranger and Joyce Carol Oates, who has recently appeared in the stranger's town on a book tour. The stranger wishes Oates to write his life story, which he hopes will be made into a film.

OTHER MAJOR WORKS

LONG FICTION: *With Shuddering Fall*, 1964; *A Garden of Earthly Delights*, 1967, revised 2003; *Expensive People*, 1968; *them*, 1969; *Wonderland*, 1971; *Do with Me What You Will*, 1973; *The Assassins: A Book of Hours*, 1975; *Childwold*, 1976; *The Triumph of the Spider Monkey*, 1976; *Son of the Morning*, 1978; *Cybele*, 1979; *Unholy Loves*, 1979; *Bellefleur*, 1980; *Angel of Light*, 1981; *A Bloodsmoor Romance*, 1982; *Mysteries of Winterthurn*, 1984; *Solstice*, 1985; *Marya: A Life*, 1986; *Lives of the Twins*, 1987 (as Rosamond Smith); *You Must Remember This*, 1987; *American Appetites*, 1989; *Soul/Mate*, 1989 (as Smith); *Because It Is Bitter, and Because It Is My Heart*, 1990; *I Lock My Door upon Myself*, 1990; *Nemesis*, 1990 (as Smith); *The Rise of Life on Earth*, 1991; *Black Water*, 1992; *Snake Eyes*, 1992 (as Smith); *Foxfire: Confessions of a Girl Gang*, 1993; *What I Lived For*, 1994; *You Can't Catch Me*, 1995 (as Smith); *Zombie*, 1995; *First Love*, 1996; *We Were the Mulvaneys*, 1996; *Man Crazy*, 1997; *My Heart Laid Bare*, 1998; *Broke Heart Blues*, 1999; *Starr Bright Will Be with You Soon*, 1999 (as Smith); *Blonde*, 2000; *Middle Age: A Romance*, 2001; *The Barrens*, 2001 (as Smith); *Beasts*, 2002; *I'll Take You There*, 2002; *Rape: A Love Story*, 2003; *The Tattooed Girl*, 2003; *The Falls*, 2004; *Missing Mom*, 2005; *Black Girl/White Girl*, 2006; *The Gravedigger's Daughter*, 2007; *My Sister, My Love: The Intimate Story of Skyler Rampike*, 2008; *A Fair Maiden*, 2009; *Little Bird of Heaven*, 2009.

POETRY: *Women in Love*, 1968; *Anonymous Sins, and Other Poems*, 1969; *Love and Its Derangements*, 1970; *Angel Fire*, 1973; *The Fabulous Beasts*, 1975; *Women Whose Lives Are Food, Men Whose Lives Are Money*, 1978; *Invisible Woman: New and Selected Poems, 1970-1982*, 1982; *The Luxury of Sin*, 1984; *The Time Traveler*, 1989; *Tenderness*, 1996.

PLAYS: *Miracle Play*, pr. 1974; *Three Plays*, pb. 1980; *I Stand Before You Naked*, pb. 1991; *In Darkest America: Two Plays*, pb. 1991; *Twelve Plays*, pb. 1991; *The Perfectionist, and Other Plays*, pb. 1995; *New Plays*, pb. 1998.

CHILDREN'S LITERATURE: *Come Meet Muffin*, 1998; *Big Mouth and Ugly Girl*, 2002; *Freaky Green Eyes*, 2003; *Sexy*, 2005; *After the Wreck, I Picked Myself Up, Spread, My Wings, and Flew Away*, 2006; *Naughty Chérie*, 2008.

EDITED TEXTS: *Scenes from American Life: Contemporary Short Fiction*, 1972; *The Best American Short Stories 1979*, 1979 (with Shannon Ravenel); *Night Walks: A Bedside Companion*, 1982; *First Person Singular: Writers on Their Craft*, 1983; *The Best American Essays*, 1991; *The Oxford Book of American Short Stories*, 1992; *American Gothic Tales*,

1996; *Snapshots: Twentieth Century Mother-Daughter Fiction*, 2000 (with Janet Berliner); *The Best American Essays of the Century*, 2000 (with Robert Atwan); *The Best American Mystery Stories*, 2005 (with Otto Penzler); *The Ecco Anthology of Contemporary American Short Fiction*, 2008 (with Christopher R. Beha).

BIBLIOGRAPHY

Bastian, Katherine. *Joyce Carol Oates's Short Stories: Between Tradition and Innovation.* Frankfurt: Verlag Peter Lang, 1983. Bastian surveys the Oatesian short story, providing occasional insights into theme and character. The focus is to place Oates in the tradition of the genre and find her links with its other masters.

Creighton, Joanne V. *Joyce Carol Oates.* Boston: Twayne, 1979. A penetrating exploration of the themes that dominate Oates's work, such as self-definition, isolation, and violent liberation. Creighton devotes a chapter to the experimentalism of five short-story collections. Includes chronology, notes, and an annotated bibliography.

Easterly, Joan. "The Shadow of a Satyr in Oates's 'Where Are You Going, Where Have You Been?'" *Studies in Short Fiction* 27 (Fall, 1990): 537-543. Interprets the character Arnold Friend as a satyr, a demigod from Greek and Roman mythology. Presents a number of arguments about the imagery and structure of the story to support this claim. Asserts Friend is the embodiment of dream, symbolizing the freedom of the imagination as opposed to the discipline of culture and intellect.

Johnson, Greg. "A Barbarous Eden: Joyce Carol Oates's First Collection." *Studies in Short Fiction* 30 (Winter, 1993): 1-14. Discusses Oates's *By the North Gate* as a microcosm of her entire career in fiction. Focuses on her Faulknerian mythmaking, her view of love as a violent force through which characters strive for power, and the similarity of her stories to those of Flannery O'Connor.

_____. *Invisible Writer: A Biography of Joyce Carol Oates.* New York: Penguin Putnam, 1998. Johnson provides a thorough analysis of Oates's work and life in this full-length authorized biography. Draws on a variety of sources, including Oates's private letters and journals.

_____, ed. *Joyce Carol Oates: Conversations, 1970-2006.* Princeton, N.J.: Ontario Review Press, 2006. This collection of interviews crossing the span of Oates's writing career is edited by her authorized biographer. Includes a lengthy interview between Oates and Greg Johnson and a chronology of biographical events.

_____. *Joyce Carol Oates: A Study of the Short Fiction.* New York: Twayne, 1994. After a general introduction to Oates's contribution to the short story, devotes separate chapters to feminism, the gothic, and postmodernism in several of Oates's short-story collections. Includes a number of comments by Oates on the short story, as well as brief excerpts from seven other critics.

_____. *Understanding Joyce Carol Oates.* Columbia: University of South Carolina Press, 1987. Geared to the general reader, this volume examines both Oates's major novels and some of her best-known stories. The focus is more on specific works than on Oates's overarching concerns. Easy to read, with a biography and bibliography.

McIntyre, Gina. "Dread Fills Oates's Tales." *Los Angeles Times*, March 14, 2011, p. D2. Review of *Give Me Your Heart* says that Oates's stories satisfy a "voyeuristic desire to watch the deeply flawed (or at least unreliable) narrators" march toward a sorry fate.

Wesley, Marilyn. *Refusal and Transgression in Joyce Carol Oates's Fiction.* Westport, Conn.: Greenwood, 1993. A feminist analysis, this work focuses on the family as portrayed in Oates's fiction. Wesley contends that the young protagonists of many of Oates's stories and novels commit acts of transgression that serve as critiques of the American family. Wesley maintains that the acts indict the society that produces and supports these unstable, dysfunctional, and often violent families.

Barry Mann; Alvin K. Benson
Updated by Nettie Farris

.

TIM O'BRIEN

Born: Austin, Minnesota; October 1, 1946

PRINCIPAL SHORT FICTION

The Things They Carried, 1990
"*Loon Point,*" 1993

OTHER LITERARY FORMS

Tim O'Brien often blurs the boundaries between genres. He began his career as a journalist, and sections of reporting are often mixed with his fiction. He develops novels, such as *Going After Cacciato* (1978; revised 1989), around successful short stories. He interlocks short fictions so closely that collections can be read as novels, although their components are published individually as short stories, as in *The Things They Carried*. He also often walks with one foot in fiction and one foot in autobiography, as in his early work *If I Die in a Combat Zone, Box Me Up and Ship Me Home* (1973; revised 1979), to which he refers as a war memoir rather than a novel. His essay "The Vietnam in Me," was the cover story for *The New York Times Magazine* of October 2, 1994. He has also written the novels *In the Lake of the Woods* (1994), *Tomcat in Love* (1998), and *July, July* (2002).

ACHIEVEMENTS

Tim O'Brien's short stories have been honored by the National Magazine Award and included in *The Pushcart Prize*, *Prize Stories: The O. Henry Awards*, and *The Best American Short Stories* collections. He was awarded the National Book Award in 1979 for *Going After Cacciato*. His collection of interrelated stories *The Things They Carried* won the *Chicago Tribune* Heartland Prize, the Melcher Book Award, and France's Prix du Meilleur Livre Étranger. His novel *In the Lake of the Woods* received the Society of American Historians' James Fenimore Cooper Prize for best

historical novel. He has also received awards from the National Endowment for the Arts, the John Simon Guggenheim Memorial Foundation, and the Vietnam Veterans of America.

BIOGRAPHY

William Timothy O'Brien was born in Minnesota in 1946 and lived there until he graduated summa cum laude from Macalester College in 1968. He was immediately drafted and, despite deep ambivalence, was inducted into the U.S. Army. The former student body president of a radical college, O'Brien served in Vietnam, first as a foot soldier and then as a typist. He was honorably discharged from the Army in 1970 with seven medals, among them the Purple Heart. He disapproved of the Vietnam War before he was drafted, while he was fighting it, and after he returned home.

Although O'Brien had done some scattered writing before the war (while he was still in college, he produced a novel that he did not publish), his real career as a writer began with Vietnam. During the summer after he was drafted, while he grappled with his conscience about serving in the war, he began to write intensely. "That horrible summer made me a writer," he recalls. O'Brien sent home accounts of the fighting in Vietnam that were first published in Minnesota newspapers and later recycled into his books.

After the war, O'Brien studied government at Harvard University and worked for *The Washington Post*. The first book he published, the 1973 war memoir *If I Die in a Combat Zone, Box Me Up and Ship Me Home*, was well received, opening the door for him to set aside both journalistic and political aspirations to build a full-time literary career.

ANALYSIS

Tim O'Brien is in essence a writer of the Vietnam War, but his relationship with that war is not simple. It is his setting, the geographical and historical reality in which his best stories are played out. It is his story, his material, the subject matter of his telling. It is also the reason he must write--because he went to Vietnam, certain things happened to him that require him to write, trying, as he says "to save Timmy's life with a story. . . . "

Vietnam also defines for him a constituency. The three and a half million people who served in Southeast Asia between 1964 and 1975 constitute the group to which he is responsible, the men and women for whom and to whom he speaks in his best work. He is sharply aware of his responsibility to this audience, which requires him to tell the truth about Vietnam--to shun oversimplifying, moralizing, or taking the easy way out. Scrupulous honesty about Vietnam--a situation where confusion, mystery, fear, uncertainty, and moral ambiguity reigned supreme--require O'Brien to shun straightforward narrative techniques, easy moralizing, or self-protective authorial distance.

Out of this need to be faithful to the deep truth about the Vietnam War experience, O'Brien developed his way of building a story like a jigsaw, out of a set of interlocking pieces. Books are built of story-pieces; stories are built of moment-pieces. In the spaces between the pieces, there is room for interpretation, for uncertainty, for mystery. Because of this structure, built up from fragments, it is impossible to categorize some of O'Brien's work as either a unitary novel or a collection of short stories, either fiction or nonfiction: He has deliberately abandoned the security of categories.

"GOING AFTER CACCIATO"

This story, which was selected for *The Best American Short Stories 1977* and *The Pushcart Prize* (and also grew into the novel *Going After Cacciato*), deals with the Vietnam draftee's terrible ambivalence about the war--the passionate desire to be someplace else, balanced against the utterly unthinkable act of leaving. O'Brien writes about this conflict in a number of his works. In this story, the two sides of the issue are embodied by the deserter Cacciato, on the one hand, and the obedient soldiers pursuing him, on the other.

Cacciato is a fool. His simplemindedness frees him to think simple, direct thoughts and take simple, direct action. His foolishness liberates him from the weight of duty, propriety, inertia, and expectation that chains the more "mature" soldiers to the war. When he wants to

be elsewhere, he simply goes. His going is a radical act that threatens the whole conceptual structure of the war because he enacts the possibility of saying no. The entire war mentality, as seen by O'Brien, depends on individual men finding it unthinkable to say no in such a way. Thus, Cacciato, always seen in the distance (like a wishing star or a mirage), becomes the image of unthinkable possibilities to the obedient soldiers still caught in the war. As one of them puts it, "Can't hump away from a war, isn't that right sir? The dummy has got to learn you can't just hump your way out of a war."

THE THINGS THEY CARRIED

Throughout his career, O'Brien continued to write short pieces for a number of magazines. One of these, his prizewinning "The Things They Carried," he later developed into a full-length book which was published in 1990 under the same title. The book is a related sequence of short pieces about the experience of a foot soldier in Vietnam. The vignettes range from one to twenty-five pages in length. In them, O'Brien mixes the techniques of the action/adventure war story with the self-doubting exploration of a contemplative. He

Tim O'Brien (AP Photo/David Pickoff)

intersplices war memories with present reflection, fact with fiction, novel with short story. This is his most successful book, telling the particular story of one soldier's war but also turning its attention to the universal questions of the nature of war, truth, healing, and courage.

O'Brien's craft in *The Things They Carried* is often compared to that of Ernest Hemingway and Joseph Heller, two other twentieth century American writers who shared the project of telling "a true war story." Like them, O'Brien creates a carefully controlled net of unstated meaning. Through understatement, oddities of style, and the juxtaposition of superficially unrelated information, O'Brien "shows" and does not "tell." Much is implied. By cooperatively reconstructing the implicit material, the reader actively participates in co-creating the story. Because of this, readers may experience themselves as more engaged, more immediately involved, than with other, more explicit, texts.

Another way in which O'Brien strives to "tell a true war story" is in his attention to physical details, the details that make up the life of a soldier. The rain, the mud, the fungus that grows in the socks, the jungle rot that attacks the skin, the precise physical sensation of bowel-loosening terror--these are the facts of a soldier's life, and these are the details that enrich the texture and reality of *The Things They Carried*. Through careful sensory detail, O'Brien attempts the impossible task of telling the true story of Vietnam so clearly that even those who were not there may stand in witness.

"THE THINGS THEY CARRIED"

The physical details of the experience of a soldier are primary in this story, which is structured as if it were a simple list of what infantrymen carried on their backs, with the exact weight added to underscore the reality of the load. It is almost as if the author had set himself a memory assignment of writing a straightforward inventory of a soldier's pack and found that the physicality of the list opened out into story because each item is needed for a reason. Those reasons tell the daily lives of the soldiers. (He also used the list format to powerful effect in "What They Didn't Know" in *Going After Cacciato*.) Some things they all carry, some things are particular to certain roles in the group, reflecting the shared and uniquely personal experience

of war. As the list develops, it begins to include the psychological and spiritual loads the men carry, things like fear and responsibility, until it becomes a full catalog of the weight that crushes humans at war.

"LOON POINT"

Published in 1993, this story is an example of an O'Brien work that does not implicitly or explicitly refer to the Vietnam War. However, much of the same confusion, mystery, fear, uncertainty, and moral ambiguity that rule his work about the war also dominate his work about the intimate conflicts between men and women. In this story, a married woman lies to her husband in order to go on a romantic getaway with her lover. During their interlude, her lover drowns before her eyes, and she returns to her husband with a wall of lies spoken and unspoken between them.

"Loon Point," like *The Things They Carried*, reflects on the simultaneous necessity and impossibility of telling the truth about the important things--love, war. Truth is necessary in order to heal, to mend the damaged heart, but it is also impossible because the inscrutable Other (the partner, the enemy) is so mysterious and the truth is so complex that putting it into words would require an oversimplification so gross as to constitute a lie. The wife elects silence because "there is nothing she could say that was entirely true"--which could also be a condensed statement of why O'Brien's work about the truth of both war and relationships is veiled in fiction, implicitness, and ambiguity.

OTHER MAJOR WORKS

LONG FICTION: *northern Lights*, 1975; *Going After Cacciato*, 1978, revised 1989; *The Nuclear Age*, 1981 (limited edition), 1985; *In the Lake of the Woods*, 1994; *Tomcat in Love*, 1998; *July, July*, 2002.

NONFICTION: *If I Die in a Combat Zone, Box Me Up and Ship Me Home*, 1973, revised 1979; "The Vietnam in Me," 1994.

BIBLIOGRAPHY

Gelfant, Blanche H., ed. *The Columbia Companion to the Twentieth-Century American Short Story*. New York: Columbia University Press, 2000. Includes a chapter in which O'Brien's short stories are analyzed.

Gilmore, Barry, and Alexander Kaplan. *Tim O'Brien in the Classroom: "This Too Is True, Stories Can Save Us."* Urbana, Ill.: National Council of Teachers of English, 2007. Provides information about O'Brien's life and works to suggest how teachers can design lessons about the author. Some of the lessons focus on the way O'Brien uses his life experience in his work, the nebulous border between fact and fiction in his writings, and his use of language. Also contains reviews and critical analyzes of his writings and interviews with O'Brien.

Harrison, Brady. "Tim O'Brien." In *A Reader's Companion to the Short Story in English*, edited by Erin Fallon, et al., under the auspices of the Society for the Study of the Short Story. Westport, Conn.: Greenwood Press, 2001. Aimed at the general reader, this essay provides a brief biography of O'Brien followed by an analysis of his short fiction.

Heberle, Mark A. *A Trauma Artist: Tim O'Brien and the Fiction of Vietnam*. Iowa City: University of Iowa Press, 2001. Argues that trauma is the central focus of O'Brien's writings, whether they are about the Vietnam War or about post-Vietnam War America. Describes how O'Brien recovers his personal experiences of war trauma to create *The Things They Carried* and other works.

Herzog, Tobey C. *Tim O'Brien*. Boston: Twayne, 1997. Critical biography addressed to informed readers from advanced high school students to university professors. Covers O'Brien's work from *If I Die in a Combat Zone, Box Me Up and Ship Me Home* through *In the Lake of the Woods*. Includes a bibliography.

Kaplan, Steven. *Understanding Tim O'Brien*. Columbia: University of South Carolina Press, 1994. Scholarly interpretation and criticism of O'Brien's work from *If I Die in a Combat Zone, Box Me Up and Ship Me Home* through *In the Lake of the Woods*. Includes a bibliography.

Lee, Don. "About Tim O'Brien." *Ploughshares* 21 (Winter, 1995-1996): 196-201. A concise and sensitive sketch of O'Brien's life and work through 1994, written on the occasion of O'Brien's guest editorship (with Mark Strand) of a volume of the literary review *Ploughshares*.

Smith, Patrick A. *Tim O'Brien: A Critical Companion*. Westport, Conn.: Greenwood Press, 2005. An introductory overview of O'Brien's life and works published from 1973 through 2002. Devotes one chapter to an analysis of *The Things They Carried*.

Tegmark, Mats. *In the Shoes of a Soldier: Communication in Tim O'Brien's Vietnam Narratives*. Uppsala: Ubsaliensis, 1998. Focuses on problematic communication in O'Brien's writings on Vietnam. Includes a bibliography and index.

Vernon, Alex. *Soldiers Once and Still: Ernest Hemingway, James Salter, and Tim O'Brien*. Iowa City: University of Iowa Press, 2004. A study of twentieth century war literature, examining how war and the military affected social and gender identities in the works of O'Brien and two other authors. Devotes four chapters to O'Brien, including "Salvation, Storytelling, and Pilgrimage in *The Things They Carried*."

Donna Glee Williams

FLANNERY O'CONNOR

Born: Savannah, Georgia; March 25, 1925
Died: Milledgeville, Georgia; August 3, 1964

"Good Country People," 1955
A Good Man Is Hard to Find, and Other Stories,
    1955
"Revelation," 1964
Everything That Rises Must Converge, 1965
The Complete Stories, 1971

OTHER LITERARY FORMS

In addition to writing thirty-one short stories, Flannery O'Connor wrote two short novels, *Wise Blood* (1952) and *The Violent Bear It Away* (1960). A collection of her essays and occasional prose entitled *Mystery and Manners* (1969) was edited by Robert and Sally Fitzgerald, and a collection of letters entitled *The Habit of Being* (1979) was edited by Sally Fitzgerald. More correspondence is collected in *The Correspondence of Flannery O'Connor and Brainard Cheneys* (1986), edited by C. Ralph Stephens. O'Connor also wrote book reviews, largely for the Catholic press; these are collected in *The Presence of Grace* (1983), which was compiled by Leo J. Zuber and edited by Carter W. Martin.

ACHIEVEMENTS

The fiction of Flannery O'Connor has been highly praised for its unrelenting irony, its symbolism, and its unique comedy. O'Connor is considered one of the most important American writers of the short story, and she is frequently compared with William Faulkner as a writer of short fiction.

For an author with a relatively small literary output, O'Connor has received an enormous amount of attention. More than twenty-five books devoted to her have

appeared beginning in the early 1960's, when significant critics worldwide began to recognize O'Connor's gifts as a fiction writer. Almost all critical works have emphasized the bizarre effects of reading O'Connor's fiction, which, at its best, powerfully blends the elements of Southwestern humor, the southern grotesque, Catholic and Christian theology and philosophy, atheistic and Christian existentialism, realism, and romance. Most critics have praised and interpreted O'Connor from a theological perspective and noted how unusual her fiction is, as it unites the banal, the inane, and the trivial with Christian, though fundamentally humorous, tales of proud Georgians fighting battles with imaginary or real agents of God sent out to shake some sense into the heads of the protagonists.

As an ironist with a satirical bent, O'Connor may be compared with some of the best in the English language, such as Jonathan Swift and Lord Byron. It is the comic irony of her stories that probably attracts most readers--from the orthodox and religious to the atheistic humanists whom she loves to ridicule in some of her best fiction. Thus, as a comedian, O'Connor's achievements are phenomenal, since through her largely Christian stories, she is able to attract readers who consider her beliefs outdated and quaint.

In her lifetime, O'Connor won recognition, but she would be surprised at the overwhelming response from literary critics that her fiction has received since her death. O'Connor won O. Henry Awards for her stories "The Life You Save May Be Your Own," "A Circle in the Fire," "Greenleaf," "Everything That Rises Must Converge," and "Revelation." *The Complete Stories,* published posthumously in 1971, won the National Book Award for Fiction. O'Connor received many other honors, including several grants and two honorary degrees.

BIOGRAPHY

Mary Flannery O'Connor's relatively short life was, superficially, rather uneventful. O'Connor was born on March 25, 1925, in Savannah, Georgia, to Regina Cline and Edward Francis O'Connor, Jr. She was their only child. O'Connor's father worked in real estate and construction, and the family lived in Savannah until 1938, when they moved to Atlanta. In that year, Edward O'Connor became a zone real estate appraiser for the Federal Housing Administration (FHA). Shortly thereafter, O'Connor and her mother moved to Milledgeville, Georgia, and her father became so ill that he had to resign from his job in Atlanta and move to Milledgeville. On February 1, 1941, Edward O'Connor died.

In her youth, O'Connor was diagnosed with the same disease that had killed her father when she was almost sixteen. Her short life would end tragically from complications related to disseminated lupus, a disease that attacks the body's vital organs. From the fall of 1938 until her death, O'Connor spent most of her life in Milledgeville, except for brief hiatuses. After graduating from the experimental Peabody High School in 1942, O'Connor entered Georgia State College for Women (subsequently renamed Georgia College) in Milledgeville, where she majored in sociology and English and was graduated with an A.B. degree in June, 1945. While in college, she was gifted both in drawing comic cartoons and in writing. In September, 1945, O'Connor enrolled at the State University of Iowa with a journalism scholarship, and in 1946, her first story, "The Geranium" (later revised several times until it became "Judgement Day," her last story), was published in *Accent*. In 1947, she received the master of fine arts degree and enrolled for postgraduate work in the prestigious Writers' Workshop. She was honored in 1948 by receiving a place at Yaddo, an artists' colony in Saratoga Springs, New York.

Planning never to return to the South, O'Connor lived briefly in New York City in 1949 but later moved to Ridgefield, Connecticut, to live with Robert and Sally Fitzgerald. Robert Fitzgerald is best known as a classics scholar and a translator of such works as the *Odyssey* and *The Theban Plays*. City life was too much for O'Connor, but she became quickly acclimated to life in slower-paced Ridgefield. In January, 1950, she underwent an operation while visiting her mother during Christmas. She remained in Milledgeville until she returned to Ridgefield in March.

In December, 1950, O'Connor became extremely ill en route to Milledgeville for Christmas. At first, it was believed that she was suffering from acute rheumatoid arthritis, but in February, after being taken to Emory University Hospital in Atlanta, O'Connor was diagnosed with disseminated lupus erythematosus. As a result of her illness, O'Connor would remain under the care of her mother for the rest of her life, and in March, 1951, she and her mother moved from the former governor's mansion in Milledgeville to Andalusia, the Cline family's farm, which was on the outskirts of town. O'Connor's mother, a Cline, was part of a family who had played a significant part in the history of the town of Milledgeville and the state of Georgia. Like many O'Connor protagonists, her mother, using hired help probably similar to the "white trash" and black field hands of O'Connor fiction, ran Andalusia as a dairy farm.

Meanwhile, O'Connor continued to write when she was not too weak. During the rest of her lifetime, she wrote fiction and befriended many people, some, such as the woman referred to in the collected letters as "A," through correspondence, others through frequent trips to college campuses for lectures, and still others through their visits to see her at Andalusia. Though her illness restricted her life considerably, she was able to achieve greatness as a writer, with a literary output that had already become a permanent part of the canon of American literature since World War II.

Physicians were able to control the effects of lupus for years through the use of cortisone and other drugs, but in early 1964, O'Connor, suffering from anemia, was diagnosed with a fibroid tumor. The operation to rid her of the tumor reactivated the lupus, and O'Connor died of kidney failure in August, 1964. In her last months, most of which were spent in hospitals, O'Connor worked slowly but conscientiously on the fiction that was to appear in her second (and posthumous) collection of short stories, *Everything That Rises Must Converge*.

Throughout her life, O'Connor remained faithful to her Catholic and Christian beliefs. Although her letters and fiction indicate frequent humor and self-mockery over her illness, it seems clear that O'Connor did not wish to be treated like an invalid, and she did not fear death because she held to the Christian belief in immortality. While some critics recognize elements of anger, bitterness, and frustration in the fiction, perhaps it was through her craft that she was able to vent her feelings in a more fruitful way. Friends and acquaintances admired her for her wit, her intelligence, and her sharpness of tongue, but they also admired her for her courage.

ANALYSIS

Flannery O'Connor is uncharacteristic of her age. In writing about the pervasive disbelief in the Christian mysteries during contemporary times, O'Connor seems better suited to the Middle Ages in her rather old-fashioned and conventional Catholic and Christian conviction that the central issue in human existence is salvation through Christ. Perhaps the recognition that such conviction in the postmodern world is rapidly fading and may soon be lost makes O'Connor's concerns for the spiritual realm, what she called the "added dimension" in her essay entitled "The Church and the Fiction Writer," more attractive for a dubious audience.

Although O'Connor completed thirty-one short stories and two novels, she is best remembered for nearly a dozen works of short fiction. These major stories may be classified as typical O'Connor short stories for a number of reasons. Each story concerns a proud protagonist, usually a woman, who considers herself beyond reproach and is boastful about her own abilities, her Christian goodness, and her property and possessions. Each central character has hidden fears that are brought to surface through an outsider figure, who serves as a catalyst to initiate a change in the protagonist's perception. O'Connor's primary theme, from her earliest to her last stories, is hubris--that is, overweening pride and arrogance--and the characters' arrogance very often takes on a spiritual dimension.

Closely connected with the theme of hubris is the enactment of God's grace (or Christian salvation). In an essay entitled "A Reasonable Use of the Unreasonable," O'Connor states that her stories are about "the action of grace in territory held largely by the devil" and points out that the most significant part of her stories is the "moment" or "action of grace," when the protagonist is confronted with her own humanity and offered, through an ironic agent of God (an outsider), and usually through violence, one last chance at salvation. O'Connor's protagonists think so highly of themselves that they are unable to recognize their own fallenness because of Original Sin, so the characters typically are brought to an awareness of their humanity (and their sinfulness) through violent confrontations with outsider figures.

"THE GERANIUM"

O'Connor's six earliest stories first appeared in her thesis at the University of Iowa. The most memorable in terms of O'Connor's later themes are "The Geranium," her first published story, and "The Turkey." "The Geranium," an early version of O'Connor's last story, "Judgement Day," deals with the experience of a southerner living in the North. In the story, an old man is treated as an equal by a black man in his apartment building but longs to return home to the South. More modernist in its pessimistic outlook than the later, more characteristic (and religious) O'Connor works, "The Geranium" shows the effects of fading southern idealism and resembles O'Connor's later stories concerned with home and displacement--other central themes of her fiction.

"THE TURKEY"

"The Turkey" describes an encounter between a young boy named Ruller and a turkey. Receiving little recognition from home, Ruller manages to capture the turkey, only to be outwitted by a leathery confidence woman, a forerunner of O'Connor's later outsider figures. Thematically, the story concerns the initiation of Ruller into adult consciousness and paves the way for O'Connor's later concern with theological issues. Ruller, who resembles the prophetlike figures of the novels and several stories, blames God for allowing him to catch the turkey and then taking it away from him.

A GOOD MAN IS HARD TO FIND

The first collection of O'Connor's fiction, *A Good Man Is Hard to Find, and Other Stories*, consists mostly of previously published short stories and a short novella, *The Displaced Person*. The title story, which may be O'Connor's most famous, deals with a Georgia family on its way to Florida for vacation. As the story opens, the main character, the grandmother, tries to convince her son, Bailey, to go to east Tennessee because she has just read about an escaped convict, The Misfit, who is heading to Florida. The next day, the family, including the nondescript mother, a baby, the other children, John Wesley and June Star, and Pitty Sing, the grandmother's cat, journeys to Florida. They stop at Red Sammy's Famous Barbeque, where the proprietor discusses his views of the changing times, saying "A good man is hard to find" to the grandmother, who has similar views.

The seemingly comic events of the day turn to disaster as the grandmother, upsetting the cat, causes an accident in which the car is wrecked. The Misfit and two men arrive at the accident scene. The grandmother recognizes The Misfit, and as a result, brings about the death of the entire family. Before she dies, however, the grandmother, who has been portrayed as a self-centered, judgmental, self-righteous, and hypocritical Protestant, sees the humanity of The Misfit and calls him "one of my babies." This section of the story represents what O'Connor calls "the action or moment of grace" in her fiction. Thematically, the story concerns religious hypocrisy, faith and doubt, and social and spiritual arrogance. The Misfit, who strikes comparison with Hazel Motes of *Wise Blood*, is a "prophet gone wrong" (from "A Reasonable Use of the Unreasonable"), tormented by doubt over whether Christ was who he said he was.

"THE LIFE YOU SAVE MAY BE YOUR OWN"

Another important story, "The Life You Save May Be Your Own," portrays a drifter named Tom T. Shiftlet, a one-armed man who covets the automobile of a widow named Lucynell Crater and marries her daughter, a deaf-mute, in an attempt to obtain it. He tells the mother that he is a man with "a moral intelligence." Shiftlet, who is searching for some explanation for the mystery of human existence, which he cannot quite comprehend, reveals himself to be just the opposite: one with amoral intelligence. An outsider figure who becomes the story's protagonist, Shiftlet leaves his wife, also named Lucynell, at a roadside restaurant, picks up a hitchhiker, and flies away to Mobile as a thunderstorm approaches. The story's epiphany concerns the irony that Shiftlet considers the hitchhiker a "slime from this earth," when in reality it is Shiftlet who fits this description. In rejecting his wife, he rejects God's grace and, the story suggests, his mother's valuation of Christianity.

"THE ARTIFICIAL NIGGER"

The next major tale, "The Artificial Nigger," is one of O'Connor's most important and complex. It has been subjected to many interpretations, including the suggestion by some critics that it contains no moment of grace on the part of Mr. Head and Nelson, the two main characters. The most Dantesque of all O'Connor stories, "The Artificial Nigger" concerns a journey to the city (hell), where Nelson is to be introduced to his first black person. As O'Connor ridicules the bigotry of the countrified Mr. Head and his grandson, she also moves toward the theological and philosophical. When Nelson gets lost in the black section of Atlanta, he identifies with a big black woman and, comparable to Saint Peter's denial of Christ, Mr. Head denies that he knows him. Nevertheless, they are reunited when they see a statue of an African American, which represents the redemptive quality of suffering and as a result serves to bring about a moment of grace in the racist Mr. Head. The difficulty of this story, other than the possibility that some may see it as racist itself, is that O'Connor's narrative is so ironic that critics are unsure whether to read the story's epiphany as a serious religious conversion or to assume that Mr. Head is still as arrogant and bigoted as ever.

Of all O'Connor's stories--with the possible exceptions of "The Life You Save May Be Your Own" and "Good Country People"-- "The Artificial Nigger" most exemplifies the influence of the humor of the Old Southwest, a tradition that included authors such as Augustus Baldwin Longstreet, Johnson Jones Hooper, and George Washington Harris. In "The Artificial Nigger," the familiar motif of the country bumpkin going to the city, which is prevalent in Southwestern humor in particular and folk tradition in general, is used.

"Good Country People"

The next important story, "Good Country People," is preceded by two lesser stories, "A Circle in the Fire" and "A Late Encounter with the Enemy," the former being a successful story about a woman's inability to comprehend the true nature of evil, and the latter being the only O'Connor portrayal of the South's attitude toward the Civil War. "Good Country People," which is frequently anthologized, concerns another major target of O'Connor's satirical fictions: the contemporary intellectual. O'Connor criticizes modern individuals who are educated and who believe that they are capable of achieving their own salvation through the pursuit of human knowledge. Hulga Hopewell, a Ph.D. in philosophy and an atheistic existentialist, resides with her mother, a banal woman who cannot comprehend the complexity of her daughter, because Hulga has a weak heart and has had an accident that caused her to lose one leg.

Believing herself to be of superior intellect, Hulga agrees to go on a picnic with a young Bible salesman and country bumpkin named Manley Pointer, hoping that she can seduce him, her intellectual inferior. Ironically, he is a confidence man with a peculiar affection for the grotesque comparable to characters in the humor of the Old Southwest. As he is about to seduce Hulga, he speeds away with her wooden leg and informs her, "I been believing in nothing since I was born," shattering Hulga's illusion that she is sophisticated and intelligent and that her atheism makes her special. As the story ends, Hulga is prepared for a spiritual recognition that her belief system is as weak and hollow as the wooden leg on which she has based her entire existence. Pointer, whose capacity for evil has been underestimated by the logical positivist Mrs. Hopewell but not by her neighbor Mrs. Freeman, crosses "the speckled lake" in an ironic allusion to Christ's walking on water.

The Displaced Person

The final piece in the collection, a novella entitled *The Displaced Person*, portrays the most positive of O'Connor's outsider figures, Mr. Guizac, a Pole. The story is divided into two sections. In the first part, to escape incarceration in the refugee camps after World War II, Mr. Guizac agrees to work for Mrs. McIntyre, a widow who runs a dairy farm. Unbeknownst to him, Mr. Guizac arouses jealousy and fear in the regular tenant farmers, the Shortleys, and the black field hands. Because Mr. Shortley is lazy and lackadaisical, he particularly resents the productivity of Mr. Guizac. The story moves toward the spiritual dimension when Mrs. Shortley, who considers herself a model Christian, begins to see Mr. Guizac and his family as agents of the devil. After Mrs. Shortley learns that her husband is to be fired the next morning, the Shortleys drive away, and Mrs. Shortley dies of a stroke and sees her "true country," which is defined in one of O'Connor's essays as "what is eternal and absolute" ("The Fiction Writer and His Country"). At the time of her death, Mrs. Shortley, displaced like the poor victims of the Holocaust, which she has witnessed in newsreels, is redeemed through displacement and enters her spiritual home.

The story's second part concerns Mrs. McIntyre's growing fear of outsiders. Mr. Shortley reappears after his wife's death and learns that Mr. Guizac is arranging a marriage for, and taking money from, Sulk, a Negro field hand, so that Mr. Guizac's niece can earn passage to the United States. The southern racial taboos are portrayed as fundamentally inhumane when confronted with the reality of human suffering, as seen in the niece, who is in a refugee camp. Father Flynn, the priest who has arranged for Mr. Guizac and his family to come to the United States to work for Mrs. McIntyre, tries to teach Mrs. McIntyre the importance of Christian charity and the fine points of Catholic theology. Unconcerned with these matters, which she considers unimportant, Mrs. McIntyre becomes neurotic about Mr. Guizac's inappropriateness and overlooks the spiritual for the material. Throughout the novella, O'Connor links the peacock, a symbol of Christ's Transfiguration, with Mr. Guizac, and in the end, Mr. Shortley "accidentally" allows a tractor to run over Mr. Guizac while Mrs. McIntyre and the other field hands watch. As the human race is complicit in the persecution and crucifixion of Christ, so are Mrs. McIntyre and the others in the death of Mr. Guizac, a Christ figure. At the story's end, Mrs. McIntyre, losing her dairy farm and all the material possessions in which she has put so much faith all her life, becomes displaced, as do the others who have participated in the "crucifixion" of Mr. Guizac.

EVERYTHING THAT RISES MUST CONVERGE

The second collection of O'Connor's short fiction, *Everything That Rises Must Converge*, shows the author's depth of vision as she moved away from stories rooted primarily in the tradition of Southwestern humor to heavily philosophical, though still quite humorous, tales of individuals in need of a spiritual experience. Most apparent is the influence of Pierre Teilhard de Chardin, the French paleontologist and Catholic theologian, on the title story, as well as the vision of the entire collection. Teilhard de Chardin argued that through the course of time, it was inevitable, even in the evolution of the species, that there was a process moving toward convergence with God.

"EVERYTHING THAT RISES MUST CONVERGE"

This idea, though perhaps used ironically, appears as the basis for "Everything That Rises Must Converge," which is considered one of O'Connor's greatest works. O'Connor once said that this story was her only one dealing with the racial issue; even so, the tale still transcends social and political commentary. The main character, Julian, is another typical O'Connor protagonist. Arrogant and unjust to his more conventional southern and racist mother, the adult college graduate Julian angrily hopes that his mother will be given a lesson in race relations by having to sit next to a black woman wearing the same hat that she is wearing. Outwardly friendly to the black woman's child, Julian's mother, with characteristic O'Connor violence, converges with the oppressed black race after she offers a penny to Carver, the child. After the black woman hits Julian's mother with her purse, Julian is as helpless, lost, and innocent as Carver is. He recognizes that his mother is dying and enters the world of "guilt and sorrow." Through this story, O'Connor reflects on the rising social status of blacks and connects this rise with a spiritual convergence between the two races.

"GREENLEAF"

"Greenleaf," also a major work, portrays still another woman, Mrs. May, attempting to run a dairy farm. Her two ungrateful bachelor sons refuse to take her self-imposed martyrdom seriously when she complains of the Greenleafs and their bull, which, at the beginning of the story, is hanging around outside her window. The Greenleafs are lower-class tenant farmers whose grown children are far more productive and successful than the bourgeois Mrs. May's. O'Connor moves to pagan mythology as she characterizes the bull as a god (compared to Zeus) and unites the Greenleaf bull symbolically with peculiarly Christian elements. The coming of grace in this story is characteristically violent. Mrs. May is gored by a bull, who, like the ancient Greek gods, is both pagan lover and deity (although a Christian deity).

"THE LAME SHALL ENTER FIRST"

The next significant story in the collection, "The Lame Shall Enter First," strikes comparison with the novel *The Violent Bear It Away*, for the main character, Rufus Johnson, a sociopathic teenage criminal, reminds readers of Francis Marion Tarwater, the hero of the novel. There is also Sheppard, the intellectual social worker who, like Tarwater's Uncle Rayber, is a secular humanist and believes that if he takes away the biblical nonsense that the adolescent protagonist has been taught, he will be saved.

Ironically, Sheppard spends all of his time trying to analyze and improve Rufus while at the same time neglecting his own son, Norton. While Rufus is clearly a demonic figure, he nevertheless believes in God and the Devil and convinces the child that he can be with his dead mother through Christian conversion. The child, misunderstanding this message, kills himself, and Sheppard is left to recognize the emptiness of his materialist philosophy. O'Connor's attitude toward the secular humanist is again satirical; without a divine source, there can be no salvation.

"REVELATION"

O'Connor's last three stories, according to most critics, ended her career at the height of her powers. "Revelation," one of the greatest pieces of short fiction in American literature, is O'Connor's most complete statement concerning the plight of the oppressed. While her fiction often uses outsiders, she seldom directly comments on her sympathies with them, but through Ruby Turpin's confrontation with the fat girl "blue with acne," who is named Mary Grace, O'Connor is able to demonstrate that in God's Kingdom the last shall be first. Mary Grace calls Mrs. Turpin, who prides herself on being an outstanding Christian lady, a "wart hog from hell," a phrase that Mrs. Turpin cannot get out of her mind. Later, Mrs. Turpin goes to "hose down" her hogs, symbols of unclean spirits, and has a vision of the oppressed souls entering heaven ahead of herself and her husband (Claud). Critical disagreement has centered largely on whether Mrs. Turpin is redeemed after her vision or whether she remains the same arrogant, self-righteous, bigoted woman she has been all of her life.

"Parker's Back"

"Parker's Back" is one of the most mysterious of O'Connor's stories. Obadiah Elihue Parker, a nonbeliever, marries Sarah Ruth, a fundamentalist bent on saving her husband's soul. After a mysterious accident in which he hits a tree, Parker gradually experiences religious conversion and, though tattooed all over the front of his body, is drawn to having a Byzantine tattoo of Christ placed on his back, thinking that his wife will be pleased. She is not, however, accusing him instead of idolatry. In reality, she is the heretic, for she is incapable of recognizing that Christ was both human and divine. Beating welts into her husband's back, Sarah Ruth fails to recognize the mystical connection between the suffering of her husband and that of the crucified Christ. By this point in her career, O'Connor was using unusual symbols to convey her sense of the mystery of God's redemptive power.

"Judgement Day"

O'Connor's last completed story, "Judgement Day," is a revised version of her first published story, "The Geranium." The central character, a displaced southerner living with his daughter in New York City, wishes to return home to die. Tanner, while an old and somewhat bigoted man, remembers fondly his relationship with a black man and hopes to befriend a black tenant in his daughter's apartment building. This story concerns Tanner's inability to recognize differences in southern and northern attitudes toward race, and, as in earlier O'Connor stories, "home" has more than a literal meaning (a spiritual destiny or heaven). Unlike almost all other O'Connor works, this story portrays racial relations as based on mutual respect. Also, Tanner, while attacked violently by the black tenant, is portrayed as a genuine believer and is sent to his eternal resting place (heaven), the destiny of a Christian. By the end of her life, O'Connor considered a return to a heavenly home much more significant than any other subject.

Other major works

LONG FICTION: *Wise Blood*, 1952; *The Violent Bear It Away*, 1960.

NONFICTION: *Mystery and Manners*, 1969; *The Habit of Being: Letters*, 1979 (Sally Fitzgerald, editor); *The Presence of Grace*, 1983; *The Correspondence of Flannery O'Connor and Brainard Cheneys*, 1986.

MISCELLANEOUS: *Collected Works*, 1988.

Bibliography

Asals, Frederick. *Flannery O'Connor: The Imagination of Extremity*. Athens: University of Georgia Press, 1982. In one of the best books on O'Connor's fiction, Asals focuses on the use of the doppelgänger (double) motif in the novels and short fiction, the most thorough and intelligent treatment of this subject. Asals also concentrates on O'Connor's religious extremity, which is evident in her fiction through her concern with polarities and extremes. Contains extensive endnotes and a good bibliography.

_____. *"A Good Man Is Hard to Find": Flannery O'Connor*. New Brunswick, N.J.: Rutgers University Press, 1993. A collection of critical essays that analyze O'Connor's story from a variety of perspectives. Critics discuss the pros and cons of O'Connor's shift in point of view from the grandmother to The Misfit, the nature of grace in a materialistic world, and the theological significance of the story's concluding confrontation.

Bacon, Jon Lance. *Flannery O'Connor and Cold War Culture*. New York: Cambridge University Press, 1993. Reads O'Connor's stories in the context of Cold War politics, popular culture, media, and consumerism that form the backdrop to her work.

Cash, Jean W. *Flannery O'Connor: A Life*. University of Tennessee, 2002. An extensively researched and painstakingly detailed account of O'Connor's life.

Darretta, John Lawrence. *Before the Sun Has Set: Retribution in the Fiction of Flannery O'Connor*. New York: Peter Lang, 2006. Examines all of O'Connor's short stories and novels to describe how her ideas about retribution changed during the period in which these works were written. Daretta argues that in her first story, "The Geranium," O'Connor's concept of individuals being paid back for their evil or kindness was personal and familiar, but by the time she completed her last story, "Judgement Day," she showed an eschatological interest in retribution.

Desmond, John F. *Risen Sons: Flannery O'Connor's Vision of History*. Athens: University of Georgia Press, 1987. Desmond argues that O'Connor's fiction reenacts Christian history and Catholic theology through an art O'Connor herself saw as an "incarnational act." Discussing several major stories and the two novels, the book focuses on the metaphysical and the Christian historical vision as observed through reading O'Connor's fiction and emphasizes that *The Violent Bear It Away* represents the fullest development of her vision. Includes an extensive bibliography and useful endnotes.

Feeley, Kathleen. *Flannery O'Connor: Voice of the Peacock*. New Brunswick, N.J.: Rutgers University Press, 1972. A useful though somewhat early study of O'Connor's fiction from a theological perspective. Contains analyses of almost all the stories and novels and focuses on the connection between the books in O'Connor's library and her own works. Feeley's primary fault is that the works are sometimes oversimplified into religious messages without enough emphasis on the humor, the sarcasm, and the satire. A bibliography of primary and secondary works is included, as is a list of some possible sources of O'Connor's fiction found in her library.

Gelfant, Blanche H., ed. *The Columbia Companion to the Twentieth-Century American Short Story*. New York: Columbia University Press, 2000. Includes a chapter in which O'Connor's short stories are analyzed.

Gooch, Brad. *Flannery: A Life of Flannery O'Connor*. New York: Little, Brown, 2009. Drawing upon letters that O'Connor wrote to friends and family and on interviews with those who knew her, Gooch develops an in-depth portrait of the writer. Her views on race and religion are discussed, as well as her relationships with men, her family, and her

community. Includes sixteen pages of black-and-white photos

Gretlund, Jan Nordby, and Karl-Heinz Westarp, eds. *Flannery O'Connor's Radical Reality*. Columbia: University of South Carolina Press, 2006. Collection of scholarly essays that assess the impact of the social, political, and religious milieu of O'Connor's time on her short stories and novels. Some of the essays examine theophany in O'Connor's stories, "mataphoric processes" in her short fiction, the collection *Everything That Rises Must Converge* and theories of the short- story sequence, the symbolism of blood in her work, and O'Connor as an American Catholic writer during the Cold War.

Hendin, Josephine. *The World of Flannery O'Connor*. Bloomington: Indiana University Press, 1970. Although this study is an early one in O'Connor scholarship, Hendin's argument that O'Connor may be read in other than religious ways makes the book worthy of consideration. Hendin offers effective analyses of most of the major O'Connor stories. While her interpretations should be approached with caution, they are nevertheless convincing as they attempt to show that O'Connor was an artist rather than a polemicist.

Hewitt, Avis, and Robert Donahoo, eds. *Flannery O'Connor in the Age of Terrorism: Essays on Violence and Grace*. Knoxville: University of Tennessee Press, 2010. Collection of essays that analyze O'Connor's depiction of violence and grace from the perspective of the twenty-first century preoccupation with terrorism. Some of the essays discuss the place of her "gory stories" in the American horror tradition, O'Connor and noir, and her stories "An Artificial Nigger" and "A Stroke of Good Fortune."

Kirk, Connie Ann. *Critical Companion to Flannery O'Connor: A Literary Reference to Her Life and Work*. New York: Facts On File, 2008. Features a biography, followed by "Works A-Z," with entries for all of O'Connor's short stories, novels, and essays; each entry provides a synopsis of the work, a critical commentary, descriptions of the characters, and suggestions for further reading. Another section provides information about people, places, and topics related to O'Connor's work. Also includes a chronology of her life and a detailed bibliography of her works.

May, Charles E., ed. *Critical Insights: Flannery O'Connor*. Pasadena, Calif.: Salem Press, 2012. Collection of original and reprinted essays providing critical readings of O'Connor's work. Also includes a biography, a chronology of major events in O'Connor's life, a complete list of her works, and a bibliography listing resources for further research.

Paulson, Suzanne Morrow. *Flannery O'Connor: A Study of the Short Fiction*. Boston: Twayne, 1988. A useful resource for the beginner. Includes primary and secondary material on O'Connor's fiction and concentrates on the predominant issues, themes, and approaches to her writings. Paulson divides O'Connor's stories into four categories: death-haunted questers, male/female conflicts, "The Mystery of Personality" and society, and good/evil conflicts. Supplemented by a chronology of O'Connor's life and a bibliography of primary and secondary works.

Rath, Sura P., and Mary Neff Shaw, eds. *Flannery O'Connor: New Perspectives*. Athens: University of Georgia Press, 1996. The new perspectives illustrated in this collection of essays are primarily feminist and Bakhtinian, with one essay using discourse theory and another focusing on race and culture. Stories discussed include "A View from the Woods," "The Artificial Nigger," and "The Crop."

Robillard, Douglas, Jr. *The Critical Response to Flannery O'Connor*. Westport, Conn.: Praeger, 2004. Compilation of forty-seven essays providing critical examinations of O'Connor's works. The collection is divided into three sections: essays written during her lifetime, essays written between 1964 and 1989, and essays that foreshadow future criticism of her writings.

Scofield, Martin. "Katherine Anne Porter, Eudora Welty, and Flannery O'Connor." In *The Cambridge Introduction to the American Short Story*. New York: Cambridge University Press, 2006. An overview and analysis of short fiction by three southern women writers. Discusses some of O'Connor's short stories, including "A Good Man Is Hard to Find," "The Artificial Nigger," and "Everything That Rises Must Converge,"

Spivey, Ted R. *Flannery O'Connor: The Woman, the Thinker, the Visionary*. Macon, Ga.: Mercer University Press, 1995. Attempts to understand O'Connor first as a southerner, then as a modernist intellect, and finally as a visionary thinker. Argues that O'Connor reflects the personal and social issues of the last decades of the twentieth century.

Walters, Dorothy. *Flannery O'Connor*. Boston: Twayne, 1973. This early but effective introduction to the works of O'Connor includes analyses of the short fiction and the novels. Walters argues perceptively and conventionally that O'Connor is predominantly a religious writer whose works can be classified as Christian tragicomedy. Walters also makes some useful observations about O'Connor's connections with earlier literary traditions. Includes a chronology of O'Connor's life, useful endnotes, and a select bibliography.

Westling, Louise Hutchings. *Sacred Groves and Ravaged Gardens: The Fiction of Eudora Welty, Carson McCullers, and Flannery O'Connor*. Athens: University of Georgia Press, 1985. The first feminist study of O'Connor's fiction. Useful for those interested in critical perspectives other than religious readings of O'Connor's fiction, as well as readers who are curious about O'Connor's relationship with Eudora Welty and Carson McCullers, two of her rivals as masters of short fiction. Westling discusses the female characters and emphasizes that O'Connor often shows female protagonists as victims of male antagonists. Contains an extensive bibliography and useful endnotes.

D. Dean Shackelford

CHRIS OFFUTT

Born: Haldeman, Kentucky; August 24, 1958

PRINCIPAL SHORT FICTION
Kentucky Straight, 1992
Out of the Woods, 1999

OTHER LITERARY FORMS

Less than a year after the publication of his first collection of short stories, Chris Offutt (AWF-iht) published *The Same River Twice: A Memoir* (1993). His first novel, *The Good Brother*, was published in 1997. The second volume of his memoir, *A Memoir of Coming Home*, was published in 2002.

ACHIEVEMENTS

Chris Offutt was named one of *Granta*'s Best Young American Fiction Writers. He has received a Whiting Writers Award, the Jean Stein Award from the American Academy of Arts and Letters, a fellowship from the National Endowment for the Arts, and a John Simon Guggenheim Memorial Foundation Fellowship. His work has been anthologized in *The Picador Book of American Short Stories* and in *The Best American Short Stories 1994.*

BIOGRAPHY

Christopher John Offutt was born in 1958 in Rowan County, Kentucky, near the tiny town of Haldeman, an area he once described as "a zip code with a creek," to Mary "Jody" Jo McCabe, a teacher, and Andrew Jefferson Offutt, a teacher-turned-science-fiction writer. Before earning a B.A. in theater arts from Morehead State University (also in Rowan County), Chris Offutt hitchhiked around the country, working at odd jobs. Among his more colorful jobs was a stint in Alabama with a circus, where he tended the elephants and played a role in one of the animal acts dressed as a walrus.

While in Boston he met Rita Lily, who later became his wife. After their plans to move back to Rowan County fell through, Offutt was accepted into the writing program at the University of Iowa, where he earned an M.F.A. in 1990. He and Rita lived in a small rented house on the Iowa River until they moved to Albuquerque and then to Montana, before completing the circle by returning to Rowan County, where Offutt took a job teaching creative writing at Morehead State University.

ANALYSIS

The ubiquitous character throughout the fiction of Chris Offutt is the hill country of eastern Kentucky. It is not just a backdrop for stories, as it so often has been for other Kentucky writers, such as James Lane Allen and Jesse Stuart. Offutt's hills live and breathe, holding the personalities in the story and often becoming the deuteragonist, the second-most important character in the story that heavily influences and motivates the protagonist. In his early fiction, eastern Kentucky, wounded, suspicious, and recovering from the damages of the coal and steel companies, which, in earlier generations, stripped it and its people of physical and spiritual worth, leaving nothing but wounds and scars, is entering a new age. New roads and innovative forms of communication are forcing connections with the rest of the world, allowing the people to move, in the words of Terry Heller in his review of *Kentucky Straight*, Offutt's first collection of stories, "from subsistence living to consumerism." Offutt deals with the growing pains of these changes without derision or mockery. He does not create stereotypical hillbillies or subhuman families that breed only within their own family. He deals with incest and other subjects often associated with the area in realistic, honest, and accurate ways.

Offutt's fiction has continued to be rife with the power of those same hills to project a siren's call for the return of those who have gone away. The later stories deal with human feelings of isolation, alienation, and disorientation; the earlier stories concentrate on the protagonists' feelings of belonging, of being connected by some mystic or metaphorical umbilical cord.

"SAWDUST"

A recurring theme in Offutt's stories is the imposing notion in eastern Kentucky that a person should never try to rise above his or her peers or elders. At the beginning of "Sawdust," Junior, the boy who serves as first-person narrator, says, "Neighbors say I think too much." When Junior makes known his intention to take an equivalency test and thus earn a high school diploma, his family acts as if they are ashamed of him, and his brother refuses to talk to him at all. When a group of boys, after hearing about his ambition, beat him, Junior's older brother, Warren, retaliates to save the family honor. He seems to accept Junior's claim that he wants the diploma for the same reason Warren wants a battery-powered television-- "To sit and look at." Once he has it, the diploma is much more than that to Junior. It is proof that his father, a lunatic who hanged himself with his belt because he was unable to heal a puppy's broken leg, was wrong when he said "a smart man wouldn't bother with town." Junior knows that he "can go there anytime." He knows that his boundaries are expandable.

"THE LEAVING ONE"

In "The Leaving One" Offutt explores the bond with the mountains felt by the natives of eastern Kentucky and the equally mysterious and mystic power of that area to call its people back to it. Vaughn, a boy who lives with his mother, meets a strange old man in the woods who claims to be Vaughn's maternal grandfather, Elijah "Lije" Boatman--a name that foreshadows the mystical journey through which he will lead Vaughn. Lije, who left the mountains to serve as a chaplain in World War I, lost his three sons in World War II and abandoned the civilized world to live in the mountains for more than forty years, until workers captured him and his daughter, Vaughn's mother, and had him committed to an asylum. Lije has returned to the mountains to die and to find his grandson and train him to replace him as mountain mystic. Lije gives Vaughn a stone that he has worn around his neck since Lije's "papaw" gave it to him just before he died, a talisman that

identifies the wearer as the inheritor and the keeper of the old ways of the hills. Lije says to Vaughn, "You be the Boatman now." At the heart of this story of maturation and succession are the beliefs, still shared by many people native to eastern Kentucky, that the hills are alive and communicate with people who can listen to them. It is also a story of preservation and of the need to integrate mystical and empirical knowledge.

"BLUE LICK"

"Blue Lick" is another of Offutt's stories narrated by a boy whose intelligence and powers of perception put him at odds with his fellow mountain folk. All of Offutt's stories are, to some extent, about limits on people's freedom, imposed by the land, by other people, or by traditions--all, at least to some extent, self-imposed. The father in this story goes to prison for car theft but is released early because his wife, who felt imprisoned by her family, ran off with the owner of the car her husband falsely was accused of stealing. With the mother gone, the father's elderly mother is saddled with the job of raising two boys she cannot possibly handle, especially because one of the boys, nicknamed Little Elvis because he makes up songs, is mentally disabled and thus requires constant supervision. When a neighbor makes cruel fun of his son and shoots his dog, the father feels that his new freedom is negated by the restrictions of his parole. His interpretation of the mountain code of manly behavior demands revenge, so he steals the man's car, takes it apart piece by piece, is caught throwing the pieces into the Blue Lick River, and is sent back to prison. Little Elvis becomes a ward of the state, and the young, unnamed narrator is left to battle his guilt. The great irony of the story is that he blames himself for his mother's leaving because he walked in on her while she was having sex with her lover. He suffers the burden of responsibility for the breakup of his family.

"NINE BALL"

It is certainly no accident that "Nine Ball" is the last story in Offutt's collection *Kentucky Straight*. Each story in this collection has as one of its themes the power of the Appalachian Mountains of eastern Kentucky to keep the people born there from abandoning them. Everett, the protagonist of "Nine Ball," may be the only major character in the book to escape successfully. He and his father make their living by raising hogs on the slop from the cafeteria of a school built fifty years ago by the Works Progress Administration. The state has announced that it will close the school the next summer. This marks the beginning of the end of their way of life, and Everett, seemingly with no plan in mind, starts severing other ties that have kept him bound there. He has a passion for the game of pool, and this leads him into a game that allows him to win enough money to leave. The sweetest part of this victory is that he wins most of the money from the local thug who has bullied him most of his life. Another tie he severs is that with his sister. Although it angers him that she has sex with virtually every man she meets, in his last moments with her he regrets that he had never had sex with her himself: "He'd missed something that everyone knew more about than him." Because his decision to leave the mountains comes at the very end of the story, it makes a perfect ending for the entire book.

OUT OF THE WOODS

Out of the Woods, Offutt's second collection of short stories, seems like a logical outgrowth of his first collection, *Kentucky Straight*. Whereas the nine stories in *Kentucky Straight* focus on the difficulties people have in escaping the mountains, the eight stories in *Out of the Woods* deal primarily with people who have left the hills of Kentucky but still feel the almost undeniable call to return to their mountain homes. The title story, the first in the collection, eases readers into this notion with two characters whose return is already built into the plot. The first to leave was Ory, one of five brothers and the only one in the family to ever move away. At the beginning of the story he has been gone for ten years, and the family has just received word that he has been shot and is in a hospital in Wahoo, Nebraska. Kay, the brothers' only sister, voices an opinion predominant in the hills of Kentucky: "Him leaving never made sense. . . . He hadn't done nothing and nobody was after him." As a means to become more accepted by Kay's family, her husband Gerald, the newcomer to the family, agrees to bring Ory home. By the time he gets there, Ory is dead. Gerald has to cut a deal with the local police to claim the body and, in a journey reminiscent of William Faulkner's *As I Lay Dying* (1930), take it back to Kentucky. The seven stories that follow

explore the insecurities and phobias many hill folk experience when they move to places where the sky, without the mountains to limit their vision of it, is disorienting, and the horizon is so far away that the distance keeps them in a fluctuating state of anxiety.

"MELUNGEONS"

The focus of "Melungeons," in the *Out of the Woods* collection, is on Deputy Ephraim Goins, who puts seventy-six-year-old Melungeon (a small mixed race of Native American, African American, and white who live in the Appalachian Mountains of Kentucky, Virginia, and Tennessee) Haze Gibson in jail at his own request for his own protection. Gibson, who had left the mountains because of a family feud, returns because he has missed every wedding and funeral his family has ever had. Goins, also a Melungeon, has suffered racial prejudice: scorned both by whites and by African Americans, Melungeons are doubly exiled and marginalized. Gibson is one of the last of the old members of his family still alive, and his nemesis, Beulah Mullins, one of the last old members of her clan, hears of his return. More than thirty people from the Mullins and the Gibson clans have died over the years in a feud that started sixty years earlier over disputed bear meat. Beulah goes into town to satisfy a bone-deep need: She enters the jail with a sawed-off shotgun hidden in her skirt, kills the last of the old Gibsons, and takes his place in the jail cell. Deputy Goins walks out of the jail toward the nearest slope, called by this primitive ritual back to the hills whence he came. The story is told in the restrained classical tones of mythic inevitability.

"MOSCOW, IDAHO"

"Moscow, Idaho," from *Out of the Woods*, focuses on a displaced eastern Kentucky ex-con. What makes the story so strong is the dialogue, for most of the story records the conversation of Tilden, the central character, and Baker, a fellow ex-con, who are unearthing coffins to make way for a new highway through the cemetery in Idaho. The men talk about prison life, which Baker misses because of the comfort of its routine and the camaraderie he felt there. However, Tilden likes the quiet, empty space of Idaho. When Baker steals a car and takes off, Tilden remains, unwilling to be on the run or to risk prison again. He lies on his back in a wheat field, wondering if he will ever find a woman he likes or a town he wants to stay in, happy that there is not a fence or a wall in sight.

"TWO-ELEVEN ALL AROUND"

The central character in this story from *Out of the Woods* is an out-of-work drunk with an alcoholic girl-friend in Casper, Wyoming "Two-Eleven All Around" is about another displaced mountain man, thirty-five years old, out of work, with no place to sleep, and with a girlfriend who is obsessed with listening to a police scanner while she is detoxing from alcohol with Prozac. The story ends when the protagonist has a sudden vision that one night he will be awakened by his son banging at the door, looking for a place to flop. A part of the drunk wants to tell his son to take a look at the empty beer cans, the beat-up furniture, and the dirty sheets, but then the father realizes that if the son does not change his ways this is where he will wind up, and the father opens the door wide and lets in his son.

OTHER MAJOR WORKS

LONG FICTION: *The Good Brother*, 1997.

NONFICTION: *The Same River Twice: A Memoir*, 1993; *No Heroes: A Memoir of Coming Home*, 2002.

BIBLIOGRAPHY

Beattie, L. Elisabeth, ed. "Chris Offutt." In *Conversations with Kentucky Writers*. Lexington: University Press of Kentucky, 1996. Extensive biographical information that reveals significant details about the sources of Offutt's stories.

Halpern, Sue. "A Zip Code with a Creek." Review of *The Same River Twice* and *Kentucky Straight*, by Chris Offutt. *The New York Times Book Review*, January 31, 1993, p. 10. Halpern describes Offutt as an exquisite storyteller, and she discusses his ear for dialect and his connection to Appalachia.

Hamilton, William L. "Learning Not to Trespass on the Gently Rolling Past." *The New York Times*, April 18, 2002. Offutt talks about how he tried to return home to live in Kentucky and why it did not work for him and his family.

Palmer, Louis H., III. "Chris Offutt Comes Home." *Appalachian Journal: A Regional Studies Review* 26, no. 1 (Fall, 1998): 22-31. Offutt shares his thoughts about connecting to the land to eastern Kentucky.

Rooke, Leon. "His Old Kentucky Home." Review of *Out of the Woods*, by Chris Offutt. *The New York Times Book Review*, March 7, 1999, p. 16. Rooke addresses Offutt's characterization and use of language, summarizing that *Out of the Woods* is a "magical book," with not one weak story.

Edmund August
Updated by Charles E. May

JOHN O'HARA

Born: Pottsville, Pennsylvania; January 31, 1905
Died: Princeton, New Jersey; April 11, 1970

PRINCIPAL SHORT FICTION

The Doctor's Son, and Other Stories, 1935
Hope of Heaven, 1938
Files on Parade, 1939
Pipe Night, 1945
Hellbox, 1947
Assembly, 1961
The Cape Cod Lighter, 1962
The Hat on the Bed, 1963
The Horse Knows the Way, 1964
Waiting for Winter, 1966
And Other Stories, 1968
The O'Hara Generation, 1969
The Time Element, and Other Stories, 1972
Good Samaritan, and Other Stories, 1974
Collected Stories of John O'Hara, 1984
John O'Hara's Hollywood: Stories, 2007 (Matthew
　　J. Bruccoli, editor)

OTHER LITERARY FORMS

John O'Hara is probably best known to American readers for his long, complex novels of manners, liberally spiced with sex and seasoned with class conflict. Most of his stories are set in that coal-mining region of Pennsylvania known as The Region by its inhabitants, an O'Hara domain which was ruled, at least fictionally, by the city of Gibbsville. He also wrote seven plays, five of them included in *Five Plays* (1961). From 1934 to 1957, he worked on treatments, adapted other fictions, and wrote original screenplays for Hollywood. He received sole credit for *Moontide* (1942) and credit in varying degrees for *I Was an Adventuress* (1940), *He Married His Wife* (1940),and *Best Things in Life Are Free* (1956). For the last title he wrote the original

story. He also wrote a series of political columns for national syndication later collected and published as *My Turn* (1966).

ACHIEVEMENTS

Although John O'Hara was perhaps best known during his lifetime as a novelist, his growing posthumous reputation appears to rest upon his shorter fiction, particularly upon the tales issued in collections nearly every Thanksgiving holiday during the last decade of the author's life; significantly, relatively few of the stories in such volumes as *Assembly*, *The Cape Cod Lighter*, *The Horse Knows the Way*, or *Waiting for Winter* had seen prior publication in magazines.

Following his depart from *The New Yorker* at the end of the 1940's, O'Hara poured most of his prodigious energies into the longer fictional form, sometimes approaching but never really matching or surpassing the accomplishment of his first novel, *Appointment in Samarra* (1934). Around 1960, with a distinct--and often expressed--premonition that time was running out, O'Hara returned to the shorter form with a vengeance, often returning for the setting of his stories to the 1920's and 1930's--as if to make good use of his vivid memory while it still served him. Following a reconciliation of sorts with *The New Yorker* on the occasion of *Sermons and Soda Water*, O'Hara resumed publication there and elsewhere, particularly in the declining *Saturday Evening Post*. It was, however, in published collections quickly reissued in paperback that O'Hara's later stories would reach their widest audiences and exercise their greatest impact. Although he continued to write and publish novels, it is clear that the best of his energies--and memories--were reserved for the stories, which accounted in large measure for the Award of Merit bestowed upon him by the American Academy of Arts and Letters in 1964.

BIOGRAPHY

John Henry O'Hara was born on January 31, 1905, the eldest child of Patrick O'Hara, M.D., and Katherine Delaney O'Hara of Pottsville, Pennsylvania. He was taught to read at the age of four and given a hand-printing set at age six. After he was refused permission to graduate from Niagara Prep, even though he was valedictorian, on the grounds of drunkenness, O'Hara went back to Pottsville. His father died shortly there-after, and O'Hara found that his father's investments had been worthless; he was never able to attend col-lege. His first job was on the *Pottsville Journal*; in 1927, he worked his way to Europe, and the next year he was in New York, working for the *Herald-Tribune*. He sold his first story to *The New Yorker* in 1928 and was published by that magazine continuously until 1949, when a review by Brendan Gill (which, James Thurber passed the word, had been written by Wolcott Gibbs) ended O'Hara's association with the magazine and, as it turned out, interrupted his career as a short-story writer for eleven years. After 1960, O'Hara made collections of stories he liked and sent them to Albert Erskine at Random House, where they were published without the intermediation of magazine editing and publication; this accounts for the greater length of the post-1960 stories.

O'Hara did most of his work in Hollywood between 1929 and 1931, before he had ever published a novel; in 1931, he married Helen R. Petit. Although he achieved some success in the next two years, O'Hara became a hard drinker, was divorced, and eventually became the victim of despair--which became an almost suicidal mood he dispelled only by locking himself in a hotel room in New York in 1933 to write *Appointment in Samarra*. In the next three years he worked again in Hollywood; published his first collection of short sto-ries, the novel *Butterfield 8* (1935), one story in *Scrib-ner's* and eleven in *The New Yorker;* and in 1938 mar-ried Belle Mulford Wylie of New York and Quogue, Long Island, to which he subsequently returned as a summer resident every year of his life. In the next few years he consolidated his reputation as a short-story writer and saw *Pal Joey* (1940) produced on Broadway with music and lyrics by Richard Rodgers and Lorenz Hart. O'Hara became a regular contributor to *Newsweek* and reviewed theater and motion pictures for that publication for the next two years. In 1944, he served as a war correspondent for *Liberty* after re-signing from the Office of Strategic Services because he did not, as he told his superiors, want to have the responsibility for killing anyone. Wylie Delaney O'Hara, his only child, was born in 1945, and in 1949 the family moved to Princeton, where he wrote *A Rage to Live* (1949).

In 1953, O'Hara almost died after his gastric ulcer hemorrhaged, and the next year his wife died after a congenital heart defect worsened; but O'Hara made both a physical and an emotional recovery from these disasters. He quit drinking and in 1955 he remarried, to Katharine (Sister) Barnes Bryan.

O'Hara published the novel *Ten North Frederick* in 1955 and received membership in the National Insti-tute of Arts and Letters two years later. The events were connected: Now his peers recognized that O'Hara was master of the large canvas as well as the small, of the sweep of history as well as the social value of one neighborhood. In the next six years, O'Hara produced

John O'Hara (Library of Congress)

two novels, *Ourselves to Know* (1960) and *Elizabeth Appleton* (1963); three novellas collected in *Sermons and Soda Water* (1960); *Five Plays* (1961); and three short-story collections, *Assembly*, with twenty-six stories, *The Cape Cod Lighter*, with twenty-three stories, and *The Hat on the Bed*, with twenty-four stories. In 1964, he received the Award of Merit for the Novel from the American Academy of Arts and Letters, an honor which then had been given to only four other novelists, and only two Americans--Ernest Hemingway and Theodore Dreiser. The next year he published *The Lockwood Concern* (1965), remarkable for its gothic atmosphere and for the linguistic and architectonic wizardry which beguiles the reader into accepting that atmosphere. He then published two novels and two short stories. He finished *The Ewings* (1972) in February, 1970, and had written seventy-four pages of a sequel when he died quietly in his sleep on April 11, 1970. He left behind an enormous achievement.

ANALYSIS

"ANDREA"

John O'Hara's "Andrea" is a wintry story first published in the collection *Waiting for Winter*. Andrea Cooper is the woman whose life is chronicled by Phil, the narrator, who met Andrea at a country club dance when she was sixteen and he was attending the University of Pennsylvania law school. She is beautiful, truthful, and a little aggressive (in the fine old tradition of O'Hara women), and he "did not often hear Andrea use a line that was not her own." During an interlude, they go out to his car. She wants to come to see him at his apartment in Philadelphia and make love to him. The dialogue that resolves this and moves the story on to all its other plateaus, indeed through its progressions from brightness to darkness and from eroticism to melodrama to tragedy, is vintage O'Hara. Over the decades, they become a couple, with Phil the responsible member. Their relationship lasts through Andrea's marriages and through Phil's rise in the legal profession. Andrea cannot stay married; Phil will not marry. Andrea is naïve about everything but sex; Phil is savvy, but perhaps not about sex. The temptation to make it neat by making him only an average lover is perhaps too overwhelming, but the implicit accusation is there in the way O'Hara presents his character.

At the end of the story, Phil goes back to Gibbsville, where the couple met, to try to head off expensive litigation in a complicated mineral rights case. Andrea's father, an unscrupulous businessman who is ruining the store he manages so that the owners will sell to a chain that has made a deal with him, has also ruined her financial security. Phil also finds out that Andrea has had another abortion, this one performed by the man she was going to marry, a doctor to whom she had come about the pregnancy before that. Phil has made her pregnant. The night before the child was conceived, they had had an argument--superficially about her marriages but really an attempt on her part to get him to marry her--and she had thrown a heavy glass at him. The event made him realize how old he was when he did not catch it; and he had been a "sensible" lover that night.

Now, on his visit to Gibbsville, she tries to pretend that she is in love with her homosexual business partner. Phil soberly refuses to believe the tale and tells her she could have killed herself with the abortion and, for the first time in their long relationship, offers immediate marriage. She gets angry at him and he leaves, for the first time without their making love. He rationalizes her promiscuity by thinking to himself that "it was her nature to pass herself around among men and she would have done so whether I was in her background or not." The problem is that Andrea is calling out for a stabilizing influence. Phil does not really know how to become one, although now an old bachelor set in his ways. Partly by design and partly because of unadmitted jealousy, he knocks down in Andrea's estimation the other men to whom she reaches out for stability.

Phil goes abroad and in Brussels avails himself of a tall blond call girl and takes to heavy drinking. Four months pass and he has to go back to Gibbsville to try again to resolve the mineral rights case. He goes out to supper with the members of the local bar association and reminisces with a few members until midnight, and then returns to his hotel room and falls asleep with the lights on. Andrea comes to see him at three o'clock in the morning. At first, she is annoyed; then he is impotent. They finally make love and, afterward, when they remember that they have been together for twenty years, Andrea says "Then it certainly isn't love. . . . Although it certainly is." Then, after inviting him to her apartment for dinner that night, she opens the windows and tells him to get some sleep. Then their affair and Phil's life--as well as hers--end:

> Then she went to the other window and opened it, and I don't know what happened next because I was not watching. But when I did look she was not there, and I did not believe that until I heard a most awful scream. Then I believed it and it is all I have left to believe.

"YOU CAN ALWAYS TELL NEWARK"

"You Can Always Tell Newark" also belongs to the post-1961, book-publication-only group of short stories. The story begins with two middle-aged men watching a singles tennis match between two young men; the outcome of both the plots run concurrently in the story, through the help of exposition which seems to be (but is not) flashback. One of the handsome young men keeps making sotto voce comments to Nance, an attractive, pregnant young woman watching them. Williams, one of the older men, offers her a seat up on the row where the spectators' backs are supported by the wall. She refuses, a little huffily. Williams and Smith, who is Williams's foil in their little expository scene, watch the young man who has been addressing Nance lose. The pair then go to the clubhouse, where Williams is even more sympathetic to the girl because he has found out that she is the daughter of his old flame. He says as much and the girl wonders why her mother did not marry him--there is a kind of empathy between them, a powerful feeling of alikeness. Then Williams figures out that Nance is probably his daughter; and Smith tells him that Nance's husband, Bud, is a brilliant medical student but she has been having an affair with Rex Ivers. Williams recalls that Nance's mother *wanted* to marry him, but that he was not "very reliable in those days" and her present husband was.

Williams finds himself on the seven o'clock train to New York with Ivers, and they begin talking. Ivers is a little high and Williams's curiosity about Nance is consuming him. Ivers talks about his affair with her, not using her name. He then says that "his girl" cannot leave her husband because he depends on her. Williams

tells him he knows the girl he is describing, and Ivers tells him what has been worrying him: that Nance wants to divorce her husband, have the child, and marry him. Rex asks him for advice. Then a wonderfully ironic scene begins. Williams says: "Well I have an ethical problem too. My ethical problem is whether to advise you one way or the other. As a matter of fact, Rex, my problem is really more difficult than yours." Rex finally, in the process of thinking out loud, which is really what he has wanted to do all along, but in the presence of someone who could be trusted to hear it, says, "It never will work out," and says that he does not want to sink the other man or be responsible for a kid growing up without a father, as he had to after his father was killed in the war.

Williams then asks him if it would make a difference if the child she was carrying was his (earlier in the story the reader learns that Nance's mother never told Williams that Nance was his child, and Smith agrees that she would probably never admit it to him). "No. It would make things tougher for me, but as long as she didn't tell Bud, her husband, she and the baby are better off." "Thank you," Williams says, and then the story is allowed to die in small talk. It is a wonderful story and shows what irony, sympathy, and drama-without-melodrama O'Hara was capable of even in the shortest stories and with the most dangerous materials--materials which could have become soap opera in the hands of anyone less magisterially in control of the story, the characters, and the style.

"THE DOCTOR'S SON"

"The Doctor's Son," which is a very long story by the standards of the 1930's and which carried O'Hara's first collection, is important to look at as part of a great writer's first efforts. The story is autobiographical, or seems to be, which is never a disadvantage for an American short story, especially at that time, when sincerity was more highly prized as one of the minor virtues and the examined life, particularly the first parts of it, was interesting to people who had just discovered psychoanalysis. The story is told by James Malloy, a young man, and not yet very experienced; in fact, he is fifteen. The year is 1919 and the world is being decimated by influenza, an apocalyptic event in O'Hara's own life. Like James Malloy, who is his fictional alter ego, his father was a doctor, and O'Hara spent a great deal of time driving him on his rounds.

Malloy's father is hit by the "flu" and has to call in Dr. Myers, a senior in medical school. James Malloy has a crush on Edith Evans, daughter of the local mine superintendent. Young Dr. Myers starts an affair with Mrs. Evans; and much of the interest of the story comes from the two little romances, one adult and one adolescent, that serve as counterpoint to the realistic scenes of how doctoring was done in the Polish and Irish bars of The Region. The plot and its subplot and theme are joined when Mr. Evans comes to see Dr. Myers at a Polish bar and makes some ambiguous remarks about the doctor's having seen his wife in the Evans home. Finally, they leave the bar following Evans in the Malloy Ford. Malloy's problem is that he is trying to make Edith feel better about the affair between the adults, which both know about, and to keep the community from having to do without the services of a doctor either because Evans has killed Dr. Myers or because Dr. Malloy has beaten him up and sent him back to Philadelphia.

Nothing is wrong, apparently, and Dr. Malloy calls the Evans house telling Dr. Myers to come to the Malloys. All is cordiality at the Malloy residence and Dr. Myers is sent off with many thanks. In the meantime, James has tried to kiss Edith and she has put him off. The doctor and his son go all over the back roads visiting patients, arguing and mumbling and visiting the Poles and the Irish. Then they hear that Mr. Evans has died. Earlier in the story, when Evans comes into the Polish bar, he says things O'Hara constructed in such a way that they were totally ambiguous, and only to be feared by the guilty--Dr. Myers and Malloy. Evans does not want a drink, but when Dr. Myers both refuses to step outside with him--fearing this is an excuse to get him alone and beat him up--and comforts Evans about his wife's condition, he takes a drink from the bottle that the sick miners have been passing around.

Dr. Myers should appeal to him as an educated person and a family man and a leader of the community not to take a drink, but he--and Malloy--are so relieved (both sigh audibly) that they do not. Evans dies, Dr. Myers leaves town, the affair between the two adolescents sours, Dr. Malloy mourns a good friend, and

ramification piles upon ramification, irony upon irony. Young Malloy thinks: "I thought of the bottle that he had shared with Steve and the other Hunkies, and Mrs. Evans's illness and Doctor Myers. It was all mixed up in my mind." The education of Malloy has begun. A perfect story is thoroughly realized and ended--sometimes the hardest part for a writer--with great restraint.

OTHER MAJOR WORKS

LONG FICTION: *Appointment in Samarra*, 1934; *Butterfield 8*, 1935; *Pal Joey*, 1940 (epistolary novel); *A Rage to Live*, 1949; *The Farmer's Hotel*, 1951; *Ten North Frederick*, 1955; *A Family Party*, 1956; *From the Terrace*, 1958; *Ourselves to Know*, 1960; *Sermons and Soda Water*, 1960; *The Big Laugh*, 1962; *Elizabeth Appleton*, 1963; *The Lockwood Concern*, 1965; *The Instrument*, 1967; *Lovey Childs: A Philadelphian's Story*, 1969; *The Ewings*, 1972; *The Novellas of John O'Hara*, 1995.

PLAYS: *Pal Joey*, pr. 1940 (pb. 1952; libretto; lyrics by Lorenz Hart, music by Richard Rodgers; based on O'Hara's novel); *Five Plays*, pb. 1961; *Two by O'Hara*, pb. 1979 (includes *Far from Heaven*, 1962, and the screenplay *The Man Who Could Not Lose*, 1959).

SCREENPLAY: *Moontide*, 1942.

NONFICTION: *Sweet and Sour*, 1954; *My Turn*, 1966; *A Cub Tells His Story*, 1974; *"An Artist Is His Own Fault": John O'Hara on Writers and Writing*, 1977 (Matthew J. Bruccoli, editor); *Selected Letters of John O'Hara*, 1978 (Bruccoli, editor).

BIBLIOGRAPHY

Bruccoli, Matthew J. *The O'Hara Concern*. New York: Random House, 1975. A carefully researched scholarly biography that reconstructs O'Hara's life and career in scrupulous detail, showing the evolution of his talent and thematic interests. Particularly authoritative in its account of O'Hara's break--and eventual reconciliation--with *The New Yorker*, and the impact of both events on his approach to short fiction. Includes an exhaustive primary and secondary bibliography.

Eppard, Philip B. *Critical Essays on John O'Hara*. New York: G. K. Hall, 1994. Collection of essays analyzing O'Hara's fiction, including some of his more than four hundred short stories. The essays range from reviews to formal academic studies of O'Hara's themes and narrative techniques.

Farr, Finis. *O'Hara.* Boston: Little, Brown, 1973. Written by a journalist of O'Hara's generation, Farr's book was the first O'Hara biography and, indeed, the first book to be written about O'Hara after his death. It includes discussion of novels and stories published during the last five years of his life. Somewhat more anecdotal in tone and scope than Bruccoli's biography, this book nevertheless includes penetrating readings of selected novels and stories, together with a brief but useful bibliography.

Gelfant, Blanche H., ed. *The Columbia Companion to the Twentieth-Century American Short Story.* New York: Columbia University Press, 2000. Includes a chapter in which O'Hara's short stories are analyzed.

Goldleaf, Steven. *John O'Hara: A Study of the Short Fiction.* New York: Twayne, 1999. This volume in the Twayne series is devoted to O'Hara's short stories. Includes bibliography and an index.

Grebstein, Sheldon Norman. *John O'Hara.* New Haven, Conn.: College and University Press, 1966. The first full-length study of O'Hara's narrative prose, prepared somewhat too soon to take in the full range of the author's later short fiction. Grebstein's volume discusses at length O'Hara's ongoing problems with the critical establishment; although Grebstein strives to achieve objectivity, it is clear that he tends to share the establishment's skeptical view of O'Hara's accomplishments. Grebstein does, however, provide incisive readings of the stories that were then available to him.

Mac Arthur, Pamela C. *The Genteel John O'Hara.* New York: Peter Lang, 2009. Focuses on O'Hara's re-creation of his hometown, Pottsville, Pennsylvania, and the nearby suburbs in his writing. Recounts the events of his life from birth until he left the "anthracite region" and moved to New York City in 1928. Considers O'Hara as an ethnographer, geographer, and social historian of Pottsville and its surrounding areas.

MacShane, Frank. Introduction to *Collected Stories of John O'Hara.* New York: Random House, 1984. MacShane has compiled a carefully prepared anthology of O'Hara's shorter fiction, preceded by a most perceptive introduction. No small part of Mac-Shane's accomplishment is the selection itself, covering the full length of O'Hara's career, yet subtly, and quite justifiably, weighted toward the stories written after 1960.

_____. *The Life of John O'Hara.* New York: E. P. Dutton, 1980. Looks at O'Hara's life through his work. A thorough study well worth reading for its valuable insights.

Quinn, Joseph L. "A Cold-Weather Journey with John O'Hara." *America* 169 (December 18-25, 1993): 17-21. Points out that throughout his career, O'Hara was preoccupied with the harsh winters and small-town atmosphere of Pottsville, Pennsylvania, the industrial coal-mining community where he was raised. Discusses O'Hara's links to F. Scott Fitzgerald and Ernest Hemingway.

Schwarz, Benjamin, and Christina Schwarz. "John O'Hara's Protectorate." *The Atlantic Monthly* 285, no. 3 (March, 2000): 108-112. A discussion of O'Hara's writing career, including information about the style and themes of his work and his depiction of his hometown, Pottsville, Pennsylvania, as the town of Gibbsville in his novels and stories. The authors maintain that O'Hara is one of the greatest social novelists of the twentieth century United States.

Wolff, Geoffrey. *The Art of Burning Bridges: A Life of John O'Hara.* New York: Knopf, 2003. A warts-and-all portrait of O'Hara. Wolff recounts the many incidents of O'Hara's bad behavior, including his alcoholism, bullying, and rages against women, editors, and critics. However, Wolff argues that these character flaws should not detract from O'Hara's literary reputation, citing the novel *Appointment in Samarra* as among his best work. Includes photographs, bibliography, and an index.

John Carr
Updated by David B. Parsell

TILLIE OLSEN

Born: Omaha, Nebraska; January 14, 1912
Died: Oakland, California; January 1, 2007
Also known as: Tillie Lerner

PRINCIPAL SHORT FICTION
Tell Me a Riddle, 1961
"Requa I," 1970

OTHER LITERARY FORMS

Besides her short stories and the novel *Yonnondio: From the Thirties* (1974), Tillie Olsen was the author of "A Biographical Interpretation"; the afterword published in Rebecca Davis's *Life in the Iron Mills* (1972; revised 1984), which Olsen edited; and *Silences* (1978), a collection of essays about women and writing. She edited two other books, *Mother to Daughter, Daughter to Mother: Mothers on Mothering--A Daybook and Reader* (1984), a collection of excerpts, and *Mothers and Daughters: That Special Quality--An Exploration in Photographs* (1987). In addition, she wrote uncollected magazine articles on women and writing and many uncollected poems, several of which appeared in *Partisan Review, Prairie Schooner, New World Writing, Ms., Harper's,* and *College English.*

ACHIEVEMENTS

Even though Tillie Olsen secured her literary reputation on the strength of one collection of short fiction, her voice as a humanist and feminist extended her influence beyond this small output. Olsen wrote about working-class people who, because of class, race, or sex, had been denied the opportunity to develop their talents. Frequently she focused on the obstacles women experienced; she understood them well. She herself was exactly such a victim of poverty during the 1930's, and then she worked and raised a family for more than twenty years until she could begin writing. Both her

fiction and her nonfiction deal with a key problem many women face: developing individual talents while combating socially imposed views.

Olsen was also known as a leading feminist educator. Her courses introduced students to forgotten writings, such as journals, to teach them about women's lives. The reading lists she developed have provided models for other women's studies courses throughout the United States. In addition to receiving the O. Henry Award for the best American short story of 1961 for "Tell Me a Riddle," Olsen won the Award for Distinguished Contribution to American Literature from the American Academy and the National Institute of Arts and Letters. Her other awards include a John Simon Guggenheim Memorial Foundation Fellowship in 1975-1976, an honorary doctorate from the University of Nebraska in 1979, a Ministry to Women Award from the Unitarian Women's Federation in 1980, a Bunting Institute Fellowship from Radcliffe College in 1985, and a Rea Award for the short story in 1994. Her short fiction appears in more than one hundred anthologies, including *The Best American Short Stories* for 1957, 1961, and 1971, and *Fifty Best American Stories, 1915-1965.*

BIOGRAPHY

Tillie Olsen, the daughter of Russian-Jewish immigrant parents, spent her youth in Nebraska and Wyoming. Her parents, Samuel and Ida (Beber) Lerner, were active union members, so political commitment, as well as economic pressures, accompanied her early years. Her father served as state secretary in the Socialist Party. In 1933, she moved to California, where, in 1936, she married printer Jack Olsen. Because she raised four daughters and worked at full-time clerical jobs, she did not publish her first book until she was in her late forties. She worked as a pork trimmer in meat-packing houses, a hotel maid, a jar-capper, and a waitress. Then, with the help of a Stanford University

Creative Writing Fellowship and a Ford Foundation grant in literature, she put together *Tell Me a Riddle*, the title story of which received the O. Henry Award for the best American short story of 1961. There followed a fellowship at the Radcliffe Institute for Independent Study, grants from the National Endowment for the Arts, and a Guggenheim Fellowship. A grant from the MacDowell Colony allowed her to complete *Yonnondio: From the Thirties*, a novel she began in the 1930's which was originally published in 1934 in the *Partisan Review*. After its revision and publication in 1974, Olsen continued writing essays and articles, as well as editing collections of women's writings. In addition, she taught at Amherst College, Stanford University, the Massachusetts Institute of Technology, and the University of Minnesota, among other colleges. In her nonfiction book *Silences*, Olsen inscribed the following dedication:

> For our silenced people, century after century, their beings consumed in the hard everyday essential work of maintaining human life. Their art, which still they made--anonymous; refused respect, recognition; lost.

She was twice arrested for her activism. Olsen died in Oakland, California, on January 1, 2007.

ANALYSIS

Tillie Olsen's *Tell Me a Riddle* contains four stories arranged chronologically in the order in which they were written: "I Stand Here Ironing," "Hey Sailor, What Ship?," "O Yes," and "Tell Me a Riddle." All but the first story contain, as major or minor characters, members of the same family, whose parents emigrated from Russia. The characters in the first story could also belong to the same family, although there is no evidence to prove it and the names of the children are different; nevertheless in "I Stand Here Ironing" the characters, situation, and tone are similar to those found in the other three stories. A difference between "I Stand Here Ironing" and the remaining stories in the volume is that the former story is told in the first person, being a kind of interior monologue (actually an imagined dialogue), whereas "Hey Sailor, What Ship?," "O Yes," and "Tell Me a Riddle" are told in varieties of the third person.

"I STAND HERE IRONING"

Exterior action in "I Stand Here Ironing" is practically nonexistent, consisting of a woman moving an iron across an ironing board. Interior action is much more complicated, being a montage of times, places, and movements involving a mother in interaction (or lack of interaction) with her firstborn, a daughter, Emily. Questions arise as to whether the montage can define or even begin to define the daughter; whether the mother or anyone else can help the daughter or whether such help is needed; whether the daughter will continue to be tormented like the mother, who identifies herself with the iron moving inexorably back and forth across the board; or whether, as the mother hopes, the daughter will be more than the dress on the ironing board, "helpless before the iron." "She will leave her seal," the mother says, the only words spoken aloud in the story; but the words could express only the mother's fervent hope for the well-being of a daughter born to a mother of nineteen, impoverished, alone, distracted, in an age of depression, war, and fear.

"HEY SAILOR, WHAT SHIP?"

"Hey Sailor, What Ship?" introduces Lennie and Helen and their children, Jeannie, Carol, and Allie. However, the story is not so much about them as it is about Whitey, the nickname of Michael Jackson, a sailor and friend of the family who seems more lost at sea than at home in any port or ship. Filtering through Whitey's consciousness, the story explores his frustrations and anger, pain and despair. At the same time, however, the living conditions of Lennie and Helen and their children and the relationships among the family and between various members of the family and Whitey are carefully delineated.

Whitey is a mariner, a perpetual wanderer whose only contact with family life is with Lennie, a boyhood friend. As the story opens, Whitey is drunk, a condition he finds himself in more and more, and with almost nothing left of his pay. His anguish, born of his desire to be with Lennie and the family and his reluctance to bear the pain of such a visit, is evident from the beginning, as are the shame and degradation he feels associated with his lifestyle. What had started out as a dream, a life of adventure on the sea, with comrades who shared the good and the bad, has become a parade of gin mills and cathouses, clip joints, hock shops, skid rows, and, lately, hospitals. Lennie's dreams, however, have also been frustrated. Lennie is a worn likeness of his former self; Helen is graying and tired from holding a job, as well as caring for house and home. The family lives in poverty in cramped quarters. Still, as Helen explains to her oldest daughter Jeannie, this house is the only place Whitey does not have to buy his way. The tragedy is that he feels he does. He comes bearing presents, distributing dollars and at the same time too drunk to share in meaningful interaction with the family he loves, where he is brother, lover, and father to a family not his own.

"O YES"

"O Yes" picks up the family several years later when Carol, the second daughter, is twelve and about to experience the pain of parting with a close friend, Parry, a black girl. Carol and her mother, Helen, have accompanied Parry and her mother, Alva, to a black church to witness Parry's baptism. Carol is uncomfortable, however, both with the surroundings and with Parry, who is growing away from her. As the services rise to a crescendo of passion, Carol asks her mother to take her home and then faints. Later Alva tries to explain to Carol that the religion is like a hope in the blood and bones and that the music offers a release to despair, but Carol will not listen.

Jeannie, Carol's older sister, tries to tell her mother that Carol and Parry are undergoing an inevitable "sorting out" process, a sorting out demanded by the culture--their environment, their peers, their teachers--a sorting out that "they" demand. The separation is hard on both girls. Nevertheless, Parry seems better equipped to handle the crisis, while Carol continues to suffer and question. Helen knows that Carol, too, has been baptized, immersed in the seas of humankind, and she suffers with her daughter. The irony is that white people have no means of catharsis through their religion; they are unable to cry "O Yes."

"TELL ME A RIDDLE"

The most haunting story in the collection *Tell Me a Riddle* is the title story. Longer than the other stories, this one focuses on Lennie's mother and father, while at the same time it brings to a culmination themes Olsen explores in the other stories: the frustration of

dreams unrealized; the despair of never having enough money; the anger and hostility of women who have had to cope with too much with too little and who have lost themselves in the process; the search for meaning and explanation; the continuing hope of the young in spite of the tensions around them; and the pain of mortality. If the story has a fault, it may be that it is too painful as it grasps readers and pulls them too close to raw feeling. "Tell me a riddle, granny," a grandchild demands. "I know no riddles, child," the grandmother answers; but she knows, and the reader knows, that the riddle is of existence itself. Why claw and scratch; why hold on? Aged and consumed by cancer, the grandmother's body will not let go.

Russian emigrants of Jewish extraction who have fled persecution to come to the American land of promise, the grandfather and grandmother have been married forty-seven years and have reared seven children, all of whom are married and have families of their own. Now the grandfather wants to sell the house and move to The Haven, a retirement community, where he will have freedom from responsibility, from fretting over money, and will be able to share in communal living, to fish or play cards or make jokes with convivial companions. The grandmother refuses, however, countering every argument her husband puts forth. She was the one who worked eighteen hours a day without sufficient money to keep the house together. Not once did he scrape a carrot or lift a dish towel or stay with the children. He is the one who needs companions; she lived a life of isolation. "You trained me well," she tells him. "I do not need others to enjoy." She is adamant: "Never again to be forced to move to the rhythms of others." The argument between them erupts continually, fanned by his desires and her anger and resentment.

Their children do not understand. How can people married forty-seven years and now at a time of life when they should be happy get themselves into a power struggle that threatens to pull them apart? Unknowingly the children take their father's side, considering their mother to be unreasonable or sick. They advise him to get her to a doctor. The doctor finds nothing seriously wrong and advises a diet and a change in lifestyle-- "start living like a human being." The grandmother continues to deteriorate; more and more she keeps to herself, stays in bed, and turns her face to the wall. One night she realizes that although the doctor said she was not sick, she feels sick, and she asks her husband to stay home with her. He refuses, once again bringing up the old argument, and as he leaves she sobs curses at him. When he returns he finds that she has left their bed and retired to a cot. They do not speak to each other for a week until one night he finds her outside in the rain singing a love song of fifty years ago. Her husband and her children bring her to a son-in-law who is a physician, and during surgery he finds cancer. The children advise their father to travel with her and visit all the children; and now begins an exodus of pain. The grandmother does not yet realize she is terminally ill, and the constant movement causes her utter despair, when all she wants is to be at home. From house to house they carry her and she refuses to participate, will not touch a baby grandchild, and retreats finally to sit in a closet when they believe she is napping. Once a granddaughter, herself upset, hauls her little body into the closet and finds her grandmother there-- "Is this where you hide, too, Grammy?"

Finally the grandfather brings her to a new apartment close to a seaside resort, dismal in the off-season and filled with the impoverished aged. The grandmother, ill in bed for several days, is tended by her granddaughter, Jeannie, daughter of Lennie and Helen, and now a visiting nurse. When she is better, the grandmother wants to go by the sea to sit in the sand. More and more now she loses control of her conscious self, sings snatches of songs, remembers pieces of quotations, tries in herself to find meaning while noticing that death, decay, and deterioration are all around her. Then she realizes that she, too, is dying and knows that she cannot tell her husband of her realization because a fiction is necessary to him, and she wants to go home.

One day Jeannie brings her a cookie in the shape of a real little girl who has died and tells her of a Spanish custom of partying at funerals, singing songs, and picnicking by the graves. From this interaction, Jeannie draws solace from what she takes to be a promise from her grandmother that at death she will go back to when she first heard music, to a wedding dance, where the flutes "joyous and vibrant tremble in the air." For the

others there is no comfort. "Too late to ask: and what did you learn with your living, Mother, and what do we need to know?"

OTHER MAJOR WORKS

LONG FICTION: *Yonnondio: From the Thirties*, 1974.
NONFICTION: "A Biographical Interpretation," 1972; *Silences*, 1978.
EDITED TEXTS: *Life in the Iron Mills*, 1972, revised 1984; *Mother to Daughter, Daughter to Mother: Mothers on Mothering---A Daybook and Reader*, 1984; *Mothers and Daughters: That Special Quality---An Exploration in Photographs*, 1987 (with others).

BIBLIOGRAPHY

Aiken, Susan Hardy, et al. *Dialogues/Dialogi: Literary and Cultural Exchanges Between (Ex)Soviet and American Women*. Durham, N.C.: Duke University Press, 1994. In this series of essays/dialogues, Susan Aiken's feminist reading of Olsen's "Tell Me a Riddle" focuses on home as a site of repression that relegates women to domestic work and child care. Argues that Olsen creates for her protagonist a free discursive space in which preestablished categories are redefined; by so doing, she contests the larger political forces of repression that divide people from themselves.

Bauer, Helen Pike. "'A Child of Anxious, Not Proud, Love': Mother and Daughter in Tillie Olsen's 'I Stand Here Ironing.'" In *Mother Puzzles: Daughters and Mothers in Contemporary American Literature*, edited by Mickey Pearlman. Westport, Conn.: Greenwood, 1989. Analyzes the story as a dialogue between a number of opposites in which the basic issues are how much of the past determines the daughter's future, how much of the mother is in the daughter, and how much responsibility the mother has for her daughter's passivity and repression.

Cardoni, Agnes Toloczko. *Women's Ethical Coming-of-Age: Adolescent Female Characters in the Prose Fiction of Tillie Olsen*. Lanham, Md.: University Press of America, 1998. A survey of Olsen's adolescent female characters, comparing and contrasting their milieux. Includes a bibliography and an index.

Coiner, Constance. *Better Red: The Writing and Resistance of Tillie Olsen and Meridel Le Sueur*. New York: Oxford University Press, 1995. Compares these two authors' activism and writing styles. Includes a bibliography and an index.

Faulkner, Mara. *Protest and Possibility in the Writing of Tillie Olsen*. Charlottesville: University Press of Virginia, 1993. Examines the themes of motherhood, relationships between men and women, community, and language in Olsen's fiction.

Frye, Joanne S. *Tillie Olsen: A Study of the Short Fiction*. New York: Twayne, 1995. One of the most extensive discussions of the four stories in *Tell Me a Riddle* and *"Requa."* Frye contends that Olsen's readings are embedded in history--both cultural and personal. The book also contains a long conversation Frye had with Olsen about her five short-fiction works.

Gelfant, Blanche H., ed. *The Columbia Companion to the Twentieth-Century American Short Story*. New York: Columbia University Press, 2000. Includes a chapter in which Olsen's short stories are analyzed.

Jacobs, Naomi. "Earth, Air, Fire, and Water in *Tell Me a Riddle*." *Studies in Short Fiction* 23 (Fall, 1986): 401-406. Jacobs analyzes the plot of Olsen's story by showing the development of a series of images derived from the four basic elements. She then relates this interpretation to Olsen's theme of spiritual rebirth.

Lisella, Julia. "I Stand Here Teaching: Tillie Olsen and Maternity in the Classroom." In *Mama Ph.D.: Women Write About Motherhood and Academic Life*, edited by Elrena Evans and Caroline Grant. New Brunswick, N.J.: Rutgers University Press, 2008. Focuses on Olsen's story "I Stand Here Ironing." Lisella analyzes the story, describing how her own life experience as a mother and a teacher altered her interpretations of its meaning.

Martin, Abigail. *Tillie Olsen*. Boise, Idaho: Boise State University, 1984. Martin sees Olsen as a writer in the Western tradition because, by advocating a change in how men and women are perceived, Olsen placed herself on a frontier in thinking. Martin interprets Olsen's work in terms of the obstacles she overcame to become a writer and compares her with

Virginia Woolf. Contains a select bibliography and a list of Olsen's poems.

Nelson, Kay Hoyle, and Nancy Huse, eds. *The Critical Response to Tillie Olsen*. Westport, Conn.: Greenwood Press, 1994. A collection of the most important articles, reviews, and excerpts of books about Olsen, arranged in chronological order; includes essays from a variety of approaches on the stories "I Stand Here Ironing," "Tell Me a Riddle," and "O Yes."

Niehus, Edward L., and Teresa Jackson. "Polar Stars, Pyramids, and *Tell Me a Riddle*." *American Notes and Queries* 24 (January/February, 1986): 77-83. Niehus and Jackson analyze one incident recalled by Eva, the dying woman, by relating it to a pole or center of life, an idea that derives from basic astronomy and late nineteenth century pyramidology. The authors explore how Olsen handles this theme when circumstances change so that the pole does not remain stable.

Olsen, Tillie. Interview by Lisa See. *Publishers Weekly* 226 (November 23, 1984): 76. Interviewed when she was almost seventy-two, Olsen focuses on her two haunting concerns, motherhood and writing, and how society continues to misunderstand these topics.

Pearlman, Mickey, and Abby H. P. Werlock. *Tillie Olsen*. Boston: Twayne, 1991. A general introduction to Olsen's life and work that tries to redress previous critical neglect and to suggest new directions for further study of her work. Includes an interview and extensive discussions of the four stories in Olsen's *Tell Me a Riddle*, especially "I Stand Here Ironing" and the title story.

Reid, Panthea. *Tillie Olsen: One Woman, Many Riddles*. New Brunswick, N.J.: Rutgers University Press, 2010. A "warts-and-all" biography of Olsen, whom Reid depicts as a narcissist who neglected her daughter and was unfaithful to her husband.

Robbins, Bruce. "Help: Tillie Olsen's 'I Stand Here Ironing' and Alan Sillitoe's 'The Loneliness of the Long-Distance Runner.'" In *Upward Mobility and the Common Good: Toward a Literary History of the Welfare State*. Princeton, N.J.: Princeton University Press, 2007. Robbins's study of upward-mobility stories includes a comparison of Olsen's story with one by Sillitoe.

Weber, Myles. "Tillie Olsen and the Question of Silenced Literature." In *Consuming Silences: How We Read Authors Who Don't Publish*. Athens: University of Georgia Press, 2005. Examines why Olsen and other authors deliberately choose to stop writing. Compares Olsen to the grandmother in

"Tell Me a Riddle" who refuses to go to a retirement home, arguing that since this story's publication, "Olsen has constructed for herself a career as an author similarly characterized by nonparticipation and a stubborn refusal to enter into the processes of writing and publishing."

Mary Rohrberger
Updated by Louise M. Stone and Nika Hoffman

JULIE ORRINGER

Born: Miami, Florida; June 12, 1973

PRINCIPAL SHORT FICTION
How to Breathe Underwater, 2003

OTHER LITERARY FORMS

In 2010, Julie Orringer (oh-ihn-gur) published *The Invisible Bridge*, an historical novel set primarily in Budapest and Paris that, against the events that culminated in World War II, details the lives and fortunes of three Hungarian Jews, the Lévi brothers: Andras, Tibor, and Matyas. Seeking opportunities unavailable in Hungary, Andras goes to Paris to study at the École Spéciale d'Architecture; he has an affair with Klara, a Hungarian ballet instructor nearly a decade his senior. The advent of the Nazis and changes in political and social events force Andras to return to Hungary. Klara accompanies him.

ACHIEVEMENTS

Before publication, two of the stories in *How to Breathe Underwater* were honored with Pushcart Prizes: "When She Is Old and I Am Famous" (1998) and "Pilgrims" (2001). In manuscript, the collection won the 2001 Joseph Henry Jackson Award, offered annually to promising young California writers. Following publication, *How to Breathe Underwater* received the northern California Book Award and was a San Francisco *Chronicle* and a *Los Angeles Times* Book of the Year for 2003 and a *New York Times*

Notable Book for 2003. The stories have been widely translated and have been dramatized and filmed.

BIOGRAPHY

Julie Orringer was born in Miami, Florida, the first of three children of medical students Carl and Agnes Orringer. In trying to establish their practices, the Orringers moved frequently, but between the ages of five and twelve, Julie Orringer lived in New Orleans, a city that she has described as an atypical southern city, adding that her family also was atypical because they were Jewish. In 1994, when Orringer was twenty, her mother died after a ten-year battle with breast cancer; the shared tragedy brought Orringer close to her younger brother and sister.

Orringer graduated from Cornell University, majoring first in child development, then in English; following graduation in 1994, she entered the M.F.A. program at the University of Iowa, holding a two-year Creative Writing Teaching Fellowship before her 1996 graduation. She moved to San Francisco, and from 1999 to 2003 was at Stanford University, first as a Stegner Fellow, then as the Marsh McCall Lecturer in Fiction. Following the publication of *How to Breathe Underwater*, she received a grant from the National Endowment for the Arts and has since received fellowships from the MacDowell Colony and from the Corporation of Yaddo; she also has been a Distinguished Visiting Writer at St. Mary's College of California and was a Visiting Professor of Creative Writing at the University of Michigan. From 2008 to 2009, she was a Rona Jaffe Foundation Fellow at the New York Public

Library, and she has since lectured at the creative writing program in Columbia University's School of the Arts. She is married to writer Ryan Harty.

ANALYSIS

None of Julie Orringer's ten published short stories were collected in *How to Breathe Underwater*. Their settings are places in which Orringer lived and has had personal experiences: New Orleans, the Midwest, and California predominate, though "When She Is Old and I Am Famous" takes place in Italy, and "What We Save" takes place in Florida's Disney World. These settings are introduced matter-of-factly and not described in any detail. Almost always, however, they are regions in which Orringer's protagonists have few connections, being either tourists or transplants to the area; they know few of the residents and fewer of the local customs. This is particularly the situation in "What We Save," "When She Is Old and I Am Famous," "Pilgrims," and "Stations of the Cross." The first two feature characters who are tourists; the latter two have as protagonists northern girls experiencing and being mystified by life in Louisiana.

In addition to the alienation caused by a protagonist experiencing and reacting to unfamiliar settings, there is frequently a compounding alienation. Sometimes this is a physical alienation: Mira, the adolescent narrator of "When She Is Old and I Am Famous," is fat, uncomfortable in her body, a discomfort that she gradually outgrows but that in the events she is recounting lead to her injuring her ankle and spending the rest of a summer vacation on crutches. At times, though, Orringer's characters experience a mental alienation, occasionally one having its roots in religious differences. The girls in "The Smoothest Way Is Full of Stones" are both Jewish, but one is a reformed Jew, while the other is Orthodox Hasidic. The northern Jewish narrator in "Stations of the Cross" recalls being nine years old and her friendship with a southern conservative Catholic who is preparing for her First Communion.

The casual and often horrible cruelties visited by children and young adults upon one another, and the ways in which the recipients of these cruelties withstand them and make moral choices are Orringer's recurrent themes and dominate the stories in *How to Breathe Underwater*. In "Pilgrims," the children encountered by young Ben and Ella are playing a twisted game in a treehouse, which involves pretending the treehouse is jail, and "in jail you get tied up" and "killed." Maddy, the fourteen-year-old protagonist of "The Isabel Fish," is verbally abused by her older brother Sage; following an automobile accident, in which Sage's girlfriend Isabel dies, the abuse escalates, accompanied by the destruction of property. Similar abuse is heaped on the recipient of the "Note to the Sixth-Grade Self": She is being bullied and abused by her classmates, and while the "Note" attempts to offer her younger self a modicum of mature comfort, it can do nothing to offset the unpleasantness that the sixth-grade narrator is experiencing.

Not all of Orringer's children are victims or accept their fates passively: Helena, the fourteen-year-old protagonist of "What We Save," actively defends herself when a sixteen-year-old attempts to fondle her as she is trapped on an amusement park ride. In "Stars of Motown Shining Bright," an even more active defense is mounted by fifteen-year-old Lucy, who has lost her virginity to young Jack Jacob, unaware that he is using her and is really interested in her naïve friend Melissa. When Jack attempts to force himself on the fully cognizant Lucy, she repels him with his gun, forces him naked into a closet, and takes the misguided Melissa home.

The cruelties demonstrated by Carney of "Stations of the Cross" are all the more horrible because her selfish actions reflect the bigotries of adults: She objects to the impending presence of her cousin Dale at her First Communion because he is a "love child . . . . He's an actual dictionary-definition bastard. And half black." In "Ask for Pain," Orringer's sole uncollected story, the young narrator has the opportunity to hurt Della, the girl who is about to become her stepsister, because Della does not know that the narrator is intimate with Javi, the young man Della loves. However, the narrator's maliciousness backfires, and the story concludes with her realizing "how small and empty" she has become.

Adults do not generally appear in the stories in *How to Breathe Underwater*. When they are glimpsed, it is through the eyes of their often uncomprehending children; readers can see that the adults are rarely happily married and are often ailing, divorced, or widowed. The children in "Pilgrims" do not recognize that their cancer-stricken mother is going to a New Age therapy session; they see only oddly behaving strangers for whom they have had to forgo their familiar Thanksgiving Day traditions. The parents in "The Isabel Fish" are well meaning but inept, persuading their daughter to take scuba lessons after she nearly drowns with her brother's girlfriend. Those in "The Smoothest Way of Stones" are either distant or clueless: Rebecca's mother is never seen; she remains in the city, recuperating from a miscarriage, while Esty's parents are concerned about the minutia of their religion and do not recognize their daughter's emergent sexuality. In "What We Save," Helena's mother has cancer and visits with a former love, a family friend, though Helena does not recognize the significance of her mother's behavior or the final gift she gives the man.

"Care" is thus far exceptional in Orringer's oeuvre. The protagonist Tessa is an adult, a young San Franciscan pill addict who is briefly responsible for the care of her six-year-old niece Olivia. In a few hours, Tessa manipulates Olivia into shoplifting, neglects her, and loses her on Pier Thirty-Nine before reclaiming her at a police station. The irresponsible Tessa is, however, convinced that Olivia would be happier with Tessa than with Olivia's mother: "she wouldn't be worried about everything she ate and everything she might step on and this rule and that rule. She'd be a girl, a little girl, not a tiny cramped adult."

"PILGRIMS"

In New Orleans, although they would prefer to be elsewhere for their Thanksgiving dinner, young Ella and her little brother Benjamin must accompany their father and their cancer-stricken mother to a stranger's house. As the adults congregate and mingle, Ella and Benjamin join the other children, who, led by the slightly older Peter, are playing a creepy game in which they are imprisoned in a treehouse and "die" by jumping from the treehouse onto a trampoline. Ella loses one of her baby teeth after jumping. One of the girls, Clarie, is obsessed with a glass of red water, believing it is her mother, and Peter steals the water and climbs into the treehouse. Clarie follows but plunges to her death. Peter conceals the body and threatens the

surviving children. Ella finds her tooth, leaves it in Clarie's dead hand, and she and Benjamin leave with their parents.

"THE SMOOTHEST WAY IS FULL OF STONES"

While her mother recuperates from a miscarriage in New York City, young Rebecca--a reformed and liberal Jew--spends the summer in the country with her Orthodox aunt and uncle and her slightly older cousin Erica, who name has been changed to Esther. While wading in a pond, they see teenage Dovid Frankel conceal a book prior to entering the house for Shabbos: It is *Essence of Persimmon: Eastern Sexual Secrets for Western Lives*. Esther takes it and, rather than destroy it or report Dovid, becomes obsessed with it, an obsession Rebecca cannot understand. The dinner conversation concerns the importance of having the household mezuzah checked and the nature of personal responsibility to Hashem, and Dovid and Rebecca briefly bond. Afterward, Esther sends Dovid a note offering the book back to him. After accompanying Esther as she gives herself to Dovid, Rebecca takes the book and walks into the pond, dropping the book into the deep water.

"WHEN SHE IS OLD AND I AM FAMOUS"

In Florence, Italy, twenty-year-old Mira is a talented artist but is fat and jealous of her beautiful sixteen-year-old cousin Aïda, who is five feet eleven inches tall, weighs 113 pounds, and is the recipient of much male attention. When Aïda arrives from Paris, she rooms with Mira and finds her condoms; this leads to a disagreement in which Mira's jealousy causes her to throw a candlestick at Aïda before telling her to move out. In the company of Drew and Joseph, two men from Mira's drawing class, the four explore a vineyard. When they see a house, Aïda pretends it is the house of her divorced mother and leads Joseph inside, leaving Mira and Drew out in the vines. As they watch, a police car arrives and Aïda and Joseph are led outside. Mira and Drew go down, Mira injuring her ankle on the way. Explanations are proffered--that Aïda is a recognizable model soothes the outraged homeowner--and Mira is treated. Later she and Aïda share life histories and tentatively bond, and Mira sells a picture and achieves some self-confidence.

"ISABEL FISH"

"Narrated by fourteen-year-old Maddy, the story begins with Maddy being unable to function in a scuba training class. As the story develops, the reader discovers that Maddy is the survivor of an automobile accident in which her sixteen-year-old brother Sage's girlfriend Isabel drowned. The accident was precipitated by Isabel taking Maddy from a pool party, at which Sage was deliberately insulting Maddy. Following the accident, Maddy's parents--who know nothing of Sage's behavior or that the teens were partying in a hot tub that was not their own--intend to take their children to St. Maarten and want Maddy and Sage to learn to scuba dive. Sage's abuse of Maddy escalates; he holds her responsible for Isabel's death and kills a number of the fish Maddy has been raising as a science project. Maddy and Sage eventually achieve a rapprochement, and Maddy successfully learns to breathe underwater.

"STATIONS OF THE CROSS"

A clipping detailing the death of Dale Fortunot in a Palestinian bombing reaches Lila, who recollects her encounter with him in Iberville Parish, Louisiana. She was nine years old and from the North, a Jewish girl in an area of Catholics. She is nevertheless friendly with Carney, who is about to have her First Communion and take the name Veronica. An estranged cousin, Marian, has been invited and has surprised everybody by accepting; she has had a love child by a black man, Dale

Carney is unhappy about this, and her comments reveal that Marian has been the subject of disapproving and bigoted conversation among the adults. When he does arrive at the ceremony, Dale is well dressed, intelligent, and articulate. Carney persuades them to play Stations of the Cross, with Dale as Jesus carrying a cross made of two-by-fours. On Carney's request, Lila ties Dale to the cross, but Carney insists that Jesus dies on the cross and begins hitting Dale much too hard, not stopping.

OTHER MAJOR WORKS

LONG FICTION: *The Invisible Bridge*, 2010.

BIBLIOGRAPHY

Benson, Heidi. "Surfacing: Julie Orringer Emerges with a Dark and Beautiful Book." A review of *How to Breathe Underwater* includes analysis of how events in Orringer's life relates to her stories.

Dierbeck, Lisa. "Survival of the Meanest." *The New York Times Book Review*, October 19, 2003, p. 18. A lengthy and perceptive review of *How to Breathe Underwater*.

Orringer, Julie. "Julie Orringer Talks with Tobias Wolff." In *The Believer Book of Writers Talking to Writers*, edited by Vendela Vida. San Francisco: Believer, 2005. Orringer discusses her work with an insightful fellow writer.

Richard Bleiler

JUDITH ORTIZ COFER

Born: Hormigueros, Puerto Rico; February 24, 1952

PRINCIPAL SHORT FICTION

The Latin Deli: Prose and Poetry, 1993

An Island Like You: Stories of the Barrio, 1995

*The Year of Our Revolution: New and Selected
    Stories and Poems,* 1998

OTHER LITERARY FORMS

Judith Ortiz Cofer (ohr-TEES KOH-fur) is recognized as an eclectic contributor to literature, creating not only short stories but also nonfiction (*Silent Dancing: A Partial Remembrance of a Puerto Rican Childhood,* 1990; *Woman in Front of the Sun: On Becoming a Writer,* 2000), poetry (*Reaching for the Mainland, and Selected New Poems,* 1995; *A Love Story Beginning in Spanish,* 2005), novels (*The Line of the Sun,* 1989; *The Meaning of Consuelo,* 2003; *Call Me María,* 2004), and a three-act play (*Latin Women Pray,* which was first performed at Georgia State University in the summer of 1984). Much of Ortiz Cofer's oeuvre is distinguished by her exploration of cultural and racial duality, rites of passage and maturity, and the influence of heritage, often presented through a mixture of genres--fiction, poetry, essays--within one work.

ACHIEVEMENTS

With the publication of *The Line of the Sun* and a nomination for a Pulitzer Prize, Judith Ortiz Cofer solidified her reputation as a distinctive voice of literature and Latina culture. Other accolades include the Pushcart Prize for nonfiction, the O. Henry Prize for short story, and the Anisfield-Wolf Award in Race Relations for *The Latin Deli.* She was named a Scholar of the English Speaking Union at Oxford University (1977) and the John Atherton Scholar of Poetry (1982). She was awarded a position on the administrative staff of the prestigious Bread Loaf Writers' Conference in 1983 and 1984, where she previously had been honored as a scholar in 1981. Ortiz Cofer has received numerous grants and fellowships for her work, including a grant from the Witter Bynner Foundation for Poetry for *Letters from a Caribbean Island* (1989) and the National Endowment for the Arts fellowship in poetry in 1989.

BIOGRAPHY

Judith Ortiz Cofer was born Judith Ortiz on February 24, 1952, in Hormigueros, Puerto Rico, where she remained a short time before immigrating to Paterson, New Jersey, when her father enlisted in the U.S. Navy in 1956. Despite calling the United States their new home, Ortiz Cofer and her family visited Puerto Rico often. Consequently, she often felt divided between two worlds. Ortiz Cofer spent her formative years attempting to balance her family's traditions with Western modernization. She considered herself an amalgamation of two cultures, and this duality would prove to be a significant influence on her work.

In 1974, Ortiz Cofer received her B.A. from Augusta College, followed by an M.A. from Florida Atlantic University three years later. She then pursued graduate studies at Oxford University. She worked as a teacher in various institutions in Florida and Georgia, before accepting a position in the English and creative-writing program at the University of Georgia in 1992.

Ortiz Cofer began to write poetry while she was a graduate student, and she published several full-length poetry collections, including *Terms of Survival* (1987), which featured highly autobiographical poems reflecting experiences of Latina women. She then decided not to limit her imagination to one genre and began to explore short fiction, novels, and autobiographical essays. In 1989, her novel *The Line of the Sun* was published to critical acclaim for its command of language and depiction of life in the barrios of Puerto Rico. It was nominated for the Pulitzer Prize in 1989. Her essay collection *Silent Dancing: A Partial Remembrance of a Puerto Rican Childhood* appeared in 1990 and presented vignettes of her parents' generation and her own, as they maneuvered their identities between American and Latin culture. This theme, also echoed in her previous poetry endeavors, would again surface in her short-story and poetry collection *The Latin Deli*, the young-adult fiction *An Island Like You: Stories of the Barrio*, and *The Year of Our Revolution: New and Selected Stories and Poems* (1998).

Her work has continued to be recognized, studied, and lauded in the twenty-first century, including her nonfiction *Woman in Front of the Sun: On Becoming a Writer*, the novels *The Meaning of Consuelo* and *Call Me María*, and her poetry collection *A Love Story Beginning in Spanish*. She also has continued to be an advocate for the consistent inclusion of Latina writers in the Western literary canon.

Analysis

Judith Ortiz Cofer is noted for her contributions to several genres--poetry, fiction, drama, essay, and autobiography--and her unique fusion of poetry and short fiction to enrich and to unify a narrative. Her work is distinguished by her examination of cultural diaspora, drawn from her experiences living in Puerto Rico and New Jersey. Through expertly drawn protagonists, based on her relatives, neighbors, and friends, Ortiz Cofer confronts issues of cultural identity with intellectual curiosity, compassion, and humor. Inspiration for her literature include her travels between Puerto Rico and New Jersey, contrasts in culture and language, generational differences (traditional values versus Western modernization), and the influence of her family's oral tradition. Although her work is largely autobiographical in nature and features the concerns of Latina women, her themes address universal issues of identity, rites of passage, family, love, and survival.

The Latin Deli

Judith Ortiz Cofer's award-winning collection of short fiction, essays, and poetry solidified her reputation as a dynamic, genuine voice of Latina literature. *The Latin Deli* centers on the experiences of Puerto Rican protagonists as they attempt to reconcile their newly defined identities in a New Jersey barrio with their past lives on their native island.

Many of the *The Latin Deli*'s stories focus on Puerto Rican young women as they come of age in the barrio, confronting the complexity of awakening sexuality while the traditional values of parents compete with a Western influence. In "Twist and Shout," the narrator is swept up in the Beatle mania of the late 1960's, which she describes as overpowering the salsa music of her parents. While her mother goes to the local bodega, the narrator leaves kidney beans cooking on the stove (to create a traditional Puerto Rican dish) to visit her teenage neighbors down the hall, who are singing and dancing to the Beatles. As she watches them gyrate against one another, a sense of excitement comes over her. When Manny starts to dance provocatively with her, his lips on her face, her excitement is tinged with fear and thoughts of her mother's disapproval. She extricates herself from Manny's arms and, heart pounding, returns to tend to the cooking of her mother's beans.

In "American History" and "The Story of My Body," the complications and stereotypes arising from bicultural relationships are examined. In "American History," the protagonist develops a crush on a Caucasian boy from the South named Eugene. Her mother tells her that to date him would only lead to heartache and degradation; in turn, Eugene's mother, believing the girl to be promiscuous because of her Puerto Rican ethnicity, sternly warns the girl to stay away from her son. In "The Story of My Body," another Puerto Rican girl is drawn to a non-Latino boy and is met with her mother's warning that she is headed for only disappointment and disillusionment. Her mother's predictions prove to be correct when the boy's father forbids him to see the girl because she is Puerto Rican and does not have fair skin.

Darker themes are evoked with a sense of nostalgia and regret in the story "Nada" when a grandmother mourns the loss of her son in the Vietnam War. Refusing all recognition from the U.S. government--medals, the U.S. flag--for her son, the inconsolable grandmother continually repeats "nada" and is disillusioned by a government offering meaningless objects as consolation for such a loss. She longs for her past life with her family in Puerto Rico, when her son was far away from the clutches of war.

AN ISLAND LIKE YOU: STORIES OF THE BARRIO

Targeting a young-adult audience, *An Island Like You: Stories of the Barrio* focuses on the awkward and often emotional transition from child to adult. Although Ortiz Cofer again uses the experiences of Puerto Rican youth living in New Jersey, this community of protagonists has universal appeal. The fictionalized barrio is representative of any neighborhood in any part of the world. As in previous collections, she explores the challenges inherent in cultural duality, as her characters attempt to forge an identity influenced by both heritage and Westernization. Often, Ortiz Cofer weaves her native Spanish into the narratives, accentuating the cultural clashes that often emerge.

In several stories, the influence of parents, grandparents, and other figures of authority factor prominently in the young protagonists' maturity and self-actualization. Although Rita, in "Bad Influence," is furious with her parents for sending her to Puerto Rico to spend time with her grandparents (to divert her growing attention to boys), she soon learns to value her grandparents' way of life and the wisdom behind her parents' decision. In "The Flea," Arturo seeks solace in a church after being taunted by his classmates for his admiration of poetry and the works of William Shakespeare. A church custodian comforts Arturo and helps him regain his confidence. He returns home, which he views as a refuge, and begins to study a sonnet his teacher had recommended.

Young protagonists learn that the adults in their lives are fallible and also deserve validation and consolation from their children. In "Abuela Invents the Zero," Constancia comes to terms with her own shortcomings after she berates her grandmother for losing her way to her seat while at church. In "Don Jose of La Mancha," although Yolanda struggles with her mother's newfound interest in another man, Yolanda discovers how to honor her deceased father's memory while still recognizing her mother's need for love and security. The young people also benefit from the richness of their parents' past, which is passed down to them through oral tradition. For example, in "The One Who Watches," Doris severs a relationship with a

friend who has proven to be a negative influence and instead reconnects with her mother, who sings in a neighborhood nightclub. Once Doris is away from her troubled friend, she recognizes the lessons--how to survive, how to be strong in the face of adversity--hidden within the stories her mother sings for her.

THE YEAR OF OUR REVOLUTION: NEW AND SELECTED STORIES AND POEMS

In *The Year of Our Revolution*, teenager Mary Ellen, drawn to the excitement of 1960's America--its music, fashion, and political debates--rebels against her parents' conservative ideals and reliance on a past life in Puerto Rico. The generational conflict and cultural duality are emphasized by her friends calling her Mary Ellen, while her parents refer to her only as María Elenita. Various short stories trace the growth of Mary Ellen as she brazenly defies her parents, experiences love and grief, and finally develops a renewed appreciation for history through the oral tradition of her parents.

In "Gravity," Mary Ellen's rebellion is symbolized by her long, unruly hair, bell-bottom jeans, tie-dyed shirts, and Indian accessories. Her bedroom remains a guarded sanctuary of books on Eastern philosophy and American music. Mary Ellen's Bob Dylan and the Beatles compete with her mother's island salsa and Tito Puente. Mary Ellen views herself as two people: by day, a good Catholic schoolgirl in uniform; after school, whomever she chooses to be. She challenges her parents by refusing to go with them to the annual New Year's Eve neighborhood party and is surprised (and almost disappointed) when her mother relents and allows her to stay home. Humbled by her mother's resignation, Mary Ellen decides to join her parents at the party. While watching them hold each other and dance, she feels the first stirrings of love, of wanting to be intimately connected with another person.

In "Making Love in Spanish, Circa 1969," Mary Ellen discovers passion, empathy, and disappointment in her first sexual experience with Pito, a wounded, unstable Vietnam soldier. Although frightened by Pito's erratic behavior, she finds herself strangely drawn to his musings on death and war and to his seductive overtures. However, when they attempt to make love, Pito is unable to because of his war injuries. Mary Ellen experiences tenderness and empathy for Pito; however, she feels robbed of an experience that, in her young mind, should be one of perfection. Her fairy-tale dreams of romance have been altered harshly by reality.

Mary Ellen's views are again drastically altered as she experiences the death of her father. In "The One Peso Prediction," she privately grieves, yet stays outwardly strong for her mother, representing her growing maturity. Although the story is framed by the death and funeral of her father, its main focus is on her mother relating stories from her past to Mary Ellen as they have tea in the kitchen. Through this oral tradition, mother and daughter finally bond. Mary Ellen learns of the intensity of her parents' love, which was forbidden by her grandparents. She empathizes with the dreams and disappointments experienced by her parents. She learns about the radical lifestyle of her grandmother as a young, revolutionary woman, who Mary Ellen presently sees in herself.

OTHER MAJOR WORKS

LONG FICTION: *The Line of the Sun*, 1989; *The Meaning of Consuelo*, 2003; *Call Me María*, 2004.

PLAY: *Latin Women Pray*, pr. 1984.

POETRY: *Peregrina*, 1986; *Terms of Survival*, 1987; *Reaching for the Mainland, and Selected New Poems*, 1995; *A Love Story Beginning in Spanish*, 2005.

NONFICTION: *Silent Dancing: A Partial Remembrance of a Puerto Rican Childhood*, 1990; *Woman in Front of the Sun: On Becoming a Writer*, 2000; *Lessons from a Writer's Life: Readings and Resources for Teachers and Students*, 2011.

EDITED TEXTS: *Letters from a Caribbean Island*, 1989; *Sleeping with One Eye Open: Women Writers and the Art of Survival*, 1999 (with Marilyn Kallet); *Riding Low on the Streets of Gold*, 2003.

BIBLIOGRAPHY

Acosta-Belen, Edna. "A *MELUS* Interview: Judith Ortiz Cofer." *MELUS* 18, no. 3 (September, 1993): 83. Ortiz Cofer relates how oral tradition influences her work and discusses her advocacy for minority writers to be recognized more fully as part of the literary canon.

Bost, Suzanne. "Transgressing Borders: Puerto Rican and Latina Mestizaje." *MELUS* 25, no. 2 (2000): 187. Analyzes the use of a chameleon as a metaphor in Ortiz Cofer's work and how it relates to cultural duality. Defines "mestiazje," which explains this synergistic philosophy of identity.

Fernandez, Roberta, ed. *In Other Words: Literature by Latinas of the United States*. Houston, Texas: Arte Publico Press, 1994. Representative collection of fiction, poetry, essays, and drama of contemporary Latina writers of the United States.

Montilla, Patricia M. "Gathering Voices: Storytelling and Collective Identity in Judith Ortiz Cofer's *Silent Dancing: A Partial Remembrance of a Puerto Rican Childhood*." *Bilingual Review* 27, no. 3 (2003): 205. Discusses the influence of Ortiz Cofer's childhood recollections of Puerto Rico and New Jersey on her development as a woman and writer.

O'Shea, Michael J. "*The Latin Deli*: Prose and Poetry." *Studies in Short Fiction* 31, no. 3 (June, 1994): 502. Presents a review of *The Latin Deli*, focusing on the eclectic nature of fiction, poetry, and essays, and comments on the universal themes evoked through the experiences of Puerto Rican protagonists.

Quintana, Alvina. *Reading U.S. Latina Writers: Remapping American Literature*. New York: Palgrave Macmillan, 2003. Argues for a shift in how the "American" writer is viewed and examines the duality of Latin and American culture experienced by Latina authors living and writing in the United States.

Vasilakis, Nancy. "*An Island Like You: Stories of the Barrio*." *The Horn Book Magazine* 71, no. 4 (1995): 464. Review of Ortiz Cofer's short fiction highlighting the author's unique characterization of Puerto Rican youth and universal themes of coming-of-age teenagers.

Michele Hardy

CYNTHIA OZICK

Born: New York, New York; April 17, 1928

PRINCIPAL SHORT FICTION

The Pagan Rabbi, and Other Stories, 1971
Bloodshed and Three Novellas, 1976
Levitation: Five Fictions, 1982
The Shawl, 1989
The Puttermesser Papers, 1997
Dictation: A Quartet, 2008

OTHER LITERARY FORMS

Cynthia Ozick (SIHN-thee-ah OH-zihk) is the author of poems, articles, reviews, essays, and short stories. She has also published several novels, including *Trust* (1966), *The Cannibal Galaxy* (1983), and *The Messiah of Stockholm* (1987). Her poems have appeared in journals such as *Epoch, Commentary, The Literary Review*, and *Judaism*. Her other short works have been published frequently in a wide variety of journals, including those mentioned. Her novel *Heir to the Glimmering World* was published in 2004. Her collection of essays *The Din in the Head* came out in 2006.

ACHIEVEMENTS

Often characterized as difficult and involved in syntax and ideas, Cynthia Ozick's works have, nevertheless, received many awards. Her short fiction especially has been judged prizeworthy, winning for her such prestigious honors as the Best American Short Stories Award (several times), the National Book Award, the American Academy of Arts and Letters Award for Fiction, the O. Henry Award, the PEN/Faulkner Award, and the Jewish Book Council Award. Immediately subsequent to the publication of "Rosa," one of her prize-winning stories, Ozick was invited to deliver the Phi Beta Kappa oration at Harvard University, and she became the first person to receive the

Michael Rea Award for career contribution to the short story. She has received a number of honorary degrees from schools such as Adelphi University, Williams College, Brandeis University, and Skidmore College as well as Yeshiva University, Hebrew Union College, and the Jewish Theological Seminary.

BIOGRAPHY

Born of Russian immigrants who took up residence in the Bronx borough in New York, Cynthia Ozick and her parents and siblings worked in the family drugstore, which kept them in comfort and relative prosperity even through the years of the Great Depression. As a female, Ozick was not considered for extensive education by her family and community. Nevertheless, she was enrolled at the age of five and a half in a Yiddish-Hebrew school, so she could take religious instruction, and her family insisted that she be allowed to stay. The rabbi giving the instruction soon found that she had what he called a "golden head." Successful as she was in religious instruction, however, her public school experiences were difficult and humiliating. It was not until her entrance into Hunter College High School in Manhattan that she was once again made to feel part of an intellectual elite. Her years at New York University, where she earned a B.A. in 1949, were followed by attendance at Ohio State University, where she received her M.A. in 1951.

In 1952, she married Bernard Hallote. A daughter, Rachel, was born in 1965. Early in her career, Ozick became interested in the Jewish textual tradition, and over the years she became an expert in it. In fiction and nonfiction, she has argued with passion concerning the vital role Judaism has played in Western culture, and she has become for many a spokesperson for the importance of art and artists in the Jewish tradition and for the role of women in Jewish culture.

ANALYSIS

Cynthia Ozick's thesis for her M.A. degree was titled "Parable in the Later Novels of Henry James," an exercise that she later thought of as a first step in an act of devotion that resulted in her belief in the exclusivity of art. In effect, as a result of studying James, she became, she believed, a worshiper at the altar of art, a devotee of the doctrine of art for art's sake. This idea--one that many believe places art before life, form before content, beauty before truth, aesthetic enjoyment before moral behavior--became the belief system that led Ozick to conclude that to worship art is to worship idols, in effect, to break the Mosaic law. This kind of understanding led Ozick to study the Jewish textual tradition and the role of Judaism in Western culture.

In the 1980's, Ozick began to realize that creative writers needed to use the highest powers of imagination to posit an incorporeal god, as exists in the Jewish faith, and to put forth a vision of moral truth rooted in the history, traditions, and literature of the Jewish people. Ozick's success in this endeavor is manifested not only in her identification as a Jewish American author but also in the number of awards she has received from representatives of the Jewish people. Perhaps most important, however, is her own satisfaction that in her writing she is serving and has continued to serve the cause of moral truth according to Mosaic law.

A highly serious approach to art as embodying moral imperatives, however, is not necessarily one that eschews metafictional techniques, repetitions, reworkings, and story sequences. Happily, in her use of self-referential devices and other dazzling postmodern presentations of the fantastic, the irreverent, and the grotesque, Ozick's techniques are relevant to the traditions and teachings of Judaism, where magic, dreams, and fantastic occurrences are ways to embody and convey truth.

"THE PAGAN RABBI"

"The Pagan Rabbi" is a case in point. It is the story of Isaac Kornfeld, a pious and intelligent man who one day hangs himself from the limb of a tree. Isaac's story is told by a friend who has known Isaac since they were classmates in the rabbinical seminary and who is a parallel character to Isaac. In the same way that the narrator and Isaac are counterparts, the fathers of both men are set up as opposites who agree on one thing only-- that philosophy is an abomination that must lead to idolatry (the worship of false gods). Though the fathers are rivals, the sons accept the apparent differences in their own personalities and remain friends. In time, their different ambitions and talents separate them. The narrator leaves the seminary, marries a Gentile, and becomes a furrier; Isaac continues his brilliant career in the seminary and achieves the peak of his renown at the time of his death, when he has almost reached the age of thirty-six. The narrator, now a bookseller separated from his wife, learns that Isaac has hanged himself with his prayer shawl from a tree in a distant park. Immediately, the narrator takes a subway to the site of the suicide; Isaac's behavior seems totally alien to his character and personality.

In the remainder of the story, Ozick attempts to explain the odd circumstances of Isaac's death, and, by means of the parallelisms, inversions, and doublings, points to the ramifications of leaving the intellectual path for the mysteries and seductions of the unknown world of fantasy, magic, and dream. Apparently Isaac,

Cynthia Ozick (AP Photo/Kathy Willens)

shortly after his marriage, began to seek different kinds of pleasure that may have been associated with the marriage bed and the beautiful Scheindel. In line with marriage customs, Scheindel covers her lustrous black hair after the wedding ceremony and subsequently bears Isaac seven daughters, one after another. As he fathers each daughter, Isaac invents bedtime stories for each, relating to such aberrations as speaking clouds, stones that cry, and pigs with souls. At the same time, Isaac shows an inordinate interest in picnics in strange and remote places.

As Isaac behaves in odder and odder ways for a rabbi, exhibiting unhealthy (because excessive) interest in the natural world, Scheindel becomes more puzzled and estranged, since she has no interest in old tales of sprites, nymphs, gods, or magic events. Scheindel's refusal to countenance anything magical is in counterpoint to her escape from the electrified fences of the concentration camp, which seemed a miracle of chance. Isaac's notebook offers little explanation for his behavior, though it is filled with romantic jottings, quotations from lyric poets, and a strange reference to his age, using the means of counting rings as for a tree. Below this unusual computation, Isaac has written a startling message: "Great Pan lives."

The narrator begins to understand more as Scheindel reads a letter written by Isaac and left tucked in his notebook. The letter makes clear that Isaac has eschewed deeply held Jewish beliefs to accept a kind of animism or pantheism, where all matter has life and, moreover, soul, although all matter except for human beings can live separate from their souls and thus are able to know everything around them. Humans cannot live separate from their souls and thus are cursed with the inability to escape from their bodies except through death. Isaac concludes that there may be another route to freedom--exaltation and ecstasy by means of coupling with a freed soul. The idea, once conceived, needs a trial, and Isaac's efforts are subsequently rewarded by the appearance of a dryad, the soul of a tree. The dryad's lovemaking brings Isaac to marvels and blisses that no man, it is said, has experienced since Adam. Isaac errs, however, in trying to trap the dryad into his own mortal condition. In so doing, he loses his own soul. His soul is set free, but Isaac's body is

doomed to death. More important, however, the soul retains the visage of the rabbi, who has been and will be the one who walks indifferently through the beauties of the fields, declaring that the sound, smells, and tastes of the law are more beautiful than anything to be found in the natural world.

Scheindel's repugnance toward, and lack of charity for, her husband's folly surprises the narrator and turns him away from her. The narrator is able to appreciate the subtlety of the rabbi's thinking and the bravery of the pursuit, but Scheindel is one who guarded the Mosaic law with her own wasted body during the Holocaust. The issue, however, is not intellectual subtlety but Scheindel--she who seemed doomed to death when she was seventeen years old, she who traded her youth and vitality for marriage to a Jewish rabbi. After his conversation with Scheindel, and as an ironic afterthought, the narrator goes home to clear his house of his three paltry houseplants. His gesture next to Isaac's forthright penetration into the forest, however, indicates something of the struggle of every Jew seduced by the pleasures of the beautiful but charged to interpret and guard the laws instead.

"THE SHAWL"

By the time of the publication of "The Shawl" in *The New Yorker* and "Rosa," also in *The New Yorker*, Ozick had come to articulate fairly clearly her recognition that imagination need not be a negative, leading to idolatry, but a positive, allowing Jews to imagine a god without image. These stories are of exceptional importance and significance in the Ozick canon. In them, Ozick deals directly with the horror of the Holocaust. Rosa is the focal character of both stories, each of which exists as a separate entity coherent in itself, and also, when juxtaposed as in a diptych or modified story sequence, each takes on added significance as the two parts interact with each other.

In "The Shawl," Rosa is a young woman with a baby in her arms wrapped in a shawl that serves not only to shelter the child, called Magda, but also to hide it, to muffle its cries, and to succor it. With Rosa in the concentration camp is her young niece, Stella, who is jealous of Magda and craves the shawl for her own comfort. Deprived of her shawl, the baby begins to cry and crawl around on the ground. Rosa's dilemma must be excruciatingly painful. She understands that her ad- olescent niece took the shawl, trying to cling to her own life, and Rosa understands that if she chances get- ting the baby without the shawl to cover it up, she is likely to lose both her life and Magda's. She chooses to go after the shawl first, and the fatal moment arrives too soon. A German officer finds the child wandering around and hurls her against the electrified fence.

Complicating the issue is the question of Magda's father. Early in the story, it is suggested that the father is no Jew, since Magda has blue eyes and blond hair and seems a pure Aryan, a situation that causes Stella to react even more bitterly. As in any nightmare, the dreaded occurs. Stella steals the shawl; the baby cries, wanders about, and is killed. Rosa survives the horrible ordeal as she has survived others, including repeated rapes by German soldiers. She knows that any action will result in her death, so she stuffs the shawl in her own mouth and drinks Magda's saliva to sustain herself.

"ROSA"

For "Rosa," Ozick won four awards. On the basis of the story's publication, she was named one of three best short-story writers in the United States. Because the story does not proceed chronologically, a brief plot summary is helpful. After Rosa and Stella are rescued from the camps, Rosa brings Stella to the United States, where Stella gets a job and Rosa opens an antiques shop. The action takes place some thirty-five years after the occurrences described in "The Shawl." Rosa is still angry with Stella for her role in Magda's death, and Rosa is able to get little personal satisfaction from her activities in the antiques shop. Apparently, her cus- tomers do not want to listen to the stories she has to tell, and one day, extremely angry and apparently insane, Rosa destroys her shop. To escape institutionalization, she agrees to move to what appears to be a poverty- stricken retirement hotel in Miami Beach. Life is diffi- cult for her. The intense heat makes it hard for her to get out into the sunlight in order to shop. When she does eat, she scavenges or makes do with tiny portions, such as a cracker with grape jelly or a single sardine. The condition of her clothes seems to indicate that she has nothing to wear.

One morning, however, Rosa makes her way to a supermarket, and there she meets Simon Persky. Persky is not a person in the ordinary mold. He notices Rosa on a personal level and insists that she respond to him. While Rosa's relationship with Persky develops, Ozick establishes two parallel plot lines, having to do with Rosa's request of Stella that she send Magda's shawl and a request from a Dr. Tree asking Stella to help him conduct research on Rosa's reaction to her imprison- ment and ill treatment.

The plot lines weave about one another, providing the matrices for the action. Rosa is responsible for saving Stella's life in the concentration camp and bringing her to the United States, and Stella is indi- rectly responsible for Magda's death, perhaps the single most horrible thing that happened to Rosa in a life full of horrors--the internment, the death of family and friends, assaults and rape by brutal Nazis, near starvation, and finally Magda's execution by electric shock. Since Magda's death, Rosa has teetered on the brink of insanity, managing to hold herself together by working and by the creative act of writing letters to an imaginary Magda, who, in Rosa's fantasy, has survived and become a professor of Greek philosophy at Co- lumbia University. Stella, too, has survived in Rosa's imagination in another guise. She is a thief, a blood- sucker, evil personified, and the Angel of Death. To Magda, Rosa writes letters in perfect Polish, literary and learned. To Stella, Rosa writes in crude English, a language she never bothered to learn. To Stella, Rosa admits that Magda is dead; to Magda, Rosa explains that Stella is unable to accept and cannot be told the truth.

The shawl, which Stella agrees to send to Rosa and which finally arrives, acted in Poland during the worst years as an umbrella covering the three people--Rosa, prepubescent Stella, and baby Magda--and providing sustenance and security, even though illusionary. After Magda's death, the shawl becomes for Rosa an icon; "idol," "false god," Stella says, since Rosa worships it and prays to it.

Dr. Tree is another threat to Rosa; he is a kind of parasite, living to feed off the horrors attached to other people's lives. He wants to interview Rosa for a book that he is writing on Holocaust survivors. His letter to

Rosa calling her a survivor is replete with jargon, with clinical terms naming the horrible conditions with neutral language and hiding the grotesque reality under the name of his own Institute for Humanitarian Context. Rosa objects to being called a "survivor" because the word dehumanizes her and every other person on the planet. Persky, on the other hand, offers Rosa a real friendship, a human relationship in concrete, not abstract, terms. Thus he emerges as winner of Rosa's attention, with Dr. Tree dismissed and memories of Magda put on hold for a while.

THE PUTTERMESSER PAPERS

The Puttermesser Papers consists of a series of five previously published short stories about Ruth Puttermesser. In the stories, it is often difficult to distinguish between what actually happens to her and what she fantasizes. In the first story, "Puttermesser: Her Work History, Her Ancestry, Her Afterlife," for example, she visits her Uncle Zindel for Hebrew lessons, but the narrator says that Uncle Zindel died before Puttermesser was born. In the second story, "Puttermesser and Xanthippe," Puttermesser creates a female golem, a person made of clay, from the dirt in the flowerpots in her apartment. The golem, named Xanthippe, helps Puttermesser get elected mayor of New York City and helps Puttermesser transform New York into a kind of paradise. The golem discovers sex, however, and as a result destroys all of the wonderful things she has helped Puttermesser achieve.

In each story, Puttermesser is a loser. She tries to achieve some kind of ideal and ends up with an unpleasant reality. In the long run, things never go right for her. In the third story, "Puttermesser Paired," she finds someone she considers to be a true soulmate, Rupert Rubeeno, a copyist. Rubeeno and Puttermesser share a love of literature, especially an interest in the British authors and lovers George Eliot, the novelist, and George Lewes, the essayist. Eventually they marry, but Rubeeno leaves her on their wedding night, apparently without consummating the marriage.

In the fourth story, "Puttermesser and the Muscovite Cousin," one of her relatives in the Soviet Union calls her and asks her to save the relative's child. The child, Lidia Klavdia Girshengornova, turns out to be a grown woman interested in making a fortune in America.

Eventually, she returns to the Soviet Union to rejoin her boyfriend. The final section, "Puttermesser in Paradise," is probably the saddest of all. In it, Puttermesser is killed by a man who rapes her after she is dead. She enters a paradise in which all things seem to go well for her, but in paradise, she ultimately finds no happiness, for even there, "nothing is permanent." She discovers the secret meaning of paradise: "It too is hell." Each thing she enjoys there disappears in turn, leaving her longing to be back on earth in spite of earth's having also been in many ways unpleasant for her.

Discussions of Ozick's fiction often include the descriptors "uncompromising," "demanding," "difficult"--characteristics that can diminish a writer's popularity and, consequently, status. For Ozick, however, no such diminution has taken place. Indeed, her reputation has grown steadily and strongly, her writings gaining more attention and Ozick more recognition. The phenomenon is not, after all, that surprising. If her protestations are stronger than those of other Jewish American writers, it is because her demands are based more clearly in moral imperatives of the Jewish tradition. Yet there is another tradition as truly her own--one commentators sometimes forget--an American literary heritage, with Nathaniel Hawthorne, Herman Melville, Edgar Allan Poe, William Faulkner, those writers who clearly work like Ozick in a realm where the "power of blackness" wrestles with all people.

DICTATION: A QUARTET

In the title story of this delightful quartet of "the blest nouvelle," one of today's finest prose stylists pays a mischievous tribute to the two prose stylists who fashioned modern fiction: Henry James and Joseph Conrad. James, the master, sees the younger Conrad as a "psychological simulacrum" of himself and recommends that Conrad follow his example and hire an amanuensis to transcribe his dictation on a monstrous Remington typewriter. James's bold assistant urges the more retiring Conrad typist to join her--"the warp and weft, the lily and the leaf that carries it"--in a devilish literary plot to stake out their claim for immortality. Readers familiar with the doppelgänger stories that the two men are writing at the time-- "The Secret Sharer" and "The Jolly Corner"--will appreciate the significance of the gambit most, but no one will be immune from the fun Ozick is having with this delicate little jeu d'esprit.

"Actors" also features doubling, as Matt Sorley, an aging character performer, gets the opportunity to play King Lear as a Jewish immigrant in the style of the old Yiddish theater. When Matt goes to visit the elderly father of the woman who wrote the play, the stage is set for an inevitable Lear-like upstaging that ends with appropriate dramatic ambiguity, as the members of the audience laugh until they weep. Although "At Fumicaro" lacks the conciseness that makes Ozick's other small works of fiction come alive, it is a complex exploration of ploy and penance. A critic, who likes being a Catholic, comes to Benito Mussolini-dominated Italy for a conference on "The Church and How It Is Known." However, in a line straight out of Bernard Malamud, "Frank Castle intended to travel to Florence first and then to Rome, but on the fourth day, entirely unexpected, he got married instead." Only a Malamud, or an Ozick, could guide you so willingly through a story of a man who, by becoming the lover of a child, learns more about how the Church is known than all his reading of Jacques Maritain and Graham Greene.

The final story-- "What Happened to the Baby?"--is about a young woman whose mother's cousin, Uncle Simon, tries to invent a wholly new universal language. The young woman's discovery of what happened to Simon's baby results in her suspicion that "lie, delusion, and deception" may indeed be the universal language that all speak. Poet Samuel Taylor Coleridge once said that in the highest literary art, the reader should be carried forward not by curiosity or a desire to arrive at the final solution but "by the pleasurable activity of mind excited by the attractions of the journey itself." Although these stories have plot and purpose, it is the perfection of Ozick's prose that makes them a pleasure to read.

OTHER MAJOR WORKS

LONG FICTION: *Trust*, 1966; *The Cannibal Galaxy*, 1983; *The Messiah of Stockholm*, 1987; *Heir to the Glimmering World*, 2004 (also known as *The Bear Boy*); *Foreign Bodies*, 2010.

PLAY: *Blue Light*, pr. 1994 (adaptation of her short story "The Shawl").

POETRY: *Epodes: First Poems*, 1992.

NONFICTION: *Art and Ardor*, 1983; *Metaphor and Memory: Essays*, 1989; *What Henry James Knew, and Other Essays on Writers*, 1993; *Fame and Folly: Essays*, 1996; *Portrait of the Artist as a Bad Character, and Other Essays on Writing*, 1996; *Quarrel and Quandary: Essays*, 2000; *The Din in the Head*, 2006.

EDITED TEXT: *The Best American Essays 1998*, 1998.

MISCELLANEOUS: *A Cynthia Ozick Reader*, 1996.

BIBLIOGRAPHY

Alkana, Joseph. "'Do We Not Know the Meaning of Aesthetic Gratification?' Cynthia Ozick's *The Shawl*, the Akedah, and the Ethics of Holocaust Literary Aesthetics." *Modern Fiction Studies* 43 (Winter, 1997): 963-990. Argues that Ozick takes a stance against universalism, the tendency to level human suffering under an all-inclusive existential or theological quandary.

Bloom, Harold, ed. *Cynthia Ozick: Modern Critical Views*. New York: Chelsea House, 1986. An excellent collection of essays, including brief book reviews as well as lengthy articles. Much of value for both the beginning student and a scholarly audience involved in an examination of complications of idea and form.

Burstein, Janet Handler. "Cynthia Ozick and the Transgressions of Art." *American Literature: A Journal of Literary History, Criticism, and Bibliography* 59 (March, 1987): 85-101. One of a number of articles on Ozick appearing in major scholarly journals. Concludes that Ozick is the most provocative of contemporary Jewish American voices. Her intelligence and stature provide her with an authoritarian voice as she speaks of literature and art and the didactic moral purpose art must display.

Cohen, Sarah Blacher. *Cynthia Ozick's Comic Art: From Levity to Liturgy*. Bloomington: Indiana University Press, 1994. Places Ozick in the context of the Jewish comic tradition but argues that levity in her fiction must serve a higher purpose than laughter for laughter's sake, usually the satiric purpose of attacking vices, follies, and stupidities.

Fisch, Harold. "Introducing Cynthia Ozick." *Response* 22 (1974): 27-34. An early article concentrating on analyses of the novel *Trust* (1966) and the story "The Pagan Rabbi." Tries to show connections between theme and techniques in both genres.

Franco, Dean. "Rereading Cynthia Ozick: Pluralism, Postmodernism, and the Multicultural Encounter. *Contemporary Literature* 49 (Spring, 2008): 56-84. Examines the central themes of Ozick, focusing on her portrayal of Jewish versus Hellenic religious aesthetics.

Friedman, Lawrence S. *Understanding Cynthia Ozick.* Columbia: University of South Carolina Press, 1991. A critical study of Ozick, which includes a bibliography and an index.

Kauvar, Elaine M. *Cynthia Ozick's Fiction: Tradition and Invention.* Bloomington: Indiana University Press, 1993. Examines the sources and contexts of Ozick's fiction, focusing on tensions between Hebraism and Hellenism, Western culture and Judaism, artistic imagination and moral responsibility; discusses Ozick's relationship to psychoanalysis, feminism, and postmodernism.

Lowin, Joseph. *Cynthia Ozick.* New York: Twayne, 1988. This excellent overview of Ozick's canon includes an annotated bibliography and full notes. Most valuable for beginning students whose knowledge of Holocaust literature and Ozick is limited. Offers perceptive and lucid analyses of all the major works.

_____. "Cynthia Ozick, Rewriting Herself: The Road from 'The Shawl' to 'Rosa.'" In *Since Flannery O'Connor: Essays on the Contemporary American Short Story*, edited by Loren Logsdon and Charles W. Mayer. Macomb: Western Illinois University Press, 1987. Contends Ozick paints not the thing itself but, like the French Symbolists, the effect produced by the thing; each of the three characters in the story uses the shawl as a life preserver.

Ozick, Cynthia. "An Interview with Cynthia Ozick." Interview by Elaine M. Kauvar. *Contemporary Literature* 26 (Winter, 1985): 375-401. Contains references to Ozick's religion, history, intelligence, feminism, postmodern techniques, and philosophy of art. A good introduction to her views, personality, and level of intelligence.

_____. "An Interview with Cynthia Ozick." *Contemporary Literature* 34 (Fall, 1993): 359-394. Ozick discusses Jewish culture, other Jewish writers, her own fiction, and the Holocaust with her friend Elaine M. Kauvar.

Pinsker, Sanford. *The Uncompromising Fiction of Cynthia Ozick.* Columbia: University of Missouri Press, 1987. A brief analysis of major works, including several of the more important short stories. Excellent for a reader new to Ozick's fiction. Emphasizes postmodern aspects of Ozick's work, particularly self-referential elements and the use of fantasy.

Socher, Abraham. "In the Image." *Commentary* 126 (September 2008):68-72. A review of *Dictation* that places it within the context of Ozick's previous work and analyzes it as a variation on Ozick's fundamental theme of art as idolatry.

Strandberg, Victor. *Greek Mind, Jewish Soul: The Conflicted Art of Cynthia Ozick.* Madison: University of Wisconsin Press, 1994. Argues that Ozick's work derives from her conflict between hating Western civilization and taking pride in the Jewish foundation of that civilization. Claims that she is an Orthodox Jewish feminist who reveres the ancient law but demands an equal rights amendment to the Torah.

Mary Rohrberger; Richard Tuerk
Updated by Charles E. May

P

ZZ Packer

Born: Chicago, Illinois; January 12, 1973
Also known as: Zuwena Packer

PRINCIPAL SHORT FICTION

Drinking Coffee Elsewhere, 2003

OTHER LITERARY FORMS

For several years ZZ Packer has researched an historical novel about slaves who escaped from the South after the Civil War to join the Buffalo Soldiers, African American regiments, headed by white officers, that guarded the western frontier. Excerpts emerged in short-story form: "Buffalo Soldiers" was published in the British magazine *Granta* in 2007, and the shattering "Dayward" was featured in *The New Yorker*'s "Summer Fiction: Twenty Under Forty" issue in 2010. Packer also has published a number of short articles and reviews in other periodicals. She edited with Kathy Pories *New Stories from the South: The Year's Best, 2008.*

ACHIEVEMENTS

In 1992, when ZZ Packer was just nineteen years old, her first short story was published in *Seventeen*. She received a Whiting Writers' Award for "Brownies" in 1993, and the Rona Jaffe Foundation Writers Award in 1997. Since then she has garnered many honors in a flourishing career. She was named a Wallace Stegner-Truman Capote Fellow in fiction at Stanford University and later a Jones lecturer, both highly competitive positions. As she continued to shape the stories that would eventually form her collection *Drinking Coffee Elsewhere*, "Brownies" was published in *Harper's* and was selected by E. L. Doctorow for *Best American Short Stories, 2000*. In 2003, *Drinking Coffee Elsewhere* was hailed as a *New York Times* Notable Book and the following year was a finalist for the PEN/Faulkner Award

in Fiction. Packer also was named a Guggenheim Fellow in fiction in 2005 and a Hodder Fellow at Princeton University in 2010.

BIOGRAPHY

Zuwena Packer was born in Chicago to middle-class parents. Her father owned a lounge and bar; her mother was a teacher and worked for the Social Security Administration. Packer grew up in Atlanta, Georgia, and, after her parents' divorce, in Louisville, Kentucky, her mother's hometown. Her first name means "good" in Swahili, but her teachers had difficulty pronouncing it. Her family was already calling her ZZ, so she adopted the nickname. She was raised in the strict Pentecostal Church, an experience that permeates several of her stories.

An Advanced Placement student in high school, Packer attended Yale University on a scholarship, thinking she would choose math or electrical engineering as a career, but English and creative writing became her passion. In 1994, she graduated from Yale with a bachelor of arts in English and then attended the Writing Seminar at Johns Hopkins University in Baltimore, Maryland, to earn a master of arts in 1995. For two years she taught English and creative writing in a Baltimore high school, until she realized that she could not successfully combine them in her life. Instead, she enrolled in the highly respected Iowa Writers' Workshop at the University of Iowa, where she received a master of fine arts degree in 1999. After that she worked at odd jobs, such as copywriting for an Internet company, while continuing with her personal writing projects.

Packer's career received a jump-start when her agent informed her that *The New Yorker* might be interested in her story "Drinking Coffee Elsewhere," if she would consider revising it. At that time, in her second year at Stanford, she had submitted work unsuccessfully to the magazine ever since college but was willing to try again. Always the perfectionist, she spent a year on the revision, yet the story was still too long; the editors wanted it for *The New Yorker*'s 2000 Debut Fiction Issue in 2000, but only if she could cut it by a fourth. She did. "Drinking Coffee Elsewhere" appeared in *The New Yorker* as scheduled, followed by "The Ant of the Self" in 2002 and "Dayward" in 2010.

Packer has been a writer-in-residence, lecturer, and visiting professor at several colleges and universities. Among many others, the eminent African American writer James Alan McPherson, who taught Packer at Iowa State, has praised her work. She moved to Pacifica, California, with her husband Michael Boros and their two sons.

ANALYSIS

ZZ Packer admits to many influences upon her writing, but the most powerful is Toni Morrison. In a 2003 interview for Barnes and Noble, Packer said that after she read Morrison's *Beloved* (1987), "I knew without a doubt that I was in the presence of greatness."

ZZ Packer (Marc Brasz/Corbis)

Packer writes with a clear eye and a generally objective tone, yet she can deftly employ humor and irony. Her language is often surprising and unforgettable: On a Baltimore street, "slow-moving junkies stuttered their way across the sidewalk." Her ear for the fervent cadences of a Pentecostal sermon is flawless: "So you can't use call-waiting on the Lord! *Jeeee-zus*, my friends, does not accept conference calls! . . . you need to PRAY!"

Packer's literary style is for the most part realistic and occasionally shades into gritty naturalism. The stories are set against a background of social change, reflecting not only the personal lives of her characters but also the development of the Civil Rights movement and its aftermath. All of her protagonists are African American, all are outsiders, but her themes are universal. While "Brownies" focuses on the uneasy interaction between African American and white children, "Doris Is Coming," with its shifting social codes, takes place during the time of the Woolworth sit-ins, when African Americans were protesting for equal treatment. However, Packer's stories are usually more humorous than depressing, with the possible exception of the early story "Geese," in which multinational expatriates struggle to survive in Japan.

Author Tessa Decarlo quotes Packer as saying: "The more race is not supposed to matter, the more it does." A different sort of prejudice appears in "Geese," in which the clash of cultures is reduced to a microcosm by the individual conflicts between multinational roommates in Japan. Most of Packer's stories deal with an initiation, a character's figurative coming of age, but not everyone achieves insight. Dina, the protagonist of the title story and of "Geese," carries a wound so deep she cannot bear to look at it and cannot cope with events around her. On the other hand, poor cross-eyed Clareese, in "Every Tongue Shall Confess," also suffers from a different sort of flawed vision that prevents her from seeing her world clearly enough to understand it.

"BROWNIES"

The ugliness of racial prejudice and the shifting relationships between whites and blacks are observed and commented upon by fourth-grader Snot, a young black girl whose real name is Laurel. Her Brownie troop from Atlanta's Woodrow Wilson Elementary is enduring a summer outing at Camp Crescendo with their leader from the African Methodist Episcopal Church, who believes her primary job is to emphasize religion. She leaves most of the actual leading to her parent helper, Octavia's mother. For this group, religion does not seem to be working.

Octavia, whose long straight hair is the envy of the other black girls, and Arnetta, the leader's pet, are the influential troublemakers of the troop. For them, the word "Caucasian" is used as an insult. Unfortunately, sharing their camp is Brownie Troop 909, composed of ten white girls with long, straight hair, who "turtled out from their bus in pairs." These girls are delayed learners, who are carefully sheltered by their leaders.

Arnetta stirs up trouble when she falsely accuses one of the white girls of insulting Daphne, a quiet African American girl, by calling her the dreaded N-word. Urging their friends to fight the intruders, Arnetta and Octavia plan to ambush the members of Troop 909, daring to haze the white girls as might not have been dared thirty years before. An outsider herself, as evidenced by her nickname, Snot compares the white girls to the quaintly dressed Mennonites, whom she and her father saw at the mall, and tries to justify his unkind actions toward them: "When you've been made to feel bad for so long, you jump at the chance to do it to others." She is aware that there is "something mean in the world that I could not stop," but she refuses to participate. Hope comes from the fact that she and the quiet Daphne know they are not alone.

"THE ANT OF THE SELF"

This story explores the ironic juxtaposition of two conflicting African American types: Ray Bivens, Jr., a shiftless con man, and Spurgeon, his responsible son, a studious, well-groomed high school debater. The first-person story takes place in October, 1995, during the Nation of Islam's Million Man March on Washington, D.C. Dutiful Spurgeon has just bailed his father out of a Louisville, Kentucky, jail on a drunk-driving charge and intends to take him back to Ray's apartment in Indiana. The boy, who lives with his mother in Louisville, is driving his mother's car.

Ray, obviously a scam artist, urges the young man to invest his debate prize money in a friend's cockfighting arena, but Spurgeon has already used it for bail. (His mother refuses to pay.) Ray decides they will first go to his girlfriend's home to pick up his exotic tropical birds, which he wants to take to the march in Washington to sell. Huckster Ray is looking for a profit any way he can get it. Spurgeon hesitates, for he has never missed a day of school or skipped a high school debate (one is scheduled for the following day), but he cannot confront his father. They put four cages of noisy tropical birds in the back seat and drive seven hundred miles to Washington. (Their frustrating odyssey suggests the doomed journey with Addie Bundren's coffin in William Faulkner's *As I Lay Dying* [1930], sad and funny at the same time.)

While many at the Million Man March are noted public figures or religious folk, Muslim and Christian, a small-town preacher offers the phrase that becomes the story's title when he says that "freedom is attained only when the ant of the self--that small, blind, crumb-seeking part of ourselves--casts off slavery and its legacy." However, after selling one bird, Ray is interested only in finding a cheap bar and a willing woman.

Spurgeon finally admits that he is glad they went to the march. Ray, who is drunk now, has found a woman and wants to borrow his ex-wife's car. Spurgeon, who is not drunk, refuses politely, but his father punches him and disappears with the woman and the car. The youth is left to pay for a broken bar window and must find his way back to Louisville. When he encounters another father and his drowsy little son at the train depot, the man offers him money for fare. Spurgeon nearly cries as he watches this father exhibit tenderness and love for his little boy.

"DRINKING COFFEE ELSEWHERE"

This psychological study is probably the most disturbing story in Packer's collection. When Dina travels from Baltimore to Yale University, where there are orientation games for new freshmen, she is asked what inanimate object she would choose to be. Her angry response, "A revolver," earns her a private room, weekly visits to the dean, and a year with the school psychiatrist. She blames her answer on the thought that most of the eighteenth century students at Yale must have owned slaves.

Dina defines herself as a misanthrope and sits naked, facing the door of her room, to discourage the counselors from coming inside, but Heidi, a lonely white freshman who is weeping copiously, will not be turned away and is admitted. Dina advises Heidi to stay in her room and avoid contact with other people, but Heidi reaches out to her. Somehow Dina can tolerate this, and they work together as dishwashers in the dining hall.

In the past, when a boy followed Dina from the grocery and politely offered to carry her bag, she ran away from him, but she lies to the psychiatrist, telling him that they became more intimate. Meanwhile, Heidi and Dina grow closer, possibly because Heidi seems safe and often sleeps in Dina's room, but when Heidi publicly declares herself a lesbian, Dina abruptly ends their friendship. Since the day of her mother's funeral, Dina has distanced herself from others, pretending that she is drinking coffee elsewhere, preferably in an Arabic country or another one far away. She believes that somehow her father caused her mother's slow death but says nothing about that to her psychiatrist. He warns her that she is pretending so much that she will be unable to communicate when she really wants to tell the truth.

Then Heidi, weeping again, informs Dina that Heidi's mother is dying of cancer. Dina offers to pay for Heidi's ticket back to Vancouver but refuses to accompany her, keeping her at arm's length. Instead, Dina returns to Baltimore, moving in with an aunt. She is still defensive, signaling everyone to stay away from her. Jean Thompson, writing in *The New York Times Book Review*, points out that "if she is a revolver, she is a weapon aimed at herself."

Some of these stories are far deeper than they appear at first and merit rereading. Not all focus on race, but they all address issues in American culture. Packer satirizes religious enthusiasts, hypocrisy, racism, and white indifference, examining these issues without pretending to solve them. Her protagonists are faced with problems that they cannot always surmount, but most of them keep trying.

OTHER MAJOR WORKS

EDITED TEXT: *New Stories from the South: The Year's Best, 2008*, 2008 (with Kathy Pories).

BIBLIOGRAPHY

DeCarlo, Tessa. "Comedienne of Manners." *Smithsonian* (Fall, 2007): 94-95. Packer's popularity is enhanced by her willingness to discuss "uncomfortable" racial issues through the use of humor.

Leyshon, Cressida. "The Aerial View." *The New Yorker* (November 25, 2002). Leyshon's interview with Packer leads to a discussion of "The Ant of the Self" and the Million Man March. Packer comments that, although "the march was an obvious metaphor for their relationship," the father and son are unable to recognize this.

Packer, ZZ. "Speaking in Tongues." In *The Workshop: Seven Decades of the Iowa Writers' Workshop*, edited by Tom Grimes. New York: Hyperion, 1999. An early version of this story, quite different from the one found in *Drinking Coffee Elsewhere*, presents an interesting comparison with the final version as an illustration of Packer's revision process.

Rakoff, Joanna Smith. "ZZ Packer: Back-story Behind the Buzz." *Poets and Writers Magazine* 31, no. 1 (2003): 55-60. Rakoff offers a superb profile of Packer's personal and professional life, examining her position as a mainstream writer and her commitment to her writing.

Thompson, Jean. "Notorious in New Haven." *The New York Times Book Review*, March 16, 2003, p. 7. Fiction writer Thompson examines several stories and finds that Packer is always superbly testing limits.

Joanne McCarthy

TOM PAINE

Born: Rhode Island; c. 1962

PRINCIPAL SHORT FICTION

Scar Vegas, and Other Stories, 2000

OTHER LITERARY FORMS

Tom Paine's reputation rests primarily on his short fiction and one novel, *The Pearl of Kuwait* (2003), a zany, romantic adventure tale set against the backdrop of the first Persian Gulf War. In the comic novel, narrated by surfer-turned-Marine Cody "Cowboy" Carmichael, his buddy Tommy Trang falls in love with a Kuwaiti princess, Lulu, and seeks to rescue her both from an unwanted marriage to Saudi Prince Fawwaz and from the invading Iraqi armies of Saddam Hussein. The volume's most memorable scene features a nude Trang outracing a camel. The novel, like Paine's short fiction, tackles sensitive and controversial political subjects with originality and humor.

ACHIEVEMENTS

Tom Paine's first published story-- "Will You Say Something, Monsieur Eliot?"--received an O. Henry Award in 1996. Paine also has won two Pushcart Prizes for "From Basra to Bethlehem" in 1997 and for "Scar Vegas" in 1998. "General Markman's Last Stand," which first appeared in *Story*, was anthologized in *The Best New Stories from the South, 1996*. Paine has been shortlisted for inclusion in *The Best American Short Stories* three times. His short-story collection, *Scar Vegas*, was honored as a finalist for the PEN/ Hemingway Award, won a Barnes and Noble Discovery Award, and was recognized by *The New York Times* as a Notable Book of the Year. In recognition of his promise, in 1999 Paine was named a "Writer on the Verge" by the *Village Voice Literary Supplement*.

BIOGRAPHY

Tom Paine grew up in Rhode Island during the 1970's. The Paines were New England Yankees dating back many generations--his father and grandfather were also named Tom Paine--but his paternal grandfather had married an Irish Catholic immigrant. Paine traces his literary instincts to that woman's father, a hard-drinking lover of women and wine, who earned his living reciting poetry and singing ballads at Catholic weddings and funerals. Paine knew he wanted to be a writer as early as the second grade, although at first he aspired to become a poet and did not take up fiction seriously until high school. He graduated from the Portsmouth Abbey School in 1980 and from Princeton University in 1984. While at Princeton, he attended Officer Candidate School and earned a commission in the Marine Corps. Although he ultimately turned down this position, during his training he acquired the military knowledge that would form the background for his first novel, *The Pearl of Kuwait*, and for several of his stories.

After college, Paine worked the night shift as an orderly at a psychiatric hospital for three years, while pursuing his writing during his off hours. He amassed enough rejection slips to blanket the doors of his apartment. He worked briefly as a copywriter and then took over the helm of the St. John *Sun-Times*, a biweekly newspaper in the United States Virgin Islands. After a stint living in Italy, during which he temporarily gave up writing for sculpting, Paine enrolled in Columbia University's M.F.A. program in creative writing, where he was awarded a prestigious Ellis Fellowship and edited the journal *Columbia*. That was when his big break occurred: Editor Deborah Garrison discovered his story "Will You Say Something, Monsieur Eliot?" in the slush pile at *The New Yorker*. The story, which appeared in that magazine in October, 2004, was Paine's first published fiction. The following year, Paine won the *Boston Review*'s annual short-story contest with

"The Milkman and I," assuring himself a place among short fiction's rising stars. Other stories quickly appeared in *Harper's*, *Story*, and *Playboy*. Paine's first ten stories were collected in *Scar Vegas* in 2000. He dedicated the work to the murdered Nigerian author and human rights activist Ken Saro-Wiwa.

Paine joined the faculty of Middlebury College in Vermont, where he taught for a decade, during which time he completed his novel, *The Pearl of Kuwait*, and several additional stories. He then began teaching writing at the University of New Hampshire and settled in North Ferrisburg, Vermont, with his wife, the internationally renowned artist Shirley Reid.

ANALYSIS

Paine's highly lyrical, voice-driven prose places him at the forefront of the maximalist or "hysterical realist" movement that arose in the 1990's as a backlash against the minimalism and "dirty realism" of writers such as Raymond Carver, Larry Brown, and Richard Ford. However, Paine avoids many of the structural innovations and postmodern gambits that one often associates with maximalism, instead preferring straightforward, linear narratives. Many of his stories contain satiric elements, and several veer directly into veiled political commentary, but beneath these observations on racism or militarism lurks a penetrating understanding of ordinary human struggle. The many voices through which Paine relates his stories and his diverse settings and subject matter reflect the author's extraordinarily wide range. Several critics have commended this ability to slip into the skin of such different characters.

"WILL YOU SAY SOMETHING, MONSIEUR ELIOT?"

"Will You Say Something, Monsieur Eliot?" is the best known of Paine's stories and his first to appear in print. It takes place against the backdrop of the Haitian coup of 1991, in which General Raoul Cédras toppled democratically elected President Jean-Bertrand Aristide, setting off a mass exodus of boat people seeking asylum in the United States. In Paine's story, one such boatload of desperate refugees rescues a Republican yachter, Eliot Swan, whose yawl has been wrecked in a hurricane. The overconfident Swan, like Paine, a Princeton graduate, is a source of hope to the refugees and

their leader, Alphonse. They believe that since Swan (whom they call "Monsieur Eliot") is a wealthy American, the U.S. president will send forces to rescue him, and that in the process they will also be saved. Although Swan is the central character in the story, the selfless Haitians around him are the clear heroes. In one memorable moment, each of the many refugees squeezes a few drops from a personal water supply into Swan's dry mouth. Paine does not shy away from depicting the horrors of life on the raft. He relates how the Haitian dead are tossed into the sea and how the living occasionally jump overboard in despair. His use of specialized nautical terminology, a vestige of his Marine training, adds a powerful authenticity to the narrative. As with many of Paine's stories, the ending is both obvious and still shocking: Swan is rescued by an American helicopter, while Alphonse and his fellow refugees are given a few jugs of water and abandoned to the open sea. If one misses the hard-hitting political implications, Paine examined them for readers in his commentary on the piece for the O. Henry Prize anthology, writing that "we are living in a corporate totalitarian state and staring one-eyed down the barrel of a fascist future." Despite Swan's shortcomings, which are many, he comes across as a fully realized human being rather than a chess piece in a battle of polemics. While not stated directly, implicit at the story's conclusion is that Swan has changed and that he does not want Alphonse and his followers to be left behind.

In "Will You Say Something, Monsieur Eliot?" Paine uses vivid and energized language to capture the effects of the storm and the power of the elements. He also displays considerable skill at controlling the pace of the narrative, slowing down the prose at its tense moments with long, lyrical passages and then speeding up quickly through snippets of dialogue that contain no quotation marks. As with many of Paine's stories, the sparse, often oblique dialogue contrasts with the rich descriptions, creating a taut rhythm that maximizes the tension of each moment.

"THE MILKMAN AND I"

Paine returns to his working-class New England roots for "The Milkman and I," a first-person narrative of a Roxbury man's relationship with his abusive and alcoholic mother. During his mother's final hospitalization for her cirrhosis, she calls out for a man named Alfred, a name that the narrator does not recognize. He phones his older sister, Peg, and she reveals that Alfred was the name of the family's African American milkman before the narrator was born. Later, when the narrator's mother dies, he finds her diary and discovers that Alfred had been his mother's lover and his own father. The story concludes with the narrator's rather overtly political realization that, in contemporary times, his mother's interracial relationship might have succeeded.

"The Milkman and I" is a traditional linear narrative, a quest story in which the protagonist seeks to understand why his mother abused him as a child. Hints of the abuse are peppered throughout the story, such as the description of the scars on his hands. (Scarring is one of Paine's preferred details, one that he returns to in "Scar Vegas" and "Ceausescu's Cat.") However, the use of the mother's diaries, which dominate the latter half of the story and serve the same structural purpose as would flashbacks, enables Paine to relate a second, earlier story within the confines of the first. "The Milkman and I" also features the wry, irreverent narrator who appears in several of Paine's works, a man who can joke that his mother, after cardiopulmonary resuscitation, looks as though she has just had sex. The verve of the voice is trademark Paine at his strongest.

"GENERAL MARKMAN'S LAST STAND"

A full-blown example of maximalism, "General Markman's Last Stand" is the story of Marine Corps General and Vietnam War hero Trevor Markman's final day of military life. Markman, who secretly enjoys wearing women's undergarments beneath his uniform, is caught stealing a brassiere from the commissary and faces possible court-martial. However, Markman's superior, General Bowles, stages a public scene in which a young woman pretending to be Markman's mistress attacks him for standing her up after promising to bring her lingerie, creating the illusion for the troops that the retiring general had been stealing the brassiere for his lover. To the Marines at Camp Lejeune, Markman is suddenly a virile hero. However, for his wife, Beatrice, who demands complete honesty, the stunt is unconvincing. She threatens to divorce Markman unless he

reveals the truth, which he finally does at a banquet in his honor, by stripping off his uniform to reveal his ladies' undergarments. By exposing himself, both literally and emotionally, Markman saves his marriage.

If "General Markman's Last Stand" lacks the plausibility of many of Paine's other stories, it serves as a powerful allegory in the vein of Nathaniel Hawthorne's "The Minister's Black Veil" and Herman Melville's "The Confidence-Man." The use of military language and detail, presumably drawn from Paine's own Marine Corps training, compensates for the outré plot. The story also exhibits a new depth in Paine's characterization, in that Markman, far more than Monsieur Eliot or the narrator of "The Milkman and I," is a deeply sympathetic and truly heroic figure, who rises above his surroundings. In that sense, "General Markman's Last Stand" is the most optimistic of Paine's shorter works.

"CEAUSESCU'S CAT"

Paine's penchant for unusual voices and locales reaches its zenith in "Ceausescu's Cat," an intricately plotted tale of twin brothers enmeshed in the political underworld of dictator Nicolae Ceausescu's Romania. The story begins when Ovidiu, an "invisible" poet in Bucharest, is summoned for a job as a film director at the Romanian state television station. Although Ovidiu has no experience in film and had not applied for the job, he suddenly finds himself making human-interest documentaries for the government to whose authority he is personally opposed. Then he is invited to the dacha of the provisional governor of Transylvania, whose daughter, Liana, attempts to seduce him. In quintessential maximalist fashion, Ovidiu discovers that Liana is actually carrying the child of his twin brother, Pavel, a disowned thief who works for the anti-Ceausescu underground. Since Pavel will not marry her, Liana wishes to marry his identical twin and escape to France. The story then takes several increasingly unlikely turns as Pavel and Ovidiu reunite and settle as political refugees in Reno, Nevada, where the absence of a political cause drives Pavel into a steep depression. The cat in the title refers to the Romanian dictator's apparent opposition to showing felines on television. In the story, Ovidiu sneaks a snippet of cat footage past the censors, footage that is later used subversively to further the anti-Ceausescu revolution of 1989.

In "Ceausescu's Cat," Paine again has returned to the international political themes and the subject of refugees, in particular, that first appeared in "Will You Say Something, Monsieur Eliot?" "Ceausescu's Cat," however, is a far less conventional and more brave story than his earlier works, one that uses multiple plot twists and reversals that force the reader to grapple with the nature of truth. The story is also among Paine's most overtly humorous, especially the false translations that Ovidiu renders during his meeting with the American ambassador to Greece. The unsolved disappearance of Pavel at the denouement of the narrative marks a departure from the more traditional and tight finales of Paine's other stories, as does the rather unexpected but brilliant poem with which the story concludes.

OTHER MAJOR WORKS
    LONG FICTION: *The Pearl of Kuwait*, 2003.

BIBLIOGRAPHY
Lamy, Nicole. "*Scar Vegas, and Other Stories*." *Review of Contemporary Fiction* 21, no. 1 (Spring, 2001): 204-205. Review praises Paine's ability to make the political personal in his geopolitical parables.
Lehmann-Haupt, Christopher. "She Stole His Kidney and Other Bad Luck Tales." *The New York Times*, January 13, 2000, p. B11. Lehmann-Haupt examines Paine's fiction through the lens of power dynamics.
Lilly, Paul P. "Male Paradigms in Thom Jones and Tom Paine." In *The Postmodern Short Story: Forms and Issues*, edited by Farhat Iftekharrudin, Joseph Boyden, Mary Rohrberger, and Jaie Claudet. Westport, Conn.: Praeger, 2003. An essay that compares Paine's work with that of another ex-Marine turned short story writer.
Henderson, Eleanor. "An Interview with Fiction Writer Tom Paine." *Poets and Writers* (December 6, 2002). Paine discusses his writing techniques and the personal nature of his subject matter.

Jacob M. Appel

GRACE PALEY

Born: Bronx, New York; December 11, 1922
Died: Thetford Hill, Vermont; August 22, 2007
Also known as: Grace Goodside

PRINCIPAL SHORT FICTION
    The Little Disturbances of Man: Stories of Men and Women in Love, 1959
    Enormous Changes at the Last Minute, 1974
    Later the Same Day, 1985
    Long Walks and Intimate Talks: Stories and Poems, 1991 (with paintings by Vera Williams)
    The Collected Stories, 1994
    Here and Somewhere Else, 2007 (with Robert Nichols)

OTHER LITERARY FORMS
In addition to her short fiction, Grace Paley published the poetry collections *Leaning Forward* (1985), *New and Collected Poems* (1992), *Begin Again: Collected Poems* (2000), and *Fidelity* (2008), and the nonfiction work *Just as I Thought* (1998). She also contributed short stories to *The New Yorker* and essays on teaching to various journals.

ACHIEVEMENTS
Grace Paley received a John Simon Guggenheim Memorial Foundation Fellowship, a National Council on the Arts grant, and a National Institute of Arts and Letters Award for short-story writing. She was elected to the American Academy of Arts and Letters in 1980, and in 1988 and 1989 she received the Edith Wharton Award. In 1993, she was awarded the Rea Award for the Short Story and the Vermont Governor's Award for

excellence in the arts. In 1994, she was a nominee for the National Book Award and a finalist for the Pulitzer Prize. In 1997, she was awarded the Lannan Foundation Literary Award.

BIOGRAPHY

Grace Paley, whose maiden name was Grace Goodside, was born and raised in New York City. Her Russian immigrant parents, Isaac Goodside, a physician, and Mary (Ridnyik) Goodside, were political exiles in their early years and passed on their political concerns to their daughter. At home they spoke Russian and Yiddish, as well as English, exposing their daughter to both old and new cultures. She studied in city schools and after graduation attended Hunter College in 1938 and later New York University. Paley, however, was not interested in formal academic study and dropped out of college. She had begun to write poetry and in the early 1940's studied with W. H. Auden at the New School for Social Research. In 1942, she married Jess Paley, a motion-picture cameraman. The couple had two children and separated three years later, although they were not legally divorced for twenty years. In the 1940's and 1950's, Paley worked as a typist while raising her children and continuing to write. At this time she began her lifelong political involvement by participating in New York City neighborhood action groups.

After many rejections, her first collection of eleven stories, *The Little Disturbances of Man*, was published in 1959. Even though the book was not widely reviewed, critics admired her work, and Paley's teaching career flourished. In the early 1960's, she taught at Columbia University and Syracuse University and also presented summer workshops. She also began writing a novel, a project which she did not complete. She increased her political activism, participating in nonviolent protests against prison conditions in New York City and the government's position on the war in Vietnam. A prominent activist in the peace movement, Paley was a member of a 1969 mission that went to Hanoi to negotiate for the release of prisoners of war. In 1973, she was a delegate to the World Peace Conference in Moscow. In 1974, her second collection of stories appeared. It received sporadic condemnation from

reviewers, partially because of her political views but also because the writing was deemed uneven in quality.

In the 1970's and 1980's, Paley continued her political activities, as well as her writing and teaching. She joined with other activists in condemning Soviet repression of human rights, and was a leader in the 1978 demonstrations in Washington, D.C., against nuclear weapons. In 1985, along with campaigning against American government policy in Central America, she visited Nicaragua and El Salvador. Her stories appeared in *The Atlantic, Esquire, Accent*, and other magazines. Paley settled in Greenwich Village in New York City, with her second husband, poet, playwright, and landscape architect Robert Nichols. In the 1990's, Paley continued to teach in the New York City area, particularly at Sarah Lawrence College, but she retired by the end of the decade. She divided her time between her home in Vermont and the Greenwich Village apartment that was so often a backdrop for her fiction. Paley died from breast cancer on August 22, 2007.

ANALYSIS

Despite her small literary output, Grace Paley's innovative style and the political and social concerns she advocates in her work enabled her to generate significant critical attention. Her stories treat traditional themes, focusing on the lives of women and the experiences of love, motherhood, and companionship that bind them together. She presents these themes, however, in inventive rather than traditional structures. Her stories are frequently fragmented and open-ended, without conventional plot or character development, structural innovations that make her work more true to life. The stories gain their vitality by Paley's use of distinctive language--the voice, idiom, tone, and rhythms of the New York City locale. She writes best when rendering the razor-tongued Jewish American urban female, with an ironic wit, who does not hesitate to voice her opinions.

To speak out is a basic theme in Paley's stories, and it reflects her own life and political principles. The women in her stories are like her; they are political activists who speak on nuclear energy, on the environment, and on all conditions that affect the world into which their children are born. This intermingling of politics and art brought Paley mixed reviews, but she continued to stretch the limits of the short story, in both form and content.

THE LITTLE DISTURBANCES OF MAN

"Goodbye and Good Luck," the first story in Grace Paley's first collection, *The Little Disturbances of Man*, shows her characteristic style and theme. The story begins, "I was popular in certain circles, says Aunt Rose. I wasn't no thinner then, only more stationary in the flesh." Aunt Rose knows what her sister--Lillie's "mama"--does not, that time rushes by relentlessly, that the old generation is quickly forgotten as the new generation supplants it, and that mama's life of stodgy domesticity (the "spotless kitchen") has meant little to her or anyone else as her life slips away. Mama, however, feels sorry for "poor Rosie" because Aunt Rose has not married or led a virtuous life.

As a young girl, Rose cannot stand her safe but boring job in a garment factory and takes instead a job selling tickets at the Russian Art Theatre, which stages Yiddish plays. The man who hires her says "Rosie Lieber, you surely got a build on you!" These attributes

Grace Paley (AP Photo/Toby Talbot)

quickly gain the attention of the Yiddish matinee idol Volodya Vlashkin, "the Valentino of Second Avenue."

Although he is much older than she and has a wife and family elsewhere, Vlashkin sets Rose up in an apartment. Their affair continues on--and off--over the years while he has many other lovers, but Rose is not lonely herself when he is gone. She never complains but worships him when she has him and is philosophical about his infidelities: An actor needs much practice if he is to be convincing on the stage. While she never asks anything from him, "the actresses . . . were only interested in tomorrow," sleeping lovelessly with wealthy producers for advancement. They get their advancement: Now they are old and forgotten. Vlashkin himself is old and retired, Aunt Rose fat and fifty, when his wife divorces him for all his past adulteries. He comes back to Rosie, the only woman who never asked anything of him, and they decide to get married. She has had her warm and love-filled life, and now she will have a bit of respectability, a husband--and, "as everybody knows, a woman should have at least one before the end of the story."

The theme is seen most clearly when Rose contrasts her life with her own mother's. Her mother had upbraided her when she moved in with Vlashkin, but her mother had "married who she didn't like. . . . He never washed. He had an unhappy smell . . . he got smaller, shriveled up little by little, till goodbye and good luck." Rosie, therefore, "decided to live for love." No amount of respectability, no husband, advancement, or wealth will save one from imminent change, decay, and death; so live for love, Aunt Rose would say, and you will have the last laugh.

The characters and tone may change in other stories, but the theme remains the same. In "The Pale Pink Roast," Anna sees her former husband and asks him to help her move into her new apartment. He is in "about the third flush of youth," a handsome, charming, but "transient" man. In the midst of hanging her curtains, he stops and makes love to her. Then, admiring her fancy apartment and stylish clothes, he asks archly who is paying for it. "My husband is," she responds. Her former husband is furious with her. The new husband, she tells him, is a "lovely" man, in the process of moving his business here. Why did you do it, then, her former husband wants to know: "Revenge? Meanness? Why?" "I did it for love," she says.

Over and over the female characters must choose between the safe but boring man and the charming but worthless lover. In "An Interest in Life," the girl has her secure but dull boyfriend yet dreams of the husband who deserted her. In "Distance," Paley tells the same story over again, but this time from the point of view of another character in the story, a bitter old woman full of destructive meanness. She was wild in youth, but she then opted for the safe, loveless marriage, and it has so soured her life that she has tried to force everyone else into the same wrong pattern. Her own very ordinary son is the analogue of the boring boyfriend from "An Interest in Life." At heart, the bitter old woman understands the young girl, and this is her redeeming humanity.

In a slight variation of theme, "Wants" demonstrates why the love relationship between man and woman must be transitory. The desirable man wants everything out of life; the loving woman wants only her man. "You'll always want nothing," the narrator's former husband tells her bitterly, suggesting a sort of ultimate biological incompatibility between the sexes. The result assuredly is sadness and loneliness, but with islands of warmth to make it endurable. In "Come On, Ye Sons of Art," Kitty is spending Sunday morning with her boyfriend ("Sunday was worth two weeks of waiting"). She is pregnant by him and already has a houseful of children by other fathers. She takes great pleasure in the fine morning she can give her boyfriend. The boyfriend, a traveling salesman, delights in his skill as a salesman. He only regrets that he is not more dishonest, like his sister, who, ignoring human relationships, has devoted herself to amassing an immense fortune by any means. Kitty's boyfriend wistfully wishes he too were corrupt, high, and mighty. They are listening to a beautiful piece of music by English composer Henry Purcell on the radio, which the announcer says was written for the queen's birthday; in reality, the music was not written for the queen, but rather for Purcell's own delight in his art, in the thing he did best, and no amount of wealth and power equals that pleasure.

In her later stories, Paley was striking out in new directions, away from the inner-city unwed mothers and the strongly vernacular idiom, to sparse, classical, universal stories. The theme, however, that there is no safe harbor against change and death, and that the only salvation is to live fully, realistically, and for the right things, has not changed. "In the Garden" has, essentially, four characters who appear to be in some country in the West Indies. Lush gardens of bright flowers and birds surround them, suggesting a particularly bountiful nature. One character is a beautiful young woman whose children were kidnapped eight months earlier and now are certainly dead, but she cannot face this fact, and her talk is constantly about "when they come home." Her husband is a rich landlord, who did not give the kidnappers their ransom money; he shouts constantly in a loud voice that everything is well. There is a vacationing Communist renting one of the landlord's houses, who, out of curiosity, asks the neighbors about the case. He learns that the landlord had once been poor but now is rich and has a beautiful wife; he could not believe that anything had the power to hurt his luck, and he was too greedy to pay the ransom. It is known that it was "his friends who did it." There is an elderly neighbor woman who is dying of a muscle-wasting disease. She had spent much time with the beautiful woman listening to her talk about when the children would return, but now she is fed up with her and cannot stand the husband's shouting. For a while, since she is too wasted to do much more, she follows with her eyes the movements of the Communist, but "sadly she had to admit that the eyes' movement, even if minutely savored, was not such an adventurous journey." Then "she had become interested in her own courage."

At first it may appear that nothing happens in the story, but it is all there. The garden is the world. The young woman with her beauty has won a rich husband; the landlord, through aggressiveness, has clawed his way to the top. Both these modes--beauty and aggressiveness--have succeeded only for a while, but inevitably whatever is gained in the world is lost because human beings are all mortal. The Communist--by being a Communist, "a tenderhearted but relentless person"--suggests someone who will try to find a political way to stave off chance and mortality, but in fact he merely leaves, having done nothing. The old woman, who realizes the fecklessness of trying to help, and who has found mere observation of process insufficient, becomes more interested in the course of her own courage in facing up to inevitable change. She and her husband are the only ones who admit to change, and this seems the right position, the tragic sense of life which makes life supportable.

THE COLLECTED STORIES

The Collected Stories gathers more than thirty years of stories from Paley's previous collections, allowing the reader to track the development of Paley's feminism and pacifism, as well as her depiction of urban family life. *The Collected Stories* also brings with it an opportunity to examine one of Paley's most enduring fictional characters, a major figure in thirteen stories, and a minor figure in several more. This character, Faith Darwin, first appeared in the "The Used Boy Raisers," where it was clear that she served as her author's alter ego, so that Faith, like Paley, is of Jewish descent, lives in Greenwich Village, has married, divorced, and remarried, has two children, and is also a writer.

In addition to paralleling Paley's own life to some degree, the Faith Darwin stories track the various political movements in which Paley was involved. For instance, in "Faith in a Tree," Faith's personal life is refrained in the light of her political principles, indicated by a demonstration against the war in Vietnam. In "Dreamer in a Dead Language," Faith's father, whom she had loved and admired uncritically, is critically reassessed in the light of her growing feminism. In later stories, however, Faith herself is subjected to criticism and revaluation. In "Listening," Faith is confronted by her lesbian friend Cassie, who accuses her of ignoring her in her fiction. Faith is also criticized by other characters in "Friends," "Zagrowsky Tells," and "Love," the last story detailing the breaking up of friendships over disagreements concerning the Soviet Union.

In these later stories, Faith must deal with changing times. In "The Long-Distance Runner," Faith faces her own aging process by returning to the old Jewish neighborhood in which she and her parents once lived

and which is now populated by African Americans. When Faith decides to live in her old apartment for three weeks with four African American children and their mother, Mrs. Luddy, she discovers that, despite their differences, they share a sense of sisterhood because they are both women and mothers. The centrality of motherhood in the life of women is a continuing theme in the Faith Darwin stories, beginning with "The Used Boy Raisers" and emerging again in such stories as "The Long Distance Runner" and "The Exquisite Moment."

Stories such as "The Long-Distance Runner," with its African American family, and "The Exquisite Moment," involving a Chinese houseguest, also remind the reader of the multicultural element in Paley's fiction. Faith's own neighborhood--a Greenwich village community of artists, left-wing political activists, and people from minority ethnic and racial groups--is different from what is considered mainstream America, but at the same time it reminds the reader that this world, too, is part of the American scene. This urban community, which blends and mixes ethnicities, religions, and radical politics, along with Faith's role as a fictional version of Paley herself, makes Faith Darwin's stories a particularly representative aspect of Grace Paley's collected work.

OTHER MAJOR WORKS
POETRY: *Leaning Forward*, 1985; *New and Collected Poems*, 1992; *Begin Again: Collected Poems*, 2000; *Fidelity*, 2008.
NONFICTION: *Conversations with Grace Paley*, 1997 (Gerhard Bach and Blaine H. Hall, editors); *Just as I Thought*, 1998.

BIBLIOGRAPHY
Aarons, Victoria. "Talking Lives: Storytelling and Renewal in Grace Paley's Short Fiction." *Studies in American Jewish Literature* 9 (1990): 20-35. Asserts that Paley empowers her characters through their penchant for telling stories. In recounting their stories, her characters try to gain some control over their lives, as if by telling they can reconstruct experience.

Arcana, Judith. *Grace Paley's Life Stories: A Literary Biography*. Urbana: University of Illinois Press, 1993. A biography of Paley which includes a bibliography and an index.

Arons, Victoria. "An Old Discussion About Feminism and Judaism: Faith and Renewal in Grace Paley's Short Fiction." In *Connections and Collisions: Identities in Contemporary Jewish-American Women's Writing*, edited by Lois E. Rubin. Newark: University of Delaware Press, 2005. Argues that Paley's "preoccupation" with equality, combined with the Jewish people's centuries of historical and current oppression, results in a fusion in her short fiction of Judaism, feminism, and political activism.

Bach, Gerhard, and Blaine Hall, eds. *Conversations with Grace Paley*. Jackson: University Press of Mississippi, 1997. A collection of interviews with Paley from throughout her career as a writer, in which she comments on the sources of her stories, her political views, her feminism, and the influences on her writing.

Baumbach, Jonathan. "Life Size." *Partisan Review* 42, no. 2 (1975): 303-306. Baumbach approaches *Enormous Changes at the Last Minute* by concentrating on the innovative narrative voice and how it enhances the themes that run throughout the stories.

Charters, Ann. "Grace Paley." In *A Reader's Companion to the Short Story in English*, edited by Erin Fallon, et al., under the auspices of the Society for the Study of the Short Story. Westport, Conn.: Greenwood Press, 2001. Aimed at the general reader, this essay provides a brief biography of Paley followed by an analysis of her short fiction.

DeKoven, Marianne. "Mrs. Hegel-Shtein's Tears." *Partisan Review* 48, no. 2 (1981): 217-223. Paley wanted to tell about everyday life but in story forms that were not the traditionally linear ones. DeKoven describes how innovative structures enable Paley to achieve uncommon empathy with her subjects.

Gelfant, Blanche H., ed. *The Columbia Companion to the Twentieth-Century American Short Story*. New York: Columbia University Press, 2000. Includes a chapter in which Paley's short stories are analyzed.

Heller, Deborah. *Literary Sisterhoods: Imagining Women Artists*. Montreal: McGill-Queen's University Press, 2005. A feminist literary critique, in which Heller examines the works of Paley and other women writers during the past two centuries to determine their varying treatments of the challenges of being both a woman and an artist. Describes how these women create female characters who are on quests for self-expression.

Iannone, Carol. "A Dissent on Grace Paley." *Commentary* 80 (August, 1985): 54-58. Iannone states that Paley's first collection of stories reveals talent. Her second, however, written when she was deeply involved in political activity, shows how a writer's imagination can become trapped by ideologies, not able to rise above them to make sense of the world. Iannone's comments on the intermingling of politics and art result in interesting interpretations of Paley's stories.

Isaacs, Neil D. *Grace Paley: A Study of the Short Fiction*. Boston: Twayne, 1990. An introduction to Paley's short fiction, providing a strong summary and critique of previous criticism. Also contains a section of Paley quotations, in which she talks about the nature of her fiction, her social commitment, and the development of her narrative language. Emphasizes Paley's focus on storytelling and narrative voice.

Marchant, Peter, and Earl Ingersoll, eds. "A Conversation with Grace Paley." *The Massachusetts Review* 26 (Winter, 1985): 606-614. A conversation with novelist Mary Elsie Robertson and writer Peter Marchant provides insights into Paley's transition from poetry to short stories, her interest in the lives of women, and the connection between her subject matter and her politics.

Meyer, Adam. "Faith and the 'Black Thing': Political Action and Self-Questioning in Grace Paley's Short Fiction." *Studies in Short Fiction* 31 (Winter, 1994): 79-89. Discusses how Paley, through the character of Faith Darwin, examines someone very much like herself while distancing herself from that person's activities.

Paley, Grace. "Grace Paley: Art Is on the Side of the Underdog." Interview by Harriet Shapiro. *Ms.* 11 (May, 1974): 43-45. This interview about Paley's life and politics succeeds in presenting her as a unique personality.

Schleifer, Ronald. "Grace Paley: Chaste Compactness." In *Contemporary American Women Writers: Narrative Strategies*, edited by Catherine Rainwater and William J. Scheick. Lexington: University Press of Kentucky, 1985. As Schleifer puts it, "Both little disturbances and enormous changes are brought together at the close of [Paley's] stories to create a sense of ordinary ongoingness that eschews the melodrama of closure."

Taylor, Jacqueline. *Grace Paley: Illuminating the Dark Lives*. Austin: University of Texas, 1990. Taylor focuses on what she calls Paley's "woman centered" point of view. Asserts that "Conversation with My Father" allows discussion of many of the narrative conventions her fiction tries to subvert; this story reveals the connection between Paley's recognition of the fluidity of life and her resistance to narrative resolution.

Norman Lavers
Updated by Louise M. Stone and Margaret Boe Birns

BREECE D'J PANCAKE

Born: South Charleston, West Virginia; June 29, 1952
Died: Charlottesville, Virginia; April 8, 1979

PRINCIPAL SHORT FICTION

The Stories of Breece D'J Pancake, 1983

OTHER LITERARY FORMS

Breece D'J Pancake (brees DEE-jay PAN-cayk) is known only for his short fiction.

ACHIEVEMENTS

Breece D'J Pancake did not live long enough to enjoy any recognition for his short fiction. In his lifetime, he received two fellowships from the University of Virginia, and he was awarded the West Virginia Library Association Annual Book Award posthumously. *The Atlantic*, which published several of his stories between 1977 and 1982, nominated his story collection for the Pulitzer Prize in 1983, the year of its publication by Little, Brown. Pancake lived to see several of his stories published, and he was solicited by *The New Yorker* for a story and by Doubleday for a novel. Pancake's sole book has gained recognition as one of the most important examples of contemporary Appalachian fiction, and his reputation continues to grow among serious short story writers.

BIOGRAPHY

Breece Dexter Pancake was born in Charleston, West Virginia, on June 29, 1952. His parents Clarence Robert Pancake and Helen Frazier chose the name Breece in the hospital the day after their son was born after seeing it in the *Charleston Gazette*'s sports section. Breece D'J Pancake's middle name, Dexter, was chosen by his father, and it was sometimes changed to David. When he became a novitiate of the Catholic Church in 1977, Pancake took "John" as his confirmation name. When the galley proof of "Trilobites," Pancake's first major publication, came back from *The Atlantic*, his middle initials were mistakenly printed as "D'J" instead of "D.J." Pancake laughed at the error and decided to let it stand, and this typographical quirk seemed to make his already curious name even more memorable.

Pancake grew up in Milton, West Virginia, originally a railroad town. Located in the Teays Valley, it was the perfect place for Pancake to hone his interest in folklore, history, and geology. Compelled to understand both the prehistoric and contemporary significance of the place that he was from, Pancake wandered around the valley, searching for secrets that the land held. He loved to hunt for arrowheads and fossils, especially the fossils of trilobites (the oldest form of life on the planet), an interest that came to define his work and led to his first major success, "Trilobites."

Pancake's interest in writing no doubt grew from his early love of storytelling and his wide exposure to the oral folk tradition of West Virginia. Early on, Pancake loved ghost stories, and he seemed to decide in high school that writing would be his vocation. He planned grand projects, including a war novel based on his father's letters and stories. An early interest in the macabre seemed to pave the way for Pancake's preoccupation with mortality. Pancake's other interests included painting and the earth sciences, and he considered going to college to study biology, hoping to become a biology teacher. He attended college at West Virginia Wesleyan in Buckhannon and shifted gears away from biology, discovering a deep interest in drama. In Buckhannon, Pancake discovered the folk songs of Phil Ochs, Woody Guthrie, and Gordon Lightfoot. Later, Pancake became fanatical about the work of Tom Waits, though it was Och's work that seemed to speak to him most of all. "Jim Dean of Indiana" was his favorite song, and John Casey quotes it at length in his foreword to an edition of *The Stories of Breece D'J Pancake.*

In 1971, after struggling at West Virginia Wesleyan, Pancake transferred to Marshall University, where he earned a B.A. in English education in 1974, aiming to become a high school English teacher. He traveled west to visit his sister and then taught at Fork Union Military Academy and Staunton Military Academy from 1974 to 1976. He attended graduate school at the University of Virginia in Charlottesville from 1976 to 1979, in the prestigious M.F.A. writing program there, studying with John Casey and James McPherson.

Pancake began attending Mass regularly in late 1976. In 1977, he became a novitiate in the Catholic Church. In Charlottesville, he distanced himself from the most cultivated students, preferring to spend his time hunting, camping, and fishing. Pancake worked on the staff of *The Virginia Quarterly Review* and formed lasting bonds with several of his teachers, including McPherson, Peter Taylor, and Richard Jones. He published several stories between 1976 and 1979, in *The Atlantic*, *Rivanna*, and *Nightwork*. He died of a self-inflicted gunshot wound on April 8, 1979, in Charlottesville. His death was ruled a suicide, though several of his family members believe it was accidental. It

is, perhaps, merely coincidental that Ochs, Pancake's hero, committed suicide on April 9, 1976, almost three years to the day before Pancake took his own life.

The Stories of Breece D'J Pancake was published in 1983 to wide acclaim, collecting his twelve stories, several of which had not been published in Pancake's lifetime. Pancake's stories were compared to Ernest Hemingway's early work in the short form, and Pancake inspired a new generation of writers to pen quiet, spare, character-driven stories deeply rooted in place. His reputation as a genius continues to grow, and the tragedy of his suicide hangs over his single collection.

ANALYSIS

Breece D'J Pancake's stories take place in the down-and-out, backwoods Appalachia region of West Virginia, and they concern desperate men, who often lead lives of isolation. Pancake's characters are emotionally distant and afraid of intimacy, sexual or otherwise. They are outsiders attempting to fill roles they feel they must to survive. Pancake's great devotion to broken characters is one of his most remarkable accomplishments as a writer. His ability to make the reader feel the suffering of prostitutes, lowlifes, wanderers, lost children, alcoholics, adulterers, and men and women of violence is uncanny; even more compelling is his great sympathy for such characters.

Pancake's stories are intense and intimate character portraits, and, thus, it is quite easy to lose track of the importance of place in his work. Even when the landscape and the history of Pancake's West Virginia seem to be secondary to character and plot, they are evident in a unique and sublime way. Pancake's world is defined by his deep-rootedness to the land. His understanding of West Virginia goes well beyond a drifter's familiarity with roads and hills. He has a real sense of the place's history, even before the time of man, and he often seems to be listening close to what the land has to say. His great love of storytelling and of sitting around and listening to people tell stories informs his style in a significant way. His spare, sharp prose is the product of a keen ear and of being raised in the oral tradition. His dialogue captures the voices of his characters without ever caricaturing their heritage, and this, too, is a product of a keen ear and of knowing what must be omitted and what must be preserved. Pancake's prose never comes close to local color, a danger often associated with regionalists. He is true to the land and his characters, aware of what they need to say and how they need to say it, and he is always faithful to the voice of the earth.

The reaction to *The Stories of Breece D'J Pancake* was immediate and zealous. A cult of readership grew up around Pancake's lone collection. Most serious students of the short story felt as if a great voice had been lost, one of the most genuine and honest voices of the twentieth century. Pancake's strong sense of place is often praised and so is his careful attention to detail in the name of evoking the distinctiveness of his oft-forgotten corner of America. Pancake's work has drawn comparisons to that of Hemingway, Flannery O'Connor, and others. Contemporary writers such as Andre Dubus III and Ann Pancake (a distant relative of Breece) count him as a major influence. If Pancake is often referred to as a regional writer, it is important to think of him in terms of a larger tradition, namely southern literature, and he has had a significant impact on writers such as Larry Brown, Bobbie Ann Mason, and Cormac McCarthy.

"TRILOBITES"

"Trilobites" is Pancake's best-known story, and it was his first major publication. Published by *The Atlantic* in 1977, "Trilobites" is the story of a young farmer named Colly, who--like Pancake--searches the hills of West Virginia for fossils. He yearns, seemingly above all else, to discover trilobites, artifacts of an age long gone. Colly is troubled by the death of his father and is deeply unsatisfied with his life on the family farm. He feels trapped and cut off from the world around him. When his mother tells him that the farm is to be sold, he feels strangely lost, knowing that he will not move with his mother to Akron. Colly's old girlfriend, Ginny, returns from college, and they have distant, mechanical sex. In the end, as Colly's world continues to collapse around him, he decides to head west, hopping a freight car and lighting out in his father's footsteps.

"Trilobites" is indicative of Pancake's work, both thematically and stylistically. A young, desperate man longs for something else, yet he is tied to his home land. He is lonely and isolated, and he dreams of a world bigger than the one he knows. The story is never predictable, as Pancake does not have Colly leave and come back, realizing that everything he needs is in his home. Colly knows that the only way to survive is to escape. In this early story, Pancake's voice appears to be fully formed, quite a remarkable achievement for such a young writer. In addition, apparent is Pancake's preoccupation with broken love, a theme that would haunt him until his death. For Colly (and for Pancake), the past is always rearing up its ugly head in the form of lost lovers and dead fathers. "Trilobites" is also typical of Pancake's work in that it is character-driven and does not rely on empty, formulaic plot techniques; instead, the reader glimpses Colly's mind in crisis mode.

"A ROOM FOREVER"

"A Room Forever" is one of Pancake's most devastating stories. It is narrated by a young man, who has just arrived in a river town from a tug called the *Delmar*. Considering the possibility of suicide, he takes up with an underage prostitute, a girl of fourteen or fifteen, for whom he feels sorry and yet uses in the same ways she is normally used. The story chronicles his futile attempts to reach out to the lost girl after the business of paid-for sex is over. The young man feels hopeless, and he recognizes the same kind of hopelessness in the girl, and he has a refrain running through is head that there are no breaks in the world, that nobody gets any breaks. After the girl leaves their hotel room, he runs into her later at a bar and sees that she is drunk, having used the money he gave her to buy booze. She disappears while he is not paying attention, and he goes out to find her slumped against a wall, her wrists cut, not yet dead. He reports that she has attempted suicide and claims not to know her.

This is familiar territory for Pancake. A depressed young man and a broken young girl come together in a thunderclap of futility and numbness. There is nothing romantic about their encounter, nothing sacred, only the everlasting promise that things often go from bad to worse. "A Room Forever," written in the last year of Pancake's life, is often cited as evidence of his state of mind, leading up to his suicide. Both characters are destitute of spirit, lost in an unforgiving world, and Pancake seems to be making some sort of comment on the hard reality of dark impulses.

"IN THE DRY"

Published in August, 1978, just a few months before Pancake's death, "In the Dry" chronicles the return of Ottie, a nonunion truck driver, to his foster family's home in Appalachia. The title is a biblical allusion (it comes from Luke 23), and the story is loaded with Pancake's quintessential concerns for the prodigal son. During the visit, Ottie's family is seemingly repulsed by him, holding on to the feeling that he was responsible for his foster brother's injuries in a car wreck. Bus, his foster brother, is not dead but paralyzed, and Ottie is haunted by his mistakes. Unlike many of Pancake's protagonists, Ottie is not ruined by a lost love, but reduced to confusion by a love he cannot have. His foster sister, Sheila, wants to sleep with him.

The real reason for Ottie's return is that he seeks redemption. He wants to be forgiven by his foster father, who had put all of his hope in Bus and blames Ottie for his accident. On a technical level, Pancake astonishes in this story, as he seems to follow Hemingway's theory of omission. The accident is the most crucial event in the story and yet the reader knows next to nothing about what actually happened. Ottie is no help, as he cannot remember. Unlike Colly in "Trilobites," Ottie is unable escape to the past for answers; instead, he must move forward into a barren and unforgiving future.

Redemption is impossible. The Gerlocks, his foster parents, are incapable of love and forgiveness. Ottie discovers that the only kind of atonement available to him is of the awful and perilous variety, a realization that many of Pancake's characters are forced to have.

BIBLIOGRAPHY

Douglass, Thomas E. *A Room Forever: The Life, Work, and Letters of Breece D'J Pancake*. Knoxville: University of Tennessee Press, 1998. The most important book on Pancake mixes biography and analysis in part 1 and includes Pancake's unpublished work, mostly letters and fragments, in part 2. An invaluable source for those interested in reading beyond Pancake's stories, and the only serious academic work wholly devoted to Pancake.

Finnegan, Brian. "Road Stories That Stay Home: Car and Driver in Appalachia and *The Stories of Breece D'J Pancake*." *southern Literary Journal* 29, no. 2 (Summer, 1997): 87-102. Focuses on the liberation of the male individual in American literature, focusing on Pancake's stories.

Harpham, Geoffrey Galt. "Short Stack: *The Stories of Breece D'J Pancake*." *Studies in Short Fiction* 23, no. 3 (Summer, 1986): 265-273. A study on the depiction of West Virginia in Pancake's stories. Examines notions of the past and the importance of background and environment on Pancake's characters.

Hunt, Samantha. "The Agony of Influence." *Poets and Writers* 37, no. 6 (November/December, 2009): 23-26. Hunt's short article deals with Pancake's influence on her, despite her seeming incompatibility with him, and focuses on several of his main themes: alcoholism, incest, adultery, and prostitution.

Kadohata, Cynthia. "Breece D'J Pancake." *Mississippi Review* 18, no. 1 (1989): 35-61. Kodohata's essays is a biographical and critical profile of Pancake's life and work.

Stevens, David. "Writing Region Across the Border: Two Stories of Breece Pancake and Alistair MacLeod." *Studies in Short Fiction* 33, no. 2 (Spring, 1996): 263-271. Consideration of Pancake and MacLeod as important regional writers.

Wilhelm, Albert E. "Poverty of Spirit in Breece Pancake's Stories." *Critique* 28, no. 1 (Fall, 1986): 39-44. Variations on the general theme of spiritual poverty in Pancake's stories. Seeks to illuminate Pancake's portrayal of men in the grip of poverty.

William Boyle

DOROTHY PARKER

Born: West End, New Jersey; August 22, 1893
Died: New York, New York; June 7, 1967
Also known as: Dorothy Parker Campbell

PRINCIPAL SHORT FICTION

"Big Blonde," 1929
Laments for the Living, 1930
After Such Pleasures, 1933
Here Lies: The Collected Stories, 1939
The Portable Dorothy Parker, 1944
The Penguin Dorothy Parker, 1977
Complete Stories, 1995

OTHER LITERARY FORMS

Dorothy Parker's principal writings, identified by Alexander Woolcott as "a potent distillation of nectar and wormwood," are short stories and verse--not serious "poetry," she claimed. Her poetic volumes include *Enough Rope* (1926), *Sunset Gun* (1928), and *Death and Taxes* (1931)--mostly lamentations for loves lost, never found, or gone awry. She wrote witty drama reviews for *Vanity Fair* (1918-1920), *Ainslee's* (1920-1933), and *The New Yorker* (1931); and terse, tart book reviews for *The New Yorker* (1927-1933) and *Esquire* (1959-1962). "Tonstant Weader Fwowed Up," her provoked, personal reaction to A. A. Milne's *The House at Pooh Corner* (1928), typifies her "delicate claws of . . . superb viciousness" (Woolcott). Parker's major plays are *The Coast of Illyria* (pr. 1949), about Charles and Mary Lamb's tortured lives, and *The Ladies of the Corridor* (pr., pb. 1953), three case studies of death-in-life among elderly women.

ACHIEVEMENTS

Dorothy Parker's career flashed brilliantly in the 1920's and early 1930's and then faded equally quickly as the world she portrayed in her stories and poems disappeared into the hardships of the Depression. Her stories are sharp, witty portraits of an age when social and sexual conventions were changing rapidly. Her dramatic monologues, usually spoken by unself-confident women, her sharp social satires, and her careful delineations of scenes and situations reveal the changing mores of the 1920's. They also, however, portray the attendants of rapid social change: anxiety, lack of communication, and differing expectations of men and women of what social and sexual roles should be. These problems continue into contemporary times, and Parker's incisive writing captures them well. Her writings are like herself--witty and sad.

Her stories, verse, and reviews appeared in, and helped to set the tone of, the newly founded *The New Yorker*, which began publication in 1925, and she remained an occasional contributor until 1955.

BIOGRAPHY

Educated at Miss Dana's School in Morristown, New Jersey, Dorothy Rothschild Parker wrote fashion blurbs and drama criticism for *Vanity Fair*, short stories for *The New Yorker* irregularly, Hollywood screenplays at intervals (1934-1954), and *Esquire* book reviews (1959-1962). Her marriage to Edwin Pond Parker (1917-1928) was succeeded by two marriages to bisexual actor-writer Alan Campbell (1934-1947; 1950-1963, when Campbell died). Campbell, Lillian Hellman, and others nurtured Parker, but they could not control her drinking and her worsening writer's block that kept her from finishing many of her literary attempts during her last fifteen years.

ANALYSIS

Dorothy Parker's best-known stories are "The Waltz," "A Telephone Call," and her masterpiece, "Big Blonde," winner of the O. Henry Memorial Prize for the best short story of 1929.

"THE WALTZ"

"The Waltz" and "A Telephone Call," both dramatic monologues, present typical Parker characters, insecure young women who derive their social and personal acceptance from the approval of men and who go to extremes, whether sincere or hypocritical, to maintain this approbation. The characters, anonymous and therefore legion, elicit from the readers a mixture of sympathy and ridicule. They evoke sympathy because each is agonizing in an uncomfortable situation which she believes herself powerless to control. The waltzer is stuck with a bad, boorish dancer-- "two stumbles, slip, and a twenty-yard dash." The other woman is longing for a telephone call from a man she loves who does not reciprocate her concern: "Please, God, let him telephone me now, Dear God, let him call me now. I won't ask anything else of You. . . ."

These predicaments are largely self-imposed as well as trivial and so they are ludicrous, unwittingly burlesqued through the narrators' hyperbolic perspectives. Both women are trapped in situations they have permitted to occur but from which they lack the resourcefulness or assertiveness to extricate themselves. The waltzer not only accepts the invitation to dance but also hypocritically flatters her partner: "Oh, they're going to play another encore. Oh, goody. Oh, that's lovely. Tired? I should say I'm not tired. I'd like to go on like this forever." These cloying words mask the truth, which she utters only to herself and to the eavesdropping audience: "I should say I'm not tired. I'm dead, that's all I am. Dead . . . and the music is never going to stop playing. . . ." Enslaved by an exaggerated code of politeness, therefore, she catches herself in the network of her own lies: "Oh, they've stopped, the mean things. They're not going to play any more. Oh, darn." Then she sets herself up for yet another round of hypocritical self-torture: "Do you really think so, if you gave them twenty dollars? . . . Do tell them to play this same thing. I'd simply adore to go on waltzing."

"A TELEPHONE CALL"

Like the waltzer, the narrator in "A Telephone Call" is her own worst enemy. Suffering from too much time on her hands--she is evidently not occupied with a job or responsibility for anyone but herself--she can afford the self-indulgence to spend hours focused exclusively on the dubious prospect of a phone call. She plays games with God; her catechism is a parody: "You see, God, if You would just let him telephone me, I wouldn't have to ask You . . . for anything more." She plays games with herself: "Maybe if I counted five hundred by fives, it might ring by that time. I'll count slowly. I won't cheat." She is totally preoccupied with herself and her futile efforts to fan the embers of a dying love; having violated the social code by phoning her former admirer at his office, by the monologue's end she is desperately preparing to violate it again by calling him at home. Nevertheless, she is ludicrous rather than pathetic because her concern is so superficial (although her concentration on the anticipated phone call is also a barrier against the more serious reality of the estrangement); her calculations so trivial ("I'll count five hundred by fives, and if he hasn't called me then, I will know God isn't going to help me, ever again"); and the stakes for which she prays so low (attempting to manipulate God's will in such a minor matter). She, like the waltzer, envisions a simplistic fairy-tale solution dependent on the agency of another.

Dorothy Parker (Library of Congress)

Thus the plots of these slight stories are as slender as the resources of the monologist narrators, for whom formulaic prayers or serial wisecracks ("I'd like to [dance] awfully, but I'm having labor pains. . . . It's so nice to meet a man who isn't a scaredy-cat about catching my beri-beri") are inadequate to alter their situations. Such narratives, with their fixed perspectives, exploitation of a single, petty issue, and simple characters, have to be short. To be any longer would be to add redundance without complexity, to bore rather than to amuse with verbal pyrotechnics.

"Big Blonde"

Although "Big Blonde" shares some of the features of the monologues, it is far more complex in narrative mode and in characterization. Rather than anatomizing a moment in time, as do the monologues, "Big Blonde" covers an indefinite span of years, perhaps a dozen. The story moves from comedy into pathos as its protagonist, Hazel Morse, moves from genuine gaiety to forced conviviality, undergirded by the hazy remorse that her name connotes.

Hazel, "a large, fair," unreflective, voluptuous blonde, has been, in her twenties, by day a "model in a wholesale dress establishment," and for "a couple of thousand evenings . . . a good sport among her [numerous] male acquaintances." Having "come to be more conscientious than spontaneous" about her enjoyment of men's jokes and drunken antics, she escapes into what she unthinkingly assumes will be a stereotype of marriage, isolation from the outer world à deux, but what instead becomes a travesty. She revels in honesty--the freedom to stop being incessantly cheerful and to indulge in the other side of the conventional feminine role that is her life's allotment, the freedom to weep sentimental tears over various manifestations, large and small, of "all the sadness there is in the world."

Her husband, Herbie, is "not amused" at her tears and impersonal sorrows: "crab, crab, crab, that was all she ever did." To transform her from "a lousy sport" into her former jocular self he encourages her to drink, "Atta girl! . . . Let's see you get boiled, baby." Having neither the intellectual, imaginative, nor domestic resources to hold her marriage together any other way, Hazel acquiesces, even though she hates "the taste of

liquor," and soon begins to drink steadily. Herbie, however, is as barren of human resources as is his wife, and alcohol only ignites their smoldering anger, despite Hazel's "thin and wordless idea that, maybe, this night, things would begin to be all right." They are not; Herbie fades out of Hazel's alcohol-blurred existence as Ed merges into it. He, too, insists "upon gaiety" and will not "listen to admissions of aches or weariness"-- nor will Ed's successors, Charley, Sydney, Fred, Billy, and others, to whom Hazel responds with forced cordiality through her alcoholic haze in which the days and years lose "their individuality."

By now perpetually "tired and blue," she becomes frightened when her "old friend" whiskey fails her, and she decides, having no ties, no talents, and no purpose in living, to commit suicide by taking twenty sleeping pills-- "Well, here's mud in your eye." In her customary vagueness she fails again, however, causing the impersonal attendants, a reluctant doctor and housemaid, more annoyance than concern. She concludes that she might as well live, but with a paradoxical prayer of diabolic self-destructiveness: "Oh, please, please, let her be able to get drunk, please keep her always drunk."

Although in both "Big Blonde" and the monologues Parker satirizes vapid, unassertive women with empty lives, her work carries with it satire's inevitable message of dissatisfaction with the status quo and an implicit plea for reform. For in subtle ways Parker makes a feminist plea even through her most passive, vacuous characters. Women ought to be open, assertive, independent; they should think for themselves and act on their own behalf, because men cannot be counted on to do it for them. They should be their own persons, like Geoffrey Chaucer's Wife of Bath, "wel at ease," instead of allowing their happiness to depend on the waxing and waning affections and attentions of inconstant men.

To the extent that Dorothy Parker was a satirist, she was also a moralist. In satirizing aimless, frivolous, or social-climbing lives, she implied a purposeful ideal. In ridiculing self-deception, hypocrisy, obsequiousness, and flattery, she advocated honesty in behavior and communication. In her epigrams, the moralist's rapiers, she could hone a razor-edge with the best. In her portraits, cameos etched in acid, the touchstone of truth shines clear.

OTHER MAJOR WORKS

PLAYS: *Nero*, pr. 1922 (with Robert Benchley); *Close Harmony: Or, The Lady Next Door*, pr. 1924 (with Elmer Rice); *The Coast of Illyria*, pr. 1949 (with Ross Evans); *The Ladies of the Corridor*, pr., pb. 1953 (with Arnaud d'Usseau).

SCREENPLAYS: *Business Is Business*, 1925 (with George S. Kaufman); *Here Is My Heart*, 1934 (with Alan Campbell); *Big Broadcast of 1936*, 1935 (with Campbell); *Hands Across the Table*, 1935; *Mary Burns, Fugitive*, 1935; *One Hour Late*, 1935 (with Campbell); *Paris in Spring*, 1935; *Lady Be Careful*, 1936 (with Campbell and Harry Ruskin); *Suzy*, 1936 (with Campbell, Horace Jackson, and Lenore Coffee); *The Moon's Our Home*, 1936; *Three Married Men*, 1936 (with Campbell); *A Star Is Born*, 1937 (with Campbell and Robert Carson); *Woman Chases Man*, 1937 (with Joe Bigelow); *Crime Takes a Holiday*, 1938; *Flight into Nowhere*, 1938; *Sweethearts*, 1938 (with Campbell); *Trade Winds*, 1938 (with Campbell and Frank R. Adams); *Five Little Peppers and How They Grew*, 1939; *The Little Foxes*, 1941; *Weekend for Three*, 1941 (with Campbell); *Saboteur*, 1942 (with Campbell, Peter Viertel, and Joan Harrison); *A Gentle Gangster*, 1943; *Mr. Skeffington*, 1944; *Smash-Up: The Story of a Woman*, 1947 (with Frank Cavett); *The Fan*, 1949 (with Walter Reisch and Ross Evans); *Queen for a Day*, 1951; *A Star Is Born*, 1954.

POETRY: *Enough Rope*, 1926; *Sunset Gun*, 1928; *Death and Taxes*, 1931; *Not So Deep as a Well*, 1936; *Not Much Fun*, 1996; *Complete Poems*, 1999.

BIBLIOGRAPHY

Calhoun, Randall. *Dorothy Parker: A Bio-Bibliography*. Westport, Conn.: Greenwood Press, 1993. A helpful guide for the student of Parker. Includes bibliographical references and an index.

Freibert, Lucy M. "Dorothy Parker." *American Short Story Writers, 1910-1945*, edited by Bobby Ellen Kimbel. Vol. 86 in *Dictionary of Literary Biography*. Detroit: Gale Research, 1989. Freibert's excellent entry on Parker provides some general biographical information and close readings of some of her most important stories. Includes a bibliography of Parker's work and a critical bibliography.

Gelfant, Blanche H., ed. *The Columbia Companion to the Twentieth-Century American Short Story*. New York: Columbia University Press, 2000. Includes a chapter in which Parker's short stories are analyzed.

Gillette, Meg. "Bedside Manners in Dorothy Parker's 'Lady with a Lamp" and Kay Boyle's *My Next Bride*." *Studies in American Fiction* 35, no. 2 (Autumn, 2007): 159-179. Compares Parker's story and Boyle's novel, both of which are abortion narratives set in the United States during the Great Depression. Discusses the social aspects of these works and how they differ from abortion narratives written in the twenty-first century.

Keats, John. *You Might as Well Live: The Life and Times of Dorothy Parker*. New York: Simon & Schuster, 1970. Keats's book was the first popular biography published on Parker and it is quite thorough and readable. Supplemented by a bibliography and an index.

Kinney, Arthur F. *Dorothy Parker, Revised*. New York: Twayne, 1998. Argues that what appears monotonal in Parker's work is a compound of complicated voices, for her work is dialogic and polyvocal. Traces the influences and sources of her work and assesses her achievements. Provides a summary survey of Parker's short-story collections, including publishing history and critical reception.

Meade, Marion. *Dorothy Parker: What Fresh Hell Is This?* London: Heinemann, 1987. Meade has produced a good, thorough biography that relates events in Parker's fiction to situations in her life. Nevertheless, Meade's focus is biographical and the discussion of Parker's work is mostly in passing. Includes notes and an index.

Melzer, Sondra. *The Rhetoric of Rage: Women in Dorothy Parker*. New York: Peter Lang, 1997. Explores Parker's depiction of female characters in her works.

Pettit, Rhonda S. ed. *The Critical Waltz: Essays on the Work of Dorothy Parker*. Madison, N.J.: Fairleigh Dickinson University Press, 2005. Collection of five new and eighteen reprinted essays analyzing Parker's written works, as well as a review of her letters to Alexander Woollcott and an interview with Parker conducted in the 1950's. Some of the essays discuss

Parker's relationship with her public, Parker as a feminist and social critic, her representation of "being and dying as a woman" in her short fiction, her political opinions, and the Freudian concepts in her work. Other essays analyze her short stories "Big Blonde" and "The Waltz."

_____, *A Gendered Collision: Sentimentalism and Modernism in Dorothy Parker's Poetry and Fiction.* Madison, N.J.: Fairleigh Dickinson, 2000. Challenges the conventional view of Parker as a humorist or a sentimentalist by reexamining her career in light of feminist scholarship. Describes how Parker's works display a collision of competing values, in which nineteenth century sentimentalism clashes with twentieth century modernism and decadence.

Simpson, Amelia. "Black on Blonde: The Africanist Presence in Dorothy Parker's 'Big Blonde.'" *College Literature* 23 (October, 1996): 105-116. Maintains that "Big Blonde" exposes how race and gender are mutually constitutive and how blackness contests and constructs the privilege of whiteness. Argues that three seemingly unimportant African figures are the key to this narrative about the subjugation of white women in America.

Walker, Nancy A. "The Remarkably Constant Reader: Dorothy Parker as Book Reviewer." *Studies in American Humor*, n.s. 3, no. 4 (1997): 1-14. A discussion of Parker's book reviews for *The New Yorker* from 1927 to 1933 and for *Esquire* from 1957 to 1962 as a reflection of her literary sensibility.

Lynn Z. Bloom
Updated by Karen M. Cleveland Marwick

EDITH PEARLMAN

Born: Providence, Rhode Island; June 26, 1936

PRINCIPAL SHORT FICTION

Vaquita, and Other Stories, 1996
Love Among the Greats, and Other Stories, 2002
How to Fall, and Other Stories, 2005
Binocular Vision: New and Selected Stories, 2011

OTHER LITERARY FORMS

While primarily a writer of short stories, Edith Pearlman also has written several articles for the travel pages of *The New York Times*, about Japan, Israel, England, and such European countries as Hungary. Her travel writing also appears in the 1998 anthology *An Inn Near Kyoto: Writing by American Women Abroad* and in the 2006 anthology *Prague and the Czech Republic: True Stories*. Other Pearlman essays have been published by *Smithsonian* and *The Atlantic*.

ACHIEVEMENTS

Edith Pearlman's short stories have received multiple awards since 1978, when she received her first O. Henry Prize for "Hanging Fire." Subsequent O. Henry Awards recognized "Conveniences" in 1984 and "The Story" in 2003. The PEN Syndicated Fiction Project, which changed its name to the Sound of Writing, selected "Boy Meets Girl" in 1987 and "Some Turbulence" for awards in 1991. In 1996, Pearlman's first collection, *Vaquita, and Other Stories*, received the Spokane Prize for Fiction and the Drue Heinz Prize for Literature. *The Writer's Handbook* selected "A Platter of Admonitions," "The Statue in the Slab," and "One Liar's Beginnings" as the best articles in 1995, 1996, and 1999. Garrison Keillor selected Pearlman's "Chance" as one of the best American short stories of the year in 1998. In 1999, "Accommodators" received the *Antioch Review* Award for Distinguished Fiction, and in 2000 "Allog" was selected as a Best American Short Story. In 2001, Pearlman's second collection, *Love Among the Greats, and Other Stories* won the Spokane Prize for Short Fiction, and her third collection, *How to Fall, and Other Stories*, was awarded the Mary McCarthy Prize in Short Fiction in 2003. Other award-winning stories have been "Mates," which won the Pushcart Prize; "Vegetarian Chili," which received the National Public Radio Award; "Madame Guralnik," which was awarded the *Boston Review* Second Prize; and "If Love Were All," which won the Moment Fiction Second Prize.

BIOGRAPHY

Edith Pearlman was born June 26, 1936, in Providence, Rhode Island, to a middle-class Jewish family. She was educated at Lincoln School, a private Quaker school for girls, and subsequently entered Radcliffe University, from which she graduated in 1957. Pearlman worked for ten years for a computer firm as a programmer before becoming a writer. She has two grown children, and has traveled extensively. With her husband, she settled in Brookline, Massachusetts, where she has been active in community governance and charity and enjoys reading and walking. Her favorite author is Charles Dickens, and her highest value is accommodation. As literary influences, Pearlman lists Colette, Sylvia Townsend Warner, and Penelope Fitzgerald. She has more than 250 published stories and essays.

ANALYSIS

While Edith Pearlman eschews autobiographical stories, the settings and characters of many of her stories reflect the people and places with whom she has been associated. Her stories, however, explore a wide variety of characters: male and female, gay and straight, young and old, American and foreign. These characters interact in eras from pre-World War II to the present and in locations from South America and Eastern Europe to Israel and the mythical town of Godolphin, Massachusetts. Several stories are linked, featuring the same characters and settings. In all of these stories' diversity, however, Pearlman's primary interest is in exploring relationships.

Pearlman's signature style is an economy of words. Her stories are short, never more than twenty pages and often less than ten. Dialogues are tightly controlled, and the actions of her characters tend to be small, believable, and ordinary, but carefully selected for significance or symbolic meaning. Pearlman enjoys using metaphorical verbs, as in "her hair foamed," and other shorthand reductions to take the place of lengthy description. She likes her characters, treating them with affection and sometimes a witty irony that is never cutting or bitter. Her vision is realistic and clearsighted, not sentimental, but even when the stories end with loss or failure, the overarching narrative attitude is affirmation and compassion for the human condition.

The lessons or morals to be derived from Pearlman's stories are subtle and sometimes elusive. Although the incidents depicted tend to be undramatic, and the tone whimsical, the themes are serious ones: illness and death, war, marriage struggles and divorce, natural disasters, hunger, disability, familial estrangement, poverty. Always the focus is on human accommodation and response to such adverse conditions, individually or collectively, and the reader comes to know the thoughts, secrets, and struggles of those who attempt to deal with these events.

Reviewers of Pearlman's stories praise her wit, her light touch, and her poignant portraits and her elegant, compact writing. Her characters have been described as off-kilter and eccentric, their characterizations as subtle and deft, her plots as restrained and simple, and her stories as buoyant and satisfying. The effect of reading them is an enhanced understanding and appreciation of human beings as they cope with the varying circumstances of their lives.

"VAQUITA"

"Vaquita" is the title story of Pearlman's first published collection. Its protagonist, Señora Marta Perera de Lefkowitz, is the elderly cigarette-smoking minister of health of a revolution-torn Latin American country. She is known as La Vaca-- "the cow"--both because of her emphasis on breast-feeding and because of an incident in her youth when, as a Polish Jew hiding from the Nazis, she had spent a year sharing a stall with a cow. Subject to imminent arrest by the revolutionaries, Señora Perera nevertheless goes about her health-inspection business via helicopter and motorbike, dealing with ignorance, shortages, and corruption in the field clinics with resignation. In the woods, she meets a teenage Indian mother with her baby, whom she counsels to continue breast-feeding as long as possible for her child's health. Acting on impulse, she gives the girl the diamond brooch, with which Señora Perera had planned to finance her escape and retirement to Israel.

This story epitomizes Pearlman's interest in people in peculiar circumstances who seek, despite opposition, to do the right thing. She does not glamorize or idealize such individuals, but presents them with their flawed pasts and problems, still trying to answer the summons of whatever force has called them into service.

"LOVE AMONG THE GREATS"

This is the first of three stories about Michal, a Jewish literary student at Harvard, who meets and marries a kindred spirit named Bellamy Berkowitz. Bellamy, who turns out to be gay, leaves her within a year, and this and her father's stroke throw Michal into an anorexic depression. Working as a framer by day, she spends all her evenings in the stacks at Widener Library, reading. On a job she meets and falls in love with Malachi, a black pediatrician, who is not interested in her. She tries dating others but, disillusioned, returns to the library. One night Malachi shows up in the stacks, looking for her. They spend a night of love among the books and marry in a hybrid civil-Jewish ceremony. Pearlman not only demonstrates humor, wit, and a light touch in describing the anguish of love and a failed marriage but also explores the universal problem of uneven levels of emotional commitment in relationships, themes that will appear in many other stories.

"VEGETARIAN CHILI"

This award-winning short-short story, included in *How to Fall*, purports to be a letter from Donna Crowninshield, manager of a women's soup kitchen in the fictional Boston suburb of Godolphin. Donna has received an ill-informed invitation from *Cuisine* to become a "guest chef" and submit a crowd-pleasing recipe for the magazine. In this letter, she replies with a tongue-in-cheek description of how she manages to put together the day's soup, while dealing with the exigencies of her establishment.

Many of Pearlman's stories are set in Godolphin, and many of these center on Donna's soup kitchen, its volunteers, and its guests. The author, who has worked in a soup kitchen, examines the ironies and problems of

charity work and the relationships of those who administer help and those who receive it. "Vegetarian Chili" humorously illustrates the gap in understanding between the urban American upper and lower classes, which mirrors the financial gap between not only the classes but also the institutions that serve them.

"THE STORY"

"The Story," first published in the *Alaska Quarterly Review*, was awarded the O. Henry Prize in 2003. It is set in the Massachusetts town of Godolphin, deprecatingly described as "not so much out of fashion as beyond its reach." Harry and Lucienne Savitsky, retired high-school teachers, are having dinner at The Hussar, an embarrassingly pathetic new Hungarian restaurant, with Justin and Judith da Costa, whose son is married to their daughter. The couples meet for dinner once a year to apportion the holiday visitations of their children between them. The unpretentious and overweight Savitskys are self-conscious around the lean, fashionable, and severe da Costas, with whom they have nothing in common but their children, and struggle to find topics of conversation. Harry is waiting for his wife to tell "the story," to relate the stark and dramatic tale of how her father, captured by the Nazis along with her twelve-year-old brother, disavowed his son as "some Goy." The lie caused the soldiers to let the boy go and enabled the youngster's escape that night along with the remainder of the family to Holland and subsequently to Argentina. Lucienne tells this story to sympathetic acquaintances as a turning point in their relationship, pointing toward intimacy, and has not yet told it to the da Costas. An approach is made to the subject of fathers--Judith's father has died--and Justin asks about Lucienne's, but she shrugs and leaves the restaurant.

The poignancy of this story lies in the parallelism between the ways in which Lucienne and her dead father deny knowledge of family relationship in order to protect that relationship from alien intrusion. The da Costas, by declining to accommodate themselves to their son's in-laws, have cut themselves off from an enhanced family relationship with the Savitskys. Just as they limit and apportion their children's holiday visits with each other, the couples will restrict their sharing of family stories and thus preclude the accompanying sympathy those stories engender.

"CHANCE"

"Chance" was selected as a Best American Short Story in 1998. It is included in *Love Among the Greats*. The narrator of the story tells of a time when, as a Jewish teenager, her synagogue was chosen at random to receive a Torah that had belonged to a destroyed village in Czechoslovakia. Bickering and quarrels among the rabbi, sexton, cantor's wife, and other members of the Committee of the Scroll finally decide that the scroll will be locked in the basement of the synagogue until a convenient time is selected to accept it officially. The narrator describes the meetings of the Torah Study Group at her home, which were really poker games, and the eccentricities, foibles, and weaknesses of the various players. She then describes the ceremony at which the Czechoslovakian Torah is formally installed. There is reverence and solemn emotion for the dead Czech congregation, but the narrator envisions them as being various and speckled in their virtues, just like their American counterparts.

This vignette considers the randomness and unpredictability of all events, drawing parallels between a poker game and human history. The tragic solemnity of a relic Torah is juxtaposed with the mundanity of a decaying Halloween pumpkin. The unwitting success of a poker bluff is considered alongside a village's genocidal extinction. Through all this, people are people, with their annoying mannerisms, their idiosyncratic beliefs, their secret yearnings, and the ways in which they cope with their various problems. While they respect the past, still death must give way to new life, just as the Torah's presentation must wait until after the Lehrman-Grossman wedding.

"ALLOG"

Pearlman's "Allog" was a Best American Short Story of 2000 and appears in *Love Among the Greats*. It is set in modern-day Jerusalem, in an apartment building occupied by an assortment of tenants, all with problems. One such tenant, eighty-five-year-old Mrs. Goldfanger, unable to care for her invalid husband, hires the services of a Southeast Asian man known as Joe. The other tenants speculate darkly about the foreigner's arrival. While Joe is hired only for elder care, he repairs Mr. Goldfanger's wheelchair and their stereo. Soon he is also repairing appliances for the Moroccan family, playing chess with the old widower and carrying his groceries upstairs, and chaperoning a schoolgirl on her walks. Eventually, when one of the tenants dies despite Joe's attempts to resuscitate her, he and his family move into the vacated apartment that the dead woman has bequeathed to his wife. Joe has become the instrument of community for the building's residents--their troubleshooter, confessor, and decision maker--in his native language, its "allog." Just as Joe has come to be not only accepted but also indispensable to his community, this word eventually comes to be part of the Israeli vocabulary.

This warm story features one of Pearlman's favorite themes: accommodation. It shows the adaptation of its characters--all with troubled Jewish pasts--to life in a new country and to the presence of an alien from an entirely different culture, who likewise adjusts to living with them in an unfamiliar nation. Whereas each character has foibles and eccentricities, Joe shows that these can be coped with and accepted, for the benefit of all.

BIBLIOGRAPHY

Kirkus Reviews. Review of *Love Among the Greats*, by Edith Pearlman. 70, no. 16 (August 15, 2002): 1170. Characterizes Pearlman's prose style and comments on her characterizations.

Pearlman, Edith. "One Fiction Writer's Beginnings." *Writer* 107, no. 2 (February, 1994). A history of how Pearlman began to write and developed into a short-story author; includes insights into what she has learned about fiction writing.

_____. "A Platter of Admonitions." *Writer* 107, no. 9 (September, 1994): 7. Pearlman gives her theory and values in writing short stories.

Summer, Joan Frank. "Book Review: *How to Fall*." *The Antioch Review* 63, no. 3 (Summer, 2005): 596. Discusses Pearlman's work as a whole and her prizes, as well as the specific collection of stories reviewed.

Sally B. Palmer

DALE PECK

Born: Bay Shore, New York; July 13, 1967

PRINCIPAL SHORT FICTION

"*Circumnavigation,*" 1990
"*The Dog Story,*" 1993
"*What We Lost,*" 1994
"*Rolling Back the Stone,*" 1997
"*Making Book,*" 1999
"*The Law of Diminishing Returns,*" 1999
"*Bliss,*" 2000
"*Cities of the Plain,*" 2002
"*Dues,*" 2004
"*Sky Writing,*" 2004
"*St. Anthony of the Vine,*" 2008

OTHER LITERARY FORMS

A successful writer in a variety of venues, Dale Peck has written five novels, including *Martin and John* (1993), *The Law of Enclosures* (1996), *Now It's Time to Say Goodbye* (1998), *The Garden of Lost and Found* (2007), and *Body Surfing* (2009). Peck has three young-adult titles to his credit: *Drift House: The First Voyage* (2005), *The Lost Cities: A Drift House Voyage* (2007), and *Sprout* (2009). Peck is the author of two nonfiction titles: *What We Lost: Based on a True Story* (2003) and *Hatchet Jobs: Writings on Contemporary Fiction* (2004).

Peck has been well known as a literary critic. His criticism has appeared in such magazines and newspapers as *The New Republic*, *The New York Times Book Review*, *The Village Voice*, and the *Los Angeles Times*. In collaboration with Calvin Baker, Peck has been an editor and developer of young-adult books. In 2000, Peck's screenplay, written with John Greyson, titled *The Law of Enclosures*, was released. Peck has been a contributing editor and columnist for *Out* magazine.

ACHIEVEMENTS

Peck's short story "Dues" won both a Pushcart Prize and an O. Henry Short Fiction Award in 2004. The short story "Bliss" won an O. Henry Short Fiction Award in 2001. Peck was awarded a John Simon Guggenheim Memorial Fellowship in 1995. Peck's 2009 young-adult novel *Sprout* won the Lambda Literary Award in the lesbian, gay, bisexual, and transgender category, for LGBT Children's-Young Adult Literature, and this work also was a finalist for the Stonewall Book Award in the Children's and Young Adult Literature Division.

BIOGRAPHY

Born on Long Island in Bay Shore to Dale and Eileen Peck, Dale Peck grew up in Kansas, where he lived from the ages of seven to eighteen. He graduated from Drew University in New Jersey in 1989. Openly gay, Peck was a member of ACT UP, an acquired immunodeficiency syndrome (AIDS) activist group in New York City. Peck's first short fiction was written soon after his college graduation, and his first novel, *Martin and John*, was published in 1993. Peck was awarded a Guggenheim Fellowship in 1995, and his short fiction has appeared in such publications as *The Nation*, *Threepenny Review*, *Granta*, *Zoetrope*, and *Tin House*. In addition to short stories, Peck is known as an author of long fiction, nonfiction, and young-adult titles.

Peck gained infamy in the literary world because of his scathing reviews, notably his review of Rick Moody's *Black Veil* (2002), for which Peck's review began with the blunt statement "Rick Moody is the worst writer of his generation." For this review and similar offerings, Peck was once known as the "most hated man in literature." Peck's reviews appearing in *The New Republic* from 2000 to 2003 and elsewhere were the focus of the author's 2004 nonfiction title *Hatchet Jobs: Writings on Contemporary*

Fiction. Peck has taught creative writing at the New School in New York City.

ANALYSIS

Dale Peck's short fiction is melodramatic, with serious themes addressed in a disarming way. The author's main characters are a blending of matter-of-fact, efficient narrators and teasing, toying, tongue-in-cheek tattlers telling stories with a smirk and a winking eye. He softens the subjects of disease, violence, and a harsh, uncaring world with a gentle but often twisted humor in the telling of each story. Disturbing things happen in Peck's short stories, and the author's method seems to be shocking the reader after first misleading the reader with either naughty innuendo or dull routine. Either way, the truth of each story seems to come quickly from around a corner, never seen from a distance to provide sufficient forewarning.

The main characters are often gay men, and a sense of loss often pervades a story. The main character has lost a love--a mother, a father, or another close family member, a dead lover--whose continued presence or influence haunts the main character. The deceased is taken too early in life, before the main character has an opportunity to know him or her better, to express fully main character's proper love and appreciation. Closure is not an option.

Whether the setting is the plains of Kansas or the streets of New York, Peck draws the reader a spare image. Much is left to the imagination, as Peck's style spends little time on the motivations of characters. The author seems to be saying, "This is just what it is, that's all." Insights and deeper meanings are left for reviewers and other writers to ponder.

"BLISS"

A five-year-old boy sat alone at home with the body of his dead twenty-six-year-old mother. The mother's killer-- a man named Shenandoah Manson--went to prison for nineteen years. The killer, terribly near-sighted, was a thief who was surprised in mid-robbery, and the boy's mother tripped and fell to her death down a flight of stairs. The killer never really saw the boy's mother because he lost his glasses in the panic. The lost glasses led to the killer's arrest.

The little boy grows into a young man, gay and living alone. He sits in his car outside the prison on the day Manson is released. The young man drives Manson to young man's home, the same home in which the young man's mother had died. The young man provides the killer, whom he calls Shen, with a room. The young man gives Shen a car. He finds Shen a job.

For the previous five years the young man had been going to group analysis, a collection of people who had been the victims of violent crime. It was a group of six to twelve people, sharing horror stories, talking about forgiveness. This is how the young man meets Shen, his mother's killer, gets to know him, and gets to like him. However, it is all too much for Shen, too fast.

The young man comes home one day to find Shen in bed with a woman. The young man bursts into the bedroom, and the woman runs out. The young man finds Shen's glasses and picks them up. The young man is jealous, both for himself and on behalf of his dead mother. His mother was pretty, much prettier than the woman Shen is with in the bedroom.

The young man, feeling betrayed, screams at Shen. Shen asks for his glasses. After a few minutes of ranting, the young man lies down next to Shen on the bed, whispers in Shen's ear, and suggests a trade in exchange for Shen's glasses.

This story, which won Peck an O. Henry Fiction Award in 2001, is an example of how the author lulls his readers into a false sense of security. A seemingly mundane story about a young man dealing with the death of his mother, learning to forgive her killer by turning the other cheek, soon takes a disturbing, eerie turn, and the reader is left in the middle of moral dilemma, abandoned in a gray area by the author and uncertain of where one's allegiance should lie.

"MAKING BOOK"

Book, the son of fanatical bridge players, is discovering his sexuality. His parents, who are waiting for their friends and fellow bridge enthusiasts, Tony and Angela Ferruci, to arrive for their weekly Tuesday-night game, have summoned Book, whom they call Boo, to the living room. With cocktail glasses in hand, Boo's parents are about to have "the sex talk" with their son. This talk has been prompted by the discovery of a pair of Boo's underwear in the laundry hamper, complete with a telltale stain near the fly.

Boo's parents are sitting on the couch, Boo's stained underwear spread out on the coffee table. Boo's parents, though they offer their support in a bizarre, creepy way, assure their son they only have his best interests at heart. Boo's parents do not know that their son, along with his best friend, Ace Ferruci, has been filming naked young women. Ace lures the young women to a secluded spot, and Boo lies in hiding with his video camera while Ace has sex with them. While Boo has been aroused by the films he has made, he has come to suspect his interest has more to do with his naked friend Ace than with the young women.

Before the Ferruci family arrives, Ace included, Boo's parents are intent on finishing their conversation with their son. Boo's father does most of the talking, while Boo's mother busies herself with making and drinking cocktails. On the coffee table, next to Boo's underwear, a videotape has appeared. This videotape is labeled "Making Book." It is a film of Boo's parents making love, apparently as their son was conceived. Fighting nausea and embarrassment, Boo watches the film of his parents and tries to focus on its clinical aspects. To his mother's horror, Boo's interest in the film manifests itself biologically. As his mother quickly exits from the living room, holding her head in her hands, it occurs to Boo that he has been concentrating on his father's video image.

As the film is ending, the Ferruci family arrives and Boo is quickly employed in helping his father create a cover-up. As the four adults make their way to the card table, Boo, whom his friends call Booker, leads his friend Ace upstairs. Booker is uncertain of what will happen next, but he is sure it will not involve a video camera.

"St. Andrew of the Vine"

Anthony DeVine lived in a mobile home park, never using the word "trailer" to describe the home he shared with his wife, Theresa. He met Theresa at the local diner in the small Texas town of Saches, where they lived in their mobile home park, not far from Mira, an older woman and a waitress at the diner. Nicky Junger lives between Mira and the DeVines, and once she had had an affair with Anthony. Once a week, Anthony uses Nicky's mobile home as a base of operations for his secret, extramarital love life.

Though skinny, balding, and possessing a degenerative eye disease, Anthony DeVine attracts a lot of women. Mira, his confidante, sees this attractiveness, and she laments that Anthony finds her too old to be a candidate for his conquests. That's how Anthony sees women, as conquests, each one to be conquered. Often, Anthony sends his afternoon conquests to Mira's mobile home, especially if the women want to talk afterward. While Theresa is away, while Nicky is at work, Mira sits at her window and watches the women arrive for their afternoon trysts with Andrew, waiting for the occasional knock at her door, offering the kind word, the understanding ear, the soft shoulder on which Anthony's more sensitive conquests drip their tears.

Out of Nicky's mobile home, across the overgrown lawn, Mira sees a woman slowly making her way across the grass to Mira's door. At first, Mira thinks it is Theresa. It is too early for Theresa to be getting home from work at the bank. No, it is Theresa's younger sister, Kennedy Albright. Mira knows it is not beneath Anthony to have an affair with his sister-in-law. As Kennedy comes closer, Mira notices Kennedy has on only one shoe, her hair is messed up, some stains covering her face and clothes. Covered in blood, Kennedy seeks Mira's help, just as Nicky Junger's car pulls up, parking in front of her home, and her screams awaken the neighborhood to the fact that Anthony DeVine is dead.

"Sky Writing"

Francis Kaplan Pelton lives in the air. Stopping only in airports, Pelton jumps from one plane to another, endlessly. Along the way, he "entertains" his fellow seatmates. Pelton's idea of entertainment includes heavy drinking, embarrassing talk, and overfamiliarity. His latest seatmate-victim, Heather Beaumont, an attractive blond from Texas, tends to say "Do what?" to Pelton's rude questions, and she matches her fellow traveler drink for drink over the Atlantic Ocean en route to London from New York.

Gavin, an airline steward in first class, familiar with Pelton from previous flights, brings drinks and flirts with Pelton, while still trying to maintain an air of decorum. Heather, a premedical student attending school in Maine, is asked by Pelton to describe in detail the physiological changes the body goes through when being choked to death by a necktie. Gavin tries to interrupt the conversation and rescue Heather from Pelton's brutish behavior, but Pelton persists in his questions. Pelton explains, to Heather and Gavin, that self-strangulation is the way Laird Swope, his lover, died.

Laird left Pelton with a fortune and an incurable disease. Pelton chooses to spend Laird's fortune in order to sustain his life in the air. Pelton loves the freedom of flight combined with the possibility of disaster that air travel affords. Laird was afraid of flying.

Pelton likes the way Heather pronounces the name Laird, the correct way, like "layered." Pelton met Laird in a restaurant, where Pelton was his waiter. In the middle of the five-course dinner, the two had sex in the men's room. It was the beginning of a short but intense relationship.

With only a few hours until landing at Heathrow, Pelton uses the plane's phone to call for booking on the next Concorde SST flight back to New York. With the speed of the Concorde, Pelton estimates, he could leave London at 10:30 a.m. and return to John F. Kennedy Airport in New York at 9 a.m., arriving before he even departed.

OTHER MAJOR WORKS

LONG FICTION: *Martin and John*, 1993; *The Law of Enclosures*, 1996; *Now It's Time to Say Goodbye*, 1998; *The Garden of Lost and Found*, 2007; *Body Surfing*, 2009.

SCREENPLAYS: *The Law of Enclosures*, 2000 (with John Greyson).

NONFICTION: *What We Lost: Based on a True Story*, 2003; *Hatchet Jobs: Writings on Contemporary Fiction*, 2004.

CHILDREN'S LITERATURE: *Drift House: The First Voyage*, 2005; *The Lost Cities: A Drift House Voyage*, 2007; *Sprout*, 2009.

EDITED TEXTS: *To Catch a Prince* by Gillian McKnight, 2005; *The Blackout Gang* by Josh McKall, 2006; *The Frog Prince* by Gillian McKnight, 2006.

BIBLIOGRAPHY

Atlas, James. "The Takedown Artist." *The New York Times Magazine*, October 26, 2003. Long profile of Peck, in which Peck discusses his troubled childhood, how he became a writer, and how he became a flame-throwing literary critic.

Epstein, Joseph. "The Axman Cometh." *Commentary* 118, no. 2 (September, 2004): 76. This article discusses Peck's nonfiction work *Hatchet Jobs*. A book concerning literary criticism and Peck's practicing of it, the article's author writes that "Peck has lowered the gauge of literary decorum beyond anything I have encountered." The reviewer adds, "But Peck is entertaining only up to a point."

Kakutani, Michiko. "New Wave of Writers Reinvents Literature." *The New York Times*, April 22, 2000, p. B9. This article places Peck in the company of writers who are "hot-wired to the gritty world around them, rendering it with uncommon spontaneity and vigor."

Mendelsohn, Daniel. "Nailed!" *The New York Review of Books*, July 15, 2004. Discusses the history of literary criticism and addresses Peck's famous literary attacks.

Randy L. Abbott

SUSAN PERABO

Born: St. Louis, Missouri; January 6, 1969

PRINCIPAL SHORT FICTION

Who I Was Supposed to Be: Short Stories, 1999
"Shelter," 2009

OTHER LITERARY FORMS

In *Writers in the Schools: A Guide to Teaching Creative Writing in the Classroom* (1998), Susan Perabo (PEHR-ah-boh) provides hands-on exercises and activities for use with students in creative writing classes.

ACHIEVEMENTS

Susan Perabo's stories have been anthologized in *New Stories from the South* and in *Best American Short Stories, 1996.* Her work has appeared in *Story, Glimmer Train, TriQuarterly,* and *The Black Warrior Review.* She was the winner of the Henfield/*Transatlantic Review* Award in 1992.

BIOGRAPHY

Susan Perabo was born on January 6, 1969, in St. Louis, Missouri. She graduated from Webster University in Missouri. Because the college did not have a women's softball team, Perabo played on the men's baseball team. Her brief career as the first woman to play National College Athletic Association (NCAA) baseball earned her a spot in the Baseball Hall of Fame in Cooperstown, New York. The following year she joined a women's club team. She received her master of fine arts degree in creative writing from the University of Arkansas, Fayetteville. She taught creative writing at Dickinson College in Carlisle, Pennsylvania, where she became an assistant professor and writer-in-residence. In addition to teaching fiction workshops, she has taught literature courses in contemporary fiction and served as a faculty adviser for the Belles Lettres Literary Society and *The Dickinson Review.* In 2001, her first novel, *The Broken Places,* was published, and her short story "Shelter," which was published in *The Iowa Review* in 2009, was nominated for the Pushcart Prize, appearing in the 2011 *Pushcart Prize XXXV.*

ANALYSIS

As an introduction to her collection of stories, Susan Perabo quotes these lines from James Baldwin's "Sonny's Blues":

> For while the tale of how we suffer, and how we are delighted, and how we may triumph is never new, it always must be heard. There isn't any other tale to tell, it's the only light we've got in all this darkness.

Perabo presents the reader with characters who suffer in various situations and in many cases achieve a type of triumph.

She tells these stores from different points of view, employing both male and female narrators of varying ages and circumstances. Typically, her stories begin with a short, attention-getting sentence, such as this opening line from "Explaining Death to the Dog": "After the baby died, I found it imperative that my German shepherd Stu understand and accept the concept of death." Another typical device is the twist that appears at the end of a number of the stories. A woman who travels to her hometown to deal with her mother's problems discovers hope for her own life. A father, who has been so distracted by his thoughts that he has lost touch with his family, is surprised by the actions of his twin sons. Perabo creates desperate characters, who often deal in unusual ways with the hardships of everyday life. In their attempts to survive painful situations, they try to escape from reality. Sharp dialogue reveals the complicated relationships between friends, parents, and children, husbands and wives. At times the snatches of dialogue add a touch of humor.

"THICK AS THIEVES"

The narrator of "Thick as Thieves," Jack, a fifty-nine-year-old Hollywood actor whose career is in a slump, is having problems with his fourth wife. The theme of alienation is dominant, as shown in Jack's failure to maintain personal relationships. His wife tells him that he makes her feel empty, and he has had little contact with his father, a retired grocer. In an attempt to connect with his father, Jack invites his father to come for a visit. Jack has seven cars, owns paintings worth forty thousand dollars, and lives in a twenty-four-room mansion in a wealthy area. When the neighbor's security camera catches his father in the act of stealing jewelry, Jack makes excuses for his father, saying that he may be a victim of Alzheimer's disease. Admitting that he has done this before, the father tells Jack that he steals for the thrill of it, that it is "the purest thrill you'd ever know." He does not sell the jewelry but gives it to the old women who live in his retirement community and bake cookies for him. When Jack returns the neighbor's jewelry, he holds back one piece, which he puts in his father's pocket. Later, when Jack attends his father's funeral, he notices that many of the old women, dressed in ordinary house dresses and worn coats, are wearing expensive jewelry. Jack recognizes some of the pieces as jewelry that belonged to his wife.

This story represents another one of Perabo's major themes, the desire to reinvent oneself. Just as Jack's career has allowed him to assume different identities, his father has chosen to live the life of a thief because it provides excitement. When Jack complains that he does not even know who his father is, the old man replies, "I'm anybody I want to be."

"COUNTING THE WAYS"

Joel and Katy, the young married couple in "Counting the Ways," inherit twenty-eight thousand dollars when Katy's mother dies. Although they might have used the money as a down payment on a house, Katy decides to purchase one of Princess Diana's dresses. They put the dress on a mannequin and prop it up in their bedroom. Katy is an example of a character who tries to reinvent herself by creating a fantasy life that allows her to escape from the pressures of her ordinary life. At first the dress provides a sense of excitement and pleasure for the young couple, but soon the

dress begins to lose its magic. When Katy hears the news of Diana's death, the dress no longer provides a sense of joy. Joel has been caught up in the fantasy but becomes more practical when he sees a chance to make a profit on the dress, thereby enabling the couple to buy a house and have a better life. The couple reaches a turning point in their lives, but Katy, unwilling to give up her fantasy life, refuses to sell the dress.

"THE MEASURE OF DEVOTION"

The narrator of "The Measure of Devotion," David Peabody, is working as an automobile tour guide at Gettysburg when Mrs. Spencer, the mother of his high school friend, Gwen, appears with Gwen's children. Mrs. Spencer introduces David to the children with the phrase, "This is the man that should have been your daddy." During the course of the tour, Mrs. Spencer tells David of the problems Gwen has experienced with drugs and failed relationships. When David insists that he and Gwen were only friends, Mrs. Spencer says she knows that he was in love with her. The theme of alienation is evident in the relationship between Gwen and her mother and in Gwen's inability to maintain relationships. When he is alone, David reflects on the night Gwen left town with another boy, while he "just lay there dying all night long while she was getting farther and farther away." Now happily married with a beautiful wife, a home of his own, and a child, David can say to himself, "She got what she deserved." Gwen has ruined her life along with the lives of her children, but David has managed to survive. The twist at the end of this story is David's reaction to the news of Gwen's misfortunes.

"THE ROCKS OVER KYBURZ"

In "The Rocks over Kyburz," Ray, a high school band director, is so dissatisfied with his job and his life that he escapes into dreams of the past when he was smoking pot and playing in bands. He spends his time thinking of ways he can change his life as he watches "images float by in his head like a memory that hadn't happened yet." He is so caught up in his own unhappiness that he has lost contact with his fifteen-year-old twin sons. When a neighbor confronts Ray with the accusation that his sons are smoking pot with her teenage daughter, Ray and his wife deny the charges. One night Ray follows the boys up the mountain path to a place where the family used to have picnics and discovers that both boys are having sex with the girl. The central image of the story is the mountain path with its twin rocks, each the size of a house, that balance precariously on a flat rock underneath. At one time there had been four rocks, but many years ago two had fallen, "crushing everything in their path." The story ends with the image of the rocks, as Ray thinks of the future, when "the steadiest thing he knew" would "shift free of its roots and roll blindly toward all of them."

"THE GREATER GRACE OF CARLISLE"

"The Greater Grace of Carlisle" opens with the following line: "My mother, beside herself with loss, spent thirty-five thousand dollars on lottery tickets in nine months." Hildy, the narrator's widowed mother, is like many of Perabo's characters who act in bizarre ways in an attempt to change their lives or to deal with loneliness and depression. Short snatches of dialogue between mother and daughter provide a touch of humor. Kathy, the daughter, learns that Hildy has sold her mother's silver, her husband's stock, and her car to finance her lottery purchases. When Kathy asks how much money is left, Hildy replies, "Enough to buy you a plane ticket back to Phoenix." Carlisle is a small town in Illinois with a sign that reads "Home of the 3A Cross Country District Champs, 1984, Go Bees." When Kathy goes to a Gamblers Anonymous meeting with her mother, Kathy meets Andy, a member of that 1984 team, who has remained in the hometown. As she sits with him on the bank of the pond in the park, Kathy feels a sense of hope for her life.

"SHELTER"

The narrator of this Pushcart Prize-winning short story is a single woman who has taken on the task of finding homes for stray and abandoned dogs and who has just discovered that she is dying. Knowing her time is short, she stops accepting new dogs and works to place the remaining dozen or so before she dies. One day she receives a call from an elderly and unusual man named Jerry, who wants a nice, fat dog to sleep on his feet. After she visits his home to make sure that it is adequate for one of her dogs, she and Jerry are unable to come to terms on placing a dog at his house. He refuses to sign the necessary paperwork, and she will not place the dog if he does not. When she is hospitalized after a dizzy spell, she finds that he has left a gift with

her sister, but in a moment of clarity, she realizes that he has given her more than one gift. He has given her the gift of hope for her dogs. As with many of Perabo's characters, both Jerry and the unnamed narrator do not approach life, in this case the end of life, in conventional ways. They are uncompromising in what they value and what they will and will not do. Ultimately, these two characters are able to find satisfactory ways to live out their remaining lives.

OTHER MAJOR WORKS

LONG FICTION: *The Broken Places*, 2001.
NONFICTION: *Writers in the Schools: A Guide to Teaching Creative Writing in the Classroom*, 1998.

BIBLIOGRAPHY

Fichtner, Margaria. "*Who I Was Supposed to Be: Short Stories* by Susan Perabo." *The Miami Herald*, August 4, 1999. In her review of Perabo's short-story collection, Fichtner provides brief summaries of several stories and credits Perabo with keen insight into the lives of her troubled characters.

Golden, Jay. "*Who I Was Supposed to Be:* Stories by Susan Perabo." *Fort Worth Star Telegram*, October 20, 1999. Sees strength in Perabo's ability to provide twists that catch the reader off guard. Golden comments on her light touch and ironic humor and calls her stories "quirky and engaging."

Pate, Nancy. "Short Stories Show Off Young Author Waiting for Growth Spurt." *Chicago Tribune*, September 10, 1999. Calling Perabo's stories "tough-minded and clever," this reviewer notes that Perabo grabs the reader's attention with intriguing first sentences. The theme that connects the stories is the characters' need for "reinvention."

Publishers Weekly. Review of *Who I Was Supposed to Be: Short Stories*, by Susan Perabo. 246 (July 9, 1999): 186. Points to Perabo's ability to narrate her stories from different points of view, using narrators of different ages and genders. Notes that Perabo relieves the tragic with the whimsical as she provides the reader with characters who face difficult situations.

Judith Barton Williamson
Updated by Kimberley M. Holloway

S. J. PERELMAN

Born: Brooklyn, New York; February 1, 1904
Died: New York, New York; October 17, 1979
Also known as: Sid Perelman

PRINCIPAL SHORT FICTION

Dawn Ginsbergh's Revenge, 1929
Parlor, Bedlam, and Bath, 1930 (with Quentin J. Reynolds)
Strictly from Hunger, 1937
Look Who's Talking, 1940
The Dream Department, 1943
Crazy Like a Fox, 1944
Keep It Crisp, 1946
Acres and Pains, 1947
Westward Ha! Or, Around the World in Eighty Clichés, 1948
Listen to the Mocking Bird, 1949
The Swiss Family Perelman, 1950
A Child's Garden of Curses, 1951
The Ill-Tempered Clavichord, 1952
Hold That Christmas Tiger!, 1954
Perelman's Home Companion, 1955
The Road to Miltown: Or, Under the Spreading Atrophy, 1957
The Most of S. J. Perelman, 1958
The Rising Gorge, 1961
Chicken Inspector No. 23, 1966
Baby, It's Cold Inside, 1970
Vinegar Puss, 1975
Eastward Ha!, 1977

OTHER LITERARY FORMS

S. J. Perelman (PEHR-uhl-muhn) published more than twenty-five books, including essays, stories, plays, and an autobiography. He also wrote screenplays for film and television, and he is best known for his work with the Marx Brothers on the films *Monkey Business* (1931) and *Horse Feathers* (1932).

ACHIEVEMENTS

S. J. Perelman was a highly successful and well-loved humorist whose best writing appeared in *The New Yorker* and then was collected in popular books for five decades, from the 1930's to the 1970's. He wrote the book upon which the Broadway hit *One Touch of Venus* (1943) was based, and he wrote one other acclaimed Broadway comedy, *The Beauty Part* (1961). For his contribution to the film adaptation of *Around the World in Eighty Days* (1956), he shared an Academy Award in 1956 and also received a New York Film Critics Award. In 1978, he received the special National Book Award for his lifetime contribution to American literature.

Perelman's influence on other writers is difficult to measure because, although he was the leader of the "dementia praecox" school of humor closely associated with *The New Yorker*, he was not the inventor of the techniques of verbal humor he used so well, and his type of writing has been on the decline. There seem to be clear mutual influences between Perelman and several of his contemporaries: James Thurber, Dorothy Parker, Groucho Marx, and Nathanael West, Perelman's brother-in-law. French Surrealists admired his style, and contemporary black humorists often use the techniques he mastered, but one hesitates to assert direct influence on writers such as Joseph Heller and Kurt Vonnegut. Perelman's type of writing seems to have been taken over by television, film, and perhaps the New Journalism. Woody Allen admired Perelman and is often mentioned as one of his disciples. In his critiques of American style, Perelman may be a predecessor of writers such as Tom Wolfe, Hunter Thompson, and Terry southern.

BIOGRAPHY

Sidney Joseph Perelman was born in Brooklyn, New York, on February 1, 1904, the son of Sophia Charren and Joseph Perelman, a Jewish poultry farmer. He briefly attended Brown University, where he edited the *College Humor* magazine. After leaving the university in 1925, he began his career as a writer and cartoonist for *Judge* magazine. Following a brief stint at *College Humor* and his marriage to Laura Weinstein on July 4, 1929, he began writing full time, and in 1931 became a regular contributor to *The New Yorker* and other major magazines. He and his wife had a son and a daughter. Perelman worked occasionally in Hollywood, writing motion-picture screenplays, but he spent most of his life in New York City and on his Pennsylvania farm. He collaborated to write several successful plays; his usual collaborator on films and plays was his wife, although on *One Touch of Venus* he worked with Ogden Nash and for a television musical, *Aladdin*, with Cole Porter.

After his wife's death in 1970, Perelman lived for two years in England but then returned to Manhattan, where he remained until his death on October 17, 1979.

ANALYSIS

Parody, satire, and verbal wit characterize S. J. Perelman's works. Most of them are very short and tend to begin as conversational essays that develop into narrative or mock dramatic episodes and sometimes return to essay. Perelman called them "feuilletons" (little leaves), "comic essays of a particular type." They seem formally related to the earliest American forms of short story, Benjamin Franklin's bagatelles and early American humor. Norris Yates best summarizes the worldview reflected in Perelman's work: Perelman values normal life, "integrity, sincerity, skepticism, taste, a respect for competence, a striving after the golden mean, and a longing for better communication and understanding among men." Yates sees Perelman's typical persona (the "I" of the pieces) as a Little Man resisting the forces of American cultural life which would "invade and corrupt his personality and impel him toward neuroses," the forces which seem determined to destroy the values Perelman holds. According to Yates, these forces manifest themselves for Perelman most decisively in "the mass media, which are, on the whole, the offspring of technology's unconsecrated marriage with Big Business."

Perelman's "autobiographical" work reveals his version of the Little Man. A favorite type of *The New Yorker* humorists, the Little Man is a caricature of a typical middle-class, early twentieth century American male, usually represented as helpless before the complexities of technological society, cowed by its crass commercialism, dominated by desperate, unfulfilled women, and sustaining himself on heroic fantasies of a bygone or imaginary era. James Thurber's Walter Mitty has become the classic presentation of this character type. Perelman's personae seem related to this type, but vary in several significant ways.

ACRES AND PAINS

In *Acres and Pains*, the major collection of his adventures on his farm, Perelman makes his persona into a city dweller who has naïvely tried to realize a romantic agrarian dream on his country estate, but who has come to see the error of his ways. Perelman uses this reversal of the rube in the city to debunk a sentimental picture of country life by exaggerating his trials. Many episodes show good country people betraying the ideal with which they are associated. Contractors, antique dealers, and barn painters rob him of purse and peace. "Perelman" differs from the Little Man type in that, although he may at any time fall victim to another illusion, he knows and admits that country life is no romance. In these sketches, he also differs from the Little Man type in his relationship to his wife and family. He is not dominated by a frustrated woman. He and his wife are usually mutual victims of pastoral illusion, although often she suffers more than he.

This "Perelman" is most like the typical Little Man when he deals with machines. For example, when his water pump goes berserk during a dinner party, he handles the problem with successful incompetence:

> By exerting a slight leverage, I succeeded in prying off the gasket or outer jacket of the pump, exactly as you would a baked potato. . . . This gave me room to poke around the innards with a sharp stick. I cleaned the pump thoroughly . . . and, as a final precaution, opened the windows to allow the water to drain down the slope.

The major difference between this persona and Walter Mitty is that the former is competent; he escapes neurosis and resists with some success his crazy world.

By splitting the narrator into a present sophisticate (a mask that often slips) and a former fool, he tends to shift the butt of humor away from the present narrator and toward the man who believes in romantic ideals and toward the people who so completely fail to live up to any admirable ideals. The latter are typified by the contractor who digs "Perelman's" pool in a bad place although he knows the best place for it. Asked why he offered his advice when the pool was dynamited rather than before it was begun, he virtuously replies. "It don't pay to poke your nose in other people's business." Implied in these tall tales of mock pastoral life are criticisms of the values which oppose those Yates lists: dishonesty, hypocrisy, greed, naïveté, incompetence, overenthusiasm, deliberately created confusion, and lying.

Looking over the full range of Perelman's first-person sketches, one sees significant variation in the presentation of the persona. In *Acres and Pains*, the narrator is much more concrete than in many other sketches in which the "I" is virtually an empty mind waiting to take shape under the power of some absurd mass-media language. Perelman is acutely sensitive to this language as a kind of oppression. Many of his sketches explore "sub-dialects" of American English in order to expose and ridicule the values that underlie them. "Tomorrow--Fairly Cloudy" is a typical example of the author's probing of a sample of American language.

"TOMORROW--FAIRLY CLOUDY"

In "Tomorrow--Fairly Cloudy," Perelman notices a new advertisement for a toothpaste which promises its users rescue from humdrum ordinary life and elevation into romance and success. In his introduction, Perelman emphasizes the absurdity of taking such ads seriously, describes the ad in detail, then introduces a dramatic scenario by observing that this ad heralds the coming demise of a desperate industry: "So all the old tactics have finally broken down--wheedling, abuse, snobbery and terror. I look forward to the last great era in advertising, a period packed with gloom, defeatism, and frustration. . . ."

In the following spectacle, the children bubble excited "adese" while father despairs over his drab life:

> Bobby--Oh, Moms, I'm so glad you and Dads decided to install a Genfeedco automatic oil burner and air conditioner with the new self-ventilating screen flaps plus finger control! It is noiseless, cuts down heating bills, and makes the air we breathe richer in vita-ray particles. . . .
>
> Mr. Bradley (tonelessly)--Well, I suppose anything is better than a heap of slag at this end of the cellar.

Soon the Fletchers arrive to sneer at their towels and to make the Bradleys aware of all the products they do not have. The sketch ends in apocalypse as their inferior plumbing gives way, and they all drown in their combination cellar and playroom. It remains unclear throughout whether this episode forecasts the forms of future advertising or its effects on the public.

Perelman exposes the absurdity of this language of conspicuous consumption by imagining its literal acceptance. In the world this language implies, happiness is possessing the right gadgets. If sales are to continue, it must be impossible for most people ever to have all the right things, and so impossible ever to be happy. The Bradleys have the right oil burner, but their towels disintegrate in two days, and they failed to use Sumwenco Super-Annealed Brass Pipe. This last omission costs them their lives. Not only their happiness but also their very survival depend on their ability to possess the right new product.

"ENTERED AS SECOND-CLASS MATTER"

Perelman's many sketches of this type culminate perhaps in "Entered as Second-Class Matter," which is apparently a montage of fragments lifted (and, one hopes, sometimes fabricated) from magazine fiction and advertising. The resulting silliness may be intended as a portrait of the mass feminine mind as perceived by American magazines, 1930-1944. It ends:

> We have scoured the fiction market to set before you *Three Million Tiny Sweat Glands Functioning* in that vibrant panorama of tomorrow so that *Your Sensitive Bowel Muscles Can* react to the inevitable realization that only by enrichment and guidance *plus a soothing depilatory* can America face its problems

confidently, unafraid, *well-groomed mouth-happy, breaking hair off at the roots without undue stench. Okay, Miss America!*

In such pieces, Perelman's values are clearly those Yates names. Especially important in these works is the humorous attempt to clear away the garbage of American language culture through ridicule. This aim is central to the series "Cloudland Revisited," in which he reexamines the popular literature of his youth. Perelman varies this formula with attacks on absurd fashion and the language of fashion, one of the best of which is "Farewell, My Lovely Appetizer."

Verbal Wit

Perelman is deservedly most admired for his faculty of verbal wit. In several of his more conventional stories which seem less restrained by satiric ends, his playfulness dazzles. Among the best of these are "The Idol's Eye," "Seedlings of Desire," and "The Love Decoy." Based on the sensational plots of teen-romance, "The Love Decoy" is narrated by a coed who seeks revenge on an instructor who once failed to make a pass and who later humiliated her before her classmates by accusing her of "galvanizing around nights." Her plan is to lure him to her room after hours, then expose him as a corrupter of undergraduates. This plan backfires in a non sequitur when a lecherous dean arrives to assault her. The reader expects the plot to complicate, but instead it is transformed when the dean is unmasked as Jim the Penman who framed the girl's father and sent him to the pen. Other identities are revealed, and the reader arrives at the end of a detective thriller. Although there is parody here of sentimental language and plot, the story seems more intent on fun than ridicule. It contains a number of Perelman's most celebrated witticisms. For example:

He caught my arm in a vice-like grip and drew me to him, but with a blow I sent him groveling. In ten minutes he was back with a basket of appetizing fresh picked grovels. We squeezed them and drank the piquant juice thirstily.

At the center of this wit is the double entendre. Multiple meanings of words suggest the multiple contexts in which they may apply. Perelman juxtaposes these contexts, makes rapid shifts between them, and sometimes

uses a suggestion to imagine a new context. The effects are sometimes surreal. The double meaning of "sent" suggests a transformation from a blow to the groin to an activity such as berrying. "Groveling" gathers an imaginary context which generates a new noun, "grovels." While this reading seems most plausible, in another reading there are no transformations, and gathering grovels becomes a euphemistic way to describe the amorous instructor's reaction to her literal attack or to her unusually expressed affection.

Perelman creates this slipperiness of meaning and encourages it to reverberate in this passage and in the language and structure of the whole work. One result is a heightened alertness in the reader to the ambiguity of language and the elusiveness of meaning, a first but important step on the way to the sort of respect for language Perelman implies in his many critiques of its abuses. This concern connects Perelman most closely with James Joyce, whom Perelman considered the greatest modern comic writer, with a number of his contemporaries, including William Faulkner and James Thurber. While Perelman has not the stature of these great writers, he shares with them a consciousness of the peculiar problems of modern life and a belief that how one uses language is important to recognizing and dealing with those problems. Among *The New Yorker* humorists with whom S. J. Perelman is associated, he is probably one of the lesser lights, showing neither the versatility, the variety, nor the universality of Dorothy Parker or of Thurber. Although critical estimates of his achievement vary, there is general agreement that his best work, done mostly before 1950, shows a marvelous gift for verbal wit.

Other Major Works

PLAYS: *The Night Before Christmas*, pr. 1941 (with Laura Perelman); *One Touch of Venus*, pr. 1943 (with Ogden Nash); *The Beauty Part*, pr. 1961.

SCREENPLAYS: *Monkey Business*, 1931; *Horse Feathers*, 1932; *Around the World in Eighty Days*, 1956.

NONFICTION: *The Last Laugh*, 1981; *Don't Tread on Me: Selected Letters of S. J. Perelman*, 1987; *Conversations with S. J. Perelman*, 1995 (Tom Teicholz, editor).

MISCELLANEOUS: *That Old Gang o' Mine: The Early and Essential S. J. Perelman*, 1984 (Richard Marschall, editor).

BIBLIOGRAPHY

Epstein, Joseph. "Sid, You Made the Prose Too Thin." *Commentary* 84 (September, 1987): 53-60. A biographical sketch of Perelman, suggesting that his best writing occurred when he was angry, as in *Acres and Pains*, a collection of stories about an idealistic city man being taken advantage of by rural hustlers; argues that elsewhere his natural penchant for gloom, suspicion, and pessimism led him merely to make wisecracks about banal subjects or unpleasantly callous pokes at barely disguised real people.

Fowler, Douglas. *S. J. Perelman*. Boston: Twayne, 1983. This critical study examines influences on Perelman, the development of his career, his relationships with his contemporaries, his technique, and his importance. Includes a chronology, a biographical sketch, and an annotated bibliography.

Gale, Steven. *S. J. Perelman: An Annotated Bibliography*. New York: Garland, 1985. Useful, annotated bibliography that lists 650 Perelman publications and 380 items written about Perelman.

_____. *S. J. Perelman: A Critical Study*. New York: Greenwood Press, 1987. Gale examines Perelman's prose, screenplays, and plays, then studies his themes and techniques. He gives special attention to Perelman's background in Jewish humor and his use of clichés and allusions. Supplemented by a chronology and a bibliographic essay.

_____, ed. *S. J. Perelman: Critical Essays*. New York: Garland, 1992. Includes more than twenty essays, articles, and critiques of Perelman from academic studies, newspapers, and popular journals over a seventy-year period of his career. Gale's introduction places Perelman in the tradition of such great humorists as Geoffrey Chaucer and Mark Twain.

Herrmann, Dorothy. *S. J. Perelman: A Life*. New York: Putnam, 1986. This complete biography makes use of recollections of Perelman's acquaintances to shed light on the life of a very private man. Includes select bibliographies of writing by and about Perelman.

Kuhlman, Thomas A. "A Passion for Words for the Witty: S. J. Perelman, Jewish-American Satirist." In *American Judaism in Popular Culture*, edited by Leonard J. Greenspoon and Ronald A. Simkins. Omaha, Nebr.: Creighton University Press, 2006. Assesses Perelman's contributions to popular culture within the broader context of the influence of Jewish culture upon American society.

Newquist, Roy. *Conversations*. New York: Rand McNally, 1967. Includes an interview in which Perelman talks about the writers he most admires, such as Mark Twain, Ring Lardner, and Robert Charles Benchley.

Perelman, S. J. *Conversations with S. J. Perelman*. Edited by Tom Teicholz. Jackson: University Press of Mississippi, 1995. A collection of interviews with Perelman.

Plimpton, George, ed. *Writers at Work: The Paris Review Interviews, Second Series*. New York: Viking, 1963. In an interview appearing on pages 241-256, Perelman offers glimpses into his creative process and his artistic purposes.

Yates, Norris Wilson. "The Sane Psychoses of S. J. Perelman." In *The American Humorist: Conscience of the Twentieth Century*. Ames: Iowa State University Press, 1964. Though this study has to some extent been superseded by more extensive and later works, it still provides a good, brief introduction to Perelman.

Terry Heller

Ann Petry

Born: Old Saybrook, Connecticut; October 12, 1908
Died: Old Saybrook, Connecticut; April 28, 1997

Principal short fiction
Miss Muriel, and Other Stories, 1971

Other literary forms

Ann Petry (PEE-tree) received her greatest critical recognition for her adult novels: *The Street* (1946), *Country Place* (1947), and *The Narrows* (1953). In 1949 she began a distinguished career as a writer of children's literature with the publication of *The Drugstore Cat,* to be followed by the now-classic biographical novels *Harriet Tubman: Conductor of the Underground Railroad* (1955) and *Tituba of Salem Village* (1964). She also published a devotional work, *Legends of the Saints* (1970), in addition to various articles for small periodicals.

Achievements

Ann Petry's receipt of a Houghton Mifflin Literary Fellowship in 1945 (and an award of twenty-five hundred dollars) enabled her to complete *The Street,* which went on to become the first novel by an African American woman to sell more than one million copies. In 1977 she was awarded a National Endowment for the Arts grant and in 1983 received a D. Litt. from Boston's Suffolk University. In 1992 the reissuing of *The Street* renewed Petry's reputation as an important American writer and introduced a new generation to her work. Her death in April, 1997, was eulogized publicly by U.S. senator Christopher Dodd, and the following year MacArthur Fellow Max Roach premiered "Theater Pieces" (December, 1998), an adaptation of Petry's tale of a jazz love triangle, "Solo on the Drums," featuring Ruby Dee and Ossie Davis along with Roach.

Biography

Ann Lane Petry was born to Peter Clarke Lane and Bertha James Lane on October 12, 1908, joining a family that had lived for several generations as the only African American citizens of the resort community of Old Saybrook, Connecticut. The descendant of a runaway Virginian slave, Petry admitted to never having felt herself to be a true New Englander; her cultural legacy was not that of the typical Yankee, and as a small child she came to know the isolating effects of racism after being stoned by white children on her first day of school. Nevertheless, her family distinguished itself within the community and boasted numerous professionals: Her grandfather was a licensed chemist; her father, aunt, and uncle became pharmacists; and her mother worked as a chiropodist. In 1902, Peter Lane opened a pharmacy in Old Saybrook, for which Ann herself trained. Inspired by the example of her many independent female relatives--women who had, she explained, "abandoned the role of housewife in the early twentieth century"--in 1931 Ann secured a degree in pharmacology from the University of Connecticut, the only black graduate in her class. She worked in family-owned pharmacies until 1938, when she met and married Louisiana-born George D. Petry and moved with him to his home in Harlem.

Petry had begun writing fiction seriously in high school after an antagonistic teacher grudgingly praised her work as having real potential, and she wrote steadily thereafter (although to no immediate success). With the move to New York City, her writing career began in earnest. She quickly secured jobs with various Harlem newspapers as a reporter, editor, and copywriter, working for the *Amsterdam News* and *The People's Voice* (the latter a weekly founded by African American clergyman and politician Adam Clayton Powell, Jr.). She also briefly acted in the American Negro Theatre and worked on a study conducted by the New York Foundation investigating the effects of segregation on black children.

Participation in a creative writing seminar at Columbia University greatly influenced Petry during this time. Her first published short story, "On Saturday the Siren Sounds at Noon," appeared in a 1943 issue of *The Crisis* (a magazine published by the National Association for the Advancement of Colored People) and not only earned her twenty dollars but also led to her discovery by an editor at Houghton Mifflin. He encouraged her to submit preliminary work on what would become *The Street*, for which Petry received the 1945 Houghton Mifflin Literary Fellowship and a stipend of twenty-five hundred dollars. Thus she was able to complete her novel, translating nearly a decade spent observing the difficulties of aspiring African Americans in the urban North into the powerful story of single mother Lutie Johnson and her star-crossed eight-year-old Bub. While her trenchant insights into the play of race and class as conjoined factors stifling Lutie's dreams recall Richard Wright's landmark *Native Son* (1940), Petry's recognition of the role of gender in the discriminatory equation made *The Street* a groundbreaking work on its own and another expression of the woman-centered ethic she had learned from her family. Published in 1946, *The Street* received both critical and popular acclaim and sold 1.5 million copies--at the time the largest audience ever reached by an African American woman. The fame accompanying that success overwhelmed Petry, however, and in 1948 she and George returned to the obscurity of Old Saybrook, where they bought the two-hundred-year-old house of an old sea captain and reared their daughter Elisabeth.

Petry's subsequent fiction did not receive the same kind of praise accorded her first novel, despite her continued willingness to tackle difficult racial themes (*The Narrows*) and explore the terrain of small-town white America from its own assumed vantage point (*Country Place*), a project seldom undertaken by black writers even today. In 1971, she published a collection of her short fiction, *Miss Muriel, and Other Stories*. She also contributed stories and essays to numerous magazines and journals. Perhaps in response to the indifference accorded her adult fiction, she began writing for children during the time she was raising Elisabeth and produced such classics as *The Drugstore Cat*, *Harriet Tubman*, and *Tituba of Salem Village*. The latter two

novels, about actual historical personages, reflect her determination to place art in the service of an honest picture of American racial history; they have become young adult classics and are perhaps more widely read than the adult fiction on which her initial reputation was built.

Petry spent the second half of her life away from the hurly-burly of publishing centers and for the most part outside the rarefied walls of the university; David Streitfeld of *The Washington Post* said that she "had little tolerance for fools or academics, two categories she regarded as essentially synonymous." She did hold a visiting professorship at the University of Hawaii in 1974-1975 and in 1977 received a grant from the National Endowment for the Arts. Boston's Suffolk University awarded her a D.Litt. degree in 1983. She had the satisfaction of seeing her daughter continue the legacy of strong female achievement by becoming an attorney.

Petry died at the age of eighty-eight in a convalescent home in the same community where she was born, still married to the man who had briefly taken her out of New England and made possible the launching of her lifelong career.

ANALYSIS

While Ann Petry's fiction typically involves African Americans struggling against the crippling impact of racism, her overarching theme involves a more broadly defined notion of prejudice that targets class and gender, as well as race. Thus her aims are consistently broader than racial critique, since she regularly exposes the consequences of America's hierarchical social systems and its capitalistic materialism. That vision explains what might otherwise seem to be inconsistencies of direction in Petry's career: her decision, for example, following the potent racial protest of *The Street* to focus her next novel, *Country Place*, on a white community's postwar crises of adjustment or her movement into the realm of children's literature. Like her contemporaries, black and white alike, who came of age in the 1930's, she adopted a social realist aesthetic committed to documenting the obstacles to human fulfillment imposed on those at the margins of American prosperity. As she explained:

I find it difficult to subscribe to the idea that art exists for art's sake. It seems to me that all truly great art is propaganda . . . [and fiction], like all other forms of art, will always reflect the political, economic, and social structure of the period in which it was created.

Her work also reveals an increasingly overt Christian existentialist vision celebrating the individual's potential for spiritual liberation, through which an entire culture might come to relinquish its crippling prejudices.

Rather than celebrating the American ideal of self-making with which her native New England is so closely associated, Petry exposes the illusions it has fostered and depicts their graphic costs to those relegated to the periphery of American possibility. Racism invites Petry's most scathing attacks, not only for the material hardship it forces upon people of color but also for the psychological and cultural distortions it produces. At her most biting, Petry lampoons the absurdist systems of human classification into which racist societies ultimately fall. Generally, her perspective is a tragic one, grounded in the recognition that confronting racism necessitates confronting history itself.

One of Petry's most insistent indictments of America's hypocrisy targets the class distinctions that parallel and overlap racism as forces negating individual hope for a better life and a more just world. Repeatedly she shows how Americans in quest of the material security, comfort, and status that propel middle-class striving acquiesce to soul-numbing labor and retreat into a moral inflexibility that blindly sanctions aggressive self-interest. In Petry's fiction the culture's high-flown rhetoric is belied by rigid social hierarchies that produce venal, grasping have-nots at the bottom, whose ambitions mimic the ruthless acquisitiveness of those at the top.

Petry's most important characters are those who reject the fallacy of the self-made individual existing independently of the world or the continuing legacy of the past. Though that perspective assumes certain mechanistic dimensions in her work, she does not concede full authority to deterministic necessity; the dice may be loaded against her protagonists, but the game is not inexorably mandated to play itself out to any single predetermined end. Her characters sometimes prove capable of personal growth that moves them toward a common humanity with the potential to fuel real and far-reaching change in the social order itself. Petry's narratives of personal transformation often grow from characters' chance movements across rigid cultural boundaries; the resulting crises test the spiritual flexibility of many others besides her protagonists.

Overlooked by academic critics, Petry's children's books offer tantalizing clues to her larger agenda. Their emphasis upon personal fearlessness in rethinking entrenched assumptions and disengaging from unjust systems invites comparison with numerous figures from her adult fiction. Moreover, in applying their new insights, these characters undertake subtly revolutionary actions that defy the cultural boundaries that had previously defined their lives. It takes a saint, perhaps, to challenge a predatory universe with an alternative vision of love, but having told children in *Legends of the Saints* that true sanctity is a function of bravery, Petry seems to evaluate her other fictional characters on their receptivity to grace as an antidote to hate.

Ann Petry (AP Photo/Jacob Harris)

MISS MURIEL, AND OTHER STORIES

While Petry's reputation rests primarily on her novels, she saw herself quite differently at the start of her career:

> I set out to be a writer of short stories and somehow ended up as a novelist--possibly because there simply wasn't room enough within the framework of the short story to do the sort of thing I wanted to do.

The pieces in *Miss Muriel, and Other Stories*, written over the course of several decades, provide a compact and provocative introduction to her imaginative concerns, chief among them her sensitivity to racism's psychological as well as material consequences.

"LIKE A WINDING SHEET"

In the prize-winning story "Like a Winding Sheet," Petry depicts the physical and mental toll exacted by the nature of work in an industrial society where laborers are treated as interchangeable machines. The story dramatizes how the corrosive humiliations of prejudice, when added to work stresses, can trigger blind and catastrophic violence. A husband's inability to challenge the string of racist assaults on his dignity delivered both during and after his exhausting night shift at a World War II defense plant not only make him incapable of imagining benign white behavior (even in the face of apologies) but also cause him to respond to his wife's affectionate teasing with the beating he is forbidden to direct at his real oppressors. While racism provides the context for his rage, however (her unwitting use of the word "nigger" echoing the hostile epithet regularly used against him by the outside world), his reaction exposes the starkness of the struggle between male and female in Petry's world and the sobering betrayals it can provoke. The title image begins as the bedsheet in which he has tossed and turned all day in a futile effort to sleep, but his wife jokingly casts it as a burial linen--a reference ironically appropriate to his sense of himself as the walking dead. By story's end that reference has assumed sinister dimensions as he feels trapped by the violence he is committing but cannot control, "and he thought it was like being enmeshed in a winding sheet."

"IN DARKNESS AND CONFUSION"

"In Darkness and Confusion" fictionalizes the Harlem Riot of 1943, an event sparked by the wounding of a black soldier whose uniform provided scant protection on his own home front. The story's protagonist, William Jones, a drugstore porter who, despite endless humiliations, has worked hard all his life to secure a better world for his son Sam, suddenly loses that son to the wartime draft and the dangers of a Jim Crow world at the southern training camp to which he is sent. When Sam, who once aspired to college and his share of the American Dream, protests an order to move to the back of the bus and then shoots the aggressive military police officer who gave it, he is court-martialed and sentenced to twenty years of hard labor.

As Jones broods over this news in a Harlem bar, he watches as another uniformed black G.I., this one standing in the supposedly more egalitarian north, tries to help a black woman being beaten by a white policeman, punches the lawman, runs, and is summarily gunned down. Jones erupts into a violence ignited by grief and rage and becomes the leader of a mob. When his churchgoing wife learns of their son's fate, she too turns to retributive action with an explosive passion that kills her: Her religion proves unable to provide her with the strength to resume her burden and go on with her life. The mob's looting of local merchants is not legitimized, for it is produced by the intoxicating siren song of white capitalist materialism, with which the culture regularly deflects attention from matters of real social justice. The riot leaves Jones more completely bereft than he had been before, for it literally costs him his heart and soul, even as it finally allows him to understand the anomie of his disaffected teenage niece, who has baldly scorned his lifetime of exhausting effort for the whites, who in the end allow them "only the nigger end of things."

"THE NEW MIRROR"

Petry as skillfully evokes the impact of racism on the black bourgeoisie as she does on the proletariat, and in several tales she demonstrates how a lifetime of belittlement and intimidation can erode one's ability to act ethically in the world. In "Miss Muriel" and "The New Mirror," Petry creates a black family much like her own--the Layens are professionals who own the pharmacy in a small New England town. The adolescent girl who narrates these tales speaks of "the training in issues of race" she has received over the years, not only through the casual bigotries she has witnessed but also through the painful self-consciousness of respectable people like her parents, whose behavior is a continual exercise in refuting cultural stereotypes while carefully preserving proudly held racial loyalties.

In "The New Mirror" the ironies are more overt and cleaner. Mr. Layen's decision to take a day off to outfit himself with a new pair of false teeth leads his unknowing wife to an excruciating encounter with police, from whom she withholds her fear that the absent Layen may have become another black man who deserts his family as a delayed response to a lifetime of indignities within the white patriarchal social order. Layen's surprising secrecy leads his daughter to realize that even securing a new set of teeth subjects a black male to humiliation, in this case taking the form of the grinning Sambos and toothless Uncle Toms he fears his dental problems will call to mind. The child learns to use the codes by which the black middle class shields itself from white contempt--just as she shoulders her own share of the burden of always acting with an eye on the reputation of "the Race." She thus learns why "all of us people with this dark skin must help hold the black island inviolate."

"MISS MURIEL"

The title story of the volume, "Miss Muriel," operates more subtly in its exploration of the racist preoccupations inculcated within and often unwillingly relinquished by its victims. The title itself refers to a white racist joke the young narrator innocently relates to one of Aunt Sophronia's black suitors--a joke in which an African American trying to buy a Muriel cigar is upbraided for not showing the proper respect for white womanhood by asking instead for a "Miss" Muriel. The child is bluntly chastised for voicing such "nigger" put-downs in one of the many moments of confusion she suffers over the inconsistent and seemingly arbitrary management of prejudices operating among the adults around her: her aunt's unpopular courtship by Bemish, a white member of their upstate New York community; the equal dismay with which Mr. Layen regards Sophronia's other suitor, the "tramp

piano player" Chink, who evokes the "low" culture of the black masses, from which the bourgeois Layen has distanced himself as part of his accommodation to a scornful white world; the contempt quietly directed against the homosexual partner of her cherished Uncle Johno; the colorist hierarchies of all the African Americans she knows (even when the lightest skinned among them eschew the opportunity to "pass"). At the end of the story, when the black men in her circle have effectively driven Bemish out of town for his persistent wooing of Sophronia, the narrator brokenheartedly confronts their hypocrisy, yelling, "You both stink. You stink like dead bats. You and your goddamn Miss Muriel." Internalizing such divisiveness as they have just enforced directly clashes with the other set of values she has been taught, and the two are starkly juxtaposed early in the story when the child muses:

> If my objections to Mr. Bemish are because he's white . . . then I have been "trained" on the subject of race just as I have been trained to be a Christian. . . .

It is one of the paradoxes of bigotry that its victims may become its emissaries, at the price of their most cherished beliefs.

"THE WITNESS"

Petry revisits this theme in a number of ways throughout the collection. Against the most aggressive forms of white hatred directed at her characters, there is no defense except a temporary abandonment of one's human dignity. "The Witness" presents the case of a retired black college professor who takes a high school teaching position in a northern white community. Called upon to assist the local pastor in counseling delinquent adolescents, he finds himself their prey as they kidnap him and force him to watch their sexual abuse of a young white woman. Having at one point coerced him to place his hand on the girl, they effectively blackmail him into complicit silence about their crime, for he is paralyzed by the specter of being publicly accused of the ultimate racial taboo. His exemplary life and professional stature cannot protect him from such sordid insinuations, and he bitterly describes himself in his moral impotence as "another poor scared black bastard who was a witness."

"THE NECESSARY KNOCKING ON THE DOOR"

In "The Necessary Knocking on the Door" a similar loss of agency is made bitingly ironic by the context in which Alice Knight's dilemma unfolds: A participant at a conference about the role of Christianity in the modern world, she finds herself unable to master her dislike for a white woman dying in the hotel room across the hall from hers--a woman who had earlier in the day refused to be seated next to a "nigger" and had thus awakened in Alice the bitterness that a lifetime of such indignities has nurtured. Her hardened heart is jolted the next day by news of the woman's death during the night--and her own guilty knowledge that she alone had heard the woman's distress but had let the hated epithet reduce her to that "animal," "outcast," "obscene" state it implies--not because it had been leveled at her but because she had let it rob her of her Christian commitment to do good to those who harm her. Even her own dreams indict Alice: "The octopus moonlight" pitilessly asserts, "Yours is the greater crime. A crime. A very great crime. It was a crime. And we were the witnesses." Like other African American writers before and since, Petry warns that prejudice delivers its most sinister harm when it saps its victims' capacity for decency and compassion and enlists them in the service of a gospel of irreparable division. In these stories Petry vividly captures the spiritual anguish of discovering that one's own grievances can weaken rather than deepen one's moral courage.

"THE BONES OF LOUELLA BROWN"

Petry's handling of white perspectives on racism is more unyielding. The absurdities into which segregationist practices lead multiracial societies (including the pseudosciences hunting frantically for physical evidence of racial "difference") are lampooned in "The Bones of Louella Brown." The most prestigious family in Massachusetts, the Bedfords, find their plans to build a chapel for their deceased members compromised when an undertaker's assistant confuses the bones of an African American maid with the sole noblewoman in their clan and, because of the "shocking" similarities of hair, teeth, height, and bone mass between the two skeletons, cannot differentiate the two. That alone is newsworthy enough to attract a Boston reporter sniffing for scandal, but the story gets juicier when it

becomes clear there is every likelihood that the segregation that has been a hallmark of the cemetery in question will be permanently breached once it can no longer guarantee that "black" bones will not commingle in the same park with "white" bones. After Mrs. Brown makes a series of ghostly visitations to principals in the story, they decide to acknowledge the truth with an epitaph explaining that either woman (or both) may lie in the crypt, along with the admission of their common humanity: "They both wore the breastplate of faith and love, and for a helmet, the hope of salvation." Here too Petry moves her reader beyond social contexts and into metaphysical ones by reminding readers that this story of dry bones (an unmistakable homage to a favorite trope of black oral tradition) is also a meditation on mortality itself, which exposes such preoccupation with earthly pecking orders for the consummate folly it is.

"THE MIGRAINE WORKERS"

"The Migraine Workers" offers another example of white protagonists brought up short in the knowledge of their moral blindness in following the unquestioned attitudes of a lifetime. Pedro Gonzalez, proud owner of a successful truck stop, suddenly finds himself staring into a trailer full of migrant laborers exuding a human misery more palpable than anything he has ever encountered. Outraged by the black driver, who blithely explains how he usually hides such scenes from public scrutiny, Pedro feeds the people with the surplus food left on his premises by other haulers. When he later discovers that an elderly man from the crew has hidden himself in the area and is living off what he can scavenge from the truckstop, his first impulse is to have the man removed by the police. It is only when his longtime assistant challenges his callousness and points to the resources they could easily spare for the man's upkeep that Pedro realizes how his own fleshy body indicts him of complicity in a system of polarized haves and have-nots: migraine-producing epiphanies indeed in the land of equal opportunity.

"MOTHER AFRICA"

Other stories in the collection evoke the mysterious private centers of grief hidden in the human heart: "Olaf and His Girl Friend" and "Solo on the Drums" show Petry's interest in African American music as an exquisite, untranslatable evocation of that pain. "Mother Africa" introduces Emanuel Turner, another of Petry's junk men, whose business indicts the acquisitive mandate of American consumer culture.

Years earlier, the loss of his wife and baby in childbirth had robbed Turner of any further desire for self-improvement; as a junk dealer he is free from anxious adherence to other people's standards of worth or accomplishment, and because he is his own man, he is a welcome figure to those around him. All that changes when a friend blesses him with the huge sculpture of a female nude being discarded by a wealthy white woman. The statue seduces Turner back into a realm of self-conscious striving as he tries to live up to its grandeur; in the process he loses his liberty and the easy rapport he has had with his neighbors. Convinced that the statue is a mythic evocation of Africa itself, he resents the prudish efforts of others to clothe her as missionaries had once done to his ancestors. Thus he is stunned to learn that this dark madonna is not a black woman at all but a white woman--the oxidized metal had misled him.

By parodying the assumed black male obsession with white women in this way, Petry implies that the real hunger at work is for authentic enunciation of the African American experience, a hunger left unsatisfied when Turner hurriedly rushes to sell the piece for scrap. In succumbing to the desire to make a world fit for his queenly companion, Turner submits himself for the first time in twenty-five years to the pressures of conformity and material acquisition. Is it love which so compromises him? Or are the statue's racial associations Petry's warnings against the lure of cultural standards derived from the spiritually bankrupt spheres of white consumer capitalism? Taken together, the stories in this collection offer tantalizing variations upon Petry's most insistent themes.

OTHER MAJOR WORKS

LONG FICTION: *The Street*, 1946; *Country Place*, 1947; *The Narrows*, 1953.

CHILDREN'S LITERATURE: *The Drugstore Cat*, 1949; *Harriet Tubman: Conductor on the Underground Railroad*, 1955; *Tituba of Salem Village*, 1964; *Legends of the Saints*, 1970.

BIBLIOGRAPHY

Bell, Bernard. "Ann Petry's Demythologizing of American Culture and Afro-American Character." In *Conjuring: Black Women, Fiction, and Literary Tradition*, edited by Marjorie Pryse and Hortense J. Spillers. Bloomington: Indiana University Press, 1985. An argument for moving Petry out of the shadow of male contemporaries like Richard Wright to permit her fiction the proper reevaluation it deserves.

Clark, Keith. "A Distaff Dream Deferred? Ann Petry and the Art of Subversion." *African-American Review* 26 (Fall, 1992): 495-505. A study of Petry's interest in the ways black women respond to the American Dream while subverting it to their own ends.

Ervin, Hazel Arnett, ed. *The Critical Response to Ann Petry*. Westport, Conn.: Praeger, 2005. A compilation of sixteen reviews and twenty-six essays that trace the literary reception of Petry's three novels in the United States from 1946 to the present.

Ervin, Hazel Arnett, and Hilary Holladay, eds. *Ann Petry's Short Fiction: Critical Essays*. Westport, Conn.: Praeger, 2004. A collection of essays addressing Petry's short stories, including issues of gender, race, and folklore. "Miss Muriel," "Solo on the Drums," "In Darkness and Confusion," "Witness," and "The Bones of Louella Brown" are among the stories analyzed.

Gross, Theodore. "Ann Petry: The Novelist as Social Critic." In *Black Fiction: New Studies in the Afro-American Novel Since 1945*, edited by A. Robert Lee. New York: Barnes & Noble, 1980. A discussion of Petry's strong commitment to an aesthetic of social realism that puts art in the service of political, economic, and societal transformation and justice.

Hernton, Calvin. "The Significance of Ann Petry." In *The Sexual Mountain and Black Women Writers*. New York: Doubleday, 1987. An analysis of the relationship between Petry's fiction and that of contemporary black women writers, particularly in its wedding of social protest and violence.

Lubin, Alex, ed. *Revising the Blueprint: Ann Petry and the Literary Left*. Jackson: University Press of Mississippi, 2007. Collection of essays that examine

Petry's relationship to left-wing political movements in the years after World War II. One of the essays focuses on her short story "New Mirror," while others discuss her three novels, the "dialectics of racial privacy" in her early career, and counter-modernity, black masculinity, and female silence in her fiction.

Petry, Elisabeth. *At Home Inside: A Daughter's Tribute to Ann Petry*. Jackson: University Press of Mississippi, 2009. Petry's daughter provides a loving portrait of her mother, describing the contradictions and complexities of her personality. Elisabeth Petry also explains how her mother used her life to create her fiction.

Washington, Gladys. "A World Made Cunningly: A Closer Look at Ann Petry's Short Fiction." *College Language Association Journal* 30 (September, 1986): 14-29. A critical argument for tracing Petry's important themes and their evolving nuances through her understudied short stories.

Wilson, Mark. "A *MELUS* Interview: Ann Petry--The New England Connection." *MELUS* 15 (Summer, 1988): 71-84. A discussion with Petry about her early life and the first decades of her writing career.

Barbara Kitt Seidman

JAYNE ANNE PHILLIPS

Born: Buckhannon, West Virginia; July 19, 1952

PRINCIPAL SHORT FICTION
Sweethearts, 1976
Counting, 1978
Black Tickets, 1979
How Mickey Made It, 1981
The Secret Country, 1982
Fast Lanes, 1987

OTHER LITERARY FORMS

Although Jayne Anne Phillips's oeuvre is dominated by her short fiction, which includes contributions to numerous anthologies, she has also written the novels *Machine Dreams* (1984), *Shelter* (1994), *MotherKind* (2000), and *Lark and Termite* (2009). *Machine Dreams* was a critical and popular success and was ultimately translated into fourteen languages.

ACHIEVEMENTS

Jayne Anne Phillips's work has been critically acclaimed throughout the world. Her honors include the Pushcart Prize for *Sweethearts*, as well as for several of her short stories in later years; the St. Lawrence Award for *Counting;* the Sue Kaufman Prize for First Fiction, awarded by the American Academy and Institute of Arts and Letters, for *Black Tickets*; the O. Henry Award in 1980 for her short story "Snow"; and a National Book Critics Circle Award nomination, an American Library Association Notable Book citation, and a *New York Times* Best Books citation for *Machine Dreams*, all in 1984. *Lark and Termite* was a finalist for the 2009 National Book Award in Fiction. In addition, Phillips is the recipient of a Guggenheim Fellowship, two National Endowment for the Arts Fellowships, and a Bunting Fellowship from the Bunting Institute of Radcliffe College.

BIOGRAPHY

Jayne Anne Phillips was born July 19, 1952, in Buckhannon, West Virginia. Her parents were Russell R. Phillips, a contractor, and Martha Jane Phillips (née Thornhill), a teacher. On May 26, 1985, Phillips married Mark Brian Stockman, a physician.

Phillips received a B.A. (magna cum laude) from West Virginia University in 1974 and an M.F.A. from the University of Iowa in 1978. In 1982, she began working as an adjunct associate professor of English at Boston University, and she also held the Fanny Howe Chair of Letters at Brandeis University, Waltham, Massachusetts, from

1986 to 1987. Despite her evidently academic career, however, Phillips has said that teaching does not really interest her and that she prefers to write.

ANALYSIS

Jayne Anne Phillips's writing style in her short fiction varies in person and in tone. For example, in *How Mickey Made It* (first published in *Rolling Stone* on February 5, 1981), the writing style suggests the rambling monologue that results from hearing only one side of a conversation. Phillips originally started her writing career as a poet, an influence that critics contend is apparent in her prose.

Many of Phillips's stories track the modern pursuit of happiness, which seems, for the most part, to be an unsuccessful quest: The main characters in stories such as "Fast Lanes" (first published in *Granta--More Dirt: The New American Fiction* in the fall of 1986) and "Bess" (first published in *Esquire* in August, 1984) are all trying to get away from their homes and families, either physically or mentally. The action often takes place around the time of the Vietnam War or soon thereafter. In "Blue Moon," the protagonist's younger brother, Billy, is told to improve his school grades, with his mother pleading, "Don't you know you'll get drafted? Vietnam is on the news every night now."

Many of Phillips's stories are drawn from observations made while traveling during a period in the 1970's that one critic called "her rootless days on the road," when she wandered from West Virginia to California and back again. "Fast Lanes" concerns the travels of a pair of post-Vietnam era "dropouts," one a self-described "hippie carpenter" named Thurman and the other an unnamed, twenty-three-year-old cocaine addict who cannot face her addiction--or the consequences of her self-destructive behavior. During a conversation about their respective pasts, Thurman says about "the old days":

> People weren't stupid; they just didn't worry. The war was over, no one was getting drafted. The girls had birth control pills . . . and everything was chummy.

However, he then negates this lotus-land vision with a cynical "Ha." Phillips's stories concentrate on the illusiveness of the sunny American Dream. Thurman's brother Barnes is killed in Vietnam, but his parents refuse to accept it; instead, his father believes that his eldest son's death was caused by drugs because he "wouldn't have died otherwise, he was an athlete." His mother, meanwhile, finds solace in alcohol, preferring to believe that Barnes is still alive, although she is upset that he never calls or writes.

Phillips does not accept "true love" as the panacea to these ills. In "Fast Lanes," the main character's addiction or self-destructive tendencies are too strong to allow her to accept healing in the form of love from Thurman. In "Blue Moon," the protagonist's mother is forever soured on football--she will not allow her son to play for the school team--when her first real love dies of a heart attack after a football game. Her marriage to someone she clearly considers second best disintegrates through the years, and she tries to break up her son's love affair with an "unsuitable" girl.

"BESS"

In "Bess," true love has become forbidden love, as it exists between a brother and a sister. It is not necessarily an incestuous love, for in this large family, each brother is described as having a favorite sister. However, as the main character, Bess, notes, "No love is innocent once it has recognized its own existence." For the title character in "Bess," the death of her brother Warwick ends her emotional life. She is left alone, with only memories of an event from years before to keep her company.

Many of Phillips's stories develop similar themes. In "Home," "The Heavenly Animal," "Souvenir," "Fast Lanes," and "Something That Happened," Phillips covers the problems of grown-up children and their aging parents. In "Home," a young woman comes home as an adult, forcing her mother to accept both her daughter's and her own sexuality. "The Heavenly Animal" addresses the failure that a father faces as he attempts to draw his adult daughter into his life as a senior citizen. "Souvenir" is the heartrending account of a mother dying of cancer who still can find the strength and courage to comfort her daughter. In "Fast Lanes," a son must accept the mental disintegration of his parents as age and emotional trauma take their toll. Conversely, "Something That Happened" deals with a mother who

Jayne Anne Phillips (AFP/Getty Images)

must accept the strange behavior of her daughter, who morbidly forces her mother to celebrate her wedding anniversary even though her parents have been divorced for five years. In fact, the mother, Kay, notes, "the last sound of the marriage was Richard (her soon-to-be-former-husband) being nervously sick in the kitchen sink."

"SOMETHING THAT HAPPENED"

Phillips's characters often seem on the verge of self-destruction or else eating themselves alive. The mother in "Something That Happened" has had to have half of her stomach removed because of ulcers; through stress and worry, she has chewed her way through her own stomach lining. In fact, she finally tells her children:

> Look, I can't worry for you anymore. If you get into trouble, don't call me. If you want someone to take care of you, take care of each other.

Since then, she has gradually resumed what she calls her "duties," although she still draws the line at attending any of her children's weddings. "Something That Happened" looks at the family from the perspective of a woman trapped by society. The main character, Kay, notes that a woman's fertile years are called "the Child-Bearing Years, as though you stand there like a blossomed pear tree and the fruit plops off." Ironically, her first three daughters become feminist vegetarians, but her fourth, Angela, is a throwback to the days of women in marital bondage. Of her mother's former wedding anniversary, Angela says to Kay: "The trouble with you . . . is that you don't care enough about yourself to remember what's been important in your life," conveniently ignoring the destructiveness of this "something that happened." In addition, Kay has to contend with her daughter trying to feed her, as though if she eats "surely something good will happen."

The perspective of this story is multifaceted; it shows the hurt and anger of a daughter who feels betrayed by her parents' divorce, while also presenting evidence that the marriage was literally eating up Kay. Kay's former husband, Richard, comes across as a selfish, sickening sort of personality. For example, after "the fourth pregnancy and first son," Richard is satisfied; he terms the fifth baby a "miscalculation" on Kay's part. This fifth pregnancy does not go as well as the others, however, and Richard feels guilty over not wanting the baby to begin with, so "he swore his love to [Angela]," giving her anything she wanted and a diamond ring on her sixteenth birthday. It is perhaps from this unhealthy aspect of the relationship that Kay is trying most to escape. She even bluntly tells Richard that Angela is his daughter, not his fiancé. The day that Richard "slipped the diamond on [Angela's] finger," Kay filed for divorce.

Dysfunctional though this family may be, it is not an obvious picture; characters are abused or degraded in very subtle ways. In fact, what Phillips writes about are the black undercurrents that slowly, inexorably drag her characters down, grinding the hope and joy out of their lives. One of the final images in "Something That Happened" is Kay's recollection of "starting oranges for ten years, piercing thick skins with a fingernail so that the kids could peel them." After a while, she continues, she "didn't want to watch the skin give way to the white ragged coat beneath."

It is this "white ragged coat" that symbolizes the raw pain inside Phillips's characters, pain that is often never resolved or ameliorated. However, these people do not necessarily give up on life; rather, they live from day to day, surviving as best they can. Phillips's stories have a realistically gritty finish.

OTHER MAJOR WORKS

LONG FICTION: *Machine Dreams*, 1984; *Shelter*, 1994; *MotherKind*, 2000; *Lark and Termite*, 2009.

BIBLIOGRAPHY

Carter, Susanne. "Variations on Vietnam: Women's Innovative Interpretations of the Vietnam War Experience." *Extrapolation* 32 (Summer, 1991): 170-183. Addresses what Carter calls "the most representative interpretation possible for a war that still begs for definition." She cites Phillips as foremost among the modern innovative writers who reach "beyond the confines of realism to expand the possibilities of interpretation in their individual novels and short stories." Although this article mainly looks at *Machine Dreams*, it casts light on similar themes that recur in many of Phillips's works. Includes a list of works cited.

Edelstein, David. "The Short Story of Jayne Anne Phillips: She Transforms Isolation and Dark Obsession into Exquisite Prose." *Esquire* 104 (December, 1985): 108-112. This article provides good biographical background, including details of Phillips's childhood and early writing career. Contains comments from one of Phillips's first writing teachers, as well as information on Phillips's close relationship with her publisher, Seymour (Sam) Lawrence. Also details Phillips's wanderings across the United States before settling in Boston.

Gelfant, Blanche H., ed. *The Columbia Companion to the Twentieth-Century American Short Story*. New York: Columbia University Press, 2000. Includes a chapter in which Phillips's short stories are analyzed.

Goldberg, G. D. "The Intimacy of Mass Culture." *New Perspectives Quarterly* 7 (Winter, 1990): 58-62. In this interview, Phillips talks about the role that television plays in the minds of children, suggesting that mass-cultural images replace myth and tradition with little sense of relationship between cultures and generations.

"Jayne Anne Phillips." *Harper's Bazaar* (October, 1984): 213. A brief biographical sketch of Phillips, commenting on her collection of short stories *Black Tickets* and her first novel, *Machine Dreams*. Notes that Phillips is dedicated to maintaining the quality of her art and has refused offers to write for Hollywood.

Lassner, Phyllis. "Jayne Anne Phillips: Women's Narrative and the Re-creation of History." In *American Women Writing Fiction: Memory, Identity, Family, Space*, edited by Mickey Pearlman. Lexington: University Press of Kentucky, 1989. Examines Phillips's work in the context of her own comments on characters and settings in her stories. Much of the chapter is devoted to stories from the collection *Fast Lanes* and includes an in-depth discussion of Phillips's writing. Complemented by primary and secondary bibliographies; the primary bibliography is especially helpful for individual publication dates and places for stories.

Phillips, Jayne Anne. "Interview with Jayne Anne Phillips." Interview by Celia Gilbert. *Publishers Weekly* 225 (June 8, 1984): 65-67. Phillips gives her views on her writing, with details about the family stories in *Black Tickets*. Contains some biographical information, as well as information on her writing career and her relationship with Seymour (Sam) Lawrence. Phillips also reveals influences on her writing and explains how she works.

Robertson, Sarah. *The Secret Country: Decoding Jayne Anne Phillips' Cryptic Fiction*. New York: Rodopi, 2007. Examines the "southern aspects" in Phillips's writing, notably the importance of place and her attachment to a regional past. Traces the family dynamics in her fiction. The majority of chapters focus on Phillip's first three novels, but Robertson devotes one chapter to the short-story collection *Fast Lanes*, and references to other short stories and collections are listed in the index.

Jo-Ellen Lipman Boon

SYLVIA PLATH

Born: Boston, Massachusetts; October 27, 1932
Died: London, England; February 11, 1963
Also known as: Victoria Lucas

PRINCIPAL SHORT FICTION

Johnny Panic and the Bible of Dreams, 1977, 1979
    (prose sketches)

OTHER LITERARY FORMS

Sylvia Plath is widely recognized as one of the strongest and most distinctive American poets of the postwar period. Her major collections include *The Colossus, and Other Poems* (1960) and a number of posthumous collections, including *Ariel* (1965), *Crossing the Water* (1971), *Collected Poems* (1981), and *Sylvia Plath: Poems* (2000). She also wrote the best-selling novel *The Bell Jar*, which first appeared in England under the pseudonym Victoria Lucas in 1963.

ACHIEVEMENTS

Sylvia Plath's *Collected Poems* won the Pulitzer Prize for poetry in 1982. She was a Fulbright scholar in England (1955-1957) and a Phi Beta Kappan.

BIOGRAPHY

Sylvia Plath was born October 27, 1932, in Boston, Massachusetts. Her father Otto, a professor of biology and renowned entomologist, died when she was a young child, leaving Plath in the care of her mother Aurelia (née Schober). A number of instances in her writings acknowledge this event as one of the most traumatic in her life, creating in her a sense of abandonment that fueled the dark, introspective character that is prominent in her work. A distinguished academic, Plath graduated summa cum laude from Smith College in 1955. She attended Newnham College, Cambridge University, on a Fulbright scholarship, receiving her

M.A. in 1957. She married renowned English poet Ted Hughes in 1956.

After completing her graduate work at Cambridge, Plath returned to the United States, where she taught for a year at Smith. Shortly thereafter, she returned with Hughes to England, where she spent the last years of her life raising two children and writing. She committed suicide in February, 1963.

Plath was briefly institutionalized after a breakdown and suicide attempt in 1953 that delayed the completion of her undergraduate work at Smith. She recounts this experience in the autobiographical novel *The Bell Jar*, which appeared shortly before her death in 1963. Plath's literary reputation is based primarily on the confessional, metaphorically dense poems she wrote during the late 1950's and early 1960's. However, she also wrote a number of short-fiction works during this period that appeared in publications as diverse as *Sewanee Review*, *The Atlantic Monthly*, *Madamoiselle*, and *Granta*. In the decades following her death much of this work has been rediscovered primarily because of the 1977 publication of *Johnny Panic and the Bible of Dreams*, a collection of Plath's more significant short prose writings.

ANALYSIS

Like her poetry, Plath's short fiction is characterized primarily by its mythic dimension. It reveals a profound fascination with dream and ritual and their connection to artistic endeavor. Similarly, both her poetry and fiction are strikingly allusive. Regardless of its subject matter or genre, the body of Plath's work concerns the aura of mystery and myth surrounding major transitions in human life. Her stories typically concern the ambivalence people feel during transformative experiences, and they seek to characterize that ambivalence.

Ted Hughes asserts in his introduction to Plath's short-fiction collection *Johnny Panic and the Bible of Dreams* that her fiction also tends to be highly autobiographical. In fact, Plath withheld much of it from publication during her lifetime, fearing the reprisals of those who might recognize themselves and disapprove of her portrayal of them in her work. Plath's protagonists are almost universally female, which also suggests that she wished to remain at the center of even her most exotic and experimental stories.

As do many fiction writers, Plath frequently recycles characters and motifs from previous works. A number of her earlier short stories in ways appear to function as prototypes for her most developed work, the later novel *The Bell Jar*. For example, both *The Bell Jar* and "Johnny Panic and the Bible of Dreams" depict traumatic experiences with electroshock therapy, although each differs significantly in style and tone. Henry in "Sunday at the Mintons'" and *The Bell Jar*'s Buddy Willard possess a similar tendency toward dogged, uninspired rationality. Both "Mothers" and *The Bell Jar* center on the experiences of a protagonist named Esther, who is often interpreted as Plath's alter ego. Similarly, Esther struggles in both works with her fears and misgivings about motherhood and female identity.

"Sunday at the Mintons'"

Plath's earliest story to merit critical attention, "Sunday at the Mintons,'" reflects in prose the stylistic tendency of her early poetry toward control and order. Written in third person to heighten its pervasive sense of restraint, the story focuses on the relationship between two parentless, retired siblings--the compulsive, "fastidious" Henry and his "impertinent," daydreaming sister Elizabeth. Having been forced late in life into each other's care, the pair confront their many differences in personality and perspective during an evening meal and stroll by the ocean.

Plath's discipline as a poet becomes markedly evident in this story, particularly toward its conclusion. In the climactic scene, Elizabeth loses a treasured brooch, given to her by her deceased mother, while leaning absently into the evening tide. When Henry treads stiffly but dutifully into the water to retrieve it, he is leveled by an unexpectedly strong "black" wave. Elizabeth, unable to deny the humor in the situation, takes the opportunity to muse lyrically about her brother, whom she compares to "Neptune sitting regally on a wave with his trident in his hand and the crown on his blown white hair." Henry, the unlikely object of her mythic fantasy, returns from the sea dripping wet, brooch in hand. His gesture underscores the story's awareness of the tension between rigidity and spontaneity in human experience.

"Johnny Panic and the Bible of Dreams"

Brazenly satirical and consciously allegorical, "Johnny Panic and the Bible of Dreams," written in 1958, differs markedly in approach from Plath's other fiction. The story was composed around the same time as *The Bell Jar* and is akin to the novel in subject matter. Like *The Bell Jar*, "Johnny Panic" concerns Plath's deep fear of electroshock therapy, with which she had a number of horrific experiences in her lifelong battle with depression. However, while the depiction of her experiences with the therapy in the novel is primarily straightforward, in "Johnny Panic" it is woven into an allegorical tapestry that is decidedly more surrealistic and Kafkaesque. The story's unnamed

Sylvia Plath (Bettmann/CORBIS)

narrator, a clerical worker in a psychiatric ward, is caught by one of her supervisors, a psychiatrist, copying accounts of patients' dreams into a secret notebook, which she fancifully calls "Johnny Panic's Bible of Dreams." A self-proclaimed "lover of dreams," she seeks what, to her mind, is a clearer understanding of the collective unconscious through these stolen dream accounts. She describes the unconscious as a "lake" into which "people's minds run at night . . . the sewage farm of the ages."

The narrator is promptly whisked away by the doctor into electroshock therapy, which she chides as an attempt "to unseat Johnny Panic from his own throne." The story ends with her first treatment, the narrator left "shaken like a leaf in the teeth of glory," her namesake Johnny Panic beckoning her in "a nimbus of arc lights on the ceiling overhead." The story's ambiguous, irresolute ending reflects the narrator's own ambivalence toward both the shame and sanctimoniousness of her illness. At some points she flaunts her condition playfully before the reader like a badge of honor; at others she hides it self-consciously like her purloined book of dreams.

"THE FIFTEEN-DOLLAR EAGLE"

Written in 1959, "The Fifteen-Dollar Eagle" contains some of Plath's boldest experiments with subject matter, description, and characterization. Written in first person, but with relatively little interpretive intrusion on the part of the narrator, the story meticulously describes the inner workings of a tattoo shop. On the insistence of her "steady man" Ned Bean, the narrator visits the shop of Carmey, a colorful and matter-of-fact tattoo artist, where she furtively explores the part-ritualistic, part-clinical exhibition of Carmey's craft.

The narrator tentatively observes Carmey as he tattoos two men--one a seasoned sailor, the other a naïve schoolboy. Each man's unique reaction to this exotic, seminal experience sets up the story's central dynamic, which involves the tension between the pride and fear associated with this archetypal but enigmatic ritual. Plath describes the ritual memorably, in a story rich and perceptive in its passion for detail and description.

"MOTHERS"

Plath's last completed story, "Mothers," written in 1962, deals with two of the most prevalent motifs in her fiction, hypocrisy and motherhood. The story concerns Esther, a young mother who, having recently moved to the English countryside, seeks to involve herself in her new community by attending a "Mothers' Union" meeting at the local church. Through a litany of disillusioning experiences with superficial and self-important "church people," Esther eventually establishes a more satisfying, meaningful relationship with Mrs. Nolan, an outspoken, endearing divorcée. Ironically, Mrs. Nolan has been summarily excluded from the Mothers' Union because of the church's disapproval of divorce. Still, she forges an unlikely but intimate bond with Esther, who shares her sense of alienation and innate sense of being tagged an "outsider."

"Mothers" is among Plath's most pointedly autobiographical stories. Written at a time when marital frictions between her and husband Ted Hughes had led to their separation, the story likewise has Esther and husband Tom "arguing loudly and freely" as the story begins. Similarly, "Mothers" presents an almost pathological preoccupation with hypocrisy. This is portrayed primarily in the character of the absentminded, solicitous village rector, who embodies the fundamental lack of sincerity and conviction Esther regards as endemic to organized religion. "Mothers" clearly reflects the struggles Plath herself endured late in her life as she fought to forge a new identity in the wake of marital conflict, single parenthood, religious skepticism, and depression.

OTHER MAJOR WORKS

LONG FICTION: *The Bell Jar*, 1963 (originally pb. under the name Victoria Lucas).

POETRY: *The Colossus, and Other Poems*, 1960; *Three Women*, 1962; *Ariel*, 1965 (revised as *Ariel: The Restored Edition*, 2004); *Uncollected Poems*, 1965; *Crossing the Water*, 1971; *Crystal Gazer*, 1971; *Fiesta Melons*, 1971; *Lyonesse*, 1971; *Winter Trees*, 1971; *Pursuit*, 1973; *The Collected Poems*, 1981 (Ted Hughes, editor); *Selected Poems*, 1985; *Sylvia Plath: Poems*, 2000 (Ted Hughes, editor).

NONFICTION: *Letters Home*, 1975; *The Journals of Sylvia Plath*, 1982 (Ted Hughes and Frances Mc-Cullough, editors); *The Unabridged Journals of Sylvia*

Plath, 1950-1962, 2000 (Karen V. Kukil, editor).
CHILDREN'S LITERATURE: *The Bed Book*, 1976.

BIBLIOGRAPHY

Alvarez, A. *The Savage God: A Study of Suicide*. New York: Random House, 1972. Probes the connections between Plath's thematic preoccupation with suicide and the inner traumas that led her to take her own life. Uses the life and work of Plath as a focal point for a broadly based discussion of the theme of self-destruction and annihilation present in the work of many artists.

Blosser, Silvianne. *A Poetics on Edge: The Poetry and Prose of Sylvia Plath, a Study of Sylvia Plath's Poetic and Poetological Developments*. New York: Peter Lang, 2001. Focuses on the language in Plath's short stories, poems, and her novel *The Bell Jar*, tracing the development of her own poetics.

Brain, Tracy. *The Other Sylvia Plath*. New York: Longman, 2001. A biographical study of Plath and her writings that argues for a distinction between Plath's "real life" and her artistic expression. Brain suggests that readers should consider even Plath's journals as less than strictly autobiographical.

Bundtzen, Lynda K. *Plath's Incarnations: Woman and the Creative Process*. Ann Arbor: University of Michigan Press, 1983. A collection of critical essays exploring various issues in Plath's poetry and fiction, particularly those related to feminine identity. Contains an exceptionally perceptive analysis of *The Bell Jar* and Plath's related, "autobiographical" fiction.

Butscher, Edward. *Sylvia Plath: Method and Madness*. New York: Seabury Press, 1976. The first major critical biography of Plath; a highly accessible account of the forces that shaped her distinctive poetic and fictive voices.

_____, ed. *Sylvia Plath: The Woman and the Work*. New York: Dodd, Mead, 1977. A collection of critical essays on the life and work of Plath compiled by her principal biographer. Opens with a biographical essay by the editor, followed by critical essays on Plath's work by a number of prominent writers and critics, including Joyce Carol Oates, Irving Howe, and Marjorie Perloff. Devotes two chapters directly to the discussion of Plath's fiction.

Gill, Jo, ed. *Cambridge Companion to Sylvia Plath*. Cambridge, England: Cambridge, 2006. A two-prong approach to Plath and her works. One section deals with "Context and Issues" and the other with "Works;" Chapter 9 examines her novel *The Bell Jar* and her other prose. The student of Plath will find both sections invaluable.

Hall, Caroline King Barnard. *Sylvia Plath, Revised*. Boston: Twayne, 1998. As the title implies, a pointedly revisionist view of Plath's work. Noting that much of the significant criticism of Plath's poetry and fiction appeared in the 1970's, this collection attempts to reinterpret Plath's works in a more contemporary context. Features one of the most detailed discussions of her short fiction to date.

Helle, Anita, ed. *The Unraveling Archive: Essays on Sylvia Plath*. Ann Arbor: University of Michigan, 2007. Eleven original essays that draw on correspondence and manuscript drafts to discuss Plath's life and writings. Includes family photographs and full-page reproductions of her paintings.

Hughes, Ted. *Birthday Letters*. New York: Farrar, Straus & Giroux, 1998. A collection of poems written by Hughes on the subject of his heavily mythologized relationship with Plath. At times joyous, at others painfully self-revealing, the book offers valuable insights into both the professional and personal relationship shared by these two literary icons.

Middlebrook, Diane. *Her Husband: Hughes and Plath -a Marriage*. New York: Viking, 2003. Middlebrook brings insight and empathy to a probing examination of the literary marriage of the century.

Stevenson, Anne. *Bitter Fame: A Life of Sylvia Plath*. Boston: Houghton Mifflin, 1989. More personal in nature than Butscher's biography, this book focuses more closely on the pathology of Plath's struggle with depression. Draws heavily on insights gained from Plath's close friends and acquaintances, making it as much a depiction of Plath the person as Plath the writer.

Gregory D. Horn

EDGAR ALLAN POE

Born: Boston, Massachusetts; January 19, 1809
Died: Baltimore, Maryland; October 7, 1849

PRINCIPAL SHORT FICTION
Tales of the Grotesque and Arabesque, 1840
The Prose Romances of Edgar Allan Poe, 1843
Tales, 1845
The Short Fiction of Edgar Allan Poe, 1976 (Stuart
  Levine and Susan Levine, editors)

OTHER LITERARY FORMS
During his short literary career, Edgar Allan Poe produced a large quantity of writing, most of which was not collected in book form during his lifetime. He published one novel, *The Narrative of Arthur Gordon Pym* (1838), and several volumes of poetry, the most famous of which is *The Raven and Other Poems* (1845). Poe earned his living primarily as a writer and as an editor of magazines. For magazines, he wrote reviews, occasional essays, meditations, literary criticism, and a variety of different kinds of journalism, as well as poetry and short fiction.

ACHIEVEMENTS
In his lifetime Edgar Allan Poe was a figure of controversy and so became reasonably well known in literary circles. Two of his works were recognized with prizes: "Manuscript Found in a Bottle" and "The Gold-Bug." "The Raven," his most famous poem, created a sensation when it was published and became something of a best seller. After his death, Poe's reputation grew steadily--though in the United States opinion remained divided--until by the middle of the twentieth century he had clear status as an author of worldwide importance. Poe's achievements may be measured in terms of what he has contributed to literature and of how his work influenced later culture.

Poe was accomplished in fiction, poetry, and criticism, setting standards in all three that distinguish him from most of his American contemporaries. In fiction, he is credited with inventing the conventions of the classical detective story, beginning the modern genre of science fiction, and turning the conventions of gothic fiction to the uses of high art in stories such as "The Fall of the House of Usher." He was also an accomplished humorist and satirist. In poetry, he produced a body of work that is respected throughout the world and a few poems that have endured as classics, notably "The Raven," as well as several poems that, in part because of their sheer verbal beauty, have persistently appealed to the popular imagination, such as "The Bells" and "Annabel Lee." In criticism, Poe was among the first to advocate and demonstrate methods of textual criticism that came into their own in the twentieth century, notably in his essay "The Philosophy of Composition," in which he analyzed with remarkable objectivity the process by which "The Raven" was built in order to produce a specified effect in its readers.

Poe's influence on later culture was pervasive. Nearly every important American writer after Poe shows signs of his influence, especially when working in the gothic mode or with grotesque humor. Only to begin to explore Poe's influence on twentieth century music and film would be a major undertaking. In terms of his world reputation, Poe stands with William Faulkner and perhaps T. S. Eliot as one of the most influential authors of the United States.

BIOGRAPHY
Edgar Allan Poe was born in Boston on January 19, 1809. His parents, David and Elizabeth Arnold Poe, were actors at a time when the profession was not widely respected in the United States. David was making a success in acting when alcohol addiction brought an end to his career. He deserted his family a year after Edgar's birth; Elizabeth died a year later in

1811, leaving Edgar an orphan in Richmond, Virginia. There, he was taken in by John Allan, who educated him well in England and the United States. Poe was a sensitive and precocious child; during his teens, his relations with his foster father declined. Stormy relations continued until Allan's first wife died and his second wife had children. Once it became unlikely that he would inherit anything significant from the wealthy Allan, Poe, at the age of twenty-one, having already published a volume of poetry, began a literary career.

From 1831 to 1835, more or less dependent on his Poe relatives, he worked in Baltimore, writing stories and poems, a few of which were published. In 1835, he secretly married his cousin, Virginia Clemm, when she was thirteen. From 1835 to 1837, he was assistant editor of *The southern Literary Messenger*, living on a meager salary, tending to drink enough to disappoint the editor, publishing his fiction, and making a national reputation as a reviewer of books. When he was fired, he moved with his wife (by then the marriage was publicly acknowledged) and her mother to New York City, where he lived in poverty, selling his writing for the next two years. Though he published *The Narrative of Arthur Gordon Pym* in 1838, it brought him no income. He moved to Philadelphia that same year and for several months continued to live on only a small income from stories and other magazine pieces. In 1839, he became coeditor of *Burton's Gentleman's Magazine*. Before drinking led to his losing this job, he wrote and published some of his best fiction, such as "The Fall of the House of Usher." He took another editing position with *Graham's Magazine* that lasted about a year. He then lived by writing and working at occasional jobs.

In 1844, he went with his family back to New York City. His wife, Virginia, had been seriously ill, and her health was declining. In New York, he wrote for newspapers. In 1845, he published "The Raven" and *Tales*, both of which were well received ("The Raven" was a popular success), though again his income from them was small. In the early nineteenth century, an author could not easily earn a satisfactory income from writing alone, in part because of the lack of international copyright laws. He was able to purchase a new weekly, the *Broadway Journal*, but it failed in 1846.

After 1845, Poe was famous, and his income, though unstable, was a little more dependable. His life, however, did not go smoothly. He was to some extent lionized in literary circles, but the combination of his desperation for financial support with alcoholism and a combative temper kept him from dealing well with being a "star." Virginia died in 1847, and Poe was seriously ill for much of the next year. In 1849, he found himself in Richmond, and for a few months he seemed quite well. His Richmond relatives received and cared for him kindly, and he stopped drinking. In October, however, while on a trip, he paused in Baltimore, became drunk, was found unconscious, and was carried to a local hospital, where he died on October 7, 1849.

ANALYSIS

The variety of Edgar Allan Poe's short fiction cannot be conveyed fully in a short introduction. Though he is best known for his classics of gothic horror, such as "The Fall of the House of Usher," and his portraits of madmen and grotesques, such as "The Tell-Tale Heart" and "The Cask of Amontillado," he is also the author of detective stories, "The Purloined Letter"; science fiction, *The Narrative of Arthur Gordon Pym*; parodies, "The Premature Burial"; satires, "The Man That Was Used Up"; social and political fiction, "The System of Dr. Tarr and Prof. Fether"; and a variety of kinds of humor, "Diddling Considered as One of the Exact Sciences" and "Hop-Frog."

Three stories that illustrate some of this variety while offering insight into Poe's characteristic themes are "A Descent into the Maelström," "The Purloined Letter," and "The Fall of the House of Usher." Among Poe's central themes is an emphasis on the mysteries of the self, of others, of nature, and of the universe. His stories usually function in part to undercut the kinds of easy optimism and certainty that were characteristic of popular thought in his time.

"A DESCENT INTO THE MAELSTRÖM"

"A Descent into the Maelström," which first appeared in *Graham's Magazine* in May, 1841, and was collected in *Tales*, opens with a declaration of mystery:

The ways of God in Nature, as in Providence, are not as our ways; nor are the models that we frame any way commensurate to the vastness, profundity, and unsearchableness of His works, which have a depth in them greater than the well of Democritus.

In using this epigraph, slightly altered from the seventeenth century English essayist Joseph Glanvill, Poe announces several motifs for the story that follows. One of these is the mystery of how God acts and, therefore, may be revealed in nature. Another is inadequacy of humanly devised models for explaining nature or God's presence in nature. Another motif is the idea of the multiple senses of depth, not merely the physical depth of a well or a maelstrom, but also the metaphorical depths of a mystery, of God, of nature, and of God's manifestation in nature.

This story is relatively simple in its outline, though interestingly complicated by its frame. In the frame, the narrator visits a remote region of Norway to look upon the famous maelstrom, an actual phenomenon described in contemporary reference books that were Poe's sources. There, he encounters an apparently retired fisherman, who guides him to a view of the whirlpool and who then tells the story of how he survived being caught in it. In the main body of the story, the guide explains how a sudden hurricane and a stopped watch caused him and his two brothers to be caught by the maelstrom as they attempted to return from a routine, if risky, fishing trip. He explains what the experience was like and how he managed to survive even though his boat and his brothers were lost. Poe carefully arranges the frame and the fisherman's narration to emphasize his themes.

The frame narrator is a somewhat comic character. The guide leads him to what he calls a little cliff and calmly leans over its edge to point out the sights, but the narrator is terrified by the cliff itself:

In truth so deeply was I excited by the perilous position of my companion, that I fell at full length upon the ground, clung to the shrubs around me, and dared not even glance upward at the sky--while I struggled in vain to divest myself of the idea that the very foundations of the mountain were in danger from the fury of the winds.

On one level this is high comedy. The narrator professes to be worried about his companion's safety but cannot help revealing that he is personally terrified, and his resulting posture contrasts humorously with the equanimity of his guide. On another level, however, Poe is also suggesting at least two serious ideas. The narrator's description of the cliff, with its sheer drop of sixteen hundred feet, should remind most readers that in a strong wind, they would feel and behave much the same as the narrator. This realization makes the next idea even more significant: The pose the narrator has adopted is pointedly a pose of worship drawn from the Old Testament of the Bible. The narrator abases himself full-length, not daring to look up while clinging to the earth. He behaves as if he is in the presence of God, and this is before the tide turns and the maelstrom forms. The same scene evokes in the narrator the awe of a mortal in a god's presence; when he sees the maelstrom, he feels he is looking into the heart of awesome, divine mystery.

Edgar Allen Poe (Library of Congress)

When the maelstrom forms, when the earth really trembles and the sea boils and the heavens shout and the guide asks him what he sees and hears, he replies, "this *can* be nothing else than the great whirlpool of the Maelström." The narrator continues to see it as a more than natural phenomenon. Unable to accept the naturalistic account of it offered by the *Encyclopædia Britannica*, he is drawn instead by the power that it exerts over his imagination to see it as a manifestation of occult powers, an eruption of supernatural power into the natural world. This view forms the context within which the guide tells his tale.

An important feature of the guide's story is the contrast between his sense of chaotic threat and his repeated perceptions that suggest an ordered purpose within this chaos. It almost seems at times as if the episode were designed to teach the fisherman a lesson that he would then pass on through the narrator to the reader, though conveying a simple moral seems not to be the fisherman's purpose. For the fisherman, it was good fortune, assisted perhaps by a kind Providence, that allowed him to find a means of escape once his fishing boat had been sucked into the gigantic whirlpool and had begun its gradual descent toward the rushing foam at the bottom of the funnel of water. The main sign of design in these events is that just as the boat is blown into the whirlpool by the sudden and violent hurricane, a circle opens in the black clouds, revealing a bright moon that illuminates the scene of terror. This event makes the weather into a symmetrical picture: An inverted funnel of clouds ascending to an opening where the moon appears, over a funnel of whirling seawater descending into an obscured opening where a rainbow appears, "like that narrow and tottering bridge which Musselmen say is the only pathway between Time and Eternity." This view of a tremendous overarching cosmic order composing a scene of mortal chaos produces other kinds of order that help to save the fisherman.

Bewitched by the beauty that he sees in this scene, the fisherman, like the narrator on the cliff-top, gains control of himself, loses his fear, and begins to look around, merely for the sake of enjoying it: "I began to reflect how magnificent a thing it was to die in such a manner . . . in view of so wonderful a manifestation of God's power." Studying the beauty, he regains his self-possession, and in possession of his faculties, no longer terrified, he begins to understand how the whirlpool works, and he learns that different shapes and sizes of objects descend its sides at different rates. Attaching himself to a cylindrical barrel, he slows his descent enough that instead of going to the bottom and so across the mystical bridge he envisions there, he is borne up until the maelstrom stops and he finds himself again in comparatively calm water.

For the fisherman, his narrow escape is a tale of wonder, luck, and divine mercy. For the reader, however, carefully prepared by the narrator and supported by elements in the fisherman's story upon which he does not comment, the story also illustrates the inscrutability of the God that may be visible in nature. This is not a God who operates nature solely for human benefit, though He has given humanity reason, aesthetic sense, and the power of faith that can allow people to survive in, and even enjoy, the terrors of nature. The fisherman's brother, who survives the onslaught of the storm to experience the maelstrom with him, is never able to move by means of faith or the appreciation of beauty beyond his terror; this makes his despair at impending death insuperable, so he cannot discover a way of escape or even attempt the one offered by the fisherman.

Though not necessarily unique in this respect, the United States has throughout its history been a nation where large groups of people tended to assume that they had discovered the one truth that explained the universe and history and where it seemed easy to believe that a benevolent God had designed a manifest destiny for the nation and, perhaps, for humankind as a whole if led by American thought. Poe was among those who distrusted such thinking deeply. "A Descent into the Maelström" is one of many Poe stories in which part of the effect is to undercut such assumptions in his readers by emphasizing the mysteries of nature and the inadequacy of human ideas to encompass them, much less encompass the divinity of which nature might be a manifestation.

"THE PURLOINED LETTER"

While "A Descent into the Maelström" emphasizes the inadequacy of human intelligence to comprehend

God's purposes in the universe, it also emphasizes the crucial importance of people using what intelligence they have to find truth and beauty in nature and experience. "The Purloined Letter," one of Poe's best detective stories, places a greater emphasis on the nature and importance of intelligence, while still pointing at mysteries of human character. This story first appeared in two magazine versions in 1844: a shorter version in *Chamber's Edinburgh Journal* and what has become the final version in *The Gift*. It was then collected in *Tales*.

The narrator and his friend C. Auguste Dupin are smoking and meditating in Dupin's darkened library, when they are interrupted by the comical Monsieur G--, the prefect of the Paris police. The prefect tries to pretend that he is merely paying a friendly call, but he cannot help making it clear that he has come to Dupin with a troubling problem. He eventually explains that the Minister D-- has managed, in the presence of an important lady, presumably the queen, to steal from her a compromising letter with which he might damage her severely by showing it to her husband. He has since been using the threat of revealing the letter to coerce the queen's cooperation in influencing policy. As the prefect repeats, to Dupin's delight, getting the letter back without publicity ought to be simple for an expert policeman. One merely finds where it is hidden and takes it back. The letter must be within easy reach of the minister to be useful, and so by minute searching of his home and by having a pretended thief waylay him, the letter should surely be found. All these things have been done with great care, and the letter has not been found. The prefect is stumped. Dupin's advice is to search again. A few weeks later, the prefect returns, still without success. Dupin then manipulates the prefect into declaring what he would pay to regain the letter, instructs him to write Dupin a check for that amount, and gives him the letter. The prefect is so astonished and gratified that he runs from the house, not even bothering to ask how Dupin has managed this feat.

The second half of the story consists of Dupin's explanation to the narrator, with a joke or two at the prefect's expense, of how he found and obtained the letter. As in Dupin's other cases, notably the famous "The Murders in the Rue Morgue," the solution involves a rigorous and seemingly miraculous application of rationality to the problem. Although in these stories Poe was establishing conventions for detection and stories about it that would flower richly in Sir Arthur Conan Doyle's tales of Sherlock Holmes, the principles upon which Dupin works are slightly but significantly different from Holmes's principles.

One key difference is the importance of poetic imagination to the process. Most of Dupin's explanation of his procedure has to do with how one goes about estimating the character and ability of one's opponent, for understanding what the criminal may do is ultimately more important to a solution than successful deduction. It requires a kind of poet to penetrate the criminal's mind, a "mere" mathematician can make competent deductions from given ideas, as the prefect has done. It takes a combination of poet and mathematician--in short, Dupin--to solve such a crime dependably. The prefect has greatly underestimated the minister because he is known to be a poet and the prefect believes poets are fools. Dupin says that the police often fail because they assume that the criminal's intelligence mirrors their own, and therefore over- or underestimate the criminal's ability. Having established that the minister is a very cunning opponent who will successfully imagine the police response to his theft, Dupin is able to deduce quite precisely how the minister will hide the letter, by placing it very conspicuously, so as not to appear hidden at all, and by disguising it. Dupin's deduction proves exactly right, and by some careful plotting, he is able to locate and regain it.

The two main portions of the story, presenting the problem and the solution, illustrate the nature and powers of human reason. The end of the story emphasizes mystery by raising questions about morality. While reason is a powerful instrument for solving problems and bringing about actions in the world, and solving problems is a satisfying kind of activity that makes Dupin feel proud and virtuous, his detecting occurs in a morally ambiguous world. The end of the story calls attention repeatedly to the relationship between Dupin and the Minister D--, a final quotation from a play even hinting that they could be brothers, though there is no other evidence that this is the case. Dupin claims intimate acquaintance and frequent association with the minister; indeed, these are the foundation of his inferences about the man's character and ability. They disagree, politically, however. The nature of this disagreement is not explained, but the story takes place in nineteenth century Paris, and Dupin's actions seem to support the royal family against a rebellious politician. Dupin, in leaving a disguised substitute for the regained letter, has arranged for the minister's fall from power and may even have endangered his life.

By providing this kind of information at the end, Poe raises moral and political questions, encouraging the reader to wonder whether Dupin's brilliant detection serves values of which the reader might approve. To those questions, the story offers no answers. In this way, Dupin's demonstration of a magnificent human intellect is placed in the context of moral mystery, quite unlike the tales of Sherlock Holmes and related classical detectives. On a moral level, who are Dupin and the minister, and what are the meanings of their actions with regard to the well-being of French citizens? While Poe invented what became major conventions in detective fiction--the rational detective, his less able associate, the somewhat ridiculous police force, the solution scene--his detective stories show greater moral complexity than those of his best-known followers.

"The Fall of the House of Usher"

"The Fall of the House of Usher" has everything a Poe story is supposed to have according to the popular view of him: a gothic house, a terrified narrator, live burial, madness, and horrific catastrophe. One of his most popular and most discussed stories, this one has been variously interpreted by critics, provoking controversy about how to read it that remains unsettled. This story was first published in 1839, and it appeared in Poe's fiction collections *Tales of the Grotesque and Arabesque* and *Tales*.

The narrator journeys to the home of his boyhood chum, Roderick Usher, a man of artistic talent and generous reputation. Usher has been seriously ill and wishes the cheerful companionship of his old friend. The narrator arrives at the grimly oppressive house in its equally grim and oppressive setting, determined to

be cheerful and helpful, but finds himself overmatched. The house and its environs radiate gloom, and though Usher alternates between a kind of creative mania and the blackest depression, he tends also on the whole to radiate gloom. Usher confides that he is upset in part because his twin sister, Madeline, is mortally ill. It develops, however, that the main reason Usher is depressed is that he has become in some way hypersensitive, and this sensitivity has revealed to him that his house is a living organism that is driving him toward madness. The narrator does not want to believe this, but the longer he stays in the house with Usher, the more powerfully Usher's point of view dominates him. Madeline dies and, to discourage grave robbers, Usher and the narrator temporarily place her in a coffin in a vault beneath the house. Once Madeline is dead, Usher's alternation of mood ceases, and he remains always deeply gloomy.

On his last evening at Usher, the narrator witnesses several events that seem to confirm Usher's view that the house is driving him mad. Furthermore, these confirmations seem to suggest that the house is just one in a nest of Chinese boxes, in a series of closed, walled-in enclosures that make up the physical and spiritual universe. This oft-repeated image is represented most vividly in one of Usher's paintings, what appears to be a burial vault unnaturally lit from within. This image conveys the idea of the flame of human consciousness imprisoned, as if buried alive in an imprisoning universe. The terrifying conviction of this view is one of the causes of Usher's growing madness. On the last evening, a storm seems to enclose the house as if it were inside a box of wind and cloud, on which the house itself casts an unnatural light. The narrator tries to comfort both himself and Usher by reading a story, but the sound effects described in the story are echoed in reality in the house. Usher, as his reason crumbles, interprets these sounds as Madeline, not really dead, breaking through various walls behind which she has been placed--her coffin and the vault--until finally, Usher claims, she is standing outside the door of the room where they are reading. The door opens, perhaps supernaturally, and there she stands. The narrator watches the twins fall against each other and collapse; he rushes outside only to see the house itself collapse into its reflection in the pool that stands before it, this last event taking place under the unnatural light of a blood-red moon.

Such a summary helps to reveal one of the main sources of conflicting interpretation. How could such events really occur? Is not this a case of an unreliable narrator, driven toward a horrific vision by some internal conflicts that might be inferred from the content of the vision? This viewpoint has tended to dominate critical discussion of the story, provoking continuous opposition from more traditionally minded readers who argue that "The Fall of the House of Usher" is a supernatural tale involving occult forces of some kind. Both modes of interpretation have their problems, and so neither has been able to establish itself as superior to the other.

One of the main difficulties encountered by both sides is accounting for the way that the narrator tells his story. He seems involved in the same sort of problem that the community of literary critics experiences. He is represented as telling the story of this experience some time after the events took place. He insists that there are no supernatural elements in his story, that everything that happened at the House of Usher can be accounted for in a naturalistic way. In this respect, he is like the narrator of "A Descent into the Maelström." He "knows" that the natural world operates according to regular "natural" laws, but when he actually sees the whirlpool, his imagination responds involuntarily with the conviction that this is something supernatural. Likewise, the narrator of "The Fall of the House of Usher" is convinced that the world can be understood in terms of natural law and, therefore, that what has happened to him at Usher either could not have happened or must have a natural explanation. Like the narrator of "The Black Cat," another of Poe's most famous stories, this narrator hopes that by telling the story, perhaps again, he will arrive at an acceptable explanation or that his listener will confirm his view of the events.

Perhaps "The Fall of the House of Usher" is a kind of trap, set to enmesh readers in the same sort of difficulty in which the narrator finds himself. If this is the case, then the story functions in a way consistent with Poe's theme of the inadequacy of models constructed by human intelligence to map the great mysteries of life and the universe. The narrator says he has had an experience that he cannot explain and that points toward an inscrutable universe, one that might be conceived as designed to drive humans mad if they find themselves compelled to comprehend it. Likewise, in reading the story, the reader has an experience that finally cannot be explained, that seems designed to drive a reader mad if he or she insists upon achieving a final view of its wholeness. The story itself may provide an experience that demonstrates the ultimate inadequacy of human reason to understand the mysteries of creation.

Although Poe wrote a variety of stories, he is best remembered for his tales of terror and madness. His popular literary reputation is probably a distorted view of Poe, both as person and as artist. While he was tragically addicted to alcohol and while he did experience considerable difficulty in a milieu that was not particularly supportive, he was nevertheless an accomplished artist whose work, especially when viewed as a whole, is by no means the mere outpouring of a half-mad, anguished soul. To look closely at any of his best work is to see ample evidence of a writer in full artistic control of his materials, calculating his effects with a keen eye. Furthermore, to examine the range and quantity of his writing, to attend to the quantity of his humor--of which there are interesting examples even in "The Fall of the House of Usher"--to notice the beauty of his poetry, to study the learned intelligence of his best criticism--in short, to see Poe whole--must lead to the recognition that his accomplishments far exceed the narrow view implied by his popular reputation.

OTHER MAJOR WORKS

LONG FICTION: *The Narrative of Arthur Gordon Pym*, 1838.

PLAY: *Politian*, pb. 1835-1836.

POETRY: *Tamerlane, and Other Poems*, 1827; *Al Aaraaf, Tamerlane, and Minor Poems*, 1829; *Poems*, 1831; *The Raven, and Other Poems*, 1845; *Eureka: A Prose Poem*, 1848; *Poe: Complete Poems*, 1959; *Poems*, 1969 (volume 1 of *Collected Works*).

NONFICTION: *The Letters of Edgar Allan Poe*, 1948; *Literary Criticism of Edgar Allan Poe*, 1965; *Essays and Reviews*, 1984.

MISCELLANEOUS: *The Complete Works of Edgar Allan Poe*, 1902 (seventeen volumes); *Collected Works of Edgar Allan Poe*, 1969, 1978 (three volumes); *The Selected Writings of Edgar Allan Poe: Authoritative Texts, Backgrounds and Contexts, Criticism*, 2004 (G. R. Thompson, editor).

BIBLIOGRAPHY

Bloom, Harold, ed. *Edgar Allan Poe's "The Tell-Tale Heart," and Other Stories*. New ed. New York: Bloom's Literary Criticism, 2009. A collection of critical essays about Poe's short fiction, including analyses of "The Cask of Amontillado," "The Tell-Tale Heart," Poe's detective fiction, and "The Fall of the House of Usher."

Brown, Arthur A. "Literature and the Impossibility of Death: Poe's 'Berenice.'" *Nineteenth-Century Literature* 50 (March, 1996): 448-463. Argues that Poe's stories of the dead coming back to life and of premature burial dramatize the horror of the impossibility of dying. In "Berenice," the reader's attention to the details of the tale reproduces the narrator's obsession with that which speaks of death and does not die, thus implicating readers in his violation of the still-living Berenice in her tomb.

Buranelli, Vincent. *Edgar Allan Poe*. 2d ed. Boston: Twayne, 1977. This study of Poe's life and works offers an excellent introduction. Includes a chronology of his life and an annotated, select bibliography.

Burluck, Michael L. *Grim Phantasms: Fear in Poe's Short Fiction*. New York: Garland, 1993. Considers the question of why Poe focused primarily on portraying weird events in his stories. Discusses the gothic conventions Poe used to achieve his effects. Argues that neither drugs nor insanity is responsible for Poe's gothic tales, but rather that the stories were a carefully thought-out literary tactic meant to appeal to current public taste and the general human reaction to fear.

Carlson, Eric, ed. *Critical Essays on Edgar Allan Poe*. Boston: G. K. Hall, 1987. This supplement to Carlson's 1966 volume offers a cross section of writing about Poe from the 1830's to the 1980's. Many of the essays deal with the short stories, illustrating a variety of interpretive strategies.

_____, ed. *The Recognition of Edgar Allan Poe*. Ann Arbor: University of Michigan Press, 1966. This selection of critical essays from 1829 to 1963 is intended to illustrate the development of Poe's literary reputation. It includes a number of the most important earlier essays on Poe, including Constance Rourke's discussion of Poe as a humorist. Also includes several essays by French and British critics.

Crisman, William. "Poe's Dupin as Professional, the Dupin Stories as Serial Text." *Studies in American Fiction* 23 (Autumn, 1995): 215-229. Part of a special section on Poe. Argues that the Dupin stories bear out Poe's mesmeric revelation that mind forms one continuum with inert substance. Poe's emphatic insistence on the role of the material and the materialistic in his detective tales makes them important psychological statements.

Fisher, Benjamin F. "Poe and the American Short Story." In *A Companion to the American Short Story*, edited by Alfred Bendixen and James Nagel. Malden, Mass.: Wiley-Blackwell, 2010. Discusses Poe's contributions to the short-story genre. Fisher explains how Poe not only wrote some of the finest short stories in the English language but also established the "first systematic principles for what constitutes true art in the short story."

Frank, Lawrence. "'The Murders in the Rue Morgue': Edgar Allan Poe's Evolutionary Reverie." *Nineteenth-Century Literature* 50 (September, 1995): 168-188. Claims that Poe's story explores the implications of the nebular hypothesis and does not reinforce the prevailing orthodoxy; rather it may have been in the service of an emerging Darwinian perspective.

Frye, Steven, ed. *Critical Insights: The Tales of Edgar Allan Poe*. Pasadena, Calif.: Salem Press, 2010. Collection of original and reprinted essays providing critical readings of Poe's short fiction. Some of the essays discuss Poe's literary cultural heritage, the reader as accomplice in his stories, elements of fantasy in his tales, his characterization of deluded detectives, and the stories "The Fall of the House of Usher," "The Cask of Amontillado," and "Ligeia." Also includes a brief biography of Poe.

Hayes, Kevin J., ed. *The Cambridge Companion to Edgar Allan Poe*. New York: Cambridge University Press, 2006. Collection of essays that examine Poe's life and works from a variety of perspectives. Includes discussions of Poe's humor, his aesthetic theory, Poe and the gothic tradition, his character C. Auguste Dupin, and his short story "The Fall of the House of Usher."

Howarth, William L. *Twentieth Century Interpretations of Poe's Tales*. Englewood Cliffs, N.J.: Prentice-Hall, 1971. Contains fifteen essays on Poe's stories, several offering general points of view on his fiction but most offering specific interpretations of tales, such as "The Fall of the House of Usher," "Ligeia," "William Wilson," "The Black Cat," and "The Tell-Tale Heart." Includes a chronology of Poe's life, a bibliography, and a helpful index to the stories discussed.

Kopley, Richard. *Edgar Allan Poe and the Dupin Mysteries*. New York: Palgrave Macmillan, 2008. Combining biographical details and literary analysis, Kopley provides detailed interpretations of three of Poe's detective stories: "The Purloined Letter," "The Mystery of Marie Rogêt," and "The Murders in the Rue Morgue." He discusses the birth of the modern detective story and establishes Poe's place within the mystery and detective genre.

Martin, Terry J. *Rhetorical Deception in the Short Fiction of Hawthorne, Poe and Melville*. Lewiston, N.Y.: Edwin Mellen Press, 1998. An original reading of "The Murders in the Rue Morgue." Martin seeks to identify this story and those by Nathaniel Hawthorne and Herman Melville as "a significant subgenre of the modern short story."

May, Charles E. *Edgar Allan Poe: A Study of the Short Fiction*. Boston: Twayne, 1991. An introduction to Poe's short stories that attempts to place them within the nineteenth century short narrative tradition and within the context of Poe's aesthetic theory. Suggests Poe's contributions to the short story in terms of his development of detective fiction, fantasy, satire, and self-reflexivity. Includes passages from Poe's narrative theory and three essays by other critics illustrating a variety of critical approaches.

Perry, Dennis R., and Carl H. Sederholm. *Poe, "The House of Usher," and the American Gothic*. New York: Palgrave Macmillan, 2009. Describes how "The Fall of the House of Usher" remains a model of American gothic literature, assessing Poe's influence on the works of Charlotte Perkins Gilman, Henry James, H. P. Lovecraft, Stephen King, and other writers.

Quinn, Arthur Hobson. *Edgar Allan Poe: A Critical Biography*. Baltimore: The Johns Hopkins University Press, 1998. A comprehensive biography of Poe, with a new introduction by Shawn Rosenheim, that describes how Poe's life and legend were misconstrued by other biographers.

Scofield, Martin. "Edgar Allan Poe." In *The Cambridge Introduction to the American Short Story*. New York: Cambridge University Press, 2006. An overview and analysis of Poe's short fiction, including his stories "The Tell-Tale Heart," "The Murders in the Rue Morgue," "Ligeia," and "The Imp of the Perverse."

Thoms, Peter. *Detection and Its Designs: Narrative and Power in Nineteenth-Century Detective Fiction*. Athens: Ohio University Press, 1998. A study of early detective fiction from readings of Poe's Dupin stories to Sir Arthur Conan Doyle's *The Hound of the Baskervilles*.

Whalen, Terence. *Edgar Allan Poe and the Masses: The Political Economy of Literature in Antebellum America*. Princeton, N.J.: Princeton University Press, 1999. A brilliant study that provides an inventive understanding of Poe's works and his standing in American literature.

Terry Heller

DONALD RAY POLLOCK

Born: Knockemstiff, Ohio; December 23, 1954

PRINCIPAL SHORT FICTION
Knockemstiff, 2008

OTHER LITERARY FORMS

Donald Ray Pollock has published poems in *River Styx* and other journals and is a frequent contributor on politics in the op-ed pages of *The New York Times* and *The Huffington Post*. He also keeps a blog, *Notes from the Holler*. He has been working on a novel set in 1965, about a serial killer named Arvin Eugene Russell.

ACHIEVEMENTS

Donald Ray Pollock is the recipient of the 2009 PEN/Robert Bingham Fellowship, an award that honors a talented fiction writer whose debut suggests great things to come and that carries a $35,000 cash prize. Pollock also won the 2009 Devil's Kitchen Award in Prose from the University of southern Illinois, Carbondale.

BIOGRAPHY

Donald Ray Pollock was born in a holler named Knockemstiff and raised in Ohio, and he has lived his entire adult life in Chillicothe, Ohio. He worked in a paper mill in Chillicothe until he was fifty and then left when he enrolled in Ohio State University's M.F.A. creative-writing program. While a student at Ohio State, Pollock, having the ability to write full time, cranked out stories that seemed to have been building up inside of him for years. He finished *Knockemstiff*, a linked story collection reminiscent of Sherwood Anderson's *Winesburg, Ohio* (1919) in subject matter (if not always in tone and delivery), and it was published by Doubleday in 2008. The book received mostly positive reviews and garnered Pollock comparisons to

Breece D'J Pancake, William Gay, Chris Offutt, and Larry Brown. Chuck Palahniuk, author of *Fight Club* (1996) and other novels, raved about Pollock's debut, giving Pollock a sort of cult following. While at Ohio State, Pollock also served as a *New York Times* political correspondent during the 2008 presidential election, in which Barack Obama was elected.

Little has been written about Pollock to this point, and whatever information is out there must be pieced together from interviews. In a 2009 interview for *Sycamore Review*, Pollock discussed his writing habits, his key influences, and the midlife crisis that forced him to quit work at the paper mill and enroll in a creative-writing program. Pollock talked about his early influences, such as classic noir films of the 1940's and 1950's, and he also credited Andrew Porter's *The Theory of Light and Matter* (2008), because the book gave him the idea to do a linked story cycle. In an interview with *Hobart*, Pollock said that he learned to write by typing out his favorite stories from authors he greatly admired: Ernest Hemingway, John Cheever, Denis Johnson, Sam Lipsyte, and Flannery O'Connor. He also credited Tom Franklin, Tobias Wolff, Jim Thompson, David Goodis, and Dawn Powell as major influences. Pollock's work has been published in *Third Coast*, *The Journal*, *Sou'wester*, *Chiron Review*, *River Styx*, *Boulevard*, *Folio*, *The Berkeley Fiction Review*, and other magazines and journals.

ANALYSIS

Donald Ray Pollock burst onto the literary scene in 2008, a fifty-four-year-old ex-paper mill worker with a debut that was part Sherwood Anderson and part Charles Bukowski. Raw and wild, *Knockemstiff* (2008) was a book that immediately stood out in a field of other new works by "sophisticated" writers from top-tier writing programs. Pollock's voice seemed unhinged, genuine to the bone, and Pollock was certainly not your typical M.F.A. graduate. His experiences in

Ohio had given him the stuff for a solid book. Unlike other writers who try to exploit the blue-collar angle, especially young writers who work a few factory jobs and then write stories or a novel about their rough experiences, Pollock had worked in the real world for almost thirty years. Thus, it was a relief to find that there was no posturing in *Knockemstiff*. Pollock is not a poseur; he is the literary descendant of such writers as Larry Brown and William Gay.

Pollock has in common with Gay and Breece D'J Pancake a deep concern for the hard and lonely world of Appalachian rural poverty. Pollock's fiction sets itself apart from other attempts to portray backwoods characters living the hard life because of his grim and spare prose and his ability to check his feelings at the door. Pollock is not trying to make a broad political statement, and he is not speaking about the problems of society as a whole; instead, he is focused on presenting with a loving brushstroke accurate portraits of broken or damaged men and women. Pollock cares for and knows his characters. They are in no way a merely a tool.

The eighteen stories in *Knockemstiff* feature a broad variety of characters, but the setting is not the only reason Pollock's book is considered a linked story cycle. Thematic continuity abounds in Pollock's world of isolation and loneliness. All of the characters have been defeated in some way, shape, or form. They are broke. Education has failed them. They live a life that is rough around the edges and filled with empty experiences. They swear. They are lonely. They are overcome with grief. They are, like the characters in the fiction of Gay and Pancake, not set up to make it in the modern world. Broken, they wander, seeking relief in booze, drugs, violence, and detached sex. They seek revenge for wrongs that have been committed against them. Many of Pollock's characters wind up failing, losing their health, their jobs, and their memory. They die or they live a life that is worse than death. Pollock's vision is complicated and sad, tragic and beautiful all at once. His characters undergo suffering and trauma, often for no apparent reason. Like O'Connor's antiheroes and antagonists, Pollock's characters are displaced in a world that will not have them.

"REAL LIFE"

Donald Ray Pollock's debut collection gets a kick-start with the first story, "Real Life." If the story operates in the terrain of writers such as Gay and Pancake, it also inhabits territory covered by Bukowski in works such as *Ham on Rye* (1982). A twist on the conventional coming-of-age story, "Real Life" chronicles a father's attempts to make his son a man through exposure to violence. The boy, Bobby, exists in a world that seems to be always on the verge of falling apart. Violence or the threat of it is everywhere. His ignorant, drunken father, Vernon, is the worst kind of example, and he is dead set on passing down to his son a legacy of violent and irrational behavior. A good kid at heart, Bobby protests, but he is swayed to have a false epiphany after his father congratulates Bobby for attacking the son of the man that Vernon has just beaten to a pulp in the bathroom of a drive-in theater. Vernon is strangely proud of his son, and Bobby is infected with a desire for more praise from his old man and for more blood.

Donald Ray Pollock (AP Photo/Matt Sullivan)

Pollock's dissection of humankind's violent nature is in full effect. Vernon is a typical antiexemplar: hungry for blood, irrational, ignorant, bad to the core. Bobby is the kind of character with whom Pollock is concerned: a boy who must overcome the odds in the face of exposure to such mindless violence and random cruelty. At the center of Pollock's work is a deep sense of pity for boys such as Bobby, who have to learn to know better on their own, who have no adult to guide them to good behavior. Pollock is also deeply preoccupied with violence against the innocent. Evil takes many forms in Pollock's book, but perhaps none more sinister than a character such as Vernon, who lashes out unprompted against a fellow human and beats him within an inch of his life.

"PILLS"

"Pills" is a story in which Robert "Bobby" Shaffer tells about an adventure from his youth. When he was sixteen, he and his buddy Frankie stole four bottles of pharmaceutical amphetamines from a bartender-drug dealer in town. They had planned on taking Frankie's car and splitting town, hoping to drive all the way to California and hide out, but instead they wind up sticking around Knockemstiff. The story chronicles their misadventures in light of the pill theft, which left them high for five days straight,. Like Pancake, Pollock is concerned with characters who see a better life for themselves somewhere else. Escape is the goal, and Bobby and Frankie fantasize about a better existence outside of their small holler. However, the fact that the story is narrated by Bobby as a middle-aged man indicates Pollock's larger message: There is no escape from the self. One either starts living where one is or ones does not live at all.

Anderson's *Winesburg, Ohio* is often (some would may mistakenly) read as a "revolt from the village" story cycle. The same could be said of Pollock's *Knockemstiff*, and "Pills" is a prime example of how the imaginations of characters stuck in small-town life begin to wander. At the end of the story, Bobby recalls looking up and seeing a plane flying overhead. He wonders if the people up there can see the fire he and Frankie have going, and he wonders what they would think of them. There is always the promise and the fear of what is happening in the larger world.

Pollock's characters are trapped in Knockemstiff, but they would be trapped anywhere; they are trapped within themselves.

"SCHOTT'S BRIDGE"

"Schott's Bridge" is another story that ties Pollock's collection to *Winesburg, Ohio*. Like Anderson, Pollock is confused by and concerned with small-town hypocrisy and narrowness. Todd Russell, an alienated gay man, befriends Frankie Johnson (the same character from "Pills"), a homophobic roughneck. Todd, wanting only to love Frankie, misjudges him, and Frankie lashes out. One of Pollock's most violent and disturbing stories, "Schott's Bridge" chronicles Frankie's brutal destruction of Todd. He beats and rapes him and then steals his car and money. Todd, seemingly left with nothing, contemplates jumping off Schott's Bridge.

This story is further evidence of Pollock's abiding concern with outsiders and outcasts. Like Wing Biddlebaum in Anderson's "Hands," Todd is someone who does not seem to fit in the place where he lives. He seeks only trust and love, but he is thwarted at every turn by hatred and narrowness. Pollock's sympathy for this character is evident as Todd stands on Schott's Bridge above the water, considering death. Instead of jumping, he throws a cigarette into the water and decides to try life, no matter how awful and difficult it is.

"ASSAILANTS"

Another tale that deals with detached and displaced characters, "Assailants" tells the story of Geraldine Murray, the wife of Del Murray. Geraldine is a notable character in Knockemstiff because she carries fish sticks around in her purse and because, after being assaulted and nearly killed in a horrifying encounter outside of a tobacco shop, she has become an agoraphobic prone to panic attacks. The man who victimized her wore a paper bag over his head. She is dismissed as an eccentric and oddball, and Del must deal with the attitude that the townsfolk have toward her. When he flirts with a young female clerk at a local shop, he is somehow upset by the girl's dismissal of Geraldine as a flake. To give validity to Geraldine's story, he decides to rob the store, with a paper bag over his head, where the young female clerk works. Unfortunately, he is too convincing. He scares the girl and she trips and falls, hitting her head, perhaps fatally. Violence is visited upon yet another innocent character in Pollock's world. More than that, Pollock is concerned with how violence begets violence, with how bad acts have a stone-thrown-in-the-lake effect, with consequences rippling out in all directions.

"I Start Over"

"I Start Over" is another story that signifies Pollock's immersion in the world of the displaced and the lonely. It also examines the violent effects of being an outcast in society. Bernie Givens, a big, sloppy man, doomed to a tragic life, cannot deal with his son's fate: The son has been damaged permanently after a seventy-two-hour binge on booze and drugs. Bernie will not accept his grief and takes it out on a coworker; as a result, Bernie is fired from his job. Things fall apart after that. Bernie turns suicidal and then homicidal. He assaults some teenagers who mock him and then goes on the lam. The story ends with him on the run, pursued by the police, jail or death very real possibilities and the only ways that Bernie can truly start over. Pollock's fascination with the crumbling life is evident. The son's mistakes are visited upon the father, just as the father's mistakes are eternally visited upon the son. Pollock's world is dark and lonesome, brutal and hard, and there is the real sense that even the strongest, most agile human being can be rendered impotent and useless at any given moment.

BIBLIOGRAPHY

Ellen, Elizabeth. "An Interview with Donald Ray Pollock." *Hobart: Another Literary Journal*, May, 2008. Available at http://www.hobartpulp.com/. In an interview, Pollock discusses the autobiographical elements in his short stories.

Fleming, Tom. "Low Life in a Small Town." *New Statesman* 137, no. 4905 (2008): 59. A positive review of Pollock's *Knockemstiff*, offering a quick critical summary of the book and some brief biographical analysis.

Pollock, Donald Ray. Interview by Christopher Feliciano Arnold. *Sycamore Review*, November 6, 2009. Available at http://www.sycamorereview.com/. An interview with Pollock that offers great insights into Pollock's life and writing, particularly in light of comparisons to Anderson, Johnson, Gay, and Pancake.

Trachtenberg, Jeffrey A. "A New American Voice." *The Wall Street Journal*, February 9, 2008, p. W1. Trachtenberg offers some background on Pollock and places him squarely in the tradition of writers such as Offutt, Daniel Woodrell, and Gay, who are firmly rooted in place and often have some sort of crime element in their fiction.

William Boyle

KATHERINE ANNE PORTER

Born: Indian Creek, Texas; May 15, 1890
Died: Silver Spring, Maryland; September 18, 1980

PRINCIPAL SHORT FICTION

Flowering Judas, and Other Stories, 1930
Hacienda, 1934
Noon Wine, 1937 (novella)
Old Mortality, 1937 (novella)
Pale Horse, Pale Rider, 1938 (novella)
Pale Horse, Pale Rider: Three Short Novels, 1939
(includes *Old Mortality, Noon Wine,* and *Pale Horse, Pale Rider*)
The Leaning Tower, and Other Stories, 1944
The Old Order, 1944
The Collected Stories of Katherine Anne Porter, 1965

OTHER LITERARY FORMS

Katherine Anne Porter wrote, in addition to short stories, one novel, *Ship of Fools* (1962), parts of which were published separately from 1947 to 1959, in such magazines and journals as *Sewanee Review, Harper's,* and *Mademoiselle.* She wrote essays of various kinds, some of which she published under the title of one of them, *The Days Before* (1952); these essays included critical analyses of Thomas Hardy's fiction and biographical studies of Ford Madox Ford and Gertrude Stein. Porter was a reporter who produced unsigned journalism for the Fort Worth weekly newspaper *The Critic* in 1917 and the Denver *Rocky Mountain News* in 1918-1919. Early in her career, she worked on a critical biography of Cotton Mather, which she never finished; she did, however, publish parts of it in 1934, 1940, 1942, and 1946. Her few poems and most of her nonfictional prose have been collected in *The Collected Essays and Occasional Writings* (1970) under the following headings: "Critical," "Personal and Particular,"

"Biographical," "Cotton Mather," "Mexican," "On Writing," and "Poems." In 1967, she published *A Christmas Story,* a personal reminiscence of her niece, who had died in 1919. Her memoir of the Sacco and Vanzetti trial, *The Never-Ending Wrong,* was published in 1977 on the fiftieth anniversary of their deaths. She was a prodigious writer of personal letters; many have been published, first, by her friend Glenway Wescott, as *The Selected Letters of Katherine Anne Porter* (1970), and later by another friend, Isabel Bayley, as *Letters of Katherine Anne Porter* (1990).

ACHIEVEMENTS

Katherine Anne Porter is distinguished by her small literary production of exquisitely composed and highly praised short fiction. Although she lived to be ninety years old, she produced and published only some twenty-five short stories and one long novel. Nevertheless, her work was praised early and often from the start of her career; some of her stories and novellas, such as "Flowering Judas," *Pale Horse, Pale Rider,* and *Old Mortality,* have been hailed as masterpieces. Sponsored by Edmund Wilson, Allen Tate, Kenneth Burke, and Elizabeth Madox Roberts, Porter won a Guggenheim Fellowship in 1931 and went to Berlin and Paris to live while she wrote such short-fiction works as "The Cracked Looking-Glass" and *Noon Wine,* for which she won a Book-of-the-Month Club award in 1937. After publication of the collection *Pale Horse, Pale Rider: Three Short Novels* in 1939, she received a gold medal for literature from the Society of Libraries of New York University, in 1940. Elected a member of the National Institute of Arts and Letters in 1943, Porter was also appointed as writer-in-residence at Stanford University in 1949, and, in the same year, she received an honorary degree, doctor of letters, from the University of North Carolina. Such awards and honors continued, with writer-in-residence appointments at the University of Michigan in 1954 and the

University of Virginia in 1958 and honorary degrees from the University of Michigan, Smith College, and La Salle College. In 1959, she received a Ford Foundation grant, in 1962 the Emerson-Thoreau gold medal from the American Academy of Arts and Sciences, and in 1966-1967, the National Book Award for Fiction, the Pulitzer Prize in fiction, and the Gold Medal for fiction, National Institute of Arts and Letters.

BIOGRAPHY

There are conflicting reports of dates from Katherine Anne Porter's life, partly because Porter herself was not consistent about her biography. Nevertheless, the main events are fairly clear. Her mother, Mary Alice, died less than two years after Katherine Anne's birth. Subsequently, her grandmother, Catherine Anne Porter, was the most important adult woman in her life. After the death of her grandmother in 1901, Katherine Anne was sent away by her father to an Ursuline convent in New Orleans and then in 1904 to the Thomas School for Girls in San Antonio. She ran away from her school in 1906 to marry John Henry Kroontz, the twenty-year-old son of a Texas rancher. She remained with him seven years (some reports say her marriage lasted only three years), and in 1911 she went to Chicago to earn her own way as a reporter for a weekly newspaper and as a bit player for a film company. From 1914 to 1916, she traveled through Texas, earning her living as a ballad singer. Then she returned to journalism, joining the staff of the Denver *Rocky Mountain News* in 1918. At about this time, Porter was gravely ill, and she thought she was going to die. Her illness was a turning point in the development of her character, and it was the basis for her novella *Pale Horse, Pale Rider*, which she finished twenty years later.

After she recovered her health, Porter lived briefly in New York and then Mexico, where she studied art while observing the Alvaro Obregón revolution in 1920. Her experiences in Mexico provided material for Porter's earliest published stories, "María Concepción" and "The Martyr" in 1922 and 1923, respectively. She married and promptly divorced Ernest Stock, a young English art student in New York, in 1925. Soon after, she participated in protests against the trial of Nicola Sacco and Bartolomeo Vanzetti, and then, in 1928, she

Katherine Anne Porter (Getty Images)

began work on her biography of Mather, which was never completed. Porter traveled often during these years, but she wrote some of her greatest stories at the same time, including "He," "The Jilting of Granny Weatherall," "Theft," and "Flowering Judas."

After publication of her collection *Flowering Judas, and Other Stories* in 1930, Porter was awarded a Guggenheim Fellowship to support her while living in Berlin and Paris from 1931 to 1937. While in Europe, she composed "The Leaning Tower" and "The Cracked Looking-Glass," and she wrote an early draft of *Noon Wine*. In 1933, she married Eugene Pressly, whom she divorced to marry Albert Erskine in 1938, when she returned to the United States to live with her new husband in Baton Rouge, Louisiana. At that time, she became a friend of Tate and his family.

In 1941, Porter appeared on television with Mark Van Doren and Bertrand Russell; in 1944, she worked on films in Hollywood; and in 1947, she undertook a lecture tour of several southern universities. The novel that she began as a story, "Promised Land," in 1936, was finally published in 1962 as *Ship of Fools* to mixed reviews. Apart from her work on this long fiction, Porter wrote little except for occasional essays and reviews, some of which she published as *The Days Before* in 1952. Porter spent most of her life after 1950 lecturing, traveling, buying and selling property, and slowly composing her novel, along with her biography of Mather. In October, 1976, she read her essay "St. Augustine and the Bullfight" at the Poetry Center in New York City, and in 1977, she published a memoir of Sacco and Vanzetti, whose trials of injustice had haunted her for fifty years. When she died in 1980 in Silver Spring, Maryland, she left behind a small canon of fiction and a great achievement of literary art.

ANALYSIS

Katherine Anne Porter's short fiction is noted for its sophisticated use of symbolism, complex exploitation of point of view, challenging variations of ambiguously ironic tones, and profound analyses of psychological and social themes. Her career can be divided into three main (overlapping) periods of work, marked by publications of her three collections: The first period, from 1922 to 1935, saw the publication of *Flowering Judas, and Other Stories*; the second, from 1930 to 1939, ended with the publication of *Pale Horse, Pale Rider: Three Short Novels*; and the third, from 1935 to 1942, shaped many of her characters that later appear in the collection *The Leaning Tower, and Other Stories*. Her two stories "Holiday" and "The Fig Tree" and her one novel were published long after the last collection of short stories, in 1960 and 1962, respectively. These constitute a coda to the body of her work in fiction.

From 1922 to 1935, Porter's fiction is concerned with the attempts of women to accommodate themselves to, or to break the bounds of, socially approved sexual roles. They usually fail to achieve the identities that they seek; instead, they ironically become victims of their own or others' ideas of what they ought to be. Violeta of "Virgin Violeta" fantasizes about her relationship with her cousin Carlos, trying to understand it according to the idealistic notions that she has learned from church and family; when Carlos responds to her sensual reality, she is shocked and disillusioned. The ironies of Violeta's situation are exploited more fully, and more artfully, in "María Concepción," "Magic," and "He."

In the first, María manages, through violence, to assert her identity through the social roles that she is expected to play in her primitive society; she kills her sensual rival, María Rosa, seizes the baby of her victim, and retrieves her wandering husband. Social norms are also triumphant over poor Ninette, the brutalized prostitute of "Magic," in which the narrator is implicated by her own ironic practice of distance from her story and her employer, Madame Blanchard. The mother of "He," however, cannot maintain her distance from the image that she has projected of her retarded son; she is willing to sacrifice him, as she had the suckling pig, to preserve the social image she values of herself toward others. In the end, however, Mrs. Whipple embraces, helplessly and hopelessly, the victim of her self-delusion: She holds her son in tragic recognition of her failures toward him, or she holds him out of ironic disregard for his essential need of her understanding. "He" does not resolve easily into reconciliation of tone and theme.

Images of symbolic importance organize the ironies of such stories as "Rope," "Flowering Judas," "Theft," and "The Cracked Looking-Glass." In the first story, a husband and wife are brought to the edge of emotional chaos by a piece of rope that the husband brought home instead of the coffee his wife wanted. As a symbol, the rope ties them together, keeps them apart, and threatens to hang them both. "Flowering Judas," one of Porter's most famous stories, develops the alienated character of Laura from her resistance to the revolutionary hero Braggioni, to her refusal of the boy who sang to her from her garden, to her complicity in the death of Eugenio in prison. At the center of the story, in her garden and in her dream, Laura is linked with a Judas tree in powerfully mysterious ways: as a betrayer and as a rebellious and independent spirit. Readers will be divided on the meaning of the tree, as they will be on the virtue of Laura's character.

"THE CRACKED LOOKING-GLASS"

The same ambivalence results from examining the symbolic function of a cracked mirror in the life of Rosaleen, the point-of-view character in "The Cracked Looking-Glass." This middle-aged Irish beauty sees herself as a monster in her mirror, but she cannot replace the mirror with a new one any more than she can reconcile her sexual frustration with her maternal affection for her aged husband, Dennis. This story twists the May-December stereotype into a reverse fairy tale of beauty betrayed, self deceived, and love dissipated. Rosaleen treats young men as the sons she never had to rear, and she represses her youthful instincts to nurse her impotent husband in his old age. She does not like what she sees when she looks honestly at herself in the mirror, but she will not replace the mirror of reality, cracked as she sees it must be.

"THEFT"

More honest and more independent is the heroine of "Theft," an artist who chooses her independence at the cost of sexual fulfillment and social gratification; she allows her possessions, material and emotional, to be taken from her, but she retains an integrity of honesty and spiritual independence that are unavailable to most of the other characters in these early stories. A similar strength of character underlies the dying monologue of Granny Weatherall, but her strength has purchased her very little certainty about meaning. When she confronts death as a second jilting, Granny condemns death's cheat as a final insult to life; she seems ironically to make meaningful in her death the emptiness that she has struggled to deny in her life.

OLD MORTALITY

In the middle period of her short fiction, Porter's characters confront powerful threats of illusion to shatter their tenuous holds on reality. Romantic ideals and family myths combine to shape the formative circumstances for Miranda in *Old Mortality*. Divided into three parts, this short novel follows the growth of the young heroine from 1885, when she is eight, to 1912, when she is recently married against her father's wishes. Miranda and her older sister, Maria, are fascinated by tales of their legendary Aunt Amy, their father's sister whose honor he had risked his life to defend in a duel, and who died soon after she married their Uncle Gabriel. The first part of the story narrates the family's anecdotes about Aunt Amy and contrasts her with her cousin Eva, a plain woman who participated in movements for women's rights. Part 2 of the story focuses on Miranda's disillusionment with Uncle Gabriel, whom she meets at a racetrack while she is immured in a church school in New Orleans; he is

impoverished, fat, and alcoholic, remarried to a bitter woman who hates his family, and he is insensitive to the suffering of his winning race horse.

Part 3 describes Miranda's encounter with cousin Eva on a train carrying them to the funeral of Uncle Gabriel. Here, Miranda's romantic image of Aunt Amy is challenged by Eva's skeptical memory, but Miranda refuses to yield her vision entirely to Eva's scornful one. Miranda hopes that her father will embrace her when she returns home, but he remains detached and disapproving of her elopement. She realizes that from now on she must live alone, separate, and alienated from her family. She vows to herself that she will know the truth about herself, even if she can never know the truth about her family's history. The story ends, however, on a note of critical skepticism about her vow, suggesting its hopefulness is based upon her ignorance.

NOON WINE

Self-delusion and selfish pride assault Mr. Thompson in *Noon Wine* until he can no longer accept their terms of compromise with his life. A lazy man who lets his south Texas farm go to ruin, he is suddenly lifted to prosperity by the energetic, methodical work of a strangely quiet Swede, Mr. Helton. This man appears one day in 1896 to ask Mr. Thompson for work, and he remains there, keeping to himself and occasionally playing the tune of "Noon Wine" on his harmonica. The turn into failure and tragedy is more sudden than the turn to prosperity had been. Mr. Hatch, an obnoxious person, comes to Mr. Thompson looking for Helton, wanted for the killing of Helton's brother in North Dakota. Thompson angrily attacks and kills Hatch, and Helton flees. Helton, however, is captured, beaten, and thrown in jail, where he dies. Thompson is acquitted of murder at his trial.

Thompson, however, cannot accept his acquittal. He believes that his neighbors think that he is really guilty. His wife is uncertain about his guilt, and his two sons not only are troubled by his part in the deaths but also accuse him of mistreating their mother. Burdened by pains of conscience, Thompson spends his days after the trial visiting neighbors and retelling the story of Hatch's visit. Thompson believes he saw Hatch knife Helton, but no one else saw it, and Helton had no knife wound. The problem for Thompson is that he cannot reconcile what he saw and what was real. All of his life has been spent in a state of delusion, and this crisis of conscience threatens to destroy his capacity to accept life on his own visionary terms. The irony of the story is that Thompson must kill himself to vindicate his innocence, but when he does so, he paradoxically accepts the consequences of his delusions even as he asserts his right to shape reality to fit his view of it.

PALE HORSE, PALE RIDER

Love and death mix forces to press Miranda through a crisis of vision in *Pale Horse, Pale Rider*. This highly experimental short novel mixes dreams with waking consciousness, present with past, and illness with health. Set during World War I, it analyzes social consequences of a military milieu, and it uses that setting to suggest a symbolic projection of the pressures that build on the imagination and identity of the central character. Miranda is a writer of drama reviews for a newspaper; her small salary is barely enough to support herself, and so when she balks at buying Liberty Bonds, she has her patriotism questioned. This worry preoccupies her thoughts and slips into her dreaming experience. In fact, the opening of the story seems to be an experience of a sleeper who is slowly coming awake from a dream of childhood in which the adult's anxieties about money are mixed. Uncertainty about Miranda's mental state grows as she mixes her memories of past with present, allowing past feelings to affect present judgments.

Miranda meets a young soldier, Adam, who will soon be sent to battle. They both know that his fate is sealed, since they are both aware of the survival statistics for soldiers who make assaults from trenches. Miranda becomes gravely ill just before Adam leaves for the war front, and he nurses her through the earliest days of her sickness. Her delirium merges her doctor with Adam, with the German enemy, and with figures of her dreams. By this process, Miranda works through her attractions to Adam, to all men, and survives to assert her independence as a professional artist. The climax of her dream, echoing certain features of Granny Weatherall's, is her refusal to follow the pale rider, who is Death. This feature of her dream is present at the beginning of the story in order to anticipate that

Miranda will have to resolve her inner battle even before the illness that constitutes her physical struggle with death. The men of her waking life enter her dreams as Death, and so when Adam actually dies in battle, Miranda is symbolically assisted in winning her battle for life. The story makes it seem that her dreaming is the reality of the men, that their lives are figments of her imagination. Her recovery of health is a triumph, therefore, of her creative energies, as well as an assertion of her independent feminine identity.

In the final, sustained period of her work in short fiction, from 1935 to 1942, Porter subjects memories to the shaping power of creative imagination as she searches out the episodes that connect to make the character of Miranda, from the stories "The Source" to "The Grave," and she traces the distorting effects of social pressures on children, wives, and artists in the remaining stories of the third collection, *The Leaning Tower, and Other Stories*. The crucial, shaping episodes of Miranda's childhood constitute the core elements of several stories in this collection. Beginning with a sequence under the title "The Old Order," Miranda's growth is shaped by her changing perceptions of life around her. Helping her to interpret events are her grandmother, Sophia Jane, and her grandmother's former black slave and lifetime companion, Aunt Nannie; in addition, Great-Aunt Eliza plays an important role in Miranda's life in the story that was later added to the sequence, "The Fig Tree." Two of the stories of this collection, "The Circus" and "The Grave," are examples of remarkable compression and, particularly in "The Grave," complex artistry.

"THE CIRCUS"

Miranda cries when she sees a clown perform high-wire acrobatics in "The Circus." Her fear is a child's protest against the clown's courtship with death. There is nothing pleasurable about it for Miranda. In fact, she seems to see through the act to recognize the threat of death itself in the white, skull-like makeup of the clown's face. The adults enjoy the spectacle, perhaps insensitive to its essential message or, on the other hand, capable of appreciating the artist's defiance of death. In any event, young Miranda is such a problem that her father sends her home with one of the servants, Dicey. The point of poignancy is in Miranda's discovery of Dicey's warm regard for her despite the fact that Dicey had keenly wanted to stay at the circus. When Miranda screams in her sleep, Dicey lies beside her to comfort her, to protect her even from the dark forces of her nightmares. This sacrifice is not understood by the child Miranda, although it should be apparent to the adult who recalls it.

"THE GRAVE"

"The Grave" is more clear about the function of time in the process of understanding. Miranda and her brother Paul explore open graves of their family while hunting. They find and exchange a coffin screw and a ring, then skin a rabbit that Paul killed, only to find that the rabbit is pregnant with several young that are "born" dead. The experience of mixing birth with death, sexual awareness with marriage and death, is suddenly illuminated for Miranda years later when she recalls her brother on that day while she stands over a candy stand in faraway Mexico.

"THE DOWNWARD PATH TO WISDOM"

Other stories of *The Leaning Tower, and Other Stories* collection have disappointed readers, but they have virtues of art nevertheless. The strangely powerful story of little Stephen in "The Downward Path to Wisdom" has painful insights that may remind one of some of the stories by Flannery O'Connor, a friend of Porter. The little boy who is the object of concern to the family in this story grows to hate his father, mother, grandmother, and uncle; in fact, he sings of his hate for everyone at the end of the tale. His hatred is understandable, since no one genuinely reaches out to love him and help him with his very real problems of adjustment. His mother hears his song, but she shows no alarm; she may think that he does not "mean" what he sings, or she may not really "hear" what he is trying to say through his "art."

A similar theme of hatred and emotional violence is treated in the heartless marital problems of Mr. and Mrs. Halloran of "A Day's Work." Here, however, the violence is borne by physical as well as emotional events, as the story ends with a deadly battle between the aging husband and wife. First one, and then the other, believes the other one is dead. The reader is not sure if either is right.

"THE LEANING TOWER"

Charles Upton, the artist hero of "The Leaning Tower," encounters emotional and physical violence during his sojourn in Berlin in 1931. When he accidentally knocks down and breaks a replica of the Leaning Tower, Charles expresses in a symbolic way his objection to values that he finds in this alien city. He must endure challenges by various other people, with their lifestyles and their foreign values, to discover an underlying humanity that he shares with them. Although he is irritated when he finds that his landlady, Rosa, has repaired the Leaning Tower, he cannot say exactly why he should be. German nationalism and decadent art have combined to shake Charles's integrity, but he searches for inner resources to survive. The story concludes with a typically ambiguous gesture of Porter's art: Charles falls into his bed, telling himself he needs to weep, but he cannot. The world is invulnerable to sorrow and pity.

"THE FIG TREE"

The coda of her work in short fiction, "The Fig Tree" and "Holiday," are revisits to earlier stories, as Porter reexamines old themes and old subjects with new emphases. "The Fig Tree" relocates Miranda in the matriarchal setting of her childhood, and "Holiday" reviews ironies of misunderstanding alien visions. In "The Fig Tree," young Miranda buries a dead baby chicken beneath a fig tree, and then she thinks she hears it chirping from beneath the earth. Frantic with anxiety, she is unable to rescue it because her grandmother forces her to leave with the family for the country. Later, Miranda's Great-Aunt Eliza, who constantly studies nature through telescopes and microscopes, explains to Miranda that she hears tree frogs when Miranda thinks she is hearing the weeping of the dead chicken. Her guilt is relieved by this, and since Miranda has emotionally mixed her burial of the chicken with burials of family members, resolution of guilt for one functions as resolution of guilt for the other.

"HOLIDAY"

The story of "Holiday" is much different in subject and setting, but its emotional profile is similar to "The Fig Tree." The narrator spends a long holiday with German immigrants in the backlands of Texas. The hardworking Müllers challenge, by their lifestyle, the values of the narrator, who only gradually comes to understand them and their ways. The most difficult experience to understand, however, is the family's attitude toward one of the daughters, Ottilie; at first, this girl seems to be only a crippled servant of the family. Gradually, however, the narrator understands that Ottilie is in fact a member of the family. She is mentally retarded and unable to communicate except in very primitive ways. Just when the narrator believes she can appreciate the seemingly heartless ways Ottilie is treated by her family, a great storm occurs and the mother dies. Most of the family follow their mother's corpse to be buried, but Ottilie is left behind. The narrator thinks Ottilie is desperate to join the funeral train with her family, and so she helps Ottilie on board a wagon and desperately drives to catch up with the family. Suddenly, however, the narrator realizes that Ottilie simply wants to be in the sunshine and has no awareness of the death of her mother. The narrator accepts the radical difference that separates her from Ottilie, from all other human beings, and resigns herself, in freedom, to the universal condition of alienation.

The critical mystery of Katherine Anne Porter's work in short fiction is in the brevity of her canon. Readers who enjoy her writing must deplore the failure of the artist to produce more than she did, but they will nevertheless celebrate the achievements of her remarkable talent in the small number of stories that she published. Whatever line of analysis one pursues in reading her stories, Porter's finest ones will repay repeated investments of reading them. They please with their subtleties of technique, from point of view to patterned images of symbolism; they inform with their syntheses of present feeling and past sensation; and they raise imaginative energy with their ambiguous presentations of alien vision. Porter's stories educate the patiently naïve reader into paths of radical maturity.

OTHER MAJOR WORKS

LONG FICTION: *Ship of Fools*, 1962.

POETRY: *Katherine Anne Porter's Poetry*, 1996 (Darlene Harbour Unrue, editor).

NONFICTION: *My Chinese Marriage*, 1921; *Outline of Mexican Popular Arts and Crafts*, 1922; *What Price Marriage*, 1927; *The Days Before*, 1952; *A Defence of Circe*, 1954; *A Christmas Story*, 1967; *The Collected Essays and Occasional Writings*, 1970; *The Selected Letters of Katherine Anne Porter*, 1970; *The Never-Ending Wrong*, 1977; *Letters of Katherine Anne Porter*, 1990.

MISCELLANEOUS: *Collected Stories and Other Writings*, 2008 (Darlene Harbour Unrue, editor).

BIBLIOGRAPHY

Alvarez, Ruth M. "Katherine M. Porter." In *A Companion to the American Short Story*, edited by Alfred Bendixen and James Nagel. Malden, Mass.: Wiley-Blackwell, 2010. Overview of Porter's short fiction, placing it in the broader context of the development of the American short story.

Arima, Hiroko. *Beyond and Alone! The Theme of Isolation in Selected Short Fiction of Kate Chopin, Katherine Anne Porter, and Eudora Welty*. Lanham, Md.: University Press of America, 2006. Focuses on the three writers' treatment of isolation in their short fiction, including their depictions of passion and isolation, family and isolation, feminine independence and isolation, social issues and isolation, and isolation and writing as resistance.

Bloom, Harold, ed. *Katherine Anne Porter*. Broomall, Pa.: Chelsea House, 2001. Provides plot summaries, lists of characters, and analytical essays about the short-fiction works "Flowering Judas," "Old Mortality, *Pale Horse, Pale Rider*, and "The Grave."

Brinkmeyer, Robert H., Jr. *Katherine Anne Porter's Artistic Development: Primitivism, Traditionalism, and Totalitarianism*. Baton Rouge: Louisiana State University Press, 1993. Applying Mikhail Bakhtin's theory of the dialogic and monologic to Porter's fiction, Brinkmeyer argues that when she created a memory-based dialogue with her southern past, she achieved her height as an artist, producing such important works of short fiction as "The Jilting of Granny Weatherall" and *Noon Wine*.

Fornataro-Neil, M. K. "Constructed Narratives and Writing Identity in the Fiction of Katherine Anne Porter." *Twentieth Century Literature* 44 (Fall,

1998): 349-361. Discusses *Old Mortality*, "He," *Noon Wine*, and "Holiday" in terms of Porter's fascination with characters who cannot or do not speak. Argues that her silent characters are alienated because they communicate by a sign system that others cannot understand.

Gelfant, Blanche H., ed. *The Columbia Companion to the Twentieth-Century American Short Story*. New York: Columbia University Press, 2000. Includes a chapter in which Porter's short stories are analyzed.

Graham, Don. "Katherine Anne Porter's Journey from Texas to the World." *Southwest Review* 84 (1998): 140-153. Argues that because the dominant figure in Texas literary mythology was the heroic cowboy, Porter, who had nothing to say about cowboys in her writing, chose instead to identify herself as a southerner.

Hartley, Lodwick, and George Core, eds. *Katherine Anne Porter: A Critical Symposium*. Athens: University of Georgia Press, 1969. A collection of seminal essays, this book includes an interview with Porter in 1963, as well as a personal assessment by Porter's friend Glenway Wescott. A group of five essays provide general surveys, and another five focus on particular stories, including "The Grave" and "Holiday." Includes select bibliography and index.

Hendrick, George. *Katherine Anne Porter*. New York: Twayne, 1965. A biographical sketch precedes studies grouped according to settings from Porter's life: the first group from Mexico, the second from Texas, and the third from New York and Europe. After a chapter on *Ship of Fools*, the book surveys Porter's essays and summarizes major themes. Notes, annotated bibliography, index, and chronology.

Liberman, M. M. *Katherine Anne Porter's Fiction*. Detroit: Wayne State University Press, 1971. In this study of Porter's methods and intentions, seven chapters offer analyses of *Ship of Fools*, *Old Mortality*, *Noon Wine*, "María Concepción," "Flowering Judas," and "The Leaning Tower." Chapter 6 examines "people who cannot speak for themselves," the central characters of "Holiday," "He," and *Noon Wine*. Includes notes and an index.

Nance, William L. *Katherine Anne Porter and the Art of Rejection*. Chapel Hill: University of North Carolina Press, 1964. Argues that an emerging thematic pattern of rejection is found in the early stories, up to "Hacienda"; variations are illustrated by the middle stories. The Miranda stories are presented as fictional autobiography, and *Ship of Fools* is closely analyzed as a failure to make a novel out of character sketches. Complemented by a bibliography and index.

Scofield, Martin. "Katherine Anne Porter, Eudora Welty, and Flannery O'Connor." In *The Cambridge Introduction to the American Short Story*. New York: Cambridge University Press, 2006. An overview and analysis of short fiction by three southern women writers. Discusses some of Porter's short fiction, including "Flowering Judas," *Noon Wine*, *Pale Horse, Pale Rider*, and "The Martyr."

Spencer, Virginia, ed. *"Flowering Judas": Katherine Anne Porter*. New Brunswick, N.J.: Rutgers University Press, 1993. This collection of critical discussions of Porter's story features background material and important essays, from Ray B. West's influential 1947 discussion of the story to debates about the character of Eugenio as a Christ figure.

Stout, Janis. *Katherine Anne Porter: A Sense of the Times*. Charlottesville: University Press of Virginia, 1995. Contains chapters on Porter's background in Texas, her view of politics and art in the 1920's, her writing and life between the two world wars, and her relationship with the southern agrarians. Addresses the issue of gender, the problem of genre in *Ship of Fools*, and the quality of Porter's "free, intransigent, dissenting mind." Includes notes and bibliography.

Titus, Mary. *The Ambivalent Art of Katherine Anne Porter*. Athens: University of Georgia Press, 2005. A look at the ways in which Porter confronted issues of gender in her work and her life, including a study of some of her unpublished papers.

Unrue, Darlene Harbour. *Katherine Anne Porter: The Life of an Artist*. Jackson: University Press of Mississippi, 2005. A comprehensive biography of Porter that offers insight into her turbulent personal life and her writing.

Walsh, Thomas F. *Katherine Anne Porter and Mexico.* Austin: University of Texas Press, 1992. Contains chapters on Porter and Mexican politics, her different periods of residence in Mexico, and *Ship of Fools.* Includes notes and bibliography.

Warren, Robert Penn. "Irony with a Center: Katherine Anne Porter." In *Selected Essays.* New York: Random House, 1951. In this important early essay on Porter's stories, Warren argues that Porter's fiction is characterized by rich surface detail apparently casually scattered and a close structure that makes such detail meaningful.

Richard D. McGhee

PADGETT POWELL

Born: Gainesville, Florida; April 25, 1952

PRINCIPAL SHORT FICTION
Typical, 1991
Aliens of Affection, 1998
Interrogative Mood: A Novel?, 2009

OTHER LITERARY FORMS

Writing is a constant with Padgett Powell (PAD-jeht POW-ehl). Even while fishing or hunting or sitting around with friends, he is thinking of stories and new ways to convey them. In addition to his short-story collections and such novels as *Edisto* (1984), *A Woman Named Drown* (1987), *Edisto Revisited* (1996), and *Mrs. Hollingworth's Men* (2000), he has written essays for national publications, including *The New Times* and *Esquire.* An essay, entitled "Whupped Before Kilt," first appeared in a 1998 issue of *The Oxford American* magazine and later served as the preface to the 1998 edition of *New Stories from the South.* It pointed out that since the South had lost the Civil War, its literature had been filled with tales of failure.

ACHIEVEMENTS

The occasion of Padgett Powell's first book, *Edisto* (1984), was greeted enthusiastically. He was a writer, in the vein of William Faulkner and Flannery O'Connor, who could tell a good story in stellar, intelligent prose. Powell lit up the literary world, was nominated for the National Book Award, and *Edisto* was included in *Time* magazine's list of that year's best fiction. In 1986, he received the Whiting Foundation Writers' Award and in 1986 and 1988 an American Academy and Institute of Arts and Letters Rome Fellowship in Literature. A 1989 Fulbright Fellowship in Turkey allowed him to develop a concept for a lengthy short story, "Mr. Irony," which appeared in *The Paris Review.* His short story "Trick or Treat" won the O. Henry Award and was anthologized in the *O. Henry Prize Stories.*

BIOGRAPHY

Padgett Powell was born in Gainesville, Florida, on April 25, 1952, to Albine Batts Powell, a trucker, labor contractor, and brewmaster, and Bettye Palmer, a teacher. Padgett Powell and his two younger brothers were uprooted frequently, living in various parts of Florida until 1968, when the family moved to Florence, South Carolina. Powell grew used to being the outsider, the new boy, attending seventeen different schools through twelfth grade. His early education showed that he had a greater proficiency in science than in literature, and in 1975 he earned a bachelor of science degree in chemistry from the College of Charleston in South Carolina. He then enrolled at the University of Tennessee in Knoxville, leaving before earning his master's degree because he became bored with his chosen course of study. He preferred reading and writing, and he spent the next few years traveling in the Southeast, working as a freight handler, a house mover, and an orthodontic technician. Powell then spent eight years as a roofer in Texas before enrolling in the master of fine arts program at the University of Houston, where he met Donald Barthelme, the man who has had the greatest influence on Powell's life and work.

Barthleme was a postmodernist, challenging long-established structures in literature. He saw in his student Powell great potential, both as an academician and a friend. Powell noted that he and Barthelme were very much alike, favoring the same writers, bars, and types of women. In 1982, Powell earned his master of fine arts degree from the University of Houston. In 1984, he married poet Sidney Wade. They moved to Gainesville and began their teaching careers at the University of Florida. They had two daughters, Amanda Dahl and Elena, and divorced in 2005.

ANALYSIS

Though Padgett Powell has experimented with various literary genres, he prefers short fiction, which requires close attention to diction and using the fewest number of words to convey the message. These words often depend upon sound or sight for inducing mood, helping Powell to avoid clichéd literary conventions and traditional forms.

Novelist Walker Percy was one of the first noted writers to recognize Powell as a major talent. Percy wrote of Powell's first book, *Edisto*, that it was "truly remarkable, both as a narrative and in its extraordinary use of language." Saul Bellow marked Powell as potentially one of the greatest writers of the generation. Powell's playfulness set him apart from other writers and, in the beginning, won him such accolades.

Much to Powell's disappointment, however, his subsequent work was not greeted with enthusiasm. While Powell has excelled at word play, at unexpected rhyming, at made-up words that fit perfectly, and his talent has been recognized, he has not yet published another widespread success.

His second novel, *A Woman Named Drown*, garnered some positive response for using extraordinary prose to convey ordinary circumstances. However, Powell was growing dissatisfied with standard forms and tones. He was so disenchanted that he did not engage in debates with fellow scholars and critics; discussions of old literary criticism and new deconstructionism seemed to him little more than scholarly self-indulgence. He needed to experiment. Powell

liked short fiction because in it he could "explore the limits of language while not rehashing tired plots and simple conflict." He produced two major collections, demonstrating that he is one of the few writers who can combine successfully postmodern absurdism with the gothic and the grotesque and that language is the driving force of his short stories

"MR. IRONY"

Typical, Powell's first collection, contained twenty-two short stories, most connected thematically, and a few longer, more traditional stories. *Typical*'s characters have a reduced capacity to "want." They wallow in their despair, expecting little else out of life. The dreary everydayness of their existence leaves them nearly paralyzed. One story, "Mr Irony," proved a seminal point in Powell's career, because it marked a shift from reality to the metafiction favored by Barthelme. Indeed, the title character is modeled on Powell's mentor, and another character, a "student of low-affected living edged with self-deprecating irony," is based on himself. Mr. Irony's skewed vision of the world, with its contradictions and absurdities, make him who he is: a traveler and a talker. "Mr. Irony" was followed by "Mr. Nefarious," "Miss Recognition," "Dr. Ordinary," "General Rancidity," and "Mr. Irony Renounces Irony," each character true to its appellation.

Powell began to see plot as incidental and characters representing extremes in human behavior. Among their ranks are the downtrodden, the mentally disturbed, the brain damaged, sociopaths; some are mean, hard-drinking southerners with a kindness common in many good old boys. They carry on the old southern traditions of dog fighting and long for the past of rebel generals, and forced gentility.

"LETTER FROM A DOGFIGHTER'S AUNT, DECEASED"

Aunt Humpy, the featured character in another story, "Letter from a Dogfighter's Aunt, Deceased," is an autodidact, a stuck-up, pedantic librarian, whose greatest pleasure comes from constantly correcting the grammar of family members. She prepares her nephew Brody for life as a procurer of dogs for fighting bouts. He excels in behavior outside the realm of decency. She admires the purity of his lawlessness.

"THE WINNOWING OF MRS. SCHUPING"

"The Winnowing of Mrs. Schuping" deals with a woman who hopes to simplify her life by divesting herself of earthly belongings and responsibilities. She gives up on travel and reading. She distrusts reality and becomes immobile, serene in watching her house deteriorate. Similarly, Powell approaches each new work by breaking down established writing traditions (winnowing) and trying new forms of expression.

Typical, in which this story appears, won the Pushcart Prize, and the title story was included in 1990's *Best American Short Stories*. Other selections were chosen for *Great Contemporary Short Stories*, the 1992 edition of *New Stories from the South*, and Anne Tyler's *The Best of the South: Ten Years of New Stories from the South* (1996).

Powell's works show the two strands of his literary influences. He grew up with southern gothic, which embraces the grotesque, the weird, and the lives of brooding, lonely people in inhospitable environments, with O'Connor and Faulkner being the most representative of the style. He deals with the ways and mores of the Old South, the hardly diminished racism, the cruelty and lack of respect for life of the good old boys, who run dog fights and shoot losers . These people are vile but capable of a strange sweetness. They cuss, booze, and whore around. They beat and walk out on their women and are in despair at what fate has dealt them. They accept no personal responsibility.

However, Powell is under the sway of Barthelme's absurdist approach, which does not require that a story have a beginning, middle, and end and is unconcerned with sentences that do not parse. Barthelme encouraged Powell to rely less on reality and to subdue his tendency to record what is. Powell found himself caught between his mentor's fanciful work and the gothic traditions of his youth. He played with language, with sounds, with nonsense rhymes that somehow, together, created sense. In combining postmodern with southern gothic, Powell developed a unique style.

Barthelme had convinced Powell that a writer must convey self-doubt, self-deprecation, and irony to keep his or her ego at bay. Not yet a master of this principle with his first book, Powell was sure that *Edisto*'s enthusiastic reception showed that he had written an outstanding book and would be deserving of such praise with subsequent works. However, he was disconcerted by the lukewarm responses afforded his next offerings. Still, he continued to be linguistically inventive and was always on the lookout for new ways to tell a story.

ALIENS OF AFFECTION

Powell's second short-story collection, *Aliens of Affection*, contains two long pieces, "Wayne" and "All Along the Watchtower," with five full-length short stories. In his prior collection, Powell had shown a closeness with the characters, but in this one he keeps them at a distance. It is hard to find a sympathetic character and a few individuals are totally despicable. They are victims of their lot and of insanity, stroke, and brain damage, and unable to adjust to modern life.

"TRICK OR TREAT"

"Trick or Treat" deserves particular attention because it is daring and explores a universal condition. A seemingly content but bored woman accepts the advances of a thirteen-year-old ruffian, whom she notes has a head that resembles a pumpkin, uncarved, making him even more vapid and foreboding. They meet needs in each other that go beyond the sexual. They develop a relationship that, under usual circumstances, would be considered pedophiliac, although the reader is called upon to accept this unacceptable relationship. *Aliens of Affection* won awards for its tales of insight and power. The title story was selected for the 1998 edition of *New Stories from the South*, and "Wayne in Love" was selected by Garrison Keillor for the 1998 edition of *The Best American Short Stories*.

Powell gets into the minds of the confused and despairing in a way that brings order out of chaos. The reader can understand the garbled thinking, the odd arrangement of words, the seeming random non sequitur, without caring about or judging what would appear to be lapses in grammar, coherence, and logic. It is the acceptance of the strange that allows the reader to hear the lyrical, the unexpected in the word arrangements. The more Powell toyed with the avant-garde, however, the more he lost readership. He says he lost his mind with Barthelme and came to see formlessness as okay. He delighted in the everyday ironies of people espousing one thing and doing another. These contradictions fascinated him and ultimately were explored in his novels and short stories.

Powell went through a period of heavy drinking that may have made him a good bar buddy but did not further his career or help his writing output. In 1996, with his return to long fiction with *Edisto Revisited*, Powell decided to give up alcohol until he made his first million dollars. The book was called a tour de force of style, but the critical response was only mildly enthusiastic.

Powell announced his retirement, but he kept observing and listening to the world around him. He continued in his academic pursuits for ten years, though not publishing until he came up with *Interrogative Mood*, a 242-page book made up of nothing but questions. When asked how he could possibly fill a book in this way, he said he'd wake up, put on his pants, realize he was depressed, and, with nothing else to do, would start writing down questions. While this book fills defies categorization, being neither long nor short fiction, it fits better with the latter because the questions sometimes create a story, other times start a train of thought, and sometimes just make the reader laugh out loud. Powell has even heard reports of its use in parlor games, with people claiming to get to know each other better through answering questions. When reminded that he wrote a piece at age thirty-five in which he said that he was "arbitrary, foolish [and confident] with a streak of petulance and defiance," he said that he could successfully change each adjective to represent his later years: "arbitrary to scattered, foolish to loutish, with a streak of trash-talking and belligerence, and finally doubtful."

OTHER MAJOR WORKS

LONG FICTION: *Edisto*, 1984; *A Woman Named Drown*, 1987; *Edisto Revisited*, 1996; and *Mrs Hollingworth's Men*, 2000.

BIBLIOGRAPHY

Barr, Brian J. " Padgett Powell." *The Believer* (September, 2006). In an interview, Powell discusses how hard labor improved his writing, what impact the South has on his

Halpern, Dan. "southern Discomfort."*The New York Times*, October 18, 2009. An enlightening discussion of Powell's life and career, complete with candid accounts of the ups and downs.

Hunt, Victoria. "Interview with Padgett Powell." *Bomb* 55 (Spring, 1996). Hunt draws an intimate portrait of Powell, in which the author, when discussing his life, pulls no punches and is candid in a way that he cannot be in his autobiographical writing. Always disarming, Powell speaks the truth, as opposed to truth seen through the eyes of fiction.

Gay Pitman Zieger

J. F. POWERS

Born: Jacksonville, Illinois; July 8, 1917
Died: Collegeville, Minnesota; June 12, 1999

PRINCIPAL SHORT FICTION

Prince of Darkness, and Other Stories, 1947
The Presence of Grace, 1956
Lions, Harts, Leaping Does, and Other Stories, 1963
Look How the Fish Live, 1975
The Old Bird: A Love Story, 1991 (a short story,
    originally pb. in *Prince of Darkness, and Other
    Stories*)
The Stories of J. F. Powers, 2000

OTHER LITERARY FORMS

J. F. Powers is the author of two novels: *Morte d'Urban* (1962), which received the National Book Award for fiction in 1962, and *Wheat That Springeth Green* (1988), a National Book Award nominee. In addition, he published essays and reviews.

ACHIEVEMENTS

Like Flannery O'Connor, a Catholic writer with whom he is often compared, J. F. Powers is widely recognized as a distinctive figure in the modern American short story despite having produced only a small body of work. A master of comedy whose range encompasses cutting satire, broad farce, and gentle humor, Powers explores fundamental moral and theological issues as they are worked out in the most mundane situations. While he is best known for stories centering on priests and parish life, Powers, in several early stories of the 1940's, was among the first to portray the circumstances of black people who had migrated from the South to Chicago and other urban centers.

BIOGRAPHY

James Farl Powers was born into a Catholic family in a town in which the "best" people were Protestant, a fact which he said "to some extent made a philosopher out of me." He attended Quincy Academy, taught by Franciscan Fathers, and many of his closest friends there later went into the priesthood. Powers himself was not attracted to clerical life, principally because of the social responsibilities, although he has said the praying would have attracted him. After graduation he worked in Marshall Field and Co., sold insurance, became a chauffeur, and clerked in Brentano's bookshop. During World War II, Powers was a conscientious objector; as a result, he spent more than a year in a federal prison. His first story was published in 1943. In 1946, he married Elizabeth Wahl, also a writer. They had five children; at the time of her death, in 1988, they had been married for forty-two years.

After the war, Powers and his family lived in Ireland, as well as in the United States. He supplemented income from writing by teaching at various colleges and universities; in addition, he received a Guggenheim Fellowship and two fellowships from the Rockefeller Foundation. In 1976, Powers settled in Collegeville, Minnesota, where he became Regents Professor of English at St. John's University.

ANALYSIS

The most frequently reprinted of J. F. Powers's short stories and therefore the best known are "Lions, Harts, Leaping Does," "The Valiant Woman," and "The Forks"--stories that are firmly rooted in social observation and realistic detail but have at their center specifically moral and theological issues. Powers was a Catholic writer, not a writer who happened to be a Catholic or one who proselytized for the Church, but rather, as Evelyn Waugh said, one whose "art is everywhere infused and directed by his Faith."

For Powers the central issue is how in the midst of a fallen world people can live up to the high ideals of the Church. Since that issue is most sharply seen in the lives of those who have chosen the religious life as their vocation, parish priests, curates, friars, nuns, and archbishops dominate Powers's stories. As might be expected of a religious writer who admires, as Powers does, the art of James Joyce and who learned the satiric mode from Sinclair Lewis and Waugh, Powers's stories are frequently ironic and often satiric portraits of clerics who fail to measure up to the ideals of their priestly vocation. Many are straightforward satires.

"Prince of Darkness"

"Prince of Darkness," for example, is the fictional portrait of a priest, Father Burner, who in his gluttony, his ambition for material rewards and professional success, and his lack of charity toward sinners in the confessional, reveals himself to be a modern incarnation of the devil himself. In opposition to Father Burner is the Archbishop, an elderly cleric in worn-out slippers who in the proper spirit of moral firmness and Christian compassion reassigns Father Burner not to the pastorate he covets but to another parish assistant's role where, presumably, his power of darkness will be held in check.

"The Devil Was the Joker"

"The Devil Was the Joker" from Powers's second collection resembles "Prince of Darkness" in theme and conception, except here the satanic figure is a layman who has been hired by a religious order to sell its publication in Catholic parishes. Mac, the salesman-- "Fat and fifty or so, with a candy-pink face, sparse orange hair, and popeyes"--hires a young former seminarian to travel about with him as his companion-driver. Myles Flynn, the former seminarian, also becomes the drinking companion and confidant of Mac, who gradually reveals himself to be totally cynical about the religious wares he is peddling, and who is, moreover, neither religious nor Catholic. Mac exploits the priests he encounters on his travels and attempts to use Myles to further his financial interests. As a way of making a sale, for example, he will frequently "take the pledge," that is, promise to refrain from alcohol. In return, he

J. F. Powers (Time & Life Pictures/Getty Images)

usually manages to extract from the priest to whom he made the pledge a large order for his wares. One day, after drunkenly confessing to Myles that he is not Catholic, Mac tries to repair the damage he imagines has been done to his position by trying to get Myles to baptize him, alleging that Myles has been responsible for his sudden conversion. It is through Myles's response that Powers provides the perspective for understanding and judging Mac. Myles perceives that Mac "was the serpent, the nice old serpent with Glen-plaid markings, who wasn't very poisonous." In conclusion, Myles not only refuses to baptize Mac but also leaves him and attempts once more to get back into the seminary.

"Prince of Darkness" and "The Devil Was the Joker" are both loosely constructed revelations of character rather than stories of conflict and action. Powers's two best-known pieces are also among the best things he has done, including those in *Look How the Fish Live*. Both are told from the point of view of a priest caught in a moral dilemma.

"THE FORKS"

In "The Forks," a young curate, Father Eudex, assistant to a Monsignor in a middle-class parish, is presented with a check from a manufacturing company that has been having labor trouble. Father Eudex, born on a farm, a reader of the *Catholic Worker*, and a sympathizer with the strikers, regards the check as hush money and therefore finds it unacceptable. His superior, the Monsignor, who drives a long black car like a politician's and is friendly with bankers and businessmen, suggests that Father Eudex use the check as down payment on a good car. The Monsignor is a man of impeccable manners, concerned with the appearance of things, with laying out a walled garden, with the perfection of his salad, and disturbed by the fact that Father Eudex strips off his shirt and helps the laborer spade up the garden, and that he uses the wrong fork at dinner. Quite clearly the Monsignor represents to Powers a modern version of the secularized church, while Father Eudex represents the traditional and, in this story, powerless Christian virtues. At the end of the story, Father Eudex, who has considered sending the check back to the company or giving it to the strikers' fund, merely tears it up and flushes it down the toilet, aware that every other priest in town will find some "good" use for it. True goodness in Powers's stories tends to be helpless in the face of such worldliness.

"THE VALIANT WOMAN"

In "The Valiant Woman," the same issue is raised in the conflict between a priest and his housekeeper. The occasion in this story is the priest's fifty-ninth birthday celebration, a dinner from which his one remaining friend and fellow priest is driven by the insistent and boorish presence of the housekeeper. The theological and moral issue is dramatized by the priest's dilemma: According to church law he can rid himself of the housekeeper, but he can only do so by violating the spirit of Christian charity. The housekeeper, being totally unconscious of the moral implications of her acts, naturally has the advantage. Like the wily mosquito who bites the priest, her acts are of the flesh only, while his, being conscious and intellectual, are of the will. The priest cannot bring himself to fire her and so in a helpless rage at being bitten by a mosquito (after having been, in effect, stung by the housekeeper), he

wildly swings a rolled up newspaper at the mosquito and knocks over and breaks a bust of Saint Joseph.

When summarized, Powers's stories sound forbidding, when, in fact, they are--despite the underlying seriousness--delightfully humorous. About the housekeeper in "The Valiant Woman," for instance, Powers has the priest think:

> [She] was clean. And though she cooked poorly, could not play the organ, would not take up the collection in an emergency and went to card parties, and told all--even so, she was clean. She washed everything. Sometimes her underwear hung down beneath her dress like a paratrooper's pants, but it and everything she touched was clean. She washed constantly. She was clean.

Not all of Powers's stories are about priests. Four of those in his first collection deal with racial and religious prejudice; three are about blacks ("The Trouble," about a race riot; "He Don't Plant Cotton," in which black entertainers in a northern nightclub are badgered by a visitor from Mississippi and quit their jobs; and "The Eye," about a lynching of an innocent black), and one about anti-Semitism ("Renner"). Two stories from *The Presence of Grace* are also not explicitly religious: "The Poor Thing" and "Blue Island." Even these apparently secular stories arise out of the same moral concern that may be seen more clearly in the overtly religious ones.

"THE POOR THING"

In "The Poor Thing," a crippled woman, Dolly, who goes through the motions of being religious, is revealed as a pious hypocrite when she slyly exploits an elderly spinster, forcing her to serve for little pay as her constant companion. The elderly woman had been talked into accepting the position in the first place and then, when she tried to leave, was falsely accused by Dolly of having stolen from her. The woman then has the choice of either returning to Dolly or having her reputation at the employment office ruined.

"BLUE ISLAND"

In "Blue Island," the oppressor is a woman who sells pots and pans by arranging "coffees" in other women's houses and then arriving to "demonstrate" her wares. Under the guise of neighborly concern for a young woman who has recently moved into the neighborhood and is unsure of herself (and ashamed of her origins), she persuades the young woman to have a coffee to which all of the important neighbor women are invited; then the saleswoman arrives with her wares. The young woman, the victim, stricken by the deception practiced on her and on the neighbors she has tried to cultivate, rushes to her bedroom and weeps, while downstairs the neighbor women file out, leaving her alone with her oppressor. In both "The Poor Thing" and "Blue Island," Powers also shows that the victims participate in their victimization, the spinster through her pride and the young woman in "Blue Island" by denying her past and attempting to be something she is not.

"LIONS, HARTS, LEAPING DOES"

Powers's best stories are undoubtedly those that bring the moral and religious issue directly into the main action. The story still most widely admired is the one written when Powers was twenty-five that established his early reputation as a master of the short story: "Lions, Harts, Leaping Does." The popularity of this story may result not only from the high level of its art but also from the way it deals so gently with the issues and creates in Father Didymus and in the simple Friar Titus two appealing characters. Indeed, one of Powers's major achievements is his ability in many of his stories to create characters with the vividness and complexity one expects only from the longer novel. For this reason, if for no other, the stories of J. F. Powers will continue to engage the attention of discriminating readers.

OTHER MAJOR WORKS

LONG FICTION: *Morte d'Urban*, 1962; *Wheat That Springeth Green*, 1988.

BIBLIOGRAPHY

Donoghue, Denis. "Bookend: The Storyteller." The *New York Times Book Review*, March 26, 2000, 35. An overview of Powers's literary career that discusses the characteristics of his writings, including some analysis of the short fiction.

Evans, Fallon, ed. *J. F. Powers*. St. Louis: Herder, 1968. A collection of essays and appreciations emphasizing the Catholic context of Powers's fiction. Among the contributors are Hayden Carruth, W. H. Gass (whose essay "Bingo Game at the Foot of the Cross" is a classic), Thomas Merton, and John Sisk. Also includes an interview with Powers and a bibliography.

Gussow, Mel. "J. F. Powers, 81, Dies." *The New York Times*, June 17, 1999, p. C23. In this tribute to Powers, Gussow traces his literary career, commenting on his first important story, "Lions, Harts, Leaping Does," and his best-known collection, *Prince of Darkness, and Other Stories*, noting his frequent focus on priests.

Hagopian, John V. *J. F. Powers*. New York: Twayne, 1968. The first book-length study of Powers, this overview comprises a biographical sketch and a survey of his work through *Morte d'Urban*. Gives extensive attention to Powers's stories. Includes a useful bibliography.

McCarthy, Colman. "The Craft of J. F. Powers." *The Washington Post*, June 12, 1993, p. A21. A brief tribute to Powers, commenting on his teaching and fiction and recounting an interview, in which Powers laments the fact that college students do not read any more.

Meyers, Jeffrey. "J. F. Powers: Uncollected Stories, Essays and Interviews, 1943-1979." *Bulletin of Bibliography* 44 (March, 1987): 38-39. Because Powers has published relatively little in his long career, it is particularly useful to have a list of his uncollected stories. The essays and interviews listed here provide valuable background.

Powers, J. F. "The Alphabet God Uses." Interview by Anthony Schmitz. *Minnesota Monthly* 22 (December, 1988): 34-39. At the time of this interview, occasioned by the publication of Powers's novel *Wheat That Springeth Green*, Schmitz himself had just published his first novel, which also deals with the Catholic clergy. Schmitz makes an ideal interviewer, and his conversation with Powers provides an excellent introduction to the man and his works.

Powers, Katherine A. "Reflections of J. F. Powers: Author, Father, Clear-Eyed Observer." *The Boston Globe*, July 18, 1999, p. K4. A reminiscence of Powers by his daughter, who discusses the writers that most influenced Powers, particularly his admiration for Evelyn Waugh, and comments on his writing and reading habits.

Preston, Thomas R. "Christian Folly in the Fiction of J. F. Powers." *Critique: Studies in Modern Fiction* 16, no. 2 (1974): 91-107. The theme of the "fool for Christ," whose actions confound the wisdom of this world, has a long tradition. Focusing on the stories "Lions, Harts, Leaping Does" and "The Forks" and the novel *Morte d' Urban*, Preston explores Powers's handling of this theme, showing how Powers uses priests as protagonists, not to dwell on concerns peculiar to the priesthood but rather to illumine the nature of the Christian life. See also *Critique: Studies in Modern Fiction* 2 (Fall, 1958), a special issue devoted to Powers and Flannery O'Connor.

Votteler, Thomas, ed. *Short Story Criticism: Excerpts from Criticism of the Works of Short Fiction Writers*. Vol. 4. Detroit: Gale Research, 1990. Contains a chapter on Powers with a good selection of criticism of his short fiction.

W. J. Stuckey

REYNOLDS PRICE

Born: Macon, North Carolina; February 1, 1933
Died: Durham, North Carolina: January 20, 2011

PRINCIPAL SHORT FICTION

The Names and Faces of Heroes, 1963
Permanent Errors, 1970
The Foreseeable Future: Three Long Stories, 1991
The Collected Stories, 1993

OTHER LITERARY FORMS

In addition to short stories, Reynolds Price's works include plays, teleplays, award-winning poetry, and the novels for which he is best known, which include *The Honest Account of a Memorable Life: An Apocryphal Gospel* (1994) and *The Promise of Rest* (1995). Price's essays and articles have been collected in several volumes, and he has also published translations from the Bible and three memoirs: *Clear Pictures: First Loves, First Guides* (1989), *Learning a Trade: A Craftsman's Notebooks, 1955-1997* (1998), and *Ardent Spirits: Leaving Home, Coming Back* (2009). His novel *The Good Priest's Son* (2005) deals with the September 11, 2001, terrorist attacks. In 2000, he published his first children's book, *A Perfect Friend.*

ACHIEVEMENTS

A Rhodes scholar at Oxford University, Reynolds Price received fellowships from the John Simon Guggenheim Memorial Foundation and the National Endowment for the Arts. His numerous honors also include a National Association of Independent Schools award, a National Institute of Arts and Letters award, a North Carolina Award, a Bellamann Foundation award, the Roanoke-Chowan Poetry Award, the Elmer H. Bobst Award, a Fund for New American Plays grant, an R. Hunt Parker Award, and the 2007 Thomas Wolfe Prize, as well as honorary doctorates from St. Andrew's Presbyterian College, Wake Forest University, Washington and Lee University, and Davidson College. His novel *A Long and Happy Life* (1962) won both the William Faulkner Foundation First Novel Award and the Sir Walter Raleigh Award. *The Surface of Earth* (1975) won the Lillian Smith Award in 1976, and *Kate Vaiden* (1986), a best seller, received the National Book Critics Circle Award for Fiction. *The Collected Stories* was a finalist for the Pulitzer Prize in Fiction. Price's books have been translated into sixteen languages.

BIOGRAPHY

The first child of William Solomon Price and Elizabeth Rodwell Price, Edward Reynolds Price was born February 1, 1933, at the Rodwell family homestead in

Macon, North Carolina. When the doctor told Will that neither his wife nor his child was likely to survive, Will made a pledge to God: If their lives were spared, he would never drink again. He kept this difficult promise, which marked the beginning of a deep bond between Reynolds and his parents. Young Reynolds heard this story many times--as he heard the other oral memories of his large extended family--and he said that these tales were his introduction to the power of narrative.

During the Depression, Will Price worked as an appliance salesman, moving his family through a succession of small North Carolina towns. Although a brother was born when Reynolds was eight, he was still essentially a solitary child, spending most of his free time reading, drawing, or playing alone in the woods. The family moved to Warrenton in 1944, where Reynolds met the farm children who served as prototypes for his early fiction. In 1947, Reynolds entered high school in Raleigh, where, during what he has called a miserable adolescence, he decided that writing would be his vocation.

In 1951, Price entered Duke University as an Angier Duke Scholar and studied English literature and history. Although he wrote relatively little fiction as an undergraduate, his story "Michael Egerton" was praised by visiting author Eudora Welty, and he was also encouraged by his professors. After graduation in 1955, Price spent three years at Merton College, Oxford, as a Rhodes scholar. While there, in addition to writing his thesis on John Milton's *Samson Agonistes* (1671), Price wrote poetry and short stories and traveled widely in Europe. In 1958, he received a B.Litt. degree and returned to Duke University to join the English faculty. Price continued to teach at Duke, interrupted only by visiting professorships and a few trips abroad.

Price's first two novels and collection of short stories, published between 1962 and 1966, were unanimously acclaimed. Some readers and critics were disturbed, however, by what they perceived as a darker tone and harsher style in his third novel, *Love and Work* (1968), and his second short-story collection, *Permanent Errors*. Price continued to publish steadily in a variety of forms: a collection of essays in 1972; another award-winning novel, *The Surface of Earth*, in 1975;

his first play in 1977; and a volume of contemporary translations of biblical stories in 1978. In 1981, he published *The Source of Light* (1981), a sequel to *The Surface of Earth*, which, like its predecessor, was praised but also criticized for its cumbersome plot.

In 1984, following surgery for spinal cancer, Price became paraplegic, but his literary output after that time had, if anything, only increased. For more than thirty years, Price's home was outside Durham, North Carolina. Situated on forty acres of land, with a pond and pine trees, it was filled with what Price called an aging boy's museum: objects as diverse as arrowheads, old 78-rpm records, numerous photographs of family and friends, and a personal letter from Dwight D. Eisenhower dated 1943. In 1977, Price became a James B. Duke Professor of English at Duke University, where he continued to teach and write. He died of a heart attack on January 20, 2011, at the age of seventy-seven.

ANALYSIS

Reynolds Price was one of the United States' most respected men of letters. After publication of his first novel in 1962, Price was instantly acclaimed as a regional writer and compared to William Faulkner. However, he resisted being called a southern writer because the label, he believed, encouraged people to focus on the surface similarities among works rather than look at their deeper truths. Price wrote out of his vision of the spirituality of all existence, particularly as expressed through the myriad interactions of family. He is known as a serious writer of rich, dense prose that is simultaneously but not incongruously infused with comic moments and homespun wisdom.

Critics have observed that it is hard to separate Price's work and literary persona from Price himself. Although events and characters in his stories and novels often bear strong resemblance to his personal circumstances, Price denied that his writing was autobiographical, saying,

> Only very occasionally and fragmentarily do I write autobiographically. My ideas come from all sorts of places, generally an exterior fact or object will precipitate an interior crystallization.

Interior crystallization is the heart of Price's fiction, which he has described as an attempt to seize territory from chaos. Price sought to uncover the natural order that he perceived as underlying the seemingly chaotic surface of daily happenings, investigating it as it manifests itself in different layers of life. Although religion has a definite presence in Price's work, it is this absolute value of existence that is paramount.

THE NAMES AND FACES OF HEROES

Price published his first volume of short fiction, *The Names and Faces of Heroes*, in 1963. Like his award-winning first novel of the year before, it was enthusiastically acclaimed. Set in Warren, North Carolina, like much of Price's work, these seven stories focus on a characteristic theme: love and its responsibilities, love that grows naturally--although sometimes crookedly--from within the nature of family, related by blood or by community. The first story, "A Chain of Love," is representative of Price's early fiction in that it presents an unsophisticated, rural, adolescent protagonist trying to make sense of the world--often through memories, often in hospitals or churches, and always moving toward a kind of healing that, without contrivance, love can bring.

"A Chain of Love" introduces Price's abiding sense of honor, almost reverence, for the power of family. It contains images and events that figure prominently in later works, including a focus on duty, the giving of gifts, the power of the name, images of light and dark, death, and the parent/child relationship--most commonly father and son. This story (published individually in 1958) is also Price's introduction of the Mustian family, who reappear in three of his novels. Rosacoke Mustian is staying in the Raleigh hospital with her Papa, who is suffering from a "tired heart." From Papa's room, Rosa can see a statue of Jesus Christ outside, and this symbol reappears in her memory of the Phelps boy, who drowned and then returned from the dead. "Papa is my duty," she says, and she tries to do more for him than his nurse does.

Rosa is also aware of the pain of others in the ward. She considers how to help--perhaps by bringing them ice water--but realizes that they "probably wouldn't want that anyhow" and that her attempts to relieve such great suffering would be "like trying to fill up No-Bottom Pond." Still, Rosa thinks, there ought to be "something you could say even in the dark that would make them know why you were standing there looking." Rosa's compassion finds a focus through a case of mistaken identity. She thinks that she sees Wesley--the boy back home--sitting in the hospital corridor and approaches him playfully, only to find that it is the boy whose father is dying of lung cancer across the hall. Embarrassed by her intrusion into his sorrow "like some big hussy," Rosa determines to get to know the Ledwell family (though she does not know their individual names) and be kind to them, but she decides to do so in secret.

The narrative dances with images of light and dark, and Rosa is first associated with the dark. As she steps toward the Ledwell boy, "bleached light" strikes her, and she drops back

> the way one of those rain snails does that is feeling its path . . . till you touch its gentle horn, and it draws itself back . . . into a tight piece you would never guess could think or move or feel, even.

Reynolds Price (AP Photo/Grant Halverson)

After much inner debate, however, Rosa decides to leave a bouquet for Mr. Ledwell, "flowers that would say better than she could how much she felt." Quietly opening Mr. Ledwell's door to deliver the anonymous gift, Rosa sees a priest administering the last rites and intends to back out unobserved. However, she is instead drawn in by the Ledwell boy, who turns and sees her "through all that dark." Rosa decides to leave because they might switch on the light and see her "looking on at this dying which was the most private thing in the world." After placing the flowers on a chair, where "in the [later] light somebody might see them and be glad that whoever it was stepped over to bring them, stepped over without saying a word," Rosa returns to Papa's room. There, in a slow voice that "cut through all the dark," she is finally able to speak her grief and acknowledge her wish that the Ledwells might have known that it was she, "that Rosacoke Mustian was sorry to see it happen."

PERMANENT ERRORS

Price's second volume of short fiction, *Permanent Errors*, was published in 1970. His introduction says that it is

> an attempt to isolate in a number of lives the central error of act, will, understanding which, once made, has been permanent, incurable, but whose diagnosis and palliation are the hopes of continuance.

The protagonists in these stories are no longer rural adolescents but rather intense, often literary individuals. Like the novel that preceded it, *Permanent Errors* sparked controversy among critics and readers, some of whom objected to what they saw as a darker perspective and new compactness, even severity, in Price's style. Price has agreed that these stories were a break with, or advance on, past work, but he also explains that people who thought his first three books were "joyous, rambunctious, yea-saying . . . found themselves abandoned in the middle of the road . . . not having seen, of course, that they'd misread the first three books."

The four pieces that form the first section, "Fool's Education," can be read independently but also form a larger wholeness when read consecutively. The first, "The Happiness of Others," introduces Charles Tamplin, a young American writer living in England who views life from a protective distance. He is referred to by his full name, but the reader knows only the first name of Sara, the woman with whom he has had a long-term relationship. Charles Tamplin and Sara are spending their last day together before they part permanently. Tamplin wants dutifully to "kill" the day "as painlessly as possible," believing that without Sara, it will be easier for him to create, to write, to get his work done. Sara, however, is still able to view the day as a sort of gift, "like a baby dumped on their doorstep, gorgeous but unwanted, condemning as an angel." Visiting a church near Oxford, they choose and recite epitaphs to each other, which reflect these differing views. Tamplin's inscription talks of love as necessarily temporary, while Sara's envisions the possibility of continuity even beyond death. Although Tamplin is not influenced by Sara's interpretation, he does realize that the ending of their relationship is not mutual, as he had supposed, and that she is accusing him of refusing to engage himself in life's changes, preferring instead to learn what he learns by watching the involvement of others.

Later, as they drive along, Tamplin feels some relief from "their airless symbiosis," thinking about how he will turn the day into a story. When their car almost collides with a flock of sheep crossing the road, Tamplin muses on the setting, which "might as easily be Galilee as Oxfordshire, before Christ." He also wonders, however, why the sheep are bothering to cross the road at all since the "grass seemed no greener there than where they had left, browner in fact." Their shepherd, "a credible David," appears almost magically, rubbing his eyes to wake himself up and apologizing for the delay soundlessly--and directly to Sara--through the windshield. She smiles at the shepherd, pardoning him, and Tamplin realizes that life's artistry, like the shepherd with "grace as natural as breath," flows simply and intimately to Sara but not to himself. He sees "a door blown fiercely open on a world, older, simpler, deeper than he'd known." Tamplin will not recover like Sara, who will grow to embrace love again. Rather, it will be his duty to write about the happiness of others, "to describe, celebrate, adore at a distance." Tamplin's error--letting Sara go, separating what he sees as art from life--is the inevitable consequence of his character up to that point.

In the second story of the section, Tamplin returns home "alone but not lonely" and agrees to witness the death of his landlady's dog. Again, he avoids intimacy and is most concerned with the ritualized rules of behavior that he creates for himself, "no word, no touch." In the third story, taking place three weeks later, Tamplin feels himself "leaned on only by the afternoon sun, the light a quiet unneedful companion." Through interactions with his landlady and her friend Mary, which evoke memories of both Sara and Tamplin's mother, it is clear that Tamplin is not really at ease. Although he is disgusted by the disorder he perceives in others' lives, thinking that "the name of all [their] stories was Scars not Seeds," Tamplin nevertheless comes to worship "their wasteful courage, ruinous choices, contingency," realizing that the name of his own story is Flight.

Written directly to Sara, the fourth story focuses on an earlier trip the couple took, but it really deals with the extent to which Tamplin has completed his fool's education. He concludes by asking Sara to come back, and some critics have suggested that Price seems to give Tamplin the benefit of the doubt here. The real question Price asks, however, is left hanging in the air: Is there sufficient space in Tamplin's life for Sara to be able to survive and grow? One may also hear its echo: Is there even space in Tamplin's life for himself? Price's work was seen by some--especially those who were disturbed by its changes after the 1962-1966 "Mustian Years"--to present the struggle between human companionship and solitude. Price, however, gave a better understanding in an interview in 1978, when he stated that he writes "books about human freedom--the limits thereof, the possibilities thereof, the impossibilities thereof." He also elaborated in a later interview that the main lens through which he has looked at human freedom has been love.

THE FORESEEABLE FUTURE

The Foreseeable Future, Price's third collection of short fiction, continues to develop this vision of love, which Price sees "as the greatest reward of human life and also one of the greatest terrors and dangers." The stories investigate moments of liberation from boundaries, moments that expand to include what Price

considers "forms of reality quite beyond those forms which we encounter in our daily routines," moments that can be used as reference points in order to navigate back into greater harmony with the inherent balance and order of life. Each of these three substantial pieces is set in North Carolina and focuses on a male protagonist who is at a spiritual crossroads. Each deals with the threat of death and includes a perceptive child who helps the protagonist make his way home.

"Fare to the Moon" takes place toward the end of World War II. Kayes is spending his last night with Leah, the "one real woman . . . who had finally cared so deep and steady as to all but fill the gully cut in him," before he joins the Army. As the story unfolds, the reader learns quietly that Leah is black, though "born nearly white and stayed that way when most children shade on off, tan or dark," and Kayes is white. One also learns that six months ago, Kayes left his wife--who still "watched him like the first angel landed"--and son for Leah, thereby alienating both of them from their communities. Driving with his brother Riley to the induction center, Kayes asks Riley to look after Leah but also admits his readiness to "leave now awhile." Riley responds that now Leah will have to leave town, too. Kayes realizes that this is true and asks, more to himself than to his brother, "How much have I broke?"

As the two men travel toward the induction center, the boy Curtis goes to help his mother retrieve Kayes's car from Leah's place. While there, he speaks with Leah briefly. Bitter about her before, Curtis now sees that Leah speaks the "clean deadlevel eye-to-eye truth" and later says to a friend, wildly and fiercely, "I flatout liked her. I saw the damned point." Curtis is thus tentatively uncovering the possibility of pardon. After passing his army physical, Kayes telephones Riley to say good-bye, telling him "I plan to live," and then tries to reach Curtis. Curtis is out, however, so Kayes speaks to Daphne, amazing himself by asking her how much she still cares. Kayes also thinks of Leah, but the "sight in his mind of Leah alone hurt too bad to watch," so he shuts his eyes and, "for the first time, asked to know how he could heal some part of the lives he'd crushed--his wife and son and Leah Birch." When no answer comes, "no word, no clue," Kayes decides to unearth his wedding ring from his shaving kit, knowing that it would be "wrong to all concerned" to wear it now but still thinking that "this empty circle might hold inside it his only chance of coming back whole . . . and starting over in decency."

Kayes wonders who on earth will ever risk Kayes Paschel again. The response comes from Curtis, who for the second time holds out the possibility of healing. Curtis dreams that night that he is with a friend but "deep gone in the dark, and losing blood." He tries to call his friend's name but finds he has forgotten it, and so he calls out his own name, "more than once," instead. Then, something pulls his hands up toward "a new light," and Curtis sees that someone "is flying there in a kind of fire that he seems to throw as he moves." Curtis sees that his friend is "moving now like a kite, and I've got the string." He reels the friend back in, until he is on the ground within reach, but "once he moves though, he's dark again," and Curtis says, "I feel the line draw tight once more." He guesses it is Kayes, "without even knowing his face or voice," and says, "I try to bet he's taking me home." Even as he dreams, Curtis realizes that he has "watched Kayes soar and wished him luck" and finds that this sight of "a useful father" will be enough to let him sleep through the night. Thus, Price concludes the story.

Such an appreciation of reality as composed of many layers--manifest and unmanifest, perceptible through the senses or in other ways--runs throughout Price's fiction. Through Price's graceful, elaborate prose, which sounds more like poetry, one is thrust into moments of truth and restoration that touch universal chords. The characters speak of love that they feel--or do not feel--for others in this collection. It is clear, however, that Price is exploring the ultimate power of love to bind one back, more securely, to oneself. This is true freedom and, ironically, the foundation for both meaningful solitude and real companionship. Characters tell of their pasts in order to know their own struggles, to heal them, and to build on them, and Price holds out the promise of the future, complete with successes and failures, based on the possibilities for freedom within each present moment. Thus, his stories are not contrived aesthetic structures separate from life (as Charles Tamplin's were), but rather are the stuff of life itself. Because people live, Price seems to say, they automatically have stories to tell. Because of the stories that Price tells, his readers will find themselves able to participate more fully, and with greater compassion, in the stories of their own lives.

THE COLLECTED STORIES

In 1993 Price published *The Collected Stories*, a complete anthology of his short fiction. Half of the fifty stories in the collection were newly published, while the remainder were culled from previous collections. Many of the stories are set in North Carolina and involve adult male characters reflecting on incidents from their past that often were shaped by "the floods of puberty." In "Deeds of Light" a fatherless young boy, starving for the presence of an adult male in his life, befriends a soldier stationed near his home, who quickly becomes "the thorough man to learn and copy in every trait and skill I lacked." In retrospect, he views the arrival of the soldier as coming at a critical stage in his youth, when hopes for a successful transition to adulthood were withering. Friends, he learns in later life, "can show you sights like nothing your kin, your lovers, God or Nature herself will ever show."

The "Enormous Door," the story of a young boy's emerging sexual awareness, reveals how the insecurities of youth often trigger imaginative reactions to inexplicable human experiences. In this case the youth, through a voyeuristic whim, observes two of his teachers engaging in sexual acts. As the scene unfolds, a rush of carnal images produce at once a sense of confusion and capabilities in the mind of the boy. His inability to fully comprehend the event sets him off on a flight of fancy intended to fill the void left in his understanding. What appears to be an "angel," cloaked in the form of a human body, intervenes to instill a sense of the sacred in a most unusual scene.

With "The Company of the Dead" and "Golden Child," Price again uses the device of an adult male ruminating on a chance incident in his youth. In the former, an adolescent boy and his friend take jobs as "setters" whose task is to sit all night by coffins of deceased family members to keep them company. It is the reactions of the living to the dead, some of them bordering on the bizarre, that provide the boy with insight into the relationships of loved ones. The ultimate lesson he learns is that love "will freeze one life and char the next; no way to predict who lives or dies." Death also becomes a reality in "Golden Child" when a young boy is subjected to unwanted comparisons with a cousin who died at a young age. At first resentful, the boy soon realizes his best hope of overcoming his own fear of death is to take up his cousin's memory and by preserving it, share in her glory.

Price's fascination with the consequences of past actions is played out in dark progression in "Truth and Lies" when a woman decides to confront her husband's young mistress, a former student of the wife. The teacher-student relationship is portrayed in ironic detail by the author, as the woman attempts to lecture her unrepentant former charge on the error of her ways but in so doing comes to the realization that the truth cannot be fixed nor the past erased. They are two lessons from which Price never strays far in his rich body of stories.

OTHER MAJOR WORKS

LONG FICTION: *A Long and Happy Life*, 1962; *A Generous Man*, 1966; *Love and Work*, 1968; *The Surface of Earth*, 1975; *The Source of Light*, 1981; *Mustian: Two Novels and a Story, Complete and Unabridged*, 1983; *Kate Vaiden*, 1986; *Good Hearts*, 1988; *The Tongues of Angels*, 1990; *Blue Calhoun*, 1992; *The Honest Account of a Memorable Life: An Apocryphal Gospel*, 1994; *The Promise of Rest*, 1995; *Roxanna Slade*, 1998; *A Great Circle: The Mayfield Trilogy*, 2001 (contains *The Surface of Earth*, *The Source of Light*, and *The Promise of Rest*); *Noble Norfleet*, 2002; *The Good Priest's Son*, 2005.

PLAYS: *Early Dark*, pb. 1977; *Private Contentment*, pb. 1984; *New Music: A Trilogy*, pr. 1989, pb. 1990; *Full Moon, and Other Plays*, pb. 1993.

TELEPLAY: *House Snake*, 1986.

POETRY: *Late Warning: Four Poems*, 1968; *Lessons Learned: Seven Poems*, 1977; *Nine Mysteries (Four Joyful, Four Sorrowful, One Glorious)*, 1979; *Vital Provisions*, 1982; *The Laws of Ice*, 1986; *The Use of Fire*, 1990; *The Collected Poems*, 1997.

NONFICTION: *Things Themselves: Essays and Scenes*, 1972; *A Common Room: Essays, 1954-1987*, 1987; *Clear Pictures: First Loves, First Guides*, 1989; *Conversations with Reynolds Price*, 1991 (Jefferson Humphries, editor); *A Whole New Life*, 1994; *Three* *Gospels*, 1996; *Learning a Trade: A Craftsman's Notebooks, 1955-1997*, 1998; *Letter to a Man in the Fire: Does God Exist and Does He Care?*, 1999; *Feasting the Heart: Fifty-Two Essays for the Air*, 2000; *A Serious Way of Wondering: The Ethics of Jesus Imagined*, 2003; *Letter to a Godchild: Concerning Faith*, 2006; *Ardent Spirits: Leaving Home, Coming Back*, 2009.

TRANSLATIONS: *Presence and Absence: Versions from the Bible*, 1973; *Oracles: Six Versions from the Bible*, 1977; *A Palpable God: Thirty Stories Translated from the Bible with an Essay on the Origins and Life of Narrative*, 1978.

CHILDREN'S LITERATURE: *A Perfect Friend*, 2000.

BIBLIOGRAPHY

Black, James T. "A Conversation with Reynolds Price." *southern Living* 27 (September, 1992): 38. A brief biographical sketch of Price's life. Discusses the ways in which families deal with crisis in his fiction.

Fodor, Sarah J. "Outlaw Christian: An Interview with Reynolds Price." *The Christian Century* 112 (November 22-29, 1995): 1128-1131. Price discusses eroticism in literature, the role of children in his fiction, the women in his novels, the importance of solitude in his life, and his views on religion and writer Flannery O'Connor.

Henry, William A. "The Mind Roams Free." *Time* 143 (May 23, 1994): 66-68. A brief biographical account, focusing on Price's struggle with spinal cancer and the significant amount of work he has written since being told a decade ago that he would not survive it.

Humphries, Jefferson, ed. *Conversations with Reynolds Price*. Jackson: University Press of Mississippi, 1991. In these fifteen interviews, which originally appeared between 1966 and 1989 in literary quarterlies, student literary journals, newspapers, and magazines, Price speaks articulately and frankly. The collection is indexed and includes a chronology and an informative introduction.

Poteet, William Mark. "One Constant Flaming Question: Men, Kinship, and Masculinity in the Fiction of Reynolds Price." In *Gay Men in Modern southern Literature: Ritual, Initiation, and the Construction of Masculinity*. New York: Peter Lang, 2006. Analyzes works by Price and two other gay southern writers to determine how these works were influenced by the authors' homosexuality and by the South's code of behavior and definitions of masculinity. Examines Price's novels *The Source of Light*, *Good Hearts*, and *The Promise of Rest*.

Price, Reynolds. Interview by Wendy Smith. *Publishers Weekly* 241 (May 9, 1994): 51-52. Price discusses his sense of malevolent fate, his troubled family history, his discovery of himself as a writer, his previous works, and the process of writing about his ordeal with cancer.

Rooke, Constance. *Reynolds Price*. Boston: Twayne, 1983. Focuses on Price's consistency of vision. After a brief biography and discussion of Price within a literary and geographical context, this study analyzes each of his first seven volumes of fiction--including his first two short-story collections--in detail. Includes a chronology and a select bibliography.

Sadler, Lynn Veach. "Reynolds Price and Religion: The 'Almost Blindlingly Lucid' Palpable World." *southern Quarterly* 26 (Winter, 1988): 1-11. Examines religious underpinnings, especially the influence of biblical narrative, in Price's fiction, and also investigates Price's perceptions of the deeper reality of life underlying what is commonly visible.

Schiff, James A., ed. *Critical Essays on Reynolds Price*. New York: G. K. Hall, 1998. A good first stop for the student of Price. Includes a bibliography and an index.

_____. *Understanding Reynolds Price*. Columbia: University of South Carolina Press, 1996. A general introduction to Price's work, focusing primarily on the novels, but also commenting on the relationship of Price's short stories to his longer fiction and memoirs.

Stevenson, John W. "The Faces of Reynolds Price's Short Fiction." *Studies in Short Fiction* 3 (1966): 300-306. Although this article deals only with the stories in Price's first collection, its perceptive insights provide a thoughtful foundation from which to approach the evolution of Price's work.

Jean C. Fulton
Updated by William Hoffman

FRANCINE PROSE

Born: Brooklyn, New York; April 1, 1947

PRINCIPAL SHORT FICTION
Women and Children First, and Other Stories, 1988
The Peaceable Kingdom, 1993
Guided Tours of Hell: Novellas, 1997 (includes *Guided Tours of Hell* and *Three Pigs in Five Days*)

OTHER LITERARY FORMS
Francine Prose's first three novels, *Judah the Pious* (1973), *The Glorious Ones* (1974), and *Marie Laveau* (1977), are historical fictions, which combine the rational and the mythic, dreaming and waking, legend and reality. The novels *Household Saints* (1981) and *Hungry Hearts* (1983) have twentieth century settings, but still focus on spiritual matters and create seemingly legendary worlds. In addition to her novels, which also include *Primitive People* (1992), *Hunters and Gatherers* (1995), *Blue Angel* (2000), *A Changed Man* (2005), and *Goldengrove* (2008), and her short stories, Prose has published nonfiction articles and essays on various subjects in a wide range of popular periodicals, such as *Redbook*, *Glamour*, *The Atlantic*, *Mademoiselle*, and *Harper's Bazaar*. She has written several children's books and translated the works of other authors, and she edited The *"Mrs. Dalloway" Reader* (2003) and *Best New American Voices, 2005* (2004).

ACHIEVEMENTS

Francine Prose won the Jewish Book Council Award in 1973 for her novel *Judah the Pious*. She won the MLLE Award from *Mademoiselle* magazine in 1975 and the Edgar Lewis Wallant Memorial Award from the Hartford Jewish Community Center in 1984 for her novel *Hungry Hearts*. In 1991, she was the recipient of a Guggenheim Fellowship. Her novel *Blue Angel* was a finalist for the 2000 National Book Award for Fiction.

BIOGRAPHY

Francine Prose was born on April 1, 1947, in Brooklyn, New York, the daughter of two doctors. She received her B.A. degree in English from Radcliffe College in 1968 and an M.A. degree in English from Harvard University in 1969. She taught creative writing at the University of Arizona in 1971-1972. She has been a visiting lecturer in fiction and a faculty member in M.F.A. programs at schools such as Warren Wilson College and Sarah Lawrence College, and she was an instructor at the Bread Loaf Writers' Conference in 1984. She married artist Howard Michels in 1976.

Prose is a professional journalist as well as a fiction writer. She has written articles and reviews for many American magazines and newspapers, including *The New York Times*, *Harper's*, *Redbook*, and *The Atlantic*. Since March, 2007, she has been the president of PEN American Center in New York City.

ANALYSIS

Francine Prose is, above all, a professional writer--competent, skilled, intelligent, and knowledgeable about the various conventions of the prose fictions and articles she writes. However, her stories, for all their surface flash and verbal cleverness, are often highly formal exercises that seldom, to quote her own character Landau in *Guided Tours of Hell*, "achieve that transcendental state" that lifts writer and reader above the realm of the ordinary world.

Prose is frequently admired for her domestic whimsy, her adroitness at satire, her offbeat and acerbic humor, and her gifts of irony and observation. However, her fictions are usually formal, well-made stories, self-consciously literary, and thus highly predictable and pat. Her use of the analogies to writer Franz Kafka

in *Guided Tours of Hell*, for example, are so carefully woven throughout the story that they get in the way of any genuine anguish that might be experienced by her characters. Just as Landau, the competent but dispassionate and disengaged writer of this story knows he is not Kafka, Francine Prose is always Landau, for her stories are mostly professional products, rather than passionate explorations.

"EVERYDAY DISORDERS"

Everyday disorders form the background of this story, and the single disruption of the everyday on which it focuses is uncommon and threatening. The story centers on the fears of Gilda, a housewife and mother of four, when her husband Nathan, a photographer and professor, brings home a glamorous and adventuresome female war photographer named Phoebe Morrow. The contrast between Gilda's own prosaic home life and Phoebe's exciting life on the road and on the battlefield establishes the story's central conflict and interest. Prose is her usual clever self in the story, establishing Gilda's domesticity and fears by having her try to imagine that Phoebe probably looks like

Francine Prose (Getty Images)

aviator Amelia Earhart but instead thinking of her as the cartoon character Snoopy, the Red Baron. Gilda's response is complicated by her knowledge that her husband, who has made his own reputation as a photographer of "everyday disorder," envies Phoebe.

While Phoebe has gone on commando raids with Sandinista guerillas, Gilda's main claim to fame seems to be the homemade mushroom soup she has prepared for dinner. The evening comes to a tragicomic climax when Gilda overhears Phoebe telling a group of admiring students a story about being wounded in a plane crash. She tells them she was cared for by a beautiful Israeli nurse who looked like Rita Hayworth and who made her homemade mushroom soup. Phoebe says she became a kind of junkie for the soup and that the nurse brought her her favorite food, linguine with steamed mussels. Gilda is not sure how to handle this revelation, as earlier she had told Phoebe that she became a kind of junkie for being pregnant and that her favorite food is linguine with steamed mussels. The story ends with Gilda's realization that Phoebe is not someone to be envied, for there is some essential component of selfhood missing in her, which she tries to patch "with borrowed scraps from other people's lives." At the end, Gilda wants to tell Nathan there is a kind of heroism in facing everyday messes.

THE PEACEABLE KINGDOM

Prose's second collection of short stories contains highly polished presentations of contemporary characters whose peaceable lives are disrupted by challenge and change. The stories in this collection are clever, well-written, highly formal fictions, complete with the conventional, vaguely dissatisfying sense of closure contemporary readers have come to expect in the well-made short story. On the surface, the characters seem ordinary enough: a young woman on her honeymoon who already questions her commitment to her husband, a reserved librarian whose fascination with a man is based on the books she reads, a teenage girl who is followed to Paris by a boy she thought she loved.

Beneath the peaceable surface of everyday life, however, Prose unearths and exposes those moments of awareness when the smooth flow of things becomes jagged and undependable. In many of these stories, characters have made what they think are reasonable

choices, only to experience an unpredicted and inexplicable disruption of that formerly comfortable decision. As in many modern short stories, things are simply not what they seem in the world of Francine Prose; the reader is always in tension with the strange and enigmatic. Even the titles of many of the stories suggest this combination of the mundane and the mysterious: "Talking Dogs," "Cauliflower Heads," "Rubber Life," "Amateur Voodoo," "Potato World," and "Dog Stories." Prose's stories in this collection are a pleasure to read, but it is a somewhat bloodless, formalist pleasure. One comes to the end of these stories full of admiration for a job well done but not always full of awe for the complex mystery of what it means to be human.

GUIDED TOURS OF HELL

Prose tackles a delicate subject in her novella *Guided Tours of Hell*--a comic, satiric treatment of the Jewish Holocaust. The way she manages this task is to focus on two characters--Jiri Krakauer, a poet whose only claim to fame is that he survived two years in a death camp where he had an affair with Franz Kafka's sister, Ottla, and Landau, a second-rate writer who has written a play entitled *To Kafka from Felice*. The novella takes place in the present time at a Kafka conference in Germany where Landau reads his play and Krakauer reads his poetry.

The central event of the story is a tour that the two men make with the conference attendees to the death camp where Krakauer was imprisoned. Landau is filled with jealousy at Krakauer's star status and angry that he has been largely ignored. Thinking there is something obscene about a guided tour of hell, unless you are the poet Dante, Landau suffers throughout the story, convinced that Krakauer never really suffered at all during his incarceration at the hands of the Nazis. The fact that Krakauer has profited from the Holocaust is more than Landau can bear.

Landau's problem, says the ironic narrator, is his falseness, his lack of depth, "the reason why, he secretly fears, his play is basically garbage, idiotic, hysterical." Throughout the novella, Landau shifts back and forth between justifying and castigating himself, between thinking that the world needs writers like Krakauer, for he has experienced the real thing, and thinking that Krakauer is a fake, posturing for praise and toadying for applause. The basic irony of the story is that Landau envies Krakauer his experience in the death camp--a fact that Krakauer understands, as he says near the end of the story: "The dirty truth is, you envy us, you wish it had happened to you. You wish you'd gotten the chance to survive Auschwitz or the Gulag."

However, this realization does not exonerate Krakauer. Landau is right about him--Krakauer is making the Holocaust into a party piece, he revels in his survival, and he lies about his experience, plagiarizing the works of other writers to create those lies. In her usual formally structured way, Prose has Landau realize at the end that they are living a Kafka story, specifically "The Judgment," reenacting the classic Kafka confrontation between father and son.

OTHER MAJOR WORKS

LONG FICTION: *Judah the Pious*, 1973; *The Glorious Ones*, 1974; *Marie Laveau*, 1977; *Animal Magnetism*, 1978; *Household Saints*, 1981; *Hungry Hearts*, 1983; *Bigfoot Dreams*, 1986; *Primitive People*, 1992; *Hunters and Gatherers*, 1995; *Blue Angel*, 2000; *A Changed Man*, 2005; *Goldengrove*, 2008.

NONFICTION: *The Lives of the Muses: Nine Women and the Artists They Inspired*, 2002; *Gluttony: The Seven Deadly Sins*, 2003; *Sicilian Odyssey*, 2003; *Caravaggio: Painter of Miracles*, 2005; *Reading Like a Writer: A Guide for People Who Love Books and for Those Who Want to Write Them*, 2006; *Anne Frank: The Book, the Life, the Afterlife*, 2009.

TRANSLATIONS: *A Scrap of Time, and Other Stories*, 1987 (with Madeline Levine; by Ida Fink); *The Journey*, 1992 (with Johanna Weschler; novel by Ida Fink).

CHILDREN'S LITERATURE: *Stories from Our Living Past*, 1974; *Dybbuk: A Story Made in Heaven*, 1996; *The Angel's Mistake: Stories of Chelm*, 1997; *You Never Know: A Legend of the Lamedvavniks*, 1998; *The Demon's Mistake: A Story from Chelm*, 2000; *After*, 2003; *Leopold, the Liar of Leipzig*, 2005; *Bullyville*, 2007; *Touch*, 2009.

EDITED TEXTS: *The "Mrs. Dalloway" Reader*, 2003; *Best New American Voices, 2005*, 2004.

BIBLIOGRAPHY

Baker, Alison. "The Bearable Lightness of Being." A review of *The Peaceable Kingdom*, by Francine Prose. *Los Angeles Times Book Review*, October 10, 1993, 3. A positive review, which describes the stories as tales of lost innocence and high hopes exposed for the common things they are. Argues that although the characters occasionally seem shallow, Prose's language lifts them out of the ordinary and allows them to redeem themselves by what they have learned.

Brown, Rosellen. "Where Love Touches Death." Review of *Guided Tours of Hell*, by Francine Prose. *New Leader* 79 (December 16, 1997): 24-27. Extended discussion of the title novella and the novella *Three Pigs in Five Days*. Argues that *Guided Tours of Hell* is motivated by the paradoxes of late twentieth century "consumer-friendly horror-gazing." Compares the central character, Landau, with Fyodor Dostoevski's Underground Man. Maintains that *Three Pigs in Five Days* is diffuse and confusing and too contrived to be compelling.

Caldwell, Gail. "Inferno of Irony." *The Boston Globe*, January 19, 1997, p. N17. A review of *Guided Tours of Hell* that focuses on Prose's ironic sensibility. Suggests that her characters are hapless romantics who revel in the despair of self-analysis. Describes *Guided Tours of Hell* and *Three Pigs in Five Days* as descents into the maelstrom that are irreverent and funny; both deal with travel abroad, where misgivings that could be minor at home have the potential to color reality.

LaPlante, Alice. *The Making of a Story: A Norton Guide to Creative Writing*. New York: W. W. Norton, 2007. LaPlante's advice about writing short stories contains numerous contributions from writers, including a brief essay in which Prose describes "What Makes a Short Story?"

Lodge, David. "Excess Baggage." *The New York Times*, January 12, 1997, p. 7. Praises the collection of two novellas in *Guided Tours of Hell*. Places these works in the tradition of the adventures of Americans in Europe, and argues that the characters' problems come to a head more urgently than they would have at home and are purged in tragic and farcical epiphanies.

Myers, D. G. "In Praise of Prose." *Commentary* 129, no. 5 (May, 2010): 51-55. Discusses Prose's life and work, examining the characters, themes, and writing style in her novels, including *Blue Angel, Hunters and Gatherers*, and *Judah the Pious*. Discusses her education at Radcliffe College and her engagement with superstitious, romantic, and satiric literary genres.

Prose, Francine. "Conversation with Francine Prose." Interview by Cara Blue Adams. *southern Review* 46, no. 3 (Summer, 2010): 376-384. In response to the interviewer's question. Prose states she has not written any short stories for a long time. She discusses her interest in films and her visit to the fiftieth anniversary exhibition of Robert Frank's book of photographs *The Americans* (1959).

_____. Interview by John Baker. *Publishers Weekly* 239 (April 13, 1992): 38-39. Prose discusses her writing career, her marriage to Howard Michels, and her nonfiction contributions to newspapers and magazines. Baker argues that in her novel *Primitive People* Prose writes more darkly than in her past fantastical novels and stories.

Reynolds, Susan Salter. "A Tour Through the Heart's Twists, the Mind's Turns." Review of *Guided Tours of Hell*, by Francine Prose. *Los Angeles Times*, January 10, 1997, p. E8. Reynolds discusses how Prose's characters combine humor and wisdom; she argues that in the two novellas shallow characters have giant revelations, feeble characters rise to historic occasions, and strong characters crumble; however, she suggests that history triumphs in the end of these two works.

Yardley, Jonathan. "Fictions About Women Writers." *The Washington Post*, June 8, 1998. p. D2. A commentary on Prose's controversial article in *Harper's*, pointing out how rarely stories by women appear in the major magazines that publish fiction, how rarely fiction by women is reviewed in serious literary journals, and how rarely work by women dominates short lists and year-end "best" lists.

Charles E. May

E. ANNIE PROULX

Born: Norwich, Connecticut; August 22, 1935

PRINCIPAL SHORT FICTION

Heart Songs, and Other Stories, 1988
Close Range: Wyoming Stories, 1999
Bad Dirt: Wyoming Stories 2, 2004
Fine Just the Way It Is: Wyoming Stories 3, 2008

OTHER LITERARY FORMS

Early in her career, E. Annie Proulx (prewl) was a freelance journalist, writing cookbooks, how-to manuals, and magazine articles on everything from making cider to building fences. Her first novel, *Postcards* (1992), received good reviews. However, it was the enthusiastic reception of her second novel, *The Shipping News* (1993), that brought her international fame and popular success. Her novel *Accordion Crimes* (1996) did not enjoy the same acclaim as her Pulitzer Prize-winning *The Shipping News*. Her nonfiction book *Red Desert: History of a Place*, with photos by Martin Stupich, was published in 2008.

ACHIEVEMENTS

For *Postcards*, E. Annie Proulx was the first woman to win the PEN/Faulkner Award for fiction. In 1993, *The Shipping News* won many awards, including the *Chicago Tribune* Heartland Prize, *The Irish Times* International Fiction Prize, the National Book Award, and the Pulitzer Prize. Four stories from her collection *Close Range: Wyoming Stories* were selected for the 1998 and 1999 editions of *The Best American Short Stories* and *Prize Stories: The O. Henry Awards*. "The Half-Skinned Deer" was selected for *The Best American Short Stories of the Century*. Proulx won the *Paris Review* Aga Khan Prize for Fiction in 2004, for her story "The Wamsutter Wolf."

BIOGRAPHY

Edna Annie Proulx was born in Norwich, Connecticut, in 1935, the oldest of five daughters. Her father worked his way up in the textile mills to the position of vice president; her mother painted landscapes in watercolors. Because her father was frequently transferred, the family moved several times when Proulx was young. She entered Colby College in the 1950's but dropped out to, as she says, "experience two terrible marriages, New York City, the Far East, and single-mother-with-two-children poverty." She returned to school in 1963, graduating Phi Beta Kappa. She entered the graduate program at Sir George Williams University (now Concordia University), in Montreal, specializing in Renaissance economic history, and she finished all the academic work for a Ph.D. except the dissertation.

By this time Proulx had been married and divorced three times and was the mother of three sons. She worked as a freelance journalist from 1975 to 1988, writing books and articles on a wide range of subjects. In the mid-1990's, Proulx moved from Vermont to Centennial, Wyoming (population 100), where she would live and write in relative isolation. She travels part of the year to Australia and Ireland and across the United States. Proulx told an interviewer for the *Los Angeles Times* in 2008 that *Fine Just the Way It Is* will be her last Wyoming book and that she plans to move away from Wyoming.

ANALYSIS

Although E. Annie Proulx's first collection, *Heart Songs, and Other Stories*, was relatively conventional in structure and language, her interest in what one of her characters calls the "rural downtrodden" is much in evidence. The stories, featuring such quaintly named characters as Albro, Eno, and Snipe, take place in rural Vermont and New Hampshire. Without condescension, Proulx describes trailer-dwelling men and women who drink, smoke, feud, and fornicate without much introspection or analysis.

CLOSE RANGE: WYOMING STORIES

In *Close Range: Wyoming Stories*, Proulx shifts her milieu to the rural West, where her characters are similarly ragged and rugged, but where, either because of

her increased confidence as a writer or because she was inspired by the landscape and the fiercely independent populace, her characters are more compellingly caught in a world that is at once grittily real and magically mythical. Claiming that her stories gainsay the romantic myth of the West, Proulx admires the independence and self-reliance she has found there, noting that the people "fix things and get along without them if they can't be fixed. They don't whine."

Place is as important as the people who populate it in *Close Range*, for the Wyoming landscape is harsh yet beautiful, real yet magical, deadly yet sustaining. In such a world, social props are worthless and folks are thrown back on their basic instincts, whether sexual, survival, or sacred. In such a world, as one character says in "Brokeback Mountain," "It's easier than you think to yield up to the dark impulse." Proulx's Wyoming is a heart of darkness both in place and in personality.

"BROKEBACK MOUNTAIN"

The remarkable thing about "Brokeback Mountain" is that although it is about a sexual relationship between

E. Annie Proulx (AP Photo/Toby Talbot)

two men, it cannot be categorized as a homosexual story; it is rather a tragic love story that happens to involve two males. The fact that the men are Wyoming cowboys rather than San Francisco urbanites makes Proulx's success in creating such a convincing and emotionally affecting story all the more wonderful.

Jack Twist and Ennis del Mar are "high-school drop-out country boys with no prospects" who, while working alone at a sheep-herding operation on Brokeback Mountain, abruptly and silently engage in a sexual encounter, after which both immediately insist, "I'm not no queer." Although the two get married to women and do not see each other for four years, when they meet again, they grab each other and hug in a gruff masculine way, and then, "as easily as the right key turns the lock tumblers, their mouths came together."

Neither has sex with other men, and both know the danger of their relationship. Twenty years pass, and their infrequent encounters are a combination of sexual passion and personal concern. The story comes to a climax when Jack, who unsuccessfully tries to convince Ennis they can make a life together, is mysteriously killed on the roadside. Although officially it was an accident, Ennis sorrowfully suspects that Jack has been murdered after approaching another man. Although "Brokeback Mountain" ends with Jack a victim of social homophobia, this is not a story about the social plight of the homosexual. The issues Proulx explores here are more basic and primal than that. Told in a straightforward, matter-of-fact style, the story elicits a genuine sympathy for a love that is utterly convincing.

"THE HALF-SKINNED STEER"

Chosen by writer John Updike for *The Best American Short Stories of the Century*, this brief piece creates a hallucinatory world of shimmering significance out of common materials. The simple event on which the story is based is a cross-country drive made by Mero, a man in his eighties, to Wyoming for the funeral of his brother. The story alternates between the old man's encounters on the road, including an accident, and his memories of his father and brother. The central metaphor of the piece is introduced in a story Mero recalls about a man who, while skinning a steer, stops for dinner, leaving the beast half skinned. When he returns,

he sees the steer stumbling stiffly away, its head and shoulders raw meat, its staring eyes filled with hate. The man knows that he and his family are doomed.

The story ends with Mero getting stuck in a snowstorm a few miles away from his destination and trying to walk back to the main highway. As he struggles through the wind and the drifts, he notices that one of the herd of cattle in the field next to the road has been keeping pace with him, and he realizes that the "half-skinned steer's red eye had been watching for him all this time." In its combination of stark realism and folktale myth, "The Half-Skinned Steer" is reminiscent of stories by Eudora Welty and Flannery O'Connor, for Mero's journey is an archetypal one toward the inevitable destiny of death.

"THE MUD BELOW"

E. Annie Proulx has said that this is her favorite story in *Close Range*, for "on-the-edge situations" and the rodeo interest her. The title refers to the mud of the rodeo arena, and the main character is twenty-three-year-old Diamond Felts, who, at five foot three has always been called "Shorty," "Kid," "Tiny," and "Little Guy." His father left when Diamond was a child, telling him, "You ain't no kid of mine." His mother taunts him about his size more than anyone else, always calling him Shorty and telling him he is stupid for wanting to be a bull rider in the rodeo.

The force of the story comes from Diamond's identification with the bulls. The first time he rides one he gets such a feeling of power that he feels as though he were the bull and not the rider; even the fright seems to fulfill a "greedy physical hunger" in him. When one man tells him that the bull is not supposed to be his role model, Diamond says the bull is his partner. The story comes to a climax when Diamond is thrown and suffers a dislocated shoulder. Tormented by the pain, he calls his mother and demands to know who his father is. Getting no answer, Diamond drives away thinking that all of life is a "hard, fast ride that ended in the mud," but he also feels the euphoric heat of the bull ride, or at least the memory of it, and realizes that if that is all there is, it must be enough.

"THE BUNCHGRASS EDGE OF THE WORLD"

Like most of the stories in *Close Range*, "The Bunchgrass Edge of the World" is about surviving. As

Old Red, a ninety-six-year-old grandfather, says at the end, "The main thing in life was staying power. That was it: stand around long enough, you'd get to sit down." Picked by Amy Tan to be included in *The Best American Short Stories 1999*, it is one of the most comic fictions in the collection. A story about a young woman named Ottaline, with a "physique approaching the size of a propane tank," being wooed by a broken-down John Deere 4030 tractor could hardly be anything else.

Ottaline's only chance for a husband seems to be the semiliterate hired man, Hal Bloom, with whom she has silent sex, that is, until she is first approached by the talking tractor, who calls her "sweetheart, lady-girl." Tired of the loneliness of listening to cellular phone conversations on a scanner, Ottaline spends more and more time with the tractor, gaining confidence until, when made to take on the responsibility of cattle trading by her ill father, she meets Flyby Amendinger, whom she soon marries. The story ends with Ottaline's father getting killed in a small plane he is flying. The ninety-six-year-old grandfather, who sees how things had to go, has the powerfully uncomplicated final word--that the main thing in life is staying power.

BAD DIRT: WYOMING STORIES 2

In her powerful 1999 collection *Close Range: Wyoming Stories*, one of Proulx's narrators says ominously, "Friend, it's easier than you think to yield up to the dark impulse." If that book painted the desperate side of rural big sky life, then *Bad Dirt: Wyoming Stories 2* is largely a lighthearted companion volume. Made up of six brief tall tales and five longer stories, *Bad Dirt* (which refers to rough country roads) is, by and large, a snort-out-loud hoot. Most of the action takes place in and around Elk Tooth, Wyoming, population eighty, worth visiting only for three bars, the most popular of which is Pee Wee's, where such stories are best told and most enjoyed. Take, for example, "The Trickle Down Effect," in which Fiesta Punch, one of the area's many desperate women ranchers, hires Deb Sipple to drive to Wisconsin to pick up some hay. However, Deb stops for too many drinks and tosses too many cigarettes out the window on the way back. When he rolls into Elk Tooth late at night, it is the closest thing to a meteor the folks have ever seen.

A similar comic story is "Summer of the Hot Tubs." When Amanda Gribb, who tends bar at Pee Wee's, hears about Willy Huson using an enormous cast-iron cooking pot for a hot tub, she grabs some frozen corn and a can of chili powder, declaring, "If he's goin cook hisself let's get some flavor in there." Then there's "The Hellhole," in which game warden Creel Zmundzinski's contempt for poachers is made clear by a fiery fissure that opens up under the obnoxious culprits he catches.

Although the long stories are more culturally complex, they still have a wry, tongue-in-cheek tone. In "What Kind of Furniture Would Jesus Pick?" Gilbert Wolfscale, born and raised on the family ranch, is caught in the downward ranching spiral of too much work, not enough money, and drought. His wife leaves him, and his two boys want nothing to do with him. Nevertheless, he has a "scalding passion" for the ranch. He knows exactly what kind of furniture Jesus would pick if he owned a place in Wyoming. In "The Indian Wars Refought," Charlie Parrott, a reservation Sioux, marries the widow Georgina Brawls, and his twenty-something daughter Linney, a real hellcat, comes to live with them. In the process of cleaning up an old commercial building, she finds letters from Buffalo Bill Cody about making a film of the battle at Wounded Knee and becomes suddenly fired up about learning of the massacre of her people. In "Man Crawling out of Trees," when Mitchell Fair and his wife Eugenie retire from the East to Wyoming, he buys an old pickup truck and drives around the prairie on his own. She gets more and more lonely, until a man crawls toward her out of the woods and she breaks the cardinal rule of the country.

In "The Wamsutter Wolf," Buddy Millar moves next door to Cheri, an overweight girl from high school, who lives with the bully who once broke Buddy's nose. Things go from bad to worse, culminating with Cheri sneaking over to Buddy's trailer and climbing into bed, late-night runs to the emergency room, fear of jealous reprisals, and guns at the ready. It is not just the imaginative plots and the cantankerous characters that make these stories so irresistible; it is the rhythm of the prose and the tone of the teller. Proulx is a tough, smart lady who is flat-out funny.

FINE JUST THE WAY IT IS: WYOMING STORIES 3

Proulx bookends the third volume of her Wyoming Stories series by citing the book's title in the first and last tale, thus locating them in time and space. In "Family Man," Ray Forkenbrock, wasting away in a home for the elderly, tells his granddaughter about his past, which she records for posterity. Even though his life was marred by hardship and a secret betrayal by his father, he is adamant that everything was "fine the way it was." In the heart-scalding final story, "Tits-Up in a Ditch," which focuses on Dakotah Lister, who loses more than her arm while serving in Iraq, her grandmother's husband Verl dismisses outsider criticism of the state by insisting that "Wyomin is fine just the way it is."

The way it was, and often still is, is vicious. The five strongest pieces in this collection are better characterized by the title of the final story, which refers to a cow that tried to climb up a deep slope and slid back down in the ditch and died. Whether the story takes place in the late nineteenth century or the early twenty-first, one slip-up in the rugged outback of Wyoming can kill. In "Them Old Cowboy Songs," Archie and Rose try to make a go of it on a modest homestead. However, the winters are bitter and the jobs are few, and Archie's decision to leave pregnant Rose in their rough-hewn little house to find work results in disaster. In "Testimony of the Monkey," a silly argument over whether to wash the lettuce splits up Marc and Catlin, two rugged outdoors enthusiasts. When, in anger and spite, she takes an ill-advised trip into harsh territory alone and catches her foot in the crevice of a rock, the rest of the story, which alternates between her painful efforts to free herself and her hallucinations about rescue, is predictable but agonizing.

Proulx indulges herself in a couple of playful fables about the devil in "I've Always Loved This Place" and "Swamp Mischief" and in a couple of serious legends about a Bermuda Triangle sagebrush and an early Indian buffalo hunt in "The Sagebrush Kid" and "Deep-Blood-Greasy-Bowl." However, the most powerful stories here are those that reverberate on the final page of the collection, when Dakotah Lister tells the parents of her husband, who has lost both legs and half his face in Iraq, "Sash is tits up in a ditch." So are they all, in this scrupulously written Proulx collection.

OTHER MAJOR WORKS

LONG FICTION: *Postcards*, 1992; *The Shipping News*, 1993; *Accordion Crimes*, 1996; *That Old Ace in the Hole*, 2002.

NONFICTION: *Great Grapes! Grow the Best Ever*, 1980; *Making the Best Apple Cider*, 1980; *Sweet and Hard Cider: Making It, Using It, and Enjoying It*, 1980 (also known as *Cider: Making, Using, and Enjoying Sweet and Hard Cider*, 1997; with Lew Nichols); *"What'll You Take for It?" Back to Barter*, 1981; *Make Your Own Insulated Window Shutters*, 1981; *The Complete Dairy Foods Cookbook: How to Make Everything from Cheese to Custard in Your Own Kitchen*, 1982 (with Nichols); *Plan and Make Your Own Fences and Gates, Walkways, Walls, and Drives*, 1983; *The Gardener's Journal and Record Book*, 1983; *The Fine Art of Salad Gardening*, 1985; *The Gourmet Gardener: Growing Choice Fruits and Vegetables with Spectacular Results*, 1987.

EDITED TEXT: *The Best American Short Stories 1997: Selected from U.S. and Canadian Magazines*, 1997 (with Katrina Kenison).

MISCELLANEOUS: *"Brokeback Mountain": Story to Screenplay*, 2006 (with Larry McMurtry and Diana Ossana).

BIBLIOGRAPHY

Cox, Christopher. "The Art of Fiction: Annie Proulx." *Paris Review* 188 (Spring, 2009): 22-49. An important long interview with Proulx about her writing career and what interests her about the nature of place and the social situation of her characters.

Elder, Richard. "Don't Fence Me In." *The New York Times*, May 23, 1999, p. 8. An extended review of *Close Range: Wyoming Stories*. Says the strength of the collection is Proulx's feeling for place and how it affects her characters. Claims Proulx's extraordinary knowledge of male behavior is most remarkable in "Brokeback Mountain." Argues that the best story in the collection is "The Mud Below."

Fitzpatrick, Andrea D. "Love's Letter Lost: Reading 'Brokeback Mountain.'" *Mosaic* 43 (March, 2010): 1-22. An analysis of the narrative strategies used in both the story and the film and how these strategies reflect the situation of the characters

Hustak, Alan. "An Uneasy Guest of Honor." *The Montreal Gazette*, June 10, 1999, p. D10. An interview-story on the occasion of Proulx's receiving an honorary degree from her alma mater, Concordia University. Provides biographical information about her education and her literary career. Proulx discusses her years as a freelance journalist, the film production based on *The Shipping News*, and the relationship of character to place in her fiction.

Liss, Barbara. "Wild, Wearying Wyoming." Review of *Close Range: Wyoming Stories*, by E. Annie Proulx. *The Houston Chronicle*, June 20, 1999, p. Z23. Praises the book's magical realism, but suggests that its "downbeat weirdness" will not be to every reader's taste. Says that "Brokeback Mountain" is the best story, with Proulx pouring a great deal of sympathy on the two young men and their passionate relationship.

Reynolds, Susan. "Writer's No Longer Home on the Range." *Los Angeles Times*, October 16, 2008, p. A1. Profile based on an interview in which Proulx talks about her plans for leaving Wyoming.

See, Carolyn. "Proulx's Wild West." *The Washington Post*, July 2, 1999, p. C2. See says she is in awe of *Close Range*, claiming that Proulx has the most amazing combination of things working for her: an exquisite sense of place, a dead-on accurate sense of working class, hard-luck Americans, and a prose style that is the best in English today.

Singleton, Janet. "Proulx's Keen Insights Focus on Life, Not Awards." *The Denver Post*, June 6, 1999, p. F3. In this interview-based story, Proulx talks about her research, her nomadic lifestyle, and the stories in *Close Range: Wyoming Stories*; says she writes stories that question the romantic myth of the West. Singleton claims Proulx's characters may live in God's country, but they seem godforsaken.

Steinbach, Alice. "E. Annie Proulx's Novel Journey to Literary Celebrity Status." *The Baltimore Sun*, May 15, 1994, p. 1K. An interview-based story that reveals Proulx's lighter side. Provides biographical information about her education, marriages, divorces, and rise to fame. Proulx discusses her love of writing, her male characters, and feminism.

Streitfeld, David. "The Stuff of a Writer." *The Washington Post*, November 16, 1993, p. B1. A long, interview-based story on Proulx on the occasion of *The Shipping News* being nominated for the National Book Award. Provides much insight into Proulx's life in rural Vermont, her preference for "the rough side of things" and her rugged independence.

Thompson, David. "The Lone Ranger." *The Independent*, May 30, 1999, pp. 4-5. An interview-story that describes Proulx's life in her Wyoming home. Thompson draws out the cantankerous Proulx better than most other interviewers. He provides some context for Proulx's life and gets her to talk about what she thinks is important.

Written and updated by Charles E. May

JAMES PURDY

Born: Fremont, Ohio; July 17, 1914
Died: Englewood, New Jersey; March 13, 2009

PRINCIPAL SHORT FICTION

Don't Call Me by My Right Name, and Other Stories,
    1956
Sixty-Three: Dream Palace, 1956
Color of Darkness: Eleven Stories and a Novella,
    1957
The Candles of Your Eyes, 1985
The Candles of Your Eyes, and Thirteen Other
    Stories, 1987
Sixty-Three: Dream Palace: Selected Stories,
    1956-1987, 1991
Moe's Villa, and Other Stories, 2000

OTHER LITERARY FORMS

James Purdy (PUR-dee), in more than four decades
of literary work, beginning in the 1950's, wrote--be-
sides his short fiction--a number of novels (including
Malcolm, published in 1959, and *In a Shallow Grave,*
published in 1976), several collections of poetry, and
numerous plays, which have been staged in the United
States and abroad.

ACHIEVEMENTS

James Purdy received a National Institute of Arts
and Letters grant in literature (1958), John Simon Guggenheim Memorial Foundation Fellowships (1958,
1962), and a Ford Foundation grant (1961). *On Glory's
Course* (1984) was a finalist for the PEN/Faulkner
Award. He also received a Rockefeller Foundation
grant, a Morton Dauwen Zabel Fiction Award from the
American Academy of Arts and Letters (1993), and an
Oscar Williams and Gene Derwood Award for poetry
and art (1995).

BIOGRAPHY

James Amos Purdy was born in Fremont, Ohio, on
July 17, 1914, the son of William and Vera Purdy.
James Purdy told many interviewers that the exact location of his birthplace is unknown, since the community no longer exists. Purdy's parents were divorced
when he was quite young. He lived, as he once said,
with his father for a time in various locations and at
other times with his mother and an aunt who had a
farm, an experience that he recalled favorably.

Purdy explained that his ethnic background was that
of a very long line of Scotch-Irish Presbyterians, but
that most of his family were deceased, as were many of
his oldest friends. Purdy's formal education began with
his attendance at the University of Chicago, where he
was to drop out during World War II to serve with the
U.S. Air Corps. He indicated that he was not the best of
soldiers but that his military service gave him the necessary background for his later novel *Eustace Chisholm
and the Works* (1967).

Purdy also attended the University of Puebla,
Mexico, for a time, and enrolled in graduate school at
the University of Chicago. He taught from 1949 to
1953 at Lawrence College in Appleton, Wisconsin, and
later worked as an interpreter in Latin America, France,
and Spain. In 1953, however, he gave up other work to
pursue a full-time career as a writer.

Although he was a prolific writer throughout his
career, Purdy's fiction, while enjoying considerable
critical success, was not successful commercially.
Purdy often attributed this fact to a conspiratorial elite
in New York that foists more commercial, but less sub-
stantive, literature on the American public.

Purdy's early work was rejected by most major
American publishing houses, and his first fiction was
published privately by friends in the United States and
later through the help of writers such as Carl Van
Vechten and, in Great Britain, Edith Sitwell. Purdy's
volumes *Sixty-Three: Dream Palace* and *Don't Call*

Me by My Right Name, and Other Stories were printed privately in 1956, and in 1957 the novella *Sixty-Three: Dream Palace* appeared with additional stories under the title *Color of Darkness*, published by Gollancz in London. These early works gained for Purdy a small, devoted following, and his allegorical novel *Malcolm* followed in 1959. In that work, Malcolm, a beautiful young man, is led by older persons through a wide range of experiences, until he finally dies of alcoholism and sexual hyperesthesia. In a way, Malcolm is a forerunner of many Purdy characters, whose driven states of being take them ultimately to disaster. (*Malcolm* was later adapted to play form by Edward Albee, an admirer of Purdy's work. The 1966 New York production, however, was not successful.)

Two Purdy novels of the 1960's expanded the author's literary audience. *The Nephew* (1960) explores small-town life in the American Midwest and centers on the attempt of an aunt to learn more about her nephew (killed in the Korean War) than she had known about him in his lifetime, and *Cabot Wright Begins* (1964) is a satirical attack on the totally materialistic American culture of consumers and competitors, where all love is either suppressed or commercialized. *Cabot Wright Begins* relates the comic adventures of a Wall Street broker-rapist who manages to seduce 366 women. The novel was sold to motion-picture firms, but the film version was never made.

The inability of people to deal with their inner desires--a major theme of Purdy's fiction--and the resultant violence provoked by that inability characterized Purdy's next novel, *Eustace Chisholm and the Works*. Another recurring Purdy theme is that of the self-destructive, cannibalistic American family, in which parents refuse to let go of their children and give them an independent life of their own. That self-destructive family theme and his earlier motif--the search for meaning in an unknown past--mark his trilogy of novels *Sleepers in Moon-Crowned Valleys*, the first volume of which, *Jeremy's Version*, appeared in 1970 to considerable critical acclaim. The second and third volumes of the trio of novels, however, *The House of the Solitary Maggot* (1974) and *Mourners Below* (1981), received little critical notice. Purdy once said that parts of the trilogy had come from stories that his

grandmother had related to him as a child at a time when he was living with her.

Perhaps the most bizarre of Purdy's novels, *I Am Elijah Thrush*, was published in 1972. Set in New York, the novel deals with an aged male dancer (once a student of Isadora Duncan and known as "the most beautiful man in the world"), who becomes obsessed with a mysterious blond, angelic child known as Bird of Heaven, a mute who communicates by making peculiar kissing sounds.

Purdy's later works reinforce these themes of lost identity and obsessive but often suppressed loves: *In a Shallow Grave* concerns a disfigured Vietnam veteran who has lost that most personal form of identity, his face; *Narrow Rooms* (1978) details the complex sexual relationships of four West Virginia boys, who cannot cope with their emotional feelings for one another and who direct their feelings into garish violence. That novel, Purdy said, was partially derived from fact; Purdy said that he frequently ran into hillbilly types in New York who told him such terrible stories of their lives.

James Purdy (AP Photo/Bebeto Matthews)

Purdy's later works include *On Glory's Course* (1984), *In the Hollow of His Hand* (1986), and the 1989 novel dealing with acquired immunodeficiency syndrome (AIDS), *Garments the Living Wear*. His novel *In a Shallow Grave* was made into a motion picture in 1988. Purdy, who remained unmarried, continued to live and write in Brooklyn, New York, until his death on March 13, 2009, at age ninety-four.

ANALYSIS

James Purdy was one of the more independent, unusual, and stylistically unique of American writers. His fiction--novels, plays, and short stories--maintained a dark vision of American life while stating that vision in a literary voice unlike any other American writer. In more than a dozen novels, several collections of short fiction, and volumes of poetry and plays, Purdy created an unrelentingly tragic view of human existence, in which people invariably are unable to face their true natures and thus violate--mentally and physically--those around them. In an interview in 1978, Purdy said:

> I think that is the universal human tragedy. We never become what we could be. I believe life is tragic. It's my view that nothing ever solves anything. Oh yes, life is full of many joys . . . but it's essentially tragic because man is imperfect. He can't find solutions by his very nature.

As a result of his tragic view of humankind, Purdy's fiction often contains unpleasant, violent, even repellent actions by his characters.

The short fiction of Purdy is marked--as are many of his novels--by the recurrence of several themes, among them the conflict in the American family unit caused by the parental inability to relinquish control over children and allow them to live their own lives, a control to which Purdy has often referred as the "cannibalization" present in the family. A second theme frequently found in Purdy's short fiction is that of obsessive love that cannot be expressed, both heterosexual and homosexual. This inability of individuals to express their emotional yearning and longing often is turned into an expression of violence against those around them. The homoerotic element in Purdy's fiction only accentuates this propensity to violence, since Purdy often sees the societal repression of the homosexual emotion of love as one of the more brutal forms of self-denial imposed on an individual. Thus, many of his stories deal with such a latent--and tension-strained--homoeroticism. These two themes are conjoined occasionally in many of his novels and short stories to produce the unspeakable sense of loss: the loss of self-identity, of a loved one, or of a wasted past.

"COLOR OF DARKNESS"

In "Color of Darkness," the title story of the collection by the same name, a husband can no longer recall the color of the eyes of his wife, who has left him. As his young son struggles with the memory of his lost mother, he begins to suck regularly on the symbol of his parents' union, their wedding ring. In a confrontation with his father--who is concerned for the boy's safety because of the metal object in his mouth--the youngster suddenly kicks his father in the groin and reduces him to a suffering, writhing object at whom the boy hurls a crude epithet.

This kind of terrible family situation--embodying loss, alienation from both a mate and a parent, and violence--is typical of the kind of intense anguish that Purdy's short stories often portray. In the world of Purdy, the American family involves a selfish, possessive, and obsessive struggle, which, over time, often becomes totally self-destructive, as individuals lash out at one another for hurts that they can no longer endure but that they cannot explain.

"DON'T CALL ME BY MY RIGHT NAME"

Elsewhere in the collection *Color of Darkness*, "Don't Call Me by My Right Name" portrays a wife who has begun using her maiden name, Lois McBane, because after six months of marriage she finds that she has grown to hate her new name, Mrs. Klein. Her loss of name is, like many such minor events in Purdy's fiction, simply a symbol for a larger loss, that of her self-identity, a theme that Purdy frequently invokes in his novels (as in his later novel *In a Shallow Grave*). The wife's refusal to accept her husband's name as her new label leads to a violent physical fight between them following a party that they both attend.

"Why Can't They Tell You Why?"

This potential for violence underlying the domestic surface of the American family is seen again in one of the author's most terrifying early stories, "Why Can't They Tell You Why?" A child, Paul, who has never known his father, finds a box of photographs. These photographs become for the boy a substitute for the absent parent, but his mother, Ethel, who appears to hate her late soldier-husband's memory, is determined to break the boy's fascination with his lost father. In a final scene of real horror, she forces the child to watch as she burns the box of photographs in the furnace, an act that drives the boy first into, a frenzy of despair and then into a state of physical and emotional breakdown, as she tries to force the child to care for her and not for his dead father. Again, Purdy has captured the awful hatreds that lie within a simple family unit and the extreme malice to which they can lead.

"Sleep Tight"

A similar tale of near-gothic horror affecting children is found in Purdy's story "Sleep Tight," which appears in his 1985 collection, *The Candles of Your Eyes*. In it, a fatally wounded burglar enters the bedroom of a child who believes in the Sandman. The child, believing the man to be the Sandman, about whom his sister, Nelle, and his mother have told him, does not report the presence of the bleeding man, who takes refuge in the child's closet. After the police have come and gone, the child enters the closet where the now-dead man has bled profusely. The child thinks the blood is watercolors and begins painting with the burglar's blood, and the child comes to believe that he has killed the Sandman with a gun.

"Cutting Edge"

Domestic violence within the family unit is but one of Purdy's terrible insights into family life in America. Subdued family tensions--beneath the surface of outright and tragic violence--appear in "Cutting Edge," in which a domineering mother, her weak-willed husband, and their son (an artist home from New York wearing a beard) form a triangle of domestic hatred. The mother is determined that her son must shave off his beard while visiting, so as to emasculate her son symbolically, the way she has emasculated his father. The son is aware of his father's reduced status at his

mother's hands and even suggests, at one point, that his father use physical violence against the woman to gain back some control over her unpleasant and demanding, dictatorial manner. Purdy directly states in the story that the three are truly prisoners of one another, seeking release but unable to find it. Purdy thus invokes once again the entrapment theme that he sees typical of American families. The father, in insisting on his son's acquiescence to the mother's demand for the removal of the beard, has lost all credibility with his son. (The father had told the son that if the offending beard was not shaved off, then the mother would mentally torture her husband for six months after their son had returned to New York.)

The story's resolution--when the son shaves off the beard and mutilates his face in the process as a rebuke to his parents--is both an act of defiance and an almost literal cutting of the umbilical cord with his family, since he tells his parents that he will not see them at Christmas and that they cannot see him in New York, since he will again have his beard. This story also introduces another theme upon which Purdy frequently touches: the contempt for artistic pursuit by the narrow and materialistic American middle class. The parents, for example, see art as causing their son's defiance of their restrictive lives.

"Dawn"

A similar mood is found in the story "Dawn," from the collection *The Candles of Your Eyes*. Outraged because his son has posed for an underwear advertisement, a father comes to New York, invades the apartment where his son Timmy lives with another actor, Freddy, and announces that he is taking Timmy home to the small town where the father still lives. The father, Mr. Jaqua, resents his son's attempt to become an actor. He has urged the boy into a more respectable profession: the law. The story turns on Timmy's inability to resist his father's demands and Timmy's ultimate acquiescence to them. After Timmy has packed and left the apartment, Freddy is left alone, still loving Timmy but aware that he will never see him again.

This inability of American middle-class culture to accept or deal logically with homosexual love as a valid expression in men's emotional makeup is also found in Purdy's novels and elsewhere in his short fiction. The theme occurs in *Eustace Chisholm and the Works* and in *The Nephew*, *In a Shallow Grave*, *Malcolm*, and *Narrow Rooms*, and this denial of one's homosexual nature often leads Purdy's characters to violent acts.

"EVERYTHING UNDER THE SUN"

A slightly suppressed homoeroticism is also found in "Everything Under the Sun," in Purdy's collection *Children Is All*. Two young men, Jesse and Cade, examples of those flat-spoken country (or hillbilly) types who often appear in Purdy's fiction, are living together in an apartment on the south end of State Street (Chicago possibly). Their basic conflict is whether Cade will work, which Jesse desires, but which Cade is unwilling to do. Cade ultimately remains in full control of the tense erotic relationship by threatening to leave permanently if Jesse does not let him have his own way. While there is talk of liquor and women, the real sexual tension is between the two men, who, when they bare their chests, have identical tattoos of black panthers. Although neither acknowledges their true relationship, their sexual attraction is seen through their ungrammatically accurate speech patterns and the subtle erotic undertones to their pairing.

"SOME OF THESE DAYS"

The stories in *The Candles of Your Eyes* exhibit a homoerotic yearning as part of their plot. In "Some of These Days," a young man (the first-person narrator of the story) is engaged in a pathetic search for the man to whom he refers as his "landlord." His quest for the elusive "landlord" (who comes to be known merely as "my lord") takes him through a series of sexual encounters in pornographic motion-picture theaters as he tries desperately to find the man whose name has been obliterated from his memory.

"SUMMER TIDINGS"

"Summer Tidings," in the same collection, portrays a Jamaican working as a gardener on an estate, where he becomes obsessed with the young blond boy whose parents own the estate. In a subtle ending, the Jamaican fancies the ecstasy of the perfume of the blond boy's shampooed hair.

"RAPTURE"

In "Rapture," an Army officer visits his sister, who is fatally ill, and she introduces the man to her young son, Brice. The soldier develops a fetish for the boy's golden hair, which he regularly removes from the boy's comb. After the boy's mother dies and her funeral is held, the uncle and his nephew are united in a wild love scene, a scene that the mother had foreseen when she thought of leaving her son to someone who would appreciate him as she had been appreciated and cared for by her bridegroom.

"LILY'S PARTY"

"Lily's Party," in the same collection, is even more explicit in its homosexual statement. In this story, Hobart, a man obsessed with his brother's wife, follows the woman to her rendezvous with a new lover, a young preacher. Hobart then watches as the woman, Lily, and the preacher make love. Then, the two men alternately make love with Lily and take occasional breaks to eat pies that Lily had cooked for a church social. Finally, the two men smear each other with pies and begin--much to Lily's consternation--to nibble at each other. As their encounter becomes more explicitly sexual, Lily is left alone, weeping in the kitchen, eating the remains of her pies, and being ignored by the two men. Purdy's fiction has a manic--almost surreal--quality, both in the short works and in the novels. In his emphasis on ordinary individuals plunging headlong into their private hells and their nightmarish lives, Purdy achieves the same kind of juxtaposition of the commonplace, seen through warped configuration of the psyche, that one finds in surrealist art.

SIXTY-THREE: DREAM PALACE

Nowhere is that quality as clearly to be found as in Purdy's most famous piece of short fiction, his early novella *Sixty-Three: Dream Palace*, a work that, by its title, conveys the grotesque vision of shattered illusion and the desperation of its characters. *Sixty-Three: Dream Palace* not only has the surreal quality of nightmare surrounding its action but also the latent homoeroticism of many of Purdy's other works and the distinctive speech rhythms, this time in the conversation of its principal character, the West Virginia boy Fenton Riddleway.

Fenton, together with his sick younger brother Claire, has come from his native West Virginia to live in an abandoned house, on what he calls "sixty-three street," in a large city. In a public park, Fenton encounters a wealthy, largely unproductive "writer" named Parkhearst Cratty. Parkhearst seeks to introduce the young man to a wealthy woman named Grainger (but who is referred to as "the great woman"). Ostensibly, both Parkhearst and Grainger are attracted to the youth, and it is suggested that he will be cared for if he will come and live in Grainger's mansion. Fenton also likes to spend time in a film theater (somewhat like Purdy's main character in "Some of These Days"). At one point in the story, Fenton is picked up by a handsome homosexual named Bruno Korsawski, who takes the boy to a production of William Shakespeare's *Othello, the Moor of Venice* (1604), starring an actor named Hayden Banks. A violent scene with Bruno serves to let readers realize Fenton's capability for violence, a potentiality that is revealed later when readers are told that he has killed his younger brother, who would not leave the abandoned house to go and live in the Grainger mansion. Faced with his younger brother's reluctance and Fenton's desire to escape from both his derelict life and the burden of caring for Claire, Fenton murdered the child, and the story's final scene has Fenton first trying to revive the dead child and then placing the body in a chest in the abandoned house.

Desperation, violence, an inability to deal with sexual longing, and the capacity to do harm even to ones who are loved are found in *Sixty-Three: Dream Palace*, and it may be the most representative of Purdy's short fiction in its use of these thematic elements, strands of which mark so many of his various short stories. The tragic vision of life that Purdy sees as the human condition thus haunts all of his short fiction, as it does his most famous story.

In 1991, Purdy published *Sixty-Three: Dream Palace, Selected Stories, 1956-1987*, a collection of reprints of twenty-six stories and one novella from the author's earlier works, including *Color of Darkness*, *Children Is All*, and *The Candles of Your Eyes*. The collection provides readers with the opportunity to reappraise the unconventional literary style and trademark blend of quirky characters and bizarre settings Purdy uses to confront racial and sexual stereotypes in American culture.

"YOU MAY SAFELY GAZE"

In "You May Safely Gaze," one of Purdy's less successful efforts, two narcissistic male exhibitionists put on an open display of affection at a beach, while a male colleague, obsessed with their behavior, complains to his disinterested female companion. The female companion appears detached, and the author, who attempts to infuse a superficiality to the entire scene, never appears to rise above the surface level in constructing a meaningful framework that would help establish the motivations behind his characters' actions.

"EVENTIDE"

Emotional voids, another favorite Purdy theme, are explored with piercing insight in "Eventide," the tale of two African American sisters grieving over lost young sons, one of whom simply disappeared, the other having died. Faced with a life without their offspring, the sisters seek solace in the darkness that surrounds them, as if life beyond it is a threat to the memory of their sons, which represents the only security they have left.

"MAN AND WIFE"

Husbands and wives fare badly in Purdy's America when faced with personal crises. In "Man and Wife," a mentally disabled husband is fired from his job for an alleged sexual deviancy, prompting his wife to accuse him of having no character because "he had never found a character to have" and the husband to bemoan a marriage invaded by "something awful and permanent that comes to everybody." Only the sense of hopelessness that pervades the marriage is left to bind them in the end. In "Sound of Talking," the reality of a marriage turned sour becomes starkly evident when a wife's patience in catering to the demands of a wheelchair-bound husband runs dry. In both stories Purdy's characters are able only to raise their voices in plaintive cries, unable to explain to their spouses or to themselves the source of their discomfort and disdain for each other. Attempts at escape often appear feeble, as in the wife's recommendation in "Sound of Talking" that she and her husband purchase a pet as a remedy for their trouble.

If the promise of marriage seems a distant memory in "Man and Wife" and "Sound of Talking," it becomes a cruel reality in the author's "Ruthanna Elder," when a young man learns his prospective bride has been violated sexually by her uncle, causing the groom-to-be to suddenly take his own life. It is a tragic tale, simply told, yet one that illustrates perhaps Purdy's most enduring theme, that of the human heart's great potential for great good or great evil.

"GERALDINE"

In Purdy's last collection of stories, entitled *Moe's Villa, and Other Stories*, "Geraldine" exhibits Purdy's insight into the conflicts in the American family unit, in this case involving a mother, Sue, her teenage son, Elmo, her mother, Belle, and Elmo's girlfriend, Geraldine. Although Belle never loved Sue, she dotes on her grandson, taking him and his girlfriend to the opera with her on a regular basis. Naturally jealous, including of the ear-piercing done by Elmo and Geraldine and their jewelry-wearing in conjunction with Belle, Sue finally buys new, expensive earrings and wears them to the opera, in the sight of her son, his girlfriend, and Belle. Her appearance prompts a quarrel between Elmo and Geraldine, who leaves with Belle, while Elmo goes to see his mother. Impressed by his mother's competing with Geraldine and Belle, Elmo reconciles with his mother and moves back in with her. The story effectively dramatizes the complex emotional struggles within a family and the cannibalization implications so prevalent in Purdy's earlier stories. The son's natural affection for his mother is presented in direct conflict with his affection for his girlfriend, and the mother succeeds at least temporarily in preventing her son from moving on with his girlfriend and living his own life.

"NO STRANGER TO LUKE"

In *Moe's Villa, and Other Stories*, "No Stranger to Luke" concerns family conflicts, but this time with economic-class conflict involved, another frequent Purdy focus. Luke and his little brother and mother are poor; the mother works because the children's father deserted them long ago. However, the three are a happy, loving family unit. Luke's mother then discovers that a small amount of money she kept in a cupboard drawer has been stolen, and Luke suspects his friend Dan, despite the fact that Dan is from a wealthy family. Luke confronts Dan about the theft, and Dan admits that he did it, saying he still has the money and that he stole it out of jealousy of the love

that Luke, his brother, and mother share. Dan says that his mother does not have ten minutes a year for him and has never called him son, making him doubt she really is his mother; moreover, his father, before he shot himself, was never home, always out at the races trying to get even more money. Dan says he wishes someone loved him enough to steal from him, but that no one ever will. Again, Purdy effectively dramatizes the lack of love within a family, this time in a materially rich but emotionally impoverished home.

"BRAWITH"

One of the briefest stories in Purdy's last collection, "Brawith" has received the most attention from critics, probably because of its powerful allegorical depiction of human disintegration and death. Brawith, injured severely in a war, moves in with his grandmother, Moira, and slowly his life seeps out of him. He always carries a roll of toilet paper with him, to soak up the moisture that keeps surfacing on his body. Finally, standing with his head and upper body inside Moira's fireplace chimney, he literally explodes, despite being totally wrapped in tissue paper, with blood and intestines showering Moira as he dies. Heavily symbolic, even allegoric, the story dramatizes human fate and the futility of the struggle to prevent that fate, despite the natural tendency to want to live as long as possible.

OTHER MAJOR WORKS

LONG FICTION: *Malcolm*, 1959; *The Nephew*, 1960; *Cabot Wright Begins*, 1964; *Eustace Chisholm and the Works*, 1967; *Jeremy's Version*, 1970; *I Am Elijah Thrush*, 1972; *The House of the Solitary Maggot*, 1974; *In a Shallow Grave*, 1976; *Narrow Rooms*, 1978; *Mourners Below*, 1981; *On Glory's Course*, 1984; *In the Hollow of His Hand*, 1986; *Garments the Living Wear*, 1989; *Out with the Stars*, 1992; *Gertrude of Stony Island Avenue*, 1997.

PLAYS: *Mr. Cough Syrup and the Phantom Sex*, pb. 1960; *Cracks*, pb. 1962, pr. 1963; *Wedding Finger*, pb. 1974; *True*, pr. 1978, pb. 1979; *Clearing in the Forest*, pr. 1978, pb. 1980; *A Day After the Fair*, pb. 1979; *Two Plays*, pb. 1979 (includes *A Day After the Fair* and *True*); *Now*, pr. 1979, pb. 1980; *What Is It, Zach?*, pr. 1979, pb. 1980; *Proud Flesh: Four Short Plays*, pb. 1980; *Strong*, pb. 1980; *Scrap of Paper*, pb. 1981; *The*

Berry-Picker, pb. 1981, pr. 1984; *In the Night of Time, and Four Other Plays*, pb. 1992 (includes *In the Night of Time, Enduring Zeal, The Paradise Circus, The Rivalry of Dolls*, and *Ruthanna Elder*); *The Rivalry of Dolls*, pr., pb. 1992.

POETRY: *The Running Sun*, 1971; *Sunshine Is an Only Child*, 1973; *She Came Out of the Mists of Morning*, 1975; *Lessons and Complaints*, 1978; *The Brooklyn Branding Parlors*, 1986.

MISCELLANEOUS: *Children Is All*, 1961 (ten stories and two plays); *An Oyster Is a Wealthy Beast*, 1967 (story and poems); *Mr. Evening: A Story and Nine Poems*, 1968; *On the Rebound: A Story and Nine Poems*, 1970; *A Day After the Fair: A Collection of Plays and Stories*, 1977.

BIBLIOGRAPHY

Adams, Don. *Alternative Paradigms of Literary Realism*. New York: St. Martin's Press, 2009. The chapter devoted to Purdy convincingly argues that Purdy's fiction can best be understood as allegorical, as an alternative to simplistic scientific "truth" and religious fundamentalism. Includes discuss of "Brawith," from *Moe's Villa, and Other Stories*.

Adams, Stephen D. *James Purdy*. New York: Barnes and Noble Books, 1976. Adams's study covers Purdy's major work from the early stories and *Malcolm* up through *In a Shallow Grave*. Of particular interest is his discussion of the first two novels in Purdy's trilogy *Sleepers in Moon* and *Crowned Valleys*.

Chudpack, Henry. *James Purdy*. Boston: Twayne, 1975. Chudpack's book is notable for students of Purdy's short fiction in that he devotes an entire chapter to the early stories of the author. He also offers an interesting introductory chapter on what he terms the "Purdian trauma."

Ladd, Jay L. *James Purdy: A Bibliography*. Columbus: Ohio State University Libraries, 1999. An annotated bibliography of works by and about Purdy.

Lane, Christopher. "Out with James Purdy: An Interview." *Critique* 40 (Fall, 1998): 71-89. Purdy discusses racial stereotypes, sexual fantasy, political correctness, religious fundamentalism, gay relationships, and the reasons he has been neglected by the literary establishment.

O'Hara, Daniel T. *Visions of Global America and the Future of Critical Reading*. Columbus: Ohio State University Press, 2009. The chapter on Purdy argues that he creates a poetics of terror, with extensive treatment of "Brawith," from *Moe's Villa, and Other Stories*, as example of the terror technique.

Peden, William. *The American Short Story: Front Line in the National Defense of Literature*. Boston: Houghton Mifflin, 1964. Peden discusses Purdy in comparison with some of the "southern gothic" writers, such as Truman Capote and Carson McCullers, and in relation to Purdy's probing of themes about the strange and perverse in American life.

Renner, Stanley. "'Why Can't They Tell You Why?' A Clarifying Echo of *The Turn of the Screw*." *Studies in American Fiction* 14 (1986): 205-213. Compares the story with Henry James's famous tale; argues that both are about a female suppressing a male's sexual identity.

Schwarzchild, Bettina. *The Not-Right House: Essays on James Purdy*. Columbia: University of Missouri Press, 1968. Although the primary focus of these essays is on Purdy's novels, there is some comparative discussion of such early works as *Sixty-Three: Dream Palace* and "Don't Call Me by My Right Name."

Skaggs, Calvin. "The Sexual Nightmare of 'Why Can't They Tell You Why?'" In *The Process of Fiction*, edited by Barbara McKenzie. New York: Harcourt, Brace & World, 1969. Argues that the mother tries to destroy the boy's masculine identification because of her own ambiguous sexual identity. Claims that in the final scene a strong female emasculates a weak male.

Tanner, Tony. Introduction to *Color of Darkness* and *Malcolm*. New York: Doubleday, 1974. Tanner's introductory essay discusses Purdy's novel *Malcolm* and *Sixty-Three: Dream Palace*. It also compares Purdy's effects with those achieved by the Russian realist Anton Chekhov.

Jere Real; William Hoffman
Updated by John L. Grigsby

THOMAS PYNCHON

Born: Glen Cove, New York; May 8, 1937

PRINCIPAL SHORT FICTION

"*Mortality and Mercy in Vienna,*" 1959
"*The Small Rain,*" 1959
"*Entropy,*" 1960
"*Low-Lands,*" 1960
"*Under the Rose,*" 1961
"*The Secret Integration,*" 1964
Slow Learner: Early Stories, 1984

OTHER LITERARY FORMS

Thomas Pynchon (PIHN-chuhn) is best known as a novelist. His novels include *V.* (1963), *The Crying of Lot 49* (1966), *Gravity's Rainbow* (1973), *Vineland* (1989), *Mason and Dixon* (1997), *Against the Day* (2006), and *Inherent Vice* (2009). After the publication of *Gravity's Rainbow*, Pynchon published nothing for seventeen years, with the exception of a few articles in *The New York Times Book Review*. In 1989, he published the novel *Vineland*, which received mixed reviews from the popular press and almost immediately was the subject of a large number of scholarly articles and papers. This dynamic was repeated in 1997 with the publication of the long-awaited opus *Mason and Dixon*. He is also the author of a nonfiction book, *Deadly Sins* (1993).

ACHIEVEMENTS

Thomas Pynchon is one of the greatest prose stylists of the twentieth century, a master of the novel, short story, and expository essay. His works have received literary acclaim and their fair share of controversy, as well as generating a remarkable amount of literary scholarship. There is even a scholarly journal entitled *Pynchon Notes* that is dedicated exclusively to the author. Pynchon has received almost every major American literary award, including the National Book Award for *Gravity's Rainbow* (shared with Isaac Bashevis Singer), the Pulitzer Prize (which was later withdrawn), the William Faulkner Foundation Award for his first novel, *V.*, the Richard and Hinda Rosenthal Foundation Award for Fiction from the National Institute of Arts and Letters for *The Crying of Lot 49*, and the Howells Medal, which Pynchon refused to accept. Pynchon also received a John D. and Catherine T. MacArthur Fellowship in 1988.

BIOGRAPHY

Thomas Ruggles Pynchon, Jr., is one of the most intensely private writers who has ever lived, even outdoing J. D. Salinger in his quest for seclusion and privacy. Only his close friends are even sure of what he looks like, and for many years the last available photograph of him was taken when he was in high school. What is known of Pynchon is available only from public records. He was graduated from high school in 1953 and entered Cornell University that year as a physics student, but in 1955 he left college and entered the U.S. Navy. He returned to Cornell in 1957, changing his major to English and was graduated in 1959. He lived in New York for a short time while working on *V.*, then moved to Seattle, where he worked for the Boeing Company, assisting in the writing of technical documents from 1960 to 1962. For several years after that, his whereabouts were uncertain, although he seems to have spent much time in California and Mexico. In the late 1980's and early 1990's, the ever-reclusive Pynchon was reported to have established residence in Northern California, the site of his novel *Vineland*. Confirmed sightings of Pynchon in New York City abounded in the late 1990's.

ANALYSIS

Not counting two excerpts from his second novel, which were printed in popular magazines, Thomas

Pynchon has published a number of short stories, one of them, "The Small Rain," in a college literary magazine, as well as the collection *Slow Learner: Early Stories*. Nevertheless, the stories are important in themselves and as aids to understanding Pynchon's novels. Most of the stories were written before the publication of Pynchon's first novel, *V.*, and share the thematic concerns of that novel. The characters of these stories live in a modern wasteland devoid of meaningful life, which they seek either to escape or to redeem. Often they feel that the world itself is about to end, either in a final cataclysm or by winding down to a state lacking energy and motion, characterized by the physical state known as entropy: the eventual "heat death" of the universe when all temperature will be the same and all molecules will be chaotically arranged, without motion or potential energy. Although the actions of the characters in the first stories vary widely, they all indicate a similar degree of hopelessness.

"THE SMALL RAIN"

Pynchon's first known short story, "The Small Rain," gives the reader insight into the author's early attempts at explicating these ideas. The story focuses on a two-day period in the life of Nathan "Lardass" Levine, a U.S. Army communications specialist from the Bronx stationed at Fort Roach, Louisiana, during the summer of 1957. After receiving a college degree from the City College of New York, Levine has refused entry into middle-class life, becoming a career enlisted soldier instead. Levine's nickname is apropos, as his Army career has consisted of attempt after attempt to avoid any and all work duties, to simply be alive but unthinking in modern life.

Levine is offered the possibility to reconsider these choices when a hurricane destroys the Louisiana village of Creole, and he is one of those assigned to reconstruct communications with the region and to find corpses in the disaster area. Basing their camp at the nearby McNeese State College, Levine is given another chance to see what he has refused--the life of upward mobility he left behind for his stagnating military existence. Rather than realizing that he may have made the wrong decisions thus far in his life, Levine blithely participates in his duties. Returning from Creole to McNeese, Levine simply gets drunk in a local campus

bar and has casual sex with a female college student, "little Buttercup." The story concludes with Levine's complaints about the weather--he hates the ever-present rain--and his refusal to consider anything but his upcoming leave in New Orleans.

Like many of the characters in *V.*, Levine accepts the idea of doing nothing. While capable of changing his chosen way of life, he is unwilling to make any effort. It is far easier for him to receive his three meals a day and his occasional leaves from duty than it is to participate in life. As Pierce, his lieutenant, suggests at one point, Levine seems content to keep extending the width of his rear end. Although limited in overall scope, this story is important to understanding a number of issues raised throughout Pynchon's texts. Like his first novel, *V.*, this first of Pynchon's stories forces readers to make their own conjunctions, to make the connections between ideas and events that Levine himself is incapable of doing. As "The Small Rain" shows, from the outset of his writing career, Pynchon was concerned with lives filled with boredom, modern life's lack of meaning, and the choices people do not make.

"MORTALITY AND MERCY IN VIENNA"

Pynchon's first nationally published short story, "Mortality and Mercy in Vienna," also illustrates many of these themes. The protagonist, a career diplomat named Cleanth Siegel, arrives at a party in Washington, D.C., only to find that the host, a look-alike named David Lupescu, is abandoning the apartment and appointing Siegel to take his place. In the course of the party, Siegel finds himself listening to the confusing details of his guests' convoluted and pointless sexual and social lives. Although he takes on the role of a father confessor and although he wants to be a healer-- "a prophet actually"--he has no cure for these people's problems. He does find a cure of sorts, however, in Irving Loon, an Ojibwa Indian who has been brought to the party. Siegel recalls that the Ojibwa are prone to a psychic disorder in which the Indian, driven by a cosmic paranoia, comes to identify with a legendary flesh-eating monster, the Windigo, and goes on a rampage of destruction, killing and eating his friends and family. Siegel speaks the word "Windigo" to Loon and watches as the Indian takes a rifle from the wall. As Loon begins shooting the members of the party, Siegel himself escapes. Like Mr. Kurtz in Joseph Conrad's *Heart of Darkness* (1899, serial; 1902, book), with whom he explicitly compares himself, Siegel finds the only possible salvation to be extermination.

The presentation of the modern world as a spiritual wasteland and the theme of paranoia continue throughout these early short stories, as well as *V.*, but none of Pynchon's other characters is able to act as forcefully as Siegel, even though his action is a negative one. The later stories, however, also demonstrate Pynchon's greater ability and growth as a writer. "Mortality and Mercy in Vienna," relying as it does on references to Conrad and T. S. Eliot and on a narrative voice which generally tells rather than shows, presents itself too self-consciously as a story even as it strives for verisimilitude. Pynchon's next story, "Low-Lands," demonstrates his growth in a short period of time.

"LOW-LANDS"

Dennis Flange, a former sailor now unhappily married, is thrown out of the house by his wife because of a surprise visit by his old Navy friend, Pig Bodine (who also later appears in *V.* and *Gravity's Rainbow*). He takes refuge with Pig in a shack in the local garbage dump, which is presided over by a black caretaker. This caretaker has barricaded his shack against gypsies who are living in the dump, but that night when Flange hears someone call him he goes outside. There he meets a young woman named Nerissa who leads him to her room in a tunnel beneath the dump. At the story's end, Flange seems prepared to stay with her.

The title of "Low-Lands" comes from an old sea chantey which causes Flange to think of the sea as "a gray or glaucous desert, a wasteland which stretches away to the horizon, . . . an assurance of perfect, passionless uniformity." This "perfect, passionless uniformity" might be an apt description of Pynchon's view of modern life, his great fear of the ultimate end to surprise and adventure. Cleanth Siegel's response to this same fear is to obliterate the problem; Dennis Flange's response is to hide from it. Flange fears the uniformity suggested by his "low-lands," but he also desires it, wishing not to be exposed and lonely on that wasteland surface, "so that he would be left sticking out like a projected radius, unsheltered and reeling across the empty lunes of his tiny sphere."

So as not to be left "sticking out," Flange has taken refuge in his marriage and his house but finds that they can no longer shelter him. He finds his surrogate for a hiding place in the gypsy girl, Nerissa. Within Nerissa's underground room, he knows he can find at least a temporary sanctuary. Like the underground refuge of Ralph Ellison's Invisible Man, this room suggests a place of recuperation and preparation to reemerge into life. In Nerissa herself, the image of the sea is restored to life: "Whitecaps danced across her eyes; sea creatures, he knew, would be cruising about in the submarine green of her heart." This ending, with its gypsies and secret tunnels, suggests the possible existence of alternatives to the wasteland of modern society, a possibility to which Pynchon was to return in *The Crying of Lot 49*; at the time, this ending made "Low-Lands" one of the most positive of Pynchon's short stories.

"ENTROPY"

A tone of hope, although somewhat more muted, can also be found in "Entropy," the best-known and perhaps most successful of Pynchon's short stories. Here Pynchon returns to the scene of "Mortality and Mercy in Vienna"--a party taking place in Washington, D.C.--but theme, characters, and plot are now handled with much more sophistication. The party itself is a lease-breaking party being hosted by one Meatball Mulligan, whose guests arrive and depart, engage in various kinds of strange behavior, and pass out at random. Upstairs, a man named Callisto lives in another apartment which he has converted into a hermetically sealed hothouse with the aid of a French-Annamese woman named Aubade. The story shifts back and forth between the two apartments, although Meatball and Callisto are connected only by the fact of living in the same building and by the theme of entropy which concerns them both.

Although there is in "Low-Lands" a brief reference to the Heisenberg principle of nuclear physics (that an event is affected by the fact of being observed), "Entropy" is the first of Pynchon's works to make sustained use of information and metaphors drawn from science and mathematics--a use which has become one of his hallmarks as a writer. Entropy manifests itself in the story in two different forms: as *physical* entropy--the tendency toward randomness and disorder within a closed system--and as *communications* entropy--a measure of the lack of information within a message or signal. In both cases, the tendency is toward stasis and confusion--lack of motion or lack of information; in either case and in human terms, the result is death.

Physical entropy is especially frightening to Callisto, which is why he has barricaded himself within his apartment. Since he fears that the "heat death" of the universe is imminent, he has built a private enclave where he can control the environment and remain safe. The concept of physical entropy can also be applied to Meatball's party as the behavior of the individual party guests becomes more and more random and disordered. Ironically, Meatball manages (at least temporarily) to avoid chaos and to reverse entropy, while Callisto fails. Realizing that he can either hide in a closet and add to the chaos and mad individualism of his party or work "to calm everybody down, one by one," Meatball chooses the latter. Callisto, on the other hand, fails to stop entropy within his own apartment. An ailing bird which he had been holding, trying to warm, dies in his hands after all; he wonders, "Has the transfer of heat ceased to work? Is there no more. . . ."

Part of the reason for Callisto's failure has to do with communications entropy. Order in communication is essential for the maintenance of order in Callisto's hothouse. Aubade brings "artistic harmony" to the apartment through a process by which all sensations "came to her reduced inevitable to the terms of sound: of music which emerged at intervals from a howling darkness of discordancy." Noise from Meatball's party threatens to plunge that music back into discord, and with the death of Callisto's bird, Aubade can no longer continue her effort. She smashes the window of the apartment with her fists and with Callisto awaits the triumph of physical entropy "and the final absence of all motion."

The fact that Meatball can bring order to his party suggests that order must be consciously created, not merely maintained as Callisto has sought to do. Even with Meatball's effort, his resolution of discord is not permanent and the final image of the party trembling "on the threshold of its third day" is not reassuring. Pynchon's message seems to be that of the physicists: Entropy is an inevitable condition although it can be

reversed for a while in some places. "Entropy" is notable for its organization and style, as well as for its subject matter. The characters and the alternation of story lines are models for Pynchon's first novel, *V.*, but the story also succeeds on its own. This "contrapuntal" structure combined with a number of references to music makes it evident that the story is structured like a musical fugue.

"UNDER THE ROSE"

"Under the Rose," Pynchon's last short story before *V.*, is also especially interesting for its style and structure. Set in Cairo at the end of the nineteenth century during the Fashoda crisis--when Britain and France nearly came to war over the colonization of the Sudan--the story is Pynchon's first re-creation of a historical setting and his first successful use of a narrative limited to the point of view of a single character. With very little authorial intrusion, Pynchon skillfully describes the activities of two spies, Porpentine and Goodfellow, in seeking to prevent the assassination of the British ambassador and the international war which would inevitably follow. The story was later reworked by Pynchon, broken up into eight vignettes seen through the eyes of outside spectators, and installed as Chapter 3 of *V.*

These early stories are generally characterized by a pessimism concerning the possibilities of human action and change. They are also marked by a sense of social isolation; with the exception of "Under the Rose," there is little or no suggestion of the political, economic, and social pressures that shape life, and even in that story, these pressures are subordinated to a suggested nameless, hostile, possibly nonhuman intelligence at work in history. Following the publication of *V.*, however, Pynchon has steadily moved back into the world, combining his imaginative perception of the condition of modern life with a recognition of the forces which can play a part in shaping that condition. That recognition is first manifested in Pynchon's "The Secret Integration."

"THE SECRET INTEGRATION"

"The Secret Integration" centers on a group of children living in the Berkshire town of Mingeborough, Massachusetts, who act in league to subvert adult institutions and encourage anarchistic liberty. The adults are seen as constantly seeking to make the children conform to their way of life: for example, Grover Snodd, "a boy genius with flaws," is certain that adults are planting Tom Swift books for him to read in order to foster a sense of competition and avarice, as well as to promote racism.

Racism is, in fact, the key theme of the story. Carl Barrington, a central member of the children's gang, is himself black, his parents having recently moved into Northumberland Estates, a new development in Mingeborough. These newcomers are resented by the white adults of the town, and the children are aware of the presence of racism in their families, even though they do not quite understand it. There is also a flashback to the night the children--one of them a nine-year-old reformed alcoholic--go to the town hotel to sit with a black jazz musician because the adults in Alcoholics Anonymous are unwilling to help a black. After a night-long vigil, the boys see the musician hauled away by the police and never learn what really happens to him. In retaliation and as an affirmation of color, the boys stage a raid on the local train at night wearing green-colored masks and costumes to scare the passengers.

Color is a threat to Mingeborough and to a white way of life which thrives on the competition, separateness, and blandness exemplified by Tom Swift. The Barringtons are a special annoyance because they live in Northumberland Estates, which seems to have been built purposely to suppress differences and encourage uniformity. This development is like the "low-lands" of Dennis Flange, but with an important difference: Rather than an abstract psychological condition, it is a real, physical place with more than enough correlatives in the nonfictional world to make it all too recognizable.

The children, however, are able to overcome this prejudice; even though Grover only understands the word "integration" as a mathematical term, they accept Carl as an equal. However, in the end, the group capitulates. They find garbage dumped on the Barringtons' front lawn and recognize it as having come from their own houses. Unable to cut themselves off from their parents and repudiated by the Barringtons themselves, they say good-bye to Carl, who, it turns out, is imaginary, "put together out of phrases, images, possibilities that grownups had somehow turned away from, repudiated, left out at the edges of town. . . ." The children return to the safety and love of their parents "and dreams that could never again be entirely safe."

"The Secret Integration" is concerned once again with the quest for possibilities and alternatives, which is the theme of *The Crying of Lot 49*, and with the prevalence of racism, which is one of the many concerns of *Gravity's Rainbow*. Although the children admit defeat, one still feels the hope that life will be somewhat better once they have grown up, that they will retain some of the lessons they have learned.

SLOW LEARNER

Pynchon's own estimation of his short stories is ambivalent and has been the subject of much scholarly discussion, especially since the publication in 1984 of *Slow Learner*, an anthology of the author's short stories. In the introduction to this book, Pynchon disparages his short stories to such an extent that it is remarkable that he permitted their republication in the first place. The first-person Thomas Pynchon of the 1984 introduction discussing the third-person Thomas Pynchon of the 1960's, however, may be no more than a fictional creation of the present Thomas Pynchon, with the introduction to *Slow Learner* being no more than another of the author's highly equivocal and extraordinarily convoluted short stories.

It is impossible to say whether Pynchon will ever return to the short-story form for its own sake, and certainly his stories are less important than his novels. Nevertheless, these works are helpful introductions to this writer's sometimes complex and baffling fictional world, and some of them--especially "Entropy" and perhaps "The Secret Integration"--will stand on their own as minor classics.

OTHER MAJOR WORKS

LONG FICTION: *V.*, 1963; *The Crying of Lot 49*, 1966; *Gravity's Rainbow*, 1973; *Vineland*, 1989; *Mason and Dixon*, 1997; *Against the Day*, 2006; *Inherent Vice*, 2009.

NONFICTION: *Deadly Sins*, 1993.

BIBLIOGRAPHY

Bloom, Harold, ed. *Thomas Pynchon*. Philadelphia: Chelsea House, 2003. Collection of essays about Pynchon's long and short fiction. David Seed's essay examines "Order in Thomas Pynchon's 'Entropy,'" while some of the other pieces discuss Pynchon's importance as a writer and analyze the characteristics of anarchy and possibility, paranoia, and "existential Gnosticism" in his works.

Chambers, Judith. *Thomas Pynchon*. New York: Twayne, 1992. A critical and interpretive examination of Pynchon's work. Includes bibliographical references and an index.

Cowart, David. *Thomas Pynchon: The Art of Allusion*. Carbondale: southern Illinois University Press, 1980. This book is one of the best volumes on Pynchon's prodigious use of allusions in his prose. Useful chapters are included on the allusive functioning of music and film in Pynchon's novels and short stories.

Curtin, Maureen F. "Skin Harvests: Automation and Chromatism in Thomas Pynchon's 'The Secret Integration' and *Gravity's Rainbow*." In *Out of Touch: Skin Tropes and Identities in Woolf, Ellison, Pynchon, and Acker*. New York: Routledge, 2003. Focuses on how skin has become a crucial element in twentieth century literature, theory, and cultural criticism by examining works by Pynchon and other authors.

Diamond, Jamie. "The Mystery of Thomas Pynchon Leads Fans and Scholars on a Quest as Bizarre as His Plots." *People Weekly* 33 (January 29, 1990): 64-66. A brief biographical sketch and discussion of Pynchon's dropping out of sight in the 1960's.

Dugdale, John. *Thomas Pynchon: Allusive Parables of Power*. New York: St. Martin's Press, 1990. Dugdale provides a critical review and interpretation of Pynchon's work. Includes thorough bibliographical references and an index.

Gelfant, Blanche H., ed. *The Columbia Companion to the Twentieth-Century American Short Story*. New York: Columbia University Press, 2000. Includes a chapter in which Pynchon's short stories are analyzed.

Gussow, Mel. "Pynchon's Letters Nudge His Mask." *The New York Times*, March 4, 1998, p. E1. Discusses the insights into Pynchon's creative process and his emotions that are evident in more than 120 letters that he sent to his agent, Candida Donadio.

Hawthorne, Mark D. "Pynchon's Early Labyrinths." *College Literature* 25 (Spring, 1998): 78-93. Discusses Pynchon's use of labyrinths in his early stories in the 1960's. Argues that while first using the labyrinth to describe escape from a confining middle-class marriage, Pynchon slowly turned it into a metaphor for the quest for self-awareness.

Holton, Robert. "'Closed Circuit': The White Male Predicament in Pynchon's Early Stories." In *Thomas Pynchon: Reading from the Margins*, edited by Niran Abbas. Madison, N.J.: Fairleigh Dickinson University Press, 2003. Argues that Pynchon's early short fiction was a response to the "problem of conformity," which was perceived as a serious issue in the 1950's. Describes how Pynchon sought to create a "renewed masculinity" in "The Small Rain," "Low-Lands," and "Mortality and Mercy in Vienna."

Hume, Kathryn. *Pynchon's Mythography: An Approach to "Gravity's Rainbow."* Carbondale: southern Illinois University Press, 1987. This excellent book examines in detail Pynchon's use of myths and legends in *Gravity's Rainbow*. The comments are also applicable to the rest of his prose works. The range of Pynchon's mythography extends from the grail and Faust legends to non-western myths.

Levine, George, and David Leverenz, eds. *Mindful Pleasures: Essays on Thomas Pynchon*. Boston: Little, Brown, 1976. A useful selection of essays on Pynchon's prose. The essays on Pynchon's use of scientific theories and terminology are particularly valuable in understanding the novel *Gravity's Rainbow* and the short story "Entropy."

McHoul, Alec, and David Wills. *Writing Pynchon: Strategies in Fictional Analysis*. Urbana: University of Illinois Press, 1990. Includes an interesting discussion (pages 131 to 160) of Pynchon's introduction to his collection of short stories *Slow Learner*.

Sales, Nancy Jo. "Meet Your Neighbor, Thomas Pynchon." *New York* 29 (November 11, 1996): 60-64. Discusses Pynchon's almost mythical status. Comments on his popularity in the 1970's and his subsequent reclusiveness.

Weisenburger, S. C. *A "Gravity's Rainbow" Companion: Sources and Contexts for Pynchon's Novel.* Athens: University of Georgia Press, 1988. This volume is an extraordinarily detailed encyclopedia of the sources for the allusions used in Pynchon's novel. Since several of the characters from Pynchon's short stories reappear in *Gravity's Rainbow*, this book is useful in order to trace the influence that Pynchon's short stories have had on his long fiction.

Donald F. Larsson
Updated by William E. Grim and Joshua Stein

Q

ELLERY QUEEN

Manfred B. Lee

Also Known As: Manfred Lepofsky
Born: Brooklyn, New York; January 11, 1905
Died: Near Waterbury, Connecticut; April 3, 1971

Frederic Danay

Also Known As: Daniel Nathan
Born: Brooklyn, New York; October 20, 1905
Died: White Plains, New York; September 3, 1982

PRINCIPAL SHORT FICTION

The Adventures of Ellery Queen, 1934
The New Adventures of Ellery Queen, 1940
The Case Book of Ellery Queen, 1945
Calendar of Crime, 1952
QBI: Queen's Bureau of Investigation, 1954
Queens Full, 1965
QED: Queen's Experiments in Detection, 1968

OTHER LITERARY FORMS

Manfred B. Lee and Frederic Dannay's career as mystery writer Ellery Queen began in 1929 with the publication of *The Roman Hat Mystery*. They went on to write more than forty other mystery novels, including four under the pseudonym Barnaby Ross, as well as their numerous short stories. During the 1940's, the pair produced weekly scripts for the long-running radio series *The Adventures of Ellery Queen*, and they worked briefly for Paramount Pictures, Columbia Pictures Entertainment, and Metro-Goldwyn-Mayer, writing screenplays featuring their namesake detective. Several of the mysteries that appeared in *Ellery Queen's Mystery Magazine* are written in play form. Dannay and Lee also produced several works of criticism on the detective story, the most important of which is perhaps *Queen's Quorum: A History of the Detective-Crime Short Story as Revealed by the 106 Most Important Books Published in This Field Since 1845* (1951).

ACHIEVEMENTS

Ellery Queen is often thought to be one of the most influential figures in the development of detective fiction, both as a writer and as an editor. "His" work was recognized several times by the Mystery Writers of America (which Dannay and Lee founded) in its annual Edgar Allan Poe Awards, and in 1960, Queen won the association's Grand Master Award. Like his contemporaries of the "golden age" of mystery and detective fiction--Agatha Christie, Rex Stout, John Dickson Carr, and others--Queen works in the puzzle tradition of Sir Arthur Conan Doyle's Sherlock Holmes, in which mysteries are solved by using a process of logical thought.

Queen's work as editor of *Ellery Queen's Mystery Magazine* has been credited with "rescuing American detective fiction from the pulps and restoring its reputation as high quality literature." From its inception in 1941, the magazine tried to publish the best in mystery fiction of all types, and it introduced new writers alongside established authors and such mainstream figures as Arthur Miller and Sinclair Lewis.

BIOGRAPHY

In 1928, two first cousins adopted the pseudonym Ellery Queen and entered a contest sponsored by *McClure's Magazine* for the best mystery story. The first prize was seventy-five hundred dollars. The cousins won but never received the money, as the magazine ceased publication before the prize was distributed. Publisher Frederick A. Stokes, who had been associated with the contest, offered to publish their entry as a novel, and *The Roman Hat Mystery* (1929) was successful enough that the cousins quit their jobs and turned to writing full-time as Ellery Queen. For approximately ten years, the cousins managed to keep the public from knowing that Ellery Queen was a pseudonym. In fact, they adopted a second pseudonym, Barnaby Ross, for four mystery novels and once staged a masked debate as Ross and Queen. After 1938, it became known that Ellery Queen was in reality Frederic Dannay and Manfred B. Lee.

Born Manfred Lepofsky, Lee was the elder of the cousins by nine months. He and Dannay, who changed his name from Daniel Nathan by adopting Frédéric Chopin's first name and creating a surname from the first syllables of his original name, went to Boys' High School in Brooklyn. Lee continued his education at New York University, where his main interest was music; he played the violin and for a time ran his own orchestra. Lee went on to become an advertising copywriter for a New York film company, while Dannay began working in an advertising agency as a copywriter and art director.

Their collaboration as Ellery Queen was highly successful. Dannay and Lee apparently alternated devising plots and doing the writing; in a 1969 interview with *The New York Times*, Dannay commented that their "clash of personalities is good for the ultimate product. . . . We're not so much collaborators as competitors. It's produced a sharper edge."

The first ten years of the collaboration were very prolific, and the novels were tightly plotted, ingenious puzzles that emphasized the logic of deduction. Indeed, twelve of the first fourteen novels are subtitled *A Problem in Deduction*. The years between the publication of *Calamity Town* (1942) and *The Finishing Stroke* (1958) are generally considered to be Queen's best. By then the logical puzzles were still tightly constructed, but Queen began giving more emphasis to elements of characterization, setting, mood, and theme. Though the plot of *The Finishing Stroke* implied an end to the Ellery Queen series, a number of other Ellery Queen novels were written after its publication.

In the 1930's, Lee and Dannay also wrote screenplays featuring Ellery Queen, and in 1939, they began writing a script per week for the radio series *The Adventures of Ellery Queen*, which lasted until 1948. In 1941, Dannay suggested to magazine publisher Lawrence Spivak that he start a magazine devoted to mystery stories. Dannay and Lee had edited *Mystery League Magazine* in 1933 and 1934, but Dannay became the sole editor of *Ellery Queen's Mystery Magazine*, which was a worldwide success. The magazine is frequently credited with raising the standard of the mystery story, and along with publishing well-established writers, it introduced numerous newcomers, many of whom went on to become successful authors. Dannay also edited scores of anthologies consisting of stories drawn from the magazine and from his and Lee's collection of detective fiction.

Lee, who was married twice and had eight children, four boys and four girls, died in 1971 of a heart attack soon after Queen's last novel, *A Fine and Private Place* (1971), was published. Dannay, who married three times and had three sons, wrote no more Ellery Queen novels after Lee's death, though he continued his work as editor of *Ellery Queen's Mystery Magazine* until his own death in 1982.

ANALYSIS

Ellery Queen's mystery stories often are a sort of animated crossword puzzle: As the puzzle solver fills in the grid according to the clues, the answers to the clues that he or she does not understand become clear through the answers to the clues that are interpreted correctly. Other stories are like riddles: The clues to the mystery must be interpreted and added together to find a logical answer. Still others are like jigsaw puzzles, where one has to fill in what is missing to get a true picture. Francis M. Nevins, Jr., in *Twentieth-Century Crime and Mystery Writers* (1980), wrote that Queen follows several motifs in most of his stories, those of "the negative clue, the dying message, the murderer as Iagoesque manipulator, the patterned series of clues deliberately left at scenes of crimes, the false answer followed by the true and devastating solution." All these techniques work well to keep the reader in suspense, yet Queen is scrupulously fair in making sure that all the clues are available to the reader as well as to Ellery Queen, the detective in all of his stories. In fact, many of Queen's stories have a formal "Challenge to the Reader" after all the clues have been presented and before Ellery solves the crime. Even the stories without this challenge, however, are structured in such a way that the reader can attempt to solve the problem before the solution is presented. Queen is not above throwing in a red herring or two, but Ellery must deal with these as must the reader. Occasionally, solutions are far-fetched, but the stories never support more than one solution.

Queen's stories are puzzles, and as such they sometimes lack any emotional punch. While police officers, doctors, and the like often do become somewhat hardened to violent death, it is nevertheless slightly shocking to the reader's sensibilities to have Ellery calmly, almost absentmindedly, stepping over bodies as he examines potential clues. When someone does react, the tone of the account often becomes rather amused: In "The Adventure of the Three R's," after Nikki Porter, Ellery's secretary, discovers that she is virtually sitting on a skeleton, she screams and draws over Ellery and two professors; the story notes that

> the top of the skull revealed a deep and ragged chasm, the result of what could only have been a tremendous blow.

> Whereupon the old pedagogue and the young took flight, joining Miss Porter, who was quietly being ill on the other side of the cabin.

Few of Queen's stories display any horror over an act of murder; instead, the tone seems to be one of faint disapproval.

Through the years, Queen gave Ellery several different foils, whose main purpose is to bring Ellery to the scene of a crime. The first and most important is his father, Inspector Richard Queen, who seems to call Ellery in on all of his difficult cases. Inspector Queen deals with the police routine, while Ellery takes the pieces that his father digs up and puts them together. Detective-Sergeant Thomas Velie is Inspector Queen's usual accompaniment, and he appears to have little intelligence but large bulk for dangerous situations. Another foil is Ellery's pretty young secretary, Nikki Porter, who can be counted on to come to the wrong conclusion. Nikki can also be depended upon to take Ellery to a party or visiting to places where something nasty is likely to happen. Ellery must have been a most unwelcome houseguest, as something disturbing seems likely to occur when he

visits. Early in his career, Ellery was also involved with Hollywood gossip columnist Paula Paris, who supplied a mild love interest and tickets to various events where disagreeable things took place. Djuna, the Queens' houseboy, appears in several stories as well. While these characters do not appear in every Queen story, the role of a foil to Ellery's intelligence is common. There is usually someone to whom the solution must be explained.

Queen's first stories were not collected until 1934, after more than half a dozen novels featuring his detective had been published. Thus, the character of Ellery Queen was already well known and popular, so Queen wastes little time in his short stories establishing characters: The reader is plunged straight into the plot. In "The African Traveller," the first story in *The Adventures of Ellery Queen*, Ellery has agreed to teach a class in applied criminology to several university students. Conveniently, Inspector Queen has just been called to the scene of a murder on the first day of the class, and he will allow Ellery and his students to examine the case and come to their own conclusions. All the clues are presented during the students' exploration of the room, and Ellery sends them off to consider the case and develop a solution. The students in this case are Ellery's foils, and though they blanch when they are first faced with the dead man, they are soon happily poking around the body. Each student later presents a coherent theory as to the killer; all are wrong. The story thus follows Nevins's pattern of the false answer followed by the true solution: Ellery tells the students where they went wrong--each ignored some clue--and lays out the logical solution, which takes into account *every* clue presented. The story is similar to a crossword puzzle: Not until all the answers to the clues have been filled in is the solution complete.

"THE BEARDED LADY"

In "The Bearded Lady," the most important clue is a painting done by the victim. The murdered man is a doctor and amateur painter who has just been willed one thousand dollars, which is to be divided between his benefactor's stepchildren upon his death. Dr. Arlen is killed in his studio and near one of his paintings, on which he has painted a beard onto a woman's face. Ellery concludes that the bearded woman is a clue to the identity of the killer:

With his murderer present, he *couldn't* paint the name; the murderer would have noticed it and destroyed it. Arlen was forced, then, to adopt a subtle means: leave a clue that would escape his killer's attention.

This story, then, falls into Nevin's category of the "dying message": Ellery must interpret this message correctly in order to solve the crime. The clue is a kind of riddle: To whom does the bearded lady refer? If it is the beard that is important, then the clue points to the stepson, who has a beard. The clue, however, could also point to the stepdaughter, whose eight-year-old son had just been punished the day before for chalking a beard onto one of Arlen's paintings. When all the other clues are taken into account, however, Ellery realizes that the killer is Mrs. Royce, a man who has dressed up as a woman in order to claim the inheritance of his sister, who was to receive from the same benefactor as Dr. Arlen two hundred thousand dollars. Dr. Arlen, the family physician, had been scheduled to examine Mrs. Royce the day after he was killed, whereupon Royce's ruse would have been discovered.

"DEAD RINGER"

The story "Dead Ringer" takes the motif of the dying message to absurdity, though the clues still hold together and the solution is logical given the clues presented. The "dead ringer" is a security agent who had been placed in a tobacconist's shop, which was suspected of being a drop for enemy agents, because he resembles the man who runs the shop. Hours after he telephoned his office to say that, in examining the shop's customer ledger, he had discovered the identities of the foreign agents, he is found dead, clutching an empty can of tobacco labeled "MIX C." Ellery deduces that, since the security agent "made his extraordinary dying effort to call your attention to the otherwise empty can," there must be something about the label that is a clue to the identities of the foreign agents. "*Every letter in MIX C is also a Roman numeral*," so the foreign agents must be numbers 1,009 and 100 in the customer ledger. While within the terms of the story this is the logical answer, it still strikes the reader as absurd. That someone would make that kind of intellectual connection while dying a painful death and still

be able to get to the can at all stretches the reader's credulity too far.

Queen recognizes that the story type of the dying message has its limitations; in "E = Murder" he writes,

> we're confronted with a dying message in the classic tradition. . . . Why couldn't he have just written the name? The classic objection. The classic reply to which is that he was afraid his killer might come back, notice it, and destroy it. . . . which I'll admit has never really satisfied me.

Nevertheless, Queen has written dozens of stories of the dying message type.

"THE INVISIBLE LOVER"

Another frequent pattern that Queen employs is what Nevins calls the "negative clue": the clue that is important because it is not there when it should be. The story "The Invisible Lover" fits this pattern, as well as embodying Nevins's category of "the murderer as Iagoesque manipulator." One of Iris Scott's suitors has been murdered, and her childhood friend and beau, Roger Bowen, has been arrested for the deed. The most damning evidence against Bowen is that the coroner has examined the bore marks on the bullet found in the dead man's body, and they match Bowen's gun. Ellery, puzzled by the rearrangement of furniture in the dead man's room, looks behind the highboy and finds a dent in the plaster that looks to have been made by a bullet. If it were made by a bullet, a loose bullet should have been found in the room, and since Bowen's bullet was found in the body, two shots should have been fired to account for the mark. No bullet was found, and two shots were not heard. Ellery thus deduces the solution to the crime because what he expected to find was not there: There was no bullet to account for the mark on the wall, and if there was no bullet, the bullet that killed the victim *must* have passed through his body and the chair on which he was sitting to make the indentation on the wall and then must have been picked up by the murderer. Ellery discovers a chair with a hole in it in the coroner's room, and when he has the body exhumed, he finds an exit wound. Therefore, the coroner must have lied about Bowen's bullet being found in the body, and his only reason for lying is that he is the murderer. All the pieces of the jigsaw have been put into place, and the true picture is revealed.

"PAYOFF" AND "THE PRESIDENT REGRETS"

Two stories that fit loosely into Nevins's category of a "patterned series of clues" are "Payoff" and "The President Regrets." "Payoff" also employs the device of the dying message: A dying man gasps out that the four men who head the racketeering organization which he did the books for, use four cities as their code names. He dies, however, before he can tell the authorities which code name belongs to the top man. Inspector Queen and Ellery know the names of the four men involved, and Ellery discovers who the boss is by matching the code names with the real names of the criminals: *Hous*ton with Hughes, *Phila*delphia with Filippo, *Berke*ley with Burke, and *Bos*ton with the boss--who must thus be the fourth man, Ewing.

"The President Regrets" is a similar puzzle, in which a screen star named Valetta Van Buren writes a letter to Ellery telling him that one of her four lovers has threatened to kill her. Without telling him the name of her potential killer, she writes that "she had something in common with three of the four, and that the fourth was the one who had threatened her." The point in common is a presidential name: Three of her lovers were called Taylor, Wilson, and Harrison, while the fourth was named Price. The patterned clues in these stories are fairly simplistic; in his novels, however, Queen used more complex ones.

Queen's stories, as well as his novels, belong to the style of the "golden age" of the formal detective story, though many of them were actually written outside that time period of the 1920's to 1940's. They are, for the most part, well written, and they are often amusing. Ellery, despite his arrogant erudition, is a likable character, but his main function is to serve the plot. The plot is king in Queen's stories: The puzzle is all. Ingenuity is the key word to the puzzle, and while some of the puzzles are so ingenious as to border on fantasy, most of them are reasonably plausible and intriguing. The stories endure because they can still involve and challenge the reader.

OTHER MAJOR WORKS

LONG FICTION: *The Roman Hat Mystery*, 1929; *The French Powder Mystery*, 1930; *The Dutch Shoe Mystery*, 1931; *The Egyptian Cross Mystery*, 1932; *The Greek Coffin Mystery*, 1932; *The Tragedy of X*, 1932 (as Barnaby Ross); *The Tragedy of Y*, 1932 (as Ross); *The American Gun Mystery*, 1933 (also as *Death at the Rodeo*, 1951); *Drury Lane's Last Case*, 1933 (as Ross); *The Siamese Twin Mystery*, 1933; *The Tragedy of Z*, 1933 (as Ross); *The Chinese Orange Mystery*, 1934; *The Spanish Cape Mystery*, 1935; *Halfway House*, 1936; *The Door Between*, 1937; *The Devil to Pay*, 1938; *The Four of Hearts*, 1938; *The Dragon's Teeth*, 1939 (also as *The Virgin Heiresses*, 1954); *Calamity Town*, 1942; *There Was an Old Woman*, 1943 (also as *The Quick and the Dead*, 1956); *The Murderer Is a Fox*, 1945; *Ten Days' Wonder*, 1948; *Cat of Many Tails*, 1949; *Double, Double*, 1950 (also as *The Case of the Seven Murders*, 1958); *The Origin of Evil*, 1951; *The King Is Dead*, 1952; *The Golden Summer*, 1953 (as Daniel Nathan); *The Scarlet Letters*, 1953; *The Glass Village*, 1954; *Inspector Queen's Own Case*, 1956; *The Finishing Stroke*, 1958; *The XYZ Murders*, 1961 (omnibus; as Ross); *A Study in Terror*, 1966 (novelization of the screenplay; also as *Sherlock Holmes vs. Jack the Ripper*, 1967); *Face to Face*, 1967; *Cop Out*, 1969 (by Frederic Dannay and Manfred Bennington Lee); *Kiss and Kill*, 1969; *The Last Woman in His Life*, 1970; *A Fine and Private Place*, 1971.

PLAY: *Danger, Men Working*, pr. c.1936 (with Lowell Brentano).

SCREENPLAY: *Ellery Queen, Master Detective*, 1940 (with Eric Taylor).

RADIO PLAY: *The Adventures of Ellery Queen*, 1939-1948.

NONFICTION: *The Detective Short Story: A Bibliography*, 1942; *Queen's Quorum: A History of the Detective-Crime Short Story as Revealed by the 106 Most Important Books Published in This Field Since 1845*, 1951, revised 1969; *In the Queen's Parlor, and Other Leaves from the Editors' Notebook*, 1957; *Ellery Queen's International Case Book*, 1964; *The Woman in the Case*, 1966 (also as *Deadlier than the Male*, 1967).

CHILDREN'S LITERATURE (AS ELLERY QUEEN, JR.): *The Black Dog Mystery*, 1941; *The Green Turtle Mystery*, 1941; *The Golden Eagle Mystery*, 1942; *The Red Chipmunk Mystery*, 1946; *The Brown Fox Mystery*, 1948; *The White Elephant Mystery*, 1950; *The Yellow Cat Mystery*, 1952; *The Blue Herring Mystery*, 1954; *The*

Mystery of the Merry Magician, 1961; *The Mystery of the Vanished Victim*, 1962; *The Purple Bird Mystery*, 1965; *The Silver Llama Mystery*, 1966.

EDITED TEXTS: *Challenge to the Reader*, 1938; *The Last Man Club*, 1940 (novelization of radio show); *Ellery Queen, Master Detective*, 1941 (novelization of the screenplay by Eric Taylor; also as *The Vanishing Corpse*); *101 Years' Entertainment: The Great Detective Stories, 1841-1941*, 1941 (revised 1946); *The Penthouse Mystery*, 1941 (novelization of a screenplay by Eric Taylor); *The Murdered Millionaire*, 1942 (novelization of the radio play); *The Perfect Crime*, 1942 (novelization of a screenplay by Eric Taylor); *Sporting Blood: The Great Sports Detective Stories*, 1942 (also as *Sporting Detective Stories*); *The Female of the Species: The Great Women Detectives and Criminals*, 1943 (also as *Ladies in Crime: A Collection of Detective Stories by English and American Writers*); *Best Stories from "Ellery Queen's Mystery Magazine,"* 1944; *The Adventures of Sam Spade, and Other Stories*, 1944 (by Dashiell Hammett; also as *They Can Only Hang You Once*); *The Misadventures of Sherlock Holmes*, 1944; *Rogues' Gallery: The Great Criminals of Modern Fiction*, 1945; *The Continental Op*, 1945 (by Dashiell Hammett); *The Return of the Continental Op*, 1945 (by Dashiell Hammett); *Hammett Homicides*, 1946 (by Dashiell Hammett); *To the Queen's Taste*, 1946; *The Queen's Awards*, 1946-1959; *Dead Yellow Women*, 1947 (by Dashiell Hammett); *Dr. Fell, Detective*, 1947 (by John Dickson Carr); *Murder by Experts*, 1947; *The Case Book of Mr. Campion*, 1947 (by Margery Allingham); *The Department of Dead Ends*, 1947 (by Roy Vickers); *The Riddles of Hildegarde Withers*, 1947 (by Stuart Palmer); *Cops and Robbers*, 1948 (by O. Henry); *Nightmare Town*, 1948 (by Dashiell Hammett); *Twentieth Century Detective Stories*, 1948, revised 1964; *The Creeping Siamese*, 1950 (by Dashiell Hammett); *The Literature of Crime: Stories by World-Famous Authors*, 1950 (also as *Ellery Queen's Book of Mystery Stories*); *The Monkey Murder, and Other Hildegarde Withers Stories*, 1950 (by Stuart Palmer); *Woman in the Dark*, 1952 (by Dashiell Hammett); *Mystery Annals*, 1958-1962; *Ellery Queen's Anthology*, 1959-1973; *Dead Man's Tale*, 1961 (by Stephen Marlowe); *Death Spins the Platter*, 1962 (by Richard

Deming); *A Man Named Thin, and Other Stories*, 1962 (by Dashiell Hammett); *To Be Read Before Midnight*, 1962; *Murder with a Past*, 1963 (by Talmage Powell); *Mystery Mix*, 1963; *Wife or Death*, 1963 (by Richard Deming); *Blow Hot, Blow Cold*, 1964; *Double Dozen*, 1964; *The Four Johns*, 1964 (also as *Four Men Called John*; by Jack Vance); *The Golden Goose*, 1964; *The Last Score*, 1964; *Twelve*, 1964; *Beware the Young Stranger*, 1965 (by Talmage Powell); *The Copper Frame*, 1965 (by Richard Deming); *The Killer Touch*, 1965; *Lethal Black Book*, 1965; *A Room to Die In*, 1965 (by Jack Vance); *Twentieth Anniversary Annual*, 1965; *All-Star Lineup*, 1966; *Crime Carousel*, 1966; *The Devil's Cook*, 1966; *Losers, Weepers*, 1966 (by Richard Deming); *The Madman Theory*, 1966 (by Jack Vance); *Shoot the Scene*, 1966 (by Richard Deming); *Where Is Bianca?*, 1966 (by Talmage Powell); *Who Spies, Who Kills?*, 1966 (by Talmage Powell); *Why So Dead?*, 1966 (by Richard Deming); *How Goes the Murder?*, 1967 (by Richard Deming); *Poetic Justice: Twenty-Three Stories of Crime, Mystery, and Detection by World-Famous Poets from Geoffrey Chaucer to Dylan Thomas*, 1967; *Which Way to Die?*, 1967 (by Richard Deming); *Guess Who's Coming to Kill You?*, 1968; *Mystery Parade*, 1968; *What's in the Dark?*, 1968 (also as *When Fell the Night*; by Richard Deming); *The Campus Murders*, 1969 (by Gil Brewer); *The Case of the Murderer's Bride, and Other Stories*, 1969 (by Erle Stanley Gardner); *Minimysteries: Seventy Short-Short Stories of Crime, Mystery, and Detection*, 1969; *Murder Menu*, 1969; *Murder--In Spades!*, 1969; *Shoot the Works!*, 1969; *The Black Hearts Murder*, 1970 (by Richard Deming); *Grand Slam*, 1970; *Mystery Jackpot*, 1970; *P as in Police*, 1970 (by Lawrence Treat); *Headliners*, 1971; *The Golden Thirteen: Thirteen First Prize Winners from "Ellery Queen's Mystery Magazine,"* 1971; *The Spy and the Thief*, 1971 (by Edward D. Hoch); *The Blue Movie Murders*, 1972 (edited and supervised by Frederic Dannay; by Edward D. Hoch); *Ellery Queen's Best Bets*, 1972; *Mystery Bag*, 1972; *Amateur in Violence*, 1973 (by Michael Gilbert); *Christmas Hamper*, 1974; *Crookbook*, 1974; *Aces of Mystery*, 1975; *Kindly Dig Your Grave, and Other Stories*, 1975 (by Stanley Ellin); *Masters of Mystery*, 1975; *Murdercade*, 1975; *Crime Wave*, 1976; *Giants of Mystery*, 1976; *Magicians of Mystery*, 1976; *Champions of Mystery*, 1977; *Faces of Mystery*, 1977; *How to Trap a Crook, and Twelve Other Mysteries*, 1977 (by Julian Symons); *Masks of Mystery*, 1977; *Searches and Seizures*, 1977; *Who's Who of Whodunits*, 1977; *A Multitude of Sins*, 1978; *Japanese Golden Dozen: The Detective Story World in Japan*, 1978; *Napoleons of Mystery*, 1978; *The Supersleuths*, 1978; *Scenes of the Crime*, 1979; *Secrets of Mystery*, 1979; *Wings of Mystery*, 1979; *Circumstantial Evidence*, 1980; *Veils of Mystery*, 1980; *Windows of Mystery*, 1980; *Crime Cruise Round the World*, 1981; *Doors to Mystery*, 1981; *Eyes of Mystery*, 1981; *Eyewitnesses*, 1981; *Book of First Appearances*, 1982 (with Eleanor Sullivan); *Maze of Mysteries*, 1982; *Lost Ladies*, 1983 (with Eleanor Sullivan); *Lost Men*, 1983 (with Eleanor Sullivan); *The Best of Ellery Queen*, 1983; *Prime Crimes*, 1984 (with Eleanor Sullivan).

BIBLIOGRAPHY

Breen, Jon L. "The Ellery Queen Mystery." *The Weekly Standard* 11, no. 4 (October 10, 2005): 41-43. A profile of Lee and Dannay that looks at their rise to fame and the reasons for their subsequent decline in popularity.

Grella, George. "The Formal Detective Novel." In *Detective Fiction: A Collection of Critical Essays*, edited by Robin W. Winks. Englewood Cliffs, N.J.: Prentice-Hall, 1980. Though Grella's essay is on the detective novel and only briefly mentions the work of Ellery Queen, the essay does discuss the characteristics of the formal detective story of the "golden age" and is thus very useful in considering Queen's stories.

Grossberger, Lewis. "Ellery Queen: A Man of Mystery and He Likes It That Way." *The Washington Post*, March 16, 1978, p. D1. A brief biographical sketch, describing how Dannay developed the Ellery Queen persona and *Ellery Queen Mystery Magazine*. Discusses Dannay's popularity in Japan and his editing work, as well as his shyness and stage fright.

Harmon, Jim. *The Great Radio Heroes*. Rev. ed. Jefferson, N.C.: McFarland, 2001. Includes a chapter on radio detectives comparing Queen to Sherlock Holmes, Sam Spade, and others. Contains a bibliography and an index.

Karnick, S. T. "Mystery Men." *National Review* 52, no. 4 (March 6, 2000): 59-61. Describes how Dannay and Lee helped establish the popularity of American mystery and detective fiction. Explains how Lee wrote the Ellery Queen stories from outlines created by Dannay, while Dannay conceived the plots, puzzles, characters and themes.

Keating, H. R. F., ed. *Whodunit? A Guide to Crime, Suspense, and Spy Fiction*, London: Windward, 1982. Keating's short entry on Ellery Queen contains some useful biographical information but has little in the way of literary criticism.

Maslin, Janet. "Critic's Notebook: Gumshoe Who Wore Pince-Nez." *The New York Times*, May 7, 2005, p. 33. Maslin reports on a gathering of a small group of "Queeniacs" who gathered at Columbia University to celebrate Ellery Queen's one hundredth birthday. In honor of the centennial, Columbia's Butler Library had mounted an exhibition of Queen memorabilia.

Nevins, Francis M., Jr. "Ellery Queen." In *Twentieth-Century Crime and Mystery Writers*, edited by John M. Reilly. 2d ed. New York: St. Martin's Press, 1985. Nevins's article on Queen is perceptive and critically useful. His discussion focuses on Queen's novels, but his delineation of story motifs applies well to the short stories. Includes a complete bibliography.

Routley, Erik. *The Puritan Pleasures of the Detective Story: A Personal Monograph*. London: Victor Gollancz, 1972. Routley's book is a highly personal survey of detective fiction, but it includes several pages on the work of Ellery Queen that are fairly perceptive about Queen's characters in the novels.

Symons, Julian. *Bloody Murder: From the Detective Story to the Crime Novel, a History*. London: Faber & Faber, 1972. Symons's history of the detective story includes several pages on Ellery Queen in the chapter entitled "The Golden Age: The Thirties." His focus is on Queen's novels, but his observations apply equally well to the short stories.

Karen M. Cleveland Marwick

R

RON RASH

Born: Chester, South Carolina; September 25, 1953

PRINCIPAL SHORT FICTION

The Night the New Jesus Fell to Earth, and Other Stories from Cliffside, North Carolina, 1994

Casualties, 2000

Chemistry, and Other Stories, 2007

Burning Bright, 2010

OTHER LITERARY FORMS

Ron Rash also writes poetry and novels, and he explores similar themes in his poetry and his fiction. His writing often begins with an image, and as he develops the image, it leads him to the appropriate form, whether poetry or fiction, or both. Sometimes one of his poems leads to a short story, or a short story leads to a novel. The story "Speckled Trout" was the genesis of *The World Made Straight* (2006), and "Pemberton's Bride" was part of *Serena* (2008).

ACHIEVEMENTS

Ron Rash has accumulated honors for his work in both poetry and fiction. Several awards have acknowledged his ability to evoke the Mountain South of North Carolina and South Carolina. Rash was recognized with the General Electric Younger Writers Award in 1987. In 1996, he received the Sherwood Anderson Award for fiction. His story "Speckled Trout" was a PEN/O. Henry Award winner in 2005. "Into the Gorge" was a PEN/O. Henry Award winner in 2010. His collection *Chemistry, and Other Stories* was one of five fiction finalists in the PEN/Faulkner Fiction Awards. It also was named one of the Notable Books of 2007 by the Story Prize Committee and was given the Thomas Wolfe Memorial Literary Award by the Western North Carolina Historical Association in 2008. Short stories by Rash have appeared in *New Stories from the South: The Year's Best* and *The Best American Short Stories*.

In 2005, Rash received the James Still Award given by the Fellowship of southern Writers for writing of the Appalachian South. He was awarded an honorary doctoral degree from Gardner-Webb University, his alma mater, in 2009.

BIOGRAPHY

Rash was born in Chester, South Carolina, where his parents worked in the textile mills. Both later completed college and became educators. Rash was mostly raised in Boiling Springs, North Carolina, where his family moved when his father became an art professor at Gardner-Webb College (now University). Both his father's and mother's families had lived in western North Carolina for more than two centuries.

Growing up, Rash spent summers on his grandmother's farm near Boone, North Carolina. He credits his time living there and roaming in the woods as developing his powers of observation for the natural details he includes in his writing. An early influence on his storytelling was his grandfather, who, although he could not read or write, would make up intriguing stories based on the pictures in the books his grandson asked him to read. Rash's awareness of language was heightened by his childhood difficulty in pronouncing certain sounds and the subsequent speech therapy to correct the problem. Those sessions made him a careful listener, a useful skill for a writer.

Rash earned a B.A. in English from Gardner-Webb College and an M.A. in English from Clemson University. He briefly taught English in high school and then taught for several years at TriCounty Technical College in Pendleton, South Carolina. He developed a disciplined approach to writing despite the demands of teaching and began to publish his poetry and fiction in literary magazines. Part of his self-discipline Rash credits to his having to develop a daily schedule of practice as a runner on high school and college track teams.

The publication of his novel *One Foot in Eden* in 2002 brought his work to the attention of a wider audience. He was appointed as Parris Distinguished Professor of Appalachian Studies at Western Carolina University in Cullowhee, North Carolina, in 2003. He is married and has two children.

ANALYSIS

Ron Rash vividly portrays the Appalachian South. It is a region that has been in transition over the past 150 years from the rural past to the early industries of lumbering and textiles and finally to the modern world of interstates, tourism, and chain stores. Although Rash's characters are set in a specific culture and landscape, they grapple with universal human concerns. Some characters try to hold to what matters from the past while confronting change; others lose the connections to their family and the land.

As John Lang notes in *Appalachia and Beyond* (2006), "Whether in fiction or poetry, Rash's work is marked by striking imagery, lively storytelling, apt figurative language, and vividly realized characters." Rash's short stories are realistic in style and subject matter, but he occasionally includes supernatural beliefs from folk culture, as in "The Corpse Bird." His style includes precise details from the natural world.

Particular threads that run through his stories include themes of displacement and of the disappearance of culture. The setting of the stories is a place where land has been taken for a national park and where dams built for electrical power have flooded home sites. Farming has become less profitable, and inhabitants have turned to factory work or have migrated away. Thus, the younger generation has begun to lose connections with family and cultural traditions.

Rash's characters are working-class men and women, who find it difficult to get ahead. The need for money, work issues, and the effects of social class are often topics of the stories. He favors first-person or third-person-limited point of view, so that the reader is taken into the mind of the characters. Rash's sharp sense of character avoids stereotyping. He says in an interview published in *Appalachia and Beyond*, "part of my responsibility is to be true to lives that were often tragic and complex, to avoid sentimentalizing those lives. We live in a culture that doesn't value an understanding of the past."

"BACK OF BEYOND"

"Back of Beyond," chosen for *New Stories from the South: The Year's Best, 2008*, embodies the theme of loss of connections found in several of Rash's stories. In this story, from *Burning Bright*, methamphetamines are the scourge that causes a break between generations, within a family, and from the past. The main character, Parson, is a pawnbroker in a small town. He feels contempt for his methamphetamine-addicted customers who pawn anything to support their habits. At the beginning of the story, a young woman pawns her great-grandmother's churn and her high school ring, symbolically disposing of both her past and her future to pay for her addiction. With a high school diploma, she could have gone on to college or found a job, but, as an addict, she can concentrate only on her next fix.

Parson has developed a cold shell to focus only on the business aspects of these transactions. He says nothing to his brother when Danny, his brother's son, brings items from the old family farm to sell to support his methamphetamine habit. However, after the sheriff comes looking for a stolen shotgun that Danny had pawned, Parson decides to act.

When Parson drives up into the mountains to the site of the old home place, he is shocked to find that Danny's parents have surrendered the house to him, and they live in a trailer on the property. The electricity has been shut off, the trailer is a mess, and the house is mostly empty because Danny has sold everything. Danny, like the young woman at the beginning of the story, had other possibilities. He had done well enough in high school. His parents had been supportive, but once he was involved with methamphetamines, nothing else mattered.

Parson tries to help. He arranges to send Danny and his girlfriend to Atlanta. However, his brother and sister-in-law, despite their fear of what Danny is involved in, are not entirely happy. They rationalize their son's behavior.

The title, "Back of Beyond" is a phrase that refers to a remote or inaccessible place. While it literally describes the old farm, it also represents Danny, who has separated himself from normal life by his addiction. Parson, too, feels isolated from his family and is repulsed by the intrusion of meth into the lives he sees.

"INTO THE GORGE"

Themes of displacement, the contrast between the present and the past, and a dilemma over money run through this story, a 2010 PEN/O. Henry Award winner and a selection for *The Best American Short Stories, 2009*. It appears in *Chemistry, and Other Stories*.

Jesse, the sixty-eight-year-old protagonist of the story, gets into trouble when he goes to harvest some ginseng his father had planted on the old family land in a gorge that belongs at present to the national park. Jesse needs the money to supplement his income from a decreasing tobacco allotment. However, an alert young park ranger finds him and arrests him. Offended by the young ranger's attitude that Jesse is an old fool and by the ranger's refusal to listen to his explanation, Jesse reacts impulsively and manages to escape by maneuvering the ranger to fall down an old well he remembers. A manhunt ensues.

As Jesse attempts to elude the pursuers by heading up the gorge, he contrasts his situation with a search for his missing great-aunt many years ago. On a cold night, she, suffering from dementia, had wandered up the gorge toward the original homestead, where she had been born. The neighbors turned out to hunt for her but found her dead, evidently from hypothermia. Jesse recalls the respect that the neighbors showed when they brought the body home and how they spoke of his great-aunt's many skills and good character. Jesse contrasts this with the lack of respect shown to him by the ranger, who is not from the area. At the end of his strength, Jesse waits out the cold night.

Like his aunt, Jesse has lost the world that he has known. The conflict reflects the different views of Jesse and the ranger toward the land. For Jesse, the ginseng patch is still his family's land, but for the ranger Jesse's actions are criminal.

CHEMISTRY, AND OTHER STORIES

The thirteen stories in *Chemistry, and Other Stories* show Rash's range from the serious to the humorous.

While the stories are rooted in the particularities of Appalachian culture and history, the subjects and themes are universal: relationships between parents and children, the theme of displacement from one's personal and historical past, the perniciousness of drug culture, the tension between outsiders and natives, the persistence of the past, and respect for nature.

The theme of displacement is seen in "Not Waving But Drowning" as a young couple travel across Lake Jocassee, formed by a power company's damming of a river. Houses, barns, and mailboxes are left and can be seen through the water by the boaters. The young husband worries about his wife's succession of miscarriages and the strain those have placed on both of them. He feels that, in a sense, he is drowning. The title alludes to Stevie Smith's poem by the same name, where a drowning person's waving for help is misinterpreted as a greeting.

A lighter tone is present in "Their Ancient, Glittering Eyes." Sightings of a monster fish are reported in the Tuckaseegee River. The county's game warden, who hails from Wisconsin, dismisses the reports as tall tales. Three elderly men decide to prove him wrong. After much effort, they manage to hook the fish. It is a very old sturgeon, a fish once common in rivers all over the country, but seldom seen lately. Out of respect, they release it. The parallels between the ancient sturgeon and the men, old in experience and knowledge, are emphasized by the title of the story, a quote from William Butler Yeats's poem "Lapis Lazuli." That poem suggests that one should face death with a heroic joy. The men in the story, like the sturgeon, refuse to surrender to old age and death. Precise imagery about the fishing expedition adds realism to the story and also suggests an environmental message about respect for an endangered species.

Several stories center on strong emotions. In "Cold Harbor," the trauma of war affects a Korean War nurse as well as a soldier whose life she saves. The title refers to a Civil War battle. "The Projectionist's Wife" is a coming-of-age story. In "Chemistry," a father seeks solace in a more emotional religion after being hospitalized for depression. The main character of "Dangerous Love" runs away to the carnival with a knife thrower and becomes part of his act, willing to risk her life for an intense relationship.

BURNING BRIGHT

This volume continues to feature the history, characters, and landscape of the Mountain South. The title alludes to William Blake's "The Tyger," a poem in which the speaker questions why or how God could create a fearsome, destructive beast such as the tiger. The stories in *Burning Bright* similarly explore the violent or destructive tendencies of human beings; yet compassion also exists in the human heart.

In the title story, "Burning Bright," a woman comes to realize that her second husband, a seemingly kind man who has brought romance back into her life, is probably the arsonist who has been setting fires in the drought-stricken county. However, she decides to keep this knowledge to herself and, instead, prays for rain.

The evils of the Great Depression, the Civil War, and methamphetamine addiction cause people to make desperate choices in, respectively, "Hard Times," "Lincolnites," and "The Ascent" (the last a selection for *New Stories from the South: The Year's Best, 2010* and *The Best American Short Stories, 2010*).

In a story with humorously macabre overtones, "Dead Confederates," money troubles cause a young man to get involved in a scheme to dig up some graves in search of Confederate relics to sell. His hospitalized mother has no health insurance, and his job on the road crew cannot pay her bills and keep up his truck payments. The initial plan goes awry, but he does find some relics to sell for the much-needed cash. He eases his conscience with the thought that the Confederates whose graves he robbed had nice tombstones and were probably rich, and so, since they are dead, it is fair enough that his mother should benefit from what they left behind. This story, like "Lincolnites," concerns the Civil War history of western North Carolina, the home of many Union supporters, and is an amusing comment on the theme of the persistence and influence of the past.

OTHER MAJOR WORKS

LONG FICTION: *One Foot in Eden*, 2002; *Saints at the River*, 2004; *The World Made Straight*, 2006; *Serena*, 2008.

POETRY: *Eureka Mill*, 1998; *Among the Believers*, 2000; *Raising the Dead*, 2002

CHILDREN'S LITERATURE: *The Shark's Tooth*, 2001

BIBLIOGRAPHY

Antopol, Molly. Review of *Chemistry, and Other Stories*, by Ron Rash. *The southern Review* 44, no. 1 (Winter, 2008): 202. Praises the craftsmanship of Rash's clear, beautiful writing style. Plots of his stories may seem familiar, but details particularize them.

Baldwin, Kara. "'Incredible Eloquence': How Ron Rash's Novels Keep the Celtic Literary Tradition Alive." *The South Carolina Review* 39, no. 1 (Fall, 2006): 37-56. Focuses mainly on Rash's first two novels, but contains an excellent bibliography up to 2006.

Brown, Joyce Compton. "Ron Rash: The Power of Blood-Memory." In *Appalachia and Beyond: Conversations with Writers from the Mountain South*, edited by John Lang. Knoxville: University of Tennessee Press, 2006. Rash reveals biographical details, his concept of himself as an Appalachian writer, his sense of the importance of the past, and his awareness of how class shapes lives.

Maslin, Janet. "Rural Pride and Poverty and a Hen's Empty Nest." *The New York Times*, March 8, 2010, p. C4. Observes Rash's precision, eye for detail, and understatement in *Burning Bright*. Common subjects are conflicting views of morality, falling out of love.

Webb, Gina. "Tales of Bleak Hopeful Lives." *The Atlanta Journal-Constitution*, March 21, 2010, p. 4E. Describes the world of *Burning Bright* as a place where human kindness has grown scarce, yet still exists, despite economic hardship and other losses. Many characters have lost almost all but their pride.

Wilhelm, Randall. Review of *Chemistry, and Other Stories*, by Ron Rash. *Appalachian Heritage* 35, no. 4 (Fall, 2007):110-112. Notes Rash's skill in portraying the Appalachian region and his precise imagery. Focus is on the human heart, where both compassion and cruelty may dwell. Stories sometimes linger on the edge of resolution rather than ending with a strong closure.

Carol J. Luther

ELWOOD REID

Born: Cleveland, Ohio; 1966

PRINCIPAL SHORT FICTION
What Salmon Know, 1999

OTHER LITERARY FORMS

Elwood Reid's 1998 first novel, *If I Don't Six*, won critical acclaim with its roughly autobiographical tale of a university football player's ultimate rejection of the culture of violence and abuse surrounding the game. He subsequently published the novels *Midnight Sun* (2000) and *D. B.* (2004). Reid also worked in television, writing scripts for and producing the series *Cold Case, Close to Home*, and *Undercovers* and writing the screenplays for the television films *The Pennsylvania Miners' Story* (2002) and *Company Town* (2006).

ACHIEVEMENTS

Elwood Reid has been hailed as a major new voice, telling stories of the world of blue-collar men. Delighted critics have compared his short stories to those of Raymond Carver.

BIOGRAPHY

Brian Elwood Reid grew up in suburban Cleveland, Ohio. His father Thomas Reid was a teacher and coach in Willoughby, Ohio, where his mother, Charlotte Reid, née Ellwood, worked as a principal's secretary. The oldest of three children, Reid earned a full four-year athletic scholarship to play football at the University of Michigan after he graduated from high school in the mid-1980's.

After two years as an offensive lineman on the team, during which he never played in a varsity game, Reid ruptured several discs in his spine, ending his athletic career. For the next ten years, Reid, who dropped his first name Brian in favor of his middle name Elwood to signal a shift in character, stayed generally around the campus at Ann Arbor, Michigan. Continuing his education while working a variety of odd jobs, including stints as a bouncer, a carpenter, and a writing instructor, Reid earned a bachelor of arts degree in general studies and then a master of fine arts from the University of Michigan.

In 1996, he submitted a first version of his short story "What Salmon Know" to the annual fiction contest of *Gentleman's Quarterly* magazine. He did not win but placed among the final five, and *Gentleman's Quarterly* published his story in its February, 1997, issue. Contacts with an agent led Reid to write and publish his first, semiautobiographical novel *If I Don't Six*. After marriage to fellow writer Nina Reid and the birth of their daughter Sophia, Reid moved to Obernburg, New York, in 1997.

ANALYSIS

What Salmon Knew, Elwood Reid's collection of short stories, seeks to give a literary voice to characters who generally would not be expected to write about their experiences themselves. They are almost all blue-collar men who battle the hardships imposed by physically demanding yet financially unsatisfactory jobs, precarious love lives, and varying degrees of alcohol abuse. Many of the narratives read like the stories one would expect to hear when talking to one of these men in a bar or beside a fish-rich river.

Critics have compared Reid to Raymond Carver and detected emotional and stylistic similarities between Carver and Reid's protagonists. Like Carver, Reid strives hard to create for his characters genuine voices and to make them react realistically to experiences and circumstances that could be those of a frustrated working-class man.

Pain and suffering, whether emotional or physical, abound in Reid's fictional universe. Most of his narrators, and their friends and enemies, have been hit hard by life. There are also adult men who have become mentally disabled as a result of car accidents, and their fate could be read as a symbolic reminder of the harshness with which contemporary society treats working-class men.

As an author, Reid has worked hard to establish his blue-collar credentials. His characters exemplify some of the roughness existing in working-class life, yet the reader may be reminded of Jack Nicholson's character Bobby Dupea in Bob Rafaelson's film, *Five Easy Pieces* (1970). Bobby tried hard to eradicate his past as a concert pianist by becoming an oil-rig worker, yet he never lost the sense of being an outside observer of his new world. Occasionally, the reader may feel that such a slight but real distance exists between Reid and some of his most successfully drawn characters.

"What Salmon Know"

The tale of two rough, drunken carpenters fishing salmon in Alaska is Reid's first published story and a powerful reflection on humanity's relationship with nature. In "What Salmon Know," Craig and Marley, co-workers in the cold wilderness of Alaska, face a crisis in their friendship when Craig, the narrator, ponders an offer to work on "a new fruit-juice plant in Hawaii." The hardened Marley scoffs at Craig for even considering a "soft" life. The choice between Alaska and Hawaii, however, becomes almost too simplistic a dramatic device to illustrate two extremes.

Marley is a character who perceives of life as a series of self-set challenges and appears to be a vulgarized version of an Ernest Hemingway character. When he and Craig start fishing, he loses expensive equipment to the harsh river and yet is satisfied to land fish after fish, demonstrating that money itself has no value to him. Marley and Craig experience a certain fall from grace when, in their haste to make it back to the beer and the warmth of a nearby bar, they fail to kill the salmon. Instead, they carry the live fish on a string over their back as they walk to the bar.

In a typically graphic scene, the dying salmon spawn sperm and eggs onto the backs of the men. Astonished, they react with humor but Craig realizes that they have somehow violated an unwritten code of conduct.

Cleaning the fish outside the bar, they are approached by two soldiers. One soldier, who has caught a large salmon, cuts two fillets out of the live fish before releasing it to die in the water. This callous conduct enrages Marley to the point that he assaults the uncomprehending soldiers. As Craig says, the salmon will not die until they have spawned, and even the mortally wounded, mutilated, and profusely bleeding fish attempts to do exactly this. The salmon's single-minded purposefulness, to swim, spawn, and die, is what Craig admires in them. The salmon live and act like Craig and Marley would want to, guided by an absolute knowledge of their purpose in life.

"Overtime"

A well-constructed story with a clear moral message, "Overtime" focuses on the ethical choices made by its protagonist Drew, literally a man in the middle. After graduating from college, Drew accepts a job as a production manager who must ensure a steady output of product for the factory owner, Big Joe. While Big Joe enjoys his life in Puerto Rico, Drew must ask unwilling workers to work overtime operating the plant's

Elwood Reid (Getty Images)

metal presses. Somewhat of a moral coward, Drew picks the easiest target, Frank Cooper, whose "good blue-collar work ethic" makes him unable to say no to a request which puts the needs of the factory above those of his family. As Drew learns the next day, Frank's daughter has been murdered because Frank was working and unable to pick her up after her volleyball game. It is this pivotal plot detail that tells the reader of the high price Drew has paid by accepting this job. The workers blame Drew, and he accepts their verdict, even though his wife tells him the murder was just a coincidence. Out of guilt, Drew stops enforcing production quotas, gets fired, starts drinking, and is left by his upset wife. The story ends with Drew in a bar, punishing himself for his moral shortcomings.

"LAURA BOREALIS"

If many of Reid's short stories are tightly constructed and offer their readers a moral, "Laura Borealis" falls into a second category of stories which end like a snapshot taken at a moment of hilarious surprise. Jim, the narrator and protagonist, is an underemployed carpenter in Alaska. One afternoon at a local bar, he meets the beautiful Linda, who seems to appear out of nowhere. When his friend Sammy Landewski tells him of a rich Texan looking to remodel a decrepit lodge and Linda fails to return from the bathroom, Jim leaves for the lodge to try to secure employment. James Jaspers, the new owner, is a buffoonish rich man, somewhat typical of the wealthy characters in Reid's stories. Recently divorced, Jaspers wants to enjoy himself and install an outside hot tub. The fact that he shares a first name with the narrator is a storytelling detail which highlights the idea that it is only money, not morals, that distinguishes rich James from poor Jim. Together with his fellow carpenter and rival Marv Stacks, Jim begins work and is asked to come back the next day.

Indicative of the subtlety with which Reid constructs clues for his plot, there is a fictional newspaper report of Japanese tourists, who "considered it good luck to consummate a marriage under the northern lights," sitting in a Jacuzzi in Alaska. When Jaspers hires some exotic dancers for a pool party, Linda reappears under the stage name Laura Borealis, "aurora borealis" being the Latin name for the northern lights. While Jaspers passes out from drink, Jim and Linda/

Laura hit it off in the tub. This lasts until Marv's smelly dog jumps in, whereupon the bouncer accompanying the women points a gun at Jim, telling Jaspers, "It's your move." Rather than being terrified, Jim feels happy in that absurd situation with Linda, and the story suddenly ends. Reid's keen eye for the occasional absurdity of life is caught nicely here, and the story provides a comical counterpart to his more graphic fiction.

"BUFFALO"

"Buffalo" features many familiar elements of Reid's short fiction. Dan, the narrator, is a carpenter fighting alcoholism and relishing his friendship with his fishing buddy Murphy. Murphy has been left by his former wife Katrina and works in a factory demanding so much overtime of him that Murphy has to ask Dan to take his adult son Jeff to the town's "Frontier Days" to see the buffalo. Like a character in another story in the collection *What Salmon Know*, Jeff has been mentally disabled ever since he got drunk, hit a patch of black ice on the road, and skidded his car into a telephone pole. At the fair, Dan becomes distracted while drinking beer with a friendly woman, and Jeff enters the buffalo pen. As Jeff is burying his face in the smelly fur of a buffalo, Dan wonders whether Jeff's disability has saved him from a worse life.

For Reid, working-class life is hard on the men who live it, and their moments of happiness or satisfaction appear to be few and far between. What distinguishes the best of his short fiction is an often tightly constructed view of a harsh life of danger and violence, in which the wealthy do not show any concern for those less fortunate.

OTHER MAJOR WORKS

LONG FICTION: *If I Don't Six*, 1998; *Midnight Sun*, 2000; *D. B.*, 2004.

BIBLIOGRAPHY

Reid, Elwood. "Elwood Reid." Interview by Barbara Hoffert. *Library Journal* 129, no. 10 (June 1, 2004): 124. Reid discusses writing about "real life people" and gives his opinion of folk heroes.

_____. "My Body, My Weapon, My Shame." *Gentleman's Quarterly* 67 (September, 1997): 360-367. Reid tells of the brutality he encountered as a college football player for the University of Michigan and how his injury forced him to rethink his life. Written for the magazine that in February, 1997, published his first short story, "What Salmon Knew," and for which Reid has continued to write short stories and nonfiction articles, this piece offers a valuable background on the life of the author. The reader realizes that Reid has worked in many of the same jobs as his characters. Reid adds that his manual labor was motivated by his desire to extinguish the image of himself as a failed athlete and that he considered himself an oddity of a football player because he loved to read literature.

Rubin, Neal. "Harsh Portrait of Schembechler Is Latest Move in Former U-M Lineman's Literary Career." *Detroit Free Press* (September 26, 1999). Extensive biographical portrait of Reid by a reporter on the occasion of Reid's negative article about his former coach in the September, 1997, issue of *Gentleman's Quarterly*. Talks about Reid's life, his sports career, and his emergence as a writer of short fiction and novels. Provides informative background on Reid; shows how he is close to the subject matter of his stories and how much emphasis he places on rewriting his work until it satisfies him.

Rungren, Lawrence. "*What Salmon Know*." Review of *What Salmon Know*, by Elwood Reid. *Library Journal* 124 (July, 1999): 139. Brief review of Reid's short-story collection, generally positive in tone. Provides one-sentence summaries of some of the stories and likens Reid to authors Raymond Carver and Thom Jones. Recommends his fiction to public libraries for acquisition.

Smothers, Bonnie. "What Salmon Know." Review of *What Salmon Know*, by Elwood Reid. *Booklist* 95 (July, 1999): p. 1924. Very brief positive review of Reid's short fiction which focuses on its male-oriented themes and his description of the plight of working-class males. Discusses the collection's title story as representative of Reid's powerful and graphic writing style.

R. C. Lutz

MARK RICHARD

Born: Lake Charles, Louisiana; November 9, 1955

PRINCIPAL SHORT FICTION

"Twenty-One Days Back," 1980
"Ditch Water Cure," 1984
"The Confrontation," 1989
"Just Name Someplace," 1989
The Ice at the Bottom of the World, 1989
Charity, 1998
"All the Trimmings," 2002

OTHER LITERARY FORMS

Although Mark Richard (ree-SHARD) is known primarily as a short-story writer, his first novel, *Fishboy* (1993), quickly became a best-selling "cult classic," and he has made a name for himself as a dramatist. His stage adaption of the Raymond Chandler novel *The Little Sister* (1949) was awarded the Joseph Jefferson Award Citation for New Work (1994). Richard's teleplay credits include such award-winning series as *Chicago Hope*, *Party of Five*, and Home Box Office's *Huff*. He also has written several "made for television" films for Columbia Broadcasting Service, Showtime, and Turner Network Television. He coproduced *Stop-Loss*, his first feature-length screenplay, in conjunction with Music Television Films in 2008. Richard is also a frequent contributor to top-tier glossies and periodicals, including *Vogue, Esquire, Gentleman's Quarterly, George, Detour, The New York Times, The Oxford American,* and *Spin*. He is best known for his gritty, immersive reportage, in which he tells a story by living the story. He is also an acclaimed music journalist and has profiled such rock icons as Tom Waits and Frank Zappa. He also has worked as a correspondent for the British Broadcasting Corporation.

ACHIEVEMENTS

Mark Richard's stories have appeared in *The New Yorker*, *Harper's*, *Anateus*, *The Quarterly*, *The Paris Review*, *The Oxford American*, *Grand Street*, *Equator*, *Esquire*, *Shenandoah*, and *The Pushcart Prize Annual*. In 1985, Richard was awarded the Virginia Prize for Fiction, and in 1987 he took top prize in the Hemingway Short Story Contest. That same year, his story "Happiness of the Garden Variety" was awarded the Goodheart Prize for Fiction by *Shenandoah*. The New York Foundation for the Arts awarded Richard a fellowship in 1989, and in 1990 his debut story collection, *The Ice at the Bottom of the World*, won the PEN/Ernest Hemingway Foundation Award for First Fiction and the Whiting Foundation's Writers' Award. The same year, Richard was awarded a National Endowment for the Arts Fellowship and the National Magazine Award for Fiction for his story "The Theory of Man." In 1992, he received a Tennessee Williams Fellowship from Sewanee: The University of the South; four years later, he was awarded the Mary Francis Hobson Medal for Arts and Letters by Chowan University.

BIOGRAPHY

The only son of Cajun Creole French parents, Mark Richard was born in 1955 in Lake Charles, Louisiana, not far from the Chennault Air Force Base, where his father, Edgar Richard, Jr., worked as an engineer for the National Aeronautics and Space Administration (NASA). Mark Richard's father resigned from his post at NASA to work as a forester, first in Kansas and Texas and later in Virginia. The family settled in Southampton County, where Richard's father worked for the Union Bag-Camp Paper Corporation.

As a child, Richard suffered from crippling hip defects and spent more than ten years in and out of charity hospitals. His family doctor misdiagnosed him as "retarded," and he was ever after referred to as a "special child" by his family and neighbors. Confined to hospital beds and body casts for months and years at time after a series of surgeries, Richard became a great lover

of books; his mother toted grocery bags full of them to his bedside from the library in Franklin.

At the age of thirteen, Richard became the youngest disc jockey ever to broadcast on American radio. At WYSR-AM in Franklin, Richard put together his own "free-form show." That meant, he told *BOMB* magazine in 1998, "knowing how to modulate. . . . You can't sustain the high pitch for very long. You need the low pitch, the dead air, you need to take breaths." Richard credits his stint as a deejay with his talent for "writing space." "You don't really learn that," he says, "unless you learn music or do something unusual where the audience has only one working sense."

Richard studied journalism and engineering at Washington and Lee University. He dropped out in his junior year and spent his early twenties crewing a string of commercial fishing trawlers and shrimpers out of North Carolina and the Florida Keys. Richard describes the experience as the most important of his young adult life; "exhilarating," "terrifying," "physically and mentally demanding," life on the water gave him the chance, rare in postmodern America, to "see what [he] was made of." What World War I was to Ernest Hemingway, the rough work of the trawlers was to Richard.

While he was digging ditches in east Texas, one of Richard's professors submitted his story "Twenty-One Days Back" to *The Atlantic*'s American Short Story Contest. It was published by *Shenandoah* in 1981. After graduating that spring, Richard rambled from one odd job to the next, making just enough to support his writing life. He sold real estate in Glouchester, wrote articles for a military newspaper in Virginia Beach and speeches and advertising copy for a doomed political campaign, and had a short stint as a private detective. Richard continued to compose stories, sending a steady stream to *Esquire*, all of which ended up in the slush pile. "But the stories always popped out," one of the magazine's fiction editors Tom Jenks said. While on vacation in the Outer Banks, Jenks dropped in on Richard and told him that if he was serious about writing, he had to move to New York. Then one day Richard sold everything he owned, went to New York, knocked on Jenks's door, and said, "Here I am. What do I do now?"

Shortly after moving to New York, Richard became a student of the famed editor Gordon Lish. It was in Lish's workshop that Richard met Jennifer Allen, a friend he would meet again when profiling Waits in Los Angeles and, not long after that, marry. With Jenks's help, Richard secured Georges Borchardt as an agent; Banks arranged for several of Richard's early stories to be published in *Esquire*. Almost five years after arriving in Manhattan in Maui shorts and sandals, Richard got an advance from Knopf for *The Ice at the Bottom of the World*.

Doubleday/Anchor collected eleven more of Richard's stories for his second collection, *Charity*, and also published his first novel, *Fishboy*. Richard moved to Los Angeles after the debut of *Fishboy* to write for television and film. He settled with his wife and their three sons in Palos Verdes, California.

ANALYSIS

Mark Richard has been called the heir apparent to William Faulkner and Flannery O'Connor, and his work is popularly conceived as a postmodern manifestation of that tradition known as the school of southern gothicism. This is a generalization many critics have made because of Richard's use of a multitude of southern settings and dialects, his prioritization of the socially outcast, and his gritty mode of realism. However, it should be said that Richard's fiction, like that of all writers who are incidentally southern, cannot be explained absolutely by the regional typecast. To classify Richard's work as "hick lit," "dirty," or "K-Mart realism" is, in some ways, to downplay the greater import of his fiction, which, if it is linked to any southern tradition, connects with that strain in Faulkner and O'Connor that speaks of a sympathy for the grotesque in humankind generally and is thereby a sign of the universality of the human experience that transcends the merely regional.

A striking characteristic of Richard's style is his attention to the musicality of language, to its ability to affect meaning inexplicably, like the shift from a major to a minor key in a melody. He has often remarked that the way a word or series of words sounds is as important as the meaning of those words. It is this emphasis of the aural sense that lends a subtle lyricism to Richard's dialogues and expositional scenes, in which

spelling and grammar are sacrificed for the sake of sound and tempo.

"HAPPINESS OF THE GARDEN VARIETY"

"Happiness of the Garden Variety" is one of the most insistently lyrical of Richard's stories, a tonal atmosphere that is reinforced by the breathless, grammatically loose, yet vaguely metrical delivery of the narrator, who recounts how he and his friend, Steve Willis, inadvertently kill their landlord's horse and, very awkwardly, try to bury the animal at sea. That narrator addresses the reader directly, as if inviting the reader into his confidence by telling the reader what the narrator and Willis "ended up having to do to Vic's horse Buster." This sense of exclusivity, of the nuance inherent in a particular oral telling, underscores the thematic through-line of the story: that meaning made with language is personal and therefore unstable.

Vic cannot read, and so he mispronounces words, lumps his possessions into groups (Vic's humans, Vic's animals, things Vic got for free or from "good deal-making"), and misuses household chemicals, which is the beginning of what happened to Buster. The fallout of Vic's illiteracy dramatizes the practical distance between what can be known by having a word "literally," that is, understanding how the shapes of the letters correspond to the sounds that denote meaning, and the having of a word through conversation, the way the word sounds. Vic's persistent mispronunciation of "aquamarine" suggests that meaning is codified individually. Vic's word "ackerine" means something to him, and so it comes to mean something to Willis and the narrator. It is this collusion of meaning that ultimately reconciles the three men as, driving home from the First Flight Lounge, Vic welcomes his two friends back into the confidence of his private language by including them in his scheme to build a shed for his good-deal washing machines and painting it-- "what color would [you] boys say would look good?"-- "Ackerine!"

"STRAYS"

Perhaps Richard's best-known story, "Strays" is the aptly titled story of two young brothers left in the care of their card-playing alcoholic uncle, also aptly named Trash. Uncle Trash arrives on the scene when the boys' mother slips away and their father must enlist the help of his brother, the nearest of the father's relatives with a car. What Uncle Trash visits upon the boys in his advantage is the sense that nothing, not even for the innocence of children, is sacred. He swindles their nickels and toy trucks, even the shirts off their backs, in a card game. "Let that be a lesson to [you]," he says, leaving the boys alone again, stark naked and with nothing to eat. It is when the children are left to themselves that the reader glimpses the shade of resilience, even love, in spite of their serial neglect. The stray mutts that gather beneath the boys' bedroom at night mirror the scavenging of the boys' hearts and come to represent, at once, their solidarity and their isolation.

At each pivot in the story, the boys act out this bizarre admixture of hope and brutality: When Uncle Trash abandons them in his search of drink, the boys catch "handfuls" of lightning bugs, and rather than collect the bugs in a Mason jar, the boys "smear bright yellow on [their] shirts." The second time Trash leaves, the older boy comforts his brother with the promise of the dogs' return, but instead of luring them into the trailer to be petted, the older boy stomps on the floorboards and watches them scatter. When their uncle deserts the boys a third and final time, they accidentally burn down the house by dousing one of the strays with bug spray and then lighting a match to the stray's ear to draw out a tick. These kinds of actions, though they are imbued with a kind of innocence, subvert the image of the boys as pitiable creatures. Poor as they are, they are agents of their own will, a point that seems to affirm that nothing being sacred does not mean that nothing can be.

"GENTLEMAN'S AGREEMENT"

The driving irony of *Charity*'s opening story, "Gentleman's Agreement," is cued by the title and describes the disjoint between a father's adult way of perceiving and understanding and his son's relative naïveté. After he breaks the "friendly family [car's]" windshield with an errant rock, the father warns the child that if he does it again, the father will nail the child's "rock-throwing hand" to the shed wall. When the father returns to fighting an out-of-control forest fire, the child is left to consider and reconsider their no-rock-throwing covenant, eventually deciding that there was nothing in the agreement about setting aside a stone in the tin shed so that "when he grew up and was older than the old man,

he could . . . shake the thing up to the old man's face and say, See? Here is a rock I didn't throw!" However, the child could not resist the volley of sound the stone made when he tossed it onto the tin shed or the promise of the explosive bang of the "Adam bomb" keystone, which he heaves, losing his balance on the rock pile, and by which he is clobbered in the head. After returning from the hospital, stitched up by a ether-addicted quack, the child willingly submits when his father takes him behind the shed, toolbox in hand. He lifts up his "rock-throwing hand," but his father goes to work, instead, on the ragged stitches. This final scene implies that though the boy does not understand value in the same way that his father does, the boy has submitted to his father, trusting his father's judgment, just as the old man has reevaluated the boy as a boy, fallible in his judgments but worthy of forgiveness.

OTHER MAJOR WORKS

LONG FICTION: *Fishboy: A Ghost's Story*, 1993.
PLAY: *The Little Sister*, pr. 1994.
SCREENPLAY: *Stop-Loss*, 2008
TELEPLAYS: *Party of Five*, 1998-1999 (three episodes); *Delta Wedding* (adaptation of Eudora Welty's novel), 2001; *Chicago Hope*, 1999-2000 (two episodes); *Huff*, 2004-2006 (fourteen episodes).
NONFICTION: "The Music of Chance," 1994; "The Ten Commandments of a Childhood," 1995; "Stumping for Jesus," 1996; "Captain Beefheart," 1998; "Who Is That Man Tied to the Mast?" (memoir), 1998; "Rolltop Mantra of the Outer Banks," 2003; *House of Prayer No. 2: A Writer's Journey Home*, 2011 (memoir).

BIBLIOGRAPHY

Conway, Martha. "Water Voices." *The San Francisco Review of Books* 18, nos. 4-5 (1993): 7-8. Includes interview with Richard in which he describes the real-life inspirations for his novel *Fishboy*.
Dolan, J. D. "Mark Richard." *BOMB* 65 (Fall, 1998). Richard discusses his influences, Magical Realism, and the musicality of language.
Harshaw, Tobin. "Fever Dreams." *The New York Times Book Review*, December 27, 1998, p. 16. Reviews *Fishboy* and argues that Richard is both a sentimentalist and a literary P. T. Barnum.

Norman, Michael. "A Book in Search of a Buzz: The Marketing of a First Novel." *The New York Times*, January 30, 1994, p. 3. Discusses Richard's rise on the American literary scene and explores some of the difficulties of marketing literary fiction in the United States.

_____. "Reader by Reader, Town by Town, a New Novelist Builds a Following." *The New York Times*, February 6. 1994, p. 3. Follows Richard on his promotional tour of *Fishboy* through the American South.

Ulin, David L. "Portrait of an Artist's Spiritual Awakening." *Los Angeles Times*, February 27, 2011, p. E10. A review of Richard's memoir *House of Prayer No. 2* offers insights into the author's early days and his success as a writer.

York, Jack Adam. "Sympathy; Or, Lines for a Book Jacket: Listening to Mark Richard." *Shenandoah* 54 no. 1 (Spring/Summer, 2004): 5-23. Discusses Richard's ability to ennoble grotesque characters through his narrators' sympathy, which he dramatizes by their acquisition of the secondary character's idiom.

M. K. Shaddix

TOMÁS RIVERA

Born: Crystal City, Texas; December 22, 1935
Died: Fontana, California; May 16, 1984

PRINCIPAL SHORT FICTION

. . . no se lo tragó la tierra/ . . . and the earth did not part, 1971 (also pb. as *This Migrant Earth,* 1985; *. . . and the earth did not devour him,* 1987).
"Eva y Daniel," 1972
"Looking for Borges," 1973
"El Pete Fonseca," 1974
"Las salamandras," 1974
"Inside the Window," 1977
The Harvest: Short Stories, 1989 (bilingual)

OTHER LITERARY FORMS

Tomás Rivera (toh-MAHS rih-VAYR-ah) wrote numerous essays, including "Into the Labyrinth: The Chicano in Literature." *Always, and Other Poems* was published in 1973 and *The Searchers: Collected Poetry* was published in 1990. Many of his essays on education and his short stories appeared in anthologies, magazines, and textbooks. A collection of Rivera's work, *Tomás Rivera: The Complete Works*, was published in 1991.

ACHIEVEMENTS

Tomás Rivera's novella *. . . and the earth did not part* won the Premo Quinto Sol National Chicano Award in 1970. As chancellor of the University of California at Riverside, Rivera is credited with bringing Chicano studies to the academic forefront. He was a founding member of the Tomás Rivera Policy Institute, which in 2010 was headquartered at the University of southern California, with a satellite office at Columbia University. The institute is considered one of the nation's premier Latino think tanks.

BIOGRAPHY

Tomás Rivera was born in Crystal City, Texas, on December 22, 1935, the son of Mexican migrant workers who were part of the influx of Mexican laborers into the United States in the 1930's and 1940's. Much of Rivera's boyhood was spent alongside his parents as they worked in the fields. Even through his junior college days, Rivera worked as a farm laborer in Texas, a fact that played a key role in his writing and, later, his work as an educational advocate on behalf of the Chicano worker.

Rivera graduated from Texas State University in San Marcos with a B.A. in English, and he earned a master's degree in English and administration at Southwest Texas State University. In 1969, Rivera received a doctorate in Spanish literature at the University of

Oklahoma. He served as vice president of administration at the University of Texas at San Antonio and executive vice president at the University of Texas at El Paso. In 1979, Rivera became the first Chicano to earn the distinction of appointment to a chancellor's post in the University of California system--a significant honor for one of such humble beginnings and a testament to the perseverance of his individualistic spirit.

ANALYSIS

Although his writing career was comparatively brief, Tomás Rivera developed a singular voice that spoke for a whole group of displaced people. It was his dual passions, academic advocacy and literature, which fueled his desire to have the Chicano experience regarded seriously by the greater academic community. In regard to his writing style, critic Juan Bruce-Novoa, commenting on . . . *and the earth did not part*, states that Rivera "achieves . . . the evocation of an environment with a minimum of words." Rivera admires Sherwood Anderson and William Faulkner and Mexican writer Juan Rulfo.

In the novella . . . *and the earth did not part* and in such stories as "The Zoo Island," Rivera conveys his characters' thoughts seemingly without editing or judgment. He even resists inclusion of how a line of dialogue is delivered, leaving the interpretation open to the reader. His style has a documentary feel to it, bearing witness to the years of migrant work Rivera did that undoubtedly honed his ear for dialogue. He admired the field-workers' spiritual strength, but he did not sentimentalize his subjects, recognizing, perhaps, the potential people have to be cruel or indifferent to even their "own kind." The idea of searching provided a compelling metaphor for Rivera, who saw in it the origin of American identity. His characters are often adolescent boys, and as such, the ones who most yearn for inclusion while fiercely protecting their turf. The young boys of his short stories struggle to remain loyal to their mothers' wishes but gravitate toward the forbidden world of sex under cover of darkness. The women are often lost, unable to pull their spouses, fathers, or sons from the wreckage of a migrant worker's transitory lifestyle. There is some indication Rivera had written another novel, "La casa grande," but no

such manuscript was found among his papers after he died of a heart attack in 1984.

. . . AND THE EARTH DID NOT PART

Although he wrote essays and short fiction, . . . *and the earth did not part*, a novella set in the 1970's in southern Texas, is the centerpiece of Rivera's literary career. It comes closest to re-creating what one would imagine the lives of field-workers to be: gritty, dismal, and rife with daily challenges to survival. Narrators in the twelve thematically connected pieces vary from an omniscient third person in "His Hand in His Pocket," concerning a boy's perilous association with a murderous Mexican couple, to a dialogue between two young Mexican students in "It Is Painful." In the latter story, one of the Mexican boys is attacked by white boys in the bathroom, but only he faces expulsion. In the title story, a boy has seen several relatives die of tuberculosis. He then grapples with an unjust God who also strikes down his father with sunstroke as he labors in the fields. After his kid brother also succumbs to the heat, the boy curses God and is later amazed when the earth does not swallow him, as he had been told would happen. While contemporary critics regard . . . *and the earth did not part* primarily as a novel narrated by one central character, it can also be viewed as a mosaic of short stories from a variety of perspectives. Regardless how one might interpret the work, there is an overwhelming sense of loss throughout; however, Rivera also celebrates the indomitable spiritual power of the Mexican field-worker.

"ZOO ISLAND"

From *The Harvest: Short Stories* collection, "Zoo Island" is a reference to Monkey Island at Brackenridge Park Zoo. The story concerns a fifteen-year-old Mexican boy, Juan, who spontaneously decides to start a census of all the migrant workers on an Iowa farm where he lives with his family. Juan discusses tactics of census-gathering with his father as they journey to a field filled with thistles they have been hired to clear. His father proudly comments that he does not use gloves, a fact he believes proves his stamina to the white bosses. Juan decides that he will post the results of the census and give the farm a name, like a real town. He counts the families who live in converted chicken coops easily, but he has a hard time getting Don Simon, an old man, to cooperate. After responding to questions about his origins rather elusively, Don Simon tells the boy that, "by counting yourself, you begin everything." Juan names the farm Zoo Island, feeling triumphant now that he has accounted for each and every one of his people, including a newborn child. The notion of the accountability of people, Rivera suggests, is what helps to give greater significance to otherwise overlooked lives. Along the way, one also understands that these human beings live in chicken coops, not houses as they should. Like chickens, they are valued only for their productivity, and not, like the human beings they are, for their spirit or character.

"THE SALAMANDERS"

"The Salamanders" is a first-person narrative from the perspective of a child migrant worker trapped penniless with his family in a small town, Crystal Lake, in northern Iowa. As the rain enters a fourth week, they are forced out of Minnesota for lack of work, arriving in yet another place with no prospects. He, his parents, and siblings drive from farm to farm in search of work. Most farmers will only say no from inside the safety of their houses. The constant rejections cause the boy to feel separated from his mother and father. When the car's wiring shorts while going through the rain, they are forced to sleep in the car by the side of a road. Seeing his sleeping family, the boy experiences further isolation. After days of no work, they finally find a farmer who tells them they can start harvesting beets from a flooded field as soon as the water level goes down. That night, sick of sleeping together in the car, the family pitches a tent at the end of the field. What most profoundly affects the boy is waking during the night to find that salamanders have infested the tent. They begin killing the salamanders, and the boy notes his strange satisfaction in squeezing the life out of them. Finally, he catches one and, looking deeply into its eyes, feels the "very pure" sensation of "original death." Like many of Rivera's stories, "The Salamanders" refrains from judging the characters, thus allowing the horror and desperation of the situation to speak for itself. The powerful emotional impact of the story lies in its minimalist approach.

"FIRST COMMUNION"

In "First Communion," Rivera tells a story imbued with an understanding of the conflict between spiritual purity and desires of the flesh. After the male adolescent in *. . . and the earth did not part* has done battle with the Devil and challenged God, he describes what happens prior to his passage from boyhood into the life of an adult Catholic. The priest talks to the gathered children about "venial sins," impelling them to confess all their sins or suffer the damnation of Hell. The boy dresses excitedly the following morning for his Communion. On his way to church, he secretly watches a man and woman making love in a tailor's shop. Disturbed and stimulated by what he has witnessed, he cannot bring himself to tell the priest. Later at home, he feels different, as though it had been he who committed the "sin of the flesh." He recalls a missionary discussing "the grace of God," and the boy finds that he now wants to know more about everything. Rivera shifts between direct, present-tense dialogue and a first-person recollection of the event, re-creating accurately how human memory works--it brings details up without warning. For a boy on the cusp of a momentous rite of passage, the sex act in particular is fraught with both allure and danger, searing itself forever into his memory.

OTHER MAJOR WORKS

POETRY: *Always, and Other Poems*, 1973; *The Searchers: Collected Poetry*, 1990.

NONFICTION: "Inside the Labyrinth: The Chicano in Literature," 1971; "Mexican American Literature," 1975; "Chicano Literature: Fiesta of the Living," 1979; CHICANO LITERATURE: The Establishment of Community," 1982.

MISCELLANEOUS: *Tomás Rivera: The Complete Works*, 1991.

BIBLIOGRAPHY

Calderón, Héctor. "The Emergence of the Chicano Novel: Tomás Rivera's *. . . y no se lo tragó la tierra* and the Community of Readers." In *Narratives of Greater Mexico: Essays on Chicano Literary History, Genre, and Borders*. Austin: University of Texas Press, 2004. Calderón examines the work of

Rivera and six other writers who created an "American Mexican literature" derived from Mexican literary traditions and genres. In addition to analyzing these writers' works, Calderón discusses their perspectives on their place in American Mexican literature.

Castañeda-Shular, Antonia, Tomás Ybarra-Frautos, and Joseph Sommers, eds. *Chicano Literature: Text and Context*. Englewood Cliffs, N.J.: Prentice-Hall, 1972. A rich source of information on Mexican American life, history, criticism, and literature, with Rivera's place in the Chicano literary canon clearly delineated.

Grajeda, Ralph F. "Tomás Rivera's Appropriation of the Chicano Past." In *Modern Chicano Writers: A Collection of Critical Essays*. Edited by Joseph Sommers and Tomás Ibarra-Frausto. Englewood Cliffs, N.J.: Prentice-Hall, 1979. Grajeda thoroughly examines and analyzes Rivera's *. . . and the earth did not part*, putting it into a historical context.

Johannessen, Lene M. "Exercises in Liminality: Tomás Rivera's *. . . and the earth did not devour him*." In *Threshold Time: Passage of Crisis in Chicano Literature*. New York: Rodopi, 2008. Analyzes the cultural, social, and political history of works of Mexican American literature, including Rivera's novella.

Kanellos, Nicolás, ed. *Short Fiction by Hispanic Writers Of the United States*. Houston, Tex.: Arte Público Press: 1993. Calling Rivera "one of the most beloved figures in Chicano literature," Kanellos offers an overview of Rivera's academic career, and an introduction to *. . . and the earth did not part*. This anthology also includes the short stories "First Communion" and "The Salamanders."

_____. "Tomás Rivera." *The Hispanic Literary Companion*. Detroit: Visible Ink, 1996. Includes quotes from other criticism of *. . . and the earth did not part*, a biography, and Rivera's short stories "Zoo Island" and "The Salamanders" from *The Harvest: Short Stories*. There is also a listing of his writings. Kanellos discusses Rivera's deep devotion to Chicano education and his belief in the ability of literature to enlighten and inform.

Leal, Luis. "Tomás Rivera." In *A Luis Leal Reader*. Edited by Ilan Stavans. Evanston, Ill.: Northwestern University Press, 2007. Leal was an internationally recognized authority on Mexican, Chicano, and Latin American literature. This collection of his essays includes a piece about Rivera.

Martínez, Manuel Luis. "Arriving at el Pueblo Libre: The Insistence of Americanismo." In *Countering the Counterculture: Rereading Postwar American Dissent from Jack Kerouac to Tomás Rivera*. Madison: University of Wisconsin Press, 2003. Analyzes the postwar works of "migrant writers," such as Rivera, and fiction by the Beats and other writers, focusing on depictions of democracy and a progressive culture. Argues that the migrant writers offered a truly radical and inclusive view of democracy.

Saldívar, Ramón. "Tomas Rivera." In *Heath Anthology of American Literature*. Vol. 1. Lexington, Mass.: D.C. Heath, 1994. A compact biography covering Rivera's life, works, and literary influences. This inclusion in a two-volume, lengthy anthology divided according to broad literary periods in America contains an excerpt from *. . . and the earth did not part*. There is a useful long essay, balancing between historical and literary details, which provides a broad background from 1945 through the 1980's.

Stavans, Ilan. *Art and Anger: Essays on Politics and the Imagination*. Albuquerque: University of New Mexico Press, 1996. Nineteen far-ranging essays with a focus on the difficulties of translating Latin American literature and the Spanish language while retaining their integrity. These essays provide a broad context, thus helping to see Rivera's position as a Chicano who bridges the gap between the North American and the Latino.

Tatum, Charles M. "Contemporary Chicano Novel." *Chicano Literature*, Boston: New Mexico State University. Twayne, 1982. 102-137. Beginning with Jose Antonio Villareal's *Pocho* (1959), this chapter places Rivera's *. . . and the earth did not part* at the forefront of modern Chicano literature.

Vigil-Piñón, Evangelina. "Un Mundo Entero: Tomás Rivera and His World." In *U.S. Latino Literature: A Critical Guide for Students and Teachers*, edited by Harold Augenbraum and Margarite

Fernández Olmos under the auspices of the Mercantile Library of New York. Westport, Conn.: Greenwood Press, 2000. Contains a short biography of Rivera, a discussion of the themes and forms in . . . *and the earth did not part*, and suggestions on how to teach this work to students.

Nika Hoffman

ELIZABETH MADOX ROBERTS

Born: Perryville, Kentucky; October 30, 1881
Died: Orlando, Florida; March 13, 1941

PRINCIPAL SHORT FICTION

The Haunted Mirror, 1932
Not by Strange Gods, 1941

OTHER LITERARY FORMS

Elizabeth Madox Roberts is best known for her novels, particularly her first, *The Time of Man* (1926), a story of Kentucky hill people, and *The Great Meadow* (1930), her epic story of American pioneers in Kentucky in the 1770's. Her other five novels were less well received and are not well known. Of her three collections of poetry, only *Under the Tree* (1922, 1930) had much success.

ACHIEVEMENTS

While still in undergraduate school, Elizabeth Madox Roberts won the Fiske Prize for a group of poems highly praised by critics. She later won the John Reed Memorial Prize in 1928 and the Poetry Society of South Carolina Prize in 1931 for her poetry. Her first novel, *The Time of Man* (1926), earned her an international reputation when it was translated into several languages. Her story "The Sacrifice of the Maidens" won second prize in the O. Henry Memorial Award contest in 1932. In 1936 and 1937, she was awarded doctor of letters degrees by Centre College in Danville, Kentucky, and by the University of Louisville. She was elected to the National Institute of Arts and Letters in 1940.

BIOGRAPHY

Elizabeth Madox Roberts was born in Perryville, Kentucky, on October 30, 1881, the second of eight children. Her family moved to Springfield, Kentucky, in 1894, where she spent most of her life. She was educated at Covington Institute, a private school in Springfield, and later attended high school in the city of Covington. After graduation, from 1900 to 1910 she taught classes both privately and in public high schools in the area.

Roberts did not enter college until she was thirty-six, when, at the urging of a family friend, she enrolled in the University of Chicago. Influenced and encouraged by the poet Harriet Monroe, Roberts concentrated on poetry, publishing *Under the Tree* in 1922. After graduation, she returned to Kentucky to devote herself full time to writing. Her first novel, *The Time of Man*, brought her several years of critical recognition, culminating in her second great success, *The Great Meadow*, in 1930.

From 1935 until her death, Roberts suffered from skin infections, nervous disorders, chronic anemia, and Hodgkins disease. In spite of failing health, she continued to work on various projects, one of which was an epic account of Daniel Boone. She died on March 13, 1941, in Orlando, Florida, and was buried in Springfield, Kentucky. Her second collection of short stories, *Not by Strange Gods*, appeared just after her death.

ANALYSIS

Although Elizabeth Madox Roberts once wrote, "I do not think that the 'short story' is a satisfactory form or that anything very good can be done with it," at least half a dozen of the stories in her two collections are haunting poetic transformations of the older regional tale into the modern lyrical short story--a genre more popularly mastered by Eudora Welty and Katherine Anne Porter. Unlike the local colorists, with whom she is often compared, Roberts does not focus on rural life to celebrate the exotic quaintness of its inhabitants, but rather, in such stories as "On the Mountainside" and "The Haunted Palace," to explore the most basic human conflicts resulting from rural life.

Moreover, her poetic style is not merely a decorative device to sentimentalize the rural world, but rather a means by which she can transform the stuff of that world into embodiments of the inner life of her characters. Although the general critical consensus is that Roberts is a competent but not a brilliant writer of short stories, this view may be the result of an unexamined bias toward the novel, as well as the failure of many critics to appreciate how she uses poetic language to create stories that, while grounded in rural reality, are haunted by the lyrical longing of their characters.

"THE HAUNTED PALACE"

Roberts's most famous story, "The Haunted Palace," whose title is derived from the poem in Edgar Allan Poe's "Fall of the House of Usher," focuses on an old antebellum mansion that sharecropper Hubert and his wife Jess plan to buy--a house so possessed by all those who have lived in it that it becomes a hallucinatory embodiment to Jess of her own inner conflicts. The most compelling scene in the story occurs when the couple bring thirty sheep into the grand rooms of the old house to give birth; surrounded by the bloody and bleating beginnings of life, Jess confronts a ghostly apparition and beats at it with her club while it beats her with identical blows: "Herself and the creature then were one. . . . She and the creature had beaten at the mirror from opposite sides." Then she knows she has been flailing at her own reflection and has broken the great mirror. The shattering of the mirror is like the breaking of a spell, and the story ends with the quiet contentment of the sheep nursing their lambs. The story thus ends in the triumph of the couple's prosaic present reality over the past romance of the old nobility.

"ON THE MOUNTAINSIDE"

Set in the Kentucky mountains, "On the Mountainside" is Roberts's poetic treatment of the classic conflict of highlands people: whether to stay in their ancestral home or to leave the hills for the cities below. The central character, Newt Reddix, having been introduced to the mysteries of book learning, feels he has received a report from the outside world and is compelled to leave to attend a school down in the settlements.

After traveling on foot through the woods for days, Newt spends the night at a house where he meets an old man on his way back to the mountains after having lived in the settlement for years. Calling himself a traitor to his God when he left the mountains, the old man describes a spring from his childhood. When Newt, "eager to enter the drama of the world," says he got a drink from that same spring a week before, the old man is astonished, cautioning Newt that the places he knew as a boy will never go out of his head. Although this prophetic warning puts terror into Newt's thoughts, making him "bereft, divided, emptied of his every wish," he watches the young wife of the house spread quilts before the fire for him and takes delight in seeing her strong body and the strange room; thus an "amorous pulse" is laid on his determination to go to the settlements to get the learning he cherishes.

"THE SACRIFICE OF THE MAIDENS"

The single scene at the heart of this story is a religious service in which several young girls take their vows to become nuns in the small chapel of a rural convent. The scene is described from the perspective of an adolescent boy, Felix Barbour, whose sister Anne is one of the postulants. The story moves back and forth between poetic descriptions of the ritual as a process of death and regeneration and Felix's half-dream reveries about his past realization of the loveliness of girls, their "soft round flesh and the shy, veiled laughter that hid under their boldness."

Over the priest's repeated intonations of "Hail Mary, full of grace, Blessed art thou among women," Felix recalls Anne and other girls as they were before taking the vows, "soft to touch . . . given to laughter, easy to come to tears, easy with pity, easy with anger" who easily became women. Fascinated by one of the girls, who enter the chapel dressed as brides, Felix longs to know her name, and wishes to "say it in his mind, to name his sense of her loveliness with a word." Ironically, this desire is fulfilled at precisely the moment when the girl becomes inaccessible to Felix's fantasies--the moment when the priest utters the name she was known by in the world, "Aurelia," and pronounces the name she will be known by henceforth--Sister Mary Dolores."

"THE SCARECROW"

Joan, the central figure of "The Scarecrow," one of Roberts's most haunting stories, can "scarcely endure to let any other flesh touch her own." One of her chores is to keep the crows out of her father's cornfield, a task she performs with the aid of a scarecrow she has made from some of her own clothes. The central scene in the story occurs when she falls asleep in the field and dreams about Tony Wright, a young man who wishes to marry her, stroking her body, bending her this way and that.

When her family arranges her marriage to Tony, he takes her to his home, where she sees into the future and rejects the place as never being her own. To protect herself from Tony's touch, much as the scarecrow has protected the corn from the crows, she hides a knife in the bosom of her dress. However, because he has seen her do it, he stays away from her until she leaves on foot and goes back to her father's house. For Joan the marriage, a mere incident, has come to an end. The story concludes with the mother crying that Joan is Mrs. Tony Wright and must return, but the father insists, "Joan, Joan! She won't marry where she's not of a mind."

OTHER MAJOR WORKS

LONG FICTION: *The Time of Man*, 1926; *My Heart and My Flesh*, 1927; *Jingling in the Wind*, 1928; *The Great Meadow*, 1930; *A Buried Treasure*, 1931; *He Sent Forth a Raven*, 1935; *Black Is My Truelove's Hair*, 1938.

POETRY: *In the Great Steep's Garden*, 1915; *Under the Tree*, 1922, 1930; *Song in the Meadow*, 1940.

BIBLIOGRAPHY

Campbell, Harry Modean, and Ruel E. Foster. *Elizabeth Madox Roberts: American Novelist*. Norman: University of Oklahoma Press, 1956. This biographical and critical study includes a chapter on the short stories that focuses on the symbolism in several of Roberts's stories, particularly "The Scarecrow," "The Sacrifice of the Maidens," and "The Haunted Palace." Also discusses analogies to music in Roberts's stories, particularly her use of musical devices in "The Shepherd's Interval."

Hall, Wade. "Place in the Short Fiction of Elizabeth Madox Roberts." *The Kentucky Review* 6 (Fall/Winter, 1986): 3-16. Discusses the ways that place affects Roberts's short fiction: in the speech of her characters, in the creative relationship between character and place, and as the landscape of one's life. Argues that in Roberts's short fiction place has a bearing on who characters are, how they behave, what happens in the stories, and how the stories are structured and written.

McDowell, Frederick P. W. *Elizabeth Madox Roberts*. New York: Twayne, 1963. In this basic introduction to Roberts's life and work, McDowell argues that her best short stories are the earliest ones, which resemble the novels in their expression of significant moments in the psychological life of their characters. Provides brief discussions of such stories as "On the Mountainside," "The Sacrifice of the Maidens," and "The Betrothed."

Rovit, Earl H. *Herald to Chaos: The Novels of Elizabeth Madox Roberts*. Lexington: University of Kentucky Press, 1960. Rovit discusses Roberts's depiction of heroic characters engaged in epic struggles against the forces of nature. He also examines her critical neglect and her role in American literature and provides a thorough analysis of her style.

Simpson, Lewis P. "The Sexuality of History." *The southern Review* 20 (October, 1984): 785-802. In this special issue of memoirs, reminiscences, and essays on Roberts, Simpson describes her as a particularly modern writer whose struggle to repudiate the philosophy of idealism is the major thematic motive of her work. He compares Roberts to William Faulkner in their awareness of the inwardness of history.

Spivey, Herman E. "The Mind and Creative Habits of Elizabeth Madox Roberts." In *All These to Teach*, edited by Robert A. Bryan, et al. Gainesville: University of Florida Press, 1965. Argues that although Roberts's achievements were greater than realized by her contemporaries, her handicaps as an artist were more than she was able to overcome. Claims that Roberts is too much concerned with humankind in general and too little with individual people in particular, that there is too little external action in her work, and that her unmastered technical experiments prevent reader understanding.

Stoneback, H. R., Nicole Camastra, and Steven Florczyk, eds. *Elizabeth Madox Roberts: Essays of Discovery and Recovery.* New York: Quincy and Harrod Press and the Elizabeth Madox Roberts Society, 2008.

Stoneback, H. R., and Steven Florczyk, eds. *Elizabeth Madox Roberts: Essays of Reassessment and Reclamation.* Nicholasville, Ky.: Wind, 2008. These two books are part of the Elizabeth Madox Roberts Society's efforts to restore Roberts reputation as a significant American writer after many years of critical neglect. They are a compilation of letters, notes, some of Roberts's unpublished fiction, a complete bibliography of primary and secondary sources, and about forty short critical pieces discussing her works. One of these pieces is Wade Hall's analysis of "Place in the Short Fiction of Elizabeth Madox Roberts," originally published in *The Kentucky Review* in 1986 and now reprinted in *Essays of Reassessment and Reclamation.*

Tate, Linda. "Elizabeth Madox Roberts: A Bibliographical Essay." *Resources for American Literary Study* 18 (1992): 22-43. A summary and critique of previous criticism of Roberts's work. Concludes that she lacks a definitive biography. Argues that her role in the southern Renaissance has not been sufficiently explored. Maintains that the major untapped appeal of her work is feminist criticism.

Charles E. May

ROXANA ROBINSON

Born: Pine Mountain, Kentucky; November 30, 1946
Also known as: Roxana Barry

PRINCIPAL SHORT FICTION

A Glimpse of Scarlet, and Other Stories, 1991
Asking for Love, and Other Stories, 1996
A Perfect Stranger, and Other Stories, 2005

OTHER LITERARY FORMS

Roxana Robinson is as recognized for her novels as for her short fiction. She is the author of four novels: *Summer Light* (1987), *This Is My Daughter* (1998), *Sweetwater* (2003), and *Cost* (2008). The last three form a loosely connected trilogy with the common theme of family, although each book's subsidiary themes are different. Her other major work is a biography of the artist Georgia O'Keeffe, published in 1989.

ACHIEVEMENTS

Recognitions of Roxana Robinson's work mostly have been fellowships or nominations for awards. Four of her books have been listed as *New York Times* Notable Books of the Year, and she has been the recipient of Guggenheim, National Endowment for the Arts, and MacDowell Colony Fellowships. Her recognition has come for her craftsmanship, her style, and her fiction's universal themes. Although her usual subject matter--emotional currents within families--has been denigrated as the stuff of "women's fiction," Robinson's spare and controlled style and the depth of her character insights have solidified for her a special place within literary fiction. It should be noted that certain of her awards are for art-related writing rather than for general fiction. This reflects her background and interests in twentieth century art, which culminated in the O'Keeffe biography.

BIOGRAPHY

Roxana Barry Robinson is the daughter of parents whose careers departed in unobtrusive ways from their families' expectations. Her father, Stuyvesant Barry, was the son of two Harvard-educated lawyers. He followed in their footsteps by attending private eastern schools before earning the obligatory Harvard degrees.

However, after law school, he gave up legal endeavors to become a teacher. Her mother, Alice Scoville, was from a Philadelphia Main Line family, with its wealth and emphasis on proper social customs, and attended Vassar. After their marriage, the couple moved to Kentucky and taught in an Appalachian school. Eventually, after Roxana's birth, the family moved to Pennsylvania, where her father became principal of the Buckingham Friends School. A gap persisted between Robinson's parents' and her grandparents' perceptions of the world. The author describes growing up among an odd mixture of the two, a situation reflected obliquely in some of her stories, especially "Family Christmas."

The young Robinson was uneasy with compliments on her writing ability; it was too much the expected thing for a girl whose parents were teachers. Nevertheless, upon enrolling in Bennington College, she took creative-writing classes. Her most memorable instructor there was Bernard Malamud, whom she credits with inspiring her with his meticulousness and passion for writing.

Before finishing a degree at Bennington, she married David Alger, who was working on a business degree in Michigan. Robinson completed her degree at the University of Michigan, earning a B.A. in English in 1969. Back in New York, a friend referred her to an opening at Sotheby's, where she spent the next four years as assistant head of the American painting department. During 1974 and 1975, she utilized this experience as exhibition director of the Terry Dintenfass Gallery.

She and Alger had a daughter; they divorced in 1975. In 1976, she married Hamilton Robinson, Jr., an investor, taking the name under which her writing would be published. In 1976, Roxana Robinson became a freelance writer. Her first published works were art-history pieces. She was working on fiction also but did not break into print with her stories until the early 1980's. While she was working on her first novel, *Summer Light*, a Harper and Row editor asked if she would be interested in doing a biography of the deceased O'Keeffe. It was too good an opportunity to turn down, because there was little in print about O'Keeffe's life. Robinson was pulled in two directions by the dual projects, but in the long term her career seems to have benefited.

The Robinsons lived in Katonah, Westchester County, a region of New York where the white Anglo-Saxon Protestant (WASP) types that featured in Robinson's stories lived. In 1997, Robinson bought an apartment on East Sixty-Seventh Street in Manhattan, where she writes in a spare eight-by-ten-foot space, a former maid's room with no view, which she chose because of its lack of distractions.

ANALYSIS

Roxana Robinson is usually described as a chronicler of events in the lives of the privileged WASP elite. This is far from unfamiliar territory in modern American literature. It is often asserted that this social class sets the country's cultural parameters and runs it, so WASP characters populate many works of fiction. Robinson is unusual because the questions of power and class that preoccupy so many who write about these characters bore her. Her interests are the play of emotions experienced by this group and the human interactions that reveal and express these emotions. The latter concern, however, which forms the subject matter of much great literature, is a subordinate feature of her writing, used mostly to highlight insights into individuals' psyches and predicaments.

The writer whose subject matter most closely parallels her own is John Updike, whom she credits with having a profound influence on her work. Updike departs from her in that his major work has followed one character, Rabbit, throughout life's ups and downs, whereas Robinson uses different characters in each story or novel.

At least one critic has described Robinson as an "ethnic writer," because of her exclusive concentration on the mores and dilemmas of WASPs. Few other character types, except for some of their Western European peers, appear in her writing. The label is a fair one, as long as the reader remembers that the term WASP cannot be applied to all Americans of Protestant faith and British ancestry.

This being said, it is fair to measure the author's fiction by the same yardsticks applied to other ethnic writers' work: How do these characters' stories illuminate universal human values and dilemmas? How well do they convey what is unique about the ethnic culture and behavior? Does the author tell a good story?

"THE TREATMENT"

"The Treatment" is unusual among Robinson's stories; it is one of the few pieces in which the focus is not on changes in domestic arrangements or the emotional currents surrounding them. The stakes are life or death. Even so, it is a quiet and inwardly focused story. The protagonist feels rage at her situation, but it is deflected onto her nurse for reminding her of facts she does not want to hear.

The story opens as a day-in-the-life account by an unnamed narrator, a woman receiving intravenous (IV) antibiotics for an unidentified disease. She describes the bulb of medicine in glowing terms: Its interior is luminous; the plastic outer covering is pearly and translucent. This medication is going to save her life.

The woman lays the bulb out to warm and waits for Ginger, her visiting nurse, to arrive. Meanwhile, the protagonist is all alone in the house. Her husband is at work, her daughter is away at college. She looks forward to Ginger's arrival, even though the IV line is to be replaced today--a frightening procedure, as it is threaded through her veins to dangle just above her heart. When Ginger arrives, they talk for a few minutes, while the nurse prepares to change the line. The woman is optimistic, although nervous. Her random pains have lessened; her current treatment, the most drastic after several rounds of oral antibiotics have failed, is surely working.

Ginger is a chatty type and keeps talking as she works. When the narrator asks about other patients who share the same condition, Ginger answers that it is a terrible disease if not caught early, because the spirochetes metastasize and migrate throughout the body. Ginger has one patient who has had it for ten years; his brain and spinal cord are involved.

The woman hears this with growing panic. Suddenly all her bright hopes turn to ash. She believes she, too, has been infected for ten years. She explodes at Ginger, telling her she should never talk this way to a patient. The woman ignores the nurse's apologies. Ginger appears as an agent of doom, working under false pretenses as a healer. The protagonist can barely hold herself together until the nurse is out the door.

"The Treatment," like many Robinson stories, uses the reversal of an emotional state to power the story and as its resolution. It differs from the majority of them, inasmuch as in most Robinson stories, the protagonist says nothing to signal her changed outlook. In true WASP style, it is revealed only by her unvoiced thoughts or through metaphor.

Does the narrator verbalize her feelings in this story because she is too upset to suppress her reaction? Or is it because the nurse is not from her social class, hence her self-protective WASP restraint can be bent?

It is also notable that neither character will give a name to the "terrible disease." Historically, this has usually been the case with cancer and with sexually transmitted diseases, but neither seems to fit the template here. Rocephin, the medication in the bulb, is an antibiotic used to treat a variety of bacterial infections. One guess, based on clues in the story, is Lyme disease. However, the author never tips her hand. Indeed, she is more interested in the patient's shifting emotions than in her long-term prognosis. The latter question is more in the territory of a different genre, the medical thriller.

"A PERFECT STRANGER"

"A Perfect Stranger" is one of Robinson's most celebrated and analyzed short stories. It describes a misunderstanding between spouses when Martha volunteers to host a visiting opera scholar in her exurban home for the weekend. She is manipulated into it by the head of the music festival's committee. This woman dislikes her, but Martha can think of no graceful way to back out. Unfortunately, she does not consult her husband Jeffrey about the offer until the arrangements are finalized. Jeffrey is not happy at the prospect of sharing his house space and weekend with "a perfect stranger." He enjoys his privacy and quiet and resents the necessity of making conversation with a person he does not even know. He does rise to the occasion and is gracious to the guest, Kingsley, in public. When Jeffrey and Martha are alone, however, he grumbles and throws small tantrums.

Most critics have focused on this story's interplay between husband and wife, contrasting their polite behavior in front of the guest with their voiced--and unspoken--complaints behind closed doors. However, when a minor emergency occurs, with the car locked up and not easily unlocked, their basic unity shines through. Both react quickly, taking steps to avoid inconveniencing or embarrassing their house guest.

There is another, equally interesting dynamic to the story. Robinson employs the unusual, for her, practice of Ping-Pong points of view; rather than telling the story from one narrator's viewpoint, she bounces back and forth between Martha's perspective and that of Kingsley, the opera expert. The result is humorous, revealing, and sometimes pathetic. Kingsley, an elderly Englishman with a collection of physical ailments, has pronounced opinions on almost everything. Martha drives him to her home, taking the longer, scenic route to show Kingsley how insulated they are from urban noise and bustle. Kingsley is not impressed. He thinks her pride in the unpaved roads is ridiculous. The beautiful swans at the reservoir appear evil-tempered to him. Later, at supper, he and Jeffrey have a good-natured and ill-informed argument about computers and novel writing.

The next day's events reveal Kingsley to be truly clueless. Outside a country restaurant, he manages to lock Martha's keys inside her car. The car can be unlocked only by a manufacturer's representative, not easily reached at this isolated location. Martha and Jeffrey take elaborate steps to keep Kingsley on schedule (he has a train to catch that evening) and to get the car opened, all without admitting what has happened. Kingsley knows the day's emotional currents suddenly have shifted, but he has no idea why. Americans are strange, women are inexplicable, and despite his supposed intellectual acuity, he does not bother inquiring any further.

Back in Britain the next day, Kingsley is relieved to have distanced himself from the mystery. Returning to his cold flat puts him back into his comfort zone. He will probably leave a string of disasters in his wake during future guest-lecture gigs. Despite the toll they take on his seventy-year-plus body, he will accept them, because his ego needs them for affirmation. Meanwhile, back in America, Martha has learned that domestic harmony is more important to her than social climbing provided by the local music festival.

"FRIENDSHIP IN A FOREIGN COUNTRY"

This early story contains several motifs that reappear in Robinson's later fiction: a colorful European setting, divorce and affairs, female friendship, and secrets kept from friends and spouses. Louisa, an Englishwoman, and Sophie, half French and half American, are sharing a much-anticipated holiday in Provence. Close friends for many years, they have taken different paths, since Louisa divorced and moved from Connecticut back to England. Their hope is that the vacation will renew their friendship and be a treat for Louisa, whose finances are strained since the divorce.

Sophie is baffled by Louisa's divorce. Louisa and Mark always seemed much happier together than Sophie in her marriage. Still, she is jealous of Louisa's newly single state. At the least, Sophie confesses, she would like to have an affair.

Louisa is aghast. She tells Sophie to have an affair if she must, but that divorce would be a big mistake. As they wander through the village streets and shops, the two women seem as close as ever. Robinson's word pictures of Provence are evocative. The reader can almost feel the hot morning air in the rented villa bedrooms and glimpse the secrets lurking in the old church. As they wander, however, Sophie becomes alarmingly aware of a gap looming between herself and her friend. Sophie loves the little church's peace and darkness; Louisa finds it boring. When they try on a fabulously expensive little black dress in a shop, Sophie is humiliated that it looks much better on Louisa, even though Louisa can hardly afford it. Finally, Louisa tells the story of her divorce. She had an affair with Tug Simmonds, she confesses. Tug is the husband of a mutual friend and a man they both considered a lecherous clown.

Sophie is horrified. Sitting across from Louisa at a café, Sophie experiences a range of reactions, from rage to ridicule. Her distress seems based at least as much on Louisa's poor taste as on moral grounds. Is it even possible, Sophie wonders, to be friends with Louisa anymore?

Then, deliberately, Sophie stirs her drink and searches within herself for the right tone and words with which to reassure Louisa that they are still friends.

With this simple story, Robinson manages to defuse the charge of petty jealousy that is often leveled at female friendships. Sophie's envy of Louisa is both completely understandable and faintly ridiculous, and Sophie is self-aware enough to realize it. The "Foreign Lands" of the title may refer to inadmissible emotional territory as well as to Provence. Once Sophie's envy is named and faced, it is not so scary after all. Perhaps unintentionally, Robinson has created in this little gem one of her most feminist stories.

OTHER MAJOR WORKS

LONG FICTION: *Summer Light*, 1987; *This Is My Daughter*, 1998; *Sweetwater*, 2003; *Cost*, 2008.
NONFICTION: *Georgia O'Keeffe: A Life*, 1989.

BIBLIOGRAPHY

Rosenblum, Constance. "For a Writer, a Home with a Hideout." *The New York Times*, July 12, 2002: p. 1L. A tour of Robinson's apartment and writing office, with her explanation of how it matches her writing needs.

Schwarz, Christina. "A Close Read: What Makes Good Writing Good." *The Atlantic* 296, no. 2 (September, 2005): 137. Detailed analysis of "Blind Man," a story in *A Perfect Stranger*. Explains what critics find praiseworthy about the author's work.

Smith, Wendy. "Roxana Robinson: Old Money, New Families." *Publishers Weekly* 245, no. 24 (June 15, 1998): 37. Informative article about Robinson's career and goals with her writing.

Emily Alward

MARY ROBISON

Born: Washington, D.C.; January 14, 1949

PRINCIPAL SHORT FICTION

Days, 1979
An Amateur's Guide to the Night, 1983
Believe Them, 1988
Tell Me: Thirty Stories, 2002

OTHER LITERARY FORMS

Mary Robison (ROH-bih-suhn) had her first novel, *Oh!*, published in 1981 by Alfred A. Knopf. The novel deals satirically with the problem of American family life. *Oh!* was followed ten years later by another novel, *Subtraction* (1991, also published by Knopf), which describes the difficulties that can arise when writers become teachers.

ACHIEVEMENTS

Mary Robison's short fiction has often been compared to that of older, more established contemporary writers, such as Raymond Carver, Ann Beattie, and Frederick Barthelme because of its spare, laconic humor and its presentation of empty lives in a hopelessly materialistic society. Her story "Yours" was anthologized in *Discovering Literature* (2000), along with the work of Carver and Sandra Cisneros. Robison received high critical praise for her early stories, which appeared in *The New Yorker*, and her first collection of short fiction, *Days*, garnered outstanding notices from many literary critics and fellow writers, even though she was only thirty years old when it was published. Though her stories embody the cool precision that has become characteristic of *The New Yorker*, her style is anything but derivative. She possesses an authentically original voice and a writing style that captures, simultaneously, the stark banality and the comic irony of the late stages of the American Dream in the last quarter of the twentieth century.

She has received fellowships from the Yaddo Writers and Artists Colony (1978) and the Breadloaf Writers Conference (1979). She has been honored with awards by the Authors Guild (1979) and PEN (1979), and she has received a grant from the John Simon Guggenheim Memorial Foundation.

BIOGRAPHY

Mary Robison was born in Washington, D.C., in 1949. Her father, Anthony Cennomo, was an attorney, and her mother, F. Elizabeth Reiss, was a psychologist and the mother of eight children. She spent most of her youth in the Midwest, but she received her M.A. at The Johns Hopkins University in Baltimore. Robison married James Robison, a writer. She was visiting lecturer (1979-1980) at Ohio University, writer-in-residence at the University of southern Mississippi, and has taught at the University of North Carolina at Greensboro, College of William and Mary, Bennington College, and Oberlin College. In 1981 she became the Briggs-Copeland assistant professor of English in the Department of Creative Writing at Harvard University.

Robinson has stated that her finest teacher at The Johns Hopkins University was the renowned novelist John Barth. She claims that she would not have taken her fiction writing seriously had it not been for The Johns Hopkins University's writing program and Barth's ability to inspire her to use her talent and publish her stories. As she put it: "John Barth charged a dead battery in me."

Robison has also judged national fiction competitions such as the one sponsored by the *Mississippi Review*. In addition, her novel *Why Did I Ever* was the winner of the 2001 *Los Angeles Times* Book Prize for Fiction. In 2009, Oprah Winfrey chose Robison's novel *One D.O.A., One on the Way* as a selection in her 2009 "Twenty-Five Books You Can't Put Down" Summer Reading List.

ANALYSIS

Mary Robison's early stories deal with the recurrent theme of the spiritual torpor at the center of a materialistic American society that is shallow, banal, boring, and bored. Her stories can be read as variations on the theme of stasis and, as such, resemble James Joyce's *Dubliners* (1914) as much as the work of Carver and Beattie. Novelist David Leavitt accurately analyzes the common dilemmas of many of her characters as their inability to move "because they're terrified of what will happen to them if they try to change." Waiting and fear of change characterize a number of her early stories, but the waiting and fear eventually

create a prevailing sense of lassitude and ennui, the desperation of a Sunday afternoon in November.

Barth describes her style as "hard-edged, fine-tooled, enigmatic super-realism," phrases that could as well describe the early Joyce. Robison, however, differs from early Joyce principally because much of her work, in spite of presenting bleak lives, is extremely comical, a quality that some overly serious critics usually miss. She is a comic writer even in the dark world of her first collection, *Days*, a pun that immediately establishes the malady of the quotidian as a major theme and also describes the "dazed" condition that many of her characters inhabit.

The gnomic titles of many of her stories are quite humorous, and when they are not ironic, they mix humor with sadness. They are, however, unerring objective correlatives, which permit plot, character, theme, and tone to coalesce comfortably. Her stories are extremely difficult to analyze with the usual literary methods because she rarely begins them at the beginning; she opens in medias res--that is, in the middle of things. Indeed, her stories are not stories in a narrative sense but rather parables of emptiness or scenes resembling the kind that the composer Robert Schumann evokes in his heartrending *Kinderszenen* (1838). In spite of the sorrow depicted in much of her work, however, Robison consistently creates stories whose titles and proper nouns can evoke comic responses: Bluey and Greer Wellman of "The Wellman Twins," Dieter and Boffo of "For Real," Sherry, Harry, and Daphne Noonan of "Coach," Ohio congressman Mel Physell, who writes poems on prosecutorial immunity, and a Great Dane named Lola from "Apostasy."

"KITE AND PAINT"

The opening of the first story in *Days*, entitled "Kite and Paint," illustrates clearly the theme of waiting, which recurs frequently throughout Robison's fiction: "It was the last day of August in Ocean City, and everybody was waiting for Hurricane Carla." Two men in their sixties, Charlie and Don, have been living together for some time. Don is not in good health but continues to care for his rose garden. He is a painter but seems to have lost interest in his craft; Charlie chides him for his unwillingness to paint anything. It is not clear whether they are lovers, though Don's former wife, Holly, has come to warn them that Hurricane Carla is imminent. The hurricane has temporarily given both men first a focus, then a purpose for action, since neither seems frightened of it. It is as though they have been waiting for a disaster such as this all their lives.

The stasis in the story has been broken. The artist, Don, draws geometric figures on six kites and names them with titles such as "Comet," "Whale," "My Beauty," and "Reddish Egret." The hurricane has mysteriously revived Don's imagination after a long hiatus and, more importantly, he decides to fly the kites as the hurricane arrives. "It'd be fun to waste them in the blow," Don declares. Robison fuses the joy of reawakened creativity with a vague death wish as the couple decides to confront "Carla," which is the feminine form of the proper name "Charles," the name itself meaning "man." By matching two important proper names, "Carla" and "Charles," Robison also invites a humorous Freudian interpretation to the possible final hours of a nearly dried-up painter and a retired junior high school shop teacher.

"PRETTY ICE"

Most of the characters in Robison's fiction live their lives unaware of their deepest motivations and remain ignorant of the power of the unconscious. One of the sources of the sardonic tone in much of Robison's fiction is observing so many characters blind to their self-destructive impulses; they literally do not know what they are doing. The perennial graduate student in plant taxonomy, Will, in the story "Pretty Ice," is a case in point: His scientific mind-set has cut him off from the potential joys of impulse and prevents him from viewing the aesthetic side of an ice storm in Columbus, Ohio. His fiancé, Belle, who holds a Ph.D. in musicology, decides at the story's conclusion that she cannot marry someone who is unable to share her and her mother's view that "an ice storm is a beautiful thing. Let's enjoy it. . . . It's twinkling like a stage set." The literal-minded taxonomist, Will, responds: "It'll make a bad-looking spring. A lot of shrubs get damaged and turn brown, and trees don't blossom right." His inability to permit his imagination to make something "pretty" becomes the final blow to a seven-year relationship that was over some time before. His icy response puts his fiancé in touch, finally, with her real unconscious feelings.

"BUD PARROT"

The long story "Bud Parrot" illustrates, if the reader observes closely, an unspoken sexual subtext upon which the narrative rests. The occasion is a wedding in Ohio, of Bud's closest friend and longtime roommate, Dean Blaines, to Gail Redding. Both men are in their middle thirties, and Bud is there to try, somehow, to win Dean back. They have probably been lovers. The tension rises as Bud, accompanied by Gail's sister, Evaline, whose constant knowing wink alerts the reader to the "real" story, impulsively surprises the newlyweds in their honeymoon suite at the Columbus Hilton. Evaline and Bud have just come from a visit to the Columbus Zoo. They find little evidence that anything sexual has occurred between husband and wife, but Dean assures Bud and Evaline that the "real" honeymoon will take place in Madrid. The tense scene ends with Bud excoriating Spain, chomping on an apple, and acting as a tempter as Dean rubs Gail's back while she glares knowingly at the handsome Bud. Once again, Robison, who trusts her reader completely, does not need to explain that some of the wedding guests probably know about the true nature of the lengthy relationship between Bud and Dean; she invites the reader to compare the "zoo" in the Honeymoon Suite at the Columbus Hilton to life in the actual Columbus Zoo.

"MAY QUEEN"

Robison can move from the sexual desperation and commercial surrealism of expensive Ohio weddings to, in "May Queen," an unconscious reenactment of human sacrifice in Indianapolis with consummate ease and assurance. Mickey and Denise observe with horror as their May queen daughter, Riva, catches fire from holy candles in St. Rose of Lima Church on a glorious spring day. The choice of the name of the parish, St. Rose of Lima, adds to the irony of the story since St. Rose was renowned for the severity of the penitential sufferings that she inflicted upon herself. The story ends with Riva's father trying to relieve his daughter's pain with promises of vacations on the shores of Lake Erie, "where we can lie around and bake in the sun all day . . . and you'll be eighteen then. You'll be able to drink, if you want to."

"HEART"

Not all Robison's stories document lives of quiet desperation so blatantly. "Heart" records the life of a lonely, aging man, Roy, who lives his life vicariously by starting conversations with teenagers at the local roller skating rink and with the friendly paperboy, whose line "Pretty soon, a new guy will be collecting" records another loss for a solitary person such as Roy. The story is an American version of British writer Katherine Mansfield's classic "Miss Brill," but without its sentimental ending. "Heart" concludes with Roy exhorting a local dog to "Wake up and live. . . . Count the Fords that pass" and telling Mrs. Kenny, who lives on the other side of Roy's duplex, that Mickey Rooney was in town with major advice: "He says you've got to have your heart in it. Every minute. . . . The dog knows." Robison's sharp ear picks up the pathetic locker-room boosterisms that many Americans exchange on empty Sunday afternoons. Mrs. Kenny notices that Roy's hands are trembling, and when she asks him why, he says he cannot sleep. She blames him for listening to the radio all night and for not trying hard enough to sleep. "Oh," he says, "that's probably it. I don't try."

Few writers capture the cruelty of the Protestant work ethic as it systematically justifies everything bad that happens to people as really being their own fault. Roy, like many lonely people, takes refuge in late-night radio to comfort him in his solitude. That sad attempt turns into proof that he does not possess the "heart" that Rooney promotes. His inability to sleep, then, becomes proof that he has not tried hard enough. Few writers are able to delineate the Calvinist circle of self-blame with the subtle but savage accuracy of Robison.

"THE NATURE OF ALMOST EVERYTHING"

The stories in Robison's next collection, *An Amateur's Guide to the Night*, are less bitter and dark principally because the humor focuses more on the absurdities of a specifically American system of values, or lack thereof. There is also a growing ability of some characters to laugh at themselves in a healthier way; the humor has become less self-deprecatory. The opening line of one of the finest stories in the book, "The Nature of Almost Everything," establishes the tone of the collection: "Tell you, at thirty-six, my goals are to stay sober and pay off my MasterCard bill." Crises are labeled clearly and dealt with directly. People have become more honest with themselves and can live vivid lives even when they must watch loved ones around them falling apart.

"AN AMATEUR'S GUIDE TO THE NIGHT"

The story "An Amateur's Guide to the Night" shows how a teenage girl, Lindy, in Terre Haute, Indiana, has worked out successful fictive defenses to help her cope with a mother who refuses to grow up and who takes refuge in pills, horror films, and pretensions that she and Lindy are really sisters. They double-date and call each other "Sis." Lindy's real spiritual center lies in her devotion to the stars and their celestial movements, which she views through her telescope at night.

"COACH"

The story "Coach" shows a good-natured midwestern football coach, Harry Noonan, enjoying early success in his first college job. His artist wife, Sherry, has carved out a life of her own with her printmaking, private studio, and a five-year plan to learn French. Their daughter, Daphne, a sexy, attractive high school girl, flirts with as many football hunks as possible. The coach's unbounded optimism centers the story in an atmosphere reminiscent of a stereotypical 1950's America. All situations and problems are analyzed and solved in the most cliché-ridden banalities. The emptiness in this story is palpable but oddly comic.

"IN JEWEL"

The story "In Jewel" is about another female artist, an art teacher educated at the Rhode Island School of Design, who has returned to teach at her old high school in Jewel, West Virginia. Though she is engaged, she takes great consolation in her gifted students and lets them get close to her. She is torn, though, between wanting to leave her hometown and her inability to do so. As she aptly puts it: "So, I like feeling at home. I just wish I didn't feel it here." Brad Foley, a student whom she helped through a family crisis and who will probably never escape Jewel, sends her a note congratulating her on her engagement and urging her to move. The final scene records in dismal detail that all she really has is what she sees before her on her desk in her room. Again, stasis wins and the fear of the unknown paralyzes even the ones who previously had an opportunity to escape.

"YOURS"

The short-short story "Yours" also deals with art but as a project that a dying thirty-five-year-old woman named Allison and her seventy-eight-year-old husband, Clark, are pursuing. It is Halloween, and they are carving jack-o'-lanterns ostensibly for the neighborhood children. Robison delicately examines the way the imagination can create what Wallace Stevens called "the violence within that protects us from the violence without"--that is, individuals create images that sum up their lives in somewhat the same way that Don in "Kite and Paint" vivified his final years. The image at the conclusion of this story is one of great iconographic mystery. Clark stares at the eight illuminated faces sitting in the darkness: "He was speaking into the phone now. He watched the jack-o'-lanterns. The jack-o'-lanterns watched him."

"I AM TWENTY-ONE"

Reassuring images that comfort and enable people to find small satisfactions are also the subject of "I Am Twenty-One." A grieving college student, whose parents had been killed in a car accident two years earlier, is trying desperately to earn good grades on her test for a course called "The Transition from Romanesque to Gothic," a phrase that could apply as well to the direction that her life seems to be taking as her isolation deepens. Though she has attempted to create a life of monastic severity and simplicity in her small room, she permits herself one picture that "wasn't of a Blessed Virgin or a detail from Amiens of the King of Judah holding a rod of the tree of Jesse. Instead, it was an eight-by-ten glossy of Rudy and Leslie, my folks." Her desire and grief have caused her to create an icon of her own genealogical tree of Jesse (the Blessed Virgin Mary's family tree): "I kept the picture around because, oddly, putting away the *idea* of my folks would have been worse than losing the real them." She has enacted the exact process by which a mere image takes on the numinous quality of an icon and so has unconsciously learned an important lesson in both her academic course and her life.

BELIEVE THEM

Robison's third collection of short fiction is entitled *Believe Them*, and the mood in these stories is definitely more upbeat than in her previous two. They also generally run longer than her earlier stories. A stronger controlling voice narrates, even though the pain of living has changed little within the stories themselves. The humor in the stories is less sardonic and bitter; the characters in some of them are actually enjoying themselves.

"SEIZING CONTROL"

The title of the volume comes from the mouth of the oldest of six children, Hazel, who is mentally challenged and cannot read, but has memorized the important facts that she needs to know for an orderly life. The first story, "Seizing Control," records what happens when five children stay up all night while their mother is having her sixth child. Hazel does not tell her parents, when asked later, any of the negative parts of the all-night party but rather lists for them everything she knows that her parents had taught her, from "Don't pet strange animals" to "Put baking soda on your bee stings" to "Whatever Mother and Father tell you, believe them."

"FOR REAL"

"For Real" is one of Robison's strongest stories. It mixes humor and pathos in the life of Boffo, the girl clown who hosts Channel 22's "Mid-day Matinee," and her handsome German boyfriend, Dieter, who works at the same television station and is several years her junior. Dieter has been trying to get Boffo to marry him so that he can remain in the United States, but she has resisted his proposals for some time. The story develops when the reader and Boffo realize that Dieter has been to his lawyer and obviously is making other plans to secure citizenship papers. Boffo realizes that she has actually enjoyed his company more than she thought, but the issue of control quickly becomes the focus of the story. As Dieter takes charge of his life and becomes less dependent on Boffo, she sees herself not only as a television clown but also possibly as a clown "For Real." She sees clearly, and for the first time, that her clown routine, for better or worse, is her life. Her three-year preoccupation with Dieter has distracted her from becoming the "best" clown she can be, and the story concludes with her realization that if she is a clown, it is worth doing right: "Excuse me, viewers? Ladies and germs? You've been being cheated, in all truth. You've been seeing a lazy job of Boffo. But stay watching. We're about to press the pedal to the floor. We're about to do it right." Her announcement is to herself as she fully understands the true nature of her life. What may seem like failure has become for her an occasion of genuine illumination, recognized and acknowledged by her fellow workers' laughter on the set.

"TRYING"

The story "Trying" is also about a clown, the class clown, Bridie O'Donnell, who has become the resident 1960's liberal at the Virginia Benedictine Convent School near Washington, D.C. Her lawyer parents are aging radicals who practice poverty law in a Washington, D.C., storefront office. Bridie spends much of her time and energy in iconoclastic wisecracking, particularly in Sister Elspeth's history class. Sister Elspeth is a six-foot, eight-inch-tall nun who suffers from giantism. Robison balances Bridie's stubborn efforts to convince her conservative classmates and teachers of the wisdom of liberal thinking against Sister Elspeth's conservative proposal of starting a "civics club." Neither character ever stops trying, though they emerge from opposite political traditions. The moment of revelation comes, however, when they recognize their mutual isolation from the rest of the community; they are grotesques, and they know it and understand each other's plight with perfect clarity.

"ADORE HER"

One of Robison's bitterest attacks on young urban professionals (called yuppies) is "Adore Her," though she has dealt with them before in "Bud Parrot," "Falling Away," and "Mirror." In a story of classic narcissism, Steve spends most of his time fawning over his girlfriend, Chloe, and polishing his Saab in the late afternoon shade. "Adore Her" is one of Robison's finest parables of emptiness, especially when Chloe explains to Steve the secret of her success: "Appearance is all." Steve is so bored with his job as a claims investigator for an insurance company that he openly tempts his very serious boss to fire him. A major issue in the story is control, as Steve begins to see himself as a slave to his job, to his yuppie materialism, and to Chloe. He becomes obsessed with finding the owner of a wallet containing many photographs of different women and spends considerable energy trying to track him down. His brief time away from attending to the beautiful but

empty Chloe has taught him that he is controlled totally by her. After seducing her into drinking a beer with him even though she has a hangover, he decides to leave her: "He would run from the unalterables: from Chloe, the apartment building, his job at Tidewater Assurance. He'd run from everything he couldn't change about what he had been calling his life." Steve is one of the few characters in Robison's fiction who sees his life paralyzed in the stasis of debilitating boredom yet seems willing to take radical and courageous steps to change the things that he can.

Robison is one of the United States' most perceptive delineators of the acedia and sterility at the center of American materialism. With flawless lucidity her highly attuned ear can expose it in the voices of the old, the bored, the desperate, and the hopeless. Her stories do not preach and never moralize. Like her teacher Barth, she presents as accurately as she can. What saves most of her characters, at least those willing to change, is their sense of humor, their lack of self-pity, and their ability to laugh at themselves.

TELL ME: THIRTY STORIES

Robison's fourth collection of short stories contains three new short stories and twenty-seven previously published stories from *The New Yorker*, *The Paris Review*, *Mississippi Review*, *Seventeen*, *Gentlemen's Quarterly*, and her earlier collections. This collection effectively illustrates her minimalist style and her often biting humor. The three new stories fit seamlessly with the older works and demonstrate that her narrative voice remains strong and her keen insight remains razor sharp.

"Father, Grandfather," the first new story in the collection, introduces three generations of a family: a father, his daughter Gloria, and her two adult daughters Cammie and Cake. Gloria, an anthropologist, has just returned from an eighteen-month assignment abroad, and her daughters are helping her to settle back in to her life at home. While the girls work on their mother's kitchen, Gloria sits motionless in an adjoining room, listening to their banter. Her father, the girls' grandfather, enters this semidomestic scene, offering the relief of small talk and fatherly advice. As the four are on the way to a cocktail party hosted by the girls, the family dynamics become more fleshed out, and by the end of the story, Gloria, her father, and her daughters resort to traditional family roles: recounting memories of long-forgotten incidents, discussing the loss of family traditions and whether they should be resurrected, and finally the passing on of family responsibilities. The father gives his war shoes to his daughter, saying, "I want each and every one of you to wear them," symbolically passing the torch of his role as family head to his daughter and implying that she, too, must do the same in due time.

In "Apostasy," Robison tells the story of two sisters, one of whom is a nun dying of cancer and the other an aide for a congressman. The story begins with Donna picking up Sister Mary Divine Heart and taking her to her convent. Their discussion of Sister Mary's cancer diagnosis is stark and emotionless, with both sisters voicing this new reality of their lives. Donna goes back to her rented home to find an odd mix of guests who have not yet left a party given by her housemate. Their conversation is not focused on life and death issues, such as Sister Mary's, but has a forlorn, detached feel that focuses on the absurdities of life, which is a jarring juxtaposition for the reader who has just learned of Sister Mary's impending death: A partygoer runs over the neighbor's dog but shows no remorse, Donna's housemate announces her intent to move out, and Donna's congressman boss pays an odd visit to her home. The last part of the story lends an atmosphere of aimlessness but, surprisingly, not hopelessness to the story.

The last new story in the collection, "Care," addresses one character's search for what she needs to do as a result of a conversation with Jack, the estranged husband of her friend Barbara, who tells her that she needs to change her life. While the story ostensibly focuses on the disintegrating marriage of Barbara and Jack, other relationships are brought into sharp focus. In fact, Leah's search to determine if she should indeed change her life subtly takes center stage in the story. By the end of the story, it is Leah's father Sweet who gives her the most insight into her own character and, presumably, the direction she should take.

OTHER MAJOR WORKS

LONG FICTION: *Oh!*, 1981; *Subtraction*, 1991; *Why Did I Ever*, 2001; *One D.O.A., One on the Way*, 2009.

BIBLIOGRAPHY

Angell, Roger, ed. *Nothing But You: Love Stories from "The New Yorker."* New York: Random House, 1997. An interesting collection of items from *The New Yorker*, with an introduction by Angell.

Bell, Madison Smartt. "Less Is Less: The Dwindling American Short Story." *Harper's* 272 (April, 1986): 64-69. Argues that writers influenced by Robison, Beattie, and Carver should resist their penchant for commercialism, homogeneity, and nihilism; critiques the "minimal" style, as characterized by obsession with surface detail, a tendency to slight distinctions, and a deterministic and even nihilistic worldview.

Birkerts, Sven. "The School of Lish." *The New Republic* 195 (October 13, 1986): 28. Discusses the writers, including Robison, nurtured by Knopf editor Gordon Lish; argues they represent a crisis in American literature, for they lack a vision of larger social connection; claims writers such as Robison falsify experience.

Flower, Dean. "An Amateur's Guide to the Night." *The Hudson Review* 37 (Summer, 1984): 307-308. Flower finds the stories in *An Amateur's Guide to the Night* narrow and turned in upon themselves, mere glimpses of domestic life. Most of them, however, are successful close-ups of middle-class young people undergoing the pangs of growing up. He praises Robison for her fine ear that accurately records the queer metaphors of everyday speech.

Guth, Hans P., and Gabriele L. Rico. *Discovering Literature*. Upper Saddle River, N.J.: Prentice-Hall, 2000. An anthology of works by various writers, including Robison. Includes a bibliography and an index.

Hallett, Cynthia Whitney. *Minimalism and the Short Story: Raymond Carver, Amy Hempel, and Mary Robison*. Lewiston, N.J.: Edwin Mellen Press, 1999. Compares the minimalist styles of these three writers. Includes a bibliography and an index.

Handler, Daniel. "Manic Oppression." *The New York Times Book Review*, March 22, 2009, p. 13. In his review of *One D.O.A., One on the Way*, Handler discusses Robison's novel as one that takes a larger view of the world as opposed to the narrower focus of her previous works.

Inness-Brown, Elizabeth. "Mary Robison, *Days.*" *Fiction International* 12 (1980): 281-283. Inness-Brown praises Robison's ability to "show" readers everything they need to know about the characters and her refusal to "tell" them anything. Inness-Brown characterizes Robison's stories as "bolts of lightning revealing ravages of a storm" and points out her strongest quality is a "beautiful precision."

Leavitt, David. "*An Amateur's Guide to the Night*." *The Village Voice* 29 (January 10, 1984): 44. Given that Robison consistently describes bleak landscapes, the vigor and enthusiasm of this collection brighten the darkness. Leavitt finds the stories in *Days* flawless because of Robison's "perfect eye for detail and ear for dialogue." He states that no short-story writer speaks to modern times "more urgently or fondly," and that her work demands critical attention.

_____. "New Voices and Old Values." *The New York Times Book Review*, May 12, 1985, p. 1. Discusses the new generation of writers, born in the 1950's and early 1960's, who write from a world in which people marry to separate, families dissolve, and loneliness and disillusionment, as their parents show them, are life's only prizes; discusses the influence of Carver, Beattie, and Robison.

Miller, Laura. "It Only Hurts When I Breathe: In Mary Robison's Stories, Characters Don't Express Emotions Directly." *The New York Times Book Review*, November 10, 2002, p. 10. Miller's review of *Tell Me* focuses on Robison's ability to subtract all unnecessary narrative from her stories and to create characters with only minimal details and in an uncomplicated style.

Pollitt, Katha. "Family and Friends." *The New York Times Book Review*, August 23, 1981, p. 14. Pollitt credits Robison's work with embodying the "unconscious surrealism of commercial America." She also finds Robison's offbeat cheerfulness and buoyancy refreshing.

Scanlon, Suzzanne. "Mary Robison: *Why Did I Ever*." *The Review of Contemporary Fiction* 22, no. 2 (2002): 239. This review looks at Robison's novel *Why Did I Ever*, which addresses the absurdities of life through the eyes of failed script doctor Money Breton.

Stokes, Geoffrey. "Uh Oh!" *The Village Voice* 26 (August 5, 1981): 32. Stokes calls Robison's *Days* the "Darwin of helplessness" and points out that most of her works are variations on the theme of stasis. He also indicates that her novel *Oh!* contains a picaresque plot with some "truly batty humor." He sees her fiction closer to British models, such as P. G. Wodehouse, than to American literary antecedents.

Patrick Meanor; Nika Hoffman
Updated by Kimberley M. Holloway

PHILIP ROTH

Born: Newark, New Jersey; March 19, 1933

PRINCIPAL SHORT FICTION

Goodbye, Columbus, and Five Short Stories, 1959

"Novotny's Pain," 1962, revised 1980

"The Psychoanalytic Special," 1963

"On the Air," 1970

"'I Always Wanted You to Admire My Fasting': Or,
Looking at Kafka," 1973

OTHER LITERARY FORMS

Philip Roth has published a number of novels, many of which were excerpted as self-contained short stories in various magazines. He has written essays of literary criticism and social commentary, dramatic works for stage and screen, and book-length works of autobiography. He also served as general editor of the Penguin series "Writers from the Other Europe" (1975-1989).

ACHIEVEMENTS

Philip Roth is first and foremost a consummate storyteller. Whether the genre is short fiction, novel, or autobiography, and whether the subject matter is serious, comic, or somewhere in between, Roth's great narrative power entertains readers. This ability to spellbind his audience stems from Roth's seemingly effortless command of the English language and his remarkable agility of mind as he maintains a rapid pace of invention, action, and ideas.

These talents have been recognized by numerous critics, and he is one of the most honored authors in contemporary American letters. In addition to his 1960 National Book Award for *Goodbye, Columbus and Five Short Stories*, Roth has won *The Paris Review*'s Aga Khan Award (1958) for "Epstein,"; a National Institute of Arts and Letters grant (1959); a John Simon Guggenheim Memorial Foundation

Fellowship (1959), the Daroff Award from he Jewish Book Council of America (1960), also for *Goodbye, Columbus and Five Other Stories*; and an O. Henry second-prize award (1960) for "Defender of the Faith." He was elected to the National Institute of Arts and Letters in 1969. Both *The Counterlife* (1986) and *Patrimony: A True Story* (1991) won the National Book Critics Circle Award (1987 and 1992, respectively), and in 1991 Roth was awarded the National Arts Club Medal of Honor for Literature. He is the only three-time winner of the Pen/Faulkner Award, which he received in 1994 for *Operation Shylock: A Confession* (1993), in 2001 for *The Human Stain* (2000), and in 2007 for *Everyman* (2006). *Sabbath's Theater* (1995) earned Roth his second National Book Award, *American Pastoral* (1997) won the Pulitzer Prize in 1998, *The Human Stain* obtained the United Kingdom's W. H. Smith Literary Award for the best book of the year in 2001, and *The Plot Against America* (2004) won the Sidewise Award for Alternate History (2005) and the Society of American Historians' James Fenimore Cooper Prize for Best Historical Fiction (2005). Roth also received the National Book Foundation's Award for Distinguished Contribution to American Letters in 2002, won the PEN/Nabokov Award in 2006, and in 2007 was chosen as the recipient of the first PEN/Saul Bellow Award for Achievement in American Fiction.

Roth has also been heavily criticized over the years. Critics accuse him of wasting his talent on a limited, self-absorbed vision of the world, having a sexist attitude toward women, portraying Jews in an unflattering light, and being needlessly pessimistic. While these charges may or may not have validity, no one doubts Roth's skills as a wordsmith. Moreover, the continuing appeal of Roth's work indicates that his apparent aimlessness and moral anguish reflect deeply felt trends in contemporary life.

BIOGRAPHY

Philip Milton Roth was reared in Newark, New Jersey, where he was influenced by the rising urban Jewish culture that dominated the intellectual and cultural life of part of that city. After graduating from Weequahic High School, he attended Newark College of Rutgers University from 1950 to 1951, finished his B.A. at Bucknell University in 1954, and earned an M.A. at the University of Chicago in 1955. After a stint in the United States Army, he returned to the University of Chicago, where he completed most of his work toward a Ph.D. and taught literature from 1956 to 1958.

Roth's stormy personal relationships and health problems have figured in much of his writing. In 1959, he was married to Margaret Martinson Williams, from whom he obtained a legal separation in 1963. She died in 1968. In 1990, Roth married his long-term companion, the actress Claire Bloom, and they divorced in 1995. Roth suffered serious appendicitis and peritonitis in 1967 and drug-induced depression following knee surgery in 1987. He underwent quintuple-bypass surgery in 1989, and he also spent time in a psychiatric hospital during his marriage to Bloom.

ANALYSIS

Some of Philip Roth's most important short stories are collected in the 1959 volume *Goodbye, Columbus*. However, Roth has produced other individual stories which have been published in such magazines as *The New Yorker, Esquire, Harper's Magazine*, and *The Atlantic Monthly*. Additionally, portions of several of his novels were first released as short stories. The shorter fiction serves to introduce the reader both to Roth's typical range of styles and to his complex themes. The author's Newark-Jewish background lends a prominent urban-ethnic flavor to his early fiction, but read in the context of his later work, which sometimes deals less directly with "Jewish" matters, it becomes clear that the Jewish elements in his work are used to exemplify larger concerns endemic to American society as a whole.

Technically, Roth's fiction runs the gamut from broad satire to somber realism to Kafkaesque surrealism. Beneath the wide range of styles, however, is the strain of social realism, which attempts to depict, often

without overt judgment, the pressures brought to bear on the modern individual searching for (or trying to recover) moral, ethical, and cultural roots in a society that prides itself on the erasure of such differences in its attempt to achieve homogeneity. Implicit in many of the stories is the problem of the leveling down into a normalcy of behavior which, although perhaps a socially acceptable way of "getting along," nevertheless mitigates against the retention of cultural eccentricities or personal individuality. While Roth's Jewish milieu provided ample opportunity to observe this phenomenon, some of his later fiction explores these matters in non-Jewish settings.

"ELI, THE FANATIC"

"Eli, the Fanatic" embodies many of Roth's themes and techniques. Taking place in suburban America, the tale concerns a young, "secularized" Jewish lawyer, Eli Peck, who is retained to convince a European Jew, who operates a resident Jewish academy in the town (aptly and symbolically named Woodenton), to close his establishment. The town is embarrassed by the presence of the yeshiva, since it calls the largely

Philip Roth (Hulton Archive/Getty Images)

Gentile residents' attention to the Jewishness of some of the inhabitants who wish to blend in peacefully with the rest of the population. Significantly, it is the Jews who hire Eli, and not the Gentiles, Jews who believe all too literally in the "melting pot" theory of assimilation. Of particular annoyance is one resident of the yeshiva--a Hasidic Jew who wears the traditional long black coat and wide-brimmed hat and walks about the town shopping for supplies for the school.

When Eli confronts the headmaster, he is touched by the old man's integrity and his fierce but philosophically stoical attachment to his cultural and religious roots--an attachment, however, which Eli cannot share. Eli realizes that the old man will never abandon his school and has no "respect" for the zoning laws which prohibit such establishments. Eli attempts a compromise. After soliciting reluctant approval from his clients, he tries to persuade the old man to insist that his Hasidic employee wear modern garb, in the hope that the visible manifestation of the enclave will be removed, thus mollifying the community. Eli is informed by the headmaster that, after the man's escape from the Holocaust, the clothes he wears are "all he's got." Eli realizes that the remark is symbolic as well as literal--that the clothes are a symbol of the identity not even the Nazis could take away from the man. Nevertheless, Eli brings to the yeshiva two of his own suits in the hope that the man will adopt the inoffensive dress.

Although he does so, much to the temporary relief of Eli and the modern Jewish community, he also leaves his old clothes on Eli's doorstep and parades about the town in Eli's ill-fitting clothes as a kind of silent reproach to a town that would rob him of his identity. Only Eli senses the meaning of the man's act. In what can only be termed a mystical transformation, Eli feels compelled to put on the Hasidic garb, and he begins to walk through the village, achieving a "conversion" to the values and sense of belonging that the man had represented. Moreover, as he literally "walks in the man's shoes," he defies the leveling and dehumanizing impetus represented by his role in enforcing the town's desires. He finally visits the hospital where his wife has recently given birth to their first son and is berated by her and several of the town's citizens and accused of having another of what has apparently been

a series of nervous breakdowns. Eli realizes that this time he is totally sane and lucid; but at the close of the story he feels the prick of a hypodermic needle, and the reader knows that he will be tranquilized and psychoanalyzed back to "normalcy."

The story illustrates the major concerns in Roth's fiction. Eli is a normally nonaggressive hero who nevertheless is prodded to assert his individuality actively and thus assuage his own guilt. The pressures of society exert a counterforce which annihilates this thrust toward individuality. The story is not really about conversion to an obscure form of Judaism so much as it is about the desire to resist the loss of cultural identity and personal individuality. In a world of diminished passions, the Rothian hero attempts to assert himself in the midst of the society which inhibits him. Unlike the "activist" heroes of much of American fiction who "light out for the territory," or who "make a separate peace," Roth's activists stand their ground and attempt to triumph over, or at least to survive within, the society--often without success.

"EPSTEIN"

Not all of Roth's heroes are activists--many become *passive* victims to these societal forces. "Epstein," an early story which appeared in *The Paris Review* and was incorporated into *Goodbye, Columbus*, illustrates this second pattern. The central character, Lou Epstein, is a financially and socially successful owner of a paper-bag company. An immigrant to America as a child, he has achieved apparent success by subscribing to the essentially Protestant work ethic of his adopted country.

Epstein's life, however, has not been happy. A son died at age eleven, and he broods about his company falling into the hands of a stranger. His wife, Goldie, a compulsive housekeeper, is aging rapidly and unattractively, and while Epstein is not young, he feels youthful sexual drives which do not tally with his wife's rejection of him or her diminished appeal. His only daughter has become fat, and her fiancé is a "chinless, lazy smart aleck." Epstein is, in short, going through a midlife crisis, surrounded by signs of unfulfilled goals and waning capacities and opportunities.

Jealous of the "zipping and unzipping" which accompany midnight teenage assignations in his living room, thus heightening the frustrations of his airless marriage, he begins an affair with the recently widowed mother of his brother's son's girlfriend. The woman represents all that his life lacks and all that his wife is not--sensuousness, lust, and adventure. The "Calvinist" gods are not mocked, however, because Epstein contracts a suspicious rash that his wife discovers to her horror, resulting in a hilarious but apocalyptic battle waged by the naked pair over the bed sheets, which Goldie seeks to burn. The next day, Epstein, seeking to confront his amour, collapses in the street with a heart attack; at the close of the story, his wife, riding in the ambulance with Epstein, assures him that he will be all right. "All he's got to do," the doctor tells her, "is live a normal life, normal for sixty." Goldie pleads, "Lou, you'll live normal, won't you? *Won't you?*"

Normal means a return to the external success and internal misery of his life before the liberating affair. The issue is not the morality of the situation but the desperate attempt to control one's life consciously and seize experience. Epstein laments,

> When they start taking things away from you, you reach out, you *grab*--maybe like a pig even, but you grab. And right, wrong, who knows! With tears in your eyes, who can even see the difference!

Epstein is returned unwillingly to the world of "normalcy." He is trapped--even biologically trapped--by a society which has adopted essentially Protestant-Calvinist values that distrust appetites, roots, and eccentric behavior, and which inculcates a sense of moral guilt, which is essentially the same as so-called Jewish guilt.

"DEFENDER OF THE FAITH"

Sergeant Nathan Marx, the Jewish protagonist of "Defender of the Faith," another story collected in *Goodbye, Columbus*, has achieved assimilated normalcy by serving honorably in World War II. After the war's end in Europe, he finds himself in charge of new soldiers in Camp Crowder, Missouri. One of his charges, Sheldon Grossbart, tries to use their shared Jewishness to gain special privileges. While his interactions with Grossbart cause Marx to rediscover his

Jewish identity, Marx also increasingly refuses to do Grossbart favors. The story's crisis occurs as Grossbart manages to have himself assigned to service in New Jersey rather than in the Pacific, where the war still rages. When Marx breaks the rules to see that Grossbart is reassigned to the Pacific, Marx considers himself a defender of American values, military values, and Jewish values, but Marx also knows that his vindictive violation of his own principles leaves him cut off from all the communities of which he longs to be a member. The story's ending leaves Marx in a richly paradoxical situation of a very Rothian sort. The story's various discussions of how lies relate to truth also raise issues of how a professional writer, as a professional teller of lies, can be a good American or a good Jew.

"NOVOTNY'S PAIN"

In another early story (with no Jewish characters) entitled "Novotny's Pain," the title character, conscripted into the army as a willing, if frightened, recruit, suffers unspecified and clearly psychosomatic lower back pain which Novotny endures in the hope that it will eventually go away. He clearly is not a "goldbricker." He is engaged to be married, and when out on a pass, he and his girlfriend enjoy a rich and acrobatic sex life despite occasional back pain.

Novotny, in desperate discomfort and moral unease, seeks medical help, but tests reveal nothing pathologically wrong. The young man admits that he fears going into battle but also sincerely asserts that if the root of the pain can be removed he will be more than willing to do his duty. The army authorities regard him, however, as a mental case, or worse, and eventually he is given a dishonorable discharge. Novotny wonders if he is being punished for all the ecstatic sex and happiness he has had with his fiancé, which his back has not prevented him from experiencing; even after he marries her, although threats that the discharge will destroy his civilian prospects turn out to be groundless, Novotny still suffers twinges of pain that correspond to his twinges of guilt. At the end, Novotny asks himself a central question: "What good was it, being good?" All of Roth's heroes try to deal with the concept of "goodness" but are impaled on the varying definitions of the term: goodness arising out of socially acceptable conformity or goodness coming from an existential attempt to define one's self satisfactorily in terms of needs, roots, and desires.

"'I ALWAYS WANTED YOU TO ADMIRE MY FASTING'"

In a later story,"'I Always Wanted You to Admire My Fasting': Or, Looking at Kafka," Roth first relates and then rewrites the last part of the life of one of Roth's favorite writers in an effort to examine what creates "goodness" in a writer. In Roth's biographical analysis, Franz Kafka died of tuberculosis at the happiest point of his life, and Roth notes signs in Kafka's late story "The Burrow" that Kafka was achieving progress toward love and toward understanding and accepting himself. However, Kafka's greatness as a writer might have never been known if Kafka had lived and been able to decide for himself whether to publish the works for which he became famous. As if to prove that advantages for others can be disadvantages for writers, the final section fancifully reimagines Kafka's life, allows him to survive until age seventy and even escape to America. Kafka becomes the nine-year-old Roth's teacher in Hebrew school in New Jersey, suffers through a romance with Roth's Aunt Rhoda--a romance that fails despite the absence of several impediments Kafka faced in real life--and finally dies unpublished. Roth concludes that one must maintain a high level of discomfort in one's society and in one's family, and one must be very lucky, to become known as a good writer.

The acerbity of Roth's vision, his honesty in portraying the deficiencies in American culture and values, and his refusal to prescribe overt solutions have led to critical charges of anti-Semitism and defeatism. His characters' valiant, if often thwarted, attempts to achieve some identity and sense of placement, however, belie the latter charge, and his honest, if not always affectionate, portrayal of both Jewish and non-Jewish characters in similar situations negates the former accusation.

OTHER MAJOR WORKS

LONG FICTION: *Letting Go*, 1962; *When She Was Good*, 1967; *Portnoy's Complaint*, 1969; *Our Gang (Starring Tricky and His Friends)*, 1971; *The Breast*, 1972, revised 1980; *The Great American Novel*, 1973; *My Life as a Man*, 1974; *The Professor of Desire*, 1977; *The Ghost Writer*, 1979; *Zuckerman Unbound*, 1981; *The Anatomy Lesson*, 1983; *Zuckerman Bound*, 1985 (includes *The Ghost Writer*, *Zuckerman Unbound*, *The Anatomy Lesson*, and *The Prague Orgy*); *The Counterlife*, 1986; *Deception*, 1990; *Operation Shylock: A Confession*, 1993; *Sabbath's Theater*, 1995; *American Pastoral*, 1997; *I Married a Communist*, 1998; *The Human Stain*, 2000; *The Dying Animal*, 2001; *The Plot Against America*, 2004; *Everyman*, 2006; *Exit Ghost*, 2007; *Indignation*, 2008; *The Humbling*, 2009; *Nemesis*, 2010.

NONFICTION: *Reading Myself and Others*, 1975, expanded 1985; *The Facts: A Novelist's Autobiography*, 1988; *Patrimony: A True Story*, 1991; *Shop Talk: A Writer and His Colleagues and Their Work*, 2001.

BIBLIOGRAPHY

Aarons, Victoria. "American-Jewish Identity in Philip Roth's Short Fiction." In *The Cambridge Companion to Philip Roth*, edited by Timothy Parrish. New York: Cambridge University Press, 2007. Aarons's analysis of the short fiction includes a discussion of the stories "Eli, the Fanatic," "Defender of the Faith," "'I Always Wanted You to Admire My Fasting,'" and the novella *Goodbye, Columbus*. Some of the other essays in this collection examine Roth's literary influence and postmodernism, and Roth and the Holocaust, Israel, ethnic identity, and gender.

Baumgarten, Murray, and Barbara Gottfried. *Understanding Philip Roth*. Columbia: University of South Carolina Press, 1990. Interpretation and discussion of Roth's fiction. Includes a bibliography and index.

Cooper, Alan. *Philip Roth and the Jews*. Albany: State University of New York Press, 1996. A carefully researched examination and consideration of Roth's work, his life, and his political views which are evident in his writing.

Gelfant, Blanche H., ed. *The Columbia Companion to the Twentieth-Century American Short Story*. New York: Columbia University Press, 2000. Includes a chapter in which Roth's short stories are analyzed.

Guttmann, Allen. *The Jewish Writer in America: Assimilation and the Crisis of Identity*. New York: Oxford University Press, 1971. Provides a broader context for interpreting Roth's work, one that a number of critics believe to be essential, particularly for some of the early short stories.

Halio, Jay L. *Philip Roth Revisited.* New York: Twayne, 1992. Discusses the critical response to Roth's fiction. Includes a bibliography and index.

Meeter, Glenn. *Philip Roth and Bernard Malamud: A Critical Essay*. Grand Rapids, Mich.: Wm. B. Eerdmans, 1968. An interesting comparison of Roth and Malamud, authors with compelling similarities, as well as important differences.

Milbauer, Asher Z., and Donald G. Watson, eds. *Reading Philip Roth*. New York: St. Martin's Press, 1988. This collection of essays is consistently insightful, examining Roth as a social critic and an exemplar of Jewish alienation. Also compares him to some prominent American novelists, as well as to Franz Kafka.

Pinsker, Sanford. *The Comedy That "Hoits": An Essay on the Fiction of Philip Roth*. Columbia: University of Missouri Press, 1975. Pinsker knows Roth inside out. In this relatively early work he does a good job of analyzing the precise relation of Roth's humor to the more serious issues addressed in his work.

_____, ed. *Critical Essays on Philip Roth*. Boston: G. K. Hall, 1982. Contains fourteen reviews of various Roth works, including his short story "The Conversion of the Jews," and an equal number of critical essays. Several of the essays deal with Roth's treatment of the Jewish American experience, and one essay compares Roth to Kafka. Pinsker provides a helpful introduction.

Rabin, Jessica G. "Still (Resonant, Relevant), and Crazy After All These Years: *Goodbye, Columbus and Five Short Stories*. In *Philip Roth: New Perspectives on an American Author*, edited by Derek Parker Royal. Westport, Conn.: Praeger, 2005. Argues that it is the "combination of ethnic particularly and American universality" that has lent this short-fiction collection "staying power for nearly forty-five years."

Rand, Naomi R. *Silko, Morrison, and Roth: Studies in Survival*. New York: Peter Lang, 1999. A study of how Silko, Morrison, and Roth each use a "survival narrative motif" as a way of defining their ethnic stance.

Rodgers, Bernard F., Jr. *Philip Roth*. Boston: Twayne, 1978. Examines a variety of Roth's works, including several of his short stories, arguing that Roth's experimentation with different literary forms should not disguise his overriding commitment to "realism" as sociomoral therapy.

Roth, Philip. *Conversations with Philip Roth*. Edited by George J. Searles. Jackson: University Press of Mississippi, 1992. In this compilation of interviews, Roth talks about his life and the influences on his fiction. Includes a bibliography and index.

Siegel, Ben, and Jay L. Halio, eds. *Playful and Serious: Philip Roth as a Comic Writer*. Newark: University of Delware Press, 2010. Collection of essays focusing on Roth's uses of humor in individual works and in his fiction generally. Two pieces focus on the short fiction: "A Comic Crisis of Faith: Philip Roth's 'The Conversion of the Jews' and 'Eli, the Fanatic,'" by Timothy Parrish, and "Philip Roth's Comic Realism in *Goodbye, Columbus*," by Victoria Aarons.

Wade, Stephen. *The Imagination in Transit: The Fiction of Philip Roth*. Sheffield, England: Sheffield Academic Press, 1996. Wade details Roth's growth as a novelist through a study of his fiction, relates the connection of Roth's work to American Jewish literary style, and lists influences on Roth's work.

David Sadkin
Updated by Ira Smolensky
and Marshall Bruce Gentry

RICHARD RUSSO

Born: Johnstown, New York; July 15, 1949

PRINCIPAL SHORT FICTION
The Whore's Child, and Other Stories, 2002

OTHER LITERARY FORMS

Richard Russo has written several novels, including the Pulitzer Prize-winning *Empire Falls* (2001), and several screenplays, including *Twilight* (1998). His short fiction has appeared in prestigious magazines and journals and has been collected in one volume of short stories, *The Whore's Child, and Other Stories*. He has written short nonfiction, including "High and Dry," a 2010 memoir of place about his native Gloversville, New York, which appeared in *Granta*.

ACHIEVEMENTS

Richard Russo (REW-soh) was a Pennsylvania Council of Arts Fellow in 1983 and received the annual award for fiction from the Society of Midland Authors in 1989 for his novel *The Risk Pool* (1988). In 1993, Paul Newman acquired the screen rights to Russo's novel *Nobody's Fool* (1993) for the film of the same name. Newman played the lead, which garnered him an Academy Award nomination. Robert Benton also received an Academy Award nomination for his screenplay for the film. Russo's 2001 *Empire Falls* won the Pulitzer Prize for Literature. Russo adapted the novel for the Home Box Office film, which aired in 2005. The film received a Golden Globe for Best Movie Mini-Series, and Newman received an Emmy Award and a Golden Globe for Best Supporting Actor in that film.

BIOGRAPHY

Richard Russo was born in Johnstown, New York, the son of Jean Findlay and construction worker James W. Russo, who left the family when Richard Russo was

a boy. Russo was raised by his mother in Gloversville, New York, a town that figures imaginatively in many of Russo's texts under different names: Mohawk, Thomaston, and Empire Falls. Though Russo left Gloversville when he went to college, he returned to New York during his college summers to work on road construction with his father.

Russo attended the University of Arizona because it was far from his hometown. He received his B.A. in English in 1971, continued his education at Arizona, and received a Ph.D. in American literature in 1980, writing his doctoral dissertation on the early American novelist Charles Brockden Brown. While working on his dissertation, he realized that he wanted to write fiction rather than study it, and he began to take creative-writing classes at the University of Arizona, eventually receiving his M.F.A. in 1981. Since then, he has taught at Arizona State University, Pennsylvania State University at Altoona, southern Connecticut State University, and southern Illinois University in Carbondale. He also has worked as a visiting writer in the Warren Wilson M.F.A. program. He began teaching at Colby College in Maine in 1991, and he retired at forty-seven in 1996 to write full time. He and Barbara, his wife of more than thirty-five years, settled in Camden, Maine. He has two adult daughters, artist Kate Russo and Emily Russo Murtagh.

ANALYSIS

Primarily known for his long fiction, Richard Russo has earned critical attention for his depictions of two distinctly different types of characters: the sardonic academic, who wears emotional blinders because of intellectualism's inability to sustain him, and the beleaguered townsman, who feels trapped by the forces that ultimately uphold him. Often, Russo places these largely male characters in juxtaposition with problematic familial members. Many of his characters inhabit variations of Russo's hometown of Gloversville, a small, deteriorating industrial town of the Northeast. The hardships and the irrepressible spirit of these people are honored, even as they are dissected and probed for clearer understanding. Russo is critical of the "organization"--often embodied in the industry that had allowed the town to be once prosperous--even as the characters in these texts often end up being sympathetic to their circumstances. Industry both pollutes and destroys, but the loss of industry offers additional, albeit different laments, as people lose their jobs and the town shrivels from economic depletion.

Russo's novels typically contain multiple, layered characterizations and subplots. Critics often have compared him to a modern-day Charles Dickens, particularly because Russo examines industry and its impact on a society and uses humor and satire as methods for delivering his messages.

Russo's short stories in the collection *The Whore's Child, and Other Stories* contain similar, albeit more condensed, versions of these themes and characters. Though some critics have characterized the stories as darker than other of his works, the condensing of the plot also allows for a more distilled version of his preoccupations concerning mortality, family dynamics, and the complicated relationship of the past to the present. By removing the expansive framework indicative of his novels, Russo gets to the essence of the situation by providing an intimate symbolic framework.

"THE WHORE'S CHILD"

The title story of the collection, "The Whore's Child," concerns a fiftyish fiction professor narrator, who has an older nun mistakenly enroll in his advanced-fiction workshop. The story the nun writes is decidedly nonfiction, but the class is compelled by its plot of a young woman (certainly the nun herself) whose life has been, essentially, reduced to what others have defined for her. Taken from her prostitute mother at an early age and placed in a convent, then orphaned from the "bad mother," the girl has nowhere else to turn except to the Church, though it is an uneasy alliance for a girl whose imagination fluctuates between an earnest love for Christ and a desire to burn down the convent. At the heart of the story is her longing for a father, who appears mysteriously in her narrative as a kind of savior who will take her away, not only from her life as a

"whore's child." Ironically, the students in the workshop identify the missing father as her mother's pimp, a fact that the nun has failed to recognize. Thus, the nun faces the realization that when one gives up a grand lie, one may have to accept a more disheartening truth.

The narrator's story runs parallel to the nun's. As a middle-aged man, he seems jaded at both the prospect of the workshop and at the possibility for any truth to ever emerge, in life or in fiction. However, by the end of the story, the larger epiphany is probably his. Something in the uncovering of the nun's central truth sets him free from the lies that he has told himself. By "telling" the truth, both the nun and the professor narrator can come to terms with stories that have haunted them.

This Russo story contains some of his key themes, in the form of the jaded academic who has lost faith in his profession and in the sanctity of marriage. Often in Russo's worlds, those who wander from marriage are haunted by their indiscretion. "The Whore's Child" also humorously critiques the concept of the fiction workshop. For example, the students find the nun's

Richard Russo (AP Photo/Pat Wellenbach)

story compelling, though it violates all of the principles of the story form that they have studied in previous workshops. This story further hints that the larger lies are not the ones in fiction but the ones people tell themselves.

"MONHEGAN LIGHT"

"Monhegan Light" is the first of two stories in this collection that concern a couple journeying to a resort island in Maine, where the main middle-aged male character must accept a difficult truth about himself. In this story, Martin, the central character, works for the film industry as a director of photography, someone who is renowned by his director friends as an "artist," who can light people well. Martin travels to the island to visit Robert Trevor, a painter, someone who also trades in light. In this case, Trevor painted Martin's former wife, Laura, many times before she died, and Martin has come to the island with his new girlfriend Beth to find out why. This story illustrates the shallow hull that surrounds the main character. Martin can train the light on others and act as an "artist," but he cannot penetrate further. Russo perhaps is commenting on the shallow nature of Hollywood when compared to other visual arts, such as painting. The painter has captured Martin's dead wife in such a way that Martin falls in love with her, a love that he reveals finally to himself and that he never had felt before he saw the painting. He never found her particularly beautiful until Trevor "lights" her for him. This story is reminiscent, in miniature, of Russo's novel *Bridge of Sighs* (2007). In that novel, part of the plot revolves around a woman and the two men who desire her, one of whom is a painter who has captured her memorably on the canvas.

"THE FARTHER YOU GO"

As in other stories in this collection, the first-person narrator of "The Farther You Go" is at both a psychological and a physical impasse. Having just undergone surgery for prostate cancer, Hank tries to cope with his throbbing genitals as he deals with his son-in-law, who seems to be abusing his daughter Julie. Though the plot suggests melodrama, "The Farther You Go" hints at the trajectories of Hank's middle-aged life that have brought him to this moment of realization: He will not live forever, nor will he remain in control. However, according to others in the story, notably Russell, his son-in-law,

Hank is the person everyone tries to emulate. Thus, the story reflects on Hank's inability to share with others the things that matter most to him, particularly his fears. In a moment of weakness, he almost hops on a plane to visit a woman with whom he once had a brief affair, in an attempt to find someone who would listen to his problems, someone who did not depend upon him. In the last scene of the story, Hank gets into a car with his wife Faye, and he suddenly realizes that he can rely on Faye to drive home, a clue that Hank may have reached a point where he can finally relinquish his control.

"JOY RIDE"

In one of two stories with a youthful main character, "Joy Ride" depicts the cross-country trip of young John Dern and his mother from their home in Camden, Maine, to John's grandparents' house in Phoenix, Arizona, though John's mother tells him that they are leaving his father and going to California to start over again. Told with Russo's characteristic wry humor, the events of the story concern John's quirky mother and her overwhelming desire to free herself from marriage. The father from whom they flee is seen as restrictive; however, over the course of the trip, the mother loses her belief in freedom when she is almost raped by a cowboy in a Western town. Eventually she and her son return home, and much later, when the boy is an adult and the father is dying, the mother inexplicably refuses to remember the journey as anything more than a trip to the grandparents' house. Thus, "Joy Ride" reinforces the value of remembering, even as it suggests that one can change or forget experiences to create a fabricated "truth" when necessary.

"BUOYANCY"

Set on a resort island in Maine, the story concerns the main character, Paul Snow, a retired academic who has written on Emily Dickinson and is fearful of many things, including his own mortality, though he refuses to acknowledge these fears. His wife has recovered from a nervous breakdown, whose parameters are not detailed until the end of the story. Snow is the worst kind of academic; certain of his intellectual importance before retirement, he begins to realize the vast unimportance of his scholarship outside of his small circle. Worse, he has stripped his wife of the opportunity to work in the field for which she trained and has had the clichéd affairs with graduate students. How ironic that he "meets death" in the form of a nude woman covered in mud. Later, when his wife Jean goes off to look for cream for his sunburn, one has the distinct impression that she might not return.

"POISON"

The poison of this title relates to the poison that the father of main character's friend, Gene, knew was being put out by the mill in the narrator's hometown. Somehow, however, this man stuck to the mill's politics, despite knowing that the mill's poisons killed many, notably the narrator's father. This story reflects closely some of Russo's personal concerns about his hometown of Gloversville and the toxins that the mill produced. At the end of the story, the narrator's friend Gene suggests that the two of them take on the town's past by telling the true story. Though the narrator does not seem compelled to take this leap, the story does hint at his fear of compromising this link between himself and Gene. Gene serves as the narrator's reminder of where he has been and what he may have sacrificed for his cushy beachfront property.

"THE MYSTERIES OF LINWOOD HART"

In this last, long story of the collection, a youthful main character named Linwood Hart must begin to accept the fact that he is not the center of the universe. Russo experiments with point of view in this story, as the limited omniscient narration traps the reader into knowing only the limited things that the main character, Linwood, knows. Lin, as he is called, believes that he is privy to all of the most important conversations that take place around him, that the "world" somehow works in a way that he automatically is given all the pieces of the puzzle to work with, that nothing is left out. In this, Lin's notion about his life is rather like the expectations readers have from stories: The author will provide all of the essential information. However, this story does leave out information. Lin does not know why his mother Evelyn and his father "Slick" Tommy are living apart, but Lin knows that his father has an apartment above the barbershop and Lin knows that the baseball coach in town, Mr. Christie, is painting Lin's house. The reader can read between the lines to some degree: The mother wants the father to be more responsible; the father wants the mother to stop believing that she is better than he is. By the end of the

story, Lin realizes that most of the story takes place outside his milieu and, thus, constructing any narrative requires him to fill in the blanks.

OTHER MAJOR WORKS

LONG FICTION: *Mohawk*, 1986; *The Risk Pool*, 1988; *Nobody's Fool*, 1993; *Empire Falls*, 2001; *Bridge of Sighs*, 2007; *That Old Cape Magic*, 2009.

SCREENPLAYS: *Keeping Mum*, 2005 (with Niall Johnson); *The Ice Harvest*, 2005 (with Robert Benton); *Twilight*, 1998 (with Benton).

TELEPLAYS: *The Flamingo Rising*, 2001 (based on Larry Baker's novel); *Brush with Fate*, 2003 (based on Susan Vreeland's novel *Girl in Hyacinth Blue*, 1999); *Empire Falls*, 2005 (based on his novel).

NONFICTION: "High and Dry," 2010.

EDITED TEXT: *Healing Touch: True Stories of Life, Death, and Hospice*, 2008.

BIBLIOGRAPHY

Case, Kristen. "Pulsating with Real Life: *The Whore's Child, and Other Stories*." *The New Leader* (July/August, 2002): 30-31. This review of the collection discusses how Russo alters his writing methods to create believable worlds in his short stories in lieu of the larger worldview of the novel.

Cooper, Rand Richards. "Bitter Harvests." *The New York Times Book Review*, July 14, 2002, p. 10. This review of *The Whore's Child, and Other Stories* suggests that the prospects in Russo's short stories seem bleaker than the outcomes in his longer fiction.

Heinegg, Peter. "You *Still* Can't Get There from Here." *America* (October 12, 2002): 26-27. This review of *The Whore's Child, and Other Stories* praises Russo's use of dialogue as part of his overall method of representing ordinary life.

Holt, Karen. "Writing What He Knows." *Publishers Weekly* (August 27, 2007): 43-44. This overview of Russo's work discusses his working-class background and the importance of place in his fiction.

Russo, Richard, and Lewis Burke Frumkes. "A Conversation with Richard Russo." *Writer* 113 (December, 2000): 19. In this interview, Russo discusses some of his inspirations and methods for writing.

Rebecca Hendrick Flannagan